Values in Conflict

Edited by
VICTOR COMERCHERO
Sacramento State College

Values in Conflict

CHRISTIANITY
MARXISM
PSYCHOANALYSIS
EXISTENTIALISM

APPLETON-CENTURY-CROFTS
EDUCATIONAL DIVISION
MEREDITH CORPORATION

New York

Copyright © 1970 by
MEREDITH CORPORATION
All rights reserved

This book, or parts thereof,
must not be used or reproduced in any manner without written permission.
For information address the publisher,
Appleton-Century-Crofts, Educational Division, Meredith Corporation,
440 Park Avenue South, New York, N.Y. 10016.

750-1

Library of Congress Card Number: 74-111099

PRINTED IN THE UNITED STATES OF AMERICA

390-20350-5

To those who gave me life

With great love

Contents

Preface	xi
General Introduction	1

AN OVERVIEW

CARL L. BECKER
from Climates of Opinion   19

CHRISTIANITY

Introduction	35
Patterns: Question-Begging	42
1. *from* THE BOOK OF JOB	45
2. THE BOOK OF ECCLESIASTES	67
3. *from* THE GOSPEL ACCORDING TO MATTHEW	79
Patterns: Emotional Appeal and Psychological Argument	85
4. *from* THE GOSPEL ACCORDING TO MARK	87
5. THE LETTER OF PAUL TO THE ROMANS	95
Patterns: Disguised Disparagement	116
6. THE FIRST LETTER OF JOHN	119
7. THOMAS AQUINAS	
from Summa contra Gentiles	127
8. JOHN CALVIN	
The Sum of the Christian Life: The Denial of Ourselves	137
9. JOHN WILSON	
Verification and Religious Language	149
Religious Experience	158
10. MAX WEBER	
Asceticism and the Spirit of Capitalism	169
11. OSCAR CULLMANN	
from The State in the New Testament	187
Patterns: Slack Definition	191

12. REINHOLD NIEBUHR
    The Social Resources of Religion — 193
    Patterns: Unsupported Assertions — 203
13. WILLIAM BARRETT
    Hebraism and Hellenism — 205

MARXISM

Introduction — 225
Patterns: Argument by Analogy — 236

14. KARL MARX & FRIEDRICH ENGELS
    from The Communist Manifesto — 239
    from The German Ideology — 259
15. KARL MARX
    Alienated Labor — 279
16. FRIEDRICH ENGELS
    from Socialism: Utopian and Scientific — 291
17. V. I. LENIN
    from The State and Revolution — 309
    Patterns: Psychological Arguments — 337
18. MAO TSE-TUNG
    Combat Liberalism — 339
    Patterns: Limited Categories — 342
    How to Study War — 343
19. LESZEK KOLAKOWSKI
    Permanent vs. Transitory Aspects of Marxism — 355
20. MILOVAN DJILAS
    Character of the Revolution — 369
    from The New Class — 385
21. ROBERT C. TUCKER
    Marx and the End of History — 389

PSYCHOANALYSIS

Introduction — 399
Patterns: Unwarranted Assumptions — 408

22. HANS HERMA
    The Unconscious — 411
23. SIGMUND FREUD
    The Technique of Psychoanalysis — 427
    Libidinal Types — 438
    Two Artificial Groups: The Church and the Army — 442
    from The Future of an Illusion — 447
    from Civilization and Its Discontents — 462

24. CARL G. JUNG
    from Analytic Psychology: Its Theory and Practice   487
    Patterns: Tonal Insinuation   519
    Marriage as a Psychological Relationship   521
25. ALFRED ADLER
    New Leading principles for the Practice of
    Individual-Psychology   533
    Individual-Psychological Treatment of Neuroses   540
    Patterns: Verbal Intimidation   548
26. KAREN HORNEY
    Morbid Dependency   549
27. ERICH FROMM
    Love and Its Disintegration in Contemporary
    Western Society   567
28. ABRAHAM H. MASLOW
    Introduction: Toward a Psychology of Health   583
    Self-Actualizing People: A Study of Psychological
    Health   588

EXISTENTIALISM

Introduction   619
Patterns: Limited and Exclusive Categories   628
29. FRIEDRICH NIETZSCHE
    from The Antichrist   631
    from The Dawn   632
    from The Gay Science   634
    from Beyond Good and Evil   636
    from The Genealogy of Morals   648
    Patterns: Limited and Exclusive Categories   675
    from Thus Spake Zarathustra   677
30. SØREN KIERKEGAARD
    from The Concept of Dread   687
    from The Sickness unto Death   691
    from Fear and Trembling   695
    Patterns: Psychological Argument (Reductio
    ad Absurdum)   706
31. FYODOR DOSTOYEVSKY
    The Grand Inquisitor   709
32. JEAN-PAUL SARTRE
    Existentialism Is a Humanism   727
33. PAUL TILLICH
    from The Courage to Be   741
34. MARTIN BUBER
    from Dialogue   749

Contents

35. ALBERT CAMUS
    The Myth of Sisyphus   771

DIALOGUE AND SYNTHESIS

36. KEITH R. BRIDSTON
    A Christian Critique of Secular Anthropologies   777
37. RICHARD LICHTMAN
    from The Marxian Critique of Christianity   789
38. ADAM SCHAFF
    The Problem of the Individual   807
    Existentialized Marxism   815
39. HERBERT MARCUSE
    A Biological Foundation for Socialism?   823
40. WILHELM REICH
    Truth versus Modju   833
    Basic Tenets on Red Fascism   838
41. VIKTOR E. FRANKL
    Basic Concepts of Logotherapy   841
42. HELEN MERRELL LYND
    from On Shame and the Search for Identity   849
43. FRANTZ FANON
    The Negro and Recognition   863
    By Way of Conclusion   871

Dictionary of Terms
Glossary of Rhetorical Devices   879
List of References   893
  907

Preface

This anthology began some few years ago when I discovered, quite by accident, that many people have no concept of inferential thought, of the need to ferret out unarticulated assumptions. Declarative sentences are simply declarative, betraying nothing about the beliefs, attitudes, and aspirations of a writer, about a writer's value structure. Applying this discovery to the learning experience, I realized that students are usually adept at reporting and summarizing events or essays, but extremely poor at interpreting them. And so I spent a day interpreting examples. "What inferences could be drawn about a girl who wants a one-carat diamond ring as opposed to one who wants a simple gold band?" (Possible inferences are that the first has more expensive tastes, is less simple than the second, values conventional expressions of love more, is more demanding, etc.) "A woman wrote a letter suggesting that a housholder reveals his moral character by how neatly he barbers his lawn. Is this accurate? What inferences can be drawn about the woman? about tidy lawn-keepers? about slack lawn-keepers?"

Gradually I came to see that students invariably depend on others as a source for their interpretations. Many of them are unable to interpret even matters concerning themselves—the behavior of their friends, the responses of their family. They not only have no context within which to interpret ideas or behavior, but they even seem to be unaware that ideas and behavior are subject to interpretation. And even among those who *are* aware of it, few sense the possibility of posing *several* interpretations and selecting the most plausible or acceptable. This anthology then, has grown out of an attempt to cope with this difficulty, to give students the rhetorical and intellectual tools they need in order to develop a rational method for interpreting ideas and behavior, for reshaping their world by perceiving it with new insight.

The organization of the anthology deserves some comment. A dictionary of terms and concepts is included so that the reader may have easily at hand a first approximation of many of the ideas that infuse the intellectual currents represented here. Only the selections themselves, however, are truly adequate to the necessary task of definition and redefinition. More important, perhaps, is the glossary of rhetorical devices, which provides the reader with some "defenses." The reader should investigate these devices before beginning the selections themselves. Although they are not analytic tools as such—for they will not help the reader penetrate to the heart of a value system—they will help protect him from manipulation and help him to identify shoddy goods. In addition, some of the devices explained in the glossary are more closely investigated under the rubric "Patterns" throughout the anthology. (In order to show that such devices are unavoidable, but not therefore excusable, most of our own introductions are analyzed for just such rhetorical patterns.) Following each independent essay is a series of problem-questions that we prefer to call "problems" rather than "questions." The term "question" tends to suggest something passive that one may regard or disregard at will, while that of "problem" conveys the desired sense of active imposition and compulsory confrontation. The latter sense also captures more adequately the problematic orientation of the anthology as a whole, its belief that learning is less the art of problem-solving than that of problem-posing. Most of the problems are brief and to the point, while some are wide-ranging and far-reaching in their implications. The reader will probably want to ask himself whether he would resolve a problem as he thinks the author under consideration would. In this way, the problem becomes not simply the author's but the reader's as well.

The essays themselves were chosen to create problems and to provoke interpretations, to lead the reader to ask, "What assumptions are implied? What consequences thereby accrue?" The art of tentative interpretation and of multiple interpretation is best served by "value systems" in conflict. Such systems can be used to comment on each other, and extrapolations can be made from them in order to demonstrate that even ostensibly innocuous assertions are subject to differing interpretations. The choice of Christianity, Marxism, psychoanalysis, and existentialism was not arbitrary. They are widespread and influential movements in the West; for, either singly or in some combination, they have been and are deeply instrumental in shaping man's structures of value and concepts of self and the world. No assumption is made, however, that these currents are the most influential, or the only ones of significance.

Within each value system, the essays were specifically chosen to show the inherent instability of ideas and to dramatize something of their evolution. To achieve either of these goals in detail and with satisfying completeness would require a far larger stage than the present one. But here the reader can at least realize that the assumptions of primary thinkers inevitably suggest possible directions and, hence, possible distortions. By including a variety of essays within a movement, we permit the reader to compare the founder with his followers, and thereby to see which elements in a founder's thought were accepted, which rejected. More importantly, such an approach permits the reader to measure his own analysis of the founder's assumptions and their possible applications against the reality of later developments. For example, just where did Christian eschatology and the body–soul dichotomy lead Calvin? Just where did Marx's dialectical materialism lead Lenin? By diversifying the essays, we also intend to show how ideas have applications never envisioned by the founder; how, for example Christianity, through Protestantism, influenced the rise of capitalism. And, by including some quite recent essays, we hope to show how evolution and counter-reaction can so drastically modify a founder's theory that contemporary theorists within a movement seem actually to have refuted his major premises.

A fifth section, "Dialogue and Synthesis," suggests the dynamic interaction of ideas, the clashing nature of values, and the inexhaustible number of syntheses possible. It makes of the reader the final combatant and last synthesizer.

Above all, we have tried to include excellent and provocative essays, as many as possible, and to present as complete a summary of each movement's primary ideas and their evolution as possible. We have, where feasible, included complete essays as more appropriate to our rhetorical and analytic aims. Fragments were included only when a thinker's thought and prevalent mode of expression make this strategy inevitable, as in the case of Nietzsche, or where a thinker is so seminal, yet so prolix, that excerpting is unavoidable, as in the cases of Marx and Freud.

The texts of the essays have not been emended except to delete references to other chapters in a book when such references made no sense within the context of the anthology. We have also taken the liberty of silently deleting editor's notes when they contributed little to our understanding of the substance of the essay. With the exception of one or two instances noted in the text, the essayist's notes are allowed to remain intact. We have, however, attempted to keep our own notes to a minimum. Where notes are necessary to translate a foreign phrase or illuminate a reference central to the author's point, we have added a brief note under the convention of asterisk (*) and dagger (†). Cross-references to other selections in the text are indicated by page and line numbers, separated by a virgule and placed in parentheses: (325/24). The first number refers to page 325 and the second to line 24 on that page. Other notations found in parentheses throughout the text are to items in the list of references given at the end of the book. For example, (29 Marcuse) refers to a work by Marcuse which is cited as the twenty-ninth item in the list beginning on page 907. Our desire throughout is to provide help to the reader where necessary and to preserve, at the same time, a text that is lean and uncluttered.

The introductions attempt painstakingly to suggest the inferential, problematic method of the anthology without revealing the underlying assumptions of a system. This ideal was an impossible one; some revelation was obviously necessary. We have attempted, however, to reveal as little as possible that directly relates to the readings. The reader is left as much as possible to confront the material alone, without an intermediary. The introductions are, thus, not intended to provide background material or a critical perspective; they are meant to demonstrate an analytic methodology. This analytic methodology, together with the anthology's informing principles, are revealed in the general introduction.

The sectional introductions, in harmony with the analytic methodology, strive to create unorthodox ways of perceiving, to reveal new perspectives. They are provocative, not definitive. The introductions to Christianity and Marxism analyze one or two assumptions of those movements, in order to establish a frame of mind conducive to asking first and last questions. They indicate how assumptions have consequences and suggest what some of these consequences might be. One or two strands of thought have been picked up and explored, not exhaustively but in some depth. The introductions are, thus, fractional; other strands of thought could easily have been explored. On the assumption that benevolent consequences need no attention while detrimental ones do, destructive implications were preferred to constructive ones.

The introduction to psychoanalysis approaches its subject from a different perspective. Based on the assumption that we become self-aware not only by unfolding our own assumptions, but by scrutinizing how others respond to us, the introduction to psychoanalysis attempts to determine what elements in psychoanalysis attract the hostility both of fundamental Christians and of party-line communists. Again only a partial analysis is offered to serve as an illustration. Finally, on the assumption that we are also revealed by how we perceive others, the introduction to existentialism analyzes aspects of the three other systems from an existential perspective.

Though we explore inward and outward, are beheld and behold others, we are involved essentially in a surveying action; we know the landscape but have not tested it. To understand truly—that is, to experience ideas in action—we need dialogue and the perception of original minds creating their own eclectic synthesis. Much of the dialogue, already begun in the various sections, is raised to the level of commentary and confrontation in the final section. There is a lesson to be learned from examining such dialogue, for how many of us have suffered the humiliation of seeing ideas won in lonely solitude defeated in public debate. Ideas that are powerless before experience, that break under bruising intellectual charges, are too fragile to support us. Even if we escape public humiliation by silence, we wither in private; fear gnaws at us; our strength is sapped; and we barter our intellectual growth and promise for a false security. The only pride that protects us is not the pride of infallibility, but that which comes from humbly aspiring toward those imperfect visionary values that most seem to us to sustain life. But even for that modest goal, we need a method.

There remains but to acknowledge my deep appreciation to Barbara Kimmel, with gratitude for her tireless efforts and invaluable aid; to Julie Ghormley, for bravely helping to prepare the finished manuscript; and to Martin Stanford, for his editorial counsel, and above all for his patience.

General Introduction

Beginnings are difficult. For they reveal in subtle ways a man's perspective even before he has had time to confess it. When a perspective differs from our own, we begin, often unintentionally, to create defensive barriers even before we discover the precise nature of the threat to ourselves. And if, as we shall try to establish, people perceive differences before they can define their significance, before they can interpret them, and hence rely on old, worn interpretations that no longer apply, then we are justified in this anthology in trying to open new perspectives in order to bring about revaluations. From this perspective, however, beginnings become doubly difficult, for the reader's perspective potentially distorts the author's intention before he has had time to argue and establish it.

We are not expressing anything very original here; we are merely acknowledging that in intellectual discourse, as in other matters, people seek to conserve energy, and to live in a state of uncertainty is more costly to the human organism than to live in one of certainty. In other words, thought consumes energy; hence, when an individual shuns thought, he is not exhibiting laziness but merely obeying a law of parsimony which enjoins the organism to conserve his energy for immediate interests at hand.

In turning his interest away from the doubtful and speculative to the immediate, the individual is, to some extent, continuing conventional patterns of what is deemed appropriate behavior. There is work to be done, and speculation is idleness. That the organism's "real" interests may differ from his immediate interests, from the work at hand, is not apparent until the organism contemplates his "real" interests, and this contemplation cannot take place unless he engages in "idle" speculation.

John Dewey has argued that what divides man from other organisms is precisely this ability to respond to the speculative and "doubtful." This vision of man responding to the "doubtful" animates Marx's concept of "species-consciousness," Freud's concept of therapy as "education for truthfulness," Nietzsche's "transvaluation of values," and it informs the organization of this book from cover to cover. Marx, Freud, Nietzsche—a host of others—would all deny that man is simply an adaptive organism, reacting to his immediate needs; and they would all be emphatic in asserting that man is not truly man until he can distinguish his "real" interests from his immediate ones. The failure to make this distinction is what, for Marx, inhibits the development of communism, for Freud, makes one neurotic, for Nietzsche, breeds herd and slave morality and prevents man from "overcoming" his limitations and fulfilling his promise.

This failure stems from man's desire for simplicity and order; from his wish for things to continue as before. But as the environment becomes more ambiguous, the individual is compelled to acknowledge its complexity and to adopt behavior that is more hesitant and anticipatory. The mind is compelled to become less reactive and adaptive and more speculative and theoretical, to make the leap from intelligence to intellect. Richard Hofstadter has defined the difference.

> Intelligence is an excellence of mind that is employed within a fairly narrow, immediate, and predictable range; it is a manipulative, adjustive, unfailingly practical quality—one of the most eminent and endearing of the animal virtues. Intelligence works within the framework of limited but clearly stated goals, and may be quick to shear away questions of thought that do not seem to help in reaching them. Finally, it is of such universal use that it can daily be seen at work and admired alike by simple or complex minds.
> Intellect on the other hand, is the critical, creative, and contemplative side of mind. Whereas intelligence seeks to grasp, manipulate, re-order, adjust, intellect examines, ponders, wonders, theorizes, criticizes, imagines. Intelligence will seize the immediate meaning in a situation and evaluate it. Intellect evaluates evaluations, and looks for the meanings of situations as a whole. Intelligence can be praised as a quality in animals; intellect, being a manifestation of human dignity, is both praised and assailed as a quality in men. When the difference is so defined, it becomes easier to understand why we sometimes say that a mind of admittedly penetrating intelligence is relatively unintellectual; and why, by the same token, we see among minds that are unmistakably intellectual a considerable range of intelligence (1 Hofstadter).

It is customary to fault intellectuals for their radical criticism—and with good reason. They are forever doubting, forever questioning, and therefore forever discovering problems just when everyone was hoping to settle into a trouble-free existence. A trouble-free existence is, of course, the antithesis of what Christ, Marx, Freud, Nietzsche, and a host of others wish for man. Indeed, in a sense we are defined by what we wish for ourselves. Dewey has commented on the behavioral consequences of the common man's desire for a careless existence.

> . . . The natural man dislikes the dis-ease which accompanies the doubtful and is ready to take almost any means to end it. Uncertainty is

got rid of by fair means or foul. Long exposure to danger breeds an overpowering love of security. Love for security, translated into desire not to be disturbed and unsettled, leads to dogmatism, to acceptance of beliefs upon authority, to intolerance and fanaticism on one side and to irresponsible dependence and sloth on the other (2 Dewey).

Freud has described this behavior in his own terms, by arguing that *"protection against* stimuli is an almost more important function for the living organism than *reception* of stimuli" (3 Freud). Simply translated, this means that the mind does not consciously suppress threatening information; it merely refuses to receive and register it. Such behavior occurs whenever the organism feels endangered, and in Freud's opinion, most people feel threatened by the truth and are not strong enough to accept it; they are not strong enough to accept the ambiguity and doubt inherent in life; they need security and certainty. Freud overstated the case. Man is probably unable to accept the problematic when he feels nothing can be done about it. Not the problematic but impotence threatens man and leads him to deny reality.

Most people, taught to be uncritical, unassertive, and dependent, feel impotent and hence threatened. But, in recent years, some of the intellectual dissent and criticism of the young suggests that medieval habits of mind—such as argument by authority—are giving way to modern scientific ones based on rational criticism, pragmatism and empiricism. Man's preference for the immediate and limited problem, rather than the potential and general one, is perhaps an inheritance of former days when the temporal sense and habitual mode of perception were more leisurely. Most of us, however, have failed to register a crucial message of our age: time is not an arithmetical constant; pragmatically it exists in inverse proportion to our problems. As these multiply geometrically (as, for example, they do in population growth), the time available to solve the problem decreases geometrically. Given man's emotional stability as rooted in habitual modes of perception, and given the utter irrelevance, even destructiveness of many of these perceptions to his immediate problems, man's interpretive processes—his ability to discern and evaluate directions and potential problems—remain inadequate to his ability to transform the world radically. The result of man's swift intelligence and sluggish intellect is crisis. Man makes techological discoveries before his intellect can apprehend their significance and even before he is truly aware that a profound discovery has been made. As a result, one to three generations usually pass before society fully absorbs the implications of a scientific breakthrough and allows this new knowledge to inform its world view and the daily lives of its members.

Given man's nostalgia for the past and his ability to reshape the future, he is going to be torn by contradictions for a long time to come.

But the contradiction between an emotional-intellectual system of values which is shaped in the past and an intelligence which is geared to the present and future is complicated by another conflict—the conflict between what we *think* we believe and what we truly believe. Both problems are interrelated and are exacerbated by our failure to appreciate the manner in which the mind works. Most of us have a very simple notion of the relationship between assent and belief. We tend to believe that once we have renounced a belief, we no longer believe it. We tend to be literal-minded in our acceptance of the power of the mind to alter convictions. We fail to understand that all convictions have multiple ramifications, and that often these ramifications are not affected initially at the moment we renounce this conviction or that. Not only our faith in man's reason—faith in the power of man's will, of his brain, or of both—leads us to our simple view of the mind but also our belief that to hold a conviction is to perceive and to understand it.

Many reasons lead us to believe that we are completely aware of our mental processes: our anxiety is thereby reduced—we are not beset by forces we cannot understand—and our reassurance grows, for we are firmly in control of our fate. Other reasons, of course, reinforce this mental model; but let us avoid speculating on its merits or demerits for the human psyche. Here we merely claim that as a functioning model little commends it other than comfort. Neither science nor art, both of which are rooted first in intuition and only thereafter in reason, support it. More to the point, it inhibits self-knowledge by making introspection a sterile exercise in the obvious—if we are aware of everything, why look for hidden connections within our psyche? Either "know thyself" is the rock upon which all education is built, or it is not; and if it is not—if education is not a form of self-discovery—one had best find out what it is, lest those of us who believe it is become totally dispensable. All of which takes us to the fundamental premise of this work, namely that education, as opposed to training, is a form of therapy which leads to self-knowledge and self-esteem, to a sense of one's unique and irreplaceable perspective on the world. And knowledge of the self is easier to come by when one appreciates the grandeur and helplessness of the human mind, come to understand that for every "monument of unaging intellect" such as the theory of relativity, there is a mass grave at Auschwitz to remind us of the inexplicable nature of man.

Albert Camus, in *The Myth of Sisyphus,* has remarked that a man's method betrays his conclusions. One can go even further and argue that a man's premises determine his conclusions; given certain premises, certain conclusions are unlikely, even impossible, while others are probable, even inevitable. No great mystery, this, unless one also discovers that many people neither know nor care to know their fundamental premises. But let me elaborate. Recently, in an attempt to moderate an impasse in a discussion, I enumerated, insofar as I was able, the assumptions underlying my argument and suggested to my opponent that his arguments presupposed an entirely different set of assumptions. My remark was greeted with a steely, correct reply: "I won't question your assumptions if you won't question mine." Obviously, to make a poor play on words, his implicit assumption in not questioning mine was that to question an assumption is equivalent to questioning a motive. Such a confusion would not be so disturbing did it not suggest other underlying assumptions, namely that a failure in reason is equivalent to a failure in morals, that all thought is at heart rationalization, that beneath all reasoning lurks a shabby motive.

What was exposed so dramatically by our exchange was not only a disagreement about the argument at hand, but an entire fabric of opposing attitudes and assumptions about life. Perhaps even more important was the revelation that a man with so many years of schooling behind him could have so little understanding of the nature of rational discourse. Apparently, to display one's thought processes is, in many eyes, unseemly self-exposure. Why?

We are not helpless before such a question. We can construct a very fine model of the mind which will not only handle this question but account for much human behavior, and even suggest ways of altering it. But useful as models are, they are not answers; they are only working hypotheses. For the moment, however, let us ignore all practical consequences and concern ourselves with creating such a model, let us try to fashion one that will permit maximum neutrality and maximum flexibility.

Thought is not a single action, but a series of actions with several steps that are clearly identifiable—perception, selection, discrimination, comparison, patterning, correlation, integration. Other actions of the intellect could be designated but this list illustrates amply the kinds of problems one encounters in trying to think.

Let us ignore the basic epistemological question of how one receives any sensation, how one "perceives" anything, and begin with what I hope is an innocuous observation: all thought deals with experience and experience is essentially the meaning one gives to one's perceptions. Observation is, thus, objective, and experience subjective. Since it is impossible, however, to give meaning to anything without being able to perceive it in an over-all context, perceptions mean nothing until one places them in a larger framework. A strange object free of associations would "mean" nothing; it would simply "be." There is nothing mysterious at work here. Phenomena, in a sense, exist to be interpreted and must be interpreted. Even a failure to interpret a phenomenon is a kind of interpretation, namely that the phenomenon is neither interesting nor important enough to be interpreted. But let me cite an example.

Until recently, if I perceived a girl stroking her hair rhythmically in the presence of a boy, I gave it no thought. It had no meaning for me because I had no frame of reference from which to view it. Indeed, my failure to have an interpretive framework probably resulted in my *failing to perceive* many a girl stroking her hair in the presence of many a boy. All this has changed. Since reading that many girls play with their hair when they are in the presence of an attractive male, I now have a contextual framework, a *model* or working hypothesis for that action. Hereafter, when I notice a girl stroking her hair—and with such an interpretive model, I can hardly fail to notice such an act—I will immediately wonder whether she fits the model. (To assume uncritically, because I have an interpretive model, that all phenomena will fit that model is to metamorphose a working hypothesis into a requirement; it is easier, of course, to have laws than to have models, easier in other words to stereotype experience than to examine and understand it.)

All of this attention to hair presupposes, of course, that I accept the model or hypothesis that women who stroke their hair are manifesting attraction for a male instead of merely scratching their scalp. I might argue the accuracy of the perception, saying a stroke is not a scratch, but that isn't the point—I needn't accept the hypothesis at all. It might even repel me. It might smack too much of Freud and sexual preoccupation. It might also imply that people are unavoidably transparent and betray themselves in subtle ways. It might even undermine my faith in man as a rational creature fully in control of his actions. It might mean any of these things and more to me. What is certain, however, is that when I accepted the hypothesis instead of rejecting it—and I did—I *did not bother to correlate this hypothesis or premise carefully with others I held*. A vague rumble of assent and I accepted it. I integrated it into my world view and it is now part of me. It seems to me that that is roughly how most of us proceed. We accept or reject models for intuitive or subjective reasons rather than for objective ones. I do not want to suggest that this is a disreputable process. Art has always been acknowledged to be intuitive, but it is too little known that scientific breakthroughs are usually the result of intuition as well. Einstein, in talking about his search for a theory that would capture his thoughts about relativity, makes graphically clear that the originating impulse was not an external discovery, but an intuitive inner hypothesis. "During all those years," he wrote "there was a feeling of direction, of going straight toward something concrete. It is, of course, very hard to express that feeling in words; but it was decidedly the case, and clearly to be distinguished from later considerations about the rational form of the solution" (4 Rogers).

Our categories seem to be breaking down. Initially we proposed the hypothesis that all thought begins with perceptions, and now we find that our perceptions are molded, if not determined, by our intuition, which itself seems to be a very complex and half-conscious set of assumptions about life, assumptions that are rooted in one's being and one's past experience. If our perceptions are necessarily colored and shaped by a complex, poorly articulated set of premises, we can only conclude that we are badly compromised by a subjectivity so intense as to make objectivity possible, if ever, only when one is consciously aware of the cast of one's subjective value system and has attempted to compensate for it. But let us illustrate the problem at close hand.

At the heart of one's view of man is the question of human innocence or guilt. Is man by nature noble, neutral, or evil? Is man free or determined by his past? Our answer to these questions will determine an entire configuration of corollary answers. More important than merely determining whether we are Christian or Marxist, conservative or liberal, classic or romantic, behaviorist or existentialist, is the impact our answer will have on what we emphasize and fail to emphasize, even on what we observe and fail to observe.

Two children, asked to bring a cold drink to their father, fight and struggle over the drink, spilling it. Their mother spanks them. Their father defends them. The mother and the father then quarrel, mother accusing father of spoiling the children, father accusing mother of being too hard on them. A far-fetched illustration? Probably not. Assuming that the parents are not habitual opponents, and that the mother is not nervous or exhausted, their response is revealing. In one variation or another this drama is enacted daily around the country. What is at issue here is a bundle of preceptions and interpretations determined by underlying but unstated assumptions. The parents have, because of their fundamental premises, observed two different events. The father, probably believing man is either good, or at least neutral, saw the children squabbling for idealistic and altruistic reasons—each wanted to serve and please him. To punish them for an accident that arose from such noble origins is to teach them in the future to guard against such spontaneous outpouring of love and helpfulness. The mother, probably believing in the inherent evil of man, either was unable to see any reason for the fight, in which case it was evil manifesting itself in a pure form, or if she did see a reason, it was a selfish one—each child fought for the prestige to be gained by the deed. Quite often such interpretations occur so instantaneously that the people making them do not understand them, do not even recognize them as interpretations, but treat them instead as *facts*. For most people, there is nothing to interpret—life is factual, objective, and patent. There is no need to question our observations for subjective bias. There is no concept even of the subjectivity of consciousness. Even when people realize they have failed to notice something, they do not give it any importance. They were "wrong" and now that they have modified this perception, they are "right." They have no framework by which to investigate Nietzsche's assertion that life is determined by one's perspective. For them the mind is not a prism refracting light into various colors; it is a mirror.

Some readers may still be wondering who was "right" in the above instance. To say both parents and neither is unsatisfying if we prefer certainty to reason. But if we prefer instead to be rational, we must content ourselves with uncertainty and an abiding sense of the ambiguity inherent in life. Does this lack of certainty mean it makes no difference how we interpret phenomena? Hardly. The difference in our example was, after all, between blame or praise, between receiving or not receiving a spanking. And over a lifetime, the accumulated differences will be great. By the time each child is eighteen, the respective parents will interpret their behavior in vastly different ways and treat them accordingly. A daughter who stays out too late will be treated with suspicion by the mother, with trust by the father. A son who complains he can't get good grades in college while working will be considered lazy or stupid by his mother, but neither by his father. In reality, of course, the flow of ongoing experience profoundly modifies everyone's beliefs and behavior, both that of parents and that of children. Which once again returns us to the fundamental premise underlying this anthology—our premises, whether conscious or unconscious, shape our beliefs and behavior so dramatically that it is absurd to talk about freedom of choice until we have some method by which to discern the premises by which we live. Most of our premises are so fundamental, so taken for granted by us, that they are, as we have argued here, undiscernible. We merely respond. We receive a low grade on an exam. We either get depressed or we do not. We say we either wanted to succeed on it or we didn't. Our response has nothing to do with our attitudes toward competition, materialism, discipline, society, to the degree to which we crave approval or to the intensity of our alienation, or does it? Our answer to this question is an unequivocal "yes." But even before we can perceive our responses, we must have developed certain patterns of mind, we must have a mind-set calculated to scrutinize and interpret ideas and behavior—that mind-set is the mind-set of reason or science.

This anthology has one deeply rooted bias, and it is that of science, namely that every existent thing manifests itself in some tangible form, either discernible with our senses alone or with our senses aided by instrumentation. Inferences may be useful, even before tangible evidence exists, but it is a basic assumption of science that ultimately all inferences will be tangibly corroborated. Thus Einstein's theory of relativity, which held that the mass of an object increases as it approaches the speed of light, was a respected and accepted theory long before evidence could be collected to verify it. In fact—and here is what makes the scientific bias of this anthology so subtle, important, and yet difficult—the theory of relativity could never have been proven without the theory itself. Cyclotrons constructed decades later to test and corroborate the theory simply will not work unless constructed to compensate for the increase in mass as the object approaches the speed of light. Science, then, often seems to be as circumlocutive as the basic argument of this anthology: premises determine conclusions, which in turn seem to reinforce the original premises.

What all this means is that this anthology operates on the assumption that a thing exists insofar as its presence is felt in one form or another, that no dichotomy separates ideas from actions, theory from practice. To state that something is true in theory but defective in practice is a contradiction in terms. If something is true in theory, it will be true in practice; if it is defective in practice, it is because it is defective in theory. This anthology is, therefore, only interested in theory as it manifests itself in practice. Ideas, insofar as they are parts of our mental framework, eventually manifest themselves in our practice; conversely, only to the extent our behavior reveals them do ideas really inhabit our minds. To maintain that one holds an idea without exhibiting in some behavioral or psychological form the consequences of such an idea, is to engage in self-deception. We thus accept Nietzsche's contention that a philosopher, to be worthy of our respect, must practice what he preaches.

Such a view is itself not without a premise, namely that life is problematic, that no ultimate answers for final ends are given to us. Life is like a Chinese puzzle in which every solution contains within its heart an unforeseen problem, which when solved, opens to our eyes a new problem hitherto unperceived. *Every* theory, *every* situation, not merely those defined as troublesome and in need of solution, will refract, if turned carefully in the glaring light of one's mind, a problematic color. But to understand this phenomenon, one must be open to experience and free from preconception.

John Keats long ago described the "problematic mind" as one possessed of "negative capability"—the capacity "of being in uncertainties, mysteries, doubts, without any irritable reaching after fact and reason" (5 Keats). Keats is speaking of artists, but there is reason to believe that self-realization, *creativity itself,* whether it be esthetic or scientific, is bound up with "negative capability" and "enjoying the doubtful."

> The creative individual . . . is an impressive person, and he is so because he has to such a large degree realized his potentialities. He has become in great measure the person he was capable of becoming . . .
> Creative persons are, to an extraordinary degree, open to experience, to the experience of their inner life as well as of their outer environment and culture. This would seem to be almost the basic condition for change, namely that one be receptive to new elements of experience. One of the most important dimensions along which persons differ is that

of the open or the closed mind. The open-minded person is keenly perceptive, the closed-minded person is strongly judgmental. Though it is an oversimplification to state it so bluntly, it is nonetheless true that whenever a person uses his mind for any purpose he performs either an act of perception (he becomes aware of something) or an act of judgment (he comes to a conclusion about something). And most persons are inclined to show a rather consistent preference for and greater pleasure in one or the other of these; preferring either to perceive or to judge.

One who emphasizes and prefers an attitude of judging will lead a life that is controlled, carefully planned, and orderly, and when the preference for judging is habitual and strong he becomes judgmental and in the extreme prone to prejudging. He is then the prejudiced person.

On the other hand, a preference for the perceptive attitude results in a life that is more open to experience both from within and from outside, and characterized by flexibility and spontaneity (6 MacKinnon).

Within the context of their age, Christ, Marx, Freud, and Nietzsche reveal heightened openness to experience and a profound penetration into the slipshod legacy of the mind—its old ideas, worn traditions, stale habits, entrenched attitudes, its habitual responses devoid of understanding. By reexamining entrenched convictions, matters of faith, everything man considers sacred, they were able to expose the irrationality of old ideas, and gradually to liberate men from the vice of their prejudices. In one of those ironic reversals which make life so problematic, and so comical or so despairing depending on one's perspective, their own ideas were later turned into prejudices. The fate of those who would open minds is to be digested by closed minds. Today's fresh air is tomorrow's stale. And so we come full circle: today's solution becomes tomorrow's problem. The starling introduced to rid the city of the pigeon becomes a greater menace; the insecticide used to clear the corn and save the strawberry passes out to sea and kills the shellfish and denudes the shore.

The inevitability of this pattern does not make our task easier. Even when the problem is linear, palpable, and inevitable—increase the span of life within a limited land area and one must decrease the rate of reproduction—our problem is not simply to find a solution but to find a solution that acknowledges the interrelatedness of human problems and that does not, in solving one problem, ignore another. It is at this point that minds reveal themselves to be problematic and intellectual or not.

John Dewey, in his essay on "The Supremacy of Method," has not only explicated the scientific method, but has expressed, in language more expressive than mine, my own intention in this anthology.

> ... The commonest fallacy is to suppose that since the state of doubt is accompanied by a feeling of uncertainty, knowledge arises when this feeling gives way to one of assurance. Thinking then ceases to be an effort to effect change in the objective situation and is replaced by

various devices which generate a change in feeling or "consciousness." Tendency to premature judgment, jumping at conclusion, excessive love of simplicity, making over of evidence to suit desire, taking the familiar for the clear, etc., all spring from confusing the feeling of certitude with a certified situation. Thought hastens toward the settled and is only too likely to force the pace. . . . A disciplined mind takes delight in the problematic, and cherishes it until a way out is found that approves itself upon examination. The questionable becomes an active questioning, a search; desire for the emotion of certitude gives place to quest for the objects by which the obscure and unsettled may be developed into the stable and clear.

. . . the first effect of experimentation [is] to reduce these things from the status of objects to that of data. . . . By data is signified subject-matter for further interpretation; something to be thought about. Objects are finalities; they are complete, finished; they call for thought only in the way of definition, classification, logical arrangement, subsumption in syllogisms, etc. But data signify "material to serve"; they are indications, evidence, signs, clues to and of something still to be reached; they are intermediate, not ultimate; means, not finalities.

The remarkable difference between the attitude which accepts the objects of ordinary perception, use and enjoyment as final, as culminations of natural processes and that which takes them as starting points for reflection and investigation, is one which reaches far beyond the technicalities of science. It marks a revolution in the whole spirit of life, in the entire attitude taken toward whatever is found in existence. When the things which exist around us, which we touch, see, hear and taste are regarded as interrogations for which an answer must be sought (and must be sought by means of deliberate introduction of changes till they are reshaped into something different), nature as it already exists ceases to be something which must be accepted and submitted to, endured or enjoyed, just as it is. It is now something to be modified, to be intentionally controlled. It is material to act upon so as to transform it into new objects which better answer our needs. Nature as it exists at any particular time is a challenge, rather than a completion; it provides possible starting points and opportunities rather than final ends (7 Dewey).

Dewey is speaking of the material world, but his remarks are as applicable to the world of ideas. Ideas are as susceptible to fossilization and reification as natural phenomena; it is only through a tenacious act of will and mind that they retain their status as "data"—as "indications, evidence, signs, clues to and of something still to be reached." What that "something" is, is obscure, a mystery in the sense in which Hamlet railed against Rosenrantz and Guildenstern for trying to "pluck out the heart of my mystery" (8 *Hamlet*). Like a sudden insight, we know it when we experience it. But we only experience insights as we learn to *look* for them and *recognize* them when we see them. Which brings us to a critical point.

Bertrand Russell has argued that the question "What can I know?"

is dependent on the prior question, "What can I ask?" The obvious answer—anything and everything—seems to beg the question; one wants to ask informed questions. But an "informed" question is a contradiction in terms. If one is informed, one has no question. Underlying this preference for "informed" questions is a preoccupation with information and a belief that accumulating is more valuable than speculating. People are taught to believe that there are intelligent questions and stupid ones, when in reality, there are only *honest* questions conveying genuine puzzlement and *dishonest* questions mouthed, not out of curiosity, but for effect. We are praised for our answers and not for our questions, and our creativity and our identity are thereby undermined. For answers are usually someone else's; questions are always ours. Questions are a perpetual affirmation of hope; answers affirm nothing, and the need for them is a negation of quest. A person is measured by the questions he asks as much as, if not more than, by the answers he gives. Therefore, we must look above all things to the questions we ask to insure asking questions in the most problematic manner.

We are accustomed, for example, to ask "What does it say?" (in other words, give me a report, describe the essay), not "What does it mean?" But the question "What does it say?" is poorly phrased and conceived; it has the effect of reifying the essay, of turning it into a self-contained object devoid of signs and implications. It assumes that an essay conveys fixed conclusions to us rather than creates new problems for us. It is not a "poor" question, but merely one that fails to draw out the full implications inherent in the essay. One could even assert that the value of an essay exists not only in the problems it resolves, but in the number of new problems it raises. An essay that creates but one problem—that of assenting or dissenting—has little value even if we assent to its thesis. The problems raised by the essay need not, of course, be problems contained within the scope of the essay itself; they may be problems of application. An essay describing the density and moisture requirements necessary to preserve giant redwood groves may contain within itself no problem. But it raises problems apart from that of agreement or disagreement with its content: Are these conditions being met? Can they be met? What must we do to meet them? Do we want to meet them? The essay has value not only because it has application, but because it has created new problems for us, problems of an altogether different kind. Prior to the essay, there was only one problem: Do we wish to preserve redwood groves? Now we have many. In life, we learn that knowledge does not reduce problems, it only redistributes them in time or liberates us to contemplate others. Thus an individual buying a car who knows nothing about them has no problem: he buys the one he likes and can afford. He may not get value for his money and he may have problems with the car later, but to insure trouble-free value, he would have to know something about cars, and would have had to confront the problem of choosing a car more carefully. Over a period of time, we assume that he would have more than recovered the initial extra expenditure of energy, but this is an assumption; we do not know it. It is, nevertheless, the underlying assumption of all learning and of this anthology. Energy expended today will be returned tomorrow; problems examined now will not be confronted later; uncertainty born in the present will yield certainty in the future.

The four value systems contained in the anthology each purport to explain man to himself and to unravel the meaning of human existence. Though there are common threads running throughout, even extreme resemblances between them at points, they are patently in conflict on major points. Clearly, then, they cannot *all* be accepted in their entirety. One can, of course, select a packaged value system, but by shifting perspectives, intensifying paradoxes, unraveling implications and revealing consequences, we hope to make such a choice unpalatable or untenable, and to show that value systems *do* make a difference, that the consequences are *real,* not only for the individual but for society.

Value systems are not self-evident and should not be accepted as such. Even the very concept of truth itself is part of a "faith system." The Christian believes truth to be absolute, immutable, eternal; Marx, on the other hand, believed it to be relative, dynamic, evolutionary. The Christian believes today's truth was yesterday's and will be tomorrow's; the Marxist believes today's truth evolves out of today's needs and practice just as yesterday's did, and that as these needs and practices change so will the truth. Sin, love, progress, freedom—everything—is subject to these same shifting perspectives. From among them we must choose our explanations. Even our attitude toward explanations is a perspective— ours being that an explanation is valuable insofar as it helps us to understand ourselves and the world around us, to liberate our energies and realize our potential, to predict more accurately our behavior and that of others.

This discussion seems to have taken us afield, but it has not; it has merely sharpened the nature of the choices confronting us. The essays contained in this anthology are strewn with problems in order to dramatize that life is problematic, that our consciousness, our very being, the beliefs we espouse, the values we affirm, the goals we cherish—all these are problematic, the product of our assumptions and aspirations working upon and being worked upon by our temperament and gifts. But before we can build, we must learn to doubt, and to say with Terence, "I am a man: I consider nothing human to be alien to me" (9 Terence).

Behind each of these value systems there is a model of man and of the universe. Our task is to gather together all the "indications, evidence, signs, clues"—all the assertions, judgments, evasions, declarations that comprise the available "data," in order to discern the hidden assumptions that more accurately reveal the model. Our primary questions must be "What assumptions are operative and what are their possible consequences?" Only then can we decide whether we favor the "model." We must gather together data that suggests not only *how* the model works, but *why* it works as it does. For only then can we decide whether the model works in practice as it is supposed to work in theory, whether the theory is defective or not.

We are builders, and "Ours is an age of reconstruction; to work in any field today is to rebuild."

The age of anxiety is behind us, and we have learned its lesson well: the universe is meaningless only so long as you have nothing you mean to do in it. If, however, you intend to play a role in inventing the Twenty-first Century, then yours is the task of conceiving and testing the models upon which this future world will be constructed. . . .

. . . The mind can create order out of disorder only in terms of the freshness and novelty of its hypothetical models of reality. . . . Man's power over his environment and thus over his future comes finally from his utmost abstractions. For it has become clear that man changes the future by inventing hypothetical models of possible worlds. . . .

But the startling paradox has emerged that the more abstract and detached man's . . . conceptions have become, the more relevant and useful they have been. . . . Strange as it sounds, our utmost abstractions have been our most valuable weapons in controlling and comprehending the world of concrete fact. . . .

How are these great abstractions arrived at? The scientist and mathematician answer with one word: intuition. Intuition in science means the ability to create a possible imaginary world, plus the ability to look then at the real world and see if there is any point of contact. The intuitive scientist makes a mathematical model. Then he examines it to see if it is beautiful, elegant, logically coherent, internally self-consistent. . . .

But the significance of all of this is that the creative scientists are making us aware that *any* man—not only a scientist—who wishes to transform his environment must operate as if he were, say, an intuitive physicist: that is, he must construct models of hypothetical worlds in the light of which he comprehends and controls his actual world. . . .

. . . There are innumerable kinds of models in all shapes and sizes. But they all have two things in common: they all embody the abstract *essence* of the problem to which they apply; they all are constructed in sequence of four basic steps:

1. First, a conceptual model of some kind of possible world is postulated.
2. Then, predictions are made, based on this model.
3. Next, these predictions are tested.

4. Finally, as a result of the tests, the model is either revised or discarded. . . .

One word of warning must accompany any look at the role of model-building in today's world. It is becoming clear that no conceptual model, however inventive and internally consistent, can guarantee relevance to the actual course of historical change. Just as no model in the sciences can guarantee its relevance to the flux of the natural world. There is nothing permanent or eternal about models. They must *always* be in the process of revision and must often (however reluctantly) be discarded. They give us no absolute certainty or security. But, even so, we must continue to use models because they offer the best means we have of freeing ourselves from the status quo and of envisioning the possibility of new worlds. It is now an inescapable fact that to live in his ever-changing society today, man must have the courage of his constructs, the courage of his never-static models-in-process. And he must also have the courage to let his most cherished models go when they have outlived their relevance and be willing to face the painful process of changing his models and beginning anew. For man knows now—unquestionably—that in changing his models, he changes his reality (10 Cozart).

Feel free to break the colored glass plates through which these four value systems view the world; choose from among the pieces and pick a few jagged pieces of Marxist red, a slender sliver or two of Christian white, three small shards of Freudian blue, a thin existential splinter of royal purple; piece them together in a pattern after your own model, and make yourself a stained glass window through which to see the world and be seen. In this age of strident dogmas and troubled loyalties, have we any other choice?

An Overview

CARL L. BECKER
from Climates of Opinion

Superstition, like many other fancies, very easily loses its power when, instead of flattering our vanity, it stands in the way of it. (Goethe)

I.

Like most men I hold certain cherished beliefs which I think valid because they follow logically from known and obvious facts. It often distresses me to find that an intimate friend of mine rejects one or other of these beliefs, even after I have laid before him all the relevant facts and have repeatedly retraced for his benefit the logical steps that ought to convince a reasonable mind. It may happen (is almost sure to, in fact) that he cannot refute my argument. No matter. Convinced against his will, he is of the same opinion still; and I realize at last that his mind is, unfortunately, not entirely open. Some perverse emotion, some deep-seated prejudice or unexamined preconception blinds him to the truth.

The disturbing prejudice which leads my friend to wrong conclusions I readily forgive because I understand it. It is a minor error into which I myself, but for the grace of some happy chance, might have fallen. In major matters we agree well enough, for it happens that we are both professors. Our experience and our interests are much the same. The facts that appear relevant and the deductions that win assent are, generally speaking, the same for him as for me. Most of our premises, and the phrases we employ without analysis, are those familiar in the schools. Agreeing so well in fundamentals, we may argue copiously throughout the night, except in opinion, as Carlyle said, not being divided.

It is less easy for us, two professors, to argue throughout the night with men of another way of life—with, let us say, politicians or preachers. The argument soon falters for want of agreement. Facts which they accept as relevant we question or regard as negligible. Processes of reasoning

From Carl L. Becker, *The Heavenly City of the Eighteenth-Century Philosophers* (New Haven: Yale University Press, 1932), pp. 1-28.

which bring conviction to us they dismiss with perverse and casual levity as academic. Before the night is well begun the discussion peters out. We see that it is useless to go on because their thought is vitiated, not merely on the surface by prejudices peculiar to them as individuals, but fundamentally by unconscious preconceptions that are common to all men of their profession.

Nevertheless, great as our differences are, all of us—professors, politicians, preachers—would no doubt find that we had much in common after all if it were possible to meet in the flesh some distinguished representatives of a former age. Let us for the moment give way to fantasy and suppose that we could, by rubbing a Mazda lamp, bring Dante and Thomas Aquinas before us. Since it would be a waste of precious time to discuss the weather, we might ask St. Thomas to define for us the concept of natural law, a phrase as much used in his time as it is in ours. Always apt at definition, St. Thomas would not hesitate. He would say:

> Since all things subject to Divine providence are ruled and measured by the eternal law . . . ; it is evident that all things partake somewhat of the eternal law, in so far as, namely, from its being imprinted on them, they derive their respective inclinations to their proper acts and ends. Now among all others, the rational creature is subject to Divine providence in the most excellent way, in so far as it partakes of a share of providence, by being provident both for itself and for others. Wherefore it has a share of the Eternal Reason, whereby it has a natural inclination to its proper act and end: and this participation of the eternal law in the rational creature is called the natural law.[1]

Having listened to this concise definition we might decide that after all a less academic subject would be better, for example, the League of Nations, something on which Dante had much to say under the caption of *De monarchia*. Being in favor of the League, Dante might support his position by the following argument:

> Mankind is a whole with relation to certain parts, and is a part with relation to a certain whole. It is a whole, of course, with relation to particular kingdoms and nations, as was shown above, and it is a part with relation to the whole universe, as is self-evident. Therefore, in the manner in which the constituent parts of . . . humanity correspond to humanity as a whole, so, we say, . . . humanity corresponds as a part to its larger whole. That the constituent parts of . . . humanity correspond to humanity as a whole through the one only principle of submission to a single Prince, can be easily gathered from what has gone before. And therefore humanity corresponds to the universe itself, or to its Prince,

---

1. *Summa theologica,* Part II (First Part), Q. XCI, art. ii.

who is God, . . . simply through one only principle, namely, the submission to a single Prince. We conclude from this that Monarchy [League of Nations] is necessary to the world for its well-being.[2]

After this the discussion would no doubt drag heavily. For what could any of us say in reply to either Dante or St. Thomas? Whatever we might say, on one side or the other, it is unlikely that either of them would find it strictly relevant, or even understand which side of the argument we were espousing. One thing only would be clear to us, namely, that the two men employed the same technique for achieving obscurity. Perhaps our first impulse would be to concede charitably that the distinguished guests were not at their best; our second, to mutter that, with all due respect, they were paying us with nonsensical rigmaroles. It may be so; to the modern mind, indeed, it is so; and it would clearly be unwise, for example, to reprint the *De monarchia* as a League of Nations propagandist tract. Nevertheless, what troubles me is that I cannot dismiss Dante or St. Thomas as unintelligent men. The judgment of posterity has placed them among the lordly ones of the earth; and if their arguments are unintelligible to us the fact cannot be attributed to lack of intelligence in them. They were at least as intelligent and learned as many who in our time have argued for or against the League of Nations—as intelligent perhaps as Clemenceau, as learned as Wilson.

Professor Whitehead has recently restored to circulation a seventeenth-century phrase—"climate of opinion." The phrase is much needed. Whether arguments command assent or not depends less upon the logic that conveys them than upon the climate of opinion in which they are sustained. What renders Dante's argument or St. Thomas' definition meaningless to us is not bad logic or want of intelligence, but the medieval climate of opinion—those instinctively held preconceptions in the broad sense, that *Weltanschauung* or world pattern—which imposed upon Dante and St. Thomas a peculiar use of the intelligence and a special type of logic. To understand why we cannot easily follow Dante or St. Thomas it is necessary to understand (as well as may be) the nature of this climate of opinion.

It is well known that the medieval world pattern, deriving from Greek logic and the Christian story, was fashioned by the church which for centuries imposed its authority upon the isolated and anarchic society of western Europe. The modern mind, which curiously notes and carefully describes everything, can indeed describe this climate of opinion although it cannot live in it. In this climate of opinion it was an unquestioned fact that the world and man in it had been created in six days by God the Father, an omniscient and benevolent intelligence, for an ultimate if in-

2. *De monarchia* (English ed., 1904), Bk. I, chap. vii, pp. 24–25.

scrutable purpose. Although created perfect, man had through disobedience fallen from grace into sin and error, thereby incurring the penalty of eternal damnation. Yet happily a way of atonement and salvation had been provided through the propitiatory sacrifice of God's only begotten son. Helpless in themselves to avert the just wrath of God, men were yet to be permitted, through his mercy, and by humility and obedience to his will, to obtain pardon for sin and error. Life on earth was but a means to this desired end, a temporary probation for the testing of God's children. In God's appointed time, the Earthly City would come to an end, the earth itself be swallowed up in flames. On that last day good and evil men would be finally separated. For the recalcitrant there was reserved a place of everlasting punishment; but the faithful would be gathered with God in the Heavenly City, there in perfection and felicity to dwell forever.

Existence was thus regarded by the medieval man as a cosmic drama, composed by the master dramatist according to a central theme and on a rational plan. Finished in idea before it was enacted in fact, before the world began, written down to the last syllable of recorded time, the drama was unalterable either for good or evil. There it was, precisely defined, to be understood as far as might be, but at all events to be remorselessly played out to its appointed end. The duty of man was to accept the drama as written, since he could not alter it; his function, to play the rôle assigned. That he might play his rôle according to the divine text, subordinate authorities—church and state—deriving their just powers from the will of God, were instituted among men to dispose them to submission and to instruct them in their proper lines. Intelligence was essential, since God had endowed men with it. But the function of intelligence was strictly limited. Useless to inquire curiously into the origin or final state of existence, since both had been divinely determined and sufficiently revealed. Useless, even impious, to inquire into its ultimate meaning, since God alone could fully understand it. The function of intelligence was therefore to demonstrate the truth of revealed knowledge, to reconcile diverse and pragmatic experience with the rational pattern of the world as given in faith.

Under the bracing influence of this climate of opinion the best thought of the time assumed a thoroughly rationalistic form. I know it is the custom to call the thirteenth century an age of faith, and to contrast it with the eighteenth century, which is thought to be preëminently the age of reason. In a sense the distinction is true enough, for the word "reason," like other words, has many meanings. Since eighteenth-century writers employed reason to discredit Christian dogma, a "rationalist" in common parlance came to mean an "unbeliever," one who denied the truth of Christianity. In this sense Voltaire was a rationalist, St. Thomas a man of faith. But this use of the word is unfortunate, since it obscures the fact that reason may be employed to support faith as well as to destroy it. There were, certainly, many differences between Voltaire and St. Thomas, but the two men had much in common for all that. What they had in common was the profound conviction that their beliefs could be reasonably demonstrated. In a very real sense it may be said of the eighteenth century that it was an age of faith as well as of reason, and of the thirteenth century that it was an age of reason as well as of faith.

This is not a paradox. On the contrary, passionate faith and an expert rationalism are apt to be united. Most men (of course I need parentheses here to take care of simple-minded folk and the genuine mystics)—most intelligent men who believe passionately that God's in his heaven and all's right with the world—feel the need of good and sufficient reasons for their faith, all the more so if a few disturbing doubts have crept in to make them uneasy. This is perhaps one of the reasons why the thought of Dante's time was so remorselessly rationalistic. The faith was still intact, surely; but it was just ceasing to be instinctively held—its ablest adherents just becoming conscious that it was held as faith. All the more need, therefore, for proving it up to the hilt. It was precisely because St. Thomas believed in a divinely ordered world that he needed, for his own peace of mind, an impregnable rational proof of a divinely ordered world. He could never have said, with Tertullian, "I believe that which is absurd." He could easily have said, with St. Anselm, "I believe in order that I may know." He might well have added, "I should be distressed indeed if I could not find a rational demonstration of what I know."

To reconcile diverse and pragmatic experience with a rational pattern of the world is a sufficiently difficult task, even if experience be limited and knowledge not too great—an impossible task unless logic proves amenable to the reasons of the heart which reason knows not of. And so the men of Dante's time found it. To devise a highly intricate dialectic was, of course, essential, but the least of their difficulties; for even with the aid of Aristotle's logic it was still not always possible to press what William James called the "irreducible brute facts" into the neat categories prescribed by the faith. It was therefore necessary, in emergencies, to seek, beneath the literal significance of authoritative texts, hidden meanings which could be elicited only by the aid of a symbolical interpretation. *Litera gesta docet; quid credas, allegoria; moralis quid agas; quo tendas, anagogia*—so runs the famous formula which the schoolmen devised for use in the schools, a formula which might be freely rendered:

> The letter teaches what we know,
> Anagogia what we hope is so;
> Faith's confirmed by allegories,
> Conduct's shaped by moral stories.

Thus it was possible for the thirteenth century, employing a highly intricate dialectic supported on occasion by a symbolical interpretation, to justify the ways of God to man. Paradise lost and paradise regained—such was the theme of the drama of existence as understood in that age; and all the best minds of the time were devoted to its explication. Theology related and expounded the history of the world. Philosophy was the science that rationalized and reconciled nature and history. Logic provided both theology and philosophy with an adequate methodology. As a result we have, among innumerable other works, the *Summa theologica,* surely one of the most amazing and stupendous products of the human mind. It is safe to say that never before or since has the wide world been so neatly boxed and compassed, so completely and confidently understood, every known detail of it fitted, with such subtle and loving precision, into a consistent and convincing whole.

We have now remained in the medieval climate of opinion as long as it is perhaps quite safe to do. Let us then descend from the peaks of the thirteenth to the lower levels of the twentieth century—to an atmosphere in which, since it is charged with a richer factual content, we can breathe with greater ease and comfort.

II.

What then can we—scientists, historians, philosophers of the twentieth century—make of the theology-history, the philosophy-science, the dialectic-methodology of the thirteenth century? We can—must, indeed, since that is our habit—peruse with infinite attention and indifference the serried, weighty folios of the *Summa* and such works now carefully preserved in libraries. We can perhaps wonder a little—although, since nothing is alien to us, we are rarely caught wondering—at the unfailing zest, the infinite patience, the extraordinary ingenuity and acumen therein displayed. We can even understand what is therein recorded well enough to translate it clumsily into modern terms. The one thing we cannot do with the *Summa* of St. Thomas is to meet its arguments on their own ground. We can neither assent to them nor refute them. It does not even occur to us to make the effort, since we instinctively feel that in the climate of opinion which sustains such arguments we could only gasp for breath. Its conclusions seem to us neither true nor false, but only irrelevant; and they seem irrelevant because the world pattern into which they are so dexterously woven is no longer capable of eliciting from us either an emotional or an aesthetic response.

With the best will in the world it is quite impossible for us to conceive of existence as a divinely ordered drama, the beginning and end of which is known, the significance of which has once for all been revealed. For good or ill we must regard the world as a continuous flux, a ceaseless and infinitely complicated process of waste and repair, so that "all things and principles of things" are to be regarded as no more than "inconstant modes or fashions," as the "concurrence, renewed from moment to moment, of forces parting sooner or later on their way." The beginning of this continuous process of change is shrouded in impenetrable mist; the end seems more certain, but even less engaging. According to J. H. Jeans:

> Everything points with overwhelming force to a definite event, or series of events, of creation at some time or times, not infinitely remote. The universe cannot have originated by chance out of its present ingredients, and neither can it have been always the same as now. For in either of these events no atoms would be left save such as are incapable of dissolving into radiation; there would be neither sunlight nor starlight but only a cool glow of radiation uniformly diffused through space. This is, indeed, so far as present-day science can see, the final end towards which all creation moves, and at which it must at long last arrive.[3]

We need not, of course, make immediate preparation for that far-off, portentous event; the universe is still a going concern and will outlast our time. But we may be reasonably curious about the relation of man to this inevitable running down of the universe. How did man enter this galley, and what is he doing in it? According to Professor Dampier-Whetham, science offers two possible answers:

> Life ... may be regarded either as a negligible accident in a bye-product of the cosmic process, or as the supreme manifestation of the high effort of creative evolution, for which the Earth alone, in the chances of time and space, has given a fitting home.[4]

Between these alternatives there is little enough to choose, since in either case man must be regarded as part of the cosmic process, fated to extinction with it. Let us listen to Bertrand Russell:

> That man is the product of causes which had no prevision of the end they were achieving; that his origin, his growth, his hopes and fears, his loves and his beliefs, are but the outcome of accidental collocations of atoms; that no fire, no heroism, no intensity of thought and feeling can preserve an individual life beyond the grave; that all the labours of all the ages, all the devotion, all the inspiration, all the noonday brightness of human genius are destined to extinction in the vast death of the solar

---

3. *Eos, or the Wider Aspects of Cosmogony,* p. 55; quoted in Dampier-Whetham, *A History of Science,* p. 483.
4. *A History of Science,* p. 482.

system, and that the whole temple of man's achievement must inevitably be buried beneath the debris of a universe in ruins—all these things, if not quite beyond dispute, are yet so nearly certain that no philosophy which rejects them can hope to stand.[5]

Edit and interpret the conclusions of modern science as tenderly as we like, it is still quite impossible for us to regard man as the child of God for whom the earth was created as a temporary habitation. Rather must we regard him as little more than a chance deposit on the surface of the world, carelessly thrown up between two ice ages by the same forces that rust iron and ripen corn, a sentient organism endowed by some happy or unhappy accident with intelligence indeed, but with an intelligence that is conditioned by the very forces that it seeks to understand and to control. The ultimate cause of this cosmic process of which man is a part, whether God or electricity or a "stress in the ether," we know not. Whatever it may be, if indeed it be anything more than a necessary postulate of thought, it appears in its effects as neither benevolent nor malevolent, as neither kind nor unkind, but merely as indifferent to us. What is man that the electron should be mindful of him! Man is but a foundling in the cosmos, abandoned by the forces that created him. Unparented, unassisted and undirected by omniscient or benevolent authority, he must fend for himself, and with the aid of his own limited intelligence find his way about in an indifferent universe.

Such is the world pattern that determines the character and direction of modern thinking. The pattern has been a long time in the weaving. It has taken eight centuries to replace the conception of existence as divinely composed and purposeful drama by the conception of existence as a blindly running flux of disintegrating energy. But there are signs that the substitution is now fully accomplished; and if we wished to reduce eight centuries of intellectual history to an epigram, we could not do better than to borrow the words of Aristophanes, "Whirl is king, having deposed Zeus."

Perhaps the most important consequence of this revolution is that we look about in vain for any semblance of the old authority, the old absolute, for any stable foothold from which to get a running start. Zeus, having been deposed, can no longer serve as a first premise of thought. It is true we may still believe in Zeus; many people do. Even scientists, historians, philosophers still accord him the customary worship. But this is no more than a personal privilege, to be exercised in private, as formerly, in Protestant countries, Papists were sometimes permitted to celebrate mass in private chapels. No serious scholar would now postulate the existence and goodness of God as a point of departure for explaining

---

5. *Mysticism and Logic*, p. 47; quoted in Dampier-Whetham, *A History of Science*, p. 487.

the quantum theory or the French Revolution. If I should venture, as certain historians once did, to expound the thought of the eigthteenth century as having been foreordained by God for the punishment of a perverse and stiff-necked generation, you would shift uneasily in your chairs, you would "register" embarrassment, and even blush a little to think that a trusted colleague should exhibit such bad taste. The fact is that we have no first premise. Since Whirl is king, we must start with the whirl, the mess of things as presented in experience. We start with the irreducible brute fact, and we must take it as we find it, since it is no longer permitted to coax or cajole it, hoping to fit it into some or other category of thought on the assumption that the pattern of the world is a logical one. Accepting the fact as given, we observe it, experiment with it, verify it, classify it, measure it if possible, and reason about it as little as may be. The questions we ask are "What?" and "How?" What are the facts and how are they related? If sometimes, in a moment of absent-mindedness or idle diversion, we ask the question "Why?" the answer escapes us. Our supreme object is to measure and master the world rather than to understand it.

Since our supreme object is to measure and master the world, we can make relatively little use of theology, philosophy, and deductive logic—the three stately entrance ways to knowledge erected in the Middle Ages. In the course of eight centuries these disciplines have fallen from their high estate, and in their place we have enthroned history, science, and the technique of observation and measurement. Theology, or something that goes under that name, is still kept alive by the faithful, but only by artificial respiration. Its functions, the services it rendered in the time of St. Thomas, have been taken over, not as is often supposed by philosophy, but by history—the study of man and his world in the time sequence. Theology in the thirteenth century presented the story of man and the world according to the divine plan of salvation. It provided the men of that age with an authentic philosophy of history, and they could afford to ignore the factual experience of mankind since they were so well assured of its ultimate cause and significance. But in the succeeding centuries men turned more and more to an investigation of the recorded story of mankind, bringing to that enterprise a remarkable attention to detail, an ever greater preoccupation with the factual event. In the light of the mass of irreducible brute facts thus accumulated, the theological vision of man and his world faded into a pale replica of the original picture. In the eighteenth century the clear-cut theological philosophy of history had degenerated into an amiable and gentlemanly "philosophy teaching by example." In the early nineteenth century, history could still be regarded as the Transcendent Idea realizing itself in the actual. In our time, history is nothing but history, the notation of what has occurred, just as it happened. The object of history, according to Santayana, is quite simply "to fix the order of events throughout past times in all places." No respectable historian any longer harbors ulterior motives; and one who should surreptitiously introduce the gloss of a transcendent interpretation into the human story would deserve to be called a philosopher and straightway lose his reputation as a scholar.

I am, of course, using the word "history" in the broad sense. It is to be understood as a method of approach rather than as a special field of study. Literature and language, government and law, economics, science and mathematics, love and sport—what is there that has not in our time been studied historically? Much of what is called science is properly history, the history of biological or physical phenomena. The geologist gives us the history of the earth; the botanist relates the life history of plants. Professor Whitehead has recently illuminated physics by tracing the history of physical concepts. To regard all things in their historical setting appears, indeed, to be an instructive procedure of the modern mind. We do it without thinking, because we can scarcely think at all without doing it. The modern climate of opinion is such that we cannot seemingly understand our world unless we regard it as a going concern. We cannot properly know things as they are unless we know "how they came to be what they are." Nor is it merely, or chiefly, the succession of external events that engages our attention. No doubt St. Thomas was aware that one thing follows another. What is peculiar to the modern mind is the disposition and the determination to regard ideas and concepts, the truth of things as well as the things themselves, as changing entities, the character and significance of which at any given time can be fully grasped only by regarding them as points in an endless process of differentiation, of unfolding, of waste and repair. Let St. Thomas ask *us* to define anything—for example, the natural law—let him ask us to tell him what it *is*. We cannot do it. But, given time enough, we can relate for him its history. We can tell him what varied forms the natural law has assumed up to now. Historical-mindedness is so much a preconception of modern thought that we can identify a particular thing only by pointing to the various things it successively was before it became that particular thing which it will presently cease to be.

Besides the historical approach to knowledge we have another to which we are even more committed—the scientific. As history has gradually replaced theology, so science has replaced philosophy. Philosophy, it is true, has managed, much better than theology, to keep up appearances in the modern world, and at the present moment signs are not wanting of refurbishings going on in its ancient and somewhat dilapidated dwelling. Yet, it is obvious that the undisputed sway which it formerly exercised has long been usurped by natural science. In the hands of St. Thomas, philosophy, with "deductive" logic as its instrument of precision, was a method of building a rational world, its aim being to reconcile experience with revealed truth. But the influences which disposed succeeding generations to examine the facts of human history, induced them also to examine the facts of natural phenomena. The rise of history and of science were but two results of a single impulse, two aspects of the trend of modern thought away from an overdone rationalization of the facts to a more careful and disinterested examination of the facts themselves.

Galileo, for example (not that he was the first by any means), did not ask what Aristotle had said about falling bodies, or whether it was reasonable to suppose that a ten-pound weight would fall to the ground more quickly than a one-pound weight. He applied to this problem the scientific method. He dropped two weights, differing as ten to one, from the leaning tower, and noted the fact that both weights reached the ground at the same time. In such a world as this, he said in effect, this is the way falling bodies behave. If that is not possible in a rational world, then the world we live in is not a rational one. Facts are primary and what chiefly concern us; they are stubborn and irreducible and we cannot get around them. They may be in accord with reason, let us hope that they are; but whether they are so or not is only a question of fact to be determined like any other.

This subtle shift in the point of view was perhaps the most important event in the intellectual history of modern times, but its implications were not at once understood. Philosophy continued to reign, and when in the eighteenth century she added a new word to her title (calling herself natural philosophy), no one noted that fact as ominous. Galileo and his successors were philosophers too, preëminently so, since their marvelous discoveries, based upon observation and experiment, uncovered so many secret places in the world, and by promising to banish mystery from the universe seemed to leave it more obviously rational than they found it. The laws of nature and nature's God appeared henceforth to be one and the same thing, and since every part of God's handiwork could all in good time be reasonably demonstrated, the intelligent man could very well do with a minimum of faith—except, of course (the exception was tremendous but scarcely noticed at the time), faith in the uniform behavior of nature and in the capacity of reason to discover its *modus operandi*.

In the course of the nineteenth century this optimistic outlook became overcast. The marriage of fact and reason, of science and the universal laws of nature, proved to be somewhat irksome, and in the twentieth century it was, not without distress, altogether dissolved. Natural philosophy was transformed into natural science. Natural science became science, and scientists rejected, as a personal affront, the title of philosopher, which formerly they had been proud to bear. The vision of man and his world as a neat and efficient machine, designed by an intelligent Author of the Universe, gradually faded away. Professors of science ceased to speak with any assurance of the laws of nature, and were content to pursue, with unabated ardor, but without any teleological implications whatever, their proper business of observing and experimenting with the something which is the stuff of the universe, of measuring and mastering its stress and movement. "Science," said Lloyd Morgan, "deals exclusively with changes of configuration, and traces the accelerations which are observed to occur, leaving to metaphysics to deal with the underlying agency, if it exist." [6]

It is well known that the result of pursuing this restricted aim (the scientific method reduced to its lowest terms) has been astounding. It is needless to say that we live in a machine age, that the art of inventing is the greatest of our inventions, or that within a brief space of fifty years the outward conditions of life have been transformed. It is less well understood that this bewildering experience has given a new slant to our minds. Fresh discoveries and new inventions are no longer the result of fortunate accidents which we are expected to note with awe. They are all a part of the day's work, anticipated, deliberately intended, and brought to pass according to schedule. Novelty has ceased to excite wonder because it has ceased to be novelty; on the contrary, the strange, so habituated have we become to it, is of the very essence of the customary. There is nothing new in heaven or earth not dreamt of in our laboratories; and we should be amazed indeed if tomorrow and tomorrow and tomorrow failed to offer us something new to challenge our capacity for readjustment. Science has taught us the futility of troubling to understand the "underlying agency" of the things we use. We have found that we can drive an automobile without knowing how the carburetor works, and listen to a radio without mastering the secret of radiation. We really haven't time to stand amazed, either at the starry firmament above or the Freudian complexes within us. The multiplicity of things to manipulate and make use of so fully engages our attention that we have neither the leisure nor the inclination to seek a rational explanation of the force that makes them function so efficiently.

In dismissing the underlying agency with a casual shrug, we are in good company. The high priest of science, even more than the common man, is a past master of this art. It is one of the engaging ironies of modern thought that the scientific method, which it was once fondly hoped would banish mystery from the world, leaves it every day more inexplicable. Physics, which it was thought had dispensed with the need of metaphysics, has been transformed by its own proper researches into the most metaphysical of disciplines. The more attentively the physicist looks at the material stuff of the world the less there is to see. Under his expert treatment the substantial world of Newtonian physics has been dissolved into a

6. *Interpretation of Nature*, p. 58.

complex of radiant energies. No efficient engineer or Prime Mover could have designed the world, since it can no longer be fully understood in terms of mechanics. "What's the sense of talking about a mechanical explanation," asks Professor Whitehead, "when you do not know what you mean by mechanics?" [7] We are told that if we ascribe position to anything it ceases to have determinable velocity; if we ascertain its velocity it ceases to have determinable position. The universe is said to be composed of atoms, an atom is said to be composed of a nucleus around which electrons revolve in determinable orbits; but experiments seem to show that an electron may, for reasons best known to itself, be moving in two orbits at the same time. To this point Galileo's common-sense method of noting the behavior of things, of sticking close to the observable facts, has brought us: it has at last presented us with a fact that common sense repudiates.

What can we do? Reason and logic cry out in pain no doubt; but we have long since learned not to bother overmuch with reason and logic. Logic was formerly visualized as something outside us, something existing independently which, if we were willing, could take us by the hand and lead us into the paths of truth. We now suspect that it is something the mind has created to conceal its timidity and keep up its courage, a hocus-pocus designed to give formal validity to conclusions we are willing to accept if everybody else in our set will too. If all men are mortal (an assumption), and if Socrates was a man (in the sense assumed), no doubt Socrates must have been mortal; but we suspect that we somehow knew all this before it was submitted to the test of a syllogism. Logics have a way of multiplying in response to the changes in point of view. First there was one logic, then there were two, then there were several; so that now, according to one authority (if a contributor to the *Encyclopaedia Britannica* who ventures to employ humor can be an authority), the state of logic is "that of Israel under the Judges, every man doeth that which is right in his own eyes." With all due allowance made for mathematical logic (which has to do with concepts, not with facts), and for the logic of probability (which Mr. Keynes assures us has a probable validity), the secure foundations of deductive and inductive logic have been battered to pieces by the ascertainable facts, so that we really have no choice; we must cling to the ascertainable facts though they slay us.

Physicists, therefore, stick to the ascertainable facts. If logic presumes to protest in the name of the law, they know how to square it, so that it complaisantly looks the other way while they go on with illicit enterprises—with the business, for example (it is Sir William Bragg who vouches for it), of teaching "the wave theory of light on Monday, Wednesday, and Friday, and the quantum theory on Tuesday, Thursday, and Saturday." It need not surprise us, then, to learn that physicists make

7. *Science and the Modern World*, p. 24.

nothing, when it suits their convenience, of regarding nucleus and electron, not as substances, but only as radiations—thus, casually dissolving the substantial world into a congeries of repellent and attractive velocities which we are invited to believe in because they can be mathematically identified and made use of. Perhaps, as Professor Jeans suggests, the world we live in was designed by a mathematician. Why not, indeed, if it can be most easily understood in terms of mathematical formulas? We know that two apples plus two apples make four apples. We have always taken it for granted that the apples exist, but we can very well understand that even if no apples are anywhere found it still remains true that two plus two make four. The mathematician gets on just as well without the apples, better indeed, since the apples have other attributes besides number. When sufficiently hard pressed, therefore, the physicist solves his difficulties by turning mathematician. As mathematician he can calculate the velocities that are observed to occur, meantime assuring us that the velocities could readily be attributed to substantial electrons, provided substantial electrons with such velocities should ever turn up. There is really no occasion for despair: our world can be computed even if it doesn't exist.

Perhaps I have said enough to suggest that the essential quality of the modern climate of opinion is factual rather than rational. The atmosphere which sustains our thought is so saturated with the actual that we can easily do with a minimum of the theoretical. We necessarily look at our world from the point of view of history and from the point of view of science. Viewed historically, it appears to be something in the making, something which can at best be only tentatively understood since it is not yet finished. Viewed scientifically, it appears as something to be accepted, something to be manipulated and mastered, something to adjust ourselves to with the least possible stress. So long as we can make efficient use of things, we feel no irresistible need to understand them. No doubt it is for this reason chiefly that the modern mind can be so wonderfully at ease in a mysterious universe.

Christianity

Introduction

One can scarcely understand the documents and institutions of Christianity without appreciating the hold that Christianity's assumptions still exercise on the imagination of people no longer professedly Christian. Years of sustained effort would be necessary to even begin to recognize, for example, the many subtle manifestations of the assumption that an ethical equation operates throughout the universe. Such a belief may manifest itself in the most trivial and perverted ways, from a *quid pro quo,* tit-for-tat, mentality about gifts and invitations through more important ones dealing with grades and wages, until finally we seize upon the fundamental ideological difference between the capitalist and communist concept of just recompense. Marx's "from each according to his ability; to each according to his need," seems to collectivize justice and rob it of its individual application: to each according to his deserts. Ultimately, however, even this assumption of an operative ethical equation is in Christianity, a secondary one. Nor is the concept of original sin the cornerstone, as is so often presupposed. The entire edifice of both the Christian and the Marxist world views is built on a belief in the objective validation of experience.[1] If we were compelled, as fortunately we are not, to isolate the bedrock premise of Christianity, we would turn to a belief in objective—that is, external—criteria: God exists and God's laws are facts as immutable as natural law; sin, though spiritualized and internalized, never lost its objective character, its categorical nature. Christianity thus immediately raised the ultimate ethical question: to what extent do intentions extenuate behavior?—raised it but never resolved it. We are compelled to walk the narrow way to the strait gate. On one side is the legalism that Christ so hated in the Pharisees, the empty ritual and dogma devoid of true spiritual understanding; on the other, feeling without awareness of what is constant and enduring in man and nature.

Paul makes it clear that we belong ultimately to God and are answerable only to him; our conscience is inviolate, the final court of

---

1. See John Wilson, "Verification and Religious Language" and "Religious Experience," pp. 149–167 below for an explication of some of the philosophical difficulties involved in validating Christian experience.

appeals. And yet, in an attempt to reconcile the differences between the letter and the spirit, between the objective act and the subjective intention, he reminds us that "love is the fulfilling of the law." This summary remark failed to put to rest the dilemma between the objective deed and the subjective spirit; the question of freedom and responsibility became a favorite topic of medieval scholastics. Man must be free to be responsible, they argued, and if, with total trust in the rightness of his act, a man acts, how can he be punished for his act without reducing his willingness to act out his freedom? The dilemma took many forms: Does God will the good, or is it good because God wills it? True freedom is doing God's will. Every form was intent upon maintaining the narrow path, and so long as God's way was intelligible to man, no serious problem arose. Difficulties began when man had trouble following God's will because he no longer knew it or no longer trusted an intermediary to define it for him.

The dilemma persists to this day. Christianity believes in the individual conscience but it also believes in objective sin, in categorical imperatives—in "thou shalt nots." The consequent tension, the possibility of making a subjective error, of making a false judgment, of following an erroneous conscience, makes the Christian liable to two perversions. The first is a sense of insecurity in following the dictates of conscience; this insecurity in turn creates a need for certification by an infallible authority, for closed systems that have an infallible certainty about them. An even more prevalent perversion—and more pernicious because so idealistic and self-destructive—is the adoption of a double standard, one for virtues and one for vices. Virtues become objective, discernible, measurable and, above all, comparative. Everyone displays them and measures himself against others. Vices become subjective, impalpable, fleeting, and particular. They are the individual's concern, hidden and his alone. The result of comparisons, of knowing one's own dark and light side, while knowing another's light side only, is self-disgust and hatred for the other's chaste luminosity. Such speculations should reveal something of how the permutations of religious ideas create seemingly remote but really closely connected consequences.

Constantly beset by heresies and schisms as one strand after another of its thought was questioned, Christianity has shifted emphasis many times. Throughout history, however—even during the Reformation when the individual conscience was accorded a special importance—Christianity has clung to its belief in the objective nature of truth, justice, and virtue, and in the existence of objective criteria by which to measure them. As Max Weber and others have suggested, Calvinists, originally ascetic, and indifferent to wealth almost accidentally accumulated as a by-product of the Protestant ethic, gradually came to accept good fortune and material wealth, or the lack thereof, as criteria of moral worth—signs of "election" to heaven or damnation to hell. The consequences of this objectification are still with us in the form of prejudice against the poor, and in programs subsidizing the wealthy instead of the poor.

Scholars have made much of the increasing humaneness and the growing spiritualization of, and application of reason to, the moral life in the transition from the Old to the New Testament. This view is somewhat oversimplified. Certainly there was a loosening of the law to make it more situational and compassionate; certainly the Mosaic spirit of *lex talionis*—eye-for-eye, tooth-for-tooth—gave way to the spirit of forgiveness and the Golden Rule—"Treat others as you would like them to treat you." But we must not overestimate the significance of this change, for it is not really a change in assumptions, but merely a change in the agent of retaliation and in its location. The principle of retribution is still present, only now God is the agent—"Vengeance is mine, says the Lord"—and the place of repayment is changed from earth to hell. A vast difference separates the Christian ethic—which even Reinhold Niebuhr, a leading Portestant theologian, admits nowhere contains any idea of genuine self-sacrifice—and the pagan Aristotelian concept of magnanimity, great-hearted, unselfish action out of a sense of what is beautiful and worthy in oneself. Dostoyevsky has gone so far as to argue that without immortality and the principle of retribution, Christianity becomes untenable and life unbearable, for then "all things are permitted." If God is not the ultimate certifier of good and evil, then good and evil cease to exist objectively; evil becomes a state of mind, and we are led to Miguel de Unamuno's belief that evil exists only in the intention and not in the act.

Dostoevsky's argument is extremely persuasive, but, as we shall see, it is only one way of looking at a complex ethical problem. We are not really interested in his argument so much as in the nature of his assumptions, for he too, as is evident by his anxiety at the elimination of rewards and punishments, shares a belief in human depravity.

Next to a belief in the objective nature of virtue, truth, and justice, a Christian's world view is determined by his consciousness of man's sinful nature. Most people, if asked to explain the concept of original sin, would murmur something about Adam and Eve, the serpent and the Fall, since the full significance of the concept is lost on them. And yet the concept of original sin sets up profound reverberations in an individual's psyche, and once exposed to it, it not only colors but to some extent predetermines one's perceptions.

The concept of "original sin" is probably as close as we can come to a direct antithesis to Jean-Paul Sartre's statement that "Existence precedes essence." By such a remark, Sartre means that man *exists*, is alive and breathes, before he defines his nature ("his essence") as either noble or ignoble. Those who accept the doctrine of "original sin," instead of maintaining with Sartre that sinners are those who sin, would insist that man sins *because he is a sinner*. Man's nature, his essence as a sinner, is thus defined even before he commits an objective sin. He is born in sin (through the Fall and Adam's lust) and has inherited it. Man is *defined*.

It was Paul who first emphasized man's sinfulness and defined him through it:

> This emphasis [on man's sinful nature] constitutes the essential matter in Paul's life and thought. He had been reared in a system [the Hebraic] where sin was regarded as transgression of law, and where repentance, forgiveness, and amendment of life were the cure. This legal estimate of sin's nature seemed to him utterly inadequate. Man's sin had deeper roots than wilful disobedience; it was, as it were, a demonic power so that it was not Paul who did evil but "sin which dwelleth in me." Deep-seated and inveterate, sinfulness was now regarded as so essentially a part of human nature that no mere forgiveness of transgressions could salve its evil or volitional amendment undo its harm. A profound, interior deliverance was needed; one must pass from the dominion of the flesh into the dominion of the spirit. Short of that, the old moral cures of repentance and forgiveness were mere palliatives, failing to deal with the real disease—"In me, that is, in my flesh, dwelleth no good thing. . . ."
> This radical estimate of the nature of sin, with accompanying demand for a radical deliverance, while phrased by Paul in terms uniquely characteristic of himself, is one of the major contributions of the New Testament (11 Fosdick).

As a concept, "original sin" obviously shapes man's sense of his relationship to God, and therefore his image of his own powers. Christianity went beyond Judaism in humanizing God, and in spiritualizing man's relation to him by making it more immediate and personal, more human and loving. From one perspective it enhanced man: God so loved man that he sacrificed his only son to free man from the bondage of sin and death; from another perspective, it diminished and impoverished him, for man's ability to work his own salvation was taken from him.

> Thus, in Christianity, the emphasis falls not only on the individual's sense of his dignity in being united with God, but also on his sinful weakness and creaturely infirmity, the sense of the need for trust in God and the help of God and the confidence in His mercy as the source of all that is good. . . . The individual, in spite of his sense of personal worth, still remains an unprofitable servant, needing forgiveness, and in expectation of a settlement of accounts with God, must in brotherly love destroy all human debit accounts, all calculations between man and man (12 Troeltsch).

This remark by Ernst Troeltsch reveals the way in which the concept of original sin divested man of any *intrinsic* qualities worthy of respect, thereby diminishing self-respect and increasing one's sense of humility. All worth was vested in a transcendent being and in salvation through him. The result is that love is made more central, and as is clearly true to life, more irrational and volitional; love is given. It cannot be earned. Still the total effect is to create a delicate balance easily gone awry, for most people want to understand why they are loved and want to feel there are objective reasons for it.[2] Failing to find any, and unable to understand or to return such unearned love, they come to doubt its existence or their capacity. Christianity well understood that love has nothing to do with justice. Thus justice, so central to the Old Testament, gives way in the New Testament to forgiveness, for as Hamlet remarks, "Use every man after his desert, and who should 'scape whipping?"

But the effect of a preoccupation with forgiveness instead of justice increases God's involvement in human affairs and thereby increases man's resistance. As Camus, speaking of metaphysical rebellion, has remarked:

> Rebellion, after all, can only be imagined in terms of opposition to someone. The only thing that gives meaning to human protest is the idea of a personal god who has created, and is therefore responsible for, everything. And so we can say, without being paradoxical, that in the Western World the history of rebellion is inseparable from the history of Christianity. . . .
>
> Only a personal god can be asked by the rebel for a personal accounting. When the personal god begins to reign, rebellion assumes its most resolutely ferocious aspect and pronounces a definitive no. With Cain, the first act of rebellion coincides with the first crime. (13 Camus).

Rebellion presupposes indignity, and, indeed, gone is the dignity implied by the Old Testament concept of justice; gone entirely are the confrontations between God and man where a Job can uphold his righteousness before God ("I desire to argue with God. . . . I know that I am innocent.") or where God is schooled by man (Genesis, 18.17-33); in return we have the Incarnation and the Crucifixion: salvation through love and suffering. Abandoned is any possibility of a covenant between man and God—for man is sinful and God is merciful—as well as any serious attempt to understand God in human, rational terms.

Instead, salvation is assumed to the faithful who uphold the law. Faith no longer means fidelity, attentive obedience to the will of God; it means trust, confidence and hope in God. Lost is independence and self-reliance; gained is the security, intimacy and assurance that comes from knowing one is loved; gained is a renewed sense of the spirit of love which should animate interpersonal relationships; gained a greater

2. For a detailed discussion of the perversion of love into a "commodity" to be bartered, see Fromm, especially paragraph 6.

sense of ethics as situational, rational, and contingent rather than absolute; gained a new sense of the order of the universe; gained a new sense of human brotherhood, of the family of man. The religion of the Patriarchs and Prophets becomes the religion of Christ, the Son of God. From Judaism, a father-oriented faith, we arrive at Christianity, a religion identified with the Son.[3]

The implications of these comparisons, rapidly sketched, are far reaching. We have neither time nor desire to undertake a closer examination of the two religions' assumptions and applications, which find their common ground in man's relation to God and the concept of sin. Sin in Judaism occurs when one violates the law; it is discrete and particular, something one has done, but something still felt to be alien and separate from the core of one's identity. Sin to the Christian is not a matter of behavior; it is a matter of essence. Man is bounded and hemmed in by it, for it is part of his very nature. The Jew feels worthy of acceptance by God when he fulfils God's law, and he explains evil as the falling away from that law. The Christian feels humble and unworthy before a God whose love far exceeds his merit.[4] For the inevitable expression of man's corruption is sin, and only faith in God and trust in his love and forgiveness can create that Spirit which "justifies" us and puts us on the right course. For the Jew sin can be avoided; for the Christian it is a living fact that is always with us, and should always be remembered with humility.

Such a belief in human depravity may persist long after a person has ostensibly "fled the faith." In fact, the great danger to those who actually seek to free themselves from Christianity is that they attack its dogmas frontally. They blaspheme and violate the sacraments while failing to recognize the substratum of beliefs that go into being a Christian. A person who maintains that "sex is ugly," that "sparing the rod spoils the child," that "men are born lazy," is still Christian, at least in one major belief—that of "original sin"—no matter what he calls himself.

"The truth shall make you free," and Christianity, which so reverences self-knowledge, is, at its best, prone to foster truth-seeking; when misunderstood, however, it is paradoxically prone to inhibit it. The great

---

3. That all these losses and gains passed with time into something new and radically different is to be expected. We can only discuss fundamentals. Still there is a philosophical problem here. Should religions be measured by their beginnings or by their endings? Is a great truth that results in great perversions less true in a sense than a lesser one that remains constant? Let us bear this question in mind as we follow the evolution of other systems.

4. While humility is perhaps an essential ingredient in loving, is it an essential ingredient in being loved? Notice how the sense of unworthiness creates a potential objectification of love into a commodity one earns. Though Christianity is explicit in saying love (grace) is freely given, the common obsession with sin and unworthiness creates puzzlement in the individual and prepares the way for love as a commercial transaction.

unsolved contradiction of Christianity, which is working itself out in our century, lies in a sublime reverence for the individual, in the glorification of personality, in an emphasis on inner spiritual renewal poorly wedded to an objective approach to external reality. Are we to be spiritual idealists or objective pragmatists? Is the measure of man objective or subjective? Does it reside in his unique spirit, or in his actual behavior?

Christianity, because of its precarious synthesis of the objective and subjective, seems doomed to an endless series of schisms. As the established church moves gradually toward objective, rigid prohibitions and further away from a living, subjective sense of its cardinal rules—"pursue the things that make for peace and build up the common life" (Romans, 89); "Love your neighbor as yourself" (Romans, 81); "The whole law is summed up in love" (Romans, 81)—it returns full circle from whence it came, and once again a reformer is needed to fight the Pharisees and bring people back to a true spiritual understanding of Christianity as disciplined duty tempered by love and understanding. This obsession with both law and spirit not only manifests itself in constant reform, but is capable of creating immeasurable schism in the average Christian psyche. Reconciliations are rarely satisfactory, but two unsatisfactory ones are obvious: (1) a man swinging toward the pragmatic and objective will not subject a conscience that is ostensibly clean to rigorous scrutiny lest it be found to be evil, which from another perspective it inevitably is; (2) a man swinging toward the unique spiritual value of his existence will subject his conscience to such vigorous scrutiny that he develops feelings of unworthiness and guilt so intense that self-love becomes impossible.[5]

In Christianity self-love is not, of course, a calculated good as it is in Aristotle's pagan ethic, as it is in many existentialisms, and as it is to some extent in psychoanalysis, where Fromm goes so far as to assert that genuine love of others is impossible without a measure of self-love. We are not interested here in speculating on which perspective has the most merit—that is a gift and burden for everyone—we are merely interested in pointing out the existence of these perspectives.

The Christian in whom the pragmatic and objective temper triumphs is often the Sunday-morning worshipper and the Monday-morning swindler, an individual whose beliefs and life are poorly fused. The Christian

5. Though we are told at least a half-dozen times—twice even by Paul—to "love your neighbour as yourself," the effective consequence of the primacy of the concept of original sin (Romans, 3.10: "There is no just man, not one") is not that one *fails* to love one's neighbour as oneself, but that one finds it difficult to love oneself, a corrupted sinner, or anyone for that matter, without numerous reservations. The love would be what Fromm calls "conditional" (hedged with conditions, earned, a commercial transaction between behavior and response) rather than "unconditional," and because so short of Christ's (Romans, 3.23: "For all alike have sinned, and are deprived of the divine splendour"), capable of increasing the spiraling sense of guilt, unworthiness and "conditional" love.

in whom the spiritual and subjective temper triumphs is often the generalist, the abstract lover of humanity, a person whose charity is reserved for all but delivered to none. The authentic Christian, on the other hand, seems to exist in that anguished world of doubt and self-scrutiny where he hammers out in the fires of his spiritual suffering the genuine humility, understanding, and empathy that are both an expression and manifestation of his own need. The rest of us can only be watchful of perversions of John's remark that "Everyone who loves is a child of God and knows God, but the unloving know nothing of God. For God is love."

Patterns: Question-Begging

The conclusion of this introduction is a classic illustration of question-begging. The final quotation and preceding remark seem to point to a middle way between two extremes; in reality they point nowhere. The *question* is not to point to love as the answer, but to define it in terms that are understandable to all. The question for us is not to be directed to love as if it were a panacea, but to learn how to love, and how to know it is truly love when we think we love. For many people the word "love" has become a cliché or a question mark.

In *Middlemarch,* George Eliot comments on love, the affectation of it and response to it. Speaking of an elderly man who decides to marry, she writes:

> Hence he determined to abandon himself to the stream of feeling, and perhaps was surprised to find what an exceedingly shallow rill it was. As in droughty regions baptism by immersion could only be performed symbolically, so Mr. Casaubon found that sprinkling was the utmost approach to a plunge which his stream would afford him; and he concluded that the poets had much exaggerated the force of masculine passion. Nevertheless, he observed with pleasure that Miss Brooke showed an ardent submissive affection which promised to fulfill his most agreeable previsions of marriage. It had once or twice crossed his mind that possibly there was some deficiency in Dorothea to account for the moderation of his abandonment; but he was unable to discern the deficiency, or to figure to himself a woman who would have pleased him better; so that there was clearly no reason to fall back upon but the exaggerations of human tradition (14 Eliot).

We once again enter one of those peculiar paradoxes that riddle life. Here a person who knows nothing of love either faults the partner or diminishes love's claims, while he continues at the same time to believe he loves. Conversely, often he who knows love most, and craves to know it most, most doubts his knowledge of it. In such a case the truest middle way is: "He who craves to love, tries to love, and is most beset by doubts as to his capacity to love, is closest to the knowledge of God; for God is infinite love." But soon doubt becomes a formula and a point of pride, something acted and not felt, and then we are again in need of new paradoxes to embrace reality.

This discussion itself has continued to beg the questions, "What is love?" and "How do we know it?", and has contented itself with noting the omission of satisfactory answers. When it has dealt with any question at all, it has been the question of what truly should have been uttered as the middle way. The question "What is love?" should be the subject of a book, not of a single paragraph—but that is not the issue. The author purported to give advice, advice that turned out upon examination to be empty, and empty because it begged the question. The remark was poetic, and poetry has its moving purposes, but poetry is not advice we can easily grapple with and follow. Is the ending, therefore however, valueless?

1

from The Book of Job

Sometimes the obvious needs restating. The Old Testament came before the New Testament. It is informed by different standards, purposes and traditions, though these standards, purposes and traditions have powerfully influenced the New Testament. It is an independent, autonomous Bible, and violence is done to it by metamorphosing it into a lengthy introduction to the New Testament. It is neither more nor less than that, merely something different. Such remarks, however, do not invalidate claims to the sacredness of either or both books if one wishes to make such claims.

Of the four divisions of the Old Testament—Pentateuch (Torah) or Law, History, Prophetic Literature, and Poetic and Wisdom Literature—Job belongs among the last. Although it is classed with the Wisdom Literature, Job is unique; it differs in literary form and it lacks the piety of the Psalms or the practical wisdom of Proverbs. It is drama, the nearest the Bible comes to Greek tragedy. The text, which is at least post-exilic but more probably dates from the fourth century B.C., *has obviously been tampered with in an attempt to make a disturbing work more orthodox. The epilogue, in which Job is rewarded, misses the point entirely and is so different in style and spirit that we can safely assume it is a later emendation. Elihu's speech (chapters 32–37), not here reproduced, is also probably an addition by a later writer, who, disturbed by the unorthodoxy of the work, attempted to make it more acceptable.*

The structure of the work in the form in which we have it consists of prologue and epilogue; three cycles consisting each of a speech or complaint by Job and a reply by each of his "comforters"; a speech by Elihu; and God's speech out of the whirlwind. We include here the prologue, first cycle, Job's last speech, God's reply, and the epilogue.

The Book of Job presents in the most direct and inspired form the question of innocent suffering. Throughout the Old Testament—from the Fall, through God's question to Cain ("If thou doest well, shalt thou not be accepted?") to the post-exilic prophets—the presumption of the Hebrews had been that God rewarded virtue and punished evil. This presumption, predicated on false rational categories instead of existential realities, makes Job's comforters so fatuous and foolish that even God's "wrath is kindled against" them. From the opening sentence ("There was a man in the land of Uz whose name was Job; and that man was perfect and upright, and one that feared God, and eschewed evil.") until the ending, when God reproves Eliphaz, Bilad and Zophar, the Book of Job challenges this presumption and all pretense to rational understanding of God's nature or ways.

1

There was a man in the land of Uz, whose name *was* Job; and that man was perfect and upright, and one that feared God, and eschewed evil. And there were born unto him seven sons and three daughters. His substance also was seven thousand sheep, and three thousand camels, and five hundred yoke of oxen, and five hundred she asses, and a very great household; so that this man was the greatest of all the men of the east. And his sons went and feasted *in their* houses, every one his day; and sent and called for their three sisters to eat and to drink with them. And it was so, when the days of *their* feasting were gone about, that Job sent and sanctified them, and rose up early in the morning, and offered burnt offerings *according* to the number of them all: for Job said, It may be that my sons have sinned, and cursed God in their hearts. Thus did Job continually.

Now there was a day when the sons of God came to present themselves before the LORD, and Satan came also among them. And the LORD said unto Satan, Whence comest thou? Then Satan answered the LORD, and said, From going to and fro in the earth, and from walking up and down in it. And the LORD said unto Satan, Hast thou considered my servant Job, that *there* is none like him in the earth, a perfect and an upright man, one that feareth God, and escheweth evil? Then Satan answered the LORD, and said, Doth Job fear God for nought? Hast not thou made an hedge about him, and about his house, and about all that he hath on every side? thou hast blessed the work of his hands, and his substance is increased in the land. But put forth thine hand now, and touch all that he hath, and he will curse thee to thy face. And the LORD said unto Satan, Behold, all that he hath *is* in thy power; only upon himself put not forth thine hand. So Satan went forth from the presence of the LORD.

And there was a day when his sons and his daughters *were* eating and drinking wine in their eldest brother's house: And there came a messenger unto Job, and said, The oxen were plowing, and the asses feeding beside them: And the Sabeans fell *upon them,* and took them away; yea, they have slain the servants with the edge of the sword; and I only am escaped alone to tell thee. While he *was* yet speaking, there came also another, and said, The fire of God is fallen from heaven, and hath burned up the sheep, and the servants, and consumed them; and I only am escaped alone to tell thee. While he *was* yet speaking, there came also another, and said, The Chaldeans made out three bands, and fell upon the camels, and have carried them away, yea, and slain the

From *The Holy Bible* (King James version).

servants with the edge of the sword; and I only am escaped alone to tell thee. While he *was* yet speaking, there came also another, and said, Thy sons and thy daughters *were* eating and drinking wine in their eldest brother's house: And, behold, there came a great wind from the wilderness, and smote the four corners of the house, and it fell upon the young men, and they are dead; and I only am escaped alone to tell thee.

Then Job arose, and rent his mantle, and shaved his head, and fell down upon the ground, and worshipped, And said, Naked came I out of my mother's womb, and naked shall I return thither: the LORD gave, and the LORD hath taken away; blessed be the name of the LORD. In all this Job sinned not, nor charged God foolishly.

2

Again there was a day when the sons of God came to present themselves before the LORD, and Satan came also among them to present himself before the LORD. And the LORD said unto Satan, From whence comest thou? And Satan answered the LORD, and said, From going to and fro in the earth, and from walking up and down in it. And the LORD said unto Satan, Hast thou considered my servant Job, that *there is* none like him in the earth, a perfect and an upright man, one that feareth God, and escheweth evil? and still he holdeth fast his integrity, although thou movedst me against him, to destroy him without cause. And Satan answered the LORD, and said, Skin for skin, yea, all that a man hath will he give for his life. But put forth thine hand now, and touch his bone and his flesh, and he will curse thee to thy face. And the LORD said unto Satan, Behold, he *is* in thine hand; but save his life.

So went Satan forth from the presence of the LORD, and smote Job with sore boils from the sole of his foot unto his crown. And he took him a potsherd to scrape himself withal; and he sat down among the ashes.

Then said his wife unto him, Dost thou still retain thine integrity? curse God, and die. But he said unto her, Thou speakest as one of the foolish women speaketh. What? shall we receive good at the hand of God, and shall we not receive evil? In all this did not Job sin with his lips.

Now when Job's three friends heard of all this evil that was come upon him, they came every one from his own place; Eliphaz the Temanite, and Bildad the Shuhite, and Zophar the Naamathite: for they had made an appointment together to come to mourn with him and to comfort him. And when they lifted up their eyes afar off, and knew him not, they lifted up their voice, and wept; and they rent every one his mantle, and sprinkled dust upon their heads toward heaven. So they sat down with him upon the ground seven days and seven nights, and none spake a word unto him: for they saw that *his* grief was very great.

3

After this opened Job his mouth, and cursed his day. And Job spake, and said, Let the day perish wherein I was born, and the night *in which* it was said, There is a man child conceived. Let that day be darkness; let not God regard it from above, neither let the light shine upon it. Let darkness and the shadow of death stain it; let a cloud dwell upon it; let the blackness of the day terrify it. As *for* that night, let darkness seize upon it; let it not be joined unto the days of the year, let it not come into the number of the months. Lo, let that night be solitary, let no joyful voice come therein. Let them curse it that curse the day, who are ready to raise up their mourning. Let the stars of the twilight thereof be dark; let it look for light, but *have* none; neither let it see the dawning of the day: Because it shut not up the doors of my *mother's* womb, nor hid sorrow from mine eyes. Why died I not from the womb? *why* did I *not* give up the ghost when I came out of the belly? Why did the knees prevent me? or why the breasts that I should suck? For now should I have lain still and been quiet, I should have slept: then had I been at rest, With kings and counsellors of the earth, which built desolate places for themselves; Or with princes that had gold, who filled their houses with silver: Or as an hidden untimely birth I had not been; as infants *which* never saw light. There the wicked cease *from* troubling; and there the weary be at rest. *There* the prisoners rest together; they hear not the voice of the oppressor. The small and great are there; and the servant *is* free from his master. Wherefore is light given to him that is in misery, and life unto the bitter *in* soul; Which long for death, but it *cometh* not; and dig for it more than for hid treasures; Which rejoice exceedingly, *and* are glad, when they can find the grave? *Why is light given* to a man whose way is hid, and whom God hath hedged in? For my sighing cometh before I eat, and my roarings are poured out like the waters. For the thing which I greatly feared is come upon me, and that which I was afraid of is come unto me. I was not in safety, neither had I rest, neither was I quiet; yet trouble came.

4

Then Eliphaz the Temanite answered and said, *If* we assay to commune with thee, wilt thou be grieved? but who can withhold himself from speaking? Behold, thou hast instructed many, and thou hast strengthened the weak hands. Thy words have upholden him that was falling, and thou hast strengthened the feeble knees. But now it is come upon thee, and thou faintest; it toucheth thee, and thou art troubled. *Is* not *this* thy fear, thy confidence, thy hope, and the uprightness of thy ways? Remember, I pray thee, who *ever* perished, being innocent? or where were the righteous cut off? Even as I have seen, they that plow iniquity, and sow wickedness, reap the same. By the blast of God they perish, and by the breath of his nostrils are they consumed. The roaring of the lion, and the voice of the fierce lion, and the teeth of the young lions, are broken. The old lion perisheth for lack of prey, and the stout lion's whelps are scattered abroad. Now a thing was secretly brought to me, and mine ear received a little thereof. In thoughts from the visions of the night, when deep sleep falleth on men, Fear came upon me, and trembling, which made all my bones to shake. Then a spirit passed before my face; the hair of my flesh stood up: It stood still, but I could not discern the form thereof: an image *was* before mine eyes, *there was* silence, and I heard a voice, *saying,* Shall mortal man be more just than God? shall a man be more pure than his maker? Behold, he put no trust in his servants; and his angels he charged with folly: How much less *in* them that dwell in houses of clay, whose foundation *is* in the dust, *which* are crushed before the moth? They are destroyed from morning to evening: they perish for ever without any regarding *it*. Doth not their excellency *which is* in them go away? they die, even without wisdom.

5

Call now, if there be any that will answer thee; and to which of the saints wilt thou turn? For wrath killeth the foolish man, and envy slayeth the silly one. I have seen the foolish taking root: but suddenly I cursed his habitation. His children are far from safety, and they are crushed in the gate, neither *is there* any to deliver *them*. Whose harvest the hungry eateth up, and taketh it even out of the thorns, and the robber swalloweth up their substance. Although affliction cometh not forth of the dust, neither doth trouble spring out of the ground; Yet man is born unto trouble, as the sparks fly upward. I would seek unto God, and unto God would I commit my cause: Which doeth great things and unsearchable; marvellous things without number: Who giveth rain upon the earth, and sendeth waters upon the fields: To set up on high those that be low; that those which mourn may be exalted to safety. He disappointeth the devices of the crafty, so that their hands cannot perform *their* enterprise. He taketh the wise in their own craftiness: and the counsel of the froward is carried headlong. They meet with darkness in the daytime, and grope in the noonday as in the night. But he saveth the poor from the sword, from their mouth, and from the hand of the mighty. So the poor hath hope, and iniquity stoppeth her mouth. Behold, happy *is* the man whom God correcteth: therefore despise not thou the chastening of the Almighty: For he maketh sore, and bindeth up: he woundeth, and his hands make whole. He shall deliver thee in six troubles: yea, in seven there shall no evil touch thee. In famine he shall redeem thee from death: and in war from the power of the sword. Thou shalt be hid from the scourge of the tongue: neither shalt thou be afraid of destruction when it cometh. At destruction and famine thou shalt laugh: neither shalt thou be afraid of the beasts of the earth. For thou shalt be in league with the stones of the field: and the beasts of the field shall be at peace with thee. And thou shalt know that thy tabernacle *shall be* in peace; and thou shalt visit thy habitation, and shalt not sin. Thou shalt know also that thy seed *shall be* great, and thine offspring as the grass of the earth. Thou shalt come to *thy* grave in a full age, like as a shock of corn cometh in in his season. Lo this, we have searched it, so it *is*; hear it, and know thou *it* for thy good.

6

But Job answered and said, Oh that my grief were throughly weighed, and my calamity laid in the balances together! For now it would be heavier than the sand of the sea: therefore my words are swallowed up. For the arrows of the Almighty *are* within me, the poison whereof drinketh up my spirit: the terrors of God do set themselves in array against me. Doth the wild ass bray when he hath grass? or loweth the ox over his fodder? Can that which is unsavoury be eaten without salt? or is there *any* taste in the white of an egg? The things *that* my soul refused to touch *are* as my sorrowful meat. Oh that I might have my request; and that God would grant *me* the thing that I long for! Even that it would please God to destroy me; that he would let loose his hand, and cut me off! Then should I yet have comfort; yea, I would harden myself in sorrow: let him not spare; for I have not concealed the words of the Holy One. What *is* my strength, that I should hope? and what *is* mine end, that I should prolong my life? *Is* my strength the strength of stones? or *is* my flesh of brass? *Is* not my help in me? and is wisdom driven quite from me? To him that is afflicted pity *should be shewed* from his friend; but he forsaketh the fear of the Almighty. My brethren have dealt deceitfully as a brook, *and* as the stream of brooks they pass away; Which are blackish by reason of the ice, *and* wherein the snow is hid: What time they wax warm, they vanish: when it is hot, they are consumed out of their place. The paths of their way are turned aside; they go to nothing, and perish. The troops of Tema looked, the companies of Sheba waited for them. They were confounded because they had hoped; they came thither, and were ashamed. For now ye are nothing; ye see *my* casting down, and are afraid. Did I say, Bring unto me? or, Give a reward for me of your substance? Or, Deliver me from the enemy's hand? or, Redeem me from the hand of the mighty? Teach me, and I will hold my tongue: and cause me to understand wherein I have erred. How forcible are right words! but what doth your arguing reprove? Do ye imagine to reprove words, and the speeches of one that is desperate, *which are* as wind? Yea, ye overwhelm the fatherless, and ye dig *a pit* for your friend. Now therefore be content, look upon me; for *it is* evident unto you if I lie. Return, I pray you, let it not be iniquity; yea, return again, my righteousness *is* in it. Is there iniquity in my tongue? cannot my taste discern perverse things?

7

Is there not an appointed time to man upon earth? *are not* his days also like the days of an hireling? As a servant earnestly desireth the shadow, and as an hireling looketh for *the reward of* his work: So am I made to possess months of vanity, and wearisome nights are appointed to me. When I lie down, I say, When shall I arise, and the night be gone? and I am full of tossings to and fro unto the dawning of the day. My flesh is clothed with worms and clods of dust; my skin is broken, and become loathsome. My days are swifter than a weaver's shuttle, and are spent without hope. O remember that my life *is* wind: mine eye shall no more see good. The eye of him that hath seen me shall me no *more:* thine eyes *are* upon me, and I *am* not. *As* the cloud is consumed and vanisheth away: so he that goeth down to the grave shall come up no *more.* He shall return no more to his house, neither shall his place know him any more. Therefore I will not refrain my mouth; I will speak in the anguish of my spirit; I will complain in the bitterness of my soul. *Am* I a sea, or a whale, that thou settest a watch over me? When I say, My bed shall comfort me, my couch shall ease my complaint; Then thou scarest me with dreams, and terrifiest me through visions: So that my soul chooseth strangling, *and* death rather than my life. I loathe *it;* I would not live alway: let me alone; for my days *are* vanity. What *is* man, that thou shouldest magnify him? and that thou shouldest set thine heart upon him? And *that* thou shouldest visit him every morning, *and* try him every moment? How long wilt thou not depart from me, nor let me alone till I swallow down my spittle? I have sinned; what shall I do unto thee, O thou preserver of men? why hast thou set me as a mark against thee, so that I am a burden to myself? And why dost thou not pardon my transgression, and take away mine iniquity? for now shall I sleep in the dust; and thou shalt seek me in the morning, but I *shall* not *be.*

8

Then answered Bildad the Shuhite, and said, How long wilt thou speak these *things?* and *how long shall* the words of thy mouth *be like* a strong wind? Doth God pervert judgment? or doth the Almighty pervert justice? If thy children have sinned against him, and he have cast them away for their transgression; If thou wouldest seek unto God betimes, and make thy supplication to the Almighty; If thou *wert* pure and upright; surely now he would awake for thee, and make the habitation of thy righteousness prosperous. Though thy beginning was small, yet thy latter end should greatly increase. For inquire, I pray thee, of the former age, and prepare thyself to the search of their fathers: (For we *are but of* yesterday, and know nothing, because our days upon earth *are* a shadow:) Shall not they teach thee, *and* tell thee, and utter words out of their heart? Can the rush grow up without mire? can the flag grow without water? Whilst it *is* yet in his greenness, *and* not cut down, it withereth before any *other* herb. So *are* the paths of all that forget God; and the hypocrite's hope shall perish: Whose hope shall be cut off, and whose trust *shall be* a spider's web. He shall lean upon his house, but it shall not stand: he shall hold it fast, but it shall not endure. He *is* green before the sun, and his branch shooteth forth in his garden. His roots are wrapped about the heap, *and* seeth the place of stones. If he destroy him from his place, then *it* shall deny him, *saying,* I have not seen thee. Behold, this *is* the joy of his way, and out of the earth shall others grow. Behold, God will not cast away a perfect *man,* neither will he help the evildoers: Till he fill thy mouth with laughing, and thy lips with rejoicing. They that hate thee shall be clothed with shame; and the dwelling place of the wicked shall come to nought.

9

Then Job answered and said, I know *it is* so of a truth: but how should man be just with God? If he will contend with him, he cannot answer him one of a thousand. *He is* wise in heart, and mighty in strength: who hath hardened *himself* against him, and hath prospered? Which removeth the mountains, and they know not: which overturneth them in his anger. Which shaketh the earth out of her place, and the pillars thereof tremble. Which commandeth the sun, and it riseth not and sealeth up the stars. Which alone spreadeth out the heavens, and treadeth upon the waves of the sea. Which maketh Arcturus, Orion, and Pleiades, and the chambers of the south. Which doeth great things past finding out; yea, and wonders without number. Lo, he goeth by me, and I see *him* not: he passeth on also, but I perceive him not. Behold, he taketh away, who can hinder him? who will say unto him, What doest thou? *If* God will not withdraw his anger, the proud helpers do stoop under him. How much less shall I answer him, *and* choose out my words *to reason* with him? Whom, though I were righteous, *yet* would I not answer, *but* I would make supplication to my judge. If I had called, and he had answered me; *yet* would I not believe that he had hearkened unto my voice. For he breaketh me with a tempest, and multiplieth my wounds without cause. He will not suffer me to take my breath, but filleth me with bitterness. If *I speak* of strength, lo, *he is* strong: and if of judgment, who shall set me a time *to plead?* If I justify myself, mine own mouth shall condemn me: *if* I say, I *am* perfect, it shall also prove me perverse. *Though* I *were* perfect, *yet* would I not know my soul: I would despise my life. This *is* one *thing,* therefore I said *it,* He destroyeth the perfect and the wicked. If the scourge slay suddenly, he will laugh at the trial of the innocent. The earth is given into the hand of the wicked: he covereth the faces of the judges thereof; if not, where, *and* who *is* he? Now my days are swifter than a post: they flee away, they see no good. They are passed away as the swift ships: as the eagle *that* hasteth to the prey. If I say, I will forget my complaint, I will leave off my heaviness, and comfort *myself:* I am afraid of all my sorrows, I know that thou wilt not hold me innocent. *If* I be wicked, why then labour I in vain? If I wash myself with snow water, and make my hands never so clean; Yet shalt thou plunge me in the ditch, and mine own clothes shall abhor me. For *he is* not a man, as I *am, that* I should answer him, *and* we should come together in judgment. Neither is there any daysman betwixt us, *that* might lay his hand upon us both. Let him take his rod away from me, and let not his fear terrify me: *Then* would I speak, and not fear him; but *it is* not so with me.

10

My soul is weary of my life; I will leave my complaint upon myself; I will speak in the bitterness of my soul. I will say unto God, Do not condemn me; shew me wherefore thou contendest with me. *Is it* good unto thee that thou shouldest oppress, that thou shouldest despise the work of thine hands, and shine upon the counsel of the wicked? Hast thou eyes of flesh? or seest thou as man seeth? *Are* thy days as the days of man? *are* thy years as man's days, That thou inquirest after mine iniquity, and searchest after my sin? Thou knowest that I am not wicked; and *there is* none that can deliver out of thine hand. Thine hands have made me and fashioned me together round about; yet thou dost destroy me. Remember, I beseech thee, that thou hast made me as the clay; and wilt thou bring me into dust again? Hast thou not poured me out as milk, and curdled me like cheese? Thou hast clothed me with skin and flesh, and hast fenced me with bones and sinews. Thou hast granted me life and favour, and thy visitation hath preserved my spirit. And these *things* hast thou hid in thine heart: I know that this *is* with thee. If I sin, then thou markest me, and thou wilt not acquit me from mine iniquity. If I be wicked, woe unto me, and *if* I be righteous, *yet* will I not lift up my head. I *am* full of confusion; therefore see thou mine affliction; For it increaseth. Thou huntest me as a fierce lion: and again thou shewest thyself marvellous upon me. Thou renewest thy witnesses against me, and increasest thine indignation upon me; changes and war *are* against me. Wherefore then hast thou brought me forth out of the womb? Oh that I had given up the ghost, and no eye had seen me! I should have been as though I had not been; I should have been carried from the womb to the grave. *Are* not my days few? cease *then, and* let me alone, that I may take comfort a little, Before I go *whence* I shall not return, *even* to the land of darkness and the shadow of death; A land of darkness, as darkness *itself; and* of the shadow of death, without any order, and *where* the light *is* as darkness.

11

Then answered Zophar the Naamathite, and said, Should not the multitude of words be answered? and should a man full of talk be justified? Should thy lies make men hold their peace? and when thou mockest, shall no man make thee ashamed? For thou hast said, My doctrine *is* pure, and I am clean in thine eyes. But oh that God would speak, and open his lips against thee; And that he would shew thee the secrets of wisdom, that *they are* double to that which is! Know therefore that God exacteth of thee *less* than thine iniquity *deserveth.* Canst thou by searching find out God? canst thou find out the Almighty unto perfection? *It is* as high as heaven; what canst thou do? deeper than hell; what canst thou know? The measure thereof *is* longer than the earth, and broader than the sea. If he cut off, and shut up, or gather together, then who can hinder him? For he knoweth vain men: he seeth wickedness also; will he not then consider *it?* For vain man would be wise, though man be born *like* a wild ass's colt. If thou prepare thine heart, and stretch out thine hands toward him; If iniquity *be* in thine hand, put it far away, and let not wickedness dwell in thy tabernacles. For then shalt thou lift up thy face without spot; yea, thou shalt be stedfast, and shalt not fear: Because thou shalt forget *thy* misery, *and* remember *it* as waters *that* pass away: And *thine* age shall be clearer than the noonday; thou shalt shine forth, thou shalt be as the morning. And thou shalt be secure, because there is hope; yea, thou shalt dig *about thee, and* thou shalt take thy rest in safety. Also thou shalt lie down, and none shall make *thee* afraid; yea, many shall make suit unto thee. But the eyes of the wicked shall fail, and they shall not escape, and their hope *shall be as* the giving up of the ghost.

12

And Job answered and said, No doubt but ye *are* the people, and wisdom shall die with you. But I have understanding as well as you; I *am* not inferior to you: yea, who knoweth not such things as these? I am *as* one mocked of his neighbour, who calleth upon God, and he answereth him: the just upright *man is* laughed to scorn. He that is ready to slip with *his* feet *is as* a lamp despised in the thought of him that is at ease. The tabernacles of robbers prosper, and they that provoke God are secure; into whose hand God bringeth *abundantly*. But ask now the beasts, and they shall teach thee, and the fowls of the air, and they shall tell thee: Or speak to the earth, and it shall teach thee: and the fishes of the sea shall declare unto thee. Who knoweth not in all these that the hand of the LORD hath wrought this? In whose hand *is* the soul of every living thing, and the breath of all mankind. Doth not the ear try words? and the mouth taste his meat? With the ancient *is* wisdom and in length of days understanding. With him *is* wisdom and strength, he hath counsel and understanding. Behold, he breaketh down, and it cannot be built again: he shutteth up a man, and there can be no opening. Behold, he withholdeth the waters, and they dry up: also he sendeth them out, and they overturn the earth. With him *is* strength and wisdom: the deceived and the deceiver *are* his. He leadeth counsellors away spoiled, and maketh the judges fools. He looseth the bond of kings, and girdeth their loins with a girdle. He leadeth princes away spoiled, and overthroweth the mighty. He removeth away the speech of the trusty, and taketh away the understanding of the aged. He poureth contempt upon princes, and weakeneth the strength of the mighty. He discovereth deep things out of darkness, and bringeth out to light the shadow of death. He increaseth the nations, and destroyeth them: he enlargeth the nations, and straiteneth them *again*. He taketh away the heart of the chief of the people of the earth, and causeth them to wander in a wilderness *where there is* no way. They grope in the dark without light, and he maketh them to stagger like *a* drunken *man*.

13

Lo, mine eye hath seen all *this,* mine ear hath heard and understood it. What ye know, *the same* do I know also: I *am* not inferior unto you. Surely I would speak to the Almighty, and I desire to reason with God. But ye *are* forgers of lies, ye *are* all physicians of no value. O that ye would altogether hold your peace! and it should be your wisdom. Hear now my reasoning, and hearken to the pleadings of my lips. Will ye speak wickedly for God? and talk deceitfully for him? Will ye accept his person? will ye contend for God? Is it good that he should search you out? or as one man mocketh another, do ye *so* mock him? He will surely reprove you, if ye do secretly accept persons. Shall not his excellency make you afraid? and his dread fall upon you? Your remembrances *are* like unto ashes, your bodies to bodies of clay. Hold your peace, let me alone, that I may speak, and let come on me what *will.* Wherefore do I take my flesh in my teeth, and put my life in mine hand? Though he slay me, yet will I trust in him: but I will maintain mine own ways before him. He also *shall be* my salvation: for an hypocrite shall not come before him. Hear diligently my speech, and my declaration with your ears. Behold now, I have ordered *my* cause; I know that I shall be justified. Who *is* he *that* will plead with me? for now, if I hold my tongue, I shall give up the ghost. Only do not two *things* unto me: then will I not hide myself from thee. Withdraw thine hand far from me: and let not thy dread make me afraid. Then call thou, and I will answer: or let me speak, and answer thou me. How many *are* mine iniquities and sins? make me to know my transgression and my sin. Wherefore hidest thou thy face, and holdest me for thine enemy? Wilt thou break a leaf driven to and fro? and wilt thou pursue the dry stubble? For thou writest bitter things against me, and makest me to possess the iniquities of my youth. Thou puttest my feet also in the stocks, and lookest narrowly unto all my paths; thou settest a print upon the heels of my feet. And he, as a rotten thing, consumeth, as a garment that is moth eaten.

14

Man *that is* born of a woman *is* of few days, and full of trouble. He cometh forth like a flower, and is cut down: he fleeth also as a shadow, and continueth not. And dost thou open thine eyes upon such an one, and bringest me into judgment with thee? Who can bring a clean *thing* out of an unclean? not one. Seeing his days *are* determined, the number of his months *are* with thee, thou hast appointed his bounds that he cannot pass; Turn from him, that he may rest, till he shall accomplish as an hireling, his day. For there is hope of a tree, if it be cut down, that it will sprout again, and that the tender branch thereof will not cease. Though the root thereof wax old in the earth, and the stock thereof die in the ground; *Yet* through the scent of water it will bud, and bring forth boughs like a plant. But man dieth, and wasteth away: yea, man giveth up the ghost, and where *is* he? *As* the waters fail from the sea, and the flood decayeth and drieth up: So man lieth down, and riseth not: till the heavens *be* no more, they shall not awake, nor be raised out of their sleep. O that thou wouldest hide me in the grave, that thou wouldest keep me secret, until thy wrath be past, that thou wouldest appoint me a set time, and remember me! If a man die, shall he live *again?* all the days of my appointed time will I wait, till my change come. Thou shalt call, and I will answer thee: thou wilt have a desire to the work of thine hands. For now thou numberest my steps: dost thou not watch over my sin? My transgression *is* sealed up in a bag, and thou sewest up mine iniquity. And surely the mountain falling cometh to nought, and the rock is removed out of his place. The waters wear the stones: thou washest away the things which grow *out* of the dust of the earth; and thou destroyest the hope of man. Thou prevailest for ever against him, and he passeth: thou changest his countenance, and sendest him away. His sons come to honour, and he knoweth *it* not; and they are brought low, but he perceiveth *it* not of them. But his flesh upon him shall have pain, and his soul within him shall mourn.

29

Moreover Job continued his parable, and said, Oh that I were as *in* months past, as *in* the days *when* God preserved me; When his candle shined upon my head, *and when* by his light I walked *through* darkness. As I was in the days of my youth, when the secret of God *was* upon my tabernacle. When the Almighty *was* yet with me, *when* my children *were* about me. When I washed my steps with butter, and the rock poured me out rivers of oil; When I went out to the gate through the city, *when* I prepared my seat in the street! The young men saw me, and hid themselves: and the aged arose, *and* stood up. The princes refrained talking, and laid *their* hand on their mouth. The nobles held their peace, and their tongue cleaved to the roof of their mouth. When the ear heard *me,* then it blessed me; and when the eye saw *me,* it gave witness to me: Because I delivered the poor that cried, and the fatherless, and *him that had* none to help him. The blessing of him that was ready to perish came upon me: and I caused the widow's heart to sing for joy. I put on righteousness, and it clothed me: my judgment *was* as a robe and a diadem. I was eyes to the blind, and feet *was* I to the lame. I *was* a father to the poor: and the cause *which* I knew not I searched out. And I brake the jaws of the wicked, and plucked the spoil out of his teeth. Then I said, I shall die in my nest, and I shall multiply *my* days as the sand. My root *was* spread out by the waters, and the dew lay all night upon my branch. My glory *was* fresh in me, and my bow was renewed in my hand. Unto me *men* gave ear, and waited, and kept silence at my counsel. After my words they spake not again; and my speech dropped upon them. And they waited for me as for the rain; and they opened their mouth wide *as* for the latter rain. *If* I laughed on them, they believed *it* not; and the light of my countenance they cast not down. I chose out their way, and sat chief, and dwelt as a king in the army, as one *that* comforteth the mourners.

30

But now *they that are* younger than I have me in derision, whose fathers I would have disdained to have set with the dogs of my flock. Yea, whereto *might* the strength of their hands *profit* me, in whom old age was perished? For want and famine *they were* solitary; fleeing into the wilderness in former time desolate and waste. Who cut up mallows by the bushes, and juniper roots *for* their meat. They were driven forth from among *men,* (they cried after them as *after* a thief.) To dwell in the cliffs of the valleys, *in* caves of the earth, and *in* the rocks. Among the bushes they brayed; under the nettles they were gathered together. *They were* children of fools, yea, children of base men: they were viler than the earth. And now am I their song, yea, I am their byword. They abhor me, they flee far from me, and spare not to spit in my face. Because he hath loosed my cord, and afflicted me, they have also let loose the bridle before me. Upon *my* right *hand* rise the youth; they push away my feet, and they raise up against me the ways of their destruction. They mar my path, they set forward my calamity, they have no helper. They came *upon me* as a wide breaking in *of water:* in the desolation they rolled themselves *upon me*. Terrors are turned upon me: they pursue my soul as the wind: and my welfare passeth away as a cloud. And now my soul is poured out upon me; the days of affliction have taken hold upon me. My bones are pierced in me in the night season: and my sinews take no rest. By the great force *of my disease* is my garment changed: it bindeth me about as the collar of my coat. He hath cast me into the mire, and I am become like dust and ashes. I cry unto thee, and thou dost not hear me: I stand up, and thou regardest me *not. Thou art become cruel to me:* with thy strong hand thou opposest thyself against me. Thou liftest me up to the wind; thou causest me to ride *upon it,* and dissolvest my substance. For I know *that* thou wilt bring me *to* death, and *to* the house appointed for all living. Howbeit he will not stretch out *his* hand to the grave, though they cry in his destruction. Did not I weep for him that was in trouble? was *not* my soul grieved for the poor? When I looked for good, then evil came *unto me:* and when I waited for light, there came darkness. My bowels boiled, and rested not: the days of affliction prevented me. I went mourning without the sun: I stood up, *and* I cried in the congregation. I am a brother to dragons, and a companion to owls. My skin is black upon me, and my bones are burned with heat. My harp also is *turned* to mourning, and my organ into the voice of them that weep.

31

I made a covenant with mine eyes; why then should I think upon a maid? For what portion of God *is there* from above? and *what* inheritance of the Almighty from on high? *Is* not destruction to the wicked? and a strange *punishment* to the workers of iniquity? Doth not he see my ways, and count all my steps? If I have walked with vanity, or if my foot hath hasted to deceit; Let me be weighed in an even balance, that God may know mine integrity. If my step hath turned out of the way, and mine heart walked after mine eyes, and if any blot hath cleaved to mine hands; *Then* let me sow, and let another eat; yea, let my offspring be rooted out. If mine heart have been deceived by a woman, or *if* I have laid wait at my neighbour's door; *Then* let my wife grind unto another, and let other bow down upon her. For this *is* an heinous crime; yea, it *is* an iniquity *to be punished by* the judges. For it *is* a fire *that* consumeth to destruction, and would root out all mine increase. If I did despise the cause of my manservant or of my maid-servant, when they contended with me; What then shall I do when God riseth up? and when he visiteth, what shall I answer him? Did not he that made me in the womb make him? and did not one fashion us in the womb? If I have withheld the poor from *their* desire, or have caused the eyes of the widow to fail; Or have eaten my morsel myself alone, and the fatherless hath not eaten thereof; (For from my youth he was brought up with me, as *with* a father, and I have guided her from my mother's womb;) If I have seen any perish for want of clothing, or any poor without covering; If his loins have not blessed me, and *if* he were *not* warmed with the fleece of my sheep; If I have lifted up my hand against the fatherless, when I saw my help in the gate: *Then* let mine arm fall from my shoulder blade, and mine arm be broken from the bone. For destruction *from* God *was* a terror to me, and by reason of his highness I could not endure. If I have made gold my hope, or have said to the fine gold, *Thou art* my confidence. If I rejoiced

because my wealth *was* great, and because mine hand had gotten much; If I beheld the sun when it shined, or the moon walking *in* brightness; And my heart hath been secretly enticed, or my mouth hath kissed my hand: This also *were* an iniquity *to be punished by* the judge: for I should have denied the God *that is* above. If I rejoiced at the destruction of him that hated me, or lifted up myself when evil found him: (Neither have I suffered my mouth to sin by wishing a curse to his soul.) If the men of my tabernacle said not, Oh that we had of his flesh! we cannot be satisfied. The stranger did not lodge in the street: *but* I opened my doors to the traveller. If I covered my transgressions as Adam, by hiding mine iniquity in my bosom: Did I fear a great multitude, or did the contempt of families terrify me, that I kept silence, *and* went not out of the door? Oh that one would hear me! behold, my desire *is, that* the Almighty would answer me, and *that* mine adversary had written a book. Surely I would take it upon my shoulder, *and* bind it *as* a crown to me. I would declare unto him the number of my steps; as a prince would I go near unto him. If my land cry against me, or that the furrows likewise thereof complain. If I have eaten the fruits thereof without money, or have caused the owners thereof to lose their life: Let thistles grow instead of wheat, and cockle instead of barley. The words of Job are ended.

38

Then the LORD answered Job out of the whirlwind, and said, Who *is* this that darkeneth counsel by words without knowledge? Gird up now thy loins like a man; for I will demand of thee, and answer thou me. Where wast thou when I laid the foundations of the earth? declare, if thou hast understanding. Who hath laid the measures thereof, if thou knowest? or who hath stretched the line upon it? Whereupon are the foundations thereof fastened? or who laid the corner stone thereof; When the morning stars sang together, and all the sons of God shouted for joy? Or *who* shut up the sea with doors when it brake forth *as if* it had issued out of the womb? When I made the cloud the garment thereof, and thick darkness a swaddling band for it, And brake up for it my decreed *place,* and set bars and doors, And said, Hitherto shalt thou come, but no further: and here shall thy proud waves be stayed? Hast thou commanded the morning since thy days *and* caused the dayspring to know his place; That it might take hold of the ends of the earth, that the wicked might be shaken out of it? It is turned as clay *to* the seal; and they stand as a garment. And from the wicked their light is withholden, and the high arm shall be broken. Hast thou entered into the springs of the sea? or hast thou walked in the search of the depth? Have the gates of death been opened unto thee? or hast thou seen the doors of the shadow of death? Hast thou perceived the breadth of the earth? declare if thou knowest it all. Where *is* the way *where* light dwelleth? and *as for* darkness, where *is* the place thereof, That thou shouldest take it to the bound thereof, and that thou shouldest know the paths *to* the house thereof? Knowest thou *it,* because thou wast then born? or *because the* number of thy days *is* great? Hast thou entered into the treasures of the snow? or hast thou seen the treasures of the hail, Which I have reserved against the time of trouble, against the day of battle and war? By what way is the light parted, *which* scattereth the east wind upon the earth? Who hath divided a watercourse for the overflowing of waters, or a way for the lightning of thunder; To cause it to rain on the earth, *where* no man is; *on* the wilderness, wherein *there is* no man; To satisfy the desolate and waste *ground:* and to cause the bud of the tender herb to spring forth? Hath the rain a father? or who hath begotten the drops of dew? Out of whose womb came the ice? and the hoary frost of heaven, who hath gendered it? The waters are hid as *with* a stone, and the face of the deep is frozen. Canst thou bind the sweet influences of Pleiades, or loose the bands of Orion? Canst thou bring forth Mazzaroth in his season? or canst thou guide Arcturus with his sons? Knowest thou the ordinances of heaven? canst thou set the dominion thereof in the earth? Canst thou lift up thy voice to the clouds, that abundance of waters may cover thee? Canst thou send lightnings, that they may go, and say unto thee, Here *we are?* Who hath put wisdom in the inward parts? or who hath given understanding to the heart? Who can number the clouds in wisdom? or who can stay the bottles of heaven, When the dust groweth into hardness, and the clods cleave fast together? Wilt thou hunt the prey for the lion? or fill the appetite of the young lions, When they couch in *their* dens, *and* abide in the covert to lie in wait? Who provideth for the raven his food? when his young ones cry unto God, they wander for lack of meat.

39

Knowest thou the time when the wild goats of the rock bring forth? *or* canst thou mark when the hinds do calve? Canst thou number the months *that* they fulfil? or knowest thou the time when they bring forth? They bow themselves, they bring forth their young ones, they cast out their sorrows. Their young ones are in good liking, they grow up with corn; they go forth, and return not unto them. Who hath sent out the wild ass free? or who hath loosed the bands of the wild ass? Whose house I have made the wilderness, and the barren land his dwellings. He scorneth the multitude of the city, neither regardeth he the crying of the driver. The range of the mountains *is* his pasture, and he searcheth after every green thing. Will the unicorn be willing to serve thee, or abide by thy crib? Canst thou bind the unicorn with his band in the furrow? or will he harrow the valleys after thee? Wilt thou trust him, because his strength *is* great? or wilt thou leave thy labour to him? Wilt thou believe him, that he will bring home thy seed, and gather *it into* thy barn? *Gavest thou* the goodly wings unto the peacocks? or wings and feathers unto the ostrich? Which leaveth her eggs in the earth, and warmeth them in dust, And forgetteth that the foot may crush them, or that the wild beast may break them. She is hardened against her young ones, as though *they were* not hers: her labour is in vain without fear; Because God hath deprived her of wisdom, neither hath he imparted to her understanding. What time she lifteth up herself on high, she scorneth the horse and his rider. Hast thou given the horse strength? hast thou clothed his neck with thunder? Canst thou make him afraid as a grasshopper? the glory of his nostrils *is* terrible. He paweth in the valley, and rejoiceth in *his* strength: he goeth on to meet the armed men. He mocketh at fear, and is not affrighted; neither turneth he back from the sword. The quiver rattleth against him, the glittering spear and the shield. He swalloweth the ground with fierceness and rage: neither believeth he that *it is* the sound of the trumpet. He saith among the trumpets, Ha, ha; and he smelleth the battle afar off, the thunder of the captains, and the shouting. Doth the hawk fly by thy wisdom, *and* stretch her wings toward the south? Doth the eagle mount up at thy command, and make her nest on high? She dwelleth and abideth on the rock, upon the crag of the rock, and the strong place. From thence she seeketh the prey, *and* her eyes behold afar off. Her young ones also suck up blood: and where the slain *are,* there *is* she.

40

Moreover the Lord answered Job, and said, Shall he that contendeth with the Almighty instruct *him?* he that reproveth God, let him answer it.

Then Job answered the LORD, and said, Behold, I am vile; what shall I answer thee? I will lay mine hand upon my mouth. Once have I spoken; but I will not answer: yea, twice; but I will proceed no further.

Then answered the LORD unto Job out of the whirlwind, and said, Gird up thy loins now like a man: I will demand of thee, and declare thou unto me. Wilt thou also disannul my judgment? wilt thou condemn me, that thou mayest be righteous? Hast thou an arm like God? or canst thou thunder with a voice like him? Deck thyself now *with* majesty and excellency; and array thyself with glory and beauty. Cast abroad the rage of thy wrath: and behold every one *that is* proud, and abase him. Look on every one *that is* proud, *and* bring him low; and tread down the wicked in their place. Hide them in the dust together, *and* bind their faces in secret. Then will I also confess unto thee that thine own right hand can save thee.

Behold now behemoth, which I made with thee; he eateth grass as an ox. Lo now, his strength *is* in his loins, and his force *is* in the navel of his belly. He moveth his tail like a cedar: the sinews of his stones are wrapped together. His bones *are as* strong pieces of brass; his bones *are* like bars of iron. He *is* the chief of the ways of God: he that made him can make his sword to approach *unto him*. Surely the mountains bring him forth food, where all the beasts of the field play. He lieth under the shady trees, in the covert of the reed, and fens. The shady trees cover him *with* their shadow; the willows of the brook compass him about. Behold, he drinketh up a river, *and* hasteth not: he trusteth that he can draw up Jordan into his mouth. He taketh it with his eyes: *his* nose pierceth through snares.

41

Canst thou draw out leviathan with an hook? or his tongue with a cord *which* thou lettest down? Canst thou put an hook into his nose? or bore his jaw through with a thorn? Will he make many supplications unto thee? will he speak soft *words* unto thee? Will he make a covenant with thee? wilt thou take him for a servant for ever? Wilt thou play with him as *with* a bird? or wilt thou bind him for thy maidens? Shall the companions make a banquet of him? shall they part him among the merchants? Canst thou fill his skin with barbed irons? or his head with fish spears? Lay thine hand upon him, remember the battle, do no more. Behold, the hope of him is in vain: shall not *one* be cast down even at the sight of him? None *is so* fierce that dare stir him up: who then is able to stand before me? Who hath prevented me, that I should repay *him?* whatsoever *is* under the whole heaven is mine. I will not conceal his parts, nor his power, nor his comely proportion. Who can discover the face of his garment? *or* who can come *to him* with his double bridle? Who can open the doors of his face? his teeth *are* terrible round about. *His* scales *are his* pride, shut up together *as with* a close seal. One is so near to another, that no air can come between them. They are joined one to another, they stick together, that they cannot be sundered. By his sneezings a light doth shine, and his eyes *are* like the eyelids of the morning. Out of his mouth go burning lamps, *and* sparks of fire leap out. Out of his nostrils goeth smoke, as *out* of a seething pot or caldron. His breath kindleth coals, and a flame goeth out of his mouth. In his neck remaineth strength, and sorrow is turned into joy before him. The flakes of his flesh are joined together: they are firm in themselves; they cannot be moved. His heart is as firm as a stone; yea, as hard as a piece of the nether *millstone*. When he raiseth up himself, the mighty are afraid: by reason of breakings they purify themselves. The sword of him that layeth at him cannot hold: the spear, the dart, nor the habergeon. He esteemeth iron as straw, *and* brass as rotten wood. The arrow cannot make him flee: slingstones are turned with him into stubble. Darts are counted as stubble: he laugheth at the shaking of a spear. Sharp stones *are* under him: he spreadeth sharp pointed things upon the mire. He maketh the deep to boil like a pot: he maketh the sea like a pot of ointment. He maketh a path to shine after him; *one* would think the deep *to be* hoary. Upon earth there is not his like, who is made without fear. He beholdeth all high *things:* he *is* a king over all the children of pride.

42

Then Job answered the LORD, and said, I know that thou canst do every *thing,* and *that* no thought can be withholden from thee. Who *is* he that hideth counsel without knowledge? therefore have I uttered that I understood not; things too wonderful for me, which I knew not. Hear, I beseech thee, and I will speak: I will demand of thee, and declare thou unto me. I have heard of thee by the hearing of the ear: but now mine eye seeth thee. Wherefore I abhor *myself,* and repent in dust and ashes.

And it was *so,* that after the LORD had spoken these words unto Job, the LORD said to Eliphaz the Temanite, My wrath is kindled against thee, and against thy two friends: for ye have not spoken of me *the thing that is* right, as my servant Job *hath.* Therefore take unto you now seven bullocks and seven rams, and go to my servant Job, and offer up for yourselves a burnt offering; and my servant Job shall pray for you: for him will I accept: lest I deal with you *after your* folly, in that ye have not spoken of me *the thing which is* right, like my servant Job. So Eliphaz the Temanite and Bildad the Shuhite *and* Zophar the Naamathite went, and did according as the LORD commanded them: the LORD also accepted Job. And the LORD turned the captivity of Job, when he prayed for his friends: also the LORD gave Job twice as much as he had before. Then came there unto him all his brethren, and all his sisters, and all they that had been of his acquaintance before, and did eat bread with him in his house: and they bemoaned him, and comforted him over all the evil that the LORD had brought upon him: every man also gave him a piece of money, and every one an earring of gold. So the LORD blessed the latter end of Job more than his beginning: for he had fourteen thousand sheep, and six thousand camels, and a thousand yoke of oxen, and a thousand she asses. He had also seven sons and three daughters. And he called the name of the first, Jemima; and the name of the second, Kezia; and the name of the third, Kerenhappuch. And in all the land were no women found *so* fair as the daughters of Job: and their father gave them inheritance among their brethren. After this lived Job an hundred and forty years, and saw his sons, and his sons' sons, *even* four generations. So Job died, *being* old and full of days.

Problems

1. What is Satan's relation to God?
2. What motivates God to lay his hand on Job? How would you describe the God of Job? Does your answer increase or decrease your sympathies for Job?
3. The confrontation between Job and his friends and comforters starts with compassion and degenerates into fierce disagreement. Why is Job enraged by the well-meaning speech of Eliphaz the Temanite which opens chapter 4? How would you have responded to such a speech?
4. Job continues to maintain his righteousness in the face of his friends' arguments. Would you describe his attitude as one of defiance or of integrity? Why?
5. How adequate or inadequate is God's reply to Job? What does Job's reply suggest about his attitude toward God? About the manner in which he receives God's answer?
6. What is the significance of God's response to Eliphaz, Bildad, and Zophar?
7. Without the epilogue, what is the point of The Book of Job? What does the tone of the epilogue and the need for such an epilogue suggest about that writer's perspective?

2

The Book of Ecclesiastes

The opening line of Ecclesiastes attributes its authorship to Solomon, but that would make it a tenth-century work, and it is too obviously influenced by Hellenic humanism to be that old. A more probable date for this work of Kohaleth, a pseudonym for an unknown author, is sometime during the second or third century B.C. *Obviously a secular work, it was accepted as scripture, partly because it was attributed to Solomon, and partly because it had a special appeal to the Jewish mind.*

Like Job, Ecclesiastes is an unorthodox work reflecting the presence of restless minds among the wise men, minds dissatisfied with the practical goals of Proverbs and intent on penetrating the great abiding issues: the meaning of existence, the purpose of creation, the mystery of evil, the confrontation with death. They probed these questions with the same observation and common sense they brought to bear on daily matters. They refused to accept on faith what reason could not demonstrate and thus, introduced for the first time a new note of skepticism.

Ecclesiastes contains some of the greatest poetry in the Old Testament and some of the most quotable lines. It has been alluded to countless times, has provided the titles for enumerable books and, with the exception of an added refrain or two, the lyrics of a folk song, "Turn! Turn! Turn!"

The author, Kohaleth, a skeptical humanist who sees himself in an impersonal, hostile, meaningless world where all things pass away, even love, and where in much wisdom is much sorrow, masks his acute, sensitive vision of suffering and futility—all is "in vain," all is "vanity"—with an apparent cynicism. Such a tough surface and tender essence reveals the complex world view, inner strength, and spiritual discipline necessary to continue the Hebraic world view once empiricism had led to an examination of the disparity between proverb and practice. Existential in its perspective, the work exposes the tension between faith, stoicism, and despair that characterized much of later Hebrew thought.

1

The words of the Preacher, the son of David, king in Jerusalem. Vanity of vanities, saith the Preacher, vanity of vanities; all *is* vanity. What profit hath a man of all his labour which he taketh under the sun? *One* generation passeth away, and *another* generation cometh: but the earth abideth for ever. The sun also ariseth, and the sun goeth down, and hasteth to his place where he arose. The wind goeth toward the south, and turneth about unto the north; it whirleth about continually, and the wind returneth again according to his circuits. All the rivers run into the sea; yet the sea *is* not full; unto the place from whence the rivers come, thither they return again. All things *are* full of labour; man cannot utter *it:* the eye is not satisfied with seeing, nor the ear filled with hearing. The thing that hath been, it *is that* which shall be; and that which is done *is* that which shall be done: and *there is* no new *thing* under the sun. Is there *any* thing whereof it may be said, See, this *is* new? it hath been already of old time, which was before us. *There is* no remembrance of former *things;* neither shall there be *any* remembrance of *things* that are to come with *those* that shall come after.

I the Preacher was king over Israel in Jerusalem. And I gave my heart to seek and search out by wisdom concerning all *things* that are done under heaven: this sore travail hath God given to the sons of man to be exercised therewith. I have seen all the works that are done under the sun; and, behold, all *is* vanity and vexation of spirit. *That which is* crooked cannot be made straight: and that which is wanting cannot be numbered.

I communed with mine own heart, saying, Lo, I am come to great estate, and have gotten more wisdom than all *they* that have been before me in Jerusalem: yea, my heart had great experience of wisdom and knowledge. And I gave my heart to know wisdom, and to know madness and folly: I perceived that this also is vexation of spirit. For in much wisdom *is* much grief: and he that increaseth knowledge increaseth sorrow.

2

I said in mine heart, Go to now, I will prove thee with mirth, therefore enjoy pleasure: and, behold, this also *is* vanity. I said of laughter, *It is* mad: and of mirth, What doeth it? I sought in mine heart to give myself unto wine, yet acquainting mine heart with wisdom; and to lay hold on folly, till I might see what *was* that good for the sons of men,

From *The Holy Bible* (King James version).

which they should do under the heaven all the days of their life. I made me great works; I builded me houses; I planted me vineyards: I made me gardens and orchards, and I planted trees in them of all *kind of* fruits: I made me pools of water, to water therewith the wood that bringeth forth trees: I got *me* servants and maidens, and had servants born in my house; also I had great possessions of great and small cattle above all that were in Jerusalem before me: I gathered me also silver and gold, and the peculiar treasure of kings and of the provinces: I gat me men singers and women singers, and the delights of the sons of men, *as* musical instruments, and that of all sorts. So I was great, and increased more than all that were before me in Jerusalem: also my wisdom remained with me. And whatsoever mine eyes desired I kept not from them, I withheld not my heart from any joy; for my heart rejoiced in all my labour: and this was my portion of all my labour. Then I looked on all the works that my hands had wrought, and on the labour that I had laboured to do: and, behold, all *was* vanity and vexation of spirit, and *there was* no profit under the sun.

And I turned myself to behold wisdom, and madness, and folly: for what *can* the man *do* that cometh after the king? *even* that which hath been already done. Then I saw that wisdom excelleth folly, as far as light excelleth darkness. The wise man's eyes *are* in his head; but the fool walketh in darkness: and I myself perceived also that one event happeneth to them all. Then said I in my heart, As it happeneth to the fool, so it happeneth even to me; and why was I then more wise? Then I said in my heart, that this also *is* vanity. For *there is* no remembrance of the wise more than of the fool for ever; seeing that which now *is* in the days to come shall all be forgotten. And how dieth the wise *man?* as the fool. Therefore I hated life; because the work that is wrought under the sun *is* grievous unto me: for all *is* vanity and vexation of spirit.

Yea, I hated all my labour which I had taken under the sun: because I should leave it unto the man that shall be after me. And who knoweth whether he shall be a wise *man* or a fool? yet shall he have rule over all my labour wherein I have laboured, and wherein I have shewed myself wise under the sun. This *is* also vanity. Therefore I went about to cause my heart to despair of all the labour which I took under the sun. For there is a man whose labour *is* in wisdom, and in knowledge, and in equity; yet to a man that hath not laboured therein shall he leave it *for* his portion. This also *is* vanity and a great evil. For what hath man of all his labour, and of the vexation of his heart, wherein he hath laboured under the sun? For all his days *are* sorrows, and his travail grief; yea, his heart taketh not rest in the night. This is also vanity.

There is nothing better for a man, *than* that he should eat and drink, and *that* he should make his soul enjoy good in his labour. This also I saw, that it *was* from the hand of God. For who can eat, or who else can hasten *hereunto,* more than I? For *God* giveth to a man that *is* good in his sight wisdom, and knowledge, and joy: but to the sinner he giveth travail, to gather and to heap up, that he may give to *him that is* good before God. This also *is* vanity and vexation of spirit.

3

To every *thing there is* a season, and a time to every purpose under the heaven: A time to be born, and a time to die; a time to plant, and a time to pluck up *that which is* planted; A time to kill, and a time to heal; a time to break down, and a time to build up; A time to weep, and a time to laugh; a time to mourn, and a time to dance; A time to cast away stones, and a time to gather stones together; a time to embrace, and a time to refrain from embracing; A time to get, and a time to lose; a time to keep, and a time to castaway; A time to rend, and a time to sew; a time to keep silence, and a time to speak; A time to love, and a time to hate; a time of war, and a time of peace. What profit hath he that worketh in that wherein he laboureth? I have seen the travail, which God hath given to the sons of men to be exercised in it. He hath made every *thing* beautiful in his time: also he hath set the world in their heart, so that no man can find out the work that God maketh from the beginning to the end. I know that *there is* no good in them, but for *a man* to rejoice, and to do good in his life. And also that every man should eat and drink, and enjoy the good of all his labour, it *is* the gift of God. I know that, whatsoever God doeth, it shall be for ever: nothing can be put to it, nor anything taken from it: and God doeth *it,* that *men* should fear before him. That which hath been is now; and that which is to be hath already been; and God requireth that which is past.

And moreover I saw under the sun the place of judgment, *that* wickedness *was* there; and the place of righteousness, *that* iniquity *was* there. I said in mine heart, God shall judge the righteous and the wicked: for *there is* a time there for every purpose and for every work. I said in mine heart concerning the estate of the sons of men, that God might manifest them, and that they might see that they themselves are beasts. For that which befalleth the sons of men befalleth beasts; even one thing befalleth them: as the one dieth, so dieth the other; yea, they have all one breath; so that a man hath no preeminence above a beast: for all *is* vanity. All go unto one place; all are of the dust, and all turn to dust again. Who knoweth the spirit of man that goeth upward, and the spirit of the beast that goeth downward to the earth? Wherefore I perceive that *there is* nothing better, than that a man should rejoice in his own works; for that *is* his portion: for who shall bring him to see what shall be after him?

4

So I returned, and considered all the oppressions that are done under the sun: and behold the tears of *such as were* oppressed, and they had no comforter; and on the side of their oppressors *there was* power but they had no comforter. Wherefore I praised the dead which are already dead more than the living which are yet alive. Yea, better *is he* than both they, which hath not yet been, who hath not seen the evil work that is done under the sun.

Again, I considered all travail, and every right work, that for this a man is envied of his neighbour. This *is* also vanity and vexation of spirit. The fool foldeth his hands together, and eateth his own flesh. Better *is* an handful *with* quietness, than both the hands full *with* travail and vexation of spirit.

Then I returned, and I saw vanity under the sun. There is one *alone,* and *there is* not a second; yea, he hath neither child nor brother: yet *is there* no end of all his labour; neither is his eye satisfied with riches; neither *saith he,* For whom do I labour, and bereave my soul of good? This *is* also vanity, yea, it *is* a sore travail.

Two *are* better than one; because they have a good reward for their labour. For if they fall, the one will lift up his fellow: but woe to him *that is* alone when he falleth; for *he hath* not another to help him up. Again, if two lie together, then they have heat: but how can one be warm *alone?* And if one prevail against him, two shall withstand him; and a threefold cord is not quickly broken.

Better *is* a poor and a wise child than an old and foolish king, who will no more be admonished. For out of prison he cometh to reign; whereas also *he that is* born in his kingdom becometh poor. I considered all the living which walk under the sun, with the second child that shall stand up in his stead. *There is* no end of all the people, *even* of all that have been before them: they also that come after shall not rejoice in him. Surely this also *is* vanity and vexation of spirit.

5

Keep thy foot when thou goest to the house of God, and be more ready to hear, than to give the sacrifice of fools: for they consider not that they do evil. Be not rash with thy mouth, and let not thine heart be hasty to utter *any* thing before God: for God *is* in heaven, and thou upon earth: therefore let thy words be few. For a dream cometh through the multitude of business; and a fool's voice *is known* by multitude of words. When thou vowest a vow unto God, defer not to pay it; for *he hath* no pleasure in fools: pay that which thou hast vowed. Better *is it* that thou shouldest not vow, than that thou shouldest vow and not pay. Suffer not thy mouth to cause thy flesh to sin; neither say thou before the angel, that it *was* an error: wherefore should God be angry at thy voice, and destroy the work of thine hands? For in the multitude of dreams and many words *there are* also *divers* vanities: but fear thou God.

If thou seest the oppression of the poor, and violent perverting of judgment and justice in a province, marvel not at the matter: for *he that is* higher than the highest regardeth; and *there be* higher than they.

Moreover the profit of the earth is for all: the king *himself* is served by the field. He that loveth silver shall not be satisfied with silver; nor he that loveth abundance with increase: this *is* also vanity. When goods increase, they are increased that eat them: and what good *is there* to the owners thereof, saving the beholding *of them* with their eyes? The sleep of a labouring man *is* sweet, whether he eat little or much: but the abundance of the rich will not suffer him to sleep. There is a sore evil *which* I have seen under the sun, *namely,* riches kept for the owners thereof to their hurt. But those riches perish by evil travail: and he begetteth a son, and *there is* nothing in his hand. As he came forth of his mother's womb, naked shall he return to go as he came, and shall take nothing of his labour, which he may carry away in his hand. And this also *is* a sore evil, *that* in all points as he came, so shall he go: and what profit hath he that hath laboured for the wind? All his days also he eateth in darkness, and *he hath* much sorrow and wrath with his sickness.

Behold *that* which I have seen: *it is* good and comely *for one* to eat and to drink, and to enjoy the good of all his labour that he taketh under the sun all the days of his life, which God giveth him: for it *is* his portion. Every man also to whom God hath given riches and wealth, and hath given him power to eat thereof, and to take his portion, and to rejoice in his labour; this *is* the gift of God. For he shall not much remember the days of his life; because God answereth *him* in the joy of his heart.

6

There is an evil which I have seen under the sun, and it *is* common among men: A man to whom God hath given riches, wealth, and honour, so that he wanteth nothing for his soul of all that he desireth, yet God giveth him not power to eat thereof, but a stranger eateth it: this *is* vanity, and it *is* an evil disease.

If a man beget an hundred *children,* and live many years, so that the days of his years be many, and his soul be not filled with good, and also *that* he have no burial; I say, *that* an untimely birth *is* better than he. For he cometh in with vanity, and departeth in darkness, and his name shall be covered with darkness. Moreover he hath not seen the sun, nor known *any thing:* this hath more rest than the other.

Yea, though he live a thousand years twice *told,* yet hath he seen no good: do not all go to one place? All the labour of man *is* for his mouth, and yet the appetite is not filled. For what hath the wise more than the fool? what hath the poor, that knoweth to walk before the living?

Better *is* the sight of the eyes than the wandering of the desire: This *is* also vanity and vexation of spirit. That which hath been is named already, and it is known that it *is* man: neither may he contend with him that is mightier than he.

Seeing there be many things that increase vanity, what *is* man the better? For who knoweth what *is* good for man in *this* life, all the days of his vain life which he spendeth as a shadow? for who can tell a man what shall be after him under the sun?

7

A good name *is* better than precious ointment; and the day of death than the day of one's birth.

It *is* better to go to the house of mourning, than to go to the house of feasting: for that *is* the end of all men; and the living will lay *it* to his heart. Sorrow *is* better than laughter: for by the sadness of the countenance the heart is made better. The heart of the wise *is* in the house of mourning; but the heart of fools *is* in the house of mirth. *It is* better to hear the rebuke of the wise, than for a man to hear the song of fools. For as the crackling of thorns under a pot, so *is* the laughter of the fool: this also *is* vanity.

Surely oppression maketh a wise man mad; and a gift destroyeth the heart. Better *is* the end of a thing than the beginning thereof: *and* the patient in spirit is better than the proud in spirit. Be not hasty in thy spirit to be angry: for anger resteth in the bosom of fools. Say not thou, What is *the cause* that the former days were better than these? for thou dost not inquire wisely concerning this.

Wisdom *is* good with an inheritance: and *by it there is* profit to them that see the sun. For wisdom *is* a defence, *and* money *is* a defence: but the excellency of knowledge *is, that* wisdom giveth life to them that have it. Consider the work of God: for who can make *that* straight, which he hath made crooked? In the day of prosperity be joyful, but in the day of adversity consider: God also hath set the one over against the other, to the end that man should find nothing after him. All *things* have I seen in the days of my vanity: there is a just *man* that perisheth in his righteousness, and there is a wicked *man* that prolongeth *his life* in his wickedness. Be not righteous over much; neither make thyself over wise: why shouldest thou destroy thyself? Be not over much wicked, neither be thou foolish: why shouldest thou die before thy time? It *is* good that thou shouldest take hold of this; yea, also from this withdraw not thine hand: for he that feareth God shall come forth of them all. Wisdom strengthened the wise more than ten mighty *men* which are in the city. For *there is* not a just man upon earth, that doeth good, and sinneth not. Also take no heed unto all words that are spoken; lest thou hear thy servant curse thee: For oftentimes also thine own heart knoweth that thou thyself likewise hast cursed others.

All this have I proved by wisdom: I said, I will be wise; but it *was* far from me. That which is far off, and exceeding deep, who can find it out? I applied mine heart to know, and to search, and to seek out wisdom, and the reason *of things,* and to know the wickedness of folly, even of foolishness *and* madness: And I find more bitter than death the woman, whose heart *is* snares and nets, *and* her hands *as* bands: whoso pleaseth God shall escape from her; but the sinner shall be taken by her. Behold, this have I found, saith the preacher, *counting* one by one, to find out the account: Which yet my soul seeketh, but I find not: one man among a thousand have I found; but a woman among all those have I not found. Lo, this only have I found, that God hath made man upright; but they have sought out many inventions.

8

Who *is* as the wise *man?* and who knoweth the interpretation of a thing? a man's wisdom maketh his face to shine, and the boldness of his face shall be changed. I *counsel thee* to keep the king's commandment, and *that* in regard of the oath of God. Be not hasty to go out of his sight: stand not in an evil thing; for he doeth whatsoever pleaseth him. Where the word of a king *is, there is* power: and who may say unto him, What doest thou? Whoso keepeth the commandment shall feel no evil thing: and a wise man's heart discerneth both time and judgment.

Because to every purpose there is time and judgment, therefore the misery of man *is* great upon him. For he knoweth not that which shall be: for who can tell him when it shall be? *There is* no man that hath power over the spirit to retain the spirit; neither *hath he* power in the day of death: and *there is* no discharge in *that* war; neither shall wickedness deliver those that are given to it. All this have I seen, and applied my heart unto every work that is done under the sun: *there is* a time wherein one man ruleth over another to his own hurt. And so I saw the wicked buried, who had come and gone from the place of the holy, and they were forgotten in the city where they had so done: this *is* also vanity. Because sentence against an evil work is not executed speedily, therefore the heart of the sons of man is fully set in them to do evil.

Though a sinner do evil an hundred times, and his *days* be prolonged, yet surely I know that it shall be well with them that fear God, which fear before him: But it shall not be well with the wicked, neither shall he prolong *his* days, *which are* as a shadow; because he feareth not before God. There is a vanity which is done upon the earth; that there be just *men,* unto whom it happeneth according to the work of the wicked; again, there be wicked *men,* to whom it happeneth according to the work of the righteous: I said that this also *is* vanity. Then I commended mirth, because a man hath no better thing under the sun, than to eat, and to drink, and to be merry: for that shall abide with him of his labour the days of his life, which God giveth him under the sun.

When I applied mine heart to know wisdom, and to see the business that is done upon the earth: (for also *there is that* neither day nor night seeth sleep with his eyes:) Then I beheld all the work of God, that a man cannot find out the work that is done under the sun: because though a man labour to seek *it* out, yet he shall not find *it;* yea further; though a wise *man* think to know *it,* yet shall he not be able to find *it.*

9

For all this I considered in my heart even to declare all this, that the righteous, and the wise, and their works, *are* in the hand of God: no man knoweth either love or hatred *by* all *that is* before them. All *things come* alike to all: *there is* one event to the righteous, and to the wicked; to the good and to the clean, and to the unclean; to him that sacrificeth, and to him that sacrificeth not: as *is* the good, so *is* the sinner; *and* he that sweareth, as *he* that feareth an oath. This *is* an evil among all *things* that are done under the sun, that *there is* one event unto all: yea, also the heart of the sons of men is full of evil, and madness *is* in their heart while they live, and after that *they go* to the dead.

For to him that is joined to all the living there is hope: for a living dog is better than a dead lion. For the living know that they shall die: but the dead know not any thing, neither have they any more a reward; for the memory of them is forgotten. Also their love, and their hatred, and their envy, is now perished; neither have they any more a portion for ever in any *thing* that is done under the sun.

Go thy way, eat thy bread with joy, and drink thy wine with a merry heart; for God now accepteth thy works. Let thy garments be always white; and let thy head lack no ointment. Live joyfully with the wife whom thou lovest all the days of the life of thy vanity, which he hath given thee under the sun, all the days of thy vanity: for that *is* thy portion in *this* life, and in thy labour which thou takest under the sun. Whatsoever thy hand findeth to do, do *it* with thy might; for *there is* no work, nor device, nor knowledge, nor wisdom, in the grave, whither thou goest.

I returned, and saw under the sun, that the race *is* not to the swift, nor the battle to the strong, neither yet bread to the wise, nor yet riches to men of understanding, nor yet favour to men of skill; but time and chance happeneth to them all. For man also knoweth not his time: as the fishes that are taken in an evil net, and as the birds that are caught in the snare; so *are* the sons of men snared in an evil time, when it falleth suddenly upon them.

This wisdom have I seen also under the sun, and it *seemed* great unto me: *There was* a little city, and few men within it; and there came a great king against it, and besieged it, and built great bulwarks against it: Now there was found in it a poor wise man, and he by his wisdom delivered the city; yet no man remembered that same poor man. Then said I, Wisdom *is* better than strength: nevertheless the poor man's wisdom *is* despised, and his words are not heard. The words of wise *men are* heard in quiet more than the cry of him that ruleth among fools. Wisdom *is* better than weapons of war: but one sinner destroyeth much good.

10

Dead flies cause the ointment of the apothecary to send forth a stinking savour: *so doth* a little folly him that is in reputation for wisdom *and* honour. A wise man's heart *is* at his right hand; but a fool's heart at his left. Yea also, when he that is a fool walketh by the way, his wisdom faileth *him,* and he saith to every one *that* he *is* a fool. If the spirit of the ruler rise up against thee, leave not thy place; for yielding pacifieth great offences. There is an evil *which* I have seen under the sun, as an error *which* proceedeth from the ruler: Folly is set in great dignity, and the rich sit in low place. I have seen servants upon horses, and princes walking as servants upon the earth. He that diggeth a pit shall fall into it; and whoso breaketh an hedge, a serpent shall bite him. Whoso removeth stones shall be hurt therewith; *and* he that cleaveth wood shall be endangered thereby. If the iron be blunt, and he do not whet the edge, then must he put to more strength: but wisdom *is* profitable to direct. Surely the serpent will bite without enchantment; and a babbler is no better. The words of a wise man's mouth *are* gracious; but the lips of a fool will swallow up himself. The beginning of the words of his mouth *is* foolishness: and the end of his talk *is* mischievous madness. A fool also is full of words: a man cannot tell what shall be; and what shall be after him, who can tell him? The labour of the foolish wearieth every one of them, because he knoweth not how to go to the city.

Woe to thee, O land, when thy king *is* a child, and thy princes eat in the morning! Blessed *art* thou, O land, when thy king *is* the son of nobles, and thy princes eat in due season, for strength, and not for drunkenness!

By much slothfulness the building decayeth; and through idleness of the hands the house droppeth through.

A feast is made for laughter, and wine maketh merry: but money answereth all *things*.

Curse not the king, no not in thy thought; and curse not the rich in thy bedchamber: for a bird of the air shall carry the voice, and that which hath wings shall tell the matter.

11

Cast thy bread upon the waters: for thou shalt find it after many days. Give a portion to seven, and also to eight; for thou knowest not what evil shall be upon the earth. If the clouds be full of rain, they empty *themselves* upon the earth: and if the tree fall toward the south, or toward the north, in the place where the tree falleth, there it shall be. He that observeth the wind shall not sow; and he that regardeth the clouds shall not reap. As thou knowest not what *is* the way of the spirit, *nor* how the bones *do grow* in the womb of her that is with child: even so thou knowest not the works of God who maketh all. In the morning sow thy seed, and in the evening withhold not thine hand: for thou knowest not whether shall prosper, either this or that, or whether they both *shall be* alike good.

Truly the light *is* sweet, and a pleasant *thing it is* for the eyes to behold the sun: But if a man live many years, *and* rejoice in them all; yet let him remember the days of darkness; for they shall be many. All that cometh *is* vanity.

Rejoice, O young man, in thy youth; and let thy heart cheer thee in the days of thy youth, and walk in the ways of thine heart, and in the sight of thine eyes: but know thou, that for all these *things* God will bring thee into judgment. Therefore remove sorrow from thy heart, and put away evil from thy flesh: for childhood and youth *are* vanity.

12

Remember now thy Creator in the days of thy youth, while the evil days come not, nor the years draw nigh, when thou shalt say, I have no pleasure in them; While the sun, or the light, or the moon, or the stars, be not darkened, nor the clouds return after the rain: In the day when the keepers of the house shall tremble, and the strong men shall bow themselves, and the grinders cease because they are few, and those that look out of the windows be darkened. And the doors shall be shut in the streets, when the sound of the grinding is low, and he shall rise up at the voice of the bird, and all the daughters of music shall be brought low; Also *when* they shall be afraid of *that which is* high, and fears *shall be* in the way, and the almond tree shall flourish, and the grasshopper shall be a burden, and desire shall fail: because man goeth to his long home, and the mourners go about the streets: Or ever the silver cord be loosed, or the golden bowl be broken, or the pitcher be broken at the fountain, or the wheel broken at the cistern. Then shall the dust return to the earth as it was: and the spirit shall return unto God who gave it.

Vanity of vanities, saith the preacher; all *is* vanity. And moreover, because the preacher was wise, he still taught the people knowledge; yea, he gave good heed, and sought out, *and* set in order many proverbs. The preacher sought to find out acceptable words: and *that which was* written *was* upright, *even* words of truth. The words of the wise *are* as goads, and as nails fastened *by* the masters of assemblies, *which* are given from one shepherd. And further, by these, my son, be admonished: of making many books *there is* no end; and much study *is* a weariness of the flesh.

Let us hear the conclusion of the whole matter: Fear God, and keep his commandments: for this *is* the whole *duty* of man. For God shall bring every work into judgment, with every secret thing, whether *it be* good, or whether *it be* evil.

Problems

1. What aspects of existence led Kohaleth to his sense of the futility of all things? What prevents Kohaleth from being a nihilist?
2. What is Kohaleth's attitude toward the life of the senses? What prevents him from adopting a philosophy of simple hedonism? What would have been his attitude toward a world view that divided man into body and soul?
3. What is Kohaleth's attitude toward justice and injustice? To what extent is he cynical about earthly justice and prone to place his trust in God for retribution? How large a role does retribution play in his world view?
4. After striving to understand the meaning of existence, Kohaleth returns to a consideration of the first principle of life. What, for him, is that principle? Is it in any way Christian?
5. In what ways might Kohaleth's world view lead to Christianity?

3
from The Gospel According to Matthew

Although Matthew appears as the first Gospel (Anglo-Saxon for "good tidings"), it is largely derived from Mark's earlier Gospel (A.D. 65–70), about ninety per cent of which Matthew reproduces. Its placement first, however, even though it was probably written after A.D. 80, gave rise to the belief that it was the oldest Gospel, and therefore contributed to its being in some ways the most influential. The aim of the author is to establish Jesus as the Messiah (Hebrew for "the anointed one," for which the Greek word is Christos) *as prophesied in the Old Testament. Chapters 5–7 from Matthew—The Sermon on the Mount wherein Jesus purifies the law in an obvious analogue to Moses receiving the law on Mount Sinai—contain the most complete single collection of Jesus's ethical teaching in the Bible. Beginning with blessings or Beatitudes, collections of which began to disseminate soon after Jesus's death, the sermon contains perhaps the most often quoted passages in the New Testament. Jesus's aim in the sermon is clear—"to complete" the law (80/30), and this intention explains the balanced antithetical structure of many of the statements: "You have learned. . . . But what I tell you. . . ."*

The portrait of Jesus that emerges in the Gospels, especially in Mark's early, more rough and realistic Gospel, is incredibly dense and scarcely prettified and sentimental; Jesus could be angry and he could be ironic. He emerges not only as a warm human being and a great theologian, but as a great psychologist and artist. Old and hallowed figures convey an undeserved impression of familiar, tired and worn ideas. This impression is unfortunate, for a close reading of the Gospels repays the reader with new understanding of what it means to be a moral man.

5

When he saw the crowds he went up the hill. There he took his seat, and when his disciples had gathered round him he began to address them. And this is the teaching he gave:

From *The New English Bible* (New York: Cambridge University Press, 1961), pp. 8–13.

'How blest are those who know that they are poor;
    the kingdom of Heaven is theirs.
How blest are the sorrowful;
    they shall find consolation.
How blest are those of a gentle spirit;
    they shall have the earth for their possession.
How blest are those who hunger and thirst to see right prevail;
    they shall be satisfied.
How blest are those who show mercy;
    mercy shall be shown to them.
How blest are those whose hearts are pure;
    they shall see God.
How blest are the peacemakers;
    God shall call them his sons.
How blest are those who have suffered persecution for the cause of right;
    the kingdom of Heaven is theirs.

'How blest you are, when you suffer insults and persecution and every kind of calumny for my sake. Accept it with gladness and exultation, for you have a rich reward in heaven; in the same way they persecuted the prophets before you.

'You are salt to the world. And if salt becomes tasteless, how is its saltness to be restored? It is now good for nothing but to be thrown away and trodden underfoot.

'You are light for all the world. A town that stands on a hill cannot be hidden. When a lamp is lit, it is not put under the mealtub, but on the lamp-stand, where it gives light to everyone in the house. And you, like the lamp, must shed light among your fellows, so that, when they see the good you do, they may give praise to your Father in heaven.

'Do not suppose that I have come to abolish the Law and the prophets; I did not come to abolish, but to complete. I tell you this: so long as heaven and earth endure, not a letter, not a stroke, will disappear from the Law until all that must happen has happened. If any man therefore sets aside even the least of the Law's demands, and teaches others to do the same, he will have the lowest place in the kingdom of Heaven, whereas anyone who keeps the Law and teaches others so will stand high in the kingdom of Heaven. I tell you, unless you show yourselves far better men than the Pharisees * and the doctors of the law, you can never enter the kingdom of Heaven.

* A group of Hasidic Jews, avowedly nationalistic and separatist, extreme in their devotion to the law, both oral and written, and to strict observance of customs and practices that had grown up out of popular practice. They were democratic in orientation, but as a result of their great emphasis on explicating scriptures, they came to influence unduly all aspects of Jewish life. Their ethical goals were elevated. Other aspects were a belief in life after death, resurrection, and the coming of the Messiah. By the time of Jesus they had become so rigid and overweening that they had alienated the common people.

'You have learned that our forefathers were told, "Do not commit murder; anyone who commits murder must be brought to judgement." But what I tell you is this: Anyone who nurses anger against his brother must be brought to judgement. If he abuses his brother he must answer for it to the court; if he sneers at him he will have to answer for it in the fires of hell.

'If, when you are bringing your gift to the altar, you suddenly remember that your brother has a grievance against you, leave your gift where it is before the altar. First go and make your peace with your brother, and only then come back and offer your gift.

'If someone sues you, come to terms with him promptly while you are both on your way to court; otherwise he may hand you over to the judge, and the judge to the constable, and you will be put in jail. I tell you, once you are there you will not be let out till you have paid the last farthing.

'You have learned that they were told, "Do not commit adultery." But what I tell you is this: If a man looks on a woman with a lustful eye, he has already committed adultery with her in his heart.

'If your right eye leads you astray, tear it out and fling it away; it is better for you to lose one part of your body than for the whole of it to be thrown into hell. And if your right hand is your undoing, cut it off and fling it away; it is better for you to lose one part of your body than for the whole of it to go to hell.

'They were told, "A man who divorces his wife must give her a note of dismissal." But what I tell you is this: If a man divorces his wife for any cause other than unchastity he involves her in adultery; and anyone who marries a woman so divorced commits adultery.

'Again, you have learned that they were told, "Do not break your oath", and, "Oaths sworn to the Lord must be kept." But what I tell you is this: You are not to swear at all—not by heaven, for it is God's throne, nor by earth, for it is his footstool, nor by Jerusalem, for it is the city of the great King, nor by your own head, because you cannot turn one hair of it white or black. Plain "Yes" or "No" is all you need to say; anything beyond that comes from the devil.

'You have learned that they were told, "An eye for an eye, and a tooth for a tooth." But what I tell you is this: Do not set yourself against the man who wrongs you. If someone slaps you on the right cheek, turn and offer him your left. If a man wants to sue you for your shirt, let him have your coat as well. If a man in authority makes you go one mile, go with him two. Give when you are asked to give; and do not turn your back on a man who wants to borrow.

'You have learned that they were told, "Love your neighbour, hate your enemy." But what I tell you is this: Love your enemies and pray for your persecutors; only so can you be children of your heavenly Father, who makes his sun rise on good and bad alike, and sends the rain on the honest and the dishonest. If you love only those who love you, what reward can you expect? Surely the tax-gatherers do as much as that. And if you greet only your brothers, what is there extraordinary about that? Even the heathen do as much. You must therefore be all goodness, just as your heavenly Father is all good.

6

'Be careful not to make a show of your religion before men; if you do, no reward awaits you in your Father's house in heaven.

'Thus, when you do some act of charity, do not announce it with a flourish of trumpets, as the hypocrites do in synagogue and in the streets to win admiration from men. I tell you this: they have their reward already. No; when you do some act of charity, do not let your left hand know what your right is doing; your good deed must be secret, and your Father who sees what is done in secret will reward you.

'Again, when you pray, do not be like the hypocrites; they love to say their prayers standing up in synagogue and at the street-corners, for everyone to see them. I tell you this: they have their reward already. But when you pray, go into a room by yourself, shut the door, and pray to your Father who is there in the secret place; and your Father who sees what is secret will reward you.

'In your prayers do not go babbling on like the heathen, who imagine that the more they say the more likely they are to be heard. Do not imitate them. Your Father knows what your needs are before you ask him.

'This is how you should pray:
"Our Father in heaven,
Thy name be hallowed;
Thy kingdom come,
Thy will be done,
On earth as in heaven.
Give us today our daily bread.
Forgive us the wrong we have done,
As we have forgiven those who have wronged us.
And do not bring us to the test,
But save us from the evil one."

For if you forgive others the wrongs they have done, your heavenly Father will also forgive you; but if you do not forgive others, then the wrongs you have done will not be forgiven by your Father.

'So too when you fast, do not look gloomy like the hypocrites: they make their faces unsightly so that other people may see that they are fasting. I tell you this: they have their reward already. But when you fast, anoint your head and wash your face, so that men may not see that you are fasting, but only your Father who is in the secret place; and your Father who sees what is secret will give you your reward.

'Do not store up for yourselves treasure on earth, where it grows rusty and moth-eaten, and thieves break in to steal it. Store up treasure in heaven, where there is no moth and no rust to spoil it, no thieves to break in and steal. For where your wealth is, there will your heart be also.

'The lamp of the body is the eye. If your eyes are sound, you will have light for your whole body; if the eyes are bad, your whole body will be in darkness. If then the only light you have is darkness, the darkness is doubly dark.

'No servant can be slave to two masters; for either he will hate the first and love the second, or he will be devoted to the first and think nothing of the second. You cannot serve God and Money.

'Therefore I bid you put away anxious thoughts about food and drink to keep you alive, and clothes to cover your body. Surely life is more than food, the body more than clothes. Look at the birds of the air; they do not sow and reap and store in barns, yet your heavenly Father feeds them. You are worth more than the birds! Is there a man of you who by anxious thought can add a foot to his height? And why be anxious about clothes? Consider how the lilies grow in the fields; they do not work, they do not spin; and yet, I tell you, even Solomon in all his splendour was not attired like one of these. But if that is how God clothes the grass in the fields, which is there today, and tomorrow is thrown on the stove, will he not all the more clothe you? How little faith you have! No, do not ask anxiously, "What are we to eat? What are we to drink? What shall we wear?" All these are things for the heathen to run after, not for you, because your heavenly Father knows that you need them all. Set your mind on God's kingdom and his justice before everything else, and all the rest will come to you as well. So do not be anxious about tomorrow; tomorrow will look after itself. Each day has troubles enough of its own.

7

'Pass no judgement, and you will not be judged. For as you judge others, so you will yourselves be judged, and whatever measure you deal out to others will be dealt back to you. Why do you look at the speck of sawdust in your brother's eye, with never a thought for the great plank in your own? Or how can you say to your brother, "Let me take the speck out of your eye", when all the time there is that plank in your own? You hypocrite! First take the plank out of your own eye, and then you will see clearly to take the speck out of your brother's.

'Do not give dogs what is holy; do not feed your pearls to pigs: they will only trample on them, and turn and tear you to pieces.

'Ask, and you will receive; seek, and you will find; knock, and the door will be opened. For everyone who asks receives, he who seeks finds, and to him who knocks, the door will be opened.

'Is there a man among you who will offer his son a stone when he asks for bread, or a snake when he asks for fish? If you, then, bad as you are, know how to give your children what is good for them, how much more will your heavenly Father give good things to those who ask him!

'Always treat others as you would like them to treat you: that is the Law and the prophets.

'Enter by the narrow gate. The gate is wide that leads to perdition, there is plenty of room on the road, and many go that way; but the gate that leads to life is small and the road is narrow, and those who find it are few.

'Beware of false prophets, men who come to you dressed up as sheep while underneath they are savage wolves. You will recognize them by the fruits they bear. Can grapes be picked from briars, or figs from thistles? In the same way, a good tree always yields good fruit, and a poor tree bad fruit. A good tree cannot bear bad fruit, or a poor tree good fruit. And when a tree does not yield good fruit it is cut down and burnt. That is why I say you will recognize them by their fruits.

'Not everyone who calls me "Lord, Lord" will enter the kingdom of Heaven, but only those who do the will of my heavenly Father. When that day comes, many will say to me, "Lord, Lord, did we not prophesy in your name, cast out devils in your name, and in your name perform many miracles?" Then I will tell them to their face, "I never knew you: out of my sight, you and your wicked ways!"

'What then of the man who hears these words of mine and acts upon them? He is like a man who had the sense to build his house on rock. The rain came down, the floods rose, the wind blew, and beat upon that house; but it did not fall, because its foundations were on rock. But what of the man who hears these words of mine and does not act upon them? He is like a man who was foolish enough to build his house on sand. The rain came down, the floods rose, the wind blew, and beat upon the house; down it fell with a great crash.'

When Jesus had finished this discourse the people were astounded at his teaching; unlike their own teachers he taught with a note of authority.

Patterns: Emotional Appeal and Psychological Argument

Jesus's utterances are often made powerful by poetic devices: syntactical parallelism, development through repetition and modified repetition, tension through reversal or inversion, colorful imagery, striking illustrations, paradox, and steady progression from the general to the particular. The opening Beatitudes (80/1-16), for all their exclamatory force, are really variations on a disguised thesis of great generality and complexity. The apparent summation, lines 80/17-20, contains not only a couple of disguised assumptions (righteousness is rewarded in Heaven; there is value in inheriting the Kingdom of Heaven), but a couple of indirect commands (you ought to suffer persecution for the cause of right, for you ought to want to be rewarded with the inheritance of Heaven).

Assumptions so fundamental and obvious seem grotesque in utterance; we therefore run the danger of permitting people to forget that it is not an absolute *given* that "You ought to want to be rewarded with the inheritance of Heaven." An atheistic existentialist such as Sartre, for example, would prefer to dispense with such rewards. For him life is more free and more heroic without God. We must remember that no matter how palpable, how trite, how inevitable an assumption may appear, it is not in itself compelling. Someone's telling us in glowing terms how much we should want Heaven does not compel us to agree.

Jesus's persuasiveness is strengthened by the use of such closely related devices as indirect assertion ("How blest are those who have suffered persecution for the cause of right; the kingdom of Heaven is theirs"), indirect command ("suffer persecution for the right"), and approval through personal compliment ("blest are those") and reward ("the kingdom of Heaven is theirs").

Jesus is here addressing his disciples (79/2), not the crowd. He, therefore, introduces an intimate tone and uses a multitude of attitudes and rhetorical devices which are calculated to increase a sense of belonging and exclusivity: special selection, ("You are salt to the world"); antitheses between society and the group ("You were told . . . but what I tell") and hence a sharpening of differences ("Do not imitate them [the hypocritically pious]"); a sense of secret advantage ("I . . . come . . . to complete [the law]", "Your good deed must be secret, and your Father who sees . . . will reward you"); a sense of the superiority of essences to appearances ("When you pray, go into a room by yourself"); exclusive and unequal categories ("You cannot serve God and Money"); anti-establishment aggression ("Do not be like the hypocrites"); the promise of a secret, rare, and precious reward for the group as a substitute for frustrated earthly hopes ("The gate that leads to life is small and the road is narrow, and those who find it are few").

Even when ostensibly direct—and Jesus far prefers the parable to the explicit moral demanded by his disciples in Mark—Jesus's method is the method of indirection, and indirection is the method of art not of science. The scientist states and hence can be refuted; the artist suggests, and suggestions, being more subtle and subliminal, are much more difficult to perceive and can only be combatted by non-acceptance. When Jesus is direct in his assertions or commands, he is prone to negate or modify a previous law, thus indirectly conveying the illusion of new freedom. And when new laws are commanded, they are usually followed sentences later by a promise of reward. The method is indirect but the message is clear: believe, be this way, do good, and you will be rewarded. There is a conflict between his ostensible message and his method: the message preaches altruism; the structure of his argument addresses itself to self-interest. Is this conflict revealing, or is it merely inevitable? Is it possible to make any other appeal and still be persuasive and widely accepted? The question is worth carrying along when reading the Marxists, the Freudians, and the existentialists.

Problems

1. To what extent do the Beatitudes imply an ethical equation operative in the universe? To what extent is Jesus's ethical system based on a belief in just recompense?
2. How great is the conflict between the Mosaic Code, "An eye for an eye, and a tooth for a tooth," and Christ's ethical injunctions to "treat others as you would like them to treat you." to "turn the other cheek"? Which is more demanding? Which more admirable? Which ethic is most acceptable to and most frequently employed by society? Why?
3. What is Christ's attitude toward the Jewish commandments, the Law? To what degree does he separate matters of the spirit from matters of behavior?
4. In the Sermon on the Mount, Christ asks us to "Pass no judgment, and you will not be judged. For as you judge others, so you will be judged; and whatever measure you deal out to others will be dealt back to you." Is Christ a moralist, as is usually thought, asking us here to avoid making judgments because if we judge harshly, we shall be judged just as harshly by God? Or is he a psychologist warning people to beware of revealing their fundamental lack of understanding and charity by harsh judgments, warning people that they reveal their spiritual state more clearly by their self-revelation, that in essence they condemn themselves? Which reading is more satisfying to you? What are the implications of such a reading for the concept of just retribution? Is Christ humanized by your reading? Do his ethics become more intelligible or less?

4

from The Gospel According to Mark

4

On another occasion he began to teach by the lake-side. The crowd that gathered round him was so large that he had to get into a boat on the lake, and there he sat, with the whole crowd on the beach right down on the water's edge. And he taught them many things by parables.

As he taught he said: 'Listen! A sower went out to sow. And it happened that as he sowed, some seed fell along the footpath; and the birds came and ate it up. Some seed fell on rocky ground, where it had little soil, and it sprouted quickly because it had no depth of earth; but when the sun rose the young corn was scorched, and as it had no proper root it withered away. Some seed fell among thistles; but the thistles shot up and choked the corn, and it yielded no crop. And some of the seed fell into good soil, where it came up and grew, and bore fruit; and the yield was thirtyfold, sixtyfold, even a hundredfold.' He added, 'If you have ears to hear, then hear.'

When he was alone, the Twelve and others who were round him questioned him about the parables. He replied, 'To you the secret of the kingdom of God has been given; but to those who are outside everything comes by way of parables, so that (as Scripture says) they may look and look, but see nothing; they may hear and hear, but understand nothing; otherwise they might turn to God and be forgiven.'

So he said, 'You do not understand this parable? How then are you to understand any parable? The sower sows the word. Those along the footpath are people in whom the word is sown, but no sooner have they heard it than Satan comes and carries off the word which has been sown in them. It is the same with those who receive the seed on rocky ground; as soon as they hear the word, they accept it with joy, but it strikes no root in them; they have no staying-power; then, when there is trouble or persecution on account of the word, they fall away at once. Others again receive the seed among thistles; they hear the word, but worldly cares and the false glamour of wealth and all kinds of evil desire

From *The New English Bible* (New York: Cambridge University Press, 1961), pp. 62–91.

come in and choke the word, and it proves barren. And there are those who receive the seed in good soil; they hear the word and welcome it; and they bear fruit thirtyfold, sixtyfold, or a hundredfold.'

He said to them, 'Do you bring in the lamp to put it under the meal-tub, or under the bed? Surely it is brought to be set on the lamp-stand? For nothing is hidden unless it is to be disclosed, and nothing put under cover unless it is to come into the open. If you have ears to hear, then hear.'

He also said, 'Take note of what you hear; the measure you give is the measure you will receive, with something more besides. For the man who has will be given more, and the man who has not will forfeit even what he has.'

He said, 'The kingdom of God is like this. A man scatters seed on the land; he goes to bed at night and gets up in the morning, and the seed sprouts and grows—how, he does not know. The ground produces a crop by itself, first the blade, then the ear, then full-grown corn in the ear; but as soon as the crop is ripe, he sets to work with the sickle, because harvest-time has come.'

He said also, 'How shall we picture the kingdom of God, or by what parable shall we describe it? It is like the mustard-seed, which is smaller than any seed in the ground at its sowing. But once sown, it springs up and grows taller than any other plant, and forms branches so large that the birds can settle in its shade.'

With many such parables he would give them his message, so far as they were able to receive it. He never spoke to them except in parables; but privately to his disciples he explained everything. . . .

7

A group of Pharisees, with some doctors of the law who had come from Jerusalem, met him and noticed that some of his disciples were eating their food with 'defiled' hands—in other words, without washing them. (For the Pharisees and the Jews in general never eat without washing the hands, in obedience to an old-established tradition; and on coming from the market-place they never eat without first washing. And there are many other points on which they have a traditional rule to maintain, for example, washing of cups and jugs and copper bowls.) Accordingly, these Pharisees and the lawyers asked him, 'Why do your disciples not conform to the ancient tradition, but eat their food with defiled hands?' He answered, 'Isaiah was right when he prophesied about you hypocrites in these words: "This people pays me lip-service, but their heart is far from me: their worship of me is in vain, for they teach as doctrines the commandments of men." You neglect the commandment of God, in order to maintain the tradition of men.'

He also said to them, 'How well you set aside the commandment of God in order to maintain your tradition! Moses said, "Honour your father and your mother", and, "The man who curses his father or mother must suffer death." But you hold that if a man says to his father or mother, "Anything of mine which might have been used for your benefit is Corban"' (meaning, set apart for God), 'he is no longer permitted to do anything for his father or mother. Thus by your own tradition, handed down among you, you make God's word null and void. And many other things that you do are just like that.'

On another occasion he called the people and said to them, 'Listen to me, all of you, and understand this: nothing that goes into a man from outside can defile him; no, it is the things that come out of him that defile a man.'

When he had left the people and gone indoors, his disciples questioned him about the parable. He said to them, 'Are you as dull as the rest? Do you not see that nothing that goes from outside into a man can defile him, because it does not enter into his heart but into his stomach, and so passes out into the drain?' Thus he declared all foods clean. He went on, 'It is what comes out of a man that defiles him. For from inside, out of a man's heart, come evil thoughts, acts of fornication, of theft, murder, adultery, ruthless greed, and malice; fraud, indecency, envy, slander, arrogance, and folly; these evil things all come from inside, and they defile the man.' . . .

10

On leaving those parts he came into the regions of Judaea and Transjordan; and when a crowd gathered round him once again, he followed his usual practice and taught them. The question was put to him: 'Is it lawful for a man to divorce his wife?' This was to test him. He asked in return, 'What did Moses command you?' They answered, 'Moses permitted a man to divorce his wife by note of dismissal.' Jesus said to them, 'It was because you were so unteachable that he made this rule for you; but in the beginning, at the creation, God made them male and female. For this reason a man shall leave his father and mother, and be made one with his wife; and the two shall become one flesh. It follows that they are no longer two individuals: they are one flesh. What God has joined together, man must not separate.'

When they were indoors again the disciples questioned him about this matter; he said to them, 'Whoever divorces his wife and marries another commits adultery against her: so too, if she divorces her husband and marries another, she commits adultery.'

They brought children for him to touch; and the disciples scolded them for it. But when Jesus saw this he was indignant, and said to them, 'Let the children come to me; do not try to stop them; for the kingdom of God belongs to such as these. I tell you, whoever does not accept the kingdom of God like a child will never enter it.' And he put his arms round them, laid his hands upon them, and blessed them.

As he was starting out on a journey, a stranger ran up, and, kneeling before him, asked, 'Good Master, what must I do to win eternal life?' Jesus said to him, 'Why do you call me good? No one is good except God alone. You know the commandments: "Do not murder; do not commit adultery; do not steal; do not give false evidence; do not defraud; honour your father and mother." ' 'But, Master,' he replied, 'I have kept all these since I was a boy.' Jesus looked straight at him; his heart warmed to him, and he said, 'One thing you lack: go, sell everything you have, and give to the poor, and you will have riches in heaven; and come, follow me.' At these words his face fell and he went away with a heavy heart; for he was a man of great wealth.

Jesus looked round at his disciples and said to them, 'How hard it will be for the wealthy to enter the kingdom of God!' They were amazed that he should say this, but Jesus insisted, 'Children, how hard it is to enter the kingdom of God! It is easier for a camel to pass through the eye of a needle than for a rich man to enter the kingdom of God.' They were more astonished than ever, and said to one another, 'Then who can be saved?' Jesus looked them in the face and said, 'For men it is impossible, but not for God; to God everything is possible.'

At this Peter spoke. 'We here', he said, 'have left everything to become your followers.' Jesus said, 'I tell you this: there is no one who has given up home, brothers or sisters, mother, father or children, or land, for my sake and for the Gospel, who will not receive in this age a hundred times as much—houses, brothers and sisters, mothers and children, and land—and persecutions besides; and in the age to come eternal life. But many who are first will be last and the last first.'

They were on the road, going up to Jerusalem, Jesus leading the way; and the disciples were filled with awe; while those who followed behind were afraid. He took the Twelve aside and began to tell them what was to happen to him. 'We are now going to Jerusalem,' he said; 'and the Son of Man will be given up to the chief priests and the doctors of the law; they will condemn him to death and hand him over to the foreign power. He will be mocked and spat upon, flogged and killed; and three days afterwards, he will rise again.'

James and John, the sons of Zebedee, approached him and said, 'Master, we should like you to do us a favour.' 'What is it you want me to do?' he asked. They answered, 'Grant us the right to sit in state with you, one at your right and the other at your left.' Jesus said to them, 'You do not understand what you are asking. Can you drink the cup that I drink, or be baptized with the baptism I am baptized with?' 'We can', they answered. Jesus said, 'The cup that I drink you shall drink, and the baptism I am baptized with shall be your baptism; but to sit at my right or left is not for me to grant; it is for those to whom it has already been assigned.'

When the other ten heard this, they were indignant with James and John. Jesus called them to him and said, 'You know that in the world the recognized rulers lord it over their subjects, and their great men make them feel the weight of authority. That is not the way with you; among you, whoever wants to be great must be your servant, and whoever wants to be first must be the willing slave of all. For even the Son of Man did not come to be served but to serve, and to surrender his life as a ransom for many.' . . .

11

He entered Jerusalem and went into the temple, where he looked at the whole scene; but, as it was now late, he went out to Bethany with the Twelve.

On the following day, after they had left Bethany, he felt hungry, and, noticing in the distance a fig-tree in leaf, he went to see if he could find anything on it. But when he came there he found nothing but leaves; for it was not the season for figs. He said to the tree, 'May no one ever again eat fruit from you!' And his disciples were listening.

So they came to Jerusalem, and he went into the temple and began driving out those who bought and sold in the temple. He upset the tables of the money-changers and the seats of the dealers in pigeons; and he would not allow anyone to use the temple court as a thoroughfare for carrying goods. Then he began to teach them, and said, 'Does not Scripture say, "My house shall be called a house of prayer for all the nations"? But you have made it a robbers' cave.' The chief priests and the doctors of the law heard of this and sought some means of making away with him; for they were afraid of him, because the whole crowd was spellbound by his teaching. And when evening came he went out of the city.

Early next morning, as they passed by, they saw that the fig-tree had withered from the roots up; and Peter, recalling what had happened, said to him, 'Rabbi, look, the fig-tree which you cursed has withered.' Jesus answered them, 'Have faith in God. I tell you this: if anyone says to this mountain, "Be lifted from your place and hurled into the sea", and has no inward doubts, but believes that what he says is happening, it will be done for him. I tell you, then, whatever you ask for in prayer, believe that you have received it and it will be yours.

'And when you stand praying, if you have a grievance against anyone, forgive him, so that your Father in heaven may forgive you the wrongs you have done.' . . .

12

. . . A number of Pharisees and men of Herod's party were sent to trap him with a question. They came and said, 'Master, you are an honest man, we know, and truckle to no man, whoever he may be; you teach in all honesty the way of life that God requires. Are we or are we not permitted to pay taxes to the Roman Emperor? Shall we pay or not?' He saw how crafty their question was, and said, 'Why are you trying to catch me out? Fetch me a silver piece, and let me look at it.' They brought one, and he said to them, 'Whose head is this, and whose inscription?' 'Caesar's', they replied. Then Jesus said, 'Pay Caesar what is due to Caesar, and pay God what is due to God.' And they heard him with astonishment.

Next Sadducees* came to him. (It is they who say that there is no resurrection.) Their question was this: 'Master, Moses laid it down for us that if there are brothers, and one dies leaving a wife but no child, then the next should marry the widow and carry on his brother's family. Now there were seven brothers. The first took a wife and died without issue. Then the second married her, and he too died without issue. So did the third. Eventually the seven of them died, all without issue. Finally the woman died. At the resurrection, when they come back to life, whose wife will she be, since all seven had married her?' Jesus said to them, 'You are mistaken, and surely this is the reason: you do not know either the scriptures or the power of God. When they rise from the dead, men and women do not marry; they are like angels in heaven.

'Now about the resurrection of the dead, have you never read in the Book of Moses, in the story of the burning bush, how God spoke to him and said, "I am the God of Abraham, the God of Isaac, and the God of Jacob"? God is not God of the dead but of the living. You are greatly mistaken.'

Then one of the lawyers, who had been listening to these discussions and had noted how well he answered, came forward and asked him, 'Which commandment is first of all?' Jesus answered, 'The first is, "Hear, O Israel: the Lord your God is the only Lord; love the Lord your God with all your heart, with all your soul, with all your mind, and with all

---

* Wealthy aristocrats who welcomed Greek thought but opposed the legalism and patriotism of the Pharisees. Their aims being more political than religious, they scorned such ideas as the resurrection, the second coming of Christ, and the last judgment. They were, more than any other group, responsible for the crucifixion of Jesus.

your strength." The second is this: "Love your neighbour as yourself." There is no other commandment greater than these.' The lawyer said to him, 'Well said, Master. You are right in saying that God is one and beside him there is no other. And to love him with all your heart, all your understanding, and all your strength, and to love your neighbour as yourself—that is far more than any burnt offerings or sacrifices.' When Jesus saw how sensibly he answered, he said to him, 'You are not far from the kingdom of God.'

After that nobody ventured to put any more questions to him; and Jesus went on to say, as he taught in the temple, 'How can the teachers of the law maintain that the Messiah is "Son of David"? David himself said, when inspired by the Holy Spirit, "The Lord said to my Lord, 'Sit at my right hand until I make your enemies your footstool.' " David himself calls him "Lord"; how can he also be David's son?'

There was a great crowd and they listened eagerly. He said as he taught them, 'Beware of the doctors of the law, who love to walk up and down in long robes, receiving respectful greetings in the street; and to have the chief seats in synagogues, and places of honour at feasts. These are the men who eat up the property of widows, while they say long prayers for appearance' sake, and they will receive the severest sentence.'

Once he was standing opposite the temple treasury, watching as people dropped their money into the chest. Many rich people were giving large sums. Presently there came a poor widow who dropped in two tiny coins, together worth a farthing. He called his disciples to him. 'I tell you this,' he said: 'this widow has given more than any of the others; for those others who have given had more than enough, but she, with less than enough, has given all that she had to live on.' . . .

Problems

1. To what extent does Jesus, in Mark, create a two-cities mentality—a city of God and a city of men? Why does he attack the powerful and the status-conscious?
2. Is Jesus attacking tradition when he attacks hand-washing, or merely trying to place tradition in another perspective? What perspective? Is the new perspective more reasonable or less?
3. Does Jesus deliberately intend a body-soul dichotomy in his remarks about uncleanliness (89/12-25), or is such a dichotomy an unwarranted and unintended extension of his concept of holiness? Where, for Jesus, does holiness most inhere—in things, deeds, or intentions?
4. In the *context* in which it is stated (90/9-27), is Jesus's remark, "It is easier for a camel to pass through the eye of a needle than for a rich man to enter the kingdom," a comment on God's attitude toward wealth or a comment on the rich man's attitude toward God?

5. To what extent does Jesus admit a double standard—the golden rule for men, a modified Mosaic code for God? If he has such a double standard, is it justifiable or intelligible in human terms? If he does not have such a double standard, how does one explain his conception of retribution? Is God humanized, aggrandized, or brutalized in human terms by Jesus's conception? To what extent does our attitude toward the limitation of salvation to the faithful ("Those who believe . . . will find salvation; those who do not believe will be condemned") affect our answer to, and our conception of, the other questions?

5

The Letter of Paul to the Romans

Paul's Letter to the Romans (A.D. 55–59), *though essentially reflective and theological in intention, suggests the splits affecting the early church, splits involving such questions as whether to admit gentiles, whether to require circumcision, whether to observe the Jewish Sabbath, whether to eat meat and observe other dietary laws. By the time Romans was written, the argument between Peter and Paul whether circumcision should be required for acceptance into the Church (see Acts, 15.1–20) had been resolved in Paul's favor, and gentile Christians already by this time probably outnumbered Jewish Christians. In Romans, Paul attempts to present the theological grounds upon which he based these arguments and his faith. The arguments speak for themselves: they are brilliant, carefully reasoned, and supported by numerous biblical allusions, but even to Paul the arguments are not entirely satisfactory. In the end, he acknowledges God's ways to be mysterious and unfathomable. "O depth of wealth, wisdom, and knowledge in God! How unsearchable his judgments, how untraceable his ways! Who knows the mind of the Lord?" Still, as a Jewish Rabbi, Paul was so steeped in the rabbinical school of close commentary, that he could not resist at least one attempt to rationalize and comprehend God's purposes. Romans, written as it was by perhaps the most influential of the Church fathers, remains one of the most important theological documents in the Christian canon.*

1

From Paul, servant of Christ Jesus, apostle by God's call, set apart for the service of the Gospel.

This gospel God announced beforehand in sacred scriptures through his prophets. It is about his Son: on the human level he was born of David's stock, but on the level of the spirit—the Holy Spirit—he was declared Son of God by a mighty act in that he rose from the dead: it is about Jesus Christ our Lord. Through him I received the privilege of a commission in his name to lead to faith and obedience men in all nations, yourselves among them, you who have heard the call and belong to Jesus Christ. 10

From *The New English Bible* (New York: Cambridge University Press, 1961), pp. 255–279.

I send greetings to all of you in Rome whom God loves and has called to be his dedicated people. Grace and peace to you from God our Father and the Lord Jesus Christ.

Let me begin by thanking my God, through Jesus Christ, for you all, because all over the world they are telling the story of your faith. God is my witness, the God to whom I offer the humble service of my spirit by preaching the gospel of his Son: God knows how continually I make mention of you in my prayers, and am always asking that by his will I may, somehow or other, succeed at long last in coming to visit you. For I long to see you; I want to bring you some spiritual gift to make you strong; or rather, I want to be among you to receive encouragement myself through the influence of your faith on me as of mine on you.

But I should like you to know, my brothers, that I have often planned to come, though so far without success, in the hope of achieving something among you, as I have in other parts of the world. I am under obligation to Greek and non-Greek, to learned and simple; hence my eagerness to declare the Gospel to you in Rome as well as to others. For I am not ashamed of the Gospel. It is the saving power of God for everyone who has faith—the Jew first, but the Greek also—because here is revealed God's way of righting wrong, a way that starts from faith and ends in faith; as Scripture says, 'he shall gain life who is justified through faith'.

For we see divine retribution revealed from heaven and falling upon all the godless wickedness of men. In their wickedness they are stifling the truth. For all that may be known of God by men lies plain before their eyes; indeed God himself has disclosed it to them. His invisible attributes, that is to say his everlasting power and deity, have been visible, ever since the world began, to the eye of reason, in the things he has made. There is therefore no possible defence for their conduct; knowing God, they have refused to honour him as God, or to render him thanks. Hence all their thinking has ended in futility, and their misguided minds are plunged in darkness. They boast of their wisdom, but they have made fools of themselves, exchanging the splendour of immortal God for an image shaped like mortal man, even for images like birds, beasts, and creeping things.

For this reason God has given them up to the vileness of their own desires, and the consequent degradation of their bodies, because they have bartered away the true God for a false one, and have offered reverence and worship to created things instead of to the Creator, who is blessed for ever; amen.

In consequence, I say, God has given them up to shameful passions. Their women have exchanged natural intercourse for unnatural, and their men in turn, giving up natural relations with women, burn with lust for one another; males behave indecently with males, and are paid in their own persons the fitting wage of such perversion.

Thus, because they have not seen fit to acknowledge God, he has given them up to their own depraved reason. This leads them to break all rules of conduct. They are filled with every kind of injustice, mischief, rapacity, and malice; they are one mass of envy, murder, rivalry, treachery, and malevolence; whisperers and scandal-mongers, hateful to God, insolent, arrogant, and boastful; they invent new kinds of mischief, they show no loyalty to parents, no conscience, no fidelity to their plighted word; they are without natural affection and without pity. They know well enough the just decree of God, that those who behave like this deserve to die, and yet they do it; not only so, they actually applaud such practices.

2

You therefore have no defence—you who sit in judgement, whoever you may be—for in judging your fellow-man you condemn yourself, since you, the judge, are equally guilty. It is admitted that God's judgement is rightly passed upon all who commit such crimes as these; and do you imagine—you who pass judgement on the guilty while committing the same crimes yourself—do you imagine that you, any more than they, will escape the judgement of God? Or do you think lightly of his wealth of kindness, of tolerance, and of patience, without recognizing that God's kindness is meant to lead you to a change of heart? In the rigid obstinacy of your heart you are laying up for yourself a store of retribution for the day of retribution, when God's just judgement will be revealed, and he will pay every man for what he has done. To those who pursue glory, honour, and immortality by steady persistence in well-doing, he will give eternal life; but for those who are governed by selfish ambition, who refuse obedience to the truth and take the wrong for their guide, there will be the fury of retribution. There will be grinding misery for every human being who is an evil-doer, for the Jew first and for the Greek also; and for every well-doer there will be glory, honour, and peace, for the Jew first and also for the Greek.

For God has no favourites: those who have sinned outside the pale of the Law of Moses will perish outside its pale, and all who have sinned under that law will be judged by the law. It is not by hearing the law, but by doing it, that men will be justified before God. When Gentiles who do not possess the law carry out its precepts by the light of nature, then, although they have no law, they are their own law, for they display the effect of the law inscribed on their hearts. Their conscience is called as witness, and their own thoughts argue the case on either side, against them or even for them, on the day when God judges the secrets of human hearts through Christ Jesus. So my gospel declares.

But as for you—you may bear the name of Jew; you rely upon the law and are proud of your God; you know his will; you are aware of moral distinctions because you receive instruction from the law; you are confident that you are the one to guide the blind, to enlighten the benighted, to train the stupid, and to teach the immature, because in the law you see the very shape of knowledge and truth. You, then, who teach your fellow-man, do you fail to teach yourself? You proclaim, 'Do not steal'; but are you yourself a thief? You say, 'Do not commit adultery'; but are you an adulterer? You abominate false gods; but do you rob their shrines? While you take pride in the law, you dishonour God by breaking it. For, as Scripture says, 'Because of you the name of God is dishonoured among the Gentiles.'

Circumcision has value, provided you keep the law; but if you break the law, then your circumcision is as if it had never been. Equally, if an uncircumcised man keep the precepts of the law, will he not count as circumcised? He may be uncircumcised in his natural state, but by fulfilling the law he will pass judgement on you who break it, for all your written code and your circumcision. The true Jew is not he who is such in externals, neither is the true circumcision the external mark in the flesh. The true Jew is he who is such inwardly, and the true circumcision is of the heart, directed not by written precepts but by the Spirit; such a man receives his commendation not from men but from God.

3

Then what advantage has the Jew? What is the value of circumcision? Great, in every way. In the first place, the Jews were entrusted with the oracles of God. What if some of them were unfaithful? Will their faithlessness cancel the faithfulness of God? Certainly not! God must be true though every man living were a liar; for we read in Scripture, 'When thou speakest thou shalt be vindicated, and win the verdict when thou art on trial.'

Another question: if our injustice serves to bring out God's justice, what are we to say? Is it unjust of God (I speak of him in human terms) to bring retribution upon us? Certainly not! If God were unjust, how could he judge the world?

Again, if the truth of God brings him all the greater honour because of my falsehood, why should I any longer be condemned as a sinner? Why not indeed 'do evil that good may come', as some libellously report me as saying? To condemn such men as these is surely no injustice.

What then? Are we Jews any better off? No, not at all! For we have already formulated the charge that Jews and Greeks alike are all under the power of sin. This has scriptural warrant:

'There is no just man, not one;
No one who understands, no one who seeks God.
All have swerved aside, all alike have become debased;
There is no one to show kindness; no, not one.

Their throat is an open grave,
They use their tongues for treachery,
Adders' venom is on their lips,
And their mouth is full of bitter curses.

Their feet hasten to shed blood,
Ruin and misery lie along their paths,
They are strangers to the high-road of peace,
And reverence for God does not enter their thoughts.'

Now all the words of the law are addressed, as we know, to those who are within the pale of the law, so that no one may have anything to say in self-defence, but the whole world my be exposed to the judgement of God. For (again from Scripture) 'no human being can be justified in the sight of God' for having kept the law: law brings only the consciousness of sin.

But now, quite independently of law, God's justice has been brought to light. The Law and the prophets both bear witness to it: it is God's way of righting wrong, effective through faith in Christ for all who have such faith—all, without distinction. For all alike have sinned, and are deprived of the divine splendour, and all are justified by God's free grace alone, through his act of liberation in the person of Christ Jesus. For God designed him to be the means of expiating sin by his sacrificial death, effective through faith. God meant by this to demonstrate his justice, because in his forbearance he had overlooked the sins of the past—to demonstrate his justice now in the present, showing that he is both himself just and justifies any man who puts his faith in Jesus.

What room then is left for human pride? It is excluded. And on what principle? The keeping of the law would not exclude it, but faith does. For our argument is that a man is justified by faith quite apart from success in keeping the law.

Do you suppose God is the God of the Jews alone? Is he not the God of Gentiles also? Certainly, of Gentiles also, if it be true that God is one. And he will therefore justify both the circumcised in virtue of their faith, and the uncircumcised through their faith. Does this mean that we are using faith to undermine law? By no means: we are placing law itself on a firmer footing.

4

What, then, are we to say about Abraham, our ancestor in the natural line? If Abraham was justified by anything he had done, then he has a ground for pride. But he has no such ground before God; for what does Scripture say? 'Abraham put his faith in God, and that faith was counted to him as righteousness.' Now if a man does a piece of work, his wages are not 'counted' as a favour; they are paid as debt. But if without any work to his credit he simply puts his faith in him who acquits the guilty, then his faith is indeed 'counted as righteousness'. In the same sense David speaks of the happiness of the man whom God 'counts' as just, apart from any specific acts of justice: 'Happy are they', he says, 'whose lawless deeds are forgiven, whose sins are buried away; happy if the man whose sins the Lord does not count against him.' Is this happiness confined to the circumcised, or is it for the uncircumcised also? Consider: we say, 'Abraham's faith was counted as righteousness'; in what circumstances was it so counted? Was he circumcized at the time, or not? He was not yet circumcised, but uncircumcised; and he later received the symbolic rite of circumcision as the hallmark of the righteousness which faith had given him when he was still uncircumcised. Consequently, he is the father of all who have faith when uncircumcised, so that righteousness is 'counted' to them; and at the same time he is the father of such of the circumcised as do not rely upon their circumcision alone, but also walk in the footprints of the faith which our father Abraham had while he was yet uncircumcised.

For it was not through law that Abraham, or his posterity, was given the promise that the world should be his inheritance, but through the righteousness that came from faith. For if those who hold by the law, and they alone, are heirs, then faith is empty and the promise goes for nothing, because law can bring only retribution; but where there is no law there can be no breach of law. The promise was made on the ground of faith, in order that it might be a matter of sheer grace, and that it might be valid for all Abraham's posterity, not only for those who hold by the law, but for those also who have the faith of Abraham. For he is the father of us all, as Scripture says: 'I have appointed you to be father of many nations.' This promise, then, was valid before God, the God in whom he put his faith, the God who makes the dead live and summons things that are not yet in existence as if they already were. When hope seemed hopeless, his faith was such that he became 'father of many nations', in agreement with the words which had been spoken to him: 'Thus shall your posterity be.' Without any weakening of faith he contemplated his own body, as good as dead (for he was about a hundred years old), and the deadness of

Sarah's womb, and never doubted God's promise, but, strong in faith, gave honour to God, in the firm conviction of his power to do what he had promised. And that is why Abraham's faith was 'counted to him as righteousness'.

Those words were written, not for Abraham's sake alone, but for our sake too: it is to be 'counted' in the same way to us who have faith in the God who raised Jesus our Lord from the dead; for he was delivered to death for our misdeeds, and raised to life to justify us.

5

Therefore, now that we have been justified through faith, let us continue at peace with God through our Lord Jesus Christ, through whom we have been allowed to enter the sphere of God's grace, where we now stand. Let us exult in the hope of the divine splendour that is to be ours. More than this: let us even exult in our present sufferings, because we know that suffering trains us to endure, and endurance brings proof that we have stood the test, and this proof is the ground of hope. Such a hope is no mockery, because God's love has flooded our inmost heart through the Holy Spirit he has given us.

For at the very time when we were still powerless, then Christ died for the wicked. Even for a just man one of us would hardly die, though perhaps for a good man one might actually brave death; but Christ died for us while we were yet sinners, and that is God's own proof of his love towards us. And so, since we have now been justified by Christ's sacrificial death, we shall all the more certainly be saved through him from final retribution. For if, when we were God's enemies, we were reconciled to him through the death of his Son, much more, now that we are reconciled, shall we be saved by his life. But that is not all: we also exult in God through our Lord Jesus, through whom we have now been granted reconciliation.

Mark what follows. It was through one man that sin entered the world, and through sin death, and thus death pervaded the whole human race, inasmuch as all men have sinned. For sin was already in the world before there was law, though in the absence of law no reckoning is kept of sin. But death held sway from Adam to Moses, even over those who had not sinned as Adam did, by disobeying a direct command—and Adam foreshadows the Man who was to come.

But God's act of grace is out of all proportion to Adam's wrongdoing. For if the wrongdoing of that one man brought death upon so many, its effect is vastly exceeded by the grace of God and the gift that came to so many by the grace of the one man, Jesus Christ. And again, the gift of God is not to be compared in its effect with that one man's sin; for the judicial action, following upon the one offence, issued in a verdict of condemnation, but the act of grace, following upon so many misdeeds, issued in a verdict of acquittal. For if by the wrongdoing of that one man death established its reign, through a single sinner, much more shall those who receive in far greater measure God's grace, and his gift of righteousness, live and reign through the one man, Jesus Christ.

It follows, then, that as the issue of one misdeed was condemnation for all men, so the issue of one just act is acquittal and life for all men. For as through the disobedience of the one man the many were made sinners, so through the obedience of the one man the many will be made righteous.

Law intruded into this process to multiply law-breaking. But where sin was thus multiplied, grace immeasurably exceeded it, in order that, as sin established its reign by way of death, so God's grace might establish its reign in righteousness, and issue in eternal life through Jesus Christ our Lord.

6

What are we to say, then? Shall we persist in sin, so that there may be all the more grace? No, no! We died to sin: how can we live in it any longer? Have you forgotten that when we were baptized into union with Christ Jesus we were baptized into his death? By baptism we were buried with him, and lay dead, in order that, as Christ was raised from the dead in the splendour of the Father, so also we might set our feet upon the new path of life.

For if we have become incorporate with him in a death like his, we shall also be one with him in a resurrection like his. We know that the man we once were has been crucified with Christ, for the destruction of the sinful self, so that we may no longer be the slaves of sin, since a dead man is no longer answerable for his sin. But if we thus died with Christ, we believe that we shall also come to life with him. We know that Christ, once raised from the dead, is never to die again: he is no longer under the dominion of death. For in dying as he died, he died to sin, once for all, and in living as he lives, he lives to God. In the same way you must regard yourselves as dead to sin and alive to God, in union with Christ Jesus.

So sin must no longer reign in your mortal body, exacting obedience to the body's desires. You must no longer put its several parts at sin's disposal, as implements for doing wrong. No: put yourselves at the disposal of God, as dead men raised to life; yield your bodies to him as implements for doing right; for sin shall no longer be your master, because you are no longer under law, but under the grace of God.

What then? Are we to sin, because we are not under law but under grace? Of course not. You know well enough that if you put yourselves at the disposal of a master, to obey him, you are slaves of the master whom you obey; and this is true whether you serve sin, with death as its result; or obedience, with righteousness as its result. But God be thanked, you, who once were slaves of sin, have yielded whole-hearted obedience to the pattern of teaching to which you were made subject, and, emancipated from sin, have become slaves of righteousness (to use words that suit your human weakness)—I mean, as you once yielded your bodies to the service of impurity and lawlessness, making for moral anarchy, so now you must yield them to the service of righteousness, making for a holy life.

When you were slaves of sin, you were free from the control of righteousness; and what was the gain? Nothing but what now makes you ashamed, for the end of that is death. But now, freed from the commands of sin, and bound to the service of God, your gains are such as make for holiness, and the end is eternal life. For sin pays a wage, and the wage is death, but God gives freely, and his gift is eternal life, in union with Christ Jesus our Lord.

7

You cannot be unaware, my friends—I am speaking to those who have some knowledge of law—that a person is subject to the law so long as he is alive, and no longer. For example, a married woman is by law bound to her husband while he lives; but if her husband dies, she is discharged from the obligations of the marriage-law. If, therefore, in her husband's lifetime she consorts with another man, she will incur the charge of adultery; but if her husband dies she is free of the law, and she does not commit adultery by consorting with another man. So you, my friends, have died to the law by becoming identified with the body of Christ, and accordingly you have found another husband in him who rose from the dead, so that we may bear fruit for God. While we lived on the level of our lower nature, the sinful passions evoked by the law worked in our bodies, to bear fruit for death. But now, having died to that which held us bound, we are discharged from the law, to serve God in a new way, the way of the spirit, in contrast to the old way, the way of a written code.

What follows? Is the law identical with sin? Of course not. But except through law I should never have become acquainted with sin. For example, I should never have known what it was to covet, if the law had not said, 'Thou shalt not covet.' Through that commandment sin found its opportunity, and produced in me all kinds of wrong desires. In the absence of law, sin is a dead thing. There was a time when, in the absence of law, I was fully alive; but when the commandment came, sin sprang to life and I died. The commandment which should have led to life proved in my experience to lead to death, because sin found its opportunity in the commandment, seduced me, and through the commandment killed me.

Therefore the law is in itself holy, and the commandment is holy and just and good. Are we to say then that this good thing was the death of me? By no means. It was sin that killed me, and thereby sin exposed its true character: it used a good thing to bring about my death, and so, through the commandment, sin became more sinful than ever.

We know that the law is spiritual; but I am not: I am unspiritual, the purchased slave of sin. I do not even acknowledge my own actions as mine, for what I do is not what I want to do, but what I detest. But if what I do is against my will, it means that I agree with the law and hold it to be admirable. But as things are, it is no longer I who perform the action, but sin that lodges in me. For I know that nothing good lodges in me—in my unspiritual nature, I mean—for though the will to do good is there, the deed is not. The good which I want to do, I fail to do; but what I do is the wrong which is against my will; and if what I do is against my will, clearly it is no longer I who am the agent, but sin that has its lodging in me.

I discover this principle, then: that when I want to do the right, only the wrong is within my reach. In my inmost self I delight in the law of God, but I perceive that there is in my bodily members a different law, fighting against the law that my reason approves and making me a prisoner under the law that is in my members, the law of sin. Miserable creature that I am, who is there to rescue me out of this body doomed to death? God alone, through Jesus Christ our Lord! Thanks be to God! In a word then, I myself, subject to God's law as a rational being, am yet, in my unspiritual nature, a slave to the law of sin.

8

The conclusion of the matter is this: there is no condemnation for those who are united with Christ Jesus, because in Christ Jesus the life-giving law of the Spirit has set you free from the law of sin and death. What the law could never do, because our lower nature robbed it of all potency, God has done: by sending his own Son in a form like that of our own sinful nature, and as a sacrifice for sin, he has passed judgment against sin within that very nature, so that the commandment of the law may find fulfilment in us, whose conduct, no longer under the control of our lower nature, is directed by the Spirit.

Those who live on the level of our lower nature have their outlook formed by it, and that spells death; but those who live on the level of the spirit have the spiritual outlook, and that is life and peace. For the outlook of the lower nature is enmity with God; it is not subject to the law of God; indeed it cannot be: those who live on such a level cannot possibly please God.

But that is not how you live. You are on the spiritual level, if only God's Spirit dwells within you; and if a man does not possess the Spirit of Christ, he is no Christian. But if Christ is dwelling within you, then although the body is a dead thing because you sinned, yet the spirit is life itself because you have been justified. Moreover, if the Spirit of him who raised Jesus from the dead dwells within you, then the God who raised Christ Jesus from the dead will also give new life to your mortal bodies through his indwelling Spirit.

It follows, my friends, that our lower nature has no claim upon us; we are not obliged to live on that level. If you do so, you must die. But if by the Spirit you put to death all the base pursuits of the body, then you will live.

For all who are moved by the Spirit of God are sons of God. The Spirit you have received is not a spirit of slavery leading you back into a life of fear, but a Spirit that makes us sons, enabling us to cry 'Abba! Father!' In that cry the Spirit of God joins with our spirit in testifying that we are God's children; and if children, then heirs. We are God's heirs and Christ's fellow-heirs, if we share his sufferings now in order to share his splendour hereafter.

For I reckon that the sufferings we now endure bear no comparison with the splendour, as yet unrevealed, which is in store for us. For the created universe waits with eager expectation for God's sons to be revealed. It was made the victim of frustration, not by its own choice, but because of him who made it so; yet always there was hope, because the universe itself is to be freed from the shackles of mortality and enter upon the liberty and splendour of the children of God. Up to the present, we know, the whole created universe groans in all its parts as if in the pangs of childbirth. Not only so, but even we, to whom the Spirit is given as firstfruits of the harvest to come, are groaning inwardly while we wait for God to make us his sons and set our whole body free. For we have been saved, though only in hope. Now to see is no longer to hope: why should a man endure and wait for what he already sees? But if we hope for something we do not yet see, then, in waiting for it, we show our endurance.

In the same way the Spirit comes to the aid of our weakness. We do not even know how we ought to pray, but through our inarticulate groans the Spirit himself is pleading for us, and God who searches our inmost being knows what the Spirit means, because he pleads for God's own people in God's own way; and in everything, as we know, he co-operates for good with those who love God and are called according to his purpose. For God knew his own before ever they were, and also ordained that they should be shaped to the likeness of his Son, that he might be the eldest among a large family of brothers; and it is these, so fore-ordained, whom he has also called. And those whom he called he has justified, and to those whom he justified he has also given his splendour.

With all this in mind, what are we to say? If God is on our side, who is against us? He did not spare his own Son, but surrendered him for us all; and with this gift how can he fail to lavish upon us all he has to give? Who will be the accuser of God's chosen ones? It is God who pronounces acquittal: then who can condemn? It is Christ—Christ who died, and, more than that, was raised from the dead—who is at God's right hand, and indeed pleads our cause. Then what can separate us from the love of Christ? Can affliction or hardship? Can persecution, hunger, nakedness, peril, or the sword? 'We are being done to death for thy sake all day long,' as Scripture says; 'we have been treated like sheep for slaughter'—and yet, in spite of all, overwhelming victory is ours through him who loved us. For I am convinced that there is nothing in death or life, in the realm of spirits or superhuman powers, in the world as it is or the world as it shall be, in the forces of the universe, in heights or depths—nothing in all creation that can separate us from the love of God in Christ Jesus our Lord.

9

I am speaking the truth as a Christian, and my own conscience, enlightened by the Holy Spirit, assures me it is no lie: in my heart there is great grief and unceasing sorrow. For I could even pray to be outcast from Christ myself for the sake of my brothers, my natural kinsfolk. They are Israelites: they were made God's sons; theirs is the splendour of the divine presence, theirs the covenants, the law, the temple worship, and the promises. Theirs are the patriarchs, and from them, in natural descent, sprang the Messiah. May God, supreme above all, be blessed for ever! Amen.

It is impossible that the word of God should have proved false. For not all descendants of Israel are truly Israel, nor, because they are Abraham's offspring, are they all his true children; but, in the words of Scripture, 'Through the line of Isaac your posterity shall be traced.' That is to say, it is not those born in the course of nature who are children of God; it is the children born through God's promise who are reckoned as Abraham's descendants. For the promise runs: 'At the time fixed I will come, and Sarah shall have a son.'

But that is not all, for Rebekah's children had one and the same father, our ancestor Isaac; and yet, in order that God's selective purpose might stand, based not upon men's deeds but upon the call of God, she was told, even before they were born, when they had as yet done nothing, good or ill, 'The elder shall be servant to the younger'; and that accords with the text of Scripture, 'Jacob I loved and Esau I hated.'

What shall we say to that? Is God to be charged with injustice? By no means. For he says to Moses, 'Where I show mercy, I will show mercy, and where I pity, I will pity.' Thus it does not depend on man's will or effort, but on God's mercy. For Scripture says to Pharaoh, 'I have raised you up for this very purpose, to exhibit my power in my dealings with you, and to spread my fame over all the world.' Thus he not only shows mercy as he chooses, but also makes men stubborn as he chooses.

You will say, 'Then why does God blame a man? For who can resist his will?' Who are you, sir, to answer God back? Can the pot speak to the potter and say, 'Why did you make me like this?'? Surely the potter can do what he likes with the clay. Is he not free to make out of the same lump two vessels, one to be treasured, the other for common use?

But what if God, desiring to exhibit his retribution at work and to make his power known, tolerated very patiently those vessels which were objects of retribution due for destruction, and did so in order to make known the full wealth of his splendour upon vessels which were objects of mercy, and which from the first had been prepared for this splendour?

Such vessels are we, whom he has called from among Gentiles as well as Jews, as it says in the Book of Hosea: 'Those who were not my people I will call My People, and the unloved nation I will call My Beloved. For in the very place where they were told "you are no people of mine", they shall be called Sons of the living God.' But Isaiah makes this proclamation about Israel: 'Though the Israelites be countless as the sands of the sea, it is but a remnant that shall be saved; for the Lord's sentence on the land will be summary and final'; as also he said previously, 'If the Lord of Hosts had not left us the mere germ of a nation, we should have become like Sodom, and no better than Gomorrah.'

Then what are we to say? That Gentiles, who made no effort after righteousness, nevertheless achieved it, a righteousness based on faith; whereas Israel made great efforts after a law of righteousness, but never attained to it. Why was this? Because their efforts were not based on faith, but (as they supposed) on deeds. They stumbled over the 'stumbling-stone' mentioned in Scripture; 'Here I lay in Zion a stumbling-stone and a rock to trip them up; but he who has faith in him will not be put to shame.'

10

Brothers, my deepest desire and my prayer to God is for their salvation. To their zeal for God I can testify; but it is an ill-informed zeal. For they ignore God's way of righteousness, and try to set up their own, and therefore they have not submitted themselves to God's righteousness. For Christ ends the law and brings righteousness for everyone who has faith.

Of legal righteousness Moses writes, 'The man who does this shall gain life by it.' But the righteousness that comes by faith says, 'Do not say to yourself, "Who can go up to heaven?"' (that is to bring Christ down), 'or, "Who can go down to the abyss?"' (to bring Christ up from the dead). But what does it say? 'The word is near you: it is upon your lips and in your heart.' This means the word of faith which we proclaim. If on your lips is the confession, 'Jesus is Lord', and in your heart the faith that God raised him from the dead, then you will find salvation. For the faith that leads to righteousness is in the heart, and the confession that leads to salvation is upon the lips.

Scripture says, 'Everyone who has faith in him will be saved from shame'—everyone: there is no distinction between Jew and Greek, because the same Lord is Lord of all, and is rich enough for the need of all who invoke him. For everyone, as it says again—'everyone who invokes the name of the Lord will be saved'. How could they invoke one in whom they had no faith? And how could they have faith in one they had never heard of? And how hear without someone to spread the news? And how could anyone spread the news without a commission to do so? And that is what Scripture affirms: 'How welcome are the feet of the messengers of good news!'

But not all have responded to the good news. For Isaiah says, 'Lord, who has believed our message?' We conclude that faith is awakened by the message, and the message that awakens it comes through the word of Christ.

But, I ask, can it be that they never heard it? Of course they did: 'Their voice has sounded all over the earth, and their words to the bounds of the inhabited world.' But, I ask again, can it be that Israel failed to recognize the message? In reply, I first cite Moses, who says, 'I will use a nation that is no nation to stir your envy, and a foolish nation to rouse your anger.' But Isaiah is still more daring: 'I was found', he says, 'by those who were not looking for me; I was clearly shown to those who never asked about me'; while to Israel he says, 'All day long I have stretched out my hands to an unruly and recalcitrant people.'

11

I ask then, has God rejected his people? I cannot believe it! I am an Israelite myself, of the stock of Abraham, of the tribe of Benjamin. No! God has not rejected the people which he acknowledged of old as his own. You know (do you not?) what Scripture says in the story of Elijah—how Elijah pleads with God against Israel: 'Lord, they have killed thy prophets, they have overthrown thine altars, and I alone am left, and they are seeking my life.' But what does the oracle say to him? 'I have left myself seven thousand men who have not done homage to Baal.' In just the same way at the present time a 'remnant' has come into being, selected by the grace of God. But if it is by grace, then it does not rest on deeds done, or grace would cease to be grace.

What follows? What Israel sought, Israel has not achieved, but the selected few have achieved it. The rest were made blind to the truth, exactly as it stands written: 'God brought upon them a numbness of spirit; he gave them blind eyes and deaf ears, and so it is still.' Similarly David says:

'May their table be a snare and a trap,
Both stumbling-block and retribution!
May their eyes be darkened so that they do not see!
Bow down their back for ever!'

I now ask, did their failure mean complete downfall? Far from it! Because they offended, salvation has come to the Gentiles, to stir Israel to emulation. But if their offence means the enrichment of the world, and if their falling-off means the enrichment of the Gentiles, how much more their coming to full strength!

But I have something to say to you Gentiles. I am a missionary to the Gentiles, and as such I give all honour to that ministry when I try to stir emulation in the men of my own race, and so to save some of them. For if their rejection has meant the reconciliation of the world, what will their acceptance mean? Nothing less than life from the dead! If the first portion of dough is consecrated, so is the whole lump. If the root is consecrated, so are the branches. But if some of the branches have been lopped off, and you, a wild olive, have been grafted in among them, and have come to share the same root and sap as the olive, do not make yourself superior to the branches. If you do so, remember that it is not you who sustain the root: the root sustains you.

You will say, 'Branches were lopped off so that I might be grafted in.' Very well: they were lopped off for lack of faith, and by faith you hold your place. Put away your pride, and be on your guard; for if God did not spare the native branches, no more will he spare you. Observe the kindness and the severity of God—severity to those who fell away, divine kindness to you, if only you remain within its scope; otherwise you too will be cut off, whereas they, if they do not continue faithless, will be grafted in; for it is in God's power to graft them in again. For if you were cut from your native wild olive and against all nature grafted into the cultivated olive, how much more readily will they, the natural olive-branches, be grafted into their native stock!

For there is a deep truth here, my brothers, of which I want you to take account, so that you may not be complacent about your own discernment: this partial blindness has come upon Israel only until the Gentiles have been admitted in full strength; when that has happened, the whole of Israel will be saved, in agreement with the text of Scripture:

> 'From Zion shall come the Deliverer;
> He shall remove wickedness from Jacob.
> And this is the covenant I will grant them,
> When I take away their sins.'

In the spreading of the Gospel they are treated as God's enemies for your sake; but God's choice stands, and they are his friends for the sake of the patriarchs. For the gracious gifts of God and his calling are irrevocable. Just as formerly you were disobedient to God, but now have received mercy in the time of their disobedience, so now, when you receive mercy, they have proved disobedient, but only in order that they too may receive mercy. For in making all mankind prisoners to disobedience, God's purpose was to show mercy to all mankind.

O depth of wealth, wisdom, and knowledge in God! How unsearchable his judgements, how untraceable his ways! Who knows the mind of the Lord? Who has been his counsellor? Who has ever made a gift to him, to receive a gift in return? Source, Guide, and Goal of all that is—to him be glory for ever! Amen.

12

Therefore my brothers, I implore you by God's mercy to offer your very selves to him: a living sacrifice, dedicated and fit for his acceptance, the worship offered by mind and heart. Adapt yourselves no longer to the pattern of this present world, but let your minds be remade and your whole nature thus transformed. Then you will be able to discern the will of God, and to know what is good, acceptable, and perfect.

In virtue of the gift that God in his grace has given me I say to everyone among you: do not be conceited or think too highly of yourself; but think your way to a sober estimate based on the measure of faith that God has dealt to each of you. For just as in a single human body there are many limbs and organs, all with different functions, so all of us, united with Christ, form one body, serving individually as limbs and organs to one another.

The gifts we possess differ as they are allotted to us by God's grace, and must be exercised accordingly: the gift of inspired utterance, for example, in proportion to a man's faith; or the gift of administration, in administration. A teacher should employ his gift in teaching, and one who has the gift of stirring speech should use it to stir his hearers. If you give to charity, give with all your heart; if you are a leader, exert yourself to lead; if you are helping others in distress, do it cheerfully.

Love in all sincerity, loathing evil and clinging to the good. Let love for your brotherhood breed warmth of mutual affection. Give pride of place to one another in esteem.

With unflagging energy, in ardour of spirit, serve the Lord.

Let hope keep you joyful; in trouble stand firm; persist in prayer. Contribute to the needs of God's people, and practise hospitality. Call down blessings on your persecutors—blessings, not curses.

With the joyful be joyful, and mourn with the mourners.

Have equal regard for one another. Do not be haughty, but go about with humble folk. Do not keep thinking how wise you are.

Never pay back evil for evil. Let your aims be such as all men count honourable. If possible, so far as it lies with you, live at peace with all men. My dear friends, do not seek revenge, but leave a place for divine retribution; for there is a text which reads, 'Justice is mine, says the Lord, I will repay.' But there is another text: 'If your enemy is hungry, feed him; if he is thirsty, give him a drink; by doing this you will heap live coals on his head.' Do not let evil conquer you, but use good to defeat evil.

13

Every person must submit to the supreme authorities. There is no authority but by act of God, and the existing authorities are instituted by him; consequently anyone who rebels against authority is resisting a divine institution, and those who so resist have themselves to thank for the punishment they will receive. For government, a terror to crime, has no terrors for good behaviour. You wish to have no fear of the authorities? Then continue to do right and you will have their approval, for they are God's agents working for your good. But if you are doing wrong, then you will have cause to fear them; it is not for nothing that they hold the power of the sword, for they are God's agents of punishment, for retribution on the offender. That is why you are obliged to submit. It is an obligation imposed not merely by fear of retribution but by conscience. That is also why you pay taxes. The authorities are in God's service and to these duties they devote their energies.

Discharge your obligations to all men; pay tax and toll, reverence and respect, to those to whom they are due. Leave no claim outstanding against you, except that of mutual love. He who loves his neighbour has satisfied every claim of the law. For the commandments, 'Thou shalt not commit adultery, thou shalt not kill, thou shalt not steal, thou shalt not covet', and any other commandment there may be, are all summed up in the one rule, 'Love your neighbour as yourself.' Love cannot wrong a neighbour; therefore the whole law is summed up in love.

In all this, remember how critical the moment is. It is time for you to wake out of sleep, for deliverance is nearer to us now than it was when first we believed. It is far on in the night; day is near. Let us therefore throw off the deeds of darkness and put on our armour as soldiers of the light. Let us behave with decency as befits the day: no revelling or drunkenness, no debauchery or vice, no quarrels or jealousies! Let Christ Jesus himself be the armour that you wear; give no more thought to satisfying the bodily appetites.

14

If a man is weak in his faith you must accept him without attempting to settle doubtful points. For instance, one man will have faith enough to eat all kinds of food, while a weaker man eats only vegetables. The man who eats must not hold in contempt the man who does not, and he who does not eat must not pass judgement on the one who does; for God has accepted him. Who are you to pass judgement on someone else's servant? Whether he stands or falls is his own Master's business; and stand he will, because his Master has power to enable him to stand.

Again, this man regards one day more highly than another, while that man regards all days alike. On such a point everyone should have reached conviction in his own mind. He who respects the day has the Lord in mind in doing so, and he who eats meat has the Lord in mind when he eats, since he gives thanks to God; and he who abstains has the Lord in mind no less, since he too gives thanks to God.

For no one of us lives, and equally no one of us dies, for himself alone. If we live, we live for the Lord; and if we die, we die for the Lord. Whether therefore we live or die, we belong to the Lord. This is why

Christ died and came to life again, to establish his lordship over dead and living. You, sir, why do you pass judgment on your brother? And you, sir, why do you hold your brother in contempt? We shall all stand before God's tribunal. For Scripture says, 'As I live, says the Lord, to me every knee shall bow and every tongue acknowledge God.' So, you see, each of us will have to answer for himself.

Let us therefore cease judging one another, but rather make this simple judgement: that no obstacle or stumbling-block be placed in a brother's way. I am absolutely convinced, as a Christian, that nothing is impure in itself; only, if a man considers a particular thing impure, then to him it is impure. If your brother is outraged by what you eat, then your conduct is no longer guided by love. Do not by your eating bring disaster to a man for whom Christ died! What for you is a good thing must not become an occasion for slanderous talk; for the kingdom of God is not eating and drinking, but justice, peace, and joy, inspired by the Holy Spirit. He who thus shows himself a servant of Christ is acceptable to God and approved by men.

Let us then pursue the things that make for peace and build up the common life. Do not ruin the work of God for the sake of food. Everything is pure in itself, but anything is bad for the man who by his eating causes another to fall. It is a fine thing to abstain from eating meat or drinking wine, or doing anything which causes your brother's downfall. If you have a clear conviction, apply it to yourself in the sight of God. Happy is the man who can make his decision with a clear conscience! But a man who has doubts is guilty if he eats, because his action does not arise from his conviction, and anything which does not arise from conviction is sin.

15

Those of us who have a robust conscience must accept as our own burden the tender scruples of weaker men, and not consider ourselves. Each of us must consider his neighbour and think what is for his good and will build up the common life. For Christ too did not consider himself, but might have said, in the words of Scripture, 'The reproaches of those who reproached thee fell upon me.' For all the ancient scriptures were written for our own instruction, in order that through the encouragement they give us we may maintain our hope with fortitude. And may God, the source of all fortitude and all encouragement, grant that you may agree with one another after the manner of Christ Jesus, so that with one mind and one voice you may praise the God and Father of our Lord Jesus Christ.

In a word, accept one another as Christ accepted us, to the glory of God. I mean that Christ became a servant of the Jewish people to maintain the truth of God by making good his promises to the patriarchs, and at the same time to give the Gentiles cause to glorify God for his mercy. As Scripture says, 'Therefore I will praise thee among the Gentiles and sing hymns to thy name'; and again, 'Gentiles, make merry together with his own people'; and yet again, 'All Gentiles, praise the Lord; let all peoples praise him.' Once again, Isaiah says, 'There shall be the Root of Jesse, the one raised up to govern the Gentiles; on him the Gentiles shall set their hope.' And may the God of hope fill you with all joy and peace by your faith in him, until, by the power of the Holy Spirit, you overflow with hope.

My friends, I have no doubt in my own mind that you yourselves are quite full of goodness and equipped with knowledge of every kind, well able to give advice to one another; nevertheless I have written to refresh your memory, and written somewhat boldly at times, in virtue of the gift I have from God. His grace has made me a minister of Christ Jesus to the Gentiles; my priestly service is the preaching of the gospel of God, and it falls to me to offer the Gentiles to him as an acceptable sacrifice, consecrated by the Holy Spirit.

Thus in the fellowship of Christ Jesus I have ground for pride in the service of God. I will venture to speak of those things alone in which I have been Christ's instrument to bring the Gentiles into his allegiance, by word and deed, by the force of miraculous signs and by the power of the Holy Spirit. As a result I have completed the preaching of the gospel of Christ from Jerusalem as far round as Illyricum. It is my ambition to bring the gospel to places where the very name of Christ has not been heard, for I do not want to build on another man's foundation; but, as Scripture says,

'They who had no news of him shall see,
And they who never heard of him shall understand.'

That is why I have been prevented all this time from coming to you. But now I have no further scope in these parts, and I have been longing for many years to visit you on my way to Spain; for I hope to see you as I travel through, and to be sent there with your support after having enjoyed your company for a while. But at the moment I am on my way to Jerusalem, on an errand to God's people there. For Macedonia and Achaia have resolved to raise a common fund for the benefit of the poor among God's people at Jerusalem. They have resolved to do so, and indeed they are under an obligation to them. For if the Jewish Christians shared their spiritual treasures with the Gentiles, the Gentiles have a clear duty to contribute to their material needs. So when I have finished this business and delivered the proceeds under my own seal, I shall set out for Spain by way of your city, and I am sure that when I arrive I shall come to you with a full measure of the blessing of Christ.

I implore you by our Lord Jesus Christ and by the love that the Spirit inspires, be my allies in the fight; pray to God for me that I may be saved from unbelievers in Judaea and that my errand to Jerusalem may find acceptance with God's people, so that by his will I may come to you in a happy frame of mind and enjoy a time of rest with you. The God of peace be with you all. Amen.

16

I commend to you Phoebe, a fellow-Christian who holds office in the congregation at Cenchreae. Give her, in the fellowship of Christ, a welcome worthy of God's people, and stand by her in any business in which she may need your help, for she has herself been a good friend to many, including myself.

Give my greetings to Prisca and Aquila, my fellow-workers in Christ. They risked their necks to save my life, and not I alone but all the gentile congregations are grateful to them. Greet also the congregation at their house.

Give my greetings to my dear friend Epaenetus, the first convert to Christ in Asia, and to Mary, who toiled hard for you. Greet Andronicus and Junias my fellow-countrymen and comrades in captivity. They are eminent among the apostles, and they were Christians before I was.

Greetings to Ampliatus, my dear friend in the fellowship of the Lord, to Urban my comrade in Christ, and to my dear Stachys. My greetings to Apelles, well proved in Christ's service, to the household of Aristobulus, and my countryman Herodion, and to those of the household of Narcissus who are in the Lord's fellowship. Greet Tryphaena and Tryphosa, who toil in the Lord's service, and dear Persis who has toiled in his service so long. Give my greetings to Rufus, an outstanding follower of the Lord, and to his mother, whom I call mother too. Greet Asyncritus, Phlegon, Hermes, Patrobas, Hermas, and all friends in their company. Greet Philologus and Julia, Nereus and his sister, and Olympas, and all God's people associated with them.

Greet one another with the kiss of peace. All Christ's congregations send you their greetings.

I implore you, my friends, keep your eye on those who stir up quarrels and lead others astray, contrary to the teaching you received. Avoid them, for such people are servants not of Christ our Lord but of their own appetites, and they seduce the minds of innocent people with smooth and specious words. The fame of your obedience has spread everywhere. This makes me happy about you; yet I should wish you to be experts in goodness but simpletons in evil; and the God of peace will soon crush Satan beneath your feet. The grace of our Lord Jesus be with you!

Greetings to you from my colleague Timothy, and from Lucius, Jason, and Sosipater my fellow-countrymen. (I Tertius, who took this letter down, add my Christian greetings.) Greetings also from Gaius, my host and host of the whole congregation, and from Erastus, treasurer of this city, and our brother Quartus.

To him who has power to make your standing sure, according to the Gospel I brought you and the proclamation of Jesus Christ, according to the revelation of that divine secret kept in silence for long ages but now disclosed, and through prophetic scriptures by eternal God's command made known to all nations, to bring them to faith and obedience—to God who alone is wise, through Jesus Christ, be glory for endless ages! Amen.

Patterns: Disguised Disparagement

Paul uses disparagement repeatedly and roughly against the Jews, and more gently against others. In his discussion of the dietary controversy for example (112/23–115/8), Paul never acknowledges his opposition to the vegetarians, but it is thinly veiled and palpable throughout. The hypothetical construction of the first two sentences allows him to reveal his bias and thereby comment unfavorably upon the vegetarians, without stating it explicitly: "If a man is weak in his faith you must accept him. . . . For instance, one man will have faith enough to eat all kinds of food, while a weaker man eats only vegetables" (112/23-26). There is no missing the implication that vegetarians are weaker in their faith. This may not have been true in the sense of intensity of faith, but in terms of their understanding of the faith *as it was understood by Paul*, it undoubtedly was. For Paul, nothing was "in itself unclean" or unholy. Because holiness or unholiness is a matter of the spirit, spiritual essence does not, therefore, inhere in foods, objects, days, or rituals. Paul's understanding of the faith is, of course, not important here. What is important is that he is mildly disparaging the vegetarians, perhaps with the hope of freeing them from a primitive conception of religion. Though the disparagement is never brutal, neither is it carefully disguised. Twice (113/9-10, 20) he announces that "nothing is impure," and just before closing, he rephrases his opening remarks, this time with enough confidence to announce his own stand: "Those of us who have a robust conscience must accept as our own burden the tender scruples of weaker men, and not consider ourselves" (113/28-30). Paul's intention here is humane, not destructive. He is trying to reconcile two divergent groups, and without feigning to neutrality, trying gently to lead one of the groups to abandon its position. Presented as it is, the disparagement becomes not chastisement, but an admonition to the vegetarians to liberate themselves from spiritually constricting, anxiety-producing formulae. Thus, even disparagement may serve constructive ends.

What is finally important for our purposes, however, is the difficulty of responding to Paul without appearing oversensitive, hypercritical, and contentious. Disguised disparagement is thus a favorite device among those who (1) wish to gain an emotional advantage by creating an undeserved illusion of fairness, (2) wish to embed commentary into their essay without providing opponents with a handle to grasp in reply, and (3) wish for one reason or another to avoid detailing their reasons. Disguised disparagement may and often does serve constructive ends; does this, however, justify its use?

Problems

1. Paul, throughout Romans, is intent on diminishing if not destroying Jewish obsession with fulfilling the Law. What are Paul's objections to the Law? Are his objections rooted in his conception of the Law, his conception of man, or his conception of the necessary relationship between the two? To what extent are his objections sound?
2. Faith for Paul means trust in God's love, putting oneself unquestioningly in his loving care; for the Hebrews it meant fidelity to the Law of God, diligence and attentiveness in fulfilling God's commands. Which of these views of faith is most optimistic about man? Most rational? Why?
3. Though Paul often speaks of divine retribution, he avoids a simple recompensatory scheme of rewards and punishments while still maintaining such a scheme for all practical purposes. Thus retribution for sin is *earned*, while salvation is *freely given*. Is the image of man ennobled or diminished by the recompensatory and highly self-reliant and individualized scheme of the Jews? What does your answer indicate about your own value system? Why would Paul have felt that such a recompensatory scheme was an indication of little faith and a mark of pride, and what does this suggest about Paul's interest? Is he more interested in justifying God to man than in justifying man? Why would he have the interest he has? Does Paul's scheme increase or diminish the claims and powers of the rational mind?
4. How does Paul try to resolve the conflict between individual responsibility and divine will and purpose?
5. Are Paul's attitudes toward Christianity and the state reasonable? What are the possible consequences of this attitude for the social order, social justice and efficiency, and for rebellion against injustice?
6. A man is measured existentially by how he acts, in another sense by the practical advice he gives. In chapters 14–15, Paul gives squabbling Christians some advice. What does the advice reveal about Paul's attitude toward (a) freedom of conscience, (b) ritual and dogma as essential elements of faith, (c) situation ethics, (d) acceptance of others as the cornerstone of Christianity? Would his attitude be conditional or unconditional, and, if so, in what way and to what extent?
7. Paul asserts, "anything which does not arise from conviction is sin" (113/ 26-27). Freud asserts that the inevitable result of a disparity between attitudes and actions is neurosis. To what extent are they asserting the same thing? To what extent is Paul's remark likely to create autonomous self-reliant indi-

viduals? To what extent is it likely to inhibit openminded introspection and experimentation and create instead a narrowminded rigidity calculated to suppress the anxiety created by an uncertain conscience? In the over-all context of Paul's remarks in Romans (14–15), what would make the difference between which path a person followed?
8. How would Job have acted had he a Pauline perspective? Would the Christian God have been angered by Eliphaz, Bildad, and Zophar?
9. Had the writer of Ecclesiastes been a Christian, in what ways would his attitude have been different?

6

The First Letter of John

The First Letter of John was written long after that of Paul, probably some time between A.D. *96 and 110 by John the Presbyter, a disciple of John the Apostle. Like the fourth Gospel, the Gospel according to John (perhaps authored by John the Apostle but probably not by John the Presbyter), the Letter of John develops a theological outlook called Johannine in opposition to that contained in the Gospels of Matthew, Mark, and Luke—the Synoptic Gospels (from the Greek word* synopsis). *John's letter, like Paul's, was written during a period when schisms were developing in the Church, in this instance as a result of the attraction of the pagan mystery cults, Hellenistic mysticism, or Gnosticism. These religions were mystical in outlook, spiritually esoteric in orientation, dichotomous in perspective, and contemptuous of the evilness of the material world. Opposed to matter was reason, which was viewed as a spiritual essence separated from God, the Eternal Light and Pure Being, and trapped by the material world of the flesh. Through revelation, supernatural knowledge or* gnosis, *man might free his spirit from its material prison and be absolved in the supernatural world of the Divine.*

The writer of the Letter, obviously aware of the schism, is intent on addressing himself to the threat posed by a religion so absorbed with enlightenment, so disdainful of the material world, and so individualistic as perhaps to weaken a sense of communal obligation rooted in the ethics of the Law. The writer is thus intent on answering this challenge to the precarious synthesis of Christianity, the concept of the Incarnation. There are characteristic Johannine emphases in his answer to gnosticism: his stress on the realizable presence of eternal life here and now as a typical quality of life that adheres to those who live in union with God; his almost pragmatic preoccupation with elucidating the practical ethical consequences of beliefs (hence his emphasis on the Incarnation as personalizing and humanizing Christianity's ethical content); his recognition that the overriding principle of Christ's life, the cardinal principle of all ethical religion, is love or charity, and that love or charity can exist and be practiced only in a community—the community of God's children.

1

It was there from the beginning; we have heard it; we have seen it with our own eyes; we looked upon it, and felt it with our own hands; and it is of this we tell. Our theme is the word of life. This life was made visible; we have seen it and bear our testimony; we here declare to you the eternal life which dwelt with the Father and was made visible to us. What we have seen and heard we declare to you, so that you and we together may share in a common life, that life which we share with the Father and his Son Jesus Christ. And we write this in order that the joy of us all may be complete.

Here is the message we heard from him and pass on to you: that God is light, and in him there is no darkness at all. If we claim to be sharing in his life while we walk in the dark, our words and our lives are a lie; but if we walk in the light as he himself is in the light, then we share together a common life, and we are being cleansed from every sin by the blood of Jesus his Son.

If we claim to be sinless, we are self-deceived and strangers to the truth. If we confess our sins, he is just, and may be trusted to forgive our sins and cleanse us from every kind of wrong; but if we say we have committed no sin, we make him out to be a liar, and then his word has no place in us.

2

My children, in writing thus to you my purpose is that you should not commit sin. But should anyone commit a sin, we have one to plead our cause with the Father, Jesus Christ, and he is just. He is himself the remedy for the defilement of our sins, not our sins only but the sins of all the world.

Here is the test by which we can make sure that we know him: do we keep his commands? The man who says, 'I know him', while he disobeys his commands, is a liar and a stranger to the truth; but in the man who is obedient to his word, the divine love has indeed come to its perfection.

Here is the test by which we can make sure that we are in him: whoever claims to be dwelling in him, binds himself to live as Christ himself lived. Dear friends, I give you no new command. It is the old command which you always had before you; the old command is the

From *The New English Bible* (New York: Cambridge University Press, 1961), pp. 408–414.

message which you heard at the beginning. And yet again it is a new command that I am giving you—new in the sense that the darkness is passing and the real light already shines. Christ has made this true, and it is true in your own experience.

A man may say, 'I am in the light'; but if he hates his brother, he is still in the dark. Only the man who loves his brother dwells in light: there is nothing to make him stumble. But one who hates his brother is in darkness; he walks in the dark and has no idea where he is going, because the darkness has made him blind.

> I write to you, my children, because your sins have been forgiven for his sake.
> I write to you, fathers, because you know him who is and has been from the beginning.
> I write to you, young men, because you have mastered the evil one.
> To you, children, I have written because you know the Father.
> To you, fathers, I have written because you know him who is and has been from the beginning.
> To you, young men, I have written because you are strong; God's word is in you, and you have mastered the evil one.

Do not set your hearts on the godless world or anything in it. Anyone who loves the world is a stranger to the Father's love. Everything the world affords, all that panders to the appetites, or entices the eyes, all the glamour of its life, springs not from the Father but from the godless world. And that world is passing away with all its allurements, but he who does God's will stands for evermore.

My children, this is the last hour! You were told that Antichrist was to come, and now many antichrists have appeared; which proves to us that this is indeed the last hour. They went out from our company but never really belonged to us; if they had, they would have stayed with us. They went out, so that it might be clear that not all in our company truly belong to it.

You, no less than they, are among the initiated; this is the gift of the Holy One, and by it you all have knowledge. It is not because you are ignorant of the truth that I have written to you, but because you know it, and because lies, one and all, are alien to the truth.

Who is the liar? Who but he that denies that Jesus is the Christ? He is Antichrist, for he denies both the Father and the Son: to deny the Son is to be without the Father; to acknowledge the Son is to have the Father too. You therefore must keep in your hearts that which you heard at the beginning; if what you heard then still dwells in you, you will yourselves dwell in the Son and also in the Father. And this is the promise that he himself gave us, the promise of eternal life.

So much for those who would mislead you. But as for you, the initiation which you received from him stays with you; you need no other teacher, but learn all you need to know from his initiation, which is real and no illusion. As he taught you, then, dwell in him.

Even now, my children, dwell in him, so that when he appears we may be confident and unashamed before him at his coming. If you know that he is righteous, you must recognize that every man who does right is his child.

3

How great is the love that the Father has shown to us! We were called God's children, and such we are; and the reason why the godless world does not recognize us is that it has not known him. Here and now, dear friends, we are God's children; what we shall be has not yet been disclosed, but we know that when it is disclosed we shall be like him, because we shall see him as he is. Everyone who has this hope before him purifies himself, as Christ is pure.

To commit sin is to break God's law: sin, in fact, is lawlessness. Christ appeared, as you know, to do away with sins, and there is no sin in him. No man therefore who dwells in him is a sinner; the sinner has not seen him and does not know him.

My children, do not be misled: it is the man who does right who is righteous, as God is righteous; the man who sins is a child of the devil, for the devil has been a sinner from the first; and the Son of God appeared for the very purpose of undoing the devil's work.

A child of God does not commit sin, because the divine seed remains in him; he cannot be a sinner, because he is God's child. That is the distinction between the children of God and the children of the devil: no one who does not do right is God's child, nor is anyone who does not love his brother. For the message you have heard from the beginning is this: that we should love one another; unlike Cain, who was a child of the evil one and murdered his brother. And why did he murder him? Because his own actions were wrong, and his brother's were right.

My brothers, do not be surprised if the world hates you. We for our part have crossed over from death to life; this we know, because we love our brothers. The man who does not love is still in the realm of death, for everyone who hates his brother is a murderer, and no murderer, as you know, has eternal life within him. It is by this that we know what love is: that Christ laid down his life for us. And we in our turn are bound to lay down our lives for our brothers. But if a man has enough to live on, and yet when he sees his brother in need shuts up his heart against him, how can it be said that the divine love dwells in him?

My children, love must not be a matter of words or talk; it must be genuine, and show itself in action. This is how we may know that we belong to the realm of truth, and convince ourselves in his sight that even if our conscience condemns us, God is greater than our conscience and knows all.

Dear friends, if our conscience does not condemn us, then we can approach God with confidence, and obtain from him whatever we ask, because we are keeping his commands and doing what he approves. This is his command: to give our allegiance to his Son Jesus Christ and love one another as he commanded. When we keep his commands we dwell in him and he dwells in us. And this is how we can make sure that he dwells within us: we know it from the Spirit he has given us.

4

But do not trust any and every spirit, my friends; test the spirits, to see whether they are from God, for among those who have gone out into the world there are many prophets falsely inspired. This is how we may recognize the Spirit of God: every spirit which acknowledges that Jesus Christ has come in the flesh is from God, and every spirit which does not thus acknowledge Jesus is not from God. This is what is meant by 'Antichrist'; you have been told that he was to come, and here he is, in the world already!

But you, my children, are of God's family, and you have the mastery over these false prophets, because he who inspires you is greater than he who inspires the godless world. They are of that world, and so therefore is their teaching; that is why the world listens to them. But we belong to God, and a man who knows God listens to us, while he who does not belong to God refuses us a hearing. That is how we distinguish the spirit of truth from the spirit of error.

Dear friends, let us love one another, because love is from God. Everyone who loves is a child of God and knows God, but the unloving know nothing of God. For God is love; and his love was disclosed to us in this, that he sent his only Son into the world to bring us life. The love I speak of is not our love for God, but the love he showed to us in sending his Son as the remedy for the defilement of our sins. If God thus loved us, dear friends, we in turn are bound to love one another. Though God has never been seen by any man, God himself dwells in us if we love one another; his love is brought to perfection within us.

Here is the proof that we dwell in him and he dwells in us: he has imparted his Spirit to us. Moreover, we have seen for ourselves, and we attest, that the Father sent the Son to be the saviour of the world, and if a man acknowledges that Jesus is the Son of God, God dwells in him and he dwells in God. Thus we have come to know and believe the love which God has for us.

God is love; he who dwells in love is dwelling in God, and God in him. This is for us the perfection of love, to have confidence on the day of judgement, and this we can have, because even in this world we are as he is. There is no room for fear in love; perfect love banishes fear. For fear brings with it the pains of judgement, and anyone who is afraid has not attained to love in its perfection. We love because he loved us first. But if a man says, 'I love God', while hating his brother, he is a liar. If he does not love the brother whom he has seen, it cannot be that he loves God whom he has not seen. And indeed this command comes to us from Christ himself: that he who loves God must also love his brother.

5

Everyone who believes that Jesus is the Christ is a child of God, and to love the parent means to love his child; it follows that when we love God and obey his commands we love his children too. For to love God is to keep his commands; and they are not burdensome, because every child of God is victor over the godless world. The victory that defeats the world is our faith, for who is victor over the world but he who believes that Jesus is the Son of God?

This is he who came with water and blood: Jesus Christ. He came, not by water alone, but by water and blood; and there is the Spirit to bear witness, because the Spirit is truth. For there are three witnesses, the Spirit, the water, and the blood, and these three are in agreement. We accept human testimony, but surely divine testimony is stronger, and this threefold testimony is indeed that of God himself, the witness he has borne to his Son. He who believes in the Son of God has this testimony in his own heart, but he who disbelieves God, makes him out to be a liar, by refusing to accept God's own witness to his Son. The witness is this: that God has given us eternal life, and that this life is found in his Son. He who possesses the Son has life indeed; he who does not possess the Son of God has not that life.

This letter is to assure you that you have eternal life. It is addressed to those who give their allegiance to the Son of God.

We can approach God with confidence for this reason: if we make requests which accord with his will he listens to us; and if we know that our requests are heard, we know also that the things we ask for are ours.

If a man sees his brother committing a sin which is not a deadly sin, he should pray to God for him, and he will grant him life—that is, when men are not guilty of deadly sin. There is such a thing as deadly sin, and I do not suggest that he should pray about that; but although all wrongdoing is sin, not all sin is deadly sin.

We know that no child of God is a sinner; it is the Son of God who keeps him safe, and the evil one cannot touch him.

We know that we are of God's family, while the whole godless world lies in the power of the evil one.

We know that the Son of God has come and given us understanding to know him who is real; indeed we are in him who is real, since we are in his Son Jesus Christ. This is the true God, this is eternal life. My children, be on the watch against false gods.

Problems

1. John, even more so than Paul, is concerned with faith manifested in action. For John, imitation of Jesus is the only sincere praise of him and the test of true faith. Is this a clear and reasonable test? In what way does this help us explain John's concern with the Incarnation, the fact that Jesus suffered as a man in the flesh?
2. The eschatological sense of impending doom is stronger in John than in Paul. Would a belief in an impending Judgment Day have a beneficial or a harmful effect on the followers of a new religion and on that religion's expansion? How could such a belief later become a liability?
3. John uses language metaphorically and symbolically, especially when talking about life and death. What is really meant by the sentence: "The man who does not love is still in the realm of death, for everyone who hates his brother is a murderer, and no murderer, as you know, has eternal life within him" (122/33-35)? Translate the metaphors into their possible psychological equivalents.
4. How does John suggest testing the spirits to see whether they are from God? In your opinion is it a meaningful test?
5. If God is action (doing, relating, creating), as was thought by the Jews, what does John mean when he twice says, "God is love"?

7
Thomas Aquinas

Scholasticism was a school of philosophy prevalent during the twelfth and thirteenth centuries. It intimately blended philosophy and theology and was characterized by a concern for theological orthodoxy, a reliance on Aristotle as the supreme authority (in the Middle Ages arguments could often be won with the simple utterance, "thus said Aristotle"), an almost total reliance on deductive, syllogistic reasoning, and finally an enormous predilection for categorizing and systematizing thought. Despite its shortcomings, which from this distance appear more and more imposing, the scholastic attempt to bring reason to bear on final questions was admirable and sincere.

Thomas Aquinas (1225–1274) is generally accepted as the greatest of the scholastics. Second only to the Summa Theologiae *(1265–1273) in importance and ambitiousness, the* Summa contra Gentiles *was written during the five years from 1259–1264. Its purpose is apparent in the title: to demonstrate, through argument, the truth of God as revealed by the Christian religion to the unbeliever. It is doubtful that the* Summa *would have been persuasive, or was ever meant to be; it was probably designed to establish, by rational argument, the truth of Christianity for those faithful who desired rational support.*

from Summa contra Gentiles

That God's providence applies immediately to all singulars

Now, some have conceded that divine providence extends to singulars, but through certain intermediary causes. Indeed, Plato asserted a threefold providence, according to Gregory of Nyssa.[1] The first of these is *that of the highest God.* Who primarily and above all provides

From Thomas Aquinas, *Summa contra Gentiles,* Book III (New York: Doubleday & Company, 1956), pp. 254–274.
1. Nemesius, *De natura hominis,* 44 (PG, 40, col. 793).

for *His own things,* that is, for all things spiritual and intellectual, but subsequently for the whole world, as far as genera and species go, and the universal causes which are the celestial bodies. Then the second type of providence is that by which provision is made for individual animals and plants, and for other generable and corruptible individuals, in respect to their generation and corruption, and other changes. Now, Plato attributes this kind of providence to the "gods that circulate about the heavens." Aristotle, on the other hand, attributes their causality to the "oblique circle."[2] Finally, he assigns a third kind of providence to things that pertain to human life. So, he attributes this function to certain "daemons living in the region of the earth" who are caretakers for human actions, according to him. But still, according to Plato, the second and third types of providence depend on the first, for the highest God has established the ones on the second and third levels as provident agents.

Now, this theory is in agreement with the Catholic faith, in so far as it traces the providence of all things back to God as its first author. But it seems incompatible with the view of the faith, in regard to this: it says that not all particulars are immediately subject to divine providence. Now, we can show from the foregoing that they are.

In point of fact, God has immediate knowledge of singulars, not merely in the sense that He knows them in their causes, but even in themselves, as we showed in Book One of this work.[3] But it would appear inappropriate for Him to know singulars and yet not to will their order, in which their chief good consists, for His will is the source of goodness in its entirety. Therefore, just as He knows singulars immediately, He must also establish order for them immediately.

Again, the order that is established by providence among things that are governed arises from the order which the provident agent decides on within his own mind. For example, the artistic form that is produced in matter proceeds from the form that is in the mind of the artist. Now, where there are many overseers, arranged one under the next, the order that is conceived by the higher one must be handed down to the lower one; just as a lower type of art receives its principles from a higher one. If, then, the second and third provident agents are claimed to be under the first provident agent, Who is the highest God, they must receive the order that is to be established in things from the highest God. Now, it is not possible for this order to be more perfect in them than in the highest God; on the contrary, all perfections come to other things from Him by way of descent, as appears from things said earlier.[4] The order of things must, then, be present in the secondary agents of providence,

2. Aristotle, *De generatione et corruptione,* II, 10 (336a 32).
3. *SCG,* I, ch. 65ff.
4. *SCG,* I, ch. 38ff.

not merely universally, but also in respect to singulars; otherwise, they could not establish order in singulars by their providence. Therefore, the ordering of singulars is much more under the control of divine providence.

Besides, in the case of things regulated by human providence we find that a certain higher overseer thinks out the way in which some of the big and universal matters are to be ordered, but he does not himself think out the ordering of the smallest details; rather, he leaves these to be planned by agents on a lower level. But, as a matter of fact, this is so because of his own deficiency, either because he does not know the circumstances for the individual details, or because he is not able to think out the order for all, by virtue of the effort and length of time that might be needed. Now, deficiencies of this kind are far removed from God, because He knows all singular things, and He does not make an effort to understand, or require any time for it; since, by understanding Himself He knows all other things, as we showed above.[5] Therefore, He plans even the order for all singular things. So, His providence applies to all singulars immediately.

Moreover, in human affairs the lower overseers, through their own efforts, plan the order for those things whose direction has been given them by the chief executive. Of course, they do not get this ability from the man who is in charge, or even its use. Indeed, if they did get it from him, the ordering would already be accomplished by the higher executive, and they would not be the agents responsible for this ordering, but simply the ones who carry it out. Now, it is obvious from things said above[6] that all wisdom and understanding are caused in intelligent beings by the highest God, and that no intellect can understand anything unless by divine power; just as no agent can perform any operation unless he act by this divine power. Therefore, God Himself is the disposer of all things immediately by His providence, and whatever beings are called agents of providence under Him are executors of His providence.

Furthermore, a higher providence gives regulations to a lower providence, just as a statesman gives regulations and laws to the leader of an army, who gives laws and regulations to the heads of larger or smaller military units. If, then, there be other providences under the first providence of the supreme God, God must give these secondary or tertiary overseers the regulations for their commands. So, He gives them either universal regulations and laws or particular ones. But, if He gives them universal regulations for their commands, since universal regulations cannot be applied in all cases to particulars, especially in the case of variable things that do not always remain the same, these secondary or tertiary

---

5. *SCG,* I, ch. 46.
6. *SCG,* II, ch. 15; III, ch. 67.

overseers would have to give orders at times that are contrary to the regulations given them for the things subject to their control. So, they would be able to pass judgment on the regulations that they have received, as to when action should accord with these regulations and when one should overlook them. Now, this could not be, for such judgment belongs to a superior. Indeed, it is the prerogative of the one who establishes the laws to interpret them and issue dispensation from them. So, this judgment over universally given regulations must be carried out by the supreme overseer. Of course, He could not do this if He refused to involve Himself immediately in the ordering of these singular things. So, according to this, He must be the immediate overseer of these things. On the other hand, if the secondary and tertiary overseers receive particular regulations and laws from the highest overseer, then it is quite obvious that the ordering of these singulars is done immediately by divine providence.

Again, the superior overseer always holds the power of judgment over the orders issued by inferior overseers, as to whether the orders are properly given or not. If, then the secondary or tertiary overseers are under God as the first overseer, God must hold the power of judgment over the things ordered by them. In fact, He could not do this if He did not consider the order of these singulars. Therefore, He Himself takes care by Himself of these singulars.

Besides, if God does not immediately by Himself take care of these inferior singular things, this can only be either because He despises them or because His dignity might be lowered by them, as some people say.[7] But this is unreasonable. It is indeed a matter of greater dignity to oversee the planning of the order for certain things than for it to be produced in them. So, if God works in all things, as we showed above,[8] and if His dignity is not diminished thereby, and if this belongs rather to His universal and supreme power, it is in no sense something to be despised by Him, or something that might besmirch His dignity, if He exercises His providence immediately over these singulars.

Moreover, every wise being who uses his power providently sets limits on the use of his power, when he acts, by ordering the objective and the extent to which it goes; otherwise, his power would not keep pace with his wisdom in such action. But it is obvious from the foregoing[9] that the divine power, in operating, reaches to the lowest things. So, the divine wisdom is in control of ordering what, how many, and what kind of effects proceed from His power, even down to the lowest things. Therefore, He is Himself planning the order for all things immediately by His providence.

7. See Averroes, *In Metaphysicam,* XII, comm. 37 and 52 (VIII, 150v and 158v).
8. See above, ch. 67ff.
9. *SCG,* II, ch. 45.

Hence it is said: "The things that are from God are well ordered" (Rom. 13:1). And again: "Thou hast done the things of old, and hast devised one thing after another; and what Thou hast willed hath been done" (Judith 9:4).

That other creatures are ruled by God by means of intellectual creatures

Since it is the function of divine providence to maintain order in things, and since a suitable order is such that there is a proportional descent from the highest things to the lowest, it must be that divine providence reaches the farthest things by some sort of proportion. Now, the proportion is like this: as the highest creatures are under God and are governed by Him, so the lower creatures are under the higher ones and are ruled by them. But of all creatures the highest are the intellectual ones, as is evident from what we said earlier.[10] Therefore, the rational plan of divine providence demands that the other creatures be ruled by rational creatures.

Again, whatever type of creature carries out the order of divine providence, it is able to do so because it participates in something of the power of the first providential being; just as an instrument does not move unless, through being moved, it participates somewhat in the power of the principal agent. So, the beings that participate more fully in the power of the divine providence are executive agents of divine providence in regard to those that participate less. But intellectual creatures participate more than others in it, because an ability to establish order which is done by cognitive power, and an ability to execute it which is done by operative power, are both required for providence, and rational creatures share in both types of power, while the rest of creatures have operative powers only. Therefore, all other creatures are ruled by means of rational creatures under divine providence.

Besides, to whomever any power is given by God, the recipient is given the power together with an ordination toward the effect of that power. For in that way all things are arranged for the best, inasmuch as each thing is ordered to all the goods that can naturally come from it. Now, the intellectual power by itself is capable of ordering and ruling; hence, we see that the operative power follows the direction of the intellective power, when they are combined in the same subject. In man, for instance, we observe that the bodily members are moved at the command of the will. The same is evident even if they are in different subjects; for instance, those men who excel in operative power must be directed by those who excel in intellectual power. Therefore, the rational plan of divine providence demands that other creatures be ruled by intellectual creatures.

10. *SCG,* II, ch. 46.

Moreover, particular powers are naturally adapted to be moved by universal powers; this is evident quite as much in the artistic as in the natural sphere. Now, it is obvious that intellectual power is more universal than any operative power, for the intellectual power contains universal forms, while each power is operative only because of some form proper to the agent. Therefore, all other creatures must be moved and regulated by means of intellectual powers.

Furthermore, in all powers arranged in an order, one is directive in relation to the next, and it knows the rational plan best. Thus, we see in the case of the arts that one art, which is concerned with the end from which the plan for the entire artistic production is derived, directs and commands another art which makes the product, as the art of navigation does in regard to shipbuilding. So, the one that introduces the form commands the one that prepares the matter. Instruments, on the other hand, which do not know the plan at all, are simply ruled. Since only intellectual creatures can know the rational plans for the ordering of creatures, it will therefore be their function to rule and govern all other creatures.

Again, that which is of itself is the cause of that which is through another. But only intellectual creatures operate by themselves, in the sense that they are masters of their operations through free choice of their will. On the other hand, other creatures are involved in operation resulting from the necessity of nature, since they are moved by something else. Therefore, intellectual creatures by their operation are motivating and regulative of other creatures.

That lower intellectual substances are ruled by higher ones

Since certain intellectual creatures are higher than others, as is clear from the foregoing,[11] the lower ones of an intellectual nature must be governed by the higher ones.

Again, more universal powers are able to move particular powers, as we said.[12] But the higher intellectual natures have more universal forms, as was shown above.[13] Therefore, they are capable of ruling the lower intellectual natures.

Besides, an intellectual potency that is nearer to the principle is always capable of ruling an intellectual power that is more removed from the principle. This is evident in both speculative and active sciences; for a speculative science which derives its principles of demonstration from another science is said to be subalternated to that other; and an active science which is nearer the end, which is the principle in matters of opera-

---

11. *SCG*, II, ch. 91 and 95.
12. See above, ch. 78.
13. *SCG*, II, ch. 98.

tion, is architectonic in regard to a more distant one. Therefore, since some intellectual substances are nearer the first principle, namely God, as was shown in Book Two,[14] they will be capable of ruling others.

Moreover, superior intellectual substances receive the influence of divine wisdom into themselves more perfectly, because each being receives something according to the being's own mode. Now, all things are governed by divine wisdom. And so, things that participate more in divine wisdom must be capable of governing those that participate less. Therefore, the lower intellectual substances are governed by the higher ones.

Thus, the higher spirits are also called *angels,* because they direct the lower spirits, as it were, by bringing messages to them; in fact, angels are spoken of as *messengers.* And they are also called *ministers,* because they carry out by their operation the order of divine providence even in the area of bodily things. Indeed, a minister is "like a living instrument," according to the Philosopher. So this is what is said in the Psalm (103: 4): "Who makest Thy angels spirits, and Thy ministers a burning fire."

On the ordering of men among themselves and to other things

As a matter of fact, human souls hold the lowest rank in relation to the other intellectual substances, because, as we said above,[15] at the start of their existence they receive a knowledge of divine providence, wherein they know it only in a general sort of way. But the soul must be brought to a perfect knowledge of this order, in regard to individual details, by starting from the things themselves in which the order of divine providence has already been established in detail. So, the soul had to have bodily organs by which it might draw knowledge from corporeal things. Yet, even with such equipment, because of the feebleness of its intellectual light, man's soul is not able to acquire a perfect knowledge of the things that are important to man unless it be helped by higher spirits, for the divine disposition requires this, that lower spirits acquire perfection through the higher ones, as we showed above.[16] Nevertheless, since man does participate somewhat in intellectual light, brute animals are subject to him by the order of divine providence, for they participate in no way in understanding. Hence it is said: "Let us make man to our own image and likeness," namely, according as he has understanding, "and let him have dominion over the fishes of the sea, and the fowls of the air, and the beasts of the earth" (Gen. 1:26).

Even brute animals, though devoid of understanding, have some knowledge; and so, in accord with the order of divine providence, they

14. *SCG,* II, ch. 95.
15. See above, ch. 80.
16. See above, ch. 79.

are set above plants and other things that lack knowledge. Hence it is said: "Behold I have given you every herb bearing seed upon the earth, and all trees that have in themselves seed of their own kind, to be your meat, and to all the beasts of the earth" (Gen. 1:29-30).

Moreover, among things utterly devoid of knowledge one thing comes under another, depending on whether the one is more powerful in acting than the other. Indeed, they do not participate in anything of the disposition of providence, but only in its execution.

Now, since man possesses intellect, sense, and bodily power, these are interrelated within him by a mutual order, according to the disposition of divine providence, in a likeness to the order which is found in the universe. In fact, corporeal power is subject to sense and intellectual power, as carrying out their command, and the sensitive power is subject to the intellectual and is included under its command.

On the same basis, there is also found an order among men themselves. Indeed, those who excel in understanding naturally gain control, whereas those who have defective understanding, but a strong body, seem to be naturally fitted for service, as Aristotle says in his *Politics*.[17] The view of Solomon is also in accord with this, for he says: "The fool shall serve the wise" (Prov. 11:29); and again: "Provide out of all the people wise men such as fear God . . . who may judge the people at all times" (Exod. 18:21-22).

Now, just as in the activities of one man disorder arises from the fact that understanding follows the lead of sensual power, while the sensual power is dragged down to the movement of the body by virtue of some disorder of the body, as is evident in the case of men who limp, so also does disorder arise in a human government, as a result of a man getting control, not because of the eminence of his understanding, but either because he usurps dominion for himself by bodily strength or because someone is set up as a ruler on the basis of sensual affection. Nor is Solomon silent on this kind of disorder, for he says: "There is an evil that I have seen under the sun, as it were by an error proceeding from the face of the prince: a fool set in high dignity" (Eccles. 10:5-6). But disorder of this kind does not exclude divine providence; it comes about, indeed, with divine permission, as a result of the deficiency of lower agents, just as we explained in connection with other evils. Nor is the natural order entirely perverted by such disorder, for the dominion of fools is weak unless strengthened by the counsel of the wise. Hence it is said in Proverbs (20:16): "Designs are strengthened by counsels, and wars are to be arranged by governments"; and again: "a wise man is strong, and a knowing man stout and valiant: because war is managed by due ordering, and there shall be safety when there are many counsels" (Prov. 24:5-6).

17. See Aristotle, *Politics*, I, 5 (1254b 25).

And since he who gives counsel rules the man who takes counsel, and in a sense governs him, it is said in Proverbs (17:2): "a wise servant shall rule over foolish sons."

So, it is evident that divine providence imposes order on all things; thus, what the Apostle says is certainly true: "the things which are of God are well ordered" (Rom. 13:1).

Problems

1. What are the advantages and disadvantages of Aquinas's deductive method?
2. How would Aquinas's concept of rational objectivity differ from ours? What would be his attitude toward modern science? In what ways does his *Summa* strengthen man's rational claims and powers or weaken them?
3. Is Aquinas's world view hierarchical and permeated with rights and prerogatives based on rank? How faithful is his world view to that contained in the Gospels or Letters? Is such a hierarchy conducive to progress or inimical to it?
4. How implicit in Aquinas's world view is the equation, "might makes right"?
5. Is Aquinas's world view quietist, that is, prone to make for passive, silent, submissive acquiescence? What are the aspects of his world view that would make for quietism? What does his world view offer man in return?

8 JOHN CALVIN

With the single exception of Martin Luther (1483–1546), who heralded the first signs of reformation in 1517 by posting his 95 theses on the castle church door in Saxony, John Calvin (1509–1564) was the greatest figure in the Protestant Reformation. After his conversion in 1533, Calvin's early study in law stood him in good stead not only when he wrote his Institutes of the Christian Religion (1534–1536), one of the world's great theological documents, but also in 1541, when he set about establishing a theocratic government (a government that subordinates state to Church) in Geneva, Switzerland.

Early Calvinism, which exerted a great influence on Puritanism and later evolved into modern Presbyterianism, differed from Lutheranism in rejecting the doctrine of consubstantiation,* in its theocratic social structure, in its concept of the irresistibility of grace, and in its emphasis on the doctrine of predestination, which stresses the absolute nature of the divine will. Only those God elects or predestines for salvation are saved; the rest are damned. Man is powerless before God's will and can do nothing to achieve his own salvation.

The Calvinist belief in election had a strange side effect. Election was gradually thought to be demonstrated by, though not equated with, earthly prosperity. Eventually, wealth and earthly blessing came to indicate a state of grace. As a result, people began to pursue prosperity, at least partly with the intention of convincing others in the community of their own election. For a more extended treatment of some of the ramifications of Calvinism, see Max Weber's essay on the relation of Protestantism to capitalism.

* The theological doctrine that both Christ and the unchanged bread and wine are present together in the consecrated Eucharistic elements. The doctrine of transubstantiation, by contrast, holds that the bread and wine are actually transformed into the body and blood of Christ.

The Sum of the Christian Life: The Denial of Ourselves

(The Christian philosophy of unworldliness and self-denial; we are not our own, we are God's, 1–3)
1. We are not our own masters, but belong to God

Even though the law of the Lord provides the finest and best-disposed method of ordering a man's life, it seemed good to the Heavenly Teacher to shape his people by an even more explicit plan to that rule which he had set forth in the law. Here, then, is the beginning of this plan: the duty of believers is "to present their bodies to God as a living sacrifice, holy and acceptable to him," and in this consists the lawful worship of him [Rom. 12:1]. From this is derived the basis of the exhortation that "they be not conformed to the fashion of this world, but be transformed by the renewal of their minds, so that they may prove what is the will of God" [Rom. 12:2]. Now the great thing is this: we are consecrated and dedicated to God in order that we may thereafter think, speak, meditate, and do, nothing except to his glory. For a sacred thing may not be applied to profane uses without marked injury to him.

If we, then, are not our own [cf. I Cor. 6:19] but the Lord's, it is clear what error we must flee, and whither we must direct all the acts of our life.

We are not our own: let not our reason nor our will, therefore, sway our plans and deeds. We are not our own: let us therefore not set it as our goal to seek what is expedient for us according to the flesh. We are not our own: in so far as we can, let us therefore forget ourselves and all that is ours.

Conversely, we are God's: let us therefore live for him and die for him. We are God's: let his wisdom and will therefore rule all our actions. We are God's: let all the parts of our life accordingly strive toward him as our only lawful goal [Rom. 14:8; cf. I Cor. 6:19]. O, how much has that man profited who, having been taught that he is not his own, has taken away dominion and rule from his own reason that he may yield it to God! For, as consulting our self-interest is the pestilence that most effectively leads to our destruction, so the sole haven of sal-

From John Calvin, *Institutes of the Christian Religion* (Philadelphia: Westminster Press, 1960), pp. 689-701.

vation is to be wise in nothing and to will nothing through ourselves but to follow the leading of the Lord alone.

Let this therefore be the first step, that a man depart from himself in order that he may apply the whole force of his ability in the service of the Lord. I call "service" not only what lies in obedience to God's Word but what turns the mind of man, empty of its own carnal sense, wholly to the bidding of God's Spirit. While it is the first entrance to life, all philosophers were ignorant of this transformation, which Paul calls "renewal of the mind" [Eph. 4:23]. For they set up reason alone as the ruling principle in man, and think that it alone should be listened to; to it alone, in short, they entrust the conduct of life. But the Christian philosophy bids reason give way to, submit and subject itself to, the Holy Spirit so that the man himself may no longer live but hear Christ living and reigning within him [Gal. 2:20].

2. Self-denial through devotion to God

From this also follows this second point: that we seek not the things that are ours but those which are of the Lord's will and will serve to advance his glory. This is also evidence of great progress: that, almost forgetful of ourselves, surely subordinating our self-concern, we try faithfully to devote our zeal to God and his commandments. For when Scripture bids us leave off self-concern, it not only erases from our minds the yearning to possess, the desire for power, and the favor of men, but it also uproots ambition and all craving for human glory and other more secret plagues. Accordingly, the Christian must surely be so disposed and minded that he feels within himself it is with God he has to deal throughout his life. In this way, as he will refer all he has to God's decision and judgment, so will he refer his whole intention of mind scrupulously to Him. For he who has learned to look to God in all things that he must do, at the same time avoids all vain thoughts. This, then, is that denial of self which Christ enjoins with such great earnestness upon his disciples at the outset of their service [cf. Matt. 16:24]. When it has once taken possession of their hearts, it leaves no place at all first either to pride, or arrogance, or ostentation; then either to avarice, or desire, or lasciviousness, or effeminacy, or to other evils that our self-love spawns [cf. II Tim. 3:2–5]. On the other hand, wherever denial of ourselves does not reign, there either the foulest vices rage without shame or if there is any semblance of virtue, it is vitiated by depraved lusting after glory. Show me a man, if you can, who, unless he has according to the commandment of the Lord renounced himself, would freely exercise goodness among men. For all who have not been possessed with this feeling have at least followed virtue for the sake of praise. Now those of the philosophers who at any time most strongly contended that virtue should be pursued for its own sake were puffed up with such great arrogance as to show they sought after virtue for no other reason than to have occasion for pride. Yet God is so displeased, both with those who court the popular breeze and with such swollen souls, as to declare that they have received their reward in this world [Matt. 6:2,5,16], and to make harlots and publicans nearer to the Kingdom of Heaven than are they [Matt. 21:31]. Yet we have still not clearly explained how many and how great are the obstacles that hinder man from a right course so long as he has not denied himself. For it was once truly said: "A world of vices is hidden in the soul of man." And you can find no other remedy than in denying yourself and giving up concern for yourself, and in turning your mind wholly to seek after those things which the Lord requires of you, and to seek them only because they are pleasing to him.

3. Self-renunciation according to Titus, ch. 2

In another place, Paul more clearly, although briefly, delineates the individual parts of a well-ordered life. "The grace of God has appeared, bringing salvation to all men, training us to renounce irreligion and worldly passions and to live sober, upright, and godly lives, in the present age; awaiting our blessed hope, and the appearing of the glory of our great God and of our Savior Jesus Christ, who gave himself for us to redeem us from all iniquity and to purify for himself a people of his own who are zealous for good deeds." [Titus 2:11–14] For, after he proffered the grace of God to hearten us, in order to pave the way for us to worship God truly he removed the two obstacles that chiefly hinder us: namely, ungodliness, to which by nature we are too much inclined; and second, worldly desires, which extend more widely. And by ungodliness, indeed, he not only means superstition but includes also whatever contends against the earnest fear of God. Worldly lusts are also equivalent to the passions of the flesh [cf. I John 2:16; Eph. 2:3; II Peter 2:18; Gal. 5:16; etc.]. Thus, with reference to both Tables of the Law, he commands us to put off our own nature and to deny whatever our reason and will dictate. Now he limits all actions of life to three parts: soberness, righteousness, and godliness. Of these, soberness doubtless denotes chastity and temperance as well as a pure and frugal use of temporal goods, and patience in poverty. Now righteousness embraces all the duties of equity in order that to each one be rendered what is his own [cf. Rom. 13:7]. There follows godliness, which joins us in true holiness with God when we are separated from the iniquities of the world. When these things are joined together by an inseparable bond, they bring about complete perfection. But, nothing is more difficult than, having bidden farewell to the reason of the flesh and having bridled our desires—nay, having put them away—to devote ourselves to God and our brethren, and to meditate, amid earth's filth, upon the life of the angels. Consequently, Paul, in order to extricate our minds from all snares, recalls us to the hope of blessed immortality, reminding us that we strive not in vain [cf. I Thess. 3:5]. For, as Christ our Redeemer once appeared, so in his final coming he will show the fruit of the salvation brought forth by him. In this way he scatters all the allurements that becloud us and prevent us from aspiring as we ought to heavenly glory. Nay, he teaches us to travel as pilgrims in this world that our celestial heritage may not perish or pass away.

(The principle of self-denial in our relations with our fellow men, 4–7)
4. Self-denial gives us the right attitude toward our fellow men

Now in these words we perceive that denial of self has regard partly to men, partly, and chiefly, to God.

For when Scripture bids us act toward men so as to esteem them above ourselves [Phil. 2:3], and in good faith to apply ourselves wholly to doing them good [cf. Rom. 12:10], it gives us commandments of which our mind is quite incapable unless our mind be previously emptied of its natural feeling. For, such is the blindness with which we all rush into self-love that each one of us seems to himself to have just cause to be proud of himself and to despise all others in comparison. If God has conferred upon us anything of which we need not repent, relying upon it we immediately lift up our minds, and are not only puffed up but almost burst with pride. The very vices that infest us we take pains to hide from others, while we flatter ourselves with the pretense that they are slight and insignificant, and even sometimes embrace them as virtues. If others manifest the same endowments we admire in ourselves, or even superior ones, we spitefully belittle and revile these gifts in order to avoid yielding place to such persons. If there are any faults in others, not content with noting them with severe and sharp reproach, we hatefully exaggerate them. Hence arises such insolence that each one of us, as if exempt from the common lot, wishes to tower above the rest, and loftily and savagely abuses every mortal man, or at least looks down upon him as an inferior. The poor yield to the rich; the common folk, to the nobles; the servants, to their masters; the unlearned, to the educated. But there is no one who does not cherish within himself some opinion of his own pre-eminence.

Thus, each individual, by flattering himself, bears a kind of kingdom in his breast. For claiming as his own what pleases him, he censures the character and morals of others. But if this comes to the point of conflict, his venom bursts forth. For many obviously display some gentleness so long as they find everything sweet and pleasant. But just how many are there who will preserve this even tenor of modesty when they are pricked and irritated? There is no other remedy than to tear out from our inward parts this most deadly pestilence of love of strife and love of self, even as it is plucked out by Scriptural teaching. For thus we are instructed to remember that those talents which God has bestowed upon us are not our own goods but the free gifts of God; and any persons who become proud of them show their ungratefulness. "Who causes you to excel?" Paul asks. "If you have received all things, why do you boast as if they were not given to you?" [I Cor. 4:7].

Let us, then, unremittingly examining our faults, call ourselves back to humility. Thus nothing will remain in us to puff us up; but there will be much occasion to be cast down. On the other hand, we are bidden so to esteem and regard whatever gifts of God we see in other men that we may honor those men in whom they reside. For it would be great depravity on our part to deprive them of that honor which the Lord has bestowed upon them. But we are taught to overlook their faults, certainly not flatteringly to cherish them; but not on account of such faults to revile men whom we ought to cherish with good will and honor. Thus it will come about that, whatever man we deal with, we shall treat him not only moderately and modestly but also cordially and as a friend. You will never attain true gentleness except by one path: a heart imbued with lowliness and with reverence for others.

5. Self-renunciation leads to proper helpfulness toward our neighbors

Now, in seeking to benefit one's neighbor, how difficult it is to do one's duty! Unless you give up all thought of self and, so to speak, get out of yourself, you will accomplish nothing here. For how can you perform those works which Paul teaches to be the works of love, unless you renounce yourself, and give yourself wholly to others? "Love," he says, "is patient and kind, not jealous or boastful, is not envious or puffed up, does not seek its own, is not irritable," etc. [I Cor. 13: 4–5 p.] If this is the one thing required—that we seek not what is our own—still we shall do no little violence to nature, which so inclines us to love of ourselves alone that it does not easily allow us to neglect ourselves and our possessions in order to look after another's good, nay, to yield willingly what is ours by right and resign it to another. But Scripture, to lead us by the hand to this, warns that whatever benefits we obtain from the Lord have been entrusted to us on this condition: that they be applied to the common good of the church. And therefore the lawful use of all benefits consists in a liberal and kindly sharing of them with others. No surer rule and no more valid exhortation to keep it could be devised than when we are taught that all the gifts we possess have been bestowed by God and entrusted to us on condition that they be distributed for our neighbors' benefit [cf. I Peter 4:10].

But Scripture goes even farther by comparing them to the powers with which the members of the human body are endowed [I Cor. 12:12 ff.]. No member has this power for itself nor applies it to its own private use; but each pours it out to the fellow members. Nor does it take any profit from its power except what proceeds from the common advantage of the whole body. So, too, whatever a godly man can do he ought to be able to do for his brothers, providing for himself in no way other than to have his mind intent upon the common upbuilding of the church. Let this, therefore, be our rule for generosity and beneficence: We are the stewards of everything God has conferred on us by which we are able to help our neighbor, and are required to render account of our stewardship. Moreover, the only right stewardship is that which is tested by the rule of love. Thus it will come about that we shall not only join zeal for another's benefit with care for our own advantage, but shall subordinate the latter to the former.

And lest perhaps we should not realize that this is the rule for the proper management of all gifts we have received from God, he also in early times applied it to the least gifts of his generosity. For he commanded that the first fruits be brought to him by which the people were to testify that it was unlawful to accept for themselves any enjoyment of benefits not previously consecrated to him [Ex. 23:19; cf. ch. 22:29, Vg.]. But if the gifts of God are only thus sanctified to us when we have dedicated them by our hand to the Author himself, that which does not savor of such dedication is clearly a corrupt abuse. Yet you wish to strive in vain to enrich the Lord by sharing your possessions; since, then, your generosity cannot extend to him, you must, as the prophet says, practice it toward the saints on earth [Ps. 16:2–3]. And alms are compared to holy sacrifices so as to correspond now to those requirements of the law [Heb. 13:16].

6. Love of neighbor is not dependent upon manner of men but looks to God

Furthermore, not to grow weary in well-doing [Gal. 6:9], which otherwise must happen immediately, we ought to add that other idea which the apostle mentions: "Love is patient . . . and is not irritable" [I Cor. 13:4–5]. The Lord commands all men without exception "to do good" [Heb. 13:16]. Yet the great part of them are most unworthy if they be judged by their own merit. But here Scripture helps in the best way when it teaches that we are not to consider that men merit of themselves but to look upon the image of God in all men, to which we owe all honor and love. However, it is among members of the household of faith that this same image is more carefully to be noted [Gal. 6:10], in so far as it has been renewed and restored through the Spirit of Christ. Therefore, whatever man you meet who needs your aid, you have no reason to refuse to help him. Say, "He is a stranger"; but the Lord has given him a mark that ought to be familiar to you, by virtue of the fact that he forbids you to despise your own flesh [Isa. 58:7, Vg.]. Say, "He is contemptible and worthless"; but the Lord shows him to be one to whom he has deigned to give the beauty of his image. Say that you owe nothing for any service of his; but God, as it were, has put him in his own place in order that you may recognize toward him the many and great benefits with which God has bound you to himself. Say that he does not deserve even your least effort for his sake; but the image of God, which recommends him to you, is worthy of your giving yourself and all your possessions. Now if he has not only deserved no good at your hand, but has also provoked you by unjust acts and curses, not even this is just reason why you should cease to embrace him in love and to perform the duties of love on his behalf [Matt. 6:14; 18:35; Luke 17:3]. You will say, "He has deserved something far different of me." Yet what has the Lord deserved? While he bids you forgive this man for all sins he has committed against you, he would truly have them charged against himself. Assuredly there is but one way in which to achieve what is not merely difficult but utterly against human nature: to love those who hate us, to repay their evil deeds with benefits, to return blessings for reproaches [Matt. 5:44]. It is that we remember not to consider men's evil intention but to look upon the image of God in them, which cancels and effaces their transgressions, and with its beauty and dignity allures us to love and embrace them.

7. The outward work of love is not sufficient, but it is intention that counts!

This mortification, then, will take place in us only if we fulfill the duties of love. Now he who merely performs all the duties of love does not fulfill them, even though he overlooks none; but he, rather, fulfills them who does this from a sincere feeling of love. For it can happen that one who indeed discharges to the full all his obligations as far as outward duties are concerned is still all the while far away from the true way of discharging them. For you may see some who wish to seem very liberal and yet bestow nothing that they do not make reprehensible with a proud countenance or even insolent words. And in this tragic and unhappy age it has come to this pass, that most men give their alms contemptuously. Such depravity ought not to have been tolerable even among the pagans; of Christians something even more is required than to show a cheerful countenance and to render their duties pleasing with friendly words. First, they must put themselves in the place of him whom they see in need of their assistance, and pity his ill fortune as if they themselves experienced and bore it, so that they may be impelled by a feeling of mercy and humaneness to go to his aid just as to their own.

He who, thus disposed, proceeds to give help to his brethren will not corrupt his own duties by either arrogance or upbraiding. Furthermore, in giving benefits he will not despise his needy brother or enslave him as one indebted to himself. This would no more be reasonable than that we should either chide a sick member that the rest of the body labors to revive or consider it especially obligated to the remaining members because it has drawn more help to itself than it can repay. Now the sharing of tasks among members is believed to have nothing gratuitous about it but, rather, to be a payment of that which, due by the law of nature, it would be monstrous to refuse. Also, in this way it will come about that he who has discharged one kind of task will not think himself free, as commonly happens when a rich man, after he has given up something of his own, delegates to other men other burdens as having nothing at all to do with him. Rather, each man will so consider with himself that in all his greatness he is a debtor to his neighbors, and that he ought in exercising kindness toward them to set no other limit than the end of his resources; these, as widely as they are extended, ought to have their limits set according to the rule of love.

(The principle of self-denial in our relation to God, 8–10)
8. Self-denial toward God: devotion to his will!

Let us reiterate in fuller form the chief part of self-denial, which, as we have said, looks to God. And indeed, many things have been said about this already that it would be superfluous to repeat. It will be enough to show how it forms us to fair-mindedness and tolerance.

To begin with, then, in seeking either the convenience or the tranquility of the present life, Scripture calls us to resign ourselves and all our possessions to the Lord's will, and to yield to him the desires of our hearts to be tamed and subjugated. To covet wealth and honors, to strive for authority, to heap up riches, to gather together all those follies which seem of make for magnificence and pomp, our lust is mad, our desire boundless. On the other hand, wonderful is our fear, wonderful our hatred, of poverty, lowly birth, and humble condition! And we are spurred to rid ourselves of them by every means. Hence we can see how uneasy in mind all those persons are who order their lives according to their own plan. We can see how artfully they strive—to the point of weariness—to obtain the goal of their ambition or avarice, while, on the other hand, avoiding poverty and a lowly condition.

In order not to be caught in such snares, godly men must hold to this path. First of all, let them neither desire nor hope for, nor contemplate, any other way of prospering than by the Lord's blessing. Upon this, then, let them safely and confidently throw themselves and rest. For however beautifully the flesh may seem to suffice unto itself, while it either strives by its own effort for honors and riches or relies upon its diligence, or is aided by the favor of men, yet it is certain that all these things are nothing; nor will we benefit at all, either by skill or by labor, except in so far as the Lord prospers them both. On the contrary, however, his blessing alone finds a way, even through all hindrances, to bring all things to a happy and favorable outcome for us; again, though entirely without it, to enable us to obtain some glory and opulence for ourselves (as we daily see impious men amassing great honors and riches), yet, inasmuch as those upon whom the curse of God rests taste not even the least particle of happiness, without this blessing we shall obtain nothing but what turns to our misfortune. For we ought by no means to desire what makes men more miserable.

9. *Trust in God's blessing only*

Therefore, suppose we believe that every means toward a prosperous and desirable outcome rests upon the blessing of God alone; and that, when this is absent, all sorts of misery and calamity dog us. It remains for us not greedily to strive after riches and honors—whether relying upon our own dexterity of wit or our own diligence, or depending upon the favor of men, or having confidence in vainly imagined fortune—but for us always to look to the Lord so that by his guidance we may be led to whatever lot he has provided for us. Thus it will first come to pass that we shall not dash out to seize upon riches and usurp honors through wickedness and by stratagems and evil arts, or greed, to the injury of our neighbors; but pursue only those enterprises which do not lead us away from innocence.

Who can hope for the help of a divine blessing amidst frauds, robberies, and other wicked arts? For as that blessing follows only him who thinks purely and acts rightly, thus it calls back from crooked thoughts and wicked actions all those who seek it. Then will a bridle be put on us that we may not burn with an immoderate desire to grow rich or ambitiously pant after honors. For with what shamelessness does a man trust that he will be helped by God to obtain those things which he desires contrary to God's Word? Away with the thought that God would abet with his blessing what he curses with his mouth! Lastly, if things do not go according to our wish and hope, we will still be restrained from impatience and loathing of our condition, whatever it may be. For we shall know that this is to murmur against God, by whose will riches and poverty, contempt and honor, are dispensed. To sum up, he who rests solely upon the blessing of God, as it has been here expressed, will neither strive with evil arts after those things which men customarily madly seek after, which he realizes will not profit him, nor will he, if things go well, give credit to himself or even to his diligence, or industry, or fortune. Rather, he will give God the credit as its Author. But if, while other men's affairs flourish, he makes but slight advancement, or even slips back, he will still bear his low estate with greater equanimity and moderation of mind than some profane person would bear a moderate success which merely does not correspond with his wish. For he indeed possesses a solace in which he may repose more peacefully than in the highest degree of wealth or power. Since this leads to his salvation, he considers that his affairs are ordained by the Lord. We see that David was so minded; while he follows God and gives himself over to his leading, he attests that he is like a child weaned from his mother's breast, and that he does not occupy himself with things too deep and wonderful for him [Ps. 131:1–2].

10. Self-denial helps us bear adversity

And for godly minds the peace and forbearance we have spoken of ought not to rest solely in this point; but it must also be extended to every occurrence to which the present life is subject. Therefore, he alone has duly denied himself who has so totally resigned himself to the Lord that he permits every part of his life to be governed by God's will. He who will be thus composed in mind, whatever happens, will not consider himself miserable nor complain of his lot with ill will toward God. How necessary this disposition is will appear if you weigh the many chance happenings to which we are subject. Various diseases repeatedly trouble us: now plague rages; now we are cruelly beset by the calamities of war; now ice and hail, consuming the year's expectation, lead to barrenness, which reduces us to poverty; wife, parents, children, neighbors, are snatched away by death; our house is burned by fire. It is on account of these occurrences that men curse their life, loathe the day of their birth, abominate heaven and the light of day, rail against God, and as they are eloquent in blasphemy, accuse him of injustice and cruelty. But in these matters the believer must also look to God's kindness and truly fatherly indulgence. Accordingly, if he sees his house reduced to solitude by the removal of his kinsfolk, he will not indeed even then cease to bless the Lord, but rather will turn his attention to this thought: nevertheless, the grace of the Lord, which dwells in my house, will not leave it desolate. Or, if his crops are blasted by frost, or destroyed by ice, or beaten down with hail, and he sees famine threatening, yet he will not despair or bear a grudge against God, but will remain firm in this trust [cf. Ps. 78:47]: "Nevertheless we are in the Lord's protection, sheep brought up in his pastures" [Ps. 79:13]. The Lord will therefore supply food to us even in extreme barrenness. If he shall be afflicted by disease, he will not even then be so unmanned by the harshness of pain as to break forth into impatience and expostulate with God; but, by considering the righteousness and gentleness of God's chastening, he will recall himself to forbearance. In short, whatever happens, because he will know it ordained of God, he will undergo it with a peaceful and grateful mind so as not obstinately to resist the command of him into whose power he once for all surrendered himself and his every possession.

Especially let that foolish and most miserable consolation of the pagans be far away from the breast of the Christian man; to strengthen their minds against adversities, they charged these to fortune. Against fortune they considered it foolish to be angry because she was blind and unthinking, with unseeing eyes wounding the deserving and the undeserving at the same time. On the contrary, the rule of piety is that God's hand alone is the judge and governor of fortune, good or bad, and that it does not rush about with heedless force, but with most orderly justice deals out good as well as ill to us.

Problems

1. Why is self-denial the essence of Christianity? What does Calvin's emphasis on self-denial suggest about human motives?
2. How central to Calvin's thought is the doctrine of original sin? How depraved is man in reason and feeling since the Fall?
3. Though Calvin stresses self-denial, he also provides compensations for it. What are they?
4. Calvin suggests a few simple rules to apply in all our dealings with our fellow men. What are they? For Calvinism, how central is empathy in interpersonal relations?
5. What would Calvin's attitude be toward a welfare state? What would it be toward collectivization of social life into great bureaucracies?
6. Geneva, Switzerland, was for all practical purposes in Calvin's day a theocracy, a city governed by a group of presbyters claiming divine authority. Is Calvinism more likely to support political liberalism or conservatism? Why?

9 JOHN WILSON

John Wilson (1928–), former Professor of Religious Knowledge, Trinity College, Toronto, is now at Oxford as Director of Farmington Trust Research on the subject of "Moral Education." The two essays below are the first chapters from Language and Christian Belief *(1958), a work that endeavors to analyze religious experience within the loose context of "logical positivism," a system of philosophy which attempts to introduce the methodology and analytic precision of the sciences into questions of philosophy. The object of philosophy thus becomes the logical clarification of language, rather than a theoretical one involving metaphysical speculation. In the following essays, Wilson attempts to analyze religious experience in order to discover what can and cannot be verified by using contemporary logical and scientific tools. His answer, contrary to some expectations, is not a wholesale dismissal of religious experience.*

Verification and Religious Language

Let us begin by taking a superficial glance at the language of religion. In religious works of literature, creeds, ritual, and so on we come across different types of sentences which have (or appear to have) different uses. On this superficial level, we can list these without difficulty:

(1) Sentences expressing commands, injunctions, exhortations, wishes, etc., such as 'Thou shalt love the Lord thy God,' 'Let us love one another,' and so on.

(2) Sentences expressing moral views, such as 'Brethren, these things ought not so to be,' 'It is not good for man to be alone,' etc.

(3) Sentences expressing factual truths, often historical, such as 'Christ was born in Bethlehem,' 'Mary was a virgin,' etc.

From John Wilson, *Language and Christian Belief* (London: Macmillan & Co., Ltd, 1958), pp. 1–31.

(4) Sentences giving information about the meanings of words, expressing analytic truths. A statement like 'A sacrament is an outward and visible sign of an inward and spiritual grace' is analytic, and should be taken as informing the hearer about the meaning of 'sacrament.'

(5) Sentences which appear to be informative, but informative about the supernatural or metaphysical rather than the natural or physical world. For instance, 'God exists,' 'Christ is the Son of God,' and so on.

So far the philosopher has not yet got to work. But when he does, it is likely that he will be tempted to make two changes in our scheme above. The first does not concern us here: it involves merging what I have called 'moral views' with 'commands, injunctions, etc.', at least to some extent. The second is to attempt to distribute sentences in (5), metaphysical sentences, among the other classes, in such a way that the possibility of supernaturally informative sentences is excluded. He could say, for instance, that some of these sentences are really analytic, and others really commands: this is one of the commonest ways in which this particular move is made.

Let us look, for example, at one of the ablest attempts to make this kind of move which have recently appeared. It has been made by Professor Braithwaite. He regards religious belief as primarily the intention or resolution to adopt a certain way of life, this intention being supported by what he calls 'stories': that is, what appear to be empirical statements of fact, statements about the world, which are however not verifiable in the way that ordinary empirical statements are verifiable. (Presumably the only sense in which they could be said to be verifiable at all is the sense in which we say that a statement in a story or work of fiction is verifiable, i.e. within the context of the work as a whole.) These statements are believed because the religious believer finds them psychologically helpful, inasmuch as they bolster up his intention to adopt the way of life which he has chosen. But they are not central to religious belief; and we should verify whether a man is to be regarded as adhering to or following a certain religion, not by seeing how many 'stories' or how much of any 'story' he accepts as true, but by seeing how far he genuinely tries to carry out his intention to adopt a religious way of life. This intention, according to Braithwaite, has a great deal in common with what is expressed in ethical statements. Religion, in fact, is an ethical outlook bolstered up with 'stories'.

I have chosen to mention this particular attempt to deal with religious statements because it is typical as well as skilful. Its typicality consists in trying to show that metaphysical statements, statements about the supernatural are other than they appear: in particular, that they cannot be regarded as genuinely informative. This in itself is not a misconceived attempt: plenty of statements are not what they appear. But it is necessary to be very careful in assigning statements to classes in this way; and I do not think that writers of this kind have always kept a firm grasp of certain necessary points in connection with the use of language.

The most important of these is the point that it is primarily people who mean, and not statements. Language does not exist in the abstract, but is used by people with certain intentions, who desire to communicate. The appropriate question, therefore, is really not 'What does such-and-such a statement mean?' but 'What does so-and-so mean by this statement?' The same point applies to verification: we should ask not 'How is this statement verified?' but 'How do people who make this statement verify it?' This point may seem trivial. But to appreciate it entails appreciating that we may get different answers to our questions. It is easy to assume that statements have single meanings and single methods of verification; and though this may be generally true of other informative statements, it may not be true of metaphysical statements. Indeed, the answers which are given to a question about the meaning of a religious belief show a remarkable variety of opinion, even amongst those who share a common religion.

It would be erroneous to suppose, therefore, that because there is no standard meaning or verification for religious statements they are meaningless and unverifiable. Nearly all philosophers today admit that they are meaningful; indeed, it was never possible to hold that they were meaningless without adopting a monopolistic and unfairly restricted sense of 'meaning'. But it is an equal mistake to suppose that because all religious believers are not agreed upon what is to count as evidence for the truth of their statements, therefore nothing counts or could ever count. It may not be at all clear how these statements are to be verified or falsified, but this does not entail that they are not verifiable or falsifiable in principle. Neither does it entail that they are not informative.

In other words, the religious believer may meet the cross-questioning of the philosopher with a straight *nolle prosequi*.* He may say simply, 'This statement is intended by me as informative.' The philosopher cannot sensibly reply, 'No, it's not.' He may point to a lack of agreed meaning and verification, show that most if not all other informative statements have agreed meaning and verification, and so on, but he cannot deny the speaker's intention: and he cannot show that the intention cannot in principle be fulfilled. For it may be possible to provide meaning and verification for the statement, or to agree on them. What the philosopher can try to do, however, is to show that whatever the intentions of the speaker, the statement is not actually informative. He will try to do this by showing that being informative, in the case of all statements, depends on the existence of agreed verification.

* Do not follow; that is, do not believe.

The religious believer is here faced with two alternatives. He can either say that his statements are not, after all, informative, thereby evading the attack altogether: or say that established meaning and verification is not in fact necessary for informative statements, thereby standing up to it. This is the crux of the matter, the rock which all metaphysics and religious belief must either escape or be wrecked on. And it seems to me tragic that religious believers do not realise that neither of the two alternatives I have mentioned are at all satisfactory.

First, the attempt to evade the attack. The attempt must fail, because it is these allegedly informative assertions which give to any religion its importance and its distinctive character. Statements which lay down language-rules ('A sacrament is an outward and visible sign of an inward and spiritual grace'), historical statements ('The man Jesus Christ was crucified in Palestine during the reign of Tiberius'), exhortations ('Brethren, let us love one another'), and moral injunctions ('Judge not'), all have obvious uses; but they would, none of them, have any peculiarly religious interest unless backed by a number of assertions about the supernatural. Thus, we are only interested in defining 'sacrament' clearly because it is held that the Son of God instituted certain sacraments: historical statements about Jesus concern us only because we believe certain metaphysical statements about Him: and exhortations and injunctions have religious force only because they derive from supernatural fact—hence we see arguments like: 'Let us love one another, for love is of God.' Most Christians, except under philosophical cross-examination, would surely regard the 'good news' of the Gospel as factually informative. To say 'There is a God' is to state a fact: God is real in the same *sense,* though not in the same way, as physical objects are real [1]: and the information which religious beliefs contain is not only supposed to be genuine, but of the utmost importance in the conduct of our lives.

The second alternative, that of claiming that statements can be informative without being verifiable in the sense required by philosophers, is more difficult to prove unsatisfactory. To begin with, many believers would hold that there was evidence for their beliefs. For some Christians, for instance, the supposed majesty and order of the natural universe is a proof of God's existence: to others, the life and personality of Christ is verification for His divinity: and so on. They might also admit that certain things counted against their beliefs: that the existence of pain and evil, for instance, counted against their belief in a loving and omnipotent God. Why is it, then, that philosophers still wish to insist that religious statements may not be verifiable? What precisely is this test of verification which they claim that all informative statements must pass?

The philosopher's point may be better made (as one or two philoso-

1. This point is of central importance to my thesis. I have tried to expand and elucidate it below [156/22–157/21].

phers have themselves suggested) in terms of falsification rather than verification; and the principle may be stated thus: 'If a statement is not decisively falsifiable, in principle as well as in practice, then the statement is not informative.' Of course this statement is itself somewhat vague: we may wonder what the phrase 'in principle' means, for instance. But the reasons for making it are tolerably clear. If you are trying to tell somebody that something is the case, this logically excludes certain other things being the case. For example, suppose I say, 'There is a tiger in the room.' Asked what evidence there was for this statement, or how it could be verified, I should mention pieces of evidence like there being a growling noise, a large striped animal with teeth and four legs, and so on. To say 'there is a tiger' entails there being a large striped animal, etc., because they are part of the meaning of the statement. The statement is vacuous without them. 'There is a tiger' is only informative if there is actually a large striped animal. Consequently, it must be decisively falsifiable: falsifiable, that is, if the pieces of evidence could not be found. Of course, the absence of only some of the evidence would not falsify it decisively: the growl might be absent, for instance, and there might still be a tiger. But there comes a time when the absence of evidence is overwhelming. An animal with three legs and no growl might still be a tiger; but an animal with no legs at all and a trunk could not be.

Moreover, statements are informative to the same degree as they are falsifiable or vulnerable. For the more precise information they give, the easier it is to upset them. 'There is something in the room' is very uninformative and not very vulnerable: 'there is an animal in the room' slightly more informative, but *ipso facto* more vulnerable: because more criteria have to be satisfied for 'animal' than for 'something'—the statement has to pass more verification-tests. 'There is a six-foot tiger exactly in the middle of the room, possessing only four teeth and pointing its tail consistently at an angle of seventy-eight degrees' is very precise, and very vulnerable. To put this more generally, any informative statement specifies that a part of reality is such-and-such: and the more precise the specification—the more the specification specifies, so to speak—then the more things there might be wrong with it.

If, then, a statement's truth is consistent with any evidence that might be forthcoming, it cannot be at all informative. Making a statement of this kind would be like saying: 'There is a tiger in the room, and nothing could count as evidence which decisively falsifies this truth.' Of course if there actually is a tiger, then the statement cannot actually be decisively falsified: for it is true. But it is still decisively falsifiable as a statement: for there is no logical compulsion about its being true. To say 'nothing could count as evidence against the existence of God' might mean 'since God exists, there can be no decisive evidence against it': but it might also mean that the statement 'God exists' is logically exempt from decisive evidence against it. And if this is true, then it cannot be informative. For saying 'God exists' is a particular instance of saying 'Such-and-such is the case'; and it is always logically possible that such-and-such is not the case. Whether it is or not precisely constitutes the test which any informative statement must pass.

Since therefore neither of these two alternatives is satisfactory, religious believers have to face up to the problem of providing their religious statements with established meaning and verification. In view of the points mentioned, they should be anxious rather than unwilling to make it clear what would decisively falsify the statements, since their informativeness corresponds to their falsifiability. Just how this process of giving verification to religious statements is to be gone through, I shall endeavour to explain in the next essay.* So far as we are here concerned, the point I wish to establish is that our fifth class of statements—those apparently informative about the supernatural world—must be claimed as genuinely informative, with all that this implies. If they are to be merged with any other class, it must be with the third: those expressing factual truths, or what are generally known as empirical statements.

Providing statements with verification, however, is not an arbitrary process; and there is one further point which must be allowed to the philosopher. Informative statements inform us about something in our experience, and must therefore be verifiable ultimately by our experience. I do not mean, of course, that they are about something which we are actually touching, seeing, feeling, etc., or which we have touched, seen, felt, etc. 'There is a tiger in the room' is informative even though we may never have seen a tiger. But they must be about something of which we could in principle have experience: for if they were not, they would not inform us about anything at all which had any connection with our lives and interests. To say 'There is a tiger in the room' would be senseless, and certainly not informative, if I added 'but nobody could ever have any experience of such a thing'. The whole interest of making such a statement is that, if we enter the room, we can expect to experience certain things—growls, stripes, being eaten, and so on. Statements which are of public interest and are informative, like this one, are based on the experiences of some people, and on the possibility that other people may also have similar experiences. This is the purpose of informative communication.

Past writers have attempted to discover many loopholes which might enable them to avoid this point also; and it is impossible to demonstrate that all of them are culs-de-sac. A typical loophole is to say that God 'transcends' human experience and that therefore we cannot expect to verify statements about God by human experience; though of course the first of these two statements need not be understood in such a way that the

* "Religious Experience," which follows on pp. 158-67 below.

second follows from it. But the same dilemma presents itself. Either 'God' stands for something at least partly within our experience, so that statements with the word 'God' in them are to that extent experimentally verifiable: or else 'God' does not stand for something within our actual or potential experience, in which case (to put it bluntly) statements about God can have no possible interest for us, and may well be meaningless. Of course this dilemma could be put more forcibly. We could say that if a descriptive word is supposed to refer to something which could not be experienced, then it seems doubtful whether it describes anything at all: since to be a thing involves the capability of being experienced, and can only be known through experience.

Nor need the Christian attempt to take evasive action over the issue of verification in any other way. Philosophers have been concerned to clarify the logical characteristics of informative assertions by various observations. They have said that they must be meaningful and verifiable: that we must know what would count as evidence for or against them: that their verification must ultimately be conducted by somebody's experience: that unless these conditions were satisfied they could not qualify for truth or falsehood, and so on. All this can be accepted; and there seems little use in trying to break out of the circle of these observations at any point, e.g. by saying that Christian assertions are 'true' in the sense of 'illuminating', or can be 'verified' 'by the Christian way of life itself.' For though the points being made here may be valid and important, they are insufficient; because Christian assertions are also supposed, by Christians themselves, to be true and verifiable in the (possibly more usual) sense in which philosophers have used these words.

This attempt to put religious assertions in the same logical boat, as it were, with straightforward empirical statements looks naïve and old-fashioned, because it suggests a naïve and old-fashioned view of religious language. We are accustomed to regard religious language as inadequate for its purposes; in particular, it is said to be 'metaphor' or 'analogy'. When challenged at every point, the metaphor becomes 'eroded' or 'evaporates', until nothing may be left. Hence the Christian and the philosopher seem both driven to the view that the metaphorical assertions cannot be informative, and must be in a different logical category from empirical statements, with a different sort of meaning and verification, if indeed they have any verification at all. But this is deceptive; because a metaphor may assert something quite as precise and informative as any other assertion. A word used metaphorically or analogically may lose something of its straightforward meaning; but it may gain some other significance. For example, 'sugar is sweet' may be a straightforward empirical assertion, and 'Mary is sweet' a metaphor; but it would be wrong to suppose that what we are saying about Mary is less definite or meaningful than what we are saying about sugar. The word 'sweet' simply means different things, and has a different method of verification, in either case. This might well be true of religious assertions. They are expressed in language borrowed from non-religious contexts, just as 'Mary is sweet' uses a word borrowed from taste-experience; but this language may well have a new and precise significance, though of course the fact that the same word is used suggests that there are points of contact between the two uses—points which might help to make the new use more comprehensible to someone who did not understand the metaphorical meaning.

One essential task which religious believers have to perform, therefore, is to give the individual words in religious language a clear and unambiguous descriptive meaning where such meaning is required. This applies both to what we might call technical religious words—words like 'God', 'soul', 'grace', and so on—and also to words used metaphorically—'love', 'father', 'kingdom', etc. Hitherto many believers have clung desperately to these words, but have been more able to say what they do not mean than what they do. Yet if religious language is ever to be genuinely and importantly informative, it is important that the criteria for the use of these words should be clear. If this task is not achieved, we shall be reduced to saying, as the Vedantist * says when asked to describe his deity, 'Not this, not this'.

To many people this might seem to imply that God is an object, much like a table or an elephant, Who can be immediately and wholly comprehended by experience: the only slight difference being that a different kind of experience is required. Yet this is plainly absurd; and a God of this kind is not the sort of God in which anybody believes. But we must be careful to understand the point. I have said earlier in this chapter that God is real in the same sense, though not in the same way, that physical objects are real. He must be real in the same sense: for the word 'real' has, in fact, only one sense—either something is real and exists, or it is unreal and does not exist. 'Real' and 'exists' are definitely not ambiguous words. But He is not (putting it roughly) real in the same *way,* because He is not the same sort of thing as a table or an elephant: indeed, we might say that He is not a *thing* at all, and certainly that He is not an object. Briefly, then, my contention is that if God is real and exists, the unambiguous logic and language of statements about existence, and the verification needed for these statements, must apply to God as much as to anything else, for these are part and parcel of what we mean by words like 'exist' and 'real'; but this is not to deny that much

* Vedantism is one of six systems of philosophy and religion which grew up in India after the Epic period, and emphasized the Upanishads, a group of poetic dialogues on metaphysics. Vedantists believe that the senses and memory are illusions. Ultimate reality is reached by excluding everything that has been imposed on it, for the imminent Atman, pure spirit, is without quality. He is, therefore, described in negative terms.

of His nature may be mysterious and uncomprehended by men. In much the same way, we might hold that love, or Martians, or the fourth dimension exist and are real: we might be able to give these words and phrases clear and unambiguous descriptive meanings and verification-methods: but they might still be very different from other things, highly mysterious, and largely uncomprehended.

Instead of the Vedantist's 'Not this, not this', Christians must be able to say, 'At least this, and at least this.' They must be able to assert definitely about God, whilst admitting that there is far more to be known about Him than we can perhaps ever hope to know. Moreover, as we come to learn more about God, there is nothing in logic to prevent our expanding the meaning of the word 'God'. In just such a way the word 'desire' has, since Freudian psychology, become expanded to include the concept of unconscious desires. In the light of new experience, words change their meaning in order to incorporate and communicate the experience. A due observance of logic, therefore, does nothing to remove the mystery of God on which Christians rightly insist; but it does serve the useful purpose of reminding us that if we are to talk meaningfully about God at any particular time, we must know what the word 'God' is agreed to mean at that time, and that we can ultimately know this only by reference to experience.

Another and equally important task for believers is to adopt a firm and unambiguous classification of the statements and sentences in their religion. Much that is spoken and written about religion is vitiated by the absence of such a classification; and it is particularly difficult for non-believers to achieve a firm grasp of the logical structure of religious doctrine. It is annoying, for instance, to argue at length about whether the soul is immortal, only to find after a time that the word 'soul' is being used to mean 'the immortal part of man'. This of course makes the statement 'The soul is immortal' analytic or tautologous, and therefore not empirically informative. In trying to assess the truth of a complex metaphysical system, such as the doctrines of the Roman church, it is essential to be clear about which statements are supposed to be informative and verifiable, and which are supposed to follow by deductive argument from other statements. For example, if we were intended to accept a number of statements on the authority of Christ, the Bible, the Church or some other source, we should be particularly interested in verifying the statements which were relevant to showing that source to be reliable, and not waste time in examining the statements deduced from its reliability.

This task of establishing meaning and verification, and classifying statements in religious belief according to their logic, has hardly been started. Hitherto Christian apologists have been chiefly interested in trying to collect and assess evidence for their beliefs, not realising the importance of the (logically prior) question of what is to count as evidence. Until this question is settled, it is unlikely that many people will be convinced by this collected 'evidence': for it may not be evidence to them at all. One cannot tell whether something is evidence for a statement or not unless one first knows what sort of statement it is supposed to be, and what sorts of things count as evidence for it. And it is this lack of clarity, if I may be permitted to conclude with a sociological sidelight, which has engendered a situation in which many intelligent people are now neither convinced of, nor hostile to, Christian belief, but merely uninterested in it.

Religious Experience

I shall now try to answer the fundamental challenge represented by the question, 'How are religious statements ultimately verified?' Briefly, my answer will be 'By religious experience': though there is much ground to be covered before we can regard that answer as philosophically satisfactory. I begin by assuming, as we saw in the last essay, that religious statements are supposed to be factually informative, like empirical statements: that when we talk of 'God', we intend to refer to something that really exists. I wish to make one more assumption: namely, that there is such a thing as religious experience. I do not wish to say that it is genuine, in the sense that it is experience *of* anything: that would make the argument circular. Neither do I wish to investigate its psychological or other causes, which would be philosophically irrelevant. I mean only, what few would surely deny, that there is such a thing as mystical or religious experience: that those who have such experience are not lying when they say that they have it.

Let it be granted, then, that some people have experiences which seem to them different in kind from any other type of experience, and that they propose to base certain assertions on these experiences. These assertions are supposed to be existential, in the sense that 'there is a God' is supposed to be like 'There are tables' rather than 'I feel happy', and 'God is love' like 'The sky is blue' rather than 'I seem to see a blue patch'. We may put precisely the same point by saying that these experiences are supposed to be cognitive: they are supposed to be experiences *of* something. We may even say, if we like, that they are meant to be 'objective' rather than 'subjective', provided we do not mislead ourselves by these words. The root of the problem, therefore, consists in determining the minimum conditions necessary for the basing of existential assertions on experience, or for regarding experiences as cognitive. The phrase 'minimum necessary conditions' is important, because I do not want to hold at all that religious assertions are so firmly based on experience as ordinary empirical assertions. There are many sufficient conditions satisfied by empirical assertions which religious assertions do not satisfy. I wish only to claim that religious assertions can satisfy all the necessary ones.

There are several conditions which are certainly sufficient, but which are not necessary. In order to show this, we have only to construct logically possible cases where we would want to say that assertions of fact or existential assertions were being made, but where these conditions are not satisfied.

(a) Ability to make scientific tests of our experience is not necessary. Thus, we would be (and in fact have been) convinced that the sky was blue and the grass green without being able to measure light-waves or assess refraction. Though it may be necessary that there should be some kind of public test for an existential assertion, it is not necessary that the test should be sophisticated.

(b) It is not necessary that the experience should be shared by a majority of people: this is not a question of counting heads. If a majority of people were colour-blind, we should still accept existential statements about colours; and though a majority of people may not be able to hear the squeak of bats, we should still be prepared to believe that bats squeak.

(c) It is not necessary that the experience should be, as it were, presented to us on a plate, whole and complete. It may be true of an experience both that it is cognitive, and that we have to learn how to have it. This has occurred in the life-history of all of us, for all infants have to learn how to use their senses: just as men who are born blind and recover their sight have to learn how to use their eyes.

(d) It is not necessary that the testing-system for assertions should be universally adopted, or that the terms figuring in the assertions should have a meaning constant for all groups of people who make them. Thus, we can imagine different ways of testing for colour in different groups of people (by simply looking at colours, by matching them, by trying them in different lights, by scientific measurement, and so on). The only common factor would be that the tests involved something which one saw—that they referred to one particular type of experience: the actual tests and methods involved might differ widely. Similarly, the meanings of colour-words differ from one society to another: Latin and Greek colour-words are notoriously unlike our own.

(e) Finally, it is often said that if an assertion is existential and true, it must afford one the ability to predict. Thus, 'I seem to see a blue expanse' allows no important prediction: but 'the sky is blue now' allows one to predict that (other things being equal) the sun will be shining outside, the weather will be right for a picnic, and so on. But we must be careful how far we extend the notion of prediction here. Prediction of a sophisticated or scientific nature—or any prediction beyond what is implied by the assertion itself—is not a necessary condition. Thus if I say 'there is a table in the next room', and you are assured of the truth of this, we may say, if we like, that you are hence able to predict that if you go into the next room you will see something solid, probably with legs, with a flat top, on which you can put things, and so on. But all this is part of what we normally mean by 'table': it is implied in the assertion itself. When I say 'there is a table' I imply that if you do certain things, you will have certain experiences: in other words, that the statement is verifiable. It is not necessary that you should be able to use my statement to 'predict' in any wider sense. We can even imagine a society which did not use its experiences of colour to predict in any but this narrow sense: a society which never connected black clouds with rain, or blue skies with sunshine, or red rags with bulls charging. To put this point in the least misleading way I can think of, it is not necessary to predict that anything will happen, though it is necessary to predict that we will be able to have certain experiences.

In what, then, does the difference between existential and non-existential ('psychological') statements consist? It is sometimes said that the former are 'corrigible' and the latter 'incorrigible'. But this will certainly not do as it stands. Statements like 'I feel happy' and 'I feel pain' are corrigible by other people. Even if we discount the possibility that I may be lying, or that I am not using the right words to describe my experience, there still remain tests which can be made by an outsider. If you assert that you feel happy, you may not be lying, but you may be deceiving yourself. That is why, if someone asks, 'Do you feel happy?' one often takes a long time to consider one's answer. The outsider can check one's answer, to some extent at least, by observing one's behaviour. If I scowl and look sullen, have frequent quarrels with my wife and detest my work, most people would agree that I was not feeling happy; but it is quite possible for me to believe the opposite. All that remains of the 'corrigible' and 'incorrigible' distinction, I think, is that if I am asserting something solely about my own experiences (and am neither a liar nor ignorant of common usage), then nobody else is likely to be in a position to refute me. There is an obvious sense in which nobody else can have my experiences. But many 'psychological' statements, like 'I feel happy' and 'I feel pain', entail far more than a verbal echo of simple experiences; and for that reason they are verifiable by other people.

This point is not essential to my case, since I should want to say, of course, that religious assertions are corrigible, and that religious experience may not be genuine (in the sense that it may not be cognitive experience). But it serves to bring out what I take to be the real difference between existential and non-existential statements, which is that the former are concerned with matters of public interest and experience to a degree that the latter are not. For example: suppose I say, in the first place, 'I feel great pain.' This is a non-existential assertion, and nobody would take exception to it. But suppose I then say, archaically, 'There is a great pain within me.' This looks like an existential assertion. If we attack this second assertion, it becomes apparent in the course of time that what I am saying refers only, or at least very largely, to my own experiences, and neither the actual or potential experiences of other people. It says nothing more than 'I feel great pain'; and it would lose nothing by adopting this, rather than the existential, form of speech. 'There is a table in the next room', on the other hand, does assert something of public interest, in the sense that it is verifiable by public experience to a far higher degree than psychological assertions.

We use these two modes of speech, existential and psychological, precisely because we wish to distinguish matters which are of public interest from matters which are not: to distinguish autobiographical remarks from common facts. Roughly, we begin thinking and talking in terms of existence or non-existence, in terms of objects or 'realities', in all cases where the experience of a sufficient number of people is coincidental: this is the easiest way of communicating our experiences to each other. I say 'There is a table': by this you are led to expect certain experiences of your own. Confident expectations of this kind are convenient to us.

We must remember, however, that if we want to talk about cognitive experience, or 'what is really there', our very language implies the possibility of non-cognitive experience in the same field, or 'what isn't really there', i.e. illusions. This implies that there must be certain tests for distinguishing reality from illusion, cognitive experience from non-cognitive, and what is really there from what is not. This is an important point, and must be met by anyone who proposes to establish any kind of object-language. Phrases like 'a sixth sense', 'something which we experience' (using 'experience' transitively), 'supernatural reality' and so on do not carry their own guarantee. But granted at least the possibility of such tests, it is not at all clear what could be meant by asking whether a whole *type* of experience is cognitive or not.

This question seems academic, in that it rests upon a misunderstanding of language. Suppose I say, 'There is an elephant in the next room.' You say, 'What do you mean by that?' I reply, 'Well, most of what I mean is that if you and other people were to enter the room, you would have such-and-such sense-experiences.' You check whether these experiences are actually to be had, and find that they are. But you are not content: you say, perhaps, 'Yes, you are right about the experiences; but surely this does not entitle you to make any existential statement: they might be "subjective", or self-induced, or non-cognitive.' Then I say: 'Well, I think I can convince you that they are not illusory: I know no scientific tests, but you will find that a large number of people have the experiences, and that they are not drunk, or subject to illusions, or liars.' You say, 'Perhaps so; but I still do not see that any number of experiences entitles you to make this existential assertion.' Then I begin to lose patience: I say, 'My dear fellow, I am no philosopher: if you don't want to call my statement "existential", then don't. All I really mean to assert is included in the experiences which you have already admitted: this is what I mean by "There is an elephant". I can't understand what you mean by asking for proof that the experiences are cognitive, or that the existential statement is justified, or that the elephant is "really" there.'

This is the point which is surely of the greatest practical importance in discussions between believers and non-believers: it comes out more clearly, perhaps, when it is not being argued by philosophers than when it is. A says: 'There is a God.' B says: 'How do you know?' A says: 'I have had certain experiences: I have seen God, talked with Him, been a changed man ever since, etc.' But this is of merely psychological or autobiographical interest to B: what B wants to know is whether there 'really' is a God, or whether A is just a dreamer. And the whole question is whether the experiences which A uses to base his assertion upon are available to B also. If they are, or even if there is any possibility of their being, then B will be interested: we have now stopped being autobiographical, and begun to deal with matters of common experience or potential experience. B will then want to know how he can have these experiences: in other words, he will want to verify and make tests for A's assertion.

A's assertion, in my view, is existential at least in the sense that it is supposed to be publicly verifiable, and that there are supposed to be tests for it. But I should want to say more than this. I should want to say that there are groups—large groups—of religious believers who do use the same system of verification for religious assertions, by means of their common experiences. These experiences are not only common (i.e. shared by all of them), but they are also co-recurrent. By this I mean that a number of numerically different experiences recur together in the same contexts. Further, having one or more of these experiences enables them to expect or predict other experiences. For instance, supposing a believer has experiences of love, grace and power, he can predict the result of a further test, e.g. what will happen if he prays, or confesses his sins. (Of course these words are technical terms to believers; if they worry non-believers we can say that experiences e, f and g allow one to predict experiences *h* and *i*.) This seems to me precisely similar in point of logic to the case with assertions like 'There is a table'. My having had certain visual experiences (seen a table) enables me to predict other experiences (touching it, putting things on it, etc.).

Religious assertions, then, do concern matters of public interest, at least within the religious groups who use the same verification-system for their assertions. They are publicly verifiable at least to a limited public. This means that there are ways of distinguishing genuine from misleading religious experience. It is admittedly unfortunate that some Christian writers should have spoken as if any kind of experience that might be labelled 'religious' or 'mystical' somehow carried its own guarantee. In fact, of course, most Christians would surely want to say that some religious believers—the worshippers of Baal, for instance—did have religious or ecstatic experiences which were not genuine or misleading: misleading, because they based on them assertions about God which were not true. Within the Christian group 'God' entails the possibility of a number of experiences (love, grace, power). If a man has only one of these, he may find it deceptive, in exactly the same way as if a man only experiences dagger-like visual images. He may find these to be unsubstantiated by the other experiences which must be available if there is really a dagger there. Further tests will show whether the single experience is deceptive or genuine.

Does this mean that religious assertions cannot be understood by those who have no religious experiences? The answer to this depends upon what is to count as understanding. In what seems to me the most important sense, religious assertions can be understood. Believers can define the terms of such assertions in terms of actual or potential experiences for the benefit of non-believers, just as a man with normal eyesight can explain the meaning of 'table' in terms of visual experiences to a blind man. An unbeliever can know what 'God' means, just as a blind man can know what 'table' means; that is, both can know how and when to use these words, what conditions must be satisfied before they can be used correctly. But in what is also an important sense, a man who has not had or cannot have any kind of experience of the *type* relevant to an assertion cannot understand the assertion. Explaining religious assertions to a non-believer is not at all like explaining the meaning of 'table' to someone who has never seen a table, but who has the use of his eyes. For here we can draw parallels: we can say, perhaps, 'Imagine something square, with legs, elevated from the ground, etc.' He would be able to appreciate the kind of experiences relevant to assertions about tables: the experiences, we might say, which make up the component parts of 'table'. It is much more like trying to explain empirical assertions to an extraterrestrial race of people who have no sense experiences at all. One could acquaint them with definitions and verification-tests, but one would get no further. Nothing one could say would seem real to them, until they were able to have at least some sense experiences.

I have avoided bringing in the debatable parallel with 'aesthetic experience' hitherto; but it is worth mentioning at this point, if only for purposes of illustration. For here too (a) we can make no scientific tests: (b) many aesthetic experiences are not shared by a majority of people: (c) it is often necessary to learn to have this experience ('musical apprecication' classes): (d) there is no universally adopted testing system for statements about works of art, and different terms ('romantic', 'baroque', etc.) have different meaning for different groups: (e) no sophisticated prediction is possible from these statements, but prediction about aesthetic experiences entailed by the statements is possible. Thus, if I say, 'Beethoven's "Eroica" is noble, dramatic and powerful,' you are entitled to assume that if you make the appropriate tests you will have certain experiences.

Tests in aesthetic experience also bear a remarkable resemblance to tests in religious experience. Neither consist in using the senses alone, or in measuring, observing, counting, etc.: we should not expect this, of course, since the statements are not intended to refer to objects or qualities of sense experience. Yet it is possible to test 'Beethoven's "Eroica" is noble'. I can acquaint myself with Beethoven's music in general, rid myself of prejudice for or against Beethoven, and above all simply listen to the 'Eroica' on many occasions over a long period of time. Religious tests have a good deal in common with this. We are told to clear the mind of prejudice, acquaint ourselves with religion in general, attempt to disregard sense experience for the moment, contemplate, meditate, and so on.

Again, we can admit ourselves mistaken about aesthetic merit. We can say, 'I thought so-and-so was a very powerful composer when I was young, but now I see that most of his work is mere bombast,' implying thereby that the tests we made when young were inadequate in some way. Similarly we can say, 'There seems to be something great about this work,' or 'There is something great about this work': and these have different meanings. We say the first, perhaps, when we have only heard it once—when we have not conducted enough tests to be sure. As with empirical statements, we preserve a distinction between autobiographical or psychological remarks ("I like this', 'This moves me greatly'), and assertions ('This is great music', 'That is a really beautiful passage').

Finally, it is noticeable that within a group whose members have common aesthetic experiences sensible and meaningful (and often helpful) conversations may be conducted which (in one sense) may be nonsense to outsiders. The group might make it plain to an outsider that when they used a word ('romantic') they referred to various aesthetic experiences (strangeness, poignancy), so that the outsider could know what the word meant; but the conversation could hardly be real to him. This frequently happens in religion also. Religious people often appear to be arguing about assertions in a way which seems quite unreal to a non-believer; and this is perfectly understandable, just as it is understandable that a discussion about music should make no sense to a man who was tone-deaf.

Both aesthetic and religious assertions refer to potential experiences, experiences which are actual within certain groups. It may be true that these experiences could become actual for a vast majority of people: that the capacity for religious experience has for some reason become repressed in modern societies. But I do not think that very much turns on this question in point of logic, though it does in point of practice. I am more concerned to discover what our attitude should be towards religious assertions. As things are, we have groups who claim to have certain experiences, on which they base verification-systems and existential assertions. What would be a rational attitude for someone who did not have these experiences?

Suppose a group of people were to lay claim to unusual experiences on which they based assertions that certain things called squmps existed. We should first want to know whether the existence of squmps was verifiable by any normal method—by sense experience, for instance. But no, this is not the case: a different type of experience is involved. Squmps have no connections with the natural world, at least in this direct way. We should then want to know whether these experiences had been properly formulated into a language-system which distinguished psychological from existential statements. Yes, this is so: it is possible for a member of the group to say 'I thought I saw a sqump yesterday, but it wasn't one', or 'That seems like a sqump, but I'm not sure', and also, 'That's definitely a sqump, it passes all the tests of experience.' At this point we must surely admit that there are existential statements about squmps. Then, surely, we should want to know just how important the whole matter was. Is there any purpose in having experiences of squmps? Or can we just shrug our shoulders when people start talking about them? In particular, if squmps are important—perhaps they illuminate our moral problems, or give us a feeling of beauty or security—can we learn to experience them?

Here, of course, the religious believer will answer with a definite 'Yes'. (It is worth noticing that the music-lover can also say 'Yes'; he can say that if you make no attempt to appreciate music, you will be missing a lot, and that once you appreciate it sufficiently, you will find it convenient to make assertions about it.) Christians at least suppose everyone to be capable of religious experience ('knowing God'), and believe it to be of immense importance and benefit to the lives of all men. Both these suppositions may be true; and it seems to me that the most rational course is to try to find out, not to shrug one's shoulders.

What we can legitimately demand of religious believers is that they should try to put forward some sort of unanimous programme for the benefit of those who want to have these experiences and test the assertions based on them. There are certain features common to the tests used by most religious groups, but it would help enormously if non-believers could be presented with a single programme. In this religion has hitherto failed; and this, together with all the other disadvantages which pertain to religious assertions as compared with assertions about sense experience, which I have described above, has made a great many people despair of ever founding religious belief on a secure logical and epistemological basis. This despair is natural but unnecessary. None of the disadvantages are fatal, and the difficulties which lie in our way are difficulties of practice, and not of logic.

It may well be asked why, if all this is acceptable, religious believers have not taken this line more clearly. But there are plenty of reasons for this. First, many believers have (mistakenly) demanded logical certainty for their assertions of fact. Secondly, their own religious experience, though sufficient for assertions, is more uncertain and fluctuating than sense experience, so that they have preferred to base their assertions on some other (illegitimate) foundation. Thirdly, they have not noticed the differences of language- and verification-systems between different religious groups. Fourthly, the structure of religious belief is not always clearly demonstrated by believers, although it is usually evident that a great many assertions may not be directly verifiable by experience, but depend logically on others: for instance, if we could verify by experience that there was a God, and that Christ always said what was true about Him, and that Christ asserted such-and-such, then we should be entitled to believe a great many other assertions. We might add to these points the desire of many believers to convert and propagandise by methods which are irrational and logically illegitimate: centuries of tradition and evangelistic zeal do not assist unbiased philosophical consideration.

All this, of course, does not mean that all or any religious assertions are actually true: this is not a philosophical question. But it does mean, I think, that they have a chance of being true along the lines suggested. What is required above all is that believers should present a solid front, at least on those assertions about which they agree. They should be able to put forward a clear and unanimous programme, describing some approved method of obtaining the experiences which are relevant to the key assertions of their faith. Whether they can learn anything from the mystics, from Wordsworth, from Mr. Huxley or from anyone else I do not know. But until they lay down some sort of agreed tests for their assertions, by means of religious experience, I do not see how they can expect anyone to place rational belief in them. What we need here, I take it, is a combination of mystic and of analytical philosopher. Perhaps this is too much to ask.

Problems

1. What, for Wilson, characterizes an "informative sentence" in religious thought? How do informative sentences differ from "commands"?
2. Wilson comments on the usual attitude toward religion as "an ethical outlook bolstered up with 'stories'." How does such an attitude make religious verification impossible? Why does such an attitude fail, therefore, to be adequate?
3. Why is Wilson trying to establish that meaning need not involve a single standard of verification?
4. Why does Wilson make a sharp distinction between people's informative intentions and agreed upon meaning and verification? How central to Wilson's argument is verification through human experience?
5. Why does Wilson feel that it is important to put "religious assertions in the same logical boat . . . with straightforward empirical statements?" Why is Wilson's analysis of metaphoric assertion so central to his argument?
6. Why is the development of a clear and unambiguous descriptive language so essential to religious assertion?
7. How does Wilson use "religious experience" to "verify" religious statements? What conditions are and are not necessary to "verify" religious assertions?
8. How will Wilson's analysis help create a program by which to experience and test religious experience?
9. Does Wilson's argument place the ultimate source of experience inside the individual psyche or in the world? As you read on, ask how acceptable his argument would be to a Marxist, a Freudian, or an existentialist.

10 MAX WEBER

Max Weber (1864–1920) begins his study of The Protestant Ethic and the Spirit of Capitalism *(1904) by asking what is to be understood by "the somewhat pretentious phrase, the* spirit *of capitalism." He then painstakingly pieces together the individual strands of thought that went into the making of "rational bourgeois capitalism."*

A sociologist of tremendous erudition and originality, Weber's great insight was into the psychological forces operative in economic society. His works repeatedly provide a critique of the interaction of idealism and economic self-interest in social change. A description of his perspective follows:

> All human action arises from a common source, in political as well as in religious life. Everywhere the first impulse to social action is given as a rule by real interests, i.e., by political and economic interests. But ideal interests lend wings to these real interests, give them a spiritual meaning, and serve to justify them. Man does not live by bread alone. He wants to have a good conscience as he pursues his life-interests. And in pursuing them he develops his capacities to the highest extent only if he believes that in so doing he serves a higher rather than a purely egoistic purpose. Interests without such 'spiritual wings' are lame; but on the other hand, ideas can win out in history only if and insofar as they are associated with real interests (15 Hintze).

The following essay, the last chapter from The Protestant Ethic, *reveals something of Weber's method and perspective, and also provides us with a dramatic illustration of how ideas have applications and consequences never foreseen by their originators and only dimly perceived by their present practitioners.*

Asceticism and the Spirit of Capitalism

In order to understand the connection between the fundamental religious ideas of ascetic Protestantism and its maxims for everyday economic conduct, it is necessary to examine with especial care such

From Max Weber, *The Protestant Ethic and the Spirit of Capitalism* (New York: Charles Scribner's Sons, 1958), pp. 155–183.

writings as have evidently been derived from ministerial practice. For in a time in which the beyond meant everything, when the social position of the Christian depended upon his admission to the communion, the clergyman through his ministry, Church discipline, and preaching, exercised an influence (as a glance at collections of *consilia, casus conscientiae,** etc., shows) which we modern men are entirely unable to picture. In such a time the religious forces which express themselves through such channels are the decisive influences in the formation of national character.

For the purposes of this chapter, though by no means for all purposes, we can treat ascetic Protestantism as a single whole. But since that side of English Puritanism which was derived from Calvinism gives the most consistent religious basis for the idea of the calling, we shall, following our previous method, place one of its representatives at the centre of the discussion. Richard Baxter stands out above many other writers on Puritan ethics, both because of his eminently practical and realistic attitude, and, at the same time, because of the universal recognition accorded to his works, which have gone through many new editions and translations. He was a Presbyterian and an apologist of the Westminster Synod, but at the same time, like so many of the best spirits of his time, gradually grew away from the dogmas of pure Calvinism. At heart he opposed Cromwell's usurpation as he would any revolution. He was unfavourable to the sects and the fanatical enthusiasm of the saints, but was very broad-minded about external peculiarities and objective towards his opponents. He sought his field of labour most especially in the practical promotion of the moral life through the Church. In the pursuit of this end, as one of the most successful ministers known to history, he placed his services at the disposal of the Parliamentary Government, of Cromwell, and of the Restoration,† until he retired from office under the last, before St. Bartholomew's day. His *Christian Directory* is the most complete compendium of Puritan ethics, and is continually adjusted to the practical experiences of his own ministerial activity. In comparison we shall make use of Spener's *Theologische Bedenken,* as representative of German Pietism, Barclay's *Apology* for the Quakers, and some other representatives of ascetic ethics, which, however, in the interest of space, will be limited as far as possible.

Now, in glancing at Baxter's *Saints' Everlasting Rest,* or his *Christian Directory,* or similar works of others, one is struck at first glance by the emphasis placed, in the discussion of wealth and its acquisition, on the ebionitic elements of the New Testament. Wealth as

---

* Counsels, cases of conscience; they were legalist, illustrating moral principles.
† At this point in the text there appeared the first of Weber's notes. Since Weber had 119 notes, totaling 29 pages, we have silently deleted them to facilitate continuity in reading.

such is a great danger; its temptations never end, and its pursuit is not only senseless as compared with the dominating importance of the Kingdom of God, but it is morally suspect. Here asceticism seems to have turned much more sharply against the acquisition of earthly goods than it did in Calvin, who saw no hindrance to the effectiveness of the clergy in their wealth, but rather a thoroughly desirable enhancement of their prestige. Hence he permitted them to employ their means profitably. Examples of the condemnation of the pursuit of money and goods may be gathered without end from Puritan writings, and may be contrasted with the late mediaeval ethical literature, which was much more open-minded on this point.

Moreover, these doubts were meant with perfect seriousness; only it is necessary to examine them somewhat more closely in order to understand their true ethical significance and implications. The real moral objection is to relaxation in the security of possession, the enjoyment of wealth with the consequence of idleness and the temptations of the flesh, above all of distraction from the pursuit of a righteous life. In fact, it is only because possession involves this danger of relaxation that it is objectionable at all. For the saints' everlasting rest is in the next world; on earth man must, to be certain of his state of grace, "do the works of him who sent him, as long as it is yet day". Not leisure and enjoyment, but only activity serves to increase the glory of God, according to the definite manifestations of His will.

Waste of time is thus the first and in principle the deadliest of sins. The span of human life is infinitely short and precious to make sure of one's own election. Loss of time through sociability, idle talk, luxury, even more sleep than is necessary for health, six to at most eight hours, is worthy of absolute moral condemnation. It does not yet hold, with Franklin, that time is money, but the proposition is true in a certain spiritual sense. It is infinitely valuable because every hour lost is lost to labour for the glory of God. Thus inactive contemplation is also valueless, or even directly reprehensible if it is at the expense of one's daily work. For it is less pleasing to God than the active performance of His will in a calling. Besides, Sunday is provided for that, and, according to Baxter, it is always those who are not diligent in their callings who have no time for God when the occasion demands it.

Accordingly, Baxter's principal work is dominated by the continually repeated, often almost passionate preaching of hard, continuous bodily or mental labour. It is due to a combination of two different motives. Labour is, on the one hand, an approved ascetic technique, as it always has been in the Western Church, in sharp contrast not only to the Orient but to almost all monastic rules the world over. It is in particular the specific defence against all those temptations which Puritanism united under the name of the unclean life, whose rôle for it was by no means small.

The sexual asceticism of Puritanism differs only in degree, not in fundamental principle, from that of monasticism; and on account of the Puritan conception of marriage, its practical influence is more far-reaching than that of the latter. For sexual intercourse is permitted, even within marriage, only as the means willed by God for the increase of His glory according to the commandment, "Be fruitful and multiply." Along with a moderate vegetable diet and cold baths, the same prescription is given for all sexual temptations as is used against religious doubts and a sense of moral unworthiness: "Work hard in your calling." But the most important thing was that even beyond that labour came to be considered in itself the end of life, ordained as such by God. St. Paul's "He who will not work shall not eat" holds unconditionally for everyone. Unwillingness to work is symptomatic of the lack of grace.

Here the difference from the mediaval view-point becomes quite evident. Thomas Aquinas also gave an interpretation of that statement of St. Paul. But for him labour is only necessary *naturali ratione* for the maintenance of individual and community. Where this end is achieved, the precept ceases to have any meaning. Moreover, it holds only for the race, not for every individual. It does not apply to anyone who can live without labour on his possessions, and of course contemplation, as a spiritual form of action in the Kingdom of God, takes precedence over the commandment in its literal sense. Moreover, for the popular theology of the time, the highest form of monastic productivity lay in the increase of the *Thesaurus ecclesiae* through prayer and chant.

Now only do these exceptions to the duty of labour naturally no longer hold for Baxter, but he holds most emphatically that wealth does not exempt anyone from the unconditional command. Even the wealthy shall not eat without working, for even though they do not need to labour to support their own needs, there is God's commandment which they, like the poor, must obey. For everyone without exception God's Providence has prepared a calling, which he should profess and in which he should labour. And this calling is not, as it was for the Lutheran, a fate to which he must submit and which he must make the best of, but God's commandment to the individual to work for the divine glory. This seemingly subtle difference had far-reaching psychological consequences, and became connected with a further development of the providential interpretation of the economic order which had begun in scholasticism.

The phenomenon of the division of labour and occupations in society had, among others, been interpreted by Thomas Aquinas, to whom we may most conveniently refer, as a direct consequence of the divine scheme of things. But the places assigned to each man in this cosmos follow *ex causis naturalibus* and are fortuitous (contingent in the Scholastic terminology). The differentiation of men into the classes and occupations established through historical development became for Luther, as we have seen, a direct result of the divine will. The perseverance of the individual in the place and within the limits which God had assigned to him was a religious duty. This was the more certainly the consequence since the relations of Lutheranism to the world were in general uncertain from the beginning and remained so. Ethical principles for the reform of the world could not be found in Luther's realm of ideas; in fact it never quite freed itself from Pauline indifference. Hence the world had to be accepted as it was, and this alone could be made a religious duty.

But in the Puritan view, the providential character of the play of private economic interests takes on a somewhat different emphasis. True to the Puritan tendency to pragmatic interpretations, the providential purpose of the division of labour is to be known by its fruits. On this point Baxter expresses himself in terms which more than once directly recall Adam Smith's well-known apotheosis of the division of labour. The specialization of occupations leads, since it makes the development of skill possible, to a quantitative and qualitative improvement in production, and thus serves the common good, which is identical with the good of the greatest possible number. So far, the motivation is purely utilitarian, and is closely related to the customary view-point of much of the secular literature of the time.

But the characteristic Puritan element appears when Baxter sets at the head of his discussion the statement that "outside of a well-marked calling the accomplishments of a man are only casual and irregular, and he spends more time in idleness than at work", and when he concludes it as follows: "and he [the specialized worker] will carry out his work in order while another remains in constant confusion, and his business knows neither time nor place . . . therefore is a certain calling the best for everyone". Irregular work, which the ordinary labourer is often forced to accept, is often unavoidable, but always an unwelcome state of transition. A man without a calling thus lacks the systematic, methodical character which is, as we have seen, demanded by wordly asceticism.

The Quaker ethic also holds that a man's life in his calling is an exercise in ascetic virtue, a proof of his state of grace through his conscientiousness, which is expressed in the care and method with which he pursues his calling. What God demands is not labour in itself, but rational labour in a calling. In the Puritan concept of the calling the emphasis is always placed on this methodical character of worldly asceticism, not, as with Luther, on the acceptance of the lot which God has irretrievably assigned to man.

Hence the question whether anyone may combine several callings is answered in the affirmative, if it is useful for the common good or one's own, and not injurious to anyone, and if it does not lead to unfaithfulness in one of the callings. Even a change of calling is by no means regarded as objectionable, if it is not thoughtless and is made for the purpose of pursuing a calling more pleasing to God, which means, on general principles, one more useful.

It is true that the usefulness of a calling, and thus its favour in the sight of God is measured primarily in moral terms, and thus in terms of the importance of the goods produced in it for the community. But a further, and, above all, in practice the most important, criterion is found in private profitableness. For if that God, whose hand the Puritan sees in all the occurrences of life, shows one of His elect a chance of profit, he must do it with a purpose. Hence the faithful Christian must follow the call by taking advantage of the opportunity. "If God show you a way in which you may lawfully get more than in another way (without wrong to your soul or to any other), if you refuse this, and choose the less gainful way, you cross one of the ends of your calling, and you refuse to be God's steward, and to accept His gifts and use them for Him when He requireth it: you may labour to be rich for God, though not for the flesh and sin."

Wealth is thus bad ethically only in so far as it is a temptation to idleness and sinful enjoyment of life, and its acquisition is bad only when it is with the purpose of later living merrily and without care. But as a performance of duty in a calling it is not only morally permissible, but actually enjoined. The parable of the servant who was rejected because he did not increase the talent which was entrusted to him seemed to say so directly. To wish to be poor was, it was often argued, the same as wishing to be unhealthy; it is objectionable as a glorification of works and derogatory to the glory of God. Especially begging, on the part of one able to work, is not only the sin of slothfulness, but a violation of the duty of brotherly love according to the Apostle's own word.

The emphasis on the ascetic importance of a fixed calling provided an ethical justification of the modern specialized division of labour. In a similar way the providential interpretation of profit-making justified the activities of the business man. The superior indulgence of the *seigneur* and the parvenu ostentation of the *nouveau riche* are equally detestable to asceticism. But, on the other hand, it has the highest ethical appreciation of the sober, middle-class, self-made man. "God blesseth His trade" is a stock remark about those good men who had successfully followed the divine hints. The whole power of the God of the Old Testament, who rewards His people for their obedience in this life, necessarily exercised a similar influence on the Puritan who, following Baxter's advice, compared his own state of grace with that of the heroes of the Bible, and in the process interpreted the statements of the Scriptures as the articles of a book of statutes.

Of course, the words of the Old Testament were not entirely without ambiguity. We have seen that Luther first used the concept of the calling in the secular sense in translating a passage from Jesus Sirach. But the book of Jesus Sirach belongs, with the whole atmosphere expressed in it, to those parts of the broadened Old Testament with a distinctly traditionalistic tendency, in spite of Hellenistic influences. It is characteristic that down to the present day this book seems to enjoy a special favour among Lutheran German peasants, just as the Lutheran influence in large sections of German Pietism has been expressed by a preference for Jesus Sirach.

The Puritans repudiated the Apocrypha as not inspired, consistently with their sharp distinction between things divine and things of the flesh. But among the canonical books that of Job had all the more influence. On the one hand it contained a grand conception of the absolute sovereign majesty of God, beyond all human comprehension, which was closely related to that of Calvinism. With that, on the other hand, it combined the certainty which, though incidental for Calvin, came to be of great importance for Puritanism, that God would bless His own in this life—in the book of Job only—and also in the material sense. The Oriental quietism, which appears in several of the finest verses of the Psalms and in the Proverbs, was interpreted away, just as Baxter did with the traditionalistic tinge of the passage in the 1st Epistle to the Corinthians, so important for the idea of the calling.

But all the more emphasis was placed on those parts of the Old Testament which praise formal legality as a sign of conduct pleasing to God. They held the theory that the Mosaic Law had only lost its validity through Christ in so far as it contained ceremonial or purely historical precepts applying only to the Jewish people, but that otherwise it had always been valid as an expression of the natural law, and must hence be retained. This made it possible, on the one hand, to eliminate elements which could not be reconciled with modern life. But still, through its numerous related features, Old Testament morality was able to give a powerful impetus to that spirit of self-righteous and sober legality which was so characteristic of the worldly asceticism of this form of Protestantism.

Thus when authors, as was the case with several contemporaries as well as later writers, characterize the basic ethical tendency of Puritanism, especially in England, as English Hebraism they are, correctly understood, not wrong. It is necessary, however, not to think of Palestinian Judaism at the time of the writing of the Scriptures, but of Judaism as it became under the influence of many centuries of formalistic, legalistic, and Talmudic education. Even then one must be very careful in drawing parallels. The general tendency of the older Judaism toward a naïve acceptance of life as such was far removed from the special characteristics of Puritanism. It was, however, just as far—and this ought not to be overlooked—from the economic ethics of mediaeval and modern Judaism, in the traits which determined the positions of both in the development of the capitalistic ethos. The Jews stood on the side of the politically and speculatively oriented adventurous capitalism; their ethos was, in a word, that of pariah-capitalism. But Puritanism carried the ethos of the rational organization of capital and labour. It took over from the Jewish ethic only what was adapted to this purpose.

To analyse the effects on the character of peoples of the penetration of life with Old Testament norms—a tempting task which, however, has not yet satisfactorily been done even for Judaism—would be impossible within the limits of this sketch. In addition to the relationships already pointed out, it is important for the general inner attitude of the Puritans, above all, that the belief that they were God's chosen people saw in them a great renaissance. Even the kindly Baxter thanked God that he was born in England, and thus in the true Church, and nowhere else. This thankfulness for one's own perfection by the grace of God penetrated the attitude toward life of the Puritan middle class, and played its part in developing that formalistic, hard, correct character which was peculiar to the men of that heroic age of capitalism.

Let us now try to clarify the points in which the Puritan idea of the calling and the premium it placed upon ascetic conduct was bound directly to influence the development of a capitalistic way of life. As we have seen, this asceticism turned with all its force against one thing: the spontaneous enjoyment of life and all it had to offer. This is perhaps most characteristically brought out in the struggle over the *Book of Sports* which James I and Charles I made into law expressly as a means of counteracting Puritanism, and which the latter ordered to be read from all the pulpits. The fanatical opposition of the Puritans to the ordinances of the King, permitting certain popular amusements on Sunday outside of Church hours by law, was not only explained by the disturbance of the Sabbath rest, but also by resentment against the intentional diversion from the ordered life of the saint, which it caused. And, on his side, the King's threats of severe punishment for every attack on the legality of those sports were motivated by his purpose of breaking the anti-authoritarian ascetic tendency of Puritanism, which was so dangerous to the State. The feudal and monarchical forces protected the pleasure seekers against the rising middle-class morality and the anti-authoritarian ascetic conventicles, just as to-day capitalistic society tends to protect those willing to work against the class morality of the proletaria and the anti-authoritarian trade union.

As against this the Puritans upheld their decisive characteristic, the principle of ascetic conduct. For otherwise the Puritan aversion to sport, even for the Quakers, was by no means simply one of principle. Sport was accepted if it served a rational purpose, that of recreation necessary for physical efficiency. But as a means for the spontaneous expression of undisciplined impulses, it was under suspicion; and in so far as it became purely a means of enjoyment, or awakened pride, raw instincts or the irrational gambling instinct, it was of course strictly condemned. Impulsive enjoyment of life, which leads away both from work in a calling and from religion, was as such the enemy of rational asceticism, whether in the form of seigneurial sports, or the enjoyment of the dance-hall or the public-house of the common man.

Its attitude was thus suspicious and often hostile to the aspects of culture without any immediate religious value. It is not, however, true that the ideals of Puritanism implied a solemn, narrow-minded contempt of culture. Quite the contrary is the case at least for science, with the exception of the hatred of Scholasticism. Moreover, the great men of the Puritan movement were thoroughly steeped in the culture of the Renaissance. The sermons of the Presbyterian divines abound with classical allusions, and even the Radicals, although they objected to it, were not ashamed to display that kind of learning in theological polemics. Perhaps no country was ever so full of graduates as New England in the first generation of its existence. The satire of their opponents, such as, for instance, Butler's *Hudibras,* also attacks primarily the pendantry and highly trained dialectics of the Puritans. This is partially due to the religious valuation of knowledge which followed from their attitude to the Catholic *fides implicita.**

But the situation is quite different when one looks at non-scientific literature, and especially the fine arts. Here asceticism descended like a frost on the life of "Merrie old England." And not only worldly merriment felt its effect. The Puritan's ferocious hatred of everything which smacked of superstition, of all survivals of magical or sacramental salvation, applied to the Christmas festivities and the May Pole and all spontaneous religious art. That there was room in Holland for a great, often uncouthly realistic art proves only how far from completely the authoritarian moral discipline of that country was able to counteract the influence of the court and the regents (a class of *rentiers*), and also the joy in life of the parvenu bourgeoisie, after the short supremacy of the Calvinistic theocracy had been transformed into a moderate national Church, and with it Calvinism had perceptibly lost in its power of ascetic influence.

The theatre was obnoxious to the Puritans, and with the strict exclusion of the erotic and of nudity from the realm of toleration, a radical view of either literature or art could not exist. The conceptions of idle talk, of superfluities, and of vain ostentation, all designations of an irrational attitude without objective purpose, thus not ascetic, and especially not serving the glory of God, but of man, were always at hand to serve in deciding in favour of sober utility as against any artistic tendencies. This was especially true in the case of decoration of the person, for instance

* Implicit faith or trust; the predisposition to believe the authority of the church irrespective of knowledge.

clothing. That powerful tendency toward uniformity of life, which to-day so immensely aids the capitalistic interest in the standardization of production, had its ideal foundations in the repudiation of all idolatry of the flesh.

Of course we must not forget that Puritanism included a world of contradictions, and that the instinctive sense of eternal greatness in art was certainly stronger among its leaders than in the atmosphere of the Cavaliers. Moreover, a unique genius like Rembrandt, however little his conduct may have been acceptable to God in the eyes of the Puritans, was very strongly influenced in the character of his work by his religious environment. But that does not alter the picture as a whole. In so far as the development of the Puritan tradition could, and in part did, lead to a powerful spiritualization of personality, it was a decided benefit to literature. But for the most part that benefit only accrued to later generations.

Although we cannot here enter upon a discussion of the influence of Puritanism in all these directions, we should call attention to the fact that the toleration of pleasure in cultural goods, which contributed to purely aesthetic or athletic enjoyment, certainly always ran up against one characteristic limitation: they must not cost anything. Man is only a trustee of the goods which have come to him through God's grace. He must, like the servant in the parable, give an account of every penny entrusted to him, and it is at least hazardous to spend any of it for a purpose which does not serve the glory of God but only one's own enjoyment. What person, who keeps his eyes open, has not met representatives of this view-point even in the present? The idea of a man's duty to his possessions, to which he subordinates himself as an obedient steward, or even as an acquisitive machine, bears with chilling weight on his life. The greater the possessions the heavier, if the ascetic attitude toward life stands the test, the feeling of responsibility for them, for holding them undiminished for the glory of God and increasing them by restless effort. The origin of this type of life also extends in certain roots, like so many aspects of the spirit of capitalism, back into the Middle Ages. But it was in the ethic of ascetic Protestantism that it first found a consistent ethical foundation. Its significance for the development of capitalism is obvious.

This worldly Protestant asceticism, as we may recapitulate up to this point, acted powerfully against the spontaneous enjoyment of possessions; it restricted consumption, especially of luxuries. On the other hand, it had the psychological effect of freeing the acquisition of goods from the inhibitions of traditionalistic ethics. It broke the bonds of the impulse of acquisition in that it not only legalized it, but (in the sense discussed) looked upon it as directly willed by God. The campaign against the temptations of the flesh, and the dependence on external things, was, as besides the Puritans the great Quaker apologist Barclay expressly says, not a struggle against the rational acquisition, but against the irrational use of wealth.

But this irrational use was exemplified in the outward forms of luxury which their code condemned as idolatry of the flesh, however natural they had appeared to the feudal mind. On the other hand, they approved the rational and utilitarian uses of wealth which were willed by God for the needs of the individual and the community. They did not wish to impose mortification on the man of wealth, but the use of his means for necessary and practical things. The idea of comfort characteristically limits the extent of ethically permissible expenditures. It is naturally no accident that the development of a manner of living consistent with that idea may be observed earliest and most clearly among the most consistent representatives of this whole attitude toward life. Over against the glitter and ostentation of feudal magnificence which, resting on an unsound economic basis, prefers a sordid elegance to a sober simplicity, they set the clean and solid comfort of the middle-class home as an ideal.

On the side of the production of private wealth, asceticism condemned both dishonesty and impulsive avarice. What was condemned as covetousness, Mammonism, etc., was the pursuit of riches for their own sake. For wealth in itself was a temptation. But here asceticism was the power "which ever seeks the good but ever creates evil"; what was evil in its sense was possession and its temptations. For, in conformity with the Old Testament and in analogy to the ethical valuation of good works, asceticism looked upon the pursuit of wealth as an end in itself as highly reprehensible; but the attainment of it as a fruit of labour in a calling was a sign of God's blessing. And even more important: the religious valuation of restless, continuous, systematic work in a worldly calling, as the highest means to asceticism, and at the same time the surest and most evident proof of rebirth and genuine faith, must have been the most powerful conceivable lever for the expansion of that attitude toward life which we have here called the spirit of capitalism.

When the limitation of consumption is combined with this release of acquisitive activity, the inevitable practical result is obvious: accumulation of capital through ascetic compulsion to save. The restraints which were imposed upon the consumption of wealth naturally served to increase it by making possible the productive investment of capital. How strong this influence was is not, unfortunately, susceptible of exact statistical demonstration. In New England the connection is so evident that it did not escape the eye of so discerning a historian as Doyle. But also in Holland, which was really only dominated by strict Calvinism for seven years, the greater simplicity of life in the more seriously religious circles, in combination with great wealth, led to an excessive propensity to accumulation.

That, furthermore, the tendency which has existed everywhere and at all times, being quite strong in Germany to-day, for middle-class fortunes to be absorbed into the nobility, was necessarily checked by the

Puritan antipathy to the feudal way of life, is evident. English Mercantilist writers of the seventeenth century attributed the superiority of Dutch capital to English to the circumstance that newly acquired wealth there did not regularly seek investment in land. Also, since it is not simply a question of the purchase of land, it did not there seek to transfer itself to feudal habits of life, and thereby to remove itself from the possibility of capitalistic investment. The high esteem for agriculture as a peculiarly important branch of activity, also especially consistent with piety, which the Puritans shared, applied (for instance in Baxter) not to the landlord, but to the yeoman and farmer, in the eighteenth century not to the squire, but the rational cultivator. Through the whole of English society in the time since the seventeenth century goes the conflict between the squirearchy, the representatives of "merrie old England", and the Puritan circles of widely varying social influence. Both elements, that of an unspoiled naïve joy of life, and of a strictly regulated, reserved self-control, and conventional ethical conduct are even to-day combined to form the English national character. Similarly, the early history of the North American Colonies is dominated by the sharp contrast of the adventurers, who wanted to set up plantations with the labour of indentured servants, and live as feudal lords, and the specifically middle-class outlook of the Puritans.

As far as the influence of the Puritan outlook extended, under all circumstances—and this is, of course, much more important than the mere encouragement of capital accumulation—it favoured the development of a rational bourgeois economic life; it was the most important, and above all the only consistent influence in the development of that life. It stood at the cradle of the modern economic man.

To be sure, these Puritanical ideals tended to give way under excessive pressure from the temptations of wealth, as the Puritans themselves knew very well. With great regularity we find the most genuine adherents of Puritanism among the classes which were rising from a lowly status, the small bourgeois and farmers, while the *beati possidentes,* even among Quakers, are often found tending to repudiate the old ideals. It was the same fate which again and again befell the predecessor of this worldly asceticism, the monastic asceticism of the Middle Ages. In the latter case, when rational economic activity had worked out its full effects by strict regulation of conduct and limitation of consumption, the wealth accumulated either succumbed directly to the nobility, as in the time before the Reformation, or monastic discipline threatened to break down, and one of the numerous reformations became necessary.

In fact the whole history of monasticism is in a certain sense the history of a continual struggle with the problem of the secularizing influence of wealth. The same is true on a grand scale of the wordly asceticism of Puritanism. The great revival of Methodism, which preceded the expansion of English industry toward the end of the eighteenth century, may well be compared with such a monastic reform. We may hence quote here a passage from John Wesley * himself which might well serve as a motto for everything which has been said above. For it shows that the leaders of these ascetic movements understood the seemingly paradoxical relationships which we have here analysed perfectly well, and in the same sense that we have given them. He wrote:

> I fear, wherever riches have increased, the essence of religion has decreased in the same proportion. Therefore I do not see how it is possible, in the nature of things, for any revival of true religion to continue long. For religion must necessarily produce both industry and frugality, and these cannot but produce riches. But as riches increase, so will pride, anger, and love of the world in all its branches. How then is it possible that Methodism, that is, a religion of the heart, though it flourishes now as a green bay tree, should continue in this state? For the Methodists in every place grow diligent and frugal; consequently they increase in goods. Hence they proportionately increase in pride, in anger, in the desire of the flesh, the desire of the eyes, and the pride of life. So, although the form of religion remains, the spirit is swiftly vanishing away. Is there no way to prevent this—this continual decay of pure religion? We ought not to prevent people from being diligent and frugal; *we must exhort all Christians to gain all they can, and to save all they can; that is, in effect, to grow rich.*

There follows the advice that those who gain all they can and save all they can should also give all they can, so that they will grow in grace and lay up a treasure in heaven. It is clear that Wesley here expresses, even in detail, just what we have been trying to point out.

As Wesley here says, the full economic effect of those great religious movements, whose significance for economic development lay above all in their ascetic educative influence, generally came only after the peak of the purely religious enthusiasm was past. Then the intensity of the search for the Kingdom of God commenced gradually to pass over into sober economic virtue; the religious roots died out slowly, giving way to utilitarian worldliness. Then, as Dowden puts it, as in *Robinson Crusoe,* the isolated economic man who carries on missionary activities on the side takes the place of the lonely spiritual search for the Kingdom of Heaven of Bunyan's pilgrim, hurrying through the market-place of Vanity.

When later the principle "to make the most of both worlds" became dominant in the end, as Dowden has remarked, a good conscience simply became one of the means of enjoying a comfortable bourgeois life, as is well expressed in the German proverb about the soft pillow.

* John Wesley (1703-91), English evangelical preacher and founder of Methodism.

What the great religious epoch of the seventeenth century bequeathed to its utilitarian successor was, however, above all an amazingly good, we may even say a pharisaically good, conscience in the acquisition of money, so long as it took place legally. Every trace of the *deplacere vix potest** has disappeared.

A specifically bourgeois economic ethic had grown up. With the consciousness of standing in the fullness of God's grace and being visibly blessed by Him, the bourgeois business man, as long as he remained within the bounds of formal correctness, as long as his moral conduct was spotless and the use to which he put his wealth was not objectionable, could follow his pecuniary interests as he would and feel that he was fulfilling a duty in doing so. The power of religious asceticism provided him in addition with sober, conscientious, and unusually industrious workmen, who clung to their work as to a life purpose willed by God.

Finally, it gave him the comforting assurance that the unequal distribution of the goods of this world was a special dispensation of Divine Providence, which in these differences, as in particular grace, pursued secret ends unknown to men. Calvin himself had made the much-quoted statement that only when the people, i.e. the mass of labourers and craftsmen, were poor did they remain obedient to God. In the Netherlands (Pieter de la Court and others), that had been secularized to the effect that the mass of men only labour when necessity forces them to do so. This formulation of a leading idea of capitalistic economy later entered into the current theories of the productivity of low wages. Here also, with dying out of the religious root, the utilitarian interpretation crept in unnoticed, in the line of development which we have again and again observed.

Mediæval ethics not only tolerated begging but actually glorified it in the mendicant orders. Even secular beggars, since they gave the person of means opportunity for good works through giving alms, were sometimes considered an estate and treated as such. Even the Anglican social ethic of the Stuarts was very close to this attitude. It remained for Puritan Asceticism to take part in the severe English Poor Relief Legislation which fundamentally changed the situation. And it could do that, because the Protestant sects and the strict Puritan communities actually did not know any begging in their own midst.

On the other hand, seen from the side of the workers, the Zinzendorf branch of Pietism, for instance, glorified the loyal worker who did not seek acquisition, but lived according to the apostolic model, and was thus endowed with the *charisma* of the disciples. Similar ideas had originally been prevalent among the Baptists in an even more radical form.

Now naturally the whole ascetic literature of almost all denominations is saturated with the idea that faithful labour, even at low wages,

* It [the acquisition of money] could barely please or satisfy [God].

on the part of those whom life offers no other opportunities, is highly pleasing to God. In this respect Protestant Asceticism added in itself nothing new. But it not only deepened this idea most powerfully, it also created the force which was alone decisive for its effectiveness: the psychological sanction of it through the conception of this labour as a calling, as the best, often in the last analysis the only means of attaining certainty of grace. And on the other hand it legalized the exploitation of this specific willingness to work, in that it also interpreted the employer's business activity as a calling. It is obvious how powerfully the exclusive search for the Kingdom of God only through the fulfilment of duty in the calling, and the strict asceticism which Church discipline naturally imposed, especially on the propertyless classes, was bound to affect the productivity of labour in the capitalistic sense of the word. The treatment of labour as a calling became as characteristic of the modern worker as the corresponding attitude toward acquisition of the business man. It was a perception of this situation, new at his time, which caused so able an observer as Sir William Petty to attribute the economic power of Holland in the seventeenth century to the fact that the very numerous dissenters in that country (Calvinists and Baptists) "are for the most part thinking, sober men, and such as believe that Labour and Industry is their duty towards God".

Calvinism opposed organic social organization in the fiscal-monopolistic form which it assumed in Anglicanism under the Stuarts, especially in the conceptions of Laud, this alliance of Church and State with the monopolists on the basis of a Christian-social ethical foundation. Its leaders were universally among the most passionate opponents of this type of politically privileged commercial, putting-out, and colonial capitalism. Over against it they placed the individualistic motives of rational legal acquisition by virtue of one's own ability and initiative. And, while the politically privileged monopoly industries in England all disappeared in short order, this attitude played a large and decisive part in the development of the industries which grew up in spite of and against the authority of the State. The Puritans (Prynne, Parker) repudiated all connection with the large-scale capitalistic courtiers and projectors as an ethically suspicious class. On the other hand, they took pride in their own superior middle-class business morality, which formed the true reason for the persecutions to which they were subjected on the part of those circles. Defoe proposed to win the battle against dissent by boycotting bank credit and withdrawing deposits. The difference of the two types of capitalistic attitude went to a very large extent hand in hand with religious differences. The opponents of the Nonconformists, even in the eighteenth century, again and again ridiculed them for personifying the spirit of shopkeepers, and for having ruined the ideals of old England. Here also lay the difference of the Puritan economic ethic from the

Jewish; and contemporaries (Prynne) knew well that the former and not the latter was the bourgeois capitalistic ethic.

One of the fundamental elements of the spirit of modern capitalism, and not only of that but of all modern culture: rational conduct on the basis of the idea of the calling, was born—that is what this discussion has sought to demonstrate—from the spirit of Christian asceticism. One has only to re-read the passage from Franklin, quoted at the beginning of this essay, in order to see that the essential elements of the attitude which was there called the spirit of capitalism are the same as what we have just shown to be the content of the Puritan worldly asceticism, only without the religious basis, which by Franklin's time had died away. The idea that modern labour has an ascetic character is of course not new. Limitation to specialized work, with a renunciation of the Faustian universality of man which it involves, is a condition of any valuable work in the modern world; hence deeds and renunciation inevitably condition each other today. This fundamentally ascetic trait of middle-class life, if it attempts to be a way of life at all, and not simply the absence of any, was what Goethe wanted to teach, at the height of his wisdom, in the *Wanderjahren*,* and in the end which he gave to the life of his *Faust*. For him the realization meant a renunciation, a departure from an age of full and beautiful humanity, which can no more be repeated in the course of our cultural development than can the flower of the Athenian culture of antiquity.

The Puritan wanted to work in a calling; we are forced to do so. For when asceticism was carried out of monastic cells into everyday life, and began to dominate worldly morality, it did its part in building the tremendous cosmos of the modern economic order. This order is now bound to the technical and economic conditions of machine production which to-day determine the lives of all the individuals who are born into this mechanism, not only those directly concerned with economic acquisition, with irresistible force. Perhaps it will so determine them until the last ton of fossilized coal is burnt. In Baxter's view the care for external goods should only lie on the shoulders of the "saint like a light cloak, which can be thrown aside at any moment". But fate decreed that the cloak should become an iron cage.

Since asceticism undertook to remodel the world and to work out its ideals in the world, material goods have gained an increasing and finally an inexorable power over the lives of men as at no previous period in history. To-day the spirit of religious asceticism—whether finally, who knows?—has escaped from the cage. But victorious capitalism, since it rests on mechanical foundations, need its support no longer. The

---

* Johann von Goethe's *Wilhelm Meister's Travels* (1821-1829), a work written late in Goethe's life which stresses, as did the sequel to *Faust,* usefulness, public service, and living for others as the key to happiness.

rosy blush of its laughing heir, the Enlightenment, seems also to be irretrievably fading, and the idea of duty in one's calling prowls about in our lives like a ghost of dead religious beliefs. Where the fulfilment of the calling cannot directly be related to the highest spiritual and cultural values, or when, on the other hand, it need not be felt simply as economic compulsion, the individual generally abandons the attempt to justify it at all. In the field of its highest development, in the United States, the pursuit of wealth, stripped of its religious and ethical meaning, tends to become associated with purely mundane passions, which often actually give it the character of sport.

No one knows who will live in this cage in the future, or whether at the end of this tremendous development entirely new prophets will arise, or there will be a great rebirth of old ideas and ideals, or, if neither, mechanized petrification, embellished with a sort of convulsive self-importance. For of the last stage of this cultural development, it might well be truly said: "Specialists without spirit, sensualists without heart; this nullity imagines that it has attained a level of civilization never before achieved."

But this brings us to the world of judgments of value and of faith, with which this purely historical discussion need not be burdened. The next task would be rather to show the significance of ascetic rationalism, which has only been touched in the foregoing sketch, for the content of practical social ethics, thus for the types of organization and the functions of social groups from the conventicle to the State. Then its relations to humanistic rationalism, its ideals of life and cultural influence; further to the development of philosophical and scientific empiricism, to technical development and to spiritual ideals would have to be analysed. Then its historical development from the mediæval beginnings of worldly asceticism to its dissolution into pure utilitarianism would have to be traced out through all the areas of ascetic religion. Only then could the quantitative cultural significance of ascetic Protestantism in its relation to the other plastic elements of modern culture be estimated.

Here we have only attempted to trace the fact and the direction of its influence to their motives in one, though a very important point. But it would also further be necessary to investigate how Protestant Asceticism was in turn influenced in its development and its character by the totality of social conditions, especially economic. The modern man is in general, even with the best will, unable to give religious ideas a significance for culture and national character which they deserve. But it is, of course, not my aim to substitute for a one-sided materialistic an equally one-sided spiritualistic causal interpretation of culture and of history. Each is equally possible, but each, if it does not serve as the preparation, but as the conclusion of an investigation, accomplishes equally little in the interest of historical truth.

Problems

1. How important is the concept of the "calling" to the spirit of capitalism? In what ways does this concept continue to manifest itself in modern society?
2. To what extent does money-making become the aim of life and the greatest good of the Protestant ethic? To what extent is this pursuit of money unrelated to the pursuit of personal happiness, unrelated in fact to any rational human considerations?
3. In what way is the Protestant ethic well-suited to a middle-class bourgeois mentality?
4. How does the evolution of the consequences of the Protestant ethic undermine the very ethic itself? Which is more hostile to the Protestant ethic and the spirit of capitalism, a welfare state or a consumer economy?
5. Max Weber makes much of the influence of Calvinism on the rise of capitalism. On the basis of your reading in the *Institutes of the Christian Religion,* in what ways might Calvinism be receptive to capitalism? In what ways hostile to it?

11 OSCAR CULLMANN

   In studying the New Testament we soon realize that the early church eschatology envisioned an imminent parousia *(Greek coming, that is, the Second Coming). The advent of the Messiah signaled the beginning of the end; Judgment Day was near at hand. It is not only Revelation that is apocalyptic. The Letters and even the Gospels convey a strong sense of the end of the world. It is this primitive eschatology that explains many of the early Christians' attitudes toward the State, such as those revealed in Romans 13. A couple of hundred years later, however, after the* parousia *had been postponed indefinitely, a new attitude toward the State began to evolve.*
  It is this tension between present and future and between Church and State that Oscar Cullmann, Professor of Early Christianity at the Sorbonne, discusses in his concluding chapter of The State in the New Testament.
  The question of the proper attitude and behavior of a Christian toward the State is an emotional issue so reverberent with prejudice and disagreement as almost to insure antagonism. Thus, while Walter Kaufmann, philosopher and literary critic, asserts flatly that "almost all of the great Christians were authoritarian" (16 Kaufmann), Cullmann obviously disagrees. It is difficult to know what the New Testament intended, for in life what is originally intended is often not effectuated, and that intention at best can only be inferred. Perhaps what was intended can never be known. Still, in reading this essay and others in this section, one can ask which of the two writers, Cullmann or Kaufmann, would most have reflected the attitude of the early Christians, the medieval Church, and the Protestant reformers.

from The State in the New Testament

   When one and the same problem is pursued through all the books of the New Testament, ordinarily one is used to finding as his final result the difference in style and method among the different

From Oscar Cullmann, *The State in the New Testament* (New York: Charles Scribner's Sons, 1956), pp. 86–92.

authors as they handle and solve the problem at hand. For the problem of the State matters are exactly reversed. Here we find at the beginning, at the initial point of our investigation, an almost radical difference apparently existing between Romans 13 and Revelation 13; but as the final result there is demonstrated a fundamental unity in the valuation of the State. The apparent contradiction comes on one side from the State itself. According as the State remains within its limits or transgresses them, the Christian will describe it as the servant of God or as the instrument of the Devil. But further: the apparent contradiction lies in the chronological dualism, the chronological tension, which characterises the New Testament situation. The conviction that the end-time has already begun and that its consummation is nevertheless still outstanding, this tension between "already fulfilled" and "not yet completed" is in no sense a contradiction in the primitive Christian eschatology; rather it is an *essential* part of it.*

And as long as this primitive Christian tension between "already fulfilled" and "not yet completed" is present, the attitude of the Christians to the State is also uniform. Since this tension is the constitutive element of all primitive Christian interpretation of the end-time, therefore also the apparent contradictions in the primitive Christian interpretation of

---

* Karl Löwith has commented at some length on the meaning for history of the Christian eschatology (that branch of theology concerned with death, the last judgment, and the salvation of the soul).

"In this theological perspective the pattern of history is a movement progressing, and at the same time returning, from alienation to reconciliation, one great detour to reach in the end the beginning through ever repeated acts of rebellion and self-surrender. Man's sin and God's saving purpose—they alone require and justify history as such, and historical time. Without original sin and final redemption the historical interim would be unnecessary and unintelligible. . . . The possibility of a Christian interpretation of history rests neither on the recognition of spiritual values nor on that of Jesus as a world-historical individual; for many such individuals have had a world-wide effect and more than one has claimed to be a savior. The Christian interpretation of history stands or falls with the acceptance of Jesus as Christ, i.e., with the doctrine of the Incarnation. . . . The Christian understanding of history and time is not a matter of theological demonstration but a concern of faith, for only by faith can one 'know' that the ultimate past and the ultimate future, the first and the last things, are converging on and represented in Jesus Christ as savior. . . . On account of this profound ambiguity of the historical fulfilment where everything is 'already' what it is 'not yet,' the Christian believer lives in a radical tension between present and future. He has faith and he does hope. Being relaxed in his present experience and straining toward the future, he confidently enjoys what he is anxiously waiting and striving for. . . .

"To illustrate the relation between the 'realized eschatology' and its future reality, we refer to O. Cullmann's comparison of the final *eschaton* with V-Day. In the course of a war the decisive battle may have been fought long before the real end of the war. Only those who realize the decisiveness of the critical battle will also be certain that victory is from now on assured. The many will only believe it when V-Day is proclaimed. Thus Calvary and the Resurrection, the decisive events in the history of salvation, assure the believer of the Day of the Lord in the ultimate future" (17 Löwith).

the State are in reality not contradictions; rather they are rooted in this chronological tension.

Primitive Christian eschatology is not merely a waiting for the future, as Albert Schweitzer and his disciples in Switzerland maintain; but neither is it merely faith in the present as already fulfilled, "realised eschatology," to use C. H. Dodd's expression. It is both. And above all, it is important to me to emphasise that this *tension* between "now" and "one day" did not make its first appearance only as a secondary solution offered by a Christianity already developing toward catholicism. It does not represent a later solution born of embarrassment, as Albert Schweitzer's disciples[1] and Rudolf Bultmann also maintain. It is rather, I emphasise, both essentially and from the beginning characteristic of the situation of the New Covenant. That the end-time is expected shortly is nothing new: it is a Jewish hope. What is new is this: that this hope in the future is combined with the faith that the end-time has already begun. And this characteristic connection between present and future is already to be found *in Jesus himself*.[2] On one hand we hear that the Kingdom of God is still expected soon; on the other, Jesus says that he has already seen Satan fall from heaven (Luke 10:18); that "The Kingdom of God has already come upon you" since he "by the Spirit of God casts out demons" (Matt. 12:28). "Go and tell John what you see and hear," he replies when the Baptist's emissaries ask whether he is the one who is coming (that is, who is to come in the future): "The blind see again, the lame walk, lepers are cleansed, the deaf hear, the dead are raised up, and the Gospel is preached to the poor!" (Matt. 11:4f).

The existence of this tension between present and future: this is what is new, what makes its appearance with Jesus. Otherwise we should still be in Judaism. If the hope in the future is more intensive than in Judaism, this is precisely because there is present the conviction that the end-time has already been inaugurated. For the "not yet consummated" is to be emphasised just as strongly as the "already inaugurated." Both together: that is the New Testament.

This is why the New Testament neither affirms nor denies the world. The dualism which we find in the New Testament is a chronological dualism between Now and the Future. It is not the hellenistic dualism between thisworldliness and otherworldliness. Therefore the Christian antithesis does not lead to the ascetic renunciation of present conditions, among which the State belongs in the first rank. It is wrong for one to deduce *only* the negative side from the saying in I Cor. 7:29ff, about the

---

1. See for example F. Buri, *Das Problem der ausgebliebenen Parusie, Schweiz. Theol. Umschau,* 1946, pp. 97ff. In answer to Buri's work, see O. Cullmann, *Das wahre durch die ausgebliebene Parusie gestellte neutestamentlichen Problem, Theol. Zeitschrift,* 1947, pp. 177ff.
2. See W. G. Kümmel, *Verheissung und Erfüllung,* 2nd. ed., 1953.

married who are to live as though they were not married, those that weep as if they did not weep, those who rejoice as if they did not rejoice, those who trade as if they possessed nothing. What is said here presupposes also that the Christians are *still* marrying, *still* weeping, *still* rejoicing, *still* trading. In this respect I agree with Amos N. Wilder when he says that the New Testament does not know "otherworldliness." [3] To be sure, however, the other side, the negative, remains in full force.

We have found this same duality also in the attitude toward the State. Indeed the genuine State of the Christians, the "politeuma," is in heaven, as Paul says in Phil. 3:20; but the earthly State is God's servant so long as it remains in the order which is willed by God. The State does not have to be Christian. The Roman State in Romans 13 was heathen. It can remain in God's present order without itself knowing that it does so, if it remains only State and does not try to be more than State. It possesses a knowledge of good and evil which is given to it even as a heathen State. The Christian, to be sure, knows about the place the State occupies in God's economy of salvation; he knows why the State is able to distinguish between good and evil. Therefore, paradoxical as it may seem, it is precisely the Christian who is able to ascribe a higher dignity to the State—even the heathen State—than the non-Christian citizen can do. To be sure, however, for just this reason the Christian will see his assignment regarding the State in these terms: that he remain in principle critical towards it, and that he watch to see that at no point does the State, whichever it may be, fall away from the divine order. And for the same reason, because on the basis of the Christian revelation he knows of the State's place within the divine order, the Christian will also be more keenly sensitive than any other citizen when a State falls away from God's order. Where others see that a State is becoming "totalitarian" the Christian sees that the powers, subjected by Christ to God's service, are once again breaking loose and becoming satanic. Heathen State and Gospel are therefore thoroughly compatible. Gospel and a totalitarian State in any guise and in any particular point are in principle incompatible.

The Church's task with regard to the State, which is posed for all time, is thus clear. First, it must loyally give the State everything necessary to its existence. It has to oppose anarchy and all Zealotism within its own ranks. Second, it has to fulfil the office of watchman over the State. That means: it must remain in principle critical toward *every* State and be ready to warn it against transgression of its legitimate limits. Third, it must deny to the State which exceeds its limits whatever such a State demands that lies within the province of religio-ideological excess; and in its preaching the Church must courageously describe this excess as opposition to God.

The Church will fulfil this assignment if it remains faithful to the

---

3. A. N. Wilder, *Otherworldliness and the New Testament*, 1954.

fundamental eschatological attitude of the New Testament. It could be shown how in the course of history the Church has always assumed a false attitude toward the State when it has forgotten that the present time is already fulfilment, but not yet consummation. Then we get such erroneous solutions as meet us ever and again in history: either that the Church tries to put itself in the place of the State: or else that the State is simply accepted uncritically in all that it does, as if there were no problem at all. Although the bearing of the Church in the two cases is radically opposite, in both cases the Church is guilty of the same fault: relinquishment of the New Testament interpretation of the end-time.

Just this interpretation is the association of Church and State in a peaceful and fruitful co-existence.

On the side of the State the stipulation is—not that it must necessarily be Christian—but indeed that it know its *limits* (and that it can do so we have heard in the Epistle to the Romans). Secondly, moreover, that it take the trouble to *understand* as much of the attitude of its Christian subjects as it is *able* to understand. In this connection the cross of Jesus should serve the State as a warning signal.

Patterns: Slack Definition

Cullmann's essay, even though it is the conclusion rather than the introduction to *The State in the New Testament*, is nevertheless prone to slack definition. Throughout the essay Cullmann dwells on the "tension" between present and future-time and establishes this tension initially with some clarity. Starting with paragraph four, however, things become opaque. The opening statement is negative—"The New Testament neither affirms nor denies the world"—and therefore fails to inform us in positive terms what the Christian attitude is. He continues to develop his argument by recourse to negatives: "It is not the hellinistic . . . The Christian antithesis does not lead . . . It is wrong for one to deduce . . ." Cullmann does not direct us to the proper deduction, however; he merely informs us that "Christians are *still* marrying, *still* weeping, *still* rejoicing, *still* trading." But such remarks are completely self-evident and tantamount to informing us that Christians *still* live. It is not Christian life that Cullmann is attempting to define, but Christian attitudes toward the state. To say that Christians are worldly merely because they continue to live, is to destroy the meaning of worldliness.

Paragraph five, in which Cullmann attempts to establish the limits of the state, remains general and abstract throughout. We are informed that the state is acceptable "if it remains only State and does not try to be more than State"; we also learn that "it possesses a knowledge of good and evil." We even learn that the Christian "knows why the State is able to distinguish between good and evil." But nowhere is a norm for the State as *State* presented; nor do we ever learn what distinguishes "good from evil." We are told the State has a "place within the divine order" and that the Christian will "be more keenly sensitive than any other citizen when a State falls away from God's order." But Cullmann never defines behavior that could be considered falling away. Is the issuing of contraceptive pills to college girls and unwed mothers falling away? Is legalized abortion? Is the Vietnam war? We are never told.

Cullmann is a great scholar, but this is not one of his better essays, for throughout the essay we dwell in the world of undefined abstraction. On the surface, the essay is strangely comforting; it asserts a healthy moral and practical relationship between church and state. The deeper perception of ambiguity, however, is troubling. What did your response to the essay reveal about your attitudes toward Church and State relations, and about the level at which you read the essay?

Problems

1. What is the Christian attitude toward historical progress?
2. What is the nature of the "tension" Cullmann speaks of? How does this tension affect the Christian's attitude toward the State?
3. Is the Christian's attitude toward the State likely to be progressive and innovative or conservative and traditional? Why?
4. Cullmann repeatedly speaks of the State being bound by "divine order" and "legitimate limits." What would be the nature of that "order" and those "limits," and how would a Christian know them?
5. Does your reading of Romans agree with Cullmann's?

12 REINHOLD NIEBUHR

A Christian existentialist and former Professor of Applied Christianity at Union Theological Seminary, Reinhold Niebuhr (1892–) is not technically a theologian. His primary concern, as indicated by the title of his professorship and of this essay, "The Social Resources of Religion," is applied Christianity, its personal relevance and social application. Like many others, Niebuhr has been troubled by the growing collectivization of human life in the pursuit of secular ideals, ideals that are so rooted in an absolute belief in progress they become corrupt. What Niebuhr and the Western World have witnessed in the twentieth century is barbarism run amuck in the name of a higher humanity. Christianity, by its incessant reminder of human sin and pride, is for Niebuhr a tonic against the assumption that man, given sufficient desire and dedication, can create a utopia. Niebuhr argues that man is both more and yet less than a passenger on a swift train to utopia, that only Christianity has captured man's true essence and those constants that mock utopian ideals. As this essay from Niebuhr's book, Does Civilization Need Religion? *(1927), suggests, religion provides man with inner resources that ultimately become social ones.*

The Social Resources of Religion

The task of analyzing and isolating the ethical limitations and the social deficiencies of religion is to no purpose if there is not in religion itself, at its best, some resources which civilization and society need for the solution of their problems. Some critics of religion discount it entirely as a social force, or at least as a force of social progress. Bertrand Russell's prejudices on this subject are too violent to make his testimony against religion particularly weighty. Yet he speaks for a large number of ethically sensitive individuals who share his critical attitude, if not his vehemence,

From Reinhold Niebuhr, *Does Civilization Need Religion?* (New York: The Macmillan Co., 1941), pp. 35–62.

when he declares: "Since the thirteenth century the church has consistently encouraged men's blood lust and avarice and discouraged every approach to human and kindly feeling. . . . Emancipation from the churches is still an essential condition of improvement, particularly in America where the churches have more influence than in Europe. . . . Of all requisites for the regeneration of society the decay of religion seems to me to have the best chance of being realized." [1] The number of people among the middle and higher classes who would subscribe to such a denunciation of organized religion is probably not very large. But there are very many who ignore the church as a force for social amelioration; and in the class of industrial workers a temper against the church exceeding even Mr. Russell's violence is very general.

Whatever may be the facts in regard to contemporary religion and to other specific types of organized religious life, it is relevant to ask whether religion as such, freed from its specific limitations, contains indispensable resources for the ethical reconstruction of society.

The first resource which would seem to be of social value is the social imagination which religion, at its best, develops upon the basis of its high evaluation of personality. A spiritual interpretation of the universe may not issue automatically in a high appreciation of human personality, but religion is never quite able to deny this ethical implication of its faith, and in occasional moments of high insight it revels in it. It persuades men to regard their fellows as their brothers because they are all children of God. It insists, in other words, that temporal circumstance and obvious differences are dwarfed before the spiritual affinities which men have through their common relation to a divine creator. Thus Jesus could deal sympathetically with the harlot of the street, the publican at the gate, the Samaritan woman at the well and the blinded fanatics and their dupes who crucified him. The apostle Paul, though he did not always understand the genius of his master, was nevertheless able to apprehend this central dogma at the heart of religion and declare: "In Christ there is neither Jew nor Greek, neither bond nor free." Celsus, the critic of the Christian church in the first century, derides the church for its failure to distinguish between outcasts and respectable citizens. The fervor and consistency with which the church has espoused the ideal of the equal worth of all personalities has not always equaled that of the early church; many compromises with the brute facts of history have been made; yet the church has never been able to betray this faith altogether. The missionary enterprise with all its weaknesses is still a revelation of this power in religion. Oceans are bridged and varying circumstances of race and environment are ignored in order that the soul inspired by God may claim kinship with other souls of every race and every clime.

The physical characteristics and outward circumstances in which

1. *Prospects of Industrial Civilization,* page 218.

men differ are sometimes not so great as they seem to the superficial observer; wherefore education may do as much as religion to cultivate and discover those profounder unities which made all men brothers. There are hatreds which are due merely to misunderstanding. They spring from the parochialism of the average mind, which knows no better than to regard with contempt what differs from the standards and values to which it has become habituated. Education and culture may emancipate men from such hatreds. Other misunderstandings which are caused by a superficial analysis of men's action may be dissipated by a profounder appreciation of the complex life of every individual out of which each action emerges. Yet understanding alone does not solve all the problems of living together. We do not hate only those whom we do not know or understand. Sometimes we hate those most whom we know best. Love does not flow inevitably out of intimacy. Intimacy may merely accentuate previous attitudes, whether they be benevolent or malevolent. Anthropologists are easily obsessed with the inequalities which men reveal in their natural state, and the very abundance of their knowledge prompts them to an ethically enervating determinism when they attempt to gauge the potentialities of so-called primitive peoples. The modern psychologists are more inclined to accept the dogma of the total depravity of man than the ancient theologians were, and they prove thereby that a profound knowledge of human nature need not incline men to regard human beings with reverence and affection. Mr. H. L. Mencken may not speak for the scientists, but he is somewhat typical of the cynicism which follows in the wake of intellectualism. His estimate of human beings is: "Man is a sick fly taking a dizzy ride on a gigantic flywheel. . . . He is lazy, improvident, unclean. . . . Life is a combat between jackals and jackasses." Love is always slightly irrational and requires an irrational urge for its support. It is at least as irrational as hatred and the same intelligence which mitigates the one may enervate the other. A highly sophisticated intelligence is generally unable to survey the human scene with any higher attitude than that of pity for human beings, and pity is a form of contempt under a thin disguise of sympathy.

The facts of human nature are sufficiently complex to validate almost any hypothesis which may be projected into them. Therefore the assumptions upon which we essay our social contacts are all important. One reason why the social sciences can never attain the scientific prestige of the physical sciences to which they aspire is that the importance of hypotheses increases with the complexity and variability of the data into which they are projected. Every assumption is an hypothesis, and human nature is so complex that it justifies almost every assumption and prejudice with which either a scientific investigation or an ordinary human contact is initiated. A vital religion not only prompts men to venture the assumption that human beings are essentially trustworthy and lovable, but it endows them with the courage and inclination to maintain their hypothesis when immediate facts contradict it until fuller facts are brought in to verify it. Mere sentiment is easily defeated by life's disappointing realities. Anatole France observed that if one started with the supposition that men are naturally good and virtuous, one inevitably ends by wishing to kill them all. Human nature is neither lovable nor trustworthy in its undisciplined state and a sentimental overestimate of its virtue may well result in the reaction to which Anatole France alludes. Yet its underdeveloped resources are always greater than either a superficial or critical intelligence is able to fathom. There must be an element of faith in love if it is to be creative. "Love," said Paul, "believes all things"; and it may be added that it saves its faith from absurdity by creating some of the evidence which justifies its assumptions. It "hopes till hope creates from its own wreck the thing it contemplates." Nothing less than a religious appreciation of personality, supported by a spiritual interpretation of the universe itself in terms of moral goodwill, will make love robust enough to overcome momentary disappointments and gain its final victory. The injunction of Jesus to his disciples to forgive not seven times, but seventy times seven, represents the natural social strategy of a robust and vital religious idealism, which subdues evil by its unswerving confidence in the good.

While it is true that religion does not issue automatically in an attitude of reverence and goodwill toward all human personalities, it nevertheless remains a fact that a religious world view does incline men to regard their fellow men from a perspective which obscures differences and imperfections and reveals affinities and potential virtue. Even if intelligence became imaginative enough to discover the affinities, it could not be courageous enough to challenge the evil in men in the name of their better selves. The art of forgiveness can be learned only in the school of religion. And it is an art which men must learn increasingly as a complex society makes human associations more and more intimate. Whatever improvement a growing social science may establish in the technique of social intercourse, men will never escape the necessity of overcoming the evil, which they inflict upon each other, by creative patience and courageous trust. A higher intelligence may mitigate our fears and an exacter justice may restrain the inclination to wreak vengeance upon the wrongdoer; but only the stubborn forces of religion will turn fear into trust and hatred into love. Sometimes mutual fear and hatred reduce themselves to such an absurdity (as in the late World War) that even a superficial intelligence can recognize it; but their absurdity does not become patent until they have issued in mutual annihilation. Even then the person with an ordinary commonsense view of life can do no better than to substitute partial trust for fear and partial understanding for hatred. So one war breeds the next. All men are potentially at once our foes and our friends. An unreflective social life assumes that they are enemies and helps to make them so. A higher social intelligence establishes a nicely balanced compromise between trust and mistrust so that the one cannot be very creative and the other not too destructive. Only the foolishness of faith knows how to assume the brotherhood of man and to create it by the help of the assumption. A religious ideal is always a little absurd because it insists on the truth of what ought to be true but is only partly true; it is however the ultimate wisdom, because reality slowly approaches the ideals which are implicit in its life. A merely realistic analysis of any given set of facts is therefore as dangerous as it is helpful. The creative and redemptive force is a faith which defies the real in the name of the ideal, and subdues it.

Love is, in short, a religious attitude. There are circumstances in which it may prosper without the inspiration of religion. In the family relation and in other intimate circles proximity and consanguinity may prompt men to regard human beings as essentially good, and direct experience validate their faith. That is why Jesus discounted love in the family as a religious achievement. "If ye love those who love you, what thanks have ye?" In the secondary relations, which are no longer secondary in the matter of importance to human welfare, the matter is not so simple. In these only a sublime assumption will persuade men to embark upon the adventure of brotherhood, and only a robust and constantly replenished faith will inure them against inevitable disappointments. The religious interpretation of the world is essentially an insistence that the ideal is real and that the real can be understood only in the light of the ideal. Since the family relation is the most ethical relation men know, religious faith interprets all life in terms of that relation. In view of many of the facts of history which seem to reveal the world of man as but a projection of the world of nature in which animal fights with animal and herd with herd, this kind of interpretation is superficially too absurd to persuade a highly sophisticated intelligence. It is the truth which is withheld from the wise and revealed to babes. Yet it is the truth without which men will not be able to build a peaceful society. It is the truth which even the physical facts of a highly complex civilization, in which space and time are being annihilated, are conspiring to make true. The races and groups of mankind are obviously not living as a family; but they ought to. And as the necessity becomes more urgent the truth of the ideal becomes more real.

It would be foolish to insist that goodwill alone will create conscience and that to detect the ethical core at the heart of man's being is all that is required to make him ethical. It is a task to persuade human beings to trust their fellows; but [it] is equally important to prompt their fellows to trustworthy action. If human nature is left unchallenged and undeveloped, it hardly qualifies the brute struggle for survival sufficiently to validate any religion or ethic of trust. Men's actions are not as free as we have imagined. The social, economic and psychological sciences have restricted the concept of freedom in the soul of man as the physical sciences have restricted it in the universe. Man is not only less free than he had once imagined, but he is not as free as he once was. If science has discredited the idea of freedom, civilization has circumscribed the fact. It is easier for man to act as an ethical individual in a comparatively simple social group, such as the family, than in a very large and complex social group when even the most robust ethical purpose must meet the resistance and the corruption of the primitive and untamed desires of the group. If man is capable of sacrificing immediate advantages for ultimate ones and his own advantages for the sake of society, this capacity is an achievement which he gains only after much effort and preserves from corruption only at the price of eternal vigilance. The first requisite of an ethical life in modern civilization is a realization of the difficulties which face the human conscience in maintaining itself against the pressure of immediate desires to which the whole emotional life of man is wedded. It is not easy to sacrifice meat for beauty, pleasure for some seemingly ephemeral value, self-interest for the sake of the family, the interest of the family for the sake of society, the interest of our generation for the society of to-morrow. Yet only by such sacrifices can man prove the reality and potency of his creative will. If such sacrifices are not actually made, all so-called morality becomes in fact a device for obscuring the bestiality of man without overcoming it.

The fact that, in spite of the pressure of the struggle for survival, man has created a kingdom of values in which truth, beauty and goodness have been made real, is proof that he is more free and more moral than the modern cynic is willing to concede. But his kingdom of values is never as uncorrupted as he imagines. The task therefore of binding men to spiritual values, and of prompting them to sacrifice immediate pleasures and physical satisfactions for them, is difficult almost to the point of desperation. Religion makes its contribution to it by giving man the assurance that the world of values really has a relevant place in the universe and that values are permanent and will be conserved. He is challenged to sacrifice in a universe in which love is a basic law. He is asked to prefer personal values to property values in a world in which personality is the highest reality. He is prompted to exercise his conscience under the scrutiny and with the sympathy of a higher conscience. Religion in its purest form does not guarantee man an immediate reward for every ethical achievement; indeed it may offer him no reward at all except the reward which inheres in the act itself. But it does give him the final satisfaction of guaranteeing the reality of a universe which is not blind to the values for which he must pay such a high price, and which is not indifferent or hostile to his struggle. It asks him to respect human personality because the universe itself, in spite of some obvious evidence to the contrary, knows how to conserve personality; and to create values in a world in which values are not an effervescence but a reality. Religion is in short the courageous logic which makes the ethical struggle consistent with world facts. In its most vital form religion validates its sublime assumptions in immediate experience and gives man an unshakable certainty. It thus becomes the dynamic of moral action as well as the logic which makes the action reasonable.

The force of its faith operates not only to preserve moral vigor but to sensitize moral judgments. The God of religious devotion is not only revealed in the moral values of the universe outside of man, but he is revealed in the aspirations of man which are beyond his achievements. God insures not only the preservation of values but their perfection. All moral achievement is qualified by the relativities of time and circumstance. The worship of a holy God saves the soul from taking premature satisfaction in its partial achievement. It subjects every moral value to comparison with a more perfect moral ideal. Of course the absolute perfection of God is itself conditioned by the imperfect human insight which conceives it. A cruel age may picture God more cruel than itself, and to a generation lusting for power God may be the supreme tyrant. Thus religion may become the sanctification of human imperfections. Yet in its highest form religion does inculcate a wholesome spirit of humility which gives the soul no peace in any virtue while higher virtue is attainable.

The force of religion in moral action and the necessity of religious assurance for the highest type of social life may be gauged by an analysis of possible alternatives to a social life which is oriented by a religious world view. There are two real alternatives to such a life. The one is based upon an ethical but unreligious world view, and the other scorns both ethics and religion in its absolute determinism. An ethical life which claims no support from religion may on occasion develop a very high type of social idealism, particularly since it escapes the ethical defects of religion even while it sacrifices religious resources. Stoicism is in many respects superior to pantheistic religions; for there are moral advantages in underestimating rather than overestimating the virtue of the universe. It is better to create a sense of tension between the conscience of man and a morally indifferent nature than to obscure the moral defects of nature by a deification of the natural order. But if men disavow all faith in a power not their own which makes for righteousness, they cannot finally save themselves from either arrogance or despair. Religion may destroy man's self-reliance by an undue sense of humility, but even that limitation is no more destructive of moral values than a self-reliance which prompts the human spirit to strut for a while on this narrow world in the consciousness of unique virtue before capitulating to a world which is too blind to know what it has destroyed. Thomas Huxley thought he would as soon worship "a wilderness of monkeys" as to give himself to the worship of humanity after the fashion of Comte. To insist too strenuously upon the uniqueness of human life in the cosmic order must inevitably issue in the pride which such a worship implies. Since the Renaissance there has been a marked decay of the spirit of humility in Western civilization which is closely associated with the secularization of its ethical idealism. The difference between the pride of secular idealism and the humility implicit in genuine religion may be gauged, as Professor Irving Babbitt suggests, by comparing Confucius with Buddha and Marcus Aurelius with Jesus. Pascal thought the stoics were guilty of "diabolical pride." The judgment may be too severe, but it must be confessed that a purely secular idealism has difficulty in escaping a morally destructive arrogance from which true religion is saved because it subjects all values and achievements to measurement, with its absolutes as the criteria. "Why callest thou me good?" said Jesus: "no one is good save God." In the religion of Jesus the perfection of God is consistently defined as an absolute love by comparison with which all altruistic achievements fall short. "I say unto you, love your enemies; bless them that curse you; do good to them that despitefully use you and persecute you; that ye may be children of your Father in heaven; for he maketh his sun to rise on the evil and the good and sendeth rain upon the just and on the unjust. For if ye love them which love you, what reward have ye? Do not even the publicans the same? . . . Be ye therefore perfect even as your Father in heaven is perfect." [2] Here the value of an absolute standard to save from undue pride in partial ethical achievements is particularly apparent. Prudential morality can hardly go beyond the encouragement of altruism within the social group, i.e. loving those "which love you." That is precisely what Stoicism did. It is just this pride in partial achievement which complicates the moral problem of modern life; for our ethical difficulties are created by the very tendency of reasonable ethics to make life within groups moral and never to aspire to the moral redemption of inter-group relations. Humility is therefore a spiritual grace which has value not only for its own sake but for its influence upon social problems. Traditional religions, which live off of original inspirations and experiences without recreating them, easily fall into a pride of their own, the pride which comes from identifying the absolute standards of their inspired source with their partial achievements and inevitable compromises. But religion in its purest and most unspoiled form is always productive of a spirit of humility which regards every moral achievement as but a vantage point from which new ventures of faith and life are to be initiated toward the alluring perfection which is in God.

An ethical idealism unsupported by religion is almost as certain to issue in final despair as in unjustified pride. A few choice spirits are some-

2. Matthew v. 43–48.

times able to imagine themselves in rebellion against the universe without finally succumbing to a temper of sullenness; but the dreadful logic of insisting upon conscience in a conscienceless world inevitably leaves its mark upon the multitude. Oswald Spengler, in his morphology of civilizations,[3] presents "religion without God" as the unvarying symptom of a dying civilization, too sophisticated to believe in the cosmic worth of its moral values but not quite ready to abandon them. The enervating effect of a moral idealism which has sacrificed its hopes with its illusions always becomes apparent in the long run, but frequently it reveals itself quite immediately in the very lives of its most robust champions.

Mr. Russell may think that the "firm foundation of unyielding despair" is an adequate basis for an ethical life, but his own growing bitterness betrays how such a philosophy corrupts moral idealism with a sense of frustration. The idealist is put into the position of sacrificing everything for values which have no guaranteed reality in the cosmic order. Even his faith in mankind is finally destroyed; for however precious personal values may seem in a given moment, his philosophy denies him the right to attribute any lasting worth to them. True religion gives man a sense of both humility and security before the holiness which is at once the source and the goal of his virtue; and thus it saves him at the same time from premature complacency and ultimate despair. The choice between irreligious and religious idealism is the choice between pride which issues in despondency and humility which becomes the basis of self-respect. There is an irrational element in either alternative; but the irreligious idealist is in error when he imagines that he has chosen the more reasonable alternative; his choice is no more reasonable and morally much less potent.

The absolute determinists who have as little confidence in the moral integrity of human nature as in any moral meaning in cosmic facts are more consistent than the Stoics, but they are involved in worse absurdities. Their cynicism robs them of both an adequate motive and an adequate method for social reconstruction. Discounting moral idealism even while they exhibit it in their social passion, they ostensibly desire social reconstruction only in the interest of the class to which they belong. But their personal interests are not frequently identical with those of the oppressed classes and they are moved as much by sympathy for the plight of the victims of our present society as by any selfish considerations. They profess to be prompted by the reflection that individual action has become useless in a capitalistic age and that it is possible to advance the interests of an individual only by making common cause with other individuals in a similar predicament. Meanwhile there is hardly an economic determinist, even among those who are actually members of the class of the oppressed, who could not gain higher advantages for

3. *The Decline of the West.*

himself by disassociating himself from his class than by making common cause with it. This is certainly true of those who are intelligent enough to evolve or elaborate the theory of absolute determinism.

Absolute determinism, when developed consistently, must disavow all other methods of social reconstruction but that of ruthless conflict. If nothing qualifies the self-interest of men, a conflict of interests becomes inevitable. This defect in method is even more important than the defect in its motive. A ruthless struggle can result in an ordered society only if the victors are able to annihilate their foes. But even in that event the interests of the members of any class engaged in a social or political struggle will cease to be identical as soon as its foes are eliminated. Thus a new and equally ruthless struggle must result between the comparatively strong and comparatively weak, the comparatively privileged and the comparatively underprivileged victors. Ultimately men cannot escape the necessity of building a stable society by the mutual compromise and the mutual sacrifice of conflicting rights. The determinists have made an important contribution to the modern social problem by revealing the brutal nature of much of man's social life. Even if the human conscience could be sensitized to a much greater degree than now seems probable, it will not be possible to eliminate conflict between various social and economic groups.[4] Good men do not easily realize how selfish they are if someone does not resist their selfishness; and they are not inclined to abridge their power if someone does not challenge their right to hold it. Religious and moral idealism cannot be expected to eliminate, but it can be expected to mitigate social warfare. The conscience of man must finally be the force which builds a new society; and a man with a conscience must be the end for which such a society is built. If there is no virtue in man which lifts him above the brute struggle for survival, there is no value in him to justify the effort of building a new and more perfect society—and he is not the stuff out of which such a society can be built. It is difficult to escape the conclusion that the reverence for personality which is implicit in religion is necessary to establish an adequate motive and an adequate method of social reconstruction. Reverence for personality qualifies the individual's will to power so that his life can be integrated with other lives with a minimum of conflict; and it saves society from sacrificing the individual to the needs of the group. In the religion of Jesus both a social and an individualistic emphasis issues from a spiritual appreciation of human personality. The

4. Stuart Mill's refutation of LePlay's thesis that the salvation of the working classes can come only through the benevolence of their superiors is worth quoting in this connection: "No times can be pointed out in which the higher classes of this or any other country performed a part even distantly resembling the one assigned to them in this theory. All privileged and powerful classes have used their power in the interest of their own selfishness. I do not affirm that what has always been must always be. This at least seems to be undeniable, that long before superior classes could be sufficiently inspired to govern in the tutelary manner supposed, the inferior classes would be too much improved to be governed."

individual is given a place and prestige which he never before possessed in society. Western civilization owes much to the high evaluation of the individual which Jesus introduced into the thought of the world. On the other hand this emphasis is saved from mere individualism by an ethic which helps the individual to realize his highest self by sacrificing personal advantages for social values.

The contribution of religion to the task of an ethical reconstruction of society is its reverence for human personality and its aid in creating the type of personality which deserves reverence. Men cannot create a society if they do not believe in each other. They cannot believe in each other if they cannot see the potential in the real facts of human nature. And they cannot have the faith which discovers potentialities if they cannot interpret human nature in the light of a universe which is perfecting and not destroying personal values.

Patterns: Unsupported Assertions

Niebuhr's essay attempts to unfold insights into the human psyche which make religion a valuable social resource. Such insights may exist and they may be persuasive, but Niebuhr's manner of conveying his insights reduces the effectiveness of an otherwise persuasive argument. He fails to recognize that an insight is a discovery, and hence must be argued or corroborated by evidence; he treats insights as if they were matters of consensus, as if one has really developed "sight into" something when there is widespread agreement that penetration has occurred. The consequence of this confusion is farreaching.

Niebuhr's essay is badly compromised by a double standard—religion at its *best*, "human nature" at its *worst*. But what we wish to argue is that his essay is strewn with unsupported assertions and with poorly supported insights. To cite a few examples of the former: "modern psychologists are more inclined to accept the dogma of the total depravity of man than the ancient theologians" (195/19-21). (Note that Niebuhr is writing in 1927 and not 1970, but the observation was questionable even then.) "Even if intelligence became imaginative enough to discover the affinities [between men], it could not be courageous enough to challenge the evil in men in the name of their better selves" (196/25-28). This is precisely what Marxism does and what some existentialists do, and it is the cornerstone of Aristotle's entire concept of the magnanimous man. "The art of forgiveness can be learned only in the school of religion" (196/28-29). Poorly supported insights abound. "Mr. H. L. Mencken . . . is somewhat typical of the cynicism which follows in the wake of intellectualism" (196/24-25). "Love is, in short, a religious attitude" (197/12). "The family relation is the most ethical relation men know . . ." (197/25). "If men disavow all faith in a power not their own which makes for righteousness, they cannot finally save themselves from either arrogance or despair" (199/37-39). One could go on, but there is no need.

In a sense, all insights are intuitive and require verification of a less rigorous sort. Moreover, in an essay, it is impossible to engage in lengthy supportive illustrations that are tangential to one's main argument. Finally, consensus does have its place in insights, for some of our fears and aspirations are, in a sense, consensus insights. We accept on faith, even before we have had time to test them, the consensus that such or such behavior is harmful or destructive or that happiness will follow a cautious pragmatism similar to this person's or that person's. But because something is common, it is not therefore acceptable.

For example, because insights are intuitive, they are capable of perversion. Witness intuitions that have led people to great speculative or gambling losses. Secondly, consensus is a very shoddy form of support. It leads to glorification of the conventional, to bromides and trite observations. In a more intense form, consensus inhibits originality; it leads to preservation of the tried and true, the unimaginative and readily comprehensible. In its most outrageous perversion, consensus insights lead to national schizophrenia, as they did in the Nazis' "insights" into racial superiority.

Much of what Niebuhr has to say is admirable and persuasive, but it is persuasive because it appeals to reader bias or reader experience. As such, it does not illuminate the new; it recapitulates the old. Insights are thus debased into commonplaces and eviscerated of creative value. The essay is genial and a rather pleasant statement, but might that not be true because we prefer to share old truths rather than be troubled by new ones?

Problems

1. What in Niebuhr's opinion are the "social resources" of religion?
2. Does Niebuhr's argument acknowledge and compensate for the disparity between religious "theory" and religious "practice"? Is this relevant to his argument? Should it affect our response?
3. What is Niebuhr's attitude toward the human intellect? Is his attitude in keeping with earlier Christian thinkers? Do you agree with his attitude?
4. Niebuhr throughout his essay makes his point by using psychological insight in the form of assertions about the human condition. How accurate are his assertions about "human nature," "human motivation," "human behavior." What, if any, are his biases?
5. Central to Niebuhr's argument is the concept of the "self-fulfilling prophesy"—a notion that beliefs have within them the power to become true merely by virtue of their existence and intensity. Why is this an important assumption for Niebuhr? To what extent do you agree with it?

13 WILLIAM BARRETT

"Hebraism and Hellenism" is the fourth chapter from William Barrett's Irrational Man *(1958), a book that, in attempting to answer the question, "What is the meaning of Existentialism?" asks another: "Is rationalism a large enough shelter in which to enclose man?" In other words, does man not lose much—perhaps the best of himself—by an obsession with an abstract or pragmatic rationalism?*

Barrett, Professor of Philosophy at New York University, is intent on analyzing "the present age" as a means of bringing us to an awareness of its uniqueness and our opportunity to shape it. This chapter discusses the origins of two major strands of Western thought: existentialism and rationalism. As such, it prepares us for the conflicts between the two as they work themselves out in modern society and also as they work themselves out in the remaining sections of this anthology.

Hebraism and Hellenism

In the celebrated chapter with this same title, in his *Culture and Anarchy,* a book about the contemporary situation in nineteenth-century England that has much to say to us even today, Matthew Arnold writes:

> We show, as a nation, laudable energy and persistence in walking according to the best light we have, but are not quite careful enough, perhaps, to see that our light be not darkness. This is only another version of the old story that energy is our strong point and favorable characteristic, rather than intelligence. But we may give to this idea a more general form still, in which it will have a yet larger range of application. We may regard this energy driving at practice, this paramount sense of the obligation of duty, self-control, and work, this earnestness in going manfully

From William Barrett, *Irrational Man* (Garden City: Doubleday & Co., 1958), pp. 69–91.

> with the best light we have, as one force. And we may regard the intelligence driving at those ideas which are, after all, the basis of right practice, the ardent sense for all the new and changing combinations of them which man's development brings with it, the indomitable impulse to know and adjust them perfectly, as another force. And these two forces we may regard as in some sense rivals—rivals not by the necessity of their own nature, but as exhibited in man and his history—and rivals dividing the empire of the world between them. And to give these forces names from two races of men who have supplied the most splendid manifestations of them, we may call them respectively the forces of Hebraism and Hellenism. Hebraism and Hellenism—between these two points of influence moves our world. At one time it feels more powerfully the attraction of one of them, at another time of the other; and it ought to be, though it never is, evenly and happily balanced between them.

Hebraism sometimes seems for Arnold to wear too markedly the stiff bewhiskered face of a British mid-Victorian member of the Dissenting Churches. We have learned a good deal about the Hebraic mind, since his day, and our picture of it will be more complicated. Nevertheless, it is well to begin with this genial and simple passage from Arnold, which so rightly perceives the distinction between the two types and sets forth their long historical battle in such clearcut terms.

The distinction, as Arnold so lucidly states it, arises from the difference between doing and knowing. The Hebrew is concerned with practice, the Greek with knowledge. Right conduct is the ultimate concern of the Hebrew, right thinking that of the Greek. Duty and strictness of conscience are the paramount things in life for the Hebrew; for the Greek, the spontaneous and luminous play of the intelligence. The Hebrew thus extols the moral virtues as the substance and meaning of life; the Greek subordinates them to the intellectual virtues, and Arnold rightly observes: "The moral virtues are with Aristotle but the porch and access to the intellectual, and with these last is blessedness." So far all this is quite simple and clear: the contrast is between practice and theory, between the moral man and the theoretical or intellectual man. But then Arnold goes on to make another point, which is somehow outside the framework with which he started:

> To get rid of one's ignorance, to see things as they are, and by seeing them as they are to see them in their beauty, is the simple and attractive ideal which Hellenism holds out before human nature; and from the simplicity and charm of this idea, Hellenism, and human life in the hands of Hellenism, is invested with a kind of aerial ease, clearness, and radiancy; they are full of what we call sweetness and light. Difficulties are kept out of view, and the beauty and rationalness of the ideal have all our thoughts.

While Arnold admires this ideal of sweetness and light, he nevertheless feels that it may not take into consideration one troubling aspect of the human condition, and he goes on to quote a remark that may or may not have been made by Thomas Carlyle:

> "Socrates," this saying goes, "is terribly *at ease in Zion.*" Hebraism —and here is the source of its wonderful strength—has always been severely preoccupied with an awful sense of the impossibility of being at ease in Zion; of the difficulties which oppose themselves to man's pursuit or attainment of that perfection of which Socrates talks so hopefully, and, as from this point of view one might almost say, so glibly. It is all very well to talk of getting rid of one's ignorance, of seeing things in their reality, seeing them in their beauty; but how is this to be done when there is something which thwarts and spoils all our efforts?
> This something is *sin.*

What Arnold perceives here is that deep within Biblical man lurks a certain *uneasiness,* which is not to be found in the conceptions of man given us by the great Greek philosophers. This uneasiness points toward another, and more central, region of human existence than the contrast between doing and knowing, morality and reason. To be sure, Arnold seeks to tie in this uneasiness of Biblical man with his main thesis, which is the distinction between moral practice and intellectual culture, by introducing the idea of sin. But the sinfulness that man experiences in the Bible—as in the Psalms or the Book of Job—cannot be confined to a supposed compartment of the individual's being that has to do with his moral acts. This sinfulness pervades the whole being of man: it *is* indeed man's being, insofar as in his feebleness and finiteness as a creature he stands naked in the presence of God. This idea of man's finiteness takes us beyond the distinctions of practice and theory, morality and knowledge, toward the center from which all such distinctions stem.

It is at this center that we must begin, in our rethinking of Arnold's distinction between Hebraism and Hellenism. We have learned a good deal not only about Hebraic thought but about the Greeks since Arnold's time, and we shall have to qualify his picture of the latter's aerial lightness and ease. The radiant and harmonious Greek Arnold depicted he had inherited from eighteenth-century classicism. We know considerably more now about Greek pessimism and the negation of life that it brought with it. We know more about the Orphic religions, which had their own powerful sense of the sinful and fallen state of man, and which exerted such an influence upon Plato. When Plato says that the body is a tomb and that to philosophize is to learn to die, he is not just tossing off a few idle rhetorical figures. From his Orphic and Pythagorean sources we can see that the whole impulse of philosophy for Plato arises from an ardent search for deliverance from the evils of the world and the curse of time.

The Greeks did not produce their tragic plays out of nothing, as Nietzsche was almost the first to observe less than a century ago. Greek tragedy comes out of an acute sense of the suffering and evil of life.

Nevertheless, Arnold is fundamentally right in his distinction between Hebrew and Greek, as is shown by the gifts bestowed on humanity by the two races: the Greeks gave us science and philosophy; the Hebrews gave us the Law. No other people—not the Chinese, not the Hindus—produced *theoretical* science, and its discovery or invention by the Greeks has been what has distinguished Western civilization from the other civilizations of the globe. In the same way, the uniqueness of Western religion is due to its Hebraic source, and the religious history of the West is the long story of the varying fortunes and mutations of the spirit of Hebraism.

1. THE HEBRAIC MAN OF EARTH

The Law, however, is not really at the center of Hebraism. At the center lies that which is the foundation and the basis of the Law, and without which the Law, even in the most Pharisaical tradition, would be but an empty shell. Here we have to think beyond Arnold. To be sure, the Law—the absolutely binding quality of its ritual and commandments—has been what has held the Jewish community together over its centuries of suffering and prevented this people from extermination. But if we go back to the Hebraic sources, to man as he is revealed to us in the Bible, we see that something more primitive and more fundamental lies at the basis of the moral law. We have to learn to reread the Book of Job in order to see this—reread it in a way that takes us beyond Arnold and into our own time, reread it with an historical sense of the primitive or primary mode of existence of the people who gave expression to this work. For earlier man, the outcome of the Book of Job was not such a foregone conclusion as it is for us later readers, for whom centuries of familiarity and forgetfulness have dulled the violence of the confrontation between man and God that is central to the narrative. For earlier man, seeing for the first time beyond the routine commandments of his religion, there was a Promethean excitement in Job's coming face to face with his Creator and demanding justification. The stage comparable to this, with the Greeks, is the emergence of critical and philosophical reflection upon the gods and their ways, the first use of rational consciousness as an instrument to examine a religion that had been up to that time traditional and ritualistic. The Hebrew, however, proceeds not by the way of reason but by the confrontation of the whole man, Job, in the fullness and violence of his passion with the unknowable and overwhelming God. And the final solution for Job lies not in the rational resolution of the problem, any more than it ever does in life, but in a change and conversion of the whole man. The relation between Job and God is a relation between an I and a Thou, to use Martin Buber's terms. Such a relation demands that each being confront the other in his completeness; it is not the confrontation of two rational minds each demanding an explanation that will satisfy reason. The relation between Job and God is on the level of existence and not of reason. Rational doubt, in the sense of the term that the later philosophic tradition of the West has made familiar to us, never enters Job's mind, even in the very paroxysm of his revolt. His relation to God remains one of faith from start to finish, though, to be sure, this faith takes on the varying shapes of revolt, anger, dismay, and confusion. Job says, *"Though he slay me, yet will I trust him,"* but he adds what is usually not brought to our attention as emphatically as the first part of his saying: *"But I will maintain my own ways before him."* Job retains his own identity ("his own ways") in confronting the Creator before whom he is as Nothing. Job in the many shades and turnings of his faith is close to those primitive peoples who may break, revile, and spit upon the image of a god who is no longer favorable. Similarly, in Psalm 89 David rebukes Yahweh for all the tribulations that He has poured upon His people, and there can be no doubt that we are here at the stage in history where faith is so real that it permits man to call God to account. It is a stage close to the primitive, but also a considerable step beyond it: for the Hebrew had added a new element, faith, and so internalized what was simply the primitive's anger against his god. When faith is full, it dares to express its anger, for faith is the openness of the whole man toward his God, and therefore must be able to encompass all human modes of being.

Faith is trust—in the sense, at least initially, in which in everday life we say we trust so-and-so. As trust it is the relation between one individual and another. Faith is trust before it is belief—belief in the articles, creeds, and tenets of a Church with which later religious history obscures this primary meaning of the word. As trust, in the sense of the opening up of one being toward another, faith does not involve any philosophical problem about its position relative to faith and reason. That problem comes up only later when faith has become, so to speak, propositional, when it has expressed itself in statements, creeds, systems. Faith as a concrete mode of being of the human person precedes faith as the intellectual assent to a proposition, just as truth as a concrete mode of human being precedes the truth of any proposition. Moreover, this trust that embraces a man's anger and dismay, his bones and his bowels—the whole man, in short—does not yet permit any separation of soul from body, of reason from man's irrational other half. In Job and the Psalms man is very much a man of flesh and blood, and his being as a creature is described time and again in images that are starkly physical:

> Remember, I beseech thee, that thou hast made me as the clay; and wilt thou bring me into the dust again?
> Hast thou not poured me out as milk, and curdled me like cheese?
> Thou hast clothed me with skin and flesh, and hast fenced me with bones and sinews.

And when Psalm 22 speaks of the sense of abandonment and dereliction, it uses not the high, rarefied language of introspection but the most powerful cry of the physical:

> My God, my God, why hast thou forsaken me? . . .
> Thou art he that took me out of the womb: thou didst make me hope when I was upon my mother's breasts.
> I was cast upon thee from the womb: thou art my God from my mother's belly . . .
> I am poured out like water, and all my bones are out of joint: my heart is like wax; it is melted in the midst of my bowels.
> My strength is dried up like a potsherd; and my tongue cleaveth to my jaws; and thou hast brought me into the dust of death.

Protestantism later sought to revive this face-to-face confrontation of man with his God, but could produce only a pallid replica of the simplicity, vigor, and wholeness of this original Biblical faith. Protestant man had thrown off the husk of his body. He was a creature of spirit and inwardness, but no longer the man of flesh and belly, bones and blood, that we find in the Bible. Protestant man would never have dared confront God and demand an accounting of His ways. That era in history had long since passed by the time we come to the Reformation.

As a man of flesh and blood, Biblical man was very much bound to the earth. "Remember, I beseech thee, that thou hast made me as the clay; and wilt thou bring me into the dust again?" Bound to the dust, he was bound to death: a creature of time, whose being was temporal through and through. The idea of eternity—eternity for man—does not bulk large in the Bible beside the power and frequency of the images of man's mortality. God is the Everlasting, who, though He meets man face to face, is altogether beyond human ken and comparison; while man, who is as Nothing before his Creator, is like all other beings of the dust a creature of a day, whose temporal substance is repeatedly compared to wind and shadow.

> Man that is born of woman is of few days, and full of trouble.
> He cometh forth like a flower, and is cut down: he fleeth also as a shadow, and continueth not.

Hebraism contains no eternal realm of essences, which Greek philosophy was to fabricate, through Plato, as affording the intellectual deliverance from the evil of time. Such a realm of eternal essences is possible only for a *detached* intellect, one who, in Plato's phrase, becomes a "spectator of all time and all existence." This ideal of the philosopher as the highest human type—the theoretical intellect who from the vantage point of eternity can survey all time and existence—is altogether foreign to the Hebraic concept of the man of faith who is passionately committed to his own mortal being. Detachment was for the Hebrew an impermissible state of mind, a vice rather than a virtue; or rather it was something that Biblical man was not yet even able to conceive, since he had not reached the level of rational abstraction of the Greek. His existence was too earth-bound, too laden with the oppressive images of mortality, to permit him to experience the philosopher's detachment. The notion of the immortality of the soul as an intellectual substance (and that that immortality might even be demonstrated rationally) had not dawned upon the mind of Biblical man. If he hoped at all to escape mortality it was on the basis of personal trust that his Creator might raise him once again from the dust.

All of this carries us beyond Arnold's simple contrasting of moral man with intellectual man, though his basic distinction is left intact and in fact deepened. To sum up:

(1) The ideal man of Hebraism is the man of faith; for Hellenism, at least as it came to ultimate philosophic expression in its two greatest philosophers, Plato and Aristotle, the ideal man is the man of reason, the philosopher who as a spectator of all time and existence must rise above these.

(2) The man of faith is the concrete man in his wholeness. Hebraism does not raise its eyes to the universal and abstract; its vision is always of the concrete, particular, individual man. The Greeks, on the other hand, were the first thinkers in history; they discovered the universal, the abstract and timeless essences, forms, and Ideas. The intoxication of this discovery (which marked nothing less than the earliest emergence and differentiation of the rational function) led Plato to hold that man lives only insofar as he lives in the eternal.

(3) There follows for the Greek the ideal of *detachment* as the path of wisdom which only the philosopher can tread. The word "theory" drives from the Greek verb *theatai,* which mean to behold, to see, and is the root of the word theater. At a theater we are spectators of an action in which we ourselves are not involved. Analogously, the man of theory, the philosopher or pure scientist, looks upon existence with detachment, as we behold spectacles at the theater; and in this way he exists, to use Kierkegaard's expression, only upon the aesthetic level of existence.

The Hebraic emphasis is on *commitment,* the passionate involvement of man with his own mortal being (at once flesh and spirit), with his offspring, family, tribe, and God; a man abstracted from such involvements would be, to Hebraic thought, but a pale shade of the actual existing human person.

(4) The eternal is a rather shadowy concept for the Hebrew except as it is embodied in the person of the unknowable and terrible God. For the Greek eternity is something to which man has ready and continuous access through his intellect.

(5) The Greek invented logic. His definition of man as the rational animal is literally as the logical animal, *to zoon logikon,* or even more literally the animal who has language, since logic derives from the verb *legein,* which means to say, speak, discourse. Man is the animal of connected logical discourse.

For the Hebrew the status of the intellect is rather typified by the silly and proud babbling of Job's friends, whose arguments never touch the core of the matter. Intellect and logic are the pride of fools and do not touch the ultimate issues of life, which transpire at a depth that language can never reach, the ultimate depth of faith. Says Job at the end of the Book: "I have heard of thee by the hearing of the ear: but now mine eye seeth thee."

(6) The Greek pursues beauty and goodness as things that are identical or at least always coincident; in fact he gives them a single name, the beautiful-and-good, *to kalokagathia.* The Hebraic sense of sin, to which Matthew Arnold alludes, is too much aware of the galling and refractory aspects of human existence to make this easy identification of the good and the beautiful. The sense of the sinfulness of Biblical man is the sense of his radical finitude in its aspect of imperfection. Hence his good must sometimes wear an ugly face, just as beauty for him may be the shining mask of evil and corruption.

It is unnecessary to extend this list. What is important is to make clear the central intuition that informs each of these two views of man. The reader probably has already divined that the features of Hebraic man are those which existential philosophy has attempted to exhume and bring to the reflective consciousness of our time, a time in which as a matter of historical happening the Hebraic religion (which means Western religion) no longer retains its unconditional validity for the mass of mankind.

This sketch of a comparison perhaps tilts the balance a little too heavily on the side of Hebraism. It is necessary, however, to correct the impression left by Matthew Arnold (and he is here a spokesman for a view that is still prevalent) that the main content of Hebraism is its energy and will toward morality. We have to insist on a noetic content in Hebraism: Biblical man too had his *knowledge,* though it is not the intellectual knowledge of the Greek. It is not the kind of knowledge that man can have through reason alone, or perhaps not through reason at all; he has it rather through body and blood, bones and bowels, through trust and anger and confusion and love and fear; through his passionate adhesion in faith to the Being whom he can never intellectually know. This kind of knowledge a man has only through living, not reasoning, and perhaps in the end he cannot even say what it is he knows; yet it is knowledge all the same, and Hebraism at its source had this knowledge. To be sure, we have stacked the cards somewhat by considering Hellenism more or less as it came to be expressed by the philosophers, and particularly the philosopher Plato; Hellas also produced the tragic poets Aeschylus and Sophocles, who had another kind of knowledge of life. But it was Greece that produced philosophy, logic, science—and also produced Plato, a figure who sums up all the ambiguity of Hellenism as it circles round the momentous issue of reason and the irrational in human life.

2. GREEK REASON

The Anglo-American philosopher Whitehead has remarked that "Twenty-five hundred years of Western philosophy is but a series of footnotes to Plato." Allowing for the disparaging irony of the word "footnotes," we can take this statement as literally accurate. The themes, the questions, and even to a great extent the terms of all subsequent Western philosophy lie in germ in the writings of Plato. All later philosophers betray a filial dependence on Plato—even Aristotle, the great hero of all anti-Platonists. And while existential philosophy is a radical effort to break with this Platonic tradition, yet paradoxically there is an existential aspect to Plato's thought. Such is the richness and ambiguity of Plato as man and philosopher.

Plato began his philosophic career as the result of a conversion. This is surely an existential beginning. He had aspired to be a dramatic poet, the biographer tells us, but after a youthful encounter with Socrates he burned all his manuscripts and dedicated himself to the search for wisdom to which Socrates had given his life. Plato was to be engaged thereafter, for the rest of his life, in a war with the poets that was first and foremost a war with the poet in himself. The steps in Plato's career, after that fateful encounter with Socrates, enact a progress, as we shall see later, that might have the title: *Death of a Poet.* Yet the poet never quite dies in Plato—revile him as he does—and at the end he returns to a great myth of creation, the *Timaeus,* though it is told as an allegory of science and metaphysics. His career is the victory of reason, or the struggle for that victory, over the poetic and mythic functions, and it is all the more remarkable in that it took place in a man who was so richly endowed with the poetic gift.

But this is more than a highly dramatic bit of personal biography:

it is an event of the greatest significance in Western history, as it could only be in a man of Plato's greatness. In Plato rational consciousness as such becomes, for the first time in human history, a differentiated psychic function. (Perhaps Socrates achieved this before him, but all we know of Socrates as a philosopher is through Plato's writings.) The momentousness of this emergence of reason can be gauged by setting Greece over against the comparably high civilizations of India and China. These latter had a great flowering of sages at a time close to that of the pre-Socratics in Greece; but neither in India nor in China was reason fully isolated and distinguished—that is, differentiated—from the rest of man's psychic being, from his feeling and intuition. Oriental man remains intuitive, not rational. Great sages like Buddha and Lao-tse rose above the mythic, but they did not become apostles of reason. The lifting of reason fully out of the primeval waters of the unconscious is a Greek achievement. And from the differentiation Western civilization takes on, subsequently, the character that distinguishes it from the civilizations of the Orient. Science itself, a peculiarly Western product, became possible only through this differentiation of reason and its exaltation as the crowning human power.

This emergence of reason that we can see taking place in the Platonic writings was a momentous historical event that spanned Plato's own lifetime. We can gauge this span by marking out at its beginning two thinkers earlier than Plato, Heraclitus and Parmenides, who were flourishing around 480 B.C., and at its end the achievement of Plato's pupil, Aristotle, who really carried the rational ideal sketched by Plato in the Later Academy to its culmination. In 399 B.C. Socrates was executed for nothing less than the crime of rationalism—an act of reason that destroyed, so the conservative Athenians thought, the gods of the tribe. These dates can be marked as points on a curve, and this curve is one of the most significant ever traced by man in his history. From 480 B.C., the time of Hercalitus and Parmenides, to the death of Aristotle in 322 B.C. is little more than a century and a half. In that century and a half man enters history as the rational animal.

Parmenides and Heraclitus were visionaries and seers. Parmenides wrote in verse, and his poem opens by describing itself as the account of a vision vouchsafed by the goddess, who has taken the poet in her chariot beyond the portals of the day and night. Heraclitus' sayings are dark and oracular, and they are meant to be taken as oracles—visionary disclosures of the real. The Greek word for "I know," *oida,* is the perfect of the verb "to see" and means "I have seen." He who knows is the man who has seen, who has had a vision. For earlier mankind, the sage, the wise man, was the reader of oracles, of dreams and entrails, the fortuneteller, the shaman. And he was the poet who, in giving expression to the "big dreams" of the tribe, voiced its hidden, its deepest and furthest wisdom. At the end of the century and a half in which Plato and Aristotle lived, this ideal sage had been transformed into the man of pure intellect, whose highest embodiment was to be found in the rational philosopher and the theoretical scientist. The vast intuitive visions of nature, as found in the pre-Socratic thinkers, gave way, in Aristotle, to the sobriety of science.

We are so used today to taking our rational consciousness for granted, in the ways of our daily life we are so immersed in its operations, that it is hard at first for us to imagine how momentous was this historical happening among the Greeks. Steeped as our age is in the ideas of evolution, we have not yet become accustomed to the idea that consciousness itself is something that has evolved through long centuries and that even today, with us, is still evolving. Only in this century, through modern psychology, have we learned how precarious a hold consciousness may exert upon life, and we are more acutely aware therefore what a precious deal of history, and of effort, was required for its elaboration, and what creative leaps were necessary at certain times to extend it beyond its habitual territory. We have seen the history of philosophy written as social history, or as economic history, or interpreted from any number of sociological points of view, but we have yet to grasp fully the history of philosophy as part of the psychic evolution of mankind. But of course the concept of evolution cannot here be interpreted in the simple and unilinear fashion of nineteenth-century thought, as in Hegel and Spencer, but rather in its full concreteness and ambiguity, as simultaneously gain and loss, advance and regress.

Nothing better illustrates this last point than the Platonic celebration of reason. The Greeks' discovery represents an immense and necessary step forward by mankind, but also a loss, for the pristine wholeness of man's being is thereby sundered or at least pushed into the background. Consider thus the famous myth of the soul: in the *Phaedrus:* the driver of the chariot, reason, holds the reins of white steeds and of black— the white steeds representing the spirited or emotional part of man, which is more docile to the dictates of reason, the black and unruly steeds representing the appetites or desires, which have to be whipped into line by the charioteer. Whips and reins convey only the idea of coercion and restraint; and the charioteer alone wears a human face while the rest of man, the non-rational part, is represented in animal form. Reason, as the divine part of man, is separated, is indeed of another nature, from the animal within him. We are a long distance here from another symbol of light and dark which early mankind, this time the Chinese, handed down to us: the famous diagram of the forces of *yin* and *yang,* in which the light and the dark lie down beside each other within the same circle, the dark area penetrated by a spot of light and the light by a spot of dark, to symbolize that each must borrow from the other, that the light has need of the dark, and conversely, in order for either to be complete. In Plato's myth first appears that cleavage between reason and the irrational that it has been the long burden of the West to carry, until the dualism makes itself felt in most violent form within modern culture.

The same superhuman, or inhuman, exaltation of reason can be seen in another of the Platonic myths, the celebrated allegory of the cave in the *Republic*. The myth begins with a very grim picture of the human condition as it actually is: Men sit in the darkness of a cave, in chains, their backs to the light and able to see only the shadows of objects cast on the wall they face. One of the prisoners becomes free, turns around to see the objects of which he had previously seen only the shadows, and the light itself that casts the shadows; he may even progress to the mouth of the cave and see the sun beyond.

This is a myth of man's progress from darkness to light, ignorance to knowledge, from dereliction to salvation. As a young man, we are told, Plato had studied the doctrines of Cratylus, a follower of Heraclitus who had taught that all things were in flux and that there was no escape anywhere from death and change; the young Plato, tormented by this vision, desired at all costs a refuge in the eternal from the insecurities and ravages of time. Hence the enormous attraction for him of the science of mathematics, which opens up a realm of eternal truths. Here at least, in pure thought, man can find an escape from time. Hence too the tremendous emotional force for him of the theory of eternal forms or Ideas, since these latter were an everlasting realm to which man has access. We have to see Plato's rationalism, not as a cool scientific project such as a later century of the European Enlightenment might set for itself, but as a kind of passionately religious doctrine—a theory that promised man salvation from the things he had feared most from the earliest days, from death and time. The extraordinary emphasis Plato put upon reason is itself a religious impulse.

Light and darkness are universal human symbols for the contrasting states of redemption and dereliction. You will find them in all cultures— in Hindu, Buddhist, Taoist, and Christian thought. The sage or saint is always the enlightened man, he who walks in the light. Plato's myth, taken simply as a story, could be adopted by any of these religions. The use that Plato makes of it, however, is altogether his own, and strikingly different from the use any religion has made of these symbols. For when he has finished the story, Plato goes on to explain it as an allegory: the progress from the cave into the light, in the myth, will correspond to the actual stages to be followed in the education of the guardians of the state, and the chief content of this education, its sole content from the age of twenty to thirty-five, is to be mathematics and dialectic. At this point we may imagine a great Eastern sage such as Buddha or Lao-tse looking somewhat askance: the enlightenment they sought, which was the redemption of the individual, would not have come through any such severely intellectual and logical training. And one's own observation of professional mathematicians hardly supports the view that they are the most whole and intact psychological specimens mankind has to offer. In Plato's extraordinary emphasis upon mathematics we see the vestiges of Pythagoreanism, in which mathematics has been given a sacred, a religious status.

Behind Plato's emphasis upon mathematics lies his theory of Ideas: the "really real" objects in the universe, *ta ontos onta,* are the universals or Ideas. Particular things are half real and half unreal—real only insofar as they participate in the eternal universals. The universal is fully real because it is eternal; the fleeting and changing particular has only a shadowy kind of reality because it passes and is then as if it had never been. Humanity, the universal, is more real than any individual man. This is the crucial emphasis of Platonism as it was passed on to all subsequent philosophy and that against which contemporary existential philosophy is in rebellion. Kierkegaard and Nietzsche in the nineteenth century were the first to reverse this Platonic scale of values and to establish the individual, the single one, precisely in the way in which he is an exception to the universal norm, as taking precedence over the universal.

Everything else in Plato follows from his identification of true Being, of "real reality," with the Ideas. Since art, for example, deals with the objects of the senses, therefore with particulars, it deals only with shadows and is itself a form of untruth. Philosophy and theoretical science have a higher value than art because in them alone truth is realized, as it is not in the arts. The earlier meaning of truth, which embraced also the utterances of the poets, has here been shifted to make it a purely intellectual concept. Psychologically speaking the significance of Plato's theory of Ideas is to transfer the weight of emphasis from sensory reality to a supersensible reality. Perhaps nothing short of this would have served historically, at that time: For man to enter history as the rational animal, it was necessary for him to be convinced that the objects of his reasoning, the Ideas, were more real than his own individual person or the particular objects that made up his world. The great step forward into rationalism required its own mythology—such perhaps is always the ambiguity of human evolution.

Plato's thought, as we have seen, values (which means, finds "really real") the eternal over the temporal, the universal over the particular reason over the non-rational other half of man. In all these valuations it is profoundly anti-existential—a philosophy of essence rather than of existence. Yet it remains existential in its conception of the activity of philosophizing as fundamentally a means of personal salvation. Plato had no conception of metaphysics as such, as a purely theoretical branch of philosophy devoted to the study of Being as Being. He was an Athenian to the end, which means that his interest in political life, the *polis,* was the one to which all other human interests were subordinate. Athens did not produce metaphysicians; these came rather from other parts of the Greek world, from Ionia, Milesia, Sicily, southern Italy; and the founder of metaphysics as a strict and separate discipline was Aristotle, a native of Stagira in Macedonia. But for Plato, the Athenian, all metaphysical speculation was simply instrumental in the passionate human search for the ideal state and the ideal way to live—in short, for a means to the redemption of man. The figure of Socrates as a living human presence dominates all the earlier dialogues because, for the young Plato, Socrates the man was the very incarnation of philosophy as a concrete way of life, a personal calling and search. It is in this sense too that Kierkegaard, more than two thousand years later, was to revive the figure of Socrates—the thinker who lived his thought and was not merely a professor in an academy—as his precursor in existential thinking. All of this adds to the richness and ambiguity of the Platonic writings. But the figure of Socrates himself undergoes some radical transformations as we follow the growth and systematization of Plato's rationalism. In the earlier so-called "Socratic," dialogues the personality of Socrates is rendered in vivid and dramatic strokes; gradually, however, he becomes merely a name, a mouthpiece for Plato's increasingly systematic views, and the dialogues tend toward monologues, mere formal essays. In the *Phaedrus* Socrates is still a friend to poets: all the greatest gifts to man, he tells us, come out of a form of inspired madness, and the poetic man, haunted by the muses, is ranked near to the philosopher in the hierarchy of human values. In *The Sophist,* however, a late dialogue, the poets are lumped together in disrepute with the Sophists as traffickers in non-being, dealers in untruth. The figure of Socrates himself by then has shrunk from a flesh-and-blood person to a shadowy abstract reasoner. In the later dialogues he even takes a back seat: the principal figure in *The Sophist* is the Eleatic Stranger; in *The Laws* it is the Athenian Stranger; and in the *Parmenides* the venerable figure of Parmenides lectures Socrates on the intricacies of dialectic. Part of this may be due simply to fading memory: the Socrates who died in 399 B.C. had stamped himself so strongly on the young man's mind that for the next thirty or forty years he virtually dominated Plato's life; but with the passage of time even this vivid figure had to grow fainter and, in unconscious compensation, Plato had to assert himself at the end against Socrates. Those unknown figures—the Eleatic Stranger and the Athenian Stranger—are simply the shadow of Plato himself, those portions of his personality which had not been able to speak through the mouth of Socrates but had at last forced themselves to be recognized. Because of his meeting with Socrates, Plato had ceased to be a poet, and finally, at the end of the trail, in his least poetic dialogue, *The Laws,* he advises the death penalty for those whose thought opposes the religious orthodoxy of the state—the very crime for which Socrates had been put to death by the Athenian orthodoxy and in revolt against which Plato himself had taken up his own career as a philosopher! Unconsciously, at the end, he took his revenge upon the figure that had dominated his life.

When we come to the end, with Aristotle, of the great historical cycle that began with the pre-Socratics, philosophy had become a purely theoretical and objective discipline. The main branches of philosophy, as we know it today as an academic subject, had been laid out. Wisdom is identified as Metaphysics, or "First Philosophy," a detached and theoretical discipline: the ghost of the existential Socrates had at last been put to rest. (The progress of this great historical curve is all the more remarkable if we consider Aristotle's own individual development, as it has been established by Werner Jaeger: as a young man and still a Platonist, Aristotle himself conceived of philosophy as the personal and passionate search for redemption from the wheel of birth and death.) The foundations of the sciences, as the West has known them, had been laid, and this was only possible because reason had detached itself from the mythic, religious, poetic impulses with which it had hitherto been mixed so that it had no distinguishable identity of its own.

The West has thought in the shadow of the Greeks; even where later Western thinkers have rebelled against Greek wisdom, they have thought their rebellion through in the terms which the Greeks laid down for them. We must therefore understand Greek rationalism in all its depth and breadth if we are to understand some of the later revolts against it, and particularly the modern effort of existential philosophy at last to think beyond it. The rationalism of the Greeks was not the mere passing salute to reason that a present-day orator might toss off before an academic audience. The Greeks were thoroughgoing, stringent, and bold in their thinking—and never more so than when they placed reason at the top of the human hierarchy. Which is greater, the artist or the thinker? Is Mozart, the creator of music, inferior to the physicist Helmholtz, the theorist who explained the nature of sound? Which is the higher life—that of Shakespeare, the greatest poet of the English language, or of Newton, the greatest English scientist? We today would hesitate to answer such questions; and in our timidity we might even reject them as meaningless. Not so the Greeks. A young Greek who felt a disposition toward both poetry and theory, and wanted to choose one for a career, would want to know which was the better life, and Plato and Aristotle would have made no bones about their reply: the theoretical life is higher than the life of the artist or that of the practical man of politics—or of the saint, for that matter, though they did not yet know of this kind of existence. In his *Nicomachean Ethics* Aristotle gives us a remarkably flexible and well-rounded picture of human nature and the many different kinds of goals, or goods, at which it may aim; but the ethical question still seems unanswered for him until he has declared which of all possible goods is the best, and in the tenth and final book of this work he expresses his own preference (stated, of course, as an objective truth) for the life of pure reason, the life of the philosopher or theoretical scientist, as the highest life. Here his own words must be observed carefully:

> It would seem, too, that this [Reason] is the true self of every man, since it is the supreme and better part. It will be strange, then, if he should choose not his own life, but some other's. . . . What is naturally proper to every creature is the highest and pleasantest for him. And so, to man, this will be the life of Reason, since Reason is, in the highest sense, a man's self. (*Eth. Nic.* X, 7.)

Reason, Aristotle tells us, is the highest part of our personality: that which the human person truly is. One's reason, then, is one's real self, the center of one's personal idenitity. This is rationalism stated in its starkest and strongest terms—*that one's rational self is one's real self*—and as such held sway over the views of Western philosophers up until very modern times. Even the Christianity of the Middle Ages, when it assimilated Aristotle, did not displace this Aristotelian principle: it simply made an uneasy alliance between faith as the supernatural center of the personality and reason as its natural center; the natural man remained an Aristotelian man, a being whose real self was his rational self.

Aristotle did not have, as Plato did, a realm of eternal essences, which is alone "really real," to guarantee the primacy of reason. Nevertheless, he too found a metaphysical ground for this primacy, in the intelligibility of all Being as it rests on a First Cause. To know, says Aristotle, is to know the cause, and human reason can ascend to knowledge of the First Cause of all things, the Unmoved Mover of the Universe, God. So long as the human intellect has held out to it the prospect of surveying the whole cosmos from its ultimate height to its lowest depth, to the end that it may see the ultimate and sufficient reason why this cosmos exists and why it exists in the manner it does —so long as such a goal is promised to the intellect, then all the spectacles afforded by art, all the worldly triumphs of the practical life, will dwindle by comparison. The value of art or of the practical life must necessarily be ranked lower than that of a theoretical vision so complete and all-encompassing. The connection between theoretical reason as the highest human function and the possible completeness of its vision of the cosmos is an intrinsic one: the latter secures the supreme value of the former. For where the ultimate reason of things may be known, who would abstain from the effort to reach it, or be distracted by other goals which partake of the finitude and incompleteness of our poor feeble human existence? "Happy is he who can know the causes of things," said the Roman poet; and the happiest man would be he who could know the ultimate causes of things.

What happens, however, to this view that the highest man is the theoretical man if we conceive of human existence as finite through and through—and if human reason, and the knowledge it can produce, is seen to be finite like the rest of man's being? Then the possibility that the system of human knowledge may be closed and completed, that all of Being may be ultimately embraced in one vision, disappears; and man is left patiently treading the endless road of knowledge that never reaches conclusion. If science were to continue its researches uninterruptedly for a thousand years, it would not disclose to us the ultimate ground of things. Being finite, we should never arrive at the highest object of knowledge, God, which this rationalist tradition has celebrated as the goal that outshines all others. This conception of human finitude places in question the supremacy that reason has traditionally been given over all other human functions in the history of Western philosophy. Theoretical knowledge may indeed be pursued as a personal passion, or its findings may have practical application; but its value above that of all other human enterprises (such as art or religion) cannot be enhanced by any claim that it will reach the Absolute. Suppose, for example, that there were a road and we were told we ought to walk it; in response to our question "Why?", we might be told that we ought to do so because the walking itself would be pleasant or useful (good for our health); but if we were told that there was a priceless treasure at the end of the road, then the imperative to walk would carry overwhelming weight with us. It is this treasure at the end of the road that has disappeared from the modern horizon, for the simple reason that the end of the road has itself disappeared.

Hence, we in our day have to come back to those old, apparently naïve questions of the Greeks from a different angle, as Nietzsche was the first to do: Which is higher, science or art? Who is the highest—the theoretical or the practical man? or the saint? or the artist? The man of faith or the man of reason? If man can no longer hold before his mind's eye the prospect of the Great Chain of Being, a cosmos rationally ordered and accessible from top to bottom to reason, what goal can philosophers set themselves that can measure up to the greatness of the old Greek ideal of the *bios theoretikos,* the theoretical life, which has fashioned the destiny of Western man for millennia?

Problems

1. What qualities does Arnold think are embodied in Hebraism and Hellenism?
2. According to Barrett, which is more problematic and less utopian in vision, Hebraism or Hellenism? Why?
3. What, according to Barrett, are the qualities that most characterize Job's encounter with God? How does Job's faith differ from that found in early Christianity and later in Protestantism?
4. Throughout the essay, Barrett tries in various ways to establish two relationships to living in order to reveal two ways of knowing. What are they? Which is more existential? Which more admirable? Why?
5. What are the respective attitudes of Hebraism and Hellenism toward (1) body and soul, (2) time and mortality, (3) the abstract universal and the concrete particular, (4) art and science, (5) man and progress? Which attitude most reflects yours? Did you choose and form your attitudes or were your attitudes formed for you?

Marxism

Introduction

So much has been made of Marxism as a secular religion that comparisons between Christianity and Marxism, between Christ and Marx, are, though unsatisfactory, perhaps inevitable. From the beginning, however, one must distinguish the innovative leader from his imitative followers. Walter Rauschenbusch, in *Christianity and the Social Crisis*, has commented eloquently on the misunderstanding that follows upon the death of a great spiritual mentor. His remarks, referring to Christ, are applicable to Marx.

> There is a gap even between the ideal cherished by any lofty mind and the realization which he can give to it in his own action. There are few men who maintain their first love unchilled to their colder age and their early purposes untarnished by policy and concession to things as they are. But as soon as the thoughts of a great spiritual leader pass to others and form the animating principle of a party or school or sect, there is an inevitable drop. The disciples cannot keep pace with the sweep of the master. They flutter where he soared. They coarsen and materialize his dreams. They put their trust in forms and organization where he dared to trust in the spirit. They repeat his words, but they make mere formulas of his prophetic figures of speech. They may join the Order of St. Francis, but they will not call the birds their sisters and the sun their brother. Belike Brother Elias becomes the head of the "little brothers" whom the poet-saint of Assisi called out to serve the Lady Poverty.[1] That is the tragedy of all who lead (18 Rauschenbusch).

1. Brother Elias (c. 1180–1253), a close friend of St. Francis, became minister general of the Franciscan order upon the resignation of St. Francis in 1221, a scant dozen or so years after Francis began the order whose members, bound to poverty and preaching, were dedicated to love, charity, and simplicity. Under Elias, who finally became head in 1232 some six years after the death of St. Francis, the order took a worldly turn, schisms were deepened, and the loose organization of friars was given an institutional structure. When the medieval Inquisition began in 1233, the Franciscan order joined the Dominicans in weeding out heresy; and Elias led the persecution of the zealots, an ascetic group within the Franciscans which, though extreme, more nearly approximated the spirit of St. Francis. The order of St. Francis was transformed from its birth as a group of wandering mendicants in 1209 into a group associated with inquisitors in little more than a generation. Brother Elias was finally excommunicated in 1239 for scandalous self-indulgence and loose living, and for flagrant abuse of power.

In similar fashion, every effort to distinguish between the lofty mind of Marx and those of his later disciples risks the danger of sentimentalizing or of patronizing Marx's ideas. Lenin, sensing the danger, opens *The State and Revolution* with an attack on these tendencies; Kolakowski, much later and from another perspective, insists on this very distinction; and, of the two, Kolakowski's grasp seems the surer. Like Christianity, the distinction between classical Marxism and modern communism appears to be rooted in the failure of the followers to perceive the essential individualism, relativism, and spirituality of its vision apart from its absolute forms. The sense of infallibility generated by Christianity and Marxism is thus capable of creating venerable certainties devoid of true understanding.

In the battle for men's minds, as we have seen in Aquinas, appeals and arguments are made and built on behalf of many things, all in the name of nature or natural reason. Throughout the Middle Ages, repeated attempts were made to reconcile natural reason with revelation. Although Marxism dispenses with revelation, it purports once again to speak in the name of natural law and natural reason. Indeed, this assumption that the laws of production and historical conflict have been discovered, together with the emphasis on truth as a "practical" rather than a theoretical matter, is the thread that unites all the early essays in this section. Even Djilas, the revisionist, alludes to history, nature, and societal relations with the confidence of one who, to some extent, has discerned natural law. The word or thought that reappears with impressive regularity throughout this section on Marxism is "inevitability."

Despite the tendency for Marxism to take on ideological overtones, Marx himself never appeals to dogma; his arguments, he repeatedly tells us, rest on empirical science, facts, immutable consequences, laws discovered. Marx and Engels state their premises at once as if they were scientific hypotheses to be established. Having done so, they then proceed to demonstrate these hypotheses historically and to analyze modern society as part of the entire historical dialectic. Finally, extrapolating from these laws, they foresee socialist society as the inevitable and predictable outcome of discernible forces in interaction.

Despite the fact that Marx did not believe in objective, immutable reality, but in reality as process, as activity and selection, the effect of a theory of reality that involved human actions in it was to create in his followers a belief that they were encountering objective reality and interacting with it. The result is not only confidence in the objective nature of reality, but in man as an instrument shaping that reality. Reality—and society is part of reality—thus becomes process and progress once its "laws" have been fully induced and understood.

This ultimate confidence rests on the objective nature of reality, on the nature of objective economic laws, on observation, reason and

Introduction 227

science as the subjective element of the interaction that provides man with the means to discover such laws, on man's ability to control such laws once discovered. In essence, the structure of Marxism is founded on the belief that man and society are part of nature and can be observed, understood and used for the common good in exactly the same way as natural law. This cornerstone of Marxism makes it positive and hopeful—thus comforting to troubled minds beset by a sense of meaninglessness. Like Christianity, it gives one something to grasp that is objective and true outside oneself; at the same time it makes one an agent of that truth. Engels' use of scientific analogies is thus not accidental:

> As long as we obstinately refuse to understand the nature and the character of these social means of action—and this understanding goes against the grain of the capitalist mode of production and its defenders—so long as these forces are at work in spite of us, in opposition to us, so long [will] they master us as we have shown above in detail.
>
> But when once their nature is understood, they can, in the hands of the producers working together, be transformed from master demons into willing servants. The difference is as that between the destructive force of electricity in the lightning of the storm, and electricity under command in the telegraph and the voltaic arc; the difference between a conflagration, and fire working in the service of man (Engels, 302/35–303/2).

Marxism, when measured against any of the three other modes of thought and value discussed in this anthology, is clearly the most optimistic. Christianity, to be sure, is even grander and more promising in its visions, but not about this world (about that, it is hopelessly pessimistic).

Marxism thus immediately creates an ontological problem of formidable dimensions. What is man's role? If man is shaped, determined, governed by inevitable societal forces, in what way can man be said to *choose* his behavior? In what way can he even be free to choose how he will perceive a phenomenon? If we are shaped by society, our perceptions are shaped by society, our reason, even our scientific tools are shaped by society. Economics, psychology, biology disappear; in their places are either bourgeois science or Marxist science. The former necessarily distorts truth because of the illusions of bourgeois society; the latter, free of illusions, constitutes true science. Freedom from illusion means, of course, the condition of being truly aware of the "dialectical" nature of the objective and the subjective. As we can see, we are once again in the middle of the scholastic argument that freedom is not rebellion, freedom is doing God's will. The concepts have not changed; only the terms are modified to fit a new system.

In point of fact, Marx rejects the above deterministic dilemma, for Marx did not believe that man was a reactive being, passively being shaped by his environment. For Marx the instrumentalist,[2] all perception involved an active interaction between subject and object, between perceiver and the thing perceived, a dialectical interplay between knower and the thing known, during which time a new synthesis is born. Truth becomes not an object of contemplation but, in part, an action of the mind. The world does not exist to be perceived, indeed cannot be perceived without dialectically altering it. If the world unavoidably must be changed, it should be changed—and for the better. Marx sums up the entire concept when he remarks:

> The question of whether objective truth can be attributed to human thinking is not a question of theory but is a *practical* question. In practice man must prove the truth, that is, the reality and power, the this-sidedness of his thinking. The dispute over the reality or non-reality of a thought which is isolated from practice, is a purely *scholastic* question (19 Marx).

The tension created by such a perspective is extremely great. On the one hand, man is determined by historical necessity (Christian: "Divine Providence"); on the other hand, man, who is part of that process, is actively engaged in shaping that necessity (Christian: "free will"), but in shaping it only when he is able to understand it (Christian: "fulfilling the law," "doing God's will"); for natural law cannot be harnessed and used for man's benefit until dialectic materialism is understood (Christian: "revelation"). One may disagree with the analogies, but they are useful in showing how both systems create a marked belief that "truth" rests on our side; "illusion" remains on yours. More important than the analogy is the impact such beliefs have on one's perceptions, not only of the future but also of science itself.

The West likes to pride itself on its rationalism and scientific objectivity. Yet, when Western thought is compared with communist theory it appears that its deepest allegiance is Christian and romantic, hence spiritualist. It is ruled by what Freud would call "illusions," and what Marx called "mystification." These charges may or may not disturb us, depending on our assumptions or our self-perceptions. The assumptions and perceptions each of us has of himself do, however, differ.

Bruce Franklin has commented on the Western concept of utopia and the communist concept of utopia in an attempt to show how much more rational and hopeful about science the communists are.

2. Instrumentalism is a philosophy that originated with John Dewey (1859–1952), American philosopher and educator. It maintains that human activity evolves out of man's attempt to solve his individual and social problems; and since problems change, the instruments dealing with them must also change. Truth is, thus, evolutionary rather than static and eternal, and is based on observable experience rather than revelation (see Dictionary of Terms for a more extended discussion).

Introduction   229

Today Soviet and American future-scene fiction offer an almost perfect—and most revealing—contrast. Whereas in the USSR future-scene fiction is a respected form of literature, in the USA it is considered offbeat, zany, and not quite respectable. Whereas in the USSR it is an almost collective fiction, an agreed-upon utopia delimited by many taboos, in the USA diversity is exalted and the demand is for as many surprises, tricks, and innovations as possible. Whereas in the USSR future-scene fiction almost always sees science as a great aid in human progress, in the USA many stories of the future see science as a destructive force, producing a society of robots or freaks or a global catastrophe. Whereas the Soviet view of the future is almost universally optimistic, envisioning a world populated by heroes, ruled by love, and ever improving, the dominant American view is profoundly pessimistic, often envisioning futures filled with extrapolations of present problems or new horrors, calamities, decay, or extinction (20 Franklin).

Obviously these differences, meant to suggest how the capitalist and communist utopias reveal the underlying fears, aspirations and attitudes of their formulators, betray deep disagreements about the nature of man and his possibilities. And it is here, despite the possible arbitrariness, that one must distinguish between Marx and present-day communist society; for there are differences. Perhaps a brief discussion of Marx's views may better reveal the "inevitable distortion" of the followers—if such exists.

Rationalism and science for Marx were tools with which man could realize his full humanity (See *The German Ideology,* 274/30–275/2; "Alienated Labor," especially 283/38–284/13, 285/1-18). Marx, like Hegel, is thus concerned with the potentialities inherent in a thing. He is one with the existentialists and psychotherapists who stress self-actualization and self-creation through one's own actions (cf. Maslow, Frankl, even Nietzsche). Marx's materialism was a set of premises, a belief with Sartre (cf. Sartre) that "existence precedes essence." In Marx's terms, in *The German Ideology,* it was a belief that:

> The production of ideas, of conceptions, of consciousness is at first directly interwoven with the material activity and the material intercourse of men, the language of real life. Conceiving, thinking, the mental intercourse of men, appear at this stage as the direct efflux of their material behavior. The same applies to mental production as expressed in the language of the politics, laws, morality, religion, metaphysics of a people. Men are the producers of their conceptions, ideas, etc.—real, active men, as they are conditioned by a definite development of their productive forces and of the intercourse corresponding to these, up to its furthest forms (Marx and Engels, [265/20-29]).

In practice what this means is that a person born in Cedar Rapids will tend to favor Christian, democratic capitalism, while one born in Moscow will smile upon atheistic, centralized, bureaucratic communism. Though this truism is obvious to most people, it is not often taken, in practice, into account.

To be a materialist in this sense is in no way to be a person who makes material prosperity the end of life. One had to await the contemporary communist bureaucracy for this distortion. Marx himself (in "Alienated Labor," (287/37–288/3) is emphatic in making clear that not only is increased material prosperity *not* the goal of life, but it may also even be destructive of life through its negation of higher values.

> In the wage system labor appears not as an end in itself but as the servant of wages. . . .
> An enforced *increase in wages* (disregarding the other difficulties, and especially that such an anomaly could only be maintained by force) would be nothing more than a *better remuneration of slaves*, and would not restore, either to the worker or to the work, their human significance and worth.
> Even the *equality of incomes* which Proudhon demands would only change the relation of the present day worker to his work into a relation of all men to work.

For Marx, alienated labor is a job, and in this sense, even a well-paid job is still a job. It is not a job that man needs, but work—work that expresses him, work that defines him, that brings him into harmony with nature and all living things. Only then is his consciousness not a consciousness directed toward wages, but a consciousness of being human; it is "species consciousness" placed in the service of his higher humanity (cf. Maslow).

Marx, from the above, is not only a rationalist and humanist, a believer in natural law, in progress through science—in other words, a creature of the Enlightenment. He is also a visionary, messianic prophet preaching a radical new "Gospel": man is good, not sinful; man is not lazy but industrious, a being who needs work, who finds and creates himself in work. The individual, far from being worthy in spirit but worthless in body, even in the lowest proletariat, is the precious incarnation of unrealized potential. The world is not damned; it is yet to be realized. The beginning of the historical end has not begun, the beginning of man's true growth in history has just started. Man who once cowered before nature's gods, has become godlike in his power over nature and no longer needs gods. The message is the same in all areas and the end of *The Communist Manifesto* proclaims it. Man is no longer a slave. Men "have nothing to lose but their chains. They have a world to win. WORKING MEN OF ALL COUNTRIES, UNITE!"

What is there in such a vision to suppose it would lead to Stalinist excesses and terror? But then, what is there in the Gospels to suggest Torquemada and the tortures of the Spanish Inquisition? The questions are not idle. Marx's thought, when coarsened and brutalized is as capable of issuing in atrocity as the obsession with the body-soul dichotomy and spiritual salvation through Christ is capable of leading to bodily torture. In ideological matters, selection and emphasis are all. Humanism and democracy can easily, and often, give way to dogmatism.

Marx's materialism is rooted in the real world. About this he is categorical. "We do not set out from . . . men as narrated, thought of, imagined, conceived. . . . We set *out* from real, active men" (*The German Ideology,* [265/36–266/1-3]). This exaltation of the actual and real as a beginning and referent point, as a methodological program, is capable of becoming not merely an inductive tool, but a means and an end. Mao Tse-tung is thus later able to assert: "Man's social practice alone is the criterion of truth . . . the epistemology of dialectical materialism raises practice to a position of primary importance." And he goes on to quote Lenin to the effect that "practice is more important than [theoretical knowledge]" (21 Mao). This emphasis on man's practice has, *in practice,* the effect of eroding away the very concept of "truth," and of causing one to accept the condition of the world and its ways as the truth and the only means of changing it; a brutal world demands brutal measures. Until the utopia, man must be taken as he is—a victim of class consciousness. Mao, in his contention that "power grows out of the barrel of a gun," not only acknowledges the dirty realities, but he is, as he readily confesses in the essay, "How to Study War," also intent on studying them. Christianity, it is true, triumphed through the intensity of its vision, with little regard for the realities of this world. But we must not ignore the possibility that it triumphed because it was not truly interested in this world. The battleground was men's hearts, not men's purses. We can only speculate on the nature of the outcome had it shifted the field of battle. The brutality with which communists pursue their goals is the result of a strictly applied rationalism placed in the service of historical necessity. To fail to be rigorous and practical is to be a "liberal," hence cowardly and irresponsible. As the young radicals like to repeat, "You're either part of the problem or part of the solution."

Communists are at great pains to defend their actions from the criticism of others. They have numerous figures to apply: "One must break eggs to make an omelette" (Khruschev). "Force is the midwife of every society pregnant with a new one" (Marx). All these figures in one way or another suggest that conflict is necessary for greater harmony, that for fear of dirty hands a new life might be lost. Unclouded certainty—stemming from the absolute sense of infallibility created by the scientific apparatus, together with an erosion through the dialectic of a belief in enduring truth—permits communists to be so confident of the justice of their extreme measures. Thus Mao can state: "The socialist system will eventually replace the capitalist system; this is an objective law independent of man's will. However much the reactionaries try to hold back the wheel of history, sooner or later revolution will take place and will inevitably triumph" (22 Mao). The sooner, of course, the better; hence the ruthlessness.[3]

What is most disconcerting and troubling about this combination of certainty, inevitability, and the erosion of "truth" as an enduring concept caused by the dialectic, is that validation by practice begins to merge and gradually becomes validation by power. Whatever is, is right by virtue of having triumphed; by virtue of its existence, it is deemed to have been part of the inevitable process. Just as medieval knights could decide truth by combat because God could not permit error to triumph, so communism gradually leads to a concept of truth by virtue of control. What is right is what is determined by power. All the schisms and reversals within the communist system are thus explainable not as errors, but as inevitable and necessary steps along the way to truth. Truth, unhappily, always eludes the critics of the system; it exists only with those who control the system, and it exists by virtue of their power; for their power is the practice, and hence the final court of appeals.

In no sense, however, are practices outside of the system ratified by virtue of their mere existence. Trial by combat among the knights of old only decided the truth within the realm of Christendom; infidels were by their very nature excluded from it. And so it is with communists. Might makes right within the system; but might outside the system can make no claims to anyone's allegiance or forbearance.

This analogy with Christendom is intentional. In a very real sense communism in its present form is like Christianity in the way it defines ground rules for criticism and explicitly silences major contentions among points of dogma. More importantly, both suppress dissent by creating a judge once removed in time from the final decisions. In Christianity, ultimate apportionment of rewards and punishments is promised on a Day of Judgment. In communism, final judgments emerge as history unfolds: either one is right and history will bear him out, or one is in error and history will reveal his shortcomings to himself and the world.

The effect, as in Christianity, is to intimidate those not possessed with a sense of infallibility or the means to assert it. Just as the possibility of an "erroneous conscience" in Christianity leads many to relinquish deci-

---

3. The communists, of course, do not have a monopoly on ruthlessness. Western behavior has been little better. It was the Germans who slew 20,000,000 Russians in World War II not the Russians who invaded and decimated Germany; and it was the United States which dropped the atomic bomb on Japan, and has dropped more tonnage on Vietnam than she did on the Axis Powers during the entire Second World War. The West also uses violence and terror as instruments of power. Restraint and limits in such matters are not rationally derived; they are ethical propositions predicated on a spiritualist conception of man. Atrocities are not performed because they affront one's sense of humanity. The mind reasons that such things just are not done. Once one despiritualizes and collectivizes man, however, man becomes, as Arthur Koestler reminds us, one one-millionth part of a million people, and anything becomes permissible in the name of necessity of the "common good."

sions involving one's conscience to others, so in communism, the possibility of impeding the revolution by anti-revolutionary or revisionist tendencies has the effect of silencing critics. Paradoxically, in view of its ostensible scientific bias, communism thus breeds a closed mind as a way of sustaining certainty and repressing anxiety. More significantly, a system that rests on discovering laws and applying them is like one that rests on interpreting revelation—it will develop an elaborate infrastructure of intermediaries dedicated to preventing error. Once it is granted that what is understood is law but so complex as to need special interpreters, communism tends, despite its desire for equality, to build a hierarchical state as certainly as Christianity does. From humble apostles grows a mighty ecclesiastical structure; from desires for a classless society grows a monolithic bureaucratic state (see Djilas).

One may argue that structure is unavoidable and inherent in life, that the structure of the communist cell has its analogue in the organic cell. But even granting the reality of this correspondence—which is not the same as granting to Aquinas or others that a hierarchical structure exists in the universe—we must acknowledge that a view such as historical materialism is capable of distortion until it diminishes the individual's life by making it not a process, not a discrete and valuable entity in itself, but part of a process, part of a larger purpose. Man thus comes to be seen almost exclusively as a "part-of-some-other" not as a "whole-unto-itself." If we are viewed as merely acting out a part of the historical dialectic, then we lose our value as ends-in-ourselves. A radical transformation occurs. We no longer have "man-as-end" as we do in Christianity;[4] we have "man-as-means" to an end—the enriched individual in a classless society.

Embedded in any clearly defined belief in progress is a sense of the disparity between what is and what should be. Marxism, with its great utopian vision, sharpens and intensifies the disparity between the two until the conflict is unendurable, and revolution results. Christianity, with its essentially static view of temporal history, creates no earthly disparity.

---

4. In Christianity, man is, of course, also "man-as-means," for man was created as a means of repopulating heaven after the Fall of Satan and the evil angels. (Notice how this concept is having consequences with respect to population control some 2,000 years later, consequences obviously never envisioned by those who emphasized the concept "Be fruitful, and multiply.") But, in point of fact, with the exception of the injunction to "Be fruitful, and multiply," and to serve God to his greater glory, man-as-means was never so important in the thinking of most Christians as man-as-end. Man as spiritual unit seems to have been the focus and center of Christianity—even during holy crusades, whether against the infidel without or the heretic within Christendom. The barbarism of religious wars must to some extent be explained, to be sure, in terms of self-interest and rationalization. But one must remember that even there rationalizations took a spiritual turn, a turn that suggests that spiritual values, at least at the conscious level, were in the forefront of Christian life. This emphasis, of course, is no longer as true today as it was then.

The disparity is strictly a disparity between this world and the next. The underlying hostility to this world, or *contemptus mundi,* of Christianity makes it less likely that one will be sacrificed for this world. (One may still be sacrificed, but for other expressed reasons. The true reasons may, of course, be the same.) Man, in Christianity, is to lead a life of "living sacrifice," not in the name of earthly progress, but for the sake of Heaven. And that state of blessedness cannot be gained by revolutions.

The tendency of communism, on the other hand, to depersonalize the individual, to see man as a force, as a social representative, to see him as symbol and personification, seems to be ironic in view of the enormous emphasis placed on seeing "real, active men." Once the visionary fervor rooted in a visceral empathy for man's plight fades, however, man's *essence* pales in the historical dialectic, and he is relegated to a behavioral mechanism, to a descriptive phenomenon. The emphasis is not even existential, for man is not free to choose truly what he does; he merely does.

Quite understandably, communism has looked with suspicion on psychoanalysis and smiled instead on behaviorism. Psychoanalysis is a depth psychology, a psychology with its own self-contained dialectic. It is introspective, subjective psychology; man is his consciousness, and he is vested with an individual dynamic, with an immutable essence, with density; he is determined but still capable of autonomy. Behaviorism on the other hand, is descriptive, objective psychology. Man is the product of external force fields, of his environment, of conditioning through habit and repetition. Man is defined not as consciousness, but as behavior. The model is man as programmed computer. And for the Marxist the programming is the programming of one's class. Thus Mao can assert, once again categorically, that "In class society everyone lives as a member of a particular class, and every kind of thinking, without exception, is stamped with the brand of a class" (23 Mao).

A preoccupation with history and class struggle, with rationalism, with man's behavior as determined, with behavior as we find it—all of these gradually inspire the creation of a new model of man. The Christian model of a coarse hairshirt worn by a gossamer spirit gives way, despite Marx's express hostility, to man as husk, man as hollow vessel to be filled either with bread or with meaningful work. And, in point of fact, this sense of man's loss, of man's alienation, of his emptiness, of his poverty and exploitation, lies at the center of much communist criticism of the unrealized, contemporary man who waits to be filled fully in the future, first with bread and work, then as species-man. That modern capitalist society has succeeded in creating many alienated husks—empty vessels—is, from this perspective, difficult to deny. Erich Fromm has commented with scarcely veiled anger on the disparity between Western attitudes toward Marxism and toward its own practices.

Among all the misunderstandings there is probably none more widespread than the idea of Marx's "materialism." Marx is supposed to have believed that the paramount psychological motive in man is his wish for monetary gain and comfort, and that this striving for maximum profit constitutes the main incentive in his personal life and in the life of the human race . . . that he had neither respect nor understanding for the spiritual needs of man, and that his "ideal" was the well-fed and well-clad, but "soulless" person. . . .

This view of Marx then goes on to discuss his socialist paradise as one of millions of people who submit to an all-powerful state bureaucracy, people who have surrendered their freedom, even though they might have achieved equality; these materially satisfied "individuals" have lost their individuality and have been successfully transformed into millions of uniform robots and automations, led by a small elite of better-fed leaders. . . .

I want to emphasize the irony which lies in the fact that the description given of the aim of Marx and of the content of his vision of socialism, fits almost exactly the reality of present-day Western capitalist society. The majority of people are motivated by a wish for greater material gain, for comfort and gadgets, and this wish is restricted only by the desire for security and the avoidance of risks. They are increasingly satisfied with a life regulated and manipulated, both in the sphere of production and of consumption, by the state and the big corporations and their respective bureaucracies; they have reached a degree of conformity which has wiped out individuality to a remarkable extent. They are, to use Marx's term, impotent "commodity men" serving virile machines. The very picture of mid-twentieth century capitalism is hardly distinguishable from the caricature of Marxist socialism as drawn by its opponents.

What is even more surprising is the fact that the people who accuse Marx most bitterly of "materialism" attack socialism for being unrealistic because it does *not* recognize that the only efficient incentive for man to work lies in his desire for material gain. Man's unbounded capacity for negating blatant contradictions by rationalizations, if it suits him, could hardly be better illustrated. The very same reasons which are said to be proof that Marx's ideas are incompatible with our religious and spiritual tradition and which are used *to defend* our present system *against* Marx, are at the same time employed by the same people to prove that capitalism corresponds to human nature and hence is far superior to an "unrealistic" socialism (24 Fromm).

What emerges clearly from our discussion is not that the communist model of man is true, or that Fromm's is false; what emerges is that, almost fifty years after T. S. Eliot wrote his poem "The Hollow Men," Western man still does not see himself as "hollow." The reason for our failure to see ourselves as "hollow men" is, of course, no guarantee that we are not. Traditional spiritualist modes of perception may still work to create an afterimage long after the sense of man's spirit has passed. Then too, we may be too busy even to look at ourselves. Perhaps, as William James suggests, we Americans truly are "cheerful nihilists" and care little about essences, "actualization," and "species-consciousness." What is important for us is not the truth, for that is difficult to glimpse, let alone perceive steadily and whole. What is important is that when we look at people, we do not see either with respect to man's present condition or to man's potentials what many communists see: we see something different.

And such fundamental differences in perspective—whatever may be the underlying realities that limit or condition them—have consequences. For us, perhaps for all people, the task is to decide whether in defiantly asserting the value of the old over the new we are expressing a rational conviction or merely reflecting a conventional bias. For we often find ourselves sadly lamenting the obstinate fear of change in others, without bothering to note that we too have our stubborn fidelities. In conflicts between the old and new, is it enough merely to assert the greater value of our position? Are there not—as this introduction attempts to show—questions one can ask to help evaluate troubled choices? Or do we ignore such questions, and by dramatizing the notion that people seek variety but fear change, prove our lack of originality?

Patterns: Argument by Analogy

Writers often betray unarticulated attitudes toward their subject matter by the progression of their argument. Thus writers who are strongly confident and outspoken, such as Marx, assert a proposition— "The history of all hitherto existing society is the history of class struggles" (*The Communist Manifesto*, [241/1-2]) —and then progress in a rather linear fashion to develop their argument. Because of the direct nature of the progression, which may be either causal or logical, the assumptions underlying their argument are usually apparent. We may not agree with the author's attitude but we are not at a great loss to discern it. We are rather more confused as to the author's attitude when, instead of asserting a proposition, he proposes an analogy. Of the logical arguments available, analogical argument is generally considered to be the least intellectual and the most emotional, for it permits an author to assert a similarity between two ideas, persons, institutions, or whatever, without defining the nature of his argument or being compelled to declare his attitude toward the analogy.

The persuasiveness of an analogy depends, of course, upon the author's ability to establish in a systematic way several corresponding points of similarity. The difficulty for the reader arises because he must necessarily so concern himself with the appropriateness of the analogy that he has little time to assess its emotional effect. An intelligent, careful reading of an essay using analogical argument is thus difficult until one has developed enough sensitivity to the emotional appeal inherent in such arguments to be able to assess the analogy's intent as well as its aptness. Thus the question, "Why was the analogy chosen?" is as important as the one, "How apt is it?" The previous essay, which compares Marxism to religion, illustrates, in addition to other matters, the manner in which analogical argument molds response.

The author opens his essay by suggesting an analogy between Marxism and Christianity—that is, between Marxism and religion. He attempts, to be sure, to disarm the reader by paying tribute to those who might feel such a comparison is "unsatisfactory." His concession is, however, only rhetorical, for he not only continues the analogy, he even informs us that it is "perhaps inevitable." This tendency to redefine preferences as obligations, to mandate interpretations as historical, scientific, or logical necessities, to transform subjective experience into something that purports to be objective reality, continues unabated not only in the essay, and especially in Marxist essays, but in life.

Until one develops a clear sense that defining an interpretation or even a conclusion as inevitable does not make it so, one can scarcely compensate for the increased intellectual passivity aroused by such assertions. Indeed, such assertions should lead to increased rather than reduced alertness. Thus a close analysis of the controlling religious analogy reveals it to be unadmittedly but continually hostile to communism. It neatly and nicely accomplishes all of the following:

(1) It offends communists who, being materialists, are hostile to religion.
(2) It tends to alienate rational humanists, who are repelled or at least vaguely put off by non-rational, quasi-mystical overtones of any kind. To define a movement, any movement, as religious in our secular age is to deal it a severe blow; for the non-communist secular humanist will more than likely respond to such an insinuation with fear, suspicion, hatred, or condescension—all of which are inimical to intellectual objectivity.
(3) It effectively excludes religious persons from an impartial investigation by inevitably making communism a competing or threatening antagonist. The analogy indirectly suggests, moreover—at least in a culture where single religion is the rule—the impossibility of being a Christian and a communist. The author implies this impossibility despite the fact that Catholic Italy possesses one of the largest communist parties outside of the communist bloc.

Though all of these consequences accrue from the analogy, they have accrued in a fashion so indirect as to make a direct charge of manipulation or bias difficult; for in making such a charge, one runs the risk of being accused of hypersensitivity or defensiveness. Indirect argument by analogy is thus an extremely effective means of molding response in imperceptible ways.

In the author's behalf, it can be said that the comparison was part of his rhetorical intention, that his profound desire to create shifting perspectives led him to the analogy with the preceding value system. One must be careful, however, not to extenuate too much. The author may have been compelled by larger aims to make analogies, but he was not compelled to make the analogies he did. He might, instead, have dwelt on the visionary affinities, the sense of human brotherhood, the self-sacrifice and altruism.

The cumulative effect of the analogy and its emphases is to establish in the reader a mind-set that is either hostile or indulgent. Either mind-set makes an objective evaluation of Marxism's intellectual merits difficult. Until the reader is aware of the prevalence of, and can recognize and compensate for, such rhetorical manipulations, he can hardly pretend to be free. He is determined, and determined in that most slavish of ways—by ignorance and insensitivity.

One last point. Readers who have begun to modify their response to communism because of this analysis of previous manipulation, have yet to realize that, in analyzing the emotional effects of analogical argument, this analysis has begged a major question: Were the analogies appropriate? The reader thus must cultivate an integrated emotional-intellectual response, lest being on the watch for emotional manipulation, he succumb to the intellectual. The reader is free to decide which fate is more to be dreaded.

14 KARL MARX & FRIEDRICH ENGELS

If the greatness of a man is measured by his effect on history, Karl Marx (1818–1883) is unquestionably one of the greatest men in history. There is about great men a living complexity and a prismatic perspective that make them extremely susceptible to misinterpretation. Like Walt Whitman, Marx also seems to "contain multitudes." Thus, Sartre sees the existentialist in him; Fromm appreciates his scientific rigor, his democratic spirit and great humanism; the communists revere Marx as dialectician and revolutionary; the typical American dwells on his hostility to bourgeois economic freedom and individuality; some even see something satanic at work.

Few of the latter have bothered to read what they so glibly damn, but reading Marx does not greatly simplify the problem: Marx wrote too much, too often under varying circumstances, over too long a period of time, and subject to too many appalling pressures, to permit us to seize upon a simple reality. A measure of his complexity—and the distortion of him by many hands—is suggested in the reluctance of the Russians to make available many of his unpublished manuscripts.

While still in his teens studying at the University of Berlin, Marx came under the influence of the leftist "Young Hegelians," a group influenced by, but opposed to Hegel, the rightist monarchist and German philosophical idealist. In 1841, at the age of 23, Marx received his doctorate in philosophy from Jena. Already by this time, his radical views had compelled him to turn to journalism, and for the next two years he edited the Rheinische Zeitung. *During these years he came under the influence of Ludwig Feuerbach, an antagonist of Hegel's view of the State as an absolute and of his concept of nature as the mirroring of an abstract Idea. But whereas Feuerbach's critique is mainly philosophical and religious, Marx is intent on analyzing the relationship of Hegel's state to civil society in order to show that the two are antagonistic, that "the State" is an abstraction, while civil society is the real-life battleground of individuals.*

When Marx's newspaper was suppressed in 1843, he went to Paris. There, in 1844, he met Friedrich Engels (1820–1895), who had elaborated views similar to Marx's. At this time, as a result of his background as the son of a wealthy German textile manufacturer, Engels may even have had a more sophisticated grasp of economics and capitalism. Their friendship deepened into a rich collaboration. The years 1843–1846, the years immediately prior to the proclamation of The Communist Manifesto *in 1848, were thus critical years in Marx's life and in the development of his thought. Though he remained* in Marx's shadow, Engels was a great man and an original mind in his own right. Very humane and generous, he lent financial support to Marx during his impoverished years of exile in England. After Marx died, he devoted the last years of his own life to editing his friend's manuscripts. Engels' relationship to Marx is a classic case of one great man humbly recognizing and serving a greater one.

Socialism: Utopian and Scientific *(1878)*, of which we present the third and final section, is one of the landmark essays in Marxism and a brilliant and simple exposition of how the contradictions inherent in capitalism doom it of historical necessity to self-destruction. The Communist Manifesto, *written two years later than* The German Ideology *(1845–1846) and four years later than "Alienated Labor" (1844), is perhaps too late a point at which to begin if one wants to understand systematically the evolution of Marx's thought and thus its full significance.* It is, however, the essay that most arouses our curiosity and interest, and it does, in hints and phrases, suggest something of the dimension of Marx's thought. While inflammatory and journalistic, it suggests both his critical and theoretical genius, and something of his visionary power. Despite his hostility to ideology, Marx becomes unavoidably both theoretician and ideologue.

The other, earlier essays are invaluable in more fully developing the ideas which were only sketched out in The Manifesto. *Contrary to their intention in that work, however, Marx and Engels in* The German Ideology *are less interested in publicizing theory than they are in explicating it in simple terms. From the opening sentence ("The premises from which we begin . . ."), and throughout the entire essay ("This method of approach is not devoid of premises. . . ."), Marx and Engels are interested in establishing the thesis that "circumstances make men just as much as men make circumstances." It is difficult for us, for whom this view is almost axiomatic some 125 years later, to realize that this discovery was truly imposing and a great change from the prevailing Idealism. More important, such a conception of consciousness gave people a complete new ontology that permitted them to envision changing their consciousness by changing their social environment. In a fundamental and significant way, man was thus liberated from his society.*

"Alienated Labor," *a section from* Economic and Philosophic Manuscripts, *the earliest of the three selections and the only one written by Marx alone, is the least general and the most extended discussion of Marx's theory of alienation that we have. In some ways a difficult and abstruse essay touching on economics and ontology, it is nevertheless essential to understanding the nature of Marx's criticism of modern capitalist society. The concept of alienation is central to Marx and to Marxism. For Marx the conflict between capital and labor, the competition between individuals and their entire preoccupation with prosperity and salary, were all the effects of the inevitable division of labor required by capitalism, of man's being alienated from his work and the products of his work, products that should have been, but were not, expressions of each individual's creative spirit. The degradation of the modern worker into a fragmentary tool, his alienation and spiritual malaise, stem thus from the mechanical nature of his work, from his indifference to it, from the fact that he is not expressed in it. Man, unable to create himself* through his work, becomes alienated from himself, becomes in his own eyes an object and a commodity. These ideas, expressed so well in The German Ideology, together with the theory of historical necessity through dialectic, fuse to form The Communist Manifesto.

A great deal has been made of Marx's personal life, his exile in England, his abject poverty, the death by starvation of his children, the arrest of his wife for begging. These ad hominem remarks which are meant to suggest the impracticability of his ideas by pointing out his inability to provide for his family, are of no concern to us. Had Marx wished, he could have prospered. But as Lewis Feuer has suggested:

> Despite his contemptuous rejection of ethical terms, Marx stands out as among the imposing ethical personalities of modern times. His action was more expressive than his word. He became the symbol of the intellectual who has not succumbed to either class or organizational pressures. He refused to be an ideologist or apologist, and he even spurned the discipline of socialist editorial boards. He was an intellectual who continued the tradition of prophetic protest. For what is a prophet? He is an intellectual who speaks with the voice of the lower classes, who articulates what they cannot say, and expresses their innermost, oftimes crushed and unconscious, aspirations. And Marx's identification with the "masses" was as total as a person's can be; free from the ordinary kinds of selfseeking, he looms as a reproach to the acquiescent, the complacent, the place hunter, the trimmer, and the smug (25 Feuer).

None of these matters are, of course, really our concern, for we are not concerned with his moral stature, but with his ideas. The following selections, both by Marx and by Engels, provide us with a sample diverse enough and long enough to suggest their power, and to make clear why Marxism has appealed to half of the peoples of the world.

from The Communist Manifesto

BOURGEOIS AND PROLETARIANS [1]

The history of all hitherto existing society is the history of class struggles.

Freeman and slave, patrician and plebeian, lord and serf, guildmaster and journeyman, in a word, oppressor and oppressed, stood in

From Karl Marx and Frederick Engels, *Selected Works* (Moscow: Progress Publishers, 1968), pp. 35–53.
1. By bourgeoisie is meant the class of modern Capitalists, owners of the means of social production and employers of wage labour. By proletariat, the class of wage-labourers who, having no means of production of their own, are reduced to selling their labour power in order to live. [*Note by Engels to the English edition of 1888.*]

constant opposition to one another, carried on an uninterrupted, now hidden, now open fight, a fight that each time ended, either in a revolutionary reconstitution of society at large, or in the common ruin of the contending classes.

In the earlier epochs of history, we find almost everywhere a complicated arrangement of society into various orders, a manifold gradation of social rank. In ancient Rome we have patricians, knights, plebeians, slaves; in the Middle Ages, feudal lords, vassals, guild-masters, journeymen, apprentices, serfs; in almost all of these classes, again, subordinate gradations.

The modern bourgeois society that has sprouted from the ruins of feudal society has not done away with class antagonisms. It has but established new classes, new conditions of oppression, new forms of struggle in place of the old ones.

Our epoch, the epoch of the bourgeoisie, possesses, however, this distinctive feature: it has simplified the class antagonisms. Society as a whole is more and more splitting up into two great hostile camps, into two great classes directly facing each other: Bourgeoisie and Proletariat.

From the serfs of the Middle Ages sprang the chartered burghers of the earliest towns. From these burgesses the first elements of the bourgeoisie were developed.

The discovery of America, the rounding of the Cape, opened up fresh ground for the rising bourgeoisie. The East-Indian and Chinese markets, the colonization of America, trade with the colonies, the increase in the means of exchange and in commodities generally, gave to commerce, to navigation, to industry, an impulse never before known, and thereby, to the revoluntionary element in the tottering feudal society, a rapid development.

The feudal system of industry, under which industrial production was monopolized by closed guilds, now no longer sufficed for the growing wants of the new markets. The manufacturing system took its place. The guild-masters were pushed on one side by the manufacturing middle class; division of labour between the different corporate guilds vanished in the face of division of labour in each single workshop.

Meantime the markets kept ever growing, the demand ever rising. Even manufacture no longer sufficed. Thereupon, steam and machinery revolutionized industrial production. The place of manufacture was taken by the giant, Modern Industry, the place of the industrial middle class, by industrial millionaires, the leaders of whole industrial armies, the modern bourgeois.

Modern industry has established the world market, for which the discovery of America paved the way. This market has given an immense development to commerce, to navigation, to communication by land. This development has, in its turn, reacted on the extension of industry; and in proportion as industry, commerce, navigation, railways extended, in the same proportion the bourgeoisie developed, increased its capital, and pushed into the background every class handed down from the Middle Ages.

We see, therefore, how the modern bourgeoisie is itself the product of a long course of development, of a series of revolutions in the modes of production and of exchange.

Each step in the development of the bourgeoisie was accompanied by a corresponding political advance of that class. An oppressed class under the sway of the feudal nobility, an armed and self-governing association in the medieval commune [2]; here independent urban republic (as in Italy and Germany), there taxable 'third estate' of the monarchy (as in France), afterwards, in the period of manufacture proper, serving either the semi-feudal or the absolute monarchy as a counterpoise against the nobility, and, in fact, corner-stone of the great monarchies in general, the bourgeoisie has at last, since the establishment of Modern Industry and of the world market, conquered for itself, in the modern representative State, exclusive political sway. The executive of the modern State is but a committee for managing the common affairs of the whole bourgeoisie.

The bourgeoisie, historically, has played a most revolutionary part.

The bourgeoisie, wherever it has got the upper hand, has put an end to all feudal, patriarchal, idyllic relations. It has pitilessly torn asunder the motley feudal ties that bound man to his 'natural superiors', and has left remaining no other nexus between man and man than naked self-interest, than callous 'cash payment'. It has drowned the most heavenly ecstasies of religious fervour, of chivalrous enthusiasm, of philistine sentimentalism, in the icy water of egotistical calculation. It has resolved personal worth into exchange value, and in place of the numberless indefeasible chartered freedoms, has set up that single, unconscionable freedom—Free Trade. In one word, for exploitation, veiled by religious and political illusions, it has substituted naked, shameless, direct, brutal exploitation.

The bourgeoisie has stripped of its halo every occupation hitherto honoured and looked up to with reverent awe. It has converted the physician, the lawyer, the priest, the poet, the man of science, into its paid wage-labourers.

The bourgeoisie has torn away from the family its sentimental veil, and has reduced the family relation to a mere money relation.

The bourgeoisie has disclosed how it came to pass that the brutal

---

2. 'Commune' was the name taken, in France, by the nascent towns even before they had conquered from their feudal lords and masters local self-government and political rights as the 'Third Estate'. Generally speaking, for the economical development of the bourgeoisie, England is here taken as the typical country; for its political development, France. [*Note by Engels to the English edition of 1888.*]

display of vigour in the Middle Ages, which Reactionists so much admire, found its fitting complement in the most slothful indolence. It has been the first to show what man's activity can bring about. It has accomplished wonders far surpassing Egyptian pyramids, Roman aqueducts, and Gothic cathedrals; it has conducted expeditions that put in the shade all former Exoduses of nations and crusades.

The bourgeoisie cannot exist without constantly revolutionizing the instruments of production, and thereby the relations of production, and with them the whole relations of society. Conservation of the old modes of production in unaltered form, was, on the contrary, the first condition of existence for all earlier industrial classes. Constant revolutionizing of production, uninterrupted disturbance of all social conditions, everlasting uncertainty and agitation distinguish the bourgeois epoch from all earlier ones. All fixed, fast-frozen relations, with their train of ancient and venerable prejudices and opinions are swept away, all new-formed ones become antiquated before they can ossify. All that is solid melts into air, all that is holy is profaned, and man is at last compelled to face with sober senses, his real conditions of life, and his relations with his kind.

The need of a constantly expanding market for its products chases the bourgeoisie over the whole surface of the globe. It must nestle everywhere, settle everywhere, establish connexions everywhere.

The bourgeoisie has through its exploitation of the world market given a cosmopolitan character to production and consumption in every country. To the great chagrin of Reactionists, it has drawn from under the feet of industry the national ground on which it stood. All old-established national industries have been destroyed or are daily being destroyed. They are dislodged by new industries, whose introduction becomes a life and death question for all civilized nations, by industries that no longer work up indigenous raw material, but raw material drawn from the remotest zones; industries whose products are consumed, not only at home, but in every quarter of the globe. In place of the old wants, satisfied by the productions of the country, we find new wants, requiring for their satisfaction the products of distant lands and climes. In place of the old local and national seclusion and self-sufficiency, we have intercourse in every direction, universal inter-dependence of nations. And as in material, so also in intellectual production. The intellectual creations of individual nations become common property. National one-sidedness and narrow-mindedness become more and more impossible, and from the numerous national and local literatures, there arises a world literature.

The bourgeoisie, by the rapid improvement of all instruments of production, by the immensely facilitated means of communication, draws all, even the most barbarian, nations into civilization. The cheap prices of its commodities are the heavy artillery with which it batters down all Chinese walls, with which it forces the barbarians' intensely obstinate hatred of foreigners to capitulate. It compels all nations, on pain of extinction, to adopt the bourgeois mode of production; it compels them to introduce what it calls civilization into their midst, i.e., to become bourgeois themselves. In one word, it creates a world after its own image.

The bourgeoisie has subjected the country to the rule of the towns. It has created enormous cities, has greatly increased the urban population as compared with the rural, and has thus rescued a considerable part of the population from the idiocy of rural life. Just as it has made the country dependent on the towns, so it has made barbarian and semi-barbarian countries dependent on the civilized ones, nations of peasants on nations of bourgeois, the East on the West.

The bourgeoisie keeps more and more doing away with the scattered state of the population, of the means of production, and of property. It has agglomerated population, centralized means of production, and has concentrated property in a few hands. The necessary consequence of this was political centralization. Independent, or but loosely connected, provinces with separate interests, laws, governments and systems of taxation, became lumped together into one nation, with one government, one code of laws, one national class-interest, one frontier and one customs-tariff.

The bourgeoisie, during its rule of scarce one hundred years, has created more massive and more colossal productive forces than have all preceding generations together. Subjection of Nature's forces to man, machinery, application of chemistry to industry and agriculture, steam-navigation, railways, electric telegraphs, clearing of whole continents for cultivation, canalization of rivers, whole populations conjured out of the ground—what earlier century had even a presentiment that such productive forces slumbered in the lap of social labour?

We see then: the means of production and of exchange, on whose foundation the bourgeoisie built itself up, were generated in feudal society. At a certain stage in the development of these means of production and of exchange, the conditions under which feudal society produced and exchanged, the feudal organization of agriculture and manufacturing industry, in one word, the feudal relations of property became no longer compatible with the already developed productive forces; they became so many fetters. They had to be burst asunder; they were burst asunder.

Into their place stepped free competition, accompanied by a social and political constitution adapted to it, and by the economical and political sway of the bourgeois class.

A similar movement is going on before our own eyes. Modern bourgeois society with its relations of production, of exchange and of property, a society that has conjured up such gigantic means of production and of exchange, is like the sorcerer, who is no longer able to control the powers of the nether world whom he has called up by his spells. For many a decade past the history of industry and commerce is but the history of the revolt of modern productive forces against modern conditions of production, against the property relations that are the conditions for the existence of the bourgeoisie and of its rule. It is enough to mention the commercial crises that by their periodical return put on its trial, each time more threateningly, the existence of the entire bourgeois society. In these crises a great part not only of the existing products, but also of the previously created productive forces, are periodically destroyed. In these crises there breaks out an epidemic that, in all earlier epochs, would have seemed an absurdity—the epidemic of over-production. Society suddenly finds itself put back into a state of momentary barbarism; it appears as if a famine, a universal war of devastation had cut off the supply of every means of subsistence; industry and commerce seem to be destroyed; and why? Because there is too much civilization, too much means of subsistence, too much industry, too much commerce. The productive forces at the disposal of society no longer tend to further the development of the conditions of bourgeois property; on the contrary, they have become too powerful for these conditions, by which they are fettered, and so soon as they overcome these fetters, they bring disorder into the whole of bourgeois society, endanger the existence of bourgeois property. The conditions of bourgeois society are too narrow to comprise the wealth created by them. And how does the bourgeoisie get over these crises? On the one hand by enforced destruction of a mass of productive forces; on the other, by the conquest of new markets, and by the more thorough exploitation of the old ones. That is to say, by paving the way for more extensive and more destructive crises, and by diminishing the means whereby crises are prevented.

The weapons with which the bourgeoisie felled feudalism to the ground are now turned against the bourgeoisie itself.

But not only has the bourgeoisie forged the weapons that bring death to itself; it has also called into existence the men who are to wield those weapons—the modern working class—the proletarians.

In proportion as the bourgeoisie, i.e., capital, is developed, in the same proportion is the proletariat, the modern working class, developed—a class of labourers, who live only so long as they find work, and who find work only so long as their labour increases capital. These labourers, who must sell themselves piecemeal, are a commodity, like every other article of commerce, and are consequently exposed to all the vicissitudes of competition, to all the fluctuations of the market.

Owing to the extensive use of machinery and to division of labour, the work of the proletarians has lost all individual character, and, consequently, all charm for the workman. He becomes an appendage of the machine, and it is only the most simple, most monotonous, and most easily acquired knack, that is required of him. Hence, the cost of production of a workman is restricted, almost entirely, to the means of subsistence that he requires for his maintenance, and for the propagation of his race. But the price of a commodity, and therefore also of labour, is equal to its cost of production. In proportion, therefore, as the repulsiveness of the work increases, the wage decreases. Nay more, in proportion as the use of machinery and division of labour increases, in the same proportion the burden of toil also increases, whether by prolongation of the working hours, by increase of the work exacted in a given time or by increased speed of the machinery, etc.

Modern industry has converted the little workshop of the patriarchal master into the great factory of the industrial capitalist. Masses of labourers, crowded into the factory, are organized like soliders. As privates of the industrial army they are placed under the command of a perfect hierarchy of officers and sergeants. Not only are they slaves of the bourgeois class, and of the bourgeois State; they are daily and hourly enslaved by the machine, by the overlooker, and, above all, by the individual bourgeois manufacturer himself. The more openly this despotism proclaims gain to be its end and aim, the more petty, the more hateful and the more embittering it is.

The less the skill and exertion of strength implied in manual labour, in other words, the more modern industry becomes developed, the more is the labour of men superseded by that of women. Differences of age and sex have no longer any distinctive social validity for the working class. All are instruments of labour, more or less expensive to use, according to their age and sex.

No sooner is the exploitation of the labourer by the manufacturer, so far, at an end, that he receives his wages in cash, then is is set upon by the other portions of the bourgeoisie, the landlord, the shopkeeper, the pawnbroker, etc.

The lower strata of the middle class—the small tradespeople, shopkeepers, and retired tradesmen generally, the handicraftsmen and peasants—all these sink gradually into the proleteriat, partly because their diminutive capital does not suffice for the scale on which Modern Industry is carried on, and is swamped in the competition with the large capitalists, partly because their specialized skill is rendered worthless by new methods of production. Thus the proletariat is recruited from all classes of the population.

The proletariat goes through various stages of development. With its birth begins its struggle with the bourgeoisie. At first the contest is carried on by individual labourers, then by the work-people of a factory, then by the operatives of one trade, in one locality, against the individual bourgeois who directly exploits them. They direct their attacks not against the bourgeois conditions of production, but against the instruments of production themselves; they destroy imported wares that compete with their labour, they smash to pieces machinery, they set factories ablaze, they seek to restore by force the vanished status of the workman of the Middle Ages.

At this stage the labourers still form an incoherent mass scattered over the whole country, and broken up by their mutual competition. If anywhere they unite to form more compact bodies, this is not yet the consequence of their own active union, but of the union of the bourgeoisie, which class, in order to attain its own political ends, is compelled to set the whole proletariat in motion, and is moreover yet, for a time, able to do so. At this stage, therefore, the proletarians do not fight their enemies, but the enemies of their enemies, the remnants of absolute monarchy, the landowners, the non-industrial bourgeois, the petty bourgeoisie. Thus the whole historical movement is concentrated in the hands of the bourgeoisie; every victory so obtained is a victory for the bourgeoisie.

But with the development of industry the proletariat not only increases in number; it becomes concentrated in greater masses, its strength grows, and it feels that strength more. The various interests and conditions of life within the ranks of the proletariat are more and more equalized, in proportion as machinery obliterates all distinctions of labour, and nearly everywhere reduces wages to the same low level. The growing competition among the bourgeois, and the resulting commercial crises, make the wages of the workers ever more fluctuating. The unceasing improvement of machinery, ever more rapidly developing, makes their livelihood more and more precarious; the collisions between individual workmen and individual bourgeois take more and more the character of collisions between two classes. Thereupon the workers begin to form combinations (Trades Unions) against the bourgeois; they club together in order to keep up the rate of wages; they found permanent associations in order to make provision beforehand for these occasional revolts. Here and there the contest breaks out into riots.

Now and then the workers are victorious, but only for a time. The real fruit of their battles lies, not in the immediate result, but in the ever-expanding union of the workers. This union is helped on by the improved means of communication that are created by modern industry and that place the workers of different localities in contact with one another. It was just this contact that was needed to centralize the numerous local struggles, all of the same character, into one national struggle between classes. But every class struggle is a political struggle. And that union, to attain which the burghers of the Middle Ages, with their miserable highways, required centuries, the modern proletarians, thanks to railways, achieve in a few years.

This organization of the proletarians into a class, and consequently into a political party, is continually being upset again by the competition between the workers themselves. But it ever rises up again, stronger, firmer, mightier. It compels legislative recognition of particular interests of the workers, by taking advantage of the divisions among the bourgeoisie itself. Thus the Ten Hours bill in England was carried.

Altogether collisions between the classes of the old society further, in many ways, the course of development of the proletariat. The bourgeoisie finds itself involved in a constant battle. At first with the aristocracy; later on, with those portions of the bourgeoisie itself, whose interests have become antagonistic to the progress of industry; at all times, with the bourgeoisie of foreign countries. In all these battles it sees itself compelled to appeal to the proletariat, to ask for its help, and thus, to drag it into the political arena. The bourgeoisie itself, therefore, supplies the proletariat with its own elements of political and general education, in other words, it furnishes the proletariat with weapons for fighting the bourgeoisie.

Further, as we have already seen, entire sections of the ruling classes are, by the advance of industry, precipitated into the proletariat, or are at least threatened in their conditions of existence. These also supply the proletariat with fresh elements of enlightenment and progress.

Finally, in times when the class struggle nears the decisive hour, the process of dissolution going on within the ruling class, in fact within the whole range of old society, assumes such a violent, glaring character, that a small section of the ruling class cuts itself adrift, and joins the revolutionary class, the class that holds the future in its hands. Just as, therefore, at an earlier period, a section of the nobility went over to the bourgeoisie, so now a portion of the bourgeoisie goes over to the proletariat, and in particular, a portion of the bourgeois ideologists, who have raised themselves to the level of comprehending theoretically the historical movement as a whole.

Of all the classes that stand face to face with the bourgeoisie today, the proletariat alone is a really revolutionary class. The other classes decay and finally disappear in the face of modern industry; the proletariat is its special and essential product.

The lower middle class, the small manufacturer, the shopkeeper, the artisan, the peasant, all these fight against the bourgeoisie, to save from extinction their existence as fractions of the middle class. They are therefore not revolutionary, but conservative. Nay more, they are reactionary, for they try to roll back the wheel of history. If by chance they are revolutionary, they are so only in view of their impending transfer into the proletariat; they thus defend not their present, but their future interests, they desert their own standpoint to place themselves at that of the proletariat.

The 'dangerous class', the social scum, that passively rotting mass thrown off by the lowest layers of old society, may, here and there, be swept into the movement by a proletarian revolution; its conditions of life, however, prepare it far more for the part of a bribed tool of reactionary intrigue.

In the conditions of the proletariat, those of old society at large are already virtually swamped. The proletarian is without property; his relation to his wife and children has no longer anything in common with the bourgeois family relations; modern industrial labour, modern subjection to capital, the same in England as in France, in America as in Germany, has stripped him of every trace of national character. Law, morality, religion, are to him so many bourgeois prejudices, behind which lurk in ambush just as many bourgeois interests.

All the preceding classes that got the upper hand sought to fortify their already acquired status by subjecting society at large to their conditions of appropriation. The proletarians cannot become masters of the productive forces of society, except by abolishing their own previous mode of appropriation, and thereby also every other previous mode of appropriation. They have nothing of their own to secure and to fortify; their mission is to destroy all previous securities for, and insurances of, individual property.

All previous historical movements were movements of minorities, or in the interest of minorities. The proletarian movement is the self-conscious, independent movement of the immense majority, in the interest of the immense majority. The proletariat, the lowest stratum of our present society, cannot stir, cannot raise itself up, without the whole superincumbent strata of official society being sprung into the air.

Though not in substance, yet in form, the struggle of the proletariat with the bourgeoisie is at first a national struggle. The proletariat of each country must, of course, first of all settle matters with its own bourgeoisie.

In depicting the most general phases of the development of the proletariat, we traced the more or less veiled civil war, raging within existing society, up to the point where that war breaks out into open revolution, and where the violent overthrow of the bourgeoisie lays the foundation for the sway of the proletariat.

Hitherto, every form of society has been based, as we have already seen, on the antagonism of oppressing and oppressed classes. But in order to oppress a class, certain conditions must be assured to it under which it can, at least, continue its slavish existence. The serf, in the period of serfdom, raised himself to membership in the commune, just as the petty bourgeois, under the yoke of feudal absolutism, managed to develop into a bourgeois. The modern labourer, on the contrary, instead of rising with the progress of industry, sinks deeper and deeper below the conditions of existence of his own class. He becomes a pauper, and pauperism develops more rapidly than population and wealth. And here it becomes evident, that the bourgeoisie is unfit any longer to be the ruling class in society, and to impose its conditions of existence upon society as an overriding law. It is unfit to rule because it is incompetent to assure an existence to its slave within his slavery, because it cannot help letting him sink into such a state, that it has to feed him, instead of being fed by him. Society can no longer live under this bourgeoisie; in other words, its existence is no longer compatible with society.

The essential condition for the existence, and for the sway of the bourgeois class, is the formation and augmentation of capital, the condition for capital is wage labour. Wage labour rests exclusively on competition between the labourers. The advance of industry, whose involuntary promoter is the bourgeoisie, replaces the isolation of the labourers, due to competition, by their revolutionary combination, due to association. The development of Modern Industry, therefore, cuts from under its feet the very foundation on which the bourgeoisie produces and appropriates products. What the bourgeoisie, therefore, produces, above all, is its own grave-diggers. Its fall and the victory of the proletariat are equally inevitable.

PROLETARIANS AND COMMUNISTS

In what relation do the Communists stand to the proletarians as a whole?

The Communists do not form a separate party opposed to other working-class parties.

They have no interests separate and apart from those of the proletariat as a whole.

They do not set up any sectarian principles of their own, by which to shape and mould the proletarian movement.

The Communists are distinguished from the other working-class parties by this only: 1. In the national struggles of the proletarians of the different countries, they point out and bring to the front the common interests of the entire proletariat, independently of all nationality. 2. In the various stages of development which the struggle of the working class against the bourgeoisie has to pass through, they always and everywhere represent the interests of the movement as a whole.

The Communists, therefore, are on the one hand, practically, the most advanced and resolute section of the working-class parties of every country, that section which pushes forward all others; on the other hand, theoretically, they have over the great mass of the proletariat the advantage of clearly understanding the line of march, the conditions, and the ultimate general results of the proletarian movement.

The immediate aim of the Communists is the same as that of all the other proletarian parties: formation of the proletariat into a class, overthrow of the bourgeois supremacy, conquest of political power by the proletariat.

The theoretical conclusions of the Communists are in no way based on ideas or principles that have been invented, or discovered, by this or that would-be universal reformer.

They merely express, in general terms, actual relations springing from an existing class struggle, from a historical movement going on under our very eyes. The abolition of existing property relations is not at all a distinctive feature of Communism.

All property relations in the past have continually been subject to historical change consequent upon the change in historical conditions.

The French Revolution, for example, abolished feudal property in favour of bourgeois property.

The distinguishing feature of Communism is not the abolition of property generally, but the abolition of bourgeois property. But modern bourgeois private property is the final and most complete expression of the system of producing and appropriating products, that is based on class antagonisms, on the exploitation of the many by the few.

In this sense, the theory of the Communists may be summed up in the single sentence: Abolition of private property.

We Communists have been reproached with the desire of abolishing the right of personally acquiring property as the fruit of a man's own labour, which property is alleged to be the ground work of all personal freedom, activity and independence.

Hard-won, self-acquired, self-earned property! Do you mean the property of the petty artisan and of the small peasant, a form of property that preceded the bourgeois form? There is no need to abolish that; the development of industry has to a great extent already destroyed it, and is still destroying it daily.

Or do you mean modern bourgeois private property?

But does wage labour create any property for the labourer? Not a bit. It creates capital, i.e., that kind of property which exploits wage labour, and which cannot increase except upon condition of begetting a new supply of wage labour for fresh exploitation. Property, in its present form, is based on the antagonism of capital and wage labour. Let us examine both sides of this antagonism.

To be a capitalist is to have not only a purely personal but a social *status* in production. Capital is a collective product, and only by the united action of many members, nay, in the last resort, only by the united action of all members of society, can it be set in motion.

Capital is, therefore, not a personal, it is a social power.

When, therefore, capital is converted into common property, into the property of all members of society, personal property is not thereby transformed into social property. It is only the social character of the property that is changed. It loses its class character.

Let us now take wage labour.

The average price of wage labour is the minimum wage, i.e., that quantum of the means of subsistence which is absolutely requisite to keep the labourer in bare existence as a labourer. What, therefore, the wage-labourer appropriates by means of his labour, merely suffices to prolong and reproduce a bare existence. We by no means intend to abolish this personal appropriation of the products of labour, an appropriation that is made for the maintenance and reproduction of human life, and that leaves no surplus wherewith to command the labour of others. All that we want to do away with is the miserable character of this appropriation, under which the labourer lives merely to increase capital, and is allowed to live only in so far as the interest of the ruling class requires it.

In bourgeois society, living labour is but a means to increase accumulated labour. In Communist society, accumulated labour is but a means to widen, to enrich, to promote the existence of the labourer.

In bourgeois society, therefore, the past dominates the present; in Communist society, the present dominates the past. In bourgeois society capital is independent and has individuality, while the living person is dependent and has no individuality.

And the abolition of this state of things is called by the bourgeois, abolition of individuality and freedom! And rightly so. The abolition of bourgeois individuality, bourgeois independence, and bourgeois freedom is undoubtedly aimed at.

By freedom is meant, under the present bourgeois conditions of production, free trade, free selling and buying.

But if selling and buying disappears, free selling and buying disappears also. This talk about free selling and buying, and all the other 'brave words' of our bourgeoisie about freedom in general, have a meaning, if any, only in contrast with restricted selling and buying, with the fettered traders of the Middle Ages, but have no meaning when opposed to the Communistic abolition of buying and selling, of the bourgeois conditions of production, and of the bourgeoisie itself.

You are horrified at our intending to do away with private property. But in your existing society, private property is already done away with for nine-tenths of the population; its existence for the few is solely due to its non-existence in the hands of those nine-tenths. You reproach us, therefore, with intending to do away with a form of property the necessary condition for whose existence is the non-existence of any property for the immense majority of society.

In one word, you reproach us with intending to do away with your property. Precisely so; that is just what we intend.

From the moment when labour can no longer be converted into

capital, money, or rent, into a social power capable of being monopolized, i.e., from the moment when individual property can no longer be transformed into bourgeois property, into capital, from that moment, you say, individuality vanishes.

You must, therefore, confess that by 'individual' you mean no other person than the bourgeois, than the middle-class owner of property. This person must, indeed, be swept out of the way, and made impossible.

Communism deprives no man of the power to appropriate the products of society; all that it does is to deprive him of the power to subjugate the labour of others by means of such appropriation.

It has been objected that upon the abolition of private property all work will cease, and universal laziness will overtake us.

According to this, bourgeois society ought long ago to have gone to the dogs through sheer idleness; for those of its members who work, acquire nothing, and those who acquire anything, do not work. The whole of this objection is but another expression of the tautology: that there can no longer be any wage labour when there is no longer any capital.

All objections urged against the Communistic mode of producing and appropriating material products, have, in the same way, been urged against the Communistic modes of producing and appropriating intellectual products. Just as, to the bourgeois, the disappearance of class property is the disappearance of production itself, so the disappearance of class culture is to him identical with the disappearance of all culture.

That culture, the loss of which he laments, is, for the enormous majority, a mere training to act as a machine.

But don't wrangle with us so long as you apply, to our intended abolition of bourgeois property, the standard of your bourgeois notions of freedom, culture, law, &c. Your very ideas are but the outgrowth of the conditions of your bourgeois production and bourgeois property, just as your jurisprudence is but the will of your class made into a law for all, a will, whose essential character and direction are determined by the economical conditions of existence of your class.

The selfish misconception that induces you to transform into eternal laws of nature and of reason, the social forms springing from your present mode of production and form of property—historical relations that rise and disappear in the progress of production—this misconception you share with every ruling class that has preceded you. What you see clearly in the case of ancient property, what you admit in the case of feudal property, you are of course forbidden to admit in the case of your own bourgeois form of property.

Abolition of the family! Even the most radical flare up at this infamous proposal of the Communists.

On what foundation is the present family, the bourgeois family, based? On capital, on private gain. In its completely developed form this family exists only among the bourgeoisie. But this state of things finds its complement in the practical absence of the family among the proletarians, and in public prostitution.

The bourgeois family will vanish as a matter of course when its complement vanishes, and both will vanish with the vanishing of capital.

Do you charge us with wanting to stop the exploitation of children by their parents? To this crime we plead guilty.

But, you will say, we destroy the most hallowed of relations, when we replace home education by social.

And your education! Is not that also social, and determined by the social conditions under which you educate, by the intervention, direct or indirect, of society, by means of schools, &c? The Communists have not invented the intervention of society in education; they do but seek to alter the character of that intervention, and to rescue education from the influence of the ruling class.

The bourgeois clap-trap about the family and education, about the hallowed co-relation of parent and child, becomes all the more disgusting, the more, by the action of Modern Industry, all family ties among the proletarians are torn asunder, and their children transformed into simple articles of commerce and instruments of labour.

But you Communists would introduce community of women, screams the whole bourgeoisie in chorus.

The bourgeois sees in his wife a mere instrument of production. He hears that the instruments of production are to be exploited in common, and, naturally, can come to no other conclusion than that the lot of being common to all will likewise fall to the women.

He has not even a suspicion that the real point aimed at is to do away with the status of women as mere instruments of production.

For the rest, nothing is more ridiculous than the virtuous indignation of our bourgeois at the community of women which, they pretend, is to be openly and officially established by the Communists. The Communists have no need to introduce community of women; it has existed almost from time immemorial.

Our bourgeois, not content with having the wives and daughters of their proletarians at their disposal, not to speak of common prostitutes, take the greatest pleasure in seducing each other's wives.

Bourgeois marriage is in reality a system of wives in common and thus, at the most, what the Communists might possibly be reproached with, is that they desire to introduce, in substitution for a hypocritically concealed, an openly legalized community of women. For the rest, it is self-evident that the abolition of the present system of production must bring with it the abolition of the community of women springing from that system, i.e., of prostitution both public and private.

The Communists are further reproached with desiring to abolish countries and nationality.

The working men have no country. We cannot take from them what they have not got. Since the proletariat must first of all acquire political supremacy, must rise to be the leading class of the nation, must constitute itself *the* nation, it is, so far, itself national, though not in the bourgeois sense of the word.

National differences and antagonisms between peoples are daily more and more vanishing, owing to the development of the bourgeoisie, to freedom of commerce, to the world market, to uniformity in the mode of production and in the conditions of life corrsponding thereto.

The supremacy of the proletariat will cause them to vanish still faster. United action, of the leading civilized countries at least, is one of the first conditions for the emancipation of the proletariat.

In proportion as the exploitation of one individual by another is put an end to, the exploitation of one nation by another will also be put an end to. In proportion as the antagonism between classes within the nation vanishes, the hostility of one nation to another will come to an end.

The charges against Communism made from a religious, a philosophical, and, generally, from an ideological standpoint, are not deserving of serious examination.

Does it require deep intuition to comprehend that man's ideas, views and conceptions, in one word, man's consciousness, changes with every change in the conditions of his material existence, in his social relations and in his social life?

What else does the history of ideas prove, than that intellectual production changes in character in proportion as material production is changed? The ruling ideas of each age have ever been the ideas of its ruling class.

When people speak of ideas that revolutionize society, they do but express the fact, that within the old society, the elements of a new one have been created, and that the dissolution of the old ideas keeps even pace with the dissolution of the old conditions of existence.

When the ancient world was in its last throes, the ancient religions were overcome by Christianity. When Christian ideas succumbed in the 18th century to rationalist ideas, feudal society fought its death battle with the then revolutionary bourgeoisie. The ideas of religious liberty and freedom of conscience, merely gave expression to the sway of free competition within the domain of knowledge.

'Undoubtedly,' it will be said, 'religious, moral, philosophical and juridical ideas have been modified in the course of historical development. But religion, morality, philosophy, political science, and law, constantly survived this change.

'There are, besides, eternal truths, such as Freedom, Justice, etc., that are common to all states of society. But Communism abolishes eternal truths, it abolishes all religion, and all morality, instead of constituting them on a new basis; it therefore acts in contradiction to all past historical experience.'

What does this accusation reduce itself to? The history of all past society has consisted in the development of class antagonisms, antagonisms that assumed different forms at different epochs.

But whatever form they may have taken, one fact is common to all past ages, viz., the exploitation of one part of society by the other. No wonder, then, that the social consciousness of past ages, despite all the multiplicity and variety it displays, moves within certain common forms, or general ideas, which cannot completely vanish except with the total disappearance of class antagonisms.

The Communist revolution is the most radical rupture with traditional property relations; no wonder that its development involves the most radical rupture with traditional ideas.

But let us have done with the bourgeois objections to Communism.

We have seen above, that the first step in the revolution by the working class, is to raise the proletariat to the position of ruling class, to win the battle of democracy.

The proletariat will use its political supremacy to wrest, by degrees, all capital from the bourgeoisie, to centralize all instruments of production in the hands of the State, i.e., of the proletariat organized as the ruling class; and to increase the total of productive forces as rapidly as possible.

Of course, in the beginning, this cannot be effected except by means of despotic inroads on the rights of property, and on the conditions of bourgeois production; by means of measures, therefore, which appear economically insufficient and untenable, but which, in the course of the movement, outstrip themselves, necessitate further inroads upon the old social order, and are unavoidable as a means of entirely revolutionizing the mode of production.

These measures will of course be different in different countries.

Nevertheless, in the most advanced countries, the following will be pretty generally applicable:

(1) Abolition of property in land and application of all rents of land to public purposes.

(2) A heavy progressive or graduated income tax.

(3) Abolition of all right of inheritance.

(4) Confiscation of the property of all emigrants and rebels.

(5) Centralization of credit in the hands of the State, by means of a national bank with State capital and an exclusive monopoly.

(6) Centralization of the means of communication and transport in the hands of the State.

(7) Extension of factories and instruments of production owned by the State; the bringing into cultivation of wastelands, and the improvement of the soil generally in accordance with a common plan.

(8) Equal liability of all to labour. Establishment of industrial armies, especially for agriculture.

(9) Combination of agriculture with manufacturing industries; gradual abolition of the distinction between town and country, by a more equable distribution of the population over the country.

(10) Free education for all children in public schools. Abolition of children's factory labour in its present form. Combination of education with industrial production, &c., &c.

When, in the course of development, class distinctions have disappeared, and all production has been concentrated in the whole nation, the public power will lose its political character. Political power, properly so called, is merely the organized power of one class for oppressing another. If the proletariat during its contest with the bourgeoisie is compelled, by the force of circumstances, to organize itself as a class, if, by means of a revolution, it makes itself the ruling class, and, as such, sweeps away by force the old conditions of production, then it will, along with these conditions, have swept away the conditions for the existence of class antagonisms and of classes generally, and will thereby have abolished its own supremacy as a class.

In place of the old bourgeois society, with its classes and class antagonisms, we shall have an association, in which the free development of each is the condition for the free development of all.

Problems

1. For Marx, class struggle ends in one of two possible results. What are they? How have the phases of western history tended either to support or to deny Marx's thesis?
2. What is the immediate aim of the communists? How do they arrive at their theoretical conclusion?
3. Why is Marx hostile toward political power vested in a class?
4. What kind of relationship does Marx accuse bourgeoisie of favoring? Can you envision another relationship equally binding but far more satisfying?
5. How do bourgeois means of production and means of exchange tend to reshape the world in their own image? In what ways does the bourgeois means of production create dependency? In what way does it create monopoly and concentration of wealth?
6. How does bourgeois society cope with the crises caused by the means of production being greater than society's capacity to absorb what is produced?
7. What forces operate together to turn the workingman into a mass, undifferentiated commodity?
8. How does increased industrialization work to destroy the lower-middle class and make it the most reactionary force in society?

9. To what extent is Marx's distinction between personal property and private property valid, useful, and appropriate?
10. For Marx, what is the distinction between the way bourgeois society and communist society use the capital gained from accumulated labor?
11. Marx is scornful of bourgois freedom and individuality. To what extent is he right or wrong in his definition of what freedom and individuality mean to the bourgeoisie?
12. Marx attacks those who "transform into eternal laws of nature" their present "mode of production and form of prosperity." Into what kinds of confusion does this lead the bourgeoisie?
13. What rhetorical devices does Marx use to give power and authority to his work?
14. How does Marx's concept of history differ from that of Christianity?

from The German Ideology*

The premises from which we begin are not arbitrary ones, not dogmas, but real premises from which abstraction can only be made in the imagination. They are the real individuals, their activity and the

From Karl Marx & Friedrich Engels, *The German Ideology*, translated from the German; edited by S. Ryazanskaya (Moscow: Progress Publishers, 1968), pp. 31–65. [All of the footnotes in this essay (except the two signed *"VC,"* 11 and 15) are present in the edition from which this text is taken.]
* *The German Ideology—Die deutsche Ideologie. Kritik der neuesten deutschen Philosophie in ihren Repräsentanten Feuerbach, B. Bauer und Stirner, und des deutschen Sozialismus in seinen verschiedenen Propheten*—written in 1845-46, is the joint work of Marx and Engels.
    In the spring of 1845 Marx and Engels decided to write the book together and set to work in earnest the following September. The manuscript, which amounted to approximately fifty printed sheets, was divided into two volumes, the first of which comprised principally an elaboration of the fundamental theses of historical materialism and a critique of the philosophical views of Ludwig Feuerbach, Bruno Bauer and Max Stirner, while the second volume was devoted to a criticism of the views of several representatives of "true" socialism.
    Work on *The German Ideology* was in the main terminated in the summer of 1846. By that time, the greater part of the first volume had been written—namely "The Leipzig Council," the chapters devoted to the criticism of the views of Bruno Bauer and Max Stirner—and the second volume for the most part too. The authors still continued to work on the first section of Volume I (the criticism of Ludwig Feuerbach's views) during the second half of 1846, but did not complete it.
    In May 1846 the major part of the manuscript of Volume I was sent from Brussels to Joseph Weydemeyer in Westphalia. Weydemeyer was to make arrangements for the publication of the book with the financial support that had been promised by two local businessmen, the "true" socialists Julius Meyer and Rudolph Rempel. But after the bulk of the manuscript of Volume II had arrived in Westphalia, Meyer and Rempel informed Marx (in their letter of July 13, 1846) that

material conditions under which they live, both those which they find already existing and those produced by their activity. These premises can thus be verified in a purely empirical way.

The first premise of all human history is, of course, the existence of living human individuals.[1] Thus the first fact to be established is the physical organisation of these individuals and their consequent relation to the rest of nature. Of course, we cannot here go either into the actual physical nature of man, or into the natural conditions in which man finds himself—geological, orohydrographical, climatic and so on.[2] The writing of history must always set out from these natural bases and their modification in the course of history through the action of men.

Men can be distinguished from animals by consciousness, by religion or anything else you like. They themselves begin to distinguish themselves from animals as soon as they begin to *produce* their means of subsistence, a step which is conditioned by their physical organization. By producing their means of subsistence men are indirectly producing their actual material life.

The way in which men produce their means of subsistence depends first of all on the nature of the actual means of subsistence they find in existence and have to reproduce. This mode of production must not be considered simply as being the reproduction of the physical existence of the individuals. Rather it is a definite form of activity of these individuals, a definite form of expressing their life, a definite *mode of life* on their part. As individuals express their life, so they are. What they

---

they were unwilling to finance the publication of *The German Ideology*. In 1846-47 Marx and Engels made repeated attempts to find a publisher in Germany for their work; their efforts were, however, unsuccessful. This was due partly to difficulties made by the police and partly to the reluctance of the publishers to print the work, since their sympathies were on the side of the representatives of the trends attacked by Marx and Engels. Only one chapter of *The German Ideology* was published during the lifetime of Marx and Engels, namely, Chapter IV of Volume II, printed in the journal *Das Westphälische Dampfboot*, August and September 1847. . . .

Neither the title of the book nor the headings of volumes I and II have survived in the manuscript. They have been inserted on the basis of Marx's note against Karl Grün, published in *Deutsche-Brüsseler-Zeitung*, April 8, 1847. . . .

The manuscript of chapters II and III of Volume II is not extant.

A number of manuscript pages have been damaged by "the gnawing criticism of the mice." Where possible the affected passages have been reconstructed on the basis of the unimpaired parts; in such cases the words inserted by the editors are enclosed in square brackets.

1. [The following passage is crossed out in the manuscript:] The first *historical* act of these individuals distinguishing them from animals is not that they think, but that they begin to *produce their means of subsistence*.
2. [The following passage is crossed out in the manuscript:] Not only the original, spontaneous organisation of men, especially racial differences, depends on these conditions but also the entire further development, or lack of development, of men up to the present time.

are, therefore, coincides with their production, both with *what* they produce and with *how* they produce. The nature of individuals thus depends on the material conditions determining their production.

This production only makes its appearance with the *increase of population*. In its turn this presupposes the *intercourse* [*Verkehr* *] of individuals with one another. The form of this intercourse is again determined by production.

The relations of different nations among themselves depend upon the extent to which each has developed its productive forces, the division of labour and internal intercourse. This statement is generally recognised. But not only the relation of one nation to others, but also the whole internal structure of the nation itself depends on the stage of development reached by its production and its internal and external intercourse. How far the productive forces of a nation are developed is shown most manifestly by the degree to which the division of labour has been carried. Each new productive force, insofar as it is not merely a quantitative extension of productive forces already known (for instance the bringing into cultivation of fresh land), causes a further development of the division of labour.

The division of labour inside a nation leads at first to the separation of industrial and commercial from agricultural labour, and hence to the separation of *town* and *country* and to the conflict of their interests. Its further development leads to the separation of commercial from industrial labour. At the same time through the division of labour inside these various branches there develop various divisions among the individuals co-operating in definite kinds of labour. The relative position of these individual groups is determined by the methods employed in agriculture, industry and commerce (patriarchalism, slavery, estates, classes). These same conditions are to be seen (given a more developed intercourse) in the relations of different nations to one another.

The various stages of development in the division of labour are just so many different forms of ownership, i.e., the existing stage in the division

---

* In *The German Ideology* the word "*Verkehr*" is used in a very wide sense, encompassing the material and spiritual intercourse of separate individuals, social groups and entire countries. Marx and Engels show that material intercourse, and above all the intercourse of men with each other in the production process, is the basis of every other form of intercourse.

The terms "*Verkehrsform*" (form of intercourse), "*Verkehrsweise*" (mode of intercourse) and "*Verkehrsverhältnisse*" (relations, or conditions, of intercourse) which we encounter in *The German Ideology* are used by Marx and Engels to express the concept "relations of production" which during that period was taking shape in their mind.

The ordinary dictionary meanings of "*Verkehr*" are traffic, intercourse, commerce. In this translation the word "*Verkehr*" has been mostly rendered as "intercourse" and occasionally as "association" or "commerce."

of labour determines also the relations of individuals to one another with reference to the material, instrument, and product of labour.

The first form of ownership is tribal [*Stammeigentum* *] ownership. It corresponds to the undeveloped stage of production at which a people lives by hunting and fishing, by the rearing of beasts or, in the highest stage, agriculture. In the latter case it presupposes a great mass of uncultivated stretches of land. The division of labour is at this stage still very elementary and is confined to a further extension of the natural division of labour existing in the family. The social structure is, therefore, limited to an extension of the family; patriarchal family chieftains, below them the members of the tribe, finally slaves. The slavery latent in the family only develops gradually with the increase of population, the growth of wants, and with the extension of external relations, both of war and of barter.

The second form is the ancient communal and State ownership which proceeds especially from the union of several tribes into a *city* by agreement or by conquest, and which is still accompanied by slavery. Beside communal ownership we already find movable, and later also immovable, private property developing, but as an abnormal form subordinate to communal ownership. The citizens hold power over their labouring slaves only in their community, and on this account alone, therefore, they are bound to the form of communal ownership. It is the communal private property which compels the active citizens to remain in this spontaneously derived form of association over against their slaves. For this reason the whole structure of society based on this communal ownership, and with it the power of the people, decays in the same measure as, in particular, immovable private property evolves. The division of labour is already more developed. We already find the antagonism of town and country; later the antagonism between those states which represent town interests and those which represent country interests, and inside the towns themselves the antagonism between industry and maritime commerce. The class relation between citizens and slaves is now completely developed.

This whole interpretation of history appears to be contradicted by

---

* The term "*Stamm*"—rendered in the present volume by the word "tribe"—played a considerably greater part in historical works written during the forties of the last century, than it does at present. It was used to denote a community of people descended from a common ancestor, and comprised the modern concepts of "gens" and "tribe." The first to define and differentiate these concepts was Lewis Henry Morgan in his work *Ancient Society; or, Researches in the Lines of Human Progress from Savagery Through Barbarism to Civilisation,* London, 1877. This outstanding American ethnographer and historian showed for the first time the significance of the gens as the nucleus of the primitive communal system and thereby laid the scientific foundations for the history of primitive society as a whole. Engels drew the general conclusions from Morgan's discoveries and made a comprehensive analysis of the meaning of the concepts "gens" and "tribe" in his work *The Origin of the Family, Private Property and the State* (1884).

the fact of conquest. Up till now violence, war, pillage, murder and robbery, etc., have been accepted as the driving force of history. Here we must limit ourselves to the chief points and take, therefore, only the most striking example—the destruction of an old civilisation by a barbarous people and the resulting formation of an entirely new organisation of society. (Rome and the barbarians; feudalism and Gaul; the Byzantine Empire and the Turks.) With the conquering barbarian people war itself is still, as indicated above, a regular form of intercourse, which is the more eagerly exploited as the increase in population together with the traditional and, for it, the only possible, crude mode of production gives rise to the need for new means of production. In Italy, on the other hand, the concentration of landed property (caused not only by buying-up and indebtedness but also by inheritance, since loose living being rife and marriage rare, the old families gradually died out and their possessions fell into the hands of a few) and its conversion into grazing-land (caused not only by the usual economic forces still operative today but by the importation of plundered and tribute-corn and the resultant lack of demand for Italian corn) brought about the almost total disappearance of the free population. The very slaves died out again and again, and had constantly to be replaced by new ones. Slavery remained the basis of the whole productive system. The plebeians, midway between freemen and slaves, never succeeded in becoming more than a proletarian rabble. Rome indeed never became more than a city; its connection with the provinces was almost exclusively political and could, therefore, easily be broken again by political events.

With the development of private property, we find here for the first time the same conditions which we shall find again, only on a more extensive scale, with modern private property. On the one hand, the concentration of private property, which began very early in Rome (as the Licinian agrarian law proves* and proceeded very rapidly from the time of the civil wars and especially under the Emperors; on the other hand, coupled with this, the transformation of the plebeian small peasantry into a proletariat, which, however, owing to its intermediate position between propertied citizens and slaves, never achieved an independent development.

The third form of ownership is feudal or estate property. If antiquity started out from the *town* and its little territory, the Middle Ages started out from the *country*. This different starting-point was determined by the sparseness of the population at that time, which was scattered over a large area and which received no large increase from the conquerors. In con-

* The *Licinian agrarian law*—the agrarian law of Licinius and Sextius, Roman tribunes of the people, passed in 367 B.C. as a result of the struggle which the plebeians waged against the patricians. According to this law a Roman citizen could not hold more than 500 Yugera (approximately 309 acres) of common land (*ager publicus*).

trast to Greece and Rome, feudal development at the outset, therefore, extends over a much wider territory, prepared by the Roman conquests and the spread of agriculture at first associated with them. The last centuries of the declining Roman Empire and its conquest by the barbarians destroyed a number of productive forces; agriculture had declined, industry had decayed for want of a market, trade had died out or been violently suspended, the rural and urban population had decreased. From these conditions and the mode of organisation of the conquest determined by them, feudal property developed under the influence of the Germanic military constitution. Like tribal and communal ownership, it is based again on a community; but the directly producing class standing over against it is not, as in the case of the ancient community, the slaves, but the enserfed small peasantry. As soon as feudalism is fully developed, there also arises antagonism to the towns. The hierarchical structure of landownership, and the armed bodies of retainers associated with it, gave the nobility power over the serfs. This feudal organisation was, just as much as the ancient communal ownership, an association against a subjected producing class; but the form of association and the relation to the direct producers were different because of the different conditions of production.

This feudal system of landownership had its counterpart in the *towns* in the shape of corporative property, the feudal organisation of trades. Here property consisted chiefly in the labour of each individual person. The necessity for association against the organised robber-nobility, the need for communal covered markets in an age when the industrialist was at the same time a merchant, the growing competition of the escaped serfs swarming into the rising towns, the feudal structure of the whole country: these combined to bring about the *guilds*. The gradually accumulated small capital of individual craftsmen and their stable numbers, as against the growing population, evolved the relation of journeyman and apprentice, which brought into being in the towns a hierarchy similar to that in the country.

Thus the chief form of property during the feudal epoch consisted on the one hand of landed property with serf labour chained to it, and on the other of the labour of the individual with small capital commanding the labour of journeymen. The organisation of both was determined by the restricted conditions of production—the small-scale and primitive cultivation of the land, and the craft type of industry. There was little division of labour in the heyday of feudalism. Each country bore in itself the antithesis of town and country; the division into estates was certainly strongly marked; but apart from the differentiation of princes, nobility, clergy and peasants in the country, and masters, journeymen, apprentices and soon also the rabble of casual labourers in the towns, no division of importance took place. In agriculture it was rendered difficult by the strip-system, beside which the cottage industry of the peasants themselves emerged. In industry there was no division of labour at all in the individual trades themselves, and very little between them. The separation of industry and commerce was found already in existence in older towns; in the newer it only developed later, when the towns entered into mutual relations.

The grouping of larger territories into feudal kingdoms was a necessity for the landed nobility as for the towns. The organisation of the ruling class, the nobility, had, therefore, everywhere a monarch at its head.

The fact is, therefore, that definite individuals who are productively active in a definite way enter into these definite social and political relations. Empirical observation must in each separate instance bring out empirically, and without any mystification and speculation, the connection of the social and political structure with production. The social structure and the State are continually evolving out of the life-process of definite individuals, but of individuals, not as they may appear in their own or other people's imagination, but as they *really* are; i.e., as they operate, produce materially, and hence as they work under definite material limits, presuppositions and conditions independent of their will.[4]

The production of ideas, of conceptions, of consciousness, is at first directly interwoven with the material activity and the material intercourse of men, the language of real life. Conceiving, thinking, the mental intercourse of men, appear at this stage as the direct efflux of their material behaviour. The same applies to mental production as expressed in the language of politics, laws, morality, religion, metaphysics, etc., of a people. Men are the producers of their conception, ideas, etc.—real, active men, as they are conditioned by a definite development of their productive forces and of the intercourse corresponding to these, up to its furthest forms. Consciousness can never be anything else than conscious existence, and the existence of men is their actual life-process. If in all ideology men and their circumstances appear upside-down as in a *camera obscura,* this phenomenon arises just as much from their historical life-process as the inversion of objects on the retina does from their physical life-process.

In direct contrast to german philosophy which descends from heaven to earth, here we ascend from earth to heaven. That is to say, we do not

---

4. [The following passage is crossed out in the manuscript:] The ideas which these individuals form are ideas either about their relation to nature or about mutual relations or about their own nature. It is evident that in all these cases their ideas are the conscious expression—real or illusory—of their real relationships and activities, of their production and intercourse and of their social and political organisation. The opposite assumption is only possible if in addition to the spirit of the real, materially evolved individuals a separate spirit is presupposed. If the conscious expression of the real relations of these individuals is illusory, if in their imagination they turn reality upsidedown, then this in its turn is the result of their limited material mode of activity and their limited social relations arising from it.

set out from what men say, imagine, conceive, nor from men as narrated, thought of, imagined, conceived, in order to arrive at men in the flesh. We set out from real, active men, and on the basis of their real life-process we demonstrate the development of the ideological reflexes and echoes of this life-process. The phantoms formed in the human brain are also, necessarily, sublimates of their material life-process, which is empirically verifiable and bound to material premises. Morality, religion, metaphysics, all the rest of ideology and their corresponding forms of consciousness, thus no longer retain the semblance of independence. They have no history, no development; but men, developing their material production and their material intercourse, alter, along with this their real existence, their thinking and the products of their thinking. Life is not determined by consciousness, but consciousness by life. In the first method of approach the starting-point is consciousness taken as the living individual; in the second method, which conforms to real life, it is the real living individuals themselves, and consciousness is considered solely as *their* consciousness.

This method of approach is not devoid of premises. It starts out from the real premises and does not abandon them for a moment. Its premises are men, not in any fantastic isolation and rigidity, but in their actual, empirically perceptible process of development under definite conditions. As soon as this active life-process is described, history ceases to be a collection of dead facts as it is with the empiricists (themselves still abstract), or an imagined activity of imagined subjects, as with the idealists.

Where speculation ends—in real life—there real, positive science begins: the representation of the practical activity, of the practical process of development of men. Empty talk about consciousness ceases, and real knowledge has to take its place. When reality is depicted, philosophy as an independent branch of knowledge loses its medium of existence. At the best its place can only be taken by a summing-up of the most general results, abstractions which arise from the observation of the historical development of men. Viewed apart from real history, these abstractions have in themselves no value whatsoever. They can only serve to facilitate the arrangement of historical material, to indicate the sequence of its separate strata. But they by no means afford a recipe or schema, as does philosophy, for neatly trimming the epochs of history. On the contrary, our difficulties begin only when we set about the observation and the arrangement—the real depiction—of our historical material, whether of a past epoch or of the present. The removal of these difficulties is governed by premises which it is quite impossible to state here, but which only the study of the actual life-process and the activity of the individuals of each epoch will make evident. We shall select here some of these abstractions, which we use in contradistinction to the ideologists, and shall illustrate them by historical examples.

[1.] HISTORY

Since we are dealing with the Germans, who are devoid of premises, we must begin by stating the first premise of all human existence and, therefore, of all history, the premise, namely, that man must be in a position to live in order to be able to "make history".[5] But life involves before everything else eating and drinking, a habitation, clothing and many other things. The first historical act is thus the production of the means to satisfy these needs, the production of material life itself. And indeed this is an historical act, a fundamental condition of all history, which today, as thousands of years ago, must daily and hourly be fulfilled merely in order to sustain human life. Even when the sensuous world is reduced to a minimum, to a stick as with Saint Bruno, it presupposes the action of producing the stick. Therefore in any interpretation of history one has first of all to observe this fundamental fact in all its significance and all its implications and to accord it its due importance. It is well known that the Germans have never done this, and they have never, therefore, had an *earthly* basis for history and consequently never a historian. The French and the English, even if they have conceived the relation of this fact with so-called history only in an extremely one-sided fashion, particularly as long as they remained in the toils of political ideology, have nevertheless made the first attempts to give the writing of history a materialistic basis by being the first to write histories of civil society, of commerce and industry.

The second point is that the satisfaction of the first need (the action of satisfying, and the instrument of satisfaction which has been acquired) leads to new needs; and this production of new needs is the first historical act. Here we recognise immediately the spiritual ancestry of the great historical wisdom of the Germans who, when they run out of positive material and when they can serve up neither theological nor political nor literary rubbish, assert that this is not history at all, but the "prehistoric era". They do not, however, enlighten us as to how we proceed from this nonsensical "prehistory" to history proper; although, on the other hand, in the historical speculation they seize upon this "prehistory" with especial eagerness because they imagine themselves safe there from interference on the part of "crude facts", and, at the same time, because there they can give full rein to their speculative impulse and set up and knock down hypotheses by the thousand.

The third circumstance which, from the very outset, enters into historical development, is that men, who daily remake their own life,

---

5. [Marginal note by Marx:] *Hegel*. Geological, hydrographical, etc., conditions. Human bodies. Needs, labour.

begin to make other men, to propagate their kind: the relation between man and woman, parents and children, the *family*. The family, which to begin with is the only social relationship, becomes later, when increased needs create new social relations and the increased population new needs, a subordinate one (except in Germany), and must then be treated and analysed according to the existing empirical data, not according to "the concept of the family", as is the custom in Germany.[6] These three aspects of social activity are not of course to be taken as three different stages, but just as three aspects or, to make it clear to the Germans, three "moments", which have existed simultaneously since the dawn of history and the first men, and which still assert themselves in history today.

The production of life, both of one's own in labour and of fresh life in procreation, now appears as a double relationship: on the one hand as a natural, on the other as a social relationship. By social we understand the co-operation of several individuals, no matter under what conditions, in what manner and to what end. It follows from this that a certain mode of production, or industrial stage, is always combined with a certain mode of co-operation, or social stage, and this mode of co-operation is itself a "productive force". Further, that the multitude of productive forces accessible to men determines the natures of society, hence, that the "history of humanity" must always be studied, and treated in relation to the history of industry and exchange. But it is also clear how in Germany it is impossible to write this sort of history, because the Germans lack not only the necessary power of comprehension and the material but also the "evidence of their senses", for across the Rhine you cannot have any experience of these things since history has stopped happening. Thus it is quite obvious from the start that there exists a materialistic connection of men with one another, which is determined by their needs and their mode of production, and which is as old as men themselves. This connection is ever taking on new forms, and thus presents a "history"

6. The building of houses. With savages each family has as a matter of course its own cave or hut like the separate family tent of the nomads. This separate domestic economy is made only the more necessary by the further development of private property. With the agricultural peoples a communal domestic economy is just as impossible as a communal cultivation of the soil. A great advance was the building of towns. In all previous periods, however, the abolition of individual economy, which is inseparable from the abolition of private property, was impossible for the simple reason that the material conditions governing it were not present. The setting-up of a communal domestic economy presupposes the development of machinery, of the use of natural forces and of many other productive forces—e.g., of water-supplies, of gas-lighting, steam-heating, etc., the removal [of the antagonism] of town and country. Without these conditions a communal economy would not in itself form a new productive force; lacking any material basis and resting on a purely theoretical foundation, it would be a mere freak and would end in nothing more than a monastic economy.—What was possible can be seen in the towns brought about by condensation and the erection of communal buildings for various definite purposes (prisons, barracks, etc.). That the abolition of individual economy is inseparable from the abolition of the family is self-evident.

independently of the existence of any political or religious nonsense which would especially hold men together.

Only now, after having considered four moments, four aspects of the primary historical relationships, do we find that man also possesses "consciousness" [7] but, even so, not inherent, not "pure" consciousness. From the start the "spirit" is afflicted with the curse of being "burdened" with matter, which here makes its appearance in the form of agitated layers of air, sounds, in short, of language. Language is as old as consciousness, language *is* practical consciousness that exists also for other men, and for that reason alone it really exists for me personally as well; language, like consciousness, only arises from the need, the necessity, of intercourse with other men.[8] Where there exists a relationship, it exists for me: the animal does not enter into "*relations*" with anything, it does not enter into any relation at all. For the animal, its relation to others does not exist as a relation. Consciousness is, therefore, from the very beginning a social product, and remains so as long as men exist at all. Consciousness is at first, of course, merely consciousness concerning the *immediate* sensuous environment and consciousness of the limited connection with other persons and things outside the individual who is growing self-conscious. At the same time it is consciousness of nature, which first appears to men as a completely alien, all-powerful and unassailable force, with which men's relations are purely animal and by which they are overawed like beasts; it is thus a purely animal consciousness of nature (natural religion).

We see here immediately: this natural religion or this particular relation of men to nature is determined by the form of society and vice versa. Here, as everywhere, the identity of nature and man appears in such a way that the restricted relation of men to nature determines their restricted relation to one another, and their restricted relation to one another determines men's restricted relation to nature, just because nature is as yet hardly modified historically; and, on the other hand, man's consciousness of the necessity of associating with the individuals around him is the beginning of the consciousness that he is living in society at all. This beginning is as animal as social life itself at this stage. It is mere herd-consciousness, and at this point man is only distinguished from sheep by the fact that with him consciousness takes the place of instinct or that his instinct is a conscious one.

This sheep-like or tribal consciousness receives its further development and extension through increased productivity, the increase of

---

7. [Marginal note by Marx:] Men have history because they must *produce* their life, and because they must produce it moreover in a *certain* way: this is determined by their physical organisation; their consciousness is determined in just the same way.
8. [The following words are crossed out in the manuscript:] My relationship to my surroundings is my consciousness.

needs, and, what is fundamental to both of these, the increase of population. With these there develops the division of labour, which was originally nothing but the division of labour in the sexual act, then that division of labour which develops spontaneously or "naturally" by virtue of natural predisposition (e.g., physical strength), needs, accidents, etc., etc. Division of labour only becomes truly such from the moment when a division of material and mental labour appears.[9] From this moment onwards consciousness *can* really flatter itself that it is something other than consciousness of existing practice, that it *really* represents something without representing something real; from now on consciousness is in a position to emancipate itself from the world and to proceed to the formation of "pure" theory, theology, philosophy, ethics, etc. But even if this theory, theology, philosophy, ethics, etc., comes into contradiction with the existing relations, this can only occur because existing social relations have come into contradiction with existing forces of production; this, moreover, can also occur in a particular national sphere of relations through the appearance of the contradiction, not within the national orbit, but between this national consciousness and the practice of other nations,[10] i.e., between the national and the general consciousness of a nation (as we see it now in Germany).

Moreover, it is quite immaterial what consciousness starts to do on its own: out of all such muck we get only the one inference that these three moments, the forces of production, the state of society, and consciousness, can and must come into contradiction with one another, because the *division of labour* implies the possibility, nay the fact that intellectual and material activity—enjoyment and labour, production and consumption—devolve on different individuals, and that the only possibility of their not coming into contradiction lies in the negation in its turn of the division of labour. It is self-evident, moreover, that "spectres", "bonds", "the higher being", "concept", "scruple", are merely the idealistic, spiritual expression, the conception apparently of the isolated individual, the image of very empirical fetters and limitations, within which the mode of production of life and the form of intercourse coupled with it move.

With the division of labour, in which all these contradictions are implicit, and which in its turn is based on the natural division of labour in the family and the separation of society into individual families opposed to one another, is given simultaneously the *distribution,* and indeed the *unequal* distribution, both quantitative and qualitative, of labour and its products, hence property: the nucleus, the first form, of which lies in the family, where wife and children are the slaves of the husband. This latent slavery in the family, though still very crude, is the first property, but even at this early stage it corresponds perfectly to the definition of

9. [Marginal note by Marx:] The first form of ideologists, *priests,* is concurrent.
10. [Marginal note by Marx:] *Religion.* The Germans and *ideology* as such.

modern economists who call it the power of disposing of the labour-power of others. Division of labour and private property are, moreover, identical expressions: in the one the same thing is affirmed with reference to activity as is affirmed in the other with reference to the product of the activity.

Further, the division of labour implies the contradiction between the interest of the separate individual or the individual family and the communal interest of all individuals who have intercourse with one another. And indeed, this communal interest does not exist merely in the imagination, as the "general interest", but first of all in reality, as the mutual interdependence of the individuals among whom the labour is divided. And finally, the division of labour offers us the first example of how, as long as man remains in natural society, that is, as long as a cleavage exists between the particular and the common interest, as long, therefore, as activity is not voluntarily, but naturally, divided, man's own deed becomes an alien power opposed to him, which enslaves him instead of being controlled by him. For as soon as the distribution of labour comes into being, each man has a particular, exclusive sphere of activity, which is forced upon him and from which he cannot escape. He is a hunter, a fisherman, a shepherd, or a critical critic, and must remain so if he does not want to lose his means of livelihood; while in communist society, where nobody has one exclusive sphere of activity but each can become accomplished in any branch he wishes, society regulates the general production and thus makes it possible for me to do one thing today and another tomorrow, to hunt in the morning, fish in the afternoon, rear cattle in the evening, criticise after dinner, just as I have a mind, without ever becoming hunter, fisherman, shepherd or critic. This fixation of social activity, this consolidation of what we ourselves produce into an objective power above us, growing out of our control, thwarting our expectations, bringing to naught our calculations, is one of the chief factors in historical development up till now.

And out of this very contradiction between the interest of the individual and that of the community the latter takes an independent form as the *State,* divorced from the real interests of individual and community, and at the same time as an illusory communal life, always based, however, on the real ties existing in every family and tribal conglomeration— such as flesh and blood, language, division of labour on a larger scale, and other interests—and especially, as we shall enlarge upon later, on the classes, already determined by the division of labour, which in every such mass of men separate out, and of which one dominates all the others. It follows from this that all struggles within the State, the struggle between democracy, aristocracy, and monarchy, the struggle for the franchise, etc., etc., are merely the illusory forms in which the real struggles of the different classes are fought out among one another (of this the

German theoreticians have not the faintest inkling, although they have received a sufficient introduction to the subject in the *Deutsch-Französische Jahrbücher* and *Die heilige Familie**).

Further, it follows that every class which is struggling for mastery, even when its domination, as is the case with the proletariat, postulates the abolition of the old form of society in its entirety and of domination itself, must first conquer for itself political power in order to represent its interest in turn as the general interest, which in the first moment it is forced to do. Just because individuals seek *only* their particular interest, which for them does not coincide with their communal interest (in fact the general is the illusory form of communal life), the latter will be imposed on them as an interest "alien" to them, and "independent" of them, as in its turn a particular, peculiar "general" interest; or they themselves must remain within this discord, as in democracy. On the other hand, too, the *practical* struggle of these particular interests, which constantly *really* run counter to the communal and illusory communal interests, makes *practical* intervention and control necessary through the illusory "general" interest in the form of the State. The social power, i.e., the multiplied productive force, which arises through the co-operation of different individuals as it is determined by the division of labour, appears to these individuals, since their co-operation is not voluntary but has come about naturally, not as their own united power, but as an alien force existing outside them, of the origin and goal of which they are ignorant, which they thus cannot control, which on the contrary passes through a peculiar series of phases and stages independent of the will and the action of man, nay even being the prime governor of these.

This *"estrangement"* [11] (to use a term which will be comprehensible

---

* *Deutsch-Französische Jahrbücher (German-French Annals)*—a magazine edited by Karl Marx and Arnold Ruge and published in German in Paris. Only the first issue, a double number, appeared (in February 1844). It included two articles by Karl Marx—"Zur Judenfrage" ("On the Jewish Question") and "Zur Kritik der Hegelschen Rechtsphilosophie. Einleitung" ("Contribution to a Critique of the Hegelian Philosophy of Law. Introduction")—and two by Frederick Engels—"Umrisse zu einer Kritik der Nationalökonomie" ("Outlines of a Critique of Political Economy") and "Die Lage Englands. 'Past and Present' by Thomas Carlyle, London 1843" ("The Position of England. 'Past and Present' by Thomas Carlyle, London 1843"). These works mark the final transition of Marx and Engels to materialism and communism. Publication of the periodical was discontinued mainly as a result of basic differences of opinion between Marx and Ruge, who was a bourgeois radical.

Friedrich Engels und Karl Marx, *Die heilige Familie, oder Kritik der kritischen Kritik. Gegen Bruno Bauer und Consorten,* Frankfurt a. M., 1845. (The English translation has been published under the title: *The Holy Family, or Critique of Critical Critique. Against Bruno Bauer and Co.,* Foreign Languages Publishing House, Moscow 1956.)

11. [This is the term preferred by Hegel, for whom the estrangement was that of mind unaccustomed to its material form. For Marx, it becomes the "alienation" of man from himself, from a fully realized humanity. See the selection that follows, Marx's essay "Alienated Labor," for a full elaboration of the concept. VC]

to the philosophers) can, of course, only be abolished given two *practical* premises. For it to become an "intolerable" power, i.e., a power against which men make a revolution, it must necessarily have rendered the great mass of humanity "propertyless", and produced, at the same time, the contradiction of an existing world of wealth and culture, both of which conditions presuppose a great increase in productive power, a high degree of its development. And, on the other hand, this development of productive forces (which itself implies the actual empirical existence of men in their *world-historical,* instead of local, being) is an absolutely necessary practical premise because without it *want* is merely made general, and with *destitution* the struggle for necessities and all the old filthy business would necessarily be reproduced; and furthermore, because only with this universal development of productive forces is a *universal* intercourse between men established, which produces in all nations simultaneously the phenomenon of the "propertyless" mass (universal competition), makes each nation dependent on the revolutions of the others, and finally has put *world-historical,* empirically universal individuals in place of local ones. Without this, (1) communism could only exist as a local event; (2) the *forces* of intercourse themselves could not have developed as *universal,* hence intolerable powers: they would have remained home-bred conditions surrounded by superstition; and (3) each extension of intercourse would abolish local communism. Empirically, communism is only possible as the act of the dominant peoples "all at once" and simultaneously, which presupposes the universal development of productive forces and the world intercourse bound up with communism.* How otherwise could for instance property have had a history at all, have taken on different forms, and landed property, for example, according to the different premises given, have proceeded in France from parcellation to centralisation in the hands of a few, in England from centralisation in the hands of a few to parcellation, as is actually the case today? Or how does it happen that trade, which after all is nothing more than the exchange of products of various individuals and countries, rules the whole world through the relation of supply and demand—a relation which, as an English economist says, hovers over the earth like the fate of the ancients, and with in-

---

* The conclusion that the proletarian revolution could only be carried through in all the advanced capitalist countries simultaneously, and hence that the victory of the revolution in a single country was impossible, which received its final expression in Engels's essay *Grundsätze des Kommunismus* (1847), was correct for the period of premonopoly capitalism.
    Lenin—who took as his starting-point the law of uneven economic and political development of capitalism in the epoch of imperialism discovered by him—came to the conclusion that, in the new historical conditions, the socialist revolution could be victorious at first in a few countries, or even in a single country, and pointed out that the victory of the revolution in all or in most countries simultaneously was impossible. This thesis was for the first time set forth in Lenin's article "On the Slogan for a United States of Europe" (1915). (Lenin, *Collected Works,* Moscow 1964, Vol. 21.)

visible hand allots fortune and misfortune to men, sets up empires and overthrows empires, causes nations to rise and to disappear—while with the abolition of the basis of private property, with the communistic regulation of production (and, implicit in this, the destruction of the alien relation between men and what they themselves produce), the power of the relation of supply and demand is dissolved into nothing, and men get exchange, production, the mode of their mutual relation, under their own control again?

Communism is for us not a *state of affairs* which is to be established, an *ideal* to which reality (will) have to adjust itself. We call communism the *real* movement which abolishes the present state of things. The conditions of this movement result from the premises now in existence. Moreover, the mass of *propertyless* workers—the utterly precarious position of labour-power on a mass scale cut off from capital or from even a limited satisfaction and, therefore, no longer merely temporarily deprived of work itself as a secure source of life—presupposes the *world market* through competition. The proletariat can thus only exist *world-historically,* just as communism, its activity, can only have a "world-historical" existence. World-historical existence of individuals, i.e., existence of individuals which is directly linked up with world history.

The form of intercourse determined by the existing productive forces at all previous historical stages, and in its turn determining these, is *civil society*. The latter, as is clear from what we have said above, has as its premises and basis the simple family and the multiple, the so-called tribe, and the more precise determinants of this society are enumerated in our remarks above. Already here we see how this civil society is the true source and theatre of all history, and how absurd is the conception of history held hitherto, which neglects the real relationships and confines itself to high-sounding dramas of princes and states.[12]

Civil society embraces the whole material intercourse of individuals within a definite stage of the development of productive forces. It embraces the whole commercial and industrial life of a given stage and, insofar, transcends the State and the nation, though, on the other hand again, it must assert itself in its foreign relations as nationality, and inwardly must organise itself as State. The term "civil society" [*bürgerliche Gesellschaft*][13] emerged in the eighteenth century, when property relationships had already extricated themselves from the ancient and medieval communal society. Civil society as such only develops with the bourgeoisie; the social organisation evolving directly out of production

---

12. [The following passage is crossed out in the manuscript:] In the main we have so far considered only one aspect of human activity, the *reshaping of nature* by men. The other aspect, the *reshaping of men by men*. . . .
    Origin of the State and the relation of the State to civil society.
13. *"Bürgerliche Gesellschaft"* can mean either "bourgeois society" or "civil society". —Ed.

and commerce, which in all ages forms the basis of the State and of the rest of the idealistic superstructure, has, however, always been designated by the same name.

[2.] CONCERNING THE PRODUCTION OF CONSCIOUSNESS

In history up to the present it is certainly an empirical fact that separate individuals have, with the broadening of their activity into world-historical activity, become more and more enslaved under a power alien to them (a pressure which they have conceived of as a dirty trick on the part of the so-called universal spirit, etc.), a power which has become more and more enormous and, in the last instance, turns out to be the *world market*. But it is just as empirically established that, by the overthrow of the existing state of society by the communist revolution (of which more below) and the abolition of private property which is identical with it, this power, which so baffles the German theoreticians, will be dissolved; and that then the liberation of each single individual will be accomplished in the measure in which history becomes transformed into world history. From the above it is clear that the real intellectual wealth of the individual depends entirely on the wealth of his real connections. Only then will the separate individuals be liberated from the various national and local barriers, be brought into practical connection with the material and intellectual production of the whole world and be put in a position to acquire the capacity to enjoy this all-sided production of the whole earth (the creations of man). *All-round* dependence, this natural form of the *world-historical* co-operation of individuals, will be transformed by this communist revolution into the control and conscious mastery of these powers, which, born of the action of men on one another, have till now overawed and governed men as powers completely alien to them. Now this view can be expressed again in speculative-idealistic, i.e., fantastic, terms as "self-generation of the species" ("society as the subject"), and thereby the consecutive series of interrelated individuals connected with each other can be conceived as a single individual, which accomplishes the mystery of generating itself. It is clear here that individuals certainly make *one another,* physically and mentally, but do not make themselves either in the nonsense of Saint Bruno, or in the sense of the "Unique", of the "made" man.

This conception of history depends on our ability to expound the real process of production, starting out from the material production of life itself, and to comprehend the form of intercourse connected with this and created by this mode of production (i.e., civil society in its various stages), as the basis of all history; and to show it in its action as State, to explain all the different theoretical products and forms of consciousness, religion, philosophy, ethics, etc. etc., and trace their origins and growth from that basis; by which means, of course, the whole thing can be depicted in its totality (and therefore, too, the reciprocal action of these various sides on one another). It has not, like the idealistic view of history, in every period to look for a category, but remains constantly on the real *ground* of history; it does not explain practice from the idea but explains the formation of ideas from material practice; and accordingly it comes to the conclusion that all forms and products of consciousness cannot be dissolved by mental criticism, by resolution into "self-consciousness" or transformation into "apparitions", "spectres", "fancies", etc., but only by the practical overthrow of the actual social relations which gave rise to this idealistic humbug; that not criticism but revolution is the driving force of history, also of religion, of philosophy and all other types of theory. It shows that history does not end by being resolved into "self-consciousness" as "spirit of the spirit", but that in it at each stage there is found a material result: a sum of productive forces, a historically created relation of individuals to nature and to one another, which is handed down to each generation from its predecessor; a mass of productive forces, capital funds and conditions, which, on the one hand, is indeed modified by the new generation, but also on the other prescribes for it its conditions of life and gives it a definite development, a special character. It shows that circumstances make men just as much as men make circumstances.

This sum of productive forces, capital funds and social forms of intercourse, which every individual and generation finds in existence as something given, is the real basis of what the philosophers have conceived as "substance" and "essence of man", and what they have deified and attacked: a real basis which is not in the least disturbed, in its effect and influence on the development of men, by the fact that these philosophers revolt against it as "self-consciousness" and the "Unique". These conditions of life, which different generations find in existence, decide also whether or not the periodically recurring revolutionary convulsion will be strong enough to overthrow the basis of the entire existing system. And if these material elements of a complete revolution are not present (namely, on the one hand the existing productive forces, on the other the formation of a revolutionary mass, which revolts not only against separate conditions of society up till then, but against the very "production of life" till then, the "total activity" on which it was based), then, as far as practical development is concerned, it is absolutely immaterial whether the *idea* of this revolution has been expressed a hundred times already, as the history of communism proves.

In the whole conception of history up to the present this real basis of history has either been totally neglected or else considered as a minor matter quite irrelevant to the course of history. History must, therefore, always be written according to an extraneous standard; the real production of life seems to be primeval history, while the truly historical appears to be separated from ordinary life, something extra-superterrestrial. With this the relation of man to nature is excluded from history and hence the antithesis of nature and history is created. The exponents of this conception of history have consequently only been able to see in history the political actions of princes and States, religious and all sorts of theoretical struggles, and in particular in each historical epoch have had to *share the illusion of that epoch*. For instance, if an epoch imagines itself to be actuated by purely "political" or "religious" motives, although "religion" and "politics" are only forms of its true motives, the historian accepts this opinion. The "idea", the "conception" of the people in question about their real practice, is transformed into the sole determining, active force, which controls and determines their practice. When the crude form in which the division of labour appears with the Indians and Egyptians calls forth the caste-system in their State and religion, the historian believes that the caste-system is the power which has produced this crude social form. While the French and the English at least hold by the political illusion, which is moderately close to reality, the Germans move in the realm of the "pure spirit", and make religious illusion the driving force of history.

The Hegelian philosophy of history is the last consequence, reduced to its "finest expression", of all this German historiography, for which it is not a question of real, nor even of political, interests, but of pure thoughts, which consequently must appear to Saint Bruno, as a series of "thoughts" that devour one another and are finally swallowed up in "self-consciousness" [14] and even more consistently the course of history appears to the Blessed Max Stirner,[15] who knows not a thing about real history, as a mere tale of "knights", robbers and ghosts, from whose visions he can, of course, only save himself by "unholiness". This conception is truly religious: it postulates religious man as the primitive man, the starting-point of history; and in its imagination puts the religious production of fancies in the place of the real production of the means of subsistence and of life itself. This whole conception of history, together with its dissolution and the scruples and qualms resulting from it, is a purely *national* affair of the Germans and has only *local* interest for the Germans, as for instance the important question treated several times of late: how really we "pass from the realm of God to the realm of Man"—as if this

14. [Marginal note by Marx:] So-called *objective* historiography just consists in treating the historical conditions independent of activity. Reactionary character.
15. [Max Stirner (1806–56) was a German social philosopher who believed that the one single reality is the independent individual. Rejecting all political, moral and traditional ties, he saw the individual as supreme, but in a social, democratic context. He is called the forefather of individualist anarchism. *VC*]

"realm of God" had ever existed anywhere save in the imagination, and the learned gentlemen, without being aware of it, were not constantly living in the "realm of Man" to which they are now seeking the way; and as if the learned pastime (for it is nothing more) of explaining the mystery of this theoretical bubble-blowing did not on the contrary lie in demonstrating its origin in actual earthly conditions. Always, for these Germans, it is simply a matter of revolving the nonsense of earlier writers into some other freak, i.e., of presupposing that all this nonsense has a special *sense* which can be discovered; while really it is only a question of explaining this theoretical talk from the actual existing conditions. The real, practical dissolution of these phrases, the removal of these notions from the consciousness of men, will, as we have already said, be effected by altered circumstances, not by theoretical deductions. For the mass of men, i.e., the proletariat, these theoretical notions do not exist and hence do not require to be dissolved, and if this mass ever had any theoretical notions, e.g., religion, etc., these have now long been dissolved by circumstances.

Problems

1. What is meant by saying Marx is a "materialist"? What is meant by saying he is "anti-idealist"? What, if anything, do either of these two words have to do with human motivation or psychology?
2. For Marx, what is the relationship of consciousness to production?
3. What is meant by Marxian dialectic, historical materialism, or dialectic materialism? What is man's relation to history?
4. To what extent, if any, does human motivation or man's psychological orientation have any significance within the context of Marxian dialectic?
5. All of the notes (except the two signed "VC," 11 and 15) are present in the edition sponsored by the Institute of Marxism-Leninism of the Central Committee of the C.P.S.U. from which this text is taken. What selective bias, if any, do you find in these footnotes? At what points, if any, in the text did you not find a note of explanation or citation when you felt one might have been helpful?

15 KARL MARX
Alienated Labor

We have begun from the presuppositions of political economy. We have accepted its terminology and its laws. We presupposed private property, the separation of labor, capital and land, as also of wages, profit and rent, the division of labor, competition, the concept of exchange value, etc. From political economy itself, in its own words, we have shown that the worker sinks to the level of a commodity, and to a most miserable commodity; that the misery of the worker increases with the power and volume of his production; that the necessary result of competition is the accumulation of capital in a few hands, and thus a restoration of monopoly in a more terrible form; and finally that the distinction between capitalist and landlord, and between agricultural laborer and industrial worker, must disappear and the whole of society divide into the two classes of property *owners* and propertyless *workers.*

Political economy begins with the fact of private property; it does not explain it. It conceives the *material process* of private property, as this occurs in reality, in general and abstract formulas which then serve it as laws. It does not *comprehend* these laws; that is, it does not show how they arise out of the nature of private property. Political economy provides no explanation of the basis of the distinction of labor from capital, of capital from land. When, for example, the relation of wages to profits is defined, this is explained in terms of the interests of capitalists; in other words, what should be explained is assumed. Similarly, competition is referred to at every point and is explained in terms of external conditions. Political economy tells us nothing about the extent to which these external and apparently accidental conditions are simply the expression of a necessary development. We have seen how exchange itself seems an accidental fact. The only moving forces which political economy recognizes are *avarice* and the *war between the avaricious, competition.*

Just because political economy fails to understand the interconnections within this movement it was possible to oppose the doctrine of competition to that of monopoly, the doctrine of freedom of the crafts to that of the guilds, the doctrine of the division of landed property to

Karl Marx, "Alienated Labor" in *Economic and Philosophical Manuscripts of Marx,* translated by T. B. Bottomore (London: C. A. Watts & Co., Ltd., 1969), pp. 93–100.

that of the great estates; for competition, freedom of crafts, and the division of landed property were conceived only as accidental consequences brought about by will and force, rather than as necessary, inevitable and natural consequences of monopoly, the guild system and feudal property.

Thus we have now to grasp the real connection between this whole system of alienation—private property, acquisitiveness, the separation of labor, capital and land, exchange and competition, value and the devaluation of man, monopoly and competition—and the system of *money*.

Let us not begin our explanation, as does the economist, from a legendary primordial condition. Such a primordial condition does not explain anything; it merely removes the question into a gray and nebulous distance. It asserts as a fact or event what it should deduce, namely, the necessary relation between two things; for example, between the division of labor and exchange. In the same way theology explains the origin of evil by the fall of man; that is, it asserts as a historical fact what it should explain.

We shall begin from a *contemporary* economic fact. The worker becomes poorer the more wealth he produces and the more his production increases in power and extent. The worker becomes an ever cheaper commodity the more goods he creates. The *devaluation* of the human world increases in direct relation with the *increase in value* of the world of things. Labor does not only create goods; it also produces itself and the worker as a *commodity,* and indeed in the same proportion as it produces goods.

This fact simply implies that the object produced by labor, its product, now stands opposed to it as an *alien being,* as a *power independent* of the producer. The product of labor is labor which has been embodied in an object and turned into a physical thing; this product is an *objectification* of labor. The performance of work is at the same time its objectification. The performance of work appears in the sphere of political economy as a *vitiation* of the worker, objectification as a *loss* and as *servitude to the object,* and appropriation as *alienation.*

So much does the performance of work appear as vitiation that the worker is vitiated to the point of starvation. So much does objectification appear as loss of the object that the worker is deprived of the most essential things not only of life but also of work. Labor itself becomes an object which he can acquire only by the greatest effort and with unpredictable interruptions. So much does the appropriation of the object appear as alienation that the more objects the worker produces the fewer he can possess and the more he falls under the domination of his product, of capital.

All these consequences follow from the fact that the worker is related to the *product of his labor* as to an *alien* object. For it is clear on this presupposition that the more the worker expends himself in work the more powerful becomes the world of objects which he creates in face of himself, the poorer he becomes in his inner life, and the less he belongs to himself. It is just the same as in religion. The more of himself man attributes to God the less he has left in himself. The worker puts his life into the object, and his life then belongs no longer to himself but to the object. The greater his activity, therefore, the less he possesses. What is embodied in the product of his labor is no longer his own. The greater this product is, therefore, the more he is diminished. The *alienation* of the worker in his product means not only that his labor becomes an object, assumes an *external* existence, but that it exists independently, *outside himself,* and alien to him, and that it stands opposed to him as an autonomous power. The life which he has given to the object sets itself against him as an alien and hostile force.

Let us now examine more closely the phenomenon of *objectification,* the worker's production and the *alienation* and *loss* of the object it produces, which is involved in it. The worker can create nothing without *nature,* without the *sensuous external world.* The latter is the material in which his labor is realized, in which it is active, out of which and through which it produces things.

But just as nature affords the *means of existence* of labor in the sense that labor cannot *live* without objects upon which it can be exercised, so also it provides the *means of existence* in a narrower sense; namely the means of physical existence for the *worker* himself. Thus, the more the worker *appropriates* the external world of sensuous nature by his labor the more he deprives himself of *means of existence,* in two respects: first, that the sensuous external world becomes progressively less an object belonging to his labor or a means of existence of his labor, and secondly, that it becomes progressively less a means of existence in the direct sense, a means for the physical subsistence of the worker.

In both respects, therefore, the worker becomes a slave of the object; first in that he receives an *object of work,* i.e., receives *work,* and secondly that he receives *means of subsistence.* Thus the object enables him to exist, first as a *worker* and secondly, as a *physical subject.* The culmination of this enslavement is that he can only maintain himself as a *physical subject* so far as he is a *worker,* and that it is only as a *physical subject* that he is a worker.

(The alienation of the worker in his object is expressed as follows in the laws of political economy: the more the worker produces the less he has to consume; the more value he creates the more worthless he becomes; the more refined his product the more crude and misshapen the worker; the more civilized the product the more barbarous the worker; the more powerful the work the more feeble the worker; the more the work manifests intelligence the more the worker declines in intelligence and becomes a slave of nature.)

Political economy conceals the alienation in the nature of labor insofar as it does not examine the direct relationship between the worker (work) and production. Labor certainly produces marvels for the rich but it produces privation for the worker. It produces palaces, but hovels for the worker. It produces beauty, but deformity for the worker. It replaces labor by machinery, but it casts some of the workers back into a barbarous kind of work and turns the others into machines. It produces intelligence, but also stupidity and cretinism for the workers.

The direct relationship of labor to its products is the relationship of the worker to the objects of his production. The relationship of property owners to the objects of production and to production itself is merely a *consequence* of this first relationship and confirms it. We shall consider this second aspect later.

Thus, when we ask what is the important relationship of labor, we are concerned with the relationship of the *worker* to production.

So far we have considered the alienation of the worker only from one aspect; namely, *his relationship with the products of his labor*. However, alienation appears not only in the result, but also in the *process,* of *production,* within *productive activity* itself. How could the worker stand in an alien relationship to the product of his activity if he did not alienate himself in the act of production itself? The product is indeed only the *résumé* of activity, of production. Consequently, if the product of labor is alienation, production itself must be active alienation—the alienation of activity and the activity of alienation. The alienation of the object of labor merely summarizes the alienation in the work activity itself.

What constitutes the alienation of labor? First, that the work is *external* to the worker, that it is not part of his nature; and that, consequently, he does not fulfill himself in his work but denies himself, has a feeling of misery rather than well being, does not develop freely his mental and physical energies but is physically exhausted and mentally debased. The worker therefore feels himself at home only during his leisure time, whereas at work he feels homeless. His work is not voluntary but imposed, *forced labor.* It is not the satisfaction of a need, but only a *means* for satisfying other needs. Its alien character is clearly shown by the fact that as soon as there is no physical or other compulsion it is avoided like the plague. External labor, labor in which man alienates himself, is a labor of self-sacrifice, of mortification. Finally, the external character of work for the worker is shown by the fact that it is not his own work but work for someone else, that in work he does not belong to himself but to another person.

Just as in religion the spontaneous activity of human fantasy, of the human brain and heart, reacts independently as an alien activity of gods or devils upon the individual, so the activity of the worker is not his own spontaneous activity. It is another's activity and a loss of his own spontaneity.

We arrive at the result that man (the worker) feels himself to be freely active only in his animal functions—eating, drinking and procreating, or at most also in his dwelling and in personal adornment—while in his human functions he is reduced to an animal. The animal becomes human and the human becomes animal.

Eating, drinking and procreating are of course also genuine human functions. But abstractly considered, apart from the environment of other human activities, and turned into final and sole ends, they are animal functions.

We have now considered the act of alienation of practical human activity, labor, from two aspects: (1) the relationship of the worker to the *product of labor* as an alien object which dominates him. This relationship is at the same time the relationship to the sensuous external world, to natural objects, as an alien and hostile world; (2) the relationship of labor the the *act of production* within *labor*. This is the relationship of the worker to his own activity as something alien and not belonging to him, activity as suffering (passivity), strength as powerlessness, creation as emasculation, the *personal* physical and mental energy of the worker, his personal life (for what is life but activity?) as an activity which is directed against himself, independent of him and not belonging to him. This is *self-alienation* as against the above-mentioned alienation of the *thing*.

We have now to infer a third characteristic of *alienated labor* from the two we have considered.

Man is a species-being [1] not only in the sense that he makes the community (his own as well as those of other things) his object both practically and theoretically, but also (and this is simply another expression for the same thing) in the sense that he treats himself as the present, living species, as a *universal* and consequently free being.

Species-life, for man as for animals, has its physical basis in the fact that man (like animals) lives from inorganic nature, and since man is more universal than an animal so the range of inorganic nature from which he lives is more universal. Plants, animals, minerals, air, light, etc. constitute, from the theoretical aspect, a part of human consciousness as objects of natural science and art; they are man's spiritual inorganic

---

1. The term "species-being" is taken from Feuerbach's *Das Wesen des Christentums* (The Essence of Christianity). Feuerbach used the notion in making a distinction between consciousness in man and in animals. Man is conscious not merely of himself as an individual but of the human species or "human essence."—*Tr. Note*

nature, his intellectual means of life, which he must first prepare for enjoyment and perpetuation. So also, from the practical aspect they form a part of human life and activity. In practice man lives only from these natural products, whether in the form of food, heating, clothing, housing, etc. The universality of man appears in practice in the universality which makes the whole of nature into his inorganic body: (1) as a direct means of life; and equally (2) as the material object and instrument of his life activity. Nature is the *inorganic body* of man; that is to say, nature excluding the human body itself. To say that man *lives* from nature means that nature is his *body* with which he must remain in a continuous interchange in order not to die. The statement that the physical and mental life of man, and nature, are interdependent means simply that nature is interdependent with itself, for man is a part of nature.

Since alienated labor: (1) alienates nature from man; and (2) alienates man from himself, from his own active function, his life activity; so it alienates him from the species. It makes *species-life* into a means of individual life. In the first place it alienates species-life and individual life, and secondly, it turns the latter, as an abstraction, into the purpose of the former, also in its abstract and alienated form.

For labor, *life activity, productive life,* now appear to man only as *means* for satisfaction of a need, the need to maintain his physical existence. Productive life is, however, species-life. It is life creating life. In the type of life activity resides the whole character of a species, its species-character; and free, conscious activity is the species-character of human beings. Life itself appears only as a *means of life.*

The animal is one with its life activity. It does not distinguish the activity from itself. It is *its activity.* But man makes his life activity itself an object of his will and consciousness. He has a conscious life activity. It is not a determination with which he is completely identified. Conscious life activity distinguishes man from the life activity of animals. Only for this reason is he a species-being. Or rather, he is only a self-conscious being, i.e. his own life is an object for him, because he is a species-being. Only for this reason is his activity free activity. Alienated labor reverses the relationship, in that man because he is a self-conscious being makes his life activity, his *being,* only a means for his *existence.*

The practical construction of an *objective world,* the *manipulation* of inorganic nature, is the confirmation of man as a conscious species-being, i.e. a being who treats the species as his own being or himself as a species-being. Of course, animals also produce. They construct nests, dwellings, as in the case of bees, beavers, ants, etc. But they only produce what is strictly necessary for themselves or their young. They produce only in a single direction, while man produces universally. They produce only under the compulsion of direct physical need, while man produces when he is free from physical need and only truly produces in freedom from such need. Animals produce only themselves, while man reproduces the whole of nature. The products of animal production belong directly to their physical bodies, while man is free in face of his product. Animals construct only in accordance with the standards and needs of the species to which they belong, while man knows how to produce in accordance with the standards of every species and knows how to apply the appropriate standard to the object. Thus man constructs also in accordance with the laws of beauty.

It is just in his work upon the objective world that man really proves himself as a *species-being*. This production is his active species life. By means of it nature appears as *his* work and his reality. The object of labor is, therefore, the *objectification of man's species life;* for he no longer reproduces himself merely intellectually, as in consciousness, but actively and in a real sense, and he sees his own reflection in a world which he has constructed. While, therefore, alienated labor takes away the object of production from man, it also takes away his *species life,* his real objectivity as a species-being, and changes his advantage over animals into a disadvantage in so far as his inorganic body, nature, is taken from him.

Just as alienated labor transforms free and self-directed activity into a means, so it transforms the species life of man into a means of physical existence.

Consciousness, which man has from his species, is transformed through alienation so that species life becomes only a means for him.

(3) Thus alienated labor turns the *species life of man,* and also nature as his mental species-property, into an *alien* being and into a *means* for his *individual existence*. It alienates from man his own body, external nature, his mental life and his *human* life.

(4) A direct consequence of the alienation of man from the product of his labor, from his life activity and from his species life is that *man* is *alienated* from other *men*. When man confronts himself he also confronts *other* men. What is true of man's relationship to his work, to the product of his work and to himself, is also true of his relationship to other men, to their labor and to the objects of their labor.

In general, the statement that man is alienated from his species life means that each man is alienated from others, and that each of the others is likewise alienated from human life.

Human alienation, and above all the relation of man to himself, is first realized and expressed in the relationship between each man and other men. Thus in the relationship of alienated labor every man regards other men according to the standards and relationships in which he finds himself placed as a worker.

We began with an economic fact, the alienation of the worker and his production. We have expressed this fact in conceptual terms as *alienated labor,* and in analyzing the concept we have merely analyzed an economic fact.

Let us now examine further how this concept of alienated labor must express and reveal itself in reality. If the product of labor is alien to me and confronts me as an alien power, to whom does it belong? If my own activity does not belong to me but is an alien, forced activity, to whom does it belong? To a being *other* than myself. And who is this being? The *gods?* It is apparent in the earliest stages of advanced production, e.g., temple building, etc. in Egypt, India, Mexico, and in the service rendered to gods, that the product belonged to the gods. But the gods alone were never the lords of labor. And no more was *nature*. What a contradiction it would be if the more man subjugates nature by his labor, and the more the marvels of the gods are rendered superfluous by the marvels of industry, he should abstain from his joy in producing and his enjoyment of the product for love of these powers.

The *alien* being to whom labor and the product of labor belong, to whose service labor is devoted, and to whose enjoyment the product of labor goes, can only be *man* himself. If the product of labor does not belong to the worker, but confronts him as an alien power, this can only be because it belongs to *a man other than the worker*. If his activity is a torment to him it must be a source of enjoyment and pleasure to another. Not the gods, nor nature, but only man himself can be this alien power over men.

Consider the earlier statement that the relation of man to himself is first realized, objectified, through his relation to other men. If therefore he is related to the product of his labor, his objectified labor, as to an *alien,* hostile, powerful and independent object, he is related in such a way that another alien, hostile, powerful and independent man is the lord of this object. If he is related to his own activity as to unfree activity, then he is related to it as activity in the service, and under the domination, coercion and yoke, of another man.

Every self-alienation of man, from himself and from nature, appears in the relation which he postulates between other men and himself and nature. Thus religious self-alienation is necessarily exemplified in the relation between laity and priest, or, since it is here a question of spiritual world, between the laity and a mediator. In the real world of practice this self-alienation can only be expressed in the real, practical relation of man to his fellow-men. The medium through which alienation occurs is itself a *practical* one. Through alienated labor, therefore, man not only produces his relation to the object and to the process of production as to alien and hostile men; he also produces the relation of other men to his production and his product, and the relation between himself and other men. Just as he creates his own production as a vitiation, a punishment, and his own product as a loss, as a product which does not belong to him, so he creates the domination of the non-producer over production and its product. As he alienates his own activity, so he bestows upon the stranger an activity which is not his own.

We have so far considered this relation only from the side of the worker, and later on we shall consider it also from the side of the non-worker.

Thus, through alienated labor the worker creates the relation of another man, who does not work and is outside the work process, to this labor. The relation of the worker to work also produces the relation of the capitalist (or whatever one likes to call the lord of labor) to work. *Private property* is therefore the product, the necessary result, of *alienated labor,* of the external relation of the worker to nature and to himself.

Private property is thus derived from the analysis of the concept of *alienated labor;* that is, alienated man, alienated labor, alienated life, and estranged man.

We have, of course, derived the concept of *alienated labor (alienated life)* from political economy, from an analysis of the *movement of private property.* But the analysis of this concept shows that although private property appears to be the basis and cause of alienated labor, it is rather a consequence of the latter, just as the gods are *fundamentally* not the cause but the product of confusions of human reason. At a later stage, however, there is a reciprocal influence.

Only in the final stage of the development of private property is its secret revealed, namely, that it is on one hand the *product* of alienated labor, and on the other hand the *means* by which labor is alienated, the *realization of the alienation.*

This elucidation throws light upon several unresolved controversies:

(1) Political economy begins with labor as the real soul of production and then goes on to attribute nothing to labor and everything to private property. Proudhon, faced by this contradiction, has decided in favor of labor against private property. We perceive, however, that this apparent contradiction is the contradiction of *alienated labor* with itself and that political economy has merely formulated the laws of alienated labor.

We also observe, therefore, that *wages* and *private property* are identical, for wages, like the product or object of labor, labor itself remunerated, are only a necessary consequence of the alienation of labor. In the wage system labor appears not as an end in itself but as the servant of wages. We shall develop this point later on and here only bring out some of the consequences.

An enforced *increase in wages* (disregarding the other difficulties, and especially that such an anomaly could only be maintained by force) would be nothing more than a *better remuneration of slaves,* and would not restore, either to the worker or to the work, their human significance and worth.

Even the *equality of incomes* which Proudhon demands would only change the relation of the present day worker to his work into a relation of all men to work. Society would then be conceived as an abstract capitalist.

(2) From the relation of alienated labor to private property it also follows that the emancipation of society from private property, from servitude, takes the political form of the *emancipation of the workers;* not in the sense that only the latter's emancipation is involved, but because this emancipation includes the emancipation of humanity as a whole. For all human servitude is involved in the relation of the worker to production, and all the types of servitude are only modifications or consequences of this relation.

As we have discovered the concept of *private property* by an *analysis* of the concept of *alienated labor,* so with the aid of these two factors we can evolve all the categories of political economy, and in every category, e.g., trade, competition, capital, money, we shall discover only a particular and developed expression of these fundamental elements.

However, before considering this structure let us attempt to solve two problems.

(1) To determine the general nature of *private property* as it has resulted from alienated labor, in its relation to *genuine human and social property.*

(2) We have taken as a fact and analyzed the *alienation of labor.* How does it happen, we may ask, that *man alienates his labor*? How is this alienation founded in the nature of human development? We have already done much to solve the problem in so far as we have *transformed* the question concerning the *origin of private property* into a question about the relation between *alienated labor* and the process of development of mankind. For in speaking of private property one believes oneself to be dealing with something external to mankind. But in speaking of labor one deals directly with mankind itself. This new formulation of the problem already contains its solution.

ad (1) *The general nature of private property and its relation to genuine human property.*

We have resolved alienated labor into two parts, which mutually determine each other, or rather constitute two different expressions of one and the same relation. *Appropriation* appears as *alienation* and *alienation* as *appropriation,* alienation as genuine acceptance in the community.

We have considered one aspect, *alienated* labor, in its bearing upon the *worker* himself, i.e., *the relation of alienated labor to itself.* And we have found as the necessary consequence of this relation the *property relation* of the *non-worker* to the *worker* and to *labor.* Private property as the material summarized expression of alienated labor includes both relations; *the relation of the worker to labor, to the product of his labor and to the non-worker,* and the relation of the *non-worker to the worker and to the product of the latter's labor.*

We have already seen that in relation to the worker, who *appropriates* nature by his labor, appropriation appears as alienation, self-activity as activity for another and of another, living as the sacrifice of life, and production of the object as loss of the object to an alien power, an alien man. Let us now consider the relation of this *alien* man to the worker, to labor, and to the object of labor.

It should be noted first that everything which appears to the worker as an *activity of alienation,* appears to the non-worker as a *condition of alienation.* Secondly, the *real, practical* attitude of the worker in production and to the product (as a state of mind) appears to the non-worker who confronts him as a *theoretical* attitude.

Thirdly, the non-worker does everything against the worker which the latter does against himself, but he does not do against himself what he does against the worker.

Let us examine these three relationships more closely.²

2. The manuscript breaks off unfinished at this point.—*Tr. Note*

Problems

1. What is alienated labor? Why is it inevitable in a capitalist society?
2. If, contrary to common belief, Marx is not interested in greater monetary gain and comfort for the worker, what is his primary concern? Why is Marx hostile to the capitalist tendency to socialize production by planned division of labor?
3. Marx is accused of having a base conception of human nature, of assuming that man is motivated only by economic factors. What are the unarticulated primary assumptions about man in this essay? Would you call those assumptions realistic or unrealistic, noble or base, hopeful or depressing? What do your answers reveal about your own assumptions about man?
4. Are charges that Marx is hostile to individualism and sympathetic to collectivism accurate? Is socialized production, in Marx's terms, collectivist or individualist? Is it in your terms?
5. To what extent is Marx interested in the equitable distribution of goods in a society? What is the nature of his primary interest in this area?
6. How accurate at the national level is Marx's assessment of the evolution of capitalism (socialized production through division of labor and private appropriation)? How accurate is it on a global level?
7. Does Marx believe in "human nature"? How do his assumptions about men or man's nature in *The German Ideology* and here again in "Alienated Labor" differ from those of Christianity?

16 FRIEDRICH ENGELS
from Socialism: Utopian and Scientific

III

    The materialist conception of history starts from the proposition that the production of the means to support human life and, next to production, the exchange of things produced, is the basis of all social structure; that in every society that has appeared in history, the manner in which wealth is distributed and society divided into classes or orders is dependent upon what is produced, how it is produced, and how the products are exchanged. From this point of view the final causes of all social changes and political revolutions are to be sought, not in men's brains, not in men's better insight into eternal truth and justice, but in changes in the modes of production and exchange. They are to be sought not in the *philosophy,* but in the *economics* of each particular epoch. The growing perception that existing social institutions are unreasonable and unjust, that reason has become unreason and right wrong,[1] is only proof that in the modes of production and exchange changes have silently taken place with which the social order, adapted to earlier economic conditions, is no longer in keeping. From this it also follows that the means of getting rid of the incongruities that have been brought to light must also be present, in a more or less developed condition, within the changed modes of production themselves. These means are not to be invented by deduction from fundamental principles, but are to be discovered in the stubborn facts of the existing system of production.

    What is, then, the position of modern socialism in this connection?

    The present structure of society—this is now pretty generally conceded—is the creation of the ruling class of today, of the bourgeoisie. The mode of production peculiar to the bourgeoisie, known, since Marx, as the capitalist mode of production, was incompatible with the feudal system, with the privileges it conferred upon individuals, entire social ranks and local corporations, as well as with the hereditary ties of subordination which constituted the framework of its social organisation. The bourgeoisie broke up the feudal system and built upon its ruins the

From Karl Marx and Frederick Engels, *Selected Works* (Moscow: Progress Publishers, 1968), pp. 417–34.
1. Mephistopheles in Goethe's *Faust,* Part I, Scene 4 (Faust's study).—*Ed.*

capitalist order of society, the kingdom of free competition, of personal liberty, of the equality, before the law, of all commodity owners, of all the rest of the capitalist blessings. Thenceforward the capitalist mode of production could develop in freedom. Since steam, machinery, and the making of machines by machinery transformed the older manufacture into modern industry, the productive forces evolved under the guidance of the bourgeoisie developed with a rapidity and in a degree unheard of before. But just as the older manufacture, in its time, and handicraft, becoming more developed under its influence, had come into collision with the feudal trammels of the guilds, so now modern industry, in its more complete development, comes into collision with the bounds within which the capitalistic mode of production holds it confined. The new productive forces have already outgrown the capitalistic mode of using them. And this conflict between productive forces and modes of production is not a conflict engendered in the mind of man, like that between original sin and divine justice. It exists, in fact, objectively, outside us, independently of the will and actions even of the men that have brought it on. Modern socialism is nothing but the reflex, in thought, of this conflict in fact; its ideal reflection in the minds, first, of the class directly suffering under it, the working class.

Now, in what does this conflict consist?

Before capitalistic production, i.e., in the Middle Ages, the system of petty industry obtained generally, based upon the private property of the labourers in their means of production; in the country, the agriculture of the small peasant, freeman or serf; in the towns, the handicrafts organised in guilds. The instruments of labour—land, agricultural implements, the workshop, the tool—were the instruments of labour of single individuals, adapted for the use of one worker, and, therefore, of necessity, small, dwarfish, circumscribed. But, for this very reason they belonged, as a rule, to the producer himself. To concentrate these scattered, limited means of production, to enlarge them, to turn them into the powerful levers of production of the present day—this was precisely the historic role of capitalist production and of its upholder, the bourgeoisie. In the fourth section of *Capital* Marx has explained in detail, how since the fifteenth century this has been historically worked out through the three phases of simple co-operation, manufacture and modern industry. But the bourgeoisie, as is also shown there, could not transform these puny means of production into mighty productive forces without transforming them, at the same time, from means of production of the individual into *social* means of production only workable by a collectivity of men. The spinning-wheel, the hand-loom, the blacksmith's hammer, were replaced by the spinning-machine, the power-loom, the steam-hammer; the individual workshop, by the factory implying the co-operation of hundreds and thousands of workmen. In like manner, production itself changed from a series of individual into a series of social acts, and the products from individual to social products. The yarn, the cloth, the metal articles that now came out of the factory, were the joint product of many workers, through whose hands they had successively to pass before they were ready. No one person could say of them: "I made that; this is *my* product."

But where, in a given society, the fundamental form of production is that spontaneous division of labour which creeps in gradually and not upon any preconceived plan, there the products take on the form of *commodities,* whose mutual exchange, buying and selling, enable the individual producers to satisfy their manifold wants. And this was the case in the Middle Ages. The peasant, e.g., sold to the artisan agricultural products and bought from him the products of handicraft. Into this society of individual producers, of commodity producers, the new mode of production thrust itself. In the midst of the old division of labour, grown up spontaneously and upon *no definite plan,* which had governed the whole of society, now arose division of labour upon a *definite plan,* as organised in the factory; side by side with *individual* production appeared *social* production. The products of both were sold in the same market, and, therefore, at prices at least approximately equal. But organisation upon a definite plan was stronger than spontaneous division of labour. The factories working with the combined social forces of a collectivity of individuals produced their commodities far more cheaply than the individual small producers. Individual production succumbed in one department after another. Socialised production revolutionised all the old methods of production. But its revolutionary character was, at the same time, so little recognised that it was, on the contrary, introduced as a means of increasing and developing the production of commodities. When it arose, it found ready-made, and made liberal use of, certain machinery for the production and exchange of commodities: merchants' capital, handicraft, wage-labour. Socialised production thus introducing itself as a new form of the production of commodities, it was a matter of course that under it the old forms of appropriation remained in full swing, and were applied to its products as well.

In the mediaeval stage of evolution of the production of commodities, the question as to the owner of the product of labour could not arise. The individual producer, as a rule, had, from raw material belonging to himself, and generally his own handiwork, produced it with his own tools, by the labour of his own hands or of his family. There was no need for him to appropriate the new product. It belonged wholly to him, as a matter of course. His property in the product was, therefore, based *upon his own labour.* Even where external help was used, this was, as a rule, of little importance, and very generally was compensated by something other than wages. The apprentices and journeymen of the guilds worked less for board and wages than for education, in order that they might become master craftsmen themselves.

Then came the concentration of the means of production and of the producers in large workshops and manufactories, their transformation into actual socialised means of production and socialised producers. But the socialised producers and means of production and their products were still treated, after this change, just as they had been before, i.e., as the means of production and the products of individuals. Hitherto, the owner of the instruments of labour had himself appropriated the product, because, as a rule, it was his own product and the assistance of others was the exception. Now the owner of the instruments of labour always appropriated to himself the product, although it was no longer *his* product but exclusively the product of the *labour of others*. Thus, the products now produced socially were not appropriated by those who had actually set in motion the means of production and actually produced the commodities, but by the *capitalists*. The means of production, and production itself, had become in essence socialised. But they were subjected to a form of appropriation which presupposes the private production of individuals, under which, therefore, everyone owns his own product and brings it to market. The mode of production is subjected to this form of appropriation, although it abolishes the conditions upon which the latter rests.[2]

This contradiction, which gives to the new mode of production its capitalistic character, *contains the germ of the whole of the social antagonisms of today*. The greater the mastery obtained by the new mode of production over all important fields of production and in all manufacturing countries, the more it reduced individual production to an insignificant residuum, *the more clearly was brought out the incompatibility of socialised production with capitalistic appropriation*.

The first capitalists found, as we have said, alongside of other forms of labour, wage-labour ready-made for them on the market. But it was exceptional, complementary, accessory, transitory wage-labour. The agricultural labourer, though, upon occasion, he hired himself out by the day, had a few acres of his own land on which he could at all events live at a pinch. The guilds were so organised that the journeyman of today became the master of tomorrow. But all this changed, as soon as the means of production became socialised and concentrated in the hands of

2. It is hardly necessary in this connection to point out that, even if the *form* of appropriation remains the same, the *character* of the appropriation is just as much revolutionised as production is by the changes described above. It is, of course, a very different matter whether I appropriate to myself my own product or that of another. Note in passing that wage-labour, which contains the whole capitalistic mode of production in embryo, is very ancient; in a sporadic, scattered form it existed for centuries alongside of slave-labour. But the embryo could duly develop into the capitalistic mode of production only when the necessary historical preconditions had been furnished. [*Note by Engels.*]

capitalists. The means of production, as well as the product, of the individual producer became more and more worthless; there was nothing left for him but to turn wage-worker under the capitalist. Wage-labour, aforetime the exception and accessory, now became the rule and basis of all production; aforetime complementary, it now became the sole remaining function of the worker. The wage-worker for a time became a wage-worker for life. The number of these permanent wage-workers was further enormously increased by the breaking-up of the feudal system that occurred at the same time, by the disbanding of the retainers of the feudal lords, the eviction of the peasants from their homesteads, etc. The separation was made complete between the means of production concentrated in the hands of the capitalists, on the one side, and the producers, possessing nothing but their labour-power, on the other. *The contradiction between socialised production and capitalistic appropriation manifested itself as the antagonism of proletariat and bourgeoisie.*

We have seen that the capitalistic mode of production thrust its way into a society of commodity-producers, of individual producers, whose social bond was the exchange of their products. But every society based upon the production of commodities has this peculiarity: that the producers have lost control over their own social interrelations. Each man produces for himself with such means of production as he may happen to have, and for such exchange as he may require to satisfy his remaining wants. No one knows how much of his particular article is coming on the market, nor how much of it will be wanted. No one knows whether his individual product will meet an actual demand, whether he will be able to make good his costs of production or even to sell his commodity at all. Anarchy reigns in socialised production.

But the production of commodities, like every other form of production, has its peculiar, inherent laws inseparable from it; and these laws work, despite anarchy, in and through anarchy. They reveal themselves in the only persistent form of social interrelations, i.e., in exchange, and here they affect the individual producers as compulsory laws of competition. They are, at first, unknown to these producers themselves, and have to be discovered by them gradually and as the result of experience. They work themselves out, therefore, independently of the producers, and in antagonism to them, as inexorable natural laws of their particular form of production. The product governs the producers.

In mediaeval society, especially in the earlier centuries, production was essentially directed towards satisfying the wants of the individual. It satisfied, in the main, only the wants of the producer and his family. Where relations of personal dependence existed, as in the country, it also helped to satisfy the want of the feudal lord. In all this there was, therefore, no exchange; the products, consequently, did not assume the character of commodities. The family of the peasant produced almost everything they wanted: clothes and furniture, as well as means of subsistence. Only when it began to produce more than was sufficient to supply its own wants and the payments in kind to the feudal lord, only then did it also produce commodities. This surplus, thrown into socialised exchange and offered for sale, became commodities.

The artisans of the towns, it is true, had from the first to produce for exchange. But they, also, themselves supplied the greatest part of their own individual wants. They had gardens and plots of land. They turned their cattle out into the communal forest, which, also, yielded them timber and firing. The women spun flax, wool, and so forth. Production for the purpose of exchange, production of commodities, was only in its infancy. Hence, exchange was restricted, the market narrow, the methods of production stable; there was local exclusiveness without, local unity within; the Mark ³ in the country; in the town, the guild.

But with the extension of the production of commodities, and especially with the introduction of the capitalist mode of production, the laws of commodity production, hitherto latent, came into action more openly and with greater force. The old bonds were loosened, the old exclusive limits broken through, the producers were more and more turned into independent, isolated producers of commodities. It became apparent that the production of society at large was ruled by absence of plan, by accident, by anarchy; and this anarchy grew to greater and greater height. But the chief means by aid of which the capitalist mode of production intensified this anarchy of socialised production was the exact opposite of anarchy. It was the increasing organisation of production, upon a social basis, in every individual productive establishment. By this, the old, peaceful, stable condition of things was ended. Wherever this organisation of production was introduced into a branch of industry, it brooked no other method of production by its side. The field of labour became a battle-ground. The great geographical discoveries,* and the colonisation following upon them, multiplied markets and quickened the transformation of handicraft into manufacture. The war did not simply break out between the individual producers of particular localities. The local struggles begot in their turn national conflicts, the commercial wars of the seventeenth and the eighteenth centuries.†

---

3. See Appendix. [*Note by Engels*.]—Here Engels refers to his work *The Mark*.—*Ed.*
* The reference is to the great discoveries made by European merchants and seafarers in the period ranging from the latter half of the 15th century to the first half of the 17th century, the most important of which were the discovery of America, Australia, of a sea route to India round Africa, etc. The great geographical discoveries contributed to the collapse of feudalism and accelerated the emergence of capitalist relations in Western Europe.
† The reference is to the wars waged in the latter half of the 17th century and the beginning of the 18th century. These were pursued by the coalitions of European powers led by France, on the one hand, and by Holland and, later, England, on the other. The underlying causes were the striving of the bourgeoisie and nobility,

Finally, modern industry and the opening of the world market made the struggle universal, and at the same time gave it an unheard-of virulence. Advantages in natural or artificial conditions of production now decide the existence or non-existence of individual capitalists, as well as of whole industries and countries. He that falls is remorselessly cast aside. It is the Darwinian struggle of the individual for existence transferred from Nature to society with intensified violence. The conditions of existence natural to the animal appear as the final term of human development. The contradiction between socialised production and capitalistic appropriation now presents itself as *an antagonism between the organisation of production in the individual workshop and the anarchy of production in society generally.*

The capitalistic mode of production moves in these two forms of the antagonism immanent to it from its very origin. It is never able to get out of that "vicious circle" which Fourier had already discovered. What Fourier could not, indeed, see in his time is that this circle is gradually narrowing; that the movement becomes more and more a spiral, and must come to an end, like the movement of the planets, by collision with the centre. It is the compelling force of anarchy in the production of society at large that more and more completely turns the great majority of men into proletarians; and it is the masses of the proletariat again who will finally put an end to anarchy in production. It is the compelling force of anarchy in social production that turns the limitless perfectibility of machinery under modern industry into a compulsory law by which every individual industrial capitalist must perfect his machinery more and more, under penalty of ruin.

But the perfecting of machinery is making human labour superfluous. If the introduction and increase of machinery means the displacement of millions of manual by a few machine-workers, improvement in machinery means the displacement of more and more of the machine-workers themselves. It means, in the last instance, the production of a number of available wage-workers in excess of the average needs of capital, the formation of a complete industrial reserve army, as I called it in 1845,[4] available at the times when industry is working at high pressure, to be cast out upon the street when the inevitable crash comes, a constant dead weight upon the limbs of the working class in its struggle for existence with capital, a regulator for the keeping of wages down to the low level that suits the interests of capital. Thus it comes

---

chiefly of France, to achieve territorial expansion and secure political and economic hegemony in Europe. These wars and the War of the Spanish Succession (1701–14) which France lost and which was the last in this series of "commercial wars" heavily undermined her economic and military positions and deprived her of vast colonial possessions.

4. *The Condition of the Working Class in England,* p. 109. [*Note by Engels.*] See Marx and Engels, *On Britain,* Moscow, 1962, p. 119.—*Ed.*

about, to quote Marx, that machinery becomes the most powerful weapon in the war of capital against the working class; that the instruments of labour constantly tear the means of subsistence out of the hands of the labourer; that the very product of the worker is turned into an instrument for his subjugation.[5] Thus it comes about that the economising of the instruments of labour becomes at the same time, from the outset, the most reckless waste of labour power, and robbery based upon the normal conditions under which labour functions;[6] that machinery, the most powerful instrument for shortening labour time, becomes the most unfailing means for placing every moment of the labourer's time and that of his family at the disposal of the capitalist for the purpose of expanding the value of his capital. Thus it comes about that the overwork of some becomes the preliminary condition for the idleness of others, and that modern industry, which hunts after new consumers over the whole world, forces the consumption of the masses at home down to a starvation minimum, and in doing thus destroys its own home market. "The law that always equilibrates the relative surplus population, or industrial reserve army, to the extent and energy of accumulation, this law rivets the labourer to capital more firmly than the wedges of Vulcan did Prometheus to the rock. It establishes an accumulation of misery, corresponding with accumulation of capital. Accumulation of wealth at one pole is, therefore, at the same time, accumulation of misery, agony of toil, slavery, ignorance, brutality, mental degradation, at the opposite pole, i.e., on the side of the class that produces *its own product in the form of capital.*" (Marx's *Capital,* p. 671.)[7] And to expect any other division of the products from the capitalistic mode of production is the same as expecting the electrodes of a battery not to decompose acidulated water, not to liberate oxygen at the positive, hydrogen at the negative pole, so long as they are connected with the battery.

We have seen that the ever-increasing perfectibility of modern machinery is, by the anarchy of social production, turned into a compulsory law that forces the individual industrial capitalist always to improve his machinery, always to increase its productive force. The bare possibility of extending the field of production is transformed for him into a similar compulsory law. The enormous expansive force of modern industry, compared with which that of gases is mere child's play, appears to us now as a *necessity* for expansion, both qualitative and quantitative, that laughs at all resistance. Such resistance is offered by consumption, by sales, by the markets for the products of modern industry. But the capacity for extension, extensive and intensive, of the markets is primarily governed by quite different laws that work much less energetically. The extension of the markets cannot keep pace with the extension of

---

5. Karl Marx, *Capital,* Vol. I, Moscow, 1965, pp. 435–87.—*Ed.*
6. Ibid., p. 462.—*Ed.*
7. Ibid., p. 645.—*Ed.*

production. The collision becomes inevitable, and as this cannot produce any real solution so long as it does not break in pieces the capitalist mode of production, the collisions become periodic. Capitalist production has begotten another "vicious circle."

As a matter of fact, since 1825, when the first general crisis broke out, the whole industrial and commercial world, production and exchange among all civilised peoples and their more or less barbaric hangers-on, are thrown out of joint about once every ten years. Commerce is at a standstill, the markets are glutted, products accumulate, as multitudinous as they are unsaleable, hard cash disappears, credit vanishes, factories are closed, the mass of the workers are in want of the means of subsistence, because they have produced too much of the means of subsistence; bankruptcy follows upon bankruptcy, execution upon execution. The stagnation lasts for years; productive forces and products are wasted and destroyed wholesale, until the accumulated mass of commodities finally filters off, more or less depreciated in value, until production and exchange gradually begin to move again. Little by little the pace quickens. It becomes a trot. The industrial trot breaks into a canter, the canter in turn grows into the head-long gallop of a perfect steeplechase of industry, commercial credit, and speculation which finally, after breakneck leaps, ends where it began—in the ditch of a crisis. And so over and over again. We have now, since the year 1825, gone through this five times, and at the present moment (1877) we are going through it for the sixth time. And the character of these crises is so clearly defined that Fourier hit all of them off when he described the first as *"crise pléthorique,"* a crisis from plethora.

In these crises, the contradiction between socialised production and capitalist appropriation ends in a violent explosion. The circulation of commodities is, for the time being, stopped. Money, the means of circulation, becomes a hindrance to circulation. All the laws of production and circulation of commodities are turned upside down. The economic collision has reached its apogee. *The mode of production is in rebellion against the mode of exchange.*

The fact that the socialised organisation of production within the factory has developed so far that it has become incompatible with the anarchy of production in society, which exists side by side with and dominates it, is brought home to the capitalists themselves by the violent concentration of capital that occurs during crises, through the ruin of many large, and a still greater number of small, capitalists. The whole mechanism of the capitalist mode of production breaks down under the pressure of the productive forces, its own creations. It is no longer able to turn all this mass of means of production into capital. They lie fallow, and for that very reason the industrial reserve army must also lie fallow. Means of production, means of subsistence, available labourers, all the elements of production and of general wealth, are present in abundance. But "abundance becomes the source of distress and want" (Fourier), because it is the very thing that prevents the transformation of the means of production and subsistence into capital. For in capitalistic society the means of production can only function when they have undergone a preliminary transformation into capital, into the means of exploiting human labour power. The necessity of this transformation into capital of the means of production and subsistence stands like a ghost between these and the workers. It alone prevents the coming together of the material and personal levers of production; it alone forbids the means of production to function, the workers to work and live. On the one hand, therefore, the capitalistic mode of production stands convicted of its own incapacity to further direct these productive forces. On the other, these productive forces themselves, with increasing energy, press forward to the removal of the existing contradiction, to the abolition of their quality as capital, to the *practical recognition of their character as social productive forces*.

This rebellion of the productive forces, as they grow more and more powerful, against their quality as capital, this stronger and stronger command that their social character shall be recognised, forces the capitalist class itself to treat them more and more as social productive forces, so far as this is possible under capitalist conditions. The period of industrial high pressure, with its unbounded inflation of credit, not less than the crash itself, by the collapse of great capitalist establishments, tends to bring about that form of the socialisation of great masses of means of production which we meet with in the different kinds of joint-stock companies. Many of these means of production and of distribution are, from the outset, so colossal that, like the railways, they exclude all other forms of capitalistic exploitation. At a further stage of evolution this form also becomes insufficient. The producers on a large scale in a particular branch of industry in a particular country unite in a trust, a union for the purpose of regulating production. They determine the total amount to be produced, parcel it out among themselves, and thus enforce the selling price fixed beforehand. But trusts of this kind, as soon as business becomes bad, are generally liable to break up, and on this very account compel a yet greater concentration of association. The whole of the particular industry is turned into one gigantic joint-stock company; internal competition gives place to the internal monopoly of this one company. This has happened in 1890 with the English alkali production, which is now, after the fusion of 48 large works, in the hands of one company, conducted upon a single plan, and with a capital of £6,000,000.

In the trusts, freedom of competition changes into its very opposite— into monopoly; and the production without any definite plan of capitalistic society capitulates to the production upon a definite plan of the invading socialistic society. Certainly this is so far still to the benefit and advantage of the capitalists. But in this case the exploitation is so palpable that it must break down. No nation will put up with production conducted by trusts, with so barefaced an exploitation of the community by a small band of dividend-mongers.

In any case, with trusts or without, the official representative of capitalist society—the state—will ultimately have to undertake the direction of production.[8] This necessity for conversion into state property is felt first in the great institutions for intercourse and communication—the post office, the telegraphs, the railways.

If the crises demonstrate the incapacity of the bourgeoisie for managing any longer modern productive forces, the transformation of the great establishments for production and distribution into joint-stock companies, trusts and state property shows how unnecessary the bourgeoisie are for that purpose. All the social functions of the capitalist are now performed by salaried employees. The capitalist has no further social function than that of pocketing dividends, tearing off coupons, and gambling on the Stock Exchange, where the different capitalists despoil one another of their capital. At first the capitalistic mode of production forces out the workers. Now it forces out the capitalists, and reduces them, just as it reduced the workers, to the ranks of the surplus population, although not immediately into those of the industrial reserve army.

But the transformation, either into joint-stock companies and trusts, or into state ownership, does not do away with the capitalistic nature

---

8. I say "have to". For only when the means of production and distribution have *actually* outgrown the form of management by joint-stock companies, and when, therefore, the taking them over by the state has become *economically* inevitable, only then—even if it is the state of today that effects this—is there an economic advance, the attainment of another step preliminary to the taking over of all productive forces by society itself. But of late, since Bismarck went in for state ownership of industrial establishments, a kind of spurious socialism has arisen, degenerating, now and again, into something of flunkeyism, that without more ado declares *all* state ownership, even of the Bismarckian sort, to be socialistic. Certainly, if the taking over by the state of the tobacco industry is socialistic, then Napoleon and Metternich must be numbered among the founders of socialism. If the Belgian state, for quite ordinary political and financial reasons, itself constructed its chief railway lines; if Bismarck, not under any economic compulsion, took over for the state the chief Prussian lines, simply to be the better able to have them in hand in case of war, to bring up the railway employees as voting cattle for the government, and especially to create for himself a new source of income independent of parliamentary votes—this was, in no sense, a socialistic measure, directly or indirectly, consciously or unconsciously. Otherwise, the Royal Maritime Company [(*Seehandlung*)—a commercial and credit society founded in Prussia in 1772. It enjoyed important government privileges and granted large loans to the Prussian Government], the Royal porcelain manufacture, and even the regimental tailor shops of the Army would also be socialistic institutions, or even, as was seriously proposed by a sly dog in Frederick William III's reign, the taking over by the state of the brothels. [*Note by Engels.*]

of the productive forces. In the joint-stock companies and trusts this is obvious. And the modern state, again, is only the organisation that bourgeois society takes on in order to support the external conditions of the capitalist mode of production against the encroachments as well of the workers as of individual capitalists. The modern state, no matter what its form, is essentially a capitalist machine, the state of the capitalists, the ideal personification of the total national capital. The more it proceeds to the taking over of productive forces, the more does it actually become the national capitalist, the more citizens does it exploit. The workers remain wage-workers—proletarians. The capitalist relation is not done away with. It is rather brought to a head. But, brought to a head, it topples over. State ownership of the productive forces is not the solution of the conflict, but concealed within it are the technical conditions that form the elements of that solution.

This solution can only consist in the practical recognition of the social nature of the modern forces of production, and therefore in the harmonising of the modes of production, appropriation, and exchange with the socialised character of the means of production. And this can only come about by society openly and directly taking possession of the productive forces which have outgrown all control except that of society as a whole. The social character of the means of production and of the products today reacts against the producers, periodically disrupts all production and exchange, acts only like a law of Nature working blindly, forcibly, destructively. But with the taking over by society of the productive forces, the social character of the means of production and of the products will be utilised by the producers with a perfect understanding of its nature, and instead of being a source of disturbance and periodical collapse, will become the most powerful lever of production itself.

Active social forces work exactly like natural forces: blindly, forcibly, destructively, so long as we do not understand, and reckon with, them. But when once we understand them, when once we grasp their action, their direction, their effects, it depends only upon ourselves to subject them more and more to our own will, and by means of them to reach our own ends. And this holds quite especially of the mighty productive forces of today. As long as we obstinately refuse to understand the nature and the character of these social means of action—and this understanding goes against the grain of the capitalist mode of production and its defenders—so long these forces are at work in spite of us, in opposition to us, so long they master us, as we have shown above in detail.

But when once their nature is understood, they can, in the hands of the producers working together, be transformed from master demons into willing servants. The difference is as that between the destructive force of electricity in the lightning of the storm, and electricity under command in the telegraph and the voltaic arc; the difference between a conflagration, and fire working in the service of man. With this recognition, at last, of the real nature of the productive forces of today, the social anarchy of production gives place to a social regulation of production upon a definite plan, according to the needs of the community and of each individual. Then the capitalist mode of appropriation, in which the product enslaves first the producer and then the appropriator, is replaced by the mode of appropriation of the products that is based upon the nature of the modern means of production; upon the one hand, direct social appropriation, as means to the maintenance and extension of production—on the other, direct individual appropriation, as means of subsistence and of enjoyment.

Whilst the capitalist mode of production more and more completely transforms the great majority of the population into proletarians, it creates the power which, under penalty of its own destruction, is forced to accomplish this revolution. Whilst it forces on more and more the transformation of the vast means of production, already socialised, into state property, it shows itself the way to accomplishing this revolution. *The proletariat seizes political power and turns the means of production into state property.*

But, in doing this, it abolishes itself as proletariat, abolishes all class distinctions and class antagonisms, abolishes also the state as state. Society thus far, based upon class antagonisms, had need of the state. That is, of an organisation of the particular class which was *pro tempore* the exploiting class, an organisation for the purpose of preventing any interference from without with the existing conditions of production, and, therefore, especially, for the purpose of forcibly keeping the exploited classes in the condition of oppression corresponding with the given mode of production (slavery, serfdom, wage-labour). The state was the official representative of society as a whole; the gathering of it together into a visible embodiment. But it was this only in so far as it was the state of that class which itself represented, for the time being, society as a whole: in ancient times, the state of slave-owning citizens; in the Middle Ages, the feudal lords; in our own time, the bourgeoisie. When at last it becomes the real representative of the whole of society, it renders itself unnecessary. As soon as there is no longer any social class to be held in subjection; as soon as class rule, and the individual struggle for existence based upon our present anarchy in production, with the collisions and excesses arising from these, are removed, nothing more remains to be repressed, and a special repressive force, a state, is no longer necessary. The first act by virtue of which the state really constitutes itself the representative of the whole of society—the taking possession of the means of production in the name of society—this is, at the same time, its last independent act as a state. State interference in social relations becomes, in one domain after another, superfluous, and then dies out of itself; the government of persons is replaced by the administration of things, and by the conduct of processes of production. The state is not "abolished." *It dies out.* This gives the measure of the value of the phrase *"a free state,"* both as to its justifiable use at times by agitators, and as to its ultimate scientific insufficiency; and also of the demands of the so-called anarchists for the abolition of the state out of hand.

Since the historical appearance of the capitalist mode of production, the appropriation by society of all the means of production has often been dreamed of, more or less vaguely, by individuals, as well as by sects, as the ideal of the future. But it could become possible, could become a historical necessity, only when the actual conditions for its realisation were there. Like every other social advance, it becomes practicable, not by men understanding that the existence of classes is in contradiction to justice, equality, etc., not by the mere willingness to abolish these classes, but by virtue of certain new economic conditions. The separation of society into an exploiting and an exploited class, a ruling and an oppressed class, was the necessary consequence of the deficient and restricted development of production in former times. So long as the total social labour only yields a produce which but slightly exceeds that barely necessary for the existence of all; so long, therefore, as labour engages all or almost all the time of the great majority of the members of society—so long, of necessity, this society is divided into classes. Side by side with the great majority, exclusively bond slaves to labour, arises a class freed from directly productive labour, which looks after the general affairs of society: the direction of labour, state business, law, science, art, etc. It is, therefore, the law of division of labour that lies at the basis of the division into classes. But this does not prevent this division into classes from being carried out by means of violence and robbery, trickery and fraud. It does not prevent the ruling class, once having the upper hand, from consolidating its power at the expense of the working class, from turning its social leadership into an intensified exploitation of the masses.

But if, upon this showing, division into classes has a certain historical justification, it has this only for a given period, only under given social conditions. It was based upon the insufficiency of production. It will be swept away by the complete development of modern productive forces. And, in fact, the abolition of classes in society presupposes a degree of historical evolution at which the existence, not simply of this or that particular ruling class, but of any ruling class at all, and, therefore, the existence of class distinction itself has become an obsolete anachronism. It presupposes, therefore, the development of production carried out to a degree at which appropriation of the means of production and of the products, and, with this, of political domination, of the monopoly of culture, and of intellectual leadership by a particular class of society, has become not only superfluous but economically, politically, intellectually, a hindrance to development.

This point is now reached. Their political and intellectual bankruptcy is scarcely any longer a secret to the bourgeoisie themselves. Their economic bankruptcy recurs regularly every ten years. In every crisis, society is suffocated beneath the weight of its own productive forces and products, which it cannot use, and stands helpless, face to face with the absurd contradiction that the producers have nothing to consume, because consumers are wanting. The expansive force of the means of production bursts the bonds that the capitalist mode of production had imposed upon them. Their deliverance from these bonds is the one precondition for an unbroken, constantly accelerated development of the productive forces, and therewith for a practically unlimited increase of production itself. Nor is this all. The socialised appropriation of the means of production does away, not only with the present artificial restrictions upon production, but also with the positive waste and devastation of productive forces and products that are at the present time the inevitable concomitants of production, and that reach their height in the crises. Further, it sets free for the community at large a mass of means of production and of products, by doing away with the senseless extravagance of the ruling classes of today and their political representatives. The possibility of securing for every member of society, by means of socialised production, an existence not only fully sufficient materially, and becoming day by day more full, but an existence guaranteeing to all the free development and exercise of their physical and mental faculties—this possibility is now for the first time here, *but it is here*.[9]

With the seizing of the means of production by society, production of commodities is done away with, and, simultaneously, the mastery of the product over the producer. Anarchy in social production is replaced by systematic, definite organisation. The struggle for individual existence disappears. Then for the first time man, in a certain sense, is finally marked off from the rest of the animal kingdom, and emerges from mere animal conditions of existence into really human ones. The whole sphere of the conditions of life which environ man, and which have hitherto ruled man, now comes under the dominion and control of man, who for the first time becomes the real, conscious lord of Nature, because he has now become master of his own social organisation. The laws of his own social

---

9. A few figures may serve to give an approximate idea of the enormous expansive force of the modern means of production, even under capitalist pressure. According to Mr. Giffen, the total wealth of Great Britain and Ireland amounted, in round numbers in 1814 to £2,200,000,000.
    1865 to £6,100,000,000.
    1875 to £8,500,000,000.

As an instance of the squandering of means of production and of products during a crisis, the total loss in the German iron industry alone, in the crisis 1873–78, was given at the second German Industrial Congress (Berlin, February 21, 1878) as £22,750,000. [*Note by Engels.*]

action, hitherto standing face to face with man as laws of Nature foreign to, and dominating him, will then be used with full understanding, and so mastered by him. Man's own social organisation, hitherto confronting him as a necessity imposed by Nature and history, now becomes the result of his own free action. The extraneous objective forces that have hitherto governed history pass under the control of man himself. Only from that time will man himself, more and more consciously, make his own history—only from that time will the social causes set in movement by him have, in the main and in a constantly growing measure, the results intended by him. It is the ascent of man from the kingdom of necessity to the kingdom of freedom.

Let us briefly sum up our sketch of historical evolution.

I. *Mediaeval Society*—Individual production on a small scale. Means of production adapted for individual use; hence primitive, ungainly, petty, dwarfed in action. Production for immediate consumption, either of the producer himself or of his feudal lord. Only where an excess of production over this consumption occurs is such excess offered for sale, enters into exchange. Production of commodities, therefore, only in its infancy. But already it contains within itself, in embryo, *anarchy in the production of society at large*.

II. *Capitalist Revolution*—Transformation of industry, at first by means of simple co-operation and manufacture. Concentration of the means of production, hitherto scattered, into great workshops. As a consequence, their transformation from individual to social means of production—a transformation which does not, on the whole, affect the form of exchange. The old forms of appropriation remain in force. The capitalist appears. In his capacity as owner of the means of production, he also appropriates the products and turns them into commodities. Production has become a *social* act. Exchange and appropriation continue to be *individual* acts, the acts of individuals. *The social product is appropriated by the individual capitalist.* Fundamental contradiction, whence arise all the contradictions in which our present-day society moves, and which modern industry brings to light.

A. Severance of the producer from the means of production. Condemnation of the worker to wage-labour for life. *Antagonism between the proletariat and the bourgeoisie.*

B. Growing predominance and increasing effectiveness of the laws governing the production of commodities. Unbridled competition. *Contradiction between socialised organisation in the individual factory and social anarchy in production as a whole.*

C. On the one hand, perfecting of machinery, made by competition compulsory for each individual manufacturer, and complemented by a constantly growing displacement of labourers. *Industrial reserve army.* On the other hand, unlimited extension of production, also compulsory under competition, for every manufacturer. On both sides, unheard-of development of productive forces, excess of supply over demand, over-production, glutting of the markets, crises every ten years, the vicious circle: excess here, of means of production and products—excess there, of labourers, without employment and without means of existence. But these two levers of production and of social well-being are unable to work together, because the capitalist form of production prevents the productive forces from working and the products from circulating, unless they are first turned into capital—which their very superabundance prevents. The contradiction has grown into an absurdity. *The mode of production rises in rebellion against the form of exchange.* The bourgeoisie are convicted of incapacity further to manage their own social productive forces.

D. Partial recognition of the social character of the productive forces forced upon the capitalists themselves. Taking over the great institutions for production and communication, first by joint-stock companies, later on by trusts, then by the state. The bourgeoisie demonstrated to be a superfluous class. All its social functions are now performed by salaried employees.

III. *Proletarian Revolution*—Solution of the contradictions. The proletariat seizes the public power, and by means of this transforms the socialised means of production, slipping from the hands of the bourgeoisie, into public property. By this act, the proletariat frees the means of production from the character of capital they have thus far borne, and gives their socialised character complete freedom to work itself out. Socialised production upon a predetermined plan becomes henceforth possible. The development of production makes the existence of different classes of society thenceforth an anachronism. In proportion as anarchy in social production vanishes, the political authority of the state dies out. Man, at last the master of his own form of social organisation, becomes at the same time the lord over Nature, his own master—free.

To accomplish this act of universal emancipation is the historical mission of the modern proletariat. To thoroughly comprehend the historical conditions and thus the very nature of this act, to impart to the now oppressed proletarian class a full knowledge of the conditions and of the meaning of the momentous act it is called upon to accomplish, this is the task of the theoretical expression of the proletarian movement, scientific socialism.

Problems

1. What is the ultimate basis of all consciousness and all social structure?
2. What consequences follow for one's concept of man and history from the belief that man does not create history but merely discovers its principles?

3. To what extent are class conflicts ideological, and to what extent factual? What is the relationship of ideology to reality?
4. How did the bourgeoisie further production by socializing it? In capitalism, what contradictions follow from socializing production but failing to socialize distribution?
5. What forces lead inevitably to greater and greater concentration of production? Why can the concentration never become too intense or apparent?
6. What changes were wrought upon the worker by socialized production? What directions did Engels foreshadow for modern industrialization, and how prophetic was he?
7. What is the suggested remedy for the anarchy created by the capitalist conflict between socializing production but capitalizing appropriation?
8. Engels suggests that without a planned economy there will be recurrent booms and depressions. How accurate has he proved in his assertion? To what extent is the United States a planned economy?
9. How accurate is Engels in predicting that capitalism would reach a time when supply would outstrip demand? Is there evidence to suggest we have reached such a time?
10. How does automation gradually lead to bureaucratic state capitalism? What are the consequences of such automation?
11. As Engels sees it, why is capitalism not able to avoid destroying itself?
12. How accurate has Engels been in his predictions at the national level? At the global level?

17 V. I. LENIN

Vladimir Ilyich Lenin (born Vladimir Ilyich Ulyanov in 1870) is the unchallenged founder and father of modern communism, which is often distinguished from classical Marxism as originated and held by Marx and Engels. In spite of ongoing ideological schisms and leadership upheavals in Russia, China, and other communist states, Lenin's position, along with that of Marx and of Engels, is everywhere secure.

Lenin's career as a revolutionary began early. In 1887, shortly after the arrest of his brother Alexander for plotting to assassinate Czar Alexander III, Lenin was admitted to and then rapidly expelled from the University of Kazan for revolutionary student activities. Banned from the University, he continued his studies alone and made use of his excellent German to read and translate Marx into Russian. Studying alone, he took the law exams in 1891 and graduated first in his class.

At St. Petersburg (renamed Leningrad in 1924) Lenin, already a Marxist, attacked both the Czar and the Narodniki, a mystical, agrarian, antimodern, anti-Western, anti-Marxist band of revolutionaries. The future of Russia, he knew, lay not with the past but with industrialization and the West. Within a short time he not only welded together a viable Marxist movement but was also arrested. For approximately two years (1895–1897) he remained in prison, and after serving an additional three-year banishment in Siberia, he left Russia for five years of self-imposed exile.

In Switzerland where he finally settled, Lenin edited a Marxist journal and also completed a major work, What Is to Be Done?, which describes his political program. In it he makes clear his intention to abolish parliamentary democracy as unworkable and untenable; in its place he proposed the dictatorship of the proletariat governed by the Communist party. His stand was instrumental in shaping the future direction of communism, for the question of whether socialism was to be democratic or centralized was a divisive issue in the movement. The rupture between the Social Democrats (democratic socialists, also called Mensheviks or "minority party") and the Leninists (communists, also called Bolsheviks or "majority party") was inevitable. As their name suggests, the Leninists won.

Developments proceeded rapidly thereafter. The Russo-Japanese War of 1904–1905 ended in a humiliating defeat for Russia. On January 9, 1905, "Bloody Sunday," peaceful petitioners who were asking redress of working conditions were massacred in front of the Czar's palace. In June of the same year there was a revolt on the battleship Potemkin. Attempts (1905–1907) at governmental reform by establishing a parliament or Duma broke down when the Czar dissolved parliament. Lenin, who had returned in 1905, was forced once again to flee in 1907.

In exile in western Europe, Lenin waited for the inevitable uprising by writing two major works, Imperialism, The Highest Stage of Capitalism *(1916)* and The State and Revolution *(1917)*. In the first of these, Lenin traces the evolution of imperialism from colonialism through a more sophisticated form which he called "parasitism," created merely by virtue of investment capital. The investment of surplus capital in underdeveloped countries soon results not only in capital ownership of those countries, but in profits being siphoned off by the mother country instead of remaining for development in the underdeveloped country. *In* State and Revolution, *Lenin rejects Western parliamentarianism and reaffirms his intention to set up a dictatorship of the proletariat. He reveals, perhaps for the first time, a new visionary strain in this work. The State will not only "wither away," but men once freed from economic constraints will be truly humanized, recreated in their full spontaneity as ethical individuals.*

During this time—World War I had been going on since 1914—Russia suffered a massive demoralizing defeat at the hands of the Germans. Early in 1917, strikes paralyzed St. Petersburg, and on February 27, the army failed to obey the Czar's order to crush the rebels. The inevitable abdication of Czar Nicholas II took place within a few days. On March 3, the monarchy was abolished and, shortly afterwards, the Social Democrats formed a provisional government.

The Germans, well aware of Lenin's belief that the war was an imperialist squabble, and of his opposition to it, hoped that by helping him seize power to end the war on the Eastern front, they in turn could concentrate their full strength on the Western front. Lenin was provided with a special railway car, and on April 3, 1917, he traveled to St. Petersburg. Six months later, the October Revolution ended the liberal Kerensky government and replaced it with a communist one. Lenin had seized power.

This brief sketch of the history of Lenin and the rise of modern communism hardly does justice to Lenin the man or the leader. He emerges as one of the great theoretical and revolutionary leaders of the twentieth century. More important perhaps, in view of his anti-democratic sentiments, are revelations coming out of Russia since the death of Joseph Stalin which suggest that Lenin sensed the danger to Russia posed by Stalin's possible ascent to power, and tried to shift his support to Leon Trotsky. But when Lenin died in 1924, Trotsky was politically outmaneuvered, and the power passed to Stalin. Thus the police state was consolidated.

Frankly authoritarian, The State and Revolution *is a blueprint and rationale for the establishment of a dictatorship of the proletariat. To assume that authoritarianism was anything but a means for Lenin is wrong. Stalin, by making it an end-in-itself, proved to be not only Lenin's tragedy, but the world's.*

from The State and Revolution

CLASS SOCIETY AND THE STATE

1. The state–a product of the irreconcilability of class antagonisms

What is now happening to Marx's theory has, in the course of history, happened repeatedly to the theories of revolutionary thinkers and leaders of oppressed classes fighting for emancipation. During the lifetime of great revoluntionaries, the oppressing classes constantly hounded them, received their theories with the most savage malice, the most furious hatred and the most unscrupulous campaigns of lies and slander. After their death, attempts are made to convert them into harmless icons, to canonise them, so to say, and to hallow their *names* to a certain extent for the "consolation" of the oppressed classes and with the object of duping the latter, while at the same time robbing the revolutionary theory of its *substance,* blunting its revolutionary edge and vulgarising it. Today, the bourgeoisie and the opportunists within the labour movement concur in this doctoring of Marxism. They omit, obscure or distort the revoluntionary side of this theory, its revolutionary soul. They push to the foreground and extol what is or seems acceptable to the bourgeoisie. All the social-chauvinists are now "Marxists" (don't laugh!). And more and more frequently German bourgeois scholars, only yesterday specialists in the annihilation of Marxism, are speaking of the "national-German" Marx, who, they claim, educated the labour unions which are so splendidly organised for the purpose of waging a predatory war!

In these circumstances, in view of the unprecedentedly widespread distortion of Marxism, our prime task is to *re-establish* what Marx really taught on the subject of the state. This will necessitate a number of long quotations from the works of Marx and Engels themselves. Of course, long quotations will render the text cumbersome and not help at all to make it popular reading, but we cannot possibly dispense with them. All, or at any rate all the most essential, passages in the works of Marx and Engels on the subject of the state must by all means be quoted as fully as possible so that the reader may form an independent opinion of the totality of the views of the founders of scientific socialism, and of the evolution of those views, and so that their distortion by the "Kaut-

From V. I. Lenin, *The State and Revolution* (Moscow: Progress Publishers, 1949), pp. 7–93.

skyism"* now prevailing may be documentarily proved and clearly demonstrated.

Let us begin with the most popular of Engels's works, *The Origin of the Family, Private Property and the State,* the sixth edition of which was published in Stuttgart as far back as 1894. We shall have to translate the quotations from the German originals, as the Russian translations, while very numerous, are for the most part either incomplete or very unsatisfactory.

Summing up his historical analysis, Engels says:

> The state is, therefore, by no means a power forced on society from without; just as little is it 'the reality of the ethical idea', 'the image and reality of reason', as Hegel maintains. Rather, it is a product of society at a certain stage of development; it is the admission that this society has become entangled in an insoluble contradiction with itself, that it has split into irreconcilable antagonisms which it is powerless to dispel. But in order that these antagonisms, these classes with conflicting economic interests might not consume themselves and society in fruitless struggle, it became necessary to have a power, seemingly standing above society, that would alleviate the conflict and keep it within the bounds of 'order'; and this power, arisen out of society but placing itself above it, and alienating itself more and more from it, is the state. (Pp. 177–78, sixth German edition.)

This expresses with perfect clarity the basic idea of Marxism with regard to the historical role and the meaning of the state. The state is a product and a manifestation of the *irreconcilability* of class antagonsims. The state arises where, when and insofar as class antagonisms objectively *cannot* be reconciled. And, conversely, the existence of the state proves that the class antagonisms are irreconcilable.

It is on this most important and fundamental point that the distortion of Marxism, proceeding along two main lines, begins.

On the one hand, the bourgeois, and particularly the petty-bourgeois, ideologists, compelled under the weight of indisputable historical facts to admit that the state only exists where there are class antagonisms and a class struggle, "correct" Marx in such a way as to make it appear that the state is an organ for the *reconciliation* of classes. According to Marx, the state could neither have arisen nor maintained itself had it been possible to reconcile classes. From what the petty-bourgeois and philistine professors and publicists say, with quite frequent and benevolent references to Marx, it appears that the state does reconcile classes. Accord-

---

* Kautsky was literary executor of the works of Marx and Engels. Leading theoretician of the German Social Democrat Party, he believed that revolution could only succeed in an industrialized society with a large proletariat. He also favored a democratic revolution and stressed the anti-totalitarian aspects of Marxism. Lenin was enraged by Kautsky's denunciation of him and thereafter tried to destroy Kautsky by violent attacks.

ing to Marx, the state is an organ of class *rule,* an organ for the *oppression* of one class by another; it is the creation of "order", which legalises and perpetuates this oppression by moderating the conflict between the classes. In the opinion of the petty-bourgeois politicians, however, order means the reconciliation of classes, and not the oppression of one class by another; to alleviate the conflict means reconciling classes and not depriving the oppressed classes of definite means and methods of struggle to overthrow the oppressors.

For instance, when, in the revolution of 1917, the question of the significance and role of the state arose in all its magnitude as a practical question demanding immediate action, and, moreover, action on a mass scale, all the Socialist-Revolutionaries and Mensheviks descended at once to the petty-bourgeois theory that the "state" "reconciles" classes. Innumerable resolutions and articles by politicans of both these parties are thoroughly saturated with this petty-bourgeois and philistine "reconciliation" theory. That the state is an organ of the rule of a definite class which *cannot* be reconciled with its antipode (the class opposite to it) is something the petty-bourgeois democrats will never be able to understand. Their attitude to the state is one of the most striking manifestations of the fact that our Socialist-Revolutionaries and Mensheviks are not socialists at all (a point that we Bolsheviks have always maintained), but petty-bourgeois democrats using near-socialist phraseology.

On the other hand, the "Kautskyite" distortion of Marxism is far more subtle. "Theoretically", it is not denied that the state is an organ of class rule, or that class antagonisms are irreconcilable. But what is overlooked or glossed over is this: if the state is the product of the irreconcilability of class antagonisms, if it is a power standing *above* society and *"alienating* itself *more and more* from it", it is obvious that the liberation of the oppressed class is impossible not only without a violent revolution, *but also without the destruction* of the apparatus of state power which was created by the ruling class and which is the embodiment of this "alienation". As we shall see later, Marx very explicitly drew this theoretically self-evident conclusion on the strength of a concrete historical analysis of the tasks of the revolution. And—as we shall show in detail further on—it is this conclusion which Kautsky has "forgotten" and distorted.

2. Special bodies of armed men, prisons, etc.

Engels continues:

> As distinct from the old gentile [tribal or clan] order, the state, first, divides its subjects *according to territory.* . . .

This division seems "natural" to us, but it cost a prolonged struggle against the old organisation according to generations or tribes.

The second distinguishing feature is the establishment of a *public power* which no longer directly coincides with the population organising itself as an armed force. This special, public power is necessary because a self-acting armed organisation of the population has become impossible since the split into classes. . . . This public power exists in every state; it consists not merely of armed men but also of material adjuncts, prisons and institutions of coercion of all kinds, of which gentile [clan] society knew nothing. . . .

Engels elucidates the concept of the "power" which is called the state, a power which arose from society but places itself above it and alienates itself more and more from it. What does this power mainly consist of? It consists of special bodies of armed men having prisons, etc., at their command.

We are justified in speaking of special bodies of armed men, because the public power which is an attribute of every state does not "directly coincide" with the armed population, with its "self-acting armed organisation".

Like all great revolutionary thinkers, Engels tries to draw the attention of the class-conscious workers to what prevailing philistinism regards as least worthy of attention, as the most habitual thing, hallowed by prejudices that are not only deep-rooted but, one might say, petrified. A standing army and police are the chief instruments of state power. But how can it be otherwise?

From the viewpoint of the vast majority of Europeans of the end of the nineteenth century whom Engels was addressing, and who had not gone through or closely observed a single great revolution, it could not have been otherwise. They could not understand at all what a "self-acting armed organisation of the population" was. When asked why it became necessary to have special bodies of armed men placed above society and alienating themselves from it (police and a standing army), the West-European and Russian philistines are inclined to utter a few phrases borrowed from Spencer or Mikhailovsky, to refer to the growing complexity of social life, the differentiation of functions, and so on.

Such a reference seems "scientific", and effectively lulls the ordinary person to sleep by obscuring the important and basic fact, namely, the split of society into irreconcilably antagonistic classes.

Were it not for this split, the "self-acting armed organisation of the population" would differ from the primitive organisation of a stick-wielding herd of monkeys, or of primitive men, or of men united in clans, by its complexity, its high technical level, and so on. But such an organisation would still be possible.

It is impossible because civilised society is split into antagonistic, and, moreover, irreconcilably antagonistic, classes whose "self-acting" arming would lead to an armed struggle between them. A state arises, a special power is created, special bodies of armed men, and every revolution, by destroying the state apparatus, shows us the naked class struggle, clearly shows us how the ruling class strives to restore the special bodies of armed men which serve *it,* and how the oppressed class strives to create a new organisation of this kind, capable of serving the exploited instead of the exploiters.

In the above argument, Engels raises theoretically the very same question which every great revolution raises before us in practice, palpably and, what is more, on a scale of mass action, namely, the question of the relationship between "special" bodies of armed men and the "self-acting armed organisation of the population". We shall see how this question is specifically illustrated by the experience of the European and Russian revolutions.

But to return to Engels's exposition.

He points out that sometimes—in certain parts of North America, for example—this public power is weak (he has in mind a rare exception in capitalist society, and those parts of North America in its pre-imperialist days where the free colonist predominated), but that, generally speaking, it grows stronger:

> It [the public power] grows stronger, however, in proportion as class antagonisms within the state become more acute, and as adjacent states become larger and more populous. We have only to look at our present-day Europe, where class struggle and rivalry in conquest have turned up the public power to such a pitch that it threatens to swallow the whole society and even the state.

This was written not later than the early nineties of the last century, Engels's last preface being dated June 16, 1891. The turn towards imperialism—meaning the complete domination of the trusts, the omnipotence of the big banks, a grand-scale colonial policy, and so forth—was only just beginning in France, and was even weaker in North America and in Germany. Since then "rivalry in conquest" has taken a gigantic stride, all the more because by the beginning of the second decade of the twentieth century the world had been completely divided up among these "rivals in conquest", i.e., among the predatory Great Powers. Since then, military and naval armaments have grown fantastically and the predatory war of 1914–17 for the domination of the world by Britain or Germany, for the division of the spoils, has brought the "swallowing" of all the forces of society by the rapacious state power close to complete catastrophe.

Engels could, as early as 1891, point to "rivalry in conquest" as one of the most important distinguishing features of the foreign policy of the Great Powers, while the social-chauvinist scoundrels have ever since 1914, when this rivalry, many times intensified, gave rise to an imperialist war, been covering up the defence of the predatory interests of "their own" bourgeoisie with phrases about "defence of the fatherland", "defence of the republic and the revolution", etc.!

3. The state—an instrument for the exploitation of the oppressed class

The maintenance of the special public power standing above society requires taxes and state loans.

> "Having public power and the right to levy taxes," Engels writes, "the officials now stand, as organs of society, *above* society. The free, voluntary respect that was accorded to the organs of the gentile [clan] constitution does not satisfy them, even if they could gain it. . . ." Special laws are enacted proclaiming the sanctity and immunity of the officials. "The shabbiest police servant" has more "authority" than the representatives of the clan, but even the head of the military power of a civilised state may well envy the elder of a clan the "unstrained respect" of society.

The question of the privileged position of the officials as organs of state power is raised here. The main point indicated is: what is it that places them *above* society? We shall see how this theoretical question was answered in practice by the Paris Commune in 1871 and how it was obscured from a reactionary standpoint by Kautsky in 1912.

> "Because the state arose from the need to hold class antagonisms in check, but because it arose, at the same time, in the midst of the conflict of these classes, it is, as a rule, the state of the most powerful, economically dominant class, which, through the medium of the state, becomes also the politically dominant class, and thus acquires new means of holding down and exploiting the oppressed class. . . ." The ancient and feudal states were organs for the exploitation of the slaves and serfs; likewise, "the modern representative state is an instrument of exploitation of wage-labour by capital. By way of exception, however, periods occur in which the warring classes balance each other so nearly that the state power as ostensible mediator acquires, for the moment, a certain degree of independence of both. . . ." Such were the absolute monarchies of the seventeenth and eighteenth centuries, the Bonapartism of the First and Second Empires in France, and the Bismarck regime in Germany.

Such, we may add, is the Kerensky government in republican Russia since it began to persecute the revolutionary proletariat, at a moment when, owing to the leadership of the petty-bourgeois democrats, the Soviets have *already* become impotent, while the bourgeoisie are not *yet* strong enough simply to disperse them.

> In a democratic republic, Engels continues, "wealth exercises its power indirectly, but all the more surely", first, by means of the "direct corruption of officials" (America); secondly, by means of an "alliance of the government and the Stock Exchange" (France and America).

At present, imperialism and the domination of the banks have "developed" into an exceptional art both these methods of upholding and giving effect to the omnipotence of wealth in democratic republics of all descriptions. Since, for instance, in the very first months of the Russian democratic republic, one might say during the honeymoon of the "socialist" S.R.s and Mensheviks joined in wedlock to the bourgeoisie, in the coalition government, Mr. Palchinsky obstructed every measure intended for curbing the capitalists and their marauding practices, their plundering of the state by means of war contracts; and since later on Mr. Palchinsky, upon resigning from the Cabinet (and being, of course, replaced by another, quite similar Palchinsky), was "rewarded" by the capitalists with a lucrative job with a salary of 120,000 rubles per annum—what would you call that? Direct or indirect bribery? An alliance of the government and the syndicates, or "merely" friendly relations? What role do the Chernovs, Tseretelis, Avksentyevs and Skobelevs play? Are they the "direct" or only the indirect allies of the millionaire treasury-looters?

The reason why the omnipotence of "wealth" is more *certain* in a democratic republic is that it does not depend on individual defects in the political machinery or on the faulty political shell of capitalism. A democratic republic is the best possible political shell for capitalism, and, therefore, once capital has gained possession of this very best shell (through the Palchinskys, Chernovs, Tseretelis and Co.), it establishes its power so securely, so firmly, that *no* change of persons, institutions or parties in the bourgeois-democratic republic can shake it.

We must also note that Engels is most explicit in calling universal suffrage an instrument of bourgeois rule. Universal suffrage, he says, obviously taking account of the long experience of German Social-Democracy, is "the gauge of the maturity of the working class. It cannot and never will be anything more in the present-day state".

The petty-bourgeois democrats, such as our Socialist-Revolutionaries and Mensheviks, and also their twin brothers, all the social-chauvinists and opportunists of Western Europe, expect just this "more" from universal suffrage. They themselves share, and instil into the minds of the people, the false notion that universal suffrage "in the *present-day* state" is really capable of revealing the will of the majority of the working people and of securing its realisation.

Here we can only indicate this false notion, only point out that Engels's perfectly clear, precise and concrete statement is distorted at every step in the propaganda and agitation of the "official" (i.e., opportunist) socialist parties. A detailed exposure of the utter falsity of this notion which Engels brushes aside here is given in our further account of the views of Marx and Engels on the *"present-day"* state.

Engels gives a general summary of his views in the most popular of his works in the following words:

> The state, then, has not existed from all eternity. There have been societies that did without it, that had no idea of the state and state power. At a certain stage of economic development, which was necessarily bound up with the split of society into classes, the state became a necessity owing to this split. We are now rapidly approaching a stage in the development of production at which the existence of these classes not only will have ceased to be a necessity, but will become a positive hindrance to production. They will fall as inevitably as they arose at an earlier stage. Along with them the state will inevitably fall. Society, which will reorganise production on the basis of a free and equal association of the producers, will put the whole machinery of state where it will then belong: into a museum of antiquities, by the side of the spinning-wheel and the bronze axe.

We do not often come across this passage in the propaganda and agitation literature of the present-day Social-Democrats. Even when we do come across it, it is mostly quoted in the same manner as one bows before an icon, i.e., it is done to show official respect for Engels, and no attempt is made to gauge the breadth and depth of the revolution that this relegating of "the whole machinery of state to a museum of antiquities" implies. In most cases we do not even find an understanding of what Engels calls the state machine.

3. Abolition of parliamentarism

> "The Commune," Marx wrote, "was to be a working, not a parliamentary, body, executive and legislative at the same time. . . .
>
> "Instead of deciding once in three or six years which member of the ruling class was to represent and repress [ver- und zertreten] the people in parliament, universal suffrage was to serve the people constituted in communes, as individual suffrage serves every other employer in the search for workers, foremen and accountants for his business."

Owing to the prevalence of social-chauvinism and opportunism, this remarkable criticism of parliamentarism, made in 1871, also belongs now to the "forgotten words" of Marxism. The professional Cabinet Ministers and parliamentarians, the traitors to the proletariat and the "practical" socialists of our day, have left all criticism of parliamentarism to the anarchists, and, on this wonderfully reasonable ground, they denounce *all* criticism of parliamentarism as "anarchism"!! It is not surprising that the proletariat of the "advanced" parliamentary countries, disgusted with such "socialists" as the Scheidemanns, Davids, Legiens, Sembats, Renaudels, Hendersons, Vanderveldes, Staunings, Brantings, Bissolatis and Co., has been with increasing frequency giving its sympathies to anarcho-syndicalism,* in spite of the fact that the latter is merely the twin brother of opportunism.

For Marx, however, revolutionary dialectics was never the empty fashionable phrase, the toy rattle, which Plekhanov, Kautsky and others have made of it. Marx knew how to break with anarchism ruthlessly for its inability to make use even of the "pigsty" of bourgeois parliamentarism, especially when the situation was obviously not revolutionary; but at the same time he knew how to subject parliamentarism to genuinely revolutionary proletarian criticism.

To decide once every few years which member of the ruling class is to repress and crush the people through parliament—this is the real essence of bourgeois parliamentarism, not only in parliamentary-constitutional monarchies, but also in the most democratic republics.

But if we deal with the question of the state, and if we consider parliamentarism as one of the institutions of the state, from the point of view of the tasks of the proletariat in *this* field, what is the way out of parliamentarism? How can it be dispensed with?

Once again we must say: the lessons of Marx, based on the study of the Commune, have been so completely forgotten that the present-day "Social-Democrat" (i.e., present-day traitor to socialism) really cannot understand any criticism of parliamentarism other than anarchist or reactionary criticism.

The way out of parliamentarism is not, of course, the abolition of representative institutions and the elective principle, but the conversion of the representative institutions from talking shops into "working" bodies. "The Commune was to be a working, not a parliamentary, body executive and legislative at the same time."

"A working, not a parliamentary, body"—this is a blow straight from the shoulder at the present-day parliamentarians and parliamentary "lap dogs" of Social-Democracy! Take any parliamentary country, from America to Switzerland, from France to Britain, Norway and so forth—in these countries the real business of "state" is performed behind the scenes and is carried on by the departments, chancelleries and General Staffs. Parliament is given up to talk for the special purpose of fooling

---

* In Sorel's detailed description of the method for overthrowing the capitalist state, the chief weapon is the "general strike" of the proletariat. He was prepared to use trade unions as the vehicle for revolution, giving rise to the term "anarchosyndicalism."

the "common people". This is so true that even in the Russian republic, a bourgeois-democratic republic, all these sins of parliamentarism came out at once, even before it managed to set up a real parliament. The heroes of rotten philistinism, such as the Skobelevs and Tseretelis, the Chernovs and Avksentyevs, have even succeeded in polluting the Soviets after the fashion of the most disgusting bourgeois parliamentarism, in converting them into mere talking shops. In the Soviets, the "socialist" Ministers are fooling the credulous rustics with phrase-mongering and resolutions. In the government itself a sort of permanent shuffle is going on in order that, on the one hand, as many Socialist-Revolutionaries and Mensheviks as possible may in turn get near the "pie", the lucrative and honourable posts, and that, on the other hand, the "attention" of the people may be "engaged". Meanwhile the chancelleries and army staffs "do" the business of "state".

Dyelo Naroda, the organ of the ruling Socialist-Revolutionary Party, recently admitted in a leading article—with the matchless frankness of people of "good society", in which "all" are engaged in political prostitution—that even in the ministries headed by the "socialists" (save the mark!), the whole bureaucratic apparatus is in fact unchanged, is working in the old way and quite "freely" sabotaging revolutionary measures! Even without this admission, does not the actual history of the participation of the Socialist-Revolutionaries and Mensheviks in the government prove this? It is noteworthy, however, that in the ministerial company of the Cadets, the Chernovs, Rusanovs, Zenzinovs and the other editors of *Dyelo Naroda* have so completely lost all sense of shame as to brazenly assert, as if it were a mere bagatelle, that in "their" ministries everything is unchanged!! Revolutionary-democratic phrases to gull the rural Simple Simons, and bureaucracy and red tape to "gladden the hearts" of the capitalists—that is the *essence* of the "honest" coalition.

The Commune substitutes for the venal and rotten parliamentarism of bourgeois society institutions in which freedom of opinion and discussion does not degenerate into deception, for the parliamentarians themselves have to work, have to execute their own laws, have themselves to test the results achieved in reality, and to account directly to their constituents. Representative institutions remain, but there is *no* parliamentarism here as a special system, as the division of labour between the legislative and the executive, as a privileged position for the deputies. We cannot imagine democracy, even proletarian democracy, without representative institutions, but we can and *must* imagine democracy without parliamentarism, if criticism of bourgeois society is not mere words for us, if the desire to overthrow the rule of the bourgeoisie is our earnest and sincere desire, and not a mere "election" cry for catching workers' votes, as it is with the Mensheviks and Socialist-Revolutionaries, and also the Scheidemanns and Legiens, the Sembats and Vanderveldes.

It is extremely instructive to note that, in speaking of the functions of *those* officials who are necessary for the Commune and for proletarian democracy, Marx compares them to the workers of "every other employer", that is, of the ordinary capitalist enterprise, with its "workers, foremen and accountants".

There is no trace of utopianism in Marx, in the sense that he made up or invented a "new" society. No, he studied the *birth* of the new society *out of* the old, and the forms of transition from the latter to the former, as a natural-historical process. He examined the actual experience of a mass proletarian movement and tried to draw practical lessons from it. He "learned" from the Commune, just as all the great revolutionary thinkers learned unhesitatingly from the experience of great movements of the oppressed classes, and never addressed them with pedantic "homilies" (such as Plekhanov's: "They should not have taken up arms", or Tsereteli's: "A class must limit itself").

Abolishing the bureaucracy at once, everywhere and completely, is out of the question. It is a utopia. But to *smash* the old bureaucratic machine at once and to begin immediately to construct a new one that will make possible the gradual abolition of all bureaucracy—this is *not* a utopia, it is the experience of the Commune, the direct and immediate task of the revoluntionary proletariat.

Capitalism simplifies the function of "state" administration; it makes it possible to cast "bossing" aside and to confine the whole matter to the organisation of the proletarians (as the ruling class), which will hire "workers, foremen and accountants" in the name of the whole of society.

We are not utopians, we do not "dream" of dispensing *at once* with all administration, with all subordination. These anarchist dreams, based upon incomprehension of the tasks of the proletarian dictatorship, are totally alien to Marxism, and, as a matter of fact, serve only to postpone the socialist revolution until people are different. No, we want the socialist revolution with people as they are now, with people who cannot dispense with subordination, control and "foremen and accountants".

The subordination, however, must be to the armed vanguard of all the exploited and working people, i.e., to the proletariat. A beginning can and must be made at once, overnight, to replace the specific "bossing" of state officials by the simple functions of "foremen and accountants", functions which are already fully within the ability of the average town dweller and can well be perfomed for "workmen's wages".

We, the workers, shall organise large-scale production on the basis of what capitalism has already created, relying on our own experience as workers, establishing strict, iron discipline backed up by the state power of the armed workers. We shall reduce the role of state officials to that of simply carrying out our instructions as responsible, revocable, modestly paid "foremen and accountants" (of course, with the aid of technicians of all sorts, types and degrees). This is *our* proletarian task, this is what we can and must *start* with in accomplishing the proletarian revolution. Such a beginning, on the basis of large-scale production, will of itself lead to the gradual "withering away" of all bureaucracy, to the gradual creation of an order—an order without inverted commas, an order bearing no similarity to wage slavery—an order under which the functions of control and accounting, becoming more and more simple, will be performed by each in turn, will then become a habit and will finally die out as the *special* functions of a special section of the population.

A witty German Social-Democrat of the seventies of the last century called the *postal service* an example of the socialist economic system. This is very true. At present the postal service is a business organised on the lines of a state-*capitalist* monopoly. Imperialism is gradually transforming all trusts into organisations of a similar type, in which, standing over the "common" people, who are over-worked and starved, one has the same bourgeois bureaucracy. But the mechanism of social management is here already to hand. Once we have overthrown the capitalists, crushed the resistance of these exploiters with the iron hand of the armed workers, and smashed the bureaucratic machine of the modern state, we shall have a splendidly-equipped mechanism, freed from the "parasite", a mechanism which can very well be set going by the united workers themselves, who will hire technicians, foremen and accountants, and pay them *all,* as indeed *all* "state" officials in general, workmen's wages. Here is a concrete, practical task which can immediately be fulfilled in relation to all trusts, a task whose fulfilment will rid the working people of exploitation, a task which takes account of what the Commune had already begun to practise (particularly in building up the state).

To organise the *whole* economy on the lines of the postal service so that the technicians, foremen and accountants, as well as *all* officials, shall receive salaries no higher than "a workman's wage", all under the control and leadership of the armed proletariat—this is our immediate aim. This is the state and this is the economic foundation we need. This is what will bring about the abolition of parliamentarism and the preservation of representative institutions. This is what will rid the labouring classes of the bourgeoisie's prostitution of these institutions.

THE ECONOMIC BASIS OF THE WITHERING AWAY OF THE STATE

Marx explains this question most thoroughly in his *Critique of the Gotha Programme* (letter to Bracke, May 5, 1875, which was not published until 1891 when it was printed in *Neue Zeit,* Vol. IX, 1, and which has appeared in Russian in a special edition). The polemical part of this remarkable work, which contains a criticism of Lassalleanism,* has, so to speak, overshadowed its positive part, namely, the analysis of the connection between the development of communism and the withering away of the state.

1. Presentation of the question by Marx

From a superficial comparison of Marx's letter to Bracke of May 5, 1875, with Engels's letter to Bebel of March 28, 1875, it might appear that Marx was much more of a "champion of the state" than Engels, and that the difference of opinion between the two writers on the question of the state was very considerable.

Engels suggested to Bebel that all chatter about the state be dropped altogether, that the word "state" be eliminated from the programme altogether and the word "community" substituted for it. Engels even declared that the Commune was no longer a state in the proper sense of the word. Yet Marx even spoke of the "future state in communist society", i.e., he would seem to recognise the need for the state even under communism.

But such a view would be fundamentally wrong. A closer examination shows that Marx's and Engels's views on the state and its withering away were completely identical, and that Marx's expression quoted above refers to the state in the process of *withering away.*

Clearly there can be no question of specifying the moment of the *future* "withering away", the more so since it will obviously be a lengthy process. The apparent difference between Marx and Engels is due to the fact that they dealt with different subjects and pursued different aims. Engels set out to show Bebel graphically, sharply and in broad outline the utter absurdity of the current prejudices concerning the state (shared to no small degree by Lassalle). Marx only touched upon *this* question in passing, being interested in another subject, namely, the *development* of communist society.

The whole theory of Marx is the application of the theory of development—in its most consistent, complete, considered and pithy form—to modern capitalism. Naturally, Marx was faced with the problem of applying this theory both to the *forthcoming* collapse of capitalism and to the *future* development of *future* communism.

---

* Ferdinand Lassalle (1825-64) organized the first German Workers Party in 1863. His aristocratic pretensions and lack of revolutionary zeal infuriated Marx, for he wanted to work within the capitalist system. As a Hegelian, he believed the state should rule society, and therefore socialism with its state ownership was his ideal state.

On the basis of what *facts,* then, can the question of the future development of future communism be dealt with?

On the basis of the fact that it *has its origin* in capitalism, that it develops historically from capitalism, that it is the result of the action of a social force to which capitalism *gave birth.* There is no trace of an attempt on Marx's part to make up a utopia, to indulge in idle guess-work about what cannot be known. Marx treated the question of communism in the same way as a naturalist would treat the question of the development of, say, a new biological variety, once he knew that it had originated in such and such a way and was changing in such and such a definite direction.

To begin with, Marx brushed aside the confusion the Gotha Programme brought into the question of the relationship between state and society. He wrote:

> 'Present-day society' is capitalist society, which exists in all civilised countries, being more or less free from medieval admixture, more or less modified by the particular historical development of each country, more or less developed. On the other hand, the 'present-day state' changes with a country's frontier. It is different in the Prusso-German Empire from what it is in Switzerland, and different in England from what it is in the United States. *'The* present-day state' is, therefore, a fiction.
>
> Nevertheless, the different states of the different civilised countries, in spite of their motley diversity of form, all have this in common, that they are based on modern bourgeois society, only one more or less capitalistically developed. They have, therefore, also certain essential characteristics in common. In this sense it is possible to speak of the 'present-day state,' in contrast with the future, in which its present root, bourgeois society, will have died off.
>
> The question then arises: what transformation will the state undergo in communist society? In other words, what social functions will remain in existence there that are analogous to present state functions? This question can only be answered scientifically, and one does not get a flea-hop nearer to the problem by a thousandfold combination of the word people with the word state.

After thus ridiculing all talk about a "people's state", Marx formulated the question and gave warning, as it were, that those seeking a scientific answer to it should use only firmly-established scientific data.

The first fact that has been established most accurately by the whole theory of development, by science as a whole—a fact that was ignored by the utopians, and is ignored by the present-day opportunists, who are afraid of the socialist revolution—is that, historically, there must undoubtedly be a special stage, or a special phase, of *transition* from capitalism to communism.

2. The transition from capitalism to communism

Marx continued:

> Between capitalist and communist society lies the period of the revolutionary transformation of the one into the other. Corresponding to this is also a political transition period in which the state can be nothing but *the revolutionary dictatorship of the proletariat.*

Marx bases this conclusion on an analysis of the role played by the proletariat in modern capitalist society, on the data concerning the development of this society, and on the irreconcilability of the antagonistic interests of the proletariat and the bourgeoisie.

Previously the question was put as follows: to achieve its emancipation, the proletariat must overthrow the bourgeoisie, win political power and establish its revolutionary dictatorship.

Now the question is put somewhat differently: the transition from capitalist society—which is developing towards communism—to communist society is impossible without a "political transition period", and the state in this period can only be the revolutionary dictatorship of the proletariat.

What, then, is the relation of this dictatorship to democracy?

We have seen that the *Communist Manifesto* simply places side by side the two concepts: "to raise the proletariat to the position of the ruling class" and "to win the battle of democracy". On the basis of all that has been said above, it is possible to determine more precisely how democracy changes in the transition from capitalism to communism.

In capitalist society, providing it develops under the most favourable conditions, we have a more or less complete democracy in the democratic republic. But this democracy is always hemmed in by the narrow limits set by capitalist exploitation, and consequently always remains, in effect, a democracy for the minority, only for the propertied classes, only for the rich. Freedom in capitalist society always remains about the same as it was in the ancient Greek republics: freedom for the slave-owners. Owing to the conditions of capitalist exploitation, the modern wage slaves are so crushed by want and poverty that "they cannot be bothered with democracy", "cannot be bothered with politics"; in the ordinary, peaceful course of events, the majority of the population is debarred from participation in public and political life.

The correctness of this statement is perhaps most clearly confirmed by Germany, because constitutional legality steadily endured there for a remarkably long time—nearly half a century (1871-1914)—and during this period the Social-Democrats were able to achieve far more than in other countries in the way of "utilising legality", and organised a larger proportion of the workers into a political party than anywhere else in the world.

What is this largest proportion of politically conscious and active wage slaves that has so far been recorded in capitalist society? One million members of the Social-Democratic Party—out of fifteen million wage-workers! Three million organised in trade unions—out of fifteen million!

Democracy for an insignificant minority, democracy for the rich—that is the democracy of capitalist society. If we look more closely into the machinery of capitalist democracy, we see everywhere, in the "petty"—supposedly petty—details of the suffrage (residential qualification, exclusion of women, etc.), in the technique of the representative institutions, in the actual obstacles to the right of assembly (public buildings are not for "paupers"!), in the purely capitalist organisation of the daily press, etc., etc.—we see restriction after restriction upon democracy. These restrictions, exceptions, exclusions, obstacles for the poor seem slight, especially in the eyes of one who has never known want himself and has never been in close contact with the oppressed classes in their mass life (and nine out of ten, if not ninety-nine out of a hundred, bourgeois publicists and politicians come under this category); but in their sum total these restrictions exclude and squeeze out the poor from politics, from active participation in democracy.

Marx grasped this *essence* of capitalist democracy splendidly when, in analysing the experience of the Commune, he said that the oppressed are allowed once every few years to decide which particular representatives of the oppressing class shall represent and repress them in parliament!

But from this capitalist democracy—that is inevitably narrow and stealthily pushes aside the poor, and is therefore hypocritical and false through and through—forward development does not proceed simply, directly and smoothly, towards "greater and greater democracy", as the liberal professors and petty-bourgeois opportunists would have us believe. No, forward development, i.e., development towards communism, proceeds through the dictatorship of the proletariat, and cannot do otherwise, for the *resistance* of the capitalist exploiters cannot be *broken* by anyone else or in any other way.

And the dictatorship of the proletariat, i.e., the organisation of the vanguard of the oppressed as the ruling class for the purpose of suppressing the oppressors, cannot result merely in an expansion of democracy. *Simultaneously* with an immense expansion of democracy, which *for the first time* becomes democracy for the poor, democracy for the people, and not democracy for the money-bags, the dictatorship of the proletariat imposes a series of restrictions on the freedom of the oppressors, the exploiters, the capitalists. We must suppress them in order to free humanity from wage slavery, their resistance must be crushed by force; it is clear that there is no freedom and no democracy where there is suppression and where there is violence.

Engels expressed this splendidly in his letter to Bebel when he said that "the proletariat needs the state, not in the interests of freedom but in order to hold down its adversaries, and as soon as it becomes possible to speak of freedom the state as such ceases to exist."

Democracy for the vast majority of the people, and suppression by force, i.e., exclusion from democracy, of the exploiters and oppressors of the people—this is the change democracy undergoes during the *transition* from capitalism to communism.

Only in communist society, when the resistance of the capitalists has been completely crushed, when the capitalists have disappeared, when there are no classes (i.e., when there is no distinction between the members of society as regards their relation to the social means of production), *only* then "the state . . . ceases to exist", and *"it becomes possible to speak of freedom"*. Only then will a truly complete democracy become possible and be realised, a democracy without any exceptions whatever. And only then will democracy begin to *wither away*, owing to the simple fact that, freed from capitalist slavery, from the untold horrors, savagery, absurdities and infamies of capitalist exploitation, people will gradually *become accustomed* to observing the elementary rules of social intercourse that have been known for centuries and repeated for thousands of years in all copybook maxims. They will become accustomed to observing them without force, without coercion, without subordination, *without the special apparatus* for coercion called the state.

The expression "the state *withers away*" is very well chosen, for it indicates both the gradual and the spontaneous nature of the process. Only habit can, and undoubtedly will, have such an effect; for we see around us on millions of occasions how readily people become accustomed to observing the necessary rules of social intercourse when there is no exploitation, when there is nothing that arouses indignation, evokes protest and revolt, and creates the need for *suppression.*

And so in capitalist society we have a democracy that is curtailed, wretched, false, a democracy only for the rich, for the minority. The dictatorship of the proletariat, the period of transition to communism, will for the first time create democracy for the people, for the majority, along with the necessary suppression of the exploiters, of the minority. Communism alone is capable of providing really complete democracy, and the more complete it is, the sooner it will become unnecessary and wither away of its own accord.

In other words, under capitalism we have the state in the proper sense of the word, that is, a special machine for the suppression of one class by another, and, what is more, of the majority by the minority. Naturally, to be successful, such an undertaking as the systematic suppression of the exploited majority by the exploiting minority calls for the utmost ferocity and savagery in the matter of suppressing, it calls for seas of blood, through which mankind is actually wading its way in slavery, serfdom and wage-labour.

Furthermore, during the *transition* from capitalism to communism suppression is *still* necessary, but it is now the suppression of the exploiting minority by the exploited majority. A special apparatus, a special machine for suppression, the "state", is *still* necessary, but this is now a transitional state. It is no longer a state in the proper sense of the word; for the suppression of the minority of exploiters by the majority of the wage slaves of *yesterday* is comparatively so easy, simple and natural a task that it will entail far less bloodshed than the suppression of the risings of slaves, serfs or wage-labourers, and it will cost mankind far less. And it is compatible with the extension of democracy to such an overwhelming majority of the population that the need for a *special machine* of suppression will begin to disappear. Naturally, the exploiters are unable to suppress the people without a highly complex machine for performing this task, but *the people* can suppress the exploiters even with a very simple "machine", almost without a "machine", without a special apparatus, by the simple *organisation of the armed people* (such as the Soviets of Workers' and Soldiers' Deputies, we would remark, running ahead).

Lastly, only communism makes the state absolutely unnecessary, for there is *nobody* to be suppressed—"nobody" in the sense of a *class,* of a systematic struggle against a definite section of the population. We are not utopians, and do not in the least deny the possibility and inevitability of excesses on the part of *individual persons,* or the need to stop *such* excesses. In the first place, however, no special machine, no special apparatus of suppression, is needed for this; this will be done by the armed people themselves, as simply and as readily as any crowd of civilised people, even in modern society, interferes to put a stop to a scuffle or to prevent a woman from being assaulted. And, secondly, we know that the fundamental social cause of excesses, which consist in the violation of the rules of social intercourse, is the exploitation of the people, their want and their poverty. With the removal of this chief cause, excesses will inevitably begin to *"wither away"*. We do not know how quickly and in what succession, but we do know they will wither away. With their withering away the state will also *wither away.*

Without building utopias, Marx defined more fully what can be defined *now* regarding this future, namely, the difference between the lower and higher phases (levels, stages) of communist-society.

3. The first phase of communist society

In the *Critique of the Gotha Programme,* Marx goes into detail to disprove Lassalle's idea that under socialism the worker will receive the "undiminished" or "full product of his labour". Marx shows that from the whole of the social labour of society there must be deducted a reserve fund, a fund for the expansion of production, a fund for the replacement of the "wear and tear" of machinery, and so on. Then, from the means of consumption must be deducted a fund for administrative expenses, for schools, hospitals, old people's homes, and so on.

Instead of Lassalle's hazy, obscure, general phrase "the full product of his labour to the worker"), Marx makes a sober estimate of exactly how socialist society will have to manage its affairs. Marx proceeds to make a *concrete* analysis of the conditions of life of a society in which there will be no capitalism, and says:

> What we have to deal with here [in analysing the programme of the workers' party] is a communist society, not as it has *developed* on its own foundations, but, on the contrary, just as it *emerges* from capitalist society; which is, therefore, in every respect, economically, morally and intellectually, still stamped with the birthmarks of the old society from whose womb it comes.

It is this communist society, which has just emerged into the light of day out of the womb of capitalism and which is in every respect stamped with the birthmarks of the old society, that Marx terms the "first", or lower, phase of communist society.

The means of production are no longer the private property of individuals. The means of production belong to the whole of society. Every member of society, performing a certain part of the socially-necessary work, receives a certificate from society to the effect that he has done a certain amount of work. And with this certificate he receives from the public store of consumer goods a corresponding quantity of products. After a deduction is made of the amount of labour which goes to the public fund, every worker, therefore, receives from society as much as he has given to it.

"Equality" apparently reigns supreme.

But when Lassalle, having in view such a social order (usually called socialism, but termed by Marx the first phase of communism), says that this is "equitable distribution", that this is "the equal right of all to an equal product of labour", Lassalle is mistaken and Marx exposes the mistake.

"Equal right," says Marx, we certainly do have here; but it is *still* a "bourgeois right", which, like every right, *implies inequality*. Every right is an application of an *equal* measure to *different* people who in fact are not alike, are not equal to one another. That is why "equal right" is a violation of equality and an injustice. In fact, everyone, having performed as much social labour as another, receives an equal share of the social product (after the above-mentioned deductions).

But people are not alike: one is strong, another is weak; one is married, another is not, one has more children, another has less, and so on. And the conclusion Marx draws is:

> With an equal performance of labour, and hence an equal share in the social consumption fund, one will in fact receive more than another, one will be richer than another, and so on. To avoid all these defects, right would have to be unequal rather than equal.

The first phase of communism, therefore, cannot yet provide justice and equality: differences, and unjust differences, in wealth will still persist, but the *exploitation* of man by man will have become impossible because it will be impossible to seize the *means of production*—the factories, machines, land, etc.—and make them private property. In smashing Lassalle's petty-bourgeois, vague phrases about "equality" and "justice" *in general,* Marx shows the *course of development* of communist society, which is *compelled* to abolish at first *only* the "injustice" of the means of production seized by individuals, and which is *unable* at once to eliminate the other injustice, which consists in the distribution of consumer goods "according to the amount of labour performed" (and not according to needs).

The vulgar economists, including the bourgeois professors and "our" Tugan, constantly reproach the socialists with forgetting the inequality of people and with "dreaming" of eliminating this inequality. Such a reproach, as we see, only proves the extreme ignorance of the bourgeois ideologists.

Marx not only most scrupulously takes account of the inevitable inequality of men, but he also takes into account the fact that the mere conversion of the means of production into the common property of the whole of society (commonly called "socialism") *does not remove* the defects of distribution and the inequality of "bourgeois right", which *continues to prevail* so long as products are divided "according to the amount of labour performed". Continuing, Marx says:

> But these defects are inevitable in the first phase of communist society as it is when it has just emerged, after prolonged birth pangs, from capitalist society. Right can never be higher than the economic structure of society and its cultural development conditioned thereby.

And so, in the first phase of communist society (usually called socialism) "bourgeois right" is *not* abolished in its entirety, but only in part, only in proportion to the economic revolution so far attained, i.e., only in respect of the means of production. "Bourgeois right" recognises them as the private property of individuals. Socialism converts them into *common* property. *To that extent*—and to that extent alone—"bourgeois right" disappears.

However, it persists as far as its other part is concerned; it persists in the capacity of regulator (determining factor) in the distribution of products and the allotment of labour among the members of society. The socialist principle, "He who does not work, shall not eat", is *already* realised; the other socialist principle, "An equal amount of products for an equal amount of labour", is also *already* realised. But this is not yet communism, and it does not yet abolish "bourgeois right", which gives unequal individuals, in return for unequal (really unequal) amounts of labour, equal amounts of products.

This is a "defect", says Marx, but it is unavoidable in the first phase of communism; for if we are not to indulge in utopianism, we must not think that having overthrown capitalism people will at once learn to work for society *without any standard of right*. Besides, the abolition of capitalism *does not immediately create* the economic prerequisites for *such* a change.

Now, there is no other standard than that of "bourgeois right". To this extent, therefore, there still remains the need for a state, which, while safeguarding the common ownership of the means of production, would safeguard equality in labour and in the distribution of products.

The state withers away insofar as there are no longer any capitalists, any classes, and, consequently, no *class* can be *suppressed*.

But the state has not yet completely withered away, since there still remains the safeguarding of "bourgeois right", which sanctifies actual inequality. For the state to wither away completely, complete communism is necessary.

4. The higher phase of communist society

Marx continues:

> In a higher phase of communist society, after the enslaving subordination of the individual to the division of labour and with it also the antithesis between mental and physical labour has vanished, after labour has become not only a livelihood but life's prime want, after the productive forces have increased with the all-round development of the individual, and all the springs of co-operative wealth flow more abundantly—only then can the narrow horizon of bourgeois right be crossed

in its entirety and society inscribe on its banners: From each according to his ability, to each according to his needs!

Only now can we fully appreciate the correctness of Engels's remarks mercilessly ridiculing the absurdity of combining the words "freedom" and "state". So long as the state exists there is no freedom. When there is freedom, there will be no state.

The economic basis for the complete withering away of the state is such a high stage of development of communism at which the antithesis between mental and physical labour disappears, at which there consequently disappears one of the principal sources of modern *social* inequality—a source, moreover, which cannot on any account be removed immediately by the mere conversion of the means of production into public property, by the mere expropriation of the capitalists.

This expropriation will make it *possible* for the productive forces to develop to a tremendous extent. And when we see how incredibly capitalism is already *retarding* this development, when we see how much progress could be achieved on the basis of the level of technique already attained, we are entitled to say with the fullest confidence that the expropriation of the capitalists will inevitably result in an enormous development of the productive forces of human society. But how rapidly this development will proceed, how soon it will reach the point of breaking away from the division of labour, of doing away with the antithesis between mental and physical labour, of transforming labour into "life's prime want"—we do not and *cannot* know.

That is why we are entitled to speak only of the inevitable withering away of the state, emphasising the protracted nature of this process and its dependence upon the rapidity of development of the *higher phase* of communism, and leaving the question of the time required for, or the concrete forms of, the withering away quite open, because there is *no* material for answering these questions.

The state will be able to wither away completely when society adopts the rule: "From each according to his ability, to each according to his needs", i.e., when people have become so accustomed to observing the fundamental rules of social intercourse and when their labour has becomes so productive that they will voluntarily work *according to their ability*. "The narrow horizon of bourgeois right", which compels one to calculate with the heartlessness of a Shylock whether one has not worked half an hour more than somebody else, whether one is not getting less pay than somebody else—this narrow horizon will then be crossed. There will then be no need for society, in distributing products, to regulate the quantity to be received by each; each will take freely "according to his needs".

From the bourgeois point of view, it is easy to declare that such a social order is "sheer utopia" and to sneer at the socialists for promising everyone the right to receive from society, without any control over the labour of the individual citizen, any quantity of truffles, cars, pianos, etc. Even to this day, most bourgeois "savants" confine themselves to sneering in this way, thereby betraying both their ignorance and their selfish defence of capitalism.

Ignorance—for it has never entered the head of any socialist to "promise" that the higher phase of the development of communism will arrive; as for the great socialists' *forecast* that it will arrive, it presupposes not the present productivity of labour and *not the present* ordinary run of people, who, like the seminary students in Pomyalovsky's stories, are capable of damaging the stocks of public wealth "just for fun", and of demanding the impossible.

Until the "higher" phase of communism arrives, the socialists demand the *strictest* control by society *and by the state* over the measure of labour and the measure of consumption; but this control must *start* with the expropriation of the capitalists, with the establishment of workers' control over the capitalists, and must be exercised not by a state of bureaucrats, but by a state of *armed workers*.

The selfish defence of capitalism by the bourgeois ideologists (and their hangers-on, like the Tseretelis, Chernovs and Co.) consists in that they *substitute* arguing and talk about the distant future for the vital and burning question of *present-day* politics, namely, the expropriation of the capitalists, the conversion of *all* citizens into workers and other employees of *one* huge "syndicate"—the whole state—and the complete subordination of the entire work of this syndicate to a genuinely democratic state, *the state of the Soviets of Workers' and Soldiers' Deputies.*

In fact, when a learned professor, followed by the philistine, followed in turn by the Tseretelis and Chernovs, talks of wild utopias, of the demagogic promises of the Bolsheviks, of the impossibility of "introducing" socialism, it is the higher stage, or phase, of communism he has in mind, which no one has ever promised or even thought to "introduce", because, generally speaking, it cannot be "introduced".

And this brings us to the question of the scientific distinction between socialism and communism which Engels touched on in his above-quoted argument about the incorrectness of the name "Social-Democrat" Politically, the distinction between the first, or lower, and the higher phase of communism will in time, probably, be tremendous. But it would be ridiculous to recognise this distinction now, under capitalism, and only individual anarchists, perhaps, could invest it with primary importance from the "Plekhanov" conversion of the Kropotkins, of Grave, Cornelissen (if there still are people among the anarchists who have learned nothing and other "stars" of anarchism into social-chauvinists or "anarchotrenchists", as Ghe, one of the few anarchists, who have still preserved a sense of honour and a conscience, has put it).

But the scientific distinction between socialism and communism is clear. What is usually called socialism was termed by Marx the "first", or lower, phase of communist society. Insofar as the means of production become *common* property, the word "communism" is also applicable here, providing we do not forget that this is *not* complete communism. The great significance of Marx's explanations is that here, too, he consistently applies materialist dialectics, the theory of development, and regards communism as something which develops *out of* capitalism. Instead of scholastically invented, "concocted" definitions and fruitless disputes over words (What is socialism? What is communism?), Marx gives an analysis of what might be called the stages of the economic maturity of communism.

In its first phase, or first stage, communism *cannot* as yet be fully mature economically and entirely free from traditions or vestiges of capitalism. Hence the interesting phenomenon that communism in its first phase retains "the narrow horizon of *bourgeois* right". Of course, bourgeois right in regard to the distribution of *consumer* goods inevitably presupposes the existence of the *bourgeois state,* for right is nothing without an apparatus capable of *enforcing* the observance of the standards of right.

It follows that under communism there remains for a time not only bourgeois right, but even the bourgeois state, without the bourgeoisie!

This may sound like a paradox or simply a dialectical conundrum, of which Marxism is often accused by people who have not taken the slightest trouble to study its extraordinary profound content.

But in fact, remnants of the old, surviving in the new, confronts us in life at every step, both in nature and in society. And Marx did not arbitrarily insert a scrap of "bourgeois" right into communism, but indicated what is economically and politically inevitable in a society emerging *out of the womb* of capitalism.

Democracy is of enormous importance to the working class in its struggle against the capitalists for its emancipation. But democracy is by no means a boundary not to be overstepped; it is only one of the stages on the road from feudalism to capitalism, and from capitalism to communism.

Democracy means equality. The great significance of the proletariat's struggle for equality and of equality as a slogan will be clear if we correctly interpret it as meaning the abolition of *classes*. But democracy means only *formal* equality. And as soon as equality is achieved for all members of society *in relation* to ownership of the means of production, that is, equality of labour and wages, humanity will inevitably be confronted with the question of advancing farther, from formal equality to actual equality, i.e., to the operation of the rule "from each according to his ability, to each according to his needs". By what stages, by means of what practical measures humanity will proceed to this supreme aim we do not and cannot know. But it is important to realise how infinitely mendacious is the ordinary bourgeois conception of socialism as something lifeless, rigid, fixed once and for all, whereas in reality *only* socialism will be the beginning of a rapid, genuine, truly mass forward movement, embracing first the *majority* and then the whole of the population, in all spheres of public and private life.

Democracy is a form of the state, one of its varieties. Consequently, it, like every state, represents on the other hand, the organised, systematic use of force against persons; but, on the other hand, it signifies the formal recognition of equality of citizens, the equal right of all to determine the structure of, and to administer, the state. This, in turn, results in the fact that, at a certain stage in the development of democracy, it first welds together the class that wages a revolutionary struggle against capitalism—the proletariat, and enables it to crush, smash to atoms, wipe off the face of the earth the bourgeois, even the republican-bourgeois, state machine, the standing army, the police and the bureaucracy and to substitute for them a *more* democratic state machine, but a state machine nevertheless, in the shape of armed workers who proceed to form a militia involving the entire population.

Here "quantity turns into quality": *such* a degree of democracy implies overstepping the boundaries of bourgeois society and beginning its socialist reorganisation. If really *all* take part in the administration of the state, capitalism cannot retain its hold. The development of capitalism, in turn, creates the *preconditions* that *enable* really "all" to take part in the administration of the state. Some of these preconditions are: universal literacy, which has already been achieved in a number of the most advanced capitalist countries, then the "training and disciplining" of millions of workers by the huge, complex, socialised apparatus of the postal service, railways, big factories, large-scale commerce, banking, etc., etc.

Given these *economic* preconditions, it is quite possible, after the overthrow of the capitalists and the bureaucrats, to proceed immediately, overnight, to replace them in the *control* over production and distribution, in the work of *keeping account* of labour and products, by the armed workers, by the whole of the armed population. (The question of control and accounting should not be confused with the question of the scientifically trained staff of engineers, agronomists and so on. These gentlemen are working today in obedience to the wishes of the capitalists, and will work even better tomorrow in obedience to the wishes of the armed workers.)

Accounting and control—that is *mainly* what is needed for the "smooth working", for the proper functioning, of the *first phase* of communist society. *All* citizens are transformed into hired employees of the state, which consists of the armed workers. *All* citizens become employees and workers of a *single* country-wide state "syndicate". All that is required is that they should work equally, do their proper share of work, and get equal pay. The accounting and control necessary for this have been *simplified* by capitalism to the utmost and reduced to the extraordinarily simple operations—which any literate person can perform—of supervising and recording, knowledge of the four rules of arithmetic, and issuing appropriate receipts.¹

When the *majority* of the people begin independently and everywhere to keep such accounts and exercise such control over the capitalists (now converted into employees) and over the intellectual gentry who preserve their capitalist habits, this control will really become universal, general and popular; and there will be no getting away from it, there will be "nowhere to go".

The whole of society will have become a single office and a single factory, with equality of labour and pay.

But this "factory" discipline, which the proletariat, after defeating the capitalists, after overthrowing the exploiters, will extend to the whole of society, is by no means our ideal, or our ultimate goal. It is only a necessary *step* for thoroughly cleaning society of all the infamies and abominations of capitalist exploitation, *and for further* progress.

From the moment all members of society, or at least the vast majority, have learned to administer the state *themselves,* have taken this work into their own hands, have organised control over the insignificant capitalist minority, over the gentry who wish to preserve their capitalist habits and over the workers who have been thoroughly corrupted by capitalism—from this moment the need for government of any kind begins to disappear altogether. The more complete the democracy, the nearer the moment when it becomes unnecessary. The more democratic the "state" which consists of the armed workers, and which is "no longer a state in the proper sense of the word", the more rapidly *every form* of state begins to wither away.

For when *all* have learned to administer and actually do independently administer social production, independently keep accounts and exercise control over the parasites, the sons of the wealthy, the swindlers and other "guardians of capitalist traditions", the escape from this popular accounting and control will inevitably become so incredibly difficult, such a rare exception, and will probably be accompanied by such swift and severe punishment (for the armed workers are practical men and not

1. When the more important functions of the state are reduced to such accounting and control by the workers themselves, it will cease to be a "political state" and "public functions will lose their political character and become mere administrative functions."

sentimental intellectuals, and they will scarcely allow anyone to trifle with them), that the *necessity* of observing the simple, fundamental rules of the community will very soon become a *habit*.

Then the door will be thrown wide open for the transition from the first phase of communist society to its higher phase, and with it to the complete withering away of the state.

Patterns: Psychological Arguments

Lenin makes clear at least one aspect of his intention: "our prime task is to reestablish what Marx really taught" (311/22-23). He acknowledges that "this will necessitate a number of long quotations from the works of Marx and Engels." But, as he insists, these quotes are necessary to counteract "the bourgeoisie and the opportunists . . . doctoring of Marxism" and thereby "robbing the revolutionary theory of its *substance,* blunting its revolutionary edge and vulgarizing it" (311/10-12). Lenin thus establishes at once, by the vehemence of his response, that he cannot allow this distortion to continue, or to ignore it, for the issue is the preservation of *authority* against those who would seek to undermine it or pervert it.

The violence of Lenin's response to the Kautskyist challenge reveals a configuration of attitudes: (1) the tendency to elevate Marx and Engels' writings to the status of "scripture"; (2) the impossibility of standing apart from such authority; (3) the requirement that the true theory be uncontaminated by heresy; (4) the necessity to discover explicit ideological support amongst Marx's writings. The diction Lenin uses throughout suggests, moreover, a hypostatization and reification of Marxism (see Glossary). Marxism becomes embodied theory, speaking with a monolithic unambiguous voice on all matters, instead of a theory subject to interpretation by and interaction with men. "This [312/10-22] expresses with perfect clarity the basic idea of Marxism . . ." (312/23). Thus Marxism becomes exempt from the dialectical process. The instrumentalist philosophy applies to everything but Marxist theory. (See Kolakowski for a more extended discussion of this point.) Lenin is not engaged in scholarly debate, but in a religious vendetta against schismatics and unbelievers. What this means, in practice, is that Marx's name takes on great psychological significance.

Nowhere is this importance more evident than in Lenin's tendency to allow Marx and Engels' quotes to stand without critical evaluation; for he is intent not on evaluating but in explicating Marx as one would Biblical commentary. The result is not a dialogue between Lenin and Marx and Engels, but a repetition and amplification. The essay has the effect of doubling arguments. A measure of the psychological importance but intellectual insignificance of the appeals to authority is the fact that Lenin's arguments are forceful enough to stand alone; indeed, one can bypass most of the quotes with little loss of continuity or understanding. But that would be tantamount to ignoring the Bible and merely reading the commentary.

There is no attempt here to disparage Lenin's analysis—that must stand or fall on its own merits. We are merely intent on noting that appeal to authority is the essay's major pattern, and that such appeal is not intended to be significant to nonadherents. Just as the words "thus said Aristotle" do not elicit from us automatic assent for what follows—or "Christ spoke these words" bring uncritical and instant agreement from a Vedantist—so we are not immediately persuaded by a quote tagged, "Engels says." Arguments that have meaning only for adherents, are, it is fair to say, primarily psychological. *The State and Revolution* thus has two levels: the authoritative or psychological level of the quotes, and the intellectual level of Lenin's commentary and argument. We must not feel smug by our indifference to authoritative appeal when we are nonadherents. For our intellectual vigor and autonomy are measured not by our indifference to authority when we are nonadherents, but by our indifference when we are adherents.

Problems

1. How does Lenin define the role of the state? How does his definition differ from that of the petty-bourgeois ideologists?
2. What place has police power in Lenin's concept of the state? In what way do class antagonisms lead to increased state power? Do you believe that preoccupation with the relation of police power to the state is accurate, or that it is merely self-revealing? Why?
3. In what ways does the state as the organ of the ruling class use its power in a democratic society to exploit the oppressed classes?
4. Why does money "talk" in a democratic republic, and why for Lenin is political freedom and the vote a charade without economic equality? To what extent do you think his assessment of United States politics is accurate?
5. Why is the abolition of parliamentarianism a fundamental concern of Lenin's? Lenin was not, by predisposition, a tyrant. What assumptions, therefore, were operative in Lenin which led him to prefer authoritarianism to parliamentary rule? Why does he exempt the bureaucracy from abolition? To what extent do you agree with his assumptions and conclusions about parliamentary rule and the need for bureaucracies?
6. Why is Lenin so eager to defend himself against the charge of utopianism? How central is the concept of the "withering away" of the State to his thought? Why does he stress the need for a transitional period, and what is the nature of that transition likely to be?
7. Why will communist injustice and inequality in the transition stage be preferable to capitalist injustice and inequality?
8. What will characterize the higher phase of communism, and what will make inequality disappear and true freedom appear? Why does Lenin cast the date so far in the future? What are the possible consequences of such distancing?
9. What assumptions lead Lenin to envision a time when the vast majority of people will have developed a community sense and will administer justice and retribution so swiftly that the State will become unnecessary?

18 MAO TSE-TUNG

Mao Tse-tung (1893–   ) fits many of the stereotypes often associated with revolutionary leaders—man of humble background; witness to the beheading and poling of starving peasants who sacked the governor's palace during a famine; superb mind (he translated Marx into Chinese); brilliant student and student revolutionary; member of the revolutionary army of 1911; harassed by authorities; heroic guerilla fighter who led his army through gruelling hardships to victory. None of these clichés captures the stature and essence of the man. Like Ho Chi Minh, Mao Tse-tung is both a poet and a military hero, something in itself so rare in the West as to be intriguing. The story of his military exploits during China's revolutionary war is epic in its scope but impossible to chronicle here; only a suggestion is possible.

The critical point of the war came during the early thirties when Chiang Kai-shek, his Kuomintang troops trained by General Wetzell from Nazi Germany, went on the offensive against the Red army of 100,000 led by Mao. In October, 1933, Chiang mobilized 900,000 troops for a major offensive. They blockaded Kiangsi, where Mao's troops were concentrated, and a million people were starved to death during the siege. In January, 1934, Mao requested help but was rebuffed by the Chinese Communist Central Committee. The result was The Long March, an ordeal of staggering proportions and heroic dimensions. Secretly, Mao prepared to evacuate Kiangsi. On the night of October 16, 1934, the march began, and it continued for twelve months over some 8,000 miles, under incessant daily attacks and bombings. Mao's army hiked over eighteen mountain ranges and crossed twenty-four rivers, averaged twenty-four marching miles a day over unbelievable terrain, and this despite constantly meeting new Kuomintang armies at every turn; ten times they were completely encircled; and yet of the 100,000, 20,000 still miraculously escaped. Mao's wife was, however, not one of them. Had these events occurred to an American, Hollywood would have made during these past thirty-five years several epic sagas based on it. The result of this March and the protracted war against the Japanese and Chiang Kai-shek was the creation of a personality somewhat strange in the West—a personality with a steely will, tough mind, a faith strong enough to move mountains and a serene poetic temperament.

Those expecting to read in these essays the outpourings of a ranting demagogue will be surprised. Mao is a thoroughgoing rationalist and almost classical in his restrained style. What emerges in these essays is disconcerting—

a warm person with a superb mind and exalted aspirations analyzes war in the most lucid and geometric way as an instrument of national policy.

In contrast to Mao's simple, fundamentally humane explication, Hitler's fascist utterances of the thirties appear to be the demonic, inhuman outpourings of a megalomaniac. The reader, of course, must decide for himself on the significance of such differences.

The essay "Combat Liberalism" dates from 1937; "How to Study War" is the first chapter of Problems of Strategy in China's Revolutionary War *written in 1936, a year after the completion of The Long March.*

Combat Liberalism

We stand for active ideological struggle because it is the weapon for ensuring unity within the Party and the revolutionary organizations in the interest of our fight. Every Communist and revolutionary should take up this weapon.

But liberalism rejects ideological struggle and stands for unprincipled peace, thus giving rise to a decadent, philistine attitude and bringing about political degeneration in certain units and individuals in the Party and the revolutionary organizations.

Liberalism manifests itself in various ways.

To let things slide for the sake of peace and friendship when a person has clearly gone wrong, and refrain from principled argument because he is an old acquaintance, a fellow townsman, a schoolmate, a close friend, a loved one, an old colleague or old subordinate. Or to touch on the matter lightly instead of going into it thoroughly, so as to keep on good terms. The result is that both the organization and the individual are harmed. This is one type of liberalism.

To indulge in irresponsible criticism in private instead of actively putting forward one's suggestions to the organization. To say nothing to people to their faces but to gossip behind their backs, or to say nothing at a meeting but to gossip afterwards. To show no regard at all for the principles of collective life but to follow one's own inclination. This is a second type.

To let things drift if they do not affect one personally; to say as little as possible while knowing perfectly well what is wrong, to be worldly wise and play safe and seek only to avoid blame. This is a third type.

Not to obey orders but to give pride of place to one's own opinions.

From Mao Tse-tung, *Selected Readings from the Works of Mao Tse-tung* (Peking: Foreign Language Press, 1967), pp. 109–111.

To demand special consideration from the organization but to reject its discipline. This is a fourth type.

To indulge in personal attacks, pick quarrels, vent personal spite or seek revenge instead of entering into an argument and struggling against incorrect views for the sake of unity or progress or getting the work done properly. This is a fifth type.

To hear incorrect views without rebutting them and even to hear counter-revolutionary remarks without reporting them, but instead to take them calmly as if nothing had happened. This is a sixth type.

To be among the masses and fail to conduct propaganda and agitation or speak at meetings or conduct investigations and inquiries among them, and instead to be indifferent to them and show no concern for their well-being, forgetting that one is a Communist and behaving as if one were an ordinary non-Communist. This is a seventh type.

To see someone harming the interests of the masses and yet not feel indignant, or dissuade or stop him or reason with him, but to allow him to continue. This is an eighth type.

To work half-heartedly without a definite plan or direction; to work perfunctorily and muddle along—"So long as one remains a monk, one goes on tolling the bell." This is a ninth type.

To regard oneself as having rendered great service to the revolution, to pride oneself on being a veteran, to disdain minor assignments while being quite unequal to major tasks, to be slipshod in work and slack in study. This is a tenth type.

To be aware of one's own mistakes and yet make no attempt to correct them, taking a liberal attitude towards oneself. This is an eleventh type.

We could name more. But these eleven are the principal types.

They are all manifestations of liberalism.

Liberalism is extremely harmful in a revolutionary collective. It is a corrosive which eats away unity, undermines cohesion, causes apathy and creates dissension. It robs the revolutionary ranks of compact organization and strict discipline, prevents policies from being carried through and alienates the Party organizations from the masses which the Party leads. It is an extremely bad tendency.

Liberalism stems from petty-bourgeois selfishness, it places personal interests first and the interests of the revolution second, and this gives rise to ideological, political and organizational liberalism.

People who are liberals look upon the principles of Marxism as abstract dogma. They approve of Marxism, but are not prepared to practise it or to practise it in full; they are not prepared to replace their liberalism by Marxism. These people have their Marxism, but they have their liberalism as well—they talk Marxism but practise liberalism; they apply Marxism to others but liberalism to themselves. They keep both kinds of goods in stock and find a use for each. This is how the minds of certain people work.

Liberalism is a manifestation of opportunism and conflicts fundamentally with Marxism. It is negative and objectively has the effect of helping the enemy; that is why the enemy welcomes its preservation in our midst. Such being its nature, there should be no place for it in the ranks of the revolution.

We must use Marxism, which is positive in spirit, to overcome liberalism, which is negative. A Communist should have largeness of mind and he should be staunch and active, looking upon the interests of the revolution as his very life and subordinating his personal interests to those of the revolution; always and everywhere he should adhere to principle and wage a tireless struggle against all incorrect ideas and actions, so as to consolidate the collective life of the Party and strengthen the ties between the Party and the masses; he should be more concerned about the Party and the masses than about any individual, and more concerned about others than about himself. Only thus can he be considered a Communist.

All loyal, honest, active and upright Communists must unite to oppose the liberal tendencies shown by certain people among us, and set them on the right path. This is one of the tasks on our ideological front.

Patterns: Limited Categories

In "Combat Liberalism," Mao Tse-tung is as usual intent on defining and classifying behavior and attitudes—in this instance, liberal behavior and the proper revolutionary attitude toward it. Given such a purpose and given the antagonism between communism and liberalism, the harsh tone of Mao's criticism of liberalism is perhaps inevitable. Liberalism is certainly guilty of many of the failings cited. But the weakness of Mao's analysis consists not in enumerating failings (though even here one may disagree with his analysis); the weakness lies rather in attempting to fit generalized human failings into one "liberal" package and thereby creating limited and artificial categories. Those aspects of human nature which are slack, indulgent, self-interested and negative are liberal; those that are tireless, dedicated, selfless and positive are Marxist. Such categories do violence to reality. Neither group has a monopoly on such characteristics. Mao is thus guilty not only of creating limited categories, but of setting up a "straw man" (see Glossary) upon whom he vents his anger.

What emerges from this analysis is a heightened sense of the tendency of people to make their hostilities concrete. Apparently it is more difficult to be angry with "human nature" itself, than it is to be angry with a specific, identifiable group of people. By investing a limited group with certain qualities, even if those qualities affront reality, one can sharpen and simplify the required response. Ambiguity is reduced; the nature of the problem shifts; the question is no longer "What does it mean?" but "What is to be done?"—and once again we live, within our hearts, in the land of trouble-free certainty.

Categories are unavoidable, for without them we are beset by confusion. But an arrogant preference for limited categories bespeaks a failure to realize that by a reversal of fortune we can become victims of the very unreal categories we create.

Problems

1. Apart from its rhetorical failings, why is Mao's definition of liberalism inadequate?
2. What is Mao's attitude toward the generous tolerance of the liberal? To what does he attribute the origin of liberalism?
3. With what category would Mao replace liberalism?
4. Why does Mao think that extenuating human frailty is a major defect that must be eradicated?
5. Which of the two, liberalism or communism, emerges as the more humane attitude? To what extent does your answer reveal laziness, slipshod standards, low aspirations, or deepseated pessimism? To what extent is your answer rooted in a belief that life is better sustained by humane understanding than by exalted aspirations and tireless idealism?

How to Study War

1. THE LAWS OF WAR ARE DEVELOPMENTAL

The laws of war are a problem which anyone directing a war must study and solve.

The laws of revolutionary war are a problem which anyone directing a revolutionary war must study and solve.

The laws of China's revolutionary war are a problem which anyone directing China's revolutionary war must study and solve.

We are now engaged in a war; our war is a revolutionary war; and our revolutionary war is being waged in this semi-colonial and semi-feudal country of China. Therefore, we must study not only the laws of war in general, but the specific laws of revolutionary war, and the even more specific laws of revolutionary war in China.

It is well known that when you do anything, unless you understand its actual circumstances, its nature and its relations to other things, you will not know the laws governing it, or know how to do it, or be able to do it well.

From Mao Tse-tung, *Problems of Strategy in China's Revolutionary War. Selected Works of Mao Tse-tung,* Vol. 1 (Peking: Foreign Language Press, 1964), pp. 179–191.

War is the highest form of struggle for resolving contradictions, when they have developed to a certain stage, between classes, nations, states, or political groups, and it has existed ever since the emergence of private property and of classes. Unless you understand the actual circumstances of war, its nature and its relations to other things, you will not know the laws of war, or know how to direct war, or be able to win victory.

Revolutionary war, whether a revolutionary class war or a revolutionary national war, has its own specific circumstances and nature, in addition to the circumstances and nature of war in general. Therefore, besides the general laws of war, it has specific laws of its own. Unless you understand its specific circumstances and nature, unless you understand its specific laws, you will not be able to direct a revolutionary war and wage it successfully.

China's revolutionary war, whether civil war or national war, is waged in the specific environment of China and so has its own specific circumstances and nature distinguishing it both from war in general and from revolutionary war in general. Therefore, besides the laws of war in general and of revolutionary war in general, it has specific laws of its own. Unless you understand them, you will not be able to win in China's revolutionary war.

Therefore, we must study the laws of war in general, we must also study the laws of revolutionary war, and, finally, we must study the laws of China's revolutionary war.

Some people hold a wrong view, which we refuted long ago. They say that it is enough merely to study the laws of war in general, or, to put it more concretely, that it is enough merely to follow the military manuals published by the reactionary Chinese government or the reactionary military academies in China. They do not see that these manuals give merely the laws of war in general and moreover are wholly copied from abroad, and that if we copy and apply them exactly without the slightest change in form or content, we shall be "cutting the feet to fit the shoes" and be defeated. Their argument is: why should knowledge which has been acquired at the cost of blood be of no use? They fail to see that although we must cherish the earlier experience thus acquired, we must also cherish experience acquired at the cost of our own blood.

Others hold a second wrong view, which we also refuted long ago. They say that it is enough merely to study the experience of revolutionary war in Russia, or, to put it more concretely, that it is enough merely to follow the laws by which the civil war in the Soviet Union was directed and the military manuals published by Soviet military organizations. They do not see that these laws and manuals embody the specific characteristics of the civil war and the Red Army in the Soviet Union, and that if we copy and apply them without allowing any change, we shall also be "cutting the feet to fit the shoes" and be defeated. Their argument is: since our war, like the war in the Soviet Union, is a revolutionary war, and since the Soviet Union won victory, how then can there be any alternative but to follow the Soviet example? They fail to see that while we should set special store by the war experience of the Soviet Union, because it is the most recent experience of revolutionary war and was acquired under the guidance of Lenin and Stalin, we should likewise cherish the experience of China's revolutionary war, because there are many factors that are specific to the Chinese revolution and the Chinese Red Army.

Still others hold a third wrong view, which we likewise refuted long ago. They say that the most valuable experience is that of the Northern Expedition of 1926–27* and that we must learn from it, or, to put it more concretely, that we must imitate the Northern Expedition in driving straight ahead to seize the big cities. They fail to see that while the experience of the Northern Expedition should be studied, it should not be copied and applied mechanically, because the circumstances of our present war are different. We should take from the Northern Expedition only what still applies today, and work out something of our own in the light of present conditions.

Thus the different laws for directing different wars are determined by the different circumstances of those wars—differences in their time, place and nature. As regards the time factor, both war and its laws develop; each historical stage has its special characteristics, and hence the laws of war in each historical stage have their special characteristics and cannot be mechanically applied in another stage. As for the nature of war, since revolutionary war and counter-revolutionary war both have their special characteristics, the laws governing them also have their own characteristics, and those applying to one cannot be mechanically transferred to the other. As for the factor of place, since each country or nation, especially a large country or nation, has its own characteristics, the laws of war for each country or nation also have their own characteristics, and here, too, those applying to one cannot be mechanically transferred to the other. In studying the laws for directing wars that occur at different historical stages, that differ in nature and that are waged in different places and by different nations, we must fix our attention on the characteristics and development of each, and must oppose a mechanical approach to the problem of war.

Nor is this all. It signifies progress and development in a commander who is initially capable of commanding only a small formation, if he

* During the first three decades of this century when China was trying to liberate herself from Western imperialist domination, the Communist and Nationalist forces of Chiang Kai-shek formed an alliance. In the summer of 1926, the united armies, led by Chiang marched northward to a great victory that drove British and U.S. business interests out of China. After the victory, Chiang led a purge of the communists and the power struggle began in earnest.

becomes capable of commanding a big one. There is also a difference between operating in one locality and in many. It likewise signifies progress and development in a commander who is initially capable of operating only in a locality he knows well, if he becomes capable of operating in many other localities. Owing to technical, tactical and strategic developments on the enemy side and on our own, the circumstances also differ from stage to stage within a given war. It signifies still more progress and development in a commander who is capable of exercising command in a war at its lower stages, if he becomes capable of exercising command in its higher stages. A commander who remains capable of commanding only a formation of a certain size, only in a certain locality and at a certain stage in the development of a war shows that he has made no progress and has not developed. There are some people who, contented with a single skill or a peep-hole view, never make any progress; they may play some role in the revolution at a given place and time, but not a significant one. We need directors of war who can play a significant role. All the laws for directing war develop as history develops and as war develops; nothing is changeless.

2. THE AIM OF WAR IS TO ELIMINATE WAR

War, this monster of mutual slaughter among men, will be finally eliminated by the progress of human society, and in the not too distant future too. But there is only one way to eliminate it and that is to oppose war with war, to oppose counter-revolutionary war with revolutionary war, to oppose national counter-revolutionary war with national revolutionary war, and to oppose counter-revolutionary class war with revolutionary class war. History knows only two kinds of war, just and unjust. We support just wars and oppose unjust wars. All counter-revolutionary wars are unjust, all revolutionary wars are just. Mankind's era of wars will be brought to an end by our own efforts, and beyond doubt the war we wage is part of the final battle. But also beyond doubt the war we face will be part of the biggest and most ruthless of all wars. The biggest and most ruthless of unjust counter-revolutionary wars is hanging over us, and the vast majority of mankind will be ravaged unless we raise the banner of a just war. The banner of mankind's just war is the banner of mankind's salvation. The banner of China's just war is the banner of China's salvation. A war waged by the great majority of mankind and of the Chinese people is beyond doubt a just war, a most lofty and glorious undertaking for the salvation of mankind and China, and a bridge to a new era in world history. When human society advances to the point where classes and states are eliminated, there will be no more wars, counter-revolutionary or revolutionary, unjust or just; that will be the era of perpetual peace for mankind. Our study of the laws of revolutionary war springs from the desire to eliminate all wars; herein lies the distinction between us Communists and all the exploiting classes.

3. STRATEGY IS THE STUDY OF THE LAWS OF A WAR SITUATION AS A WHOLE

Wherever there is war, there is a war situation as a whole. The war situation as a whole may cover the entire world, may cover an entire country, or may cover an independent guerrilla zone or an independent major operational front. Any war situation which acquires a comprehensive consideration of its various aspects and stages forms a war situation as a whole.

The task of the science of strategy is to study those laws for directing a war that govern a war situation as a whole. The task of the science of campaigns and the science of tactics is to study those laws for directing a war that govern a partial situation.

Why is it necessary for the commander of a campaign or a tactical operation to understand the laws of strategy to some degree? Because an understanding of the whole facilitates the handling of the part, and because the part is subordinate to the whole. The view that strategic victory is determined by tactical successes alone is wrong because it overlooks the fact that victory or defeat in a war is first and foremost a question of whether the situation as a whole and its various stages are properly taken into account. If there are serious defects or mistakes in taking the situation as a whole and its various stages into account, the war is sure to be lost. "One careless move loses the whole game" refers to a move affecting the situation as a whole, a move decisive for the whole situation, and not to a move of a partial nature, a move which is not decisive for the whole situation. As in chess, so in war.

But the situation as a whole cannot be detached from its parts and become independent of them, for it is made up of all its parts. Sometimes certain parts may suffer destruction or defeat without seriously affecting the situation as a whole, because they are not decisive for it. Some defeats or failures in tactical operations or campaigns do not lead to deterioration in the war situation as a whole, because they are not of decisive significance. But the loss of most of the campaigns making up the war situation as a whole, or of one or two decisive campaigns, immediately changes the whole situation. Here, "most of the campaigns" or "one or two campaigns" are decisive. In the history of war, there are instances where defeat in a single battle nullified all the advantages of a series of victories, and there are also instances where victory in a single battle after many defeats opened up a new situation. In those instances the "series of victories" and the "many defeats" were partial in nature and not decisive for the situation as a whole, while "defeat in a single battle" or "victory in a single battle" played the decisive role. All this explains the importance of taking into account the situation as a whole. What is most important for the person in over-all command is to concentrate on attending to the war situation as a whole. The main point is that, according to the circumstances, he should concern himself with the problems of the grouping of his military units and formations, the relations between campaigns, the relations between various operational stages, and the relations between our activities as a whole and the enemy's activities as a whole—all these problems demand his greatest care and effort, and if he ignores them and immerses himself in secondary problems, he can hardly avoid setbacks.

The relationship between the whole and the part holds not only for the relationship between strategy and campaign but also for that between campaign and tactics. Examples are to be found in the relation between the operations of a division and those of its regiments and battalions, and in the relation between the operations of a company and those of its platoons and squads. The commanding officer at any level should centre his attention on the most important and decisive problem or action in the whole situation he is handling, and not on other problems or actions.

What is important or decisive should be determined not by general or abstract considerations, but according to the concrete circumstances. In a military operation the direction and point of assault should be selected according to the actual situation of the enemy, the terrain, and the strength of our own forces at the moment. One must see to it that the soldiers do not overeat when supplies are abundant, and take care that they do not go hungry when supplies are short. In the White areas the mere leakage of a piece of information may cause defeat in a subsequent engagement, but in the Red areas such leakage is often not a very serious matter. It is necessary for the high commanders to participate personally in certain battles but not in others. For a military school, the most important question is the selection of a director and instructors and the adoption of a training programme. For a mass meeting, the main thing is mobilizing the masses to attend and putting forward suitable slogans. And so on and so forth. In a word, the principle is to centre our attention on the important links that have a bearing on the situation as a whole.

The only way to study the laws governing a war situation as a whole is to do some hard thinking. For what pertains to the situation as a whole is not visible to the eye, and we can understand it only by hard thinking; there is no other way. But because the situation as a whole is made up of parts, people with experience of the parts, experience of campaigns and tactics, can understand matters of a higher order provided they are willing to think hard. The problems of strategy include the following:

Giving proper consideration to the relation between the enemy and ourselves.

Giving proper consideration to the relation between various campaigns or between various operational stages.

Giving proper consideration to those parts which have a bearing on (are decisive for) the situation as a whole.

Giving proper consideration to the special features contained in the general situation.

Giving proper consideration to the relation between the front and the rear.

Giving proper consideration to the distinction as well as the connection between losses and replacements, between fighting and resting, between concentration and dispersion, between attack and defense, between advance and retreat, between concealment and exposure, between the main attack and supplementary attacks, between assault and containing action, between centralized command and decentralized command, between protracted war and war of quick decision, between positional war and mobile war, between our own forces and friendly forces, between one military arm and another, between higher and lower levels, between cadres and the rank and file, between old and new soldiers, between senior and junior cadres, between old and new cadres, between Red areas and White areas, between old Red areas and new ones, between the central district and the borders of a given base area, between the warm season and the cold season, between victory and defeat, between large and small troop formations, between the regular army and the guerilla forces, between destroying the enemy and winning over the masses, between expanding the Red Army and consolidating it, between military work and political work, between past and present tasks, between present and future tasks, between tasks arising from one set of circumstances and tasks arising from another, between fixed fronts and fluid fronts, between civil war and national war, between one historical stage and another, etc., etc.

None of these problems of strategy is visible to the eye, and yet, if we think hard, we can comprehend, grasp and master them all, that is, we can raise the important problems concerning a war or concerning military operations to the higher plane of principle and solve them. Our task in studying the problems of strategy is to attain this goal.

4. THE IMPORTANT THING IS TO BE GOOD AT LEARNING

Why have we organized the Red Army? For the purpose of defeating the enemy. Why do we study the laws of war? For the purpose of applying them in war.

To learn is no easy matter and to apply what one has learned is even harder. Many people appear impressive when discoursing on military science in classrooms or in books, but when it comes to actual fighting, some win battles and others lose them. Both the history of war and our own experience in war have proved this point.

Where then does the crux lie?

In real life, we cannot ask for "ever-victorious generals", who are few and far between in history. What we can ask for is generals who are brave and sagacious and who normally win their battles in the course of a war, generals who combine wisdom with courage. To become both wise and courageous one must acquire a method, a method to be employed in learning as well as in applying what has been learned.

What method? The method is to familiarize ourselves with all aspects of the enemy situation and our own, to discover the laws governing the actions of both sides and to make use of these laws in our own operations.

The military manuals issued in many countries point both to the necessity of a "flexible application of principles according to circumstances" and to the measures to be taken in case of defeat. They point to the former in order to warn a commander against subjectively committing mistakes through too rigid an application of principles, and to the latter in order to enable him to cope with the situation after he has committed subjective mistakes or after unexpected and irresistible changes have occurred in the objective circumstances.

Why are subjective mistakes made? Because the way the forces in a war or a battle are disposed or directed does not fit the conditions of the given time and place, because subjective direction does not correspond to, or is at variance with, the objective conditions, in other words, because the contradiction between the subjective and the objective has not been resolved. People can hardly avoid such situations whatever they are doing, but some people prove themselves more competent than others. As in any job we demand a comparatively high degree of competence, so in war we demand more victories or, conversely, fewer defeats. Here the crux is to bring the subjective and the objective into proper correspondence with each other.

Take an example in tactics. If the point chosen for attack is on one of the enemy's flanks and it is located precisely where his weak spot happens to be, and in consequence the assault succeeds, then the subjective corresponds with the objective, that is, the commander's reconnaissance, judgement and decision have corresponded with the enemy's actual situation and dispositions. If the point chosen for attack is on another flank or in the centre and the attack hits a snag and makes no headway, then such correspondence is lacking. If the attack is properly timed, if the reserves are used neither too late nor too early, and if all the other dispositions and operations in the battle are such as to favour us and not the enemy, then the subjective direction throughout the battle completely corresponds with the objective situation. Such complete correspondence is extremely rare in a war or a battle, in which the belligerents are groups of live human beings bearing arms and keeping their secrets from each other; this is quite unlike handling inanimate objects or routine matters. But if the direction given by the commander corresponds in the main with the actual situation, that is, if the decisive elements in the direction correspond with the actual situation, then there is a basis for victory.

A commander's correct dispositions stem from his correct decisions, his correct decisions stem from his correct judgements, and his correct judgements stem from a thorough and necessary reconnaissance and from pondering on and piecing together the data of various kinds gathered through reconnaissance. He applies all possible and necessary methods of reconnaissance, and ponders on the information gathered about the enemy's situation, discarding the dross and selecting the essential, eliminating the false and retaining the true, proceeding from one thing to another and from the outside to the inside; then, he takes the conditions on his own side into account, and makes a comparative study of both sides and their interrelations, thereby forming his judgments, making up his mind and working out his plans. Such is the complete process of knowing a situation which a military man goes through before he formulates a strategic plan, a campaign plan or a battle plan. But instead of doing this, a careless military man bases his military plans on his own wishful thinking, and hence his plans are fanciful and do not correspond with reality. A rash military man relying solely upon enthusiasm is bound to be tricked by the enemy, or lured on by some superficial or partial aspect of the enemy's situation, or swayed by irresponsible suggestions from subordinates that are not based on real knowledge or deep insight, and so he runs his head against a brick wall, because he does not know or does not want to know that every military plan must be based on the necessary reconnaissance and on careful consideration of the enemy's situation, his own situation, and their interrelations.

The process of knowing a situation goes on not only before the formulation of a military plan but also after. In carrying out the plan from the moment it is put into effect to the end of the operation, there is another process of knowing the situation, namely, the process of practice. In the course of this process, it is necessary to examine anew whether the plan worked out in the preceding process corresponds with reality. If it does not correspond with reality, or if it does not fully do so, then in the light of our new knowledge, it becomes necessary to form new judgements, make new decisions and change the original plan so as to meet the new situation. The plan is partially changed in almost every operation, and sometimes it is even changed completely. A rash man who does not understand the need for such alterations or is unwilling to make them, but who acts blindly, will inevitably run his head against a brick wall.

The above applies to a strategic action, a campaign or a battle. Provided he is modest and willing to learn, an experienced military man will be able to familiarize himself with the character of his own forces (commanders, men, arms, supplies, etc., and their sum total), with the character of the enemy forces (likewise, commanders, men, arms, supplies, etc., and their sum total) and with all other conditions related to the war, such as politics, economics, geography and weather; such a military man will have a better grasp in directing a war or an operation and will be more likely to win victories. He will achieve this because, over a long period of time, he has come to know the situation on the enemy side and his own, discovered the laws of action, and resolved the contradictions between the subjective and the objective. This process of knowing is extremely important; without such a long period of experience, it would be difficult to understand and grasp the laws of an entire war. Neither a beginner nor a person who fights only on paper can become a really able high-ranking commander; only one who has learned through actual fighting in war can do so.

All military laws and military theories which are in the nature of principles are the experience of past wars summed up by people in former days or in our own times. We should seriously study these lessons, paid for in blood, which are a heritage of past wars. That is one point. But there is another. We should put these conclusions to the test of our own experience, assimilating what is useful, rejecting what is useless, and adding what is specifically our own. The latter is very important, for otherwise we cannot direct a war.

Reading is learning, but applying is also learning and the more important kind of learning at that. Our chief method is to learn warfare through warfare. A person who has had no opportunity to go to school can also learn warfare—he can learn through fighting in war. A revolutionary war is a mass undertaking; it is often not a matter of first learning and then doing, but of doing and then learning, for doing is itself learning. There is a gap between the ordinary civilian and the soldier, but it is no Great Wall, and it can be quickly closed, and the way to close it is to take part in revolution, in war. By saying that it is not easy to learn and to apply, we mean that it is hard to learn thoroughly and to apply skilfully. By saying that civilians can very quickly become soldiers, we mean that it is not difficult to cross the threshold. To put the two statements together, we may cite the Chinese adage, "Nothing in the world is difficult for one who sets his mind to it." To cross the threshold is not difficult, and mastery, too, is possible provided one sets one's mind to the task and is good at learning.

The laws of war, like the laws governing all other things, are reflections in our minds of objective realities; everything outside of the mind is objective reality. Consequently what has to be learned and known includes the state of affairs on the enemy side and that on our side, both of which should be regarded as the object of study, while the mind (the capacity to think) alone is the subject performing the study. Some people are good at knowing themselves and poor at knowing their enemy, and some are the other way round; neither can solve the problem of learning and applying the laws of war. There is a saying in the book of Sun Wu Tzu, the great military scientist of ancient China, "Know the enemy and know yourself, and you can fight a hundred battles with no danger of defeat",[2] which refers both to the stage of learning and to the stage of application, both to knowing the laws of the development of objective reality and to deciding on our own action in accordance with these laws in order to overcome the enemy facing us. We should not take this saying lightly.

War is the highest form of struggle between nations, states, classes, or political groups, and all the laws of war are applied by warring nations, states, classes, or political groups for the purpose of achieving victory for themselves. Unquestionably, victory or defeat in war is determined mainly by the military, political, economic and natural conditions on both sides. But not by these alone. It is also determined by each side's subjective ability in directing the war. In his endeavour to win a war, a military man cannot overstep the limitations imposed by the material conditions; within these limitations, however, he can and must strive for victory. The stage of action for a military man is built upon objective material conditions, but on that stage he can direct the performance of many a drama, full of sound and colour, power and grandeur. Therefore, given the objective material foundations, *i.e.*, the military, political, economic and natural conditions, our Red Army commanders must display their prowess and marshal all their forces to crush the national and class enemies and to transform this evil world. Here is where our subjective ability in directing war can and must be exercised. We do not permit any of our Red Army commanders to become a blundering hothead; we decidedly want every Red Army commander to become a hero who is both bold and clear-headed, who possesses both all-conquering courage and the ability to remain master of the situation throughout the changes and vicissitudes of the entire war. Swimming in the ocean of war, he not only must not flounder but must make sure of reaching the opposite shore with measured strokes. The laws for directing war constitute the art of swimming in the ocean of war.

So much for our methods.

Problems

1. What aspects of Mao's argument betray his Marxist bias?
2. What is, for Mao, the purpose of war? How, in his view, does one distinguish a just war from an unjust one?
3. What significance is there in the fact that Mao stresses rational, methodological understanding rather than fanatical devotion? What does your answer suggest about the manner in which Mao's mind works?
4. How does Mao define the subjective and the objective? Why is it essential to replace subjectivity with objectivity? By Mao's definitions, are we objective or subjective toward Mao and China? Justify your answer.
5. How doctrinaire is Mao? Does he favor rigid adherence or flexible adherence to the lessons of past wars?
6. These two essays by Mao, the first written in 1937 and the latter a year earlier, are quite different in tone and appeal. How would you assess this difference, and what explanation can you give for it?

19 LESZEK KOLAKOWSKI

Leszek Kolakowski (1927–), one of the leading Polish philosophers of this generation, is what orthodox communists call a "revisionist." Initially, the term referred to one who attempted to revise Marx's doctrine of dialectical materialism; but with the growing uncertainty as to what Marx really intended, it has come to mean any lapse from orthodoxy. Expulsion from the Communist Party is the usual result; and in fact Kolakowski has recently been expelled from the Polish Communist Party.

This essay, one of several in the collection Toward a Marxist Humanism *(1958), undertakes a sustained reinterpretation of Marxism. As the title of the essay, "Permanent vs. Transitory Aspects of Marxism," suggests, the essay is intent on distinguishing between what is essentially Marxist and what is institutionalized Stalinism. Like many Polish thinkers, Kolakowski has been influenced by Sartrean existentialism with its emphasis on freedom, choice, and individual responsibility. He is, thus, indirectly part of the dialogue between Polish Marxist intellectuals and French intellectual existentialists.*

Anthony Quinton, writing in the New York Review of Books, *sums up Kolakowski's new synthesis. "His final conclusion is that as agents we cannot predict our own choices; for the individual, only the past is inevitable; to regard oneself as fated to act in a fixed way is to treat oneself as dead" (26 Quinton).*

Permanent vs. Transitory Aspects of Marxism

A few days after the Greatest Philologist in the World (Stalin) published in a daily newspaper his opus announcing that Marr's theory was false,[1] I had the opportunity to attend a congress of philologists on this very subject. In the course of the discussion one of the participants made a most tactless step. He produced a pamphlet issued several weeks

From Leszek Kolakowski, *Toward a Marxist Humanism* (New York: Grove Press, 1968), pp. 173-87.
1. N. J. Marr (1864-1934) was a Soviet linguist whose "japhetic theory" of languages was dogma in the Soviet Union until Stalin's pronouncement.—*Trans.*

earlier by one of his colleagues who was present and read an extract that ran roughly as follows: "It is quite obvious that in linguistics Marr's theory is the only genuine Marxist-Leninist theory of language, that it alone is compatible with the principles of Marxism-Leninism, that it is the sole infallible instrument of Marxist-Leninist research," etc. Then the malicious fellow produced the current issue of the daily newspaper and quoted sections from an article by the same author that said, more or less: "It is obvious that Marr's theory has nothing in common with Marxism-Leninism, that it is a striking vulgarization of Marxism-Leninism, that the Marxist-Leninist conception of language must be firmly opposed to Marr's theory," etc. "What is the meaning of this?" raged the critic. "Of such a change of view within a few weeks? What a chameleon!" Confounded, the author of the quoted passages remained silent while everyone laughed merrily, until a Party activist pointed out that they should not laugh because every man had a right to change his mind and this should not in itself be considered a disgrace.

As I listened, my first impression was that the critic had been right in showing up the opportunism of the philologist and his shameful readiness to reverse his opinions with lightning speed to conform to the judgment delivered by the Greatest Philologist in the World. Only later, much later, did I realize that the embarrassed author of the pamphlet was the genuine Marxist, whereas the critic had shown himself to be completely ignorant. Because—and this is the core of the question I wish to consider—Marr's theory was truly compatible with Marxism two days before the publication of the Greatest Philologist's work, and truly incompatible with Marxism on the day this work appeared. Since the author of the pamphlet was an authentic Marxist he had no reason to be ashamed, but ought to have prided himself on his unshakable faithfulness to the principles of Marxism.

Principles? Perhaps this is an awkward choice of words. The point is that the term "Marxism" did not designate a doctrine with a specific content. It meant a doctrine defined purely formally, its content being in every case supplied by the decrees of the Infallible Institution which, during a certain phase, was the Greatest Philologist, the Greatest Economist, the Greatest Philosopher, and the Greatest Historian in the World.

In short, "Marxism" became a concept of institutional, rather than intellectual, content—which, by the way, happens to every doctrine connected with a church. Similarly, the word "Marxist" does not describe a man who believes in a specific world view whose content is defined. It refers to a man with a mental attitude characterized by a willingness to adopt institutionally approved opinions. From this point of view, the current content of Marxism does not matter. A man is a Marxist if he is always ready to accept as its content each recommendation of the Office. This is why, until February, 1956, the only real Marxist (which also means a revolutionary, a dialectician, a materialist) was one who agreed that there was no way to socialism except through revolutionary violence. An anti-Marxist (that is, a reformer, a metaphysician, an idealist) was anyone who thought other means could be found. As we know, after February, 1956, the reverse became true: since then the only real Marxist has been one who recognizes the possibility of a peaceful transition to socialism in certain countries. It is difficult to predict accurately who will, in regard to this problem, be a Marxist next year. But we will not be the ones to decide—the Office will settle the matter.

It is precisely for this reason, because of the institutional rather than the intellectual character of Marxism, that a true Marxist will profess beliefs he does not necessarily understand. The 1950 Marxist knew that Lysenko's theory of heredity was correct, that Hegel represented the aristocratic reaction to the French Revolution, that Dostoevski was a decadent and Babaeyski a great writer, that Suvorov served the cause of progress, and also that the resonance theory in chemistry was reactionary nonsense. Every 1950 Marxist knew these things even if he had never heard of chromosomes, had no idea what century Hegel lived in, had never read one of Dostoevski's books or studied a high-school chemistry textbook. To a Marxist all this is absolutely unnecessary so long as the content of Marxism is determined by the Office.

In this way the concept of Marxism was defined very precisely, without any possibility of error, although the definition was purely formal; that is, it merely indicated where to look for the current content of Marxism, without actually specifying that content.

Chronologically, this appears to be the second concept of Marxism. The original one simply meant the sum total of views and theories characteristic of Karl Marx. This first, historical concept of Marxism still retains its validity and precision (in the same sense that the concepts of "Platonism," "Freudianism," and "Cartesianism" do) irrespective of whether any Marxist—meaning, in this context, a believer in Marx's views—exists in the world.

We are thus faced with a question: If the sort of Marxism in which doctrine was continuously established by the Office is now dead in the minds of most intellectuals who considered themselves Marxists, has the concept of Marxism retained any meaning at all? If so, what meaning, other than the historical one connected with the work of the man who gave his name to the doctrine? What sense is there in slogans urging the "development of Marxism," and what meaning remains in the division between Marxists and non-Marxists in science?

Before the Office was born, and with it a new concept of Marxism, the reply to this question was not very difficult. Outstanding theoreticians—Russian revolutionaries like Lenin, Trotsky, and Bukharin—when analyzing, for example, the social conditions and history of Russia, applied Marx's conceptual framework to situations Marx himself never considered. They used the Marxist concept of class—undoubtedly a theoretical novelty that distinguished Marxism from other doctrines—to describe the relations of forces in Russian society. Here it is clear what is meant by "development of Marxism": the application of Marx's method and conceptual apparatus to new subjects of study. Let us suppose, however, that certain social processes arise for which this conceptual apparatus is no longer adequate. We can admit the adequacy of this apparatus as applied to the capitalist societies so scrupulously analyzed by Marx, and also recognize the basic accuracy of such analyses, while at the same time maintaining that this conceptual scheme is not applicable to the study of new, noncapitalist societies, where new concept must be used to study basic social stratification. (This problem, among others, is discussed by Stanislaw Ossowski in his still unpublished work *Concepts of Class Structure in the Social Consciousness,* which I had an opportunity to see in manuscript.) Can the attempt to build such a new apparatus aspire to be called "Marxist"? It is contradictory to Marxism, therefore "non-Marxist," if we assume that Marx's original conceptual categories are all that is necessary to describe and analyze every social phenomenon that might ever occur. Marx, of course, never made any such assumption; it is an original contribution of his Stalinist Epigoni.* Yet if such an attempt is merely not contradictory to Marxism, does this mean that it becomes Marxist?

Obviously we might agree to call all the achievements of science and all scientific truths by the name of "Marxism," but then we would have to consider as Marxist all discoveries in astro-botany, every new physiological law, and every new proposition in topology. In this sense, which has sometimes been specifically postulated, the world "Marxism" is stripped of meaning and becomes a superfluous synonym for "truth" or "scientific knowledge." This synonym is not simply superfluous but also mystifying, because it deviously suggests that all human knowledge is either inspired by Karl Marx or else progresses only thanks to the method he formulated—which is obviously false.

And yet, to return to our example, if we wish to develop a new conceptual apparatus to analyze social stratification in types of societies unknown to Marx, we must fall back upon a certain methodological rule which he not only consistently observed but applied so forcefully and universally that it is typical of his work. According to this rule, all

* *Epigoni* means sons, followers; literally, in Greek mythology, the sons of the Seven against Thebes. Joseph Stalin (1879–1953) gained unquestioned power in Russian politics after the death of Lenin in 1924. There was a brief power struggle between Stalin and Leon Trotsky (1879–1940), which ended with Trotsky, a more liberal and classical Marxist who favored world revolution, fleeing the country. Stalin favored consolidating the revolution at home, heavy emphasis on forced industrialization, collectivization of farms, bureaucratic rule, despotic purges, and police terror. He has come to signify everything oppressive in communism.

analyses of social life should proceed by seeking the basic divisions that separate societies into antagonistic groups. Even if it turns out that in certain societies these divisions are based on other criteria than the ones Marx formulated for the nineteenth-century bourgeois world, still the very fact of applying this extremely general rule leads the scholar to adopt Marx's characteristic methodology. From this point of view it can be said that the sociological research he is engaged in is "Marxist."

It happens, though, that the progress of knowledge requires us not only to enrich our supply of conceptual tools and methodological rules as compared with those found in Marx's works, but also to question and revise some of his concrete statements. The Office itself once proclaimed that some of Engels' assumptions about the origin of the state were false. In accordance with its usual procedures, it did not bother to justify this revision, but for the purposes of our discussion that is of secondary importance. Moreover, the Office disavowed Marx's thesis that it was impossible to build a socialist society in one isolated country. When Stalin came out with his concept of socialism in one country, Trotsky, as an orthodox and classical Marxist, rebuked him for deviating from the principles of Marxism and was, in turn, called an anti-Marxist by Stalin. Refraining for the moment from judging who was right in this dispute and whose view was verified by historical developments, we can nevertheless clearly see the scholastic sterility of a dispute conducted this way. If we say, as Stalin did, that the international situation has changed since Marx's time and that Marx himself recommended that the future of socialism be weighed in terms of the current structure of class power on an international scale, we are taking recourse to a way of thinking employed by Marx but so generalized and so common to all those who want to analyze reality rationally that it is not specifically symptomatic of "Marxist" thinking. On the other hand, if we maintain, as Lenin and Trotsky did, that Marx's analysis in this realm is not obsolete, we are falling back on the distinguishing features of Marx's method and on the concrete results of his analyses. From this point of view, although the second position may be considered Marxist, the first (regardless of whether it is factually true or false) is neither peculiarly "Marxist" nor "anti-Marxist." Although it expresses a thesis obviously contradictory to the results of Marx's own research, it is based, legitimately or not, on a rule which, though Marx used it, is not unique to his work. In other cases it is possible to question certain of Marx's theses by applying methodological rules that he not only used but used in a particular and distinctive way We may call an analysis of this kind "Marxist" in a legitimate sense of the term.

Thus we come to the formulation of the problem under discussion. Marx's work contains essential features that are not peculiar to him and his followers, and that do not suffice to distinguish a separate school of thought: a relentlessly rationalist orientation, a sense of radical criticism, a distaste for sentimentality in social research, a deterministic method. Social scientists who fail to observe these principles—as the majority of people who called themselves Marxists notoriously and demonstrably did, in breach of the elementary rules of methodological rationalism—are surely not Marxists. (Instead, they easily may, and did, discredit the very idea of Marxism by associating it inseparably with their own methods of thinking and with the activities of the Office. At the same time, they made those who apply Marx's scientific contributions to their work ashamed of being called Marxist.) On the other hand, those who respect these principles do not thereby become Marxists, for these principles are not uniquely characteristic of Marx's work.

Yet there are many aspects of his work which constitute an original contribution to the development of the social sciences. They are, above all, certain methodological rules that enable man to know and master social material. The principle of determinism—and determinism becomes more intelligible if it is understood as a rule of thinking and not as a metaphysical theory—is certainly not specifically Marxist. It does not state simply that "In the same conditions the same phenomena occur," and still less that "all events are causally conditioned," because in such a formulation determinism becomes an empty generalization, unverifiable and fruitless in scientific research. Broadly speaking, this principle requires that we try to analyze every phenomenon as thoroughly as possible—given the tools and tasks at hand—by situating it within the framework of every kind of relationship with other phenomena. On the other hand, what is distinctively Marxist is a certain more specific conception of determinism, as expressed by the fundamental idea of historical materialism: the requirement that in a genetic analysis of political institutions and various forms of social consciousness we should look for the relationships that link them with social divisions arising from the system of ownership, or more generally, from the system of production; and for these we should seek the relationships connecting them with technical progress.

To be scientifically useful, such a principle must be formulated in general terms. It is, for instance, extremely harmful to interpret this principle as holding that fundamental class structure (in Marx's sense) determines unequivocally all other divisions in the social institutions and intellectual life of society throughout the entire history of mankind.

As we have said, what is typical of Marx is the tendency to emphasize the primary divisions in society that most influence the development of history. Also typical is his awareness of the limitations and distortions imposed on the social sciences by the pressures of societal conditions that shape the minds of researchers, as well as his fight to destroy ideological myths in science, a fight we never expected to have to resume most forcefully against a doctrine disguised under his name. Typical, too, is a certain type of historicism which not only rejects attempts to evaluate historical phenomena from the viewpoint of a moralistic keeper of eternal values, but which is based on the general principle of the historical relativity of the subjects under study, and also on the conviction that human nature is the product of man's social history and that our entire conception of the world is "socially subjective." This means it is a product of collective activity, which creatively organizes reality to adapt it to man's biological and social orientation in the world, and only thus formed does it remain in our minds. In this sense, then, the whole extra-human world is created by man.

Another typical trait is Marx's practical orientation in the social sciences. He selected problems to be dealt with according to whether they served the cause of an egalitarian society, the cause of abolishing class divisions and of emancipating the exploited and oppressed. Equally typical is his conviction that, on the strength of historical law, the capitalist economy and the political rule of the bourgeoisie will inevitably change into a socialist system, and that this transformation will take place as a result of the proletariat's rise to power. In time, the proletariat will abolish itself as a class, which will mean the abolition of classes as such and of the state as an instrument of class rule.

And so we have an enumeration—only as illustrations, of course—of the principles and conclusions that are connected specifically with the name of Marx in the history of science. We are speaking here exclusively about matters dealing with the methodology of the social sciences, for there is no typical Marxist methodology which has affected the development of the natural sciences (with the exception of Marxist methodology in the official meaning of the term, which successfully helped deter progress).

It is not difficult to see that many of these rules have been permanently assimilated into the social sciences as practiced by groups totally independent of official Marxism, and therefore considered by the Office as non-Marxist, anti-Marxist, bourgeois, and so on. Many of Marx's ideas entered into the bloodstream of scientific life and thus ceased to distinguish Marx—and those who regarded themselves as orthodox believers in his doctrine—from others. From this point of view, then, dividing scientists into Marxists and non-Marxists became entirely meaningless. Still, there are other significant elements of Marx's method which have not become so widely accepted and at least appear to provide that basis for making such a distinction. But the question is not that simple, and for several reasons.

First of all, the word "Marxism," as it is commonly used and most deeply rooted in today's social consciousness, is linked with an intellectual activity that is notorious in philosophy and sociology. I mean it is used in the first of the two meanings discussed above—the institutional sense associated with the activity of the Office. It is clear that no lay sociologist or philosopher with scientific aspirations has the slightest wish to have anything in common with Marxism thus conceived because he does not like to be accused of religiosity. Therefore, even if his scientific work is most profoundly inspired by Marx, he is either very reluctant to describe his outlook as Marxist or else he must, in each instance, define precisely his use of the term.

That is why in order to revitalize the distinction between Marxists and non-Marxists the first condition would be to disseminate a concept of Marxism different from the current one. The possibility of such a revision, however, depends on certain social facts. This is so because the meaning of words is a social fact and cannot be established arbitrarily by simply declaring that we wish to practice "true" Marxism, while up till now the majority of Marxists were really pseudo-Marxists, Marxists in quotation marks. (This explains why, in speaking of intellectual Stalinism, I am not trying to present it as a sort of pseudo-Marxism in contradistinction to some kind of genuine Marxism. For Stalinism created a socially vital concept of Marxism that was an institutional and not an intellectual phenomenon, and this concept did function successfully in reality. There was only one element of mystification in it: the name of Karl Marx, from which the term was originally derived. But as time passes, etymological associations die out or at least grow fainter in the minds of people using a given term.)

Second, and even more important, outside and independently of the existence and functioning of institutional Marxism, there emerged in the social sciences a variety of conceptual categories, methodological rules, and new—now highly developed—branches of study. Therefore, in the intellectual sense of Marxism, there are whole areas of research where the division between Marxists and non-Marxists never assumed any significance. Obviously we should not infer from this that Marx's method, even today, would be irrelevant and unable to provide a vigorous and dynamic inspiration for research in these fields. If, for example, sociological investigations of public opinion developed almost entirely outside the sphere of influence of the Marxist tradition, still it is very likely that new perspectives for study in this realm could be opened if its fundamental stock of categories were enriched by the introduction of Marx's concept of class. Since logical semantics has made use of tools that ignore the social aspect of meaning, here Marx's method of analysis could probably contribute in many ways to its progress. In many fields of research, particularly in political and economic history as well as in the history of various areas of culture, Marx's theoretical achievements have played a significantly creative role, and this in spite of institutional Marxism. Hence it would obviously be absurd, merely because of the long existence of institutional

Marxism, to advocate a return to Ranke's type of historiography, Kallenbach's history of literature, and Zeller's history of philosophy.

Third and finally, we must note that if the decision whether a given doctrine, theory, or historical interpretation is Marxist or non-Marxist is to make any sense at all, that decision can be based only on a consideration of the very general methodological assumptions used to construct that doctrine or theory. Of course, the borderline between a "fact" and an "interpretation" is flexible and defies precise definition in the social sciences, just as in the natural ones. Nonetheless, there does exist a great mass of knowledge whose "factual" character is beyond any doubt, and to call it "Marxist" is nonsense.

On the other hand, the history of science teaches us that problems of interpretation are never settled with any finality. The best proof of this is provided by an obvious fact that casts doubt on the primitive belief that it is possible to achieve complete objectivity in the social sciences—the fact that nearly every human generation rewrites the history of the world. What is noteworthy is that this is very often done successfully. And this means that the same, or nearly the same, stock of factual knowledge lends itself to a great number of *well-founded* and rationally justified—though radically different—interpretations. Is it worthwhile to take the trouble to determine whether they are Marxist or not, and if so, in which cases?

From the point of view of institutional Marxism, the matter is clear: In 1945 the only Marxist evaluation of Hegel was that he was a German chauvinist, an apologist for war, an enemy of the Slavic peoples, and a precursor of fascism; in 1954 Hegel had become an eminent dialectician, an idealist who played an important role in shaping Marx's philosophy. From the standpoint of an intellectual conception of Marxism, the problem looks somewhat different. There does not exist, and never will, one "truly Marxist" interpretation of Stoic philosophy, or a particular interpretation of Mickiewicz's poetry that would be "the only one compatible with Marxism." One can speak of interpreting Stoic philosophy with the help of general Marxist rules of historical methodology, but the same method may yield widely differing results. For the hope that the methodology of the social sciences may come to resemble a logarithmic table or a computer that will always enable us to proceed from a given set of facts to the same unequivocal answers is a chimera. Moreover, it is far from certain that the most rigorous application of this methodology would necessarily lead to conclusions in agreement with some particular remarks of Friedrich Engels about Stoicism—nor can it exhaust the possibilities of scientific study of the subject.

That is why disputes in which scholars try to snatch from each other the exclusive privilege of using "genuine Marxism" and to monopolize the honorable title of "consistent Marxist" are sterile verbalism. One can argue whether a given theory fulfills more or less well the requirements of scientific thinking, which include the essential rules of the method worked out by Marx. These rules, however, must be of a very general nature, and they do not contain any specific instructions on how to evaluate one or another historical phenomenon. Moreover, they always allow for many possible interpretations: the rule of historical materialism itself does not determine the type, intensity, or degree of uniformity of the influence exerted by the sum total of material conditions of life on the social thinking of people in all the epochs of history. And, *a forteriori*, historical materialism does not determine whether, for example, Pascal's philosophy is to be taken as an expression of the decadent tendencies of declining feudalism, or a representation of bourgeois thought, or something else again. In sociological investigations, and even more so in philosophical ones, there is hardly a single perfectly unambiguous term. Vacillations in meaning are inherited by even the most fundamental theses of a doctrine; none can be regarded as precise. If terms such as "matter," "social consciousness," "cognition," "superstructure," "causal determination," "relations of production," and so on are not clear, it follows that no methodological rules and no assertions of the theory in which they are involved have a precisely defined meaning.

Therefore, what we call Marxism, as understood in its intellectual function and as a method of thinking, can vary greatly in content within the limits of a very general framework. We know that it would be difficult to develop a Marxist angelology, and that we certainly could not present Bossuet's philosophy of history as Marxist. To know this, however, is not very useful, since our primary purpose in using the word "Marxist" is not to distinguish scientific thinking from the notorious irrationalism of theologians. The fact is that within the boundaries of science, where various styles of thinking and various types of methodology can very well coexist and compete, the borderline between Marxism and non-Marxism is extremely fluid.

It is obvious that it cannot be otherwise in view of at least two circumstances mentioned earlier—the insufficiency for contemporary scholarship of the rules Marx formulated, as well as their ambiguity; and also the fluidity of the limits of their validity. Thus to speak of a "compact and uniform Marxist camp," in contradistinction to the rest of the world, defining by its very existence a basic line of division in science, or to proclaim shibboleths about the "purity of Marxist doctrine"—all this makes no sense in the intellectual conception of Marxism. It may have a certain utility, but only when Marxism is considered as a political or religious phenomenon rather than as a science. In circumstances where we must venture to separate knowledge from faith, as the Averroists did against orthodoxy in the thirteenth century, and where political tactics become less and less able to exert their destructive pressure on the content of scientific knowledge, the Marxist "camp" in science will increasingly assume an ethereal shape instead of remaining the monolithic mass it once was. Of course, the tradition of the old, rigid division into Marxists and non-Marxists is not defunct, and will certainly influence scientific life for a long time to come, even where institutional Marxism is dead and discredited in the social consciousness. It is equally certain, though, that the pressure of this tradition will continue to decrease in direct proportion to the gradual elimination of institutional Marxism from the realm of science.

This does not in the least imply that in the humanistic sciences—those inevitably most influenced by social conditions—all divisions caused by differing world views have ceased to exist. But the most significant division is not that between orthodox Marxists guarding the purity of the doctrine against any admixture of heathen blood on the one hand, and everyone else on the other. It is—to use political language for a moment—the division between the Right and the Left in the humanities. This cleavage is most often characterized less by a concrete methodology than by an intellectual attitude. By the intellectual Left in the humanities we mean intellectual activity distinguished by: radical rationalism in thinking; steadfast resistance to any invasion of myth into science; an entirely secular view of the world; criticism pushed to its utmost limits; distrust of all closed doctrines and systems; striving for open-mindedness, that is, readiness to revise accepted theses, theories, and methods; esteem for scientific innovation; tolerance toward differing scientific standpoints, together with a simultaneous preparedness for war—even one of aggression—against every manifestation of irrationalism; and above all, a belief in the cognitive values of science and in the possibility of social progress.

Like all such delimitations, this one is less exact than, say, a national boundary. Still, it seems to me incomparably more significant than the division that the traditional Marxist camp has traditionally accepted. Wherever these attitudes prevail, they are enough to guarantee that all Marx's scientific contributions—whose importance for the humanities cannot be overrated—will be preserved and perpetuated in scientific thought. These attitudes also make it possible to decide what is obsolete in Marx's doctrine and what is rash generalization, disproved by subsequent history. For today it is clear that several of Marx's ideas have not survived the merciless test of time. His predictions as to the future course of history, especially, were as fallible as most predictions are. Such ideas retain only the significance of utopias, that of moral stimulus rather than scientific theory.

Moreover, we can assume that with the gradual refinement of research techniques in the humanities, the concept of Marxism as a separate school of thought will in time become blurred and ultimately disappear altogether, just as there is no "Newtonism" in physics, no "Linnaeism" in botany, no "Harveyism" in physiology, and no "Gaussism" in mathematics. What is permanent in Marx's work will be assimilated in the natural course of scientific development. In the process some of his theses will surely be restricted in scope, others will be more precisely formulated, still others discarded. But the greatest triumph of an eminent scholar comes when his achievements cease to define a separate school of thought, when they merge into the very tissue of scientific life and become an elemental part of it, losing their disparate existence. This process is obviously different and much slower in the humanities, but even there it is an essential part of progress.

It is otherwise in the field of philosophy, taken as a discursive expression of a view of the world. There, names of great creative thinkers live through the centuries in the names of trends and schools of thought—yet they change character. When we use the term "Platonism" to describe a particular contemporary tendency in philosophy, we are not referring to orthodox believers in the whole Platonic doctrine, because there are none. "Platonism" in the current philosophical context applies to a more or less distant affinity with the particular ideas that have survived as the most distinctive and characteristic features of Plato's thought: belief in the primacy of the species over the individual; belief in the double existence of things—one sensate and forever changing, the other inaccessible to direct observation, immutable.

In the history of world views one can scarcely imagine a total disappearance of doctrinal variety and a rigid monopoly by one system. That is why terms derived from the names of those who introduced into philosophy original and revealing perspectives or formulated widely accepted points of view will surely survive. "Marxism" in this sense does not denote a doctrine that must be accepted or rejected as a whole. It does not mean a universal system, but a vital philosophical inspiration affecting our whole outlook on the world, a constant stimulus to the social intelligence and social memory of mankind. It owes its permanent validity to the new and invaluable points of view it opened before our eyes, enabling us to look at human affairs through the prism of universal history; to see, on the one hand, how man in society is formed by the struggle against nature and, on the other hand, the simultaneous process by which man's work humanizes nature; to consider thinking as a product of practical activity; to unmask myths of consciousness as resulting from ever recurring alienations in social existence and to trace them back to their real sources. These perspectives enable us, furthermore, to analyze social life in its incessant conflicts and struggles which, through countless multitudes of individual goals and desires, individual suffering and disappointments, individual defeats and victories, together compose a picture of uniform evolution that—we have every right to believe—signifies, on the grand scale of history, not retrogression but progress.

Problems

1. What are the "permanent" and the "transitory" aspects of Marxism?
2. Does Kolakowski create a dichotomy between theory and practice or merely between Marxist methodology and Soviet institutionalism? What are the implications of his dichotomy?
3. What is Kolakowski's attitude toward attempts to make Marxism a metaphysics, or to equate it with science and progress?
4. In what sense can Marxist methodology be used to analyze communist society? If such an analysis were undertaken, what difference would it make if it were a permanent Marxist analysis or a transitory one?
5. Why is Kolakowski so concerned with disseminating a concept of Marxism different from the current one?
6. Why is it difficult to apply Marxist ideas without paradoxically undermining Marxist methodology?
7. What future does Kolakowski envision for Marxism in the social sciences? What are the implications of this vision?
8. From your reading of Lenin, do you think he would have favored the "permanent" aspects of Marxism or the "transitory" aspects? Justify your answer.

20 MILOVAN DJILAS

Probably no work coming out of Eastern Europe since World War II has made an impact on the world to match that of The New Class *(1957) by Milovan Djilas. It is common to describe the work as a "shattering analysis of communism," "a crushing indictment of communist rule," "a work that could shake the communist world." Djilas himself describes it simply as "an analysis of the Communist system," as the "reflective observation" of an intellectual—part history, part opinion, part confession of a revolutionary. He makes clear in the Preface that he is not "engaged in detailed criticism of Communist theory," that "it is gratuitous to criticize Communism as an idea."*

> *The ideas of equality and brotherhood among men, which have existed in varying forms since human society began—and which contemporary Communism theoretically accepts—are principles which fighters for progress and freedom will always try to achieve. To criticize these ideals would not only be reactionary and ugly, but futile and foolish as well. The wish to attain them for mankind is inextinguishable.*

Such remarks reveal the tone: The New Class *is one of those great works of the human intellect which perceive so well that which has been before us, and express it so clearly, that we are appalled we had not seen it before. It has the shaping power of truth suddenly and simply glimpsed. Djilas's thesis is brief: communism has created not a classless society, but a "new class"— bureaucratic, power-oriented, rigid.*

The story of Djilas's career as a former Vice President of Yugoslavia; of his expulsion from the Communist Party for having appealed for "democratization"; of his solitary confinement for ten years; of The New Class *being written on toilet paper and smuggled out of prison; of his release after seven years in 1961 and his rearrest a year later for writing* Conversations with Stalin *after having been warned to remain silent—all this is history. Those who have heard or read Djilas do not need history to tell them that Djilas is one of those humane giants who holds the mirror up to man and shows him what, with vision and devotion, he may become.*

Character of the Revolution

1.

History shows that in countries where Communist revolutions have taken place other parties too have been dissatisfied with existing conditions. The best example is Russia, where the party which accomplished the Communist revolution was not the only revolutionary party.

However, only the Communist parties were both revolutionary in their opposition to the *status quo* and staunch and consistent in their support of the industrial transformation. In practice, this meant a radical destruction of established ownership relations. No other party went so far in this respect. None was "industrial" to that degree.

It is less clear why these parties had to be socialist in their program. Under the backward conditions existing in Czarist Russia, capitalist private ownership not only showed itself incapable of rapid industrial transformation, but actually obstructed it. The private property class had developed in a country in which extremely powerful feudal relationships still existed, while monopolies of more developed countries retained their grip on this enormous area abounding in raw materials and markets.

Czarist Russia, according to its history, had to be a latecomer with respect to the industrial revolution. It is the only European country which did not pass through the Reformation and the Renaissance. It did not have anything like the medieval European city-states. Backward, semifeudal, with absolutist monarchy and a bureaucratic centralism, with a rapid increase of the proletariat in several centers, Russia found herself in the whirlpool of modern world capitalism, and in the snares of the financial interests of the gigantic banking centers.

Lenin states in his work *Imperialism, the Final Stage of Capitalism* that three-fourths of the capital of the large banks in Russia was in the hands of foreign capitalists. Trotsky in his history of the Russian revolution emphasizes that foreigners controlled forty per cent of the shares of industrial capital in Russia, and that this percentage was even greater in some leading industries. As for Yugoslavia, foreigners had a decisive influence in the most important branches of Yugoslav economy. These facts alone do not prove anything. But they show that foreign capitalists used their power to check progress in these countries, to develop them

From Milovan Djilas, *The New Class* (New York: Frederick A. Praeger, Inc., 1957), pp. 15–36.

exclusively as their own sources of raw materials and cheap labor, with the result that these nations became unprogressive and even began to decline.

The party which had the historic task of carrying out the revolution in these countries had to be anti-capitalistic in its internal policy and anti-imperialistic in its foreign policy.

Internally, domestic capital was weak, and was largely an instrument or affiliate of foreign capital. It was not the capitalist class but another class, the proletariat which was arising from the increasing poverty of the peasantry, that was vitally interested in the industrial revolution. Just as the elimination of outrageous exploitation was a matter of life and death for those who already were proletarians, so was industrialization a matter of survival for those who in their turn were about to become proletarians. The movement which represented both of these had to be anti-capitalistic, that is, socialistic in its ideas, slogans and pledges.

The revolutionary party could not seriously contemplate execution of an industrial revolution unless it concentrated all domestic resources in its own hands, particularly those of native capitalists against whom the masses were also embittered because of severe exploitation and the use of inhumane methods. The revolutionary party had to take a similar stand against foreign capital.

Other parties were unable to follow a similar program. All of them either aspired to a return to the old system, to preservation of vested, static relationships; or at best, to gradual and peaceful development. Even the parties which were anti-capitalistic, as for example the SRs (Socialist-Revolutionary Party) in Russia, aspired toward returning society to idyllic primitive peasant life. Even the socialist parties such as the Mensheviks in Russia did not go farther than to push for the violent overthrow of the barriers to free capitalist development. They took the point of view that it was necessary to have fully developed capitalism in order to arrive at socialism later. However, the problem here was different; both a return to the old system and unhampered development of capitalism were impossible for these countries. Neither solution was capable, under the given international and internal conditions, of resolving the urgent problem of further development of these countries, i.e., their industrial revolutions.

Only the party which was in favor of the anti-capitalist revolution and rapid industrialization had prospects for success. Obviously that party had to be, in addition, socialist in its convictions. But since it was obliged to operate under prevailing conditions in general, and in the labor or socialist movements, such a party had to depend ideologically on the concept of the inevitability and usefulness of modern industry as well as on the tenet that revolution was unavoidable. This concept already existed, it was necessary only to modify it. The concept was Marxism—its revolutionary aspect. Association with revolutionary Marxism, or with the European socialist movement, was natural for the party then. Later, with the development of the revolution and with the organizational changes in the developed countries, it became just as essential for it to separate itself from the reformism of European socialism.

The inevitability of revolution and of rapid industrialization, which exacted enormous sacrifices and involved ruthless violence, required not only promises but faith in the possibility of the kingdom of heaven on earth. Advancing, as others also do, along the line of least resistance, the supporters of revolution and industrialization often departed from established Marxist and socialist doctrine. However, it was impossible for them to shed the doctrine entirely.

Capitalism and capitalist relationships were the proper and at the given moment the inevitable forms and techniques by which society expressed its needs and aspirations for improving and expanding production. In Great Britain, in the first half of the nineteenth century, capitalism improved and expanded production. And just as the industrialists in Britain had to destroy the peasantry in order to attain a higher degree of production, the industrialists, or the bourgeoisie, in Russia had to become a victim of the industrial revolution. The participants and the forms were different, but the law was the same in both cases.

In both instances socialism was inevitable—as a slogan and pledge, as a faith and a lofty ideal, and, in fact, as a particular form of government and ownership which would facilitate the industrial revolution and make possible improvement and expansion of production.

2.

All the revolutions of the past originated after new economic or social relationships had begun to prevail, and the old political system had become the sole obstacle to further development.

None of these revolutions sought anything other than the destruction of the old political forms and an opening of the way for already mature social forces and relationships existing in the old society. Even in those cases where the revolutionists desired something else, such as the building of economic and social relationships by means of force, as did the Jacobins* in the French revolution, they had to accept failure and be swiftly eliminated.

* The French name for the Dominican order; it was applied to a group of the French revolutionaries when they rented offices from the Dominicans. The Jacobins, for the most part bourgeois and republican, were the minority party against the Girondists and their aims were moderate. Gradually they were led to extremism under Robespierre 1758–94) and initiated the Reign of Terror in 1793. Their influence ended when Robespierre was guillotined in 1794.

In all previous revolutions, force and violence appeared predominantly as a consequence, as an instrument of new but already prevailing economic and social forces and relationships. Even when force and violence surpassed proper limits during the course of a revolution, in the final analysis the revolutionary forces had to be directed toward a positive and attainable goal. In these cases terror and despotism might have been inevitable but solely temporary manifestations.

All so-called *bourgeois* revolutions, whether achieved from below, i.e., with participation of the masses as in France, or from above, i.e., by *coup d'état* * as in Germany under Bismarck † had to end up in political democracy. That is understandable. Their task was chiefly to destroy the old despotic political system, and to permit the establishment of political relationships which would be adequate for already existing economic and other needs, particularly those concerning the free production of goods.

The case is entirely different with contemporary Communist revolutions. These revolutions did not occur because new, let us say socialist, relationships were already existing in the economy, or because capitalism was "overdeveloped." On the contrary. They did occur because capitalism was not fully developed and because it was not able to carry out the industrial transformation of the country.

In France capitalism had already prevailed in the economy, in social relationships, and even in the public conscience prior to inception of the revolution. The case is hardly comparable with socialism in Russia, China, or Yugoslavia.

The leaders of the Russian revolution themselves were aware of this fact. Speaking at the Seventh Congress of the Russian Communist Party on March 7, 1918, while the revolution was still in progress, Lenin said:

> . . . One of the fundamental differences between bourgeois and socialist revolutions is that in a bourgeois revolution, which arises from feudalism, new economic organizations which gradually change all aspects of feudal society are progressively created in the midst of the old order. In accomplishing this task, every bourgeois revolution accomplishes all that is required of it: it hastens the growth of capitalism.
>
> A socialist revolution is in an entirely different situation. To the extent that a country which had to begin a socialist revolution, because of the vagaries of history, is backward, the transition from old capitalist relations to socialist relations is increasingly difficult. . . .
>
> The difference between socialist revolutions and bourgeois revolutions lies specifically in the fact that, in the latter case, established forms of capitalist relations exist, while the soviet power—the proletariat—does

---
* The overthrow of a government by a sudden seizure of power.
† Otto von Bismarck (1811–98) engineered a *coup d'état* in Prussia in 1862 when, after being appointed premier by King William I, he dissolved parliament in contravention of the constitution over the issues of taxes for the army.

not attain such relations, if we exclude the most developed forms of capitalism, which actually encompassed a small number of top industries and only very scantily touched agriculture.

I quote Lenin, but I could quote any leader of the Communist revolution and numerous other authors, as confirmation of the fact that settled relationships did not exist for the new society, but that someone, in this case the "soviet power," must therefore build them. If the new "socialist" relationships had been developed to the fullest in the country in which Communist revolution was able to emerge victorious, there would have been no need for so many assurances, dissertations, and efforts embracing the "building of socialism."

This leads to an apparent contradiction. If the conditions for a new society were not sufficiently prevalent, then who needed the revolution? Moreover, how was the revolution possible? How could it survive in view of the fact that the new social relationships were not yet in the formative process in the old society?

No revolution or party had ever before set itself to the task of building social relationships or a new society. But this was the primary objective of the Communist revolution.

Communist leaders, though no better acquainted than others with the laws which govern society, discovered that in the country in which their revolution was possible, industrialization was also possible, particularly when it involved a transformation of society in keeping with their ideological hypothesis. Experience—the success of revolution under "unfavorable" conditions—confirmed this for them; the "building of socialism" did likewise. This strengthened their illusion that they knew the laws of social development. In fact, they were in the position of making a blueprint for a new society, and then of starting to build it, making corrections here and leaving out something there, all the while adhering closely to their plans.

Industrialization, as an inevitable, legitimate necessity of society, and the Communist way of accomplishing it, joined forces in the countries of Communist revolutions.

However, neither of these, though they progressed together and on parallel tracks, could achieve success overnight. After the completion of the revolution, someone had to shoulder the responsibility for industrialization. In the West, this role was taken over by the economic forces of capitalism liberated from the despotic political chains, while in the countries of Communist revolutions no similar forces existed and, thus, their function had to be taken over by the revolutionary organs themselves, the new authority, that is, the revolutionary party.

In earlier revolutions, revolutionary force and violence became a hindrance to the economy as soon as the old order was overthrown. In

Communist revolutions, force and violence are a condition for further development and even progress. In the words of earlier revolutionaries, force and violence were only a necessary evil and a means to an end. In the words of Communists, force and violence are elevated to the lofty position of a cult and an ultimate goal. In the past, the classes and forces which made up a new society already existed before the revolution erupted. The Communist revolutions are the first which have had to create a new society and new social forces.

Even as the revolutions in the West had inevitably to end in democracy after all the "aberrations" and "withdrawals," in the East, the revolutions had to end in despotism. The methods of terror and violence in the West became needless and ridiculous, and even a hindrance in accomplishing the revolution for the revolutionaries and revolutionary parties. In the East, the case was the opposite. Not only did despotism continue in the East because the transformation of industry required so much time, but, as we shall see later, it lasted long after industrialization had taken place.

3.

There are other basic differences between Communist revolutions and earlier ones. Earlier revolutions, though they had reached the point of readiness in an economy and a society, were unable to break out without advantageous conditions. We now know the general conditions necessary for the eruption and success of a revolution. However, every revolution has, in addition to these general conditions, its peculiarities which make its planning and execution possible.

War, or more precisely, national collapse of the state organization, was unnecessary for past revolutions, at least for the larger ones. Until now, however, this has been a basic condition for the victory of Communist revolutions. This is even valid for China; true, there the revolution began prior to the Japanese invasion, but it continued for an entire decade to spread and finally to emerge victorious with the end of the war. The Spanish revolution of 1936, which could have been an exception, did not have time to transform itself into a purely Communist revolution, and, therefore, never emerged victorious.

The reason war was necessary for the Communist revolution, or the downfall of the state machinery, must be sought in the immaturity of the economy and society. In a serious collapse of a system, and particularly in a war which has been unsuccessful for the existing ruling circles and state system, a small but well-organized and disciplined group is inevitably able to take authority in its hands.

Thus at the time of the October Revolution the Communist Party had about 80,000 members. The Yugoslav Communist Party began the 1941 revolution with about 10,000 members. To grasp power, the support and active participation of at least a part of the people is necessary, but in every case the party which leads the revolution and assumes power is a minority group relying exclusively on exceptionally favorable conditions. Furthermore, such a party cannot be a majority group until it becomes the permanently established authority.

The accomplishment of such a grandiose task—the destruction of a social order and the building of a new society when conditions for such an undertaking are not propitious in the economy or society—is a task able to attract only a minority, and at that, only those who believe fanatically in its possibilities.

Special conditions and a particular party are basic characteristics of Communist revolutions.

The achievement of every revolution, as well as of every victory in war, demands centralization of all forces. According to Mathiez's theory, the French Revolution was the first in which "all the resources of a people at war were placed in the hands of the authorities: people, food, clothing." This must be the case to an even greater degree in a Communist "immature" revolution: not only all material means but all intellectual means must fall into the hands of the party, and the party itself must become politically, and as an organization, centralized to the fullest extent. Only Communist parties, politically united, firmly grouped around the center, and possessing identical ideological viewpoints, are able to carry out such a revolution.

Centralization of all forces and means as well as some kind of political unity of the revolutionary parties are essential conditions for every successful revolution. For the Communist revolution these conditions are even more important, since from the very beginning the Communists exclude every other independent political group or party from being an ally of their party. At the same time they demand uniformity of all viewpoints, including practical political views as well as theoretical, philosophical, and even moral views. The fact that the left-of-center SR's (Socialist-Revolutionaries) participated in the October Revolution, and that individuals and groups from other parties participated in the revolutions in China and Yugoslavia, does not disprove but rather confirms this proposition: these groups were only collaborators of the Communist Party, and only to a fixed degree in the struggle. After the revolution these collaborating parties were dispersed, or they dissolved of their own accord and merged with the Communist Party. The Bolsheviks routed the left-of-center SR's as soon as the latter wished to become independent, while the non-Communist groups in Yugoslavia and China that had supported the revolution had, in the meantime, renounced every one of their political activities.

The earlier revolutions were not carried out by a single political group. To be sure, in the course of a revolution individual groups pressured and destroyed one another; but, taken as a whole, the revolution was not the work of only one group. In the French revolution the Jacobins succeeded in maintaining their dictatorship for a brief period only. Napoleon's dictatorship, which emerged from the revolution, signified both the end of the Jacobin revolution and the beginning of the rule of the bourgeoisie. In every case, although one party played a decisive role in the earlier revolutions, the other parties did not surrender their independence. Although suppression and dispersion existed, they could be enforced only for a brief time. The parties could not be destroyed and would always emerge anew. Even the Paris Commune, which the Communists take as a forerunner of their revolution and their state, was a multi-party revolution.

A party may have played the chief, and even an exclusive, role in a particular phase of a revolution. But no previous party was ideologically, or as an organization, centralized to the degree that the Communist Party was. Neither the Puritans in the English revolution nor the Jacobins in the French revolution were bound by the same philosophical and ideological views, although the first belonged to a religious sect. From the organizational point of view the Jacobins were a federation of clubs; the Puritans were not even that. Only contemporary Communist revolutions pushed compulsory parties to the forefront, which were ideologically and organizationally monolithic.

In every case one thing is certain: in all earlier revolutions the necessity for revolutionary methods and parties disappeared with the end of civil war and of foreign intervention, and these methods and parties had to be done away with. After Communist revolutions, the Communists continue with both the methods and the forms of the revolution, and their party soon attains the fullest degree of centralism and ideological exclusiveness.

Lenin expressly emphasized this during the revolution itself in enumerating his conditions for acceptance in the Comintern: [1]

> In the present epoch of acute civil war, a Communist Party will be able to perform its duty only if it is organized in the most centralized manner, only if iron discipline bordering on military discipline prevails in it, and if its party center is a powerful and authoritative organ, wielding wide powers and enjoying the universal confidence of the members of the party.

And to this, Stalin appended, in *Foundations of Leninism:*

---

1. *Selected Works,* Vol. X; New York, International Publishers, 1936.

This is the position in regard to discipline in the party in the period of struggle preceding the achievement of the dictatorship.

The same, but to an even greater degree, must be said about discipline in the party after the dictatorship has been achieved.

The revolutionary atmosphere and vigilance, insistence on ideological unity, political and ideological exclusiveness, political and other centralism do not cease after assuming control. On the contrary, they become even more intensified.

Ruthlessness in methods, exclusiveness in ideas, and monopoly in authority in the earlier revolutions lasted more or less as long as the revolutions themselves. Since revolution in the Communist revolution was only the first act of the despotic and totalitarian authority of a group, it is difficult to forecast the duration of that authority.

In earlier revolutions, including the Reign of Terror in France, superficial attention was paid to the elimination of real oppositionists. No attention was paid to the elimination of those who might become oppositionists. The eradication and persecution of some social or ideological groups in the religious wars of the Middle Ages was the only exception to this. From theory and practice, Communists know that they are in conflict with all other classes and ideologies, and behave accordingly. They are fighting against not only actual but also potential opposition. In the Baltic countries,* thousands of people were liquidated overnight on the basis of documents indicating previously held ideological and political views. The massacre of several thousand Polish officers in the Katyń Forest † was of similar character. In the case of Communism, long after the revolution is over, terrorist and oppressive methods continue to be used. Sometimes these are perfected and become more extensive than in the revolution, as in the case of the liquidation of the Kulaks.‡ Ideological exclusiveness and intolerance are intensified after the revolution.

---

* The Baltic states were Lithuania, Latvia and Estonia, until they were annexed by Russia in 1940 after the Russian invasion of Poland in September 1939. Their value to Russia lay in the fact that they provided warm water ports to the Baltic Sea.
† After the Russian invasion of Poland in September, 1938, as part of the Russo-German Pact, thousands of Poles were taken prisoner and placed in camps. Three of these camps were designated for intellecuals, who were also Polish Army Reserve Officers. Sometime in the spring of 1940, approximately 15,000 of these intellectual Polish officers disappeared. After the war it was discovered that they had been massacred in the Katyn Forest and buried in mass graves as part of the liquidation of the Polish intelligentsia by the Soviet NKVD (The People's Commissariat of Internal Affairs, the equivalent of the Nazi Gestapo; our closest equivalent would be the C.I.A. or the F.B.I.).
‡ Late in 1929 an all-out farm collectivization drive began in Russia. The official policy of liquidating the Kulaks (small farmers refusing collectivization) as a class resulted in the confiscation of their property and mass deportations in which over 5,000,000 peasant families were sent to forced labor camps. After the Kulaks engaged in large scale destruction of their own property and crops in order to avoid collectivization, Stalin created delays in alleviating their suffering and many starved to death.

Even when it is able to reduce physical oppression, the tendency of the ruling party is to strengthen the prescribed ideology—Marxism-Leninism.

Earlier revolutions, particularly the so-called bourgeois ones, attached considerable significance to the establishment of individual freedoms immediately following cessation of the revolutionary terror. Even the revolutionaries considered it important to assure the legal status of the citizenry. Independent administration of justice was an inevitable final result of all these revolutions. The Communist regime in the U.S.S.R. is still remote from independent administration of justice after forty years of tenure. The final results of earlier revolutions were often greater legal security and greater civil rights. This cannot be said of the Communist revolution.

There is another vast difference between the earlier revolutions and contemporary Communist ones. Earlier revolutions, especially the greater ones, were a product of the struggles of the working classes, but their ultimate results fell to another class under whose intellectual and often organizational leadership the revolutions were accomplished. The bourgeoisie, in whose name the revolution was carried out, to a considerable extent harvested the fruits of the struggles of the peasants and *sans-culottes*.* The masses of a nation also participated in a Communist revolution; however, the fruits of revolution do not fall to them, but to the bureaucracy. For the bureaucracy is nothing else but the party which carried out the revolution. In Communist revolutions, the revolutionary movements which carried out the revolutions are not liquidated. Communist revolutions may "eat their own children," but not all of them.

In fact, on completion of a Communist revolution, ruthless and underhanded deals inevitably are made between various groups and factions which disagree about the path of the future.

Mutual accusations always revolve around dogmatic proof as to who is "objectively" or "subjectively" a greater counter-revolutionary or agent of internal and foreign "capitalism." Regardless of the manner in which these disagreements are resolved, the group that emerges victorious is the one that is the most consistent and determined supporter of industrialization along Communist principles, i.e., on the basis of total party monopoly, particularly of state organs in control of production. The Communist revolution does not devour those of its children who are needed for its future course—for industrialization. Revolutionaries who accepted the ideas and slogans of the revolution literally, naïvely believing in their materialization, are usually liquidated. The group which understood that revolution would secure authority, on a social-political-Communist basis, as an instrument of future industrial transformation, emerges victorious.

---

* Literally, "without knee breeches," a term applied to extreme republicans after 1793. At that time they gave up wearing knee breeches, an article of clothing associated with the Old Regime, in favor of trousers *(pantalons)*.

The Communist revolution is the first in which the revolutionaries and their allies, particularly the authority-wielding group, survived the revolution. Similar groups inevitably failed in earlier ones. The Communist revolution is the first to be carried out to the advantage of the revolutionaries. They, and the bureaucracy which forms around them, harvest its fruits. This creates in them, and in the broader echelons of the party, the illusion that theirs is the first revolution that remained true to the slogans on its banners.

4.

The illusions which the Communist revolution creates about its real aims are more permanent and extensive than those of earlier revolutions because the Communist revolution resolves relationships in a new way and brings about a new form of ownership. Earlier revolutions, too, inevitably resulted in major or minor changes in property relationships. But in those revolutions one form of private ownership superseded the others. In the Communist revolution this is not the case; the change is radical and deep-rooted, and a collective ownership suppresses private ownership.

The Communist revolution, while still in process of development, destroys capitalist, land-holding, private ownership, i.e., that ownership which makes use of foreign labor forces. This immediately creates the belief that the revoluntionary promise of a new realm of equality and justice is being fulfilled. The party, or the state authority under its control, simultaneously undertakes extensive measures for industrialization. This also intensifies the belief that the time of freedom from want has finally arrived. Despotism and oppression are there, but they are accepted as temporary manifestations, to last only until the opposition of the expropriated authorities and counter-revolutionaries is stifled, and the industrial transformation is completed.

Several essential changes occur in the very process of industrialization. Industrialization in a backward country, especially if it has no assistance and is hindered from abroad, demands concentration of all material resources. Nationalization of industrial property and the land is the first concentration of property in the hands of a new regime. However, it does not, and can not, stop at this.

The newly originated ownership inevitably comes in conflict with other forms of ownership. The new ownership imposes itself by force on smaller owners who do not employ someone else's manpower, or to whom such manpower is unessential, i.e., on craftsmen, workers, small commercial merchants, and peasants. This expropriation of small property owners is effected even when it is not done for economic motives, i.e., in order to attain a higher degree of productivity.

In the course of industrialization, the property of those elements who were not opposed to, or even assisted, the revolution is taken over. As a matter of form, the state also becomes the owner of this property. The state administers and manages the property. Private ownership ceases, or decreases to a role of secondary importance, but its complete disappearance is subject to the whim of the new men in authority.

This is experienced by the Communists and by some members of the masses as a complete liquidation of classes and the realization of a classless society. In fact, the old pre-revolutionary classes do disappear with the completion of industrialization and collectivization. There remains the spontaneous and unorganized displeasure of the mass of the people—a displeasure which neither ceases nor abates. Communist delusions and self-deceit about the "remnants" and "influence" of the "class enemy" still persist. But the illusion that the long-dreamed classless society arises by these means is complete, at least for the Communists themselves.

Every revolution, and even every war, creates illusions and is conducted in the name of unrealizable ideals. During the struggle the ideals seem real enough for the combatants; by the end they often cease to exist. Not so in the case of a Communist revolution. Those who carry out the Communist revolution as well as those among the lower echelons persist in their illusions long after the armed struggle. Despite oppression, despotism, unconcealed confiscations, and privileges of the ruling echelons, some of the people—and especially the Communists—retain the illusions contained in their slogans.

Although the Communist revolution may start with the most idealistic concepts, calling for wonderful heroism and gigantic effort, it sows the greatest and the most permanent illusions.

Revolutions are inevitable in the lifetime of nations. They may result in despotism, but they also launch nations on paths previously blocked to them.

The Communist revolution cannot attain a single one of the ideals named as its motivating force. However, Communist revolution has brought about a measure of industrial civilization to vast areas of Europe and Asia. In this way, material bases have actually been created for a future freer society. Thus while bringing about the most complete despotism, the Communist revolution has also created the basis for the abolition of despotism. As the nineteenth century introduced modern industry to the West, the twentieth century will introduce modern industry to the East. The shadow of Lenin extends over the vast expanse of Eurasia in one way or another. In despotic form in China, in democratic form in India and Burma, all of the remaining Asiatic and other nations are inevitably entering an industrial revolution. The Russian revolution initiated this process. The process remains the incalculable and historically significant fact of the revolution.

5.

It might appear that Communist revolutions are mostly historical deceptions and chance occurrences. In a sense this is true: no other revolutions have required so many exceptional conditions; no other revolutions promised so much and accomplished so little. Demagoguery and misrepresentation are inevitable among the Communist leaders since they are forced to promise the most ideal society and "abolition of every exploitation."

However, it cannot be said that the Communists deceived the people, that is, that they purposely and consciously did something different from what they had promised. The fact is simply this: they were unable to accomplish that in which they so fanatically believed. They cannot acknowledge this even when forced to execute a policy contrary to everything promised before and during the revolution. From their point of view, such acknowledgment would be an admission that the revolution was unnecessary. It would also be an admission that they had themselves become superfluous. Anything of the sort is impossible for them.

The ultimate results of a social struggle can never be of the kind envisaged by those who carry it out. Some such struggles depend on an infinite and complex series of circumstances beyond the controllable range of human intellect and action. This is most true of revolutions that demand superhuman efforts and that effect hasty and radical changes in society. They inevitably generate absolute confidence that the ultimate in human prosperity and liberty will appear after their victories. The French revolution was carried out in the name of common sense, in the belief that liberty, equality, and fraternity would eventually appear. The Russian revolution was carried out in the name of "a purely scientific view of the world," for the purpose of creating a classless society. Neither revolution could possibly have been created if the revolutionaries, along with a part of the people, had not believed in their own idealistic aims.

Communist illusions as to post-revolutionary possibilities were more preponderant among the Communists than among those who followed them. The Communists should have known and, in fact, did know about the inevitability of industrialization, but they could only guess about its social results and relationships.

Official Communist historians in the U.S.S.R. and Yugoslavia describe the revolution as if it were the fruit of the previously planned actions of its leaders. But only the course of the revolution and the armed struggle was consciously planned, while the forms which the revolution took stemmed from the immediate course of events and from the direct action taken. It is revealing that Lenin, undoubtedly one of the greatest revolutionaries in history, did not foresee when or in what form the revolution would erupt until it was almost upon him. In January 1917, one month before the February Revolution, and only ten months before the October Revolution which brought him to power, he addressed a meeting of Swiss Socialist youths:

"We, the older generation, perhaps will not live to see the decisive battles of the approaching revolution. But, I can, it seems to me, express with extreme confidence the hope that the youth, who work in the wonderful socialist movement of Switzerland and of the whole world, will have the good fortune not only to fight but also to emerge victorious in the approaching revolution of the proletariat."

How can it then be said that Lenin, or anyone else, was able to foresee the social results arising after the long and complex struggle of the revolution?

But even if Communist aims per se were unreal, the Communists, as distinct from earlier revolutionaries, were fully realistic in creating those things that were possible. They carried it out in the only way possible—by imposing their absolute totalitarian authority. Theirs was the first revolution in history in which the revolutionaries not only remain on the political scene after victory but, in the most practical sense, build social relationships completely contrary to those in which they believed and which they promised. The Communist revolution, in the course of its later industrial duration and transformation, converts the revolutionaries themselves into creators and masters of a new social state.

Marx's concrete forecasts proved inaccurate. To an even greater degree, the same can be said for Lenin's expectations that a free or classless society would be created with the aid of the dictatorship. But the need that made the revolution inevitable—industrial transformation on the basis of modern technology—is fulfilled.

6.

Abstract logic would indicate that the Communist revolution, when it achieves, under different conditions and by state compulsion, the same things achieved by industrial revolutions and capitalism in the West, is nothing but a form of state-capitalist revolution. The relationships which are created by its victory are state-capitalist. This appears to be even more true because the new regime also regulates all political, labor, and other relationships and, what is more important, distributes the national income and benefits and distributes material goods which actually have been transformed into state property.

Discussion on whether or not the relationships in the U.S.S.R. and in other Communist countries are state-capitalist, socialist, or perhaps something else, is dogmatic to a considerable degree. However, such discussion is of fundamental importance.

Even if it is presumed that state capitalism is nothing other than the "antechamber of socialism," as Lenin emphasized, or that it is the first phase of socialism, it is still not one iota easier for the people who live under Communist despotism to endure. If the character of property and social relationships brought about by the Communist revolution is strengthened and defined, the prospects for liberation of the people from such relationships become more realistic. If the people are not conscious of the nature of the social relationships in which they live, or if they do not see a way in which they can alter them, their struggle cannot have any prospect of success.

If the Communist revolution, despite its promises and illusions, is state-capitalist in its undertakings with state-capitalist relationships, the only lawful and positive actions its functionaries can take are the ones that improve their work and reduce the pressure and irresponsibility of state administration. The Communists do not admit in theory that they are working in a system of state capitalism, but their leaders behave this way. They continually boast about improving the work of the administration and about leading the struggle "against bureaucratism."

Moreover, actual relationships are not those of state capitalism; these relationships do not provide a method of improving the system of state administration basically.

In order to establish the nature of relationships which arise in the course of the Communist revolution and ultimately become established in the process of industrialization and collectivization, it is necessary to peer further into the role and manner of operation of the state under Communism. At present, it will be sufficient to point out that in Communism the state machinery is not the instrument which really determines social and property relationships; it is only the instrument by which these relationships are protected. In truth, everything is accomplished in the name of the state and through its regulations. The Communist Party, including the professional party bureaucracy, stands above the regulations and behind every single one of the state's acts.

It is the bureaucracy which formally uses, administers, and controls both nationalized and socialized property as well as the entire life of society. The role of the bureaucracy in society, i.e., monopolistic administration and control of national income and national goods, consigns it to a special privileged position. Social relations resemble state capitalism. The more so, because the carrying out of industrialization is effected not with the help of capitalists but with the help of the state machine. In fact, this privileged class performs that function, using the state machine as a cover and as an instrument.

Ownership is nothing other than the right of profit and control. If one defines class benefits by this right, the Communist states have seen, in the final analysis, the origin of a new form of ownership or of a new ruling and exploiting class.

In reality, the Communists were unable to act differently from any ruling class that preceded them. Believing that they were building a new and ideal society, they built it for themselves in the only way they could. Their revolution and their society do not appear either accidental or unnatural, but appear as a matter of course for a particular country and for prescribed periods of its development. Because of this, no matter how extensive and inhuman Communist tyranny has been, society, in the course of a certain period—as long as industrialization lasts—has to and is able to endure this tyranny. Furthermore, this tyranny no longer appears as something inevitable, but exclusively as an assurance of the depredations and privileges of a new class.

In contrast to earlier revolutions, the Communist revolution, conducted in the name of doing away with classes, has resulted in the most complete authority of any single new class. Everything else is sham and an illusion.

from The New Class

1.

Everything happened differently in the U.S.S.R. and other Communist countries from what the leaders—even such prominent ones as Lenin, Stalin, Trotsky, and Bukharin—anticipated. They expected that the state would rapidly wither away, that democracy would be strengthened. The reverse happened. They expected a rapid improvement in the standard of living—there has been scarcely any change in this respect and, in the subjugated East European countries, the standard has even declined. In every instance, the standard of living has failed to rise in proportion to the rate of industrialization, which was much more rapid. It was believed that the differences between cities and villages, between intellectual and physical labor, would slowly disappear; instead these differences have increased. Communist anticipations in other areas—including their expectations for developments in the non-Communist world—have also failed to materialize.

From Milovan Djilas, *The New Class* (New York: Frederick A. Praeger, Inc., 1957), pp. 15–36.

The greatest illusion was that industrialization and collectivization in the U.S.S.R., and destruction of capitalist ownership, would result in a classless society. In 1936, when the new Constitution was promulgated, Stalin announced that the "exploiting class" had ceased to exist. The capitalist and other classes of ancient origin had in fact been destroyed, but a new class, previously unknown to history, had been formed.

It is understandable that this class, like those before it, should believe that the establishment of its power would result in happiness and freedom for all men. The only difference between this and other classes was that it treated the delay in the realization of its illusions more crudely. It thus affirmed that its power was more complete than the power of any other class before in history, and its class illusions and prejudices were proportionally greater.

This new class, the bureaucracy, or more accurately the political bureaucracy, has all the characteristics of earlier ones as well as some new characteristics of its own. Its origin had its special characteristics also, even though in essence it was similar to the beginnings of other classes.

Other classes, too, obtained their strength and power by the revolutionary path, destroying the political, social, and other orders they met in their way. However, almost without exception, these classes attained power *after* new economic patterns had taken shape in the old society. The case was the reverse with new classes in the Communist systems. It did not come to power to *complete* a new economic order but to *establish* its own and, in so doing, to establish its power over society.

In earlier epochs the coming to power of some class, some part of a class, or of some party, was the final event resulting from its formation and its development. The reverse was true in the U.S.S.R. There the new class was definitely formed after it attained power. Its consciousness had to develop before its economic and physical powers, because the class had not taken root in the life of the nation. This class viewed its role in relation to the world from an idealistic point of view. Its practical possibilities were not diminished by this. In spite of its illusions, it represented an objective tendency toward industrialization. Its practical bent emanated from this tendency. The promise of an ideal world increased the faith in the ranks of the new class and sowed illusions among the masses. At the same time it inspired gigantic physical undertakings.

Because this new class had not been formed as a part of the economic and social life before it came to power, it could only be created in an organization of a special type, distinguished by a special discipline based on identical philosophic and ideological views of its members. A unity of belief and iron discipline was necessary to overcome its weaknesses.

The roots of the new class were implanted in a special party, of the Bolshevik type. Lenin was right in his view that his party was an exception in this history of human society, although he did not suspect that it would be the beginning of a new class.

To be more precise, the initiators of the new class are not found in the Bolshevik type as a whole but in that stratum of professional revolutionaries who made up its core even before it attained power. It was not by accident that Lenin asserted after the failure of the 1905 revolution that only professional revolutionaries—men whose sole profession was revolutionary work—could build a new party of the Bolshevik type. It was still less accidental that even Stalin, the future creator of a new class, was the most outstanding example of such a professional revolutionary. The new ruling class has been gradually developing from this very narrow stratum of revolutionaries. These revolutionaries composed its core for a long period. Trotsky noted that in pre-revolutionary professional revolutionaries was the origin of the future Stalinist bureaucrat. What he did not detect was the beginning of a new class of owners and exploiters.

This is not to say that the new party and the new class are identical. The party, however, is the core of that class, and its base. It is very difficult, perhaps impossible, to define the limits of the new class and to identify its members. The new class may be said to be made up of those who have special privileges and economic preference because of the administrative monopoly they hold.

Since administration is unavoidable in society, necessary administrative functions may be coexistent with parasitic functions in the same person. Not every member of the party is a member of the new class, any more than every artisan or member of a middle-class party is a bourgeois.

In loose terms, as the new class becomes stronger and attains a more perceptible physiognomy, the role of the party diminishes. The core and the basis of the new class is created in the party and at its top, as well as in the state political organs. The once live, compact party, full of initiative, is disappearing to become transformed into the traditional oligarchy of the new class, irresistibly drawing into its ranks those who aspire to join the new class and repressing those who have any ideals.

The party makes the class, but the class grows as a result and uses the party as a basis. The class grows stronger, while the party grows weaker; this is the inescapable fate of every Communist party in power.

If it were not materially interested in production or if it did not have within itself the potentialities for the creation of a new class, no party could act in so morally and ideologically foolhardy a fashion, let alone stay in power for long. Stalin declared, after the end of the First Five-Year Plan: "If we had not created the apparatus, we would have failed!" He should have substituted "new class" for the word "apparatus," and everything would have been clearer.

It seems unusual that a political party could be the beginning of a new class. Parties are generally the product of classes and strata which have become intellectually and economically strong. However, if one grasps the actual conditions in pre-revolutionary Russia and in other countries in which Communism prevailed over national forces it will be clear that a party of this type is the product of specific opportunities and that there is nothing unusual or accidental in this being so. Although the roots of Bolshevism reach far back into Russian history, the party is partly the product of the unique pattern of international relationships in which Russia found itself at the end of the nineteenth and the beginning of the twentieth century. Russia was no longer able to live in the modern world as an absolute monarchy, and Russia's capitalism was too weak and too dependent on the interests of foreign powers to make it possible to have an industrial revolution. This revolution could only be implemented by a new class, or by a change in the social order. As yet, there was no such class.

In history, it is not important who implements a process, it is only important that the process be implemented. Such was the case in Russia and other countries in which Communist revolutions took place. The revolution created forces, leaders, organizations, and ideas which were necessary to it. The new class came into existence for objective reasons, and by the wish, wits, and action of its leaders. . . .

Problems

1. What is the illusion of every ruling class? Why is this illusion even greater for the "new class," the bureaucrats of a Communist country?
2. Compare the psychological outlook of the old professional revolutionary of Czarist Russia with that of the new-class bureaucrat of the U.S.S.R. as seen in Djilas's discussion.
3. According to Djilas, what are the essential differences between earlier (bourgeois-type) revolutions and later (communist-type) revolutions?
4. Show how Djilas "stands Marxism on its head" by finding in Russia, as well as in China and Yugoslavia, historical evidence to deny "historical materialism."
5. Djilas asserts that Marx and Lenin were inaccurate in their "forecasts" (383/25). Does Djilas construct his own analysis and critique from starting points (principles) that can be classed as Marxist or as non-Marxist? Explain. In answering this question, consider carefully your answer to the previous question.
6. What are the consequences for Marxist metaphysics—for dialectical materialism—of Djilas' analysis of the creation of a "new class"?
7. If a Marxist accepts Djilas's analysis, what Marxist assumptions about man must he abandon? How would he avoid creating a schism in his outlook between Marxist aspirations and possible non-Marxist assumptions?

21 ROBERT C. TUCKER

> *This essay by Robert C. Tucker, professor of politics and Director of Russian Studies at Princeton University, is the concluding essay from his book* The Marxian Revolutionary Idea *(1969). Subtitled, "Essays on Marxist Thought and the Impact on Radical Movements," the book deals, in Tucker's own words, "with Marxism in two fundamental aspects. First, as theory—as a body of theory about man, history, society, and politics. Second, as ideology—as a radical social philosophy offering a vision of the good society and directions for its attainment." In this essay, Tucker lays down his "own credo concerning Marx:" Marx's "enduring value lies especially in his 'futurology,' " in his "vision of a matured humanity dwelling in a transformed world" (27 Tucker). Coming at the end of this section on Marxism, after the reader has read the primary works, and attempting as it does to extract the essence of Marx's message to us now, one hundred and fifty years after his death, this essay provides the reader with an opportunity not only to summarize what has gone before, but to test his own understanding of Marx against another's.*

Marx and the End of History

The hundred-and-fiftieth anniversary of Marx's birth is a more propitious occasion for commemoration of him than the hundreth would have been.[1] In May 1918, the world was at war, and not much concerned with such ceremonies. A party of Marxist revolutionaries had just taken power in Russia, but the future of that revolution, and others like it, was still unclear. And some early philosophical writings of Marx, knowledge of which was destined greatly to deepen our understanding of the genesis and meaning of Marxism, were still lying in archives and unknown to all but a very few. It was still too soon to assess the historical

From Robert C. Tucker, *The Marxian Revolutionary Idea* (New York: W. W. Norton, 1969), pp. 215–25.
1. An address presented at a symposium held in Trier on May 5, 1968, by the German UNESCO Commission to commemorate the hundred-and-fiftieth anniversary of Marx's birth.

significance of Marx. Now we are better situated in time to make the assessment.

The most important of the early writings published since 1918 are the *Economic and Philosophical Manuscripts of 1844.* Here the young Marx set down a first systematic sketch of Marxism in concepts largely derived from post-Kantian German philosophy, Hegel's in particular. Deciphering what he conceived to be the "esoteric" meaning of Hegel's *Phenomenology of Mind,* he formulated his own conception of history as a process of self-development of the human species culminating in communism. Man, according to this conception, is essentially a producer; and material production is the primary form of his producing activity, industry being the externalized productive powers of the species. In the course of his history, which Marx described as a "history of production," a world of created objects gradually arises around man. Original nature is overlaid with a man-made "anthropological nature" or "nature produced by history." And Marx believed that this was the true or scientific restatement of the Hegelian conception. For had not Hegel seen the history of the world as a production-history on the part of the world-spirit? His error had been to mystify the process by treating the productive activity as *mental* activity primarily. To move from mystification to reality, from philosophy to science, one had only to turn Hegel on his head. Then it appeared that the Hegelian image of spirit creating a world was simply a philosopher's distorted picture of the reality of history, namely, that man—working man—creates a world in *material* productive activities over the centuries. Inevitably, therefore, Marx later named his transformed Hegelianism the "materialist conception of history."

Still following Hegel's basic scheme, Marx in the manuscripts visualized the human history of production as being also a history of estrangement *(Entfremdungsgeschichte).* Man's nature, he postulated, was to be a "free conscious producer," but so far he had not been able to express himself freely in productive activity. He had been driven to produce by need and greed, by a passion for accumulation which in the modern bourgeois age becomes accumulation of capital. His productive activity had always, therefore, been involuntary; it had been "labor." And since man, when he produces involuntarily, is estranged from his human nature, labor is "alienated labor." Escape from alienated labor finally becomes materially possible in the stage of technological development created by modern machine industry. The way of escape lies in the revolutionary seizure and socialization of the productive powers by the workers. Repossessed through revolution of his organs of material production externalized in industry, man will at last be able to produce in freedom. To Marx communism did not mean a new economic system. It meant the end of economics in a society where man, liberated from labor, would realize his creative nature in a life of leisure. So Marx defined communism in his manuscripts as "transcendence of human self-alienation," and saw it as the real future situation that Hegel had depicted in a mystified manner at the close of his *Phenomenology,* where spirit, having attained absolute knowledge, returns to itself out of its alienation and is fully "at home with itself in its otherness."

Such, very briefly, was Marxism as originally expounded; and it was this view of history that Marx and Engels elaborated in their voluminous later writings. Naturally, much was added and refined. Marx's thought, however, like that of most powerfully original thinkers, showed an underlying continuity. Indeed, *Capital,* published in 1867, was simply the form in which he finally finished and published the book he set out to write in his manuscripts of 1844.

Consequently, we are now able to see in him, far more clearly than anyone could easily have done a half-century ago, an heir and representative of the great age of German philosophy that started with Kant and ran its course through Schelling, Fichte, and Hegel to its diverse later outcomes. I do not mean to say that we should see him only as a philosopher, or Marxism itself exclusively as a philosophical phenomenon. For Marx, as perhaps befitted a descendant of rabbinical forbears, had a prophetic mission. The teaching that he derived from philosophy and saw as science was received widely as a new faith. It became the party ideology of movements for revolution and, in our century, regimes of revolution acting in Marx's name. Here, however, I am not concerned with Marxism as a party ideology, but with Marx as an intellectual and Marxism as *he* understood it. My question is this: What is his most important message to us now? The answer I wish to suggest is that the aspect of Marx with the greatest enduring significance and relevance for our time is the utopian aspect, the part that we today might call his "futurology." In order to explain this view, let me go a few steps further in identifying his position.

If we ask ourselves what kind of philosopher Marx basically was, it is easy to answer that he was a philosopher of history. For all his various attempts at a general definition of his position were statements about the historical process. Yet to describe Marx as a philosopher of history is to express a rather superficial truth, because history per se was not the primary object of his theorizing. The primary object was man, man as a species and "species-being" (*Gattungswesen*); and the theory of man is the matrix of Marx's theory of history. He defines history as the *growth-process* of the human species. In his own succinct statement in the 1844 manuscripts: "And just as all things natural must *become,* man, too, has his act of becoming—*history.* . . ."

Now this way of thinking carried the interesting implication that history has an end. Not in the sense of the world's ending, for Marx assumed, in his pre-nuclear innocence, that man and his world would exist indefinitely if not forever. The end of history meant the end of the growth-process of humanity, its emergence into adulthood. Although life and its vicissitudes would go on, and presumably some sorts of change would still occur, the historical agony of growing up, the long struggle of the species to *become* man—a class struggle in large part—would finally be over. The developmental stages of history, which Marx linked with successive "modes of production" from slave labor in antiquity through serf labor in the feudal period to wage labor in the bourgeois era, would be superseded by a radically new mode of productive activity and, along with it, an entirely new form of human community not subject to the dialectical dissolution and breakdown that had necessarily overtaken all historical forms of society. It was with this central idea in mind that Marx wrote in the preface to *The Critique of Political Economy* that the existing bourgeois social formation would bring to a close the prehistory of human society. It was another way of saying that the coming great revolution would usher in the post-historical phase of man's existence on this planet.

The notion of the adulthood of the species was meant by Marx with utmost philosophical seriousness. History as man's protracted "act of becoming" would give way in post-history to man's *being*, to his maturity on both a collective and individual scale. Only at the end could this occur, although the material conditions for it were developing all along. For alienation dogged humanity in every historical cycle of the growth-process, and indeed reached its lowest depth in the bourgeois era when man in the form of the wretched proletarian factory worker became a totally abased dehumanized being, an *Unmensch*. Thus, self-realization, or becoming fully human, was not for Marx a problem that an individual person could solve on his own. It could be solved only within the framework of the self-realization of the species at the end of history.

The normative concept of man implicit in this theory has already been touched upon. Man was seen as a spontaneously productive being with a need to express himself along a multitude of lines, and as tending in all his productive activities, material production included, to construct things "according to the laws of beauty." Marx's vision of the post-historical future was governed by this idea. Not only would machine industry be liberated to produce enough goods to meet the needs of all, but man himself would be liberated from the acquisitive drive, the obsession with wealth that had made him an alienated being. He would consequently be emancipated from the twin tyranny of need and specialization, from his age-old imprisonment in a life of labor and from the various enslaving forms of division of labor inherent in that life. The radically new mode of production coming in post-history would be the free creativity of individuals producing in cooperative association.

Marx not only conceived man as an artistic being in essence, but envisaged his post-historical relationship with "anthropological nature" in artistic terms. Unlike most modern Western philosophers, for whom the subject-object relation has presented primarily the problem of knowing, Marx hardly recognized this problem. Having translated Hegel materialistically, he saw the objects outside man as so many congealments of human productive activity combined with the stuff that the earth provided wherewith to make things. Consequently, their existence and knowability were not really in question. The posture of Cartesian doubt was not for Marx. How could it be for one whose imperative need was not to establish that a world exists but to explain why it appeared so unbearably ugly and oppressive—and to change it? Marx approached the problem of the subject-object relation from an aesthetic viewpoint.

The self-realization of the species would involve the humanization of the world that man had created, the "resurrection of nature." Having been produced in alienated labor and appropriated as private property, the world of objects made by human hand and machine confronted its makers during history as an "alienated world." The end of history would bring its de-alienation. After acquiring mastery of his productive powers and freedom to produce in a human way, man would refashion his own objectified nature according to the laws of beauty. Instead of confronting him as negations of himself, alien and hostile beings, the objects of his production would bring him self-confirmation. In addition to developing his productive talents in all directions, he would develop his capacity for aesthetic experience. His five senses would be cleansed gradually of the possessiveness, the "sense of having," that had always in the past defiled them and prevented him from perceiving and appreciating the intrinsic aesthetic quality of objects outside him. Consequently, reasoned Marx in his manuscripts of 1844, post-historical man would finally leave even communism behind. For communism, too, was a kind of ownership and possession—communal possession. With the complete humanization of man, even this form of possessiveness would be transcended. So we read in the manuscripts that "communism is the necessary form and energetic principle of the immediate future, but communism is not as such the goal of human development, the form of human society." Not communism as such but "positive humanism" was the goal of human development.

The idea of history having an end is not something new with Marx. In essence it as an eschatological idea with roots extending deep into the Judeo-Christian tradition. The heavenly afterlife was brought down to earth in the utopias of the Renaissance, the eighteenth-century Enlightenment, and the early nineteenth-century socialists. Marx built upon these foundations as well as upon German philosophy. But because of the Hegelian philosophical perspective from which he worked, and of the genius that he brought to the task, he created one of the most *relevant* of modern utopias.

What makes his futurology so pertinent to present problems is, I think, first of all the world scope of his conception of man's post-historical future. Marx was not a community-builder. He had no use for small-scale utopian community ventures carried out, as he once scornfully put it, "behind the back of society." That, to him, was utopianism in the pejorative sense. Being a philosopher of Hegelian formation, for whom history was meaningful only as world-history, he insisted from the start of his theorizing that the goal of human development could only be a new state of the world (*Weltzustand*). So he envisaged utopia on a global scale: man fully matured, master at last of his own powers and those of nature, exercising conscious control of the collective life-process, living the freely creative life in a universal human society.

Marx has been critized for having little to say about community structures and institutional arrangements in post-historical society.[2] But such criticism may be misdirected in the final analysis, and in any event there is something to be said on the other side. A growing number of human problems have become or are fast becoming world problems, not resolvable within the confines of a single community or country or region, however large, although solutions may and should often *begin* locally. Not only war and arms-competition fall in this category, but also unchecked population growth, economic lag and food shortage, racialism, denial of human rights and freedoms, the squandering of mineral resources, the pollution of soil, water, and the earth's atmosphere, and so on. Progress can be made on such problems in nations and regions, but adequate solutions cannot be found within any national or hemispheric or European or Atlantic or communist community but only within a universal human community. In our time, any serious utopia must be, like Marx's, a new state of the world.

His futurology also has relevance for us in its concrete envisagement of a future human life-style. Marx's concept of the "abolition of labor" in post-historical society anticipated certain present developments that are taking place owing to a technological revolution rather than the proletarian revolution forecast in the *Communist Manifesto*. Automation and the unlocking of the productive powers of the atom have begun to pose the question of a profound reorientation of man's existence, a reorientation from the work-centered life to a different kind of life. With the elimination of a great deal of economic labor, the problem of the *good* life may become inescapable for a growing proportion of mankind. What kind of living will then take the place of a large part of what has been called working for a living?

2. For example, by Martin Buber, in *Paths in Utopia*, ch. 8, and in my *Philosophy and Myth in Karl Marx*, ch. 13.

Marx's aesthetic utopia, his vision of a post-historical world where human existence takes on the character of creative leisure and artistic expression, represents at least one conceivable answer. Since men in the mass may not have as much artistic bent as he imputed to human nature and may not regard leisure as the unmitigated blessing he thought it would be, we cannot take his utopia as a statement of the inevitable. It still has value, however, as a preview of what is possible. And his notion of the entire environment as a field for aesthetic effort, of "anthropological nature" itself as man's supreme work of art, is particularly pertinent in an age that has seen so much spoliation of nature, destruction of natural beauty, and spread of urban blight. Who in our time, living in big cities, can doubt the imperative need for what Marx called the "true resurrection of nature"?

There is possible guidance for us, finally, in his fundamental concept of the growing up of the race, the graduation of man from his historical growth-process into adulthood. Not that we can take a happy ending of history for granted any longer. Living in the final third of the twentieth century, with great tragedies behind and dangers ahead, we cannot anticipate the future in a Marxian spirit of millenarian optimism. We can see that man may not achieve a universal community, that he may not gain mastery of his powers, that the world's population may go on exploding, that racialism and nationalism may continue to flourish, that life may grow poorer in an increasingly crowded, impersonal, coercive, and regimented society, and that—in the warning words of Erik H. Erikson—"Reactionary rage equipped with atomic weapons may mean the end of man just when for the first time he has a chance to become one species."[3] But the very hugeness of these dangers suggests that *without* some such breakthrough to human maturity as Marx was talking about, the cause may be lost. What I mean to say is that the least likely future may be one in which man muddles through more or less as he has been doing, governments show no more imagination and moral leadership than they have been showing, and history goes on as usual.

The precondition of successful human adaptation and even survival may be radical change—not so much in the organizational arrangements for living as in the consciousness of people, their attitudes to others and themselves, their sense of responsibility to distant peoples and future generations, their patterns of feeling and identity. This is to say that further growth is essential, that the species may now be in a "maturation crisis." If so, one of the most serious aspects of the crisis is the general lack of awareness of it, the tendency of most people and even the leaders of nations to assume that no great change is called for, that no enlargement of the human spirit is necessary, that we immature humans are

3. R. I. Evans, *Dialogue with Erik Erikson* (New York, Evanston, and London: Harper and Row, 1967), p. 33.

already grown up. Marx therefore may be at his most relevant in telling us that this is not so, that the species is still engaged in its historical act of becoming and has not yet fully achieved the condition of *being* human.

It must be said, in conclusion, that he was far more effective in grasping these fundamentals and envisaging a fully human future than he was in specifying the means of bringing it about. He greatly overestimated material and technological development as the prerequisite of human maturation, failing to see the immense psychological difficulties and the consequent critical role of leadership and education in the process. He imagined, mistakenly, that revolutionary force and violence could be the means of achieving not only a new society but the new adult human being as its inhabitant; and so he left to such teachers as Gandhi and Martin Luther King, Jr., the task of showing men how to change society, nonviolently, by changing themselves. Finally, and as a result, Marx thought that the revolutionary process of man's maturation could take place very rapidly once the conditions were ripe. He did not understand that the growing up of collective man is bound to be—like the growing up of individuals—a protracted process marked by partial advances, occasional breakthroughs, inevitable setbacks, and only eventual success.

But he was not the first prophet to be more successful in pointing out the promised land than in leading people to it. His genius lay in his powers of visualizing the end. In an age when utopianism has become the only realism, these powers are needed as never before.

Problems

1. To what extent does Tucker see early Marx as concerned with the self-development of the human species? What is history?
2. Why were production and communism central to Marx's vision?
3. To what extent, in Tucker's opinion, is Marx fundamentally evolutionary rather than revolutionary in theory?
4. Why did Marx believe self-realization must be a collective rather than an individual problem?
5. Marx is often cited as being scientific and objective. To what extent is his vision normative and artistic instead?
6. Compare and contrast Marx and Paul as visionaries.
7. How tenable or untenable do you find Marx's vision? Are your objections rooted in his aspirations or his assumptions? What would you replace them with?

Psychoanalysis

Introduction

Psychoanalysis is hardly a monolithic movement. Like Christianity and Marxism, it has its schisms, its "new theologies," its revisionists, its unrecognizable modifications. As Philip Rieff has observed, "The battle to remain orthodox is always lost. Orthodoxy, as a shrewd Huguenot pastor observed long ago, is successful heresy" (28 Rieff).

From its inception, Freudian psychoanalysis was beset by hostility; and in recent years, it has become a commonplace in some analytic circles to attack classical Freudian theory for a host of shortcomings. The "cultural school" or "dynamic culturalists" (to which loose classification Karen Horney and Erich Fromm belong) attack it for neglecting cultural factors in neurosis, and for a too static view of civilization. The existential psychotherapists (to which group Viktor E. Frankl may be loosely associated), criticize it for its failure to consider the unique, self-creative nature of each human being and the individual's search for meaning as a motivating force. Client-centered therapists like Carl Rogers are put off by the cold, aloof, dogmatic authoritarianism of Freudian therapy, its failure to create a warm, accepting climate between therapist and patient. Abraham H. Maslow in particular would fault Freudian theory for its pessimism about man, for failing to see man's goodness and inherent potential. All these criticisms come from within the broad psychotherapeutic movement, and all are intent on "liberalizing" Freudian theory and practice.

What is strange and peculiar about Freud is that he also should have been so successful in alienating even those outside the movement. Freud is almost ignored by the communists; Hitler, at the other end of the political spectrum, was utterly paranoid in his antagonism to psychoanalysis. Right-wing conservatives view the entire mental health movement as a left-wing plot (which is most ironic in view of communist hostility); behaviorists dismiss his theories as unscientific speculations, and sometimes speak of him as "Papa Fraud"; fundamentalist Christians are repelled for a host of reasons, especially for his apparent "pan-sexualism." As Herbert Marcuse has noted, Freud's theories have been so modified that the revision "constitutes a blank discarding of his fundamental theoretical conceptions" (29 Marcuse).

It is difficult to isolate the origin and genesis of this widespread hostility. Freud is accused of pessimism, but then what could be more pessimistic than the concept of original sin? Freud, of course, never thought of himself as a pessimist. "Seventy years have taught me to accept life with a cheerful humility. . . . I am not a pessimist. I permit no philosophic reflection to spoil my enjoyment of the simple things of life" (30 Jones).

It is part of the American folkway to dismiss ideas that appear on the surface to be pessimistic, without adequately asking, with Nietzsche, whether our judgment in these matters is not an act of unreason, a reflection and expression of the prevalent faith and morality of the society, and thus deeply problematic. Hence, while some persons view Freud's inquiries into infantile sexuality and the Oedipus complex, his theory of instinctual aggression, his probing of the unconscious for neurotic sexual conflicts as signs of his morbid mind, others see his suspicions of moralism, of self-aggrandizing concepts, of simplistic and naïve beliefs in steady painless progress as proofs of his pessimism.

This readiness on the part of many Americans to reject or to restructure anything unpleasant or pessimistic leads to a Pollyanna world view [1] predicated on "looking for the silver lining," on boosting, moralizing, positive thinking. People within such a system seem to believe that optimism and pessimism reside in attitudes themselves, which, of course, they do not. They are rather the *products* of our interpretations, and any interpretation is dependent on our assumptions, on our value system. It is, therefore, possible to reinterpret the above attitudes and conclude that

> . . . Pollyanna is the only true pessimist. Pollyanna secretly feels that things are so bad that the only way to make life endurable is by pretending that the badness does not exist and by finding consolation in sentimentality. The only optimist whose optimism is a creative force and not just soothing syrup is the person who can face just how bad and how inadequate the past has been, out of a sturdy hope that with hard thinking better ways can be found. . . . The greatest optimist . . . is the pathologist who has the courage to study our mistakes at the autopsy table (31 Kubie).

What is it in our prevalent world view that leads us to see Freud, the great mental pathologist, as a pessimist? From the Freudian perspective the question is less problematic.

Freud, like Jesus, thought judgments were symptomatic and revela-

---

1. *Pollyanna* (1913) by Eleanor Hodgman Porter is, in a sense, the summation of American sentimental literature. A sample of the little girl's "glad" mentality follows. In a raffle for a Church bazaar, she wishes for a doll carriage but instead wins some old crutches. When told that she ought to be thankful she doesn't need them, she suddenly sees this new truth and brightens up with gladness. The sentimental unreality of this mentality is revealed in its sustained effort to find *immediate* consolation in almost any area of great disappointment or suffering.

tory—"as you judge so shall you be judged." He thought of the neurotic as an incompletely socialized or "uncivilized" individual,[2] as one who rebelled out of weakness rather than from a position of strength. Unable or unwilling to adapt, to accept the sacrifices required by civilization, the neurotic refuses to confront reality and instead attempts to deny it. Thus, from the Freudian perspective, those who charge Freud with pessimism are revealing neurotic anxiety. Such individuals need therapy, for therapy is "education for truthfulness."

One cannot assert, from the above argument, that Freud would have recommended therapy to Pollyanna. He believed that some people could not tolerate the burden of truth, and that for them illusion was preferable. We cannot, by any means, however, conclude that the sterner one's world-view, the more truth and the less illusion it contains. For, if that were so, the harshest world view commensurate with rational coherence would be the truest; and that as a primary assumption is patent nonsense, not to speak of such harsh consequences as whipping the "devil" out of children, or putting "evil ones" to death for any non-conformity. We must acknowledge the possibility that "self-fulfilling prophecies" are operative; that positive thought can easily become real merely by virtue of its positiveness; that a spirit of defeatism, and perhaps real defeat, follows upon reduced hope. One cannot conclude from this new line of thought, however, that "positive thinking" is the better course. Positive thinking led to Hitler's invasion of Russia and to his defeat. There is, of course, a third course: those who neither hope nor fear, who try to see reality as it is, who work because they are "civilized" and, therefore, must work.

We are not interested here in arriving at the truth, or even at the objective nature of Freudian theory; we are intent on analyzing some of the possible implications involved in the hostility to Freudian theory. Instead of drawing inferences about Freudian theory, then, we shall use Freudian theory to draw inferences about ourselves.

Hostility to Freud, it becomes obvious at a glance, is by no means always coherent or carefully reasoned. Freud is a materialist, in the sense Marx was, but that does not make his theory congenial to the communists. His determinism is not thoroughgoing enough for the behaviorists, nor as socially induced as the communists would like. His emphasis on the unique individual personality, his humanism, his unworldliness,

2. Socialization or the act of becoming civilized was not, for Freud, a matter of teaching conformity; it was a matter of psychological health, of ethics. In *The Future of an Illusion* (452/32–454/6), in *Civilization and Its Discontents* (480/34–481/39), and in "Why War?", a letter to Einstein, Freud makes clear that a man is "civilized" when his instincts have been so tamed that he is *biologically* incapable of committing an anti-social or unethical act. Thus he would, for example, be unable to seduce a woman because he would be unable to perform the sexual act; or to commit murder because he physically could not pull the trigger (cf. Marcuse's use of the word "biological").

and his preference for spiritualized expression should please Christians, while his exposé of social exploitation and religious illusions should please communists; the result in both cases is otherwise.

Already a partial answer to our question is beginning to emerge. While there is something to please everyone, there is also something to offend everyone; and people seem to be more sensitive to offense than to pleasure, and apt to treasure painful memories longer. In the hope of reaching a more complete answer, let us sort out our own responses more clearly and dramatically by developing Freud's theories in broadstroke.

Freud's theory, like Marx's, is dynamic and dialectic. Man is neither a freely acting nor a totally reactive being: he is worked upon by the interaction of forces from within and from without. He is determined both by his hereditary disposition and by his environment. These hereditary and environmental forces are not imaginary; they are "real" (in the sense that anger or a habit is "real," or a taste for one food over another is "real"). Any change in the nature or energy of these forces, some of which are unconscious, creates a corresponding change in another area. The result is a new dynamic balance. These forces, both conscious and unconscious, involve the instincts (id), society (ego), and one's conscience (superego), and prove to be either uncontrollable or controllable only by a concession or compromise in some area. The basic motivating force of human behavior is sex, but there is also an innate impulse to aggression. These instincts cannot be eliminated, only channeled and used. Man desires gratification; society demands repression. The result is conflict. A healthy person is one who has balanced the conflicting claims of his instincts (id), the society in which he is raised (ego), and his ideals (superego), without being tyrannized by one or another of these forces, and without resenting the sacrifices society imposes upon him in its service. For civilization gives us numerous compensations and we must not harm it. The entire process is summed up in Freud's remark "Where id is, there ego shall be" (32 Freud); where the unconscious, irrational, demonic instincts are, there, through therapy, conscious reason and a sense of reality—a "reality principle"—shall rule.

Neurotic conflict for Freud is not a conflict between opposing impulses on the conscious level. That is normal conflict, and is to be expected.

> It is a battle between two forces of which one has succeeded in coming to the level of the preconscious and conscious part of the mind, while the other has been confined on the unconscious level. That is why the conflict can never have a final outcome one way or the other . . . The sole task of the treatment . . . is the substitution of something conscious for something unconscious, the transformation of the unconscious thoughts into conscious thoughts. . . . By extending the unconscious into the consciousness the repressions are raised, the conditions of symptom-

Introduction 403

formation are abolished, and the pathogenic [neurotic] conflict exchanged for a normal one which must be decided one way or the other. We do nothing for our patients but enable this one mental change to take place in them; the extent to which it is achieved is the extent of the benefit we do them. Where there is no repression or mental process analogous to it to be undone there is nothing for our therapy to do (33 Freud).

Freud here makes it clear that therapy does not abolish conflict, but merely enables the patient to choose consciously his course of action. His choice may, of course, be unconventional. Freud notes:

> ... anyone who has successfully undergone the training of learning and recognizing the truth about himself is henceforth strengthened against the dangers of immorality, even if his standard of morality should in some respect deviate from the common one (34 Freud).

To a conservative Christian, Freud's last remark is unintelligible—there is no morality *apart* from the "common one." In Freud we once again have a messianic voice upholding a new spiritualized vision of morality against the literal one of the Pharisees. Freud's remark makes eminent good sense to a Marxist in a capitalist society, for he believes capitalist morality to be corrupt. It would, however, make little sense to a communist in a communist society; he would accept the "common" morality, as would a conservative Christian in a Christian one. For both, morality is more than an attitude, an abiding concern for others, a deep sense of responsibility, or a rational sense of what is good for one's brother; it is a series of rituals and taboos (cf. Romans). We are confronted once again with the vegetarians against Paul in Romans, with a new tendency to reify spiritual states until morality resides in the action itself instead of in the entire matrix of intention–action–consequence.

What emerges from this analysis is a series of questions. Who believes in human freedom, in man's spiritual state and potential, in the sanctity of the human conscience, in an evolutionary, instrumentalist attitude toward truth? Who sees evil in such freedom, questions man's rational powers, takes refuge in authority? Who is freer, and in the sense that Paul used it, "stronger in his faith": the one who is disturbed by the anti-legalistic implications of Freud's remark, or the person who accepts the notion that "no thing is impure in itself" (Rom. 14.14). Like Christ and Marx, Freud is intent on rationalizing ethics; he is an instrumentalist, and his ethics are situational.

The psychoanalytic situation, it is true, is therefore dependent on an attitude of liberal toleration. But it is false to infer from this dependency that psychoanalysis breeds permissiveness or, in Freud's words, "free living." Freud is emphatic in his denial. "It is out of the question that part of the analytic treatment should consist of advice to 'live freely'" (35 Freud). Indeed, Freud has been criticized by others for moral attitudes that are too middle class; and it is true that his theories are concerned, essentially, not with the squandering of sexuality but with the conservation of emotion, and hence of energy, both of which he considers necessary to health. What, then, could lead one to conclude that Freud's theory breeds loose living?

A strong belief in "original sin" and human depravity can obviously lead one to suspect any morality that is *not* repressive. Though Christ is, in the main, and for his time, situational, tolerant (Mary Magdalene), self-critical— "Why do you look at the speck of sawdust in your brother's eye, with never a thought for the great plank in your own? . . . First take the plank out of your own eye and then you will see clearly to take the speck out of your brother's" (Matt. 7.3-5)—and non-repressive (perhaps because original sin is not central to his thought), he is at times capable of uttering statements that are brutally repressive—"If your right eye leads you astray, tear it out and fling it away; it is better for you to lose one part of your body than for the whole of it to be thrown into hell. And if your right hand is your undoing, cut it off and fling it away; it is better for you to lose one part of your body than for the whole of it to go to hell" (Matt. 5.29-30). A preference for the latter, legalistic, repressive morality places one in that line of Christian thought which is authoritarian; a preference for the former, tolerant, situational, self-critical and non-repressive morality places one in the line of Christian humanism. Erich Fromm has described the two elements.

> The essential element in authoritarian religion and in the authoritarian religious experience is the surrender to a power transcending man. The main virtue of this type of religion is obedience, its cardinal sin is disobedience. Just as the deity is conceived as omnipotent or omniscient, man is conceived as being powerless and insignificant. Only as he can gain grace or help from the deity by complete surrender can he feel strength. Submission . . . of the mind overwhelmed by its own poverty, is the very essence of all authoritarian religions whether they are couched in secular or in theological language. . . . To such ideals as "life after death" or "the future of mankind" the life and happiness of persons living here and now may be sacrificed; the alleged ends justify every means and become symbols in the names of which religious or secular "elites" control the lives of their fellow men.
>
> Humanistic religion, on the contrary, is centered around man and his strength. Man must develop his power of reason in order to understand himself, his relationship to his fellow men and his position in the universe. He must recognize the truth, both with regard to his limitations and his potentialities. He must develop his powers of love for others as well as for himself and experience the solidarity of all living beings. . . .

Man's aim in humanistic religion is to achieve the greatest strength, not the greatest powerlessness; virtue is self-realization, not obedience. Faith is certainty of conviction based on one's experience of thought and feeling, not assent to propositions on credit of the proposer. The prevailing mood is that of joy, while the prevailing mood in authoritarian religion is that of sorrow and of guilt (36 Fromm).

Despite charges of authoritarianism against psychoanalysis, it is the authoritarian Christian who most fears any slackening of the superego's repressive power even if this creates a dynamic imbalance between his conscience, his id, and his perception of reality. Indeed, from a psychoanalytic perspective, he suffers from that very imbalance, hence the anxiety and authoritarianism. One could attribute his fear to his belief in "original sin," were it not that he is also repelled by the entire Freudian sexual model. Attitudinal contradictions are thus evident. If the original sin was pride—and lust a major manifestation of it—then sexuality is the condition of sinfulness. The intellectually consistent position of an authoritarian Christian would be to accept the Freudian sexual model—perhaps even the existence of the unconscious as well, for reason was considered to have been impaired by the Fall (Calvin thought it was totally depraved) —but to disagree with his therapeutic techniques. But such a criticism rarely materializes. If the ground for the objection to Freudian theory does not lie with original sin, where does it lie?

The Christian model, as we have suggested earlier, is not dynamic, but static; it involves a simple dualism of body and soul, will and reason, with the soul and reason being the higher principles whose function it is to control the lower principles for the sake of the higher. The body is corrupt, the will depraved by lustful desires; reason has as its task to chasten and control the depraved will and thereby preserve the soul from corruption. It is a simple model, but it has served the West nicely for nearly two thousand years.

Freudian theory attacks the very heart of the Christian system—reason —by complicating the forces at work and by making it a feeble instrument inadequate to its task unless properly educated. Rational control in therapy is often revealed to be little more than unconscious compulsion; free will and an entire configuration of self-congratulatory attitudes for one's righteousness are thereby called into question. One is exposed in one's nakedness as a borderline neurotic. And since in Freud's eyes, as we have seen, mental health and morality are associated concepts, normality becomes not a state but an ethical ideal, and neurosis becomes the Freudian equivalent of Christian sin (Christianity having no equivalent for mental illness). Those who like their world neatly dichotomized— right–wrong, good–evil, sick–well—and tightly ordered, will be disturbed by the Freudian tendency to blur the sharp distinction between neurotic and normal.[3] It will unsettle an authoritarian Christian because it humanizes *all* men, destroys traditional distinctions and hierarchies based on sinner and sinless, and makes it impossible for one to hide (see the Reich essays dealing with secrecy and authoritarianism); there is no refuge in an austere, aloof distance, for man becomes transparent. The unapproachable mystery of personality is unraveled, and we must become humble and tolerant before the reality of human frailty and inadequacy.

It would be difficult for an individual raised in the tyrannical shadow of authoritarian Christianity to realize that for Freud neurosis was not a normative matter. It was an illness, but not itself a moral failing. It might, of course, lead to immoral behavior just as physical ill health might lead to shoddy work; but just as ill health is not poor work so neurosis is not immorality. But Freud's disinterested pursuit of understanding is alien to authoritarian Christians for whom almost all things are normative. The difference is the difference mentioned previously, between preferring to perceive and understand, and preferring, despite Christ's advice against it, to judge.

These differing preferences offer us a clue to the hostility. Not merely fine points of dogma and differing models of the human psyche disturb the authoritarian, but the upheaval Freudian theory works upon his certitudes. Unlike the humanistic Christian who is situational and self-critical, the authoritarian mind needs orderly categories to suppress internal turmoil, and requires sharp dichotomies to reduce ambivalence. The authoritarian is compelled to seek psychological closure in order to reduce anxiety, for he is terrified of his own precarious balance and coherence; he is, therefore, hardly going to smile upon a theory that declassifies the world and leaves much of it tentative, open, and insoluble. A mind that needs external props in the way of divine sanctions and civil laws, that is frightened of its own precarious ethical control and so projects that precariousness outward in the form of suspicion and harsh judgment of others, is going to resist any movement that undermines external authority and attempts to substitute in its place rational, internal controls. Freud offers nothing but self-reliance, autonomy, and the anxiety of analysis; the authoritarian prefers dependence, certainty, and the satisfaction of prejudgment.

3. Thus, in *Leonardo da Vinci: A Study in Psychosexuality* (1910), after making clear that "it was doubtful whether Leonardo ever embraced a woman in love" (37 Freud), that Leonardo was sexually deeply repressed, that his sexual life was non-existent and was "restricted to so-called ideal homosexuality" (38 Freud), Freud concludes: "Let us expressly emphasize that we have never considered Leonardo as a neurotic or as a 'nervous person' in the sense of this awkward term. . . . We no longer believe that health and disease, normal and nervous, are sharply distinguished from each other, and that neurotic traits must be considered as proofs of a general inferiority" (39 Freud). For Freud, not eccentricity but creative sterility, psychological unreality, and behavioral irresponsibility mark the neurotic.

Introduction 407

If Reich is correct in his analysis (see 833/1–835/29, 838/8-31), these factors may be operative in the communist hostility as well, but some deeper disagreement is at work. It is probably political, despite the fact that Freud was quite harsh in his criticism of the middle class and of middle-class morality—he felt it was an exhausted class, populated by enervated Prufrocks, who as a result of the strain of modern urban life suffered from "increasing nervousness" and "exhausted nerves." Psychotherapy, as Marcuse has noted with condemnation, nevertheless often works for adjustment and hence indirectly for the status quo and against revolution.

Freud was aware of the failure of the world of the bourgeoisie, but he did not, as a consequence, become an active ally of social reform. He knew how shoddy, irrational, and destructive middle-class values are and has indirectly exerted an influence in rationalizing them by educating people for truthfulness and thereby teaching them to recognize when their happiness is dependent on the wretchedness of others. But this fact is not enough to endear him to the Marxists. One can only conclude then, that hostility to the bourgeoisie is not the main ingredient in contemporary communist ideology. The roots of communist hostility lie, more probably, in Freud's suspicion of politics, in his belief that it is inevitably authoritarian in nature, that the irrationality of the mass makes it susceptible to manipulation by a demogogue. If for Kierkegaard the crowd is "untruth," for Freud the crowd is irrationality. By their very nature, groups are unreasoning, for it is love or libido, not self-interest as the Marxists suppose, that binds the members of a group together. In politics, man is in a heightened state akin to emotional frenzy or love.

An attitude so skeptical of the value of man's political life clashes sharply with the communist messianic belief in political man and in politics as the battlefield where opposing interests are fought out. Freud was, by temperament, suspicious of all social idealisms, especially those couched in the idiom of nationalistic or melioristic rhetoric, for he believed they inevitably masked power drives. Freud was also suspicious of violent political appeals based on group interests; at most, these were rationalizations for passions to be unleashed, reasons put forward to disguise the irrational impulses that are operative in a given situation.

Freud, it is obvious from the above, is resolutely individualist and anti-collectivist. He refuses to acknowledge national interest as a final cause and prefers instead to probe human motives. No emotions are public initially; they begin privately and are then projected outward and made public. Politics thus masks unconscious guilts, anxieties, compulsions. Even in his analysis of politics, Freud reveals his suspicion of moral self-deception. The result is a tendency to obliterate ethical positions and social aspirations in politics. Obviously Freud was more afraid of a ruthless messianic aggressor acting in the belief that he was possessed of truth than he was of unresolved evils—perhaps because he believed that much evil is done in the name of good and in the name of redressing previous evil. Moreover, Freud feared collective violence, for he believed it expressed man's most naked barbarism. Collective violence is always more shameless and cruel than individual violence. In the final analysis, Freud did not believe in a perfect society; since conflict between the individual and society is inevitable, all revolutions are of dubious value.

Freud's critique of politics thus starts from assumptions totally different from those of the Marxists, and by means of their hostility, one can assess the relative weight they give to various aspects of Marxist theory. Utopianism, rational self-interest, political revolution as vehicle and answer, progress through control and power—these loom as central aspects of communist thought. On the other hand, Freud's emphasis on self-criticism and introspection can only undermine anyone's sense of infallibility.

One can compose a Marxist critique with little difficulty, but our purpose, as we stated earlier; is to suggest, not to explicate. The primary irreducible difference upon which the entire previous edifice is built seems to be that between individualism and collectivism. Despite Marx's hope for man once he is liberated from wage slavery, his view of man is finally collectivist. Man alone cannot realize his full potential; all that has humanized man has been collective endeavor. Man is socially conditioned and determined; his consciousness is shaped by society and should be used to reshape it. The public man, man as socio-political organism, is the ultimate reality and hope. Only by accepting his relatedness, by accepting himself as part of something greater than himself, can man find salvation from his present misery.

For Freud, the irreducible unit is man, the single individual; and his profound allegiance is to preserving the inner life of the individual, his psychological freedom and integrity, from the encroachments and onslaughts made upon it by society. Religious man is an illusion, political man a fraud, social man superficial. The only reality is the reality of the individual psyche beset by conflict from within and without, precariously trying, between the demands of the id and of society, to sustain the energy and freedom necessary to create its own harmonious dance of life.

Patterns: Unwarranted Assumptions

Even granting the complexity of the author's task—to analyze psychoanalysis without being too revelatory, by reflecting Christian and Marxist perspectives—the essay is guilty of glaring over-assumption. The author, it is true, makes clear the tentative nature of his conclusions; but we must remember that an admission of a deficiency does not thereby remove it.

The opening begins rather explicitly with concrete references, but this feeling for the particular soon passes, and by the fifth paragraph we are already in the world of questionable generalization and hypothetical construction. We are introduced to a "value system" that is described as part of the American folkway. Such an assumption, which is really the creation of a "straw man", remains, in view of the evidence supporting it, unwarranted within the context of the essay. The tendency to create "straw men" is continued later in the essay when we are introduced to a mythical authoritarian Christian. The author simplifies his task of comparing two value systems by comparing one in all its complexity—the Freudian—against another in all its simplicity—the Christian. Nowhere does the author feel called upon to establish the widespread existence of such "Christians." It does little good to assert that they are common knowledge. Until the author is prepared to establish or at least argue his stereotype, we are free to question it and indeed scarcely have any other choice.

The brief section at the end on Marxism and psychoanalysis degenerates into a set of rather sweeping, abstract, and highly elliptical remarks. From these swift statements we are asked to accept the author's conclusion that "the primary irreducible difference . . . seems to be that between individualism and collectivism." But the conclusion itself is defective for it is not a conclusion at all, merely the culminating assumption of a whole chain.

The extenuations made on behalf of the essay to the effect that it was intended to be suggestive, provocative, and of manageable length, are not persuasive. In matters of intellect, kindly indulgence is perhaps necessary, but it should never lead one to confuse that which is suggestive with that which is persuasive. The essay, as a piece of persuasion, is unfinished. The house has been framed, but in its present form is unlivable. It is a beginning—as are all assumptions—that the reader will have to complete.

22 HANS HERMA

The following essay from Hans Herma's A Handbook of Psychoanalysis *(1950), serves as an admirable introduction to Freud. In this essay, Herma defines key psychoanalytic terms and concepts in a simple fashion, and indicates something of the complexity of the Freudian dynamic without creating confusion in the reader. The terms and concepts are arranged, moreover, to permit easy reference; the reader is thereby able to avoid the necessity of immediate memorization of a number of new concepts.*

The Unconscious

When we watch people in their many daily pursuits, it is easy enough to understand what they are doing and why. Sometimes, however, we have to turn to science when we are confronted with an inner experience the nature of which puzzles us and makes us aware of the fact that we are at a loss to explain it.

Such experiences may appear to be of minor or no significance, like slips of the tongue, forgetting to do things, not remembering the name of our best friend, in short, what we have come to know as "Freudian errors." Or they may be so bizarre as to seemingly defy any attempt at a rational explanation, as is the case with our dreams. But we cannot pass over as inconsequential certain strange phenomena such as neurotic symptoms, since they do make people suffer, for example the terror which some people experience when they have to take an elevator or subway. Confronted with such facts we must admit that we have no self-evident explanation and are in need of one from science. Yet we are reluctant to give credence to an explanation science has to offer when it offends our tender feelings, readily dismissing it as "mere theory."

In the natural sciences we have gradually come to accept certain

From Hans Herma, *A Handbook of Psychoanalysis* (Cleveland: The World Publishing Co., 1950), pp. 4–19.

things as true even though they are contrary to our habitual train of thought. But when it comes to psychological matters we still behave as though common sense is all that is necessary to reject or "disprove" a statement concerning ourselves, no matter how true science may have proven it to be.

The concept of unconscious mental processes, basic to psychoanalysis, is taken by many as a figure of speech, merely indicating vagueness or dim awareness. But it is meant literally. It is indeed true, as Ernest Jones says: "To assume the existence of mental processes of which we are totally unaware, i.e., an unconscious mind, is to take a serious step in thought which has far-reaching consequences."[1] This step was taken by Freud, and not in a casual manner. It was based on a detailed and painstaking investigation of observable facts and in the face of overwhelming evidence; he was fully aware of the far-reaching consequences. Actually, it was not the assumption of unconscious mental processes which made his discoveries so important—for this assumption had been made by others before him—but the fact that he could show the effects of the unconscious upon the conscious psychic processes.

. . . We have set ourselves the task of describing briefly the conclusions which Freud drew from the observation of a great number of psychological facts as to how the psychic system works, presenting what might be called the picture of the mind or of the psychic system. We may refer to this as the structure of the total personality as conceived by psychoanalysis.

THE STRUCTURE OF PERSONALITY

What we call the structure of personality is a construct, something like a mathematical formula which describes concrete, observable facts, such as the falling of an object, in abstract terms. More aptly, it may be compared to the way physics depicts the structure of an atom by making a model of what goes on between the particles that make it up—their pathways, their energy charges and modes of interaction.

There is nothing arbitrary about such a construct, nor is the fact that it is always open to revision an indication that it is not "true" or is merely "hypothetical." It may be modified because it is an abstraction, a set of generalizations about demonstrable facts of psychic life. We must, therefore, always keep in mind that it is a highly simplified version of the real state of affairs, not to be taken too literally.

It will be easier to describe Freud's construct of the psychic sys-

---

1. Ernest Jones, *What Is Psychoanalysis?* (New York: International Universities Press, 1947), p. 25.

tem if we reverse the steps that led historically to its development and simply describe his final formulations.

THE ID AND THE EGO

To begin with, we must distinguish between two basically different types of psychic functions which are involved in any given action. Suppose we come home from work, find some food in the refrigerator and cook and eat it. We ascribe the fact that we want to eat to a need arising from the body, it varies in intensity depending on how long we have gone without food or how hard we have been working. Such a need we may also call an instinct, an instinctual tendency or a drive. It makes us act but does not tell us how. If the food happens to be in a can our instinct does not even tell us that it is food. Here we have to rely on our memory, the skills we have acquired and, if we cannot find a can opener, the resistant metal box may present a challenge to our ability, i.e., intelligence, to solve problems. None of these activities are controlled by those inborn tendencies we called instincts.

They do not tell us to open the refrigerator, nor how; they do not tell us how to open the can and cook the contents, nor how to season it, nor even to make sure that it is not spoiled. What are these actions controlled by if not by instincts? We have no trouble in identifying the control as coming from ourselves. We say: "I open the can, I do this or that, I think, I act or feel." We ascribe, in other words, the function of control to the self, the "ego," Latin for "I." Our language is so constructed as to show that we like to take full responsibility—and credit—for all such acts and accomplishments.

On the other hand, there is a linguistic reluctance on our part to identify ourselves as clearly with certain other acts, although they are no less a part of ourselves.

We talk as though we ("I") were somehow passively subjected to some forces outside ourselves, or outside our control. If we can't get an idea clear in our mind, or can't remember something, we say, "It does not come to me." When we are angry we may also say, "It burns me up," not, "I burn myself up." Similarly: "It gets me down, and "It occurs to me." (The original Latin meaning of this word puts it even clearer: "Occurrere" means running against or towards.) "It makes me mad" can double for "I am mad." But "It is exasperating" can be linked to the "I" only in the passive voice; the same is true for "It is disappointing." There is some possibility, however, for saying: "I drive myself crazy with . . ." although the usual version is "It drives me crazy." But why give more examples? They do not prove anything except that the language reflects a certain awareness of some vague and undefinable forces in us which seem to impinge upon the "ego." All these expressions have in common some element of lack or loss of control on the part of the ego, or an unwillingness on its part to be held responsible for them. On the other hand, where the ego wants to take credit for its own activity our language does not lend itself to attributing the ego's accomplishments to anything but itself. We cannot substitute "It thinks, does, or acts," when we mean that *we* are doing it. It was this feature of our language which suggested the term "id" (Latin for "it") to denote those forces outside of the ego, of which the instincts are the most important part.

THE INSTINCTS AND THE PLEASURE PRINCIPLE

The outstanding feature of the instinctual needs (the id tendencies) is that they press for immediate satisfaction. They will not rest until they are satisfied, and if the satisfaction is not forthcoming they will become more insistent and bothersome, no matter what the external conditions are. It is just because reality does not always provide all the things we crave that we are equipped with such tools as memory, intelligence, etc., in short the ego functions, which enable us to secure them. If the world were organized in such a way that all possible satisfactions were available at all times, we would not need any of these special functions, just as we do not (usually) have to call upon them in order to secure a sufficient supply of oxygen; we are always surrounded by plenty of air which is freely available without any effort on our part. In such a world we could survive with the instincts alone. Such a world does not exist, alas, for any living creature.

However, the id tendencies show another remarkable quality: they are not amenable to any considerations as to whether or not it is possible to get satisfaction. Hunger does not cease because there is no food around; if anything, it becomes more demanding. The id tendencies behave like the child who "wants what it wants when it wants it," disregarding all the arguments or pleadings of the helpless mother who cannot satisfy his desires. These instinctual tendencies—if such metaphoric language will be excused—know only the pain or displeasure of want, and the pleasure when satisfaction is forthcoming, they act as though pleasure were the only principle in the world that counts, and as though the world "owed them a living," as though all one has to do to get pleasure is to seek it. Hence, it has been said that they function in accordance with the pleasure principle. The behavior of children is largely under the sway of this principle and it takes a long time and a lot of education before they are able and ready to give it up—in part at least, because it never is dispensed with fully.

THE EGO AND THE REALITY PRINCIPLE

The ego, on the other hand, cannot afford such extravagant behavior. If it is to be successful in its task of securing the satisfaction which the id demands, it will have to take into account under what conditions it can get it. It must know the world, deal with its dangers and opportunities and often enough change and master it. The ego must "work" to make the world yield what the id wants. It acts in accordance with the conditions prevailing in the external reality, in short, in terms of the reality principle. If children afford a good example of behavior dominated by id forces and the pleasure principle, adults show—or ought to—behavior under the domination of the reality principle. While we are equipped by birth with a full set of id tendencies, the ego develops in a person only gradually in the process of growing up, and through education.

THE EGO—SERVANT AND MASTER

We have not as yet mentioned what these instinctual tendencies are, and do not intend to say more than this: they can be classified into two basic groups, the sexual and the aggressive tendencies. It is more important to consider the ego's relationship to them.

We have mentioned that the ego functions in their service. It must now be added that the ego can perform its tasks efficiently only if it is not overwhelmed by the id forces. Everybody knows that it is hard to concentrate on one's work (an ego-function) when one gets hungry. If the desire for food were to flood our conscious experience completely, we would be unable to perform any work—not even preparing the food we wanted to eat. This is shown impressively in an experiment with two dogs. One dog was placed before a fence on the other side of which there was a piece of meat. Immediately he tried to get around the fence (open at both ends) and finally succeeded. He was able to make the detour necessary because he could postpone the satisfaction for which the id tendencies were pressing. The other dog, however, had been starved for several days. When placed before the fence behind which he saw the meat, he could not take his eyes off it, the seemed to be glued to the attractive sight. He was unable to change the direction of his activity, explore the situation and find a way to get the meat. He could not withstand the pressure of hunger long enough to use his intelligence. A less serious and only in part comparable example for the human species is the overthrow of reason in those who want to lose weight, when they are confronted with a tempting cake or ice cream sundae.

To sum up, the ego must be able not only to deal efficiently with the external world but must also be able to control the id tensions. This it accomplishes in either of two ways: through understanding the reasons for postponing gratification or renouncing them altogether, or by developing more or less automatic controls—emotional barriers which simply prevent unwelcome impulses from coming through and by entering consciousness making their presence known to the ego. These barriers are called defenses.

THE DEFENSES OF THE EGO

In order to stress the automatic, involuntary action of the ego which can exclude id tendencies from being consciously experienced, these barriers are also referred to as mechanisms. The most important and most widely known is repression, an emotional block that keeps us from remembering something even if we make a conscious effort.

In his lectures at Clark University in 1909 Freud described its mode of operation in a graphic manner. Assuming that some students in a class misbehave and make noise, becoming a disturbing and undesirable element in the classroom, the teacher expels ("represses") them. But because they are out of the classroom they do not cease to exist. In fact they may try to come back, and some students inside the room may have to block the door to keep them out. If the ones outside, out of malice or revenge, pound at the door, we have in them a parallel to repressed ideas: they try to return. Here the comparison ends, however, for while the teacher can change his mind or accept the expelled students' promises to behave themselves and re-admit them, the usual case is that the ego is not free to do the same. It can re-admit repressed ideas only if they are sufficiently disguised so as to be no longer recognizable.

Of the long list of defense mechanisms which are at the disposal of the ego, we want to mention, in addition to repression, only the most important:

Projection—perceiving in another person (or the outer world in general) what is actually within oneself, e.g., in the words of the Bible seeing the mote in another's eye but not the beam in one's own.

Regression—expressing an instinctual impulse belonging to a later stage of development in a form which is characteristic of an earlier stage, e.g., a toilet-trained child who, on the arrival of a new baby, expresses his need for love by reverting to wetting the bed, instead of demanding more affection from the parents or being satisfied with less.

Identification—feeling and behaving as though one were the person (or one with him) whom one loves or fears instead of having a conscious feeling of love or fear of him.

Rationalization—advancing for one's behavior (or thought) an inadequate reason which serves to hide an unacceptable motive.

Sublimation—channelizing a crude instinctual impulse into socially acceptable forms of activity and thus giving expression to fit in a more refined ("sublimated") form. We shall discuss later why the ego needs so many rather subtle means of self-protection.

An amendment to our picture of the personality becomes imperative if we are to fit the mechanisms of defense into it. These are, as we said, unconscious, yet they are developed and employed by the ego. It follows, then, that the ego, too, is in part unconscious, notwithstanding the fact that its very tools are what we mean by the term "consciousness": orientation in time and space, perception and thinking, memory and learning, and control over our bodily movements.

THE NEUROTIC SYMPTOM

With the exception of sublimation, defense mechanisms require more or less permanent efforts on the part of the ego to keep them in operation, and therefore they absorb some of the ego's energies, a fact which accounts for the fatigue or exhaustion experienced as a result of an emotional strain or disturbance. Because defenses operate automatically, and that means unconsciously, thoughts, feelings or impulses can no longer be readmitted into conscious experience. They remain split off from consciousness and, unlike ordinary memories, do not respond to our will. But like the debarred students, they do not cease to exist. Like any of the original id impulses, they press for expression by demanding readmission to consciousness in order to be discharged: what is repressed tends to return. Since they cannot return directly because access to the conscious part of the ego is blocked by the defenses, they force their way out in a disguised form. For instance instead of getting angry with another person the anger is turned against oneself and one gets a headache. In this form the objectionable impulse is acceptable to the ego which no longer recognizes the real nature of the impulse. The impulse which has been excluded from conscious experience (repressed or warded off) may seek a disguised expression, in dreams, in errors of speech and in similar transitory loss of conscious control over speech or action. If the repression of an impulse or thought is not temporary, its disguised expression is called a neurotic symptom. Repression is a basic condition for symptom formation.

In view of the foregoing we have to add to our description of the id. We have characterized it heretofore as merely the reservoir of instinctual impulses or energies. Now we see in it also the repository for all those memories, thoughts, feelings or impulses which were once conscious but which have later been repressed. This brings us to the point where we can understand why the symptomatic forms of discharge repeat themselves time and again ("repetition compulsion"). The discharge of instinctual impulses through symptoms is never sufficient, because discharge actions in the disguised form are a gesture rather than the real thing, that is to say, they are only symbolic. They are as unsuitable for a complete discharge as looking at a love scene in the movie which does not satisfy the need for a sex partner although, in itself, the screen spectacle may be quite enjoyable.

There is another reason for the repetitive nature of symptomatic, that is, neurotic, behavior. The ideas which we have formed as children about people or events which we could not correctly understand cannot be corrected in the light of new experience by the more mature mind, once they have been split off from the conscious part of the ego and, through repression or other defense mechanisms, relegated to the unconscious. Many misconceptions of sexual matters, such as the anatomical difference of the sexes or the origin of children, cannot be modified in the light of later knowledge because, being represented [sic], they are excluded from conscious re-evaluation.

But it is primarily through the repression of our early experiences that we become incapable of realizing the promise of the future—the satisfactions of maturity. Like Lot's wife in the Biblical story, who, not heeding the Lord's command, looked back on Sodom and Gomorrah, turned into a pillar of salt, so we become prisoners of the past through the rigid defenses maintained by the ego against the memories of our childhood.

FANTASY AND REALITY

We mentioned before that id tendencies—whether they are directly instinctual or whether they are repressed ideas or wishes—can seek an outlet in dreams. This is a warning to us not to disregard an aspect of the mind which is of fundamental importance: namely, that satisfaction of impulses can be obtained, to a certain degree, through mere fantasy. This is possible not only in sleep but also in the waking state. We engage in fleeting fantasies, sometimes hardly noticed by ourselves, or in more elaborate ones known as "daydreams." These fantasies are important because they provide us with an outlet for id impulses when their direct discharge is not possible, e.g., hurting someone whom we do not dare to hurt. But they, too, can in turn become pushed out of consciousness by the ego if it finds them disturbing and unacceptable. In our clumsy language—the only kind at our disposal to describe these strange mental processes—we call them "unconscious fantasies." They, together with memories of actual experiences, make up the main body of repressed material which has become part of the id.

The fact that id tendencies can find at least a partial satisfaction through imagination presents a potential danger to the ego. If it were to let itself be fooled into taking for real, satisfactions which are only imaginary, it could not properly carry out its task of assuring the safety and survival of the organism. Hence it must be able to distinguish between what is fantasy and what is reality, that is to say, it must put its own experiences to the test of "reality." In the state of sleep, when most of the ego functions are rudimentary or out of commission, the fantasy productions we call dreams are experienced by us as real, often frighteningly so, and only on awakening do we recognize them for what they are. In children the "reality testing" function of the ego is still rather weak, and this allows fantasies to assume so important a role in childhood and in turn makes childhood so significant for later life. In the adult this function ordinarily becomes stronger but it can be lost in part or, in more severe forms of mental disturbance, altogether.

The abandonment of reality testing on the part of the ego is dangerous only where clear separation of fantasy and reality is called for to insure that its dealings with reality are appropriate. In the absence of such a necessity, the ego can very well afford a partial relaxation of its vigilance and indulge in the free play of fantasy. Daydreaming is a source of pleasure which no one is willing to forego. And if we expose ourselves to the blandishments of the world of the movies, of literature and the arts, the ego enjoys the deception of the senses in the firm knowledge that their appearance of reality is nothing but an illusion. Our fun is spoiled if we must forcefully remind ourselves that a gruesome scene on the screen or stage is "only make-believe."

THE SUPEREGO

Our description of the structure of personality, far from being complete, has yet to take into account another set of mental operations: the conscience, as we say in common language, or technically, the superego.

In our earlier considerations we have accounted for the ego's need to institute defense against id impulses. They are required by the ego in order to remain free from their interfering with carrying out its tasks. However, if the defenses served merely the purpose of postponing the satisfaction of id impulses until the ego could procure them, there would be no need for further defensive measures on its part, once the needs were met. This is the case for some impulses but not for all. In the first place, there are some impulses which cannot be satisfied for a very long time (e.g., a child's wish to be a grownup or to have a child), and some never (e.g., to be a boy rather than a girl, or vice versa). In the second place, the satisfaction of one wish or impulse may be possible only if another, perhaps more important, remains unsatisfied (e.g., the impulse to hurt someone whom one loves). But there is still another reason why the ego must have checks on the strivings of the Id. The truth is that the ego is not as free an agent as we have pictured it.

Let us return to the example which served as a starting point. Let us suppose we have finished the preparation of the food and are ready to eat it. We suddenly realize that the child presently coming home from school will find nothing left for him. We may be hungry and not have time to prepare anything else, but a sense of responsibility for the youngster compels restraint. The ego here acts not in obedience to the id (hunger) nor to the requirements of the reality situation (the availability of food) but to a moral standard, something that is not part of itself, but which is superior to it: the *"superego."* If we are carried away by our hunger, disregarding the moral standard, i.e., the demands of the superego, and eat the meal anyhow, we are ashamed or guilty or feel self-reproach. We would not only offend our moral standards but we would also impair our ideal of wanting to be a good parent. Or to put it in another way, we would not be living up to our "ego ideal." Our moral standards and our ego ideal are what constitute the superego. Obviously we could not live in peace if we were to carry out just any of the impulses coming from the id at whatever time reality affords an opportunity for satisfaction. We would offend against the standards of the superego.

THE ORIGIN OF THE SUPEREGO

Without the regulative influence of the superego a person could not really be a social being. The reality principle restricts the ego to what is possible but has nothing to say about what is permissible. In a general way it can be said that permissible is what is socially acceptable. Logically it would follow that an individual acquires the superego through a process of learning or training from society. But this is only partly true. The individual must have motives for learning, and these motives are emotional—in the last analysis, id tendencies. We may therefore expect the superego to be a mixture of rational and irrational elements. It would be difficult, for example, to find a rational basis for the ego ideal which we have developed for ourselves and

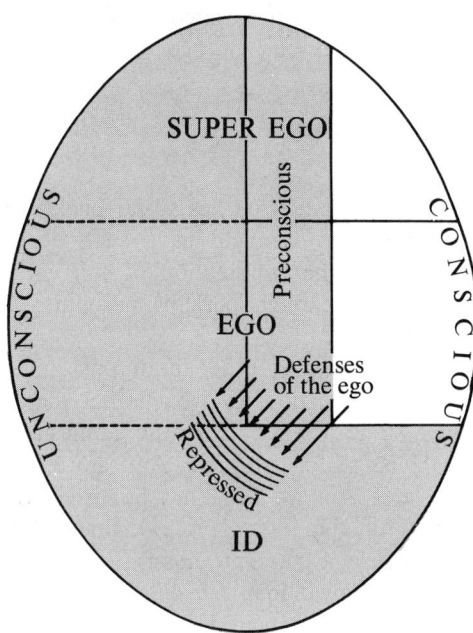

This is a simplified diagram depicting the structure of the psychiatric apparatus. No meaning attaches to the relative size of the divisions. "Preconscious" is any material which we can make conscious through a mere effort of will such as simple remembering.

which we so strenuously try to live up to. For one thing, it shows clearly discernible traces of self-love (narcissism). For another, what does the ego ideal "to be a good parent" really entail? If we should feel guilty in depriving a child of a pleasure (to safeguard his health, for example), our ego ideal reveals itself as being at odds with our rational judgment. Our moral standards, too, show a peculiar resistance to revision in the light of critical thinking. We may feel guilty for acts which we can fully justify on grounds of reason; stranger still, mere thoughts which are not carried out and do not hurt anyone, may cause us to feel as guilty as if we had committed a serious crime. These contradictions cannot be understood unless we assume that there are aspects of the superego which are totally unconscious. (See *figure*.)

The explanation of this fact lies in the origin of the superego. It is acquired by the individual not solely through the simple process of learning, but also through the operation of one of the defense mechanisms of the ego we mentioned before. The child takes over from his parents (and from other adults who are important to him) certain prohibitions, attitudes and values, by identifying himself with his parents. This is a continuous process throughout his development, but those which are most decisive for his later development are the prohibitions and attitudes of his parents, appropriated as his own during a critical period of internal conflict, between the ages of three and six.

THE OEDIPUS CONFLICT

Even though this period lies so far back in our early history that it seems hard to believe it could have such deep significance for our later life, actually it is the culmination of still earlier events in our life of no less importance—though perhaps not quite so spectacular in their outward appearance. . . .

The fact that we remember little about this time is no argument against its significance. We do not veil what is not there but what we do not want to be seen. The veil of "infantile amnesia" shrouds painful experiences with the bliss of forgetfulness. And as to the import of these early happenings in later life, we need not be troubled to find true for the soul what is true for the body: prick a man's little finger and it will heal in a day; prick a nascent embryo and it will turn into a monster. A wound to a grown man's feelings is the shattering blow to a child's. And what is true for pain is true for pleasure. What to the man is mere passing fancy, to the child becomes fateful involvement.

What, then, happens in this period of life? Let us speak first of the boy. For the first time in his life, he forms emotional relationships comparable to those of the adult. Up to this point his mother has been the purveyor to all his needs and protector against all danger and every threat. She does for him all he cannot do by himself—an extension of himself, as it were, not clearly differentiated as yet as a person distinct from himself, due to the symbiosis existing between them. She is as much a part of himself as is his hand, only better: she will provide where his own hand as yet falters or fails. But a hand, too, on whose ministrations he is utterly dependent. No matter how willing, it may not act as his will and command, and what is more, it may rudely interfere with his wishes. Worse still, it can be withdrawn. If it be sudden, it endangers his existence and becomes a threat of annihilation. But if the withdrawal be gradual, each withdrawal is also a promise of return when in need. It is the promise of the future which turns the threat into a source of security. A long series of such experiences brings gradual recognition that it is really another person that provides it. Thus a differentiation takes place between the mother and the self. As long as the mother is considered a part of himself, loving her is not basically different from loving himself. It is only when she, in his eyes, becomes a person in her own right that loving her really means loving another person. This step in seeing the mother as an object outside himself coincides with another development that has been taking place in another sphere, the experience of pleasurable sensations in the body. While as a baby all of the pleasure was centered in the region of the mouth, through intermediary stages it has now come to pass to the genital area. It is from this meeting of the new sensual excitement with the recognition of the mother as a separate entity that his emotional attachment to her takes on a truly sexual character, sexual in the sense that pleasurable genital sensations and genital play are stimulated by the feelings for the mother. This is the first form of an "object-relationship" comparable to those of adults when they fall in love with each other.

As in the adult, a wish for exclusive possession of the beloved one arouses jealousy and antagonism against anyone who seems to make similar demands on her attention. The father is one of them, and not the least important one at that. Hence the boy develops an increasingly hostile attitude to the father whom previously he had only loved and admired and whom he had tried to imitate in every way. These new feelings toward him make the boy deeply divided (ambivalent). This in itself is disconcerting enough; but through a misunderstanding, peculiar to his primitive mind, he adds to his discomfort and conflict. He believes that his father harbors exactly the same feelings toward him as he himself has toward his father. In this he follows the primitive law, "an eye for an eye, a tooth for a tooth," believing that his father could not but hate him, since he hates his father. It is on this basis that direct threats or subtle hints about his tendency to manipulate his genitals for the pleasure this affords (infantile masturbation) give rise to apprehension and fear. Children are good observers but bad interpreters. When now the discovery of the anatomical differences of the sexes is made or remembered, and when it is fitted into the new context, the vague anxiety becomes focused on the notion that he may be punished by his father by being deprived of his genitals, the very organs which have taken on heightened importance as a source of new feelings of pleasure ("castration fear"). This makes his fear altogether unbearable. Not realizing on account of his intellectual immaturity that his fears are a fantasy, he arrives at a solution of his conflict and mastery of his fear which has far-reaching consequences. He believes that this threat of his father's is due to his impassioned feelings for his mother and his genital play (masturbation). By taking what he believes to be prohibitions of his father as his own, he begins to act in accordance with them: he abandons the manipulation of his sexual organs and he withdraws the sexual component of his feelings for his mother, reducing them to tender affection. He can now be without fear of retribution on the part of the father and may act without fear of repudiation by the mother. We say the child identifies himself with the father because, in acting as he thinks his father wishes him to, he does so on his own accord, as though the demands of his father were now within himself; in fact, they are: they have been internalized.

It goes without saying that this is a schematized description of what in reality is a highly complex process, with many ramifications and variations. It holds true for the girl as well as the boy, except that the object of her love is the father rather than the mother. There is this difference though: the girl, in the usual case, misinterprets her lack of a penis as a deprivation, for which she holds her mother responsible and, out of resentment, she turns to the father.

The constellation of the conflict we described is reminiscent of the Greek mythological story of King Oedipus, cast in the form of a drama by Sophocles. In it King Oedipus, acting under the spell of preordained fate which he cannot escape, unknowingly kills his father and marries his mother. He is no less free of guilt for his crimes by committing them unwittingly and under compulsion of forces beyond his control than is the youngster who, equally unconscious and beyond his control, is given to impulses and fantasies of the same nature, though on a different plane: his deeds remain in the sphere of feeling and fantasy, since he is but a child.

Though his crime is only imaginary, he emerges from his conflict a different being. Whereas before, he could act in compliance with external demands and, if they were unpleasant, only out of fear of punishment, he is now capable of feelings of guilt and of acting in the absence of external compulsion. The basis is thus established for what we have called the superego. Its origin reveals its essence: it is the "heir" of the parents. It threatens and punishes in the way the parents did, and—so as not to make our description too fragmentary—let us add that it also provides reassuring love and protection the way the parents did. Even the ego ideal is fashioned on the model of the parents. It is they whom the boy emulates as a child and it is the expectations they have of him that he tries to live up to. He wants to be what they are and what they want him to be. He incorporates his image of his parents and their image of himself and makes it part of himself—his ego ideal. He now tries to live up to his ego ideal as he once tried to live up to his parents' ideals and wishes.

PERSONALITY AND DEVELOPMENT

We have looked at a complex set of forces which interact in the personality, in a cross-sectional view, as it were. We have come to realize that the greater part of them is the product of the interaction between two sets of factors. One of these is the original equipment of the individual, his instinctual urges and rudimentary dispositions for adaptation to the environment, the other the influences and demands made upon him by the environment, both physical and social. A concrete and detailed understanding of this interaction and its consequences requires a careful description of the individual's development. . . . The importance of the early history of the human being has always been recognized in the practical tasks of education. It is reported that a Greek philosopher was requested by some parents to assume responsibility for the education of their son. "How old is he?" asked the savant of antiquity. "Three years," answered the parents. "I am sorry I can't accept him," said he, "it is too late."

It is only since the discoveries of Freud that we can fully appreciate the answer of the wise old man—and know the reasons thereof.

Problems

1. How does the unconscious manifest itself?
2. What are the elements in Freud's psychic system and how do they manifest themselves?
3. How does the id differ from the ego, and what are their respective relationships to external reality?
4. Why are the conscious ways the ego copes with the id preferable to unconscious, automatic ways? Why might speed of handling and efficiency of handling be in opposition?
5. Of the defenses used by the ego to protect itself from the id, which is least effective and most prone to lead to neurosis? Why?
6. How amenable to rational modification is the superego? What would the "ideal" superego be?
7. Why are the early years of life so formative?

23 SIGMUND FREUD

Erich Fromm has remarked that *"the most striking and probably the strongest emotional force in Freud was* his passion for truth and his uncompromising faith in reason; *for him reason was the only human capacity which could help to solve the problem of existence or at least, ameliorate the suffering which is inherent in human life"* (40 Fromm). *How paradoxical, at least on the surface, that someone so devoted to reason and truth should develop a theory that has as its cardinal assumption a concept of dynamic psychic determinism which is largely unconscious and irrational. Paradoxical, perhaps; but an examination of Freud's background indicates the many forces that were working upon him to create his intellectual discipline in search of human irrationality.*

Born in Moravia in 1856, Freud lived most of his life in Vienna, the capital of the disintegrating Austro-Hungarian Empire, which was riddled with grandiose lies and pompous affectations. This environment probably contributed to his sense of the hollowness of public opinion, of the indifferent penetration of "common sense"; it must also have contributed to his belief that social conventions were often nothing more than euphemisms papered over a sordid reality.

Four years after receiving his medical degree in 1881, Freud began a collaboration with Josef Breuer (1842–1925), a Viennese physician. Through this collaboration, he became confirmed in his suspicion that behavior was ruled by unconscious forces. As a result of their work with people suffering from hysteria (the term is now obsolete)—a psychosomatic disorder that caused blindness, paralysis, etc.—Breuer and Freud proved that hysteria had no organic cause, for under hypnosis the patient could see and walk. The hidden sexual content unearthed in therapy, however, and the tendency of patients to develop strong feelings for the therapist led Breuer gradually to abandon the psychotherapeutic method. His decision to withdraw was accelerated by the heavy criticism leveled at their book Studies in Hysteria *(1895).*

Freud continued his investigations alone. He published in rather rapid succession three seminal works that transformed man's self-concept: The Interpretation of Dreams *(1900),* The Psychopathology of Everyday Life *(1901), and* Three Contributions to the Theory of Sexuality *(1905). In 1906 he was joined by Jung, Adler, and others. The group was rapidly beset by conflicts, and the story of Freud's friction and eventual rupture with his followers— Alfred Adler, Wilhelm Stekel, Carl Jung, Otto Rank, Sandor Fereszi, and Wilhelm Reich—over various psychotherapeutic techniques reveals the strange tension in Freud between a mind open to modification from within but re-*

sistant to influence from without. In fairness to Freud, whose dogmatism has been exaggerated almost beyond endurance, many of the conflicts centered around the role of sexuality in human behavior. Freud, as a result of heavy opposition and fierce criticism, had invested much of himself in such theories and, in the case of Jung, at least, he saw compromise operating to mitigate an unpalatable truth. In addition, Freud was an extremely courageous man and thoroughly persuaded that time would vindicate him. Thus, in explaining his concept of libido in 1921, he wrote:

> Libido is an expression taken from the theory of the emotions. . . .
> Psychoanalysis, then, gives these love instincts the name of sexual instincts, a potiori [as following] and by reason of their origin. The majority of "educated" people have regarded this nomenclature as an insult, and have taken their revenge by retorting upon psychoanalysis with the reproach of "pan-sexualism." Anyone who considers sex as something mortifying and humiliating to human nature is at liberty to make use of the more genteel expressions "Eros" and "erotic." I might have done so myself from the first and thus have spared myself much opposition. But I did not want to, for I like to avoid concessions to faintheartedness. One can never tell where that road may lead one; one gives way first in words, and then little by little in substance too. I cannot see any merit in being ashamed of sex; the Greek word "Eros," which is to soften the affront, is in the end nothing more than a translation of our German word Liebe [love]; and finally, he who knows how to wait need make no concessions (41 Freud).

The evolution of Freud's psychoanalytic theories: his psychic topography (conscious, unconscious, preconscious), his structural hypothesis (id, ego, superego), his theories of libido, of infantile sexuality (oral and anal) leading to mature (phallic) sexuality, the Oedipal complex, bisexuality and ambivalance, repression as the heart of neurosis, sublimation and displacement, Eros and the death instinct as opposing drives—these and other theories have just been suggested and discussed in Hans Herma's clear and simple presentation. Freud's essay from An Outline of Psychoanalysis (1940), continues the presentation of his theories by describing the technique of psychoanalysis. Freud, however, never considered his theories final; the Freudian system is not a closed one, and Freud continued to modify his theories to the last. As he aged, his interests became less clinical and more cultural and anthropological. This shift in orientation is revealed in his later works, three of which, Group Psychology and the Analysis of the Ego (1921) from which "Two Artificial Groups" is taken, The Future of an Illusion (1927), and Civilization and Its Discontents (1930), are included below. Freud, who was notoriously self-demanding and who may have been ironic, dismissed the latter two works as the speculative writings of an old man who wrote because he had nothing better to do. "Libidinal Types" (1931) is a slender summation of some of his discoveries. When Hitler, who considered psychoanalysis a degenerate Jewish cult, seized Austria in 1938, Freud, who was suffering from cancer of the jaw, fled to England, where he died in 1939.

It is impossible to do justice to Freud the man in what must at best be a pastiche of biography, history, and psychoanalytic theory. Philip Rieff, in his preface to Freud: The Mind of the Moralist, *captures something of Freud the man:*

> Freud's greatness of character comes through his letters. . . . Told from the inside, Freud's life takes on depth, even heroic proportion, not because of the external pace of events, which is in fact steady, but, rather, because of the heavy burden of knowingness about life that Freud carried from the beginning, on his back, as it were. Yet he never bent over in defeat; difficult as he found the task, he forced himself to remain emotionally and morally upright to the last, "defiant" of his corrupting knowledge—although as he himself admitted, in a letter splendid with modesty, he did not know quite why he thus maintained his integrity (42 Rieff).

As the quote suggests, even with respect to himself, Freud, like Marx, avoided self-aggrandizing moralisms. Such was the nature of their humility and their humanism.

The Technique of Psychoanalysis

A dream, then, is a psychosis, with all the absurdities, delusions and illusions of a psychosis. No doubt it is a psychosis which has only a short duration, which is harmless and even performs a useful function, which is brought about with the subject's consent and is ended by an act of his will. Nevertheless it *is* a psychosis, and we learn from it that even so deep-going a modification of mental life as this can be undone and can give place to normal functioning. Is it too bold, then, to hope that it must also be possible to submit the dreaded spontaneous illnesses of the mind to our control and bring about their cure?

We already possess much knowledge preliminary to such an undertaking. We have postulated that it is the ego's task to meet the demands of the three forces upon which it is dependent—reality, the id and the superego—and meanwhile to preserve its own organization and maintain its own autonomy. The necessary condition for the pathological states we have mentioned can only be a relative or absolute weakening of the ego which prevents it from performing its tasks. The severest demand upon the ego is probably the keeping down of the instinctual

From Sigmund Freud, *An Outline of Psychoanalysis* (New York: W. W. Norton & Company, Inc., 1949), pp. 61–79.

claims of the id, and for this end the ego is obliged to maintain great expenditures of energy upon anti-cathexes.* But the claims made by the superego, too, may become so powerful and so remoreseless that the ego may be crippled, as it were, for its other tasks. We may suspect that, in the economic conflicts which now arise, the id and the superego often make common cause against the hard-pressed ego, which, in order to retain its normal state, clings on to reality. But if the other two are too strong, they may succeed in loosening the organization of the ego and altering it so that its proper relation to reality is disturbed or even abolished. We have seen it happen in dreams: when the ego is detached from the reality of the external world, then, under the influence of the internal world, it slips down into psychosis.

Our plan of cure is based upon these views. The ego has been weakened by the internal conflict; we must come to its aid. The position is like a civil war which can only be decided by the help of an ally from without. The analytical physician and the weakened ego of the patient, basing themselves upon the real external world, are to combine against the enemies, the instinctual demands of the id, and the moral demands of the superego. We form a pact with each other. The patient's sick ego promises us the most complete candor, promises, that is, to put at our disposal all of the material which his self-perception provides; we, on the other hand, assure him of the strictest discretion and put at his service our experience in interpreting material that has been influenced by the unconscious. Our knowledge shall compensate for his ignorance and shall give his ego once more mastery over the lost provinces of his mental life. This pact constitutes the analytic situation.

No sooner have we taken this step than we meet with a first disappointment, a first warning against complacency. If the patient's ego is to be a useful ally in our common work, it must, however hard it may be pressed by the hostile powers, have retained a certain degree of coherence, a fragment at least of understanding for the demands of reality. But this is not to be expected from the ego of a psychotic; it cannot carry out a pact of this sort, indeed it can scarcely engage in it. It will very soon toss us away and the help we offer it, to join the portions of the external world that no longer mean anything to it. Thus we learn that we must renounce the idea of trying our plan of cure upon psychotics—renounce it forever, perhaps, or only for the moment, until we have discovered some other plan better suited for that purpose.

But there is another class of psychological patients who evidently resemble the psychotics very closely, the immense number of sufferers

* Cathexis is the concentration or fixation of psychic energy upon an idea, person, object, or fantasy, with the consequence that the idea, etc. is charged with emotional significance. Anti-cathexes are, hence, the attachment of energy to an object that is opposite to the original impulse, as when unconscious hate is expressed as conscious love.

from severe neuroses. The causes as well as the pathogenic mechanisms of their illness must be the same or at least very similar. Their ego, however, has proved more resistant and has become less disorganized. Many of them, in spite of their troubles and of their consequent inadequacy, are none the less able to maintain their position in real life. It may be that these neurotics will show themselves ready to accept our help. We will confine our interest to them and see how far and by what means we can "cure" them.

We conclude our pact then with the neurotics: complete candor on one side, strict discretion on the other. This looks as though we were aiming at the post of a secular father confessor. But there is a great difference, for what we want to hear from our patient is not only what he knows and conceals from other people, but what he does not know. With this end in view we give him a more detailed definition of what we mean by candor. We impose upon him the *fundamental rule* of analysis, which is henceforward to govern his behavior to us. He must tell us not only what he can say intentionally and willingly, what will give him relief like a confession, but everything else besides that his self-observation presents him with—everything that comes into his head, even if it is *disagreeable* to say it, even if it seems *unimportant* or positively *meaningless*. If he can succeed after this injunction in putting his self-criticism out of action, he will provide us with a mass of material—thoughts, ideas, recollections—which already lie under the influence of the unconscious, which are often its direct derivatives, and which thus put us in a position to conjecture the nature of his repressed unconscious material and to extend, by the information we give him, his ego's knowledge of his unconscious.

But nothing could be further from the truth than that his ego is content to play the part of obediently and passively bringing us the material we require and of believing and accepting our translation of it. Very different things happen in fact, some of which we might have foreseen but others of which are bound to astonish us. The most remarkable is this. The patient is not satisfied with regarding the analyst in the light of reality as a helper and adviser who, moreover, is remunerated for the trouble he takes and who would himself be content with some such rôle as that of an Alpine guide on a difficult climb; on the contrary, the patient sees in his analyst the return—the reincarnaion—of some important figure out of his childhood or past, and consequently transfers on to him feelings and reactions that undoubtedly applied to this model. It soon becomes evident that this fact of transference is a factor of undreamed-of importance—on the one hand an instrument of irreplaceable value and on the other a source of serious dangers. This transference is *ambivalent:* it comprises positive and affectionate as well as negative and hostile attitudes toward the analyst, who, as a rule, is put in the place of one or other of the patient's parents, his father or his mother. So long as it is positive it serves us admirably. It alters the whole analytic situation and sidetracks the patient's rational aim of becoming well and free from his troubles. Instead of it there emerges the aim of pleasing the analyst, of winning his applause and his love. This becomes the true motive-force for the patient's collaboration; the weak ego becomes strong; under the influence of this aim the patient achieves things that would otherwise be beyond his power, his symptoms disappear and he seems to have recovered—all of this simply out of love for his analyst. The analyst must shamefacedly admit to himself that he set out upon a difficult undertaking without any suspicion of the extraordinary powers that would be at his command.

Moreover, the relation of transference carries with it two further advantages. If the patient puts the analyst in the place of his father (or mother), he is also giving him the power which his superego exercises over his ego, since his parents were, as we know, the origin of his superego. The new superego now has an opportunity for a sort of *after-education* of the neurotic; it can correct blunders for which his parental education was to blame. But at this point a warning must be given against misusing this new influence. However much the analyst may be tempted to act as teacher, model and ideal to other people and to make men in his own image, he should not forget that that is not his task in the analytic relationship, and indeed that he will be disloyal to his task if he allows himself to be led on by his inclinations. He will only be repeating one of the mistakes of the parents, when they crushed their child's independence, and he will only be replacing one kind of dependence by another. In all his attempts at improving and educating the patient the analyst must respect his individuality. The amount of influence which he may legitimately employ will be determined by the degree of inhibition in development present in the patient. Many neurotics have remained so infantile that in analysis too they can only be treated as children.

Another advantage of transference is that in it the patient produces before us with plastic clarity an important part of his life history, of which he would otherwise have probably given us only an unsatisfactory account. It is as though he were acting it in front of us instead of reporting it to us.

And now for the other side of the question. Since transference reproduces the patient's relation with his parents, it takes over the ambivalence of that relation as well. It almost inevitably happens that one day his positive attitude toward the analyst changes over into a negative and hostile one. This too is as a rule a repetition of the past. His obedience to his father (if it is his father that is in question), his wooing his father's favor, have their roots in an erotic wish directed toward him. Sometime or other this demand will press its way up in the transference as well and insist upon satisfaction. But in the analytic situation it must necessarily meet with frustration. Real sexual relations between patients and analysts are impossible, and even subtler methods of satisfaction, such as favors, intimacy, and so on, will be only sparingly granted by the analyst. A humiliation of this kind is taken as the occasion for the change-over; the same thing probably occurred in the patient's childhood.

Therapeutic successes that take place under the sway of the positive transference are under the suspicion of being of a *suggestive* nature. If the negative transference gains the upper hand they are blown away like spray before the wind. We perceive with horror that all our trouble and labor hitherto have been vain. Indeed, even what we had taken for a permanent intellectual gain by the patient, his understanding of psychoanalysis and his reliance upon its efficacy, suddenly vanishes. He behaves like a child who has no power of judgment of his own but blindly believes whoever he loves and no one else. The danger of these states of transference evidently consists in the possibility of the patient misunderstanding their nature and taking them for fresh real experiences instead of reflections of the past. If he (or she) perceives the strong erotic desire that lies concealed behind the positive transference, he believes that he has fallen passionately in love; if the transference changes over, then he feels himself insulted and neglected, he hates the analyst as an enemy and is ready to abandon the analysis. In both of these extreme cases he has forgotten the pact into which he entered at the beginning of the treatment and has become disqualified for continuing the common work. It is the analyst's task to tear the patient away each time from the menacing illusion, to show him again and again that what he takes to be new real life is a reflection of the past. And, to prevent him from falling into a state in which he will be inaccessible to all evidence, the analyst takes care that neither the love nor the hostility reach extreme heights. This is achieved by forewarning the patient in good time of these possibilities and by not overlooking the first signs of their appearance. Careful handling of the transference is as a rule richly rewarded. If we succeed, as we usually can, in persuading the patient of the true nature of the phenomena of transference, we have struck a powerful weapon out of the hand of his resistance and have converted dangers into gains. For the patient never forgets again what he has experienced in the form of transference; it has a greater force of conviction for him than anything that he can acquire in other ways.

It is a most undesirable thing if the patient *acts* outside the transference instead of remembering. The ideal conduct for our purposes would be that he should behave as normally as possible outside the treatment and express his abnormal reactions only in the transference.

The method by which we strengthen the patient's weakened ego has as its starting point an increase in the ego's self-knowledge. No doubt this is not the whole story, but it is a first step. The loss of such knowledge means for the ego a surrender of power and influence; it is the first tangible sign that the ego is being constricted and hampered by the demands of the id and of the superego. Thus the first part of the help we have to offer is intellectual work on our side and encouragement of the patient to collaborate in it. We are aware that this first kind of activity must pave the way to another more difficult problem. We shall not lose sight of the dynamic side of that problem even during our preliminary work. We obtain our material from a variety of sources—from what is provided by the information given by the patient and by his free associations, from what he shows us in his transferences, from what we gather by interpreting his dreams and from what he betrays by slips or *parapraxes*.* All of this material helps us to make constructions in regard to what happened to him but has been forgotten, as well as in regard to what is now happening in him without his understanding it. But we never fail in all this to make a severe distinction between *our* knowledge and *his* knowledge. We avoid telling him at once things that we have often discovered quite early, or we avoid telling him the whole of what we think we have discovered. We consider carefully the moment at which we shall impart the knowledge of our constructions to him; we wait for what seems to be a suitable occasion—a judgment which it is not always easy to make. As a rule we put off telling him of a construction or explanation until he himself has so nearly arrived at it that only a single step remains to be taken, though that step is in fact the decisive synthesis. If we proceeded in another way and overwhelmed him with our interpretations before he was prepared for them, our information would either produce no effect or it would arouse a violent outbreak of *resistance* which would make the further progress of our work more difficult or might even threaten to stop it altogether. But if we have prepared everything properly, it often happens that our patient will immediately confirm our construction and himself recollect the internal or external event which he had forgotten. The more exactly the construction coincides with the details of what has been forgotten the easier will be his assent. As regards this particular matter *our* knowledge will then have become *his* knowledge as well.

With the mention of resistance we have reached the second and more important part of our task. We have already heard that the ego

* A paraprax is a faulty action, a blunder or lapse, as of memory, which reveals unconscious material.

protects itself against the incursion of undesirable elements from the unconscious and repressed id by means of anti-cathexes, which must remain intact if it is to function normally. The more hardly the ego feels itself pressed, the more convulsively it clings (in terror, as it were) to these anti-cathexes, in order to protect what remains of it from further irruptions. But such defensive trends do not by any means harmonize with the aims of our treatment. We desire, on the contrary, that the ego, emboldened by the certainty of our help, shall dare to take the offensive in order to reconquer what has been lost. And it is at this point that we become aware of the strength of these anti-cathexes in the form of *resistances* against our work. The ego shrinks from undertakings that seem dangerous and threaten unpleasure; it must be constantly spurred on and soothed down if it is not to fail us. This resistance, which persists through the whole treatment and is renewed with every fresh piece of work, has been named, though not quite correctly, *repression-resistance*. We shall hear that it is not the only kind of resistance that meets us. It is interesting to notice that in this situation the allegiance of the different parties is in a sense reversed: for the ego is struggling against our appeal, while the unconscious, which is in general our opponent, comes to our help, since it has a natural "upward drive" and desires nothing better than to press forward across its ordained frontiers into the ego and into consciousness. The struggle which develops, if we gain our point and can persuade the ego to overcome its resistances, is carried through under our direction and with our assistance. Its outcome is a matter of indifference: whether it results in the ego accepting, after having made a fresh examination, an instinctual demand which it has hitherto repudiated, or whether it once more rejects it, this time finally. In either case a permanent danger has been disposed of, the compass of the ego has been extended and a wasteful expenditure of energy has been made unnecessary.

The overcoming of resistances is the part of our work which requires the greatest time and the greatest trouble. But it is worth while, since it brings about a favorable modification of the ego which will be maintained whatever the fate of the transference and will persist through the patient's life. And we have at the same time worked in the direction of undoing the modification which had been brought about under the influence of the unconscious; for whenever we have been able to detect its derivatives in the ego, we have drawn attention to their illegitimate origin and have urged the ego to eject them. It will be remembered that one of the essential conditions of our pact of assistance was that modifications of the ego of this kind, due to the intrusion of unconscious elements, should not have gone beyond a certain degree.

The further our work proceeds and the deeper our knowledge of the mental life of neurotics penetrates, the more clearly two new factors force themselves upon our notice which demand the closest attention as sources of resistance. Both of them are completely unknown to the patient, neither of them could be taken into account when our pact was made; nor do they arise from the patient's ego. They can both be included under the one description of "need to be ill" or "need to suffer"; but they are of different origins, though in other respects of a similar nature. The first of these two factors is the sense of guilt or consciousness of guilt, as it is called in disregard of the fact that the patient does not feel it and is not aware of it. It is evidently the portion of the resistance contributed by a superego that has grown peculiarly severe and cruel. The patient must not be healthy, he must remain ill, for he deserves no better. This resistance does not actually interfere with our intellectual work, but it makes it ineffective; indeed, it often allows us to remove one form of neurotic suffering but is ready to replace it at once by another one, or perhaps by an organic illness. The sense of guilt also offers an explanation of the cure or improvement of severe neuroses which we sometimes observe after real accidents: all that matters is that the patient should be wretched—in what way is of no consequence. The uncomplaining resignation with which such people often put up with their hard fate is most remarkable but also most revealing. In dealing with this resistance we are obliged to restrict ourselves to making it conscious and attempting the gradual demolition of the hostile superego.

It is not so easy to demonstrate the existence of yet another form of resistance, our means of combating which are especially inadequate. There are some neurotics in whom, to judge by all their reactions, the instinct of self-preservation has actually been reversed. They seem to have nothing in view but self-injury and self-destruction. It is possible that people who in the end do in fact commit suicide belong to this group. It must be supposed that in such people far-reaching defusions of instinct have taken place, as a result of which there have been set free excessive quantities of the destructive instinct directed inwards. These patients cannot tolerate the possibility of being cured by our treatment and fight against it with all their force. But it must be confessed that these are cases which we have not yet succeeded in explaining completely.

Let us once more glance over the situation which we have reached in our attempt at bringing help to the patient's neurotic ego. That ego is no longer able to fulfill the task set to it by the external world (including human society). It has not access to all of its experiences, a large proportion of its fund of memories have escaped it. Its activity is inhibited by the strict prohibitions of the superego, its energy is consumed in vain attempts at fending off the demands of the id. Beyond this, as a result of the constant inroads of the id, its organization is impaired, it is internally split apart, it is no longer capable of any proper synthesis, it is torn by discordant impulses, unappeased conflicts and unsolved doubts. To begin with, we induce the patient's thus enfeebled ego to take part in the purely intellectual work of interpretation, which aims at provisionally filling the gaps in his mental resources, and to transfer to us the authority of his superego; we stimulate his ego to take up the struggle over each individual demand made by the id and to defeat the resistances which arise in connection with it. At the same time, we restore order in his ego, by detecting the material and impulses which have forced their way in from the unconscious, and expose them to criticism by tracing them back to their origin. We serve the patient in various functions as an authority and a substitute for his parents, as a teacher and educator; and we have done the best for him if, as analysts, we raise the mental processes in his ego to a normal level, transform what had become unconscious and repressed into preconscious material and thus return it once more to the possession of his ego. On the patient's side certain rational factors operate in our favor, such as the need for recovery which arises from his sufferings and the intellectual interest that we may awaken in him in the theories and revelations of psychoanalysis; but of far greater force is the positive transference with which he meets us. On the other side there are fighting against us the negative transference, the ego's repression-resistance (that is, the unpleasure felt by it at undertaking the severe work imposed upon it), the sense of guilt arising from its relation to the superego, and the need to be ill caused by deep-going modifications in its instinctual economy. Whether we regard a case as slight or severe depends upon the share taken by the last two of these factors. Apart from these, there are a few other factors that may be mentioned as having a favorable or unfavorable influence. A particular kind of psychological inertia, a sluggishness of the libido, which is unwilling to abandon its fixations, is by no means welcome to us; the patient's capacity for sublimating his instincts plays an important part and the same is true of his capacity for rising superior to the crude life of the instincts as well as the relative power of his intellectual functions.

We shall not be disappointed, but on the contrary we shall find it entirely intelligible, if we are led to the conclusion that the final outcome of the struggle which we have engaged in depends upon *quantitative* relations, upon the amount of energy which we can mobilize in the patient to our advantage, in comparison with the amount of energy of the forces working against us. Here once more God is on the side of the big battalions. It is true that we do not always succeed in winning, but at least we can usually see why it is that we have not won. Those who have been following our discussion only out of therapeutic interest will perhaps turn away in contempt after this admission. But we are here concerned with therapy only in so far as it works by psychological methods; and for the time being we have no other. The future may teach us how to exercise a direct influence, by means of particular chemical substances, upon the amounts of energy and their distribution in the apparatus of the mind. It may be that there are other undreamed-of possibilities of therapy. But for the moment we have nothing better at our disposal than the technique of psychoanalysis, and for that reason, in spite of its limitations, it is not to be despised.

Problems

1. How does "transference" complicate the psychotherapeutic situation and yet at the same time serve it?
2. Why does the analyst have access to the superego while the patient does not? What is the nature of the power this gives the therapist, and how might he abuse it?
3. How does Freud explain the phenomenon of resistance in therapy? To what extent does such an explanation appear consistent and satisfactory to you?
4. Why does Freud seem so concerned with the preservation of energy? How important to his theory is the implicit assumption that there is a fixed energy pool? In what ways could this theory of sex-economy or conservation of libidinal energy manifest itself?
5. How does Freud explain resistance caused by the "need to suffer"?
6. What is meant by a "neurotic ego"?
7. Why would Freud prefer the word "transference" to "love" when he acknowledges that the patient recovers "out of love for his analyst" (432/10)?
8. To what extent does Freud's theory reveal a value system and disguised moralisms? What are they? To what extent could the theory be described as a rationale for established Judeo-Christian moralisms?

Libidinal Types

Observation teaches us that in individual human beings the general features of humanity are embodied in almost infinite variety. If we follow the promptings of a legitimate desire to distinguish particular types in this multiplicity, we must begin by selecting the characteristics to look for and the points of view to bear in mind in making our differentiation. For this purpose physical qualities will be no less

From Sigmund Freud, *Character and Culture* (New York: Collier Books, 1963), pp. 210–14.

useful than mental; it will be most valuable of all if we can make our classification on the basis of a regularly occurring combination of physical and mental characteristics.

It is doubtful whether we are as yet able to discover types of this order, although we shall certainly be able to do so sometime on a basis of which we are still ignorant. If we confine our efforts to defining certain purely psychological types, the libidinal situation will have the first claim to serve as the basis of our classification. It may fairly be demanded that this classification should not merely be deduced from our knowledge or our conjectures about the libido, but that it should be easily verified in actual experience and should help to clarify the mass of our observations and enable us to grasp their meaning. Let it be admitted at once that there is no need to suppose that, even in the psychical sphere, these libidinal types are the only possible ones; if we take other characteristics as our basis of classification we might be able to distinguish a whole series of other psychological types. But there is one rule which must apply to all such types: they must not coincide with specific clinical pictures. On the contrary, they should embrace all the variations which according to our practical standards fall within the category of the normal. In their extreme developments, however, they may well approximate to clinical pictures and so help to bridge the gulf which is assumed to exist between the normal and the pathological.

Now we can distinguish three main libidinal types, according as the subject's libido is mainly allocated to one or another region of the mental apparatus. To name these types is not very easy; following the lines of our depth-psychology, I should be inclined to call them the *erotic*, the *narcissistic* and the *obsessional* type.

The *erotic* type is easily characterized. Erotics are persons whose main interest—the relatively largest amount of their libido—is focused on love. Loving, but above all being loved, is for them the most important thing in life. They are governed by the dread of loss of love, and this makes them peculiarly dependent on those who may withhold their love from them. Even in its pure form this type is a very common one. Variations occur according as it is blended with another type and as the element of aggression in it is strong or weak. From the social and cultural standpoint this type represents the elementary instinctual claims of the id, to which the other psychical agencies have become docile.

The second type is that which I have termed the *obsessional*—a name which may at first seem rather strange; its distinctive characteristic is the supremacy exercised by the super-ego, which is segregated from the ego with great accompanying tension. Persons of this type are governed by anxiety of conscience instead of by the dread of losing love; they exhibit, we might say, an inner instead of an outer dependence; they develop a high degree of self-reliance, from the social standpoint they are the true upholders of civilization, for the most part in a conservative spirit.

The characteristics of the third type, justly called the *narcissistic*, are in the main negatively described. There is no tension between ego and super-ego—indeed, starting from this type one would hardly have arrived at the notion of a super-ego; there is no preponderance of erotic needs; the main interest is focused on self-preservation; the type is independent and not easily overawed. The ego has a considerable amount of aggression available, one manifestation of this being a proneness to activity; where love is in question, loving is preferred to being loved. People of this type impress others as being "personalities"; it is on them that their fellow-men are specially likely to lean; they readily assume the role of leader, give a fresh stimulus to cultural development or break down existing conditions.

These pure types will hardly escape the suspicion of being deduced from the theory of the libido. But we feel that we are on the firm ground of experience when we turn to the mixed types which are to be found so much more frequently than the unmixed. These new types: the *erotic-obsessional,* the *erotic-narcissistic* and the *narcissistic-obsessional* do really seem to provide a good grouping of the individual psychical structures revealed in analysis. If we study these mixed types we find in them pictures of characters with which we have long been familiar. In the *erotic-obsessional* type the preponderance of the instincts is restricted by the influence of the super-ego: dependence on persons who are *contemporary* objects and, at the same time, on the residues of *former* objects—parents, educators and ideal figures—is carried by this type to the furthest point. The *erotic-narcissistic* type is perhaps the most common of all. It combines contrasting characteristics which are thus able to moderate one another; studying this type in comparison with the other two erotic types, we can see how aggressiveness and activity go with a predominance of narcissism. Finally, the *narcissistic-obsessional* type represents the variation most valuable from the cultural standpoint, for it combines independence of external factors and regard for the requirements of conscience with the capacity for energetic action, and it reinforces the ego against the super-ego.

It might be asked in jest why no mention has been made of another mixed type which is theoretically possible: the *erotic-obsessional-narcissistic*. But the answer to this jest is serious: such a type would no longer be a type at all, but the absolute norm, the ideal harmony. We thereupon realize that the phenomenon of different *types* arises just in so far as one or two of the three main modes of expending the libido in the mental economy have been favoured at the cost of the others.

Another question that may be asked is what is the relation of these libidinal types to pathology, whether some of them have a special disposition to pass over into neurosis and, if so, which types lead to which forms of neurosis. The answer is that the hypothesis of these libidinal types throws no fresh light on the genesis of the neuroses. Experience testifies that persons of all these types can live free from neurosis. The pure types marked by the undisputed predominance of a single psychical agency seem to have a better prospect of manifesting themselves as pure character-formations, while we might expect that the mixed types would provide a more fruitful soil for the conditioning factors of neurosis. But I do not think that we should make up our mind on these points until they have been carefully submitted to appropriate tests.

It seems easy to infer that when persons of the erotic type fall ill they will develop hysteria, just as those of the obsessional type will develop obsessional neurosis; but even this conclusion partakes of the uncertainty to which I have just alluded. People of the narcissistic type, who, being otherwise independent, are exposed to frustration from the external world, are peculiarly disposed to psychosis; and their mental composition also contains some of the essential conditioning factors which make for criminality.

We know that we have not as yet exact certainty about the aetiological conditions of neurosis. The precipitating occasions are frustrations and inner conflicts: conflicts between the three great physical agencies, conflicts arising in the libidinal economy by reason of our bisexual disposition, conflicts between the erotic and the aggressive instinctual components. It is the endeavour of the psychology of the neurosis to discover what imparts a pathogenic character to these processes, which are a part of the normal course of mental life.

Problems

1. What bases does Freud give for laying down his typology? How exclusive and categorical is he in his presentation?
2. What are the dynamics (not the description) of the three types?
3. Amplify at length upon the implications that can be drawn from Freud's remark that "the *erotic–obsessional–narcissistic* . . . would no longer be a type at all, but the absolute norm, the ideal harmony" (440/38-40). What is the relation of these types to neurosis?
4. How would one adapt the concept of original sin to this typology?
5. Which libidinal type would a devout Christian most likely be? Why? Which type would a communist be? Why? Which type do you think Freud was? Why? Which type are you?

Two Artificial Groups: The Church and the Army

We may recall from what we know of the morphology of groups that it is possible to distinguish very different kinds of groups and opposing lines in their development. There are very fleeting groups and extremely lasting ones; homogeneous ones, made up of the same sorts of individuals, and unhomogeneous ones; natural groups, and artificial ones, requiring an external force to keep them together; primitive groups, and highly organized ones with a definite structure. But for reasons which remain to be explained we should like to lay particular stress upon a distinction to which writers on the subject have been inclined to give too little attention; I refer to that between leaderless groups and those with leaders. And, in complete opposition to the usual practice, we shall not choose a relatively simple group formation as our point of departure, but shall begin with highly organized, lasting and artificial groups. The most interesting example of such structures are Churches—communities of believers—and armies.

A Church and an army are artificial groups—that is, a certain external force is employed to prevent them from disintegrating [1] and to check alterations in their structure. As a rule a person is not consulted, or is given no choice, as to whether he wants to enter such a group; any attempt at leaving it is usually met with persecution or with severe punishment, or has quite definite conditions attached to it. It is quite outside our present interest to inquire why these associations need such special safeguards. We are only attracted by one circumstance, namely that certain facts, which are far more concealed in other cases, can be observed very clearly in those highly organized groups which are protected from dissolution in the manner that has been mentioned.

In a Church (and we may with advantage take the Catholic Church as a type) as well as in an army, however different the two may be in other respects, the same illusion * holds good of there being a head—in the Catholic Church Christ, in an army its Commander-in-Chief—

From Sigmund Freud, *Group Psychology and the Analysis of the Ego* (New York: Bantam Books, Inc., 1960), pp. 32–39.
1. [*Footnote added* 1923:] In groups, the attributes "stable" and "artificial" seem to coincide or at least to be intimately connected.
* For a definition of "illusion," see *The Future of an Illusion*, 459/35–460/27.

who loves all the individuals in the group with an equal love. Everything depends upon this illusion; if it were to be dropped, then both Church and army would dissolve, so far as the external force permitted them to. This equal love was expressly enunciated by Christ: "'Inasmuch as ye have done it unto one of the least of these my brethren, ye have done it unto me." He stands to the individual members of the group of believers in the relation of a kind elder brother; he is their substitute father. All the demands that are made upon the individual are derived from this love of Christ's. A democratic strain runs through the Church, for the very reason that before Christ everyone is equal, and that everyone has an equal share in his love. It is not without a deep reason that the similarity between the Christian community and a family is invoked, and that believers call themselves brothers in Christ, that is, brothers through the love which Christ has for them. There is no doubt that the tie which unites each individual with Christ is also the cause of the tie which unites them with one another. The like holds good of an army. The Commander-in-Chief is a father who loves all soldiers equally, and for that reason they are comrades among themselves. The army differs structurally from the Church in being built up of a series of such groups. Every captain is, as it were, the Commander-in-Chief and the father of his company, and so is every non-commissioned officer of his section. It is true that a similar hierarchy has been constructed in the Church, but it does not play the same part in it economically;[2] for more knowledge and care about individuals may be attributed to Christ than to a human Commander-in-Chief.

An objection will justly be raised against this conception of the libidinal structure of an army on the ground that no place has been found in it for such ideas as those of one's country, of national glory, etc., which are of such importance in holding an army together. The answer is that that is a different instance of a group tie, and no longer such a simple one; for the examples of great generals, like Caesar, Wallenstein, or Napoleon, show that such ideas are not indispensable to the existence of an army. We shall presently touch upon the possibility of a leading idea being substituted for a leader and upon the relations between the two. The neglect of this libidinal factor in an army, even when it is not the only factor operative, seems to be not merely a theoretical omission but also a practical danger. Prussian militarism which was just as unpsychological as German science may have had to suffer the consequences of this in the [first] World War. We know that the war neuroses which ravaged the German army have been recognized as being a protest of the individual against the part he was expected to play in the army; and according to the communication of Simmel (1918), the hard treatment of the men by their superiors

2. [I.e. in the quantitative distribution of the psychical forces involved.]

may be considered as foremost among the motive forces of the disease. If the importance of the libido's claims on this score had been better appreciated, the fantastic promises of the American President's Fourteen Points would probably not have been believed so easily, and the splendid instrument would not have broken in the hands of the German leaders.³

It is to be noticed that in these two artificial groups each individual is bound by libidinal ties on the one hand to the leader (Christ, the Commander-in-Chief) and on the other hand to the other members of the group. How these two ties are related to each other, whether they are of the same kind and the same value, and how they are to be described psychologically—these questions must be reserved for subsequent inquiry. But we shall venture even now upon a mild reproach against earlier writers for not having sufficiently appreciated the importance of the leader in the psychology of the group, while our own choice of this as a first subject for investigation has brought us into a more favorable position. It would appear as though we were on the right road toward an explanation of the principal phenomenon of group psychology—the individual's lack of freedom in a group. If each individual is bound in two directions by such an intense emotional tie, we shall find no difficulty in attributing to that circumstance the alteration and limitation which have been observed in his personality.

A hint to the same effect, that the essence of a group lies in the libidinal ties existing in it, is also to be found in the phenomenon of panic, which is best studied in military groups. A panic arises if a group of that kind becomes disintegrated. Its characteristics are that none of the orders given by superiors are any longer listened to, and that each individual is only solicitous on his own account, and without any consideration for the rest. The mutual ties have ceased to exist, and a gigantic and senseless fear is set free. At this point, again, the objection will naturally be made that it is rather the other way round; and that the fear has grown so great as to be able to disregard all ties and all feelings of consideration for others. McDougall * (1920, 24) has even made use of panic (though not of military panic) as a typical instance of that intensification of emotion by contagion ("primary induction") on which he lays so much emphasis. But nevertheless this rational method of explanation is here quite inadequate. The very question that needs explanation is why the fear has become so gigantic. The greatness of the danger cannot be responsible, for the same army

3. [By Freud's wish this paragraph was printed as a footnote in the English translation of 1922. It appears in the text in all the German editions, however, both before and after that date.]
* William McDougall (1871–1938), an American psychologist who pioneered in physiological and social psychology.

which now falls a victim to panic may previously have faced equally great or greater danger with complete success; it is of the very essence of panic that it bears no relation to the danger that threatens, and often breaks out on the most trivial occasions. If an individual in panic fear begins to be solicitous only on his own account, he bears witness in so doing to the fact that the emotional ties, which have hitherto made the danger seem small to him, have ceased to exist. Now that he is by himself in facing the danger, he may surely think it greater. The fact is, therefore, that panic fear presupposes a relaxation in the libidinal structure of the group and reacts to that relaxation in a justifiable manner, and the contrary view—that the libidinal ties of the group are destroyed owing to fear in the face of the danger—can be refuted.

The contention that fear in a group is increased to enormous proportions through induction (contagion) is not in the least contradicted by these remarks. McDougall's view meets the case entirely when the danger is a really great one and when the group has no strong emotional ties—conditions which are fulfilled, for instance, when a fire breaks out in a theatre or a place of amusement. But the truly instructive case and the one which can be best employed for our purposes is that mentioned above, in which a body of troops breaks into a panic although the danger has not increased beyond a degree that is usual and has often been previously faced. It is not to be expected that the usage of the word '"panic" should be clearly and unambiguously determined. Sometimes it is used to describe any collective fear, sometimes even fear in an individual when it exceeds all bounds, and often the name seems to be reserved for cases in which the outbreak of fear is not warranted by the occasion. If we take the word "panic" in the sense of collective fear, we can establish a far-reaching analogy. Fear in an individual is provoked either by the greatness of a danger or by the cessation of emotional ties (libidinal cathexes); the latter is the case of neurotic fear or anxiety.[4] In just the same way panic arises either owing to an increase of the common danger or owing to the disappearance of the emotional ties which hold the group together; and the latter case is analogous to that of neurotic anxiety.[5]

Anyone who, like McDougall (1920), describes a panic as one of the plainest functions of the "group mind," arrives at the paradoxical position that this group mind does away with itself in one of its most striking manifestations. It is impossible to doubt that panic means the disintegration of a group; it involves the cessation of all the feelings

---

4. See Lecture XXV of my *Introductory Lectures* (1916–17). [See also, however, *Inhibitions, Symptoms and Anxiety* (1926).]
5. Compare Béla von Felszeghy's interesting though somewhat overimaginative paper "Panik und Pankomplex" (1920).

of consideration which the members of the group otherwise show one another.

The typical occasion of the outbreak of a panic is very much as it is represented in Nestroy's parody of Hebbel's play about Judith and Holofernes.* A soldier cries out: "The general has lost his head!" and thereupon all the Assyrians take to flight. The loss of the leader in some sense or other, the birth of misgivings about him, brings on the outbreak of panic, though the danger remains the same; the mutual ties between the members of the group disappear, as a rule, at the same time as the tie with their leader. The group vanishes in dust, like a Prince Rupert's drop when its tail is broken off.

The dissolution of a religious group is not so easy to observe. A short time ago there came into my hands an English novel of Catholic origin, recommended by the Bishop of London, with the title *When It was Dark*.[6] It gave a clever and, as it seems to me, a convincing picture of such a possibility and its consequences. The novel, which is supposed to relate to the present day, tells how a conspiracy of enemies of the person of Christ and of the Christian faith succeed in arranging for a sepulchre to be discovered in Jerusalem. In this sepulchre is an inscription, in which Joseph of Arimathaea confesses that for reasons of piety he secretly removed the body of Christ from its grave on the third day after its entombment and buried it in this spot. The resurrection of Christ and his divine nature are by this means disproved, and the result of this archaeological discovery is a convulsion in European civilization and an extraordinary increase in all crimes and acts of violence, which only ceases when the forgers' plot has been revealed.

The phenomenon which accompanies the dissolution that is here supposed to overtake a religious group is not fear, for which the occasion is wanting. Instead of it ruthless and hostile impulses toward other people make their appearance, which, owing to the equal love of Christ, they had previously been unable to do.[7] But even during the kingdom of Christ those people who do not belong to the community of believers, who do not love him, and whom he does not love, stand outside this tie. Therefore a religion, even if it calls itself the religion of love, must be hard and unloving to those who do not belong to it. Fundamentally indeed every religion is in this same way a religion of love for all those whom it embraces; while cruelty and intolerance

---

* *Judith* is a book of the Apocrypha which tells the story of how Judith, a Jewish widow of great beauty, enters the enemy camp of Holofernes, gains his favor, and beheads him in his bed.

6. [A book by "Guy Thorne" (pseudonym of C. Ranger Gull) which enjoyed extremely large sales at the time of its publication in 1903.]

7. Compare the explanation of similar phenomena after the abolition of the paternal authority of the sovereign given in Federn's *Die vaterlose Gesellschaft* (1919).

toward those who do not belong to it are natural to every religion. However difficult we may find it personally, we ought not to reproach believers too severely on this account; people who are unbelieving or indifferent are much better off psychologically in this matter [of cruelty and intolerance]. If today that intolerance no longer shows itself so violent and cruel as in former centuries, we can scarcely conclude that there has been a softening in human manners. The cause is rather to be found in the undeniable weakening of religious feelings and the libidinal ties which depend upon them. If another group tie takes the place of the religious one—and the socialistic tie seems to be succeeding in doing so—then there will be the same intolerance toward outsiders as in the age of the Wars of Religion; and if differences between scientific opinions could ever attain a similar significance for groups, the same result would again be repeated with this new motivation.

Problems

1. Which of the distinctions among groups is, for Freud, the most significant?
2. What does Freud mean by an "artificial group"? How does such a group manifest authoritarian behavior with respect to membership? Why do you think such groups respond as they do?
3. What is the illusion that holds the group together?
4. Why is the leader important in uniting the group?
5. How does Freud's libidinal theory explain internal harmony and external aggression?
6. What phenomena occur upon the dissolution of a group?
7. Why is Freud's theory anti-utopian? What objections would a Christian have to it? What objections would a communist have?

from The Future of an Illusion

I

When one has lived for quite a long time in a particular civilization and has often tried to discover what its origins were and along what path it has developed, one sometimes also feels tempted to take a glance in the other direction and to ask what further fate lies before it and what transformations it is destined to undergo. But one soon finds that the value of such an enquiry is diminished from

From Sigmund Freud, *The Future of an Illusion* (Garden City: Doubleday & Company, Inc., 1964), pp. 5-33.

the outset by several factors. Above all, because there are only a few people who can survey human activity in its full compass. Most people have been obliged to restrict themselves to a single, or a few, fields of it. But the less a man knows about the past and the present the more insecure must prove to be his judgement of the future. And there is the further difficulty that precisely in a judgement of this kind the subjective expectations of the individual play a part which it is difficult to assess; and these turn out to be dependent on purely personal factors in his own experience, on the greater or lesser optimism of his attitude to life, as it has been dictated for him by his temperament or by his success or failure. Finally, the curious fact makes itself felt that in general people experience their present naïvely, as it were, without being able to form an estimate of its contents; they have first to put themselves at a distance from it—the present, that is to say, must have become the past—before it can yield points of vantage from which to judge the future.

Thus anyone who gives way to the temptation to deliver an opinion on the probable future of our civilization will do well to remind himself of the difficulties I have just pointed out, as well as of the uncertainty that attaches quite generally to any prophecy. It follows from this, so far as I am concerned, that I shall make a hasty retreat before a task that is too great, and shall promptly seek out the small tract of territory which has claimed my attention hitherto, as soon as I have determined its position in the general scheme of things.

Human civilization, by which I mean all those respects in which human life has raised itself above its animal status and differs from the life of beasts—and I scorn to distinguish between culture and civilization—, presents, as we know, two aspects to the observer. It includes on the one hand all the knowledge and capacity that men have acquired in order to control the forces of nature and extract its wealth for the satisfaction of human needs, and, on the other hand, all the regulations necessary in order to adjust the relations of men to one another and especially the distribution of the available wealth. The two trends of civilization are not independent of each other: firstly, because the mutual relations of men are profoundly influenced by the amount of instinctual satisfaction which the existing wealth makes possible; secondly, because an individual man can himself come to function as wealth in relation to another one, in so far as the other person makes use of his capacity for work, or chooses him as a sexual object; and thirdly, moreover, because every individual is virtually an enemy of civilization, though civilization is supposed to be an object of universal human interest.[1] It is remarkable that, little as men are able to exist

---

1. [The hostility of human individuals to civilization plays a large part in the earlier chapters of this work. Freud returned to the subject and discussed it still more fully two years later in his *Civilization and its Discontents* (1930a).]

in isolation, they should nevertheless feel as a heavy burden the sacrifices which civilization expects of them in order to make a communal life possible. Thus civilization has to be defended against the individual, and its regulations, institutions and commands are directed to that task. They aim not only at effecting a certain distribution of wealth but at maintaining that distribution; indeed, they have to protect everything that contributes to the conquest of nature and the production of wealth against men's hostile impulses. Human creations are easily destroyed, and science and technology, which have built them up, can also be used for their annihilation.

One thus gets an impression that civilization is something which was imposed on a resisting majority by a minority which understood how to obtain possession of the means to power and coercion. It is, of course, natural to assume that these difficulties are not inherent in the nature of civilization itself but are determined by the imperfections of the cultural forms which have so far been developed. And in fact it is not difficult to indicate those defects. While mankind has made continual advances in its control over nature and may expect to make still greater ones, it is not possible to establish with certainty that a similar advance has been made in the management of human affairs; and probably at all periods, just as now once again, many people have asked themselves whether what little civilization has thus acquired is indeed worth defending at all. One would think that a re-ordering of human relations should be possible, which would remove the sources of dissatisfaction with civilization by renouncing coercion and the suppression of the instincts, so that, undisturbed by internal discord, men might devote themselves to the acquisition of wealth and its enjoyment. That would be the golden age, but it is questionable if such a state of affairs can be realized. It seems rather that every civilization must be built up on coercion and renunciation of instinct; it does not even seem certain that if coercion were to cease the majority of human beings would be prepared to undertake to perform the work necessary for acquiring new wealth. One has, I think, to reckon with the fact that there are present in all men destructive, and therefore anti-social and anti-cultural, trends and that in a great number of people these are strong enough to determine their behaviour in human society.

This psychological fact has a decisive importance for our judgement of human civilization. Whereas we might at first think that its essence lies in controlling nature for the purpose of acquiring wealth and that the dangers which threaten it could be eliminated through a suitable distribution of that wealth among men, it now seems that the emphasis has moved over from the material to the mental. The decisive question is whether and to what extent it is possible to lessen the burden of the instinctual sacrifices imposed on men, to reconcile men to those which must necessarily remain and to provide a compensation for them. It is just as impossible to do without control of the mass [2] by a minority as it is to dispense with coercion in the work of civilization. For masses are lazy and unintelligent; they have no love for instinctual renunciation, and they are not to be convinced by argument of its inevitability; and the individuals composing them support one another in giving free rein to their indiscipline. It is only through the influence of individuals who can set an example and whom masses recognize as their leaders that they can be induced to perform the work and undergo the renunciations on which the existence of civilization depends. All is well if these leaders are persons who possess superior insight into the necessities of life and who have risen to the height of mastering their own instinctual wishes. But there is a danger that in order not to lose their influence they may give way to the mass more than it gives way to them, and it therefore seems necessary that they shall be independent of the mass by having means to power at their disposal. To put it briefly, there are two widespread human characteristics which are responsible for the fact that the regulations of civilization can only be maintained by a certain degree of coercion—namely, that men are not spontaneously fond of work and that arguments are of no avail against their passions.

I know the objections which will be raised against these assertions. It will be said that the characteristic of human masses depicted here, which is supposed to prove that coercion cannot be dispensed with in the work of civilization, is itself only the result of defects in the cultural regulations, owing to which men have become embittered, revengeful and inaccessible. New generations, who have been brought up in kindness and taught to have a high opinion of reason, and who have experienced the benefits of civilization at an early age, will have a different attitude to it. They will feel it as a possession of their very own and will be ready for its sake to make the sacrifices as regards work and instinctual satisfaction that are necessary for its preservation. They will be able to do without coercion and will differ little from their leaders. If no culture has so far produced human masses of such a quality, it is because no culture has yet devised regulations which will influence men in this way, and in particular from childhood onwards.

It may be doubted whether it is possible at all, or at any rate as yet, at the present stage of our control over nature, to set up cultural regulations of this kind. It may be asked where the number of superior, unswerving and disinterested leaders are to come from who are to act as educators of the future generations, and it may be alarming to think of the enormous amount of coercion that will inevitably be

2. ['*Masse.*' The German word has a very wide meaning. It is translated 'group' for special reasons in Freud's *Group Psychology* (1921c). See *Standard Ed.*, 18, 69n. Here 'mass' seems more appropriate.]

required before these intentions can be carried out. The grandeur of the plan and its importance for the future of human civilization cannot be disputed. It is securely based on the psychological discovery that man is equipped with the most varied instinctual dispositions, whose ultimate course is determined by the experiences of early childhood. But for the same reason the limitations of man's capacity for education set bounds to the effectiveness of such a transformation in his culture. One may question whether, and in what degree, it would be possible for a different cultural environment to do away with the two characteristics of human masses which make the guidance of human affairs so difficult. The experiment has not yet been made. Probably a certain percentage of mankind (owing to a pathological disposition or an excess of instinctual strength) will always remain asocial; but if it were feasible merely to reduce the majority that is hostile towards civilization to-day into a minority, a great deal would have been accomplished—perhaps all that *can* be accomplished.

I should not like to give the impression that I have strayed a long way from the line laid down for my enquiry [see opening paragraphs]. Let me therefore give an express assurance that I have not the least intention of making judgements on the great experiment in civilization that is now in progress in the vast country that stretches between Europe and Asia.[3] I have neither the special knowledge nor the capacity to decide on its practicability, to test the expediency of the methods employed or to measure the width of the inevitable gap between intention and execution. What is in preparation there is unfinished and therefore eludes an investigation for which our own long-consolidated civilization affords us material.

II

We have slipped unawares out of the economic field into the field of psychology. At first we were tempted to look for the assets of civilization in the available wealth and in the regulations for its distribution. But with the recognition that every civilization rests on a compulsion to work and a renunciation of instinct and therefore inevitably provokes opposition from those affected by these demands, it has become clear that civilization cannot consist principally or solely in wealth itself and the means of acquiring it and the arrangements for its distribution; for these things are threatened by the rebelliousness and destructive mania of the participants in civilization. Alongside of wealth

3. [See, however, some remarks in Chapter V of *Civilization and Its Discontents* (1930*a*), and at two points in *Why War?* (1933*b*) and a long discussion in the last of the *New Introductory Lectures* (1933*a*).]

we now come upon the means by which civilization can be defended—measures of coercion and other measures that are intended to reconcile men to it and to recompense them for their sacrifices. These latter may be described as the mental assets of civilization.

For the sake of a uniform terminology we will describe the fact that an instinct cannot be satisfied as a 'frustration', the regulation by which this frustration is established as a 'prohibition' and the condition which is produced by the prohibition as a 'privation'. The first step is to distinguish between privations which affect everyone and privations which do not affect everyone but only groups, classes or even single individuals. The former are the earliest; with the prohibitions that established them, civilization—who knows how many thousands of years ago?—began to detach man from his primordial animal condition. We have found to our surprise that these privations are still operative and still form the kernel of hostility to civilization. The instinctual wishes that suffer under them are born afresh with every child; there is a class of people, the neurotics, who already react to these frustrations with asocial behaviour. Among these instinctual wishes are those of incest, cannibalism and lust for killing. It sounds strange to place alongside one another wishes which everyone seems united in repudiating and others about which there is so much lively dispute in our civilization as to whether they shall be permitted or frustrated; but psychologically it is justifiable to do so. Nor is the attitude of civilization to these oldest instinctual wishes by any means uniform. Cannibalism alone seems to be universally proscribed and—to the non-psycho-analytic view—to have been completely surmounted. The strength of the incestuous wishes can still be detected behind the prohibition against them; and under certain conditions killing is still practised, and indeed commanded, by our civilization. It is possible that cultural developments lie ahead of us in which the satisfaction of yet other wishes, which are entirely permissible to-day, will appear just as unacceptable as cannibalism does now.

These earliest instinctual renunciations already involve a psychological factor which remains important for all further instinctual renunciations as well. It is not true that the human mind has undergone no development since the earliest times and that, in contrast to the advances of science and technology, it is the same to-day as it was at the beginning of history. We can point out one of these mental advances at once. It is in keeping with the course of human development that external coercion gradually becomes internalized; for a special mental agency, man's super-ego, takes it over and includes it among its commandments.[4] Every child presents this process of transformation to us; only by that means does it become a moral and social being. Such a strengthening of the super-ego is a most precious cultural asset in the

4. [See Chapter III of *The Ego and the Id* (1923b), *Standard Ed.*, 19, 28 ff.]

psychological field. Those in whom it has taken place are turned from being opponents of civilization into being its vehicles. The greater their number is in a cultural unit the more secure is its culture and the more it can dispense with external measures of coercion. Now the degree of this internalization differs greatly between the various instinctual prohibitions. As regards the earliest cultural demands, which I have mentioned, the internalization seems to have been very extensively achieved, if we leave out of account the unwelcome exception of the neurotics. But the case is altered when we turn to the other instinctual claims. Here we observe with surprise and concern that a majority of people obey the cultural prohibitions on these points only under the pressure of external coercion—that is, only where that coercion can make itself effective and so long as it is to be feared. This is also true of what are known as the *moral* demands of civilization, which likewise apply to everyone. Most of one's experiences of man's moral untrustworthiness fall into this category. There are countless civilized people who would shrink from murder or incest but who do not deny themselves the satisfaction of their avarice, their aggressive urges or their sexual lusts, and who do not hesitate to injure other people by lies, fraud and calumny, so long as they can remain unpunished for it; and this, no doubt, has always been so through many ages of civilization.

If we turn to those restrictions that apply only to certain classes of society, we meet with a state of things which is flagrant and which has always been recognized. It is to be expected that these underprivileged classes will envy the favoured ones their privileges and will do all they can to free themselves from their own surplus of privation. Where this is not possible, a permanent measure of discontent will persist within the culture concerned and this can lead to dangerous revolts. If, however, a culture has not got beyond a point at which the satisfaction of one portion of its participants depends upon the suppression of another, and perhaps larger, portion—and this is the case in all present-day cultures—it is understandable that the suppressed people should develop an intense hostility towards a culture whose existence they make possible by their work, but in whose wealth they have too small a share. In such conditions an internalization of the cultural prohibitions among the suppressed people is not to be expected. On the contrary, they are not prepared to acknowledge the prohibitions, they are intent on destroying the culture itself, and possibly even on doing away with the postulates on which it is based. The hostility of these classes to civilization is so obvious that it has caused the more latent hostility of the social strata that are better provided for to be overlooked. It goes without saying that a civilization which leaves so large a number of its participants unsatisfied and drives them into revolt neither has nor deserves the prospect of a lasting existence.

The extent to which a civilization's precepts have been internalized—to express it popularly and unpsychologically: the moral level of its participants—is not the only form of mental wealth that comes into consideration in estimating a civilization's value. There are in addition its assets in the shape of ideals and artistic creations—that is, the satisfactions that can be derived from those sources.

People will be only too readily inclined to include among the psychical assets of a culture its ideals—its estimates of what achievements are the highest and the most to be striven after. It will seem at first as though these ideals would determine the achievements of the cultural unit; but the actual course of events would appear to be that the ideals are based on the first achievements which have been made possible by a combination of the culture's internal gifts and external circumstances, and that these first achievements are then held on to by the ideal as something to be carried further. The satisfaction which the ideal offers to the participants in the culture is thus of a narcissistic nature; it rests on their pride in what has already been successfully achieved. To make this satisfaction complete calls for a comparison with other cultures which have aimed at different achievements and have developed different ideals. On the strength of these differences every culture claims the right to look down on the rest. In this way cultural ideals become a source of discord and enmity between different cultural units, as can be seen most clearly in the case of nations.

The narcissistic satisfaction provided by the cultural ideal is also among the forces which are successful in combating the hostility to culture within the cultural unit. This satisfaction can be shared in not only by the favoured classes, which enjoy the benefits of the culture, but also by the suppressed ones, since the right to despise the people outside it compensates them for the wrongs they suffer within their own unit. No doubt one is a wretched plebeian, harassed by debts and military service; but, to make up for it, one is a Roman citizen, one has one's share in the task of ruling other nations and dictating their laws. This identification of the suppressed classes with the class who rules and exploits them is, however, only part of a larger whole. For, on the other hand, the suppressed classes can be emotionally attached to their masters; in spite of their hostility to them they may see in them their ideals; unless such relations of a fundamentally satisfying kind subsisted, it would be impossible to understand how a number of civilizations have survived so long in spite of the justifiable hostility of large human masses.

A different kind of satisfaction is afforded by art to the participants in a cultural unit, though as a rule it remains inaccessible to the masses, who are engaged in exhausting work and have not enjoyed any personal education. As we discovered long since, art offers substitutive satisfactions for the oldest and still most deeply felt cultural renunciations, and for that reason it serves as nothing else does to reconcile a man to the sacrifices he has made on behalf of civilization. On the other hand, the creations of art heighten his feelings of identification, of which every cultural unit stands in so much need, by providing an occasion for sharing highly valued emotional experiences. And when those creations picture the achievements of his particular culture and bring to his mind its ideals in an impressive manner, they also minister to his narcissistic satisfaction.

No mention has yet been made of what is perhaps the most important item in the psychical inventory of a civilization. This consists in its religious ideas in the widest sense—in other words (which will be justified later) in its illusions.

V

Let us now take up the thread of our enquiry. What, then, is the psychological significance of religious ideas and under what heading are we to classify them? The question is not at all easy to answer immediately. After rejecting a number of formulations, we will take our stand on the following one. Religious ideas are teachings and assertions about facts and conditions of external (or internal) reality which tell one something one has not discovered for oneself and which lay claim to one's belief. Since they give us information about what is most important and interesting to us in life, they are particularly highly prized. Anyone who knows nothing of them is very ignorant; and anyone who has added them to his knowledge may consider himself much the richer.

There are, of course, many such teachings about the most various things in the world. Every school lesson is full of them. Let us take geography. We are told that the town of Constance lies on the Bodensee.[5] A student song adds: 'if you don't believe it, go and see.' I happen to have been there and can confirm the fact that that lovely town lies on the shore of a wide stretch of water which all those who live round it call the Bodensee; and I am now completely convinced of the correctness of this geographical assertion. In this connection I am reminded of another, very remarkable, experience. I was already a man of mature years when I stood for the first time on the hill of the Acropolis in Athens, between the temple ruins, looking out over the blue sea. A feeling of astonishment mingled with my joy. It seemed to say: 'So it really *is* true, just as we learnt at school!' How shallow and weak must have been the belief I then acquired in the real truth of

---

5. [The German name for what we call the Lake of Constance.]

what I heard, if I could be so astonished now! But I will not lay too much stress on the significance of this experience; for my astonishment could have had another explanation, which did not occur to me at the time and which is of a wholly subjective nature and has to do with the special character of the place.[6]

All teachings like these, then, demand belief in their contents, but not without producing grounds for their claim. They are put forward as the epitomized result of a longer process of thought based on observation and certainly also on inferences. If anyone wants to go through this process himself instead of accepting its result, they show him how to set about it. Moreover, we are always in addition given the source of the knowledge conveyed by them, where that source is not self-evident, as it is in the case of geographical assertions. For instance, the earth is shaped like a sphere; the proofs adduced for this are Foucault's pendulum experiment,[7] the behaviour of the horizon and the possibility of circumnavigating the earth. Since it is impracticable, as everyone concerned realizes, to send every schoolchild on a voyage round the world, we are satisfied with letting what is taught at school be taken on trust; but we know that the path to acquiring a personal conviction remains open.

Let us try to apply the same test to the teachings of religion. When we ask on what their claim to be believed is founded, we are met with three answers, which harmonize remarkably badly with one another. Firstly, these teachings deserve to be believed because they were already believed by our primal ancestors; secondly, we possess proofs which have been handed down to us from those same primaeval times; and thirdly, it is forbidden to raise the question of their authentication at all. In former days anything so presumptuous was visited with the severest penalties, and even to-day society looks askance at any attempt to raise the question again.

This third point is bound to rouse our strongest suspicions. After all, a prohibition like this can only be for one reason—that society is very well aware of the insecurity of the claim it makes on behalf of its religious doctrines. Otherwise it would certainly be very ready to put the necessary data at the disposal of anyone who wanted to arrive at conviction. This being so, it is with a feeling of mistrust which it is hard to allay that we pass on to an examination of the other two grounds of proof. We ought to believe because our forefathers believed. But these ancestors of ours were far more ignorant than we are. They believed in things we could not possibly accept to-day; and the pos-

6. [This had happened in 1904, when Freud was almost fifty. He wrote a full account of the episode in an open letter to Romain Rolland some ten years after the present work (1936a).]
7. [J. B. L. Foucault (1819–68) demonstrated the diurnal motion of the earth by means of a pendulum in 1851.]

sibility occurs to us that the doctrines of religion may belong to that class too. The proofs they have left us are set down in writings which themselves bear every mark of untrustworthiness. They are full of contradictions, revisions and falsifications, and where they speak of factual confirmations they are themselves unconfirmed. It does not help much to have it asserted that their wording, or even their content only, originates from divine revelation; for this assertion is itself one of the doctrines whose authenticity is under examination, and no proposition can be a proof of itself.

Thus we arrive at the singular conclusion that of all the information provided by our cultural assets it is precisely the elements which might be of the greatest importance to us and which have the task of solving the riddles of the universe and of reconciling us to the sufferings of life—it is precisely those elements that are the least well authenticated of any. We should not be able to bring ourselves to accept anything of so little concern to us as the fact that whales bear young instead of laying eggs, if it were not capable of better proof than this.

This state of affairs is in itself a very remarkable psychological problem. And let no one suppose that what I have said about the impossibility of proving the truth of religious doctrines contains anything new. It has been felt at all times—undoubtedly, too, by the ancestors who bequeathed us this legacy. Many of them probably nourished the same doubts as ours, but the pressure imposed on them was too strong for them to have dared to utter them. And since then countless people have been tormented by similar doubts, and have striven to suppress them, because they thought it was their duty to believe; many brilliant intellects have broken down over this conflict, and many characters have been impaired by the compromises with which they have tried to find a way out of it.

If all the evidence put forward for the authenticity of religious teachings originates in the past, it is natural to look round and see whether the present, about which it is easier to form judgements, may not also be able to furnish evidence of the sort. If by this means we could succeed in clearing even a single portion of the religious system from doubt, the whole of it would gain enormously in credibility. The proceedings of the spiritualists meet us at this point; they are convinced of the survival of the individual soul and they seek to demonstrate to us beyond doubt the truth of this one religious doctrine. Unfortunately they cannot succeed in refuting the fact that the appearance and utterances of their spirits are merely the products of their own mental activity. They have called up the spirits of the greatest men and of the most eminent thinkers, but all the pronouncements and information which they have received from them have been so foolish and so wretchedly meaningless that one can find nothing credible in them but the capacity of the spirits to adapt themselves to the circle of people who have conjured them up.

I must now mention two attempts that have been made—both of which convey the impression of being desperate efforts—to evade the problem. One, of a violent nature, is ancient; the other is subtle and modern. The first is the *'Credo quia absurdum'* of the early Father of the Church.[8] It maintains that religious doctrines are outside the jurisdiction of reason—are above reason. Their truth must be felt inwardly, and they need not be comprehended. But this *Credo* is only of interest as a self-confession. As an authoritative statement it has no binding force. Am I to be obliged to believe *every* absurdity? And if not, why this one in particular? There is no appeal to a court above that of reason. If the truth of religious doctrines is dependent on an inner experience which bears witness to that truth, what is one to do about the many people who do not have this rare experience? One may require every man to use the gift of reason which he possesses, but one cannot erect, on the basis of a motive that exists only for a very few, an obligation that shall apply to everyone. If one man has gained an unshakable conviction of the true reality of religious doctrines from a state of ecstasy which has deeply moved him, of what significance is that to others?

The second attempt is the one made by the philosophy of 'As if'. This asserts that our thought-activity includes a great number of hypotheses whose groundlessness and even absurdity we fully realize. They are called 'fictions', but for a variety of practical reasons we have to behave 'as if' we believed in these fictions. This is the case with religious doctrines because of their incomparable importance for the maintenance of human society.[9] This line of argument is not far removed from the *'Credo quia absurdum'*. But I think the demand made by the 'As if' argument is one that only a philosopher could put forward. A man whose thinking is not influenced by the artifices of philosophy will never be able to accept it; in such a man's view, the admission that something is absurd or contrary to reason leaves no more to be said. It cannot be expected of him that precisely in treating his most important interests he shall forgo the guarantees he requires for all his ordinary activities. I am reminded of one of my children who was distinguished at an early age by a peculiarly marked matter-of-factness.

---

8. ['I believe because it is absurd.' This is attributed to Tertullian.]
9. I hope I am not doing him an injustice if I take the philosopher of 'As if' as the representative of a view which is not foreign to other thinkers: 'We include as fictions not merely indifferent theoretical operations but ideational constructs emanating from the noblest minds, to which the noblest part of mankind cling and of which they will not allow themselves to be deprived. Nor is it our object so to deprive them—for as *practical fictions* we leave them all intact; they perish only as *theoretical truths*.' (Hans Vaihinger, 1922, 68 [C. K. Ogden's translation, 1924, 48–49].)

When the children were being told a fairy story and were listening to it with rapt attention, he would come up and ask: 'Is that a true story?' When he was told it was not, he would turn away with a look of disdain. We may expect that people will soon behave in the same way towards the fairy tales of religion, in spite of the advocacy of 'As if'.

But at present they still behave quite differently; and in past times religious ideas, in spite of their incontrovertible lack of authentication, have exercised the strongest possible influence on mankind. This is a fresh psychological problem. We must ask where the inner force of those doctrines lies and to what it is that they owe their efficacy, independent as it is of recognition by reason.

VI

I think we have prepared the way sufficiently for an answer to both these questions. It will be found if we turn our attention to the psychical origin of religious ideas. These, which are given out as teachings, are not precipitates of experience or end-results of thinking: they are illusions, fulfilments of the oldest, strongest and most urgent wishes of mankind. The secret of their strength lies in the strength of those wishes. As we already know, the terrifying impression of helplessness in childhood aroused the need for protection—for protection through love —which was provided by the father; and the recognition that this helplessness lasts throughout life made it necessary to cling to the existence of a father, but this time a more powerful one. Thus the benevolent rule of a divine Providence allays our fear of the dangers of life; the establishment of a moral world-order ensures the fulfilment of the demands of justice, which have so often remained unfulfilled in human civilization; and the prolongation of earthly existence in a future life provides the local and temporal framework in which these wish-fulfilments shall take place. Answers to the riddles that tempt the curiosity of man, such as how the universe began or what the relation is between body and mind, are developed in conformity with the underlying assumptions of this system. It is an enormous relief to the individual psyche if the conflicts of its childhood arising from the father-complex—conflicts which it has never wholly overcome—are removed from it and brought to a solution which is universally accepted.

When I say that these things are all illusions, I must define the meaning of the word. An illusion is not the same thing as an error; nor is it necessarily an error. Aristotle's belief that vermin are developed out of dung (a belief to which ignorant people still cling) was an error; so was the belief of a former generation of doctors that *tabes dorsalis* * is

---

* A disease of the spinal column, usually caused by syphilis, and resulting in the inability to coordinate one's movements.

the result of sexual excess. It would be incorrect to call these errors illusions. On the other hand, it was an illusion of Columbus's that he had discovered a new sea-route to the Indies. The part played by his wish in this error is very clear. One may describe as an illusion the assertion made by certain nationalists that the Indo-Germanic race is the only one capable of civilization; or the belief, which was only destroyed by psycho-analysis, that children are creatures without sexuality. What is characteristic of illusions is that they are derived from human wishes. In this respect, they come near to psychiatric delusions. But they differ from them, too, apart from the more complicated structure of delusions. In the case of delusions, we emphasize as essential their being in contradiction with reality. Illusions need not necessarily be false—that is to say, unrealizable or in contradiction to reality. For instance, a middle-class girl may have the illusion that a prince will come and marry her. This is possible; and a few such cases have occurred. That the Messiah will come and found a golden age is much less likely. Whether one classifies this belief as an illusion or as something analogous to a delusion will depend on one's personal attitude. Examples of illusions which have proved true are not easy to find, but the illusion of the alchemists that all metals can be turned into gold might be one of them. The wish to have a great deal of gold, as much gold as possible, has, it is true, been a good deal damped by our present-day knowledge of the determinants of wealth, but chemistry no longer regards the transmutation of metals into gold as impossible. Thus we call a belief an illusion when a wish-fulfilment is a prominent factor in its motivation, and in doing so we disregard its relations to reality, just as the illusion itself sets no store by verification.

Having thus taken our bearings, let us return once more to the question of religious doctrines. We can now repeat that all of them are illusions and insusceptible of proof. No one can be compelled to think them true, to believe in them. Some of them are so improbable, so incompatible with everything we have laboriously discovered about the reality of the world, that we may compare them—if we pay proper regard to the psychological differences—to delusions. Of the reality value of most of them we cannot judge; just as they cannot be proved, so they cannot be refuted. We still know too little to make a critical approach to them. The riddles of the universe reveal themselves only slowly to our investigation; there are many questions to which science to-day can give no answer. But scientific work is the only road which can lead us to a knowledge of reality outside ourselves. It is once again merely an illusion to expect anything from intuition and introspection; they can give us nothing but particulars about our own mental life, which are hard to interpret, never any information about the questions which religious doctrine finds it so easy to answer. It would be insolent to let one's own arbitrary will step into the breach and, according to one's personal estimate, declare this or that part of the religious system to be less or more acceptable. Such questions are too momentous for that; they might be called too sacred.

At this point one must expect to meet with an objection. 'Well then, if even obdurate sceptics admit that the assertions of religion cannot be refuted by reason, why should I not believe in them, since they have so much on their side—tradition, the agreement of mankind, and all the consolations they offer?' Why not, indeed? Just as no one can be forced to believe, so no one can be forced to disbelieve. But do not let us be satisfied with deceiving ourselves that arguments like these take us along the road of correct thinking. If ever there was a case of a lame excuse we have it here. Ignorance is ignorance; no right to believe anything can be derived from it. In other matters no sensible person will behave so irresponsibly or rest content with such feeble grounds for his opinions and for the line he takes. It is only in the highest and most sacred things that he allows himself to do so. In reality these are only attempts at pretending to oneself or to other people that one is still firmly attached to religion, when one has long since cut oneself loose from it. Where questions of religion are concerned, people are guilty of every possible sort of dishonesty and intellectual misdemeanour. Philosophers stretch the meaning of words until they retain scarcely anything of their original sense. They give the name of 'God' to some vague abstraction which they have created for themselves; having done so they can pose before all the world as deists, as believers in God, and they can even boast that they have recognized a higher, purer concept of God, notwithstanding that their God is now nothing more than an insubstantial shadow and no longer the mighty personality of religious doctrines. Critics persist in describing as 'deeply religious' anyone who admits to a sense of man's insignificance or impotence in the face of the universe, although what constitutes the essence of the religious attitude is not this feeling but only the next step after it, the reaction to it which seeks a remedy for it. The man who goes no further, but humbly acquiesces in the small part which human beings play in the great world—such a man is, on the contrary, irreligious in the truest sense of the word.

To assess the truth-value of religious doctrines does not lie within the scope of the present enquiry. It is enough for us that we have recognized them as being, in their psychological nature, illusions. But we do not have to conceal the fact that this discovery also strongly influences our attitude to the question which must appear to many to be the most important of all. We know approximately at what periods and by what kind of men religious doctrines were created. If in addition we discover the motives which led to this, our attitude to the problem of religion will undergo a marked displacement. We shall tell ourselves that it would be very nice if there were a God who created the world and was a benevolent Providence, and if there were a moral order in the universe and an after-life; but it is a very striking fact that all this is exactly as we are bound to wish it to be. And it would be more remarkable still if our wretched, ignorant and downtrodden ancestors had succeeded in solving all these difficult riddles of the universe.

Problems

1. Why are analyses of the probable future of a civilization so difficult?
2. What does Freud mean by civilization? Why must it be defended against the individual?
3. How does the cultural ideal cement society together? What compensations does it provide? When does it break down?
4. Why and how does Freud's view of man in civilization place him in conflict with Marxist assumptions?
5. What is Freud's attitude toward the arguments and evidence offered in support of religious ideas?
6. How does Freud define an illusion? In what ways are some of the distinctions he makes in this area useful? What are illusions a reaction to?
7. What is Freud's attitude toward intuition as a source of knowledge? What are the possible consequences for his value system of his attitude?

from Civilization and Its Discontents

II

In my *Future of an Illusion* [1927c] I was concerned much less with the deepest sources of the religious feeling than with what the common man understands by his religion—with the system of doctrines and promises which on the one hand explains to him the riddles of this world with enviable completeness, and, on the other, assures him that a careful Providence will watch over his life and will compensate him in a future existence for any frustrations he suffers here. The common man cannot imagine this Providence otherwise than in the figure

From Sigmund Freud, *Civilization and Its Discontents* (New York: W. W. Norton & Company, Inc., 1962), pp. 21–67.

of an enormously exalted father. Only such a being can understand the needs of the children of men and be softened by their prayers and placated by the signs of their remorse. The whole thing is so patently infantile, so foreign to reality, that to anyone with a friendly attitude to humanity it is painful to think that the great majority of mortals will never be able to rise above this view of life. It is still more humiliating to discover how large a number of people living to-day, who cannot but see that this religion is not tenable, nevertheless try to defend it piece by piece in a series of pitiful rearguard actions. One would like to mix among the ranks of the believers in order to meet these philosophers, who think they can rescue the God of religion by replacing him by an impersonal, shadowy and abstract principle, and to address them with the warning words: 'Thou shalt not take the name of the Lord thy God in vain!' And if some of the great men of the past acted in the same way, no appeal can be made to their example: we know why they were obliged to.

Let us return to the common man and to his religion—the only religion which ought to bear that name. The first thing that we think of is the well-known saying of one of our great poets and thinkers concerning the relation of religion to art and science:

Wer Wissenschaft und Kunst besitzt, hat auch Religion;
Wer jene beide nicht besitzt, der habe Religion![1]

This saying on the one hand draws an antithesis between religion and the two highest achievements of man, and on the other, asserts that, as regards their value in life, those achievements and religion can represent or replace each other. If we also set out to deprive the common man, [who has neither science nor art] of his religion, we shall clearly not have the poet's authority on our side. We will choose a particular path to bring us nearer an appreciation of his words. Life, as we find it, is too hard for us; it brings us too many pains, disappointments and impossible tasks. In order to bear it we cannot dispense with palliative measures. 'We cannot do without auxiliary constructions', as Theodor Fontane tells us.[2] There are perhaps three such measures: powerful deflections, which cause us to make light of our misery; substitutive satisfactions, which diminish it; and intoxicating substances, which make us insensitive to it. Something of the kind is indispensable.[3] Voltaire has

---

1. ['He who possesses science and art also has religion; but he who possesses neither of those two, let him have religion!']—Goethe, *Zahme Xenien* IX (Gedichte aus dem Nachlass).
2. [It has not been possible to trace this quotation.]
3. In *Die Fromme Helene* Wilhelm Busch has said the same thing on a lower plane: 'Wer Sorgen hat, hat auch Likör.' ['He who has cares has brandy too.']

deflections in mind when he ends *Candide* with the advice to cultivate one's garden; and scientific activity is a deflection of this kind, too. The substitutive satisfactions, as offered by art, are illusions in contrast with reality, but they are none the less psychically effective, thanks to the role which phantasy has assumed in mental life. The intoxicating substances influence our body and alter its chemistry. It is no simple matter to see where religion has its place in this series. We must look further afield.

The question of the purpose of human life has been raised countless times; it has never yet received a satisfactory answer and perhaps does not admit of one. Some of those who have asked it have added that if it should turn out that life has *no* purpose, it would lose all value for them. But this threat alters nothing. It looks, on the contrary, as though one had a right to dismiss the question, for it seems to derive from the human presumptuousness, many other manifestations of which are already familiar to us. Nobody talks about the purpose of the life of animals, unless, perhaps, it may be supposed to lie in being of service to man. But this view is not tenable either, for there are many animals of which man can make nothing, except to describe, classify and study them; and innumerable species of animals have escaped even this use, since they existed and became extinct before man set eyes on them. Once again, only religion can answer the question of the purpose of life. One can hardly be wrong in concluding that the idea of life having a purpose stands and falls with the religious system.

We will therefore turn to the less ambitious question of what men themselves show by their behaviour to be the purpose and intention of their lives. What do they demand of life and wish to achieve in it? The answer to this can hardly be in doubt. They strive after happiness; they want to become happy and to remain so. This endeavour has two sides, a positive and a negative aim. It aims, on the one hand, at an absence of pain and unpleasure, and, on the other, at the experiencing of strong feelings of pleasure. In its narrower sense the word 'happiness' only relates to the last. In conformity with this dichotomy in his aims, man's activity develops in two directions, according as it seeks to realize—in the main, or even exclusively—the one or the other of these aims.

As we see, what decides the purpose of life is simply the programme of the pleasure principle. This principle dominates the operation of the mental apparatus from the start. There can be no doubt about its efficacy, and yet its programme is at loggerheads with the whole world, with the macrocosm as much as with the microcosm. There is no possibility at all of its being carried through; all the regulations of the universe run counter to it. One feels inclined to say that the intention that man should be 'happy' is not included in the plan of 'Creation'. What we call happiness in the strictest sense comes from the (preferably sudden) satisfaction of needs which have been dammed up to a high degree, and it is from its nature only possible as an episodic phenomenon. When any situation that is desired by the pleasure principle is prolonged, it only produces a feeling of mild contentment. We are so made that we can derive intense enjoyment only from a contrast and very little from a state of things.[4] Thus our possibilities of happiness are already restricted by our constitution. Unhappiness is much less difficult to experience. We are threatened with suffering from three directions: from our own body, which is doomed to decay and dissolution and which cannot even do without pain and anxiety as warning signals; from the external world, which may rage against us with overwhelming and merciless forces of destruction; and finally from our relations to other men. The suffering which comes from this last source is perhaps more painful to us than any other. We tend to regard it as a kind of gratuitous addition, although it cannot be any less fatefully inevitable than the suffering which comes from elsewhere.

It is no wonder if, under the pressure of these possibilities of suffering, men are accustomed to moderate their claims to happiness—just as the pleasure principle itself, indeed, under the influence of the external world, changed into the more modest reality principle—, if a man thinks himself happy merely to have escaped unhappiness or to have survived his suffering, and if in general the task of avoiding suffering pushes that of obtaining pleasure into the background. Reflection shows that the accomplishment of this task can be attempted along very different paths; and all these paths have been recommended by the various schools of wordly wisdom and put into practice by men. An unrestricted satisfaction of every need presents itself as the most enticing method of conducting one's life, but it means putting enjoyment before caution, and soon brings its own punishment. The other methods, in which avoidance of unpleasure is the main purpose, are differentiated according to the source of unpleasure to which their attention is chiefly turned. Some of these methods are extreme and some moderate; some are one-sided and some attack the problem simultaneously at several points. Against the suffering which may come upon one from human relationships the readiest safeguard is voluntary isolation, keeping oneself aloof from other people. The happiness which can be achieved along

---

4. Goethe, indeed, warns us that 'nothing is harder to bear than a succession of fair days.'
>   [Alles in der Welt lässt sich ertragen,
>   Nur nicht eine Reihe von schönen
>   Tagen.
>   (Weimar, 1810–12.)]

But this may be an exaggeration.

this path is, as we see, the happiness of quietness. Against the dreaded external world one can only defend oneself by some kind of turning away from it, if one intends to solve the task by oneself. There is, indeed, another and better path: that of becoming a member of the human community, and, with the help of a technique guided by science, going over to the attack against nature and subjecting her to the human will. Then one is working with all for the good of all. But the most interesting methods of averting suffering are those which seek to influence our own organism. In the last analysis, all suffering is nothing else than sensation, it only exists in so far as we feel it, and we only feel it in consequence of certain ways in which our organism in regulated.

The crudest, but also the most effective among these methods of influence is the chemical one—intoxication. I do not think that anyone completely understands its mechanism, but it is a fact that there are foreign substances which, when present in the blood or tissues, directly cause us pleasurable sensations; and they also so alter the conditions governing our sensibility that we become incapable of receiving unpleasurable impulses. The two effects not only occur simultaneously, but seem to be intimately bound up with each other. But there must be substances in the chemistry of our own bodies which have similar effects, for we know at least one pathological state, mania, in which a condition similar to intoxication arises without the administration of any intoxicating drug. Besides this, our normal mental life exhibits oscillations between a comparatively easy liberation of pleasure and a comparatively difficult one, parallel with which there goes a diminished or an increased receptivity to unpleasure. It is greatly to be regretted that this toxic side of mental processes has so far escaped scientific examination. The service rendered by intoxicating media in the struggle for happiness and in keeping misery at a distance is so highly prized as a benefit that individuals and peoples alike have given them an established place in the economics of their libido. We owe to such media not merely the immediate yield of pleasure, but also a greatly desired degree of independence from the external world. For one knows that, with the help of this 'drowner of cares' one can at any time withdraw from the pressure of reality and find refuge in a world of one's own with better conditions of sensibility. As is well known, it is precisely this property of intoxicants which also determines their danger and their injuriousness. They are responsible, in certain circumstances, for the useless waste of a large quota of energy which might have been employed for the improvement of the human lot.

The complicated structure of our mental apparatus admits, however, of a whole number of other influences. Just as a satisfaction of instinct spells happiness for us, so severe suffering is caused us if the external world lets us starve, if it refuses to sate our needs. One may therefore hope to be freed from a part of one's sufferings by influencing the instinctual impulses. This type of defence against suffering is no longer brought to bear on the sensory apparatus; it seeks to master the internal sources of our needs. The extreme form of this is brought about by killing off the instincts, as is prescribed by the worldly wisdom of the East and practised by Yoga. If it succeeds, then the subject has, it is true, given up all other activities as well—he has sacrificed his life; and, by another path, he has once more only achieved the happiness of quietness. We follow the same path when our aims are less extreme and we merely attempt to *control* our instinctual life. In that case, the controlling elements are the higher psychical agencies, which have subjected themselves to the reality principle. Here the aim of satisfaction is not by any means relinquished; but a certain amount of protection against suffering is secured, in that non-satisfaction is not so painfully felt in the case of instincts kept in dependence as in the case of uninhibited ones. As against this, there is an undeniable diminution in the potentialities of enjoyment. The feeling of happiness derived from the satisfaction of a wild instinctual impulse untamed by the ego is incomparably more intense than that derived from sating an instinct that has been tamed. The irresistibility of perverse instincts, and perhaps the attraction in general of forbidden things finds an economic explanation here.

Another technique for fending off suffering is the employment of the displacements of libido which our mental apparatus permits of and through which its function gains so much in flexibility. The task here is that of shifting the instinctual aims in such a way that they cannot come up against frustration from the external world. In this, sublimation of the instincts lends its assistance. One gains the most if one can sufficiently heighten the yield of pleasure from the sources of psychical and intellectual work. When that is so, fate can do little against one. A satisfaction of this kind, such as an artist's joy in creating, in giving his phantasies body, or a scientist's in solving problems or discovering truths, has a special quality which we shall certainly one day be able to characterize in metapsychological terms. At present we can only say figuratively that such satisfactions seem 'finer and higher'. But their intensity is mild as compared with that derived from the sating of crude and primary instinctual impulses; it does not convulse our physical being. And the weak point of this method is that it is not applicable generally: it is accessible to only a few people. It presupposes the possession of special dispositions and gifts which are far from being common to any practical degree. And even to the few who do possess them, this method cannot give complete protection from suffering. It creates no impenetrable armour against the arrows of fortune, and it habitually fails when the source of suffering is a person's own body.[5]

While this procedure already clearly shows an intention of making oneself independent of the external world by seeking satisfaction in internal, psychical processes, the next procedure brings out those features yet more strongly. In it, the connection with reality is still further loosened; satisfaction is obtained from illusions, which are recognized as such without the discrepancy between them and reality being allowed to interfere with enjoyment. The region from which these illusions arise is the life of the imagination; at the time when the development of the sense of reality took place, this region was expressly exempted from the demands of reality-testing and was set apart for the purpose of fulfilling wishes which were difficult to carry out. At the head of these satisfactions through phantasy stands the enjoyment of works of art—an enjoyment which, by the agency of the artist, is made accessible even to those who are not themselves creative.[6] People who are receptive to the influence of art cannot set too high a value on it as a source of pleasure and consolation in life. Nevertheless the mild narcosis induced in us by art can do no more than bring about a transient withdrawal from the pressure of vital needs, and it is not strong enough to make us forget real misery.

Another procedure operates more energetically and more thoroughly. It regards reality as the sole enemy and as the source of all suffering, with which it is impossible to live, so that one must break off all relations with it if one is to be in any way happy. The hermit turns his back on the world and will have no truck with it. But one can do more than that; one can try to re-create the world, to build up in its stead another world

---

5. When there is no special disposition in a person which imperatively prescribes what direction his interests in life shall take, the ordinary professional work that is open to everyone can play the part assigned to it by Voltaire's wise advice. It is not possible, within the limits of a short survey, to discuss adequately the significance of work for the economics of the libido. No other technique for the conduct of life attaches the individual so firmly to reality as laying emphasis on work; for his work at least gives him a secure place in a portion of reality, in the human community. The possibility it offers of displacing a large amount of libidinal components, whether narcissistic, aggressive, or even erotic, on to professional work and on to the human relations connected with it lends it a value by no means second to what it enjoys as something indispensible to the preservation and justification of existence in society. Professional activity is a source of special satisfaction if it is a freely chosen one—if, that is to say, by means of sublimation, it makes possible the use of existing inclinations, of persisting or constitutionally reinforced instinctual impulses. And yet, as a path to happiness, work is not highly prized by men. They do not strive after it as they do after other possibilities of satisfaction. The great majority of people only work under the stress of necessity, and this natural human aversion to work raises most difficult social problems.
6. Cf. 'Formulations on the Two Principles of Mental Functioning' (1911*b*), and Lecture XXIII of my *Introductory Lectures* (1916–17).

in which its most unbearable features are eliminated and replaced by others that are in conformity with one's own wishes. But whoever, in desperate defiance, sets out upon this path to happiness will as a rule attain nothing. Reality is too strong for him. He becomes a madman, who for the most part finds no one to help him in carrying through his delusion. It is asserted, however, that each one of us behaves in some one respect like a paranoic, corrects some aspect of the world which is unbearable to him by the construction of a wish and introduces this delusion into reality. A special importance attaches to the case in which this attempt to procure a certainty of happiness and a protection against suffering through a delusional remoulding of reality is made by a considerable number of people in common. The religions of mankind must be classed among the mass-delusions of this kind. No one, needless to say, who shares a delusion ever recognizes it as such.

I do not think that I have made a complete enumeration of the methods by which men strive to gain happiness and keep suffering away and I know, too, that the material might have been differently arranged. One procedure I have not yet mentioned—not because I have forgotten it but because it will concern us later in another connection. And how could one possibly forget, of all others, this technique in the art of living? It is conspicuous for a most remarkable combination of characteristic features. It, too, aims of course at making the subject independent of Fate (as it is best to call it), and to that end it locates satisfaction in internal mental processes, making use, in so doing, of the displaceability of the libido of which we have already spoken [¶10]. But it does not turn away from the external world; on the contrary, it clings to the objects belonging to that world and obtains happiness from an emotional relationship to them. Nor is it content to aim at an avoidance of unpleasure—a goal, as we might call it, of weary resignation; it passes this by without heed and holds fast to the original, passionate striving for a positive fulfilment of happiness. And perhaps it does in fact come nearer to this goal than any other method. I am, of course, speaking of the way of life which makes love the centre of everything, which looks for all satisfaction in loving and being loved. A psychical attitude of this sort comes naturally enough to all of us; one of the forms in which love manifests itself—sexual love—has given us our most intense experience of an overwhelming sensation of pleasure and has thus furnished us with a pattern for our search for happiness. What is more natural than that we should persist in looking for happiness along the path on which we first encountered it? The weak side of this technique of living is easy to see; otherwise no human being would have thought of abandoning this path to happiness for any other. It is that we are never so defenceless against suffering as when we love, never so helplessly unhappy as when we have lost our loved object or its love. But this does not dispose of the technique of living based on the value of love as a means to happiness. There is much more to be said about it.

We may go on from here to consider the interesting case in which happiness in life is predominantly sought in the enjoyment of beauty, wherever beauty presents itself to our senses and our judgement—the beauty of human forms and gestures, of natural objects and landscapes and of artistic and even scientific creations. This aesthetic attitude to the goal of life offers little protection against the threat of suffering, but it can compensate for a great deal. The enjoyment of beauty has a peculiar, mildly intoxicating quality of feeling. Beauty has no obvious use; nor is there any clear cultural necessity for it. Yet civilization could not do without it. The science of aesthetics investigates the conditions under which things are felt as beautiful, but it has been unable to give any explanation of the nature and origin of beauty, and, as usually happens, lack of success is concealed beneath a flood of resounding and empty words. Psychoanalysis, unfortunately, has scarcely anything to say about beauty either. All that seems certain is its derivation from the field of sexual feeling. The love of beauty seems a perfect example of an impulse inhibited in its aim. 'Beauty' and 'attraction' [7] are originally attributes of the sexual object. It is worth remarking that the genitals themselves, the sight of which is always exciting, are nevertheless hardly ever judged to be beautiful; the quality of beauty seems, instead, to attach to certain secondary sexual characters.

In spite of the incompleteness [of my enumeration, ¶13], I will venture on a few remarks as a conclusion to our inquiry. The programme of becoming happy, which the pleasure principle imposes on us [¶6], cannot be fulfilled; yet we must not—indeed, we cannot—give up our efforts to bring it nearer to fulfilment by some means or other. Very different paths may be taken in that direction, and we may give priority either to the positive aspect of the aim, that of gaining pleasure, or to its negative one, that of avoiding unpleasure. By none of these paths can we attain all that we desire. Happiness, in the reduced sense in which we recognize it as possible, is a problem of the economics of the individual's libido. There is no golden rule which applies to everyone: every man must find out for himself in what particular fashion he can be saved.[8] All kinds of different factors will operate to direct his choice. It is a question of how much real satisfaction he can expect to get from the external world, how far he is led to make himself independent of it, and, finally, how much strength he feels he has for

---

7. [The German *'Reiz'* means 'stimulus' as well as 'charm' or 'attraction'. Freud had argued on the same lines in the first edition of his *Three Essays* (1905d), *Standard Ed.*, 7, 209, as well as in a footnote added to that work in 1915, ibid., 156.]

8. [The allusion is to a saying attributed to Frederick the Great: 'in my State every man can be saved after his own fashion.' Freud had quoted this a short time before, in *Lay Analysis* (1926e), *Standard Ed.*, 20, 236.]

altering the world to suit his wishes. In this, his psychical constitution will play a decisive part, irrespectively of the external circumstances. The man who is predominantly erotic will give first preference to his emotional relationships to other people; the narcissistic man, who inclines to be self-sufficient, will seek his main satisfactions in his internal mental processes; the man of action will never give up the external world on which he can try out his strength.[9] As regards the second of these types, the nature of his talents and the amount of instinctual sublimation open to him will decide where he shall locate his interests. Any choice that is pushed to an extreme will be penalized by exposing the individual to the dangers which arise if a technique of living that has been chosen as an exclusive one should prove inadequate. Just as a cautious business-man avoids tying up all his capital in one concern, so, perhaps, worldly wisdom will advise us not to look for the whole of our satisfaction from a single aspiration. Its success is never certain, for that depends on the convergence of many factors, perhaps on none more than on the capacity of the psychical constitution to adapt its function to the environment and then to exploit that environment for a yield of pleasure. A person who is born with a specially unfavourable instinctual constitution, and who has not properly undergone the transformation and rearrangement of his libidinal components which is indispensable for later achievements, will find it hard to obtain happiness from his external situation, especially if he is faced with tasks of some difficulty. As a last technique of living, which will at least bring him substitutive satisfactions, he is offered that of a flight into neurotic illness—a flight which he usually accomplishes when he is still young. The man who sees his pursuit of happiness come to nothing in later years can still find consolation in the yield of pleasure of chronic intoxication; or he can embark on the desperate attempt at rebellion seen in a psychosis.[10]

Religion restricts this play of choice and adaptation, since it imposes equally on everyone its own path to the acquisition of happiness and protection from suffering. Its technique consists in depressing the value of life and distorting the picture of the real world in a delusional manner—which presupposes an intimidation of the intelligence. At this price, by forcibly fixing them in a state of psychical infantilism and by drawing them into a mass-delusion, religion succeeds in sparing many people an individual neurosis. But hardly anything more. There are, as we have

---

9. [Freud further develops his ideas on these different types in his paper on 'Libidinal Types' (1931*a*).]

10. [*Footnote added* 1931:] I feel impelled to point out one at least of the gaps that have been left in the account given above. No discussion of the possibilities of human happiness should omit to take into consideration the relation between narcissism and object libido. We require to know what being essentially self-dependent signifies for the economics of the libido.

said, many paths which *may* lead to such happiness as is attainable by men, but there is none which does so for certain. Even religion cannot keep its promise. If the believer finally sees himself obliged to speak of God's 'inscrutable decrees', he is admitting that all that is left to him as a last possible consolation and source of pleasure in his suffering is an unconditional submission. And if he is prepared for that, he could probably have spared himself the *détour* he has made.

III

Our enquiry concerning happiness has not so far taught us much that is not already common knowledge. And even if we proceed from it to the problem of why it is so hard for men to be happy, there seems no greater prospect of learning anything new. We have given the answer already [¶6] by pointing to the three sources from which our suffering comes: the superior power of nature, the feebleness of our own bodies and the inadequacy of the regulations which adjust the mutual relationships of human beings in the family, the state and society. In regard to the first two sources, our judgement cannot hesitate long. It forces us to acknowledge those sources of suffering and to submit to the inevitable. We shall never completely master nature; and our bodily organism, itself a part of that nature, will always remain a transient structure with a limited capacity for adaptation and achievement. This recognition does not have a paralysing effect. On the contrary, it points the direction for our activity. If we cannot remove all suffering, we can remove some, and we can mitigate some: the experience of many thousands of years has convinced us of that. As regards the third source, the social source of suffering, our attitude is a different one. We do not admit it at all; we cannot see why the regulations made by ourselves should not, on the contrary, be a protection and a benefit for every one of us. And yet, when we consider how unsuccessful we have been in precisely this field of prevention of suffering, a suspicion dawns on us that here, too, a piece of unconquerable nature may lie behind—this time a piece of our own psychical constitution.

When we start considering this possibility, we come upon a contention which is so astonishing that we must dwell upon it. This contention holds that what we call our civilization is largely responsible for our misery, and that we should be much happier if we gave it up and returned to primitive conditions. I call this contention astonishing because, in whatever way we may define the concept of civilization, it is a certain fact that all the things with which we seek to protect ourselves against the threats that emanate from the sources of suffering are part of that very civilization.

How has it happened that so many people have come to take up this strange attitude of hostility to civilization?[11] I believe that the basis of it was a deep and long-standing dissatisfaction with the then existing state of civilization and that on that basis a condemnation of it was built up, occasioned by certain specific historical events. I think I know what the last and the last but one of those occasions were. I am not learned enough to trace the chain of them far back enough in the history of the human species; but a factor of this kind hostile to civilization must already have been at work in the victory of Christendom over the heathen religions. For it was very closely related to the low estimation put upon earthly life by the Christian doctrine. The last but one of these occasions was when the progress of voyages of discovery led to contact with primitive peoples and races. In consequence of insufficient observation and a mistaken view of their manners and customs, they appeared to Europeans to be leading a simple, happy life with few wants, a life such as was unattainable by their visitors with their superior civilization. Later experience has corrected some of those judgements. In many cases the observers had wrongly attributed to the absence of complicated cultural demands what was in fact due to the bounty of nature and the ease with which the major human needs were satisfied. The last occasion is especially familiar to us. It arose when people came to know about the mechanism of the neuroses, which threaten to undermine the modicum of happiness enjoyed by civilized men. It was discovered that a person becomes neurotic because he cannot tolerate the amount of frustration which society imposes on him in the service of its cultural ideals, and it was inferred from this that the abolition or reduction of those demands would result in a return to possibilities of happiness.

There is also an added factor of disappointment. During the last few generations mankind has made an extraordinary advance in the natural sciences and in their technical application and has established his control over nature in a way never before imagined. The single steps of this advance are common knowledge and it is unnecessary to enumerate them. Men are proud of those achievements, and have a right to be. But they seem to have observed that this newly-won power over space and time, this subjugation of the forces of nature, which is the fulfilment of a longing that goes back thousands of years, has not increased the amount of pleasurable satisfaction which they may expect from life and has not made them feel happier. From the recognition of this fact we ought to be content to conclude that power over nature is

11. [Freud had discussed this question at considerable length two years earlier, in the opening chapters of *The Future of an Illusion* (1927c).]

not the *only* precondition of human happiness, just as it is not the *only* goal of cultural endeavour; we ought not to infer from it that technical progress is without value for the economics of our happiness. One would like to ask: is there, then, no positive gain in pleasure, no unequivocal increase in my feeling of happiness, if I can, as often as I please, hear the voice of a child of mine who is living hundreds of miles away or if I can learn in the shortest possible time after a friend has reached his destination that he has come through the long and difficult voyage unharmed? Does it mean nothing that medicine has succeeded in enormously reducing infant mortality and the danger of infection for women in childbirth, and, indeed, in considerably lengthening the average life of a civilized man? And there is a long list that might be added to benefits of this kind which we owe to the much-despised era of scientific and technical advances. But here the voice of pessimistic criticism makes itself heard and warns us that most of these satisfactions follow the model of the 'cheap enjoyment' extolled in the anecdote—the enjoyment obtained by putting a bare leg from under the bedclothes on a cold winter night and drawing it in again. If there had been no railway to conquer distances, my child would never have left his native town and I should need no telephone to hear his voice; if travelling across the ocean by ship had not been introduced, my friend would not have embarked on his sea-voyage and I should not need a cable to relieve my anxiety about him. What is the use of reducing infantile mortality when it is precisely that reduction which imposes the greatest restraint on us in the begetting of children, so that, taken all round, we nevertheless rear no more children than in the days before the reign of hygiene, while at the same time we have created difficult conditions for our sexual life in marriage, and have probably worked against the beneficial effects of natural selection? And, finally, what good to us is a long life if it is difficult and barren of joys, and if it is so full of misery that we can only welcome death as a deliverer?

It seems certain that we do not feel comfortable in our present-day civilization, but it is very difficult to form an opinion whether and in what degree men of an earlier age felt happier and what part their cultural conditions played in the matter. We shall always tend to consider people's distress objectively—that is, to place ourselves, with our own wants and sensibilities, in *their* conditions, and then to examine what occasions we should find in them for experiencing happiness or unhappiness. This method of looking at things, which seems objective because it ignores the variations in subjective sensibility, is, of course, the most subjective possible, since it puts one's own mental states in the place of any others, unknown though they may be. Happiness, however, is something essentially subjective. No matter how much we may shrink with horror from certain situations—of a galley-slave in antiquity, of a peasant during the Thirty Years' War,* of a victim of the Holy Inquisition, of a Jew awaiting a pogrom †—it is nevertheless impossible for us to feel our way into such people—to divine the changes which original obtuseness of mind, a gradual stupefying process, the cessation of expectations, and cruder or more refined methods of narcotization have produced upon their receptivity to sensations of pleasure and unpleasure. Moreover, in the case of the most extreme possibility of suffering, special mental protective devices are brought into operation. It seems to me unprofitable to pursue this aspect of the problem any further.

It is time for us to turn our attention to the nature of this civilization on whose value as a means to happiness doubts have been thrown. We shall not look for a formula in which to express that nature in a few words, until we have learned something by examining it. We shall therefore content ourselves with saying once more that the word 'civilization' describes the whole sum of the achievements and the regulations which distinguish our lives from those of our animal ancestors and which serve two purposes—namely to protect men against nature and to adjust their mutual relations.[12] In order to learn more, we will bring together the various features of civilization individually, as they are exhibited in human communities. In doing so, we shall have no hesitation in letting ourselves be guided by linguistic usage or, as it is also called, linguistic feeling, in the conviction that we shall thus be doing justice to inner discernments which still defy expression in abstract terms.

The first stage is easy. We recognize as cultural all activities and resources which are useful to men for making the earth serviceable to them, for protecting them against the violence of the forces of nature, and so on. As regards this side of civilization, there can be scarcely any doubt. If we go back far enough, we find that the first acts of civilization were the use of tools, the gaining of control over fire and the construction of dwellings. Among these, the control over fire stands out as a quite extraordinary and unexampled achievement,[13] while the others opened

---

* The Thirty Years War (1618–48), which began as a political and religious conflict among the German states, proved to be "not one war but a series of contests in which the issues changed and the parties to the quarrel changed with them." Austria, Sweden, Denmark, France, England, The Netherlands, and Spain all participated at different times for various reasons. The prolonged and harsh fortunes of war devastated the German countryside and reduced the population from about sixteen to six million inhabitants. (See G. N. Clark, *The Seventeenth Century,* 2nd ed. [Oxford: Clarendon, 1945], pp. 4, 159–62).
† In Czarist Russia, periodic pogroms led to the slaughter of thousands of Jews.
12. See *The Future of an Illusion.*
13. Psycho-analytic material, incomplete as it is and not susceptible to clear interpretation, nevertheless admits of a conjecture—a fantastic-sounding one—about the origin of this human feat. It is as though primal man had the habit, when he came in contact with fire, of satisfying an infantile desire connected with it, by putting it out with a stream of his urine. The legends that we possess leave no doubt about the originally phallic view taken of tongues of flame as they shoot upwards. Putting

up paths which man has followed ever since, and the stimulus to which is easily guessed. With every tool man is perfecting his own organs, whether motor or sensory, or is removing the limits to their functioning. Motor power places gigantic forces at his disposal, which, like his muscles, he can employ in any direction; thanks to ships and aircraft neither water nor air can hinder his movements; by means of spectacles he corrects defects in the lens of his own eye; by means of the telescope he sees into the far distance; and by means of the microscope he overcomes the limits of visibility set by the structure of his retina. In the photographic camera he has created an instrument which retains the fleeting visual impressions, just as a gramophone disc retains the equally fleeting auditory ones; both are at bottom materializations of the power he possesses of recollection, his memory. With the help of the telephone he can hear at distances which would be respected as unattainable even in a fairy tale. Writing was in its origin the voice of an absent person; and the dwelling-house was a substitute for the mother's womb, the first lodging, for which in all likelihood man still longs, and in which he was safe and felt at ease.

These things that, by his science and technology, man has brought about on this earth, on which he first appeared as a feeble animal organism and on which each individual of his species must once more make its entry ('oh inch of nature!') as a helpless suckling—these things do not only sound like a fairy tale, they are an actual fulfilment of every—or of almost every—fairy-tale wish. All these assets he may lay claim to as his cultural acquisition. Long ago he formed an ideal conception of omnipotence and omniscience which he embodied in his gods. To these gods he attributed everything that seemed unattainable to his wishes, or that was forbidden to him. One may say, therefore, that these gods were cultural ideals. To-day he has come very close to the attainment of this ideal, he has almost become a god himself. Only, it is true, in the fashion in which ideals are usually attained according to the general judgement of humanity. Not completely; in some respects not

---

out fire by micturating—a theme to which modern giants, Gulliver in Lilliput and Rabelais' Gargantua, still hark back—was therefore a kind of sexual act with a male, an enjoyment of sexual potency in a homosexual competition. The first person to renounce this desire and spare the fire was able to carry it off with him and subdue it to his own use. By damping down the fire of his own sexual excitation, he had tamed the natural force of fire. This great cultural conquest was thus the reward for his renunciation of instinct. Further, it is as though woman had been appointed guardian of the fire which was held captive on the domestic hearth, because her anatomy made it impossible for her to yield to the temptation of this desire. It is remarkable, too, how regularly analytic experience testifies to the connection between ambition, fire and urethral erotism.—[Freud had pointed to the connection between urination and fire as early as in the 'Dora' case history (1905e [1901]). The connection with ambition came rather later. A full list of references will be found in the Editor's Note to the later paper on the subject, 'The Acquisition and Control of Fire' (1932a).]

at all, in others only half way. Man has, as it were, become a kind of prosthetic [14] God. When he puts on all his auxiliary organs he is truly magnificent; but those organs have not grown on to him and they still give him much trouble at times. Nevertheless, he is entitled to console himself with the thought that this development will not come to an end precisely with the year 1930 A.D. Future ages will bring with them new and probably unimaginably great advances in this field of civilization and will increase man's likeness to God still more. But in the interests of our investigations, we will not forget that present-day man does not feel happy in his Godlike character.

We recognize, then, that countries have attained a high level of civilization if we find that in them everything which can assist in the exploitation of the earth by man and in his protection against the forces of nature—everything, in short, which is of use to him—is attended to and effectively carried out. In such countries rivers which threaten to flood the land are regulated in their flow, and their water is directed through canals to places where there is a shortage of it. The soil is carefully cultivated and planted with the vegetation which it is suited to support; and the mineral wealth below ground is assiduously brought to the surface and fashioned into the required implements and utensils. The means of communication are ample, rapid and reliable. Wild and dangerous animals have been exterminated and the breeding of domesticated animals flourishes. But we demand other things from civilization besides these, and it is a noticeable fact that we hope to find them realized in these same countries. As though we were seeking to repudiate the first demand we made, we welcome it as a sign of civilization as well if we see people directing their care too to what has no practical value whatever, to what is useless—if, for instance, the green spaces necessary in a town as playgrounds and as reservoirs of fresh air are also laid out with flower-beds, or if the windows of the houses are decorated with pots of flowers. We soon observe that this useless thing which we expect civilization to value is beauty. We require civilized man to reverence beauty wherever he sees it in nature and to create it in the objects of his handiwork so far as he is able. But this is far from exhausting our demands on civilization. We expect besides to see the signs of cleanliness and order. We do not think highly of the cultural level of an English country town in Shakespeare's time when we read that there was a big dung-heap in front of his father's house in Stratford; we are indignant and call it 'barbarous' (which is the opposite of civilized) when we find the paths in the Wiener Wald [15] littered with paper. Dirtiness of any kind seems to us incompatible with civilization. We extend our

---

14. [A prosthesis is the medical term for an artificial adjunct to the body, to make up for some missing or inadequate part: e.g. false teeth or a false leg.]
15. [The wooded hills on the outskirts of Vienna.]

demand for cleanliness to the human body too. We are astonished to
learn of the objectionable smell which emanated from the *Roi Soleil;* [16]
and we shake our heads on the Isola Bella [17] when we are shown the
tiny wash-basin in which Napoleon made his morning toilet. Indeed, we
are not surprised by the idea of setting up the use of soap as an actual
yardstick of civilization. The same is true of order. It, like cleanliness,
applies solely to the works of man. But whereas cleanliness is not to be
expected in nature, order, on the contrary, has been imitated from her.
Man's observation of the great astronomical regularities not only furnished him with a model for introducing order into his life, but gave him
the first points of departure for doing so. Order is a kind of compulsion to repeat which, when a regulation has been laid down once and for
all, decides when, where and how a thing shall be done, so that in every
similar circumstance one is spared hesitation and indecision. The benefits of order are incontestable. It enables men to use space and time to
the best advantage while conserving their psychical forces. We should
have a right to expect that order would have taken its place in human
activities from the start and without difficulty; and we may well wonder
that this has not happened—that, on the contrary, human beings exhibit an inborn tendency to carelessness, irregularity and unreliability
in their work, and that a laborious training is needed before they learn
to follow the example of their celestial models.

Beauty, cleanliness and order obviously occupy a special position
among the requirements of civilization. No one will maintain that they
are as important for life as control over the forces of nature or as
some other factors with which we shall become acquainted. And yet no
one would care to put them in the background as trivialities. That
civilization is not exclusively taken up with what is useful is already
shown by the example of beauty, which we decline to omit from among
the interests of civilization. The usefulness of order is quite evident.
With regard to cleanliness, we must bear in mind that it is demanded
of us by hygiene as well, and we may suspect that even before the days
of scientific prophylaxis the connection between the two was not altogether strange to man. Yet utility does not entirely explain these efforts;
something else must be at work besides.

No feature, however, seems better to characterize civilization than
its esteem and encouragement of man's higher mental activities—his
intellectual, scientific and artistic achievements—and the leading role
that it assigns to ideas in human life. Foremost among those ideas are
the religious systems, on whose complicated structure I have en-

---

16. [Louis XIV of France.]
17. [The well-known island in Lake Maggiore, visited by Napoleon a few days before the battle of Marengo.]

deavoured to throw light elsewhere.[18] Next come the speculations of philosophy; and finally what might be called man's 'ideals'—his ideas of a possible perfection of individuals, or of peoples or of the whole of humanity, and the demands he sets up on the basis of such ideas. The fact that these creations of his are not independent of one another, but are on the contrary closely interwoven, increases the difficulty not only of describing them but of tracing their psychological derivation. If we assume quite generally that the motive force of all human activities is a striving towards the two confluent goals of utility and a yield of pleasure, we must suppose that this is also true of the manifestations of civilization which we have been discussing here, although this is easily visible only in scientific and aesthetic activities. But it cannot be doubted that the other activities, too, correspond to strong needs in men—perhaps to needs which are only developed in a minority. Nor must we allow ourselves to be misled by judgements of value concerning any particular religion, or philosophic system, or ideal. Whether we think to find in them the highest achievements of the human spirit, or whether we deplore them as aberrations, we cannot but recognize that where they are present, and, in especial, where they are dominant, a high level of civilization is implied.

The last, but certainly not the least important, of the characteristic features of civilization remains to be assessed: the manner in which the relationships of men to one another, their social relationships, are regulated—relationships which affect a person as a neighbour, as a source of help, as another person's sexual object, as a member of a family and of a State. Here it is especially difficult to keep clear of particular ideal demands and to see what is civilized in general. Perhaps we may begin by explaining that the element of civilization enters on the scene with the first attempt to regulate these social relationships. If the attempt were not made, the relationships would be subject to the arbitrary will of the individual: that is to say, the physically stronger man would decide them in the sense of his own interests and instinctual impulses. Nothing would be changed in this if this stronger man should in his turn meet someone even stronger than he. Human life in common is only made possible when a majority comes together which is stronger than any separate individual and which remains united against all separate individuals. The power of this community is then set up as 'right' in opposition to the power of the individual, which is condemned as 'brute force'. This replacement of the power of the individual by the power of a community constitutes the decisive step of civilization. The essence of it lies in the fact that the members of the community restrict themselves in their possibilities of satisfaction, whereas the individual knew no such restrictions. The first requisite of civilization, therefore, is

---

18. [Cf. *The Future of an Illusion* (1927c).]

that of justice—that is, the assurance that a law once made will not be broken in favour of an individual. This implies nothing as to the ethical value of such a law. The further course of cultural development seems to tend towards making the law no longer an expression of the will of a small community—a caste or a stratum of the population or a racial group—which, in its turn, behaves like a violent individual towards other, and perhaps more numerous, collections of people. The final outcome should be a rule of law to which all—except those who are not capable of entering a community—have contributed by a sacrifice of their instincts, and which leaves no one—again with the same exception—at the mercy of brute force.

The liberty of the individual is no gift of civilization. It was greatest before there was any civilization, though then, it is true, it had for the most part no value, since the individual was scarcely in a position to defend it. The development of civilization imposes restrictions on it, and justice demands that no one shall escape those restrictions. What makes itself felt in a human community as a desire for freedom may be their revolt against some existing injustice, and so may prove favourable to a further development of civilization; it may remain compatible with civilization. But it may also spring from the remains of their original personality, which is still untamed by civilization and may thus become the basis in them of hostility to civilization. The urge for freedom, therefore, is directed against particular forms and demands of civilization or against civilization altogether. It does not seem as though any influence could induce a man to change his nature into a termite's. No doubt he will always defend his claim to individual liberty against the will of the group. A good part of the struggles of mankind centre round the single task of finding an expedient accommodation—one, that is, that will bring happiness—between this claim of the individual and the cultural claims of the group; and one of the problems that touches the fate of humanity is whether such an accommodation can be reached by means of some particular form of civilization or whether this conflict is irreconcilable.

By allowing common feeling to be our guide in deciding what features of human life are to be regarded as civilized, we have obtained a clear impression of the general picture of civilization; but it is true that so far we have discovered nothing that is not universally known. At the same time we have been careful not to fall in with the prejudice that civilization is synonymous with perfecting, that it is the road to perfection pre-ordained for men. But now a point of view presents itself which may lead in a different direction. The development of civilization appears to us as a peculiar process which mankind undergoes, and in which several things strike us as familiar. We may characterize this process with reference to the changes which it brings about in the familiar instinctual dispositions of human beings, to satisfy which is, after all, the economic task of our lives. A few of these instincts are used up in such a manner that something appears in their place which, in an individual, we describe as a character-trait. The most remarkable example of such a process is found in the anal erotism of young human beings. Their original interest in the excretory function, its organs and products, is changed in the course of their growth into a group of traits which are familiar to us as parsimony, a sense of order and cleanliness— qualities which, though valuable and welcome in themselves, may be intensified till they become markedly dominant and produce what is called the anal character. How this happens we do not know, but there is no doubt about the correctness of the finding.[19] Now we have seen that order and cleanliness are important requirements of civilization, although their vital necessity is not very apparent, any more than their suitability as sources of enjoyment. At this point we cannot fail to be struck by the similarity between the process of civilization and the libidinal development of the individual. Other instincts [besides anal erotism] are induced to displace the conditions for their satisfaction, to lead them into other paths. In most cases this process coincides with that of the *sublimation* (of instinctual aims) with which we are familiar, but in some it can be differentiated from it. Sublimation of instinct is an especially conspicuous feature of cultural development; it is what makes it possible for higher psychical activities, scientific, artistic or ideological, to play such an important part in civilized life. If one were to yield to a first impression, one would say that sublimation is a vicissitude which has been forced upon the instincts entirely by civilization. But it would be wiser to reflect upon this a little longer. In the third place,[20] finally, and this seems the most important of all, it is impossible to overlook the extent to which civilization is built up upon a renunciation of instinct, how much it presupposes precisely the non-satisfaction (by suppression, repression or some other means?) of powerful instincts. This 'cultural frustration' dominates the large field of social relationships between human beings. As we already know, it is the cause of the hostility against which all civilizations have to struggle. It will also make severe demands on our scientific work, and we shall have much to explain here. It is not easy to understand how it can become possible to deprive an instinct of satisfaction. Nor is doing so without danger. If the loss is not compensated for economically, one can be certain that serious disorders will ensue.

But if we want to know what value can be attributed to our view

---

19. Cf. my 'Character and Anal Erotism' (1908*b*), and numerous further contributions, by Ernest Jones [1918] and others.
20. [Freud had already mentioned two other factors playing a part in the 'process' of civilization: character-formation and sublimation.]

that the development of civilization is a special process, comparable to the normal maturation of the individual, we must clearly attack another problem. We must ask ourselves to what influences the development of civilization owes its origin, how it arose, and by what its course has been determined.

VI

In none of my previous writings have I had so strong a feeling as now that what I am describing is common knowledge and that I am using up paper and ink and, in due course, the compositor's and printer's work and material in order to expound things which are, in fact, self-evident. For that reason I should be glad to seize the point if it were to appear that the recognition of a special, independent aggressive instinct means an alteration of the psycho-analytic theory of the instincts.

We shall see, however, that this is not so and that it is merely a matter of bringing into sharper focus a turn of thought arrived at long ago and of following out its consequences. Of all the slowly developed parts of analytic theory, the theory of the instincts is the one that has felt its way the most painfully forward.[21] And yet that theory was so indispensable to the whole structure that something had to be put in its place. In what was at first my utter perplexity, I took as my starting-point a saying of the poet-philosopher, Schiller, that 'hunger and love are what moves the world'.[22] Hunger could be taken to represent the instincts which aim at preserving the individual; while love strives after objects, and its chief function, favoured in every way by nature, is the preservation of the species. Thus, to begin with, ego-instincts and object-instincts confronted each other. It was to denote the energy of the latter and only the latter instincts that I introduced the term 'libido'.[23] Thus the antithesis was between the ego-instincts and the 'libidinal' instincts of love (in its widest sense [24]) which were directed to an object. One of these object-instincts, the sadistic instinct, stood out from the rest, it is true, in that its aim was so very far from being loving. Moreover it was obviously in some respects attached to the ego-instincts: it could not hide its close affinity with instincts of mastery which have no libidinal

---

21. [Some account of the history of Freud's theory of the instincts will be found in the Editor's Note to his paper 'Instincts and their Vicissitudes' (1915c), *Standard Ed.*, 14, 113 ff.]
22. ['Die Weltweisen.']
23. [In Section II of the first paper on anxiety neurosis (1895b).]
24. [I.e. as used by Plato. See Chapter IV of *Group Psychology* (1921c), *Standard Ed.*, 18, 99.]

purpose. But these discrepancies were got over; after all, sadism was clearly a part of sexual life, in the activities of which affection could be replaced by cruelty. Neurosis was regarded as the outcome of a struggle between the interest of self-preservation and the demands of the libido, a struggle in which the ego had been victorious but at the price of severe sufferings and renunciations.

Every analyst will admit that even to-day this view has not the sound of a long-discarded error. Nevertheless, alterations in it became essential, as our enquiries advanced from the repressed to the repressing forces, from the object-instincts to the ego. The decisive step forward was the introduction of the concept of narcissism—that is to say, the discovery that the ego itself is cathected with libido, that the ego, indeed, is the libido's original home, and remains to some extent its headquarters.[25] This narcissistic libido turns towards objects, and thus becomes object-libido; and it can change back into narcissistic libido once more. The concept of narcissism made it possible to obtain an analytic understanding of the traumatic neuroses and of many of the affections bordering on the psychoses, as well as of the latter themselves. It was not necessary to give up our interpretation of the transference neuroses as attempts made by the ego to defend itself against sexuality; but the concept of libido was endangered. Since the ego-instincts, too, were libidinal, it seemed for a time inevitable that we should make libido coincide with instinctual energy in general, as C. G. Jung had already advocated earlier. Nevertheless, there still remained in me a kind of conviction, for which I was not as yet able to find reasons, that the instincts could not all be of the same kind. My next step was taken in *Beyond the Pleasure Principle* (1920g), when the compulsion to repeat and the conservative character of instinctual life first attracted my attention. Starting from speculations on the beginning of life and from biological parallels, I drew the conclusion that, besides the instinct to preserve living substance and to join it into ever larger units,[26] there must exist another, contrary instinct seeking to dissolve those units and to bring them back to their primaeval, inorganic state. That is to say, as well as Eros there was an instinct of death.* The phenomena of life could be explained from the concurrent or mutually opposing action of these two instincts. It was not easy, however, to demonstrate the activities of this supposed death instinct. The manifestations of Eros were conspicuous and noisy enough. It might be assumed that the death instinct operated silently within the organism towards its dissolution, but

---

25. [Cf. in this connection the editorial Appendix B to *The Ego and the Id, Standard Ed.*, 19, 63.]
26. The opposition which thus emerges between the ceaseless trend by Eros towards extension and the general conservative nature of the instincts is striking, and it may become the starting-point for the study of further problems.
* ["Eros" understood in the broad sense.]

that, of course, was no proof. A more fruitful idea was that a portion of the instinct is diverted towards the external world and comes to light as an instinct of aggressiveness and destructiveness. In this way the instinct itself could be pressed into the service of Eros, in that the organism was destroying some other thing, whether animate or inanimate, instead of destroying its own self. Conversely, any restriction of this aggressiveness directed outwards would be bound to increase the self-destruction, which is in any case proceeding. At the same time one can suspect from this example that the two kinds of instinct seldom—perhaps never —appear in isolation from each other, but are alloyed with each other in varying and very different proportions and so become unrecognizable to our judgement. In sadism, long since known to us as a component instinct of sexuality, we should have before us a particularly strong alloy of this kind between trends of love and the destructive instinct; while its counterpart, masochism, would be a union between destructiveness directed inwards and sexuality—a union which makes what is otherwise an imperceptible trend into a conspicuous and tangible one.

The assumption of the existence of an instinct of death or destruction has met with resistance even in analytic circles; I am aware that there is a frequent inclination rather to ascribe whatever is dangerous and hostile in love to an original bipolarity in its own nature. To begin with it was only tentatively that I put forward the views I have developed here,[27] but in the course of time they have gained such a hold upon me that I can no longer think in any other way. To my mind, they are far more serviceable from a theoretical standpoint than any other possible ones; they provide that simplification, without either ignoring or doing violence to the facts, for which we strive in scientific work. I know that in sadism and masochism we have always seen before us manifestations of the destructive instinct (directed outwards and inwards), strongly alloyed with erotism; but I can no longer understand how we can have overlooked the ubiquity of non-erotic aggressivity and destructiveness and can have failed to give it its due place in our interpretation of life. (The desire for destruction when it is directed *inwards* mostly eludes our perception, of course, unless it is tinged with erotism.) I remember my own defensive attitude when the idea of an instinct of destruction first emerged in psycho-analytic literature, and how long it took before I became receptive to it. That others should have shown, and still show, the same attitude of rejection surprises me less. For 'little children do not like it'[28] when there is talk of the inborn human inclination to 'badness', to aggressiveness and destructiveness, and so to cruelty as well. God has made them in the image of His own perfection;

27. [Cf. *Beyond the Pleasure Principle* (1920g), *Standard Ed.*, 18, 59.]
28. ['Denn die Kindlein, Sie hören es nicht gerne.' A quotation from Goethe's poem 'Die Ballade vom vertriebenen und heimgekehrten Grafen'.]

nobody wants to be reminded how hard it is to reconcile the undeniable existence of evil—despite the protestations of Christian Science—with His all-powerfulness or His all-goodness. The Devil would be the best way out as an excuse for God; in that way he would be playing the same part as an agent of economic discharge as the Jew does in the world of the Aryan ideal. But even so, one can hold God responsible for the existence of the Devil just as well as for the existence of the wickedness which the Devil embodies. In view of these difficulties, each of us will be well advised, on some suitable occasion, to make a low bow to the deeply moral nature of mankind; it will help us to be generally popular and much will be forgiven us for it.²⁹

29. In Goethe's Mephistopheles we have a quite exceptionally convincing identification of the principle of evil with the destructive instinct: "For all things from the Void / Called forth, deserve to be destroyed . . . / Thus, all which you as Sin have rated— / Destruction,—aught with Evil blent,— / That is my proper element." The Devil himself names as his adversary, not what is holy and good, but Nature's power to create, to multiply life—that is, Eros: "From Water, Air, and Earth unfolding, / A thousand germs break forth and grow, / In dry, and wet, and warm, and chilly: / And had I not the flame reserved, why, really, / There's nothing special of my own to show." Both passages are from Goethe's *Faust,* Part I, Scene 3. Translated by Bayard Taylor. There is a passing allusion to the second passage in Chapter I (G) of *The Interpretation of Dreams* (1900a), Standard Ed., 4, 78.

Problems

1. What are the three modes and the specific expressions with which people make life bearable? What are the consequences of each method? Which do you find more attractive, the positive or the negative? Why?
2. Why does Freud say, "the idea of life having a purpose stands and falls with the religious system" (464/23-24)? What does he think is the purpose of life?
3. What are the total implications for man and the concept of utopia in Freud's remark that "we are so made that we can derive intense enjoyment only from a contrast and very little from a state of things" (465/5-7)? What is Freud's attitude toward progress? How would it place him in conflict with Marxists? Which view do you find more persuasive?
4. Freud is sometimes accused of reducing love to sex. What passages suggest the falseness of this charge?
5. What are the implications of Freud's remark that "Happiness . . . is a problem of the economics of the individual's libido" (470/32-34)? Why is the remark hostile to religion?
6. How have science and technology undermined religion?
7. What, for Freud, are the characteristics and attitudes of countries with a high level of civilization?
8. What is the relationship of civilization to individual liberty for Freud? By Freud's definition, are communists or non-communists more civilized?

24 CARL G. JUNG

Carl G. Jung (1875–1961) was the third and the greatest of Freud's followers to break with him over matters of emphasis and interpretation. The rupture was made irreparable in 1912 after the publication of The Psychology of the Unconscious, *a work that expounded a new desexualized theory of libidinal energy. Freud, who had become extremely sensitive to the charge of "pan-sexualism" leveled against psychoanalysis, and who resisted any change in terminology as an attempt to "soften the affront" to people's sensibility, accused Jung of desexualizing libido merely to make it more palatable to others and the better to harmonize it with his own religious interests.*

Unlike many in the psychoanalytic circle who were Austrian, Jewish, and prone to rationalism, Jung was Swiss, Christian, and prone to mysticism. As a result of this predisposition, his early contributions to psychotherapeutic technique, such as "free association" word tests, soon gave way to a vague, symbolic mysticism. Unlike Freud, who, as a rationalist and scientist, was interested in discovering motivations and deterministic roots of behavior, Jung was interested in life goals and purposes, in the hidden religious strivings of the individual. In a real sense then, despite the coinage "Analytic Psychology," Jung's interests are less analytical and more metaphysical, less personal and more universal, and hence more attractive to individuals who wish to weave religion and psychology into a new synthesis. For a similar intent with existential overtones, see the essay by Viktor E. Frankl, "Basic Concepts of Logotherapy."

The following essays consist of two of five lectures which Jung delivered in 1935. These lectures expound his theories in a relatively direct way, and the essay, "Marriage as a Psychological Relationship," reveals something of their application.

from Analytic Psychology: Its Theory and Practice

LECTURE ONE

As you know, my purpose is to give you a short outline of certain fundamental conceptions of psychology. If my demonstration is chiefly concerned with my own principles or my own point of view, it is not that I overlook the value of the great contributions of other workers in this field. I do not want to push myself unduly into the foreground, but I can surely expect my audience to be as much aware of Freud's and Adler's merits as I am.

Now as to our procedure, I should like to give you first a short idea of my programme. We have two main topics to deal with, namely, on the one side the concepts concerning the *structure of the unconscious mind* and its *contents;* on the other, the *methods* used in the *investigation* of contents originating in the unconscious psychic processes. The second topic falls into three parts, first, the word-association method; second, the method of dream-analysis; and third, the method of active imagination.

I know, of course, that I am unable to give you a full account of all there is to say about such difficult topics as, for instance, the philosophical, religious, ethical and social problems peculiar to the collective consciousness of our time, or the processes of the collective unconscious and the comparative mythological and historical researches necessary for their elucidation. These topics, although apparently remote, are yet the most potent factors in making, regulating, and disturbing the personal mental condition, and they also form the root of disagreement in the field of psychological theories. Although I am a medical man and therefore chiefly concerned with psychopathology, I am nevertheless convinced that this particular branch of psychology can only be benefited by a considerably deepened and more extensive knowledge of the normal psyche in general. The doctor especially should never lose sight of the fact that diseases are disturbed normal processes and not *entia per se* * with a psychology exclusively their own. *Similia similibus curantur* † is a remarkable truth of the old medicine, and as a great truth it is also

---

From Carl G. Jung, *Analytical Psychology: Its Theory & Practice* (New York: Random House, Inc., 1968), pp. 3–61.
* Entities in themselves.
† From similar things are things cured.

liable to become great nonsense. Medical psychology, therefore, should be careful not to become morbid itself. One-sidedness and restriction of horizon are well-known neurotic peculiarities.

Whatever I may be able to tell you will undoubtedly remain a regrettably unfinished torso. Unfortunately I take little stock of new theories, as my empirical temperament is more eager for new facts than for what one might speculate about them, although this is, I must admit, an enjoyable intellectual pastime. Each new case is almost a new theory to me, and I am not quite convinced that this standpoint is a thoroughly bad one, particularly when one considers the extreme youth of modern psychology, which to my mind has not yet left its cradle. I know, therefore, that the time for general theories is not yet ripe. It even looks to me sometimes as if psychology had not yet understood either the gigantic size of its task, or the perplexingly and distressingly complicated nature of its subject-matter: the psyche itself. It seems as if we were just waking up to this fact, and that the dawn is still too dim for us to realize in full what it means that the psyche, being the *object* of scientific observation and judgment, is at the same time its *subject*, the *means* by which you make such observations. The menace of so formidably vicious a circle has driven me to an extreme of caution and relativism which has often been thoroughly misunderstood.

I do not want to disturb our dealings by bringing up disquieting critical arguments. I only mention them as a sort of anticipatory excuse for seemingly unnecessary complications. I am not troubled by theories, but a great deal by facts; and I beg you therefore to keep in mind that the shortness of time at my disposal does not allow me to produce all the circumstantial evidence which would substantiate my conclusions. I especially refer here to the intricacies of dream-analysis and to the comparative method of investigating the unconscious processes. In short, I have to depend a great deal upon your goodwill, but I realize naturally it is my own task in the first place to make things as plain as possible.

Psychology is a science of consciousness, in the very first place. In the second place, it is the science of the products of what we call the unconscious psyche. We cannot directly explore the unconscious psyche because the unconscious is just unconscious, and we have therefore no relation to it. We can only deal with the conscious products which we suppose have originated in the field called the unconscious, that field of 'dim representations' which the philosopher Kant in his *Anthropology* speaks of as being half a world. Whatever we have to say about the unconscious is what the conscious mind says about it. Always the unconscious psyche, which is entirely of an unknown nature, is expressed by consciousness and in terms of consciousness, and that is the only thing we can do. We cannot go beyond that, and we should always keep it in mind as an ultimate critique of our judgment.

Consciousness is a peculiar thing. It is an intermittent phenomenon. One-fifth, or one-third, or perhaps even one-half of our human life is spent in an unconscious condition. Our early childhood is unconscious. Every night we sink into the unconscious, and only in phases between waking and sleeping have we a more or less clear consciousness. To a certain extent it is even questionable how clear that consciousness is. For instance, we assume that a boy or girl ten years of age would be conscious, but one could easily prove that it is a very peculiar kind of consciousness, for it might be a consciousness without any consciousness of the *ego*. I know a number of cases of children eleven, twelve, and fourteen years of age, or even older, suddenly realizing 'I am'. For the first time in their lives they know that they themselves are experiencing, that they are looking back over a past in which they can remember things happening but cannot remember that they were in them.

We must admit that when we say 'I' we have no absolute criterion whether we have a full experience of 'I' or not. It might be that our realization of the ego is still fragmentary and that in some future time people will know very much more about what the ego means to man than we do. As a matter of fact, we cannot see where that process might ultimately end.

Consciousness is like a surface or a skin upon a vast unconscious area of unknown extent. We do not know how far the unconscious rules because we simply know nothing of it. You cannot say anything about a thing of which you know nothing. When we say 'the unconscious' we often mean to convey something by the term, but as a matter of fact we simply convey that we do not know what the unconscious is. We have only indirect proofs that there is a mental sphere which is subliminal. We have some scientific justification for our conclusion that it exists. From the products which that unconscious mind produces we can draw certain conclusions as to its possible nature. But we must be careful not to be too anthropomorphic in our conclusions, because things might in reality be very different from what our consciousness makes them.

If, for instance, you look at our physical world and if you compare what our consciousness makes of this same world, you find all sorts of mental pictures which do not exist as objective facts. For instance, we see colour and hear sound, but in reality they are oscillations. As a matter of fact, we need a laboratory with very complicated apparatus in order to establish a picture of that world apart from our senses and apart from our psyche; and I suppose it is very much the same with our unconscious—we ought to have a laboratory in which we could establish by objective methods how things really are when in an unconscious condition. So any conclusion or any statement I make in the course of my lectures about the unconscious should be taken with that critique in mind. It is always *as if,* and you should never forget that restriction.

The conscious mind moreover is characterized by a certain narrowness. It can hold only a few simultaneous contents at a given moment. All the rest is unconscious at the time, and we only get a sort of continuation or a general understanding or awareness of a conscious world through the *succession* of conscious moments. We can never hold an image of totality because our consciousness is too narrow; we can only see flashes of existence. It is always as if we were observing through a slit so that we only see a particular moment; all the rest is dark and we are not aware of it at that moment. The area of the unconscious is enormous and always continuous, while the area of consciousness is a restricted field of momentary vision.

Consciousness is very much the product of perception and orientation in the *external* world. It is probably localized in the cerebrum, which is of ectodermic origin and was probably a sense organ of the skin at the time of our remote ancestors. The consciousness derived from that localization in the brain therefore probably retains these qualities of sensation and orientation. Peculiarly enough, the French and English psychologists of the early seventeenth and eighteenth centuries tried to derive consciousness from the senses as if it consisted solely of sense data. That is expressed by the famous formula *Nihil est in intellectu quod non fuerit in sensu.*[1] You can observe something similar in modern psychological theories. Freud, for instance, does not derive the conscious from sense data, but he derives the unconscious from the conscious, which is along the same rational line.

I would put it the reverse way: I would say the thing that comes first is obviously the unconscious and that consciousness really arises from an unconscious condition. In early childhood we are unconscious; the most important functions of an instinctive nature are unconscious, and consciousness is rather the product of the unconscious. It is a condition which demands a violent effort. You get tired from being conscious. You get exhausted by consciousness. It is an almost unnatural effort. When you observe primitives, for instance, you will see that on the slightest provocation or with no provocation whatever they doze off, they disappear. They sit for hours on end, and when you ask them, 'What are you doing? What are you thinking?' they are offended, because they say, 'Only a man that is crazy thinks—he has thoughts in his head. We do not think'. If they think at all, it is rather in the belly or in the heart. Certain Negro tribes assure you that thoughts are in the belly because they only realize those thoughts which actually dis-

1. ['There is nothing in the mind that was not in the senses'. Cf. Leibniz. *Nouveaux Essais sur l'Entendement humain,* Bk. II, ch. 1, sec. 2, in response to Locke. The formula was scholastic in origin; cf. Duns Scotus, *Super universalibus Porphyrii,* qu. 3.]

turb the liver, intestines, or stomach. In other words, they are conscious only of emotional thoughts. Emotions and affects are always accompanied by obvious physiological innervations.

The Pueblo Indians told me that all Americans are crazy, and of course I was somewhat astonished and asked them why. They said, 'Well, they say they think in their heads. No sound man thinks in the head. *We* think in the heart'. They are just about in the Homeric age, when the diaphragm (*phren* = mind, soul) was the seat of psychic activity. That means a psychic localization of a different nature. *Our* concept of consciousness supposes thought to be in our most dignified head. But the Pueblo Indians derive consciousness from the intensity of feeling. Abstract thought does not exist for them. As the Pueblo Indians are sun-worshippers, I tried the argument of St. Augustine on them. I told them that God is not the sun but the one who made the sun. They could not accept this because they cannot go beyond the perceptions of their senses and their feelings. Therefore consciousness and thought to them are localized in the heart. To us, on the other hand, psychic activities are nothing. We hold that dreams and fantasies are localized 'down below,' therefore there are people who speak of the *sub*-conscious mind, of the things that are *below* consciousness.

These peculiar localizations play a great role in so-called primitive psychology, which is by no means primitive. For instance if you study Tantric Yoga and Hindu psychology you will find the most elaborate system of psychic layers, of localizations of consciousness up from the region of the perineum to the top of the head. These 'centres' are the so-called *chakras,* and you not only find them in the teachings of yoga but can discover the same idea in old German alchemical books, which surely do not derive from a knowledge of yoga.

The important fact about consciousness is that nothing can be conscious without an ego to which it refers. If something is not related to the ego then it is not conscious. Therefore you can define consciousness as a relation of psychic facts to the ego. What is that ego? The ego is a complex datum which is constituted first of all by a general awareness of your body, of your existence, and secondly by your memory data; you have a certain idea of having been, a long series of memories. Those two are the main constituents of what we call the ego. Therefore you can call the ego a complex of psychic facts. This complex has a great power of attraction, like a magnet; it attracts contents from the unconscious, from that dark realm of which we know nothing; it also attracts impressions from the outside, and when they enter into association with the ego they are conscious. If they do not, they are not conscious.

My idea of the ego is that it is a sort of complex. Of course, the nearest and dearest complex which we cherish is our ego. It is always in the centre of our attention and of our desires, and it is the absolutely indispensable centre of consciousness. If the ego becomes split up, as in schizophrenia, all sense of values is gone, and also things become inaccessible for voluntary reproduction because the centre has split and certain parts of the psyche refer to one fragment of the ego and certain other contents to another fragment of the ego. Therefore, with a schizophrenic, you often see a rapid change from one personality into another.

You can distinguish a number of functions in consciousness. They enable consciousness to become oriented in the field of ectopsychic facts and endopsychic facts. What I understand by the *ectopsyche* is a system of relationship between the contents of consciousness and facts and data coming in from the environment. It is a system of orientation which concerns my dealing with the external facts given to me by the function of my senses. The *endopsyche,* on the other hand, is a system of relationship between the contents of consciousness and postulated processes in the unconscious.

In the first place we will speak of the ectopsychic functions. First of all we have *sensation,* our sense function. By sensation I understand what the French psychologists call 'la fonction du réel',* which is the sum-total of my awareness of external facts given to me through the function of my senses. So I think that the French term 'la fonction du réel' explains it in the most comprehensive way. Sensation tells me that something *is*: it does not tell me *what* it is and it does not tell me other things about that something; it only tells me that something is.

The next function that is distinguishable is *thinking.* Thinking, if you ask a philosopher, is something very difficult, so never ask a philosopher about it because he is the only man who does not know what thinking is. Everybody else knows what thinking is. When you say to a man, 'Now think properly', he knows exactly what you mean, but a philosopher never knows. Thinking in its simplest form tells you *what* a thing is. It gives a name to the thing. It adds a concept because thinking is perception and judgment. (German psychology calls it apperception.)

The third function you can distinguish and for which ordinary language has a term is *feeling.* Here minds become very confused and people get angry when I speak about feeling, because according to their view I say something very dreadful about it. Feeling informs you through its feeling-tones of the *values* of things. Feeling tells you for instance whether a thing is acceptable or agreeable or not. It tells you what a thing is *worth* to you. On account of that phenomenon, you cannot perceive and you cannot apperceive without having a certain feeling reaction. You always have a certain feeling-tone, which you can even demonstrate by experiment. We will talk of these things later on. Now

* The function of the real.

the 'dreadful' thing about feeling is that it is, like thinking, a *rational* function. All men who think are absolutely convinced that feeling is never a rational function but, on the contrary, most irrational. Now I say: Just be patient for a while and realize that man cannot be perfect in every respect. If a man is perfect in his thinking he is surely never perfect in his feeling, because you cannot do the two things at the same time; they hinder each other. Therefore when you want to think in a dispassionate way, really scientifically or philosophically, you must get away from all feeling-values. You cannot be bothered with feeling-values at the same time, otherwise you begin to feel that it is far more important to think about the freedom of the will than, for instance, about the classification of lice. And certainly if you approach from the point of view of feeling the two objects are not only different as to *facts* but also as to *value*. Values are no anchors for the intellect, but they exist and giving value is an important psychological function. If you want to have a complete picture of the world you must necessarily consider values. If you do not, you will get into trouble. To many people feeling appears to be most irrational, because you feel all sorts of things in foolish moods: therefore everybody is convinced, in this country particularly, that you should control your feelings. I quite admit that this is a good habit and wholly admire the English for that faculty. Yet there are such things as feelings, and I have seen people who control their feelings marvellously well and yet are terribly bothered by them.

Now the fourth function. Sensation tells us that a thing *is*. Thinking tells us *what* that thing is, feeling tells us what it is *worth* to us. Now what else could there be? One would assume one has a complete picture of the world when one knows there *is* something, *what* it is, and what it is *worth*. But there is another category, and that is time. Things have a past and they have a future. They come from somewhere, they go to somewhere, and you cannot see where they came from and you cannot know where they go to, but you get what the Americans call a hunch. For instance, if you are a dealer in art or in old furniture you get a hunch that a certain object is by a very good master of 1720, you get a hunch that it is good work. Or you do not know what shares will do after a while, but you get the hunch that they will rise. That is what is called *intuition,* a sort of divination, a sort of miraculous faculty. For instance, you do not know that your patient has something on his mind of a very painful kind, but you 'get an idea', you 'have a certain feeling', as we say, because ordinary language is not yet developed enough for one to have suitably defined terms. But the word intuition becomes more and more a part of the English language, and you are very fortunate because in other languages that word does not exist. The Germans cannot even make a linguistic distinction between sensation and feeling. It is different in French; if you speak French you cannot possibly say that you have a certain 'sentiment dans l'estomac',* you will say 'sensation'; in English you also have your distinctive words for sensation and feeling. But you can mix up *feeling* and *intuition* easily. Therefore it is an almost artificial distinction I make here, though for practical reasons it is most important that we make such a differentiation in scientific language. We must define what we mean when we use certain terms, otherwise we talk an unintelligible language, and in psychology this is always a misfortune. In ordinary conversation, when a man says feeling, he means possibly something entirely different from another fellow who also talks about feeling. There are any number of psychologists who use the word *feeling*, and they define it as a sort of crippled thought. 'Feeling is nothing but an unfinished thought'—that is the definition of a well-known psychologist. But feeling is something genuine, it is something real, it is a function, and therefore we have a word for it. The instinctive natural mind always finds the words that designate things which really have existence. Only psychologists invent words for things that do not exist.

The last-defined function, intuition, seems to be very mysterious, and you know I am 'very mystical,' as people say. This then is one of my pieces of mysticism! Intuition is a function by which you see round corners, which you really cannot do; yet the fellow will do it for you and you trust him. It is a function which normally you do not use if you live a regular life within four walls and do regular routine work. But if you are on the Stock Exchange or in Central Africa, you will use your hunches like anything. You cannot, for instance, calculate whether when you turn round a corner in the bush you will meet a rhinoceros or a tiger—but you get a hunch, and it will perhaps save your life. So you see that people who live exposed to natural conditions use intuition a great deal, and people who risk something in an unknown field, who are pioneers of some sort, will use intuition. Inventors will use it and judges will use it. Whenever you have to deal with strange conditions where you have no established values or established concepts, you will depend upon that faculty of intuition.

I have tried to describe that function as well as I can, but perhaps it is not very good. I say that intuition is a sort of perception which does not go exactly by the senses, but it goes via the unconscious, and at that I leave it and say 'I don't know how it works'. I do not know what is happening when a man knows something he definitely should not know. I do not know how he has come by it, but he has it all right and he can act on it. For instance, anticipatory dreams, telepathic phenomena, and all that kind of thing are intuitions. I have seen plenty of them, and I am convinced that they do exist. You can see these things also with primitives. You can see them everywhere if you pay attention to these perceptions that somehow work through the subliminal data, such as

* Feeling in my stomach.

sense-perceptions so feeble that our consciousness simply cannot take them in. Sometimes, for instance, in cryptomnesia,* something creeps up into consciousness; you catch a word which gives you a suggestion, but it is always something that is unconscious until the moment it appears, and so presents itself as if it had fallen from heaven. The Germans call this an *Einfall,* which means a thing which falls into your head from nowhere. Sometimes it is like a revelation. Actually, intuition is a very natural function, a perfectly normal thing, and it is necessary, too, because it makes up for what you cannot perceive or think or feel because it lacks reality. You see, the past is not real any more and the future is not as real as we think. Therefore we must be very grateful to heaven that we have such a function which gives us a certain light on those things which are round the corners. Doctors, of course, being often presented with the most unheard-of situations, need intuition a great deal. Many a good diagnosis comes from this 'very mysterious' function.

Psychological functions are usually controlled by the will, or we hope they are, because we are afraid of everything that moves by itself. When the functions are controlled they can be excluded from use, they can be suppressed, they can be selected, they can be increased in intensity, they can be directed by willpower, by what we call intention. But they also can function in an involuntary way, that is, they think for you, they feel for you—very often they do this and you cannot even stop them. Or they function unconsciously so that you do not know what they have done, though you might be presented, for instance, with the result of a feeling process which has happened in the unconscious. Afterwards somebody will probably say, 'Oh, you were very angry, or you were offended, and therefore you reacted in such and such a way'. Perhaps you are quite unconscious that you have felt in that way, nevertheless it is most probable that you have. Psychological functions, like the sense functions, have their specific energy. You cannot dispose of feeling, or of thinking, or of any of the four functions. No one can say, 'I will not think'—he will think inevitably. People cannot say, 'I will not feel'—they will feel because the specific energy invested in each function expresses itself and cannot be exchanged for another.

Of course, one has preferences. People who have a good mind prefer to think about things and to adapt by thinking. Other people who have a good feeling function are good social mixers, they have a great sense of values; they are real artists in creating feeling situations and living by feeling situations. Or a man with a keen sense of objective observation will use his sensation chiefly, and so on. The dominating function gives each individual his particular kind of psychology. For example, when a man uses chiefly his intellect, he will be of an unmistakable type, and you can deduce from that fact the condition of his

---

* A mental condition in which old ideas based on past experiences are forgotten and seem new upon reentry.

feeling. When thinking is the dominant or superior function, feeling is necessarily in an inferior condition. The same rule applies to the other three functions. But I will show you that with a diagram which will make it clear.

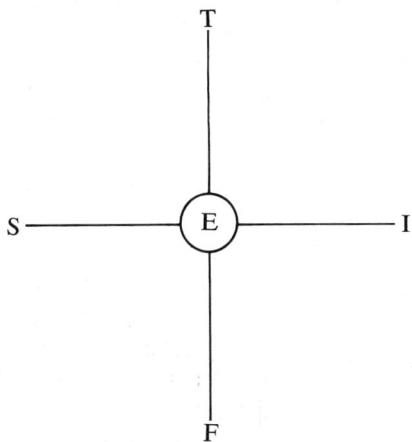

Figure 1 The Functions

You can make the so-called cross of the functions (Figure 1). In the centre is the *ego* (E), which has a certain amount of energy at its disposal, and that energy is the will-power. In the case of the thinking type, that will-power can be directed to *thinking* (T). Then we must put *feeling* (F) down below, because it is, in this case, the *inferior function*. That comes from the fact that when you think you must exclude feelings just as when you feel you must exclude thinking. If you are thinking, leave feeling and feeling-values alone, because feeling is most upsetting to your thoughts. On the other hand people who go by feeling-values leave thinking well alone, and they are right to do so, because these two different functions contradict each other. People have sometimes assured me that their thinking was just as differentiated as their feeling, but I could not believe it, because an individual cannot have the two opposites in the same degree of perfection at the same time.

The same is the case with *sensation* (S) and *intuition* (I). How do they affect each other? When you are observing physical facts you cannot see round corners at the same time. When you observe a man who is working by his sense function you will see, if you look at him attentively, that the axes of his eyes have a tendency to converge and to come together at one point. When you study the expression or the eyes of intuitive people, you will see that they only glance at things—they do not look, they radiate at things because they take in their fullness, and among the many things they perceive they get one point on the periphery of their field of vision and that is the *hunch*. Often you can tell from the eyes whether people are intuitive or not. When you have an intuitive attitude you usually do not observe the details. You try always to take in the whole of a situation, and then suddenly something crops up out of this wholeness. When you are a sensation type you will observe facts as they are, but then you have no intuition, simply because the two things cannot be done at the same time. It is too difficult, because the principle of the one function excludes the principle of the other function. That is why I put them here as opposites.

Now, from this simple diagram you can arrive at quite a lot of very important conclusions as to the structure of a given consciousness. For instance, if you find that *thinking* is highly differentiated, then feeling is undifferentiated. What does that mean? Does it mean these people have no feelings? No, on the contrary. They say, 'I have very strong feelings. I am full of emotion and temperament'. These people are under the sway of their emotions, they are caught by their emotions, they are overcome by their emotions at times. If, for instance, you study the private life of professors it is a very interesting study. If you want to be fully informed as to how the intellectual behaves at home, ask his wife and she will be able to tell you a story!

The reverse is true of the *feeling* type. The feeling type, if he is natural, never allows himself to be disturbed by thinking; but when he gets sophisticated and somewhat neurotic he is disturbed by thoughts. Then thinking appears in a compulsory way, he cannot get away from certain thoughts. He is a very nice chap, but he has extraordinary convictions and ideas, and his thinking is of an inferior kind. He is caught by this thinking, entangled in certain thoughts; he cannot disentangle because he cannot reason, his thoughts are not movable. On the other hand, an intellectual, when caught by his feelings, says, 'I feel just like that,' and there is no argument against it. Only when he is thoroughly boiled in his emotion will he come out of it again. He cannot be reasoned out of his feeling, and he would be a very incomplete man if he could.

The same happens with the *sensation* type and the *intuitive* type. The intuitive is always bothered by the reality of things; he fails from the standpoint of realities; he is always out for the possibilities of life. He is the man who plants a field and before the crop is ripe is off again to a new field. He has ploughed fields behind him and new hopes ahead all the time, and nothing comes off. But the sensation type remains with things. He remains in a given reality. To him a thing is true when it is real. Consider what it means to an intuitive when something is real. It is just the wrong thing; it should not be, something else should be. But when a sensation type does not have a given reality—four walls in which to be—he is sick. Give the intuitive type four walls in which to be, and the only thing is how to get out of it, because to him a given situation is a prison which must be undone in the shortest time so that he can be off to new possibilities.

These differences play a very great role in practical psychology. Do not think I am putting people into this box or that and saying, 'He is an intuitive', or 'He is a thinking type'. People often ask me, 'Now, is So-and-So not a thinking type?' I say, 'I never thought about it,' and I did not. It is no use at all putting people into drawers with different labels. But when you have a large empirical material, you need critical principles of order to help you to classify it. I hope I do not exaggerate, but to me it is very important to be able to create a kind of order in my empirical material, particularly when people are troubled and confused or when you have to explain them to somebody else. For instance, if you have to explain a wife to a husband or a husband to a wife, it is often very helpful to have these objective criteria, otherwise the whole thing remains 'He said'—'She said'.

As a rule, the inferior function does not possess the qualities of a conscious differentiated function. The conscious differentiated function can as a rule be handled by intention and by the will. If you are a real thinker, you can direct your thinking by your will, you can control your thoughts. You are not the slave of your thoughts, you can think of something else. You can say, 'I can think something quite different, I can think the contrary'. But the feeling type can never do that because he cannot get rid of his thought. The thought possesses him, or rather he is possessed by thought. Thought has a fascination for him, therefore he is afraid of it. The intellectual type is afraid of being caught by feeling because his feeling has an archaic quality, and there he is like an archaic man—he is the helpless victim of his emotions. It is for this reason that primitive man is extraordinarily polite, he is very careful not to disturb the feelings of his fellows because it is dangerous to do so. Many of our customs are explained by that archaic politeness. For instance, it is not the custom to shake hands with somebody and keep your left hand in your pocket, or behind your back, because it must be visible that you do not carry a weapon in that hand. The Oriental greeting of bowing with hands extended palms upward means 'I have nothing in my hands'. If you kowtow you dip your head to the feet of the other man so that he sees you are absolutely defenceless and that you trust him completely. You can still study the symbolism of manners with primitives, and you can also see why they are afraid of the other fellow. In a similar way, we are afraid of our inferior functions. If you take a typical intellectual who is terribly afraid of falling in love, you will think his fear very foolish. But he is most probably right, because he will very likely make foolish nonsense when he falls in love. He will be caught most certainly, because his feeling only reacts to an archaic or to a dangerous type of woman. This is why many intellectuals are inclined to marry beneath them. They are caught by the landlady perhaps, or by the cook, because they are unaware of their archaic feeling through which they get caught. But they are right to be afraid, because their undoing will be in their feeling. Nobody can attack them in their intellect. There they are strong and can stand alone, but in their feelings they can be influenced, they can be caught, they can be cheated, and they know it. Therefore never force a man into his feeling when he is an intellectual. He controls it with an iron hand because it is very dangerous.

The same law applies to each function. The inferior function is always associated with an archaic personality in ourselves; in the inferior function we are all primitives. In our differentiated functions we are civilized and we are supposed to have free will; but there is no such thing as free will when it comes to the inferior function. There we have an open wound, or at least an open door through which anything might enter.

Now I am coming to the *endopsychic functions* of consciousness. The functions of which I have just spoken rule or help our conscious orientation in our relations with the environment; but they do not apply to the relation of things that are as it were below the ego. The ego is only a bit of consciousness which floats upon the ocean of the dark things. The dark things are the inner things. On that inner side there is a layer of psychic events that forms a sort of fringe of consciousness round the ego. I will illustrate it by a diagram (Figure 2).

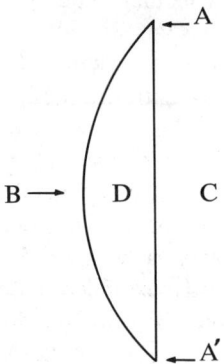

Figure 2 The Ego

If you suppose AA′ to be the threshold of consciousness, then you would have in D an area of consciousness referring to the ectopsychic world B, the world ruled by those functions of which we were just speaking. But on the other side, in C, is the *shadow-world*. There the ego is somewhat dark, we do not see into it, we are an enigma to ourselves. We only know the ego in D, we do not know it in C. Therefore we are always discovering something new about ourselves. Almost every year something new turns up which we did not know before. We always think we are now at the end of our discoveries. We never are. We go on discovering that we are this, that, and other things, and sometimes we have astounding experiences. That shows there is always a part of our personality which is still unconscious, which is still becoming; we are unfinished; we are growing and changing. Yet that future personality which we are to be in a year's time is already here, only it is still in the shadow. The ego is like a moving frame on a film. The future personality is not yet visible, but we are moving along, and presently we come to view the future being. These potentialities naturally belong to the dark side of the ego. We are well aware of what we have been, but we are not aware of what we are going to be.

Therefore the *first* function on that endopsychic side is *memory*. The function of memory, or reproduction, links us up with things that have faded out of consciousness, things that became subliminal or were cast away or repressed. What we call memory is this faculty to reproduce unconscious contents, and it is the first function we can clearly distinguish in its relationship between our consciousness and the contents that are actually not in view.

The *second* endopsychic function is a more difficult problem. We are now getting into deep waters because here we are coming into darkness. I will give you the name first: *the subjective components of conscious functions*. I hope I can make it clear. For instance, when you meet a man you have not seen before, naturally you think something about him. You do not always think things you would be ready to tell him immediately; perhaps you think things that are untrue, that do not really apply. Clearly, they are subjective reactions. The same reactions take place with things and with situations. Every application of a conscious function, whatever the object might be, is always accompanied by subjective reactions which are more or less inadmissible or unjust or inaccurate. You are painfully aware that these things happen in you, but nobody likes to admit that he is subject to such phenomena. He prefers to leave them in the shadow, because that helps him to assume that he is perfectly innocent and very nice and honest and straightforward and 'only too willing', etc. - you know all these phrases. As a matter of fact, one is not. One has any amount of subjective reactions, but it is not quite becoming to admit these things. These reactions I call the subjective components. They are a very important part of our relations to our own inner side. There things get definitely painful. That is why we dislike entering this shadow-world of the ego. We do not like to look at the shadow-side of ourselves; therefore there are many people in our civilized society who have lost their shadow altogether, they have got rid of it. They are only two-dimensional; they have lost the third dimension, and with it they have usually lost the body. The body is a most doubtful friend because it produces things we do not like; there are too many things about the body which cannot be mentioned. The body is very often the personification of this shadow of the ego. Sometimes it forms the skeleton in the cupboard, and everybody naturally wants to get rid of such a thing. I think this makes sufficiently clear what I mean by subjective components. They are usually a sort of disposition to react in a certain way, and usually the disposition is not altogether favourable.

There is one exception to this definition: a person who is not, as we suppose we all are, living on the positive side, putting the right foot forward and not the wrong one, etc. There are certain individuals whom we call in our Swiss dialect 'pitch-birds' [*Pechvögel*]; they are always getting into messes, they put their foot in it and always cause trouble, because they *live* their own shadow, they live their own negation. They are the sort of people who come late to a concert or a lecture, and because they are very modest and do not want to disturb other people, they sneak in at the end and then stumble over a chair and make a hideous racket so that everybody has to look at them. Those are the 'pitch-birds'.

Now we come to the *third* endopsychic component—I cannot say function. In the case of memory you can speak of a function, but even your memory is only to a certain extent a voluntary or controlled function. Very often it is exceedingly tricky; it is like a bad horse that cannot be mastered. It often refuses in the most embarrassing way. All the more is this the case with the subjective components and reactions. And now things begin to get worse, for this is where the *emotions* and *affects* come in. They are clearly not functions any more, they are just events, because in an emotion, as the word denotes, you are moved away, you are cast out, your decent ego is put aside, and something else takes your place. We say, 'He is beside himself', or 'The devil is riding him', or 'What has gotten into him today', because he is like a man who is possessed. The primitive does not say he got angry beyond measure; he says a spirit got into him and changed him completely. Something like that happens with emotions; you are simply possessed, you are no longer yourself, and your control is decreased practically to zero. That is a condition in which the inner side of a man takes hold of him, he cannot prevent it. He can clench his fists, he can keep quiet, but it has him nevertheless.

The *fourth* important endopsychic factor is what I call *invasion*. Here the shadow-side, the unconscious side, has full control so that it can break into the conscious condition. Then the conscious control is at its lowest. Those are the moments in a human life which you do not necessarily call pathological; they are pathological only in the old sense of the word when pathology meant the science of the passions. In that sense you can call them pathological, but it is really an extraordinary condition in which a man is seized upon by his unconscious and when anything may come out of him. One can lose one's mind in a more or less normal way. For instance, we cannot assume that the cases our ancestors knew very well are abnormal, because they are perfectly normal phenomena among primitives. They speak of the devil or an incubus or a spirit going into a man, or of his soul leaving him, one of his separate souls—they often have as many as six. When his soul leaves him, he is in an altered condition because he is suddenly deprived of himself; he suffers a loss of self. That is a thing you can often observe in neurotic patients. On certain days, or from time to time, they suddenly lose their energy, they lose themselves, and they come under a strange influence. These phenomena are not in themselves pathological; they belong to the ordinary phenomenology of man, but if they become habitual we rightly speak of a neurosis. These are the things that lead to neurosis; but they are also exceptional conditions among normal people. To have overwhelming emotions is not in itself pathological, it is merely undesirable. We need not invent such a word as pathological for an undesirable thing, because there are other undesirable things in the world which are not pathological, for instance, tax-collectors.

LECTURE TWO

We cannot deal with unconscious processes directly because they are not reachable. They are not directly apprehended; they appear only in their products, and we postulate from the peculiar quality of those products that there must be something behind them from which they originate. We call that dark sphere the unconscious psyche.

The ectopsychic contents of consciousness derive in the first place from the environment, through the data of the senses. Then the contents also come from other sources, such as memory and processes of judgment. These belong to the endopsychic sphere. A third source for conscious contents is the dark sphere of the mind, the unconscious. We approach it through the peculiarities of the endopsychic functions, those functions which are not under the control of the will. They are the vehicle by which unconscious contents reach the surface of consciousness.

The unconscious processes, then, are not directly observable, but those of its products that cross the threshold of consciousness can be divided into two classes. The first class contains recognizable material of a definitely personal origin; these contents are individual acquisitions or products of instinctive processes that make up the personality as a whole. Furthermore, there are forgotten or repressed contents, and creative contents. There is nothing specially peculiar about them. In other people such things may be conscious. Some people are conscious of things of which other people are not. I call that class of contents the subconscious mind or the *personal unconscious,* because, as far as we can judge, it is entirely made up of personal elements, elements that constitute the human personality as a whole.

Then there is another class of contents of definitely unknown origin, or at all events of an origin which cannot be ascribed to individual acquisition. These contents have one outstanding peculiarity, and that is their mythological character. It is as if they belong to a pattern not peculiar to any particular mind or person, but rather to a pattern peculiar to *mankind in general.* When I first came across such contents I wondered very much whether they might not be due to heredity, and I thought they might be explained by racial inheritance. In order to settle that question I went to the United States and studied the dreams of pure-blooded Negroes, and I was able to satisfy myself that these images have nothing to do with so-called blood or racial inheritance, nor are they personally acquired by the individual. They belong to mankind in general, and therefore they are of a *collective* nature.

These collective patterns I have called *archetypes,* using an expression of St Augustine's. An archetype means a *typos* [imprint], a definite grouping of archaic character containing, in form as well as in meaning, *mythological motifs.* Mythological motifs appear in pure form in fairytales, myths, legends, and folklore. Some of the well-known motifs are: the figures of the Hero, the Redeemer, the Dragon (always connected with the Hero, who has to overcome him), the Whale or the Monster who swallows the Hero. Another variation of the motif of the Hero and the Dragon is the Katabasis, the Descent into the Cave, the Nekyia. You remember in the Odyssey where Ulysses descends *ad inferos* * to consult Tiresias,† the seer. This motif of the Nekyia is found everywhere in antiquity and practically all over the world. It expresses the psychological mechanism of introversion of the conscious mind into the deeper layers of the unconscious psyche. From these layers derive the contents of an impersonal, mythological character, in other words, the archetypes, and I call them therefore the impersonal or *collective unconscious.*

I am perfectly well aware that I can give you only the barest outline of this particular question of the collective unconscious. But I will give you an example of its symbolism and of how I proceed in order to discriminate it from the personal unconscious. When I went to America to investigate the unconscious of Negroes I had in mind this particular problem: are these collective patterns racially inherited, or are they 'a priori categories of imagination', as two Frenchmen, Hubert and Mauss,

---
* Into Hades.
† Tiresias, the long-lived blind prophet who appears in Sophocles' Oedipus *Rex.*

quite independently of my own work, have called them. A Negro told me a dream in which occurred the figure of a man crucified on a wheel. I will not mention the whole dream because it does not matter. It contained of course its personal meaning as well as allusions to impersonal ideas, but I picked out only that one motif. He was a very uneducated Negro from the South and not particularly intelligent. It would have been most probable, given the well-known religious character of the Negroes, that he should dream of a man crucified on a *cross*. The cross would have been a personal acquisition. But it is rather improbable that he should dream of the man crucified on a *wheel*. That is a very uncommon image. Of course I cannot prove to you that by some curious chance the Negro had not seen a picture or heard something of the sort and then dreamt about it; but if he had not had any model for this idea it would be an *archetypal image,* because the crucifixion on the wheel is a *mythological motif*. It is the ancient sun-wheel, and the crucifixion is the sacrifice to the sun-god in order to propitiate him, just as human and animal sacrifices formerly were offered for the fertility of the earth. The sun-wheel is an exceedingly archaic idea, perhaps the oldest religious idea there is. We can trace it to the Mesolithic and Paleolithic ages, as the sculptures of Rhodesia prove. Now there were real wheels only in the Bronze Age; in the Paleolithic Age the wheel was not yet invented. The Rhodesian sun-wheel seems to be contemporary with very naturalistic animal-pictures, like the famous rhino with the tick-birds, a masterpiece of observation. The Rhodesian sun-wheel is therefore an original vision, presumably an archetypal sun-image. But this image is not a naturalistic one, for it is always divided into four or eight partitions (Figure 3). This

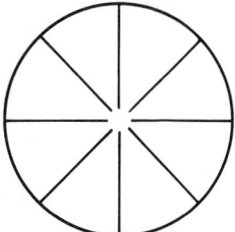

Figure 3 Sun-wheel

image, a sort of divided circle, is a symbol which you find throughout the whole history of mankind as well as in the dreams of modern individuals. We might assume that the invention of the actual wheel started from this vision. Many of our inventions came from mythological anticipations and primordial images. For instance, the art of alchemy is the mother of modern chemistry. Our conscious scientific mind started in the matrix of the unconscious mind.

In the dream of the Negro, the man on the wheel is a repetition of the Greek mythological motif of Ixion, who, on account of his offence against men and gods, was fastened by Zeus upon an incessantly turning wheel. I give you this example of a mythological motif in a dream merely in order to convey to you an idea of the collective unconscious. One single example is of course no conclusive proof. But one cannot very well assume that this Negro had studied Greek mythology, and it is improbable that he had seen any representation of Greek mythological figures. Furthermore, figures of Ixion are pretty rare.

I could give you conclusive proof of a very elaborate kind of the existence of these mythological patterns in the unconscious mind. But in order to present my material I should need to lecture for a fortnight. I would have first to explain to you the meaning of dreams and dream-series and then give you all the historical parallels and explain fully their importance, because the symbolism of these images and ideas is not taught in public schools or universities, and even specialists very rarely know of it. I had to study it for years and to find the material myself, and I cannot expect even a highly educated audience to be *au courant* with such abstruse matters. When we come to the technique of dream-analysis I shall be forced to enter into some of the mythological material and you will get a glimpse of what this work of finding parallels to unconscious products is really like. For the moment I have to content myself with the mere statement that there are mythological patterns in that layer of the unconscious, that it produces contents which cannot be ascribed to the individual and which may even be in strict contradiction to the personal psychology of the dreamer. For instance, you are simply astounded when you observe a completely uneducated person producing a dream which really should not occur with such a person because it contains the most amazing things. And children's dreams often make you think to such a degree that you must take a holiday afterwards in order to recover from the shock, because these symbols are so tremendously profound, and you think: How on earth is it possible that a child should have such a dream?

It is really quite simple to explain. Our mind has its history, just as our body has its history. You might be just as astonished that man has an appendix, for instance. Does he know he ought to have an appendix? He is just born with it. Millions of people do not know they have a thymus, but they have it. They do not know that in certain parts of their anatomy they belong to the species of the fishes, and yet it is so. Our unconscious mind, like our body, is a storehouse of relics and memories of the past. A study of the structure of the unconscious collective mind would reveal the same discoveries as you make in comparative anatomy. We do not need to think that there is anything mystical about it. But because I speak of a collective unconscious, I have been accused of obscurantism. There is nothing mystical about the collective unconscious. It is just a new branch of science, and it is really common sense to admit the existence of unconscious collective processes. For, though a child is not born conscious, his mind is not a *tabula rasa.** The child is born with a definite brain, and the brain of an English child will work not like that of an Australian blackfellow but in the way of a modern English person. The brain is born with a finished structure, it will work in a modern way, but this brain has its history. It has been built up in the course of millions of years and represents a history of which it is the result. Naturally it carries with it the traces of that history, exactly like the body, and if you grope down into the basic structure of the mind you naturally find traces of the archaic mind.

The idea of the collective unconscious is really very simple. If it were not so, then one could speak of a miracle, and I am not a miracle-monger at all. I simply go by experience. If I could tell you the experiences you would draw the same conclusions about these archaic motifs. By chance, I stumbled somehow into mythology and have read more books perhaps than you. I have not always been a student of mythology. One day, when I was still at the clinic, I saw a patient with schizophrenia who had a peculiar vision, and he told me about it. He wanted me to see it and, being very dull, I could not see it. I thought, 'This man is crazy and I am normal and his vision should not bother me'. But it did. I asked myself: What does it mean? I was not satisfied that is was just crazy, and later I came on a book by a German scholar, Dieterich, who had published part of a magic papyrus. I studied it with great interest, and on page 7 I found the vision of my lunatic 'word for word'. That gave me a shock. I said: 'How on earth is it possible that this fellow came into possession of that vision?' It was not just one image, but a series of images and a literal repetition of them. I do not want to go into it now because it would lead us too far. It is a highly interesting case: as a matter of fact, I published it.[2]

This astonishing parallelism set me going. You probably have not come across the book of the learned professor Dieterich, but if you had read the same books and observed such cases you would have discovered the idea of the collective unconscious.

The deepest we can reach in our exploration of the unconscious mind is the layer where man is no longer a distinct individual, but where his mind widens out and merges into the mind of mankind—not the conscious mind, but the unconscious mind of mankind, where we are all the same. As the body has its anatomical conformity in its two eyes and two ears and one heart and so on, with only slight individual differences, so has the mind its basic conformity. On this collective level we are no longer

---

* Blank tablet. The primary assumption of John Locke (1632–1704), English philosopher and founder of empiricism, was that the mind was born blank and that everything contained in it had been inscribed there by means of sensations through the five senses.
2. *How Natives Think,* trans. by Lilian A. Clare.

separate individuals, we are all one. You can understand this when you study the psychology of primitives. The outstanding fact about the primitive mentality is this lack of distinctiveness between individuals, this oneness of the subject with the object, this *participation mystique,** as Lévy-Bruhl terms it. Primitive mentality expresses the basic structure of the mind, that psychological layer which with us is the collective unconscious, that underlying level which is the same in all. Because the basic structure of the mind is the same in everybody, we cannot make distinctions when we experience on that level. There we do not know if something has happened to you or to me. In the underlying collective level there is a wholeness which cannot be dissected. If you begin to think about participation as a fact which means that fundamentally we are identical with everybody and everything, you are led to very peculiar theoretical conclusions. You should not go further than those conclusions because these things get dangerous. But some of the conclusions you should explore, because they can explain a lot of peculiar things that happen to man.

I want to sum up: I have brought a diagram (Figure 4). It looks very complicated but as a matter of fact it is very simple. Suppose our mental sphere to look like a lighted globe. The surface from which the light emanates is the function by which you chiefly adapt. If you are a person who adapts chiefly by thinking, your surface if the surface of a thinking man. You will tackle things with your thinking, and what you will show to people will be your thinking. It will be another function if you are of another type.[3]

In the diagram, *sensation* is given as the peripheral function. By it man gets information from the world of external objects. In the second circle, *thinking,* he gets what his senses have told him; he will give things a name. Then he will have a *feeling* about them; a feeling-tone will accompany his observation. And in the end he will get some consciousness of where a thing comes from, where it may go, and what it may do. That is *intuition,* by which you see round corners. These four functions form the ectopsychic system.

The next sphere in the diagram represents the conscious ego-complex to which the functions refer. Inside the endopsyche you first notice *memory,* which is still a function that can be controlled by the will; it is under the control of your ego-complex. Then we meet the *subjective components of the functions.* They cannot be exactly directed by the will but they still can be suppressed, excluded, or increased in intensity by will-power. These components are no longer as controllable as memory, though even memory is a bit tricky as you know. Then we come to the

---

* Mystical participation.
3. For a general description of types and functions, see *Psychological Types,* Chap. X.

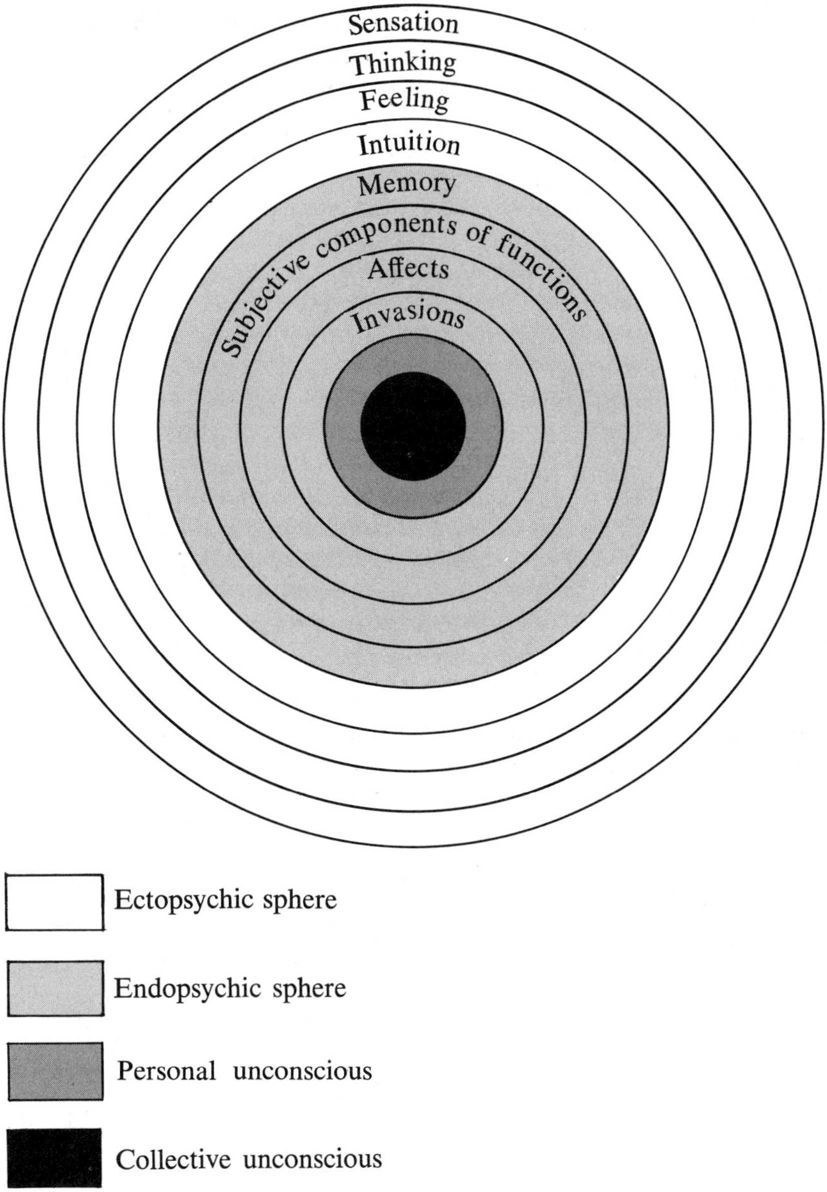

Sensation
Thinking
Feeling
Intuition
Memory
Subjective components of functions
Affects
Invasions

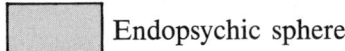 Ectopsychic sphere

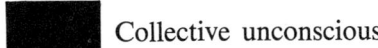 Endopsychic sphere

Personal unconscious

Collective unconscious

Figure 4 The Psyche

affects and *invasions*, which are only controllable by sheer force. You can suppress them, and that is all you can do. You have to clench your fists in order not to explode because they are apt to be stronger than your ego-complex.

This psychic system cannot really be expressed by such a crude diagram. The diagram is rather a scale of values showing how the energy or intensity of the ego-complex which manifests itself in will-power gradually decreases as you approach the darkness that is ultimately at the bottom of the whole structure—the *unconscious*. First we have the personal subconscious mind. The *personal unconscious* is that part of the psyche which contains all the things that could just as well be conscious. You know that many things are termed unconscious, but that is only a relative statement. There is nothing in this particular sphere that is necessarily unconscious in everybody. There are people who are conscious of almost anything of which man can be conscious. Of course we have an extraordinary amount of unconsciousness in our civilization, but if you go to other races, to India or to China, for example, you discover that these people are conscious of things for which the psychoanalyst in our countries has to dig for months. Moreover, simple people in natural conditions often have an extraordinary consciousness of things of which people in towns have no knowledge and of which townspeople begin to dream only under the influence of psychoanalysis. I noticed this at school. I had lived in the country among peasants and with animals, and I was fully conscious of a number of things of which other boys had no idea. I had the chance and I was not prejudiced. When you analyse dreams or symptoms or fantasies of neurotic or normal people, you begin to penetrate the unconscious mind, and you can abolish its artificial threshold. The personal unconscious is really something very relative, and its circle can be restricted and become so much narrower that it touches zero. It is quite thinkable that a man can develop his consciousness to such an extent that he can say: *Nihil humanum a me alienum puto.*[4]

Finally we come to the ultimate kernel which cannot be made conscious at all—the sphere of the archetypal mind. Its presumable contents appear in the form of images which can be understood only by comparing them with historical parallels. If you do not recognize certain material as historical and if you do not possess the parallels, you cannot integrate these contents into consciousness and they remain projected. The contents of the *collective unconscious* are not subject to any arbitrary intention and are not controllable by the will. They actually behave as if they did not exist in yourself—you see them in your neighbours but not in yourself. When the contents of the collective unconscious become activated,

---

4. [Cf. Terence, *Heauton Timorumenos,* 1.1.25: 'Homo sum; humani nil a me alienum puto' (I am a man; I count nothing human alien to me).]

we become aware of certain things in our fellow men. For instance, we begin to discover that the bad Abyssinians are attacking Italy. You know the famous story by Anatole France. Two peasants were always fighting each other, and there was somebody who wanted to go into the reasons for it, and he asked one man: 'Why do you hate your neighbour and fight him like this?' He replied: 'Mais il est de l'autre côté de la rivière!'* That is like France and Germany. We Swiss people, you know, had a very good chance during the Great War to read newspapers and to study that particular mechanism which behaved like a great gun firing on one side of the Rhine and in exactly the same way on the other side, and it was very clear that people saw in their neighbours the thing they did not recognize in themselves.

As a rule, when the collective unconscious becomes really constellated in larger social groups, the result is a public craze, a mental epidemic that may lead to revolution or war or something of the sort. These movements are exceedingly contagious—almost overwhelmingly contagious because, when the collective unconscious is activated, you are no longer the same person. You are not only *in* the movement—you *are* it. If you lived in Germany or were there for a while, you would defend yourself in vain. It gets under your skin. You are human, and wherever you are in the world you can defend yourself only by restricting your consciousness and making yourself as empty, as soulless, as possible. Then you lose your soul, because you are only a speck of consciousness floating on a sea of life in which you do not participate. But if you remain yourself you will notice that the collective atmosphere gets under your skin. You cannot live in Africa or any such country without having that country under your skin. You cannot prevent it, because somewhere you are the same as the Negro or the Chinese or whoever you live with, you are all just human beings. In the collective unconscious you are the same as a man of another race, you have the same archetypes, just as you have, like him, eyes, a heart, a liver, and so on. It does not matter that his skin is black. It matters to a certain extent, sure enough—he has probably a whole historical layer less than you. The different strata of the mind correspond to the history of the races.

If you study races as I have done you can make very interesting discoveries. You can make them, for instance, if you analyse North Americans. The American, on account of the fact that he lives on virgin soil, has the Red Indian in him. The Red man, even if he has never seen one, and the Negro, though he may be cast out and the tram-cars reserved for white men only, have got into the American and you will realize that he belongs to a partly coloured nation.[5] These things are

* But it's the other way around!
5. [*Civilization in Transition* (C. W., vol. 10), pars. 94 ff and 946 ff.]

wholly unconscious, and you can only talk to very enlightened people about them. It is just as difficult to talk to Frenchmen or Germans when you have to tell them why they are so much against each other.

A little while ago I had a nice evening in Paris. Some very cultivated men had invited me, and we had a pleasant conversation. They asked me about national differences, and I thought I would put my foot in it, so I said: 'What you value is *la clarté latine, la clarté de l'esprit latin.** That is because your thinking is inferior. The Latin thinker is inferior in comparison to the German thinker.' They cocked their ears, and I said: 'But your feeling is unsurpassable, it is absolutely differentiated'. They said: 'How is that?' I replied: 'Go to a café or a vaudeville or a place where you hear songs and stage-plays and you will notice a very peculiar phenomenon. There are any number of very grotesque and cynical things and then suddenly something sentimental happens. A mother loses her child, there is a lost love, or something marvellously patriotic, and you must weep. For you, the salt and the sugar have to go together. But a German can stand a whole evening of sugar only. The Frenchman must have some salt in it. You meet a man and say: *Enchanté de faire votre connaissance.*† You are not *enchanté de faire sa connaissance* at all; you are really feeling: Oh go to the devil. But you are not disturbed, nor is he. But do not say to a German: *Enchanté de faire votre connaissance,* because he will believe it. A German will sell you a pair of sock-suspenders and not only expect, as is natural, to be paid for it. He also expects to be loved for it'.

The German nation is characterized by the fact that its feeling function is inferior, it is not differentiated. If you say that to a German he is offended. I should be offended too. He is very attached to what he calls *Gemütlichkeit.*‡ A room full of smoke in which everybody loves everybody —that is *gemütlich* and that must not be disturbed. It has to be absolutely clear, just one note and no more. That is *la clarté germanique du sentiment,*§ and it is inferior. On the other hand, it is a gross offense to a Frenchman to say something paradoxical, because it is not clear. An English philosopher has said, 'A superior mind is never quite clear'. That is true, and also superior feeling is never quite clear. You will only enjoy a feeling that is above board when it is slightly doubtful, and a thought that does not have a slight contradiction in it is not convincing.

Our particular problem from now on will be: How can we approach the dark sphere of man? As I have told you, this is done by three methods of analysis: the word-association test, dream-analysis, and the method of active imagination. First of all I want to say something about *word-*

---

* Latin clarity; the lucidity of the Latin mind.
† Pleased to make your acquaintance.
‡ Comfort, coziness.
§ The Germanic transparency of feeling.

association tests.[6] To many of you perhaps these seem old-fashioned, but since they are still being used I have to refer to them. I use this test now not with patients but with criminal cases.

The experiment is made—I am repeating well-known things—with a list of say a hundred words. You instruct the test person to react with the first word that comes into his mind as quickly as possible after having heard and understood the stimulus word. When you have made sure that the test person has understood what you mean you start the experiment. You mark the time of each reaction with a stop-watch. When you have finished the hundred words you do another experiment. You repeat the stimulus words and the test person has to reproduce his former answers. In certain places his memory fails and reproduction becomes uncertain to faulty. These mistakes are important.

Originally the experiment was not meant for its present application at all; it was intended to be used for the study of mental association. That was of course a most Utopian idea. One can study nothing of the sort by such primitive means. But you can study something else when the experiment fails, when people make mistakes. You ask a simple word that a child can answer, and a highly intelligent person cannot reply. Why? That word has hit on what I call a complex, a conglomeration of psychic contents characterized by a peculiar or perhaps painful feeling-tone, something that is usually hidden from sight. It is as though a projectile struck through the thick layer of the *persona*[7] into the dark layer. For instance, somebody with a money complex will be hit when you say: 'To buy', 'to pay', or 'money'. That is a disturbance or reaction.

We have about twelve or more categories of disturbance and I will mention a few of them so that you will get an idea of their practical value. The prolongation of the reaction time is of the greatest practical importance. You decide whether the reaction time is too long by taking the average mean of the reaction times of the test person. Other characteristic disturbances are: reaction with more than one word, against the instructions; mistakes in reproduction of the word; reaction expressed by facial expression, laughing, movement of the hands or feet or body, coughing, stammering, and such things; insufficient reactions like 'yes' or 'no'; not reacting to the real meaning of the stimulus word; habitual use of the same words; use of foreign languages—of which there is not a great danger in England, though with us it is a great nuisance; defective reproduction, when memory begins to fail in the reproduction experiment; total lack of reaction.

All these reactions are beyond the control of the will. If you submit to the experiment you are done for, and if you do not submit to it you are done for too, because one knows why you are unwilling to do so. If you

---

6. *Studies in Word Association,* tr. Eder.
7. *Two Essays on Analytical Psychology* (C. W., vol. 7), pars. 245 f., 304 f.

put it to a criminal he can refuse, and that is fatal because one knows why he refuses. If he gives in he hangs himself. In Zurich I am called in by the Court when they have a difficult case; I am the last straw.

The results of the association test can be illustrated very neatly by a diagram (Figure 5). The height of the columns represents the actual

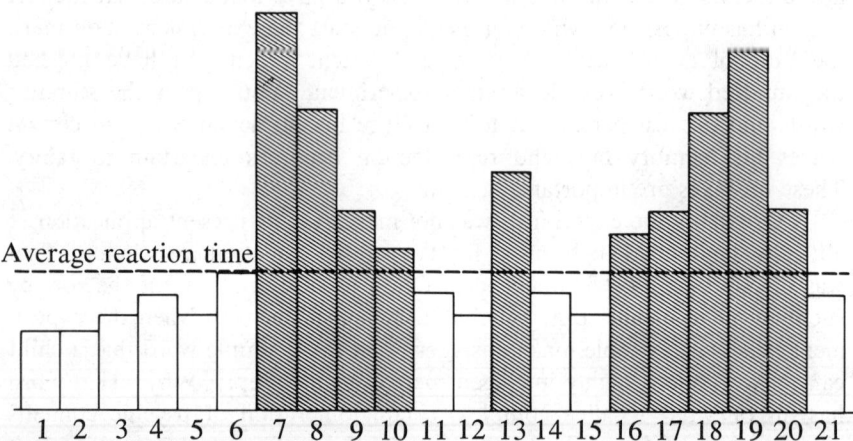

Stimulus words: 7 knife; 13 lance (=spear); 16 to beat; 18 pointed; 19 bottle.

Figure 5 Association Test

reaction time of the test person. The dotted horizontal line represents the average mean of reaction times. The unshaded columns are those reactions which show no signs of disturbance. The shaded columns show disturbed reactions. In reactions 7, 8, 9, 10, you observe for instance a whole series of disturbances: the stimulus word at 7 was a critical one, and without the test person noticing it at all three subsequent reaction times are overlong on account of the perseveration of the reaction to the stimulus word. The test person was quite unconscious of the fact that he had an emotion. Reaction 13 shows an isolated disturbance, and in 16-20 the result is again a whole series of disturbances. The strongest disturbances are in reactions 18 and 19. In this particular case we have to do with a so-called intensification of sensitiveness through the sensitizing effect of an unconscious emotion: when a critical stimulus word has aroused a perseverating emotional reaction, and when the next critical stimulus word happens to occur within the range of that perseveration, then it is apt to produce a greater effect than it would have been expected to produce if it had occurred in a series of indifferent associations. This is called the sensitizing effect of a perseverating emotion.

In dealing with criminal cases we can make use of the sensitizing effect, and then we arrange the critical stimulus words in such a way that they occur more or less within the presumable range of perseveration. This can be done in order to increase the effect of critical stimulus words. With a suspected culprit as a test person, the critical stimulus words are words which have a direct bearing upon the crime.

The test person for Figure 5 was a man about 35, a decent individual, one of my normal test persons. I had of course to experiment with a great number of normal people before I could draw conclusions from pathological material. If you want to know what it was that disturbed this man, you simply have to read the words that caused the disturbances and fit them together. Then you get a nice story. I will tell you exactly what it was.

To begin with, it was the word *knife* that caused four disturbed reactions. The next disturbance was *lance* (or *spear*) and then *to beat,* then the word *pointed* and then *bottle*. That was in a short series of fifty stimulus words, which was enough for me to tell the man point-blank what the matter was. So I said: 'I did not know you had had such a disagreeable experience'. He stared at me and said: 'I do not know what you are talking about'. I said, 'You know you were drunk and had a disagreeable affair with sticking your knife into somebody'. He said: 'How do you know?' Then he confessed the whole thing. He came of a respectable family, simple but quite nice people. He had been abroad and one day got into a drunken quarrel, drew a knife and stuck it into somebody, and got a year in prison. That is a great secret which he does not mention because it would cast a shadow on his life. Nobody in his town or surroundings knows anything about it and I am the only one who by chance stumbled upon it. In my seminar in Zurich I also make these experiments. Those who want to confess are of course welcome to. However, I always ask them to bring some material of a person *they* know and *I* do not know, and I show them how to read the story of that individual. It is quite interesting work; sometimes one makes remarkable discoveries.

I will give you other instances. Many years ago, when I was quite a young doctor, an old professor of criminology asked me about the experiment and said he did not believe in it. I said: 'No, Professor? You can try it whenever you like'. He invited me to his house and I began. After ten words he got tired and said: 'What can you make of it? Nothing has come of it'. I told him he could not expect a result with ten or twelve words; he ought to have a hundred and then we would see something. He said: 'Can you do something with these words?' I said: 'Little enough, but I can tell you something. Quite recently you have had worries about money, you have too little of it. You are afraid of dying of heart disease. You must have studied in France, where you had a love affair, and it has come back to your mind, as often, when one has thoughts of dying, old sweet memories come back from the womb of time'. He said: 'How do you know?' Any child could have seen it! He was a man of 72 and he had associated *heart* with *pain*—fear that he would die of heart failure. He associated *death* with *to die*—a natural reaction—and with *money* he associated *too little*, a very usual reaction. Then things became rather startling to me. To *pay*, after a long reaction time, he said *La Semeuse*, though our conversation was in German. That is the famous figure on the French coin. Now why on earth should this old man say *La Semeuse*? When he came to the word *kiss* there was a long reaction time and there was a light in his eyes and he said: *Beautiful*. Then of course I had the story. He would never have used French if it had not been associated with a particular feeling, and so we must think why he used it. Had he had losses with the French franc? There was no talk of inflation and devaluation in those days. That could not be the clue. I was in doubt whether it was money or love, but when he came to *kiss|beautiful* I knew it was love. He was not the kind of man to go to France in later life, but he had been a student in Paris, a lawyer, probably at the Sorbonne. It was relatively simple to stitch together the whole story.

But occasionally you come upon a real tragedy. Figure 6 is the case of a woman of about thirty years of age. She was in the clinic, and the diagnosis was schizophrenia of a depressive character. The prognosis was correspondingly bad. I had this woman in my ward, and I had a peculiar feeling about her. I felt I could not quite agree with the bad prognosis, because already schizophrenia was a relative idea with me. I thought that we are all relatively crazy, but this woman was peculiar, and I could not accept the diagnosis as the last word. In those days one knew precious little. Of course I made an anamnesis, but nothing was discovered that threw any light on her illness. Therefore I put her to the association test and finally made a very peculiar discovery. The first disturbance was caused by the word *angel*, and a complete lack of reaction by the word *obstinate*. Then there were *evil, rich, money, stupid, dear* and *to marry*. Now this woman was the wife of a well-to-do man in a very fine position and apparently happy. I had questioned her husband, and the only thing he could tell me, as she also did, was that the depression came on about two months after her eldest child had died—a little girl four years old. Nothing else could be found out about the aetiology of the case. The association test confronted me with a most baffling series of reactions which I could not put together. You will often be in such a situation, particularly if you have no routine with that kind of diagnosis. Then you first ask the test person about the words which are not going directly to the kernel. If you asked directly about the strongest disturbances you would get wrong answers, so you begin with relatively harmless words and you are likely to get an honest reply. I said: 'What about *angel*? Does that word mean something to you?' She replied: 'Of course, that is my child whom I have lost'. And then came a great flood of tears. When the storm had blown over I asked: 'What does *obstinate* mean to you?' She said: 'It means nothing to

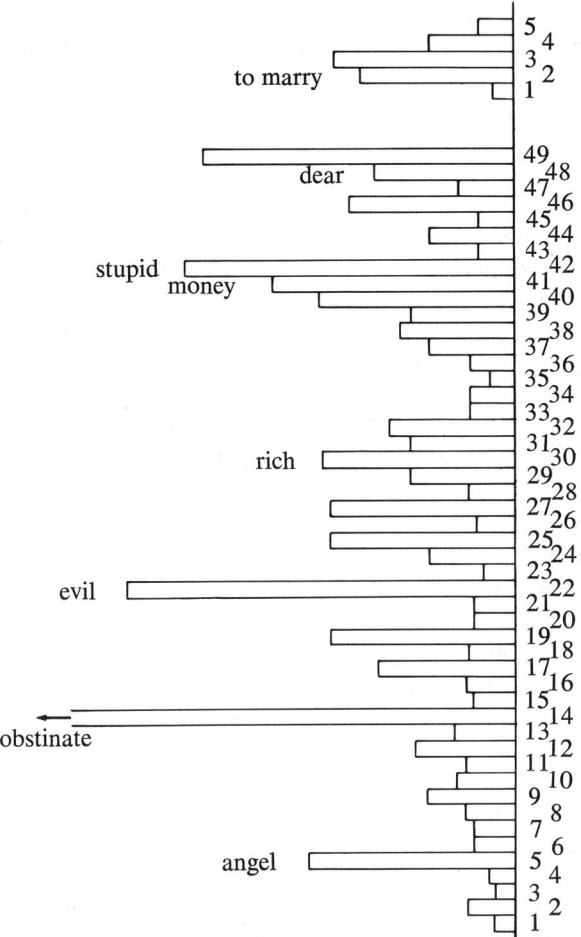

Figure 6 Association Test

me'. But I said: 'There was a big disturbance with the word and it means there is something connected with it'. I could not penetrate it. I came to the word *evil* and could get nothing out of her. There was a severely negative reaction which showed that she refused to answer. I went on to *blue,* and she said: 'Those are the eyes of the child I have lost'. I said: 'Did they make a particular impression on you?' She said: 'Of course. They were so wonderfully blue when the child was born'. I noticed the expression on her face, and I said: 'Why are you upset?' and she replied: 'Well, she did not have the eyes of my husband'. Finally it came out that the child had had the eyes of a former lover of hers. I said: 'What is upsetting you with regard to that man?' And I was able to worm the story out of her.

In the little town in which she grew up there was a rich young man. She was of a well-to-do family but nothing grand. The man was of the moneyed aristocracy and the hero of the little town, and every girl dreamed of him. She was a pretty girl and thought she might have a chance. Then she discovered she had no chance with him, and her family said: 'Why think of him? He is a rich man and does not think of you. Here is Mr So-and So, a nice man. Why not marry him?' She married him and was perfectly happy ever after until the fifth year of her marriage, when a former friend from her native town came to visit her. When her husband left the room he said to her: 'You have caused pain to a certain gentleman' (meaning the hero). She said: 'What? I caused pain?' The friend replied: 'Didn't you know he was in love with you and was disappointed when you married another man?' That set fire to the roof. But she repressed it. A fortnight later she was bathing her boy, two years, and her girl, four years old. The water in the town—it was not in Switzerland—was not above suspicion, in fact it was infected with typhoid fever. She noticed that the little girl was sucking a sponge. But she did not interfere, and when the little boy said, 'I want to drink some water', she gave him the possibly infected water. The little girl got typhoid fever and died, the little boy was saved. Then she had what she wanted—or what the devil in her wanted—the denial of her marriage in order to marry the other man. To this end she had committed murder. She did not know it: she only told me the facts and did not draw the conclusion that she was responsible for the death of the child since she knew the water was infected and there was danger. I was faced with the question whether I should tell her she had committed murder, or whether I should keep quiet. (It was only a question of telling *her*, there was no threat of a criminal case.) I thought that if I told her it might make her condition much worse, but there was a bad prognosis anyhow, whereas, if she could realize what she had done, the chance was that she might get well. So I made up my mind to tell her point-blank: 'You killed your child'. She went up in the air in an emotional state, but then she came down to the facts. In three weeks we were able to discharge her, and she never came back. I traced her for fifteen years, and there was no relapse. That depression fitted her case psychologically: she was a murderess and under other circumstances would have deserved capital punishment. Instead of going to jail she was sent to the lunatic asylum. I practically saved her from the punishment of insanity by putting an enormous burden on her conscience. For if one can accept one's sin one can live with it. If one cannot accept it, one has to suffer the inevitable consequences.

Patterns: Tonal Insinuation

Tonal insinuation (see glossary) in Jung's lectures is nuanced to suit the "persona" he wishes to project. But the nature of the persona itself is ambiguous and deeply tied to the subject matter. The result is coloration of the subject matter and manipulation of the audience with the consequent diminution of its critical power.

Jung opens his lecture with generous tribute to Freud and Adler, but the tribute is so extended and hedged by explanation that it draws attention not to Freud and Adler, but to Jung. Immediately he is cast as fair and open-minded. The modest, seeming apologetic manner is continued in (488/16–489/21), but the *substance* as opposed to the tone, is emphatically self-laudatory: "I take little stock of new theories, as my empirical temperament is more eager for new facts than for what one might speculate about them, although this is, I must admit, an enjoyable intellectual pastime." In one sentence Jung grounds his theories in empirical science and disparages the worth of "intellectual speculation" and criticism. Warning us of the complexity of the subject, informing us that "the menace of so formidably vicious a circle has driven me to an extreme of caution and relativism" (489/19-21), he continues in this vein. He closes the paragraph by telling us that he has "often been thoroughly misunderstood." Thus, within one paragraph the following advantages have been insinuated: (1) the empirical, factual nature of his findings; (2) the enjoyable but rather unserious nature of intellectual criticism; (3) the complexity of the subject; (4) the great caution of Jung; (5) the great misunderstanding his scientific caution has created. It is difficult to maintain a critical perspective under such insinuated attacks, for they seriously undermine one's position. Nor does the advantageous insinuation abate.

In the very next paragraph he tells us: "I am not troubled by theories, but a great deal by facts; . . . keep in mind that the shortness of time . . . does not allow me to . . . substantiate my conclusions. . . . I have to depend a great deal on your good will." His closing remark, "it is my own task in the first place to make things as plain as possible," has the effect of suggesting that he will make serious efforts in this area, and that failure to understand will be the fault of the listeners. In the remainder of the lecture, however, he alludes to Kant, quotes a scholastic formula in Latin without translating it, tells of a conversation with a "homeric age" Pueblo Indian with whom he "tried the argument of St. Augustine" (without telling us what it was), alludes to the study of the Tantric Yoga, Hindu psychology and old German alchemical books, quotes French, and otherwise demonstrates erudition which seems to pass for incidental learning. But it is hardly likely that Jung believed such learning to be widespread.

The essay is replete with intimidating insinuations. Things are "really quite simple" (506/34); "The idea of the collective unconscious is really very simple. If it were not so, then one could speak of a miracle, and I am not a miracle-monger at all. I simply go by experience" (507/12-14). There are allusions to esoteric books, compliments paid to himself (507/29, 511/35); and throughout the tone is one of humor that disarms opposition while deadening it.

One could go on at length, but the point is clear. Jung, whose ideas can stand alone, manipulates his tone to create an even more favorable ambiance. The result is greater receptivity to his ideas. A comparison of Jung's tone or even Adler's with Freud's is revealing. The reader is left to assess the significance of the simple directness, the lack of jargon or allusion in the writings of Freud as opposed to those of Jung and Adler.

Problems

1. What elements of Jung's theory are descriptive rather than analytical? Is his explanation of the functions of the mind descriptive or analytical? In what way does descriptive theory have less application than analytic theory?
2. What are the possible disadvantages of Jung's tendency to divide matters into hierarchical, polar opposites? What is the significance of Jung's tendency to create limited or exclusive categories? Of Freud and Jung, which seems more tolerant and accepting? Why? Which is potentially more authoritarian? Why?
3. How does Jung's tendency to "type" people differ from Freud's? Which of the two is more flexible? Which is more analytic and explanatory? Which is more prone to stereotyping? Give reasons.
4. How does Jung's concept of the unconscious differ from Freud's? Which theory more adequately preserves the unique autonomy of the individual?
5. Does Jung believe self-knowledge is indispensable to control? Does he believe the individual can know as much about himself as Freud does? Which of the two seems to give the individual more potential "rational" control over himself? Why?
6. Freud's mental model is extremely dynamic, involving forces in action and counteraction. Is Jung's mental model more or less dynamic than Freud's?

Marriage as a Psychological Relationship

Regarded as a psychological relationship, marriage is a highly complex structure made up of a whole series of subjective and objective factors, mostly of a very heterogeneous nature. As I wish to confine myself here to the purely psychological problems of marriage, I must disregard in the main the objective factors of a legal and social nature, although these cannot fail to have a pronounced influence on the psychological relationship between the marriage partners.

Whenever we speak of a "psychological relationship" we presuppose one that is *conscious,* for there is no such thing as a psychological relationship between two people who are in a state of unconsciousness. From the psychological point of view they would be wholly without relationship. From any other point of view, the physiological for example, they could be regarded as related, but one could not call their relationship psychological. It must be admitted that though such total unconsciousness as I have assumed does not occur, there is nevertheless a not inconsiderable degree of partial unconsciousness, and the psychological relationship is limited in the degree to which that unconsciousness exists.

In the child, consciousness rises out of the depths of unconscious psychic life, at first like separate islands, which gradually unite to form a "continent," a continuous land-mass of consciousness. Progressive mental development means, in effect, extension of consciousness. With the rise of a continuous consciousness, and not before, psychological relationship becomes possible. So far as we know, consciousness is always ego-consciousness. In order to be conscious of myself, I must be able to distinguish myself from others. Relationship can only take place where this distinction exists. But although the distinction may be made in a general way, normally it is incomplete, because large areas of psychic life still remain unconscious. As no distinction can be made with regard to unconscious contents, on this terrain no relationship can be established; here there still reigns the original unconscious condition of the ego's primitive identity with others, in other words a complete absence of relationship.

The young person of marriageable age does, of course, possess an ego-consciousness (girls more than men, as a rule), but, since he has only

From C. G. Jung, "Marriage as a Psychological Relationship," from *The Collected Works of C. G. Jung,* Bollingen Series XX, Vol. 17 (New York: Pantheon Books, Inc., 1954), pp. 189–201.

recently emerged from the mists of original unconsciousness, he is certain to have wide areas which still lie in the shadow and which preclude to that extent the formation of psychological relationship. This means, in practice, that the young man (or woman) can have only an incomplete understanding of himself and others, and is therefore imperfectly informed as to his, and their, motives. As a rule the motives he acts from are largely unconscious. Subjectively, of course, he thinks himself very conscious and knowing, for we constantly overestimate the existing content of consciousness, and it is a great and surprising discovery when we find that what we had supposed to be the final peak is nothing but the first step in a very long climb. The greater the area of unconsciousness, the less is marriage a matter of free choice, as is shown subjectively in the fatal compulsion one feels so acutely when one is in love. The compulsion can exist even when one is not in love, though in less agreeable form.

Unconscious motivations are of a personal and of a general nature. First of all, there are the motives deriving from parental influence. The relationship of the young man to his mother, and of the girl to her father is the determining factor in this respect. It is the strength of the bond to the parents that unconsciously influences the choice of husband or wife, either positively or negatively. Conscious love for either parent favours the choice of a like mate, while an unconscious tie (which need not by any means express itself consciously as love) makes the choice difficult and imposes characteristic modifications. In order to understand them, one must know first of all the cause of the unconscious tie to the parents, and under what conditions it forcibly modifies, or even prevents, the conscious choice. Generally speaking, all the life which the parents could have lived, but of which they thwarted themselves for artificial motives, is passed on to the children in substitute form. That is to say, the children are driven unconsciously in a direction that is intended to compensate for everything that was left unfulfilled in the lives of their parents. Hence it is that excessively moral-minded parents have what are called "unmoral" children, or an irresponsible wastrel of a father has a son with a positively morbid amount of ambition, and so on. The worst results flow from parents who have kept themselves artificially unconscious. Take the case of a mother who deliberately keeps herself unconscious so as not to disturb the pretence of a "satisfactory" marriage. Unconsciously she will bind her son to her, more or less as a substitute for a husband. The son, if not forced directly into homosexuality, is compelled to modify his choice in a way that is contrary to his true nature. He may, for instance, marry a girl who is obviously inferior to his mother and therefore unable to compete with her; or he will fall for a woman of a tyrannical and overbearing disposition, who may perhaps succeed in tearing him away from his mother. The choice of a mate, if the instincts have not been vitiated, may remain free from these influences, but sooner or later they will make themselves felt as obstacles.

A more or less instinctive choice might be considered the best from the point of view of maintaining the species, but it is not always fortunate psychologically, because there is often an uncommonly large difference between the purely instinctive personality and one that is individually differentiated. And though in such cases the race might be improved and invigorated by a purely instinctive choice, individual happiness would be bound to suffer. (The idea of "instinct" is of course nothing more than a collective term for all kinds of organic and psychic factors whose nature is for the most part unknown.)

If the individual is to be regarded solely as an instrument for maintaining the species, then the purely instinctive choice of a mate is by far the best. But since the foundations of such a choice are unconscious, only a kind of impersonal liaison can be built upon them, such as can be observed to perfection among primitives. If we can speak here of a "relationship" at all, it is, at best, only a pale reflection of what we mean, a very distant state of affairs with a decidedly impersonal character, wholly regulated by traditional customs and prejudices, the prototype of every conventional marriage.

So far as reason or calculation or the so-called loving care of the parents does not arrange the marriage, and the pristine instincts of the children are not vitiated either by false education or by the hidden influence of accumulated and neglected parental complexes, the marriage choice will normally follow the unconscious motivations of instinct. Unconsciousness results in non-differentiation, or unconscious identity. The practical consequence of this is that one person presupposes in the other a psychological structure similar to his own. Normal sex life, as a shared experience with apparently similar aims, further strengthens the feeling of unity and identity. This state is described as one of complete harmony, and is extolled as a great happiness ("one heart and one soul")—not without good reason, since the return to that original condition of unconscious oneness is like a return to childhood. Hence the childish gestures of all lovers. Even more is it a return to the mother's womb, into the teeming depths of an as yet unconscious creativity. It is, in truth, a genuine and incontestable experience of the Divine, whose transcendent force obliterates and consumes everything individual; a real communion with life and the impersonal power of fate. The individual will for self-possession is broken: the woman becomes the mother, the man the father, and thus both are robbed of their freedom and made instruments of the life urge.

Here the relationship remains within the bounds of the biological instinctive goal, the preservation of the species. Since this goal is a collective nature, the psychological link between husband and wife will also be essentially collective, and cannot be regarded as an individual relationship in the psychological sense. We can only speak of this when the nature of the unconscious motivations has been recognized and the original identity broken down. Seldom or never does a marriage develop into an individual relationship smoothly and without crises. There is no birth of consciousness without pain.

The ways that lead to conscious realization are many, but they follow definite laws. In general, the change begins with the onset of the second half of life. The middle period of life is a time of enormous psychological importance. The child begins its psychological life within very narrow limits, inside the magic circle of the mother and the family. With progressive maturation it widens its horizon and its own sphere of influence; its hopes and intentions are directed to extending the scope of personal power and possessions; desire reaches out to the world in ever-widening range; the will of the individual becomes more and more identical with the natural goals pursued by unconscious motivations. Thus man breathes his own life into things, until finally they begin to live of themselves and to multiply; and imperceptibly he is overgrown by them. Mothers are overtaken by their children, men by their own creations, and what was originally brought into being only with labour and the greatest effort can no longer be held in check. First it was passion, then it became duty, and finally an intolerable burden, a vampire that battens on the life of its creator. Middle life is the moment of greatest unfolding, when a man still gives himself to his work with his whole strength and his whole will. But in this very moment evening is born, and the second half of life begins. Passion now changes her face and is called duty; "I want" becomes the inexorable "I must," and the turnings of the pathway that once brought surprise and discovery become dulled by custom. The wine has fermented and begins to settle and clear. Conservative tendencies develop if all goes well; instead of looking forward one looks backward, most of the time involuntarily, and one begins to take stock, to see how one's life has developed up to this point. The real motivations are sought and real discoveries are made. The critical survey of himself and his fate enables a man to recognize his peculiarities. But these insights do not come to him easily; they are gained only through the severest shocks.

Since the aims of the second half of life are different from those of the first, to linger too long in the youthful attitude produces a division of the will. Consciousness still presses forward, in obedience, as it were, to its own inertia, but the unconscious lags behind, because the strength and inner resolve needed for further expansion have been sapped. This disunity with oneself begets discontent, and since one is not conscious of the real state of things one generally projects the reasons for it upon one's partner. A critical atmosphere thus develops, the necessary prelude to conscious realization. Usually this state does not begin simultaneously for both partners. Even the best of marriages cannot expunge individual differences so completely that the state of mind of the partners is absolutely identical. In most cases one of them will adapt to marriage more quickly than the other. The one who is grounded on a positive relationship to the parents will find little or no difficulty in adjusting to his or her partner, while the other may be hindered by a deep-seated unconscious tie to the parents. He will therefore achieve complete adaptation only later, and, because it is won with greater difficulty, it may even prove the more durable.

These differences in tempo, and in the degree of spiritual development, are the chief causes of a typical difficulty which makes its appearance at critical moments. In speaking of "the degree of spiritual development" of a personality, I do not wish to imply an especially rich or magnanimous nature. Such is not the case at all. I mean, rather, a certain complexity of mind or nature, comparable to a gem with many facets as opposed to the simple cube. There are many-sided and rather problematical natures burdened with hereditary traits that are sometimes very difficult to reconcile. Adaptation to such natures, or their adaptation to simpler personalities, is always a problem. These people, having a certain tendency to dissociation, generally have the capacity to split off irreconcilable traits of character for considerable periods, thus passing themselves off as much simpler than they are; or it may happen that their many-sidedness, their very versatility, lends them a peculiar charm. Their partners can easily lose themselves in such a labyrinthine nature, finding in it such an abundance of possible experiences that their personal interests are completely absorbed, sometimes in a not very agreeable way, since their sole occupation then consists in tracking the other through all the twists and turns of his character. There is always so much experience available that the simpler personality is surrounded, if not actually swamped, by it; he is swallowed up in his more complex partner and cannot see his way out. It is an almost regular occurrence for a woman to be wholly contained, spiritually, in her husband, and for a husband to be wholly contained, emotionally, in his wife. One could describe this as the problem of the "contained" and the "container."

The one who is contained feels himself to be living entirely within the confines of his marriage; his attitude to the marriage partner is undivided; outside the marriage there exist no essential obligations and no binding interests. The unpleasant side of this otherwise ideal partnership is the disquieting dependence upon a personality that can never be seen in its entirety, and is therefore not altogether credible or dependable. The great advantage lies in his own undividedness, and this is a factor not to be underrated in the psychic economy.

The container, on the other hand, who in accordance with his tendency to dissociation has an especial need to unify himself in undivided love for another, will be left far behind in this effort, which is naturally very difficult for him, by the simpler personality. While he is seeking in the latter all the subtleties and complexities that would complement and correspond to his own facets, he is disturbing the other's simplicity. Since in normal circumstances simplicity always has the advantage over complexity, he will very soon be obliged to abandon his efforts to arouse subtle and intricate reactions in a simpler nature. And soon enough his partner, who in accordance with her [1] simpler nature expects simple answers from him, will give him plenty to do by constellating his complexities with her everlasting insistence on simple answers. Willynilly, he must withdraw into himself before the suasions of simplicity. Any mental effort, like the conscious process itself, is so much of a strain for the ordinary man that he invariably prefers the simple, even when it does not happen to be the truth. And when it represents at least a half-truth, then it is all up with him. The simpler nature works on the more complicated like a room that is too small, that does not allow him enough space. The complicated nature, on the other hand, gives the simpler one too many rooms with too much space, so that she never knows where she really belongs. So it comes about quite naturally that the more complicated contains the simpler. The former cannot be absorbed in the latter, but encompasses it without being itself contained. Yet, since the more complicated has perhaps a greater need of being contained than the other, he feels himself outside the marriage and accordingly always plays the problematical role. The more the contained clings, the more the container feels shut out of the relationship. The contained pushes into it by her clinging, and the more she pushes, the less the container is able to respond. He therefore tends to spy out of the window, no doubt unconsciously at first; but with the onset of middle age there awakens in him a more insistent longing for that unity and undividedness which is especially necessary to him on account of his dissociated nature. At this juncture things are apt to occur that bring the conflict to a head. He becomes conscious of the fact that he is seeking completion, seeking the contentedness and undividedness that have always been lacking. For the contained this is only a confirmation of the insecurity she has always felt so painfully; she discovers that in the rooms which apparently belonged to her there dwell other, unwished-for guests. The hope of security vanishes, and this disappointment drives her in on herself, unless by desperate and violent efforts she can succeed in forcing her partner to capitulate, and in extorting a confession that his longing for unity was nothing but a childish or morbid fantasy. If these tactics do not succeed, her acceptance of failure may do her a real good, by

1. [In translating this and the following passages, I have, for the sake of clarity, assumed that the container is the man and the contained the woman. This assumption is due entirely to the exigencies of English grammar, and is not implied in the German text. Needless to say, the situation could just as easily be reversed.—Trans.]

forcing her to recognize that the security she was so desperately seeking in the other is to be found in herself. In this way she finds herself and discovers in her own simpler nature all those complexities which the container had sought for in vain.

If the container does not break down in face of what we are wont to call "unfaithfulness," but goes on believing in the inner justification of his longing for unity, he will have to put up with his self-division for the time being. A dissociation is not healed by being split off, but by more complete disintegration. All the powers that strive for unity, all healthy desire for selfhood, will resist the disintegration, and in this way he will become conscious of the possibility of an inner integration, which before he had always sought outside himself. He will then find his reward in an undivided self.

This is what happens very frequently about the midday of life, and in this wise our miraculous human nature enforces the transition that leads from the first half of life to the second. It is a metamorphosis from a state in which man is only a tool of instinctive nature, to another in which he is no longer a tool, but himself: a transformation of nature into culture, of instinct into spirit.

One should take great care not to interrupt this necessary development by acts of moral violence, for any attempt to create a spiritual attitude by splitting off and suppressing the instincts is a falsification. Nothing is more repulsive than a furtively prurient spirituality; it is just as unsavoury as gross sensuality. But the transition takes a long time, and the great majority of people get stuck in the first stages. If only we could, like the primitives, leave the unconscious to look after this whole psychological development which marriage entails, these transformations could be worked out more completely and without too much friction. So often among so-called "primitives" one comes across spiritual personalities who immediately inspire respect, as though they were the fully matured products of an undisturbed fate. I speak here from personal experience. But where among present-day Europeans can one find people not deformed by acts of moral violence? We are still barbarous enough to believe both in asceticism and its opposite. But the wheel of history cannot be put back; we can only strive towards an attitude that will allow us to live out our fate as undisturbedly as the primitive pagan in us really wants. Only on this condition can we be sure of not perverting spirituality into sensuality, and vice versa; for both must live, each drawing life from the other.

The transformation I have briefly described above is the very essence of the psychological marriage relationship. Much could be said about the illusions that serve the ends of nature and bring about the transformations that are characteristic of middle life. The peculiar harmony that characterizes marriage during the first half of life—provided the adjustment is successful—is largely based on the projection of certain archetypal images, as the critical phase makes clear.

Every man carries within him the eternal image of woman, not the image of this or that particular woman, but a definite feminine image. This image is fundamentally unconscious, an hereditary factor of primordial origin engraved in the living organic system of the man, an imprint or "archetype" of all the ancestral experiences of the female, a deposit, as it were, of all the impressions ever made by woman-in short, an inherited system of psychic adaptation. Even if no women existed, it would still be possible, at any given time, to deduce from this unconscious image exactly how a woman would have to be constituted psychically. The same is true of the woman: she too has her inborn image of man. Actually, we know from experience that it would be more accurate to describe it as an image of *men,* whereas in the case of the man it is rather the image of *woman.* Since this image is unconscious, it is always unconsciously projected upon the person of the beloved, and is one of the chief reasons for passionate attraction or aversion. I have called this image the "anima," and I find the scholastic question *Habet mulier animam?* * especially interesting, since in my view it is an intelligent one inasmuch as the doubt seems justified. Woman has no anima, no soul, but she has an *animus.* The anima has an erotic, emotional character, the animus a rationalizing one. Hence most of what men say about feminine eroticism, and particularly about the emotional life of women, is derived from their own anima projections and distorted accordingly. On the other hand, the astonishing assumptions and fantasies that women make about men come from the activity of the animus, who produces an inexhaustible supply of illogical arguments and false explanations.

Anima and animus are both characterized by an extraordinary many-sidedness. In a marriage it is always the contained who projects this image upon the container, while the latter is only partially able to project his unconscious image upon his partner. The more unified and simple this partner is, the less complete the projection. In which case, this highly fascinating image hangs as it were in mid air, as though waiting to be filled out by a living person. There are certain types of women who seem to be made by nature to attract anima projections; indeed one could almost speak of a definite "anima type." The so-called "sphinx-like" character is an indispensable part of their equipment, also an equivocalness, an intriguing elusiveness—not an indefinite blur that offers nothing, but an indefiniteness that seems full of promises, like the speaking silence of a Mona Lisa. A woman of this kind is both old and young, mother and daughter, of more than doubtful chastity, childlike, and yet

* Does woman have a soul?

endowed with a naïve cunning that is extremely disarming to men.[2] Not every man of real intellectual power can be an animus, for the animus must be a master not so much of fine ideas as of fine words—words seemingly full of meaning which purport to leave a great deal unsaid. He must also belong to the "misunderstood" class, or be in some way at odds with his environment, so that the idea of self-sacrifice can insinuate itself. He must be a rather questionable hero, a man with possibilities, which is not to say that an animus projection may not discover a real hero long before he has become perceptible to the sluggish wits of the man of "average intelligence." [3]

For man as well as for woman, in so far as they are "containers," the filling out of this image is an experience fraught with consequences, for it holds the possibility of finding one's own complexities answered by a corresponding diversity. Wide vistas seem to open up in which one feels oneself embraced and contained. I say "seem" advisedly, because the experience may be two-faced. Just as the animus projection of a woman can often pick on a man of real significance who is not recognized by the mass, and can actually help him to achieve his true destiny with her moral support, so a man can create for himself a *femme inspiratrice* by his anima projection. But more often it turns out to be an illusion with destructive consequences, a failure because his faith was not sufficiently strong. To the pessimists I would say that these primordial psychic images have an extraordinarily positive value, but I must warn the optimists against blinding fantasies and the likelihood of the most absurd aberrations.

One should on no account take this projection for an individual and conscious relationship. In its first stages it is far from that, for it creates a compulsive dependence based on unconscious motives other than the biological ones. Rider Haggard's *She* gives some indication of the curious world of ideas that underlies the anima projection. They are in essence spiritual contents, often in erotic disguise, obvious fragments of a primitive mythological mentality that consists of archetypes, and whose totality constitutes the collective unconscious. Accordingly, such a relationship is at bottom collective and not individual. (Benoît, who created in *L'Atlantide* a fantasy figure similar even in details to "She," denies having plagiarized Rider Haggard.)

If such a projection fastens on to one of the marriage partners, a collective spiritual relationship conflicts with the collective biological one

---

2. There are excellent descriptions of this type in H. Rider Haggard's *She* (London, 1887) and Pierre Benoît's *L'Atlantide* (Paris, 1920; trans. by Mary C. Tongue and Mary Ross as *Atlantida,* New York, 1920).
3. A passably good account of the animus is to be found in Marie Hay's book *The Evil Vineyard* (New York, 1923), also in Elinor Wylie's *Jennifer Lorn* (New York, 1923) and Selma Lagerlöf's *Gösta Berlings Saga* (1891; English trans. by P. B. Flach, *The Story of Gösta Berling,* 1898).

and produces in the container the division or disintegration I have described above. If he is able to hold his head above water, he will find himself through this very conflict. In that case the projection, though dangerous in itself, will have helped him to pass from a collective to an individual relationship. This amounts to full conscious realization of the relationship that marriage brings. Since the aim of this paper is a discussion of the psychology of marriage, the psychology of projection cannot concern us here. It is sufficient to mention it as a fact.

One can hardly deal with the psychological marriage relationship without mentioning, even at the risk of misunderstanding, the nature of its critical transitions. As is well known, one understands nothing psychological unless one has experienced it oneself. Not that this ever prevents anyone from feeling convinced that his own judgment is the only true and competent one. This disconcerting fact comes from the necessary over-valuation of the momentary content of consciousness, for without this concentration of attention one could not be conscious at all. Thus it is that every period of life has its own psychological truth, and the same applies to every stage of psychological development. There are even stages which only the few can reach, it being a question of race, family, education, talent, and passion. Nature is aristocratic. The normal man is a fiction, although certain generally valid laws do exist. Psychic life is a development that can easily be arrested on the lowest levels. It is as though every individual had a specific gravity, in accordance with which he either rises, or sinks down, to the level where he reaches his limit. His views and convictions will be determined accordingly. No wonder, then, that by far the greater number of marriages reach their upper psychological limit in fulfilment of the biological aim, without injury to spiritual or moral health. Relatively few people fall into deeper disharmony with themselves. Where there is a great deal of pressure from outside, the conflict is unable to develop much dramatic tension for sheer lack of energy. Psychological insecurity, however, increases in proportion to social security, unconsciously at first, causing neuroses, then consciously, bringing with it separations, discord, divorces, and other marital disorders. On still higher levels, new possibilities of psychological development are discerned, touching on the sphere of religion where critical judgment comes to a halt.

Progress may be permanently arrested on any of these levels, with complete unconsciousness of what might have followed at the next stage of development. As a rule graduation to the next stage is barred by violent prejudices and superstitious fears. This, however, serves a most useful purpose, since a man who is compelled by accident to live at a level too high for him becomes a fool and a menace.

Nature is not only aristocratic, she is also esoteric. Yet no man of understanding will thereby be induced to make a secret of what he knows, for he realizes only too well that the secret of psychic development can never be betrayed, simply because that development is a question of individual capacity.

Problems

1. What, for Jung, distinguishes a "psychological relationship" from any other?
2. Why do parents ironically get results in children opposite to those expected? What is revealed about parents who get such opposite results?
3. What is revealed about Jung's assumptions about man and what is good for him by his favorable attitude toward instinctual choice as being beneficial for the species but not for the individual?
4. To what extent does Jung tend to prefer the collective to the individual? Would his world view in its totality be more appealing to a Christian or to a Marxist?
5. Running throughout the essay is a theory of life cycles, of stages in life. Do you believe such cycles are basically organic, or are they socially compelled?
6. In what ways does Jung's pervasive polarity manifest itself in the essay? Jung, however, is always seeking a unity: what is that unity in this essay?
7. What are the implications of Jung's remark, "Nature is aristocratic" (530/20) and of his conclusion? Could Freud have made such a remark or written such an ending? Why?

25 ALFRED ADLER

Alfred Adler (1870–1937), the first of Freud's pupils to break with him, did so in 1911 because he rejected the sexual etiology of neurosis. In its place, he posited, as the root cause of neurosis, feelings of inferiority. With this concept, the term "inferiority complex" was born.

Adler, like Nietzsche, contended that individuals are motivated by the search for power. But whereas Nietzsche stressed power over self, power as strength and self-control, Adler stressed power as control over others. In his theory, Adler distinguished between masculine aggressive strivings for power, and feminine strivings which are usually manifested in passive or submissive ways, such as hypersensitivity, defensiveness, projection, or fantasy. Perhaps of more importance, though of an indirect sort, was Adler's emphasis on the individual and his "life style" (hence the title "Individual Psychology"), on the need for the therapist to respect the autonomy of the individual and, thereby, to provide a model of quiet considerateness for the patient, who, suffering from feelings of deprivation and inferiority, is unable to care sufficiently for the feelings of others. The result of these emphases was a start in that steady movement toward greater concern with the patient's present problems and with improving the relationship between therapist and patient.

The two essays below are, respectively, Chapter III and the Introduction from Adler's The Practice and Theory of Individual Psychology *(1955). As indicated by their titles, they suggest the outlines of his theory and its application.*

New Leading Principles for the Practice of Individual-Psychology

I. Every neurosis can be understood as an attempt to free oneself from a feeling of inferiority in order to gain a feeling of superiority.

II. The path of the neurosis does not lead in the direction of social

From Alfred Adler, *The Practice and Theory of Individual Psychology* (London: Humanities Press, 1955), pp. 23–31.

functioning, nor does it aim at solving given life-problems but finds an outlet for itself in the small family circle, thus achieving the isolation of the patient.

III. The larger unit of the social group is either completely or very extensively pushed aside by a mechanism consisting of hyper-sensitiveness and intolerance. Only a small group is left over for the manoeuvres aiming at the various types of superiority to expend themselves upon. At the same time protection and the withdrawal from the demands of the community and the decisions of life are made possible.

IV. Thus estranged from reality, the neurotic man lives a life of imagination and phantasy and employs a number of devices for enabling him to side-step the demands of reality and for reaching out toward an ideal situation which would free him from any service for the community and absolve him from responsibility.

V. These exemptions and the privileges of illness and suffering give him a substitute for his original hazardous goal of superiority.

VI. Thus the neurosis and the psyche represent an attempt to free oneself from all the constraints of the community by establishing a counter compulsion. This latter is so constituted that it effectively faces the peculiar nature of the surroundings and their demands. Both of these convincing inferences can be drawn from the manner in which this counter compulsion manifests itself and from the neuroses selected.

VII. The counter-compulsion takes on the nature of a revolt, gathers its material either from favourable affective experiences or from observations. It permits thoughts and affects to become preoccupied either with the above-mentioned stirrings or with unimportant details, as long as they at least serve the purpose of directing the eye and the attention of the patient away from his life-problems. In this manner, depending upon the needs of the situation, he prepares anxiety-and compulsion-situations, sleeplessness, swooning, perversions, hallucinations, slightly pathological affects, neurasthenic * and hypochondriacal complexes and psychotic pictures of his actual condition, all of which are to serve him as excuses.

VIII. Even logic falls under the domination of the counter-compulsion. As in psychosis this process may go as far as the actual nullification of logic.

IX. Logic, the will to live, love, human sympathy, co-operation and language, all arise out of the needs of human communal life. Against the latter are directed automatically all the plans of the neurotic individual striving for isolation and lusting for power.

X. To cure a neurosis and a psychosis it is necessary to change

---

* Neurasthenia is a neurosis marked by fatigue, weakness, depression and bodily disturbances.

completely the whole upbringing of the patient and turn him definitely and unconditionally back upon human society.

XI. All the volition and all the strivings of the neurotic are dictated by his prestige-seeking policy, which is continually looking for excuses which will enable him to leave the problems of life unsolved. He consequently automatically turns against allowing any community-feeling to develop.

XII. If therefore we may regard the demand for a complete and unified understanding of man and for a comprehension of his (undivided) individuality as justified—a view to which we are forced both by the nature of reason and the individual-psychological knowledge of the urge toward an integration of the personality—then the method of *comparison,* the main tool of our method, enables us to arrive at some conception of the power-lines along which an individual strives to attain superiority. The following will serve as the two contrasting-poles for comparison:

(1) Our own attitude in a situation similar to that of a patient hard-pressed by some demand. In such a case it is essential for the practitioner to possess, in a considerable degree, the gift of *putting himself in the other person's place.*

(2) The patient's attitudes and anomalies dating from early childhood. These can always be shown as dominated by the relation of the child to his environment, by his erroneous and in the main generalized evaluation (of himself), by his obstinate and deep-rooted feeling of inferiority and by his striving after power.

(3) Other types of individuals, particularly those specifically neurotic. In these cases we shall come upon the patent discovery that what one type attains by means of neurasthenic troubles, another endeavours to obtain by means of fear, hysteria, neurotic-compulsion or psychosis. Traits of character, affects, principles and nervous symptoms, pointing toward the same goal and, when torn from their context, frequently giving a contrary significance, all these serve as a protection against the shock caused by the demands of the community.

(4) Those very demands of the community which the nervous individual, in varying degrees, sidesteps, such as co-operation, fellow-feeling, love, social adaptation and the responsibilities of the community.

By means of this individual-psychological investigation we realize that the neurotic individual, far more than the ordinary normal man, arranges his psychic-life in accordance with the desire for power over his fellow-men. His longing for superiority enables him continually and extensively to reject all outside compulsion, the demands made upon him by others and the responsibilities imposed by Society. The realization of this basic fact in the psychic life of the neurotic, so lightens the task of obtaining an insight into psychic inter-connections that it is bound to become the most useful working-hypothesis in the investigation and curing of neurotic diseases, until a more profound understanding of the individual enables us to disentangle and grasp in their full significance, the real factors involved in each case.

What irritates the healthy man in this type of argument and the conclusions drawn therefrom, is the suggestion that an imagined goal constructed by an emotionally-conditioned superiority, can possess greater force than rational deliberation. But we can find this inversion of an ideal frequently enough both in the life of healthy individuals as in that of whole nations. War, political abuses, crimes, suicide, ascetic penances, provide us with similar surprises. A good many of our sufferings and tortures we ourselves originate and take upon ourselves under the influence of some idea.

That a cat should catch mice, that without ever having been taught to do so, should be prepared for it even in the first days of its existence, is no more remarkable than that the neurotic individual, according to his nature and destiny, his position and his self-evaluation, should evade and find unbearable every form of compulsion; that he should secretly or openly, consciously or unconsciously look for excuses to free himself, frequently originating them himself.

The reason for the intolerance of the neurotics toward the constraints of society, as the history of their childhood shows, is to be sought in the continuous conflict-attitude that has been practised for many years against the environment. This is forced upon the child, without there being any real justification for its expressing itself in just such a reaction, by the bodily or psychically conditioned position it occupies and from which the child receives either lasting or intensified feelings of inferiority. The object of the conflict-attitude is the conquest of power and importance, an ideal of superiority constructed with an infant's incapacity and over-evaluation and the fulfilment of which presents compensations and super-compensations of a most general kind, in the pursuit of which there always occurs a victory over the constraints of society and over the will of the environment. As soon as this conflict has taken on more acute forms it evolves, from within itself, an antagonism against compulsions of all kinds, whether they be education, reality, common interest, external force, personal weakness, as well as all the compulsions presented by such factors as work, cleanliness, acceptance of nourishment, normal urination and defecation, sleep, treatment of disease, love, tenderness, friendship, loneliness and its opposite, sociability. In toto we get the picture of a man who does not want to play the game, a dog in the manger. Where antagonism is directed against the awakening of feelings of love and comradeship there arises a fear of love and marriage that can assume many and manifold degrees and forms. At this place let me call attention to a number of forms of compulsion hardly perceivable to the normal individual, which are nevertheless almost regularly prevented from developing by the appearance of a nervous or psychotic condition. These compulsions are:—to recognize this compulsion, to be attentive, to subordinate oneself, to tell the truth, to study or to pass examinations, to be punctual, to entrust oneself to a person, a carriage, the railroad; to confide the household, business, children, spouse, or oneself to other people; to become a landlord or adopt a profession; to marry, to acknowledge the correctness of the other man's view, to be grateful, to bring children into the world, to play a proper sexual role or recognize proper love-responsibilities; to rise in the morning, to sleep at night, to recognize the equal rights and equality of others, the rights of women, to keep a measure in everything, to be loyal, etc. All these idiosyncrasies may be conscious or unconscious but they are never grasped by the patient in all their bearings.

This examination teaches us two things:

(1) The concept of compulsion in the neurotic has been tremendously enlarged and embraces relationships, even if only from a logical point of view, that a normal individual does not include under the category of compulsion.

(2) The antagonism is no final-phenomena but extends further. It has a continuation and is followed by a state of fermentation. It signifies at all times a conflict-attitude and shows us as though at an apparent resting point, the striving of the neurotic to triumph over others, the striving for a directed violent twisting of the logical inferences drawn from human communal life. "Non me rebus, sed mihi res subigere conor." * In this passage taken from a letter of Horace to Maecenas, the former shows in what this infuriated lust for importance ends: in a headache and sleeplessness.

A patient, thirty-five years old, complained to me that he had for a number of years been suffering from sleeplessness, from brooding and masturbation-compulsions. The latter symptom was particularly significant, for the patient was married, the father of two children and on excellent marital relations with his wife. Among other torturing phenomena he spoke of a kind of "rubber-fetichism". From time to time, in any exciting situation, the word "rubber" forced itself to his lips.

The results of an extensive individual-psychological examination led to the following facts: starting from a period in childhood characteristized by marked depression, at a time when the patient used to wet his bed and was regarded as a stupid child because of his clumsiness, he had developed *along the guiding-line of ambition* to such an extent that the latter had grown into a *megalomania*. The pressure of his environment,

---

* I do not try to subject myself to things, but to subject things to me.

which actually did exist in a very high degree, brought close to him the picture of a *definitely inimical external world* and invested him with a permanently pessimistic outlook upon life. In such a mood he felt all the demands of the external world as unbearable compulsions and retorted by wetting his bed and by clumsiness, until he met a teacher in whom, for the first time in his life, he came into contact with the counterpart of a good fellowman. He then began to mitigate his defiance and rage at the demands of others and his conflict-attitude toward the community, to the extent of it becoming possible for him to stop wetting his bed, of developing into a "gifted" student and to work for the highest of ideals in life. His hostility against the compulsion of others he solved, in the manner of a poet and a philosopher, by a flight into the transcendental. He developed an emotionally-steeped idea as if *he were the only human being in existence,* and that everything else, particularly human beings, were merely appearances. The relationship with the ideas of Schopenhauer, Fichte, Kant * is not to be dismissed. The deeper purpose, however, lay in his robbing existence of value in order to obtain a feeling of security, and escape "the scorn and questionings of our times". All of this was to have been accomplished by *magic,* comparable to that which unreliant children use when they wish to deprive facts of their power. In this way the *rubber-erasure* became the symbol and sign of his power, because to the child, as the destroyer of the visible, the rubber appeared like a possibility fulfilled. The whole situation called for over-evaluation and generalization, and thus the word and concept "rubber" became the conquering watchword, whenever school, the parental household and later on man or woman, wife or child, presented any difficulties or threatened him with coercion.

So, in a well-nigh poetical manner, he arrived at the goal of the isolated hero, fulfilled his striving after power and renounced society. His steadily improving position in the world prevented him, however, from entirely pushing aside the actual and ever-present communal feelings. Little was consequently lost *of the love and the logic that binds us all together,* and so he was spared the fate of developing a *paranoiac disease.*† He went only as far as a compulsion-neurosis.

His love was not based upon pure communal feeling. In fact it came under the attraction of the main line of his striving after power. Since the concept and the feeling "power" were united with the magic word "rubber", he sought and found a catchword that would free him from his sexuality in the picture of a *rubber-girdle.* Not a woman but a rubber girdle, in other words, not a personal but an impersonal object influenced

* German philosophers who were Idealists, in opposition to Materialists. They were concerned with the relationship of mind and self to cognition and modes of experience, and with exploring the role the mind plays in shaping experience.
† A psychosis characterized by marked delusions of persecution and sudden outbreaks of violence.

him. And thus while making his power-intoxication and his derogatory attitude toward women secure, he became a fetichist, for these traits are found regularly as the starting point of fetichism. Had the belief in his own virility been slighter we would have seen suggestions of homosexuality, gerontophily,* necrophily † and similar traits appear.

His masturbation-compulsion had the same basic character. It likewise served to enable him to escape from the compulsion of love, from the "magic" of women.

The sleeplessness was directly caused by his brooding-compulsion, the latter struggling against the constraint of sleep. An unquenchable ambition compelled him to spend the night solving the problems of the day. Has he not like another Alexander accomplished so little as yet? This sleeplessness had however another side to it. It weakened his energy and his power of action; became the justification for his disease. What he had so far accomplished had been done so to speak with one hand, had been done despite his sleeplessness. What might he not have done had he been able to sleep! But he was not able to sleep and in this way, by means of this nocturnal brooding-compulsion, he obtained an alibi. Thus he rescued his uniqueness and his god-likeness. All blame for any deficiency could now no more be attributed to his character but to the puzzling and fatal circumstance of his not having been able to sleep. Thus his invalid state had become a disagreeable accident, and for its continuation not he but the insufficient knowledge of the physicians, was responsible. If he is not able to prove his greatness, it will be the concern of the physicians to do so. As can be seen it was of no small importance to him to remain an invalid and he was not going to make the task of the physicians easy.

It is interesting to see how he solves the problem of life and death in order to save his god-likeness. He still has the feeling that his mother, who has been dead for twelve years, is alive. But there is a marked uncertainty about this assumption, manifesting itself more strongly than that tender feeling which so frequently appears shortly after the death of a near relative. This doubt concerning his wild assumption does not at all emanate from cold logic. It is to be explained through the insight given by individual-psychology. If everything is but appearance then his mother has not died. If she is alive, however, then the idea of his being unique falls to the ground. He has no more solved this problem than philosophy has the idea of the universe as an appearance. He answers the compulsion and mischief of death with a doubt.

The interconnection of all the manifestations of his disease he regards as a justification for securing all his privileges as against his wife, his relatives and his inferiors. His high opinion of himself can

---

* Neurotic obsession with, and sexual attraction to, the aged.
† A neurotic erotic attraction to corpses.

never come to harm, for taking his sufferings into consideration, he is always greater than he appears to be and he can always evade difficult undertakings by pointing to his disease. But he can also act differently. Toward his superiors he can be the most conscientious, the most industrious and the most obedient official and enjoy their complete approbation although secretly always aspiring to surpass them.

This over-intense striving after the sensation of power had made him ill. His emotional and sensational life, his initiative and his capacity for work, even his power of reasoning, fell under the self-imposed compulsion of his lust for omnipotence, so that his feelings for humanity and with it love, friendship and adjustment to society, all disappeared. A cure could only have been attained by dismantling his whole prestige-mechanism and by inducing the development of a feeling for society.

Problems

1. For Adler, what is the cause of neurosis, and how does it manifest itself?
2. Which kinds of situations does the individual seek out and which does he avoid? Why is compulsion especially repellent? How does it divide the neurotic from the "normal"?
3. How can a flight from compulsion lead paradoxically to obsessive-compulsive behavior?
4. How persuasive do you find Adler's model of man? Do you find it more useful than Jung's? Why?

Individual-Psychological Treatment of Neuroses

To treat the extensive field of psycho-therapy concisely at a time when the discussion concerning the value of its principles are still so rife, is a fairly hazardous enterprise. Permit me consequently to refer to the basis for my views given in the material containing my experiences, that has been at the disposal of the public since 1907. In 1907 I proved in my book on Organ Inferiority (Vienna) that the inherited constitutional anomalies are not to be regarded as manifesting themselves merely in degenerative processes, but as causing the appearance likewise of compensatory and hyper-compensatory activities and significant

From Alfred Adler, *The Practice and Theory of Individual Psychology* (London: Humanities Press, 1955), pp. 1–16.

correlation-phenomena to which the reinforced psychic activity essentially contributed. This compensatory psychic exertion in order to conquer the psychic tensions, frequently strikes out along new and different lines. To the observer this compensatory activity appears to be of a well-tested nature, thus fulfilling its purpose of covering up some imagined deficiency in a most wonderful manner. The most widely distributed method adopted by the *feeling of inferiority,* appearing during childhood, to prevent its being unmasked, is the creation of a compensatory psychic superstructure, *the neurotic modus vivendi.* This seeks to regain, by means of fully tested preparations and defences, a point of vantage and superiority in life. Any departure from the normal can subsequently be explained either by a greater ambition or by a more marked degree of precaution. All the devices and arrangements, including therein the neurotic character, traits and symptoms, derive their value from previous attempts, experiences, identifications and imitations that are not entirely unknown even to a healthy individual. The language they speak, rightly understood, makes it evident that an individual is here struggling for recognition, actually attempting to force it; that he is aspiring ceaselessly to a godlike domination over his environment from out the region of his insecurity and his sense of inferiority.

Placing on one side this, the root of neurotic behaviour, we find the latter to consist of a variegated assortment of incitements and potentialities for incitement, which do not represent *the cause,* but rather the consequences of the neurosis. I have tried to present this frequently intensified "affective activity" and to show how, in order either to achieve some purpose or escape some danger, it is often converted into an apparent "aggression-check". What is customarily known as "disposition to neurosis" (*neurotic disposition*) is a real neurosis already, the more suitable neurotic symptoms appearing more definitely and as proofs of disease, only on those actual occasions when *an inward need demands the calling forth of strengthened devices.* This demonstration of illness and the "arrangements" associated with it, are specifically needed for the following purposes:

(1) To serve as excuses if life denies the longed-for triumphs.

(2) So that all *decisions may be postponed.*

(3) To permit those goals already attained to appear in an intenser light, since they have been gained *in spite of suffering.* These and other devices clearly exhibit the striving of the neurotic *for the semblance of things.*

The inference to be drawn is in each case simple. The neurotic in order to ensure success for his actions, in all of which he has been guided by an imagined goal, keeps to lines of direction typical for him and which he actually follows literally and unwaveringly. In this manner, by means of definite and adapted traits of character, tested affect-preparations, and a neurotic perspective of the past, present and future, the neurotic personality gains its fixed form. The urge to ensure security for this superiority operates with such strength that every psychic phenomenon, when analysed from the comparative psychological view, discloses superficially the similar characteristic, namely, to free itself from a feeling of weakness that it may reach the summit of its ambition; to lift itself from "below" to "above" and by the use of devices not always easily intelligible, become completely supreme. In order that by planning, thinking and a grasp of the world, he may be able to obtain a pedantic kind of order and *security,* the neurotic resorts to every rule and helping-formula he knows, the most important of which correspond to the primitive antithetic scheme. He consequently attaches importance only to affect-values that correspond to an upper and lower and attempts—as far as I can make out—to relate these to the contrast between "masculine" and "feminine" that appears so real to him. Through falsification of conscious and unconscious judgments, there is thus given, as if by means of some psychic accumulator, an occasion for *affect-disturbances* * and these latter are in turn adapted to the personal life-line of the patient. Those traits of his psyche felt as "feminine", *e.g.* passive attitude, obedience, softness, cowardice, memory of defeat, ignorance, lack of capacity, tenderness, he attempts to push with an exaggerated orientation towards the "masculine", thus developing hatred, defiance, cruelty, egoism. He seeks triumph in every human relation. He may, however, on the contrary markedly emphasize his weakness and, in this way, force upon others the burden of serving him. This procedure increases the patient's precautions and prevision enormously and leads to planned evasions of impending decisions. Where the patient believes it incumbent upon him in life to bring evidence of "masculine excellences", for instance, in struggles of every nature, in professions, in love, or in those cases where he fears he may become "effeminate" through defeat, (and this applies also to the masculine sex), he will even, when far removed, try to approach the problem circuitously. We shall then always succeed in finding a life-line, deviating from the direct path, which, on account of fear of mistakes and defeat, is searching for safe side-paths. The falsification of his sexual rôle results, in consequence of which the neurotic seems to exhibit a tendency toward "psychical hermaphrodism",† which he actually believes himself to possess. Viewed from this side the neurosis might easily be suspected of having a sexual causation. In reality, however, the same struggle takes place within the sexual domain that we have found within our entire psychic life; the original inferiority-feeling forces itself forward along by-paths (in sexual life along the road of masturbation, homosexuality,

* Emotional disturbances.
† An individual possessed with a marked degree of male and female sexual characteristics.

fetichism, algolagny,* over-evaluation of sexuality, etc.), so as not to lose its orientation toward the goal of superiority. The schematic formula, "I wish to be a complete man", then serves as the abstract and concretistic goal of the neurotic. It is a compensating termination for the basic feeling of an inferiority interpreted as feminine. The scheme that has been apperceived in this manner and upon which the individual has proceeded, is antithetic throughout and it has, in conscious falsification, been interpreted as containing within itself *hostile elements*. We can consequently always recognize as the unconscious premises of the neurotic goal-striving, the following two facts:

(1) *Human relations in all circumstances represent a struggle.*

(2) *The feminine sex is inferior and by its reaction serves as the measure of masculine strength.*

These two unconscious presuppositions that both masculine and feminine patients reveal in equal degree, are at the bottom of the distortion and poisoning of all human relationships, of the appearance of affect-disturbances and strengthenings, and the occurrence of permanent dissatisfaction instead of frankness. Dissatisfaction generally becomes lightened after intensification of the symptoms and after a successful demonstration of the existence of a disease. *The symptom is a substitute, in a way, for the neurotic lust for superiority with its associated affect.* In the patient's emotional life it leads more certainly to a sham-victory over the environment than would be true in the case of a straightforward battle, a definite trait of character, or resistance. *For me the understanding of the symptom-language has become the main condition for the success of the psycho-therapeutic cure.*

Since the purpose of the neurosis is to help an individual in the securing of the end-goal of superiority and since the feeling of inferiority apparently, excludes the possibility of direct aggression, circuitous routes which possess vaguely active, sometimes masochistic and always self-torturing characteristics, are preferred. Generally we encounter a mixture of psychic stirrings and disease-symptoms making their appearance either synchronously during the same period of illness, or following one another. When torn from their context in the disease-mechanism, they at times give the impression of being contradictory or of indicating a split in personality. The context shows that the patient can draw from two contradictory lines to reach his *ideal situation of imagined superiority,* just as he actually, with the same object in view, will argue correctly or incorrectly, and judge and feel quite independently of his goal. We must, on all occasions, expect the neurotic to possess those view-points, sensations, memories, affects, character-traits and symptoms that are to be presupposed in him by reason of his recognized life-line and goal.

* Sado-masochism.

Thus the neurotic in order to conquer along the line of obedience, submissiveness, "hysterical impressionability", in order to chain other people down through his weakness, fear, passivity, need for tenderness—has at his hand all kinds of reminders, of fear-inspiring pictures of horror, affect-preparations and identifications with properly adapted feelings and character-traits, in the same way that a neurotic, subject to compulsions, possesses definite principles, laws and prohibitions supposed to apply to himself only, but which in reality invest his sense of personality with a god-like power. As a goal we always find the acquisition of some ideal "income" for which the patient battles with the means his immediate experiences have shown to be the most suitable, just as tenaciously as a neurotic suffering from compulsion of meeting with accident, struggles for his material "income". The same holds true in those cases where active affects like rage, anger and jealousy make the path to pre-eminence secure. These latter are frequently represented by attacks of pain, fainting-spells or epileptic seizures. All neurotic symptoms have as their object the task of ensuring the safety of the patient's feeling of personality and the life-line with which he has identified himself. In order to prove his ability to cope with life, all the "arrangements" and neurotic symptoms necessary for the patient come into existence, as an aid in necessity, as an unduly developed coefficient-of-security against the dangers he anticipates and toward whose prevention he has been unceasingly working when, under the influence of his inferiority feeling, he has been constructing his plans for the future.

THE "ARRANGEMENT" OF THE NEUROSIS

The feeling of inferiority, afterwards purposely adhered to and emphasized, developing from the impressions of reality, incites the patient continuously in his childhood, to fix some goal for his striving, a goal extending beyond human limits, one which approaches a deification and which coerces an individual to march along lines rigidly determined. The neurotic system, *the life-plan of the nervous man,* lies between these two points—his feeling of inferiority and his striving for superiority. This compensatory psychical structure, this nervous "willing", utilizes all of one's own and foreign experience, purposefully distorting them, it is true, and falsifying their value at times, yet, on the other hand, employing their correct content whenever it suffices for the neurotic objective.

On closer inspection we find a perfectly explicable phenomenon, namely that all these lines of direction are provided, on numerous sides, with warning-signs and encouragement, with reminders and summons to action, so that it is really possible to speak of the existence of a widely ramifying safety-net. Everywhere we encounter the neurotic psychic life forming a super-structure built over a threatening infantile situation, a super-structure, changing in the course of years and adapting itself to reality more than would have been the case in the child's ordinary evolution. It is not to be wondered at then, if every psychic phenomenon of the neurotic is permeated by this rigid system and appears *like an analogy* in which the lines of direction always stand out in relief. Such phenomena are: the neurotic character, the nervous symptom, the demeanour, every device used in life, the evasions and deviations that occur as soon as decisions are about to threaten the god-like state of the neurotic, and finally his view-of-the-world, his attitude to men and women and his dreams. I presented my interpretation of the last-named phenomenon in 1911. Bringing my views upon dreams into harmony with those on neuroses, I found their *main function to consist of simplified early trials, and of warnings and encouragements favourable to the life-plan; and to have as their object the solution of some future problem.*

How does this striking similarity in psychic phenomena arise, where everything seems to be permeated with and guided by the same tendency —a striving upwards, a striving toward the masculine, toward the feeling of god-likeness?

The answer can be easily extracted from the above-mentioned work. The hypnotic nature of the goal of the neurotic, forces his whole psychic life into an integrated adaptation. As soon as the patient's life-line has been recognized, he will always be found at that particular place where we should expect to find him according to his presuppositions and previous history. The strong urge toward the integration of his personality, flows from an inward necessity and has been created by his tendency to safeguard himself. The path is made secure and unalterable by the proper schematic "arrangements" of character-traits, affect-preparations and symptoms. At this point let me append some remarks about "affect-disturbances", and neurotic "sensibility" in order to prove the existence of an unconscious "arrangement" for the purpose of keeping them within the life-line, thus employing them both as a *means to an end and as an artifice of the neurosis.*

For example, a patient with agoraphobia, in order by a complicated mechanism, to raise his prestige at home and force his environment into his service and to prevent himself likewise from losing, while on the street or in open places, the "resonance" so fervently desired, unites unconsciously and emotionally into a "junktim", the thought of being alone, of strange people, of purchases, search for the theatre, society, etc., and the phantasy of an apoplectic stroke, a confinement on the street, disease infection through germs on the street.[1] The exaggerated

---

1. "Junktim": purposive connection of two thoughts and affect-complexes that have in reality little or nothing to do with one another, in order to strengthen the affect. The metaphor has a similar origin.

size of the *safety-coefficient as contrasted with the thought potentialities* is clearly seen. In this way the discernible purpose can be followed to its final objective and the life-line recognized. Similarly the neurotic precaution of a patient subject to attacks of anxiety, who wishes furthermore to withdraw from making a decision, be it in an examination, a love-affair or an undertaking, will force him by thus establishing a proof of illness, to connect his situation with that of an execution, a prison, a shoreless sea, being buried alive and with death. In order to evade a decision about the success of a love-affair, the following connection of ideas may be resorted to as serving the desired purpose: a man, a murderer or a burglar, a woman, sphinx, demon or vampire. Every defeat is felt as all the more threatening because of being brought together with the thought of death or pregnancy, (encountered among neurotic men also). The transferred affect compels the patient to avoid a certain undertaking. Father and mother are at times invested by phantasy with the rôle of lover or spouse until the bond is firm enough to secure an evasion of the marriage problem. Religious and ethical feelings of guilt are, as is so frequently the case in compulsion-neurosis, constructed and utilized in order to attain a sensation of power, (*e.g.* "if I do not pray at night my mother will die"; the statement should be made positively in order to understand the fiction of god-likeness: "if I pray she will not die").

Together with the exaggerated personality-ideal and the "anxieties" of a neurotic type designed to secure it, we also find exaggerated "expectations" whose certainty of disappointment leads the patient to reinforced and definitely conditioned affects of mourning, hatred, dissatisfaction, jealousy, etc. In these cases the insistence upon principles, ideals, dreams, castles in the air, etc., plays a tremendous rôle and the neurotic can, by connecting these with some person or situation, deprive everything of its inherent value and so exhibit his superiority. The great importance of love in human life and the neurotic's search for superhuman influence and importance in love, bring about the frequent occurrence of an "arrangement" like that of disappointed expectation, so that the patient may in this manner evade the sexual problem. Masturbation compulsion, impotence, perversions and fetishism are found to lie along some indirect route of such a main line.

As a third type of construction designed to prevent defeat or a marked inferiority feeling, I shall briefly mention the *anticipation* of sensations, feelings and apperceptions, that have the significance, in connection with threatening situations, of acting as preparations, warnings, and encouragements such as occur in dreams, hypochondriac and melancholic conditions, in illusions in particular, in psychosis, in neurasthenia and in hallucinations.[2] A good example is provided by the dream of

---

2. This view-point has since then, in consequence of the study of war-neuroses, been accepted by practically all writers.

children who wet their bed, picturing themselves in the toilet so that they may be able to develop their generally revengeful and obstinate enuretic attitude, *uninfluenced by the intellect*. Similarly, images derived from tabes, paralysis, true epilepsy, paranoia, heart and lung affections etc. can be employed to produce fears or secure safety.

In order to present an intelligible, but admittedly schematic picture of the peculiar orientation of neurotics and psychotics, I suggest that we present the common attitude towards nervousness in a formula and then compare that formula with another representing the above views and corresponding better with reality. The first formula would appear as follows:

*Individual + experience + environment + demands
of life = a neurosis.*

In this formula the individual is regarded as weakened either by a feeling of inferiority, by heredity, by "sexual constitution", by emotionality or by his character. Furthermore his experiences, the environment and the external demands weigh upon the patient so heavily that they induce him to "take refuge in sickness". This interpretation is manifestly wrong and gains no support from the secondary hypothesis that the deficiency in wish-fulfilments or the "libido" that exists, in reality, is corrected by the neurosis.

A better formula would read as follows:—

Evaluation $(I + E + M)$* + *Arrangement* (*Experiences + Character + Emotionality + Symptoms*) = *Personality-ideal.*

In other words the only *definite and fixed point conceived of is the personality-ideal*. In order to approximate more nearly to his godlikeness, the neurotic makes a tendentious evaluation of his individuality, his experiences and his environment. But since this does not by any means suffice to bring him to his life-line or nearer to his goal, he *provokes experiences* which his previously determined favourable applications make easier—of feeling set-back, deceived, suffering—all of which give him the trusted and desired basis of aggression. That he constructs so much from real experiences and from possibilities and builds just the type of *character-traits and affect-preparations* that fit into his personality-ideal, follows from the above description and has been discussed by me in detail. In a similar fashion the patient identifies himself with his symptoms, all his experiences taking the form that appears necessary and useful for the heightening of his feeling of personality. Not the slighest trace of a predetermined autochthonous teleology * is to be found in this modus vivendi,† projected and tenaciously adhered

* I = individual; E = experiences; M = milieu or environment.
* Indigenous cosmology; aboriginal theory of final causes.
† A workable compromise, an accomodation, between two opposing parties or sides.

to by means of a self-suggested principal goal. The neurotic life-plan is maintained and teleologically arranged only by the urge toward superiority, by the careful evasion of dangerous-looking decisions, by previously tested wanderings along a few clearly determined lines of direction and the enormously increased safety-net. In consequence, the questions relating to the conservation or loss of psychic energy lose all their meaning. The patient will create just so much psychic energy as will enable him to remain on his path of superiority and express his masculine protest and god-likeness.

Patterns: Verbal Intimidation

Alfred Adler obviously had no intention of intimidating his audience and, within a psychoanalytic context, his language is really quite free of jargon. But it is not free of threatening mannerisms. The net effect of his language is, therefore, to intimidate the general reader.

A brief examination of his diction reveals it to be heavily latinate instead of anglo-saxon—it tends to polysyllabic words. Adler reveals, moreover, a propensity to compress abstract concepts instead of explaining them in simple terms. The combination of long words and compressed construction, instead of short words and simple construction, undermines the reader's confidence. At first glance—and every reader takes in a page at a glance in order to get his bearings—the impression is: (1) long latinate words, (2) frequent employment of italics and quotation marks, (3) jargon, (4) repeated high-level abstractions without concrete illustration, (5) very long paragraphs. As a result, the reader either is depressed into acceptance, or else he feels so threatened that he either stops reading, or fails, despite the lack of difficulty, to understand what he reads.

Verbal intimidation thus has the effect not of creating a favorable response, but of diminishing communication. Even argumentative intimidation is less effective than persuasion that guides and reassures.

Problems

1. How does the need for superiority lead to rationalization?
2. Why are impaired human relations and sexual rivalry intricately tied up with neurosis?
3. Why does the deviousness of the neurotic lead to self-destructive behavior?
4. How does the neurotic need for superiority lead the neurotic to perceive reality selectively?
5. How do the false premises of the neurotic, formulated as a "personality ideal," ultimately become the means of perpetuating his neurosis? How does the entire fabric of defenses become an imprisoning life plan?

26 KAREN HORNEY

Karen Horney (1885–1952), together with Harry Stack Sullivan, Erich Fromm, and others, is a "dynamic-culturalist," one of the "culture school," a group of psychoanalytic "revisionists" who tend to stress interpersonal relations and social rather than sexual factors in the genesis of neurosis.

After coming to this country from Germany in 1932, she began to deviate from orthodox Freudian theory by rejecting Freud's libidinal theory and his structural theory of the mind. In place of Freud's instinctual needs, Eros and Thanatos (the death instinct), she substituted the need for security, and elaborated ten strategies the neurotic develops in order to cope with anxiety. These strategies—the striving for affection, approval, power, prestige, admiration, independence, etc.—are, however, mutually exclusive (for example, power–affection, or approval–independence) and therefore create violent inner conflicts which the individual attempts to resolve by creating a false idealized image in opposition to his real self. This idealized self gradually erodes the individual's real self and creates, instead of authentic human self-confidence, a godlike idealized self victimized by pride and ensnared by the "search for glory."

"Morbid Dependency," from Neurosis and Human Growth (1950), suggests in a very common interpersonal context how the "pride system" creates irreconcilable conflicts and tormenting ambivalences.

Morbid Dependency

Among the three major solutions of the inner conflict within the pride system the self-effacing seems the least satisfactory one. Besides having the drawback entailed in every neurotic solution, it makes for a greater subjective feeling of unhappiness than the others. The genuine suffering of the self-effacing type may not be greater than in other kinds of neurosis, but subjectively he feels miserable more often and more intensely than others because of the many functions suffering has assumed for him.

From Karen Horney, *Neurosis and Human Growth* (New York: W. W. Norton & Company, Inc., 1950), pp. 239–58.

Besides, his needs and expectations of others make for a too great dependency upon them. And, while every enforced dependency is painful, this one is particularly unfortunate because his relation to people cannot but be divided. Nevertheless love (still in its broad meaning) is the only thing that gives a positive content to his life. Love, in the specific sense of erotic love, plays so peculiar and significant a role in his life that its presentation warrants a separate chapter. Although this unavoidably makes for certain repetitions, it also gives us a better opportunity to bring into clearer relief certain salient factors of the whole structure.

Erotic love lures this type as the supreme fulfillment. Love must and does appear as the ticket to paradise, where all woe ends: no more loneliness; no more feeling lost, guilty, and unworthy; no more responsibility for self; no more struggle with a harsh world for which he feels hopelessly unequipped. Instead love seems to promise protection, support, affection, encouragement, sympathy, understanding. It will give him a feeling of worth. It will give meaning to his life. It will be salvation and redemption. No wonder then that for him people often are divided into the haves and have-nots, not in terms of money and social status but of being (or not being) married or having an equivalent relationship.

Thus far the significance of love lies primarily in all he expects from being loved. Because psychiatric writers who have described the love of dependent persons have put a one-sided emphasis on this aspect, they have called it parasitic, sponging, or "oral-erotic." And this aspect may indeed be in the foreground. But for the typical self-effacing person (a person with prevailing self-effacing trends) the appeal is as much in loving as in being loved. To love, for him, means to lose, to submerge himself in more or less ecstatic feelings, to merge with another being, to become one heart and one flesh, and in this merger to find a unity which he cannot find in himself. His longing for love thus is fed by deep and powerful sources: the longing for surrender and the longing for unity. And we cannot understand the depth of his emotional involvement without considering these sources. The search for unity is one of the strongest motivating forces in human beings and is even more important to the neurotic, with his inner division. The longing to surrender to something bigger than we are seems to be the essential element in most forms of religion. And although the self-effacing surrender is a caricature of the healthy yearning, it nevertheless has the same power. It appears not only in the craving for love but also in many other ways.[1]

---

1. *Cf.* Karen Horney, *The Neurotic Personality of Our Time*, W. W. Norton, 1936, "The Problem of Masochism." In that book I suggested the longing for self-extinction as the basic explanatory principle for what I then still called masochistic phenomena. I would think now that this longing arises from the background of the special self-effacing structure.

It is one factor in his propensity to lose himself in all kinds of feelings: in a "sea of tears"; in ecstatic feelings about nature; in wallowing in guilt-feelings; in his yearning for oblivion in orgasm or in fading out in sleep; and often in his longing for death as the ultimate extinction of self.

Going still another step deeper: the appeal love has for him resides not only in his hopes for satisfaction, peace, and unity, but love also appears to him as the only way to actualize his idealized self. In loving, he can develop to the full the lovable attributes of his idealized self; in being loved he obtains the supreme confirmation of it.

Because love has for him a unique value, *lovableness* ranks first among all the factors determining his self-evaluation. I have already mentioned that the cultivation of lovable qualities started in this type with his early need for affection. It becomes all the more necessary the more crucial others become for his peace of mind; and all the more encompassing, the more expansive moves are suppressed. Lovable qualities are the only ones invested with a kind of subdued pride, the latter showing in his hypersensitivity to any criticism or questioning on this score. He feels deeply hurt if his generosity or his attentiveness to the needs of others is not appreciated or even, on the contrary, irritates them. Since these lovable qualities are the only factors he values in himself, he experiences any rejection of them as a total rejection of himself. Accordingly his fear of rejection is poignant. Rejection to him means not only losing all the hopes he had attached to somebody but also being left with a feeling of utter worthlessness.

In analysis we can study more closely how lovable attributes are enforced through a system of rigorous shoulds. He should not only be sympathetic but also attain the *absolute* in understanding. He should never feel personal hurts because everything of this sort should be wiped out by such understanding. To feel hurt, in addition to being painful, arouses self-condemnatory reproaches for being petty or selfish. Particularly he should not be vulnerable to the pangs of jealousy—a dictate entirely impossible of fulfillment for a person whose fear of rejection and desertion is bound to be aroused easily. All he can do at best is to insist upon a pretense of "broad-mindedness." Any friction that arises is his fault. He should have been more serene, more thoughtful, more forgiving. The extent to which he feels his shoulds as his own varies. Usually some are externalized to the partner. What he is aware of then is an anxiety to measure up to the latter's expectations. The two most relevant shoulds on this score are that he should be able to develop any love relationship into a state of absolute harmony and that he should be able to make the partner love him. When enmeshed in an untenable relation and having enough sense to know that it would be all for his own good to end it, his pride presents this solution as a disgraceful failure and demands that he should make the relation work. On the other hand, just because the lovable qualities—no matter how spurious—are invested with a secret pride, they also become a basis for his many hidden claims. They entitle him to exclusive devotion, and to the fulfillment of his many needs which we discussed in the last chapter. He feels entitled to be loved not only for his attentiveness, which may be real, but also for his very weakness and helplessness, for his very suffering and self-sacrificing.

Between these shoulds and claims conflicting currents can arise in which he may get inextricably caught. One day he is all abused innocence and may resolve to tell the partner off. But then he becomes frightened of his own courage, both in terms of demanding anything for himself and of accusing the other. He also becomes frightened at the prospect of losing him. And so the pendulum swings to the other extreme. His shoulds and self-reproaches get the upper hand. He should not resent anything, he should be unruffled, he should be more loving and understanding—and it all is his fault anyway. Similarly he wavers in his estimate of the partner, who sometimes seems strong and adorable, sometimes incredibly and inhumanly cruel. Thus everything is befogged and any decision out of the question.

Although the inner conditions in which he enters a love relationship are always precarious, they do not necessarily lead to disaster. He can reach a measure of happiness, provided he is not too destructive and provided he finds a partner who is either fairly healthy or, for neurotic reasons of his own, rather cherishes his weakness and dependency. Although such a partner may feel his clinging attitude burdensome at times, it may also make him feel strong and safe to be the protector and to arouse so much personal devotion—or what he conceives as such. Under these circumstances the neurotic solution might be called a successful one. The feeling of being cherished and sheltered brings out the very best qualities of the self-effacing person. Such a situation, however, will inevitably prevent him from outgrowing his neurotic difficulties.

How often such fortuitous circumstances occur is not in the analyst's domain to judge. What comes to his attention are the less fortunate relations, in which the partners torment each other and in which the dependent partner is in danger of destroying himself, slowly and painfully. In these instances we speak of a morbid dependency. Its occurrence is not restricted to sexual relations. Many of its characteristic features may operate in nonsexual friendships between parent and child, teacher and pupil, doctor and patient, leader and follower. But they are most pronounced in love relations, and having once grasped them therein one will easily recognize them in other relations when they may be clouded over by such rationalizations as loyalty or obligation.

Morbidly dependent relations are initiated by the unfortunate choice of a partner. To be more accurate, we should not speak of choice. The self-effacing person actually does not choose but instead is "spellbound" by certain types. He is naturally attracted by a person of the same or opposite sex who impresses him as stronger and superior. Leaving out of consideration here the healthy partner, he may easily fall in love with a detached person, provided the latter has some glamour through wealth, position, reputation, or particular gifts; with an outgoing narcissistic type possessing a buoyant self-assurance similar to his own; with an arrogant-vindictive type who dares to make open claims and is unconcerned about being haughty and offensive. Several reasons combine for his being easily infatuated with these personalities. He is inclined to overrate them because they all seem to possess attributes which he not only bitterly misses in himself but ones for the lack of which he despises himself. It may be a question of independence, of self-sufficiency, of an invincible assurance of superiority, a boldness in flaunting arrogance or aggressiveness. Only these strong, superior people—as he sees them—can fulfill all his needs and take him over. To follow the fantasies of one woman patient: only a man with strong arms can save her from a burning house, a shipwreck, or threatening burglars.

But what accounts specifically for being fascinated or spellbound—i.e., for the compulsive element in such an infatuation—is the suppression of his expansive drives. As we have seen, he must go to any length to disavow them. Whatever hidden pride and drives for mastery he has, remain foreign to him—while, conversely, he experiences the subdued helpless part of his pride system as the very essence of himself. But on the other hand, because he suffers under the results of his shrinking process, the capacity to master life aggressively and arrogantly also appears to him to be most desirable. Unconsciously and even—when he feels free enough to express it—consciously, he thinks that if only he could be as proud and ruthless as the Spanish conquistadors he would be "free," with the world at his feet. But since this quality is out of reach for him, he is fascinated by it in others. He externalizes his own expansive drives and admires them in others. It is their pride and arrogance that touch him to the core. Not knowing that he can solve his conflict in himself only, he tries to solve it by love. To love a proud person, to merge with him, to live vicariously through him would allow him to participate in the mastery of life without having to own it to himself. If in the course of the relationship he discovers that the god has feet of clay, he may sometimes lose interest because he can no longer transfer his pride to him.

On the other hand a person with self-effacing trends does not appeal to him as a sexual partner. He may like him as a friend because he finds in him more sympathy, understanding, or devotion than in others. But when starting a more intimate relationship with him, he may feel even repelled. He sees in him, as in a mirror, his own weakness and despises him for it or at least is irritated by it. He is also afraid of the clinging-vine attitude of such a partner because the mere idea that he himself must be the stronger one terrifies him. These negative emotional responses then may render it impossible to value existing assets in such a partner.

Among the obviously proud people those of the arrogant-vindictive type as a rule exert the greatest fascination on the dependent person although, in terms of his real self-interest, he has stringent reasons to be afraid of them. The cause of the fascination lies in part in their pride in the most conspicuous way. But even more crucial is the fact that they are most likely to knock his own pride out from under him. The relationship may start indeed with some crude offense on the part of the arrogant person. Somerset Maugham in *Of Human Bondage* had described this in the first meeting between Philip and Mildred. Stefan Zweig has a similar instance in his *Amok*. In both cases the dependent person responds first with anger and an impulse to get back at the offender—in each case a woman—but almost simultaneously is so fascinated that he "falls" for her hopelessly and passionately and has thereafter but the one driving interest: to win her love. Thereby he ruins, or almost ruins, himself. Insulting behavior frequently precipitates a dependent relationship. It need not always be as dramatic as in *Of Human Bondage* or *Amok*. It may be much more subtle and insidious. But I wonder if it is ever entirely missing in such a relationship. It may consist of a mere lack of interest or an arrogant reserve, of paying attention to others, of joking or facetious remarks, of being unimpressed by whatever assets in the partner usually impress others—such as name, profession, knowledge, beauty. These are "insults" because they are felt as rejections, and—as I have mentioned—a rejection is an insult for anybody whose pride is largely invested in making everybody love him. The frequency of such occurrences throws light upon the appeal detached people have for him. Their very aloofness and unavailability constitute the insulting rejection.

Incidents such as these seem to lend weight to the notion that the self-effacing person merely craves for suffering and avidly seizes the prospect of it offered by the insults. Actually nothing has more blocked a real understanding of morbid dependency than this notion. It is all the more misleading since it contains a grain of truth. We know that suffering has manifold neurotic values for him and it is also true that insulting behavior attracts him magnetically. The error lies in establishing a too neat causal connection between these two facts by assuming that the magnetic attraction is determined by the prospect of suffering. The reason lies in two other factors, both of which we mentioned separately:

the fascination that arrogance and aggressiveness in others exert on him, and his own need for surrender. We now can see that these two factors are more closely interlinked than we have hitherto realized. He craves to surrender himself body and soul, but can do so only if his pride is bent or broken. In other words the initial offense is not so much intriguing because it hurts as because it opens the possibility for self-riddance and self-surrender. To use a patient's words: "The person who shakes my pride from under me releases me from my arrogance and pride." Or: "If he can insult me, then I am just an ordinary human being"—and, one might add, "only then can I love." We may think here too of Bizet's Carmen, whose passion was inflamed only if she were not loved.

No doubt the abandoning of pride as a rigid condition for love-surrender is pathological, particularly (as we shall see presently) since the pronounced self-effacing type can love only if he feels, or is, degraded. But the phenomenon ceases to seem unique and mysterious if we remember that for the healthy person love and *true* humility go together. It also is not quite as widely different from what we have seen in the expansive type as we might at first be led to believe. The latter's fear of love is mainly determined by his unconscious realization that he would have to relinquish much of his neurotic pride for the sake of love. To put it succinctly: *neurotic pride is the enemy of love.* Here the difference between the expansive and the self-effacing type is that the former does not need love in any vital way but, on the contrary, shuns it as a danger; while for the latter love-surrender appears as a solution for everything, and hence as a vital necessity. The expansive type, too, can surrender only if his pride is broken, but then may become passionately enslaved. Stendhal has described this process in the proud Mathilde's passion for Julien in *The Red and the Black*. It shows that the arrogant person's fear of love is well founded—for him. But mostly he is too much on his guard to allow himself to fall in love.

Although we can study the characteristics of a morbid dependency in any relationship, they come into clearest relief in the sexual relationship between a self-effacing and an arrogant-vindictive type. The conflicts generated here are more intense, and can develop more fully, since for reasons residing in both partners the relationship is usually of longer duration. The narcissistic or detached partner more easily becomes tired of the implicit demands made upon him and is liable to quit,[2] while the sadistic partner is more prone to fasten himself onto his victim. For the dependent person, in turn, it is much more difficult to extricate himself from a relation with an arrogant-vindictive type. With his peculiar weakness, he is as unequipped for such an involvement as a ship built for navigation in still waters is for crossing a rough, stormy ocean.

2. *Cf.* Flaubert's *Madame Bovary*. Both her lovers become tired of her and break away. *Cf.* also Karen Horney, *Self-Analysis*, Claire's self-analysis.

Her whole lack of sturdiness, every weak spot in her structure will then make itself felt and may mean ruin. Similarly a self-effacing person may have functioned fairly well in life, but when tossed into the conflicts involved in such a relationship every hidden neurotic factor in him will come into operation. I shall describe the process here primarily from the standpoint of the dependent person. For the sake of simplifying the presentation I shall assume that the self-effacing partner is a woman and the aggressive one a man. Actually this combination seems to be more frequent in our civilization although, as many instances show, self-effacement has nothing to do with femininity nor aggressive arrogance with masculinity. Both are exquisitely neurotic phenomena.

The first characteristic to strike us is such a woman's total absorption in the relationship. The partner becomes the sole center of her existence. Everything revolves around him. Her mood depends upon whether his attitude toward her is more positive or negative. She does not dare make any plans lest she might miss a call or an evening with him. Her thoughts are centered on understanding or helping him. Her endeavors are directed toward measuring up to what she feels he expects. She has but one fear—that of antagonizing and losing him. Conversely her other interests subside. Her work, unless connected with him, becomes comparatively meaningless. This may even be true of professional work otherwise dear to her heart, or productive work in which she has accomplished things. Naturally the latter suffers most.

Other human relations are neglected. She may neglect or leave her children, her home. Friendships serve more and more merely to fill the time when he is not available. Engagements are dropped at a moment's notice when he appears. The impairment of other relations often is fostered by the partner because he in turn wants to make her more and more dependent upon him. Also she starts to look at her relatives or friends through his eyes. He scorns her trust in people and instills his own suspiciousness in her. So she loses roots and becomes more and more impoverished. In addition her self-interest, always at a low ebb, sinks. She may incur debts, risk her reputation, her health, her dignity. If she is in analysis or used to analyzing herself, the interest in self-recognition gives way to a concern for understanding *his* motivations and helping *him*.

The trouble may set in, full fledged, right at the beginning. But sometimes things look fairly auspicious for a while. In certain neurotic ways the two seem to fit together. He needs to be the master; she needs to surrender. He is openly demanding, she complying. She can surrender only if her pride is broken, and for many reasons of his own he cannot fail to do so. But sooner or later clashes are bound to occur between two temperaments—or, more accurately, between two neurotic structures—which in all essentials are diametrically opposed. The main clashes occur on the issue of feelings, of "love." She insists upon love, affection, closeness. He is desperately afraid of positive feelings. Their display seems indecent to him. Her assurances of love seem like pure hypocrisy to him—and indeed, as we know, it is actually more a need to lose herself and merge with him that motivates her than personal love for him. He cannot keep from striking out against her feelings, and hence against her. This in turn makes her feel neglected or abused, arouses anxiety, and reinforces her clinging attitudes. And here another collision occurs. Although he does everything to make her dependent upon him, her clinging to him terrifies and repels him. He is afraid and contemptuous of any weakness in himself and despises it in her. This means another rejection for her, provoking more anxiety and more clinging. Her implicit demands are felt as coercion, and he has to hit out in order to retain his feelings of mastery. Her compulsive helpfulness offends his pride in self-sufficiency. Her insistence upon "understanding" him likewise hurts his pride. And actually, with all her often sincere attempts, she does not really understand him—hardly can do so. Besides in her "understanding" there is too much need to excuse and to forgive, for she feels all *her* attitudes as good and natural. He in turn senses her feeling morally superior and feels provoked to tear down the pretenses involved. There is but scant possibility for a good talk about these matters because at bottom they are both self-righteous. So she starts to see him as a brute and he her as a moral prig. The tearing down of her pretenses could be eminently helpful if it were done in a constructive way. But as it is mostly done in a sarcastic, derogatory way, it merely hurts her and makes her more insecure and more dependent.

It is an idle speculation to ask whether or not, with all these clashes, they might be helpful to each other. Certainly he could stand some softening and she some toughening. But mostly they are both too deeply entrenched in their particular neurotic needs and aversions. Vicious circles which bring out the worst in both keep operating, and can result only in mutual tormenting.

The frustrations and limitations to which she is exposed vary not so much in kind as in being more or less civilized, more or less intense. There is always some cat-and-mouse play of attracting and repulsing, binding and withdrawing. Satisfactory sexual relations may be followed by crude offenses; an enjoyable evening by forgetting a date; eliciting confidences by sarcastically using them against her. She may try to play the same game, but is too inhibited to do it well. But she is always a good instrument on which to play, since his attacks make her despondent and his seemingly positive moods throw her into fallacious hopes that from now on everything will be better. There are always plenty of things he feels entitled to do without allowing any questioning. His claims may concern financial support or gifts for himself and his friends or relatives; work to be done for him, like housework or typing; furthering his career; strict consideration of his needs. These latter may, for instance, concern time arrangements, undivided and uncritical interest in his pursuits, having or not having company, remaining unruffled when he is sulky or irritable, and so on and so forth.

Whatever he demands is his self-evident due. There is no appreciation forthcoming but much nagging irritability when his wishes are not fulfilled. He feels and declares in no uncertain terms that he is not at all demanding but that she is stingy, sloppy, inconsiderate, unappreciative— and that he has to put up with all sorts of abuse. On the other hand he is astute at spotting her claims, which he finds altogether neurotic. Her need for affection, time, or company is possessive, her wanting sex or good food, overindulgence. So when he frustrates her needs, which he must do for reasons of his own, it is in his mind no frustration at all. It is better to disregard her needs because she should be ashamed of having them. Actually his frustrating techniques are highly developed. They include dampening joy by sulkiness, making her feel unwelcome and unwanted, withdrawing physically or psychically. The most harmful and, for her, least tangible part is his pervasive attitude of disregard and contempt. Whatever actual regard he may have for her faculties or qualities is seldom expressed. On the other hand, as I have already said, he does despise her for her softness and for her caginess and indirectness. But in addition, because of his need for active externalization of his self-hate, he is faultfinding and derogatory. If she in turn dares to criticize him, he discards what she says in a highhanded manner or proves that she is vindictive.

We find the greatest variation in sexual matters. Sexual relations may stand out as the only satisfactory contact. Or, in case he is inhibited in enjoying sex, he may frustrate her in this regard too, which is felt all the more keenly since in view of his lack of tenderness sex may mean for her the only assurance of love. Or sex may be a means of degrading and humiliating her. He may make it clear that for him she is nothing but a sexual object. He may flaunt sexual relations with other women, intermingled with derogatory comments about her being less attractive or responsive than these others. Sexual intercourse may be degrading because of any tenderness or because he uses sadistic techniques.

Her attitudes toward such maltreatment are full of contradictions. As we shall see presently, it is not a static set of reactions but a fluctuating process leading her into more and more conflicts. To begin with, she is simply helpless, as she always has been toward aggressive people. She never could assert herself against them and fight back in any effective way. Complying has always been easier for her. And, being prone to feel guilty anyhow, she rather agrees with his many reproaches, particularly since they often contain a good grain of truth.

But her compliance now assumes greater proportions and also changes in quality. It remains an expression of her need to please and appease but in addition is determined now by her longing for total surrender. This, as we have seen, she can do only when most of her pride has been broken. Thus part of her secretly welcomes his behavior and most actively collaborates with him. He is obviously—though unconsciously—out to crush her pride; she secretly has a complementary irresistible urge to immolate it. In sexual performances this urge may come into full awareness. With orgiastic lust she may prostrate herself, assume humiliating positions, be beaten, bitten, insulted. And sometimes these are the only conditions under which she can reach a full satisfaction. This urge for total surrender by means of self-degradation seems to account more fully than other explanations for the masochistic perversions.

Such frank expressions of a lust to degrade herself are evidence of the enormous power such a drive can assume. It may also show in fantasies—often connected with masturbation—of degrading sexual orgies, of being publicly exposed, raped, tied, beaten. Finally, this drive may be expressed in dreams of lying destitute in a gutter and being lifted up by the partner, of being treated by him like a prostitute, of groveling at his feet.

The drive toward self-degradation may be too disguised to come into clear relief. But for the experienced observer it shows in many other ways, such as her eagerness—or rather urgency—to whitewash him and to take upon herself the blame for his misdemeanor; or in her abjectness in serving and deferring to him. She is not aware of it, because in her mind such deference registers as humility or love, or humility in loving, since as a rule the urge to prostrate herself—except in sexual matters—is most deeply suppressed. Yet the urge is there and enforces a compromise, which is to let the degradation occur without being aware that it happens. This explains why for a long time she may not even notice his offensive behavior although it is flagrantly obvious to others. Or, if she takes cognizance of it, she does not experience it emotionally and does not really mind it. Sometimes a friend may call it to her attention. But even though she may be convinced of its truth and of her friend's interest in her welfare, it may merely irritate her. In fact it must do so, because it touches too closely upon her conflict in this respect. Even more telling are her own attempts at a time when she tries to struggle out of the situation. Over and over again she may then recall all his insulting and humiliating attitudes, hoping that this will help her to take a stand against him. And only after long futile attempts of this kind will she realize, with surprise, that they simply do not carry any weight.

Her need for total surrender also makes it necessary to idealize the partner. Because she can find her unity only with somebody to whom she has delegated her pride, he should be the proud one and she the subdued.

I have mentioned the initial fascination that his arrogance has for her. Although this conscious fascination may subside, her glorification of him persists in more subtle ways. She may see him more clearly in many details later on, but she does not get a sober total picture of him until she has actually made the break—and even then the glorification may linger on. She is meanwhile inclined to think, for instance, that notwithstanding his difficulties he is mostly right and knows better than anybody else. Both her need to idealize him and her need to surrender operate here hand in hand. She has extinguished her personal self to the extent of seeing him, others, and herself through his eyes—another factor that makes the breaking away so difficult.

So far all plays in with the partner. But there is a turning point, or rather a long-drawn-out turning process, as the stake she is gambling for fails to materialize. Her self-degradation is largely (although not altogether) after all a means to an end: that of finding inner unity through surrender of self and merging with the partner. In order for her to reach this fulfillment the partner has to accept her love-surrender and return her love. But on exactly this decisive point he fails her—as we know, he is bound to do so by dint of his own neurosis. Therefore, while she does not mind—or rather secretly welcomes—his arrogance, she fears and resents bitterly the rejections as well as the implicit and explicit frustrations in matters of love. There are involved here both her deep longing for salvation and that part of her pride which demands in its service that she should be able to make him love her and to make a go of the relation. Besides, like most people, she cannot easily relinquish a goal in which she has invested so heavily. And so she responds to his maltreatment with becoming anxious, despondent, or desperate, only to regain hope soon after, clinging—against evidence to the contrary—to the belief that one day he will love her.

At this very point conflicts set in, at first short lived and quickly surmounted but gradually deepening and becoming permanent. On the one hand she tries desperately to improve the relationship. To her this appears as a commendable way of putting efforts into cultivating it; to him as increased clinging. Both are right up to a point; but both also miss the essential issue, which is her fighting for what appears to her as the ultimate good. More than ever she stands on tiptoe to please, to measure up to his expectations, to see the fault in herself, to overlook or not to resent any crudeness, to understand, to smooth over. Not realizing that all these efforts are in the service of radically wrong goals, she evaluates these efforts as "improvements." Similarly she typically adheres to the usually fallacious belief that he "improves" too.

On the other hand she starts to hate him. At first this is repressed altogether because it would annihilate her hopes. Then it may become conscious in flashes. She now starts to resent his offensive treatment, again hesitating to admit it to herself. With this turn vindictive trends come to the fore. There are blowups in which her true resentment appears, but still without her knowing how true it is. She becomes more critical, is less willing to let herself be exploited. Characteristically most of this vindictiveness appears in indirect ways, in complaints, suffering, martyrdom, increased clinging. The vindictive elements also creep into her goal. They were always there in a latent form but now they spread like a cancerous growth. Though the longing to make him love her persists, it becomes more strongly a matter of a vindictive triumph.

This is unfortunate for her in every way. Although it remains unconscious, to be sharply divided in so crucial an issue makes for genuine unhappiness. Also, for the very reason that it is unconscious, this vindictiveness serves to tie her more closely to him because it supplies her with another strong incentive to work toward a "happy ending." And even when she succeeds and he does fall in love with her after all—which he may, if he is not too rigid and she is not too self-destructive—she does not reap the benefits. Her need for triumph is fulfilled and dwindles, her pride has its due but she is no longer interested. She may be grateful, appreciative for love given, but she feels it is now too late. Actually she cannot love with her pride satisfied.

If, however, her redoubled efforts do not essentially change the picture, she may turn more vehemently against herself and thereby come into a cross fire. Since the idea of surrender gradually loses its value, and since therefore she becomes aware of tolerating too much abuse, she feels exploited and hates herself for it. Also she begins to realize at last that her "love" is in actual fact a morbid dependency (whatever term she may use). This is a healthy recognition, but at first she reacts to it with self-contempt. In addition, condemning the vindictive trends in herself, she hates herself for having them. And finally she runs herself down mercilessly for failing to elicit his love. She is aware of some of this self-hate, but usually most of it is externalized in the passive way characteristic of the self-effacing type. This means that there is now a massive and pervasive feeling of being abused by him. This makes for a new split in her attitude toward him. The increased resentment stemming from this feeling of being abused drives her away. But also the very self-hate either is so frightening that it calls for reassuring affection or reinforces on a purely self-destructive basis her receptiveness to maltreatment. The partner then becomes the executor of her own self-destruction. She is driven to be tormented and humiliated because she hates and despises herself.

The self-observations of two patients, both about to extricate themselves from a dependent relationship, may illustrate the role of self-hate in this period. The first patient, a man, decided to go on a brief vacation alone in order to find out what his true feelings were toward the woman upon whom he was dependent. Attempts of this kind, although understandable, mostly prove futile—partly because compulsive factors befog the issue and partly because the individual is usually not really concerned with his own problems and their relation to the situation but only with "finding out," in a vacuum, whether or not he loves the other person.

In this case his very determination to go to the root of the trouble did bear fruit, although he could not of course find the answer to his question. Feelings did emerge; in fact, he got into a hurricane of feelings. First he became immersed in feeling that the woman was so inhumanly cruel that no punishment was drastic enough. Soon after, he felt just as intensely that he would give everything for a friendly move on her part. These extreme feelings alternated several times, and each of them felt so real that for the time being he forgot the opposite feeling. Only after he had gone through this process three times did he realize that his feelings were contradictory. Only then did he realize that none of these extremes represented his true feelings and only then did he see clearly that both were compulsive. This realization relieved him. Instead of being swept helplessly from one emotional experience into its opposite, he could now start to regard both as a problem to be understood. The following piece of analysis brought about the surprising realization that both feelings, at bottom, had less to do with the partner than with his own inner processes.

Two questions helped to clarify the emotional upheaval: Why did he have to exaggerate her offenses to the extent of making her an inhuman monster? Why did it take him so long to recognize the apparent contradiction in his mood-swings? The first question led us to see the following sequences: increased self-hate (for several reasons), increased feeling of being abused by the woman, and responding to his externalized self-hate with vindictive hate toward her. After having seen this process the answer to the second question was easy. His feelings were contradictory only when taken at their face value as expressing love and hate for the woman. Actually he was frightened by the vindictiveness expressed in the idea of no punishment being drastic enough, and he tried to allay this anxiety by longing for the woman in order to reassure himself.

The other illustration concerns a woman patient who at the particular period wavered between feeling rather independent and feeling an almost irresistible urge to call up her partner. Once when she was about to reach for the telephone—knowing full well she only made things harder for herself by a renewed contact—she thought: "I wish somebody would tie me to a mast like Ulysses . . . like Ulysses? But he needed to be tied in order to resist the lure of Circe who turned men into swine! [3] So that is what drives me: a violent urge to degrade myself and to be humiliated by him." This felt right, and the spell was broken. Being able at this time to

---

3. The patient in question confused the incident of the Sirens with those about Circe. This did not of course affect the validity of her discovery.

analyze herself, she then asked herself the pertinent question: what made this urge so strong just now? She then experienced considerable self-hate and self-contempt of which she had not been aware. Incidents of previous days emerged, ones which had caused her to turn against herself. After this she felt relieved and on more solid ground, for at this period she wanted to leave him and through this self-analysis she did get hold of one of the strings that still tied her to him. She started the next analytic session by saying: "We have to work more at my self-hate."

There is thus a crescendo of inner turmoil through all the factors mentioned: the dwindling hope for fulfillment, the redoubled efforts, the emerging of hate and vindictiveness with their repercussions and the violence against self. The inner situation becomes increasingly untenable. She is actually at the point where it becomes a proposition of sink or swim. Two moves set in now and it all depends on which wins. The one to go under—as we have discussed before—has for this type the appeal of a final solution of all conflicts. She may contemplate suicide, threaten it, attempt it, do it. She may fall ill and succumb to her illness. She may become morally sloppy and for instance plunge into meaningless affairs. She may hit out vindictively against her partner, usually injuring herself more than him. Or without knowing it she may simply lose her zest for living, become indolent, neglect her appearance, her work, and put on weight.

The other move is in the direction of health, and consists in efforts to get out of the situation. Sometimes it is the very realization of being actually in danger of going to pieces that gives her the necessary courage. Sometimes the two moves go on intermittently. The process of struggling out is eminently painful. Incentive and strength to do so come from both healthy and neurotic sources. There is an awakening constructive self-interest; there is also an increasing resentment against him, not only for actual alleged abuse but also for making her feel "cheated"; there is hurt pride over having played a losing game. On the other hand she is up against terrific odds. She has cut herself off from so many things and people and, being as torn as she is, is petrified at the idea of being thrown on her own. Also to break away would mean to declare herself defeated, and another kind of pride rebels against that. There are usually ups and downs—times when she feels she is able to leave him and others when she would rather suffer any indignity than get out. It is largely as it were a struggle between one pride and another with herself, terrified, in the middle. The outcome depends on many factors. Most of them are in herself, but many also are in her whole life situation—and, to be sure, the help of a friend or analyst may be of considerable importance.

Assuming that she does manage to struggle out of her involvement, the value of her action would depend upon these questions: did she, by hook or crook, get out of the one dependency only sooner or later to rush into another one? Or did she get so wary of her feelings that she tended to deaden all of them? She may then appear "normal" but actually be scarred for life. Or has she changed in a more radical way and come out a really stronger person? Any of these possibilities may be realized. Naturally an analysis offers the best chance to outgrow the neurotic difficulties which led her into distress and danger. Then provided she can mobilize sufficient constructive forces during her struggle and has matured through the real suffering involved, plain ordinary honesty with self and efforts to get on her own feet can go far toward attaining a measure of inner freedom.

Morbid dependency is one of the most complicated phenomena with which we have to deal. We cannot hope to understand it as long as we are unreconciled to the complexities of human psychology and insist upon a simple formula to explain it. We cannot explain the total picture as manifold branches of sexual masochism. If it is present at all, it is an *outcome* of many other factors and not their root. Nor is it all the inverted sadism of a weak and hopeless person. Nor do we grasp its essentials when focusing on the parasitic or symbiotic aspects, or on the neurotic's drive to lose himself. Nor does self-destructiveness with the urge to inflict suffering upon self, alone suffice as an explanatory principle. Nor, finally, can we regard the whole condition as being merely an externalization of pride and hate. When we regard one or another factor as *the* deep root of the whole phenomenon we cannot help getting a one-sided picture which fails to embrace all the peculiarities involved. Moreover all such explanations give too static a picture. Morbid dependency is not a static condition but a process in which all or most of these factors come into play—coming to the fore, receding in importance, one determining or reinforcing the other or conflicting with it.

And, finally, all the factors mentioned, though relevant to the total picture, are, as it were, too negative to account for the passionate character of the involvment. For a passion it is, when it flares up or smolders. But there is no passion without an expectation of some vital fulfillment. And it makes no difference whether or not these expectations arise on neurotic premises. This factor, which in its turn cannot be isolated but may be grasped only in the framework of the whole self-effacing stature, is the drive for total surrender and the longing to find unity through merging with the partner.

Problems

1. Which of Freud's three libidinal types tends to become morbidly dependent? Why? In what way do Adler's theories throw light on the problem of morbid dependency?
2. What is the self-effacing person's concept of love? What are the possible consequences of such a concept? Conceive of a less destructive concept.
3. Why is fear of rejection the cornerstone of morbid dependency? What assumptions can create such a fear? What tyrannical consequences can follow from this fear?
4. What types are most attractive to self-effacing persons, and to what extent is the attraction a compulsion? What "illusions" follow the establishment of a new relationship?
5. What are the factors that lead one to seek punishing relationships? Why does the partner come to consume the self-effacing person's thoughts?
6. What dynamics operate to create contradictory and conflicting emotions? What are these emotions, and why does pride play such a large role in the creation of conflicting emotions?

Problems

1. ...

27 ERICH FROMM

Erich Fromm (1900–   ), though trained as a Freudian, is less a Freudian "revisionist"—despite Marcuse's strictures against him for "revisionism" in Eros and Civilization *(1955),—than he is a psychoanalytic eclectic. A "dynamic culturalist" like Horney, he is probably even more concerned than she is with the interrelationship between the individual and the social condition in which he finds himself. In a sense, Fromm is a psychoanalyst writing social psychology. His works are hardly descriptive or theoretical; they are lyrical statements, with a strong visionary strain, a pronounced social consciousness and an abiding faith that man, through love and understanding, can throw off his suffocating individuality and use his freedom to find meaning and self-fulfillment in the community of men. There is much hope and much beauty in his writing, but there is also an underlying fear that man may fail to develop his power to love and to care, and may instead flee from freedom with all its risks and take refuge in authoritarian forms.*

This essay, the third chapter from his book, The Art of Loving *(1956), enlarges the scope of his introductory analysis and thereby shows, in contrast to the Horney essay, how the culture school perceives the dynamic interaction between society and the individual.*

Love and Its Disintegration in Contemporary Western Society

If love is a capacity of the mature, productive character, it follows that the capacity to love in an individual living in any given culture depends on the influence this culture has on the character of the average person. If we speak about love in contemporary Western culture, we mean to ask whether the social structure of Western civilization and the spirit resulting from it are conducive to the development of love. To raise the question is to answer it in the negative. No objective observer of our Western life can doubt that love—brotherly love, motherly love,

From Erich Fromm, *The Art of Loving* (New York: Harper & Row, 1956), pp. 83–106.

and erotic love—is a relatively rare phenomenon, and that its place is taken by a number of forms of pseudo-love which are in reality so many forms of the disintegration of love.

Capitalistic society is based on the principle of political freedom on the one hand, and of the market as the regulator of all economic, hence social relations, on the other. The commodity market determines the conditions under which commodities are exchanged, the labor market regulates the acquisition and sale of labor. Both useful things and useful human energy and skill are transformed into commodities which are exchanged without the use of force and without fraud under the conditions of the market. Shoes, useful and needed as they may be, have no economic value (exchange value) if there is no demand for them on the market; human energy and skill are without exchange value if there is no demand for them under existing market conditions. The owner of capital can buy labor and command it to work for the profitable investment of his capital. The owner of labor must sell it to capitalists under the existing market conditions, unless he is to starve. This economic structure is reflected in a hierarchy of values. Capital commands labor; amassed things, that which is dead, are of superior value to labor, to human powers, to that which is alive.

This has been the basic structure of capitalism since its beginning. But while it is still characteristic of modern capitalism, a number of factors have changed which give contemporary capitalism its specific qualities and which have a profound influence on the character structure of modern man. As the result of the development of capitalism we witness an ever-increasing process of centralization and concentration of capital. The large enterprises grow in size continuously, the smaller ones are squeezed out. The ownership of capital invested in these enterprises is more and more separated from the function of managing them. Hundreds of thousands of stockholders "own" the enterprise; a managerial bureaucracy which is well paid, but which does not own the enterprise, manages it. This bureaucracy is less interested in making maximum profits than in the expansion of the enterprise, and in their own power. The increasing concentration of capital and the emergence of a powerful managerial bureaucracy are paralleled by the development of the labor movement. Through the unionization of labor, the individual worker does not have to bargain on the labor market by and for himself; he is united in big labor unions, also led by a powerful bureaucracy which represents him vis-à-vis the industrial colossi. The initiative has been shifted, for better or worse, in the fields of capital as well as in those of labor, from the individual to the bureaucracy. An increasing number of people cease to be independent, and become dependent on the managers of the great economic empires.

Another decisive feature resulting from this concentration of capital, and characteristic of modern capitalism, lies in the specific way of the organization of work. Vastly centralized enterprises with a radical division of labor lead to an organization of work where the individual loses his individuality, where he becomes an expendable cog in the machine. The human problem of modern capitalism can be formulated in this way:

Modern capitalism needs men who co-operate smoothly and in large numbers; who want to consume more and more; and whose tastes are standardized and can be easily influenced and anticipated. It needs men who feel free and independent, not subject to any authority or principle or conscience—yet willing to be commanded, to do what is expected of them, to fit into the social machine without friction; who can be guided without force, led without leaders, prompted without aim—except the one to make good, to be on the move, to function, to go ahead.

What is the outcome? Modern man is alienated from himself, from his fellow men, and from nature.[1] He has been transformed into a commodity, experiences his life forces as an investment which must bring him the maximum profit obtainable under existing market conditions. Human relations are essentially those of alienated automatons, each basing his security on staying close to the herd, and not being different in thought, feeling or action. While everybody tries to be as close as possible to the rest, everybody remains utterly alone, pervaded by the deep sense of insecurity, anxiety and guilt which always results when human separateness cannot be overcome. Our civilization offers many palliatives which help people to be consciously unaware of this aloneness: first of all the strict routine of bureaucratized, mechanical work, which helps people to remain unaware of their most fundamental human desires, of the longing for transcendence and unity. Inasmuch as the routine alone does not succeed in this, man overcomes his unconscious despair by the routine of amusement, the passive consumption of sounds and sights offered by the amusement industry; furthermore by the satisfaction of buying ever new things, and soon exchanging them for others. Modern man is actually close to the picture Huxley describes in his *Brave New World:* well fed, well clad, satisfied sexually, yet without self, without any except the most superficial contact with his fellow men, guided by the slogans which Huxley formulated so succinctly, such as: "When the individual feels, the community reels"; or "Never put off till tomorrow the fun you can have today," or, as the crowning statement: "Everybody is happy nowadays." Man's happiness today consists in "having fun." Having fun lies in the satisfaction of consuming and "taking in" commodities, sights, food, drinks, cigarettes, people, lectures, books, movies—all are consumed, swallowed. The world is one great object for our appetite, a big apple, a big bottle, a big breast; we are the sucklers, the eternally expectant ones, the hopeful ones—and

---

1. Cf. a more detailed discussion of the problem of alienation and of the influence of modern society on the character of man in *The Sane Society,* E. Fromm, Rinehart and Company, New York, 1955.

the eternally disappointed ones. Our character is geared to exchange and to receive, to barter and to consume; everything, spiritual as well as material objects, becomes an object of exchange and of consumption.

The situation as far as love is concerned corresponds, as it has to by necessity, to this social character of modern man. Automatons cannot love; they can exchange their "personality packages" and hope for a fair bargain. One of the most significant expressions of love, and especially of marriage with this alienated structure, is the idea of the "team." In any number of articles on happy marriage, the ideal described is that of the smoothly functioning team. This description is not too different from the idea of a smoothly functioning employee; he should be "reasonably independent," co-operative, tolerant, and at the same time ambitious and aggressive. Thus, the marriage counselor tells us, the husband should "understand" his wife and be helpful. He should comment favorably on her new dress, and on a tasty dish. She, in turn, should understand when he comes home tired and disgruntled, she should listen attentively when he talks about his business troubles, should not be angry but understanding when he forgets her birthday. All this kind of relationship amounts to is the well-oiled relationship between two persons who remain strangers all their lives, who never arrive at a "central relationship," but who treat each other with courtesy and who attempt to make each other feel better.

In this concept of love and marriage the main emphasis is on finding a refuge from an otherwise unbearable sense of aloneness. In "love" one has found, at last, a haven from aloneness. One forms an alliance of two against the world, and this egoism *à deux* is mistaken for love and intimacy.

The emphasis on team spirit, mutual tolerance and so forth is a relatively recent development. It was preceded, in the years after the First World War, by a concept of love in which mutual sexual satisfaction was supposed to be the basis for satisfactory love relations, and especially for a happy marriage. It was believed that the reasons for the frequent unhappiness in marriage were to be found in that the marriage partners had not made a correct "sexual adjustment"; the reason for this fault was seen in the ignorance regarding "correct" sexual behavior, hence in the faulty sexual technique of one or both partners. In order to "cure" this fault, and to help the unfortunate couples who could not love each other, many books gave instructions and counsel concerning the correct sexual behavior, and promised implicitly or explicitly that happiness and love would follow. The underlying idea was that love is the child of sexual pleasure, and that if two people learn how to satisfy each other sexually, they will love each other. It fitted the general illusion of the time to assume that using the right techniques is the solution not only to technical problems of industrial production, but of all human problems as well. One ignored the fact that the contrary of the underlying assumption is true.

Love is not the result of adequate sexual satisfaction, but sexual happiness—even the knowledge of the so-called sexual technique—is the result of love. If aside from everyday observation this thesis needed to be proved, such proof can be found in ample material of psychoanalytic data. The study of the most frequent sexual problems—frigidity in women, and the more or less severe forms of psychic impotence in men—shows that the cause does not lie in a lack of knowledge of the right technique, but in the inhibitions which make it impossible to love. Fear of or hatred for the other sex are at the bottom of those difficulties which prevent a person from giving himself completely, from acting spontaneously, from trusting the sexual partner in the immediacy and directness of physical closeness. If a sexually inhibited person can emerge from fear or hate, and hence become capable of loving, his or her sexual problems are solved. If not, no amount of knowledge about sexual techniques will help.

But while the data of psychoanalytic therapy point to the fallacy of the idea that knowledge of the correct sexual technique leads to sexual happiness and love, the underlying assumption that love is the concomitant of mutual sexual satisfaction was largely influenced by the theories of Freud. For Freud, love was basically a sexual phenomenon. "Man having found by experience that sexual (genital) love afforded him his greatest gratification, so that it became in fact a prototype of all happiness to him, must have been thereby impelled to seek his happiness further along the path of sexual relations, to make genital eroticism the central point of his life." [2] The experience of brotherly love is, for Freud, an outcome of sexual desire, but with the sexual instinct being transformed into an impulse with "inhibited aim." "Love with an inhibited aim was indeed originally full of sensual love, and in man's unconscious mind is so still." [3] As far as the feeling of fusion, of oneness ("oceanic feeling"), which is the essence of mystical experience and the root of the most intense sense of union with one other person or with one's fellow men, is concerned, it was interpreted by Freud as a pathological phenomenon, as a regression to a state of an early "limitless narcissism." [4]

It is only one step further that for Freud love is in itself an irrational phenomenon. The difference between irrational love, and love as an expression of the mature personality does not exist for him. He pointed out in a paper on transference love,[5] that transference love is essentially not different from the "normal" phenomenon of love. Falling in love always verges on the abnormal, is always accompanied by blindness to reality, compulsiveness, and is a transference from love objects of childhood. Love

---

2. S. Freud, *Civilization and Its Discontents*, translated by J. Riviere, The Hogarth Press, Ltd., London, 1953, p. 69.
3. *Ibid.*, p. 69.
4. *Ibid.*, p. 21.
5. Freud, *Gesamte Werke*, London, 1940–52, Vol. X.

as a rational phenomenon, as the crowning achievement of maturity, was, to Freud, no subject matter for investigation, since it had no real existence.

However, it would be a mistake to overestimate the influence of Freud's ideas on the concept that love is the result of sexual attraction, or rather that it is the *same* as sexual satisfaction, reflected in conscious feeling. Essentially the causal nexus proceeds the other way around. Freud's ideas were partly influenced by the spirit of the nineteenth century; partly they became popular through the prevailing spirit of the years after the First World War. Some of the factors which influenced both the popular and the Freudian concepts were, first, the reaction against the strict mores of the Victorian age. The second factor determining Freud's theories lies in the prevailing concept of man, which is based on the structure of capitalism. In order to prove that capitalism corresponded to the natural needs of man, one had to show that man was by nature competitive and full of mutual hostility. While economists "proved" this in terms of the insatiable desire for economic gain, and the Darwinists in terms of the biological law of the survival of the fittest, Freud came to the same result by the assumption that man is driven by a limitless desire for the sexual conquest of all women, and that only the pressure of society prevented man from acting on his desires. As a result men are necessarily jealous of each other, and this mutual jealousy and competition would continue even if all social and economic reasons for it would disappear.[6]

Eventually, Freud was largely influenced in his thinking by the type of materialism prevalent in the nineteenth century. One believed that the substratum of all mental phenomena was to be found in physiological phenomena; hence love, hate, ambition, jealousy were explained by Freud as so many outcomes of various forms of the sexual instinct. He did not see that the basic reality lies in the totality of human existence, first of all in the human situation common to all men, and secondly in the practice of life determined by the specific structure of society. (The decisive step beyond this type of materialism was taken by Marx in his "historical materialism," in which not the body, nor an instinct like the need for food or possession, serves as the key to the understanding of man, but the total life process of man, his "practice of life"). According to Freud, the full and uninhibited satisfaction of all instinctual desires would create mental health and happiness. But the obvious clinical facts demonstrate that men—and women—who devote their lives to unrestricted sexual satisfaction do not attain happiness, and very often suffer from severe neurotic conflicts or symptoms. The complete satisfaction of all instinctual needs is not only not a basis for happiness, it does not even guarantee sanity. Yet Freud's idea could only have become so popular in the period after the

---

6. The only pupil of Freud who never separated from the master, and yet who in the last years of his life changed his views on love, was Sándor Ferenczi. For an excellent discussion on this subject see *The Leaven of Love* by Izette de Forest, Harper & Brothers, New York, 1954.

First World War because of the changes which had occurred in the spirit of capitalism, from the emphasis on saving to that on spending, from self-frustration as a means for economic success to consumption as the basis for an ever-widening market, and as the main satisfaction for the anxious, automatized individual. Not to postpone the satisfaction of any desire became the main tendency in the sphere of sex as well as in that of all material consumption.

It is interesting to compare the concepts of Freud, which correspond to the spirit of capitalism as it existed, yet unbroken, around the beginning of this century, with the theoretical concepts of one of the most brilliant contemporary psychoanalysts, the late H. S. Sullivan. In Sullivan's psychoanalytic system we find, in contrast to Freud's, a strict division between sexuality and love.

What is the meaning of love and intimacy in Sullivan's concept? "Intimacy is that type of situation involving two people which permits validation of all components of personal worth. Validation of personal worth requires a type of relationship which I call collaboration, by which I mean clearly formulated adjustments of one's behavior to the expressed needs of the other person in pursuit of increasingly identical—that is, more and more nearly mutual satisfactions, and in the maintenance of increasingly similar security operations."[7] If we free Sullivan's statement from its somewhat involved language, the essence of love is seen in a situation of collaboration, in which two people feel: "We play according to the rules of the game to preserve our prestige and feeling of superiority and merit."[8]

Just as Freud's concept of love is a description of the experience of the patriarchal male in terms of nineteenth-century capitalism, Sullivan's description refers to the experience of the alienated, marketing personality of the twentieth century. It is a description of an "egotism *à deux*," of two people pooling their common interests, and standing together against a hostile and alienated world. Actually his definition of intimacy is in principle valid for the feeling of any cooperating team, in which everybody "adjusts his behavior to the expressed needs of the other person in the pursuit of common aims" (it is remarkable that Sullivan speaks here of *expressed* needs, when the least one could say about love is that it implies a reaction to *unexpressed* needs between two people).

Love as mutual sexual satisfaction, and love as "teamwork" and as

---

7. H. S. Sullivan, *The Interpersonal Theory of Psychiatry*, W. W. Norton Co., New York, 1953, p. 246. It must be noted that although Sullivan gives this definition in connection with the strivings of pre-adolescence, he speaks of them as integrating tendencies, coming out during pre-adolescence, "which when they are completely developed, we call love," and says that this love in pre-adolescence "represents the beginning of something very like full-blown, psychiatrically defined *love*."

8. *Ibid.*, p. 246. Another definition of love by Sullivan, that love begins when a person feels another person's needs to be as important as his own, is less colored by the marketing aspect than the above formulation.

a haven from aloneness, are the two "normal" forms of the disintegration of love in modern Western society, the socially patterned pathology of love. There are many individualized forms of the pathology of love, which result in conscious suffering and which are considered neurotic by psychiatrists and an increasing number of laymen alike. Some of the more frequent ones are briefly described in the following examples.

The basic condition for neurotic love lies in the fact that one or both of the "lovers" have remained attached to the figure of a parent, and transfer the feelings, expectations and fears one once had toward father or mother to the loved person in adult life; the persons involved have never emerged from a pattern of infantile relatedness, and seek for this pattern in their affective demands in adult life. In these cases, the person has remained, affectively, a child of two, or of five, or of twelve, while intellectually and socially he is on the level of his chronological age. In the more severe cases, this emotional immaturity leads to disturbances in his social effectiveness; in the less severe ones, the conflict is limited to the sphere of intimate personal relationships.

Referring to our previous discussion of the mother- or father-centered personality, the following example for this type of neurotic love relation to be found frequently today deals with men who in their emotional development have remained stuck in an infantile attachment to mother. These are men who have never been weaned as it were from mother. These men still feel like children; they want mother's protection, love, warmth, care, and admiration; they want mother's unconditional love, a love which is given for no other reason than that they need it, that they are mother's child, that they are helpless. Such men frequently are quite affectionate and charming if they try to induce a woman to love them, and even after they have succeeded in this. But their relationship to the woman (as, in fact, to all other people) remains superficial and irresponsible. Their aim is to be loved, not to love. There is usually a good deal of vanity in this type of man, more or less hidden grandiose ideas. If they have found the right woman, they feel secure, on top of the world, and can display a great deal of affection and charm, and this is the reason why these men are often so deceptive. But when, after a while, the woman does not continue to live up to their phantastic expectations, conflicts and resentment start to develop. If the woman is not always admiring them, if she makes claims for a life of her own, if she wants to be loved and protected herself, and in extreme cases, if she is not willing to condone his love affairs with other women (or even have an admiring interest in them), the man feels deeply hurt and disappointed, and usually rationalizes this feeling with the idea that the woman "does not love him, is selfish, or is domineering." Anything short of the attitude of a loving mother toward a charming child is taken as proof of a lack of love. These men usually confuse their affectionate behavior, their wish to please, with genuine love and thus arrive at the conclusion that they are being treated quite unfairly; they imagine themselves to be the great lovers and complain bitterly about the ingratitude of their love partner.

In rare cases such a mother-centered person can function without any severe disturbances. If his mother, in fact, "loved" him in an overprotective manner (perhaps being domineering, but without being destructive), if he finds a wife of the same motherly type, if his special gifts and talents permit him to use his charm and be admired (as is the case sometimes with successful politicians), he is "well adjusted" in a social sense, without ever reaching a higher level of maturity. But under less favorable conditions—and these are naturally more frequent—his love life, if not his social life, will be a serious disappointment; conflicts, and frequently intense anxiety and depression arise when this type of personality is left alone.

In a still more severe form of pathology the fixation to mother is deeper and more irrational. On this level, the wish is not, symbolically speaking, to return to mother's protecting arms, nor to her nourishing breast, but to her all-receiving—and all-destroying—womb. If the nature of sanity is to grow out of the womb into the world, the nature of severe mental disease is to be attracted by the womb, to be sucked back into it—and that is to be taken away from life. This kind of fixation usually occurs in relation to mothers who relate themselves to their children in this swallowing-destroying way. Sometimes in the name of love, sometimes of duty, they want to keep the child, the adolescent, the man, within them; he should not be able to breathe but through them; not be able to love, except on a superficial sexual level—degrading all other women; he should not be able to be free and independent but an eternal cripple or a criminal.

This aspect of mother, the destructive, engulfing one, is the negative aspect of the mother figure. Mother can give life, and she can take life. She is the one to revive, and the one to destroy; she can do miracles of love—and nobody can hurt more than she. In religious images (such as the Hindu goddess Kali) and in dream symbolism the two opposite aspects of mother can often be found.

A different form of neurotic pathology is to be found in such cases where the main attachment is that to father.

A case in point is a man whose mother is cold and aloof, while his father (partly as a result of his wife's coldness) concentrates all his affection and interest on the son. He is a "good father," but at the same time authoritarian. Whenever he is pleased with the son's conduct he praises him, gives him presents, is affectionate; whenever the son displeases him, he withdraws, or scolds. The son, for whom father's affection is the only one he has, becomes attached to father in a slavish way. His main aim in life is to please father—and when he succeeds he feels happy, secure and satisfied. But when he makes a mistake, fails, or does not succeed in pleasing father, he feels deflated, unloved, cast out. In later life such a man will try to find a father figure to whom he attaches himself in a similar fashion. His whole life becomes a sequence of ups and downs depending on whether he has succeeded in winning father's praise. Such men are often very successful in their social careers. They are conscientious, reliable, eager—provided their chosen father image understands how to handle them. But in their relationships to women they remain aloof and distant. The woman is of no central significance to them; they usually have a slight contempt for her, often masked as the fatherly concern for a little girl. They may have impressed a woman initially by their masculine quality, but they become increasingly disappointing, when the woman they marry discovers that she is destined to play a secondary role to the primary affection for the father figure who is prominent in the husband's life at any given time; that is, unless the wife happens to have remained attached to her father—and thus is happy with a husband who relates to her as to a capricious child.

More complicated is the kind of neurotic disturbance in love which is based on a different kind of parental situation, occurring when parents do not love each other, but are too restrained to quarrel or to indicate any signs of dissatisfaction outwardly. At the same time, remoteness makes them also unspontaneous in their relationship to their children. What a little girl experiences is an atmosphere of "correctness," but one which never permits a close contact with either father or mother, and hence leaves the girl puzzled and afraid. She is never sure of what the parents feel or think; there is always an element of the unknown, the mysterious, in the atmosphere. As a result the girl withdraws into a world of her own, day-dreams, remains remote, and retains the same attitude in her love relationships later on.

Furthermore the withdrawal results in the development of intense anxiety, a feeling of not being firmly grounded in the world, and often leads to masochistic tendencies as the only way to experience intense excitement. Often such women would prefer having the husband make a scene and shout, to his maintaining a more normal and sensible behavior, because at least it would take away the burden of tension and fear from them; not so rarely they unconsciously provoke such behavior, in order to end the tormenting suspense of affective neutrality.

Other frequent forms of irrational love are described in the following paragraphs, without going into an analysis of the specific factors in childhood development which are at their roots:

A form of pseudo-love which is not infrequent and is often experienced (and more often described in moving pictures and novels) as the "great love" is *idolatrous love*. If a person has not reached the level where he has a sense of identity, of I-ness, rooted in the productive unfolding of his own powers, he tends to "idolize" the loved person. He is alienated from his own powers and projects them into the loved person, who is worshiped as the *summum bonum,* the bearer of all love, all right, all bliss. In this process he deprives himself of all sense of strength, loses himself in the loved one instead of finding himself. Since usually no person can, in the long run, live up to the expectations of her (or his) idolatrous worshiper, disappointment is bound to occur, and as a remedy a new idol is sought for, sometimes in an unending circle. What is characteristic for this type of idolatrous love is, at the beginning, the intensity and suddenness of the love experience. This idolatrous love is often described as the true, great love; but while it is meant to portray the intensity and depth of love, it only demonstrates the hunger and despair of the idolator. Needless to say it is not rare that two persons find each other in a mutual idolatry which, sometimes, in extreme cases, represents the picture of a *folie à deux.*

Another form of pseudo-love is what may be called *"sentimental love."* Its essence lies in the fact that love is experienced only in phantasy and not in the here-and-now relationship to another person who is real. The most widespread form of this type of love is that to be found in the vicarious love satisfaction experienced by the consumer of screen pictures, magazine love stories and love songs. All the unfulfilled desires for love, union, and closeness find their satisfaction in the consumption of these products. A man and a woman who in relation to their spouses are incapable of ever penetrating the wall of separateness are moved to tears when they participate in the happy or unhappy love story of the couple on the screen. For many couples, seeing these stories on the screen is the only occasion on which they experience love—not for each other, but together, as spectators of other people's "love." As long as love is a day dream, they can participate; as soon as it comes down to the reality of the relationship between two real people—they are frozen.

Another aspect of sentimental love is the abstractification of love in terms of time. A couple may be deeply moved by memories of their past love, although when this past was present no love was experienced—or the phantasies of their future love. How many engaged or newly married couples dream of their bliss of love to take place in the future, while at the very moment at which they live they are already beginning to be bored with each other? This tendency coincides with a general attitude characteristic of modern man. He lives in the past or in the future, but not in the present. He remembers sentimentally his childhood and his mother—or he makes happy plans for the future. Whether love is experienced vicariously by participating in the fictitious experiences of others, or whether it is shifted away from the present to the past or the future, this abstractified and alienated form of love serves as an opiate which alleviates the pain of reality, the aloneness and separateness of the individual.

Still another form of neurotic love lies in the use of *projective mechanisms* for the purpose of avoiding one's own problems, and being concerned with the defects and frailties of the "loved" person instead. Individuals behave in this respect very much as groups, nations or religions do. They have a fine appreciation for even the minor shortcomings of the other person, and go blissfully ahead ignoring their own—always busy trying to accuse or to reform the other person. If two people both do it—as is so often the case—the relationship of love becomes transformed into one of mutual projection. If I am domineering or indecisive, or greedy, I accuse my partner of it, and depending on my character, I either want to cure him or to punish him. The other person does the same—and both thus succeed in ignoring their own problems and hence fail to undertake any steps which would help them in their own development.

Another form of projection is the projection of one's own problems on the children. First of all such projection takes place not infrequently in the wish for children. In such cases the wish for children is primarily determined by projecting one's own problem of existence on that of the children. When a person feels that he has not been able to make sense of his own life, he tries to make sense of it in terms of the life of his children. But one is bound to fail within oneself *and* for the children. The former because the problem of existence can be solved by each one only for himself, and not by proxy; the latter because one lacks in the very qualities which one needs to guide the children in their own search for an answer. Children serve for projective purposes also when the question arises of dissolving an unhappy marriage. The stock argument of parents in such a situation is that they cannot separate in order not to deprive the children of the blessings of a unified home. Any detailed study would show, however, that the atmosphere of tension and unhappiness within the "unified family" is more harmful to the children than an open break would be—which teaches them at least that man is able to end an intolerable situation by a courageous decision.

One other frequent error must be mentioned here. The illusion, namely, that love means necessarily the absence of conflict. Just as it is customary for people to believe that pain and sadness should be avoided under all circumstances, they believe that love means the absence of any conflict. And they find good reasons for this idea in the fact that the struggles around them seem only to be destructive interchanges which bring no good to either one of those concerned. But the reason for this lies in the fact that the "conflicts" of most people are actually attempts to avoid the *real* conflicts. They are disagreements on minor or superficial matters which by their very nature do not lend themselves to clarification or solution. Real conflicts between two people, those which do not serve to cover up or to project, but which are experienced on the deep level of inner reality to which they belong, are not destructive. They lead to clarification, they produce a catharsis from which both persons emerge with more knowledge and more strength. This leads us to emphasize again something said above.

Love is possible only if two persons communicate with each other from the center of their existence, hence if each one of them experiences himself from the center of his existence. Only in this "central experience" is human reality, only here is aliveness, only here is the basis for love. Love, experienced thus, is a constant challenge; it is not a resting place, but a moving, growing, working together; even whether there is harmony or conflict, joy or sadness, is secondary to the fundamental fact that two people experience themselves from the essence of their existence, that they are one with each other by being one with themselves, rather than by fleeing from themselves. There is only one proof for the presence of love: the depth of the relationship, and the aliveness and strength in each person concerned; this is the fruit by which love is recognized.

Just as automatons cannot love each other they cannot love God. The *disintegration of the love of God* has reached the same proportions as the disintegration of the love of man. This fact is in blatant contradiction to the idea that we are witnessing a religious renaissance in this epoch. Nothing could be further from the truth. What we witness (even though there are exceptions) is a regression to an idolatric concept of God, and a transformation of the love of God into a relationship fitting an alienated character structure. The regression to an idolatric concept of God is easy to see. People are anxious, without principles or faith, they find themselves without an aim except the one to move ahead; hence they continue to remain children, to hope for father or mother to come to their help when help is needed.

True, in religious cultures, like that of the Middle Ages, the average man also looked at God as to a helping father and mother. But at the same time he took God seriously also, in the sense that the paramount goal of his life was to live according to God's principles, to make "salvation" the supreme concern to which all other activities were subordinated. Today, nothing of such effort is present. Daily life is strictly separated from any religious values. It is devoted to the striving for material comforts, and for success on the personality market. The principles on which our secular efforts are built are those of indifference and egotism (the latter often labeled as "individualism," or "individual initiative"). Man of truly religious cultures may be compared with children at the age of eight, who need father as a helper, but who begin to adopt his teachings and principles in their lives. Contemporary man is rather like a child of three, who cries for father when he needs him, and otherwise is quite self-sufficient when he can play.

In this respect, in the infantile dependence on an anthropomorphic picture of God without the transformation of life according to the principles of God, we are closer to a primitive idolatric tribe than to the religious culture of the Middle Ages. In another respect our religious situation shows features which are new, and characteristic only of contemporary Western capitalistic society. Modern man has transformed himself into a commodity; he experiences his life energy as an investment with which he should make the highest profit, considering his position and the situation on the personality market. He is alienated from himself, from his fellow men and from nature. His main aim is profitable exchange of his skills, knowledge, and of himself, his "personality package" with others who are equally intent on a fair and profitable exchange. Life has no goal except the one to move, no principle except the one of fair exchange, no satisfaction except the one to consume.

What can the concept of God mean under these circumstances? It is transformed from its original religious meaning into one fitting the alienated culture of success. In the religious revival of recent times, the belief in God has been transformed into a psychological device to make one better fitted for the competitive struggle.

Religion allies itself with auto-suggestion and psychotherapy to help man in his business activities. In the twenties one had not yet called upon God for purposes of "improving one's personality." The best-seller in the year 1938, Dale Carnegie's *How to Win Friends and Influence People*, remained on a strictly secular level. What was the function of Carnegie's book at that time is the function of our greatest best-seller today, *The Power of Positive Thinking* by the Reverend N. V. Peale. In this religious book it is not even questioned whether our dominant concern with success is in itself in accordance with the spirit of monotheistic religion. On the contrary, this supreme aim is never doubted, but belief in God and prayer is recommended as a means to increase one's ability to be successful. Just as modern psychiatrists recommend happiness of the employee, in order to be more appealing to the customers, some ministers recommend love of God in order to be more successful. "Make God your partner" means to make God a partner in business, rather than to become one with Him in love, justice and truth. Just as brotherly love has been replaced by impersonal fairness, God has been transformed into a remote General Director of Universe, Inc.; you know that he is there, he runs the show (although it would probably run without him too), you never see him, but you acknowledge his leadership while you are "doing your part."

Problems

1. Why is the social structure of Western capitalist civilization not conducive to the development of love?
2. How does alienation lead to the inability to love?
3. What is the proper relationship of sex to love?
4. Why does Fromm take issue with Freud's concept of love? Which of the two do you agree with? Why?
5. What perverted assumptions about the nature of true love does Fromm describe? Why would people have these assumptions? What better model would you suggest?
6. For Fromm, what is the final proof of love? What does your agreement or disagreement signify?
7. For Fromm, how does the disintegration of love lead to the destruction of religious feeling?

28 ABRAHAM H. MASLOW

Abraham H. Maslow (1908–), a former professor at Brandeis University, is neither a psychoanalyst nor a psychiatrist; he is a psychologist who, together with Carl Rogers and others, belongs to what Maslow himself calls a "third force" between behaviorism and psychoanalysis. This third force is characterized by "a new conception of human sickness and human health" which recognizes the intrinsic inadequacy and implicit moralism of these terms, and stresses man's inherent goodness and man's striving for self-fulfillment. It emphasizes "full-humanness," "the development of the biologically based nature of man, and therefore is (empirically) normative for the whole species rather than for particular times and places, i.e., it is less culturally relative. . . . [than] the terms 'health and illness' often are" (46 Maslow).

The first of these two essays, "Toward a Psychology of Health" (1962), expresses the basic assumptions of the self-actualizing school. The second essay, "Self-Actualizing People" (1954), develops a model drawn from empirical observation. Maslow is, of course, dismayed by those who persist in treating his "empirical description of the characteristics of self-actualizing people as if . . . [he] had arbitrarily invented these characteristics instead of discovering them" (47 Maslow). The dates of the two essays indicate clearly that the assumptions are not presuppositions, as some would think, but empirically induced inferences.

Introduction: Toward a Psychology of Health

There is now emerging over the horizon a new conception of human sickness and of human health, a psychology that I find so thrilling and so full of wonderful possibilities that I yield to the temptation to present it publicly even before it is checked and confirmed, and before it can be called reliable scientific knowledge.

The basic assumptions of this point of view are:

From Abraham H. Maslow, *Toward a Psychology of Being* (Princeton, N.J.: D. Van Nostrand Co., Inc., 1962), pp. 3–8.

(1) We have, each of us, an essential biologically based inner nature, which is to some degree "natural," intrinsic, given, and, in a certain limited sense, unchangeable, or, at least, unchanging.

(2) Each person's inner nature is in part unique to himself and in part species-wide.

(3) It is possible to study this inner nature scientifically and to discover what it is like—(not *invent*—*discover*).

(4) This inner nature, as much as we know of it so far, seems not to be intrinsically evil, but rather either neutral or positively "good." What we call evil behavior appears most often to be a secondary reaction to frustration of this intrinsic nature.

(5) Since this inner nature is good or neutral rather than bad, it is best to bring it out and to encourage it rather than to suppress it. If it is permitted to guide our life, we grow healthy, fruitful, and happy.

(6) If this essential core of the person is denied or suppressed, he gets sick sometimes in obvious ways, sometimes in subtle ways, sometimes immediately, sometimes later.

(7) This inner nature is not strong and overpowering and unmistakable like the instincts of animals. It is weak and delicate and subtle and easily overcome by habit, cultural pressure, and wrong attitudes toward it.

(8) Even though weak, it rarely disappears in the normal person—perhaps not even in the sick person. Even though denied, it persists underground forever pressing for actualization.

(9) Somehow, these conditions must all be articulated with the necessity of discipline, deprivation, frustration, pain, and tragedy. To the extent that these experiences reveal and foster and fulfill our inner nature, to that extent they are desirable experiences.

Observe that if these assumptions are proven true, they promise a scientific ethics, a natural value system, a court of ultimate appeal for the determination of good and bad, of right and wrong. The more we learn about man's natural tendencies, the easier it will be to tell him how to be good, how to be happy, how to be fruitful, how to respect himself, how to love, how to fulfill his highest potentialities. This amounts to automatic solution of many of the personality problems of the future. The thing to do seems to be to find out what *you* are *really* like inside, deep down, as a member of the human species and as a particular individual.

The study of such healthy people can teach us much about our own mistakes, our shortcomings, the proper directions in which to grow. Every age but ours has had its model, its ideal. All of these have been given up by our culture; the saint, the hero, the gentleman, the knight, the mystic. About all we have left is the well-adjusted man without problems, a very pale and doubtful substitute. Perhaps we shall soon be able to use as our guide and model the fully growing and self-fulfilling human being, the one in whom all his potentialities are coming to full development, the one whose inner nature expresses itself freely, rather than being warped, suppressed, or denied.

The serious thing for each person to recognize vividly and poignantly, each for himself, is that every falling away from species-virtue, every crime against one's own nature, every evil act, *every one without exception records itself* in our unconscious and makes us despise ourselves. Karen Horney had a good word to describe this unconscious perceiving and remembering; she said it "registers." If we do something we are ashamed of, it "registers" to our discredit, and if we do something honest or fine or good, it "registers" to our credit. The net results ultimately are either one or the other—either we respect and accept ourselves or we despise ourselves and feel contemptible, worthless, and unlovable. Theologians used to use the word "*accidie*" to describe the sin of failing to do with one's life all that one knows one could do.

This point of view in no way denies the usual Freudian picture. But it does add to it and supplement it. To oversimplify the matter somewhat, it is as if Freud supplied to us the sick half of psychology and we must now fill it out with the healthy half. Perhaps this health psychology will give us more possibility for controlling and improving our lives and for making ourselves better people. Perhaps this will be more fruitful than asking "how to get *unsick*."

How can we encourage free development? What are the best educational conditions for it? Sexual? Economic? Political? What kind of world do we need for such people to grow in? What kind of world will such people create? Sick people are made by a sick culture; healthy people are made possible by a healthy culture. But it is just as true that sick individuals make their culture more sick and that healthy individuals make their culture more healthy. Improving individual health is one approach to making a better world. To express it in another way, encouragement of personal growth is a real possibility; cure of actual neurotic symptoms is far less possible without outside help. It is relatively easy to try deliberately to make oneself a more honest man; it is very difficult to try to cure one's own compulsions or obsessions.

The classical approach to personality problems considers them to be problems in an undesirable sense. Struggle, conflict, guilt, bad conscience, anxiety, depression, frustration, tension, shame, self-punishment, feeling of inferiority or unworthiness—they all cause psychic pain, they disturb efficiency of performance, and they are uncontrollable. They are therefore automatically regarded as sick and undesirable and they get "cured" away as soon as possible.

But all of these symptoms are found also in healthy people, or in people who are growing toward health. Supposing you *should* feel guilty and don't? Supposing you have attained a nice stabilization of forces and you *are* adjusted? Perhaps adjustment and stabilization, while good because it cuts your pain, is also bad because development toward a higher ideal ceases?

Erich Fromm, in a very important book,[1] attacked the classical Freudian notion of a superego because this concept was entirely authoritarian and relativistic. That is to say, your superego or your conscience was supposed by Freud to be primarily the internalization of the wishes, demands, and ideals of the father and mother, whoever they happen to be. But supposing they are criminals? Then what kind of conscience do you have? Or supposing you have a rigid moralizing father who hates fun? Or a psychopath? This conscience exists—Freud was right. We do get our ideals largely from such early figures and not from Sunday School books read later in life. But there is also another element in conscience, or, if you like, another kind of conscience, which we all have either weakly or strongly. And this is the "intrinsic conscience." This is based upon the unconscious and preconscious perception of our own nature, of our own destiny, or our own capacities, of our own "call" in life. It insists that we be true to our inner nature and that we do not deny it out of weakness or for advantage or for any other reason. He who belies his talent, the born painter who sells stockings instead, the intelligent man who lives a stupid life, the man who sees the truth and keeps his mouth shut, the coward who gives up his manliness, all these people perceive in a deep way that they have done wrong to themselves and despise themselves for it. Out of this self-punishment may come only neurosis, but there may equally well come renewed courage, righteous indignation, increased self-respect, because of thereafter doing the right thing; in a word, growth and improvement can come through pain and conflict.

In essence I am deliberately rejecting our present easy distinction between sickness and health, at least as far as surface symptoms are concerned. Does sickness mean having symptoms? I maintain now that sickness might consist of *not* having symptoms when you should. Does health mean being symptom-free? I deny it. Which of the Nazis at Auschwitz or Dachau were healthy? Those with stricken conscience or those with a nice, clear, happy conscience? Was it possible for a profoundly human person not to feel conflict, suffering, depression, rage, etc?

In a word if you tell me you have a personality problem I am not certain until I know you better whether to say "Good!" or "I'm sorry." It depends on the reasons. And these, it seems, may be bad reasons, or they may be good reasons.

An example is the changing attitude of psychologists toward pop-

1. Fromm, Erich, *Man For Himself* (Rinehart, 1947).

ularity, toward adjustment, even toward delinquency. Popular with whom? Perhaps it is better for a youngster to be *unpopular* with the neighboring snobs or with the local country club set. Adjusted to what? To a bad culture? To a dominating parent? What shall we think of a well-adjusted slave? A well-adjusted prisoner? Even the behavior problem boy is being looked upon with new tolerance. *Why* is he delinquent? Most often it is for sick reasons. But occasionally it is for good reasons and the boy is simply resisting exploitation, domination, neglect, contempt, and trampling upon.

Clearly what will be called personality problems depends on who is doing the calling. The slave owner? The dictator? The patriarchal father? The husband who wants his wife to remain a child? It seems quite clear that personality problems may sometimes be loud protests against the crushing of one's psychological bones, of one's true inner nature. What is sick then is *not* to protest while this crime is being committed. And I am sorry to report my impression that most people do not protest under such treatment. They take it and pay years later, in neurotic and psychosomatic symptoms of various kinds, or perhaps in some cases never become aware that they are sick, that they have missed true happiness, true fulfillment of promise, a rich emotional life, and a serene, fruitful old age, that they have never known how wonderful it is to be creative, to react aesthetically, to find life thrilling.

The question of desirable grief and pain or the necessity for it must also be faced. Is growth and self-fulfillment possible at all without pain and grief and sorrow and turmoil? If these are to some extent necessary and unavoidable, then to what extent? If grief and pain are sometimes necessary for growth of the person, then we must learn not to protect people from them automatically as if they were always bad. Sometimes they may be good and desirable in view of the ultimate good consequences. Not allowing people to go through their pain, and protecting them from it, may turn out to be a kind of overprotection, which in turn implies a certain lack of respect for the integrity and the intrinsic nature and the future development of the individual.

Problems

1. In what way might Maslow's primary assumptions conflict with those of Freud? In what way might they conflict with those of Christianity?
2. Which of the thinkers we have read thus far most share Maslow's conception of man? Why? Why do you share or deny Maslow's assumptions? What assumptions would you propose in their place?
3. Maslow does not explain how one comes to have a knowledge of "good and evil" to "register". What assumptions does he therefore make about the nature of good and evil?

4. Why, for Maslow, might adjustment and stabilization be harmful? Do you agree?
5. What is the place of pain, conflict, and suffering in Maslow's theory? What arguments might one use to defend their role? With what arguments might one attack it?

Self-Actualizing People: A Study of Psychological Health

PERSONAL FOREWORD

The study to be reported in this chapter is unusual in various ways. It was not planned as an ordinary research; it was not a social venture but a private one, motivated by my own curiosity and pointed toward the solution of various personal moral, ethical, and scientific problems. I sought only to convince and to teach myself (as is quite proper in a personal quest) rather than to prove or to demonstrate to others.

Quite unexpectedly, however, these studies have proved to be so enlightening to me, and so laden with exciting implications, that it seems fair that some sort of report should be made to others in spite of its methodological shortcomings.

In addition, I consider the problem of psychological health to be so pressing, that *any* suggestions, *any* bits of data, however moot, are endowed with great heuristic value. This kind of research is in principle so difficult—involving as it does a kind of lifting oneself by one's axiological bootstraps—that if we were to wait for conventionally reliable data, we should have to wait forever. It seems that the only manly thing to do is not to fear mistakes, to plunge in, to do the best that one can, hoping to learn enough from blunders to correct them eventually. At present the only alternative is simply to refuse to work with the problem. Accordingly, for whatever use can be made of it, the following report is presented with due apologies to those who insist on conventional reliability, validity, sampling, etc.

SUBJECTS AND METHODS

The subjects were selected from among personal acquaintances and friends, and from among public and historical figures. In

From Abraham H. Maslow, *Motivation and Personality* (New York: Harper & Row, Inc., 1954), pp. 199–234.

addition, in a first research with young people, three thousand college students were screened, but yielded only one immediately usable subject and a dozen or two possible future subjects.

I had to conclude that self-actualization of the sort I had found in my older subjects was not possible in our society for young, developing people.

Accordingly, in collaboration with Dr. Evelyn Raskin and Dan Freedman, a search was begun for a panel of *relatively* healthy college students. We arbitrarily decided to choose the healthiest 1 percent of the college population. This research, pursued over a two-year period as time permitted, had to be interrupted before completion, but it was, of course, very instructive at the clinical level. It is hoped that the subjects selected may yet be followed up for our further instruction.

It was also hoped that figures created by novelists or dramatists could be used for demonstration purposes, but none were found that were usable in our culture and our time (in itself a thought-provoking finding).

The first clinical definition, on the basis of which subjects were finally chosen or rejected, had a positive as well as a merely negative side. The negative criterion was an absence of neurosis, psychopathic personality, psychosis, or strong tendencies in these directions. Possibly psychosomatic illness called forth closer scrutiny and screening. Wherever possible, Rorschach tests were given, but turned out to be far more useful in revealing concealed psychopathology than in selecting healthy people. The positive criterion for selection was positive evidence of self-actualization (SA), as yet a difficult syndrome to describe accurately. For the purposes of this discussion, it may be loosely described as the full use and exploitation of talents, capacities, potentialities, etc. Such people seem to be fulfilling themselves and to be doing the best that they are capable of doing, reminding us of Nietzsche's exhortation, "Become what thou art!" They are people who have developed or are developing to the full stature of which they are capable. These potentialities may be either idiosyncratic or species-wide, so that the self in self-actualization must not have too individualistic a flavor.

This criterion implies also either gratification, past or present, of the basic emotional needs for safety, belongingness, love, respect, and self-respect, and of the cognitive needs for knowledge and understanding or in a few cases, conquest of these needs. This is to say that all subjects felt safe and unanxious, accepted, loved and loving, respect-worthy and respected, and that they had worked out their philosophical, religious, or axiological bearings. It is still an open question as to whether this basic gratification is a sufficient or only a prerequisite condition of self-actualization. It may be that self-actualization means basic gratification plus at least minimum talent, capacity, or richness.

In general, the technique of selection used was that of *iteration,* previously used in studies of the personality syndromes of self-esteem and of security. This [technique] consists briefly in starting with the personal or cultural nontechnical state of belief, collating the various extant usages and definitions of the syndrome, and then defining it more carefully, still in terms of actual usage (what might be called the lexicographical stage), with, however, the elimination of the logical and factual inconsistencies customarily found in folk definitions.

On the basis of the corrected folk definition, the first groups of subjects are selected, a group who are high in the quality and a group who are low in it. These people are studied as carefully as possible in the clinical style, and on the basis of this empirical study the original corrected folk definition is further changed and corrected as required by the data now in hand. This gives the first clinical definition. On the basis of this new definition, the original group of subjects is reselected, some being retained, some being dropped, and some new ones being added. This second level group of subjects is then in its turn clinically, and if possible, experimentally and statistically studied, which in turn causes modification, correction, and enrichment of the first clinical definition, with which in turn a new group of subjects is selected and so on. In this way an originally vague and unscientific folk concept can become more and more exact, more and more operational in character, and therefore more scientific.

Of course, external, theoretical, and practical considerations may intrude into this spiral-like process of self-correction. For instance, early in this study, it was found that folk usage was so unrealistically demanding that no living human being could possibly fit the definition. We had to stop excluding a possible subject on the basis of single foibles, mistakes, or foolishness; or to put it in another way, we could not use perfection as a basis for selection, since no subject was perfect.

Another such problem was presented by the fact that in all cases it was impossible to get full and satisfactory information of the kind usually demanded in clinical work. Possible subjects, when informed of the purpose of the research, became self-conscious, froze up, laughed off the whole effort, or broke off the relationship. As a result, since this early experience, all older subjects have been studied indirectly, indeed almost surreptitiously. Only younger people can be studied directly.

Since living people were studied whose names could not be divulged, two desiderata or even requirements of ordinary scientific work became impossible to achieve: namely, repeatability of the investigation and public availability of the data upon which conclusions were made. These difficulties are partly overcome by the inclusion of public and historical figures, and by the supplementary study of young people and children who could conceivably be used publicly.

The subjects have been divided into the following categories:

Cases: 3 fairly sure and 2 highly probable contemporaries
2 fairly sure historical figures (Lincoln in his last years and Thomas Jefferson)
6 highly probable public and historical figures (Einstein, Eleanor Roosevelt, Jane Addams, William James, and Spinoza)

Partial Cases: 5 contemporaries who fairly certainly fall short somewhat but who can yet be used for study
7 historical figures who probably or certainly fall short, but who can yet be used for study (Walt Whitman, Henry Thoreau, Beethoven, F. D. Roosevelt, Freud)

Potential or Possible Cases: 20 younger people who seem to be developing in the direction of self-actualization, and G. W. Carver, Eugene V. Debs, Albert Schweitzer, Thomas Eakins, Fritz Kreisler, Goethe

GATHERING AND PRESENTATION OF THE DATA

Data here consist not so much in the usual gathering of specific and discrete facts as in the slow development of a global or holistic impression of the sort that we form of our friends and acquaintances. It was rarely possible to set up a situation, to ask pointed questions, or to do any testing with my older subjects (although this *was* possible and was done with younger subjects). Contacts were fortuitous and of the ordinary social sort. Friends and relatives were questioned where this was possible.

Because of this and also because of the small number of subjects as well as the incompleteness of the data for many subjects, any quantitative presentation is impossible: only composite impressions can be offered for whatever they may be worth (and of course they are worth much less than controlled objective observation, since the investigator is never *quite* certain about what is description and what is projection).

The holistic analysis of these total impressions yields, as the most important and useful whole characteristics of self-actualizing people for further clinical and experimental study, the following:

MORE EFFICIENT PERCEPTION OF REALITY AND MORE COMFORTABLE RELATIONS WITH IT

The first form in which this capacity was noticed was as an unusual ability to detect the spurious, the fake, and the dishonest in personality, and in general to judge people correctly and efficiently. In an informal experiment with a group of college students, a clear tendency was discerned for the more secure (the more healthy) to judge their professors more accurately than did the less secure students.

As the study progressed, it slowly became apparent that this efficiency extended to many other areas of life—indeed *all* areas that were tested. In art and music, in things of the intellect, in scientific matters, in politics and public affairs, they seemed as a group to be able to see concealed or confused realities more swiftly and more correctly than others. Thus an informal experiment indicated that their predictions of the future from whatever facts were in hand at the time seemed to be more often correct, because less based upon wish, desire, anxiety, fear, or upon generalized character-determined optimism or pessimism.

At first this was phrased as good taste or good judgment, the implication being relative and not absolute. But for many reasons (some to be detailed below), it has become progressively more clear that this had better be called perception (not taste) of something that was absolutely there (reality, not a set of opinions). It is hoped that this conclusion—or hypothesis—can soon be put to the experimental test.

If this is so, it would be impossible to overstress its importance. Recently Money-Kyrle, an English psychoanalyst, has indicated that he believes it possible to call a neurotic person not only *relatively* but *absolutely* inefficient, simply because he does not perceive the real world so accurately or so efficiently as does the healthy person. The neurotic is not only emotionally sick—he is cognitively *wrong!* If health and neurosis are, respectively, correct and incorrect perceptions of reality, propositions of fact and propositions of value merge in this area, and in principle, value propositions should then be empirically demonstrable rather than merely matters of taste or exhortation. For those who have wrestled with this problem it will be clear that we may have here a partial basis for a true science of values, and consequently of ethics, social relations, politics, religion, etc.

It is definitely possible that maladjustment or even extreme neurosis would disturb perception enough to affect acuity of perception of light or touch or odor. But it is *probable* that this effect can be demonstrated in spheres of perception removed from the merely physiological. It should also follow that the effects of wish, desire, prejudice, upon perception as in many recent experiments should be very much less in healthy people than in sick. A priori considerations encourage the hypothesis that this superiority in the perception of reality eventuates in a superior ability to reason, to perceive the truth, to come to conclusions, to be logical and to be cognitively efficient, in general.

It was found that self-actualizing people distinguished far more easily than most the fresh, concrete, and idiographic from the generic, abstract, and rubricized. The consequence is that they live more in the real world of nature than in the man-made mass of concepts, abstractions, expectations, beliefs, and stereotypes that most people confuse with the world. They are therefore far more apt to perceive what is there rather than their own wishes, hopes, fears, anxieties, their own theories and beliefs, or those of their cultural group. "The innocent eye," Herbert Read has very effectively called it.

The relationship with the unknown seems to be of exceptional promise as another bridge between academic and clinical psychology. Our healthy subjects are uniformly unthreatened and unfrightened by the unknown, being therein quite different from average men. They accept it, are comfortable with it, and, often are even *more* attracted by it than by the known. They not only tolerate the ambiguous and unstructured, they like it. Quite characteristic is Einstein's statement, "The most beautiful thing we can experience is the mysterious. It is the source of all art and science."

These people, it is true, are the intellectuals, the researchers, and the scientists, so that perhaps the major determinant here is intellectual power. And yet we all know how many scientists with high IQ, through timidity, conventionality, anxiety, or other character defects, occupy themselves exclusively with what is known, with polishing it, arranging and rearranging it, classifying it, and otherwise puttering with it instead of discovering, as they are supposed to do.

Since, for healthy people, the unknown is not frightening, they do not have to spend any time laying the ghost, whistling past the cemetery, or otherwise protecting themselves against imagined dangers. They do not neglect the unknown, or deny it, or run away from it, or try to make believe it is really known, nor do they organize, dichotomize, or rubricize it prematurely. They do not cling to the familiar, nor is their quest for the truth a catastrophic need for certainty, safety, definiteness, and order, such as we see in an exaggerated form in Goldstein's brain-injured or in the compulsive-obsessive neurotic. They can be, when the total objective situation calls for it, comfortably disorderly, sloppy, anarchic, chaotic, vague, doubtful, uncertain, indefinite, approximate, inexact, or inaccurate (all, at certain moments in science, art, or life in general, quite desirable).

Thus it comes about that doubt, tentativeness, uncertainty, with the consequent necessity for abeyance of decision, which is for most a torture, can be for some a pleasantly stimulating challenge, a high spot in life rather than a low.

ACCEPTANCE (SELF, OTHERS, NATURE)

A good many personal qualities that can be perceived on the surface and that seem at first to be various and unconnected may be understood as manifestations or derivatives of a more fundamental single attitude, namely, of a relative lack of overriding guilt, of crippling shame, and of extreme or severe anxiety. This is in direct contrast with the neurotic person who in every instance may be described as crippled by guilt and/or shame and/or anxiety. Even the normal member of our culture feels unnecessarily guilty or ashamed about too many things and has anxiety in too many unnecessary situations. Our healthy individuals find it possible to accept themselves and their own nature without chagrin or complaint or, for that matter, even without thinking about the matter very much.

They can accept their own human nature in the stoic style, with all its shortcomings, with all its discrepancies from the ideal image without feeling real concern. It would convey the wrong impression to say that they are self-satisfied. What we must say rather is that they can take the frailties and sins, weaknesses, and evils of human nature in the same unquestioning spirit with which one accepts the characteristics of nature. One does not complain about water because it is wet, or about rocks because they are hard, or about trees because they are green. As the child looks out upon the world with wide, uncritical, innocent eyes, simply noting and observing what is the case, without either arguing the matter or demanding that it be otherwise, so does the self-actualizing person look upon human nature in himself and in others. This is of course not the same as resignation in the eastern sense, but resignation too can be observed in our subjects, especially in the face of illness and death.

Be it observed that this amounts to saying in another form what we have already described; namely, that the self-actualized person sees reality more clearly: our subjects see human nature as it *is* and not as they would prefer it to be. Their eyes see what is before them without being strained through spectacles of various sorts to distort or shape or color the reality.

The first and most obvious level of acceptance is at the so-called animal level. Those self-actualizing people tend to be good and lusty animals, hearty in their appetites and enjoying themselves mightily without regret or shame or apology. They seem to have a uniformly good appetite for food; they seem to sleep well; they seem to enjoy their sexual lives without unnecessary inhibition and so on for all the relatively physiological impulses. They are able to accept themselves not only on these low levels, but at all levels as well; e.g., love, safety, belongingness, honor, self-respect. All of these are accepted without question as worth while, simply because these people are inclined to accept the work of nature rather than to argue with her for not having constructed things to a different pattern. This shows itself in a relative lack of the disgusts and aversions seen in average people and especially in neurotics, e.g., food annoyances, disgust with body products, body odors, and body functions.

Closely related to self-acceptance and to acceptance of others is (1) their lack of defensiveness, protective coloration, or pose, and (2) their distaste for such artificialities in others. Cant, guile, hypocrisy, front, face, playing a game, trying to impress in conventional ways: these are all absent in themselves to an unusual degree. Since they can live comfortably even with their own shortcomings, these finally come to be perceived, especially in later life, as not shortcomings at all, but simply as neutral personal characteristics.

This is not an absolute lack of guilt, shame, sadness, anxiety, defensiveness; it is a lack of unnecessary (because unrealistic) guilt, etc. The animal processes, e.g., sex, urination, pregnancy, menstruation, growing old, etc., are part of reality and so must be accepted. Thus no healthy woman feels guilty or defensive about being female or about any of the female processes.

What healthy people *do* feel guilty about (or ashamed, anxious, sad, or defensive) are (1) improvable shortcomings, e.g., laziness, thoughtlessness, loss of temper, hurting others; (2) stubborn remnants of psychological ill health, e.g., prejudice, jealousy, envy; (3) habits, which, though relatively independent of character structure, may yet be very strong, or (4) shortcomings of the species or of the culture or of the group with which they have identified. The general formula seems to be that healthy people will feel bad about discrepancies between what is and what might very well be or ought to be.

SPONTANEITY

Self-actualizing people can all be described as relatively spontaneous in behavior and far more spontaneous than that in their inner life, thoughts, impulses, etc. Their behavior is marked by simplicity and naturalness, and by lack of artificiality or straining for effect. This does not necessarily mean consistently unconventional behavior. If we were to take an actual count of the number of times that the self-actualizing person behaved in an unconventional manner the tally would not be high. His unconventionality is not superficial but essential or internal. It is his impulses, thought, consciousness that are so unusually unconventional, spontaneous, and natural. Apparently recognizing that the world of people in which he lives could not understand or accept this, and since he has no wish to hurt them or to fight with them over every triviality, he will go through the ceremonies and rituals of convention with a good-humored shrug and with the best possible grace. Thus I have seen a man accept an honor he laughed at and even despised in private, rather than make an issue of it and hurt the people who thought they were pleasing him.

That this conventionality is a cloak that rests very lightly upon his shoulders and is easily cast aside can be seen from the fact that the self-actualizing person practically never allows convention to hamper him or inhibit him from doing anything that he considers very important or basic. It is at such moments that his essential lack of conventionality appears, and not as with the average Bohemian or authority-rebel, who makes great issues of trivial things and who will fight against some unimportant regulation as if it were a world issue.

This same inner attitude can also be seen in those moments when the person becomes keenly absorbed in something that is close to one of his main interests. He can then be seen quite casually to drop off all sorts of rules of behavior to which at other times he conforms; it is as if he has to make a conscious effort to be conventional; as if he were conventional voluntarily and by design.

Finally, this external habit of behavior can be voluntarily dropped when in the company of people who do not demand or expect routine behavior. That this relative control of behavior is felt as something of a burden is seen by our subjects' preference for such company as allows them to be more free, natural, and spontaneous, and that relieves them of what they find sometimes to be effortful conduct.

One consequence or correlate of this characteristic is that these people have codes of ethics that are relatively autonomous and individual rather than conventional. The unthinking observer might sometimes believe them to be unethical, since they can break not only conventions but laws when the situation seems to demand it. But the very opposite is the case. They are the most ethical of people even though their ethics are not necessarily the same as those of the people around them. It is this kind of observation that leads us to understand very assuredly that the ordinary ethical behavior of the average person is largely conventional behavior rather than truly ethical behavior, e.g., behavior based on fundamentally accepted principles.

Because of this alienation from ordinary conventions and from the ordinarily accepted hypocrisies, lies, and inconsistencies of social life, they sometimes feel like spies or aliens in a foreign land and sometimes behave so.

I should not give the impression that they try to hide what they are like. Sometimes they let themselves go deliberately, out of momentary irritation with customary rigidity or with conventional blindness. They may, for instance, be trying to teach someone or they may be trying to protect someone from hurt or injustice or they may sometimes find emotions bubbling up from within them that are so pleasant or even ecstatic that it seems almost sacrilegious to suppress them. In such instances I have observed that they are not anxious or guilty or ashamed of the impression that they make on the onlooker. It is their claim that they usually behave in a conventional fashion simply because no great issues are involved or because they know people will be hurt or embarrassed by any other kind of behavior.

Their ease of penetration to reality, their closer approach to an animal-like or childlike acceptance and spontaneity imply a superior awareness of their own impulses, desires, opinions, and subjective reactions in general. Clinical study of this capacity confirms beyond a doubt the opinion, e.g., of Fromm that the average normal, well-adjusted person often has not the slightest idea of what he is, of what he wants, of what his own opinions are.

It was such findings as these that led ultimately to the discovery of a most profound difference between self-actualizing people and others; namely, that the motivational life of self-actualizing people is not only quantitatively different but also qualitatively different from that of ordinary people. It seems probable that we must construct a profoundly different psychology of motivation for self-actualizing people, e.g., expression motivation or growth motivation, rather than deficiency motivation. Perhaps it will be useful to make a distinction between living and *preparing* to live. Perhaps the concept of motivation should apply *only* to non-self-actualizers. Our subjects no longer strive in the ordinary sense, but rather develop. They attempt to grow to perfection and to develop more and more fully in their own style. The motivation of ordinary men is a striving for the basic need gratifications that they lack. But self-actualizing people in fact lack none of these gratifications; and yet they have impulses. They work, they try, and they are ambitious, even though in an unusual sense. For them motivation is just character growth, character expression, maturation, and development; in a word self-actualization. Could these self-actualizing people be more human, more revealing of the original nature of the species, closer to the species type in the taxonomical sense? Ought a biological species to be judged by its crippled, warped, only partially developed specimens, or by examples that have been overdomesticated, caged, and trained?

PROBLEM CENTERING

Our subjects are in general strongly focused on problems outside themselves. In current terminology they are problem centered rather than ego centered. They generally are not problems for themselves and are not generally much concerned about themselves; e.g., as contrasted with the ordinary introspectiveness that one finds in insecure people. These individuals customarily have some mission in life, some task to fulfill, some problem outside themselves which enlists much of their energies.

This is not necessarily a task that they would prefer or choose for themselves; it may be a task that they feel is their responsibility, duty, or obligation. This is why we use the phrase "a task that they must do" rather than the phrase "a task that they want to do." In general these tasks are nonpersonal or unselfish, concerned rather with the good of mankind in general, or of a nation in general, or of a few individuals in the subject's family.

With a few exceptions we can say that our subjects are ordinarily concerned with basic issues and eternal questions of the type that we have learned to call philosophical or ethical. Such people live customarily in the widest possible frame of reference. They seem never to get so close to the trees that they fail to see the forest. They work within a framework of values that are broad and not petty, universal and not local, and in terms of a century rather than the moment. In a word, these people are all in one sense or another philosophers, however homely.

Of course, such an attitude carries with it dozens of implications for every area of daily living. For instance, one of the main presenting symptoms originally worked with (bigness, lack of smallness, triviality, pettiness) can be subsumed under this more general heading. This impression of being above small things, of having a larger horizon, a wider breadth of vision, of living in the widest frame of reference, *sub specie aeternitatis*,* is of the utmost social and interpersonal importance; it seems to impart a certain serenity and lack of worry over immediate concerns that make life easier not only for themselves but for all who are associated with them.

THE QUALITY OF DETACHMENT; THE NEED FOR PRIVACY

For all my subjects it is true that they can be solitary without harm to themselves and without discomfort. Furthermore, it is true for almost all that they positively *like* solitude and privacy to a definitely greater degree than the average person. The dichotomy introvert-extrovert applies hardly at all to these people, and will not be used here. The term that seems to be most useful is detachment.

It is often possible for them to remain above the battle, to remain unruffled, undisturbed by that which produces turmoil in others. They find it easy to be aloof, reserved, and also calm and serene; thus it becomes possible for them to take personal misfortunes without reacting violently as the ordinary person does. They seem to be able to retain their dignity even in undignified surroundings and situations. Perhaps this comes in part from their tendency to stick by their own interpretation of a situation rather than to rely upon what other people feel

* As in a kind of eternity.

or think about the matter. This reserve may shade over into austerity and remoteness.

This quality of detachment may have some connection with certain other qualities as well. For one thing it is possible to call my subjects more objective (in *all* senses of that word) than average people. We have seen that they are more problem centered than ego centered. This is true even when the problem concerns themselves, their own wishes, motives, hopes, or aspirations. Consequently, they have the ability to concentrate to a degree not usual for ordinary men. Intense concentration produces as a by-product such phenomena as absent-mindedness, the ability to forget and to be oblivious of outer surroundings. Examples are the ability to sleep soundly, to have undisturbed appetite, to be able to smile and laugh through a period of problems, worry, and responsibility.

In social relations with most people, detachment creates certain troubles and problems. It is easily interpreted by "normal" people as coldness, snobbishness, lack of affection, unfriendliness, or even hostility. By contrast, the ordinary friendship relationship is more clinging, more demanding, more desirous of reassurance, compliment, support, warmth, and exclusiveness. It is true that self-actualizing people do not need others in the ordinary sense. But since this being needed or being missed is the usual earnest of friendship, it is evident that detachment will not easily be accepted by average people.

AUTONOMY; INDEPENDENCE OF CULTURE AND ENVIRONMENT

One of the characteristics of self-actualizing people, which to a certain extent crosscuts much of what we have already described, is their relative independence of the physical and social environment. Since they are propelled by growth motivation rather than by deficiency motivation, self-actualizing people are not dependent for their main satisfactions on the real world, or other people or culture or means to ends or, in general, on extrinsic satisfactions. Rather they are dependent for their own development and continued growth on their own potentialities and latent resources. Just as the tree needs sunshine and water and food, so do most people need love, safety, and the other basic need gratifications that can come only from without. But once these external satisfiers are obtained, once these inner deficiencies are satiated by outside satisfiers, the true problem of individual human development begins, e.g., self-actualization.

This independence of environment means a relative stability in the face of hard knocks, blows, deprivations, frustrations, and the like. These people can maintain a relative serenity and happiness in the midst of circumstances that would drive other people to suicide; they have also been described as "self-contained."

Deficiency-motivated people *must* have other people available, since most of their main need gratifications (love, safety, respect, prestige, belongingness) can come only from other human beings. But growth-motivated people may actually be *hampered* by others. The determinants of satisfaction and of the good life are for them now inner-individual and *not* social. They have become strong enough to be independent of the good opinion of other people or even of their affection. The honors, the status, the rewards, the prestige, and the love they can bestow must have become less important than self-development and inner growth. We must remember that the best technique we know, even though not the only one, for getting to this point of independence from love and respect, is to have been given plenty of this very same love and respect in the past.

CONTINUED FRESHNESS OF APPRECIATION

Self-actualizing people have the wonderful capacity to appreciate again and again, freshly and naïvely, the basic goods of life, with awe, pleasure, wonder, and even ecstasy, however stale these experiences may have become to others. Thus for such a person, any sunset may be as beautiful as the first one, any flower may be of breath-taking loveliness, even after he has seen a million flowers. The thousandth baby he sees is just as miraculous a product as the first one he saw. He remains as convinced of his luck in marriage thirty years after his marriage and is as surprised by his wife's beauty when she is sixty as he was forty years before. For such people, even the casual workaday, moment-to-moment business of living can be thrilling, exciting, and ecstatic. These intense feelings do not come all the time; they come occasionally rather than usually, but at the most unexpected moments. The person may cross the river on the ferry ten times and at the eleventh crossing have a strong recurrence of the same feelings, reaction of beauty, and excitement as when he rode the ferry for the first time.

There are some differences in choice of beautiful objects. Some subjects go primarily to nature. For others it is primarily children, and for a few subjects it has been primarily great music; but it may certainly be said that they derive ecstasy, inspiration, and strength from the basic experiences of life. No one of them, for instance, will get this same sort of reaction from going to a night club or getting a lot of money or having a good time at a party.

Perhaps one special experience may be added. For several of my subjects the sexual pleasures and particularly the orgasm provided, not passing pleasure alone, but some kind of basic strengthening and revivifying that some people derive from music or nature. I shall say more about this in the section on the mystic experience.

It is probable that this acute richness of subjective experience is an aspect of closeness of relationship to the concrete and fresh, *per se* reality discussed above. Perhaps what we call staleness in experience is a consequence of ticketing off a rich perception into one or another category or rubric as it proves to be no longer advantageous, or useful, or threatening or otherwise ego involved.

THE MYSTIC EXPERIENCE; THE OCEANIC FEELING

Those subjective expressions that have been called the mystic experience and described so well by William James are a fairly common experience for our subjects. The strong emotions described in the previous section sometimes get strong enough, chaotic, and widespread enough to be called mystic experiences. My interest and attention in this subject was first enlisted by several of my subjects who described their sexual orgasms in vaguely familiar terms which later I remembered had been used by various writers to describe what *they* called the mystic experience. There were the same feelings of limitless horizons opening up to the vision, the feeling of being simultaneously more powerful and also more helpless than one ever was before, the feeling of great ecstasy and wonder and awe, the loss of placing in time and space with, finally, the conviction that something extremely important and valuable had happened, so that the subject is to some extent transformed and strengthened even in his daily life by such experiences.

It is quite important to dissociate this experience from any theological or supernatural reference, even though for thousands of years they have been linked. None of our subjects spontaneously made any such tie-up, although in later conversation some semireligious conclusions were drawn by a few, e.g., "life must have a meaning," etc. Because this experience is a natural experience, well within the jurisdiction of science, it is probably better to use Freud's term for it, e.g., the oceanic feeling.

We may also learn from our subjects that such experiences can occur in a lesser degree of intensity. The theological literature has generally assumed an absolute, qualitative difference between the mystic experience and all others. As soon as it is divorced from supernatural reference and studied as a natural phenomenon, it becomes possible to place the mystic experience on a quantitative continuum from intense to mild. We discover then that the *mild* mystic experience occurs in many, perhaps even most individuals, and that in the favored individual it occurs dozens of times a day.

Apparently the acute mystic experience is a tremendous intensification of *any* of the experiences in which there is loss of self or transcendance of it, e.g., problem centering, intense concentration, muga behavior, as described by Benedict, intense sensuous experiences, self-forgetful and intense enjoyment of music or art.

GEMEINSCHAFTSGEFÜHL

This word,* invented by Alfred Adler, is the only one available that describes well the flavor of the feelings for mankind expressed by self-actualizing subjects. They have for human beings in general a deep feeling of identification, sympathy, and affection in spite of the occasional anger, impatience, or disgust described below.* Because of this they have a genuine desire to help the human race. It is as if they were all members of a single family. One's feelings toward his brothers would be on the whole affectionate, even if these brothers were foolish, weak, or even if they were sometimes nasty. They would still be more easily forgiven than strangers.

If one's view is not general enough and if it is not spread over a long period of time, then one may not see this feeling of identification with mankind. The self-actualizing person is after all very different from other people in thought, impulse, behavior, emotion. When it comes down to it, in certain basic ways he is like an alien in a strange land. Very few really understand him, however much they may like him. He is often saddened, exasperated, and even enraged by the shortcomings of the average person, and while they are to him ordinarily no more than a nuisance they sometimes become bitter tragedy. However far apart he is from them at times, he nevertheless feels a basic underlying kinship with these creatures whom he must regard with, if not condescension, at least the knowledge that he can do many things better than they can, that he can see things that they cannot see, that the truth that is so clear to him is for most people veiled and hidden. This is what Adler called the older-brotherly attitude.

INTERPERSONAL RELATIONS

Self-actualizing people have deeper and more profound interpersonal relations than any other adults (although not necessarily deeper than those of children). They are capable of more fusion, greater love, more perfect identification, more obliteration of the ego

---

* *Gemein:* common, mutual; *-schaft:* (-ship) suffix denoting state, condition, or quality; *Gefühl:* sentiment, feeling; hence, "fellow-feeling."

boundaries than other people would consider possible. There are, however, certain special characteristics of these relationships. In the first place, it is my observation that the other members of these relationships are likely to be healthier and closer to self-actualization than the average, often *much* closer. There is high selectiveness here, considering the small proportion of such people in the general population.

One consequence of this phenomenon and of certain others as well is that self-actualizing people have these especially deep ties with rather few individuals. Their circle of friends is rather small. The ones that they love profoundly are few in number. Partly this is for the reason that being very close to someone in this self-actualizing style seems to require a good deal of time. Devotion is not a matter of a moment. One subject expressed it so: "I haven't got time for many friends. Nobody has, that is, if they are to be *real* friends." The only possible exception in my group was one woman who seemed to be especially equipped socially. It was almost as if her appointed task in life was to have close and warm and beautiful relations with all the members of her family and their families as well as all her friends and theirs. Perhaps this was because she was an uneducated woman who had no formal task or career. This exclusiveness of devotion can and does exist side by side with a widespreading *Gemeinschaftsgefühl*, benevolence, affection, and friendliness (as qualified above). These people *tend* to be kind or at least patient to almost everyone. They have an especially tender love for children and are easily touched by them. In a very real even though special sense, they love or rather have compassion for all mankind.

This love does not imply lack of discrimination. The fact is that they can and do speak realistically and harshly of those who deserve it, and especially of the hypocritical, the pretentious, the pompous, or the self-inflated. But the face-to-face relationships even with these people do not always show signs of realistically low evaluations. One explanatory statement was about as follows: "Most people, after all, do not amount to much but they *could* have. They make all sorts of foolish mistakes and wind up being miserable and not knowing how they got that way when their intentions were good. Those who are not nice are usually paying for it in deep unhappiness. They should be pitied rather than attacked."

Perhaps the briefest possible description is to say that their hostile reactions to others are (1) deserved, (2) for the good of the person attacked or for someone else's good. This is to say, with Fromm, that their hostility is not character based, but is reactive or situational.

All the subjects for whom I have data show in common another characteristic that is appropriate to mention here, namely, that they attract at least some admirers, friends or even disciples or worshippers. The relation between the individual and his train of admirers is apt to be rather one-sided. The admirers are apt to demand more than our individual is willing to give. And furthermore, these devotions are apt to be rather embarrassing, distressing, and even distasteful to the self-actualizing person, since they often go beyond ordinary bounds. The usual picture is of our subject being kind and pleasant when forced into these relationships, but ordinarily trying to avoid them as gracefully as possible.

THE DEMOCRATIC CHARACTER STRUCTURE

All my subjects without exception may be said to be democratic people in the deepest possible sense. I say this on the basis of a previous analysis of authoritarian and democratic character structures that is too elaborate to present here; it is possible only to describe some aspects of this behavior in short space. These people have all the obvious or superficial democratic characteristics. They can be and are friendly with anyone of suitable character regardless of class, education, political belief, race, or color. As a matter of fact it often seems as if they are not even aware of these differences, which are for the average person so obvious and so important.

They have not only this most obvious quality but their democratic feeling goes deeper as well. For instance they find it possible to learn from anybody who has something to teach them—no matter what other characteristics he may have. In such a learning relationship they do not try to maintain any outward dignity or to maintain status or age prestige or the like. It should even be said that my subjects share a quality that could be called humility of a certain type. They are all quite well aware of how little they know in comparison with what *could* be known and what *is* known by others. Because of this it is possible for them without pose to be honestly respectful and even humble before people who can teach them something that they do not know or who have a skill they do not possess. They give this honest respect to a carpenter who is a good carpenter; or for that matter to anybody who is a master of his own tools or his own craft.

The careful distinction must be made between this democratic feeling and a lack of discrimination in taste, of an undiscriminating equalizing of any one human being with any other. These individuals, themselves elite, select for their friends elite, but this is an elite of character, capacity, and talent, rather than of birth, race, blood, name, family, age, youth, fame, or power.

Most profound, but also most vague is the hard-to-get-at tendency to give a certain quantum of respect to *any* human being just because he is a human individual; our subjects seem not to wish to go beyond a certain minimum point, even with scoundrels, of demeaning, of derogating, of robbing of dignity.

DISCRIMINATION BETWEEN MEANS AND ENDS

I have found none of my subjects to be chronically unsure about the difference between right and wrong in his actual living. Whether or not they could verbalize the matter, they rarely showed in their day-to-day living the chaos, the confusion, the inconsistency, or the conflict that are so common in the average person's ethical dealings. This may be phrased also in such terms as: these individuals are strongly ethical, they have definite moral standards, they do right and do not do wrong. Needless to say, their notions of right and wrong are often not the conventional ones.

One way of expressing the quality I am trying to describe was suggested by Dr. David Levy, who pointed out that a few centuries ago these would have been described as men who walk in the path of God or as godly men. So far as religion is concerned, none of my subjects is orthodoxly religious, but on the other hand I know of only one who describes himself as an atheist (four of the total group studied). The few others for whom I have information hesitate to call themselves atheists. They say that they believe in a God, but describe this God more as a metaphysical concept than as a personal figure. Whether or not they could be called religious people as a group must then depend entirely on the concept or definition of religion that we choose to use. If religion is defined only in social-behavioral terms, then these are all religious people, the atheists included. But if more conservatively we use the term religion so as to include and stress the supernatural element and institutional orthodoxy (certainly the more common usage) then our answer must be quite different, for then almost none of them is religious.

Self-actualizing people most of the time behave as though, for them, means and ends are clearly distinguishable. In general, they are fixed on ends rather than on means, and means are quite definitely subordinated to these ends. This, however, is an over-simple statement. Our subjects make the situation more complex by often regarding as ends in themselves many experiences and activities that are, for other people, only means to ends. Our subjects are somewhat more likely to appreciate for its own sake, and in an absolute way, the doing itself; they can often enjoy for its own sake the getting to some place as well as the arriving. It is occasionally possible for them to make out of the most trivial and routine activity an intrinsically enjoyable game or dance or play. Wertheimer pointed out that most children are so creative that they can transform hackneyed routine, mechanical, and rote experiences, e.g., as in one of his experiments, transporting books from one set of shelves to another, into a structured and amusing game of a sort by doing this according to a certain system or with a certain rhythm.

PHILOSOPHICAL, UNHOSTILE SENSE OF HUMOR

One very early finding that was quite easy to make, because it was common to all my subjects, was that their sense of humor is not of the ordinary type. They do not consider funny what the average man considers to be funny. Thus they do not laugh at hostile humor (making people laugh by hurting someone) or superiority humor (laughing at someone else's inferiority) or authority-rebellion humor (the unfunny, smutty joke). Characteristically what they consider humor is more closely allied to philosophy than to anything else. It may also be called the humor of the real because it consists in large part in poking fun at human beings in general when they are foolish, or forget their place in the universe, or try to be big when they are actually small. This can take the form of poking fun at themselves, but this is not done in any masochistic or clownlike way. Lincoln's humor can serve as a suitable example. Probably Lincoln never made a joke that hurt anybody else; it is also likely that many or even most of his jokes had something to say, had a function beyond just producing a laugh. They often seemed to be education in a more palatable form, akin to parables or fables.

On a simple quantitative basis, our subjects may be said to be humorous less often than the average of the population. Punning, joking, witty remarks, gay repartee, persiflage of the ordinary sort is much less often seen than the rather thoughtful, philosophical humor that elicits a smile more usually than a laugh, that is intrinsic to the situation rather than added to it, that is spontaneous rather than planned, and that very often can never be repeated. It should not be surprising that the average man, accustomed as he is to joke books and belly laughs, considers our subjects to be rather on the sober and serious side.

CREATIVENESS

This is a universal characteristic of all the people studied or observed. There is no exception. Each one shows in one way or another a special kind of creativeness or originality or inventiveness that has certain peculiar characteristics. These special characteristics can be understood more fully in the light of discussion later in this chapter. For one thing, it is different from the special-talent creativeness of the Mozart type. We may as well face the fact that the so-called geniuses display ability that we do not understand. All we can say of them is that they seem to be specially endowed with a drive and a capacity that may have rather little relationship to the rest of the personality and with which, from all evidence, the individuals seem to be born. Such talent we have no concern with here since it does not rest upon psychic health or basic satisfaction. The creativeness of the self-actualized man seems rather to be kin to the naïve and universal creativeness of unspoiled children. It seems to be more a fundamental characteristic of common human nature—a potentiality given to all human beings at birth. Most human beings lose this as they become enculturated, but some few individuals seem either to retain this fresh and naïve, direct way of looking at life, or if they have lost it, as most people do, they later in life recover it.

This creativeness appears on some of our subjects not in the usual forms of writing books, composing music, or producing artistic objects, but rather may be much more humble. It is as if this special type of creativeness, being an expression of healthy personality, is projected out upon the world or touches whatever activity the person is engaged in. In this sense there can be creative shoemakers or carpenters or clerks. Whatever one does can be done with a certain attitude, a certain spirit that arises out of the nature of the character of the person performing the act. One can even *see* creatively as the child does.

This quality is differentiated out here for the sake of discussion, as if it were something separate from the characteristics that precede it and follow it, but this is not actually the case. Perhaps when we speak of creativeness here we are simply describing from another point of view, namely, from the point of view of consequences, what we have described above as a greater freshness, penetration, and efficiency of perception. These people seem to see the true and the real more easily. It is because of this that they seem to other more limited men creative.

Furthermore, as we have seen, these individuals are less inhibited, less constricted, less bound, in a word, less enculturated. In more positive terms, they are more spontaneous, more natural, more human. This too would have as one of its consequences what would seem to other people to be creativeness. If we assume, as we may from our study of children, that all people were once spontaneous, and perhaps in their deepest roots still are, but that these people have in addition to their deep spontaneity a superficial but powerful set of inhibitions, then this spontaneity must be checked so as not to appear very often. If there were no choking-off forces, we might expect that every human being would show this special type of creativeness.

RESISTANCE TO ENCULTURATION

Self-actualizing people are not well adjusted (in the naïve sense of approval of and identification with the culture). They get along with the culture in various ways, but of all of them it may be said that in a certain profound and meaningful sense they resist enculturation and maintain a certain inner detachment from the culture in which they are immersed. Since in the culture-and-personality literature very little has been said about resistance to molding by the culture, and since, as Riesman has clearly pointed out, the saving remnant is especially important for American society, even our meager data are of some importance.

On the whole the relationship of these healthy people with their much less healthy culture is a complex one; from it can be teased out at least the following components.

1. All these people fall well within the limits of apparent conventionality in choice of clothes, of language, of food, of ways of doing things in our culture. And yet they are not *really* conventional, certainly not fashionable or smart or chic.

The expressed inner attitude is usually that it is ordinarily of no great consequence which folkways are used, that one set of traffic rules is as good as any other set, that while they make life smoother they do not really matter enough to make a fuss about. Here again we see the general tendency of these people to accept most states of affairs that they consider unimportant or unchangeable or not of primary concern to them as individuals. Since choice of shoes, or style of haircut or politeness, or manner of behaving at a party are not of primary concern to any of the individuals studied, they are apt to elicit as a reaction only a shrug of the shoulders.

But since this tolerant acceptance is not warm approval with identification, their yielding to convention is apt to be rather casual and perfunctory, with cutting of corners in favor of directness, honesty, saving of energy, etc. In the pinches, when yielding to conventions is too annoying or too expensive, the apparent conventionality reveals itself for the superficial thing that it is, and is tossed off as easily as a cloak.

2. Hardly any of these people can be called authority rebels in the adolescent or hot sense. They show no active impatience or moment-to-moment, chronic, long-time discontent with the culture or preoccupation with changing it quickly, although they often enough show bursts of indignation with injustice. One of these subjects, who was a hot rebel in his younger days, a union organizer in the days when this was a highly dangerous occupation, has given up in disgust and hopelessness. As he became resigned to the slowness of social change (in this culture and in this era) he turned finally to education of the young. All the others show what might be called a calm, long-time concern with culture improvement that seems to me to imply an acceptance of slowness of change along with the unquestioned desirability and necessity of such change.

This is by no means a lack of fight. When quick change is possible or when resolution and courage are needed, it is available in these people. Although they are not a radical group of people in the ordinary sense, I think they easily *could* be. First of all, this is primarily an intellectual group (it must be remembered who selected them), most of whom already have a mission, and feel that they are doing something really important to improve the world. Second, they are a realistic group and seem to be unwilling to make great but useless sacrifices. In a more drastic situation it seems very likely that they would be willing to drop their work in favor of radical social action, e.g., the anti-Nazi underground in Germany or in France. My impression is that they are not against fighting but only against ineffective fighting.

Another point that came up very commonly in discussion was the desirability of enjoying life and having a good time. This seems to all but one to be incompatible with hot and full-time rebelliousness. Furthermore, it seems to them that this is too great a sacrifice to make for the small returns expected. Most of them have had their episodes of fighting, impatience, and eagerness in youth, and in most cases have learned that their optimism about quick change was unwarranted. What they settled down to as a group was an accepting, calm, good-humored everyday effort to improve the culture, usually from within, rather than to reject it and fight it from without.

3. An inner feeling of detachment from the culture is not necessarily conscious but is displayed by almost all, particularly in discussions of the American culture as a whole, in various comparisons with other cultures, and in the fact that they very frequently seem to be able to stand off from it as if they did not quite belong to it. The mixture of varying proportions of affection or approval and hostility or criticism indicated that they select from American culture what is good in it by their lights and reject what they think bad in it. In a word they weigh it, assay it, taste it, and then make their own decisions.

This is certainly very different from the ordinary sort of passive yielding to cultural shaping displayed for instance by the ethnocentric subjects of the many studies of authoritarian personalities.

Detachment from the culture is probably also reflected in our self-actualizing subjects' detachment from people and their liking for privacy, which has been described above, as also in their lesser than average need for and liking for the familiar and customary.

4. For these and other reasons they may be called autonomous, i.e., ruled by the laws of their own character rather than by the rules of society. It is in this sense that they are not only or merely Americans, but also to a greater degree than others, members at large of the human species. To say that they are above or beyond the American culture would be misleading if interpreted strictly, for after all they speak American, act American, have American characters, etc.

And yet if we compare them with the oversocialized, the robotized, or the ethnocentric, we are irresistibly tempted to hypothesize that this group is not simply another subcultural group, but rather less enculturated, less flattened out, less molded. This implies degree, and placing on a continuum that ranges from relative acceptance of the culture to relative detachment from it.

If this turns out to be a tenable hypothesis, at least one other hypothesis can be deduced from it, that those individuals in different cultures who are more detached from their own culture should not only have less national character but also should be more like each other in certain respects than they are like the less developed members of their own societies. Of course this raises questions about what constitutes the good American.

In summary the perennial question, Is it possible to be a good or healthy man in an imperfect culture? has been answered by the observation that it *is* possible for relatively healthy people to develop in the American culture. They manage to get along by a complex combination of inner autonomy and outer acceptance that of course will be possible only so long as the culture remains tolerant of this kind of detached withholding from complete cultural identification.

Of course this is not ideal health. Our imperfect society clearly forces inhibitions and restraints upon our subjects. To the extent that they have to maintain their little secrecies, to that extent is their spontaneity lessened and to that extent are some of their potentialities not actualized. And since only few people can attain health in our culture, those who do attain it are lonely for their own kind and therefore again less spontaneous and less actualized.[1]

THE IMPERFECTIONS OF SELF-ACTUALIZING PEOPLE

The ordinary mistake that is made by novelists, poets, and essayists about the good human being is to make him so good that he is a caricature, so that nobody would like to be like him. The individual's own wishes for perfection, and his guilt and shame about shortcomings are projected upon various kinds of people from whom the average man demands much more than he himself gives. Thus teachers and ministers are ordinarily conceived to be rather joyless people who have no mundane desires and who have no weaknesses. It is my belief that most of the novelists who have attempted to portray good (healthy) people did this sort of thing, making them into stuffed shirts or marionettes or unreal projections of unreal ideals, rather than into the robust, hearty, lusty individuals they really are. Our subjects show many of the lesser human failings. They too are equipped with silly, wasteful, or thoughtless habits. They can be boring, stubborn, irritating. They are by no means free from a rather superficial vanity, pride, partiality to their own productions, family, friends, and children. Temper outbursts are not rare.

Our subjects are occasionally capable of an extraordinary and unexpected ruthlessness. It must be remembered that they are very strong

1. I am indebted to Dr. Tamara Dembo for her help with this problem.

people. This makes it possible for them to display a surgical coldness when this is called for, beyond the power of the average man. The man who found that a long-trusted acquaintance was dishonest cut himself off from this friendship sharply and abruptly and without any pangs whatsoever. Another woman who was married to someone she did not love, when she decided on divorce, did it with a decisiveness that looked almost like ruthlessness. Some of them recover so quickly from the death of people close to them as to seem heartless.

Not only are these people strong but also they are independent of the opinions of other people. One woman, extremely irritated by the stuffy conventionalism of some individuals she was introduced to at a gathering, went out of her way to shock these people by her language and behavior. One might say it was all right for her to react to irritation in this way, but another result was that these people were completely hostile not only to the woman but to the friends in whose home this meeting took place. While our subject *wanted* to alienate these people, the host and hostess did not.

We may mention one more example that arises primarily from the absorption of our subjects in an impersonal world. In their concentration, in their fascinated interest, in their intense concentration on some phenomenon or question, they may become absent-minded or humorless and forget their ordinary social politeness. In such circumstances, they are apt to show themselves more clearly as essentially not interested in chatting, gay conversation, party-going, or the like, they may use language or behavior that may be very distressing, shocking, insulting, or hurtful to others. Other undesirable (at least from the point of view of others) consequences of detachment have been listed above.

Even their kindness can lead them into mistakes, e.g., marrying out of pity, getting too closely involved with neurotics, bores, unhappy people, and then being sorry for it, allowing scoundrels to impose on them for a while, giving more than they should so that occasionally they encourage parasites and psychopaths, etc.

Finally, it has already been pointed out that these people are *not* free of guilt, anxiety, sadness, self-castigation, internal strife, and conflict. The fact that these arise out of nonneurotic sources is of little consequence to most people today (even to most psychologists) who are therefore apt to think them *un*healthy for this reason.

VALUES AND SELF-ACTUALIZATION

A firm foundation for a value system is automatically furnished to the self-actualizer by his philosophic acceptance of the nature of his self, of human nature, of much of social life, and of nature and physical reality. These acceptance values account for a high percentage of the total of his individual value judgments from day to day. What he approves of, disapproves of, is loyal to, opposes or proposes, what pleases him or displeases him can often be understood as surface derivations of this source trait of acceptance.

Not only is this foundation automatically (and universally) supplied to *all* self-actualizers by their intrinsic dynamics (so that in at least this respect fully developed human nature may be universal and cross-cultural); other determiners are supplied as well by these same dynamics. Among these are (1) his peculiarly comfortable relationships with reality, (2) his *Gemeinschaftsgefühl,* (3) his basically satisfied condition from which flow, as epiphenomena, various consequences of surplus, of wealth, overflowing abundance, (4) his characteristically discriminating relations to means and ends etc. (see above).

One most important consequence of this attitude toward the world—as well as a validation of it—is the fact that conflict and struggle, ambivalence and uncertainty over choice lessen or disappear in many areas of life. Apparently "morality" is largely an epiphenomenon of nonacceptance or dissatisfaction. Many problems are seen to be gratuitous and fade out of existence in the atmosphere of pagan acceptance. It is not so much that the problem is solved as that it becomes clearly seen that it never was an intrinsic problem in the first place, but only a sick-man created one, e.g., card-playing, dancing, wearing short dresses, exposing the head (in some churches) or *not* exposing the head (in others), drinking wine, or eating some meats and not others, or eating them on some days but not on others. Not only are such trivialities deflated; the process also goes on at a more important level, e.g., the relations between the sexes, attitudes toward the structure of the body and toward its functioning, and toward death itself.

The pursuit of this finding to more profound levels has suggested to the writer that much else of what passes for morals, ethics, and values may be the gratuitous epiphenomena of the pervasive psychopathology of the average. Many conflicts, frustrations, and threats (which force the kind of choice in which value is expressed), evaporate or resolve for the self-actualizing person in the same way as do, let us say, conflicts over dancing. For him the seemingly irreconcilable battle of the sexes becomes no conflict at all but rather a delightful collaboration. The antagonistic interests of adults and children turn out to be not so antagonistic after all. Just as with sex and age differences, so also is it with natural differences, class and caste differences, political differences, role differences, religious differences, etc. As we know, these are each fertile breeding grounds for anxiety, fear, hostility, aggression, defensiveness, and jealousy. But it begins to appear that they *need not be,* for our subjects' reaction to differences is much less often of this undesirable type.

To take the teacher-student relationship as a specific paradigm; our teacher subjects behaved in a very unneurotic way simply by interpreting the whole situation differently, e.g., as a pleasant collaboration rather than as a clash of wills, of authority, of dignity, etc.; the replacement of artificial dignity—that is easily and inevitably threatened—with the natural simplicity that is *not* easily threatened; the giving up of the attempt to be omniscient and omnipotent; the absence of student-threatening authoritarianism; the refusal to regard the students as competing with each other or with the teacher; the refusal to assume the professor stereotype and the insistence of remaining as realistically human as, say, a plumber or a carpenter; all of these created a classroom atmosphere in which suspicion, wariness, defensiveness, hostility, and anxiety disappeared. So also do similar threat responses tend to disappear in marriages, in families and in other interpersonal situations when threat itself is reduced.

The principles and the values of the desperate man and of the psychologically healthy man must be different in at least some ways. They have profoundly different perceptions (interpretations) of the physical world, the social world and the private psychological world, whose organization and economy is in part the responsibility of the person's value system. For the basically deprived man the world is a dangerous place, a jungle, an enemy territory populated by (1) those whom he can dominate and (2) those who can dominate him. His value system is of necessity, like that of any jungle denizen, dominated and organized by the lower needs, especially the creature needs and the safety needs. The basically satisfied person is in a different case. He can afford out of his abundance to take these needs and their satisfaction for granted and can devote himself to higher gratifications. This is to say that their value systems are different, in fact *must* be different.

The topmost portion of the value system of the self-actualized person is entirely unique and idiosyncratic-character structure-expressive. This must be true by definition, for self-actualization is actualization of a self, and no two selves are altogether alike. There is only one Renoir, one Brahms, one Spinoza. Our subjects had very much in common, as we have seen, and yet at the same time were more completely individualized, more unmistakably themselves, less easily confounded with others than any average control group could possibly be. That is to say, they are simultaneously very much alike and very much unlike each other. They are more completely individual than any group that has ever been described, and yet are also more completely socialized, more identified with humanity than any other group yet described.

THE RESOLUTION OF DICHOTOMIES IN SELF-ACTUALIZATION

At this point we may finally allow ourselves to generalize and underscore a very important theoretical conclusion derivable from the study of self-actualizing people. At several points in this chapter—and in other chapters as well—it was concluded that what had been considered in the past to be polarities or opposites or dichotomies were so *only in unhealthy people*. In healthy people, these dichotomies were resolved, the polarities disappeared, and many oppositions thought to be intrinsic merged and coalesced with each other to form unities.

For example the age-old opposition between heart and head, reason and instinct, or cognition and conation was seen to disappear in healthy people where they become synergic rather than antagonists, and where conflict between them disappears because they say the same thing and point to the same conclusion. In a word in these people, desires are in excellent accord with reason. St. Augustine's "Love God and do as you will" can easily be translated, "Be healthy and then you may trust your impulses."

The dichotomy between selfishness and unselfishness disappears altogether in healthy people because in principle every act is *both* selfish and unselfish. Our subjects are simultaneously very spiritual and very pagan and sensual. Duty cannot be contrasted with pleasure nor work with play when duty *is* pleasure, when work *is* play, and the person doing his duty and being virtuous is simultaneously seeking his pleasure and being happy. If the most socially identified people are themselves also the most individualistic people, of what use is to retain the polarity? If the most mature are also childlike? And if the most ethical and moral people are also the lustiest and most animal?

Similar findings have been reached for kindness-ruthlessness, concreteness-abstractness, acceptance-rebellion, self-society, adjustment-maladjustment, detachment from others-identification with others, serious-humorous, Dionysian-Apollonian, introverted-extraverted, intense-casual, serious-frivolous, conventional-unconventional, mystic-realistic, active-passive, masculine-feminine, lust-love, and Eros-Agape. In these people the id, the ego, and the supergo are collaborative and synergic; they do not war with each other nor are their interests in basic disagreement as they are in neurotic people. So also do the cognitive, the conative, and the emotional coalesce into an organismic unity and into a non-Aristotelian interpenetration. The higher and the lower are not in opposition but in agreement, and a thousand serious philosophical dilemmas are discovered to have more than two horns, or, paradoxically, no horns at all. If the war between the sexes turns out to be no war at all in matured people, but only a sign of crippling, and stunting of growth, who then would wish to choose sides? Who would deliberately and knowingly choose psychopathology? Is it necessary to choose between the good woman and the bad, as if they were mutually exclusive, when we have found that the really healthy woman is both at the same time?

In this, as in other ways, healthy people are so different from average ones, not only in degree but in kind as well, that they generate two different kinds of psychology. It becomes more and more clear that the study of crippled, stunted, immature, and unhealthy specimens can yield only a cripple psychology and a cripple philosophy. The study of self-actualizing people must be the basis for a more universal science of psychology.

Problems

1. What was the positive criterion for inclusion in Maslow's study? What do you think of his methodology?
2. What are the assumptive implications and consequences of Maslow's finding that "folk usage was so unrealistically demanding that no living human being could possibly fit the definition" (590/26-27)?
3. Do you believe a "self-actualizing" person as described would be loved and admired or envied and resented? Is your answer based on experience or on belief; and what are your underlying assumptions?
4. In what ways would the self-actualizing person be attractive or repellent to a Christian? To what extent does he resemble Marx's "species man"?
5. In what ways are independence, freshness, and openness to life experience without prejudgment the key to self-actualization? Is Christ saying the same thing when he tells us to "pass no judgement" (Matthew, 7.1)?
6. In what way do Maslow's conclusions that there is no conflict between individuality and species humanity—that dichotomies between selfish–unselfish, lust–love, work–play, and so forth, can be resolved—suggest the artificiality of these conflicts?
7. In the section on Christianity, we discovered that John, like Paul, is convinced of the need to acknowledge sinfulness. Can an admission of sinfulness and unworthiness have any psychological value? If so, what? Can consciousness of sinfulness be psychologically debilitating? If so, when?

Existentialism

Introduction

John tells us "The truth shall make you free"—believe and salvation is yours. Marx preaches the same message, only now the revelation is dialectical materialism, and the liberation comes from realizing how man's consciousness can be freed from wage slavery by modifying his environment. And the psychoanalysts, painfully unraveling the tortured knot in the human psyche, urge the same message upon us: bring to light the unconscious, behold it, and you are freed from its domination and now control it. But from their mountain heights or underground depths, the existentialists announce that such programs are all a fraud. Not "The truth shall make you free," but "you are free" is the truth. Nothing need be done, no faith accepted, no dialectic mastered, no therapy undergone, just a simple truth affirmed: I am free. Life is an unclear gift, and therefore a burden; for meaning is not predetermined from without but created from within.

When one has said that man exists, that he is free—compelled to freedom, ceaselessly free—one has exhausted all healthy generalizations. Friedrich Nietzsche did not create existentialism by having Zarathustra proclaim, "God is dead," thereby reminding us that we exist alone. Nor is existentialism a philosophy; still less is it a school or system. It is an attitude, a way of perceiving man and the world. As such, it has existed since man confronted his frailty and the meaning of his existence. Job, bemoaning his fate and affirming the reality of his existence before his comforters, is existential. Ecclesiastes, commenting on the vanity of all things and trying from amidst his sorrow to unravel the meaning of life, is existential. Hamlet, in his soliloquies and perplexed extenuations, is existential. To be aware of life, life as snowflake—precious, lovely, unique, fleeting—is to be existential. To be anguished by inexplicabilities and yet glory in possibilities, as does Nietzsche, is to be existential. To dwell in the subjective realm of the mind, savoring sensations and cherishing experiences because they are *your* experiences, is to be existential. Existentialism is a state of being—a matter of the mind and heart.

To say that one is an existentialist is, therefore, a contradiction in terms; it is, as Søren Kierkegaard has noted, to order and abrogate, to fix experience, and existence by its very nature is ongoing, fluid, not thing but process, "the opposite of finality." A biography is not to be confused with a person, for one is a timeless immutable object, the other a subject living in time and subject to its sway; one is perceived, the other both perceives and is perceived.

Albert Camus has remarked that "beginning to think is beginning to be undermined" (48 Camus), and existentialism is the process of being so undermined. Man has become a question mark, and existentialists wish, with a terrible intensity, to unravel that question. They wish to dispense with the smothering simplicities, the tidy proprieties, the packaged answers that really put aside questions; they wish to penetrate the "pasteboard mask." Thus, for them too, answers are only as good as the questions asked, and a solution that ignores an extreme situation has not addressed itself to the real problem, a problem that is so dreadfully complex as to defy the efforts of systematizers. Existentialists are, thus, creatures of the exception, and they condemn systematizers who create regularity by pruning away all that is irregular and inconvenient.

Existentialism is thus a radical perspective—radical in the sense of getting to the root, to that which is fundamental. An existentialist would maintain that none of the previous value systems touched the root of the problems, "Who am I? What do I do with my freedom?"

Institutional Christianity has a ready-made set of answers which can be learned. We are the children of God. Through Adam's Fall we suffered all and were cut off from God's saving grace, until, through Christ who died for our sins, we won the hope of eternal salvation. In addition, there are commandments to be obeyed, sacraments to observe, duties to perform. But an existentialist presented with such a package, might ask: Where do I fit in? And where is my freedom and my choice? The institutional Christian might answer that one fits in by belonging to the Church, by developing faith, that one has freedom to practice the faith or not.

The existentialist would probably question the adequacy of these answers, for they are concerned with externals. Existential belonging does not mean being part of a group; for proximity is not intimacy. Loneliness and alienation are matters of the spirit, and cannot be assuaged by creating an "artificial group" sense of belonging that nowhere addresses itself to the spiritual reality of existential isolation. If members born within the same family are capable of a lifetime devoid of experienced intimacy or relatedness, how can a larger "artificial" family hope to create it? Only a disciplined evasion can lead one to escape the existential reality that souls meet but are not tied together.

Obviously, from an existential perspective, the institutional concept of belonging is shallow and superficial; it fails, Martin Buber would argue, to address itself to the individual's longing to transcend his subjectivity, to respond to and meet the other in a transcendent unmediated presence. Belonging as defined by membership is little more than surface pleasantry

Introduction 621

without spiritual exchange. One relates to the other as an object, a thing, as an "it" instead of a "thou."

A Christian, such as John, might argue that once one is informed by the religious spirit, one will feel a deep sense of communion. But such an answer begs the question. If one feels the religious spirit so keenly, why, as Kierkegaard suggests, belong to the institutionalized Church at all? What function does it serve? One is, by virtue of one's feelings, what the Church, by its forms, hopes to create. If in addition to placing oneself in God's hands, one must, moreover, submit to Church practice, how can one be said to be free? By submitting to another, hasn't one abdicated one's responsibility for oneself? Can intimacy bought at the expense of self be real?

Pressed by existential questions, the institutional Church is compelled to declare that belonging to the Church is irrelevant to religious belief or to declare that the Church is not really concerned with "human belonging" but with religious truth. (There are, of course, other possibilities—Church as social gathering—but such an answer is improbable). The effect of either conclusion is to remove the Church from the human realm; as a vehicle for human brotherhood it breaks down. Not because human brotherhood is impossible, but because it becomes consequent upon an existential encounter with God and not prior to it. The Church then becomes a gathering place for men of good will, and not itself a vehicle of good will.

The argument shifts radically when the existentialist asks how the practice of the institutional church contributes to the existential encounter with God. By the answer, one can discern how much reification the Church has undergone. The answer reveals not only the speaker's theology but his attitude toward institutional forms as opposed to existential confrontations. At one extreme Kierkegaard contends that the institutions are not simply unnecessary intermediaries; they actively interfere with the encounter between man and his god.

> But what then is "Christendom"? Is not "Christendom" the most colossal attempt at serving God, not by following Christ, as He required, and suffering for the doctrine, but instead of that, by "building the sepulchers of the prophets and garnishing the tombs of the righteous" and saying, "If we had been in the days of our fathers, we should not have been partakers with them in the blood of the prophets"?
>
> It is of this sort of divine service I used the expression that, in comparison with the Christianity of the New Testament, it is playing Christianity. . . .
>
> However, this expression, "to play Christianity," could not be used by the Authoritative Teacher; He has a different way of talking about it.
>
> Christ calls it (O give heed!), He calls it "hypocrisy." And not only that, but He says (now shudder!), He says that this guilt of hypocrisy is

as great, precisely as great a crime as that of killing the prophets, so it is blood-guilt. Yea, if one could question Him, He would perhaps make answer that this guilt of hypocrisy, precisely because it is adroitly hidden and deliberately carried on through a whole lifetime, is a greater crime than theirs who in an outburst of rage killed the prophets (49 Kierkegaard).

At the other extreme there is Fyodor Dostoyevsky's Grand Inquisitor who calls Christ, the existentialist, a troublemaker who upsets the well-ordered, comfortable life people truly desire.

We cannot know with certainty where Christ would have stood. There is strong reason to suggest that it was his intense existential attitude that angered the legalistic, highly institutionalized Pharisees and Sadducees. Walter Rauschenbusch has uttered some provocative remarks with respect to Christ and the Church.

> Jesus was not a mere social reformer. Religion was the heart of his life. ... He was the first real man, the inaugurator of a new humanity. ... He was too great to be the Saviour of a fractional part of human life. His redemption extends to all human needs and powers and relations. Theologians have felt no hesitation in founding a system of speculative thought on the teachings of Jesus, and yet Jesus was never an inhabitant of the realm of speculative thought [i.e., he was an existentialist]. He has been made the founder and organizer of a great ecclesiastical machine, which derives authority for its offices and institutions from him, and yet "hardly any problem of exegesis is more difficult than to discover in the gospels an administrative or organizing or ecclesiastical Christ" (50 Rauschenbusch).

The conflict between existential Christianity and the institutionalized Church is a very real and a very deep one. Its main outlines are revealed in Dostoyevsky's "The Grand Inquisitor."

Under no conditions, of course, does an existentialist debate whether God is a fact or not. In this respect, existentialists are more Johannine than Pauline, though even Paul has been debased from an exalted situational spiritualist into a legalist preoccupied with forms and order. The existentialist argues that God is not described or justified; he is experienced. One does not explain him; one addresses him. He is not spoken of, he is spoken to. In this emphasis on the secret stirrings of the self, existentialists are like Shakespeare in his later years; they sense the greater reality of the felt, unarticulated life. Thus, to illustrate the change and difference, the 70-line, unreal, ornate, poetic outbursts of Juliet's parents at her imagined death (*Romeo and Juliet,* IV, v, 20-90) give place to the mute gestures and strangled questions of Macduff when he hears his wife and children have been slain: "My children too? ... My wife killed too? ... All my pretty ones?/ Did you say all? O Hellkite! All? What, all my pretty chickens and their dam/ At one fell swoop?" (*Macbeth,* IV, iii, 210-218)

Before the existential reality, words fall away as inadequate vessels to carry so much emotion. And before the "wordless depths" and awesome majesty of God's felt presence, the ritualized gestures and ceremonial trappings pale into insignificance; for the final mediator of truth is not outside oneself, but *is* oneself.

This emphasis on the subjective experience inevitably places existentialists in opposition to Marxists, for whom subjectivity is a defect to be weeded out (cf. Mao, "How to Study War"). Despite Sartre's strenuous attempts to reconcile existentialism and Marxism, and the great receptivity to such an attempt by revisionists like Leszek Kolakowski, the two movements seem to contain value systems that can scarcely be reconciled.

The Marxist dialectic is so deterministic and so devoid, finally, of human free will, that the existentialist scoffs at it as one more neat system that creates order, *after the fact,* by reshaping our interpretation of those facts. He argues that, for all their ostensible scientific rationality, the Marxist's desire to give the irrational and anarchical nature of reality a spurious order is, at heart, completely subjective. The Marxist belief that the universe is lawful is predicated on selective perception. To argue that the universe is ordered because science has discovered some order within it, the existentialist adds, is to assume that every beautiful child grows into a handsome adult—a non-sequitur based on an unwarranted assumption. There are limits to the extent to which extrapolations can be made about anything. And Marxism, in its zeal for order and reason, denies those limits. Though it is fair to say that a Swede may be taller than a Sicilian, it is an unfair extrapolation to say that all Swedes are taller than all Sicilians. To do so, the existentialist concludes, is to leap into the world of stereotypy.

A Marxist can, with some justification, reply that Marxism does not deny the exception; it merely asserts its insignificance for, statistically, Swedes are taller than Sicilians. Nor are such statistics devoid of value, for they reveal laws that are acted upon by all thinking men. Thus, when statistical probabilities reach alarming rates, as they do for example between smoking and lung cancer, we assume that *objective, rational* persons will give up smoking. For a law has been suggested by the statistics, a law whose nature we will soon understand through reason and science.

The existentialist cannot deny such logic, he can merely emphasize the dual nature of existence—the *en-soi* (in-itself) and *pour-soi* (for-itself) of Jean-Paul Sartre. Some "being" involves objects, for example, a table, which exists "in-itself"; it has no purpose outside itself; it is sufficient; it has a fixed essence. The essence of a table is to be a table. Another kind of "being," however, is aware of itself and hence can live "for-itself": man. Man is both being "in-itself" and being "for-itself." The color of a man's hair, the contour of his face, thus exist "in-themselves"; they have no purpose. When we talk of a man in this sense, we mean that the essence of John Doe is to be short and blue-eyed, or of Mary Roland is to be slim and blonde. We are not referring to that part of them that is free, that part of being which exists "for-itself," which is self-directive and purposeful. Where the purposive "for-itself" is concerned, it is impossible to talk about essence, for it is not fixed, but changing, not determined but freely directive.

When one understands this distinction, the existentialist argues, one understands that statistics have revelatory value only with respect to the "in-itself," for they are not free but determined. We can unravel causal determinants when something is determined, but we cannot do so with respect to that which is free. The Marxist is thus, with certain statistics, obviously not unraveling cause, but imposing artificial order. One can give the wildest chance phenomena an artificial order in this fashion; ashes thrown to the wind, soldiers killed by booby traps, waves irregularly lapping away at a sandbar—all can be made to look determined, *after the fact*.

The Marxist preference for scientific predictability based on statistics, ignores, moreover, the fact that science is concerned not with absolutes but with *probabilities*. A scientific theory must have general applicability and substantial predictability, or it is not a useful theory. When existential facts and theory do not mesh well, facts are retained and theory discarded; but, the existentialist contends, this is not done in Marxism. When existential facts and theory do not work for them, facts are either rewritten, reinterpreted, or set aside for "reinterpretation" when more "facts" are available—facts that will obviously reveal the scientific basis of Marxist theory. But the entire exercise is not scientific; it is scholastic. The modern Marxist is like Aquinas; he accepts the truth of his theory in advance and uses evidence and argument to support it. Marxist science, by preferring theory to fact, is medieval. At best, the existentialist notes, it is rooted in nineteenth century deterministic models of science and is totally unaware of the twentieth-century theory of indeterminacy or contrariety—the notion that things may have contradiction and uncertainty built into them. The delay that Marxists like to think is scientific caution is thus nothing but sloppy methodology and postponement.

One could scarcely hope for better, the existentialist suggests, from a system that considers dialectical truth to be superior to psychological truth, for truth then becomes inhuman. Man is no longer "the measure of all things," man becomes a victim of force fields, of weighted factors determining his course of action by their relative mass. The center of meaning thereby shifts radically. Meaning is no longer something man invests things and experience with; it is something he discovers or has interpreted for him. Man is thus emptied of all content and becomes a passive receptor. Existential ambiguity gives way to a dubious scientific clarity wherein contradictions between fact and theory are denied, and any attempt to point them out leads to attacks on the critic for lack of faith, precipitous judgment, or incorrect interpretation. The tired answer that we are still in an early stage and that, when all the facts are in, our sacrifices shall have been worth the cost, becomes a bromide to placate suffering humanity.

> If it is certain that the kingdom will come, what does time matter? Suffering is never provisional for the man who does not believe in the future. But one hundred years of suffering are fleeting in the eyes of the man who prophesies, for the hundred and first year, the definitive city. In the perspective of the Marxist prophecy, nothing matters. In any event, when the bourgeois class has disappeared, the proletariat will establish the rule of the universal man at the summit of production, by the very logic of productive development. What does it matter that this should be accomplished by dictatorship and violence? In this New Jerusalem, echoing with the roar of miraculous machinery, who will still remember the cry of the victim? (51 Camus)

The cavalier dismissal by the Marxist of the exception, of the existent individual for the sake of a collective mass creates that most cruel and insensitive evil—man suffering from the tyranny of the abstraction. How often has man been tortured for ideals—as witness The Holy Inquisition. Where one loses feeling for man's existential reality, the way is opened to power in the name of abstract good.

> The will to power, the nihilist struggle for domination and authority, have done considerably more than sweep away the Marxist Utopia. This has become in its turn a historic fact destined to be put to use like all the other historic facts. This idea, which was supposed to dominate history, has become lost in history; the concept of abolishing means has been reduced to a means in itself and cynically manipulated for the most banal and bloody ends. . . .
> How could a so-called scientific socialism conflict to such a point with facts? The answer is easy; it was not scientific. On the contrary, its defect resulted from a method ambiguous enough to wish to be simultaneously determinist and prophetic, dialectic and dogmatic (52 Camus).

Despite all of its pretense to science, Marxism, too, leads us back to existential ambiguity. Those who thought they were interpreting reality, were, in good existential fashion, shaping it to their will. Only they were guilty of "bad faith"—self-deception. Like Freud, they had raised self-deception to the level of theory.

Psychoanalysis, however, differs from Marxism. Where Marxism employs self-deception as a means to power, psychoanalysis creates a mental model that is self-deceived in order to liberate people from power.

But it is not liberating; in fact, the existentialist can argue that Freudian determinism is offensive. Freud's notion of the coexistent mind, with layers of the past and present coexisting, as if, to use an analogy with cities, London of the fourteenth, seventeenth, and twentieth centuries all inhabited the same ground, seems to deny real change. More disturbing is the entire concept of the unconscious and of the superego, the vision of man as beset by ineradicable forces. For inherent in both is a kind of escape from freedom, choice, and commitment. Man is driven not only by past forces he can neither control nor understand, he is driven to pursue ideals he never chose. Between the libidinal and aggressive drives of the id and the censorious model of the superego, man is deprived of freedom and choice and bound by parental commitments. Man is no longer the architect of his existence; possibility, praise, blame for his identity—these alternatives vanish before the reality of human dynamics. There are no heroes, only men. For the existentialist, this condition seems to destroy human responsibility. Man can move neither forward nor backward; every gain has its commensurate loss. "Progress" is bought at the expense of self, civilization at the expense of libido. Man becomes a machine with shifting gears, not a free, self-creating being.

Sartre would argue that such a model creates a false dichotomy in man between conscious choice and unconscious drive, and that such a dichotomy involves self-deception; for that which is unconscious must once have been conscious. In repressing something and pushing it into the unconscious, I am thus hiding the truth from myself.

A vast difference intervenes between telling a lie to oneself and telling it to another. A lie told to another is known by the deceiver to be a lie, and hence involves deception of another. But a lie told to oneself obliterates the distinction between "deceiver and deceived." A deceived person receives a lie as if it were truth, but how, when one is deceiver can one also be deceived? The truth one wants to hide from oneself, must have been known in order to have been hidden. One must know where and how one hid it, lest not knowing what that truth was, one accidentally encounter it. The result is immobility, for spontaneous movement may lead to discovery.

Freud's model of man ignores the *conscious* evasion, the willful nature of neurosis, the obstinate tenacious flight from purposeful being into static being; he fails to see the exact nature of the fear—fear of self, of freedom, of choosing and of committing oneself. By denying that one knows the truth one is excused. That one has deliberately hidden it is ignored. Moreover, self-deception clouds the critical and analytic powers and permits one to create a comfortable new value system based on false, fractional perceptions. Self-deception permits cowardly synthesis, for a person who dreads the possibilities of life, the rigors of choice, and the anguish of disciplined commitment, is bound to bring together unreal strands of thought that reassure him. A neurotic, instead of being a rebel who rejects social demands, as Freud suggests, is a coward hiding from himself, one who tries to turn man into a thing, and thereby to end the agony of always "becoming" by finally "being"—anything, something, but it must be *final,* fixed, immutable. There can be no question here of ignorance. Freud permits the self-deceived person, out of misguided tolerance, to escape his cowardly choice, which is the exchange of freedom and creativity for the *security* of mediocrity and group identity.

Freud is too kind, existentialists like Sartre would argue, for it is not sex that drives such people; indeed, they are not moving forward at all. What motivates them is flight. Neurosis is not frustrated sexuality, for it is not a sexual outlet that the neurotic wants, but the desire to lose himself in something larger than himself, some higher group or cause. In his analysis of the anti-semite as self-deceived, Sartre remarks:

> I quoted some statements made by antisemites, all of them absurd: "I hate Jews because they teach indiscipline to servants, because a Jewish furrier robbed me, etc." Do not think that antisemites are completely unaware of the absurdity of these answers. They know that their statements are empty and contestable; but it amuses them to make such statements: it is their adversary whose duty it is to choose his words seriously because he believes in words. They have a right to play. They even like to play with speech because by putting forth ridiculous reasons, they discredit the seriousness of their interlocutor; they are enchanted with their unfairness because for them it is not a question of persuading by good argument but of intimidating or disorienting. If you insist too much they close up, they point out with one superb word that the time to argue has passed. Not that they are afraid of being convinced: their only fear is that they will look ridiculous or that their embarrassment will make a bad impression on a third party whom they want to get on their side. Thus if the antisemite is impervious, as everyone has been able to observe, to reason and experience, it is not because his conviction is so strong, but rather his conviction is strong because he has chosen to be impervious (53 Sartre).

We have come full circle. From Kierkegaard excoriating religious institutions for playing at Christianity, through Camus attacking Marxist contradiction, to Sartre attacking the self-deceived playing at reason, we end up at the same point—all suffer from existential unawareness. They do not understand the meaning of life, or are so fearful of it, that they take refuge in groups or systems. They play at life or try to order it, instead of living and experiencing it. Before the terrible freedom, the dreadful possibility, the shame of exposure through mutual discovery in dialogue, they flee, and thereby deny the loneliness and power, the fragility and preciousness of existence. They cannot "imagine Sisyphus happy."

Patterns: Limited and Exclusive Categories

The author, throughout this essay, creates sharp dichotomies and clear categories; on the one hand there are existentialists, on the other systematizers of one sort or another. The possibility of eclectic synthesis, of a middle ground, is ignored by dramatizing differences. Camus' highly rationalistic, quasi-existentialism is thus opposed not to classical Marxism but to the extreme materialism of modern communism. Sartrean voluntarism is opposed, not to neo-Freudianism, but to the Freudian deterministic model. Those elements of the Marxist dialectic which stress process and the creative interaction between man and his environment are slighted just as are the aspects of Freudianism which stress free choice. The author is not intent on a rounded presentation; he is concerned with creating neat antitheses, antitheses that are made possible by ignoring resemblances, by "limiting" the spectrum of items compared so as to sharpen the opposition, and by ignoring resemblances. By this method, one can create a neat and total antithesis between blacks and whites by limiting one's discussion to hair and pigmentation.

The categories are created, however, not merely by limiting the items contained within each category but by limiting the number of categories presented. Because only two categories are presented, the real spectrum of possibilities is omitted. The reader is made to assume that these alternatives are the only ones and that they are mutually exclusive.

Limited and exclusive categories sharpen and clarify differences and thus serve a useful rhetorical function, especially in pedagogy. On the other hand, when the complexity of the problem is not acknowledged, these same categories can be used to create a deceptive simplicity. In addition, since the problem is defined in a way that insists upon certain questions and excludes others, the reader is placed in a reactive rather than an active role. He is denied a major premise (rhetorical or otherwise) of combat: pick favorable terrain. Limited and exclusive categories usurp choice and thereby compel him to battle on a terrain chosen by the author.

29 FRIEDRICH NIETZSCHE

Walter Kaufmann has issued a timely warning, which warrants repeating here, to anyone who reads selections from Nietzsche:

> An anthologist can easily re-create Nietzsche in his own image, even as writers of lives of Jesus present us, perhaps as often as not, with wishful self-portraits. Doubtless Nietzsche has attracted crackpots and villains, but perhaps the percentage is no higher than in the case of Jesus. As Maritain has said: "If books were judged by the bad uses man can put them to, what book has been more misused than the Bible?" (54 Kaufmann)

No modern philosopher—unless one accepts Marx as a philosopher—has been so misunderstood and so vilified by masses of individuals who have only heard of him but never bothered to read him. For some, damnation follows once they have identified him with the superman theory and recalled that the Nazis incorporated in their ideology such a theory. That the Nazis perverted him by just that scrupulous editing Kaufmann warns of, is forgotten, if it was ever known. Of such shoddy associations are reputations made and destroyed.

Nietzsche was born near Leipzig, Germany, in 1844. His father, a Lutheran minister, died when Nietzsche was five, and so he grew up in a household composed of women—his mother, a sister, a grandmother and two spinster aunts. It was an environment destined to develop in him a lifelong sense of lonely isolation.

His academic career in classical philology was marked by spectacular brilliance: at the prodigious age of 24 he was appointed professor at the University of Basel in Switzerland. Four years later, in 1872, he wrote **The Birth of Tragedy**, *a work that explores the genesis of tragedy through music and dance, and its death at the withering touch of Socratic rationalism. The work, in its exploration of the clashing Dionysian and Apollonian impulses and in its radical perspectives linking tragic beauty to affirmation and suffering, already suggests a penetrating insight into the essence of values. The process of revaluation begun in* **The Birth of Tragedy** *is continued and amplified in his later works.*

In 1889 Nietzsche went insane. Many have used this fact to dismiss his thought as the work of a madman. Nietzsche's defect, however, was not faulty vision; if anything he saw too clearly. In all probability—though there is no certainty—his tortured insanity was not tied to his vision, to his loneliness, to the poor reception given his works, but to complications caused by syphilis. The last ten years of his life were spent in mental darkness, with only sporadic moments of illumination. He died in 1900.

Some men take their great genius as license for a petty spirit; others, gifted with small talent take it upon themselves to cultivate a great heart; and some rare spirits are given both great gifts and great souls. One can scarcely understand Nietzsche if one does not understand that his writings were informed by this vision of great-souled men of great gifts. Freud, who thought little of most men and was little prone to compliment, has remarked of Nietzsche that "he had a more penetrating knowledge of himself than any other man who ever lived or was ever likely to live" (55 Freud). Nietzsche's contempt for pretentiousness, for cowardly evasions, for fear-ridden rationalizations and tawdry aspirations, informs almost everything he wrote. The mark of the superior man was the desire to "overcome" himself; and the "will to power" was the will to increase one's own strength, beauty, and control, to increase one's own powers.

Chronologically, Nietzsche post-dates Kierkegaard, but there is a soaring and plunging movement, a sense of existential freedom and spaciousness which utterly defy Kierkegaard, and make Nietzsche a more sweeping and congenial introduction to the existentialist vision. Moreover, Nietzsche is beginning to loom as one of the greatest and most influential figures of the nineteenth century. And so we begin with this prismatic genius teeming with difficult paradoxes. The works included below all date from the middle years, the years of great outpouring, 1881–1888. With the exception of the preface to, and selection from, The Antichrist *(written in 1888, published in 1895), which serve admirably as a preface to all Nietzsche's writings, and* Thus Spake Zarathustra *(1883–5), which as the poetic summation and the most cryptic and difficult of his works is given its proper place at the end, the works are presented in the order in which they were written:* The Dawn *(1881),* The Gay Science *(1882),* Beyond Good and Evil *(1886),* The Genealogy of Morals *(1887).*

This headnote began with a few words of caution about misreading Nietzsche. Nietzsche himself was so saddened and angered by the distortions of his thought that it is only fitting to end with his half-prideful, half-sorrowful words of warning.

> In the end, nobody hears more out of things, including books, than he knows already. For that to which one lacks access from experience, one has no ears. Let us then imagine an extreme case: that a book speaks of all sorts of experiences which lie utterly beyond any possibility of frequent, or even rare, experiences—that it represents the first language for a new sequence of experiences. In that case, simply nothing is heard; and people have the acoustic illusion that where nothing is heard there is *nothing.*
>
> This has been my usual experience and, if you will, the originality of my experience. Whoever thought that he had understood something of me had merely construed something out of me, after his own image. Not infrequently, it was an antithesis of me . . . (56 Nietzsche).

from The Antichrist

TRANSVALUATION OF ALL VALUES

This book belongs to the very few. Perhaps not one of them is even living yet. Maybe they will be the readers who understand my *Zarathustra:* how *could* I mistake myself for one of those for whom there are ears even now? Only the day after tomorrow belongs to me. Some are born posthumously.

The conditions under which I am understood, and then of *necessity*—I know them only too well. One must be honest in matters of the spirit to the point of hardness before one can even endure my seriousness and my passion. One must be skilled in living on mountains—seeing the wretched ephemeral babble of politics and national self-seeking *beneath* oneself. One must have become indifferent; one must never ask if the truth is useful or if it may prove our undoing. The predilection of strength for questions for which no one today has the courage; the courage for the *forbidden;* the predestination to the labyrinth. An experience of seven solitudes. New ears for new music. New eyes for what is most distant. A new conscience for truths that have so far remained mute. *And* the will to the economy of the great style: keeping our strength, our *enthusiasm* in harness. Reverence for oneself; love of oneself; unconditional freedom before oneself.

Well then! Such men alone are my readers, my right readers, my predestined readers: what matter the *rest?* The rest—that is merely mankind. One must be above mankind in strength, in *loftiness* of soul—in contempt.

54

One should not be deceived: great spirits are skeptics. Zarathustra is a skeptic. Strength, *freedom* which is born of the strength and overstrength of the spirit, proves itself by skepticism. Men of conviction are not worthy of the least consideration in fundamental questions of value and disvalue. Convictions are prisons. Such men do not look far

From Friedrich Nietzsche, *The Antichrist, The Portable Nietzsche* (New York: The Viking Press, 1954), pp. 568–69.

enough, they do not look *beneath* themselves: but to be permitted to join in the discussion of value and disvalue, one must see five hundred convictions *beneath* oneself—*behind* oneself.

A spirit who wants great things, who also wants the means to them, is necessarily a skeptic. Freedom from all kinds of convictions, to be able to see freely, is part of strength. Great passion, the ground and the power of his existence, even more enlightened, even more despotic than he is himself, employs his whole intellect; it makes him unhesitating; it gives him courage even for unholy means; under certain circumstances it does not begrudge him convictions. Conviction as a *means:* many things are attained only by means of a conviction. Great passion uses and uses up convictions, it does not succumb to them—it knows itself sovereign. . . .

from The Dawn

76

If you think it evil, you make it evil.—The passions become evil and malignant when regarded with evil and malignant eyes. It is in this way that Christianity has succeeded in transforming Eros and Aphrodite—sublime powers, capable of idealisation—into hellish genii and phantom goblins, by means of the pangs which every sexual impulse was made to raise in the conscience of the believers. Is it not a dreadful thing to transform necessary and regular sensations into a source of inward misery, and thus arbitrarily to render interior misery necessary and regular *in the case of every man!* Furthermore, this misery remains secret, with the result that it is all the more deeply rooted; for it is not all men who have the courage, which Shakespeare shows in his sonnets, of making public their Christian gloom on this point.

Must a feeling, then, always be called evil against which we are forced to struggle, which we must restrain even within certain limits, or, in given cases, banish entirely from our minds? Is it not the habit of vulgar souls always to call an *enemy* evil! and must we call Eros an enemy? The sexual feelings, like the feelings of pity and adoration, possess the particular characteristic that, in their case, one being gratifies another by the pleasure he enjoys—it is but rarely that we meet with such a benevolent arrangement in nature. And yet we calumniate and corrupt

From Friedrich Nietzsche, *The Dawn of Day, The Complete Works of Friedrich Nietzsche,* vol. 9 (New York: Russell & Russell, 1964), pp. 77–177.

it all by our bad conscience! We connect the procreation of man with a bad conscience!

But the outcome of this diabolisation of Eros is a mere farce: the "demon" Eros becomes an object of greater interest to mankind than all the angels and saints put together, thanks to the mysterious Mumbo-Jumboism of the Church in all things erotic: it is due to the Church that love stories, even in our own time, have become the one common interest which appeals to all classes of people—with an exaggeration which would be incomprehensible to antiquity, and which will not fail to provoke roars of laughter in coming generations. All our poetising and thinking, from the highest to the lowest, is marked, and more than marked, by the exaggerated importance bestowed upon the love story as the principal item of our existence. Posterity may perhaps, on this account, come to the conclusion that its entire legacy of Christian culture is tainted with narrowness and insanity.

104

Our valuations.—All actions may be referred back to valuations, and all valuations are either one's own or adopted, the latter being by far the more numerous. Why do we adopt them? Through fear, *i.e.* we think it more advisable to pretend that they are our own, and so well do we accustom ourselves to do so that it at last becomes second nature to us. A valuation of our own, which is the appreciation of a thing in accordance with the pleasure or displeasure it causes us and no one else, is something very rare indeed!—But must not our valuation of our neighbour—which is prompted by the motive that we adopt his valuation in most cases—proceed from ourselves and by our own decision? Of course, but then we come to these decisions during our childhood, and seldom change them. We often remain during our whole lifetime the dupes of our childish and accustomed judgments in our manner of judging our fellowmen (their minds, rank, morality, character, and reprehensibility), and we find it necessary to subscribe to their valuations.

105

Pseudo-egoism.—The great majority of people, whatever they think and say about their "egoism," do nothing for their ego all their life long, but only for a phantom of this ego which has been formed in regard to them by their friends and communicated to them. As a consequence, they all live in a haze of impersonal and half-personal opinions and of arbitrary and, as it were, poetic valuations: the one always in the head of another, and this head, again, in the head of somebody else—a queer world of phantoms which manages to give itself a rational appearance! This haze of opinions and habits grows in extent and lives almost independently of the people it surrounds; it is it which gives rise to the immense effect of general judgments on "man"—all those men, who do not know themselves, believe in a bloodless abstraction which they call "man," *i.e.* in a fiction; and every change caused in this abstraction by the judgments of powerful individualities (such as princes and philosophers) produces an extraordinary and irrational effect on the great majority,—for the simple reason that not a single individual in this haze can oppose a real ego, an ego which is accessible to and fathomed by himself, to the universal pale fiction, which he could thereby destroy.

from The Gay Science

[*283*]

Preparatory men. I welcome all signs that a more manly, a warlike, age is about to begin, an age which, above all, will give honor to valor once again. For this age shall prepare the way for one yet higher, and it shall gather the strength which this higher age will need one day—this age which is to carry heroism into the pursuit of knowledge and *wage wars* for the sake of thoughts and their consequences. To this end we now need many preparatory valorous men who cannot leap into being out of nothing—any more than out of the sand and slime of our present civilization and metropolitanism: men who are bent on seeking for that aspect in all things which must be *overcome;* men characterized by cheerfulness, patience, unpretentiousness, and contempt for all great vanities, as well as by magnanimity in victory and forbearance regarding the small vanities of the vanquished; men possessed of keen and free judgment concerning all victors and the share of chance in every victory and every fame; men who have their own festivals, their own weekdays, their own periods of mourning, who are accustomed to command with assurance and are no less ready to obey when necessary, in both cases equally proud and serving their own cause; men who are in greater danger, more fruitful, and happier! For, believe me, the secret of the greatest fruitfulness and the greatest enjoyment of existence is: to *live*

From Friedrich Nietzsche, *The Gay Science, The Portable Nietzsche* (New York: The Viking Press, 1954), pp. 97–99.

dangerously! Build your cities under Vesuvius! Send your ships into uncharted seas! Live at war with your peers and yourselves. Be robbers and conquerors, as long as you cannot be rulers and owners, you lovers of knowledge. Soon the age will be past when you could be satisfied to live like shy deer, hidden in the woods! At long last the pursuit of knowledge will reach out for its due: it will want to *rule* and *own*, and you with it!

[290]

One thing is needful. "Giving style" to one's character—a great and rare art! It is exercised by those who see all the strengths and weaknesses of their own natures and then comprehend them in an artistic plan until everything appears as art and reason and even weakness delights the eye. Here a large mass of second nature has been added; there a piece of original nature has been removed: both by long practice and daily labor. Here the ugly which could not be removed is hidden; there it has been reinterpreted and made sublime. . . . It will be the strong and domineering natures who enjoy their finest gaiety in such compulsion, in such constraint and perfection under a law of their own; the passion of their tremendous will relents when confronted with stylized, conquered, and serving nature; even when they have to build palaces and lay out gardens, they demur at giving nature a free hand. Conversely, it is the weak characters without power over themselves who *hate* the constraint of style. . . . They become slaves as soon as they serve; they hate to serve. Such spirits—and they may be of the first rank—are always out to interpret themselves and their environment as *free* nature—wild, arbitrary, fantastic, disorderly, astonishing; and they do well because only in this way do they please themselves. For one thing is needful: that a human being attain his satisfaction with himself—whether it be by this or by that poetry and art; only then is a human being at all tolerable to behold. Whoever is dissatisfied with himself is always ready to revenge himself therefore; we others will be his victims, if only by always having to stand his ugly sight. For the sight of the ugly makes men bad and gloomy.

Problems

1. Why does Nietzsche reserve certain truths for the very few? What characterizes these few?
2. Why, for Nietzsche, do freedom and strength prove themselves in skepticism?
3. What are the implications of Nietzsche's remark, "If you think it evil, you

make it evil" (632/13)? Analyze the thought of the following thinkers with the above model in mind: Paul, Marx, Freud, Maslow.
4. How, for Nietzsche, are we revealed by our valuations? What other thinkers have shared the same thought? In what way is this resemblance significant?
5. What is pseudo-egoism? Why would people suffer from it?
6. Who are the preparatory men and what are they characterized by?

from Beyond Good and Evil

PART ONE

2

"How *could* anything originate out of its opposite? For example, truth out of error? or the will to truth out of the will to deception? or selfless deeds out of selfishness? or the pure and sunlike gaze of the sage out of lust? Such origins are impossible; whoever dreams of them is a fool, indeed worse; the things of the highest value must have another, *peculiar* origin—they cannot be derived from this transitory, seductive, deceptive, paltry world, from this turmoil of delusion and lust. Rather from the lap of Being, the intransitory, the hidden god, the 'thing-in-itself'—there must be their basis, and nowhere else."

This way of judging constitutes the typical prejudgment and prejudice which give away the metaphysicians of all ages; this kind of valuation looms in the background of all their logical procedures; it is on account of this "faith" that they trouble themselves about "knowledge," about something that is finally baptized solemnly as "the truth." The fundamental faith of the metaphysicians is *the faith in opposite values*.[1] It has not even occurred to the most cautious among them that one might have a doubt right here at the threshold where it was surely most necessary—even if they vowed to themselves, *"de omnibus dubitandum."* [2]

For one may doubt, first whether there are any opposites at all, and secondly whether these popular valuations and opposite values on which the metaphysicians put their seal, are not perhaps merely foreground estimates, only provisional perspectives, perhaps even from some nook, per-

From Friedrich Nietzsche, *Beyond Good and Evil* (New York: Random House, Inc., 1966), pp. 9–221.
1. Nietzsche's attack on this faith is prefigured in the title of the book. This aphorism invites comparison with the first aphorism of *Human, All-Too-Human*.
2. "All is to be doubted." Descartes.

haps from below, frog perspectives, as it were, to borrow an expression painters use. For all the value that the true, the truthful, the selfless may deserve, it would still be possible that a higher and more fundamental value for life might have to be ascribed to deception, selfishness, and lust, It might even be possible that what constitutes the value of these good and revered things is precisely that they are insidiously related, tied to, and involved with these wicked, seemingly opposite things—maybe even one with them in essence. Maybe!

But who has the will to concern himself with such dangerous maybes? For that, one really has to wait for the advent of a new species of philosophers, such as have somehow another and converse taste and propensity from those we have known so far—philosophers of the dangerous "maybe" in every sense.

And in all seriousness: I see such new philosophers coming up.

4

The falseness of a judgment is for us not necessarily an objection to a judgment; in this respect our new language may sound strangest. The question is to what extent it is life-promoting, life-preserving, species-preserving, perhaps even species-cultivating. . . . To recognize untruth as a condition of life—that certainly means resisting accustomed value feelings in a dangerous way; and a philosophy that risks this would by that token alone place itself beyond good and evil.

29

Independence is for the very few; it is a privilege of the strong. And whoever attempts it even with the best right but without inner constraint proves that he is probably not only strong, but also daring to the point of recklessness. He enters into a labyrinth, he multiplies a thousandfold the dangers which life brings with it in any case, not the least of which is that no one can see how and where he loses his way, becomes lonely, and is torn piecemeal by some minotaur of conscience. Supposing one like that comes to grief, this happens so far from the comprehension of men that they neither feel it nor sympathize. And he cannot go back any longer. Nor can he go back to the pity of men.—

30

Our highest insights must—and should—sound like follies and sometimes like crimes when they are heard without permission by those who are not predisposed and predestined for them.³ The difference between the exoteric and the esoteric, formerly known to philosophers—among the Indians as among the Greeks, Persians, and Muslims, in short, wherever one believed in an order of rank and *not* in equality and equal rights—does not so much consist in this, that the exoteric approach comes from outside and sees, estimates, measures, and judges from the outside, not the inside: what is much more essential is that the exoteric approach sees things from below, the esoteric looks *down from above*. There are heights of the soul from which even tragedy ceases to look tragic; and rolling together all the woe of the world—who could dare to decide whether its sight would *necessarily* seduce us and compel us to feel pity and thus double this woe?

What serves the higher type of men as nourishment or delectation must almost be poison for a very different and inferior type. The virtues of the common man might perhaps signify vices and weaknesses in a philosopher. It could be possible that a man of a high type, when degenerating and perishing, might only at that point acquire qualities that would require those in the lower sphere into which he had sunk to begin to venerate him like a saint. There are books that have opposite values for soul and health, depending on whether the lower soul, the lower vitality, or the higher and more vigorous ones turn to them: in the former case, these books are dangerous and lead to crumbling and disintegration; in the latter, heralds' cries that call the bravest to *their* courage. Books for all the world are always foul-smelling books: the smell of small people clings to them. Where the people eat and drink, even where they venerate, it usually stinks. One should not go to church if one wants to breathe *pure* air.

202

Let us immediately say once more what we have already said a hundred times, for today's ears resist such truths—*our* truths. We know well enough how insulting it sounds when anybody counts man, unadorned and without metaphor, among the animals; but it will be charged against us as almost a *guilt* that precisely for the men of "modern

---

3. This theme is taken up again in several later sections, where the concept of the mask is discussed.

ideas" we constantly employ such expressions as "herd," "herd instincts," and so forth. What can be done about it? We cannot do anything else; for here exactly lies our novel insight. We have found that in all major moral judgments Europe is now of one mind, including even the countries dominated by the influence of Europe: plainly, one now *knows* in Europe what Socrates thought he did not know and what that famous old serpent once promised to teach—today one "knows" what is good and evil.[4]

Now it must sound harsh and cannot be heard easily when we keep insisting: that which here believes it knows, that which here glorifies itself with its praises and reproaches, calling itself good, that is the instinct of the herd animal, man, which has scored a breakthrough and attained prevalence and predominance over other instincts—and this development is continuing in accordance with the growing physiological approximation and assimilation of which it is the symptom. *Morality in Europe today is herd animal morality*—in other words, as we understand it, merely *one* type of human morality beside which, before which, and after which many other types, above all *higher* moralities, are, or ought to be, possible. But this morality resists such a "possibility," such an "ought" with all its power: it says stubbornly and inexorably, "I am morality itself, and nothing besides is morality." Indeed, with the help of a religion which indulged and flattered the most sublime herd-animal desires, we have reached the point where we find even in political and social institutions an ever more visible expression of this morality: the *democratic* movement is the heir of the Christian movement.

But there are indications that its tempo is still much too slow and sleepy for the more impatient, for the sick, the sufferers of the instinct mentioned: witness the ever madder howling of the anarchist dogs who are baring their fangs more and more obviously and roam through the alleys of European culture. They seem opposites of the peacefully industrious democrats and ideologists of revolution, and even more so of the doltish philosophasters and brotherhood enthusiasts who call themselves socialists and want a "free society"; but in fact they are at one with the lot in their thorough and instinctive hostility to every other form of society except that of the *autonomous* herd (even to the point of repudiating the very concepts of "master" and "servant"—*ni dieu ni maître*[5]

---

4. Cf. *Zarathustra,* "On Old and New Tablets," section 2: "When I came to men I found them sitting on an old conceit: the conceit that they have long known what is good and evil for man . . . whoever wanted to sleep well still talked of good and evil before going to sleep."

And in Shaw's *Major Barbara* (Act III) Undershaft says: "What! no capacity for business, no knowledge of law, no sympathy with art, no pretension to philosophy; only a simple knowledge of the secret that has puzzled all the philosophers, baffled all the lawyers. . . : the secret of right and wrong. Why, man, you are a genius, a master of masters, a god! At twenty-four, too!"

5. "Neither god nor master."

runs a socialist formula). They are at one in their tough resistance to every special claim, every special right and privilege (which means in the last analysis, *every* right: for once all are equal nobody needs "rights" any more). They are at one in their mistrust of punitive justice (as if it were a violation of those who are weaker, a wrong against the *necessary consequence* of all previous society). But they are also at one in the religion of pity, in feeling with all who feel, live, and suffer (down to the animal, up to "God"—the excess of a "pity with God" belongs in a democratic age). They are at one, the lot of them, in the cry and the impatience of pity, in their deadly hatred of suffering generally, in their almost feminine inability to remain spectators, to *let* someone suffer. They are at one in their involuntary plunge into gloom and unmanly tenderness under whose spell Europe seems threatened by a new Buddhism. They are at one in their faith in the morality of *shared* pity, as if that were morality in itself being the height, the *attained* height of man, the sole hope of the future, the consolation of present man, the great absolution from all former guilt. They are at one, the lot of them, in their faith in the community as the *savior,* in short, in the herd, in "themselves"—

212

More and more it seems to me that the philosopher, being *of necessity* a man of tomorrow and the day after tomorrow, has always found himself, and *had* to find himself, in contradiction to his today: his enemy was ever the ideal of today. So far all these extraordinary furtherers of man whom one calls philosophers, though they themselves have rarely felt like friends of wisdom but rather like disagreeable fools and dangerous question marks, have found their task, their hard, unwanted, inescapable task, but eventually also the greatness of their task, in being the bad conscience of their time.

By applying the knife vivisectionally to the chest of the very *virtues of their time* they betrayed what was their own secret: to know of a *new* greatness of man, of a new untrodden way to his enhancement. Every time they exposed how much hypocrisy, comfortableness, letting oneself go and letting oneself drop, how many lies lay hidden under the best honored type of their contemporary morality, how much virtue was *outlived.* Every time they said: "We must get there, that way, where *you* today are least at home."

Facing a world of "modern ideas" that would banish everybody into a corner and "specialty," a philosopher—if today there could be philosophers—would be compelled to find the greatness of man, the concept of "greatness," precisely in his range and multiplicity, in his wholeness in manifoldness. He would even determine value and rank in accordance with how much and how many things one could bear and take upon himself, how *far* one could extend his responsibility.

Today the taste of the time and the virtue of the time weakens and thins down the will; nothing is as timely as weakness of the will. In the philosopher's ideal, therefore, precisely strength of the will, hardness, and the capacity for long-range decisions must belong to the concept of "greatness"—with as much justification as the opposite doctrine and the ideal of a dumb, renunciatory, humble, selfless humanity was suitable for an opposite age, one that suffered, like the sixteenth century, from its accumulated energy of will and from the most savage floods and tidal waves of selfishness.

In the age of Socrates among men of fatigued instincts, among the conservatives of ancient Athens who let themselves go—"toward happiness," as they said; toward pleasure, as they acted—and who all the while still mouthed the ancient pompous words to which their lives no longer gave them any right, *irony* may have been required for greatness of soul,[6] that Socratic sarcastic assurance of the old physician and plebeian who cut ruthlessly into his own flesh, as he did into the flesh and heart of the "noble," with a look that said clearly enough: "Don't dissemble in front of me! Here—we are equal."

Today, conversely, when only the herd animal receives and dispenses honors in Europe, when "equality of rights" could all too easily be changed into equality in violating rights—I mean, into a common war on all that is rare, strange, privileged, the higher man, the higher soul,

---

6. Aristotle's discussion of greatness of soul (*megalopsychia*) is worth quoting here, at least in part, because it evidently influenced Nietzsche. The valuations that find expression in Aristotle's account are exceedingly remote from those of the New Testament and help us understand Nietzsche's contrast of master morality and slave morality, introduced below (section 260). Moreover, in his long discussion of "what is noble," Nietzsche emulates Aristotle's descriptive mode.

"A person is thought to be great-souled if he claims much and deserves much [as Socrates did in the *Apology* when he said he deserved the greatest honor Athens could bestow]. . . . He that claims less than he deserves is small-souled. . . . The great-souled man is justified in despising other people—his estimates are correct; but most proud men have no good ground for their pride. . . . He is fond of conferring benefits, but ashamed to receive them, because the former is a mark of superiority and the latter of inferiority. . . . It is also characteristic of the great-souled men never to ask help from others, or only with reluctance, but to render aid willingly; and to be haughty towards men of position and fortune, but courteous towards those of moderate station. . . . He must be open both in love and in hate, since concealment shows timidity; and care more for the truth than for what people will think; . . . he is outspoken and frank, except when speaking with ironical self-depreciation, as he does to common people. . . . He does not bear a grudge, for it is not a mark of greatness of soul to recall things against people, especially the wrongs they have done you, but rather to overlook them. He is . . . not given to speaking evil himself, even of his enemies, except when he deliberately intends to give offence. . . . Such then being the great-souled man, the corresponding character on the side of deficiency is the small-souled man, and on that of excess the vain man" (*Nicomachean Ethics* IV.3, Rackham translation Cambridge, Mass., Harvard University Press, 1947).

The whole passage is relevant and extremely interesting.

the higher duty, the higher responsibility, and the abundance of creative power and masterfulness—today the concept of greatness entails being noble, wanting to be by oneself, being able to be different, standing alone and having to live independently. And the philosopher will betray something of his own ideal when he posits: "He shall be greatest who can be loneliest, the most concealed, the most deviant, the human being beyond good and evil, the master of his virtues, he that is overrich in will. Precisely this shall be called *greatness:* being capable of being as manifold as whole, as ample as full." And to ask it once more: today—is greatness *possible?*

260

Wandering through the many subtler and coarser moralities which have so far been prevalent on earth, or still are prevalent, I found that certain features recurred regularly together and were closely associated—until I finally discovered two basic types and one basic difference.

There are *master morality* and *slave morality*[7]—I add immediately that in all the higher and more mixed cultures there also appear attempts at mediation between these two moralities, and yet more often the interpenetration and mutual misunderstanding of both, and at times they occur directly alongside each other—even in the same human being, within a *single* soul.[8] The moral discrimination of values has originated either among a ruling group whose consciousness of its difference from the ruled group was accompanied by delight—or among the ruled, the slaves and dependents of every degree.

In the first case, when the ruling group determines what is "good," the exalted, proud states of the soul are experienced as conferring distinction and determining the order of rank. The noble human being separates from himself those in whom the opposite of such exalted, proud states finds expression: he despises them. It should be noted immediately that in this first type of morality the opposition of "good" and *"bad"* means approximately the same as "noble" and "contemptible." (The opposition of "good" and *"evil"* has a different origin.) One feels contempt for the cowardly, the anxious, the petty, those intent on narrow utility; also

---

7. While the ideas developed here, and explicated at greater length a year later in the first part of the *Genealogy of Morals,* had been expressed by Nietzsche in 1878 in section 45 of *Human, All-Too-Human,* this is the passage in which his famous terms "master morality" and "slave morality" are introduced.

8. These crucial qualifications, though added immediately, have often been overlooked. "Modern" moralities are clearly mixtures; hence their manifold tensions, hypocrisies, and contradictions.

for the suspicious with their unfree glances, those who humble themselves, the doglike people who allow themselves to be maltreated, the begging flatterers, above all the liars: it is part of the fundamental faith of all aristocrats that the common people lie. "We truthful ones"—thus the nobility of ancient Greece referred to itself.

It is obvious that moral designations were everywhere first applied to *human beings* and only later, derivatively, to actions. Therefore it is a gross mistake when historians of morality start from such questions as: why was the compassionate act praised? The noble type of man experiences *itself* as determining values; it does not need approval; it judges, "what is harmful to me is harmful in itself"; it knows itself to be that which first accords honor to things; it is *value-creating*. Everything it knows as part of itself it honors: such a morality is self-glorification. In the foreground there is the feeling of fullness, of power that seeks to overflow, the happiness of high tension, the consciousness of wealth that would give and bestow: the noble human being, too, helps the unfortunate, but not, or almost not, from pity, but prompted more by an urge begotten by excess of power. The noble human being honors himself as one who is powerful, also as one who has power over himself, who knows how to speak and be silent, who delights in being severe and hard with himself and respects all severity and hardness. "A hard heart Wotan put into my breast," says an old Scandinavian saga: a fitting poetic expression, seeing that it comes from the soul of a proud Viking. Such a type of man is actually proud of the fact that he is *not* made for pity, and the hero of the saga therefore adds as a warning: "If the heart is not hard in youth it will never harden." Noble and courageous human beings who think that way are furthest removed from that morality which finds the distinction of morality precisely in pity, or in acting for others, or in *désintéressement;* * faith in oneself, pride in oneself, a fundamental hostility and irony against "selflessness" belong just as definitely to noble morality as does a slight disdain and caution regarding compassionate feelings and a "warm heart."

It is the powerful who *understand* how to honor; this is their art, their realm of invention. The profound reverence for age and tradition—all law rests on this double reverence—the faith and prejudice in favor of ancestors and disfavor of those yet to come are typical of the morality of the powerful; and when the men of "modern ideas," conversely, believe almost instinctively in "progress" and "the future" and more and more lack respect for age, this in itself would sufficiently betray the ignoble origin of these "ideas."

A morality of the ruling group, however, is most alien and embarrassing to the present taste in the severity of its principle that one has duties

---

* Disinterestedness; being without a vested interest; objective.

only to one's peers; that against beings of a lower rank, against everything alien, one may behave as one pleases or "as the heart desires," and in any case "beyond good and evil"—here pity and like feelings may find their place.[9] The capacity for, and the duty of, long gratitude and long revenge—both only among one's peers—refinement in repaying, the sophisticated concept of friendship, a certain necessity for having enemies (as it were, as drainage ditches for the affects of envy, quarrelsomeness, exuberance—at bottom, in order to be capable of being good *friends*): all these are typical characteristics of noble morality which, as suggested, is not the morality of "modern ideas" and therefore is hard to empathize with today, also hard to dig up and uncover.[10]

It is different with the second type of morality, *slave morality*. Suppose the violated, oppressed, suffering, unfree, who are uncertain of themselves and weary, moralize: what will their moral valuations have in common? Probably, a pessimistic suspicion about the whole condition of man will find expression, perhaps a condemnation of man along with his condition. The slave's eye is not favorable to the virtues of the powerful: he is skeptical and suspicious, *subtly* suspicious, of all the "good" that is honored there—he would like to persuade himself that even their happiness is not genuine. Conversely, those qualities are brought out and flooded with light which serve to ease existence for those who suffer: here pity, the complaisant and obliging hand, the warm heart, patience, industry, humility, and friendliness are honored—for here these are the most useful qualities and almost the only means for enduring the pressure of existence. Slave morality is essentially a morality of utility.

Here is the place for the origin of that famous opposition of "good" and "evil": into evil one's feelings project power and dangerousness, a certain terribleness, subtlety, and strength that does not permit contempt to develop. According to slave morality, those who are "evil" thus inspire

---

9. The final clause that follows the dash, omitted in the Cowan translation, is crucial and qualifies the first part of the sentence: a noble person has no *duties* to animals but treats them in accordance with his feelings, which means, if he is noble, with pity.

The ruling masters, of course, are not always noble in this sense, and this is recognized by Nietzsche in *Twilight of the Idols,* in the chapter "The 'Improvers' of Mankind," in which he gives strong expression to his distaste for Manu's laws concerning outcasts. Indeed, in *The Antichrist,* section 57, Nietzsche contradicts outright his formulation above: "When the exceptional human being treats the mediocre more tenderly than himself and his peers, this is not mere courtesy of the heart—it is simply his *duty*."

More important: Nietzsche's obvious distaste for slave morality and the fact that he makes a point of liking master morality better does not imply that he endorses master morality.

10. Clearly, master morality cannot be discovered by introspection nor by the observation of individuals who are "masters" rather than "slaves." Both of these misunderstandings are widespread. What is called for is rather a rereading of, say, the *Iliad* and, to illustrate "slave morality," the New Testament.

fear; according to master morality it is precisely those who are "good" that inspire, and wish to inspire, fear, while the "bad" are felt to be contemptible.

The opposition reaches its climax when, as a logical consequence of slave morality, a touch of disdain is associated also with the "good" of this morality—this may be slight and benevolent—because the good human being has to be *undangerous* in the slaves' way of thinking: he is good-natured, easy to deceive, a little stupid perhaps, *un bonhomme*.[11] Wherever slave morality becomes preponderant, language tends to bring the words "good" and "stupid" closer together.

One last fundamental difference: the longing for *freedom,* the instinct for happiness and the subtleties of the feeling of freedom belong just as necessarily to slave morality and morals as artful and enthusiastic reverence and devotion are the regular symptom of an aristocratic way of thinking and evaluating.

This makes plain why love *as passion*—which is our European specialty—simply must be of noble origin: as is well known, its invention must be credited to the Provençal knight-poets, those magnificent and inventive human beings of the *"gai saber"* [12] to whom Europe owes so many things and almost owes itself.—

261

Among the things that may be hardest to understand for a noble human being is vanity: he will be tempted to deny it, where another type of human being could not find it more palpable. The problem for him is to imagine people who seek to create a good opinion of themselves which they do not have of themselves—and thus also do not "deserve"— and who nevertheless end up *believing* this good opinion themselves. This strikes him half as such bad taste and lack of self-respect, and half as so baroquely irrational, that he would like to consider vanity as exceptional, and in most cases when it is spoken of he doubts it.

He will say, for example: "I may be mistaken about my value and nevertheless demand that my value, exactly as I define it, should be acknowledged by others as well—but this is no vanity (but conceit or,

---

11. Literally "a good human being," the term is used for precisely the type described here.
12. "Gay science": in the early fourteenth century the term was used to designate the art of the troubadours, codified in *Leys d'amors.* Nietzsche subtitled his own *Fröhliche Wissenschaft* (1882), *"la gaya scienza,"* placed a quatrain on the title page, began the book with a fifteen-page "Prelude in German Rhymes," and in the second edition (1887) added, besides a Preface and Book V, an "Appendix" of further verses.

more frequently, what is called 'humility' or 'modesty')." Or: "For many reasons I may take pleasure in the good opinion of others: perhaps because I honor and love them and all their pleasures give me pleasure; perhaps also because their good opinion confirms and strengthens my faith in my own good opinion; perhaps because the good opinion of others, even in cases where I do not share it, is still useful to me or promises to become so—but all that is not vanity."

The noble human being must force himself, with the aid of history, to recognize that, since time immemorial, in all somehow dependent social strata the common man *was* only what he was *considered:* not at all used to positing values himself, he also attached no other value to himself than his masters attached to him (it is the characteristic *right of masters* to create values).

It may be understood as the consequence of an immense atavism that even now the ordinary man still always *waits* for an opinion about himself and then instinctively submits to that—but by no means only a "good" opinion; also a bad and unfair one (consider, for example, the great majority of the self-estimates and self-underestimates that believing women accept from their father-confessors, and believing Christians quite generally from their church).

In accordance with the slowly arising democratic order of things (and its cause, the intermarriage of masters and slaves), the originally noble and rare urge to ascribe value to oneself on one's own and to "think well" of oneself will actually be encouraged and spread more and more now; but it is always opposed by an older, ampler, and more deeply ingrained propensity—and in the phenomenon of "vanity" this older propensity masters the younger one. The vain person is delighted by *every* good opinion he hears of himself (quite apart from all considerations of its utility, and also apart from truth or falsehood), just as every bad opinion of him pains him: for he submits to both, he *feels* subjected to them in accordance with that oldest instinct of submission that breaks out in him.

It is "the slave" in the blood of the vain person, a residue of the slave's craftiness—and how much "slave" is still residual in woman, for example!—that seeks to *seduce* him to good opinions about himself; it is also the slave who afterwards immediately prostrates himself before these opinions as if he had not called them forth.

And to say it once more: vanity is an atavism.

270

The spiritual haughtiness and nausea of every man who has suffered profoundly—it almost determines the order of rank *how* profoundly human beings can suffer—his shuddering certainty, which permeates and colors him through and through, that by virtue of his suffering he *knows more* than the cleverest and wisest could possibly know, and that he knows his way and has once been "at home" in many distant, terrifying worlds of which "*you* know nothing"—this spiritual and silent haughtiness of the sufferer, this pride of the elect of knowledge, of the "initiated," of the almost sacrificed, finds all kinds of disguises necessary to protect itself against contact with obtrusive and pitying hands and altogether against everything that is not its equal in suffering. Profound suffering makes noble; it separates.

One of the most refined disguises is Epicureanism, and a certain ostentatious courage of taste which takes suffering casually and resists everything sad and profound. There are "cheerful people" who employ cheerfulness because they are misunderstood on its account—they *want* to be misunderstood. There are "scientific men" who employ science because it creates a cheerful appearance, and because being scientific suggests that a human being is superficial—they *want* to seduce others to this false inference. There are free, insolent spirits who would like to conceal and deny that they are broken, proud, incurable hearts (the cynicism of Hamlet—that case of Galiani),[13] and occasionally even foolishness is the mask for an unblessed all-too-certain knowledge.

From which it follows that it is characteristic of more refined humanity to respect "the mask" and not to indulge in psychology and curiosity in the wrong place.

13. The parenthesis is not found in the first four editions, but in most subsequent editions, including Schlechta's. In *Nietzsche contra Wagner* we read, instead of the parenthesis: "—the case of Hamlet."

Problems

1. Compare and contrast Nietzsche and the previous value systems in the light of Nietzsche's remark that "the falseness of a judgment is for us not necessarily an objection. . . . The question is to what extent it is life-promoting, life-preserving, species-preserving, perhaps even species-cultivating" (637/16-19).
2. Why does Nietzsche propose to apply a "knife . . . to the chest of the very virtues" of our time (640/28)?
3. What are master morality and slave morality? How do they manifest themselves in behavior? Which do you tend to prefer? Why? Analyze the other value systems from this new perspective.

from The Genealogy of Morals

FIRST ESSAY

10

The slave revolt in morality begins when *ressentiment* [1] itself becomes creative and gives birth to values: the *ressentiment* of natures that are denied the true reaction, that of deeds, and compensate themselves with an imaginary revenge. While every noble morality develops from a triumphant affirmation of itself, slave morality from the outset says No to what is "outside," what is "different," what is "not itself"; and *this* No is its creative deed. This inversion of the value-positing eye—this *need* to direct one's view outward instead of back to oneself—is of the essence of *ressentiment:* in order to exist, slave morality always first needs a hostile external world; it needs, physiologically speaking, external stimuli in order to act at all—its action is fundamentally reaction.

The reverse is the case with the noble mode of valuation: it acts and grows spontaneously, it seeks its opposite only so as to affirm itself more gratefully and triumphantly—its negative concept "low," "common," "bad" is only a subsequently-invented pale, contrasting image in relation to its positive basic concept—filled with life and passion through and through—"we noble ones, we good, beautiful, happy ones!" When the noble mode of valuation blunders and sins against reality, it does so in respect to the sphere with which it is *not* sufficiently familiar, against a real knowledge of which it has indeed inflexibly guarded itself: in some circumstances it misunderstands the sphere it despises, that of the common man, of the lower orders; on the other hand, one should remember that, even supposing that the affect of contempt, of looking down from a superior height, *falsifies* the image of that which it despises, it will at any rate still be a much less serious falsification than that perpetrated on its opponent—*in effigie* of course—by the submerged hatred, the vengefulness of the impotent. There is indeed too much carelessness, too much taking lightly, too much looking away and impatience involved in contempt, even too much joyfulness, for it to be able to transform its object into a real caricature and monster.

One should not overlook the almost benevolent nuances that the Greek nobility, for example, bestows on all the words it employs to

From Friedrich Nietzsche, *The Genealogy of Morals* (New York: Random House, Inc., 1967), pp. 36–129.
1. Resentment. [See Dictionary: *ressentiment*.]

distinguish the lower orders from itself; how they are continuously mingled and sweetened with a kind of pity, consideration, and forbearance, so that finally almost all the words referring to the common man have remained as expressions signifying "unhappy," "pitiable" (compare *deilos*,[2] *deilaios*,[3] *ponēros*,[4] *mochthēros*,[5] the last two of which properly designate the common man as work-slave and beast of burden)—and how on the other hand "bad," "low," "unhappy" have never ceased to sound to the Greek ear as one note with a tone-color in which "unhappy" preponderates: this as an inheritance from the ancient nobler aristocratic mode of evaluation, which does not belie itself even in its contempt (—philologists should recall the sense in which *oïzyros*,[6] *anolbos*,[7] *tlēmōn*,[8] *dystychein*,[9] *xymphora*[10] are employed). The "well-born" *felt* themselves to be the "happy"; they did not have to establish their happiness artificially by examining their enemies, or to persuade themselves, *deceive* themselves, that they were happy (as all men of *ressentiment* are in the habit of doing); and they likewise knew, as rounded men replete with energy and therefore *necessarily* active, that happiness should not be sundered from action—being active was with them necessarily a part of happiness (whence *eu prattein*[11] takes its origin)—all very much the opposite of "happiness" at the level of the impotent, the oppressed, and those in whom poisonous and inimical feelings are festering, with whom it appears as essentially narcotic, drug, rest, peace, "sabbath," slackening of tension and relaxing of limbs, in short *passively*.

While the noble man lives in trust and openness with himself (*gennaios*[12] "of noble descent" underlines the nuance "upright" and probably also "naïve"), the man of *ressentiment* is neither upright nor naïve nor honest and straightforward with himself. His soul *squints;* his spirit loves hiding places, secret paths and back doors, everything covert entices him as *his* world, *his* security, *his* refreshment; he understands how to keep silent, how not to forget, how to wait, how to be provisionally self-deprecating and humble. A race of such men of *ressentiment* is bound to become eventually *cleverer* than any noble race; it will also honor cleverness to a far greater degree: namely, as a condition of

2. All of the footnoted words in this section are Greek. The first four mean *wretched,* but each has a separate note to suggest some of its other connotations. *Deilos:* cowardly, worthless, vile.
3. Paltry.
4. Oppressed by toils, good for nothing, worthless, knavish, base, cowardly.
5. Suffering hardship, knavish.
6. Woeful, miserable, toilsome; wretch.
7. Unblest, wretched, luckless, poor.
8. Wretched, miserable.
9. To be unlucky, unfortunate.
10. Misfortune.
11. To do well in the sense of faring well.
12. High-born, noble, high-minded.

existence of the first importance; while with noble men cleverness can easily acquire a subtle flavor of luxury and subtlety—for here it is far less essential than the perfect functioning of the regulating *unconscious* instincts or even than a certain imprudence, perhaps a bold recklessness whether in the face of danger or of the enemy, or that enthusiastic impulsiveness in anger, love, reverence, gratitude, and revenge by which noble souls have at all times recognized one another. *Ressentiment* itself, if it should appear in the noble man, consummates and exhausts itself in an immediate reaction, and therefore does not *poison:* on the other hand, it fails to appear at all on countless occasions on which it inevitably appears in the weak and impotent.

To be incapable of taking one's enemies, one's accidents, even one's misdeeds seriously for very long—that is the sign of strong, full natures in whom there is an excess of the power to form, to mold, to recuperate and to forget (a good example of this in modern times is Mirabeau,[13] who had no memory for insults and vile actions done him and was unable to forgive simply because he—forgot). Such a man shakes off with a *single* shrug much vermin that eats deep into others; here alone genuine "love of one's enemies" is possible—supposing it to be possible at all on earth. How much reverence has a noble man for his enemies!—and such reverence is a bridge to love.—For he desires his enemy for himself, as his mark of distinction; he can endure no other enemy than one in whom there is nothing to despise and *very much* to honor! In contrast to this, picture "the enemy" as the man of *ressentiment* conceives him—and here precisely is his deed, his creation: he has conceived "the evil enemy," *"the Evil One,"* and this in fact is his basic concept, from which he then evolves, as an afterthought and pendant, a "good one"—himself!

11

This, then, is quite the contrary of what the noble man does, who conceives the basic concept "good" in advance and spontaneously out of himself and only then creates for himself an idea of "bad"! This "bad" of noble origin and that "evil" out of the cauldron of unsatisfied hatred—the former an after-production, a side issue, a contrasting shade, the latter on the contrary the original thing, the beginning, the distinctive *deed* in the conception of a slave morality—how different these words "bad" and "evil" are, although they are both apparently the opposite of the same concept "good." But it is *not* the same concept "good": one should ask rather precisely *who* is "evil" in the sense of the morality of *ressentiment*. The answer, in all strictness, is: *precisely* the "good man" of the other morality, precisely the noble, powerful man, the

---

13. Honoré Gabriel Riqueti, Comte de Mirabeau (1749–91), was a celebrated French Revolutionary statesman and writer.

ruler, but dyed in another color, interpreted in another fashion, seen in another way by the venomous eye of *ressentiment*.

Here there is one thing we shall be the last to deny: he who knows these "good men" only as enemies knows only *evil enemies,* and the same men who are held so sternly in check *inter pares* [14] by custom, respect, usage, gratitude, and even more by mutual suspicion and jealousy, and who on the other hand in their relations with one another show themselves so resourceful in consideration, self-control, delicacy, loyalty, pride, and friendship—once they go outside, where the strange, the *stranger* is found, they are not much better than uncaged beasts of prey. There they savor a freedom from all social constraints, they compensate themselves in the wilderness for the tension engendered by protracted confinement and enclosure within the peace of society, they go *back* to the innocent conscience of the beast of prey, as triumphant monsters who perhaps emerge from a disgusting procession of murder, arson, rape, and torture, exhilarated and undisturbed of soul, as if it were no more than a students' prank, convinced they have provided the poets with a lot more material for song and praise. One cannot fail to see at the bottom of all these noble races the beast of prey, the splendid *blond beast* [15] prowling about avidly in search of spoil and victory; this hidden core needs to erupt from time to time, the animal has to get out again

14. Among equals.
15. This is the first appearance in Nietzsche's writings of the notorious "blond beast." It is encountered twice more in the present section; a variant appears in section 17 of the second essay; and then the *blonde Bestie* appears once more in *Twilight,* "The 'Improvers' of Mankind," section 2. That is all. For a detailed discussion of these passages see Kaufmann's *Nietzsche,* Chapter 7, section III: ". . . The 'blond beast' is not a racial concept and does not refer to the 'Nordic race' of which the Nazis later made so much. Nietzsche specifically refers to Arabs and Japanese . . . —and the 'blondness' presumably refers to the beast, the lion."

Francis Golffing, in his free translation of the *Genealogy,* deletes the blond beast three times out of four; only where it appears the second time in the original text, he has "the blond Teutonic beast." This helps to corroborate the myth that the blondness refers to the Teutons. Without the image of the lion, however, we lose not only some of Nietzsche's poetry as well as any chance to understand one of his best known coinages; we also lose an echo of the crucial first chapter of *Zarathustra,* where the lion represents the second stage in "The Three Metamorphoses" of the spirit—above the obedient camel but below the creative child.

Arthur Danto has suggested that if lions were black and Nietzsche had written "Black Beast," the expression would "provide support for African instead of German nationalists" (*Nietzsche as Philosopher,* New York, Macmillan, 1965, p. 170). Panthers *are* black and magnificent animals, but anyone calling Negroes black beasts and associating them with "a disgusting procession of murder, arson, rape, and torture," adding that "the animal has to get out again and go back to the wilderness," and then going on to speak of "their hair-raising cheerfulness and profound joy in all destruction," would scarcely be taken to "provide support for . . . nationalists." On the contrary, he would be taken for a highly prejudiced critic of the Negro.

No other German writer of comparable stature has been a more extreme critic of German nationalism than Nietzsche. For all that, it is plain that in this section he sought to describe the behavior of the ancient Greeks and Romans, the Goths and the Vandals, not that of nineteenth-century Germans.

and go back to the wilderness: the Roman, Arabian, Germanic, Japanese nobility, the Homeric heroes, the Scandinavian Vikings—they all shared this need.

It is the noble races that have left behind them the concept "barbarian" wherever they have gone; even their highest culture betrays a consciousness of it and even a pride in it (for example, when Pericles says to his Athenians in his famous funeral oration "our boldness has gained access to every land and sea, everywhere raising imperishable monuments to its goodness *and wickedness*"). This "boldness" of noble races, mad, absurd, and sudden in its expression, the incalculability, even incredibility of their undertakings—Pericles specially commends the *rhathymia*[16] of the Athenians—their indifference to and contempt for security, body, life, comfort, their hair-raising cheerfulness and profound joy in all destruction, in all the voluptuousness of victory and cruelty—all this came together, in the minds of those who suffered from it, in the image of the "barbarian," the "evil enemy," perhaps as the "Goths," the "Vandals." The deep and icy mistrust the German still arouses today whenever he gets into a position of power is an echo of that inextinguishable horror with which Europe observed for centuries that raging of the blond Germanic beast (although between the old Germanic tribes and us Germans there exists hardly a conceptual relationship, let alone one of blood).

I once drew attention to the dilemma in which Hesiod found himself when he concocted his succession of cultural epochs and sought to express them in terms of gold, silver, and bronze: he knew no way of handling the contradiction presented by the glorious but at the same time terrible and violent world of Homer except by dividing one epoch into two epochs, which he then placed one behind the other—first the epoch of the heroes and demigods of Troy and Thebes, the form in which that world had survived in the memory of the noble races who were those heroes' true descendants, then the bronze epoch, the form in which that same world appeared to the descendants of the downtrodden, pillaged, mistreated, abducted, enslaved: an epoch of bronze, as aforesaid, hard, cold, cruel, devoid of feeling or conscience, destructive and bloody.

Supposing that what is at any rate believed to be the "truth" really is true, and the *meaning of all culture* is the reduction of the beast of prey "man" to a tame and civilized animal, a *domestic animal,* then one would undoubtedly have to regard all those instincts of reaction and *ressentiment* through whose aid the noble races and their ideals were finally confounded and overthrown as the actual *instruments of culture;*

16. Thucydides, 2.39. In *A Historical Commentary on Thucydides,* vol. II (Oxford, Clarendon Press, 1956; corrected imprint of 1966), p. 118, A. W. Gomme comments on this word: "in its original sense, 'ease of mind,' 'without anxiety' . . . But ease of mind can in certain circumstances become carelessness, remissness, frivolity: Demosthenes often accused the Athenians of *rhathymia* . . ."

which is not to say that the *bearers* of these instincts themselves represent culture. Rather is the reverse not merely probable—no! today it is *palpable!* These bearers of the oppressive instincts that thirst for reprisal, the descendants of every kind of European and non-European slavery, and especially of the entire pre-Aryan populace—they represent the *regression* of mankind! These "instruments of culture" are a disgrace to man and rather an accusation and counterargument against "culture" in general! One may be quite justified in continuing to fear the blond beast at the core of all noble races and in being on one's guard against it: but who would not a hundred times sooner fear where one can also admire than *not* fear but be permanently condemned to the repellent sight of the ill-constituted, dwarfed, atrophied, and poisoned? [17] And is that not *our* fate? What today constitutes *our* antipathy to "man"?—for we *suffer* from man, beyond doubt.

Not fear; rather that we no longer have anything left to fear in man; that the maggot [18] "man" is swarming in the foreground; that the "tame man," the hopelessly mediocre and insipid man, has already learned to feel himself as the goal and zenith, as the meaning of history, as "higher man"—that he has indeed a certain right to feel thus, insofar as he feels himself elevated above the surfeit of ill-constituted, sickly, weary and exhausted people of which Europe is beginning to stink today, as something at least relatively well-constituted, at least still capable of living, at least affirming life.

13

But let us return: the problem of the *other* origin of the "good," of the good as conceived by the man of *ressentiment,* demands its solution.

That lambs dislike great birds of prey does not seem strange: only it gives no ground for reproaching these birds of prey for bearing off little lambs. And if the lambs say among themselves: "these birds of prey are evil; and whoever is least like a bird of prey, but rather its opposite, a lamb—would he not be good?" there is no reason to find fault with this institution of an ideal, except perhaps that the birds of prey might view it a little ironically and say: *"we* don't dislike them at all, these good little lambs; we even love them: nothing is more tasty than a tender lamb."

17. If the present section is not clear enough to any reader, he might turn to *Zarathustra's* contrast of the *overman* and the *last man* (Prologue, sections 3–5) and, for good measure, read also the first chapter or two of Part One. Then he will surely see how Aldous Huxley's *Brave New World* and George Orwell's *1984*—but especially the former—are developments of Nietzsche's theme. Huxley, in his novel, uses Shakespeare as a foil; Nietzsche, in the passage above, Homer.
18. *Gewürm* suggests wormlike animals; *wimmelt* can mean swarm or crawl but is particularly associated with maggots—in a cheese, for example.

To demand of strength that it should *not* express itself as strength, that it should *not* be a desire to overcome, a desire to throw down, a desire to become master, a thirst for enemies and resistances and triumphs, is just as absurd as to demand of weakness that it should express itself as strength. A quantum of force is equivalent to a quantum of drive, will, effect—more, it is nothing other than precisely this very driving, willing, effecting, and only owing to the seduction of language (and of the fundamental errors of reason that are petrified in it) which conceives and misconceives all effects as conditioned by something that causes effects, by a "subject," can it appear otherwise. For just as the popular mind separates the lightning from its flash and takes the latter for an *action,* for the operation of a subject called lightning, so popular morality also separates strength from expressions of strength, as if there were a neutral substratum behind the strong man, which was *free* to express strength or not to do so. But there is no such substratum; there is no "being" behind doing, effecting, becoming; "the doer" is merely a fiction added to the deed—the deed is everything. The popular mind in fact doubles the deed; when it sees the lightning flash, it is the deed of a deed: it posits the same event first as cause and then a second time as its effect. Scientists do no better when they say "force moves," "force causes," and the like—all its coolness, its freedom from emotion notwithstanding, our entire science still lies under the misleading influence of language and has not disposed of that little changeling, the "subject" (the atom, for example, is such a changeling, as is the Kantian "thing-in-itself"); no wonder if the submerged, darkly glowering emotions of vengefulness and hatred exploit this belief for their own ends and in fact maintain no belief more ardently than the belief that *the strong man is free* to be weak and the bird of prey to be a lamb—for thus they gain the right to make the bird of prey *accountable* for being a bird of prey.

When the oppressed, downtrodden, outraged exhort one another with the vengeful cunning of impotence: "let us be different from the evil, namely good! And he is good who does not outrage, who harms nobody, who does not attack, who does not requite, who leaves revenge to God, who keeps himself hidden as we do, who avoids evil and desires little from life, like us, the patient, humble, and just"—this, listened to calmly and without previous bias, really amounts to no more than: "we weak ones are, after all, weak; it would be good if we did nothing *for which we are not strong enough*"; but this dry matter of fact, this prudence of the lowest order which even insects possess (posing as dead, when in great danger, so as not to do "too much"), has, thanks to the counterfeit and self-deception of impotence, clad itself in the ostentatious garb of the virtue of quiet, calm resignation, just as if the weakness of the weak—that is to say, their *essence,* their effects, their sole ineluctable, irremovable reality—were a voluntary achievement, willed, chosen, a *deed,* a *merito-*

rious act. This type of man *needs* to believe in a neutral independent "subject," prompted by an instinct for self-preservation and self-affirmation in which every lie is sanctified. The subject (or, to use a more popular expression, the *soul*) has perhaps been believed in hitherto more firmly than anything else on earth because it makes possible to the majority of mortals, the weak and oppressed of every kind, the sublime self-deception that interprets weakness as freedom, and their being thus-and-thus as a *merit*.

14

Would anyone like to take a look into the secret of how *ideals are made* on earth? Who has the courage?—Very well! Here is a point we can see through into this dark workshop. But wait a moment or two, Mr. Rash and Curious: your eyes must first get used to this false iridescent light.—All right! Now speak! What is going on down there? Say what you see, man of the most perilous kind of inquisitiveness—now I am the one who is listening.—

—"I see nothing, but I hear the more. There is a soft, wary, malignant muttering and whispering coming from all the corners and nooks. It seems to me one is lying; a saccharine sweetness clings to every sound. Weakness is being lied into something *meritorious,* no doubt of it—so it is just as you said"—

—Go on!

—"and impotence which does not requite into 'goodness of heart'; anxious lowliness into 'humility'; subjection to those one hates into 'obedience' (that is, to one of whom they say he commands this subjection—they call him God). The inoffensiveness of the weak man, even the cowardice of which he has so much, his lingering at the door, his being ineluctably compelled to wait, here acquire flattering names, such as 'patience,' and are even called virtue itself; his inability for revenge is called unwillingness to revenge, perhaps even forgiveness ('for *they* know not what they do—we alone know what *they* do!'). They also speak of 'loving one's enemies'—and sweat as they do so."

—Go on!

—"They are miserable, no doubt of it, all these mutterers and nook counterfeiters, although they crouch warmly together—but they tell me their misery is a sign of being chosen by God; one beats the dogs one likes best; perhaps this misery is also a preparation, a testing, a schooling, perhaps it is even more—something that will one day be made good and recompensed with interest, with huge payments of gold, no! of happiness. This they call 'bliss.' "

—Go on!

—"Now they give me to understand that they are not merely better than the mighty, the lords of the earth whose spittle they have to lick (*not* from fear, not at all from fear! but because God has commanded them to obey the authorities) [19]—that they are not merely better but are also 'better off,' or at least will be better off someday. But enough! enough! I can't take any more. Bad air! Bad air! This workshop where *ideals are manufactured*—it seems to me it stinks of so many lies."

—No! Wait a moment! You have said nothing yet of the masterpiece of these black magicians, who make whiteness, milk, and innocence of every blackness—haven't you noticed their perfection of refinement, their boldest, subtlest, most ingenious, most mendacious artistic stroke? Attend to them! These cellar rodents full of vengefulness and hatred—what have they made of revenge and hatred? Have you heard these words uttered? If you trusted simply to their words, would you suspect you were among men of *ressentiment?* . . .

—"I understand; I'll open my ears again (oh! oh! oh! and *close* my nose). Now I can really hear what they have been saying all along: 'We good men—*we are the just*'—what they desire they call, not retaliation, but 'the triumph of *justice*'; what they hate is not their enemy, no! they hate 'injustice,' they hate 'godlessness'; what they believe in and hope for is not the hope of revenge, the intoxication of sweet revenge (—'sweeter than honey' Homer called it), but the victory of God, of the *just* God, over the godless; what there is left for them to love on earth is not their brothers in hatred but their 'brothers in love,' as they put it, all the good and just on earth."

—And what do they call that which serves to console them for all the suffering of life—their phantasmagoria of anticipated future bliss?

—"What? Do I hear aright? They call that 'the Last Judgment,' the coming of *their* kingdom, of the 'Kingdom of God'—meanwhile, however, they live 'in faith,' 'in love,' 'in hope.'"

—Enough! Enough!

SECOND ESSAY

2

This precisely is the long story of how *responsibility* originated. The task of breeding an animal with the right to make promises evidently embraces and presupposes as a preparatory task that one first *makes* men to a certain degree necessary, uniform, like among like, regular, and consequently calculable. The tremendous labor of that which I have called "morality of mores" (*Dawn,* sections 9, 14, 16)—the labor performed by man upon himself during the greater part of the existence of the human race, his entire *prehistoric* labor, finds in this its meaning,

---

19. Allusion to Romans 13:1–2.

its great justification, notwithstanding the severity, tyranny, stupidity, and idiocy involved in it: with the aid of the morality of mores and the social straitjacket, man was actually *made* calculable.

If we place ourselves at the end of this tremendous process, where the tree at last brings forth fruit, where society and the morality of custom at last reveal *what* they have simply been the means to: then we discover that the ripest fruit is the sovereign individual, like only to himself, liberated again from morality of custom, autonomous and supramoral (for "autonomous" and "moral" are mutually exclusive),[20] in short, the man who has his own independent, protracted will and the *right to make promises*—and in him a proud consciousness, quivering in every muscle, of *what* has at length been achieved and become flesh in him, a consciousness of his own power and freedom, a sensation of mankind come to completion. This emancipated individual, with the actual *right* to make promises, this master of a *free* will, this sovereign man—how should he not be aware of his superiority over all those who lack the right to make promises and stand as their own guarantors, of how much trust, how much fear, how much reverence he arouses—he *"deserves"* all three—and of how this mastery over himself also necessarily gives him mastery over circumstances, over nature, and over all more short-willed and unreliable creatures? The "free" man, the possessor of a protracted and unbreakable will, also possesses his *measure of values:* looking out upon others from himself, he honors or he despises; and just as he is bound to honor his peers, the strong and reliable (those with the *right* to make promises)—that is, all those who promise like sovereigns, reluctantly, rarely, slowly, who are chary of trusting, whose trust is a mark of *distinction,* who give their word as something that can be relied on because they know themselves strong enough to maintain it in the face of accidents, even "in the face of fate"—he is bound to reserve a kick for the feeble windbags who promise without the right to do so, and a rod for the liar who breaks his word even at the moment he utters it. The proud awareness of the extraordinary privilege of *responsibility,* the consciousness of this rare freedom, this power over oneself and over fate, has in his case penetrated to the profoundest depths and become instinct, the dominating instinct. What will he call this dominating instinct, supposing he feels the need to give it a name? The answer is beyond doubt: this sovereign man calls it his *conscience.*

20. The parenthetical statement is the contrary of Kant's view. When it was written, it must have struck most readers as paradoxical, but in the twentieth century it is apt to seem *less* paradoxical than Kant's view. *The Lonely Crowd* (by David Riesman, with Nathan Glazer and Reuel Denney; New Haven, Conn.: Yale University Press, 1950) has popularized a Nietzschean, non-Kantian conception of the autonomous individual, who is contrasted with the tradition-directed (Nietzsche's morality of mores), the inner-directed (Kant, for example), and the other-directed (Nietzsche's "last man").

4

But how did that other "somber thing," the consciousness of guilt, the "bad conscience," come into the world?—And at this point we return to the genealogists of morals. To say it again—or haven't I said it yet?—they are worthless. A brief span of experience that is merely one's own, merely modern; no knowledge or will to knowledge of the past; even less of historical instinct, of that "second sight" needed here above all—and yet they undertake history of morality: it stands to reason that their results stay at a more than respectful distance from the truth. Have these genealogists of morals had even the remotest suspicion that, for example, the major moral concept *Schuld* [guilt] has its origin in the very material concept *Schulden* [debts]? [21] Or that punishment, as requital, evolved quite independently of any presupposition concerning freedom or non-freedom of the will?—to such an extent, indeed, that a *high* degree of humanity had to be attained before the animal "man" began even to make the much more primitive distinctions between "intentional," "negligent," "accidental," "accountable," and their opposites and to take them into account when determining punishments. The idea, now so obvious, apparently so natural, even unavoidable, that had to serve as the explanation of how the sense of justice ever appeared on earth—"the criminal deserves punishment *because* he could have acted differently"—is in fact an extremely late and subtle form of human judgment and inference: whoever transposes it to the beginning is guilty of a crude misunderstanding of the psychology of more primitive mankind. Throughout the greater part of human history punishment was *not* imposed *because* one held the wrongdoer responsible for his deed, thus *not* on the presupposition that only the guilty one should be punished: rather, as parents still punish their children, from anger at some harm or injury, vented on the one who caused it—but this anger is held in check and modified by the idea that every injury has its *equivalent* and can actually be paid back, even if only through the *pain* of the culprit. And whence did this primeval, deeply rooted, perhaps by now ineradicable idea draw its power—this idea of an equivalence between injury and pain? I have already divulged it: in the contractual relationship between *creditor* and *debtor,* which is as old as the idea of "legal subjects" and in turn points back to the fundamental forms of buying, selling, barter, trade, and traffic.

21. The German equivalent of "guilt" is *Schuld;* and the German for "debt(s)" is *Schuld(en)*. "Innocent" is *unschuldig;* "debtor" is *Schuldner;* and so forth. This obviously poses problems for an English translation of this essay; but once the point has been clearly stated, no misunderstandings need result. Nietzsche's claims obviously do not *depend* on the double meaning of a German word; nor are they weakened by the fact that in English there are two different words, one derived from an Anglo-Saxon root, the other from Latin.

8

To return to our investigation: the feeling of guilt, of personal obligation, had its origin, as we saw, in the oldest and most primitive personal relationship, that between buyer and seller, creditor and debtor: it was here that one person first encountered another person, that one person first *measured himself* against another. No grade of civilization, however low, has yet been discovered in which something of this relationship has not been noticeable. Setting prices, determining values, contriving equivalences, exchanging—these preoccupied the earliest thinking of man to so great an extent that in a certain sense they constitute thinking *as such:* here it was that the oldest kind of astuteness developed; here likewise, we may suppose, did human pride, the feeling of superiority in relation to other animals, have its first beginnings. Perhaps our word "man" (*manas*) still expresses something of precisely *this* feeling of self-satisfaction: man designated himself as the creature that measures values, evaluates and measures, as the "valuating animal as such."

Buying and selling, together with their psychological appurtenances, are older even than the beginnings of any kind of social forms of organization and alliances: it was rather out of the most rudimentary form of personal legal rights that the budding sense of exchange, contract, guilt, right, obligation, settlement, first *transferred* itself to the coarsest and most elementary social complexes (in their relations with other similar complexes), together with the custom of comparing, measuring, and calculating power against power. The eye was now focused on this perspective; and with that blunt consistency characteristic of the thinking of primitive mankind, which is hard to set in motion but then proceeds inexorably in the same direction, one forthwith arrived at the great generalization, "everything has its price; *all* things can be paid for"—the oldest and naïvest moral canon of *justice,* the beginning of all "good-naturedness," all "fairness," all "good will," all "objectivity" on earth. Justice on this elementary level is the good will among parties of approximately equal power to come to terms with one another, to reach an "understanding" by means of a settlement—and to *compel* parties of lesser power to reach a settlement among themselves.—

9

Still retaining the criteria of prehistory (this prehistory is in any case present in all ages or may always reappear) [22]: the community, too, stands to its members in that same vital basic relation, that of the creditor to his debtors. One lives in a community, one enjoys the ad-

22. A prophetic parenthesis.

vantages of a communality (oh what advantages! we sometimes underrate them today), one dwells protected, cared for, in peace and trustfulness, without fear of certain injuries and hostile acts to which the man *outside,* the "man without peace," is exposed—a German will understand the original connotations of *Elend*[23]—since one has bound and pledged oneself to the community precisely with a view to injuries and hostile acts. What will happen *if this pledge is broken?* The community, the disappointed creditor, will get what repayment it can, one may depend on that. The direct harm caused by the culprit is here a minor matter; quite apart from this, the lawbreaker is above all a "breaker," a breaker of his contract and his word *with the whole* in respect to all the benefits and comforts of communal life of which he has hitherto had a share. The lawbreaker is a debtor who has not merely failed to make good the advantages and advance payments bestowed upon him but has actually attacked his creditor: therefore he is not only deprived henceforth of all these advantages and benefits, as is fair—he is also reminded *what these benefits are really worth.* The wrath of the disappointed creditor, the community, throws him back again into the savage and outlaw state against which he has hitherto been protected: it thrusts him away—and now every kind of hostility may be vented upon him. "Punishment" at this level of civilization is simply a copy, a *mimus,* of the normal attitude toward a hated, disarmed, prostrated enemy, who has lost not only every right and protection, but all hope of quarter as well; it is thus the rights of war and the victory celebration of the *vae victis!*[24] in all their mercilessness and cruelty—which explains why it is that war itself (including the warlike sacrificial cult) has provided all the *forms* that punishment has assumed throughout history.

10

As its power increases, a community ceases to take the individual's transgressions so seriously, because they can no longer be considered as dangerous and destructive to the whole as they were formerly: the malefactor is no longer "set beyond the pale of peace" and thrust out; universal anger may not be vented upon him as unrestrainedly as before—on the contrary, the whole from now on carefully defends the malefactor against this anger, especially that of those he has directly harmed, and takes him under its protection. A compromise with the anger of those directly injured by the criminal; an effort to localize the affair and to prevent it from causing any further, let alone a general, disturbance; attempts to discover equivalents and to settle the whole matter

23. Misery. Originally, exile.
24. Woe to the losers!

(*compositio*); above all, the increasingly definite will to treat every crime as in some sense *dischargeable,* and thus at least to a certain extent to *isolate* the criminal and his deed from one another—these traits become more and more clearly visible as the penal law evolves. As the power and self-confidence of a community increase, the penal law always becomes more moderate; every weakening or imperiling of the former brings with it a restoration of the harsher forms of the latter. The "creditor" always becomes more humane to the extent that he has grown richer; finally, how much injury he can endure without suffering from it becomes the actual *measure* of his wealth. It is not unthinkable that a society might attain such a *consciousness of power* that it could allow itself the noblest luxury possible to it—letting those who harm it go *unpunished*. "What are my parasites to me?" it might say. "May they live and prosper: I am strong enough for that!"

The justice which began with, "everything is dischargeable, everything must be discharged," ends by winking and letting those incapable of discharging their debt go free: it ends, as does every good thing on earth, by *overcoming itself*.[25] This self-overcoming of justice: one knows the beautiful name it has given itself—*mercy;* it goes without saying that mercy remains the privilege of the most powerful man, or better, his— beyond the law.[26]

11

Here a word in repudiation of attempts that have lately been made to seek the origin of justice in quite a different sphere—namely in that of *ressentiment.* To the psychologists first of all, presuming they would like to study *ressentiment* close up for once, I would say: this plant blooms best today among anarchists and anti-Semites—where it has always bloomed, in hidden places, like the violet, though with a different odor. And as like must always produce like, it causes us no surprise to see a repetition in such circles of attempts often made before— see above, section 14—to sanctify *revenge* under the name of *justice*—as if justice were at bottom merely a further development of the feeling of

---

25. *Sich selbst aufhebend.* And in the next sentence *Selbstaufhebung* has been translated as self-overcoming.
26. The theme sounded here is one of the central motifs of Nietzsche's philosophy ". . . Let us eliminate the concept of *sin* from the world—and let us soon dispatch the concept of *punishment* after it! May these exiled monsters live somewhere else henceforth and not among men—if they insist on living and will not perish of disgust with themselves! . . . Shouldn't we be mature enough yet for the opposite view? Shouldn't we be able to say yet: every 'guilty' person is sick?—No, the hour for that has not yet come. As yet the physicians are lacking above all . . . As yet no thinker has had the courage of measuring the health of a society and of individuals according to how many parasites they can stand . . ."

being aggrieved—and to rehabilitate not only revenge but all *reactive affects* in general. To the latter as such I would be the last to raise any objection: in respect to the entire biological problem (in relation to which the value of these affects has hitherto been underrated) it even seems to me to constitute a *service*. All I draw attention to is the circumstance that it is the spirit of *ressentiment* itself out of which the new nuance of scientific fairness (for the benefit of hatred, envy, jealousy, mistrust, rancor, and revenge) proceeds. For this "scientific fairness" immediately ceases and gives way to accents of deadly enmity and prejudice once it is a question of dealing with another group of affects, affects that, it seems to me, are of even greater biological value than those reactive affects and consequently deserve even more to be *scientifically* evaluated and esteemed: namely, the truly *active* affects, such as lust for power, avarice, and the like. (E. Dühring: [27] *The Value of Life; A Course in Philosophy;* and, fundamentally, *passim.*)

So much against this tendency in general: as for Dühring's specific proposition that the home of justice is to be sought in the sphere of the reactive feelings, one is obliged for truth's sake to counter it with a blunt antithesis: the *last* sphere to be conquered by the spirit of justice is the sphere of the reactive feelings! When it really happens that the just man remains just even toward those who have harmed him (and not merely cold, temperate, remote, indifferent: being just is always a *positive* attitude), when the exalted, clear objectivity, as penetrating as it is mild, of the eye of justice and *judging* is not dimmed even under the assault of personal injury, derision, and calumny, this is a piece of perfection and supreme mastery on earth—something it would be prudent not to expect or to *believe* in too readily. On the average, a small dose of aggression, malice, or insinuation certainly suffices to drive the blood into the eyes—and fairness out of the eyes—of even the most upright people. The active, aggressive, arrogant man is still a hundred steps closer to justice than the reactive man; for he has absolutely no need to take a false and prejudiced view of the object before him in the way the reactive man does and is bound to do. For that reason the aggressive man, as the stronger, nobler, more courageous, has in fact also had at all times a *freer* eye, a *better* conscience on his side: conversely, one can see who has the invention of the "bad conscience" on his conscience—the man of *ressentiment!*

Finally, one only has to look at history: in which sphere has the entire administration of law hitherto been at home—also the need for law? In the sphere of reactive men, perhaps? By no means: rather in

27. Eugen Dühring (1833–1901), a prolific German philosopher and political economist, was among other things an impassioned patriot and anti-Semite and hated the cosmopolitan Goethe and the Greeks. He is remembered chiefly as the butt of polemical works by Karl Marx and Friedrich Engels and of scattered hostile remarks in Nietzsche's writings.

that of the active, strong, spontaneous, aggressive. From a historical point of view, law represents on earth—let it be said to the dismay of the above-named agitator (who himself once confessed: "the doctrine of revenge is the red thread of justice that runs through all my work and efforts")—the struggle *against* the reactive feelings, the war conducted against them on the part of the active and aggressive powers who employed some of their strength to impose measure and bounds upon the excesses of the reactive pathos and to compel it to come to terms. Wherever justice is practiced and maintained one sees a stronger power seeking a means of putting an end to the senseless raging of *ressentiment* among the weaker powers that stand under it (whether they be groups or individuals)—partly by taking the object of *ressentiment* out of the hands of revenge, partly by substituting for revenge the struggle against the enemies of peace and order, partly by devising and in some cases imposing settlements, partly by elevating certain equivalents for injuries into norms to which from then on *ressentiment* is once and for all directed. The most decisive act, however, that the supreme power performs and accomplishes against the predominance of grudges and rancor—it always takes this action as soon as it is in any way strong enough to do so—is the institution of *law,* the imperative declaration of what in general counts as permitted, as just, in its eyes, and what counts as forbidden, as unjust; once it has instituted the law, it treats violence and capricious acts on the part of individuals or entire groups as offenses against the law, as rebellion against the supreme power itself, and thus leads the feelings of its subjects away from the direct injury caused by such offenses; and in the long run it thus attains the reverse of that which is desired by all revenge that is fastened exclusively to the viewpoint of the person injured: from now on the eye is trained to an ever more *impersonal* evaluation of the deed, and this applies even to the eye of the injured person himself (although last of all, as remarked above).

"Just" and "unjust" exist, accordingly, only after the institution of the law (and *not,* as Dühring would have it, after the perpetration of the injury). To speak of just or unjust *in itself* is quite senseless; *in itself,* of course, no injury, assault, exploitation, destruction can be "unjust," since life operates *essentially,* that is in its basic functions, through injury, assault, exploitation, destruction and simply cannot be thought of at all without this character. One must indeed grant something even more unpalatable: that, from the highest biological standpoint, legal conditions can never be other than *exceptional conditions,* since they constitute a partial restriction of the will of life, which is bent upon power, and are subordinate to its total goal as a single means: namely, as a means of creating *greater* units of power. A legal order thought of as sovereign and universal, not as a means in the struggle between power-complexes but as a means of *preventing* all struggle in general—perhaps after the communistic cliché of Dühring, that every will must consider every other will its equal—would be a principle *hostile to life,* an agent of the dissolution and destruction of man, an attempt to assassinate the future of man, a sign of weariness, a secret path to nothingness.—

16

At this point I can no longer avoid giving a first, provisional statement of my own hypothesis concerning the origin of the "bad conscience": it may sound rather strange and needs to be pondered, lived with, and slept on for a long time. I regard the bad conscience as the serious illness that man was bound to contract under the stress of the most fundamental change he ever experienced—that change which occurred when he found himself finally enclosed within the walls of society and of peace. The situation that faced sea animals when they were compelled to become land animals or perish was the same as that which faced these semi-animals, well adapted to the wilderness, to war, to prowling, to adventure: suddenly all their instincts were disvalued and "suspended." From now on they had to walk on their feet and "bear themselves" whereas hitherto they had been borne by the water: a dreadful heaviness lay upon them. They felt unable to cope with the simplest undertakings; in this new world they no longer possessed their former guides, their regulating, unconscious and infallible drives: they were reduced to thinking, inferring, reckoning, co-ordinating cause and effect, these unfortunate creatures; they were reduced to their "consciousness," their weakest and most fallible organ! I believe there has never been such a feeling of misery on earth, such a leaden discomfort—and at the same time the old instincts had not suddenly ceased to make their usual demands! Only it was hardly or rarely possible to humor them: as a rule they had to seek new and, as it were, subterranean gratifications.

All instincts that do not discharge themselves outwardly *turn inward*—this is what I call the *internalization* [28] of man: thus it was that man first developed what was later called his "soul." The entire inner world, originally as thin as if it were stretched between two membranes, expanded and extended itself, acquired depth, breadth, and height, in the same measure as outward discharge was *inhibited.* Those fearful bulwarks with which the political organization protected itself against the old instincts of freedom—punishments belong among these bulwarks—brought about that all those instincts of wild, free, prowling man turned backward *against man himself.* Hostility, cruelty, joy in persecuting, in attacking, in change, in destruction—all this turned against the possessors of such instincts: *that* is the origin of the "bad conscience."

28. *Verinnerlichung.* Cf. Freud.

The man who, from lack of external enemies and resistances and forcibly confined to the oppressive narrowness and punctiliousness of custom, impatiently lacerated, persecuted, gnawed at, assaulted, and maltreated himself; this animal that rubbed itself raw against the bars of its cage as one tried to "tame" it; this deprived creature, racked with homesickness for the wild, who had to turn himself into an adventure, a torture chamber, an uncertain and dangerous wilderness—this fool, this yearning and desperate prisoner became the inventor of the "bad conscience." But thus began the gravest and uncanniest illness, from which humanity has not yet recovered, man's suffering *of man, of himself*—the result of a forcible sundering from his animal past, as it were a leap and plunge into new surroundings and conditions of existence, a declaration of war against the old instincts upon which his strength, joy, and terribleness had rested hitherto.

Let us add at once that, on the other hand, the existence on earth of an animal soul turned against itself, taking sides against itself, was something so new, profound, unheard of, enigmatic, contradictory, *and pregnant with a future* that the aspect of the earth was essentially altered. Indeed, divine spectators were needed to do justice to the spectacle that thus began and the end of which is not yet in sight—a spectacle too subtle, too marvelous, too paradoxical to be played senselessly unobserved on some ludicrous planet! From now on, man is *included* among the most unexpected and exciting lucky throws in the dice game of Heraclitus' "great child," be he called Zeus or chance; he gives rise to an interest, a tension, a hope, almost a certainty, as if with him something were announcing and preparing itself, as if man were not a goal but only a way, an episode, a bridge, a great promise.—

17

Among the presuppositions of this hypothesis concerning the origin of the bad conscience is, first, that the change referred to was not a gradual or voluntary one and did not represent an organic adaptation to new conditions but a break, a leap, a compulsion, an ineluctable disaster which precluded all struggle and even all *ressentiment*. Secondly, however, that the welding of a hitherto unchecked and shapeless populace into a firm form was not only instituted by an act of violence but also carried to its conclusion by nothing but acts of violence—that the oldest "state" thus appeared as a fearful tyranny, as an oppressive and remorseless machine, and went on working until this raw material of people and semi-animals was at last not only thoroughly kneaded and pliant but also *formed*.

I employed the word "state": it is obvious what is meant—some pack of blond beasts of prey,[29] a conqueror and master race which, organized for war and with the ability to organize, unhesitatingly lays its terrible claws upon a populace perhaps tremendously superior in numbers but still formless and nomad. That is after all how the "state" began on earth: I think that sentimentalism which would have it begin with a "contract" has been disposed of. He who can command, he who is by nature "master," he who is violent in act and bearing—what has he to do with contracts!

20

History shows that the consciousness of being in debt to the deity did not by any means come to an end together with the organization of communities on the basis of blood relationship. Even as mankind inherited the concepts "good and bad" from the tribal nobility (along with its basic psychological propensity to set up orders of rank), it also inherited, along with the tribal and family divinities, the burden of still unpaid debts and of the desire to be relieved of them. (The transition is provided by those numerous slave and dependent populations who, whether through compulsion or through servility and mimicry, adapted themselves to their masters' cult of the gods: this inheritance then overflows from them in all directions.) The guilty feeling of indebtedness to the divinity continued to grow for several millennia—always in the same measure as the concept of God and the feeling for divinity increased on earth and was carried to the heights. (The entire history of ethnic struggle, victory, reconciliation, fusion, everything that precedes the definitive ordering of rank of the different national elements in every great racial synthesis, is reflected in the confused genealogies of their gods, in the sagas of the gods' struggles, victories, and reconciliations; the advance toward universal empires is always also an advance toward universal divinities; despotism with its triumph over the independent nobility always prepares the way for some kind of monotheism.)

The advent of the Christian God, as the maximum god attained so far, was therefore accompanied by the maximum feeling of guilty indebtedness on earth. Presuming we have gradually entered upon the *reverse* course, there is no small probability that with the irresistible decline of faith in the Christian God there is now also a considerable decline in mankind's feeling of guilt, indeed, the prospect cannot be dismissed that the complete and definitive victory of atheism might free mankind of this whole feeling of guilty indebtedness toward its origin, its *causa prima*. Atheism and a kind of *second innocence* belong together.—

29. *Irgendein Rudel blonder Raubtiere, eine Eroberer- und Herren-Rasse:* Francis Golffing, in his translation, spirits away both the blond beasts of prey and the master race by rendering these words "a pack of savages, a race of conquerors." Cf. section 11 of the first essay, above, with its three references to the *blonde Bestie.*

22

You will have guessed *what* has really happened here, *beneath* all this: that will to self-tormenting, that repressed cruelty of the animal-man made inward and scared back into himself, the creature imprisoned in the "state" so as to be tamed, who invented the bad conscience in order to hurt himself after the *more natural* vent for this desire to hurt had been blocked—this man of the bad conscience has seized upon the presupposition of religion so as to drive his self-torture to its most gruesome pitch of severity and rigor. Guilt before *God:* this thought becomes an instrument of torture to him. He apprehends in "God" the ultimate antithesis of his own ineluctable animal instincts; he reinterprets these animal instincts themselves as a form of guilt before God (as hostility, rebellion, insurrection against the "Lord," the "father," the primal ancestor and origin of the world); he stretches himself upon the contradiction "God" and "Devil"; he ejects from himself all his denial of himself, of his nature, naturalness, and actuality, in the form of an affirmation, as something existent, corporeal, real, as God, as the holiness of God, as God the Judge, as God the Hangman, as the beyond, as eternity, as torment without end, as hell, as the immeasurability of punishment and guilt.

In this psychical cruelty there resides a madness of the will which is absolutely unexampled: the *will* of man to find himself guilty and reprehensible to a degree that can never be atoned for; his *will* to think himself punished without any possibility of the punishment becoming equal to the guilt; his *will* to infect and poison the fundamental ground of things with the problem of punishment and guilt so as to cut off once and for all his own exit from this labyrinth of "fixed ideas"; his *will* to erect an ideal—that of the "holy God"—and in the face of it to feel the palpable certainty of his own absolute unworthiness. Oh this insane, pathetic beast—man! What ideas he has, what unnaturalness, what paroxysms of nonsense, what *bestiality of thought* erupts as soon as he is prevented just a little from being a *beast in deed!*

All this is interesting, to excess, but also of a gloomy, black, unnerving sadness, so that one must forcibly forbid oneself to gaze too long into these abysses. Here is *sickness,* beyond any doubt, the most terrible sickness that has ever raged in man; and whoever can still bear to hear (but today one no longer has ears for this!) how in this night of torment and absurdity there has resounded the cry of *love,* the cry of the most nostalgic rapture, of redemption through *love,* will turn away, seized by invincible horror.—There is so much in man that is hideous!—Too long, the earth has been a madhouse!—

24

I end up with three question marks; that seems plain. "What are you really doing, erecting an ideal or knocking one down?" I may perhaps be asked.

But have you ever asked yourselves sufficiently how much the erection of *every* ideal on earth has cost? How much reality has had to be misunderstood and slandered, how many lies have had to be sanctified, how many consciences disturbed, how much "God" sacrificed every time? If the temple is to be erected *a temple must be destroyed:* that is the law— let anyone who can show me a case in which it is not fulfilled!

We modern men are the heirs of the conscience-vivisection and self-torture [30] of millennia: this is what we have practiced longest, it is our distinctive art perhaps, and in any case our subtlety in which we have acquired a refined taste. Man has all too long had an "evil eye" for his natural inclinations, so that they have finally become inseparable from his "bad conscience." An attempt at the reverse would *in itself* be possible— but who is strong enough for it?—that is, to wed the bad conscience to all the *unnatural* inclinations, all those aspirations to the beyond, to that which runs counter to sense, instinct, nature, animal, in short all ideals hitherto, which are one and all hostile to life and ideals that slander the world. To whom should one turn today with *such* hopes and demands?

One would have precisely the *good* men against one; and, of course, the comfortable, the reconciled, the vain, the sentimental, the weary.

What gives greater offense, what separates one more fundamentally, than to reveal something of the severity and respect with which one treats oneself? And on the other hand—how accommodating, how friendly all the world is toward us as soon as we act as all the world does and "let ourselves go" like all the world!

The attainment of this goal would require a *different* kind of spirit from that likely to appear in this present age: spirits strengthened by war and victory, for whom conquest, adventure, danger, and even pain have become needs; it would require habituation to the keen air of the heights, to winter journeys, to ice and mountains in every sense; it would require even a kind of sublime wickedness, an ultimate, supremely self-confident mischievousness in knowledge that goes with great health; it would require, in brief and alas, precisely this *great health!*

Is this even possible today?—But some day, in a stronger age than this decaying, self-doubting present, he must yet come to us, the *redeeming*

---

30. *Selbsttierquälerei: Tierquälerei* really means cruelty to animals or, literally, animal torture; hence Nietzsche's coinage suggests that this kind of self-torture involves mortification of the animal nature of man.

man of great love and contempt, the creative spirit whose compelling strength will not let him rest in any aloofness or any beyond, whose isolation is misunderstood by the people as if it were flight *from* reality— while it is only his absorption, immersion, penetration *into* reality, so that, when he one day emerges again into the light, he may bring home the *redemption* of this reality: its redemption from the curse that the hitherto reigning ideal has laid upon it. This man of the future, who will redeem us not only from the hitherto reigning ideal but also from that which was bound to grow out of it, the great nausea, the will to nothingness, nihilism; this bell-stroke of noon and of the great decision that liberates the will again and restores its goal to the earth and his hope to man; this Antichrist and antinihilist; this victor over God and nothingness—*he must come one day.*—

THIRD ESSAY

14

The more normal sickliness becomes among men—and we cannot deny its normality—the higher should be the honor accorded the rare cases of great power of soul and body, man's *lucky hits;* the more we should protect the well-constituted from the worst kind of air, the air of the sickroom. Is this done?

The sick represent the greatest danger for the healthy; it is *not* the strongest but the weakest who spell disaster for the strong. Is this known?

Broadly speaking, it is not fear of man that we should desire to see diminished; for this fear compels the strong to be strong, and occasionally terrible—it *maintains* the well-constituted type of man. What is to be feared, what has a more calamitous effect than any other calamity, is that man should inspire not profound fear but profound *nausea;* also not great fear but great *pity.* Suppose these two were one day to unite, they would inevitably beget one of the uncanniest monsters: the "last will" of man, his will to nothingness, nihilism. And indeed a great deal points to this union. Whoever can smell not only with his nose but also with his eyes and ears, scents almost everywhere he goes today something like the air of madhouses and hospitals—I am speaking, of course, of the cultural domain, of every kind of "Europe" on this earth. The *sick* are man's greatest danger; *not* the evil, *not* the "beasts of prey." Those who are failures from the start, downtrodden, crushed—it is they, the *weakest,* who must undermine life among men, who call into question and poison most dangerously our trust in life, in man, and in ourselves. Where does one not encounter that veiled glance which burdens one with a profound sadness, that inward-turned glance of the born failure which betrays how such a man speaks to himself—that glance which is a sigh! "If only I were someone else," sighs this glance: "but there is no hope of that. I am who I am: how could I ever get free of myself? And yet—*I am sick of myself!*"

It is on such soil, on swampy ground, that every weed, every poisonous plant grows, always so small, so hidden, so false, so saccharine. Here the worms of vengefulness and rancor swarm; here the air stinks of secrets and concealment; here the web of the most malicious of all conspiracies is being spun constantly—the conspiracy of the suffering against the well-constituted and victorious, here the aspect of the victorious is *hated*. And what mendaciousness is employed to disguise that this hatred is hatred! What a display of grand words and postures, what an art of "honest" calumny! These failures: what noble eloquence flows from their lips! How much sugary, slimy, humble submissiveness swims in their eyes! What do they really want? At least to *represent* justice, love, wisdom, superiority—that is the ambition of the "lowest," the sick. And how skill-full such an ambition makes them! Admire above all the forger's skill with which the stamp of virtue, even the ring, the golden-sounding ring of virtue, is here counterfeited. They monopolize virtue, these weak, hopelessly sick people, there is no doubt of it: "we alone are the good and just," they say, "we alone are *homines bonae voluntatis.*" [31] They walk among us as embodied reproaches, as warnings to us—as if health, well-constitutedness, strength, pride, and the sense of power were in themselves necessarily vicious things for which one must pay some day, and pay bitterly: how ready they themselves are at bottom to *make* one pay; how they crave to be *hangmen*. There is among them an abundance of the vengeful disguised as judges, who constantly bear the word "justice" in their mouths like poisonous spittle, always with pursed lips, always ready to spit upon all who are not discontented but go their way in good spirits. Nor is there lacking among them that most disgusting species of the vain, the mendacious failures whose aim is to appear as "beautiful souls" and who bring to market their deformed sensuality, wrapped up in verses and other swaddling clothes, as "purity of heart": the species of moral masturbaters and "self-gratifiers." The will of the weak to represent *some* form of superiority, their instinct for devious paths to tyranny over the healthy—where can it not be discovered, this will to power of the weakest!

The sick woman especially: no one can excel her in the wiles to dominate, oppress, and tyrannize. The sick woman spares nothing, living or dead; she will dig up the most deeply buried things (the Bogos say: "woman is a hyena").

Examine the background of every family, every organization, every commonwealth: everywhere the struggle of the sick against the healthy—a silent struggle as a rule, with petty poisons, with pinpricks, with sly long-suffering expressions, but occasionally also with that invalid's Phari-

31. Men of good will.

seeism of *loud* gestures that likes best to pose as "noble indignation." This hoarse, indignant barking of sick dogs, this rabid mendaciousness and rage of "noble" Pharisees, penetrates even the hallowed halls of science (I again remind readers who have ears for such things of that Berlin apostle of revenge, Eugen Dühring, who employs moral mumbo-jumbo more indecently and repulsively than anyone else in Germany today: Dühring, the foremost moral bigmouth today—unexcelled even among his own ilk, the anti-Semites).

They are all men of *ressentiment,* physiologically unfortunate and worm-eaten, a whole tremulous realm of subterranean revenge, inexhaustible and insatiable in outbursts against the fortunate and happy [32] and in masquerades of revenge and pretexts for revenge: when would they achieve the ultimate, subtlest, sublimest triumph of revenge? Undoubtedly if they succeeded in *poisoning the consciences* of the fortunate with their own misery, with all misery, so that one day the fortunate began to be ashamed of their good fortune and perhaps said one to another: "it is disgraceful to be fortunate: *there is too much misery!*"

But no greater or more calamitous misunderstanding is possible than for the happy, well-constituted, powerful in soul and body, to begin to doubt their *right to happiness* in this fashion. Away with this "inverted world"! Away with this shameful emasculation of feeling! That the sick should *not* make the healthy sick—and this is what such an emasculation would involve—should surely be our supreme concern on earth; but this requires above all that the healthy should be *segregated* from the sick, guarded even from the sight of the sick, that they may not confound themselves with the sick. Or is it their task, perhaps, to be nurses or physicians? [33]

But no worse misunderstanding and denial of *their* task can be imagined: the higher *ought* not to degrade itself to the status of an instrument of the lower, the pathos of distance *ought* to keep their tasks eternally separate! Their right to exist, the privilege of the fulltoned bell over the false and cracked, is a thousand times greater: they alone are our *warranty* for the future, they alone are *liable* for the future of man. The sick can never have the ability or obligation to do what *they* can do, what *they* ought to do: but if they are to be able to do what *they* alone ought to do, how can they at the same time be physicians, consolers, and "saviors" of the sick?

And therefore let us have fresh air! fresh air! and keep clear of the

---

32. "Fortunate and happy": *die Glücklichen.* In the next sentence the word is rendered "the fortunate," and *Glück* as "good fortune"; but in the next paragraph "happy" and "happiness" have been used, as Nietzsche evidently means both.
33. Cf. Goethe's letter to Frau von Stein, June 8, 1787: "Also, I must say myself, I think it true that humanity will triumph eventually, only I fear that at the same time the world will become a large hospital and each will become the other's humane nurse." In a letter to Rée, April 17, 1877, Nietzsche writes, "each the other's 'humane nurse.'"

madhouses and hospitals of culture! And therefore let us have good company, *our* company! Or solitude, if it must be! But away from the sickening fumes of inner corruption and the hidden rot of disease! ... So that we may, at least for a while yet, guard ourselves, my friends, against the two worst contagions that may be reserved just for us—against the *great nausea at man!* against *great pity for man!* [34]

15

If one has grasped in all its profundity—and I insist that precisely this matter requires *profound* apprehension and comprehension—how it cannot be the task of the healthy to nurse the sick and to make them well, then one has also grasped one further necessity—the necessity of doctors and nurses *who are themselves sick;* and now we understand the meaning of the ascetic priest and grasp it with both hands.

We must count the ascetic priest as the predestined savior, shepherd, and advocate of the sick herd: only thus can we understand his tremendous historical mission. *Dominion over the suffering* is his kingdom, that is where his instinct directs him, here he possesses his distinctive art, his mastery, his kind of happiness. He must be sick himself, he must be profoundly related to the sick—how else would they understand each other?—but he must also be strong, master of himself even more than of others, with his will to power intact, so as to be both trusted and feared by the sick, so as to be their support, resistance, prop, compulsion, taskmaster, tyrant, and god. He has to defend his herd—against whom? Against the healthy, of course, and also against envy of the healthy; he must be the natural opponent *and despiser* of all rude, stormy, unbridled, hard, violent beast-of-prey health and might. The priest is the first form of the more *delicate* animal that despises more readily than it hates. He will not be spared war with the beasts of prey, a war of cunning (of the "spirit") rather than one of force, as goes without saying; to fight it he will under certain circumstances need to evolve a virtually new type of preying animal out of himself, or at least he will need to *represent* it—a new kind of animal ferocity in which the polar bear, the supple, cold, and patient tiger, and not least the fox seem to be joined in a unity at once enticing and terrifying. If need compels him, he will walk among the other beasts of prey with bearlike seriousness and feigned superiority, venerable, prudent, and cold, as the herald and mouthpiece of more mysterious powers, determined to sow this soil with misery, discord, and self-contradiction wherever he can and, only too certain of his art, to dominate the *suffering* at all times. He brings salves and balm with him,

34. The dangers of the great nausea and the great pity are among the central motifs of *Thus Spoke Zarathustra.*

no doubt; but before he can act as a physician he first has to wound; when he then stills the pain of the wound *he at the same time infects the wound*—for that is what he knows to do best of all, this sorcerer and animal-tamer, in whose presence everything healthy necessarily grows sick, and everything sick tame.

Indeed, he defends his sick herd well enough, this strange shepherd—he also defends it against itself, against the baseness, spite, malice, and whatever else is natural to the ailing and sick and smolders within the herd itself; he fights with cunning and severity and in secret against anarchy and ever-threatening disintegration within the herd, in which the most dangerous of all explosives, *ressentiment,* is constantly accumulating. So to detonate this explosive that it does not blow up herd and herdsman is his essential art, as it is his supreme utility; if one wanted to express the value of the priestly existence in the briefest formula it would be: the priest *alters the direction of ressentiment.*

For every sufferer instinctively seeks a cause for his suffering; more exactly, an agent; still more specifically, a *guilty* agent who is susceptible to suffering—in short, some living thing upon which he can, on some pretext or other, vent his affects, actually or in effigy: for the venting of his affects represents the greatest attempt on the part of the suffering to win relief, *anaesthesia*—the narcotic he cannot help desiring to deaden pain of any kind. This alone, I surmise, constitutes the actual physiological cause of *ressentiment,* vengefulness, and the like: a desire to *deaden pain by means of affects.* This cause is usually sought, quite wrongly in my view, in defensive retaliation, a mere reactive protective measure, a "reflex movement" set off by sudden injury or peril, such as even a beheaded frog still makes to shake off a corrosive acid. But the difference is fundamental: in the one case, the desire is to prevent any further injury, in the other it is to *deaden,* by means of a more violent emotion of any kind, a tormenting, secret pain that is becoming unendurable, and to drive it out of consciousness at least for the moment: for that one requires an affect, as savage an affect as possible, and, in order to excite that, any pretext at all. "Someone or other must be to blame for my feeling ill"—this kind of reasoning is common to all the sick, and is indeed held the more firmly the more the real cause of their feeling ill, the physiological cause, remains hidden. (It may perhaps lie in some disease of the *nervus sympathicus,** or in an excessive secretion of bile, or in a deficiency of potassium sulphate and phosphate in the blood, or in an obstruction in the abdomen which impedes the blood circulation, or in degeneration of the ovaries, and the like).

The suffering are one and all dreadfully eager and inventive in discovering occasions for painful affects; they enjoy being mistrustful and dwelling on nasty deeds and imaginary slights; they scour the entrails of

---

* Sympathetic nervous system.

their past and present for obscure and questionable occurrences that offer them the opportunity to revel in tormenting suspicions and to intoxicate themselves with the poison of their own malice: they tear open their oldest wounds, they bleed from long-healed scars, they make evildoers out of their friends, wives, children, and whoever else stands closest to them.³⁵ "I suffer: someone must be to blame for it"—thus thinks every sickly sheep. But his shepherd, the ascetic priest, tells him: "Quite so, my sheep! someone must be to blame for it: but you yourself are this someone, you alone are to blame for it—*you alone are to blame for yourself!*"— This is brazen and false enough: but one thing at least is achieved by it, the direction of *ressentiment* is *altered*.

16

You will guess what, according to my idea, the curative instinct of life has at least *attempted* through the ascetic priest, and why it required for a time the tyranny of such paradoxical and paralogical concepts as "guilt," "sin," "sinfulness," "depravity," "damnation": to render the sick to a certain degree *harmless,* to work the self-destruction of the incurable, to direct the *ressentiment* of the less severely afflicted sternly back upon themselves, ("one thing is needful")—and in this way to *exploit* the bad instincts of all sufferers for the purpose of self-discipline, self-surveillance, and self-overcoming.

It goes without saying that a "medication" of this kind, a mere affect medication, cannot possibly bring about a real cure of sickness in a physiological sense; we may not even suppose that the instinct of life contemplates or intends any sort of cure. A kind of concentration and organization of the sick on one side (the word "church" is the most popular name for it), a kind of provisional safeguarding of the more healthily constituted, the more fully achieved, on the other, and the creation of a *chasm* between healthy and sick—for a long time that was all! And it was much! *very much!*

(It is plain that in this essay I proceed on a presupposition that I do not first have to demonstrate to readers of the kind I need: that man's "sinfulness" is not a fact, but merely the interpretation of a fact, namely of physiological depression—the latter viewed in a religio-moral per-

---

35. The most striking illustration of this sentence is found in Dostoevsky's *Notes from Underground*—and on February 23, 1887, not quite nine months before the publication of the *Genealogy,* Nietzsche wrote Overbeck about his accidental discovery of Dostoevsky in a bookstore, where he had chanced upon a French translation of that work: "my joy was extraordinary" (*Portable Nietzsche,* pp. 454 f). In 1888 he wrote in section 45 of *Twilight of the Idols:* "The testimony of Dostoevsky is relevant to this problem—Dostoevsky, the only psychologist, incidentally, from whom I had something to learn; he ranks among the most beautiful strokes of fortune in my life, even more than my discovery of Stendhal. . . ." (*ibid.,* p. 549.)

spective that is no longer binding on us.—That someone *feels* "guilty" or "sinful" is no proof that he is right, any more than a man is healthy merely because he feels healthy. Recall the famous witch trials: the most acute and humane judges were in no doubt as to the guilt of the accused; the "witches" *themselves did not doubt it*—and yet there was no guilt. —To express this presupposition in a more general form: I consider even "psychological pain" to be not a fact but only an interpretation—a causal interpretation—of facts that have hitherto defied exact formulation—too vague to be scientifically serious—a fat word replacing a very thin question mark. When someone cannot get over a "psychological pain," that is *not* the fault of his "psyche" but, to speak crudely, more probably even that of his belly (speaking crudely, to repeat, which does not mean that I want to be heard crudely or understood crudely—). A strong and well-constituted man digests his experiences (his deeds and misdeeds included) as he digests his meals, even when he has to swallow some tough morsels. If he cannot get over an experience and have done with it, this kind of indigestion is as much physiological as is the other—and often in fact merely a consequence of the other.—With such a conception one can, between ourselves, still be the sternest opponent of all materialism.—)

Patterns: Limited and Exclusive Categories

It is sometimes useful to re-analyze a rhetorical device in order to dramatize the dual nature of rhetoric—it may disguise the truth or it may intensify our awareness of it. Unlike the author of the introduction, who seemed to take refuge in limited and exclusive categories in order to evade the difficulties inherent in his task, Nietzsche uses such categories to dramatize the difficulties that follow from our present "slave" morality. We are not interested, of course, in assessing the accuracy of his implied consequences; we are concerned only with demonstrating how starkly he conveys the nature of those consequences by means of such rhetorical devices.

Such categories, as indicated in the glossary, have the effect of reducing options and destroying subtlety. This reduction and destruction is, however, precisely what Nietzsche intends, for his purpose throughout is to dramatize the cowardice of denying the mutability of opinions and truth.

. . . it is still most suitable for every individual *to give* to his character and business *the appearance* of unalterableness, —even when they are not so in reality. "One can rely on him, he remains the same" —that is the praise which has most significance in all dangerous conditions of society. Society feels with satisfaction that it has a reliable *tool* ready at all times in the virtue of this one, in the ambition of that one, and in the reflection and passion of a third one, —it honours this *tool-like nature,* this self-constancy, this unchangeableness in opinions, efforts, and even in faults, with the highest honours. Such a valuation, which prevails and has prevailed everywhere simultaneously with the morality of custom, educates "characters," and brings all changing, re-learning, and self-transforming into *disrepute*. Be the advantage of this mode of thinking ever so great otherwise, it is in any case the mode of judging which is most injurious *to knowledge:* for precisely the good-will of the knowing one ever to declare himself unhesitatingly as *opposed* to his former opinions, and in general to be distrustful of all that wants to be fixed in him— is here condemned and brought into disrepute. The disposition of the thinker, as incompatible with a "fixed reputation," is regarded as *dishonourable,* while the petrifaction of opinions has all the honour to itself. . . . (50a Nietzsche)

Nietzsche, by his rigid categories, is intent on showing that moralities too have consequences—perhaps "the petrification of opinions"—and that antithetical moralities will have antithetical consequences.

In "First Essay, Section 10," for example, Nietzsche plays off one category— "master morality" —against another— "slave morality." The two are presented as differing both in origin and in consequence; one begins in self-affirmation, in action, the other in negation and reaction; one issues in nobility, "trust and openness," the other issues in *ressentiment,* in love of "hiding places, secret paths and back doors, everything covert." By playing one assumption off against another, by spelling out one consequence from another, Nietzsche hopes through rigid categories, to produce a strange paradox— flexibility of allegiance, a morality predicated on the end produced—the creation of "preparatory men," precursers to the "overman." The very rigidity of exclusive categories is used by Nietzsche to dramatize the effect of rigidity. The hope is that the very reaction provoked by the personal subject matter will not only destroy the exclusive categories but destroy "slave morality," itself. For emotions hostile to rigidity, though deliberately aroused by the author's rhetoric, do not end with the author's rhetoric; they continue on in life. By attacking the exaggeration and rigidity of the categories, one is, moreover, compelled to think about the actual consequences of morality. And by being compelled to defend oneself against the charge of thoughtless allegiance, one is paradoxically defeated by thought.

Problems

1. What is *ressentiment?* How does it lead to slave morality? How does it manifest itself?
2. How does the noble person's concept of good and bad differ from that of the man of *ressentiment?*
3. What justifies the historical process for Nietzsche? How does his attitude toward history and cultural progress differ from that of Christianity or Marxism?
4. What is the origin of guilt and "bad conscience"? How does it reflect a

commercial mentality? And how does it manifest itself? What, according to Nietzsche, is the relation of Christianity to guilt, and what effect will the decline of Christianity have on our sense of guilt? Do you agree?
5. What are the implications of Nietzsche's remark that "mercy remains the privilege of the most powerful man" (661/20)? How does this compel us to rethink the Christian fusion of humility and mercy?
6. What elements in Nietzsche's value system place him in violent conflict with both Christianity and Marxism?
7. What are the consequences of the battle of the sick against the healthy? Who are the sick, who the healthy? With what value systems does this place each in conflict?
8. What is the role of suffering in Nietzsche's concept of man? How does a man's attitude and response to suffering define him?
9. How is Nietzsche's method summed up in the remark that "man's 'sinfulness' is not a fact, but merely the interpretation of a fact. . . . That someone *feels* 'guilty' or 'sinful' is no proof that he is right"? What for Nietzsche is the final criterion of the "rightness" of an interpretation? Do you agree?

from Thus Spake Zarathustra

ON THE PALE CRIMINAL

You do not want to kill, O judges and sacrificers, until the animal has nodded? Behold, the pale criminal has nodded: out of his eyes speaks the great contempt.

"My ego is something that shall be overcome: my ego is to me the great contempt of man," that is what his eyes say.

That he judged himself, that was his highest moment; do not let the sublime return to his baseness! There is no redemption for one who suffers so of himself, except a quick death.

Your killing, O judges, shall be pity and not revenge. And as you kill, be sure that you yourselves justify life! It is not enough to make your peace with the man you kill. Your sadness shall be love of the overman:* thus you shall justify your living on.

From Friedrich Nietzsche, *Thus Spake Zarathustra,* in *The Portable Nietzsche* (New York: The Viking Press, 1954), pp. 149–228.

* "Overman" is a more just term for the "Superman," that future man who is free, fully realized, autonomous—who reflects the values Nietzsche has been articulating. Nietzsche intends no Darwinian evolution. The "Overman" is the product of the individual self-overcoming, of the individual strenuously and ceaselessly pushing at the outer limits of his being.

"Enemy" you shall say, but not "villain"; "sick" you shall say, but not "scoundrel"; "fool" you shall say, but "not sinner."

And you, red judge, if you were to tell out loud all that you have already done in thought, everyone would cry, "Away with this filth and this poisonous worm!"

But thought is one thing, the deed is another, and the image of the deed still another: the wheel of causality does not roll between them.

An image made this pale man pale. He was equal to his deed when he did it; but he could not bear its image after it was done. Now he always saw himself as the doer of one deed. Madness I call this: the exception now became the essence for him. A chalk streak stops a hen; the stroke that he himself struck stopped his poor reason: madness *after* the deed I call this.

Listen, O judges: there is yet another madness, and that comes *before* the deed. Alas, you have not yet crept deep enough into this soul.

Thus speaks the red judge, "Why did this criminal murder? He wanted to rob." But I say unto you: his soul wanted blood, not robbery; he thirsted after the bliss of the knife. His poor reason, however, did not comprehend this madness and persuaded him: "What matters blood?" it asked; "don't you want at least to commit a robbery with it? To take revenge?" And he listened to his poor reason: its speech lay upon him like lead; so he robbed when he murdered. He did not want to be ashamed of his madness.

And now the lead of his guilt lies upon him, and again his poor reason is so stiff, so paralyzed, so heavy. If only he could shake his head, then his burden would roll off: but who could shake this head?

What is this man? A heap of diseases, which, through his spirit, reach out into the world: there they want to catch their prey.

What is this man? A ball of wild snakes, which rarely enjoy rest from each other: so they go forth singly and seek prey in the world.

Behold this poor body! What is suffered and coveted this poor soul interpreted for itself: it interpreted it as murderous lust and greed for the bliss of the knife.

Those who become sick today are overcome by that evil which is evil today: they want to hurt with that which hurts them. But there have been other ages and another evil and good. Once doubt was evil and the will to self. Then the sick became heretics or witches: as heretics or witches they suffered and wanted to inflict suffering.

But your ears do not want to accept this: it harms your good people, you say to me. But what matter your good people to me? Much about your good people nauseates me; and verily, it is not their evil. Indeed, I wish they had a madness of which they might perish like this pale criminal.

Verily, I wish their madness were called truth or loyalty or justice:

but they have their virtue in order to live long and in wretched contentment.

I am a railing by the torrent: let those who can, grasp me! Your crutch, however, I am not.

Thus spoke Zarathustra.

ON THE PREACHERS OF DEATH

There are preachers of death; and the earth is full of those to whom one must preach renunciation of life. The earth is full of the superfluous; life is spoiled by the all-too-many. May they be lured from this life with the "eternal life"! Yellow the preachers of death wear, or black. But I want to show them to you in still other colors.

There are the terrible ones who carry around within themselves the beast of prey and have no choice but lust or self-laceration. And even their lust is still self-laceration. They have not even become human beings yet, these terrible ones: let them preach renunciation of life and pass away themselves!

There are those with consumption of the soul: hardly are they born when they begin to die and to long for doctrines of weariness and renunciation. They would like to be dead, and we should welcome their wish. Let us beware of waking the dead and disturbing these living coffins!

They encounter a sick man or an old man or a corpse, and immediately they say, "Life is refuted." But only they themselves are refuted, and their eyes, which see only this one face of existence. Shrouded in thick melancholy and eager for the little accidents that bring death, thus they wait with clenched teeth. Or they reach for sweets while mocking their own childishness; they clutch the straw of their life and mock that they still clutch a straw. Their wisdom says, "A fool who stays alive—but such fools are we. And this is surely the most foolish thing about life."

"Life is only suffering," others say, and do not lie: see to it, then, that *you* cease! See to it, then, that the life which is only suffering ceases!

And let this be the doctrine of your virtue: "Thou shalt kill thyself! Thou shalt steal away!"

"Lust is sin," says one group that preaches death; "let us step aside and beget no children."

"Giving birth is troublesome," says another group; "why go on giving birth? One bears only unfortunates!"

And they too are preachers of death.

"Pity is needed." says the third group. "Take from me what I have! Take from me what I am! Life will bind me that much less!"

If they were full of pity through and through, they would make life insufferable for their neighbors. To be evil, that would be their real goodness. But they want to get out of life: what do they care that with their chains and presents they bind others still more tightly?

And you, too, for whom life is furious work and unrest—are you not very weary of life? Are you not very ripe for the preaching of death? All of you to whom furious work is dear, and whatever is fast, new, and strange—you find it hard to bear yourselves; your industry is escape and the will to forget yourselves. If you believed more in life you would fling yourselves less to the moment. But you do not have contents enough in yourselves for waiting—and not even for idleness.

Everywhere the voice of those who preach death is heard: and the earth is full of those to whom one must preach death. Or "eternal life"—that is the same to me, if only they pass away quickly.

Thus spoke Zarathustra.

ON WAR AND WARRIORS

We do not want to be spared by our best enemies, nor by those whom we love thoroughly. So let me tell you the truth!

My brothers in war, I love you thoroughly; I am and I was of your kind. And I am also your best enemy. So let me tell you the truth!

I know of the hatred and envy of your hearts. You are not great enough not to know hatred and envy. Be great enough, then, not to be ashamed of them.

And if you cannot be saints of knowledge, at least be its warriors. They are the companions and forerunners of such sainthood.

I see many soldiers: would that I saw many warriors! "Uniform" one calls what they wear: would that what it conceals were not uniform!

You should have eyes that always seek an enemy—*your* enemy. And some of you hate at first sight. Your enemy you shall seek, your war you shall wage—for your thoughts. And if your thought be vanquished, then your honesty should still find cause for triumph in that. You should love peace as a means to new wars—and the short peace more than the long. To you I do not recommend work but struggle. To you I do not recommend peace but victory. Let your work be a struggle. Let your peace be a victory! One can be silent and sit still only when one has bow and arrow: else one chatters and quarrels. Let your peace be a victory!

You say it is the good cause that hallows even war? I say unto you: it is the good war that hallows any cause. War and courage have accomplished more great things than love of the neighbor. Not your pity but your courage has so far saved the unfortunate.

"What is good?" you ask. To be brave is good. Let the little girls say, "To be good is what is at the same time pretty and touching."

They call you heartless: but you have a heart, and I love you for being ashamed to show it. You are ashamed of your flood, while others are ashamed of their ebb.

You are ugly? Well then, my brothers, wrap the sublime around you, the cloak of the ugly. And when your soul becomes great, then it becomes prankish; and in your sublimity there is sarcasm. I know you.

In sarcasm the prankster and the weakling meet. But they misunderstand each other. I know you.

You may have only enemies whom you can hate not enemies you despise. You must be proud of your enemy: then the successes of your enemy are your successes too.

Recalcitrance—that is the nobility of slaves. Your nobility should be obedience. Your very commanding should be an obeying. To a good warrior "thou shalt" sounds more agreeable than "I will." And everything you like you should first let yourself be commanded to do.

Your love of life shall be love of your highest hope; and your highest hope shall be the highest thought of life. Your highest thought, however, you should receive as a command from me—and it is: man is something that shall be overcome.

Thus live your life of obedience and war. What matters long life? What warrior wants to be spared?

I do not spare you; I love you thoroughly, my brothers in war!

Thus spoke Zarathustra.

THE DRUNKEN SONG

9

You vine! Why do you praise me? Did I not cut you? I am cruel, you bleed; what does your praise of my drunken cruelty mean?

"What has become perfect, all that is ripe—wants to die"—thus you speak. Blessed, blessed be the vintager's knife! But all that is unripe wants to live: woe!

Woe entreats: Go! Away, woe! But all that suffers wants to live, that it may become ripe and joyous and longing—longing for what is farther, higher, brighter. "I want heirs"—thus speaks all that suffers; "I want children, I do not want *myself*."

Joy, however, does not want heirs, or children—joy wants itself, wants eternity, wants recurrence, wants everything eternally the same.

Woe says, "Break, bleed, heart! Wander, leg! Wing, fly! Get on! Up, Pain!" Well then old heart: *Woe implores, "Go!"*

10

You higher men, what do you think? Am I a soothsayer? A dreamer? A drunkard? An interpreter of dreams? A midnight bell? A drop of dew? A haze and fragrance of eternity? Do you not hear it? Do you not smell it? Just now my world became perfect; midnight too is noon; pain too is a joy; curses too are a blessing; night too is a sun—go away or you will learn: a sage too is a fool.

Have you ever said Yes to a single joy! O my friends, then you said Yes too to *all* woe. All things are entangled, ensnared, enamored; if ever you wanted one thing twice, if ever you said, "You please me, happiness! Abide, moment!" then you wanted *all* back. All anew, all eternally, all entangled, ensnared, enamored—oh, then you *loved* the world. Eternal ones, love it eternally and evermore; and to woe, too, you say: go, but return! *For all joy wants—eternity.*

11

All joy wants the eternity of all things, wants honey, wants lees, wants drunken midnight, wants tombs, wants tomb-tears' comfort, wants gilded evening glow.

What does joy not want? It is thirstier, more cordial, hungrier, more terrible, more secret than all woe; it wants *itself*, it bites into *itself*, the ring's will strives in it; it wants love, it wants hatred, it is overrich, gives, throws away, begs that one might take it, thanks the taker, it would like to be hated; so rich is joy that it thirsts for woe, for hell, for hatred, for disgrace, for the cripple, for *world*—this world, oh, you know it!

You higher men, for you it longs, joy, the intractable blessed one—for your woe, you failures. All eternal joy longs for failures. For all joy wants itself, hence it also wants agony. O happiness, O pain! Oh, break, heart! You higher men, do learn this, joy wants eternity. Joy wants the eternity of *all* things, *wants deep, wants deep eternity.*

12

Have you now learned my song? Have you guessed its intent? Well then, you higher men, sing me now my round. Now you yourselves sing me the song whose name is "Once More" and whose meaning is "into all eternity"—sing, you higher men, Zarathustra's round!

O man, take care!
What does the deep midnight declare?
"I was asleep—
From a deep dream I woke and swear:
The world is deep,
Deeper than day had been aware.
Deep is its woe;
Joy—deeper yet than agony:
Woe implores: Go!
But all joy wants eternity—
Wants deep, wants deep eternity."

ON SELF-OVERCOMING

"Will to truth," you who are wisest call that which impels you and fills you with lust?

A will to the thinkability of all things: this *I* call your will. You want to *make* all being thinkable, for you doubt with well-founded suspicion that it is already thinkable. But it shall yield and bend for you. Thus your will wants it. It shall become smooth and serve the spirit as its mirror and reflection. That is your whole will, you who are wisest: a will to power—when you speak of good and evil too, and of valuations. You still want to create the world before which you can kneel: that is your ultimate hope and intoxication.

The unwise, of course, the people—they are like a river on which a bark drifts; and in the bark sit the valuations, solemn and muffled up. Your will and your valuations you have placed on the river of becoming; and what the people believe to be good and evil, that betrays to me an ancient will to power.

It was you who are wisest who placed such guests in this bark and gave them pomp and proud names—you and your dominant will. Now the river carries your bark farther; it *has* to carry it. It avails nothing that the broken wave foams and angrily opposes the keel. Not the river is your danger and the end of your good and evil, you who are wisest, but that will itself, the will to power—the unexhausted procreative will of life.

But to make you understand my word concerning good and evil, I shall now say to you my word concerning life and the nature of all the living.

I pursued the living; I walked the widest and the narrowest paths that I might know its nature. With a hundredfold mirror I still caught its glance when its mouth was closed, so that its eyes might speak to me. And its eyes spoke to me.

But wherever I found the living, there I heard also the speech on obedience. Whatever lives, obeys.

And this is the second point: he who cannot obey himself is commanded. That is the nature of the living.

This, however, is the third point that I heard: that commanding is harder than obeying; and not only because he who commands must carry the burden of all who obey, and because this burden may easily crush him. An experiment and hazard appeared to me to be in all commanding; and whenever the living commands, it hazards itself. Indeed, even when it commands *itself,* it must still pay for its commanding. It must become the judge, the avenger, and the victim of its own law. How does this happen? I asked myself. What persuades the living to obey and command, and to practice obedience even when it commands?

Hear, then, my word, you who are wisest. Test in all seriousness whether I have crawled into the very heart of life and into the very roots of its heart.

Where I found the living, there I found will to power; and even in the will of those who serve I found the will to be master.

That the weaker should serve the stronger, to that it is persuaded by its own will, which would be master over what is weaker still: this is the one pleasure it does not want to renounce. And as the smaller yields to the greater that it may have pleasure and power over the smallest, thus even the greatest still yields, and for the sake of power risks life. That is the yielding of the greatest: it is hazard and danger and casting dice for death.

And where men make sacrifices and serve and cast amorous glances, there too is the will to be master. Along stealthy paths the weaker steals into the castle and into the very heart of the more powerful—and there steals power.

And life itself confided this secret to me: "Behold," it said, "I am *that which must always overcome itself.* Indeed, you call it a will to procreate or a drive to an end, to something higher, farther, more manifold: but all this is one, and one secret.

"Rather would I perish than forswear this; and verily, where there is perishing and a falling of leaves, behold, there life sacrifices itself—for power. That I must be struggle and a becoming and an end and an opposition to ends—alas, whoever guesses what is my will should also guess on what *crooked* paths it must proceed.

"Whatever I create and however much I love it—soon I must oppose it and my love; thus my will wills it. And you too, lover of knowledge, are only a path and footprint of my will; verily, my will to power walks also on the heels of your will to truth.

"Indeed, the truth was not hit by him who shot at it with the word of the 'will to existence': that will does not exist. For, what does not exist cannot will; but what is in existence, how could that still want existence? Only where there is life is there also will: not will to life but—thus I teach you—will to power.

"There is much that life esteems more highly than life itself; but out of the esteeming itself speaks the will to power."

Thus life once taught me; and with this I shall yet solve the riddle of your heart, you who are wisest.

Verily, I say unto you: good and evil that are not transitory, do not exist. Driven on by themselves, they must overcome themselves again and again. With your values and words of good and evil you do violence when you value; and this is your hidden love and the splendor and trembling and overflowing of your soul. But a more violent force and a new overcoming grow out of your values and break egg and eggshell.

And whoever must be a creator in good and evil, verily, he must first be an annihilator and break values. Thus the highest evil belongs to the highest goodness: but this is creative.

Let us speak of this, you who are wisest, even if it be bad. Silence is worse; all truths that are kept silent become poisonous.

And may everything be broken that cannot brook our truths! There are yet many houses to be built!

Thus spoke Zarathustra.

Problems

1. Who are the "pale criminals"? What motivates them?
2. From your knowledge of the nature of Nietzsche's past hostilities, define the nature of the war he wages and why he would appear to glorify it.
3. Who are the higher men, the overmen or the supermen, and what are they like? Which of the writers you have previously read described similar men? What are the implications of the resemblances?
4. What is self-overcoming, and why is it so central to Nietzsche's thought? How does the concept of self-overcoming place him in a line of moralists and visionaries starting with Christ?
5. Why does life esteem most highly the "will to power"?

30 SØREN KIERKEGAARD

The work of Danish philosopher Søren Kierkegaard (1813–1855), rejecting, as it does, abstract Hegelian systems, is almost stifling and claustrophobic in its obsession with the existing, isolated individual. For Kierkegaard, rationalism is an evasion, and aestheticism a distraction from the essential ethical substance of life. Subjectivism is absolute; the individual is alone, living a perpetual dark night of the soul in which he must hammer out his own truth. It was these beliefs that led to Kierkegaard's hostility to institutionalized Christianity—which he called Christendom. Christendom pretends to give one truth; but only a consciously affirmed truth, one's own truth, can give life meaning and make it endurable—and Christendom makes this impossible.

Nothing informs Kierkegaard's thought more than his hostility to those who pretend to be ruled by reason, for reason devoid of initial faith is a sham. All thought involves the act of taking, as its beginning, an initial assumption; it involves a "leap of faith," for the chasm between one's limited understanding and the ground of one's initial assumption is an absolute abyss. Kierkegaard has nothing but laughter for Hegel and other systematizers who deny the inherent contradiction of life. He writes:

> System and finality correspond to one another, but existence is precisely the opposite of finality. It may be seen, from a purely abstract point of view, that system and existence are incapable of being thought together; because in order to think existence at all, systematic thought must think it as abrogated, and hence as not existing. Existence separates and holds the various moments of existence discretely apart; systematic thought consists of the finality which brings them together (57 Kierkegaard).

There is undeniable courage involved in this emphasis on the individual resolutely carving truth from within his being, but there is also something terrifyingly relativistic as well. As demonstrated by the three selections below, from The Concept of Dread (1844), The Sickness Unto Death (1849), and Fear and Trembling (1843), Kierkegaard well understood "dread," "despair" and "trial"; he is thus able to cut away the prettified deceits, the pleasant pretenses of rationality, the complex conventions by which we hide from ourselves, and reveal us to ourselves as we are—naked before the abyss. But there is a strain of irrationality, of a solipsism so absolute that the shudder created in us is not only of the abyss, but of the possible implications as well.

from The Concept of Dread

In one of Grimm's Fairy Tales there is the story of a youth who went out in search of adventures for the sake of learning what it is to fear or be in dread. We will let that adventurer go his way without troubling ourselves to learn whether in the course of it he encountered the dreadful. On the other hand I would say that learning to know dread is an adventure which every man has to affront if he would not go to perdition either by not having known dread or by sinking under it. He therefore who has learned rightly to be in dread has learned the most important thing.

If a man were a beast or an angel, he would not be able to be in dread. Since he is a synthesis he can be in dread, and the greater the dread, the greater the man. This, however, is not affirmed in the sense in which men commonly understand dread, as related to something outside a man, but in the sense that man himself produces dread. Only in this sense can we interpret the passage where it is said of Christ that he was in dread [*aengstes*] even unto death and the place also where he says to Judas, "What thou doest, do quickly." Not even the terrible word upon which even Luther dreaded to preach, "My God, my God, why hast thou forsaken me?"—not even this expresses suffering so strongly. For this word indicates a situation in which Christ actually is; the former sayings indicate a relation to a situation which is not yet actual.

Dread is the possibility of freedom. Only this dread is by the aid of faith absolutely educative, laying bare as it does all finite aims and discovering all their deceptions. And no Grand Inquisitor has in readiness such terrible tortures as has dread, and no spy knows how to attack more artfully the man he suspects, choosing the instant when he is weakest, nor knows how to lay traps where he will be caught and ensnared, as dread knows how, and no sharpwitted judge knows how to interrogate, to examine the accused, as dread does, which never lets him escape, neither by diversion nor by noise, neither at work nor at play, neither by day nor by night.

He who is educated by dread is educated by possibility, and only the man who is educated by possibility is educated in accordance with his infinity. Possibility is therefore the heaviest of all categories. One often

From Søren Kierkegaard, *The Concept of Dread* (Princeton: Princeton University Press, 1944), pp. 139–42.

hears, it is true, the opposite affirmed, that possibility is so light but reality is heavy. But from whom does one hear such talk? From a lot of miserable men who never have known what possibility is, and who, since reality showed them that they were not fit for anything and never would be, mendaciously bedizened a possibility which was so beautiful, so enchanting; and the only foundation of this possibility was a little youthful tomfoolery of which they might rather have been ashamed. Therefore by this possibility which is said to be light one commonly understands the possibility of luck, good fortune, etc. But this is not possibility, it is a mendacious invention which human depravity falsely embellishes in order to have reason to complain of life, of providence, and as a pretext for being self-important. No, in possibility everything is possible, and he who truly was brought up by possibility has comprehended the dreadful as well as the smiling. When such a person, therefore, goes out from the school of possibility, and knows more thoroughly than a child knows the alphabet that he can demand of life absolutely nothing, and that terror, perdition, annihilation, dwell next door to every man, and has learned the profitable lesson that every dread which alarms [*aengste*] may the next instant become a fact, he will then interpret reality differently, he will extol reality, and even when it rests upon him heavily he will remember that after all it is far, far lighter than the possibility was. Only thus can possibility educate; for finiteness and the finite relationships in which the individual is assigned a place, whether it be small and commonplace or world-historical, educate only finitely, and one can always talk them around, always get a little more out of them, always chaffer, always escape a little way from them, always keep a little apart, always prevent oneself from learning absolutely from them; and if one is to learn absolutely, the individual must in turn have the possibility in himself and himself fashion that from which he is to learn, even though the next instant it does not recognize that it was fashioned by him, but absolutely takes the power from him.

But in order that the individual may thus absolutely and infinitely be educated by possibility, he must be honest towards possibility and must have faith. By faith I mean what Hegel in his fashion calls very rightly "the inward certainty which anticipates infinity." When the discoveries of possibility are honestly administered, possibility will then disclose all finitudes and idealize them in the form of infinity in the individual who is overwhelmed by dread, until in turn he is victorious by the anticipation of faith.

What I say here appears perhaps to many an obscure and foolish saying, since they even boast of never having been in dread. To this I would reply that doubtless one should not be in dread of men, of finite things, but that only the man who has gone through the dread of possibility is educated to have no dread—not because he avoids the dreadful things of life, but because they always are weak in comparison with those of possibility. If on the other hand the speaker means that the great thing about him is that he has never been in dread, then I shall gladly initiate him into my explanation, that this comes from the fact that he is spirit-less.

If the individual cheats the possibility by which he is to be educated, he never reaches faith; his faith remains the shrewdness of finitude, as his school was that of finitude. But men cheat possibility in every way—if they did not, one has only to stick one's head out of the window, and one would see enough for possibility to begin its exercises forthwith. There is an engraving by Chodowiecki which represents the surrender of Calais as viewed by the four temperaments, and the theme of the artist was to let the various impressions appear mirrored in the faces which express the various temperaments. The most commonplace life has events enough, no doubt, but the question is whether the possibility in the individuality is honest towards itself. It is recounted of an Indian hermit who for two years had lived upon dew, that he came once to the city, tasted wine, and then became addicted to drink. This story, like every other of the sort, can be understood in many ways, one can make it comic, one can make it tragic; but the man who is educated by possibility has more than enough to occupy him in such a story. Instantly he is absolutely identified with that unfortunate man, he knows no finite evasion by which he might escape. Now the dread of possibility holds him as its prey, until it can deliver him saved into the hands of faith. In no other place does he find repose, for every other point of rest is mere nonsense, even though in men's eyes it is shrewdness. This is the reason why possibility is so absolutely educative. No man has ever become so unfortunate in reality that there was not some little residue left to him, and, as common sense observes quite truly, if a man is canny, he will find a way. But he who went through the curriculum of misfortune offered by possibility lost everything, absolutely everything, in a way that no one has lost it in reality. If in this situation he did not behave falsely towards possibility, if he did not attempt to talk around the dread which would save him, then he received everything back again, as in reality no one ever did even if he received everything double, for the pupil of possibility received infinity, whereas the soul of the other expired in the finite. No one ever sank so deep in reality that he could not sink deeper, or that there might not be one or another sunk deeper than he. But he who sank in the possibility has an eye too dizzy to see the measuring rod which Tom, Dick, and Harry hold out as a straw to the drowning man; his ear is closed so that he cannot hear what the market price for men is in his day, cannot hear that he is just as good as most of them. He sank absolutely, but then in turn he floated up from the depth of the abyss, lighter now than all that is oppressive and dreadful in life. Only I do not deny that he who is educated by possibility is exposed—not to the danger of bad company and dissoluteness of various sorts, as are those who are educated by the finite, but—to one danger of downfall, and that is self-slaughter. If at the beginning of his education he misunderstands the anguish of dread, so that it does not lead him to faith but away from faith, then he is lost. On the other hand, he who is educated by possibility remains with dread, does not allow himself to be deceived by its countless counterfeits, he recalls the past precisely; then at last the attacks of dread, though they are fearful, are not such that he flees from them. For him dread becomes a serviceable spirit which against its will leads him whither he would go. Then when it announces itself, when it craftily insinuates that it has invented a new instrument of torture far more terrible than anything employed before, he does not recoil, still less does he attempt to hold it off with clamor and noise, but he bids it welcome, he hails it solemnly, as Socrates solemnly flourished the poisoned goblet, he shuts himself up with it, he says, as a patient says to the surgeon when a painful operation is about to begin, "Now I am ready." Then dread enters into his soul and searches it thoroughly, constraining out of him all the finite and the petty, and leading him hence whither he would go.

Problems

1. What is dread?
2. What is the relation of possibility to empathy? How does possibility educate a person?
3. Why do people shun possibility? What are the consequences for their development of this avoidance?

from The Sickness unto Death

DESPAIR IS "THE SICKNESS UNTO DEATH"

The concept of the sickness unto death must be understood, however, in a peculiar sense. Literally it means a sickness the end and outcome of which is death. Thus one speaks of a mortal sickness as synonymous with a sickness unto death. In this sense despair cannot be called the sickness unto death. But in the Christian understanding of it death itself is a transition unto life. In view of this, there is from the Christian standpoint no earthly, bodily sickness unto death. For death is doubtless the last phase of the sickness, but death is not the last thing. If in the strictest sense we are to speak of a sickness unto death, it must be

From Søren Kierkegaard, *The Sickness Unto Death* (Princeton: Princeton University Press, 1951), pp. 24–31.

one in which the last thing is death, and death the last thing. And this precisely is despair.

Yet in another and still more definite sense despair is the sickness unto death. It is indeed very far from being true that, literally understood, one dies of this sickness, or that this sickness ends with bodily death. On the contrary, the torment of despair is precisely this, not to be able to die. So it has much in common with the situation of the moribund when he lies and struggles with death, and cannot die. So to be sick *unto* death is, not to be able to die—yet not as though there were hope of life; no, the hopelessness in this case is that even the last hope, death, is not available. When death is the greatest danger, one hopes for life; but when one becomes acquainted with an even more dreadful danger, one hopes for death. So when the danger is so great that death has become one's hope, despair is the disconsolateness of not being able to die.

It is in this last sense that despair is the sickness unto death, this agonizing contradiction, this sickness in the self, everlastingly to die, to die and yet not to die, to die the death. For dying means that it is all over, but dying the death means to live to experience death; and if for a single instant this experience is possible, it is tantamount to experiencing it forever. If one might die of despair as one dies of a sickness, then the eternal in him, the self, must be capable of dying in the same sense that the body dies of sickness. But this is an impossibility; the dying of despair transforms itself constantly into a living. The despairing man cannot die; no more than "the dagger can slay thoughts" can despair consume the eternal thing, the self, which is the ground of despair, whose worm dieth not, and whose fire is not quenched. Yet despair is precisely *self*-consuming, but it is an impotent self-consumption which is not able to do what it wills; and this impotence is a new form of self-consumption, in which again, however, the despairer is not able to do what he wills, namely, to consume himself. This is despair raised to a higher potency, or it is the law for the potentiation. This is the hot incitement, or the cold fire in despair, the gnawing canker whose movement is constantly inward, deeper and deeper, in impotent self-consumption. The fact that despair does not consume him is so far from being any comfort to the despairing man that it is precisely the opposite, this comfort is precisely the torment, it is precisely this that keeps the gnawing pain alive and keeps life in the pain. This precisely is the reason why he despairs—not to say despaired—because he cannot consume himself, cannot get rid of himself, cannot become nothing. This is the potentiated formula for despair, the rising of the fever in the sickness of the self.

A despairing man is in despair over *something*. So it seems for an instant, but only for an instant; that same instant the true despair manifests itself, or despair manifests itself in its true character. For in the fact that he despaired of *something,* he really despaired of himself, and now would be rid of himself. Thus when the ambitious man whose watchword was "Either Caesar or nothing" does not become Caesar, he is in despair thereat. But this signifies something else, namely, that precisely because he did not become Caesar he now cannot endure to be himself. So properly he is not in despair over the fact that he did not become Caesar, but he is in despair over himself for the fact that he did not become Caesar. This self which, had he become Caesar, would have been to him a sheer delight (though in another sense equally in despair), this self is now absolutely intolerable to him. In a profounder sense it is not the fact that he did not become Caesar which is intolerable to him, but the self which did not become Caesar is the thing that is intolerable; or, more correctly, what is intolerable to him is that he cannot get rid of himself. If he had become Caesar he would have been rid of himself in desperation, but now that he did not become Caesar he cannot in desperation get rid of himself. Essentially he is equally in despair in either case, for he does not possess himself, he is not himself. By becoming Caesar he would not after all have become himself but have got rid of himself, and by not becoming Caesar he falls into despair over the fact that he cannot get rid of himself. Hence it is a superficial view (which presumably has never seen a person in despair, not even one's own self) when it is said of a man in despair, "He is consuming himself." For precisely this it is he despairs of, and to his torment it is precisely this he cannot do, since by despair fire has entered into something that cannot burn, or cannot burn up, that is, into the self.

So to despair over something is not yet properly despair. It is the beginning, or it is as when the physician says of a sickness that it has not yet declared itself. The next step is the declared despair, despair over oneself. A young girl is in despair over love, and so she despairs over her lover, because he died, or because he was unfaithful to her. This is not a declared despair; no, she is in despair over herself. This self of hers, which, if it had become "his" beloved, she would have been rid of in the most blissful way, or would have lost, this self is now a torment to her when it has to be a self without "him"; this self which would have been to her her riches (though in another sense equally in despair) has now become to her a loathsome void, since "he" is dead, or it has become to her an abhorrence, since it reminds her of the fact that she was betrayed. Try it now, say to such a girl, "Thou art consuming thyself," and thou shalt hear her reply, "Oh, no, the torment is precisely this, that I cannot do it."

To despair over oneself, in despair to will to be rid of oneself, is the formula for all despair, and hence the second form of despair (in despair at willing to be oneself) can be followed back to the first (in despair at not willing to be oneself), just as in the foregoing we resolved the first into the second. A despairing man wants despairingly to be himself. But if he despairingly wants to be himself, he will not want to get rid of himself. Yes, so it seems; but if one inspects more closely, one perceives that after all the contradiction is the same. That self which he despairingly wills to be is a self which he is not (for to will to be that self which one truly is, is indeed the opposite of despair); what he really wills is to tear his self away from the Power which constituted it. But notwithstanding all his despair, this he is unable to do, notwithstanding all the efforts of despair, that Power is the stronger, and it compels him to be the self he does not will to be. But for all that he wills to be rid of himself, to be rid of the self which he is, in order to be the self he himself has chanced to choose. To be *self* as he wills to be would be his delight (though in another sense it would be equally in despair), but to be compelled to be *self* as he does not will to be is his torment, namely, that he cannot get rid of himself.

Socrates proved the immortality of the soul from the fact that the sickness of the soul (sin) does not consume it as sickness of the body consumes the body. So also we can demonstrate the eternal in man from the fact that despair cannot consume his self, that this precisely is the torment of contradiction in despair. If there were nothing eternal in a man, he could not despair; but if despair could consume his self, there would still be no despair.

Thus it is that despair, this sickness in the self, is the sickness unto death. The despairing man is mortally ill. In an entirely different sense than can appropriately be said of any disease, we may say that the sickness has attacked the noblest part; and yet the man cannot die. Death is not the last phase of the sickness, but death is continually the last. To be delivered from this sickness by death is an impossibility, for the sickness and its torment . . . and death consist in not being able to die.

This is the situation in despair. And however thoroughly it eludes the attention of the despairer, and however thoroughly the despairer may succeed (as in the case of that kind of despair which is characterized by unawareness of being in despair) in losing himself entirely, and losing himself in such a way that it is not noticed in the least—eternity nevertheless will make it manifest that his situation was despair, and it will so nail him to himself that the torment nevertheless remains that he cannot get rid of himself, and it becomes manifest that he was deluded in thinking that he succeeded. And thus it is eternity must act, because to have a self, to be a self, is the greatest concession made to man, but at the same time it is eternity's demand upon him.

Problems

1. What is the sickness unto death?
2. What is its relation to actual death?

3. What is the relationship of despair to alienation? Is despair rooted in the self or in society?
4. What would Kierkegaard think of Marx's analysis of alienation?

from Fear and Trembling

PRELUDE

I

"And God tempted Abraham and said unto him, Take Isaac, thine only son, whom thou lovest, and get thee into the land of Moriah, and offer him there for a burnt offering upon the mountain which I will show thee." *

It was early in the morning, Abraham arose betimes, he had the asses saddled, left his tent, and Isaac with him, but Sarah looked out of the window after them until they had passed down the valley and she could see them no more. They rode in silence for three days. On the morning of the fourth day Abraham said never a word, but he lifted up his eyes and saw Mount Moriah afar off. He left the young men behind and went on alone with Isaac beside him up to the mountain. But Abraham

From Søren Kierkegaard, *Fear and Trembling* (Princeton: Princeton University Press, 1954), pp. 10–100.
* Genesis 22: 1–12, from *The King James Bible* follows:
  And it came to pass after these things, that God did tempt Abraham, and said unto him, Abraham: and he said, Behold, *here* I *am*. And he said, Take now thy son, thine only *son* Isaac, whom thou lovest, and get thee into the land of Moriah; and offer him there for a burnt offering upon one of the mountains which I will tell thee of. And Abraham rose up early in the morning, and saddled his ass, and took two of his young men with him, and Isaac his son, and clave the wood for the burnt offering, and rose up, and went unto the place of which God had told him. Then on the third day Abraham lifted up his eyes, and saw the place afar off. And Abraham said unto his young men, Abide ye here with the ass; and I and the lad will go yonder and worship, and come again to you. And Abraham took the wood of the burnt offering, and laid *it* upon Isaac his son; and he took the fire in his hand, and a knife; and they went both of them together. And Isaac spake unto Abraham his father, and said, My father: and he said, Here *am* I, my son. And he said, Behold the fire and the wood: but where *is* the lamb for a burnt offering? And Abraham said, My son, God will provide himself a lamb for a burnt offering: so they went both of them together.
  And they came to the place which God had told him of; and Abraham built an altar there, and laid the wood in order, and bound Isaac his son, and laid him on the altar upon the wood. And Abraham stretched forth his hand, and took the knife to slay his son. And the angel of the Lord called unto him out of heaven, and said, Abraham, Abraham: and he said, Here *am* I. And he said, Lay not thine hand upon the lad, neither do thou any thing unto him: for now I know that thou fearest God, seeing thou hast not withheld thy son, thine only *son* from me.

said to himself, "I will not conceal from Isaac whither this course leads him." He stood still, he laid his hand upon the head of Isaac in benediction, and Isaac bowed to receive the blessing. And Abraham's face was fatherliness, his look was mild, his speech encouraging. But Isaac was unable to understand him, his soul could not be exalted; he embraced Abraham's knees, he fell at his feet imploringly, he begged for his young life, for the fair hope of his future, he called to mind the joy in Abraham's house, he called to mind the sorrow and loneliness. Then Abraham lifted up the boy, he walked with him by his side, and his talk was full of comfort and exhortation. But Isaac could not understand him. He climbed Mount Moriah, but Isaac understood him not. Then for an instant he turned away from him, and when Isaac again saw Abraham's face it was changed, his glance was wild, his form was horror. He seized Isaac by the throat, threw him to the ground, and said, "Stupid boy, dost thou then suppose that I am thy father? I am an idolater. Dost thou suppose that this is God's bidding? No, it is my desire." Then Isaac trembled and cried out in his terror, "O God in heaven, have compassion upon me. God of Abraham, have compassion upon me. If I have no father upon earth, be Thou my father!" But Abraham in a low voice said to himself, "O Lord in heaven, I thank Thee. After all it is better for him to believe that I am a monster, rather than that he should lose faith in Thee."

PROBLEM I

Is there such a thing as a teleological * suspension of the ethical?

The ethical as such is the universal, and as the universal it applies to everyone, which may be expressed from another point of view by saying that it applies every instant. It reposes immanently in itself, it has nothing without itself which is its *telos,* but is itself *telos* for everything outside it, and when this has been incorporated by the ethical it can go no further. Conceived immediately as physical and psychical, the particular individual is the individual who has his *telos* in the universal, and his ethical task is to express himself constantly in it, to abolish his particularity in order to become the universal. As soon as the individual would assert himself in his particularity over against the universal he sins, and only by

---

* Teleology is the theory of final ends, a way of perceiving life, natural processes, historical events as if they were purposeful and working toward a final end. The theory of divine providence is an example of a teleological theory. To say the heart beats *to pump* blood, or that cows eat grass *to give* milk, is to speak teleologically; all we know for certain is that the heart beats *and* that it pumps blood. The question, and the entire essay, asks—Can God suspend human ethics for teleological reasons that man cannot know?

recognizing this can he again reconcile himself with the universal. Whenever the individual after he has entered the universal feels an impulse to assert himself at the particular, he is in temptation (*Anfechtung*), and he can labor himself out of this only by abandoning himself as the particular in the universal. If this be the highest thing that can be said of man and of his existence, then the ethical has the same character as man's eternal blessedness, which to all eternity and at every instant is his *telos,* since it would be a contradiction to say that this might be abandoned (i.e. teleologically suspended), inasmuch as this is no sooner suspended than it is forfeited, whereas in other cases what is suspended is not forfeited but is preserved precisely in that higher thing which is its *telos.*

If such be the case, then Hegel is right when in his chapter on "The Good and the Conscience," he characterizes man merely as the particular and regards this character as "a moral form of the evil" which is to be annulled in the teleology of the moral, so that the individual who remains in this stage is either sinning or subjected to temptation (*Anfechtung*). On the other hand, he is wrong in talking of faith, wrong in not protesting loudly and clearly against the fact that Abraham enjoys honor and glory as the father of faith, whereas he ought to be prosecuted and convicted of murder.

For faith is this paradox, that the particular is higher than the universal—yet in such a way, be it observed, that the movement repeats itself, and that consequently the individual, after having been in the universal, now as the particular isolates himself as higher than the universal. If this be not faith, then Abraham is lost, then faith has never existed in the world . . . because it has always existed. For if the ethical (i.e. the moral) is the highest thing, and if nothing incommensurable remains in man in any other way but as the evil (i.e. the particular which has to be expressed in the universal), then one needs no other categories besides those which the Greeks possessed or which by consistent thinking can be derived from them. This fact Hegel ought not to have concealed, for after all he was acquainted with Greek thought.

One not infrequently hears it said by men who for lack of losing themselves in studies are absorbed in phrases that a light shines upon the Christian world whereas a darkness broods over paganism. This utterance has always seemed strange to me, inasmuch as every profound thinker and every serious artist is even in our day rejuvenated by the eternal youth of the Greek race. Such an utterance may be explained by the consideration that people do not know what they ought to say but only that they must say something. It is quite right for one to say that paganism did not possess faith, but if with this one is to have said something, one must be a little clearer about what one understands by faith, since otherwise one falls back into such phrases. To explain the whole of existence and faith along with it, without having a conception of what faith is, is easy, and that man does not make the poorest calculation in life who reckons upon admiration when he possesses such an explanation; for, as Boileau says, *"un sot trouve toujours un plus sot qui l'admire."* *

Faith is precisely this paradox, that the individual as the particular is higher than the universal, is justified over against it, is not subordinate but superior—yet in such a way, be it observed, that it is the particular individual who, after he has been subordinated as the particular to the universal, now through the universal becomes the individual who as the particular is superior to the universal, for the fact that the individual as the particular stands in an absolute relation to the absolute. This position cannot be mediated, for all mediation comes about precisely by virtue of the universal; it is and remains to all eternity a paradox, inaccessible to thought. And yet faith is this paradox—or else (these are the logical deductions which I would beg the reader to have *in mente* at every point, though it would be too prolix for me to reiterate them on every occasion)—or else there never has been faith . . . precisely because it always has been. In other words, Abraham is lost.

That for the particular individual this paradox may easily be mistaken for a temptation (*Anfechtung*) is indeed true, but one ought not for this reason to conceal it. That the whole constitution of many persons may be such that this paradox repels them is indeed true, but one ought not for this reason to make faith something different in order to be able to possess it, but ought rather to admit that one does not possess it, whereas those who possess faith should take care to set up certain criteria so that one might distinguish the paradox from a temptation (*Anfechtung*).

Now the story of Abraham contains such teleological suspension of the ethical. There have not been lacking clever pates and profound investigators who have found analogies to it. Their wisdom is derived from the pretty proposition that at bottom everything is the same. If one will look a little more closely, I have not much doubt that in the whole world one will not find a single analogy (except a later instance which proves nothing), if it stands fast that Abraham is the representative of faith, and that faith is normally expressed in him whose life is not merely the most paradoxical that can be thought but so paradoxical that it cannot be thought at all. He acts by virtue of the absurd, for it is precisely absurd that he as the particular is higher than the universal. This paradox cannot be mediated; for as soon as he begins to do this he has to admit that he was in temptation (*Anfechtung*), and if such was the case, he never gets to the point of sacrificing Isaac, or, if he has sacrificed Isaac, he must turn back repentantly to the universal. By virtue of the absurd he gets Isaac again. Abraham is therefore at no instant a tragic hero but something quite different, either a murderer or a believer. The middle term which saves the tragic hero, Abraham has not. Hence it is that I can

* An idiot always finds a greater idiot to admire him.

understand the tragic hero but cannot understand Abraham, though in a certain crazy sense I admire him more than all other men.

Abraham's relation to Isaac, ethically speaking, is quite simply expressed by saying that a father shall love his son more dearly than himself. Yet within its own compass the ethical has various gradations. Let us see whether in this story there is to be found any higher expression for the ethical such as would ethically explain his conduct, ethically justify him in suspending the ethical obligation toward his son, without in this search going beyond the teleology of the ethical.

When an undertaking in which a whole nation is concerned is hindered,[1] when such an enterprise is brought to a standstill by the disfavor of heaven, when the angry deity sends a calm which mocks all efforts, when the seer performs his heavy task and proclaims that the deity demands a young maiden as a sacrifice—then will the father heroically make the sacrifice. He will magnanimously conceal his pain, even though he might wish that he were "the lowly man who dares to weep,"[2] not the king who must act royally. And though solitary pain forces its way into his breast, he has only three confidants among the people, yet soon the whole nation will be cognizant of his pain, but also cognizant of his exploit, that for the welfare of the whole he was willing to sacrifice her, his daughter, the lovely young maiden. O charming bosom! O beautiful cheeks! O bright golden hair! And the daughter will affect him by her tears, and the father will turn his face away, but the hero will raise the knife.—When the report of this reaches the ancestral home, then will the beautiful maidens of Greece blush with enthusiasm, and if the daughter was betrothed, her true love will not be angry but be proud of sharing in the father's deed, because the maiden belonged to him more feelingly than to the father.

When the intrepid judge[3] who saved Israel in the hour of need in one breath binds himself and God by the same vow, then heroically the young maiden's jubilation, the beloved daughter's joy, he will turn to sorrow, and with her all Israel will lament her maiden youth; but every free-born man will understand, and every stout-hearted woman will admire Jephtha, and every maiden in Israel will wish to act as did his daughter. For what good would it do if Jephtha were victorious by reason of his vow if he did not keep it? Would not the victory again be taken from the nation?

---

1. The Trojan war. When the Greek fleet was unable to set sail from Aulis because of an adverse wind the seer Calchas announced that King Agamemnon had offended Artemis and that the goddess demanded his daughter Iphigenia as a sacrifice of expiation.
2. See Euripides, *Iphigenia in Aulis*, v. 448 in Wilster's translation. Agamemnon says, "How lucky to be born in lowly station where one may be allowed to weep." The confidants mentioned below are Menelaus, Calchas and Ulysses.
3. Jephtha. Judges 11:30–40.

When a son is forgetful of his duty,[4] when the state entrusts the father with the sword of justice, when the laws require punishment at the hand of the father, then will the father heroically forget that the guilty one is his son, he will magnanimously conceal his pain, but there will not be a single one among the people, not even the son, who will not admire the father, and whenever the law of Rome is interpreted, it will be remembered that many interpreted it more learnedly, but none so gloriously as Brutus.

If, on the other hand, while a favorable wind bore the fleet on with swelling sails to its goal, Agamemnon had sent that messenger who fetched Iphigenia in order to be sacrificed; if Jephtha, without being bound by any vow which decided the fate of the nation, had said to his daughter, "Bewail now thy virginity for the space of two months, for I will sacrifice thee"; if Brutus had had a righteous son and yet would have ordered the lictors to execute him—who would have understood them? If these three men had replied to the query why they did it by saying, "It is a trial in which we are tested," would people have understood them better?

When Agamemnon, Jephtha, Brutus at the decisive moment heroically overcome their pain, have heroically lost the beloved and have merely to accomplish the outward sacrifice, then there never will be a noble soul in the world who will not shed tears of compassion for their pain and of admiration for their exploit. If, on the other hand, these three men at the decisive moment were to adjoin to their heroic conduct this little word, "But for all that it will not come to pass," who then would understand them? If as an explanation they added, "This we believe by virtue of the absurd," who would understand them better? For who would not easily understand that it was absurd, but who would understand that one could then believe it?

The difference between the tragic hero and Abraham is clearly evident. The tragic hero still remains within the ethical. He lets one expression of the ethical find its *telos* in a higher expression of the ethical; the ethical relation between father and son, or daughter and father, he reduces to a sentiment which has its dialectic in its relation to the idea of morality. Here there can be no question of a teleological suspension of the ethical.

With Abraham the situation was different. By his act he overstepped the ethical entirely and possessed a higher *telos* outside of it, in relation to which he suspended the former. For I should very much like to know how one would bring Abraham's act into relation with the universal, and whether it is possible to discover any connection whatever between what Abraham did and the universal . . . except the fact that he transgressed it. It was not for the sake of saving a people, not to maintain the

---

4. The son of Brutus while his father was Consul took part in a conspiracy to restore the king Rome had expelled, and Brutus ordered him to be put to death.

idea of the state, that Abraham did this, and not in order to reconcile angry deities. If there could be a question of the deity being angry, he was angry only with Abraham, and Abraham's whole action stands in no relation to the universal, is a purely personal undertaking. Therefore, whereas the tragic hero is great by reason of his moral virtue, Abraham is great by reason of a personal virtue. In Abraham's life there is no higher expression for the ethical than this, that the father shall love his son. Of the ethical in the sense of morality there can be no question in this instance. In so far as the universal was present, it was indeed cryptically present in Isaac, hidden as it were in Isaac's loins, and must therefore cry out with Isaac's mouth, "Do it not! Thou art bringing everything to naught."

Why then did Abraham do it? For God's sake, and (in complete identity with this) for his own sake. He did it for God's sake because God required this proof of his faith; for his own sake he did it in order that he might furnish the proof. The unity of these two points of view is perfectly expressed by the word which has always been used to characterize this situation: it is a trial, a temptation (*Fristelse*).[5] A temptation—but what does that mean? What ordinarily tempts a man is that which would keep him from doing his duty, but in this case the temptation is itself the ethical . . . which would keep him from doing God's will. But what then is duty? Duty is precisely the expression for God's will.

Here is evident the necessity of a new category if one would understand Abraham. Such a relationship to the deity paganism did not know. The tragic hero does not enter into any private relationship with the deity, but for him the ethical is the divine, hence the paradox implied in his situation can be mediated in the universal.

Abraham cannot be mediated, and the same thing can be expressed also by saying that he cannot talk. So soon as I talk I express the universal, and if I do not do so, no one can understand me. Therefore if Abraham would express himself in terms of the universal, he must say that his situation is a temptation (*Anfechtung*), for he has no higher expression for that universal which stands above the universal which he transgresses.

Therefore, though Abraham arouses my admiration, he at the same time appalls me. He who denies himself and sacrifices himself for duty gives up the finite in order to grasp the infinite, and that man is secure enough. The tragic hero gives up the certain for the still more certain, and the eye of the beholder rests upon him confidently. But he who gives up the universal in order to grasp something still higher which is not the universal—what is he doing? Is it possible that this can be anything else but a temptation (*Anfechtung*)? And if it be possible . . . but the individual was mistaken—what can save him? He suffers all the pain of the tragic hero, he brings to naught his joy in the world, he renounces every-

---

5. This is temptation in the sense we ordinarily attach to the word.

thing . . . and perhaps at the same instant debars himself from the
sublime joy which to him was so precious that he would purchase it at any
price. Him the beholder cannot understand nor let his eye rest confidently
upon him. Perhaps it is not possible to do what the believer proposes,
since it is indeed unthinkable. Or if it could be done, but if the individual
had misunderstood the deity—what can save him? The tragic hero has
need of tears and claims them, and where is the envious eye which would
be so barren that it could not weep with Agamemnon; but where is the
man with a soul so bewildered that he would have the presumption to
weep for Abraham? The tragic hero accomplishes his act at a definite
instant in time, but in the course of time he does something not less
significant, he visits the man whose soul is beset with sorrow, whose breast
for stifled sobs cannot draw breath, whose thoughts pregnant with tears
weigh heavily upon him, to him he makes his appearance, dissolves the
sorcery of sorrow, loosens his corslet, coaxes forth his tears by the fact that
in his sufferings the sufferer forgets his own. One cannot weep over
Abraham. One approaches him with a *horror religiosus,** as Israel
approached Mount Sinai.—If then the solitary man who ascends Mount
Moriah, which with its peak rises heaven-high above the plain of Aulis,
if he be not a somnambulist who walks securely above the abyss while
he who is stationed at the foot of the mountain and is looking on
trembles with fear and out of reverence and dread dare not even call to
him—if this man is disordered in his mind, if he had made a mistake!
Thanks and thanks again to him who proffers to the man whom the
sorrows of life have assaulted and left naked—proffers to him the fig-leaf
of the word with which he can cover his wretchedness. Thanks be to thee,
great Shakespeare, who art able to express everything, absolutely everything, precisely as it is—and yet why didst thou never pronounce this
pang? Didst thou perhaps reserve it to thyself—like the loved one whose
name one cannot endure that the world should mention? For the poet
purchases the power of words, the power of uttering all the dread secrets
of others, at the price of a little secret he is unable to utter . . . and a poet
is not an apostle, he casts out devils only by the power of the devil.

But now when the ethical is thus teleologically suspended, how does
the individual exist in whom it is suspended? He exists as the particular
in opposition to the universal. Does he then sin? For this is the form of
sin, as seen in the idea. Just as the infant, though it does not sin,
because it is not as such yet conscious of its existence, yet its existence
is sin, as seen in the idea, and the ethical makes its demands upon it
every instant. If one denies that this form can be repeated [in the adult]
in such a way that it is not sin, then the sentence of condemnation is
pronounced upon Abraham. How then did Abraham exist? He believed.
This is the paradox which keeps him upon the sheer edge and which he

* Religious horror; awe.

cannot make clear to any other man, for the paradox is that he as the individual puts himself in an absolute relation to the absolute. Is he justified in doing this? His justification is once more the paradox; for if he is justified, it is not by virtue of anything universal, but by virtue of being the particular individual.

How then does the individual assure himself that he is justified? It is easy enough to level down the whole of existence to the idea of the state or the idea of society. If one does this, one can also mediate easily enough, for then one does not encounter at all the paradox that the individual as the individual is higher than the universal—which I can aptly express also by the thesis of Pythagoras, that the uneven numbers are more perfect than the even. If in our age one occasionally hears a rejoinder which is pertinent to the paradox, it is likely to be to the following effect: "It is to be judged by the result." A hero who has become a σκάνδαλον [6] to his contemporaries because they are conscious that he is a paradox who cannot make himself intelligible, will cry out defiantly to his generation, "The result will surely prove that I am justified." In our age we hear this cry rather seldom, for as our age, to its disadvantage, does not produce heroes, it has also the advantage of producing few caricatures. When in our age one hears this saying, "It is to be judged according to the result," a man is at once clear as to who it is he has the honor of talking with. Those who talk thus are a numerous tribe, whom I will denominate by the common name of *Docents*.[7] In their thoughts they live secure in existence, they have a *solid* position and *sure* prospects in a well-ordered state, they have centuries and even millenniums between them and the concussions of existence, they do not fear that such things could recur—for what would the police say to that! and the newspapers! Their lifework is to judge the great, and to judge them according to the result. Such behavior toward the great betrays a strange mixture of arrogance and misery: of arrogance, because they think they are called to be judges; of misery because they do not feel that their lives are even in the remotest degree akin to the great. Surely a man who possesses even a little *erectioris ingenii* * has not become entirely a cold and clammy mollusk, and when he approaches what is great it can never escape his mind that from the creation of the world it has been customary for the result to come last, and that, if one would truly learn anything from great actions, one must pay attention precisely to the beginning. In case he who should act were to judge himself according to the result, he would never get to the point of beginning. Even though the result may give joy to the whole world, it cannot help the hero, for he would get

---

6. This is the Scriptural word which we translate by "offense" or "stumbling block."
7. *Docents* and *Privatdocents* (both of them German titles for subordinate teachers in the universities) were very frequently the objects of S. K.'s satire. He spoke more frequently of "the professor" after Martensen had attained that title.
* More alertness of mind.

to know the result only when the whole thing was over, and it was not by this he became a hero, but he was such for the fact that he began.

Moreover, the result (inasmuch as it is the answer of finiteness to the infinite query) is in its dialectic entirely heterogeneous with the existence of the hero. Or is it possible to prove that Abraham was justified in assuming the position of the individual with relation to the universal . . . for the fact that he got Isaac by *miracle?* If Abraham had actually sacrificed Isaac, would he then have been less justified?

But people are curious about the result, as they are about the result in a book—they want to know nothing about dread, distress, the paradox. They flirt aesthetically with the result, it comes just as unexpectedly but also just as easily as a prize in the lottery; and when they have heard the result they are edified. And yet no robber of temples condemned to hard labor behind iron bars, is so base a criminal as the man who pillages the holy, and even Judas who sold his Master for thirty pieces of silver is not more despicable than the man who sells greatness.

It is abhorrent to my soul to talk inhumanly about greatness, to let it loom darkly at a distance in an indefinite form, to make out that it is great without making the human character of it evident—wherewith it ceases to be great. For it is not what happens to me that makes me great, but it is what I do, and there is surely no one who thinks that a man became great because he won the great prize in the lottery. Even if a man were born in humble circumstances, I would require of him nevertheless that he should not be so inhuman toward himself as not to be able to think of the King's castle except at a remote distance, dreaming vaguely of its greatness and wanting at the same time to exalt it and also to abolish it by the fact that he exalted it meanly. I require of him that he should be man enough to step forward confidently and worthily even in that place. He should not be unmanly enough to desire impudently to offend everybody by rushing straight from the street into the King's hall. By that he loses more than the King. On the contrary, he should find joy in observing every rule of propriety with a glad and confident enthusiasm which will make him frank and fearless. This is only a symbol, for the difference here remarked upon is only a very imperfect expression for spiritual distance. I require of every man that he should not think so inhumanly of himself as not to dare to enter those palaces where not merely the memory of the elect abides but where the elect themselves abide. He should not press forward impudently and impute to them kinship with himself; on the contrary, he should be blissful every time he bows before them, but he should be frank and confident and always be something more than a charwoman, for if he will not be more, he will never gain entrance. And what will help him is precisely the dread and distress by which the great are tried, for otherwise, if he has a bit of pith in him, they will merely arouse his justified envy. And what distance alone makes great, what people would make great by empty and hollow phrases, that they themselves reduce to naught.

Who was ever so great as that blessed woman, the Mother of God, the Virgin Mary? And yet how do we speak of her? We say that she was highly favored among women. And if it did not happen strangely that those who hear are able to think as inhumanly as those who talk, every young girl might well ask, "Why was not I too the highly favored?" And if I had nothing else to say, I would not dismiss such a question as stupid, for when it is a matter of favor, abstractly considered, everyone is equally entitled to it. What they leave out is the distress, the dread, the paradox. My thought is as pure as that of anyone, and the thought of the man who is able to think such things will surely become pure—and if this be not so, he may expect the dreadful; for he who once has evoked these images cannot be rid of them again, and if he sins against them, they avenge themselves with quiet wrath, more terrible than the vociferousness of ten ferocious reviewers. To be sure, Mary bore the child miraculously, but it came to pass with her after the manner of women, and that season is one of dread, distress and paradox. To be sure, the angel was a ministering spirit, but it was not a servile spirit which obliged her by saying to the other young maidens of Israel, "Despise not Mary. What befalls her is the extraordinary." But the Angel came only to Mary, and no one could understand her. After all, what woman was so mortified as Mary? And is it not true in this instance also that one whom God blesses He curses in the same breath? This is the spirit's interpretation of Mary, and she is not (as it shocks me to say, but shocks me still more to think that they have thoughtlessly and coquettishly interpreted her thus)—she is not a fine lady who sits in state and plays with an infant god. Nevertheless, when she says, "Behold the handmaid of the Lord"—then she is great, and I think it will not be found difficult to explain why she became the Mother of God. She has no need of worldly admiration, any more than Abraham has need of tears, for she was not a heroine, and he was not a hero, but both of them became greater than such, not at all because they were exempted from distress and torment and paradox, but they became great through these.

It is great when the poet, presenting his tragic hero before the admiration of men, dares to say, "Weep for him, for he deserves it." For it is great to deserve the tears of those who are worthy to shed tears. It is great that the poet dares to keep the crowd in awe, dares to castigate men, requiring that every man examine himself whether he be worthy to weep for the hero. For the waste-water of blubberers is a degradation of the holy.—But greater than all this is that the knight of faith dares to say even to the noble man who would weep for him, "Weep not for me, but weep for thyself."

One is deeply moved, one longs to be back in those beautiful times, a sweet yearning conducts one to the desired goal, to see Christ wandering in the promised land. One forgets the dread, the distress, the paradox. Was it so easy a matter not to be mistaken? Was it not dreadful that this man who walks among the others—was it not dreadful that He was God? Was it not dreadful to sit at table with Him? Was it so easy a matter to become an Apostle? But the result, eighteen hundred years—that is a help, it helps to the shabby deceit wherewith one deceives oneself and others. I do not feel the courage to wish to be contemporary with such events, but hence I do not judge severely those who were mistaken, nor think meanly of those who saw aright.

I return, however, to Abraham. Before the result, either Abraham was every minute a murderer, or we are confronted by a paradox which is higher than all mediation.

The story of Abraham contains therefore a teleological suspension of the ethical. As the individual he became higher than the universal. This is the paradox which does not permit of mediation. It is just as inexplicable how he got into it as it is inexplicable how he remained in it. If such is not the position of Abraham, then he is not even a tragic hero but a murderer. To want to continue to call him the father of faith, to talk of this to people who do not concern themselves with anything but words, is thoughtless. A man can become a tragic hero by his own powers—but not a knight of faith. When a man enters upon the way, in a certain sense the hard way of the tragic hero, many will be able to give him counsel; to him who follows the narrow way of faith no one can give counsel, him no one can understand. Faith is a miracle, and yet no man is excluded from it; for that in which all human life is unified is passion,[8] and faith is a passion.

Patterns: Psychological Argument (Reductio ad Absurdum)

Kierkegaard, like Nietzsche, is a philosopher of the extreme—his analyses are pushed to their outer limits. When he carries an argument to what most people would consider an absurd degree, he is not trying to amuse

8. Lessing has somewhere given expression to a similar thought from a purely aesthetic point of view. What he would show expressly in this passage is that sorrow too can find a witty expression. To this end he quotes a rejoinder of the unhappy English king, Edward II. In contrast to this he quotes from Diderot a story of a peasant woman and a rejoinder of hers. Then he continues: "That too was wit, and the wit of a peasant at that; but the situation made it inevitable." Consequently one must not seek to find the excuse for the witty expressions of pain and of sorrow in the fact that the person who uttered them was a superior person, well educated, intelligent, and witty withal, *for the passions make all men again equal*—but the explanation is to be found in the fact that in all probability everyone would have said the same thing in the same situation. The thought of a peasant woman a queen could have had and must have had, just as what the king said in that instance a peasant too would have been able to say and doubtless would have said.

the reader; he is merely trying to point out that, in ethical and religious matters, if an argument is not acceptable at its extremes, it should not be acceptable at all.

Throughout his analysis of the Abraham and Isaac story, Kierkegaard is intent on developing extreme answers to a series of logical questions: Why did God tempt Abraham? How does Abraham's trial differ from the trial of a tragic hero? Would it have made any difference if God had not intervened to save Isaac? Kierkegaard's method is dialectical and relentless. He hunts up questions, stalks answers, raises objections, and gradually carries everything to extremes. But Kierkegaard is not intent on pointing out the absurdity of a position so that we will deny it; he is intent on pointing out the absurdity of a position so that we will feel its terror. For only then can we existentially feel the nature of Abraham's ordeal, only then can we experience how shallow our faith is and how short it falls from true belief. For where faith exists, reason has no place.

What should emerge from this analysis is a sense of the complexity of rhetoric. For although rhetoric as manipulation has been emphasized throughout this work, rhetoric is not itself a vice; it is an instrument of persuasion, and may have tawdry uses or poetic ones. We are grateful for analysis that preserves us from succumbing to the negative, but often we are less grateful for that which analyzes positive feelings. In this suspicion of criticism, we betray hidden assumptions that criticism is a cutting tool but not a creative force, that it undermines rather than enhances emotional appreciation. Is it really true, as Carl Jung suggests, that the heart and the head cannot coexist? Or is Abraham Maslow closer to the truth when he argues that such dichotomies are in fact synthesized in self-actualizing persons? Are such fears really rooted in self-doubt? In fears of emotional poverty? If so, should we give in to fears whose side effect is a gradual but real impoverishment? For analysis is only conscious at first; imperceptibly it becomes a comfortable second nature, until finally we are left with a ripened experience, intense with emotion and made wise through understanding.

Problems

1. What is a temptation and how must it involve some violation or suspension of the ethical order of things?
2. What is the relationship of reason to faith when one is undergoing a temptation? What are the possible consequences of such an attitude?
3. How does the "knight of faith" differ from the "tragic hero"? Which do you find more comprehensible? Which do you find more admirable? What does this reveal about your attitude to this world, and toward man's relation to God?
4. What assumptions about the nature of man's relation to other men and about man's relation to God are revealed by Kierkegaard's analysis? Do you share those assumptions? Do any of the writers we have read, Christian or otherwise, share those assumptions?

31 FYODOR DOSTOYEVSKY

Fyodor Dostoyevsky (1821–1881) was arrested in 1849 for revolutionary activities and sentenced to be shot on December 22, 1849. At the last minute, the czar exhibited a macabre sense of humor, and after all the prisoners had been lined up in the snow before a firing squad, he ordered a reprieve. On Christmas eve, Dostoyevsky was shipped in irons to Siberia. His arrest profoundly affected him, and his encounter with heroic criminals made him a conservative and a messianic nationalist, increased his interest in the souls of suffering and self-willed types, and led him to view man as ruled by a perverse impulse to freedom, which man can only manifest by asserting his will over his reason.

In Notes from the Underground *(1864), Dostoyevsky develops an elaborate underground character, wretched and self-conscious, lucid and self-pitying, suffocating in his individuality yet intent on defiantly asserting it despite his knowledge of its absurdity and his recognition of the suffering it causes him. Utopian systems bent on creating harmonious conformity and superficial happiness have failed to account for the underground man in us, that dark perverse part of our being that prefers the noble suffering of a nuanced individuality to the ignoble happiness of the utopian systematizers.*

This conflict between freedom and individuality on the one hand and rationality and order on the other absorbs Dostoyevsky's thought and informs many of his novels. This chapter from The Brothers Karamazov *(1880), finished about three months before his death, suggests the existential fabric of his thought and analyzes, in the confrontation between Jesus and The Grand Inquisitor, the eternal conflict between heroic freedom and comfortable happiness, between individualism and collectivism.*

The Grand Inquisitor

'I'm afraid here, too, it's impossible to begin without an introduction, that is, a literary introduction—oh, dear,' Ivan laughed 'what a rotten author I'd make! You see the action of my poem takes place in the

From Fyodor Dostoyevsky, *The Brothers Karamazov* (Baltimore: Penguin Books, 1958), pp. 288–308.

sixteenth century and in those days, as you no doubt know from your lessons at school, it was the custom in poetical works to bring heavenly powers down to earth. Not to mention Dante, in France court clerks as well as monks in monasteries performed plays in which the Madonna, the angels, the saints, Christ, and even God himself were brought on the stage. In those days it was all done very artlessly. In Victor Hugo's *Notre Dame de Paris,* an edifying play, to which the people were admitted without charge, was performed at the Paris town hall in the reign of Louis XI to celebrate the birth of the French Dauphin. It was called *Le bon jugement de la trés sainte et gracieuse Vierge Marie,** and she appeared in person and pronounced her *bon jugement*. We occasionally had almost identical performances of plays, based on Old Testament stories, in Moscow before the time of Peter the Great. But in addition to plays, there were in those days a great many stories and "poems" in which, whenever required, holy angels and all the heavenly powers took part. In our monasteries monks were also occupied with translating, copying, and even composing such poems—and even under the Tartars. There is, for instance, one such monastery poem (translated from the Greek, of course): *The Holy Virgin's Journey Through Hell,* with descriptions as bold as those of Dante's. Our Lady visits hell and is shown round "the torments" by the archangel Michael. She sees the sinners and their sufferings. There is there, incidentally, a highly diverting category of sinners in a burning lake: those who are thrown into this lake can never swim out of it, and these "God forgets"—an expression of extraordinary depth and force. And so the Mother of God, shocked and weeping, kneels before the throne of God and begs for a free pardon for all in hell, for all she has seen there, without distinction. Her conversation with God is extraordinarily interesting. She beseeches, she refuses to go away, and when God points to the stigmata on the hands and feet of her Son and asks her: "How am I to forgive his torturers?"—she bids all the saints, all the martyrs, all the angels and archangels to kneel with her and pray for a free pardon for all without distinction. It ends by her obtaining from God a respite from torments every year from Good Friday to Trinity Sunday; † and the sinners in hell at once give thanks to the Lord and cry out to him: "Thou art just, O Lord, in that judgement!" Well, then, my little poem would also have been of that kind had it appeared at that time. In my poem he appears, though, it is true, he says nothing, but only appears and passes on. Fifteen centuries have passed since he gave the promise to come into his kingdom, fifteen centuries since his prophet wrote: "Behold I come quickly." "Of that day and hour knoweth no man, not the angels of heaven, but my Father only," as he said himself while still on earth. But mankind awaits him with the same faith and the same yearning. Oh, with

* The good judgment of the very saintly and gracious Virgin Mary.
† Approximately 59 days.

greater faith even, for fifteen centuries have passed since the pledges given to man from heaven have ceased:

> Trust what thy heart doth tell thee,
> Trust no pledges from above.

'And only the faith in what your heart tells you remains! It is true there were many miracles in those days. There were saints who worked miraculous cures; according to their "lives", the Holy Mother of God herself came to visit some holy men. But the devil does not slumber, and many people were already beginning to doubt the truth of those miracles. Just then there appeared in the north of Germany a dreadful new heresy. A great star, "burning as it were a lamp" (that is, the church), "fell upon the fountains of waters and they became wormwood". Those heresies began impiously to deny the existence of miracles. But those who remained faithful believed all the more ardently. The tears of mankind rose up to him as before, they waited for him, they loved him, they put their hope in him, they yearned to suffer and die for him as before. . . . And for countless ages mankind prayed with fiery faith, "Oh Lord our God, appear unto us." They called upon him for so many ages that he, in his infinite mercy, longed to come down to those who prayed to him. He had come down and had visited before that day some saints, martyrs, and holy hermits while they were still on earth, as is written in their "lives". In our own country, the poet Tyutchev, who believed sincerely in the truth of his words, proclaimed that:

> In slavish habit, the Heavenly King,
> By the burden of the Cross weighed down,
> Through my native land went wandering,
> Showering blessings upon village and town.

And I can assure you that it really was so. And now the time came when he wished to appear to the people, if only for a moment—to the tormented, suffering people, to the people sunk in filthy iniquity, but who loved him like innocent children. The action of my poem takes place in Spain, in Seville, during the most terrible time of the Inquisition, when fires were lighted every day throughout the land to the glory of God and

> In the splendid autos-da-fé *
> Wicked heretics were burnt.

Oh, of course, this was not the second coming when, as he promised, he would appear at the end of time in all his heavenly glory, and which would

---

* Literally, "act of the faith" (Port.); the ceremony accompanying the pronouncement of judgment by the Inquisition and followed by the execution of sentence by the secular authorities; broadly, the burning of a heretic.

be as sudden "as the lightning cometh out of the east, and shineth even unto the west". No, all he wanted was to visit his children only for a moment and just where the stakes of the heretics were crackling in the flames. In his infinite mercy he once more walked among men in the semblance of man as he had walked among men for thirty-three years fifteen centuries ago. He came down into the hot "streets and lanes" of the southern city just at the moment when, a day before, nearly a hundred heretics had been burnt all at once by the cardinal, the Grand Inquisitor, *ad majorem gloriam Dei* * in "a magnificent auto da fé", in the presence of the king, the court, the knights, the cardinals, and the fairest ladies of the Court and the whole population of Seville. He appeared quietly, inconspicuously, but everyone—and that is why it is so strange—recognized him. That might have been one of the finest passages in my poem—I mean, why they recognized him. The people are drawn to him by an irresistible force, they surround him, they throng about him, they follow him. He walks among them in silence with a gentle smile of infinite compassion. The sun of love burns in his heart, rays of Light, of Enlightenment, and of Power stream from his eyes and, pouring over the people, stir their hearts with responsive love. He stretches forth his hands to them, blesses them, and a healing virtue comes from contact with him, even with his garments. An old man, blind from childhood, cries out to him from the midst of the crowd "O Lord, heal me so that I may see thee", and it is as though scales fell from his eyes, and the blind man sees him. The people weep and kiss the ground upon which he walks. Children scatter flowers before him, sing and cry out to him: "Hosannah!" "It is he, it is he himself," they all repeat. "It must be he, it can be no one but he." He stops on the steps of the Cathedral of Seville at the moment when a child's little, open white coffin is brought in with weeping into the church: in it lies a girl of seven, the only daughter of a prominent citizen. The dead child is covered with flowers. "He will raise up your child", people shout from the crowd to the weeping mother. The canon, who has come out to meet the coffin, looks on perplexed and knits his brows. But presently a cry of the dead child's mother is heard. She throws herself at his feet. "If it is thou," she cries, holding out her hands to him, "then raise my child from the dead!" The funeral cortége halts. The coffin is lowered on to the steps at his feet. He gazes with compassion and his lips once again utter softly the words, "Talitha cumi"—"and the damsel arose". The little girl rises in the coffin, sits up, and looks around her with surprise in her smiling, wide-open eyes. In her hands she holds the nosegay of white roses with which she lay in her coffin. There are cries, sobs, and confusion among the people, and it is at that very moment that the Cardinal himself, the Grand Inquisitor, passes by the cathedral in the

* "To the greater glory of God"; the motto of the Jesuit order.

square. He is an old man of nearly ninety, tall and erect, with a shrivelled face and sunken eyes, from which though, a light like a fiery spark still gleams. Oh, he is not wearing his splendid cardinal robes in which he appeared before the people the day before, when the enemies of the Roman faith were being burnt—no, at that moment he is wearing only his old, coarse, monk's cassock. He is followed at a distance by his sombre assistants and his slaves and his "sacred" guard. He stops in front of the crowd and watches from a distance. He sees everything. He sees the coffin set down at *his* feet, he sees the young girl raised from the dead, and his face darkens. He knits his grey, beetling brows and his eyes flash with an ominous fire. He stretches forth his finger and commands the guards to seize *him*. And so great is his power and so accustomed are the people to obey him, so humble and submissive are they to his will, that the crowd immediately makes way for the guards and, amid the death-like hush that descends upon the square, they lay hands upon *him* and lead him away. The crowd, like one man, at once bows down to the ground before the old Inquisitor, who blesses them in silence and passes on. The guards take their Prisoner to the dark, narrow, vaulted prison in the old building of the Sacred Court and lock him in there. The day passes and night falls, the dark, hot and "breathless" Seville night. The air is "heavy with the scent of laurel and lemon". Amid the profound darkness, the iron door of the prison is suddenly opened and the old Grand Inquisitor himself slowly enters the prison with a light in his hand. He is alone and the door at once closes behind him. He stops in the doorway and gazes for a long time, for more than a minute, into his face. At last he approaches him slowly, puts the lamp on the table and says to him:

' "Is it you? You?"

'But, receiving no answer, he adds quickly: "Do not answer, be silent. And, indeed, what can you say? I know too well what you would say. Besides, you have no right to add anything to what you have said already in the days of old. Why, then, did you come to meddle with us? For you have come to meddle with us, and you know it. But do you know what is going to happen tomorrow? I know not who you are and I don't want to know: whether it is you or only someone who looks like him, I do not know, but tomorrow I shall condemn you and burn you at the stake as the vilest of heretics, and the same people who today kissed your feet, will at the first sign from me rush to rake up the coals at your stake tomorrow. Do you know that? Yes, perhaps you do know it," he added after a moment of deep reflection without taking his eyes off his prisoner for an instant.'

'I'm afraid I don't quite understand it, Ivan,' said Alyosha, who had been listening in silence all the time, with a smile. 'Is it just a wild fantasy, or has the old man made some mistake, some impossible *qui pro quo?*'*

'You can assume it to be the latter,' laughed Ivan, 'if our modern realism has spoilt you so much that you can't bear anything fantastic. If you prefer a *qui pro quo,* then let it be so. It is true,' he laughed again, 'the old man was ninety and he might have long ago gone mad about his fixed idea. He might, too, have been struck by the Prisoner's appearance. It might, finally, have been simply delirium. A vision the ninety-year-old man had before his death, particularly as he had been greatly affected by the burning of a hundred heretics at the auto-da-fé the day before. What difference does it make to us whether it was a *qui pro quo* or a wild fantasy? The only thing that matters is that the old man should speak out, that at last he does speak out and says aloud what he has been thinking in silence for ninety years.'

'And is the Prisoner also silent? Does he look at him without uttering a word?'

'Yes,' Ivan laughed again, 'that's how it should be in all such cases. The old man himself tells him that *he* has no right to add anything to what had already been said before. If you like, this is the most fundamental feature of Roman Catholicism, in my opinion at any rate: "Everything," he tells him, "has been handed over by you to the Pope and, therefore, everything is now in the Pope's hands, and there's no need for you to come at all now—at any rate, do not interfere for the time being." They not only speak, but also write in that sense. The Jesuits do at any rate. I've read it myself in the works of their theologians. "Have you the right to reveal to us even one of the mysteries of the world you have come from?" my old man asks him and he replies for him himself. "No, you have not. So that you may not add anything to what has been said before and so as not to deprive men of the freedom which you upheld so strongly when you were on earth. All that you might reveal anew would encroach on men's freedom of faith, for it would come as a miracle, and their freedom of faith was dearer to you than anything even in those days, fifteen hundred years ago. Was it not you who said so often in those days, 'I shall make you free'? But now you have seen those 'free' men," the old man adds suddenly with a pensive smile. "Yes, this business has cost us a great deal," he goes on, looking sternly at him, "but we've completed it at last in your name. For fifteen centuries we've been troubled by this freedom, but now it's over and done with for good. You don't believe that it is all over? You look meekly at me and do not deign even to be indignant with me? I want you to know that now—yes, today—these men are more than ever convinced that they are absolutely free, and yet they themselves have brought their freedom to us and humbly

---

* Literally, "he for him," that is, confusing the identities of two persons.

laid it at our feet. But it was we who did it. And was that what you wanted? Was that the kind of freedom you wanted?"'

'I'm afraid I don't understand again,' Alyosha interrupted. 'Is he being ironical, is he laughing?'

'Not in the least. You see, he glories in the fact that he and his followers have at last vanquished freedom and have done so in order to make men happy. "For," he tells him, "it is only now (he is, of course, speaking of the Inquisition), that it has become possible for the first time to think of the happiness of men. Man is born a rebel, and can rebels be happy? You were warned," he says to him. "There has been no lack of warnings and signs, but you did not heed the warnings. You rejected the only way by which men might be made happy, but, fortunately, in departing, you handed on the work to us. You have promised and you have confirmed it by your own word. You have given us the right to bind and unbind, and of course you can't possibly think of depriving us of that right now. Why, then, have you come to interfere with us?"

'And what's the meaning of "there has been no lack of warnings and signs"?' asked Alyosha.

'That, you see, is the chief thing about which the old man has to speak out.

' "The terrible and wise spirit, the spirit of self-destruction and non-existence," the old man went on, "the great spirit talked with you in the wilderness and we are told in the books that he apparently 'tempted' you. Is that so? And could anything truer have been said than what he revealed to you in his three questions and what you rejected, and what in the books are called 'temptations'? And yet if ever there has been on earth a real, prodigious miracle, it was on that day, on the day of the three temptations. Indeed, it was in the emergence of those three questions that the miracle lay. If it were possible to imagine, for the sake of argument, that those three questions of the terrible spirit had been lost without leaving a trace in the books and that we had to rediscover, restore, and invent them afresh and that to do so we had to gather together all the wise men of the earth—rulers, high priests, scholars, philosophers, poets—and set them the task of devising and inventing three questions which would not only correspond to the magnitude of the occasion, but, in addition, express in three words, in three short human sentences, the whole future history of the world and of mankind, do you think that the entire wisdom of the earth, gathered together, could have invented anything equal in depth and force to the three questions which were actually put to you at the time by the wise and mighty spirit in the wilderness? From those questions alone, from the miracle of their appearance, one can see that what one is dealing with here is not the human, transient mind, but the absolute and everlasting one. For in those three questions the whole future history of mankind is, as it were, anticipated and combined in one whole and three images are presented in which all the insoluble historical contradictions of human nature all over the world will meet. At the time it could not be so clearly seen, for the future was still unknown, but now, after fifteen centuries have gone by, we can see that everything in those three questions was so perfectly divined and foretold and has been so completely proved to be true that nothing can be added or taken from them.

' "Decide yourself who was right—you or he who questioned you then? Call to your mind the first question; its meaning, though not in these words, was this: 'You want to go into the world and you are going empty-handed, with some promise of freedom, which men in their simplicity and their innate lawlessness cannot even comprehend, which they fear and dread—for nothing has ever been more unendurable to man and to human society than freedom! And do you see the stones in this parched and barren desert? Turn them into loaves, and mankind will run after you like a flock of sheep, grateful and obedient, though for ever trembling with fear that you might withdraw your hand and they would no longer have your loaves.' But you did not want to deprive man of freedom and rejected the offer, for, you thought, what sort of freedom is it if obedience is bought with loaves of bread? You replied that man does not live by bread alone, but do you know that for the sake of that earthly bread the spirit of the earth will rise up against you and will join battle with you and conquer you, and all will follow him, crying 'Who is like this beast? He has given us fire from heaven!' Do you know that ages will pass and mankind will proclaim in its wisdom and science that there is no crime and, therefore, no sin, but that there are only hungry people. 'Feed them first and then demand virtue of them!'—that is what they will inscribe on their banner which they will raise against you and which will destroy your temple. A new building will rise where your temple stood, the dreadful Tower of Babel will rise up again, and though, like the first one, it will not be completed, yet you might have prevented the new tower and have shortened the sufferings of men by a thousand years—for it is to us that they will come at last, after breaking their hearts for a thousand years with their tower! Then they will look for us again under the ground, hidden in the catacombs (for we shall again be persecuted and tortured), and they will find us and cry out to us, 'Feed us, for those who have promised us fire from heaven have not given it to us!' And then we shall finish building their tower, for he who feeds them will complete it, and we alone shall feed them in your name, and we shall lie to them that it is in your name. Oh, without us they will never, never feed themselves. No science will give them bread so long as they remain free. But in the end they will lay their freedom at our feet and say to us, 'We don't mind being your slaves so long as you feed us!' They will, at last, realize themselves that there cannot be enough freedom and bread for everybody, for they will never, never be able to let everyone have his fair share! They will also be convinced that they can never be free because they are weak, vicious, worthless, and rebellious. You promised them bread from heaven, but, I repeat again, can it compare with earthly bread in the eyes of the weak, always vicious and always ignoble race of man? And if for the sake of the bread from heaven thousands and tens of thousands will follow you, what is to become of the millions and scores of thousands of millions of creatures who will not have the strength to give up the earthly bread for the bread of heaven? Or are only the scores of thousands of the great and strong dear to you, and are the remaining millions, numerous as the sand of the sea, who are weak but who love you, to serve only as the material for the great and the strong? No, to us the weak, too, are dear. They are vicious and rebellious, but in the end they will become obedient too. They will marvel at us and they will regard us as gods because, having become their masters, we consented to endure freedom and rule over them—so dreadful will freedom become to them in the end! But we shall tell them that we do your bidding and rule in your name. We shall deceive them again, for we shall not let you come near us again. That deception will be our suffering, for we shall be forced to lie. That was the meaning of the first question in the wilderness, and that was what you rejected in the name of freedom, which you put above everything else. And yet in that question lay hidden the great secret of this world. By accepting 'the loaves', you would have satisfied man's universal and everlasting craving, both as an individual and as mankind as a whole, which can be summed up in the words 'whom shall I worship?' Man, so long as he remains free, has no more constant and agonizing anxiety than to find as quickly as possible someone to worship. But man seeks to worship only what is incontestable, so incontestable, indeed, that all men at once agree to worship it all together. For the chief concern of those miserable creatures is not only to find something that I or someone else can worship, but to find something that all believe in and worship, and the absolutely essential thing is that they should do so *all together*. It is this need for *universal* worship that is the chief torment of every man individually and of mankind as a whole from the beginning of time. For the sake of that universal worship they have put each other to the sword. They have set up gods and called upon each other, 'Give up your gods and come and worship ours, or else death to you and to your gods!' And so it will be to the end of the world, even when the gods have vanished from the earth: they will prostrate themselves before idols just the same. You knew, you couldn't help knowing this fundamental mystery of human nature, but you rejected the only absolute banner, which was offered to you, to make all men worship you alone incontestably—the banner of earthly bread, which you rejected in the name of freedom and the bread from heaven. And look what you have done further—and all again in the name of freedom! I tell you man has no more agonizing anxiety than to find someone to whom he can hand over with all speed the gift of freedom with which the unhappy creature is born. But only he can gain possession of men's freedom who is able to set their conscience at ease. With the bread you were given an incontestable banner: give him bread and man will worship you, for there is nothing more incontestable than bread; but if at the same time someone besides yourself should gain possession of his conscience—oh, then he will even throw away your bread and follow him who has ensnared his conscience. You were right about that. For the mystery of human life is not only in living, but in knowing why one lives. Without a clear idea of what to live for man will not consent to live and will rather destroy himself than remain on the earth, though he were surrounded by loaves of bread. That is so, but what became of it? Instead of gaining possession of men's freedom, you gave them greater freedom than ever! Or did you forget that a tranquil mind and even death is dearer to man than the free choice in the knowledge of good and evil? There is nothing more alluring to man than this freedom of conscience, but there is nothing more tormenting, either. And instead of firm foundations for appeasing man's conscience once and for all, you chose everything that was exceptional, enigmatic, and vague, you chose everything that was beyond the strength of men, acting, consequently, as though you did not love them at all—you who came to give your life for them! Instead of taking possession of men's freedom you multiplied it and burdened the spiritual kingdom of man with its sufferings for ever. You wanted man's free love so that he should follow you freely, fascinated and captivated by you. Instead of the strict ancient law, man had in future to decide for himself with a free heart what is good and what is evil, having only your image before him for guidance. But did it never occur to you that he would at last reject and call in question even your image and your truth, if he were weighed down by so fearful a burden as freedom of choice? They will at last cry aloud that the truth is not in you, for it was impossible to leave them in greater confusion and suffering than you have done by leaving them with so many cares and insoluble problems. It was you yourself, therefore, who laid the foundation for the destruction of your kingdom and you ought not to blame anyone else for it. And yet, is that all that was offered to you? There are three forces, the only three forces that are able to conquer and hold captive for ever the conscience of these weak rebels for their own happiness—these forces are: miracle, mystery, and authority. You rejected all three and yourself set the example for doing so. When the wise and terrible spirit set you on a pinnacle of the temple and said to you: 'If thou be the Son of God, cast thyself down: for it is written, He shall give his angels charge concerning thee: and in their hands they shall bear thee up, lest at any time thou dash thy foot against a stone, and thou shalt prove then how great is thy faith in thy father.' But having heard him, you rejected his proposal and did not give way and did not cast yourself down. Oh, of course, you acted proudly and magnificently, like God. But men, the weak, rebellious race of men, are they gods? Oh, you understood perfectly then that in taking one step, in making a move to cast yourself down, you would at once have tempted God and have lost all your faith in him, and you would have been dashed to pieces against the earth which you came to save, and the wise spirit that tempted you would have rejoiced. But, I repeat, are there many like you? And could you really assume for a moment that men, too, could be equal to such a temptation? Is the nature of man such that he can reject a miracle and at the most fearful moments of life, the moments of his most fearful, fundamental, and agonizing spiritual problems, stick to the free decision of the heart? Oh, you knew that your great deed would be preserved in books, that it would go down to the end of time and the extreme ends of the earth, and you hoped that, following you, man would remain with God and ask for no miracle. But you did not know that as soon as man rejected miracle he would at once reject God as well, for what man seeks is not so much God as miracles. And since man is unable to carry on without a miracle, he will create new miracles for himself, miracles of his own, and will worship the miracle of the witch-doctor and the sorcery of the wise woman, rebel, heretic and infidel though he is a hundred times over. You did not come down from the cross when they shouted to you, mocking and deriding you: 'If thou be the Son of God, come down from the cross.' You did not come down because, again, you did not want to enslave man by a miracle and because you hungered for a faith based on free will and not on miracles. You hungered for freely given love and not for the servile raptures of the slave before the might that has terrified him once and for all. But here, too, your judgement of men was too high, for they are slaves, though rebels by nature. Look round and judge: fifteen centuries have passed, go and have a look at them: whom have you raised up to yourself? I swear, man has been created a weaker and baser creature than you thought him to be! Can he, can he do what you did? In respecting him so greatly, you acted as though you ceased to feel any compassion for him, for you asked too much of him—you who have loved him more than yourself! Had you respected him less, you would have asked less of him, and that would have been more like love, for his burden would have been lighter. He is weak and base. What does it matter if he does rebel against our authority everywhere now and is proud of his rebellion? It is the pride of a child and of a schoolboy. They are little children rioting in class and driving out their teacher. But an end will come to the transports of the children, too. They will pay dearly for it.

They will tear down the temples and drench the earth with blood. But they will realize at last, the foolish children, that although they are rebels, they are impotent rebels who are unable to keep up with their rebellion. Dissolving into foolish tears, they will admit at last that he who created them rebels must undoubtedly have meant to laugh at them. They will say so in despair, and their utterance will be a blasphemy which will make them still more unhappy, for man's nature cannot endure blasphemy and in the end will always avenge it on itself. And so, unrest, confusion, and unhappiness—this is the present lot of men after all you suffered for their freedom! Your great prophet tells in a vision and in an allegory that he saw all those who took part in the first resurrection and that there were twelve thousand of them from each tribe. But if there were so many then, they too, were not like men, but gods. They had borne your cross, they had endured scores of years of the hungry and barren wilderness, feeding on locusts and roots—and you can indeed point with pride to those children of freedom, freely given love, and free and magnificent sacrifice in your name. But remember that there were only a few thousand of them, and they, too, gods. But what of the rest? And why are the rest, the weak ones, to blame if they were not able to endure all that the mighty ones endured? Why is the weak soul to blame for being unable to receive gifts so terrible? Surely, you did not come only to the chosen and for the chosen? But if so, there is a mystery here and we cannot understand it. And if it is a mystery, then we, too, were entitled to preach a mystery and to teach them that it is neither the free verdict of their hearts nor love that matters, but the mystery which they must obey blindly, even against their conscience. So we have done. We have corrected your great work and have based it on *miracle, mystery, and authority.* And men rejoiced that they were once more led like sheep and that the terrible gift which had brought them so much suffering had at last been lifted from their hearts. Were we right in doing and teaching this? Tell me. Did we not love mankind when we admitted so humbly its impotence and lovingly lightened its burden and allowed men's weak nature even to sin, so long as it was with our permission? Why, then, have you come to meddle with us now? And why are you looking at me silently and so penetratingly with your gentle eyes? Get angry, I do not want your love because I do not love you myself. And what have I to hide from you? Or don't I know to whom I am speaking? All I have to tell you is already known to you. I can read it in your eyes. And would I conceal our secret from you? Perhaps it is just what you want to hear from my lips. Well, then, listen. We are not with you but with *him:* that is our secret! It's a long time—eight centuries—since we left you and went over to *him.* Exactly eight centuries ago we took from him what you rejected with scorn, the last gift he offered you, after having shown you all the kingdoms of the earth: we took from him Rome and the sword of Caesar and proclaimed ourselves the rulers of the earth, the sole rulers, though to this day we have not succeeded in bringing our work to total completion. But whose fault is it? Oh, this work is only beginning, but it has begun. We shall have to wait a long time for its completion and the earth will have yet much to suffer, but we shall reach our goal and be Caesars and it is then that we shall think about the universal happiness of man. And yet even in those days you could have taken up the sword of Caesar. Why did you reject that last gift? By accepting that third counsel of the mighty spirit, you would have accomplished all that man seeks on earth, that is to say, whom to worship, to whom to entrust his conscience and how at last to unite all in a common, harmonious, and incontestable ant-hill, for the need of universal unity is the third and last torment of men. Mankind as a whole has always striven to organize itself into a world state. There have been many great nations with great histories, but the more highly developed they were, the more unhappy they were, for they were more acutely conscious of the need for the world-wide union of men. The great conquerors, the Timurs and Ghenghis-Khans, swept like a whirlwind over the earth, striving to conquer the world, but, though unconsciously, they expressed the same great need of mankind for a universal and world-wide union. By accepting the world and Caesar's purple, you would have founded the world state and given universal peace. For who is to wield dominion over men if not those who have taken possession of the consciences and in whose hands is their bread? And so we have taken the sword of Caesar and, having taken it, we of course rejected you and followed *him*. Oh, many more centuries are yet to pass of the excesses of their free mind, of their science and cannibalism, for, having begun to build their Tower of Babel without us, they will end up with cannibalism. But then the beast will come crawling up to us and will lick our feet and will bespatter them with tears of blood from its eyes. And we shall sit upon the beast and raise the cup, and on it will be written: 'Mystery!' And then, and only then, will the reign of peace and happiness come to men. You pride yourself upon your chosen ones, but you have only the chosen ones, while we will bring peace to all. But that is not all: how many of those chosen ones, of those mighty ones who could have become the chosen ones, have at last grown tired of waiting for you and have carried and will go on carrying the powers of their spirit and the ardours of their hearts to another field and will end by raising their *free* banner against you? But you raised that banner yourself. With us, however, all will be happy and will no longer rise in rebellion nor exterminate one another, as they do everywhere under your freedom. Oh, we will convince them that only then will they become free when they have resigned their freedom to us and have submitted to us. And what do you think? Shall we be right or shall we be lying? They will themselves be convinced that we are right, for they will remember the horrors of slavery and confusion to which your freedom brought them. Freedom, a free mind and science will lead them into such a jungle and bring them face to face with such marvels and insoluble mysteries that some of them, the recalcitrant and the fierce, will destroy themselves, others, recalcitrant but weak, will destroy one another, and the rest, weak and unhappy, will come crawling to our feet and cry aloud: 'Yes, you were right, you alone possessed his mystery and we come back to you—save us from ourselves!' In receiving loaves from us, they will, of course, see clearly that we are taking the loaves made by their own hands in order to distribute them among themselves, without any miracle. They will see that we have not made stones into loaves, but they will, in truth, be more pleased with receiving them from our hands than with the bread itself! For they will remember only too well that before, without us, the bread they made turned to stones in their hands, but that when they came back to us, the very stones turned to bread in their hands. They will appreciate only too well what it means to submit themselves to us for ever! And until men understand this, they will be unhappy. And who, pray, was more than anyone responsible for that lack of understanding? Who divided the flock and scattered it on unknown paths? But the flock will be gathered together again and will submit once more, and this time it will be for good. Then we shall give them quiet, humble happiness, the happiness of weak creatures, such as they were created. Oh, we shall at last persuade them not to be proud, for you raised them up and by virtue of that taught them to be proud; we shall prove to them that they are weak, that they are mere pitiable children, but that the happiness of a child is the sweetest of all. They will grow timid and begin looking up to us and cling to us in fear as chicks to the hen. They will marvel at us and be terrified of us and be proud that we are so mighty and so wise as to be able to tame such a turbulent flock of thousands of millions. They will be helpless and in constant fear of our wrath, their minds will grow timid, their eyes will always be shedding tears like women and children, but at the slightest sign from us they will be just as ready to pass to mirth and laughter, to bright-eyed gladness and happy childish song. Yes, we shall force them to work, but in their leisure hours we shall make their life like a children's game, with children's songs, in chorus, and with innocent dances. Oh, we shall permit them to sin, too, for they are weak and helpless, and they will love us like children for allowing them to sin. We shall tell them that every sin can be expiated, if committed with our permission; that we allow them to sin because we love them all and as for the punishment for their sins—oh well, we shall take it upon ourselves. And we shall take it upon ourselves, and they will adore us as benefactors who have taken their sins upon ourselves before God. And they will have no secrets from us. We shall allow or forbid them to live with their wives and mistresses, to have or not have children—everything according to the measure of their obedience—and they will submit themselves to us gladly and cheerfully. The most tormenting secrets of their conscience—everything, everything they will bring to us, and we shall give them our decision for it all, and they will be glad to believe in our decision, because it will relieve them of their great anxiety and of their present terrible torments of coming to a free decision themselves. And they will all be happy, all the millions of creatures, except the hundred thousand who rule over them. For we alone, we who guard the mystery, we alone shall be unhappy. There will be thousands of millions of happy infants and one hundred thousand sufferers who have taken upon themselves the curse of knowledge of good and evil. Peacefully they will die, peacefully will they pass away in your name, and beyond the grave they will find nothing but death. But we shall keep the secret and for their own happiness will entice them with the reward of heaven and eternity. For even if there were anything at all in the next world, it would not of course be for such as they. They declare and prophesy that you will come and be victorious again, that you will come with your chosen ones, with your proud and mighty ones, but we shall declare that they have only saved themselves, while we have saved all. It is said that the whore, who sits upon the beast and holds in her hands the *mystery,* will be put to shame, that the weak will rise up again, that they will rend her purple and strip naked her 'vile' body. But then I will rise and point out to you the thousands of millions of happy babes who have known no sin. And we who, for their happiness, have taken their sins upon ourselves, we shall stand before you and say, 'Judge us if you can and if you dare.' Know that I am not afraid of you. Know that I, too, was in the wilderness, that I, too, fed upon locusts and roots, that I, too, blessed freedom, with which you have blessed men, and that I, too, was preparing to stand among your chosen ones, among the strong and mighty, thirsting 'to make myself of the number'. But I woke up and refused to serve madness. I went back and joined the hosts of those who have *corrected your work.* I went away from the proud and returned to the meek for the happiness of the meek. What I say to you will come to pass and our kingdom will be established. I repeat, tomorrow you will behold the obedient flock which at a mere sign from me will rush to heap up the hot coals against the stake at which I shall burn you because you have come to meddle with us. For if anyone has ever deserved our fire, it is you. Tomorrow I shall burn you. *Dixi!"* *

Ivan stopped. He had got worked up as he talked and he spoke with enthusiasm; but when he had finished, he suddenly smiled.

Alyosha, who had listened to him in silence, tried many times towards

* I have spoken.

the end to interrupt him, restraining his great agitation with an effort. But now he suddenly burst into speech, as though carried away beyond control.

'But,' he cried, reddening, 'this is absurd! Your poem is in praise of Jesus and not in his disparagement as—as you wanted it to be. And who will believe you about freedom? Is that the way to understand it? Is that the way it is understood by the Greek Orthodox Church? It's Rome, and not the whole of Rome, either—it's not true. They are the worst among the Catholics—the Inquisitors, the Jesuits! . . . And, besides, there could never have been such a fantastic person as your Inquisitor. What are those sins of men they take upon themselves? Who are these keepers of the mystery who have taken some sort of curse upon themselves for the happiness of men? When have they been seen? We know the Jesuits, people speak ill of them—do you really think they are the people in your poem? They are certainly not the same at all. . . . They are simply the Romish army for the future establishment of a universal government on earth, with the Emperor—the Pontiff of Rome—at its head. That is their ideal, but without any mystery or lofty sadness about it. . . . It's the most ordinary lust for power, for filthy earthly gains, enslavement—something like a future regime of serfdom with them as the landowners—that is all they are after. Perhaps they don't even believe in God. Your suffering Inquisitor is nothing but a fantasy. . . .'

'Wait, wait,' Ivan laughed, 'don't be so excited! You say it's a fantasy—very well, I don't deny it. Of course it's a fantasy. But, look here, you don't really think that the Catholic movement in the last few centuries is really nothing but a lust for power for the sake of some filthy gains. . . . It isn't by any chance Father Paissy's teachings, is it?'

'No, no, on the contrary, Father Paissy once said something of the same kind as you, but,' Alyosha suddenly recollected himself, 'of course, it's not the same thing at all. Not the same thing at all!'

'A very valuable piece of information all the same in spite of your "not the same thing at all". What I'd like to ask you is why your Jesuits and Inquisitors have united only for some vile material gains? Why shouldn't there be among them a sufferer tormented by great sorrow and loving humanity? You see, let us suppose that among all those who are only out for filthy material gains there's one, just one, who is like my old Inquisitor, who had himself fed on roots in the wilderness a man possessed, who was eager to mortify his flesh so as to become free and perfect; and yet one who had loved humanity all his life and whose eyes were suddenly opened and who saw that it was no great moral felicity to attain complete control over his will and at the same time achieve the conviction that millions of other God's creatures had been created as a mockery, that they would never be able to cope with their freedom, that no giants would ever arise from the pitiful rebels to complete the tower, that the great idealist had not in mind such boobies when he dreamt of his harmony. Realizing that, he returned and joined—the clever fellows. That could have happened, couldn't it?

'Whom did he join? What clever fellows?' cried Alyosha, almost passionately. 'They are not so clever and they have no such mysteries and secrets. Except perhaps only godlessness, that's all their secret. Your inquisitor doesn't believe in God—that's all his secret!'

'Well, suppose it is so! At last you've guessed it! And, in fact, it really is so. That really is his whole secret. But is that not suffering, particularly for a man like him who had sacrificed his whole life for a great cause in the wilderness and has not cured himself of his love of humanity? In his last remaining years he comes to the clear conviction that it is only the advice of the great and terrible spirit that could bring some sort of supportable order into the life of the feeble rebels, "the unfinished experimental creatures created as a mockery". And so, convinced of that, he sees that one has to follow the instructions of the wise spirit, the terrible spirit of death and destruction. He therefore accepts lies and deceptions and leads men consciously to death and destruction. Keeps deceiving them all the way, so that they should not notice where they are being led, for he is anxious that those miserable, blind creatures should at least on the way think themselves happy. And, mind you, the deception is in the name of him in whose ideal the old man believed so passionately all his life! Is not that a calamity? And even if there were only one such man at the head of the whole army of men "craving for power for the sake of filthy gains"—would not even one such man be sufficient to make a tragedy? Moreover, one man like that, standing at the head of the movement, is enough for the emergence of a real leading idea of the entire Roman Church with all its armies and Jesuits—the highest idea of this Church. I tell you frankly it's my firm belief that there was never any scarcity of such single individuals among those who stood at the head of the movement. Who knows, there may have been many such individuals among the Roman Pontiffs, too. Who knows, perhaps this accursed old man, who loves humanity so obstinately in his own particular way, still exists even now in the form of a whole multitude of such individual old men, and not by chance, either, but by agreement, as a secret society formed long ago to guard the mystery. To guard it from the weak and unhappy, so as to make them happy. I'm sure it exists and, indeed, it must be so. I can't help feeling that something of the same kind of mystery exists also among the freemasons at the basis of their organization. That is why the Catholics hate the freemasons so much, for they regard them as their competitors who are breaking up the unity of their idea, while there should be only one flock and one shepherd. However, I feel that in defending my theory I must appear to you as an author who resents your criticism. Let's drop it.'

'You're probably a freemason yourself!' Alyosha cried, unable to restrain himself. 'You don't believe in God,' he added, but this time in great sorrow. He imagined, besides, that his brother was looking mockingly at him. 'How does your poem end?' he asked suddenly, his eyes fixed on the ground. 'Or was that the end?'

'I intended to end it as follows: when the Inquisitor finished speaking, he waited for some time for the Prisoner's reply. His silence distressed him. He saw that the Prisoner had been listening intently to him all the time, looking gently into his face and evidently not wishing to say anything in reply. The old man would have liked him to say something, however bitter and terrible. But he suddenly approached the old man and kissed him gently on his bloodless, aged lips. That was all his answer. The old man gave a start. There was an imperceptible movement at the corners of his mouth; he went to the door, opened it and said to him: "Go, and come no more—don't come at all—never, never!" And he let him out into "the dark streets and lanes of the city". The Prisoner went away.'

'And the old man?'

'The kiss glows in his heart, but the old man sticks to his idea.'

Problems

1. What are The Grand Inquisitor's assumptions about man? Of the writers we have read, whose do they most approximate? Compare and contrast your own value system.
2. What are the Prisoner's assumptions about man? Of the writers we have read, whose do they most approximate? Compare and contrast your own value system.
3. What are the three questions put to Christ in the wilderness? Why does freedom become the major conflict between the Prisoner and the Inquisitor?
4. What is meant by "miracle, mystery and authority"? Do you agree that this is what people crave? How does the Inquisitor's analysis resemble Freud's? Which side would Marx be on? Lenin? Paul? Kierkegaard?
5. Erich Fromm in *The Art of Loving* asserts that before one can love another one must first love oneself. In Dostoyevsky's *The Brothers Karamazov*, Father Zossima offers his formula for faith: "Active love. Strive to love your neighbour actively and indefatigably. In as far as you advance in love you will grow surer of the reality of God and of the immortality of your soul. If you attain to perfect self-forgetfulness in the love of your neighbour, then you will believe without doubt, and no doubt can possibly enter your soul" (14 Dostoyevsky). For Fromm, love of self leads to love of others. For Zossima, love of others leads to love of God. Which perspective most commends itself to you as the primary step? Why?

32 JEAN-PAUL SARTRE

Jean-Paul Sartre (1905–   ) is a French writer and existentialist philosopher who has contributed greatly to the popularization of existentialism through the sound and color of his aphorisms and through the power of his plays and novels. He is thus rare in being both an influential philosopher and a successful writer.

*"Existentialism is a Humanism," a famous lecture given by Sartre in 1946, was not intended to be a definitive statement of existentialism. In it, however, starting with the assumption that "existence precedes essence"—that one exists before one creates an identity—Sartre explores the groundwork of Sartrean ontology. Man is defined as a subjective consciousness in flux, striving to attain objective permanence; man is thus ever evolving and never static. Only "self-deception" (*mauvaise foi; *literally, "bad faith") and cowardice can lead one to believe one has a fixed identity; man is condemned to freedom, to perpetual choice and discovery, burdened with the possibility at every moment of carving out a new identity.*

The importance of freedom, choice, and engagement *or commitment took on increased importance in Sartre's thought while he was a member of the French underground during World War II. His experience there taught him that life has meaning when men invest it with meaning, that self-deception is making cowardly excuses for acting badly or without conviction; that risking death for one's conviction is the final measure not only of one's commitment, but of the meaning of one's life. He sums up these thoughts in an essay written at the time of the Liberation of France.*

> We were never more free than under the Nazi Occupation. We had lost all our rights, beginning with the right to speak. We were insulted daily and had to bear those insults in silence. On one pretext or another—as workers, Jews, political prisoners—Frenchmen were deported. . . . And because of all this we were free: precisely because the Nazi poison was seeping in our thoughts, every true thought was a victory. . . . Every instant we lived to the full the meaning of that banal little phrase "All men are mortal." The choice that each of us made of his life and his being was a genuine choice because it was made in the presence of death; because it could always have been expressed in the form "Rather death than . . ." Everyone of us who knew the truth about the Resistance asked himself anxiously "If they torture me, shall I be able to keep silent?" Thus the basic question of freedom was set before

us; and we were brought to the point of the deepest knowledge a man can have of himself. The secret of man is not his Oedipus complex or his inferiority complex; it is the limit of his own freedom; his capacity for standing up to torture and death (58 Sartre).

In 1964, in keeping with his existentialist hostility to awards and prizes, Sartre returned the Nobel Prize for literature. In recent years, he has attempted a Marxist-existentialist synthesis with mixed success. Kolakowski has acknowledged Sartre's influence, but Sartre has also been attacked. For a commentary on Sartre's attempted synthesis by a Marxist philosopher, see the two essays by Adam Schaff.

Existentialism Is a Humanism

I should like on this occasion to defend existentialism against some charges which have been brought against it.

First, it has been charged with inviting people to remain in a kind of desperate quietism because, since no solutions are possible, we should have to consider action in this world as quite impossible. We should then end up in a philosophy of contemplation; and since contemplation is a luxury, we come in the end to a bourgeois philosophy. The Communists in particular have made these charges.

On the other hand, we have been charged with dwelling on human degradation, with pointing up everywhere the sordid, shady, and slimy, and neglecting the gracious and beautiful, the bright side of human nature; for example, according to Mlle. Mercier, a Catholic critic, with forgetting the smile of the child. Both sides charge us with having ignored human solidarity, with considering man as an isolated being. The Communists say that the main reason for this is that we take pure subjectivity, the *Cartesian I think*,* as our starting point; in other words, the moment in which man becomes fully aware of what it means to him to be an isolated being; as a result, we are unable to return to a state of solidarity with the men who are not ourselves, a state which we can never reach in the *cogito*.

From the Christian standpoint, we are charged with denying the reality and seriousness of human undertakings, since, if we reject God's

From Jean-Paul Sartre, *Existentialism* (New York: Philosophical Library, Inc., 1947), pp. 11–61.
* The reference is to French philosopher and mathematician René Descartes (1596–1650), whose *Discourse on Method* (1637) has as its initial assumption, *Cogito, ergo sum:* "I think, therefore I am."

commandments and the eternal verities, there no longer remains anything but pure caprice, with everyone permitted to do as he pleases and incapable, from his own point of view, of condemning the points of view and acts of others.

I shall try today to answer these different charges. Many people are going to be surprised at what is said here about humanism. We shall try to see in what sense it is to be understood. In any case, what can be said from the very beginning is that by Existentialism we mean a doctrine which makes human life possible and, in addition, declares that every truth and every action implies a human setting and a human subjectivity.

As is generally known, the basic charge against us is that we put the emphasis on the dark side of human life. Someone recently told me of a lady who, when she let slip a vulgar word in a moment of irritation, excused herself by saying, "I guess I'm becoming an Existentialist." Consequently, Existentialism is regarded as something ugly; that is why we are said to be naturalists; and if we are, it is rather surprising that in this day and age we cause so much more alarm and scandal than does naturalism, properly so called. The kind of person who can take in his stride such a novel as Zola's *The Earth* is disgusted as soon as he starts reading an Existentialist novel; the kind of person who is resigned to the wisdom of the ages—which is pretty sad—finds us even sadder. Yet, what can be more disillusioning than saying "true charity begins at home" or "a scoundrel will always return evil for good?"

We know the commonplace remarks made when this subject comes up, remarks which always add up to the same thing: we shouldn't struggle against the powers that be; we shouldn't resist authority; we shouldn't try to rise above our station; any action which doesn't conform to authority is romantic; any effort not based on past experience is doomed to failure; experience shows that man's bent is always toward trouble, that there must be a strong hand to hold him in check, if not, there will be anarchy. There are still people who go on mumbling these melancholy old saws, the people who say, "It's only human!" whenever a more or less repugnant act is pointed out to them, the people who glut themselves on *chansons réalistes;** these are the people who accuse Existentialism of being too gloomy, and to such an extent that I wonder whether they are complaining about it, not for its pessimism, but much rather its optimism. Can it be that what really scares them in the doctrine I shall try to present here is that it leaves to man a possibility of choice? To answer this question, we must reexamine it on a strictly philosophical plane. What is meant by the term *Existentialism?*

Most people who use the word would be rather embarrassed if they had to explain it, since, now that the word is all the rage, even the work of a musician or painter is being called "existentialist." A gossip colum-

---

* Realistic, satiric songs commenting on contemporary persons or events.

nist in *Clartés* signs himself *The Existentialist*, so that by this time the word has been so stretched and has taken on so broad a meaning, that it no longer means anything at all. It seems that for want of an advance-guard doctrine analogous to surrealism, the kind of people who are eager for scandal and flurry turn to this philosophy, which in other respects does not at all serve their purposes in this sphere.

Actually, it is the least scandalous, the most austere of doctrines. It is intended strictly for specialists and philosophers. Yet it can be defined easily. What complicates matters is that there are two kinds of Existentialist; first, those who are Christian, among whom I would include Jaspers and Gabriel Marcel, both Catholic; and on the other hand the atheistic Existentialists, among whom I class Heidegger, and then the French Existentialists and myself. What they have in common is that they think that existence precedes essence, or, if you prefer, that subjectivity must be the starting point.

Just what does that mean? Let us consider some object that is manufactured, for example, a book or a paper cutter: here is an object which has been made by an artisan whose inspiration came from a concept. He referred to the concept of what a paper cutter is and likewise to a known method of production, which is part of the concept, something which is, by and large, a routine. Thus, the paper cutter is at once an object produced in a certain way and, on the other hand, one having a specific use; and one cannot postulate a man who produces a paper cutter but does not know what it is used for. Therefore, let us say that, for the paper cutter, essence—that is, the ensemble of both the production routines and the properties which enable it to be both produced and defined—precedes existence. Thus, the presence of the paper cutter or book in front of me is determined. Therefore, we have here a technical view of the world whereby it can be said that production precedes existence.

When we conceive God as the Creator, He is generally thought of as a superior sort of artisan. Whatever doctrine we may be considering, whether one like that of Descartes or that of Leibnitz, we always grant that will more or less follows understanding or, at the very least, accompanies it, and that when God creates He knows exactly what He is creating. Thus, the concept of man in the mind of God is comparable to the concept of paper cutter in the mind of the manufacturer, and, following certain techniques and a conception, God produces man, just as the artisan, following a definition and a technique, makes a paper cutter. Thus, the individual man is the realization of a certain concept in the divine intelligence.

In the eighteenth century, the atheism of the *philosophes* discarded the idea of God, but not so much for the notion that essence precedes existence. To a certain extent, this idea is found everywhere; we find it in Diderot, in Voltaire, and even in Kant. Man has a human nature; this human nature, which is the concept of the human, is founded in all men, which means that each man is a particular example of a universal concept, man. In Kant, the result of this universality is that the wild man, the natural man, as well as the bourgeois, are circumscribed by the same definition and have the same basic qualities. Thus, here too the essence of man precedes the historical existence that we find in nature.

Atheistic Existentialism, which I represent, is more coherent. It states that if God does not exist, there is at least one being in whom existence precedes essence, a being who exists before he can be defined by any concept, and that this being is man, or, as Heidegger says, human reality. What is meant here by saying that existence precedes essence? It means that, first of all, man exists, turns up, appears on the scene, and, only afterwards, defines himself. If man, as the Existentialist conceives him, is indefinable, it is because at first he is nothing. Only afterward will he be something, and he himself will have made what he will be. Thus, there is no human nature, since there is no God to conceive it. Not only is man what he conceives himself to be, but he is also only what he wills himself to be after this thrust toward existence.

Man is nothing else but what he makes of himself. Such is the first principle of Existentialism. It is also what is called "subjectivity," the name we are labeled with when charges are brought against us. But what do we mean by this, if not that man has a greater dignity than a stone or table? For we mean that man first exists, that is, that man first of all is the being who hurls himself toward a future and who is conscious of imagining himself as being in the future. Man is at the start a plan which is aware of itself, rather than a patch of moss, a piece of garbage, or a cauliflower; nothing exists prior to this plan; there is nothing in heaven; man will be what he will have planned to be. Not what he will want to be. Because by the word "will" we generally mean a conscious decision, which is subsequent to what we have already made of ourselves. I may want to belong to a political party, write a book, get married; but all that is only a manifestation of an earlier, more spontaneous choice that is called "will." But if existence really does precede essence, man is responsible for what he is. Thus, Existentialism's first move is to make every man aware of what he is and to make the full responsibility of his existence rest on him. And when we say that a man is responsible for himself, we do not only mean that he is responsible for his own individuality, but that he is responsible for all men.

The word "subjectivism" has two meanings, and our opponents play on the two. Subjectivism means, on the one hand, that an individual chooses and makes himself; and, on the other, that it is impossible for man to transcend human subjectivity. The second of these is the essential meaning of Existentialism. When we say that man chooses his own self, we mean that every one of us does likewise; but we also mean by that that in making this choice he also chooses all men. In fact, in creating the man that we want to be, there is not a single one of our acts which does not at the same time create an image of man as we think he ought to be. To choose to be this or that is to affirm at the same time the value of what we choose, because we can never choose evil. We always choose the good, and nothing can be good for us without being good for all.

If, on the other hand, existence precedes essence, and if we grant that we exist and fashion our image at one and the same time, the image is valid for everybody and for our whole age. Thus, our responsibility is much greater than we might have supposed, because it involves all mankind. If I am a workingman and choose to join a Christian trade union rather than be a Communist, and if by being a member I want to show that the best thing for man is resignation, that the kingdom of man is not of this world, I am not only involving my own case—I want to be resigned for everyone. As a result, my action has involved all humanity. To take a more individual matter, if I want to marry, to have children, even if this marriage depends solely on my own circumstances or passion or wish, I am involving all humanity in monogamy and not merely myself. Therefore, I am responsible for myself and for everyone else. I am creating a certain image of man of my own choosing. In choosing myself, I choose man.

This helps us understand what the actual content is of such rather grandiloquent words as anguish, forlornness, despair. As you will see, it's all quite simple.

First, what is meant by "anguish"? The Existentialists say at once that man is anguish. What that means is this: the man who involves himself and who realizes that he is not only the person he chooses to be, but also a lawmaker who is, at the same time, choosing all mankind as well as himself, cannot escape the feeling of his total and deep responsibility. Of course, there are many people who are not anxious; but we claim that they are hiding their anxiety, that they are fleeing from it. Certainly, many people believe that when they do something, they themselves are the only ones involved, and when someone says to them, "What if everyone acted that way?" they shrug their shoulders and answer, "Everyone doesn't act that way." But really, one should always ask himself, "What would happen if everybody looked at things that way?" There is no escaping this disturbing thought except by a kind of double-dealing. A man who lies and makes excuses for himself by saying "not everybody does that," is someone with an uneasy conscience, because the act of lying implies that a universal value is conferred upon the lie.

Anguish is evident even when it conceals itself. This is the anguish that Kierkegaard called the "anguish of Abraham." You know the story:

an angel has ordered Abraham to sacrifice his son; if it really were an angel who has come and said, "You are Abraham, you shall sacrifice your son," everything would be all right. But everyone might first wonder, "Is it really an angel, and am I really Abraham? What proof do I have?"

There was a madwoman who had hallucinations; someone used to speak to her on the telephone and give her orders. Her doctor asked her, "Who is it who talks to you?" She answered, "He says it's God." What proof did she really have that it was God? If an angel comes to me, what proof is there that it's an angel? And if I hear voices, what proof is there that they come from heaven and not from hell, or from the subconscious, or a pathological condition? What proves that they are addressed to me? What proof is there that I have been appointed to impose my choice and my conception of man on humanity? I'll never find any proof or sign to convince me of that. If a voice addresses me, it is always for me to decide that this is the angel's voice; if I consider that such an act is a good one, it is I who will choose to say that it is good rather than bad.

Now, I'm not being singled out as an Abraham, and yet at every moment I'm obliged to perform exemplary acts. For every man, everything happens as if all mankind had its eyes fixed on him and were guiding itself by what he does. And every man ought to say to himself, "Am I really the kind of man who has the right to act in such a way that humanity might guide itself by my actions?" And if he does not say that to himself, he is masking his anguish.

There is no question here of the kind of anguish which would lead to quietism, to inaction. It is a matter of a simple sort of anguish that anybody who has had responsibilities is familiar with. For example, when a military officer takes the responsibility for an attack and sends a certain number of men to death, he chooses to do so, and in the main he alone makes the choice. Doubtless, orders come from above, but they are too broad; he interprets them, and on this interpretation depend the lives of ten or fourteen or twenty men. In making a decision he cannot help having a certain anguish. All leaders know this anguish. That doesn't keep them from acting; on the contrary, it is the very condition of their action. For it implies that they envisage a number of possibilities, and when they choose one, they realize that it has value only because it is chosen. We shall see that this kind of anguish, which is the kind that Existentialism describes, is explained, in addition, by a direct responsibility to the other men whom it involves. It is not a curtain separating us from action, but is part of action itself.

When we speak of "forlornness," a term Heidegger was fond of, we mean only that God does not exist and that we have to face all the consequences of this. The Existentialist is strongly opposed to a certain kind of secular ethics which would like to abolish God with the least possible expense. About 1880, some French teachers tried to set up a secular ethics which went something like this: God is a useless and costly hypothesis; we are discarding it; but, meanwhile, in order for there to be an ethics, a society, a civilization, it is essential that certain values be taken seriously and that they be considered as having an *a priori* existence. It must be obligatory, *a priori,* to be honest, not to lie, not to beat your wife, to have children, etc., etc. So we're going to try a little device which will make it possible to show that values exist all the same, inscribed in a heaven of ideas, though otherwise God does not exist. In other words—and this, I believe, is the tendency of everything called "reformism" in France—nothing will be changed if God does not exist. We shall find ourselves with the same norms of honesty, progress, and humanism, and we shall have made of God an outdated hypothesis which will peacefully die off by itself.

The Existentialist, on the contrary, thinks it very distressing that God does not exist, because all possibility of finding values in a heaven of ideas disappears along with Him; there can no longer be an *a priori* Good, since there is no infinite and perfect consciousness to think it. Nowhere is it written that the Good exists, that we must be honest, that we must not lie; because the fact is we are on a plane where there are only men. Dostoyevsky said, "If God didn't exist, everything would be possible." That is the very starting point of Existentialism. Indeed, everything is permissible if God does not exist, and as a result man is forlorn, because neither within him nor without does he find anything to cling to. He can't start making excuses for himself.

If existence really does precede essence, there is no explaining things away by reference to a fixed and given human nature. In other words, there is no determinism, man is free, man is freedom. On the other hand, if God does not exist, we find no values or commands to turn to which legitimize our conduct. So, in the bright realm of values, we have no excuse behind us, nor justification before us. We are alone, with no excuses.

That is the idea I shall try to convey when I say that man is condemned to be free. Condemned, because he did not create himself, yet, in other respects is free; because, once thrown into the world, he is responsible for everything he does. The Existentialist does not believe in the power of passion. He will never agree that a sweeping passion is a ravaging torrent which fatally leads a man to certain acts and is therefore an excuse. He thinks that man is responsible for his passion.

The Existentialist does not think that man is going to help himself by finding in the world some omen by which to orient himself. Because he thinks that man will interpret the omen to suit himself. Therefore, he thinks that man, with no support and no aid, is condemned every moment to invent man. Ponge, in a very fine article, has said, "Man is the future of man." That's exactly it. But if it is taken to mean that this future is recorded in heaven, that God sees it, then it is false, because it would really no longer be a future. If it is taken to mean that, whatever a man may be, there is a future to be forged, a virgin future before him, then this remark is sound. But then we are forlorn.

To give you an example which will enable you to understand forlornness better, I shall cite the case of one of my students who came to see me under the following circumstances: his father was on bad terms with his mother, and, moreover, was inclined to be a collaborationist; his older brother had been killed in the German offensive of 1940, and the young man, with somewhat immature but generous feelings, wanted to avenge him. His mother lived alone with him, very much upset by the half-treason of her husband and the death of her older son; the boy was her only consolation.

The boy was faced with the choice of leaving for England and joining the Free French Forces—that is, leaving his mother behind—or remaining with his mother and helping her to carry on. He was fully aware that the woman lived only for him and that his going off—and perhaps his death—would plunge her into despair. He was also aware that every act that he did for his mother's sake was a sure thing, in the sense that is was helping her to carry on, whereas every effort he made toward going off and fighting was an uncertain move which might run aground and prove completely useless; for example, on his way to England he might, while passing through Spain, be detained indefinitely in a Spanish camp; he might reach England or Algiers and be stuck in an office at a desk job. As a result, he was faced with two very different kinds of action: one, concrete, immediate, but concerning only one individual; the other concerned an incomparably vaster group, a national collectivity, but for that very reason was dubious, and might be interrupted en route. And, at the same time, he was wavering between two kinds of ethics. On the one hand, an ethics of sympathy, of personal devotion; on the other, a broader ethics, but one whose efficacy was more dubious. He had to choose between the two.

Who could help him choose? Christian doctrine? No. Christian doctrine says, "Be charitable, love your neighbor, take the more rugged path, etc., etc." But which is the more rugged path? Whom should he love as a brother? The fighting man or his mother? Which does the greater good, the vague act of fighting in a group, or the concrete one of helping a particular human being to go on living? Who can decide *a priori*? Nobody. No book of ethics can tell him. The Kantian ethics says, "Never treat any person as a means, but as an end." Very well, if I stay with my mother, I'll treat her as an end and not as a means; but by virtue of this very fact, I'm running the risk of treating the people around me who are fighting, as means; and, conversely, if I go to join those who are fighting, I'll be treating them as an end, and, by doing that, I run the risk of treating my mother as a means.

If values are vague, and if they are always too broad for the concrete and specific case that we are considering, the only thing left for us is to trust our instincts. That's what this young man tried to do; and when I saw him, he said, "In the end, feeling is what counts. I ought to choose whichever pushes me in one direction. If I feel that I love my mother enough to sacrifice everything else for her—my desire for vengeance, for action, for adventure—then I'll stay with her. If, on the contrary, I feel that my love for my mother isn't enough, I'll leave."

But how is the value of a feeling determined? What gives his feeling for his mother value? Precisely the fact that he remained with her. I may say that I like so-and-so well enough to sacrifice a certain amount of money for him, but I may say so only if I've done it. I may say, "I love my mother well enough to remain with her" if I have remained with her. The only way to determine the value of this affection is, precisely, to perform an act which confirms and defines it. But, since I require this affection to justify my act, I find myself caught in a vicious circle.

On the other hand, Gide has well said that a mock feeling and a true feeling are almost indistinguishable; to decide that I love my mother and will remain with her, or to remain with her by putting on an act, amount somewhat to the same thing. In other words, the feeling is formed by the acts one performs; so, I cannot refer to it in order to act upon it. Which means that I can neither seek within myself the true condition which will impel me to act, nor apply to a system of ethics for concepts which will permit me to act. You will say, "At least, he did go to a teacher for advice." But if you seek advice from a priest, for example, you have chosen this priest; you already knew, more or less, just about what advice he was going to give you. In other words, choosing your adviser is involving yourself. The proof of this is that if you are a Christian, you will say, "Consult a priest." But some priests are collaborating, some are just marking time, some are resisting. Which to choose? If the young man chooses a priest who is resisting or collaborating, he has already decided on the kind of advice he's going to get. Therefore, in coming to see me he knew the answer I was going to give him, and I had only one answer to give: "You're free, choose, that is, invent." No general ethics can show you what is to be done; there are no omens in the world. The Catholics will reply, "But there are." Granted—but, in any case, I myself choose the meaning they have.

When I was a prisoner, I knew a rather remarkable young man who was a Jesuit. He had entered the Jesuit order in the following way: he had had a number of very bad breaks; in childhood, his father died, leaving him in poverty, and he was a scholarship student at a religious institution where he was constantly made to feel that he was being kept out of charity; then, he failed to get any of the honors and distinctions that children like; later on, at about eighteen, he bungled a love affair; finally, at twenty-two, he failed in military training, a childish enough matter, but it was the last straw.

This young fellow might well have felt that he had botched everything. It was a sign of something, but of what? He might have taken refuge in bitterness or despair. But he very wisely looked upon all this as a sign that he was not made for secular triumphs, and that only the triumphs of religion, holiness, and faith were open to him. He saw the hand of God in all this, and so he entered the order. Who can help seeing that he alone decided what the sign meant?

Some other interpretation might have been drawn from this series of setbacks; for example, that he might have done better to turn carpenter or revolutionist. Therefore, he is fully responsible for the interpretation. Forlornness implies that we ourselves choose our being. Forlornness and anguish go together.

As for "despair," the term has a very simple meaning. It means that we shall confine ourselves to reckoning only with what depends upon our will, or on the ensemble of probabilities which make our action possible. When we want something, we always have to reckon with probabilities. I may be counting on the arrival of a friend. The friend is coming by rail or streetcar; this supposes that the train will arrive on schedule, or that the streetcar will not jump the track. I am left in the realm of possibility; but possibilities are to be reckoned with only to the point where my action comports with the ensemble of these possibilities, and no further. The moment the possibilities I am considering are not rigorously involved by my action, I ought to disengage myself from them, because no God, no scheme, can adapt the world and its possibilities to my will. When Descartes said, "Conquer yourself rather than the world," he meant essentially the same thing.

The Marxists to whom I have spoken reply, "You can rely on the support of others in your action, which obviously has certain limits, because you're not going to live forever. That means: rely on both what others are doing elsewhere to help you, in China, in Russia, and what they will do later on, after your death, to carry on the action and lead it to its fulfillment, which will be the revolution. You even *have* to rely upon that, otherwise you're immortal." I reply at once that I will always rely on fellow fighters insofar as these comrades are involved with me in a common struggle, in the unity of a party or a group in which I can more or less make my weight felt; that is, one whose ranks I am in as a fighter and whose movements I am aware of at every moment. In such a situation, relying on the unity and will of the party is exactly like counting on the fact that the train will arrive on time or that the car won't jump the track. But, given that man is free and that there is no human nature for me to depend on, I cannot count on men whom I do not know by relying on human goodness or man's concern for the good of society. I don't know what will become of the Russian revolution; I may make an example of it to the extent that at the present time it is apparent that the proletariat plays a part in Russia that it plays in no other nation. But I can't swear that this will inevitably lead to a triumph of the proletariat. I've got to limit myself to what I see.

Given that men are free and that tomorrow they will freely decide what man will be, I cannot be sure that, after my death, fellow fighters will carry on my work to bring it to its maximum perfection. Tomorrow, after my death, some men may decide to set up fascism, and the others may be cowardly and muddled enough to let them do it. Fascism will then be the human reality, so much the worse for us.

Actually, things will be as man will have decided they are to be. Does that mean that I should abandon myself to quietism? No. First, I should involve myself; then, act on the old saw, "Nothing ventured, nothing gained." Nor does it mean that I shouldn't belong to a party, but rather that I shall have no illusions and shall do what I can. For example, suppose I ask myself, "Will socialization, as such, ever come about?" I know nothing about it. All I know is that I'm going to do everything in my power to bring it about. Beyond that, I can't count on anything. Quietism is the attitude of people who say, "Let others do what I can't do." The doctrine I am presenting is the very opposite of quietism, since it declares, "There is no reality except in action." Moreover, it goes further, since it adds, "Man is nothing else than his plan; he exists only to the extent that he fulfills himself; he is therefore nothing else than the ensemble of his acts, nothing else than his life." . . .

I've been reproached for asking whether Existentialism is humanistic. It's been said, "But you said in *Nausea* that the humanists were all wrong. You made fun of a certain kind of humanist. Why come back to it now?" Actually, the word "humanism" has two very different meanings. By "humanism" one can mean a theory which takes man as an end and as a higher value. Humanism in this sense can be found in Cocteau's tale *Around the World in Eighty Hours,* when a character, because he is flying over some mountains in an airplane, declares, "Man is simply amazing." That means that I, who did not build the airplanes, shall personally benefit from these particular inventions, and that I, as man, shall personally consider myself responsible for, and honored by, acts of a few particular men. This would imply that we ascribe a value to man on the basis of the highest deeds of certain men. This humanism is absurd, because only the dog or the horse would be able to make such an overall judgment about man, which they are careful not to do, at least to my knowledge.

But it cannot be granted that a man may make a judgment about man. Existentialism spares him from any such judgment. The Existentialist will never consider man as an end because he is always in the making. Nor should we believe that there is a mankind to which we might set up a cult in the manner of Auguste Comte. The cult of mankind ends in the self-enclosed humanism of Comte, and, let it be said, of fascism. This kind of humanism we can do without.

But there is another meaning of humanism. Fundamentally it is this: man is constantly outside of himself; in projecting himself, in losing himself outside of himself, he makes for man's existing; and, on the other hand, it is by pursuing transcendent goals that he is able to exist; man, being this state of passing beyond, and seizing upon things only as they bear upon this passing beyond, is at the heart, at the center of this passing beyond. There is no universe other than a human universe, the universe of human subjectivity. This connection between transcendency, as a constituent element of man—not in the sense that God is transcendent, but in the sense of passing beyond—and subjectivity, in the sense that man is not closed in on himself but is always present in a human universe, is what we call "Existentialist humanism." Humanism, because we remind man that there is no lawmaker other than himself, and that in his forlornness he will decide by himself; because we point out that man will fulfill himself as man, not in turning toward himself, but in seeking outside of himself a goal which is just this liberation, just this particular fulfillment.

From these few reflections it is evident that nothing is more unjust than the objections that have been raised against us. Existentialism is nothing else than an attempt to draw all the consequences of a coherent atheistic position. It isn't trying to plunge man into despair at all. But if one calls every attitude of unbelief despair, like the Christians, then the word is not being used in its original sense. Existentialism isn't so atheistic that it wears itself out showing that God doesn't exist. Rather, it declares that even if God did exist, that would change nothing. There you've got our point of view. Not that we believe that God exists, but we think that the problem of His existence is not the issue. In this sense Existentialism is optimistic, a doctrine of action, and it is plain dishonesty for Christians to make no distinction between their own despair and ours and then to call us despairing.

Problems

1. What are the charges usually leveled against existentialism?
2. What is Sartre's reply to these charges?
3. What are Sartre's primary assumptions? Why does he find them so attractive?
4. What are the implications of existential subjectivism? In what way does it

put existentialism in opposition to Marxism? Are reconciliations between existentialism and Christianity possible? How? Between existentialism and psychoanalysis? How?
5. To what extent would Sartre's arguments that man is not determined, that choice is unavoidable, be persuasive to a Marxist or a psychoanalyst? How would they counter his argument?
6. Faith for Paul, as we discovered earlier, means trust in God's love, the putting of oneself unquestioningly in his loving care; for the ancient Hebrews it means fidelity to the Law of God, diligence and attentiveness in fulfilling God's commands. Which of these views of faith is most existential? Which do people need more: self-respect, or a feeling of being loved? Why?
7. Fromm makes much of Marx's existentialism. In re-examining Marx's *The German Ideology* and "Alienated Labor," what proof of an existential perspective can you find there? To what extent does Marx's remark, "As individuals express their life, so they are," mean the same thing as Sartre's "Existence precedes essence"?

33 PAUL TILLICH

Paul Tillich (1886–1965) was born in Germany and ordained a Lutheran minister in 1912. Following his expulsion from his professorship of philosophy at Frankfurt University in 1933 for his opposition to the Nazis, he came to this country at the invitation of Reinhold Niebuhr, and joined the faculty of the Union Theological Seminary. In 1954 he became a professor at Harvard University.

One of the world's leading contemporary theologians, Tillich was instrumental in reintroducing ontology, philosophical existentialism, and depth psychology into theology. Unlike Kierkegaard, who maintained the inherent incompatibility of faith and reason, Tillich accepts reason as a necessary but finite tool; he is thus intent on bringing reason to bear on existential questions. For Tillich, the ultimate question is how man gives meaning to his existence. Life for Tillich is not self-justifying (cf. Maslow); meaning can only be found from whole-hearted commitment to something transcending self (cf. Frankl). Faith is caring, "ultimate concern"; and God becomes "Being-Itself," "Being" which can only be perceived through symbols, of which Jesus, or Christ, is the ultimate symbol. Religion thus shifts from a concern with dogma, institutions, and ultimate truth to a concern with spiritual renewal, with harmonizing that which man is with that which he ought to and can be, with "New Being" as revealed in Christ.

Rationalist and existentialist that he is, Tillich is concerned with the situation in which the individual finds himself. Faith cannot reiterate sterile formulae; it must address itself to the questions men ask as a result of the condition in which they find themselves, and that condition today is anxiety and alienation. Religion, to be meaningful, must show men that no human truth will satisfy, that only Christ as man and symbol shows men the way and the truth of an "ultimate concern" which frees them from the burden of themselves, and teaches them not only to "accept" others but to "accept" themselves. For the message of Christ is that we are "accepted."

This essay is from Tillich's The Courage To Be *(1952), a book that draws upon politics, economics, and depth psychology in its analysis of self-acceptance and the kinds of courage necessary to transcend anxiety, alienation, and loneliness.*

from The Courage to Be

The rise of modern individualism and the courage to be as oneself

Individualism is the self-affirmation of the individual self as individual self without regard to its participation in its world. As such it is the opposite of collectivism, the self-affirmation of the self as part of a larger whole without regard to its character as an individual self. Individualism has developed out of the bondage of primitive collectivism and medieval semicollectivism. It could grow under the protective cover of democratic conformity, and it has come into the open in moderate or radical forms within the Existentialist movement.

Primitive collectivism was undermined by the experience of personal guilt and individual question-asking. Both were effective at the end of the ancient world and led to the radical nonconformism of the cynics and skeptics, to the moderate nonconformism of the Stoics, and to the attempt to reach a transcendent foundation for the courage to be in Stoicism, mysticism, and Christianity. All these motives were present in medieval semicollectivism, which came to an end like early collectivism with the experience of personal guilt and the analytic power of radical question-asking. But it did not immediately lead to individualism. Protestantism, in spite of its emphasis on the individual conscience, was established as a strictly authoritarian and conformist system, similar to that of its adversary, the Roman Church of the Counter-reformation. There was no individualism in either of the great confessional groups. And there was only hidden individualism outside them, since they had drawn the individualistic trends of the Renaissance into themselves and adapted them to their ecclesiastical conformity.

This situation lasted for 150 years but no more. After this period, that of confessional orthodoxy, the personal element came again to the fore. Pietism and methodism* re-emphasized personal guilt, personal

From Paul Tillich, *The Courage to Be* (New Haven: Yale University Press, 1952), pp. 113–23.

* Pietism, with its attempted substitution of the devotional elements (repentance, faith) for the intellectual elements of Christianity, was practiced by the German Pietists in the 17th century. Methodism as a sect began with John Wesley at Oxford University in 1729 and stressed such personal elements as the state of grace (an individual free choice), redemption through Christ and renewal through the Holy Spirit.

experience, and individual perfection. They were not intended to deviate from ecclesiastical conformity, but unavoidably they did deviate; subjective piety became the bridge of the victorious reappearance of autonomous reason. Pietism was the bridge to Enlightenment.* But even Enlightenment did not consider itself individualistic. One believed not in a conformity which is based on biblical revelation but on one which should be based on the power of reason in every individual. The principles of practical and theoretical reason were supposed to be universal among men and able to create, with the help of research and education, a new conformity.

The whole period believed in the principle of "harmony"—harmony being the law of the universe according to which the activities of the individual, however individualistically conceived and performed, lead "behind the back" of the single actor to a harmonious whole, to a truth in which at least a large majority can agree, to a good in which more and more people can participate, to a conformity which is based on the free activity of every individual. The individual can be free without destroying the group. The functioning of economic liberalism seemed to confirm this view: the laws of the market produce, behind the backs of the competitors in the market, the greatest possible amount of goods for everybody. The functioning of liberal democracy showed that the freedom of the individual to decide politically does not necessarily destroy political conformity. Scientific progress showed that individual research and the freedom for individual scientific convictions do not prevent a large measure of scientific agreement. Education showed that emphasis on the free development of the individual child does not reduce the chances of his becoming an active member of a conformist society. And the history of Protestantism confirmed the belief of the Reformers that the free encounter of everybody with the Bible can create an ecclesiastical conformity—in spite of individual and even denominational differences. Therefore it was by no means absurd when Leibnitz † formulated the law of pre-established harmony by teaching that the monads of which all things consist, although they have no doors and windows that open toward each other, participate in the same world which is present in each of them, whether it be dimly or clearly perceived. The problem of individualization and participation seemed to be solved philosophically as well as practically.

Courage to be as oneself, as this is understood in the Enlightenment,

---

* The mainstream of 18th-century thought, which was rationalist, pantheist, empiricist, and which believed in natural law and the efficacy of reason, was termed the Enlightenment.
† Gottfried Wilhelm von Leibnitz (1646–1716) was a German idealist philosopher. He was the object of Voltaire's scathing satire in *Candide,* where he becomes Pangloss, the unflagging philosophic optimist, who after disaster and catastrophe can still proclaim, "All is for the best in the best of all possible worlds!"

is a courage in which individual self-affirmation includes participation in universal, rational, self-affirmation. Thus it is not the individual self as such which affirms itself but the individual self as the bearer of reason. The courage to be as oneself is the courage to follow reason and to defy irrational authority. In this respect—but only in this respect—it is Neo-Stoicism. For the courage to be of the Enlightenment is not a resigned courage to be. It dares not only to face the vicissitudes of fate and the inescapability of death but to affirm itself as transforming reality according to the demands of reason. It is a fighting, daring courage. It conquers the threat of meaninglessness by courageous action. It conquers the threat of guilt by accepting errors, shortcomings, misdeeds in the individual as well as in social life as unavoidable and at the same time to be overcome by education. The courage to be as oneself within the atmosphere of Enlightenment is the courage to affirm oneself as a bridge from a lower to a higher state of rationality. It is obvious that this kind of courage to be must become conformist the moment its revolutionary attack on that which contradicts reason has ceased, namely in the victorious bourgeoisie.

The romantic and naturalistic forms of the courage to be as oneself

The romantic movement has produced a concept of individuality which is equally to be distinguished from the medieval concept and from that of the Enlightenment and contains elements of both. The individual is emphasized in his uniqueness, as an incomparable and infinitely significant expression of the substance of being. Not conformity but differentiation is the end of the ways of God. Self-affirmation of one's uniqueness and acceptance of the demands of one's individual nature are the right courage to be. This does not necessarily mean willfulness and irrationality, because the uniqueness of one's individuality lies in its creative possibilities. But the danger is obvious. The romantic irony elevated the individual beyond all content and made him empty: he was no longer obliged to participate in anything seriously. In a man like Friedrich von Schlegel the courage to be as an individual self produced complete neglect of participation, but it also produced, in reaction to the emptiness of this self-affirmation, the desire to return to a collective. Schlegel, and with him many extreme individualists in the last hundred years, became Roman Catholics. The courage to be as oneself broke down, and one turned to an institutional embodiment of the courage to be as a part. Such a turn was prepared by the other side of romantic thought, the emphasis on the collectives and semicollectives of the past, the ideal of the "organic society." Organism, as has so often happened in the past, became the symbol of a balance between individualization and participation. However, its historical function in the early 19th century was to express not the need for a balance but the longing for the collectivist pole. It was used by all reactionary groups of this period who, be it for political or for spiritual reasons or both, tried to re-establish a "new Middle Ages." In this way the romantic movement produced both a radical form of the courage to be as oneself and the (unfulfilled) desire for a radical form of the courage to be as a part. Romanticism as an attitude has outlived the romantic movement. So-called Bohemianism was a continuation of the romantic courage to be as oneself. Bohemianism continued the romantic attack on the established bourgeoisie and its conformism. Both the romantic movement and its Bohemian continuation have decisively contributed to present-day Existentialism.

But Bohemianism and Existentialism have received elements of another movement in which the courage to be as oneself was pronounced: naturalism. The word naturalism is used in many different ways. For our purpose it suffices to deal with that type of naturalism in which the individualistic form of the courage to be as oneself is effective. Nietzsche is an outstanding representative of such a naturalism. He is a romantic naturalist and, at the same time, one of the most important—perhaps *the* most important—forerunner of the Existentialist courage to be as oneself. The phrase "romantic naturalist" seems to be a contradiction in terms. The self-transcendence of romantic imagination and the naturalistic self-restriction to the empirically given appear to be separated by a deep gap. But naturalism means the identification of being with nature and the consequent rejection of the supernatural. This definition leaves the question of the nature of the natural wide open. Nature can be described mechanistically. It can be described organologically. It can be described in terms of a necessary progressive integration or of creative evolution. It can be described as a system of laws or of structures or as a mixture of both. Naturalism can take its pattern from the absolutely concrete, the individual self as we find it in man, or from the absolutely abstract, the mathematic equations which determine the character of power fields. All this and much more can be naturalism.

But not all of these types of naturalism are expressions of courage to be as oneself. Only if the individualistic pole in the structure of the natural is decisive can naturalism be romantic and amalgamate with Bohemianism and Existentialism. This is the case in the voluntaristic types of naturalism. If nature (and for naturalism this means "being") is seen as the creative expression of an unconscious will or as the objectivation of the will to power or as the product of the *élan vital,** then the centers of will, the individual selves, are decisive for the movement of the whole. In individuals' self-affirmation life affirms itself or negates itself. Even if

* Life force.

the selves are subject to an ultimate cosmic destiny they determine their own being in freedom. A large section of American pragmatism belongs to this group. In spite of American conformism and its courage to be as a part, pragmatism shared many concepts with that perspective more widely known in Europe as the "philosophy of life." Its ethical principle is growth, its educational method is self-affirmation of the individual self, its preferred concept is creativity. The pragmatist philosophers are not always aware of the fact that courage to create implies the courage to replace the old by the new—the new for which there are no norms and criteria, the new which is a risk and which, measured by the old, is incalculable. Their social conformity hides from them what in Europe was expressed openly and consciously. They do not realize that pragmatism in its logical consequence (if not restricted by Christian or humanistic conformity) leads to that courage to be as oneself which is proclaimed by the radical Existentialists. The pragmatist type of naturalism is in its character, though not in its intention, a follower of romantic individualism and a predecessor of Existentialist independentism. The nature of the undirected growth is not different from the nature of the will to power and of the élan vital. But the naturalists themselves are different. The European naturalists are consistent and self-destructive; the American naturalists are saved by a happy inconsistency: they still accept the conformist courage to be as a part.

The courage to be as oneself in all these groups has the character of the self-affirmation of the individual self as individual self in spite of the elements of nonbeing threatening it. The anxiety of fate is conquered by the self-affirmation of the individual as an infinitely significant microcosmic representation of the universe. He mediates the powers of being which are concentrated in him. He has them within himself in knowledge and he transforms them in action. He directs the course of his life, and he can stand tragedy and death in a "heroic affect" and a love for the universe which he mirrors. Even loneliness is not absolute loneliness because the contents of the universe are in him. If we compare this kind of courage with that of the Stoics we find that the main point of difference is in the emphasis on the uniqueness of the individual self in the line of thought which starts in the Renaissance and runs over the romantics to the present. In Stoicism it is the wisdom of the wise man which is essentially equal in everyone out of which his courage to be arises. In the modern world it is the individual as individual. Behind this change lies the Christian valuation of the individual soul as eternally significant. But it is not this doctrine which gives the courage to be to modern man but the doctrine of the individual in his quality as mirror of the universe.

Enthusiasm for the universe, in knowing as well as in creating, also answers the question of doubt and meaninglessness. Doubt is the necessary tool of knowledge. And meaninglessness is no threat so long as enthusiasm for the universe and for man as its center is alive. The anxiety of guilt is removed: the symbols of death, judgment, and hell are put aside. Everything is done to deprive them of their seriousness. The courage of self-affirmation will not be shaken by the anxiety of guilt and condemnation.

In later romanticism another dimension of the anxiety of guilt and its conquest was opened up. The destructive trends in the human soul were discovered. The second period of the romantic movement, in philosophy as well as in poetry, broke away from the ideas of harmony which were decisive from the Renaissance to the classicists and early romantics. In this period, which is represented in philosophy by Schelling and by Schopenhauer, in literature by men like E. T. A. Hoffman, a kind of demonic realism was born, which was tremendously influential on Existentialism and depth psychology. The courage to affirm oneself must include the courage to affirm one's own demonic depth. This contradicted radically the moral conformism of the average Protestant and even of the average humanist. But it was avidly accepted by the Bohemian and the romantic naturalists. The courage to take the anxiety of the demonic upon oneself in spite of its destructive and often despairing character was the form in which the anxiety of guilt was conquered. But this was possible only because the personal quality of evil had been removed by the preceding development and could now be replaced by the cosmic evil, which is structural and not a matter of personal responsibility. The courage to take the anxiety of guilt upon oneself has become the courage to affirm the demonic trends within oneself. This could happen because the demonic was not considered unambiguously negative but was thought to be part of the creative power of being. The demonic as the ambiguous ground of the creative is a discovery of the later period of romanticism, which over the bridges of Bohemianism and naturalism was brought to the Existentialism of the 20th century. Its confirmation in scientific terms was depth psychology.

In some respects all these forms of the individualistic courage to be are forerunners of the radicalism of the 20th century, in which the courage to be as oneself was brought to most powerful expression in the Existentialist movement. The survey given in this chapter shows that the courage to be as oneself is never completely separated from the other pole, the courage to be as a part; and even more, that overcoming isolation and facing the danger of losing one's world in the self-affirmation of oneself as an individual are a way toward something which transcends both self and world. Ideas like the microcosm mirroring the universe, or the monad representing the world, or the individual will to power expressing the character of will to power in life itself—all these point to a solution which transcends the two types of the courage to be.

Problems

1. What arguments does Tillich use to suggest that individualism is a recent phenomenon?
2. What forces were operative to bring it about?
3. How might extreme romantic individualism lead to its own collapse and to a return to collectivism?
4. How does Tillich's analysis of romanticism lead to an understanding of the clashing values of Marxism and existentialism?
5. Why are Americans torn by conflicting pulls—one collectivist, the other individualist?
6. What are the various ways in which the "courage to be as oneself" manifests itself?

34 MARTIN BUBER

The five works which I have brought together for English readers in this volume have arisen in connexion with my little book I and Thou *(1923), as filling out and applying what was said there, with particular regard to the needs of our time.*

The first of these works, Dialogue *(1929), proceeded from the desire to clarify the "dialogical" principle presented in* I and Thou, *to illustrate it and to make precise its relation to essential spheres of life.*

With these words, Martin Buber (1878–1965), a Jewish philosopher who has influenced the psychologist Carl Rogers, as well as numerous contemporary philosophers and theologians, introduces Between Man and Man. *This collection of essays firmly establishes Buber among those existentialists like Gabriel Marcel and Karl Jaspers who stress dialogue, transcendence of one's subjectivity, and* meeting *in I–Thouness as the existential and ontological condition in which the self is truly realized and authenticated; and it places him in opposition to existentialists like Søren Kierkegaard, Martin Heidegger, and Jean-Paul Sartre who, even in their concepts of intersubjectivity, deny man's ability to transcend his own subjectivity and to know and experience another person outside himself. When Buber writes in* I and Thou, *that "all real living is meeting," he is stressing his belief that man is defined by his relations, which are either isolating and hollow, mere subject–object relations, exploitive relations—I–It relations where people are turned into things—or relations which are sweet and clean, which are devoid of implicit or overt comparisons. They are mutual meetings that are open, direct, liberating, and enriching; they are relations between full and unique subjects in which the precious otherness of the other person is experienced and felt. This is the world of I–Thou, of dialogue.*

Though we are all doomed to alternate between the suffering and loss of I–It relations and the fullness and ecstacy of I–Thou relations, Martin Buber takes his stand against those who postulate intrinsic, irreparable loneliness, and with those who believe that people, through care for and openness to each other, have the power to transcend their loneliness and experience true communion.

from Dialogue

Just as the most eager speaking at one another does not make a conversation (this is most clearly shown in that curious sport, aptly termed discussion, that is, "breaking apart", which is indulged in by men who are to some extent gifted with the ability to think), so for a conversation no sound is necessary, not even a gesture. Speech can renounce all the media of sense, and it is still speech.

Of course I am not thinking of lovers' tender silence, resting in one another, the expression and discernment of which can be satisfied by a glance, indeed by the mere sharing of a gaze which is rich in inward relations. Nor am I thinking of the mystical shared silence, such as is reported of the Franciscan Aegidius and Louis of France (or, almost identically, of two rabbis of the Hasidim) who, meeting once, did not utter a word, but "taking their stand in the reflection of the divine Face" experienced one another. For here too there is still the expression of a gesture, of the physical attitude of the one to the other.

What I am thinking of I will make clear by an example.

Imagine two men sitting beside one another in any kind of solitude of the world. They do not speak with one another, they do not look at one another, not once have they turned to one another. They are not in one another's confidence, the one knows nothing of the other's career, early that morning they got to know one another in the course of their travels. In this moment neither is thinking of the other; we do not need to know what their thoughts are. The one is sitting on the common seat obviously after his usual manner, calm, hospitably disposed to everything that may come. His being seems to say it is too little to be ready, one must also be really *there*. The other, whose attitude does not betray him, is a man who holds himself in reserve, withholds himself. But if we know about him we know that a childhood's spell is laid on him, that his withholding of himself is something other than an attitude, behind all attitude is entrenched the impenetrable inability to communicate himself. And now—let us imagine that this is one of the hours which succeed in bursting asunder the seven iron bands about our heart—imperceptibly the spell is lifted. But even now the man does not speak a word, does not stir a finger. Yet he does something. The lifting of the spell has happened to him—no matter from

From Martin Buber, *Between Man and Man* (New York: Macmillan, 1965), pp. 3–25.

where—without his doing. But this is what he does now: he releases in himself a reserve over which only he himself has power. Unreservedly communication streams from him, and the silence bears it to his neighbour. Indeed it was intended for him, and he receives it unreservedly as he receives all genuine destiny that meets him. He will be able to tell no one, not even himself, what he has experienced. What does he now "know" of the other? No more knowing is needed. For where unreserve has ruled, even wordlessly, between men, the word of dialogue has happened sacramentally.

Opinions and the factual

Human dialogue, therefore, although it has its distinctive life in the sign, that is in sound and gesture (the letters of language have their place in this only in special instances, as when, between friends in a meeting, notes describing the atmosphere skim back and forth across the table), can exist without the sign, but admittedly not in an objectively comprehensible form. On the other hand an element of communication, however inward, seems to belong to its essence. But in its highest moments dialogue reaches out even beyond these boundaries. It is completed outside contents, even the most personal, which are or can be communicated. Moreover it is completed not in some "mystical" event, but in one that is in the precise sense factual, thoroughly dovetailed into the common human world and the concrete time-sequence.

One might indeed be inclined to concede this as valid for the special realm of the erotic. But I do not intend to bring even this in here as an explanation. For Eros is in reality much more strangely composed than in Plato's genealogical myth, and the erotic is in no way, as might be supposed, purely a compressing and unfolding of dialogue. Rather do I know no other realm where, as in this one (to be spoken of later), dialogue and monologue are so mingled and opposed. Many celebrated ecstasies of love are nothing but the lover's delight in the possibilities of his own person which are actualized in unexpected fulness.

I would rather think of something unpretentious yet significant—of the glances which strangers exchange in a busy street as they pass one another with unchanging pace. Some of these glances, though not charged with destiny, nevertheless reveal to one another two dialogical natures.

But I can really show what I have in mind only by events which open into a genuine change from communication to communion, that is, in an embodiment of the word of dialogue.

What I am here concerned with cannot be conveyed in ideas to a reader. But we may represent it by examples—provided that, where the matter is important, we do not eschew taking examples from the inmost recesses of the personal life. For where else should the like be found?

My friendship with one now dead arose in an incident that may be described, if you will, as a broken-off conversation. The date is Easter 1914. Some men from different European peoples had met in an undefined presentiment of the catastrophe, in order to make preparations for an attempt to establish a supra-national authority. The conversations were marked by that unreserve, whose substance and fruitfulness I have scarcely ever experienced so strongly. It had such an effect on all who took part that the fictitious fell away and every word was an actuality. Then as we discussed the composition of the larger circle from which public initiative should proceed (it was decided that it should meet in August of the same year) one of us, a man of passionate concentration and judicial power of love, raised the consideration that too many Jews had been nominated, so that several countries would be represented in unseemly proportion by their Jews. Though similar reflections were not foreign to my own mind, since I hold that Jewry can gain an effective and more than merely stimulating share in the building of a steadfast world of peace only in its own community and not in scattered members, they seemed to me, expressed in this way, to be tainted in their justice. Obstinate Jew that I am, I protested against the protest. I no longer know how from that I came to speak of Jesus and to say that we Jews knew him from within, in the impulses and stirrings of his Jewish being, in a way that remains inaccessible to the peoples submissive to him. "In a way that remains inaccessible to you"— so I directly addressed the former clergyman. He stood up, I too stood, we looked into the heart of one another's eyes. "It is gone," he said, and before everyone we gave one another the kiss of brotherhood.

The discussion of the situation between Jews and Christians had been transformed into a bond between the Christian and the Jew. In this transformation dialogue was fulfilled. Opinions were gone, in a bodily way the factual took place.

Disputations in religion

Here I expect two objections, one weighty and one powerful.

One argument against me takes this form. When it is a question of essential views, of views concerning *Weltanschauung*,* the conversation *must* not be broken off in such a way. Each must expose himself wholly, in a real way, in his humanly unavoidable partiality, and thereby experience himself in a real way as limited by the other, so that the two suffer together the destiny of our conditioned nature and meet one another in it.

* World view; one's unique perspective on the world.

To this I answer that the experience of being limited is included in what I refer to; but so too is the experience of overcoming it together. This cannot be completed on the level of *Weltanschauung,* but on that of reality. Neither needs to give up his point of view; only, in that unexpectedly they do something and unexpectedly something happens to them which is called a covenant, they enter a realm where the law of the point of view no longer holds. They too suffer the destiny of our conditioned nature, but they honour it most highly when, as is permitted to us, they let themselves run free of it for an immortal moment. They had already met one another when each in his soul so turned to the other that from then on, making him present, he spoke really to and towards him.

The other objection, which comes from a quite different, in fact from the opposite, side is to the effect that this may be true so far as the province of the point of view reaches, but it ceases to be true for a confession of faith. Two believers in conflict about their doctrines are concerned with the execution of the divine will, not with a fleeting personal agreement. For the man who is so related to his faith that he is able to die or to slay for it there can be no realm where the law of the faith ceases to hold. It is laid on him to help truth to victory, he does not let himself be misled by sentiments. The man holding a different, that is a false, belief must be converted, or at least instructed; direct contact with him can be achieved only outside the advocacy of the faith, it cannot proceed from it. The thesis of religious disputation cannot be allowed to "go".

This objection derives its power from its indifference to the nonbinding character of the relativized spirit—a character which is accepted as a matter of course. I can answer it adequately only by a confession.

I have not the possiblity of judging Luther, who refused fellowship with Zwingli * in Marburg, or Calvin who furthered the death of Servetus.† For Luther and Calvin believe that the Word of God has so descended among men that it can be clearly known and must therefore be exclusively advocated. I do not believe that; the Word of God crosses my vision like a falling star to whose fire the meteorite will bear witness without making it light up for me, and I myself can only bear witness to the light but not produce the stone and say "This is it". But this difference of faith is by no means to be understood merely as a subjective one. It is not based on the fact that we who live to-day are weak in faith, and it will remain even if our faith is ever so much strengthened. The situation of the world itself, in the most serious sense, more precisely the relation between God and man, has changed. And this change is certainly not comprehended in its essence by our thinking only of the darkening, so familiar to

---

* Ulrich Zwingli (1484–1531) was a German Swiss reformer.
† Michael Servetus was a reformer who was put to death in Geneva in 1553.

us, of the supreme light, only of the night of our being, empty of revelation. It is the night of an expectation—not of a vague hope, but of an expectation. We expect a theophany of which we know nothing but the place, and the place is called community. In the public catacombs of this expectation there is no single God's Word which can be clearly known and advocated, but the words delivered are clarified for us in our human situation of being turned to one another. There is no obedience to the coming one without loyalty to his creature. To have experienced this is our way.

A time of genuine religious conversations is beginning—not those so-called but fictitious conversations where none regarded and addressed his partner in reality, but genuine dialogues, speech from certainty to certainty, but also from one open-hearted person to another open-hearted person. Only then will genuine common life appear, not that of an identical content of faith which is alleged to be found in all religions, but that of the situation, of anguish and of expectation.

Setting of the question

The life of dialogue is not limited to men's traffic with one another; it is, it has shown itself to be, a relation of men to one another that is only represented in their traffic.

Accordingly, even if speech and communication may be dispensed with, the life of dialogue seems, from what we may perceive, to have inextricably joined to it as its minimum constitution one thing, the mutuality of the inner action. Two men bound together in dialogue must obviously be turned to one another, they must therefore—no matter with what measure of activity or indeed of consciousness of activity—have turned to one another.

It is good to put this forward so crudely and formally. For behind the formulating question about the limits of a category under discussion is hidden a question which bursts all formulas asunder.

Observing, looking on, becoming aware

We may distinguish three ways in which we are able to perceive a man who is living before our eyes. (I am not thinking of an object of scientific knowledge, of which I do not speak here.) The object of our perception does not need to know of us, of our being there. It does not matter at this point whether he stands in a relation or has a standpoint towards the perceiver.

The *observer* is wholly intent on fixing the observed man in his mind, on "noting" him. He probes him and writes him up. That is, he is diligent to write up as many "traits" as possible. He lies in wait for them, that none may escape him. The object consists of traits, and it is known what lies behind each of them. Knowledge of the human system of expression constantly incorporates in the instant the newly appearing individual variations, and remains applicable. A face is nothing but physiognomy, movements nothing but gestures of expression.

The *onlooker* is not at all intent. He takes up the position which lets him see the object freely, and undisturbed awaits what will be presented to him. Only at the beginning may he be ruled by purpose, everything beyond that is involuntary. He does not go around taking notes indiscriminately, he lets himself go, he is not in the least afraid of forgetting something ("Forgetting is good," he says). He gives his memory no tasks, he trusts its organic work which preserves what is worth preserving. He does not lead in the grass as green fodder, as the observer does; he turns it and lets the sun shine on it. He pays no attention to traits ("Traits lead astray," he says). What stands out for him from the object is what is not "character" and not "expression" ("The interesting is not important," he says). All great artists have been onlookers.

But there is a perception of a decisively different kind.

The onlooker and the observer are similarly orientated, in that they have a position, namely, the very desire to perceive the man who is living before our eyes. Moreover, this man is for them an object separated from themselves and their personal life, who can in fact for this sole reason be "properly" perceived. Consequently what they experience in this way, whether it is, as with the observer, a sum of traits, or, as with the onlooker, an existence, neither demands action from them nor inflicts destiny on them. But rather the whole is given over to the aloof fields of aesthesis.

It is a different matter when in a receptive hour of my personal life a man meets me about whom there is something, which I cannot grasp in any objective way at all, that "says something" to me. That does not mean, says to me what manner of man this is, what is going on in him, and the like. But it means, says something *to me,* addresses something to me, speaks something that enters my own life. It can be something about this man, for instance that he needs me. But it can also be something about myself. The man himself in his relation to me has nothing to do with what is said. He has no relation to me, he has indeed not noticed me at all. It is not he who says it to me, as that solitary man silently confessed his secret to his neighbour on the seat; but *it* says it.

To understand "say" as a metaphor is not to understand. The phrase "that doesn't say a thing to me" is an outworn metaphor; but the saying I am referring to is real speech. In the house of speech are many mansions, and this is one of the inner.

The effect of having this said to me is completely different from that of looking on and observing. I cannot depict or denote or describe the man in whom, through whom, something has been said to me. Were I to attempt it, that would be the end of saying. This man is not my object; I have got to do with him. Perhaps I have to accomplish something about him; but perhaps I have only to learn something, and it is only a matter of my "accepting". It may be that I have to answer at once, to this very man before me; it may be that the saying has a long and manifold transmission before it, and that I am to answer some other person at some other time and place, in who knows what kind of speech, and that it is now only a matter of taking the answering on myself. But in each instance a word demanding an answer has happened to me.

We may term this way of perception *becoming aware*.

It by no means needs to be a man of whom I become aware. It can be an animal, a plant, a stone. No kind of appearance or event is fundamentally excluded from the series of the things through which from time to time something is said to me. Nothing can refuse to be the vessel for the Word. The limits of the possibility of dialogue are the limits of awareness.

The signs

Each of us is encased in an armour whose task is to ward off signs. Signs happen to us without respite, living means being addressed, we would need only to present ourselves and to perceive. But the risk is too dangerous for us, the soundless thunderings seem to threaten us with annihilation, and from generation to generation we perfect the defence apparatus. All our knowledge assures us, "Be calm, everything happens as it must happen, but nothing is directed at you, you are not meant; it is just 'the world', you can experience it as you like, but whatever you make of it in yourself proceeds from you alone, nothing is required of you, you are not addressed, all is quiet."

Each of us is encased in an armour which we soon, out of familiarity, no longer notice. There are only moments which penetrate it and stir the soul to sensibility. And when such a moment has imposed itself on us and we then take notice and ask ourselves, "Has anything particular taken place? Was it not of the kind I meet every day?" then we may reply to ourselves, "Nothing particular, indeed, it is like this every day, only we are not there every day."

The signs of address are not something extraordinary, something that steps out of the order of things, they are just what goes on time and again, just what goes on in any case, nothing is added by the address. The waves of the aether roar on always, but for most of the time we have turned off our receivers.

What occurs to me addresses me. In what occurs to me the world-happening addresses me. Only by sterilizing it, removing the seed of address from it, can I take what occurs to me as a part of the world-happening which does not refer to me. The interlocking sterilized system into which all this only needs to be dovetailed is man's titanic work. Mankind has pressed speech too into the service of this work.

From out of this tower of the ages the objection will be levelled against me, if some of its doorkeepers should pay any attention to such trains of thought, that it is nothing but a variety of primitive superstition to hold that cosmic and telluric happenings have for the life of the human person a direct meaning that can be grasped. For instead of understanding an event physically, biologically, sociologically (for which I, inclined as I always have been to admire genuine acts of research, think a great deal, when those who carry them out only know what they are doing and do not lose sight of the limits of the realm in which they are moving), these keepers say, an attempt is being made to get behind the event's alleged significance, and for this there is no place in a reasonable world continuum of space and time.

Thus, then, unexpectedly I seem to have fallen into the company of the augurs, of whom, as is well-known, there are remarkable modern varieties.

But whether they haruspicate or cast a horoscope their signs have this peculiarity that they are in a dictionary, even if not necessarily a written one. It does not matter how esoteric the information that is handed down: he who searches out the signs is *well up in* what life's juncture this or that sign means. Nor does it matter that special difficulties of separation and combination are created by the meeting of several signs of different kinds. For you can "look it up in the dictionary". The common signature of all this business is that it is for all time: things remain the same, they are discovered once for all, rules, laws, and analogical conclusions may be employed throughout. What is commonly termed superstition that is, perverse faith, appears to me rather as perverse knowledge. From "superstition" about the number 13 an unbroken ladder leads into the dizziest heights of gnosis. This is not even the aping of a real faith.

Real faith—if I may so term presenting ourselves and perceiving—begins when the dictionary is put down, when you are done with it. What occurs to me says something to me, but what it says to me cannot be revealed by any esoteric information; for it has never been said before nor is it composed of sounds that have ever been said. It can neither be interpreted nor translated, I can have it neither explained nor displayed; it is not a *what* at all, it is said into my very life; it is no experience that can be remembered independently of the situation, it remains the address of that moment and cannot be isolated, it remains the question of a questioner and will have its answer.

(It remains the question. For that is the other great contrast between all the business of interpreting signs and the speech of signs which I mean here: this speech never gives information or appeasement.)

Faith stands in the stream of "happening but once" which is spanned by knowledge. All the emergency structures of analogy and typology are indispensable for the work of the human spirit, but to step on them when the question of the questioner steps up to you, to me, would be running away. Lived life is tested and fulfilled in the stream alone.

With all deference to the world continuum of space and time I know as a living truth only concrete world reality which is constantly, in every moment, reached out to me. I can separate it into its component parts, I can compare them and distribute them into groups of similar phenomena, I can derive them from earlier and reduce them to simpler phenomena; and when I have done all this I have not touched my concrete world reality. Inseparable, incomparable, irreducible, now, happening once only, it gazes upon me with a horrifying look. So in Stravinsky's ballet the director of the wandering marionette show wants to point out to the people at the annual fair that a pierrot who terrified them is nothing but a wisp of straw in clothes: he tears it asunder—and collapses, gibbering, for on the roof of the booth the *living* Petrouchka sits and laughs at him.

The true name of concrete reality is the creation which is entrusted to me and to every man. In it the signs of address are given to us.

A conversion

In my earlier years the "religious" was for me the exception. There were hours that were taken out of the course of things. From somewhere or other the firm crust of everyday was pierced. Then the reliable permanence of appearances broke down; the attack which took place burst its law asunder. "Religious experience" was the experience of an otherness which did not fit into the context of life. It could begin with something customary, with consideration of some familiar object, but which then became unexpectedly mysterious and uncanny, finally lighting a way into the lightning-pierced darkness of the mystery itself. But also, without any intermediate stage, time could be torn apart—first the firm world's structure then the still firmer self-assurance flew apart and you were delivered to fulness. The "religious" lifted you out. Over there now lay the accustomed existence with its affairs, but here illumination and ecstasy and rapture held, without time or sequence. Thus your own being encompassed a life here and a life beyond, and there was no bond but the actual moment of the transition.

The illegitimacy of such a division of the temporal life, which is streaming to death and eternity and which only in fulfilling its temporality can be fulfilled in face of these, was brought home to me by an everyday event, an event of judgment, judging with that sentence from closed lips and an unmoved glance such as the ongoing course of things loves to pronounce.

What happened was no more than that one forenoon, after a morning of "religious" enthusiasm, I had a visit from an unknown young man, without being there in spirit. I certainly did not fail to let the meeting be friendly, I did not treat him any more remissly than all his contemporaries who were in the habit of seeking me out about this time of day as an oracle that is ready to listen to reason. I conversed attentively and openly with him—only I omitted to guess the questions which he did not put. Later, not long after, I learned from one of his friends—he himself was no longer alive—the essential content of these questions; I learned that he had come to me not casually, but borne by destiny, not for a chat but for a decision. He had come to me, he had come in this hour. What do we expect when we are in despair and yet go to a man? Surely a presence by means of which we are told that nevertheless there is meaning.

Since then I have given up the "religious" which is nothing but the exception, extraction, exaltation, ecstasy; or it has given me up. I possess nothing but the everyday out of which I am never taken. The mystery is no longer disclosed, it has escaped or it has made its dwelling here where everything happens as it happens. I know no fulness but each mortal hour's fulness of claim and responsibility. Though far from being equal to it, yet I know that in the claim I am claimed and may respond in responsibility, and know who speaks and demands a response.

I do not know much more. If that is religion then it is just *everything*, simply all that is lived in its possibility of dialogue. Here is space also for religion's highest forms. As when you pray you do not thereby remove yourself from this life of yours but in your praying refer your thought to it, even though it may be in order to yield it; so too in the unprecedented and surprising, when you are called upon from above, required, chosen, empowered, sent, you with this your mortal bit of life are referred to, this moment is not extracted from it, it rests on what has been and beckons to the remainder which has still to be lived, you are not swallowed up in a fulness without obligation, you are willed for the life of communion.

Who speaks?

In the signs of life which happens to us we are addressed. Who speaks?

It would not avail us to give for reply the word "God", if we do not give it out of that decisive hour of personal existence when we had to forget everything we imagined we knew of God, when we dared to keep nothing handed down or learned or self-contrived, no shred of knowledge, and were plunged into the night.

When we rise out of it into the new life and there begin to receive the signs, what can we know of that which—of him who gives them to us? Only what we experience from time to time from the signs themselves. If we name the speaker of this speech God, then it is always the God of a moment, a moment God.

I will now use a *gauche* comparison, since I know no right one.

When we really understand a poem, all we know of the poet is what we learn of him in the poem—no biographical wisdom is of value for the pure understanding of what is to be understood: the *I* which approaches us is the subject of this single poem. But when we read other poems by the poet in the same true way their subjects combine in all their multiplicity, completing and confirming one another, to form the one polyphony of the person's existence.

In such a way, out of the givers of the signs, the speakers of the words in lived life, out of the moment Gods there arises for us with a single identity the Lord of the voice, the One.

Above and below

Above and below are bound to one another. The word of him who wishes to speak with men without speaking with God is not fulfilled; but the word of him who wishes to speak with God without speaking with men goes astray.

There is a tale that a man inspired by God once went out from the creaturely realms into the vast waste. There he wandered till he came to the gates of the mystery. He knocked. From within came the cry: "What do you want here?" He said, "I have proclaimed your praise in the ears of mortals, but they were deaf to me. So I come to you that you yourself may hear me and reply." "Turn back," came the cry from within. "Here is no ear for you. I have sunk my hearing in the deafness of mortals."

True address from God directs man into the place of lived speech, where the voices of the creatures grope past one another, and in their very missing of one another succeed in reaching the eternal partner.

Responsibility

The idea of responsibility is to be brought back from the province of specialized ethics, of an "ought" that swings free in the air, into that of lived life. Genuine responsibility exists only where there is real responding.

Responding to what?

To what happens to one, to what is to be seen and heard and felt. Each concrete hour allotted to the person, with its content drawn from the world and from destiny, is speech for the man who is attentive. Attentive, for no more than that is needed in order to make a beginning with the reading of the signs that are given to you. For that very reason, as I have already indicated, the whole apparatus of our civilization is necessary to preserve men from this attentiveness and its consequences. For the attentive man would no longer, as his custom is, "master" the situation the very moment after it stepped up to him: it would be laid upon him to go up to and into it. Moreover, nothing that he believed he possessed as always available would help him, no knowledge and no technique, no system and no programme; for now he would have to do with what cannot be classified, with concretion itself. This speech has no alphabet, each of its sounds is a new creation and only to be grasped as such.

It will, then, be expected of the attentive man that he faces creation as it happens. It happens as speech, and not as speech rushing out over his head but as speech directed precisely at him. And if one were to ask another if he too heard and he said he did, they would have agreed only about an experiencing and not about something experienced.

But the sounds of which the speech consists—I repeat it in order to remove the misunderstanding, which is perhaps still possible, that I referred to something extraordinary and larger than life—are the events of the personal everyday life. In them, as they now are, "great" or "small", we are addressed, and those which count as great, yield no greater signs than the others.

Our attitude, however, is not yet decided through our becoming aware of the signs. We can still wrap silence about us—a reply characteristic of a significant type of the age—or we can step aside into the accustomed way; although both times we carry away a wound that is not to be forgotten in any productivity or any narcotism. Yet it can happen that we venture to respond, stammering perhaps—the soul is but rarely able to attain to surer articulation—but it is an honest stammering, as when sense and throat are united about what is to be said, but the throat is too horrified at it to utter purely the already composed sense. The words of our response are spoken in the speech, untranslatable like the address, of doing and letting—whereby the doing may behave like a letting and the letting like a doing. What we say in this way with the being is our entering upon the situation, into the situation, which has at this moment stepped up to us, whose appearance we did not and could not know, for its like has not yet been.

Nor are we now finished with it, we have to give up that expectation: a situation of which we have become aware is never finished with, but we subdue it into the substance of lived life. Only then, true to the moment, do we experience a life that is something other than a sum of moments. We respond to the moment, but at the same time we respond on its behalf, we answer for it. A newly-created concrete reality has been laid in our arms; we answer for it. A dog has looked at you, you answer for its glance, a child has clutched your hand, you answer for its touch, a host of men moves about you, you answer for their need.[1]

Morality and religion

Responsibility which does not respond to a word is a metaphor of morality. Factually, responsibility only exists when the court is there to which I am responsible, and "self-responsibility" has reality only when the "self" to which I am responsible becomes transparent into the absolute. But he who practises real responsibility in the life of dialogue does not need to name the speaker of the word to which he is responding—he knows him in the word's substance which presses on and in, assuming the cadence of an inwardness, and stirs him in his heart of hearts. A man can ward off with all his strength the belief that "God" is there, and he tastes him in the strict sacrament of dialogue.

Yet let it not be supposed that I make morality questionable in order to glorify religion. Religion, certainly, has this advantage over morality, that it is a phenomenon and not a postulate, and further that it is able to include composure as well as determination. The reality of morality, the demand of the demander, has a place in religion, but the reality of religion, the unconditioned being of the demander, has no place in morality. Nevertheless, when religion does itself justice and asserts itself, it is much more dubious than morality, just because it is more actual and inclusive. Religion as risk, which is ready to give itself up, is the nourishing stream of the arteries; as system, possessing, assured and assuring, religion which believes in religion is the veins' blood, which ceases to circulate. And if there is nothing that can so hide the face of our fellow-man as morality can, religion can hide from us as nothing else can the face of God. Prin-

---

1. The significance of *responsibility* (and the point of the whole section, indeed of the whole of *Dialogue*) is brought out more acutely in the German than in the English. *Wort, Antwort, antworten, verantworten,* etc., are part of a closely interrelated situation in which speech and response, answering for and being responsible for, and so on, are more intimately connected than the English version can hope to show. If the reader will remember that "responsibility" carries in itself the root sense of being "answerable", then the significance of the "word" in actual life will not be lost. Buber's teaching about the "word" always carries a strict reference to "lived life", and is very far from being an abstraction, theological or other.

ciple there, dogma here, I appreciate the "objective" compactness of dogma, but behind both there lies in wait the—profane or holy—war against the situation's power of dialogue, there lies in wait the "once-for-all" which resists the unforeseeable moment. Dogma, even when its claim of origin remains uncontested, has become the most exalted form of invulnerability against revelation. Revelation will tolerate no perfect tense, but man with the arts of his craze for security props it up to perfectedness.

SECTION TWO: LIMITATION

The realms

The realms of the life of dialogue and the life of monologue do not coincide with the realms of dialogue and monologue even when forms without sound and even without gesture are included. There are not merely great spheres of the life of dialogue which in appearance are not dialogue, there is also dialogue which is not the dialogue of life, that is, it has the appearance but not the essence of dialogue. At times, indeed, it seems as though there were only this kind of dialogue.

I know three kinds. There is genuine dialogue—no matter whether spoken or silent—where each of the participants really has in mind the other or others in their present and particular being and turns to them with the intention of establishing a living mutual relation between himself and them. There is technical dialogue, which is prompted solely by the need of objective understanding. And there is monologue disguised as dialogue, in which two or more men, meeting in space, speak each with himself in strangely tortuous and circuitous ways and yet imagine they have escaped the torment of being thrown back on their own resources. The first kind, as I have said, has become rare; where it arises, in no matter how "unspiritual" a form, witness is borne on behalf of the continuance of the organic substance of the human spirit. The second belongs to the inalienable sterling quality of "modern existence". But real dialogue is here continually hidden in all kinds of odd corners and, occasionally in an unseemly way, breaks surface surprisingly and inopportunely—certainly still oftener it is arrogantly tolerated than downright scandalizing— as in the tone of a railway guard's voice, in the glance of an old newspaper vendor, in the smile of the chimney-sweeper. And the third....

A *debate* in which the thoughts are not expressed in the way in which they existed in the mind but in the speaking are so pointed that they may strike home in the sharpest way, and moreover without the men that are spoken to being regarded in any way present as persons; a *conversation* characterized by the need neither to communicate something, nor to learn something, nor to influence someone, nor to come into connexion with someone, but solely by the desire to have one's own self-reliance confirmed by marking the impression that is made, or if it has become unsteady to have it strengthened; a *friendly chat* in which each regards himself as absolute and legitimate and the other as relativized and questionable; a *lovers' talk* in which both partners alike enjoy their own glorious soul and their precious experience—what an underworld of faceless spectres of dialogue!

The life of dialogue is not one in which you have much to do with men, but one in which you really have to do with those with whom you have to do. It is not the solitary man who lives the life of monologue, but he who is incapable of making real in the context of being the community in which, in the context of his destiny, he moves. It is, in fact, solitude which is able to show the innermost nature of the contrast. He who is living the life of dialogue receives in the ordinary course of the hours something that is said and feels himself approached for an answer. But also in the vast blankness of, say, a companionless mountain wandering that which confronts him, rich in change, does not leave him. He who is living the life of monologue is never aware of the other as something that is absolutely not himself and at the same time something with which he nevertheless communicates. Solitude for him can mean mounting richness of visions and thoughts but never the deep intercourse, captured in a new depth, with the incomprehensibly real. Nature for him is either an *état d' âme,* hence a "living through" in himself, or it is a passive object of knowledge, either idealistically brought within the soul or realistically alienated. It does not become for him a word apprehended with senses of beholding and feeling.

Being, lived in dialogue, receives even in extreme dereliction a harsh and strengthening sense of reciprocity; being, lived in monologue, will not, even in the tenderest intimacy, grope out over the outlines of the self.

This must not be confused with the contrast between "egoism" and "altruism" conceived by some moralists. I know people who are absorbed in "social activity" and have never spoken from being to being with a fellow-man. I know others who have no personal relation except to their enemies, but stand in such a relation to them that it is the enemies' fault if the relation does not flourish into one of dialogue.

Nor is dialogic to be identified with love. I know no one in any time who has succeeded in loving every man he met. Even Jesus obviously loved of "sinners" only the loose, lovable sinners, sinners against the Law; not those who were settled and loyal to their inheritance and sinned against him and his message. Yet to the latter as to the former he stood in a direct relation. Dialogic is not to be identified with love. But love without dialogic, without real outgoing to the other, reaching to the other, and companying with the other, the love remaining with itself—this is called Lucifer.

Certainly in order to be able to go out to the other you must have the starting place, you must have been, you must be, with yourself. Dialogue between mere individuals is only a sketch, only in dialogue between persons is the sketch filled in. But by what could a man from being an individual so really become a person as by the strict and sweet experiences of dialogue which teach him the boundless contents of the boundary?

What is said here is the real contrary of the cry, heard at times in twilight ages, for universal unreserve. He who can be unreserved with each passer-by has no substance to lose; but he who cannot stand in a direct relation to each one who meets him has a fulness which is futile. Luther is wrong to change the Hebrew "companion" (out of which the Seventy had already made one who is near, a neighbour) into "nearest". If everything concrete is equally near, equally nearest, life with the world ceases to have articulation and structure, it ceases to have human meaning. But nothing needs to mediate between me and one of my companions in the companionship of creation, whenever we come near one another, because we are bound up in relation to the same centre.

The basic movements

I term basic movement an essential action of man (it may be understood as an "inner" action, but it is not there unless it is there to the very tension of the eyes' muscles and the very action of the foot as it walks), round which an essential attitude is built up. I do not think of this happening in time, as though the single action preceded the lasting attitude; the latter rather has its truth in the accomplishing, over and over again, of the basic movement, without forethought but also without habit. Otherwise the attitude would have only aesthetic or perhaps also political significance, as a beautiful and as an effective lie. The familiar maxim, "An attitude must first be adopted, the rest follows of itself" ceases to be true in the circle of essential action and essential attitude—that is, where we are concerned with the wholeness of the person.

The basic movement of the life of dialogue is the turning towards the other. That, indeed, seems to happen every hour and quite trivially. If you look at someone and address him you turn to him, of course with the body, but also in the requisite measure with the soul, in that you direct your attention to him. But what of all this is an essential action, done with the essential being? In this way, that out of the incomprehensibility of what lies to hand this one person steps forth and becomes a presence. Now to our perception the world ceases to be an insignificant multiplicity of points to one of which we pay momentary attention. Rather it is a limitless tumult round a narrow breakwater, brightly outlined and able to bear heavy loads—limitless, but limited by the breakwater, so that, though not engirdled, it has become finite in itself, been given form, released from its own indifference. And yet none of the contacts of each hour is unworthy to take up from our essential being as much as it may. For no man is without strength for expression, and our turning towards him brings about a reply, however imperceptible, however quickly smothered, in a looking and sounding forth of the soul that are perhaps dissipating in mere inwardness and yet do exist. The notion of modern man that this turning to the other is sentimental and does not correspond to the compression of life today is a grotesque error, just as his affirmation that turning to the other is impractical in the bustle of this life today is only the masked confession of his weakness of initiative when confronted with the state of the time. He lets it dictate to him what is possible or permissible, instead of stipulating, as an unruffled partner, what is to be stipulated to the state of *every* time, namely, what space and what form it is bound to concede to creaturely existence.

The basic movement of the life of monologue is not turning away as opposed to turning towards; it is "reflexion".[2]

When I was eleven years of age, spending the summer on my grandparents' estate, I used, as often as I could do it unobserved, to steal into the stable and gently stroke the neck of my darling, a broad dapple-grey horse. It was not a casual delight but a great, certainly friendly, but also deeply stirring happening. If I am to explain it now, beginning from the still very fresh memory of my hand, I must say that what I experienced in touch with the animal was the Other, the immense otherness of the Other, which, however, did not remain strange like the otherness of the ox and the ram, but rather let me draw near and touch it. When I stroked the mighty mane, sometimes marvellously smooth-combed, at other times just as astonishingly wild, and felt the life beneath my hand, it was as though the element of vitality itself bordered on my skin, something that was not I, was certainly not akin to me, palpably the other, not just another, really the Other itself; and yet it let me approach, confided itself to me, placed itself elementally in the relation of *Thou* and *Thou* with me. The horse, even when I had not begun by pouring oats for him into the manger, very gently raised his massive head, ears flicking, then snorted quietly, as a conspirator gives a signal meant to be recog-

---

2. "Reflexion" for *Rückbiegung* is by no means a perfect rendering. Buber, however, makes clear that he is here describing the essence of the "monological" life, in which the other is not really met as the other, but merely as a part of the monological self, in an *Erlebnis* or inner experience which has no objective import: what happens is that the self "curves back on itself."

nizable only by his fellow-conspirator; and I was approved. But once—I do not know what came over the child, at any rate it was childlike enough—it struck me about the stroking, what fun it gave me, and suddenly I became conscious of my hand. The game went on as before, but something had changed, it was no longer the same thing. And the next day, after giving him a rich feed, when I stroked my friend's head he did not raise his head. A few years later, when I thought back to the incident, I no longer supposed that the animal had noticed my defection. But at the time I considered myself judged.

Reflexion is something different from egoism and even from "egotism." It is not that a man is concerned with himself, considers himself, fingers himself, enjoys, idolizes and bemoans himself; all that can be added, but it is not integral to reflexion. (Similarly, to the turning towards the other, completing it, there can be added the realizing of the other in his particular existence, even the encompassing of him, so that the situations common to him and oneself are experienced also from his, the other's, end.) I term it reflexion when a man withdraws from accepting with his essential being another person in his particularity—a particularity which is by no means to be circumscribed by the circle of his own self, and though it substantially touches and moves his soul is in no way immanent in it—and lets the other exist only as his own experience, only as a "part of myself". For then dialogue becomes a fiction, the mysterious intercourse between two human worlds only a game, and in the rejection of the real life confronting him the essence of all reality begins to disintegrate.

The wordless depths

Sometimes I hear it said that every *I and Thou* is only superficial, deep down word and response cease to exist, there is only the one primal being unconfronted by another. We should plunge into the silent unity, but for the rest leave its relativity to the life to be lived, instead of imposing on it this absolutized *I* and absolutized *Thou* with their dialogue.

Now from my own unforgettable experience I know well that there is a state in which the bonds of the personal nature of life seem to have fallen away from us and we experience an undivided unity. But I do not know—what the soul willingly imagines and indeed is bound to imagine (mine too once did it)—that in this I had attained to a union with the primal being or the godhead. That is an exaggeration no longer permitted to the responsible understanding. Responsibly—that is, as a man holding his ground before reality—I can elicit from those experiences only that in them I reached an undifferentiable unity of myself without form or content. I may call this an original pre-biographical unity and suppose that it is hidden unchanged beneath all biographical change, all development and complication of the soul. Nevertheless, in the honest and sober account of the responsible understanding this unity is nothing but the unity of this soul of mine, whose "ground" I have reached, so much so, beneath all formations and contents, that my spirit has no choice but to understand it as the groundless. But the basic unity of my own soul is certainly beyond the reach of all the multiplicity it has hitherto received from life, though not in the least beyond individuation, or the multiplicity of all the souls in the world of which it is one—existing but once, single, unique, irreducible, this creaturely one: one of the human souls and not the "soul of the All"; a defined and particular being and not "Being"; the creaturely basic unity of a creature, bound to God as in the instant before release the creature is to the *creator spiritus,* not bound to God as the creature to the *creator spiritus* in the moment of release.

The unity of his own self is not distinguishable in the man's feeling from unity in general. For he who in the act or event of absorption is sunk beneath the realm of all multiplicity that holds sway in the soul cannot experience the cessation of multiplicity except as unity itself. That is, he experiences the cessation of his own multiplicity as the cessation of mutuality, as revealed or fulfilled absence of otherness. The being which has become one can no longer understand itself on this side of individuation nor indeed on this side of *I and Thou.* For to the border experience of the soul "one" must apparently mean the same as "the One".

But in the actuality of lived life the man in such a moment is not above but beneath the creaturely situation, which is mightier and truer than all ecstasies. He is not above but beneath dialogue. He is not nearer the God who is hidden above *I and Thou,* and he is farther from the God who is turned to men and who gives himself as the *I* to a *Thou* and the *Thou* to an *I,* than that other who in prayer and service and life does not step out of the position of confrontation and awaits no wordless unity, except that which perhaps bodily death discloses.

Nevertheless, even he who lives the life of dialogue knows a lived unity: the unity of *life,* as that which once truly won is no more torn by any changes, not ripped asunder into the everyday creaturely life and the "deified" exalted hours; the unity of unbroken, raptureless perseverance in concreteness, in which the word is heard and a stammering answer dared.

Problems

1. What is silent communication?
2. What are signs? Why is a response to signs so indispensable for dialogue?
3. What is the present relation between God and man as Buber sees it?
4. What is the difference between observing, looking on, and becoming aware?

5. What happened to the "convert" Buber, to make him give up the "religious"? What has he replaced it with?
6. Why is dialogue without responsibility impossible?
7. How does dialogue lead not to a belief in God but to a deep sense of him?
8. How does dialogue differ from monologue?
9. What are the basic movements and the wordless depths?
10. Compare and contrast Buber's value system to those of Christ, of Marx, of Maslow, and of Nietzsche. Which does he most resemble? Which do you most prefer?

35 ALBERT CAMUS

Albert Camus (1913-1960), in good existential fashion, has disavowed being an existentialist; and, in fact, he is more aptly described as a post-rationalist. Nevertheless, he reveals sufficient affinities with existentialism to warrant inclusion here. A close associate of Sartre in the underground during the Occupation, he triggered a violent falling-out between them by his grim analysis of Marxism in The Rebel *(1951).*

Camus has evolved through two clear stages. The earlier is marked by an obsession with absurdity—that state of mind when one poses rational questions and confronts the silence that is the only answer. It is the confrontation with the silent abyss. But the absurd heroes in The Myth of Sisyphus *(1942),* The Stranger *(1942), and* Caligula *(1944), can be seen as heralds of a new and later vision, in* The Plague *(1947), of man engaging in strenuous dialogue with absurdity, trying heroically to combat inexplicable evil, and thereby giving dignity and meaning to life. Despite the stark sense of evil and a deep feeling for the senselessness of life, a stoicism that is almost untouched by gloom appears throughout his writings.*

Camus was a man of profound humanity—to some, the intellectual conscience of an age—but above all he was a man of joy, a Mediterranean pagan whose soul was moved by the curve of a North African sun as it dropped toward the sea.

The Myth of Sisyphus

The gods had condemned Sisyphus to ceaselessly rolling a rock to the top of a mountain, whence the stone would fall back of its own weight. They had thought with some reason that there is no more dreadful punishment than futile and hopeless labor.

If one believes Homer, Sisyphus was the wisest and most prudent

From Albert Camus, *The Myth of Sisyphus* (New York: Random House, 1955), pp. 88–91.

of mortals. According to another tradition, however, he was disposed to practice the profession of highwayman. I see no contradiction in this. Opinions differ as to the reasons why he became the futile laborer of the underworld. To begin with, he is accused of a certain levity in regard to the gods. He stole their secrets. Aegina, the daughter of Aesopus, was carried off by Jupiter. The father was shocked by that disappearance and complained to Sisyphus. He, who knew of the abduction, offered to tell about it on condition that Aesopus would give water to the citadel of Corinth. To the celestial thunderbolts he preferred the benediction of water. He was punished for this in the underworld. Homer tells us also that Sisyphus had put Death in chains. Pluto could not endure the sight of his deserted, silent empire. He dispatched the god of war, who liberated Death from the hands of her conqueror.

It is said also that Sisyphus, being near to death, rashly wanted to test his wife's love. He ordered her to cast his unburied body into the middle of the public square. Sisyphus woke up in the underworld. And there, annoyed by an obedience so contrary to human love, he obtained from Pluto permission to return to earth in order to chastise his wife. But when he had seen again the face of this world, enjoyed water and sun, warm stones and the sea, he no longer wanted to go back to the infernal darkness. Recalls, signs of anger, warnings were of no avail. Many years more he lived facing the curve of the gulf, the sparkling sea, and the smiles of earth. A decree of the gods was necessary. Mercury came and seized the impudent man by the collar and, snatching him from his joys, led him forcibly back to the underworld, where his rock was ready for him.

You have already grasped that Sisyphus is the absurd hero. He *is,* as much through his passions as through his torture. His scorn of the gods, his hatred of death, and his passion for life won him that unspeakable penalty in which the whole being is exerted toward accomplishing nothing. This is the price that must be paid for the passions of the earth. Nothing is told us about Sisyphus in the underworld. Myths are made for the imagination to breathe life into them. As for this myth, one sees merely the whole effort of a body straining to raise the huge stone, to roll it and push it up a slope a hundred times over; one sees the face screwed up, the cheek tight against the stone, the shoulder bracing the clay-covered mass, the foot wedging it, the fresh start with arms outstretched, the wholly human security of two earth-clotted hands. At the very end of his long effort measured by skyless space and time without depth, the purpose is achieved. Then Sisyphus watches the stone rush down in a few moments toward that lower world whence he will have to push it up again toward the summit. He goes back down to the plain.

It is during that return, that pause, that Sisyphus interests me. A face that toils so close to stones is already stone itself! I see that man going back down with a heavy yet measured step toward the torment of which he will never know the end. That hour like a breathing-space which returns as surely as his suffering, that is the hour of consciousness. At each of those moments when he leaves the heights and gradually sinks toward the lairs of the gods, he is superior to his fate. He is stronger than his rock.

If this myth is tragic, that is because its hero is conscious. Where would his torture be, indeed, if at every step the hope of succeeding upheld him? The workman of today works every day in his life at the same tasks, and this fate is no less absurd. But it is tragic only at the rare moments when it becomes conscious. Sisyphus, proletarian of the gods, powerless and rebellious, knows the whole extent of his wretched condition: it is what he thinks of during his descent. The lucidity that was to constitute his torture at the same time crowns his victory. There is no fate that cannot be surmounted by scorn.

If the descent is thus sometimes performed in sorrow, it can also take place in joy. This word is not too much. Again I fancy Sisyphus returning toward his rock, and the sorrow was in the beginning. When the images of earth cling too tightly to memory, when the call of happiness becomes too insistent, it happens that melancholy rises in man's heart: this is the rock's victory, this is the rock itself. The boundless grief is too heavy to bear. These are our nights of Gethsemane. But crushing truths perish from being acknowledged. Thus, Oedipus at the outset obeys fate without knowing it. But from the moment he knows, his tragedy begins. Yet at the same moment, blind and desperate, he realizes that the only bond linking him to the world is the cool hand of a girl. Then a tremendous remark rings out: "Despite so many ordeals, my advanced age and the nobility of my soul make me conclude that all is well." Sophocles' Oedipus, like Dostoevsky's Kirilov, thus gives the recipe for the absurd victory. Ancient wisdom confirms modern heroism.

One does not discover the absurd without being tempted to write a manual of happiness. "What! by such narrow ways—?" There is but one world, however. Happiness and the absurd are two sons of the same earth. They are inseparable. It would be a mistake to say that happiness necessarily springs from the absurd discovery. It happens as well that the feeling of the absurd springs from happiness. "I conclude that all is well," says Oedipus, and that remark is sacred. It echoes in the wild and limited universe of man. It teaches that all is not, has not been, exhausted. It drives out of this world a god who had come into it with dissatisfaction and a preference for futile sufferings. It makes a fate a human matter, which must be settled among men.

All Sisyphus' silent joy is contained therein. His fate belongs to him. His rock is his thing. Likewise, the absurd man, when he contemplates his torment, silences all the idols. In the universe suddenly restored to its silence, the myriad wondering little voices of the earth rise up. Unconscious, secret calls, invitations from all the faces, they are the necessary reverse and price of victory. There is no sun without shadow, and it is essential to know the night. The absurd man says yes and his effort will henceforth be unceasing. If there is a personal fate, there is no higher destiny, or at least there is but one which he concludes is inevitable and despicable. For the rest, he knows himself to be the master of his days. At that subtle moment when man glances backward over his life, Sisyphus returning toward his rock, in that light pivoting he contemplates that series of unrelated actions which becomes his fate, created by him, combined under his memory's eye and soon sealed by his death. Thus, convinced of the wholly human origin of all that is human, a blind man eager to see who knows that the night has no end, he is still on the go. The rock is still rolling.

I leave Sisyphus at the foot of the mountain! One always finds one's burden again. But Sisyphus teaches the higher fidelity that negates the gods and raises rocks. He too concludes that all is well. This universe henceforth without a master seems to him neither sterile nor futile. Each atom of that stone, each mineral flake of that night-filled mountain, in itself forms a world. The struggle itself toward the heights is enough to fill a man's heart. One must imagine Sisyphus happy.

Problems

1. Why did Sisyphus defy the gods and refuse to return to Hades? Why is he an absurd hero?
2. To what extent does Camus equate consciousness with the tragic?
3. How does victory emerge out of a sense of the absurd?
4. Why must one "imagine Sisyphus happy"?

Dialogue
and Synthesis

36 KEITH R. BRIDSTON
A Christian Critique of Secular Anthropologies

Any "Christian critique" of modern secular anthropologies must be entered into with the greatest trepidation, indeed humility. Herbert Butterfield in *Christianity and History* has pointed out that Christians have all too often stood on the wrong side of controversies in which ecclesiastical authorities felt the "Christian" cause was at stake: "Sometimes, indeed, as in the case of freedom of conscience, the Church has bitterly fought the world, and I am confronted by the anomaly that it was the world which stood for the cause now regarded as the right one even by the clergy themselves." [1]

This is a peculiarly subtle temptation when questions having to do with the nature of man and his destiny are under consideration. Christians, I suppose, have every right to make statements, even dogmatic affirmations, about man. But the proper biblical preface to these is a searching question: "What is man?" And the ultimate answer to that question lies not in our affirmations, but in God's answer. That, of course, lies in the mystery of God himself, in his love and grace. Thus, to a certain extent, man—even Christian man—cannot finally and definitively answer the Psalmist's question: "What is man?" Only God really knows.

To compare Christian anthropology with secular anthropology or anthropologies therefore, is not to compare the absolute with relatives. If there is indeed a "true" Christian anthropology, there is no guarantee that Christians are the ones articulating it at the moment. Our problem is to find who is, and then to appropriate it.

The first clue, and perhaps the decisive one, is the concern for man as man. Presumably in the Christian tradition this might be taken for granted. Ironically it cannot be. Particularly since the time of the Reformation, and especially within the Western Christian tradition, the doctrine of sin has been so understood and interpreted as to cast doubt on the worth and meaning of man as man. The extreme form of this doctrinal bias is contained in the idea of "total depravity," but the

From Keith R. Bridston, "A Christian Critique of Secular Anthropologies," in *Conflicting Images of Man*, ed. William Nicholls (New York: The Seabury Press, 1966), pp. 71–88.
1. Herbert Butterfield, *Christianity and History* (London: Fontana, 1957), p. 173.

fundamental pessimism of this anthropological perspective is largely shared in Western Christianity and may have infected the whole of the Church's view of man in all parts of Christendom today.

This radical pessimism in regarding man is, of course, a "protestant" corrective, but like all correctives it tends itself to become absolutized. To say that man is sinful is to say the obvious. Sometimes, to be sure, the obvious needs to be stated. This has often been true in the history of Christianity: a great many reform movements, not to speak of revolutions, are so explainable. Unfortunately, the idea crept in that to assert the sinfulness of man was necessary to uphold the authority, power, and majestic holiness of God. Christian theologians began to be protective about God, and they paternalistically defended him by deprecating man. What could be more futile, or what could demonstrate more effectively the subtlety of sin itself in inflating human pretensions! But above all, this compulsive concern to protect God by denying man resulted in a denial of two of the most basic foundation stones of the Christian tradition: first, that God created man, and in his own image; second, that God so loved man, even as sinful and fallen, that he gave himself to restore man to his true and proper state.

In short, Christian anthropology has been in its present forms largely informed by the doctrine of sin, at the expense of the doctrine of creation, and determined by an obsession with justification without adequate grounding in the Incarnation. Hendrik Kraemer, the great missiologist, has described Islam as "super-heated" monotheism,[2] but the same inclination toward an exaggerated theocentricity may be found in Christian thought as well. The New Testament itself bears ample witness to the fact that to love God who is not seen is easier for most than to love man who is seen. That is particularly true when it is thought that to love God somehow makes the love of neighbor only relatively important.

Against this background, it may perhaps be more understandable why so-called "secular" anthropologies have to be taken with the utmost seriousness by any Christian who wishes to know what "true" anthropology is. Insofar as they are concerned with man as man they may already have exceeded the rightness of much that passes for "Christian anthropology" in many of the theologies of the Church, both past and present.

Furthermore, besides being correctives to defective and inadequate "Christian" anthropologies, secular views of man may in themselves

---

2. "Islam is theocentric, but in a super-heated state. Allah in Islam becomes white-hot Majesty, white-hot Omnipotence, white-hot Uniqueness. His personality vanishes in the burning heat of His aspects . . . Man is entirely absorbed in the greatness and majesty of God and vanishes away" (*Christian Message in a Non-Christian World* [Grand Rapids, Mich.: Kregel, 1961], pp. 221–22).

incarnate and articulate essential elements necessary for the recovery of the full image of man revealed in the Bible, but elements which have been lost or forgotten in the Christian tradition down through the centuries. This does not mean that the spokesmen for such positions are always conscious of the anthropological implications of their insights. Indeed, one of the weaknesses of many secular anthropologies is their fragmentary and "sectarian" character. They discover a truth, or a valid interpretation, but often emphasize it to the exclusion of all others. The "truth" about man must be catholic; that is, it must incorporate all valid insights into one anthropology. Unless the Christian doctrine of man has this catholic character it cannot be "true" in the full and complete sense of that word, however well it is attested by tradition or bolstered by dogmatic authority.

It would take much more space than is available here merely to describe, to say nothing of criticizing, the various secular anthropologies that are current today. In examining these contemporary views of man, nevertheless, it is apparent that the most vital and important of them have their origins in some of the great pivotal thinkers of the nineteenth century: Darwin, Marx, and Freud. It is perhaps worth noting that, considered in the perspectives of universal history, these great "originals" who are the architects of our modern thought-world are intimately related to the Christian tradition, however alienated they may have been from the religious establishments of their day. In fact, the growth of the "new mentality" of science which all three so brilliantly represent and which, as Whitehead puts it, "has practically recoloured our mentality," in a very real sense finds its source, to use John Baillie's words, in "the Christian doctrine of creation" and "the Christian doctrine that the order of nature is contingent upon the divine Will." [3]

Deny it as they will, secular thinkers are indelibly marked with the Christian stamp and this is most transparent in their anthropological views. It is another reason, of course, why what they have to say is so important in reconstructing a modern Christian doctrine of man. These great "outsiders" represent the primitive Christian memory like a multifaceted mirror held up before the Christian community of today. The reflections of the various mirrors, distorted and obscure in different ways, together help to indicate the true Christian anthropological image.

It may be that the chief criticism which can be leveled against the secular anthropologies of our day is not that they fail to take "Christian" anthropology seriously, or even that they are "unreligious," but that they are subconsciously inhibited from working out the full logic of their discoveries because they *think* (or, better, unconsciously *feel*) that their insights are "unchristian" or "unreligious"; for in the marrow of their

3. John Baillie, *Natural Science and the Spiritual Life* (London: Oxford University Press, 1951), p. 22.

spiritual bones they are religious and Christian. The theological framework which they have accepted as orthodox, and which has been confirmed by the attacks of Christian critics, has no place for the truths which they have found. And, as a result, both they and the Christian intellectual community have been poorer for it; they have been intellectually excommunicated and they have accepted that excommunication as valid. If the advocates of secular anthropologies have tended to be sectarian, it is partly because Christian defenders have refused to let them be catholic.

This may be illustrated by returning to the great germinal thinkers already mentioned. Each of those named (and there are others almost equally worthy of mention were space to permit) has many aspects to his thought. All that can be done here is to suggest the chief contribution which each has made to current anthropological views.

MAN AS NATURAL

Darwin has made the point that man is natural. The Copernican and Cartesian revolutions had destroyed the "bandbox affair" of the neatly ordered medieval world, including its angelic hosts and prankish devils, and the result was that "man was alone, quite alone, in a vast and complex cosmic machine." [4] But there was still place for a faith that man was special, that he was somehow not a part of the machine, and that God had made it all for him. Darwin, however, along with Spencer, Thomas Huxley, and the other evolutionists shattered even that thin remnant of faith in man's natural uniqueness. Man was simply the highest and most complicated form of life resulting from an evolutionary process starting from the simplest protozoon. As Darwin himself put it:

> Not only the various domestic races, but the most distinct genera and orders within the same great class—for instance, mammals, birds, reptiles, and fishes—are all the descendants of one common progenitor, and we must admit that the whole vast amount of difference between forms has primarily arisen from simple variability. To consider the subject under this point of view is enough to strike one dumb with amazement.[5]

Darwin did not devote much time to the metaphysical implications of his theory, but there were many who did. And it was not so much the facts of evolution as the theory of it which, in various forms and

---

4. J. H. Randall, *The Making of the Modern Mind* (Boston: Houghton Mifflin, rev. ed., 1940), p. 227.
5. Charles Darwin, *The Variations of Animals and Plants under Domestication* (New York: D. Appleton & Co., 1896), pp. 425–26.

applied to many fields, has made an enormous impact on intellectual history since that time. As has been mentioned, the apparent reduction of man to one integral element in the general evolution of life struck defenders of the Christian faith with amazement, but not dumbness. In Roman Catholicism, for example, only recently through Teilhard de Chardin has this basic hostility and defensiveness given way to an attempt to appropriate evolutionary theory as a fundamental structure for theological speculation.

But if Darwinism seemed to reduce man's spiritual stature and uniqueness, modern physics carried this undermining of traditional Christian anthropology even further—so far, in fact, that the circle may have been completed. Evolutionary theory, after all, could be viewed as a vivid testimony to the intellectual powers of man, whatever his biological origins. Modern physics, however, has thrown doubts on even that. It is not only that man appears much smaller and more insignificant when looked at in a cosmic perspective. Even more significant, physicists' cosmological speculations deriving from Einstein have ended in a radical skepticism about the ability of man to comprehend the natural universe. P. W. Bridgman says of this development:

> Finally, I come to what seems to me may well be from the long range point of view the most revolutionary of the insights to be derived from our recent experiences in physics, more revolutionary than the insights afforded by the discoveries of Galileo and Newton, or of Darwin. This is the insight that it is impossible to transcend the human reference point.... The new insight comes from the realization that the structure of nature may eventually be such that our processes of thought do not correspond to it sufficiently to permit us to think about it all. We have already had an intimation of this in the behavior of very small things in the quantum domain.... There can be no difference of opinion with regard to the dilemma that now confronts us in the direction of the very small. We are now approaching a bound beyond which we are forever stopped from pushing our inquiries, not by the construction of the world, but by the construction of ourselves. The world fades out and eludes us because it becomes meaningless. We cannot even express this in the way we would like. We cannot say that there exists a world beyond any knowledge possible to us because of the nature of knowledge. The very concept of existence becomes meaningless. It is literally true that the only way of reacting to this is to shut up. We are confronted with something truly ineffable. We have reached the limit of vision of the great pioneers of science, namely that we live in a sympathetic world, in that it is comprehensible by our minds.[6]

Is this saying somewhat the same thing that Christian theologians

---

6. P. W. Bridgman, quoted in James B. Conant, *Modern Science and Modern Man* (New York: Columbia University Press, 1952), pp. 86–87.

mean when they speak of the mystery of God's creation? Groups of physicists and theologians in Germany have begun a dialogue on precisely this question. Though it is premature to suggest that at long last the thought-worlds of science and theology have begun to meet, one physicist-theologian seems to believe a confluence is immanent, particularly in regard to their respective views of man. As C. F. von Weizsäcker suggests in *The History of Nature* the skepticism and nihilism reflected in the words of Bridgman are in some sense "the negative counterpole of Christianity" and "when this experience faces its own situation fully, it is perhaps the most honest self-appraisal of the modern world."[7] Or to put it another way, a full recognition of man's identity with the natural universe has eventually led not to a pretentious magnification of man, but to a recognition that man in a microcosmic way is "truly ineffable." He is to himself a mystery. It may be cause for reflection that the empirical scientists are saying this with more conviction than some theologians for whom the question "What is man?" apparently has been exhaustively answered by their theomonistic dogmatic categories.

MAN AS SOCIAL

Marx has made the point that man is social. Herbert Spencer's application of Darwinism to society and history suggests the easy compatibility between Darwin's empirical evolutionary data and the general climate of optimistic progressivism of the nineteenth century. Marx was both a product and a creator of that philosophical spirit of inevitable human advance. Darwin, Marx, and Freud were all concerned with the dynamics of life and, though their theories were not directly connected with one another, they had this in common: "Each emphasized the extent to which the human being is the product of forces outside his control."[8] In this sense they were all—implicitly or explicitly—protesting against the Hegelian idealism dominating the preceding era which tended to explain all human dynamics as derivative from reason.

Marxism accepts Hegelian rationalism to the extent of borrowing its dialectical method but, as Marx himself proclaimed, he had taken the thesis-antithesis-synthesis pyramid which Hegel had foolishly tried to balance on its idealistic point and placed it squarely on its base: materialistic historical determinism. Darwin indicated that man was formed by his biological origins, and Marx supplemented this environmental

---

7. C. F. von Weizsäcker, *The History of Nature* (Chicago: University of Chicago Press, 1949), p. 190.
8. Joseph Wood Krutch, *The Measure of Man* (New York: Grosset Universal Library, 1956), p. 36.

determinism by focusing on the economic factor, "the means of production," as decisive in the formation of man. Marxist theory is largely occupied with the riddle of social change—a riddle which the economic and technological revolution of the nineteenth century imposed on every perceptive thinker of the time, however different their answers to it. My old friend David Carmichael's *bon mot,* "Read Marx and inwardly digest," is particularly appropriate for Christians because, of all the answers given to the nineteenth century's riddle of change, the Church's tended to be the most romantic and individualistic. Though there were some notable exceptions (such as F. D. Maurice), through its hymns, tracts, sermons, and theological books the nineteenth-century Christian community taken as a whole reflects two extremes: utopian idealism and spiritualized pietism. In both cases, it is man as an individual who is the center of attention and upon whom the theological fulcrum rests. It may be the world which is to be saved, or man himself, but in either case it depends upon the efforts of individuals. Man understood in a corporate sense is almost entirely missing.

The idea of individuality "which is the most unique emphasis of modern culture," according to Reinhold Niebuhr, and has deep Christian roots, is a "tragically abortive concept" when it becomes ideologically rationalized into secular individualism.[9] But this is precisely the distinguishing mark of nineteenth-century Christian anthropology. And though it may have passed in theological circles, this individualistic understanding of man still remains potent in the Christian community in a vestigial way through "popular" religion in local congregations. The fact that man cannot be understood apart from his fellows, that his corporate environment determines his individual significance, that his social setting and relationships define his manhood—points which St. Paul makes with some force to the Church in Corinth—has yet fully to penetrate the mentality of the Christian community even though the secular community has mainly accepted and absorbed it. Needless to say, Marx's social anthropology may be all too congenial to the collectivist tendencies of modern life whether that is seen in political dictatorship or communal conformism. But any Christian critique to be made of these centripetal forces on the basis of man's dignity and integrity as an individual can only be undertaken if the essential social and corporate character of the Christian message is affirmed at the same time.

The increased attention being given by theologians to ecclesiology in recent years may indicate a change toward a more social orientation in Christian anthropology as well. Nevertheless, the forming and deforming impact of corporate "principalities and powers" on man's being

9. Reinhold Niebuhr, *The Nature and Destiny of Man* (London: Nisbet, 1941), Vol. I, p. 97.

has been given much more perceptive analyses by social critics such as William Whyte in *The Organization Man,* C. Northcote Parkinson in his tongue-in-cheek *Parkinson's Law,* Vance Packard, C. Wright Mills, and other "popular" sociologists in their various writings than by the theological moralists representing the religious Establishment. Only recently have Christian spokesmen such as Gibson Winter and James M. Gustafson and Liston Pope shown evidence of having absorbed the anthropological insight of man as social thoroughly enough to *think* Christian ethics naturally in sociological terms. But this natural sociological-theological integration has not yet affected the general anthropological ethos of the churches. Social problems are increasingly being recognized as social, but the criteria used to judge them and the antidotes being suggested are largely individualistic. And so the pressing moral issues being imposed by a collectivist age—from invasion of privacy to automation—are being denied relevant Christian analysis. This discrepancy between the social form in which modern man is meeting his most excruciating moral crises and the individualistic anthropological bias of local "folk" Christianity may be one of the chief explanations why ministers are facing traumatic frustrations in effectively communicating through their preaching today.

MAN AS VISCERAL

Freud has made the point that man is visceral. In considering the revolutionary implications of his work, Freud compared himself to both Copernicus and Darwin; and in his writings he not infrequently mentioned Marx and referred to his concepts. Whether Freud, as an intellectual revolutionary, will eventually be ranked as a true Copernican is probably premature to say; nevertheless, his own estimate of the tremendous impact of his theories on the imagination of twentieth-century man is difficult to dismiss. In fact, there are those who argue: "Two figures stand out massively as the architects of our present-day conception of man: Darwin and Freud." [10] And as with Darwin, the empirical biologist, so with Freud, the practicing neurologist, his influence may be ascribed as much—perhaps even more—to the conclusions drawn from, and the philosophical meaning attached to, his laboriously achieved research data than the scientific theories he himself developed from it.

Freud's work is too rich and multidimensioned to be quickly and briefly summarized. In thinking of its impact on our modern secular view of man, however, one thing stands out: Freud made crystal clear

---

10. J. R. Bruner, in *Freud and the 20th Century,* ed. by Benjamin Nelson (New York: Meridian Books, 1957), p. 279.

the incalculable significance of the largely submerged portion of human nature for a proper understanding of man. Whatever names one wishes to attach to that hidden realm—passion, emotion, instinct, unconscious force—Freud branded upon the popular mind the fact that this mysterious, hidden world was "reality," that it actually existed, and that it was mightily determinative of who men were and what they were and how they were as human beings.

The word "sex" is commonly associated with Freud. Symbolically, at least, that word may be as apt as any in epitomizing Freud's anthropological contribution, however oversimplified it may be to describe his whole thought. For it was through his isolation of sexuality as an "energy of equal dignity," as the power behind a neurosis, that "Freud would soon be able to describe psychic reality systematically as the domain of phantasy, dream and mythology, and as the imagery and language of a universal unconscious, and thus adding as a scientific dimension to the image of man what had been an age-old intuitive knowledge." [11] In short, Freud broke through the inhibitions, prudery, and hypocrisy of the Victorian mentality camouflaging the true nature of man and subjected it to naked scientific examination and inquiry.

If Freud's theory of sex tended to overshoot its mark, or to be too simplistic, nevertheless it was, in the religious reaction it provoked, a vivid reminder of the fact that "it was only too easy to do what had become civilization's 'second nature,' that is, in the face of man's sexual and aggressive drives ever again to beat a hasty retreat into romanticism and religionism, into secrecy, ridicule, and lechery," as Erik Erikson says. That is, Freud's insights into human nature are a perennial warning against anthropological falsifications in the name of supposed religious or theological principles or scruples.

It is all too easy to understand why the Church found Freudian anthropology difficult to digest, and may still find it so. For one thing, Christian theology since the time of the Reformation has tended to be docetic. That can be seen in Christology as well as ecclesiology. The incarnational affirmation that the "Word became flesh" does not come easily to those who presuppose a basic and unalterable dichotomy between spirit and matter. When this dualistic mentality applies itself to a description of man, the outcome is foreordained: *essential* man is a spirit or—as in idealism—a mind. At the same time, the churches on the whole are Marcionite—in practice if not in theory. The "earthiness" of the Old Testament has little attraction for spiritualized Christians, and the liturgical (as well as the educational and homiletical) practice of the churches bears witness to this fact. Phrases such as "I long after you all in the bowels of Christ" fall on deaf ears; and if not deaf, faintly scandalized. "Bowels," after all, are hardly proper and certainly

11. Erik H. Erikson, in *Freud and the 20th Century,* ed. by Benjamin Nelson, p. 91.

not to be thought of as the abode of religious "spiritual" feelings. "Well, the early Christians were somewhat crude and primitive in other ways as well." So we are inclined to leave speculation about bowels and their relation to the nature of man to the psychologists and cultural anthropologists in their theories of infantile sexuality and toilet training.

This Marcionite-docetic truncation of Christian anthropology has had disastrous consequences.* Christian theology itself, cut off from the emotional warmth, the vivid imagery, and the essential humanity of the Jewish tradition as found in the Old Testament, becomes dry, dogmatic, and unimaginative; it is an exercise of the head, a cerebral enterprise which in its scholastic rigidity cannot comprehend a Joseph whose "bowels did yearn upon his brother" or whose rough intellectual instruments cannot discern the intricate human interplay between Saul, David, and Jonathan. Such spiritualized and rationalized "Christian" anthropology is incapable of coping with man as man; it can only do so when man has been reduced to its cramped theological measure.

Is it surprising, then, that "no one can count the number of people who now think of any crisis as a personal failure, and who turn to a psychoanalyst or to a psychonanalytical literature for an explanation of their suffering where once they would have turned to a minister or to the Bible for consolation"? [12] Beyond these more immediate pastoral implications, the shriveled anthropology falsely called "Christian" has led our whole culture to seek elsewhere than in the Church for the meaning of life and of man. Modern man does not go to hear a sermon if he is perplexed about his nature and being: he goes to see Bergman's or Fellini's films, he sees Albee's or Osborne's plays, he reads Camus, Faulkner, Joyce, or Sartre. This is not to say that he is going to find in Fellini's "8½" or in Williams' *Night of the Iguana* the final answer to his perplexities; but at least he knows that his question "What is man?" is also theirs and that they are willing to be open to all the paradoxical dimensions of human existence in searching out a viable answer. The same cannot be said for many sermons.

In much the same way, in the field of science and in the political sphere, so-called "Christian" anthropology has by its diminutive character forced out both honest speculation and rigorous action from the religious community. In view of this melancholy history, the Christian critique of secular anthropologies must, as was mentioned at the beginning of this essay, be preceded by radical repentance. That in turn must be followed by the recognition that the very idea of a "Christian" anthropology set over against "secular" views is a false understanding

---

* The Marcionites were second-century anti-Judaic gnostics; the Docetae were an early heretical sect which held that Christ's body was not human but celestial. This phrase, then, refers to the damage done to Christian anthropology by the beliefs of these two sects.

12. Alfred Kazin, in *Freud and the 20th Century*, ed. by Benjamin Nelson, p. 15.

of the problem. The Christian view of man, if it is true, cannot be one among many. Its truth lies precisely in its catholicity: that is, in its ability to comprehend all valid anthropological truths and see them as a whole. The fact that the elemental anthropological insights "man is natural," "man is social," "man is visceral" have had such tardy recognition by Christians (especially when these particular insights are so intimately related to the mainstream of the Judaeo-Christian theological tradition) should be an evident warning against complacency about the ease with which this synthesizing and integrating task may be accomplished.

Ernst Cassirer in *An Essay on Man* expresses dismay that the variety of empirical treatments of man resulted in a situation in which "our modern theory of man lost its intellectual center. We acquired instead a complete anarchy of thought." In the past, he writes, metaphysics, theology, mathematics, and biology successively gave guidance in integrating anthropological thought, but the "real crisis of this problem manifested itself when such a central power capable of directing all individual efforts ceased to exist; . . . an established authority to which one might appeal no longer existed. Theologians, scientists, politicians, sociologists, biologists, psychologists, ethnologists, economists all approached the problem from their own viewpoint. To combine or unify all these particular aspects and perspectives was impossible." [13] Cassirer finds it ironical that precisely at the time when we have a superabundance of facts derived from scientific investigation, when our instruments for observation and experimentation have become sharper, and in general when we have a more favorable position than any other age for a penetrating view of man, we appear "nevertheless, not yet to have found a method for the mastery and organization of this material."

Cassirer quotes Max Scheler to the same effect: "In no other period of human knowledge has man ever become more problematic to himself than in our own days. We have a scientific, a philosophical, and a theological anthropology that know nothing of each other. Therefore we no longer possess any clear and consistent idea of man. The ever-growing multiplicity of the particular sciences that are engaged in the study of men has much more confused and obscured than elucidated our concept of man." [14]

What are Christians to say, then, when confronted by a Julian Huxley who says that "man represents the culmination of that process of organic evolution which has been proceeding on this planet for over a thousand million years" and that his unique value ultimately lies in

---

13. Ernst Cassirer, *An Essay on Man* (New Haven, Conn.: Yale University Press, 1944), pp. 39–40.
14. Max Scheler, *Die Stellung des Menschen im Kosmos* (Darmstadt: Reichl, 1928), pp. 13 f.

the fact that "man has now become the sole representative of life in that progressive aspect and its sole trustee for any progress in the future"?[15] Or when Marx speaks through one of his disciples, saying, "Man is an ensemble of social relations"? Or when a D. H. Lawrence proclaims, "My great religion is a belief in the blood, the flesh, as being wiser than the intellect. We can go wrong in our minds. But what our blood feels and believes, and says, is always true"? What is the Christian response?

As has been suggested, the first inclination is simply to disprove such anthropological positions, critically to undermine and dismember them, and then to substitute the "true" doctrine in their place. Or it is to try to synthesize them within a grander and more comprehensive conceptual framework. It may be, however, that this assumption of intellectual superiority is not only outmoded but actually futile for Christian theologians. Cassirer and Scheler may be quite right in placing theology as one among many competing anthropological viewpoints, none of which can hope to provide the intellectual integrating center for the rest. Theology as a scientific discipline cannot expect to be given a special intellectual edge in open scientific competition.

But is the Christian image of man ultimately a conceptual framework, an intellectual idea, a doctrine? Is there, in fact, a Christian anthropology at all? The Christian view of man is derived from an image, not an idea. It is drawn from and projected by a person, not a dogma. When Christians confess "true man," they do not define him, they behold him. They do not intellectualize about him, they believe in him.

This, of course, is not anthropology but faith. It is probably absurd to think that faith can be a critique of all other anthropologies. But is it more absurd than to think that man ultimately can be his own measure? Or to believe that any anthropology, even a theological anthropology, can ever take the full measure of this True Man?

He came to fulfill, not to destroy, the law and the prophets. He still comes to do the same. That is his final human critique. And it must be ours.

15. Julian Huxley, *Man in the Modern World* (New York: Mentor Books, 1948), p. 27.

37 RICHARD LICHTMAN
from The Marxian Critique of Christianity

Marx and Engels were deeply impressed by Feuerbach's analysis and never denied that their own interpretation was heavily dependent upon it. But they did not believe it had gone far enough in its dissection of the motive of the religious projection or in its comprehension of the particular social circumstances from which that projection derived. Feuerbach had traced religion to anthropology, but his anthropology was too abstract, and had itself to be rooted in a detailed sociology. In particular, Marx did not believe that Feuerbach had penetrated the source of human dependency from which the compensatory illusion of religion sprang. As Marx wrote in his *Theses on Feuerbach:*

> Feuerbach starts out from the fact of religious self-alienation, the duplication of the world into a religious, imaginary world and a real one. His work consists in the dissolution of the religious world into its secular bases . . . the chief thing still remains to be done. For the fact that the secular foundation detaches itself from itself and establishes itself in the clouds as an independent realm is really to be explained only by the self-cleavage and self-contradictoriness of this secular basis. . . .
> Feuerbach, consequently, does not see that the "religious sentiment" is itself a *social product,* and that the abstract individual whom he analyzes belongs in reality to a particular form of society.[1]

Marx was unwilling to accept any pure religious sentiment operating in an abstract human nature. It should be clear that the materialist theory of history and the particular theory of ideology demand this conclusion. For the forms of consciousness are reflections of the social relations of production existing in a given society at a specific moment in time. It is consequently to social structure that we must turn to reach the roots of religious ideology. The heart of Marx's position is contained in the following passage, which deserves to be quoted at some length because of its crucial importance to the theory as a whole, and because it is not possible to do justice to it in paraphrase:

From Richard Lichtman, "The Marxian Critique of Christianity," in *Marxism and Christianity,* ed. Herbert Aptheker (New York: Humanities Press, 1968), pp. 76–94.
1. Feuer, 244–45.

For Germany the criticism of religion is in the main complete, and criticism of religion is the premise of all criticism.

The profane existence of error is discredited after its heavenly *oratio pro aris et focis* (speech for the altars and hearths) has been rejected. Man, who looked for a superman in the fantastic reality of heaven and found nothing there but the reflexion of himself, will no longer be disposed to find but the semblance of himself, the non-human (unmensch) where he seeks and must seek his true reality.

The basis of irreligious criticism is: Man makes religion, religion does not make man. In other words, religion is the self-consciousness and self-feeling of man who has either not yet found himself or has already lost himself again. But man is no abstract being squatting outside the world. Man is the world of man, the state, society. This state, this society, produce religion, a reversed world-consciousness, because they are a reversed world. Religion is the general theory of that world, . . . its universal ground for consolation and justification. It is the fantastic realization of the human essence because the human essence has no true reality. The true struggle against religion is therefore mediately the fight against the other world, of which religion is the spiritual aroma.

Religious distress is at the same time the expression of real distress and the protest against real distress. Religion is the sigh of the oppressed creature, the heart of a heartless world, just as it is the spirit of a spiritless situation. It is the opium of the people.

The abolition of religion as the illusory happiness of the people is required for their real happiness. The demand to give up the illusions about its condition is the demand to give up a condition which needs illusions. The criticism of religion is therefore in embryo the criticism of the vale of woe, the halo of which is religion.

Criticism has plucked the imaginary flowers from the chain not so that man will wear the chain without any fantasy or consolation but so that he will shake off the chain and cull the living flower. . . . Religion is only the illusory sun which revolves round man as long as he does not revolve around himself.

The task of history, therefore, once the world beyond the truth has disappeared, is to establish the truth of this world. The immediate task of philosophy, which is at the service of history, once the saintly form of human self-alienation has been unmasked, is to unmask self-alienation in its unholy forms. Thus the criticism of heaven turns into the criticism of the earth, the criticism of religion into the criticism of right and the criticism of theology into the criticism of politics.[2]

In the context of Marx's large system, this very dense and brilliant passage can be viewed as affirming the following important propositions:

(1) Feuerbach has completed the criticism of religion itself, and established it as distorted projection of man's being.

(2) Religion is either the expression of a society too primitive to

---

2. *On Religion*—Karl Marx and Frederich Engels—Foreign Languages Publishing House, Moscow, 1955. Pp. 41-42.

grant man an awareness of his independence from nature, or too corrupt to permit him autonomous control of his own being.

(3) Religion is the reversal of the world in the sense that the corruption of social existence finds its purported validation in re-religious doctrine.

(4) Religion is a consolation for misery—an opiate. It is a cry against real degradation, but an expression of human impotence which confirms and enhances the very distress against which it arises.

(5) If man is to grow in dignity, the narcotic of religious illusion must be wrenched from him. But this is only the beginning of man's task. It is subsequently necessary to discover the perversion in man's social being that led him to find this crippling distortion attractive.

(6) It is finally necessary to eradicate the source of this perversion, an act that can only be fulfilled by a revolutionary restructuring of the human society.

This is the essential thrust of Marx's position; it remains now to fill in its outline and draw the implications it entails. We must first locate more concretely the nature of the social corruption which forms the basis of religious projection. We may best begin by contrasting present religiosity with its primitive varieties. All religion reflects the fact that man's life is controlled by external power over which he has no control; but in primitive society it was the power of nature which so constrained man, while in the modern world, it is the force of the social system which exercises this external dominance. So Engels wrote in an interesting passage in *Anti-Dühring:*

> ... it was not long before, side by side with the forces of nature, social forces begin to be active—forces which confront man as equally alien and at first equally inexplicable dominating him with the same apparent natural necessity as the forces of nature themselves. The fantastic figures, which at first only reflected the mysterious forces of nature, at this point acquire social attributes, become representative of the forces of history.[3]

The "fetishism of commodities" comes to replace the original fetishism of nature.

The root source of religion is alienation and the illusory attempt to overcome it. For the primitive the dominating external force is in nature, while for developing man it lies in society itself; this is the dialectical foundation of human history for it means that man is the source of his own disfigurement and the vehicle of his own restoration. It is man himself whom man must overcome in the process of his transformation. The hand that inflicts the wound is the hand that cures

3. Ibid. Pp. 147–48.

it. This contention is at the heart of everything that Marx and Engels wrote, and is not, as has recently been maintained, a youthful enthusiasm of Marx which he came with maturity to abandon.

But how is it possible for human activity to confront man as "an alien power opposed to him, which enslaves him instead of being controlled by him?" [4] In a word, the answer for Marx is that human society is not a free, conscious, purposefully-planned product of human cooperation, but a class divided, antagonistic and therefore, irrational form of existence. In this latter circumstance, the decisions of multitudes of men combine to establish a realm in which they cannot achieve mutual realization. In this Marxian vision, the invisible hand of Adam Smith is stood on its head, for while Smith viewed social reason as the result of the interplay of individually reasonable acts (defining "reasonable" as "efficiently egoistic") Marx viewed social irrationality as the medium in which individual rationality was necessarily aborted:

> This crystallization of social activity, this consolidation of what we ourselves produce into an objective power above us, growing out of our control, thwarting our expectations, bringing to naught our calculations, is one of the chief factors in historical development up to now. . . . The social power, i.e., the multiplied productive force, which arises through the cooperation of different individuals as it is determined within the division of labor, appears to these individuals, since their cooperation is not voluntary but natural, not as their own united power, but as an alien force existing outside them, of the origin and end of which they are ignorant, which they thus cannot control, which, on the contrary, passes through a peculiar series of phases and stages independent of the will and action of man, nay even being the prime governor of these.[5]

In alienated society the product of human labor confronts man as natural, not voluntary, that is, as imposed upon him as an unalterable fact, rather than as chosen by him in response to human requirements. At first sight, society is qualitatively different from nature, for in the natural realm, nothing at all occurs as the result of conscious intention. But with closer inspection the difference begins to disappear, and we discover that while the agents of history work deliberately for the satisfaction of conscious goals, it is not the case that the joint effort of their individual purposes can prove satisfactory to them as purposeful men. For within any society characterized by class division "a cleavage exists between the particular and the common interest," [6] and the course of history, though it is the resultant, in some sense, of the intentions of human beings, is in no sense the resultant at which any of those con-

---

4. Feuer, 254.
5. Feuer, 254–256.
6. Feuer, 254.

scious agents aimed. History is therefore, the outcome of human intention while it is simultaneously, the negation of human intention:

> That which is willed happens but rarely; in the majority of instances the numerous desired ends cross and conflict with one another, or these ends themselves are from the outset incapable of realization, or the means of attaining them insufficient. Thus the conflicts of innumerable individual wills and individual actions in the domain of history produce a state of affairs entirely analogous to that prevailing in the realm of unconscious nature . . . Historical events thus appear on the whole to be likewise governed by chance. But where on the surface accident holds sway, there actually it is always governed by inner, hidden laws, and it is only a matter of discovering these laws.[7]

These last lines point in the direction of genuine human liberation. For if society is like nature in the fact that its accidental facade masks a realm of law, it is also like nature in that the understanding of law makes man the potential master of the forces which have previously oppressed him. To the primitive, with overwhelming effect, and to historical man in continually diminishing effect, nature is destructive precisely because it cannot be understood and mastered for human ends. The understanding of nature brings with it power over natural forces. The same is true of social existence, for once we understand the forces active in society:

> when once we grasp their action, their direction, their effects, it depends only upon ourselves to subject them more and more to our own will, and by means of them to reach our own ends. And this holds quite especially of the mighty productive forces of today.[8]

With the socialization of the productive forces of society it becomes possible for man to overcome his alienation. At this moment he emerges fully from the realm of mere nature, for his existence is now in his own control, and whatever suffering and defeat he experiences in this new life will bear the characteristics of tragedy rather than farce. His objectified activity will no longer constrict him of necessity in an alien mold, but will constitute the free environment in which he manifests his essential humanity. In this circumstance he will achieve mastery over history, and in Engels' markedly Kantian words "pass from the kingdom of necessity to the kingdom of freedom." [9]

It is of the greatest significance, however, to note that this overcoming of alienation is not achieved in thought, but in action. For, as

---

7. Feuer, 230.
8. Feuer, 105.
9. Feuer, 109.

we recall, it is not thought that determines social existence, but social existence that determines thought:

> Mere knowledge ... is not enough to bring social forces under the domination of society. What is above all necessary for this is a social act. And when this act has been accomplished, when society, by taking possession of all means of production and using them on a planned basis, has freed itself and all its members from the bondage in which they themselves have produced but which confront them as an irresistible alien force ... only then will the last alien force which is still reflected in religion vanish; and with it will also vanish the religious reflection itself, for the simple reason that then there will be nothing left to reflect.[10]

So long as man remains under the control of alien forces, religion will persist. So long as economic power continues to confront man as an inexorable destiny which he is helpless to oppose, rendering him thereby incapable of eradicating the social evils which afflict him, or even of understanding the crucial fact that human degradation is the work of man, the result of institutions which he himself has created and which he is equally capable of remaking for his own fulfillment, so long will the need for illusory compensation remain. The only redemption open to man is that which he will render through his own labor. He must make himself autonomous. When he does so he will realize that the ideals which are rooted in his nature need no longer be projected beyond society and history into an unearthly realm, dependent for fruition upon the mysterious intervention of some heavenly savior. Man will come to realize that he has been the source and agency of his own corruption, and that he possesses the power to establish the conditions of his own dignity. To hold that the evil of this world will be redeemed by an agency beyond man and time is to destroy the motive for secular transformation. But significantly, to accomplish the needed social transformation is to destroy the foundation upon which religious illusion flourishes. The religious illusion is ingredient in a corrupt superstructure which will wither of itself with the revolution in man's social existence.

The obvious implication of this position is that religion will disappear independently of any external pressure. Here, again, the similarity with Freud is interesting. For just as a psychoanalyst could never advocate the destruction of a patient's illusion through violence or terror, neither can an intelligent disciple of Marx. Social illusion will disappear as an individual hysterical symptom disappears, with the cure of its cause. Nor is it irrelevant that for both these great traditions the cure is effected by extending the rational autonomy of man. Man's object for Marx ought to be the transformation of his social existence; those who repress religion only assure its martyrdom and its prolongation. These who understand religion can afford to await its natural death.

10. *On Religion* op. cit. P. 149.

What has been said thus far, constitutes the basic tendency in the views of Marx and Engels; but there is a countertendency which appears late in the works of Engels which should also be noted. In an essay in which Engels is discussing the role of labor in the evolution of mankind he makes the following observation:

> Let us not flatter ourselves overmuch on account of our human conquest over nature. For each such *conquest takes its revenge on us.* Each of them, it is true, has in the first place the consequences on which we counted, but in the second and third places it has quite different, unforeseen effects which only too often cancel out the first. The people who, in Mesopotamia, Greece, Asia Minor, and elsewhere, destroyed the forests to obtain cultivable land, never dreamed that they were laying the basis for the present devastated condition of these countries, by removing along with the forests the collecting centers and reservoirs of moisture. (emphasis added)
>
> But if it has already required the labor of thousands of years for us to learn to some extent to calculate the more remote *natural* consequences of our actions aiming at production, it has been still more difficult in regard to the more remote *social* consequences of these actions. (emphasis in the original.) [11]

Engels does not deny that there has been steady progress in discovering the remote effects of social behavior, but he underscores too, the laboriousness of the effort. If it has taken thousands of years to learn of the more remote natural consequences of our actions and if the situation is still more difficult in regard to the social consequences of our actions, there cannot be any realistic prospect of an early mastery of social existence. It will apparently continue to be true for a very long time, and even under a system of socialism, that the indirect consequences of our social actions will remain unknown to us. But if that be the case, alienation will continue into a quite distant future and can hardly be expected to disappear even with the advent of socialism. For alienation results essentially from the fact that human labor produces a world opaque to man and destructive of his purpose.

If the remote consequences of his acts cannot be predicted, then some element of opacity is built into man's social existence in the foreseeable future, and if his social world is opaque, it will only be some happy miracle that will prevent some of the unforeseen results of his actions from returning to man in a destructive form. But in so far as alienation is the fundamental cause of religion, man's inability to master the remote effects of his social actions will produce a tendency toward religion in any society, socialist or otherwise, which man can realistically envision in the course of history. It is, in fact, not even clear that the

---

11. *The Dialectics of Nature*—New World Paperback—Pp. 291–292.

notion of a thoroughly transparent social existence is even intelligible, since it would seem to imply that all of men's future actions are predictable, while the implication of this consequence is that I can predict my own future action, a conception which seems to invalidate any meaningful notion of what human action is.

It is now possible to turn to the specific character of Christianity. And the first thing we must note about the Christian religion is that it made its original appeal to the miserable, oppressed and rejected orders of men that languished in despair as the Roman Empire sank into oblivion. Christianity promised an other-worldly compensation to those who suffered most from the evils of earthly existence. Christianity bears the essential imprint of that populace of the slaves, the subjugated, the poor and the impotent to whom it made its original appeal. So, when Professor Anton Menger wondered why with the enormous concentration of ownership and widespread misery of the oppressed that existed at the time of Rome's decline, socialism did not follow, Engels answered that:

> ... this "socialism" did in fact, as far as it was possible at the time, exist and even become dominant—in Christianity. Only this Christianity, as was bound to be the case in the historic conditions, did not want to accomplish the social transformation in this world, but beyond it, in heaven, in eternal life after death, in the impending "millennium." [12]

Christianity appealed to an alienated agglomeration of men for whom a truly human existence was impossible in this world, and who were therefore seduced by the projection of a fantasied fulfillment. The fact of worldly degradation is masked by the dream of eternal beatitude. For all the varied components in the mass who embraced the Christian dream, earthly salvation was a thing of the past:

> for the ruined free men it was the former polis, the town and the state at the same time, of which their forefathers had been free citizens; for the war-captive slaves the time of freedom before their subjugation and captivity; for the small peasants the abolished gentile social system and communal landownership ... Where was the way out, salvation, for the enslaved, oppressed and impoverished, a way out common to all these groups of people whose interests were mutually alien or even opposed? And yet it had to be found if a great revolutionary movement was to embrace them all.
>
> This way out was found. But not in this world. In the state in which things were it could only be a religious way out. Then a new world was disclosed. The continued life of the soul after the death of the body had gradually become a recognized article of faith throughout the Roman

---

12. *On Religion* op. cit. P. 316–317.

world . . . Then came Christianity, which took recompense and punishment in the world beyond seriously and created heaven and hell, and a way out was found which would lead the laboring and burdened from this vale of woe to eternal paradise.[13]

Crucial to their interpretation is the view of Marx and Engels that Christianity is grounded not in a political, but in an eschatological vision. The thrust of Christianity is toward escape, not transformation, and the end of history—the second coming of Christ and the establishment of the Kingdom of God—was something which Jesus and his earthly disciples fully expected to be realized quickly, within the lifetime of their own generation. Engels refers in some detail to John's vision of the Apocalypse to support his contention that the whole meaning of Christian preparation is for a vision which negates the life of earthly man, a vision which is immanent, and soon to occur.

But if Christianity is preparation for eternity rather than secular change, it is not surprising that it contains no ethic upon which human society can be established. The function of the teaching of Jesus was to prepare men for the second coming, and not to root them in an existence whose nature, no matter how improved by secular means, was an essential corruption to be radically cancelled by the redemption of the divine kingdom. The root of Christian morality is the denial of this world for the sake of another, and the negation of human society for a beatific community. If the suggestions which the Gospels contain for the transition to a realm beyond secular history were mistakenly applied within history the result could only be chaotic. Marx seems thoroughly to enjoy the point when he asks:

> Do you offer your right cheek when you are struck upon the left, or do you not institute proceedings for assault? Yet the Gospel forbids that. . . . Are not most of your court proceedings and the majority of civil laws concerned with property? But you have been told that your treasure is not in this world.[14]

It followed that when the paradise failed to materialize, Christianity was left to accommodate itself to earthly existence without an intrinsic criterion in terms of which it might discriminate among the social systems of men. So, Marx contends, Christians find themselves living in states with radically different governments and constitutions accepting their given lot in the conviction that one is to render under Caesar what is his own, and submitting to authority since it is "ordained by God." [15]

13. Ibid Pp. 334–336.
14. Ibid P. 35.
15. Ibid Pp. 83–84.

But as a result of its normative vacuousness and its willingness to comply with any secular authority which would protect its own religious practice, Christianity ended by accommodating itself through history to everything vile and degrading in man's social existence.

> The social principles of Christianity justified the slavery of Antiquity, glorified the serfdom of the Middle Ages and equally know when necessary, how to defend the oppression of the proletariat, although they make a pitiful face over it.
> The social principles of Christianity preach the necessity of a ruling and an oppressed class, and all they have for the latter is the pious wish the former will be charitable.
> The social principles of Christianity transfer the . . . adjustment of all infamies to heaven and thus justify the further existence of those infamies on earth.
> The social principles of Christianity declare all vile acts of the oppressors against the oppressed to be either the just punishment of original sin and other sins or trials that the Lord in his infinite wisdom imposes on those redeemed.
> The social principles of Christianity preach cowardice, self-contempt, abasement, submission, dejection, in a word all the qualities of the canaille; and the proletariat, not wishing to be treated as canaille, needs its courage, its self-feeling, its pride and its sense of independence more than its bread.[16]

There is one additional consequence of the origin of Christian ethics that must be noted; the inherent hypocrisy of Christian ideals. For if the original counsels, admonishments and preachings of Jesus were designed to prepare men for a release from their worldly existence, and if in fact that monumental expectation was never realized, what could become of the ideals originally proposed? One might argue that they should have been discarded and replaced by other standards pertinent to the mundane life of men. But in fact, given the ostensive nature of Jesus and his relation to the institutionalized Church that followed him, this was impossible. Some pretense had to be made of adopting [sic] the eschatological vision of the founder to the wholly unforeseen and disparate conditions which actually prevailed. But those conditions, man's continued historical existence, were incompatible with the profession vision. The result could only have been an internal disruption and falsification of the ideal itself. Some variant of the original ideal was professed, but one so opposed to its original intention, that the norm was reconstituted as a denial of itself. It is against such a process that the following contention of Engels acquires full meaning:

> . . . Christianity knew only *one* point in which all men were equal: that

16. Ibid P. 145.

all were equally born in original sin—which corresponded perfectly to its character as the religion of the slaves and the oppressed. Apart from this it recognized, at most, the equality of the elect, which however was only stressed at the very beginning. The traces of common ownership which are also found in the early stages of the new religion can be ascribed to solidarity among the proscribed rather than to real equalitarian ideals. Within a very short time the establishment of the distinction between priests and laymen put an end even to this incipient Christian equality.[17]

But while actual equality disappears under the development of Christianity, one continues to hear innumerable sermons about God's equal love for all of men.

Marx and Engels never tire of noting the baseness of organized religion and the extent of its hypocrisy. Whatever the pretentious piety in which religion dresses the justification of its enslavement of man through the illusion of impotence and compensatory solace, its historical place has been at the side of the oppressor. Marx rarely misses the opportunity to vent his sarcasm at the self-seeking of this institution, as when he notes in *Capital* that the "English Established Church will more readily pardon an attack on 38 of its 39 articles than 1/39 of its income." [18] The same sneer is carried in the following passage and in the whole thrust of Marx's work:

> In England even now occasionally in rural districts a laborer is condemned to imprisonment for desecrating the Sabbath by working in his front garden. The same laborer is punished for breach of contract if he remains away from his metal, paper, or glass works on the Sunday, even if it be from a religious whim. The orthodox Parliament will hear nothing of Sabbath-breaking if it occurs in the process of expanding capital.[19]

It is now possible to say something about the development of specific Christian churches and doctrines, that is, about Christianity and the economic system of which it was a reflection. Here, the role of class plays a very large part, for if the economic interpretation of history and the theory of ideology are correct, religion has no independent history, and its internal conflicts must finally express more ultimate conflicts, among economic interests, that is, among the rising and falling economic classes in society.

> Even the so-called religious wars of the sixteenth century involved primarily positive material class interests; those were class wars, too, just as the later internal collisions in England and France were. Although

---

17. Ibid P. 145.
18. *Capital*—Karl Marx—The Modern Library, New York. P. 15.
19. Ibid P. 291 note.

the class struggles of that day were carried on under religious shibboleths, and though the interests, requirements, and demands of the various classes were concealed behind a religious screen, this changed nothing in the matter and is easily explained by the conditions of the time.[20]

When Christianity is examined in the Middle Ages it is readily seen to be an institution bearing the heavy imprint of class power and prestige. This fact was born at the time of Constantine when Christianity was made the official religion of the State. The Church grew as "the most general synthesis and sanction of the existing feudal domination." [21] The clergy obtained a monopoly on learning and education, both of which became essentially theological. Politics and jurisprudence bore the same mark. In time the Church passed from a persecuted minority to a powerful oppressor of the dissenting beliefs of others. It had "partaken of the fruits of slavery in the Roman empire for centuries, and later did nothing to prevent the slave trade of Christians, either of the Germans in the North, or of the Venetians on the Mediterranean . . ." [22] It came to mirror exactly the practice of the nobles, requiring the small farmer to transfer to its growing power the title to his land and his independence. In this way it helped to reduce the free farmer to a serf. In these circumstances, "all the generally voiced attacks against feudalism were above all attacks against the Church, and all social and political, revolutionary doctrines were necessarily at the same time and mainly theological heresies." [23] Since the Church stood as the ideological sanction of the feudal system, it was necessary to de-mythologize that system before it could be directly destroyed. It was in the context of this need that the Protestant Reformation occurred.

Vigorous opposition to the system of feudalism existed throughout the Middle Ages in the form of mysticism, heresy or actual insurrection. Some of these heresies were the expression of patriarchal shepherds resisting the spread of feudalism, but these were of minor importance. Much more significant was the opposition to feudalism that developed in the towns that had already outgrown it, and among the plebeians that stood outside it. In this bifurcated opposition one can see the roots of the fundamental antagonism between bourgeoisie-burgher and peasant-plebeian opposition that was to break out again at the time of the Peasant War.

The original form of heresy, that of the Albigenses in France, appeared in the 12th century as an expression of the interest of town burghers in a "cheap church." Its demands included the revival of simple

20. Ibid P. 98.
21. Ibid P. 99.
22. *The Origin of the Family, Private Property and the State*—Engels—Foreign Languages Publishing House, Moscow. P. 247.
23. *On Religion*, P. 99.

early Christianity and the abolition of exclusive priesthood, a demand not unlike that of later bourgeoisie for simple and cheap government. But this heresy was paralleled by another which, while it shared burgher interest in the elimination of Church authority, went much further.

> It demanded the restoration of early Christian equality among members of the community and the recognition of this equality as a prescript for the burgher world as well. From "equality of the children of God" it inferred civil equality, and partly even equality of property. Equality of nobleman and peasant, of patrician, privileged burgher and plebeian, abolition of the corvee, ground-rents, taxes, privileges, and at least the most crying differences in property . . .[24]

At first these different strands were not clearly distinguished from each other, but by the 14th and 15th century their distinctive forms were more clearly marked. So John Ball stood alongside the Wycliffe movement and the Taborites beside the Calixtines in Bohemia. What was appearing, of course, was the incipient class structure which would in times emerge in full reality in the distinction between bourgeoisie and proletariat. And just as the process was to repeat itself later, so it was the burgher class itself that brought forth "an appendage of propertyless urban plebeians, day laborers and servants of all kinds, belonging to no recognized social Estate . . ."[25] These were the ranks that stood outside of official feudal society, without privilege or property, without rights, burdened by heavy taxes, the most obvious manifestation of the breakdown of feudal society. It was understandable that a group so thoroughly exploited and miserable and without real historical hope should produce the chiliastic vision of common ownership, absolute equality and elimination of authority, which derived its violent fantasy from the impossibility of its aspiration. But this plebeian element was also to give rise to the movement of Thomas Munzer and the Anabaptists, the precursors of the later proletariat, and to merge with the free peasants, serfs and bondsmen all of whom sought the overthrow of the feudal system. At the time of the Reformation, then, Engels saw society as divided among three significant classes:

> While the first of the three large camps, the *conservative Catholic camp,* embraced all the elements interested in maintaining the existing conditions, i.e., the imperial authorities, the ecclesiastical and a section of the lay princes, the richer nobility, the prelates and the city patricians, the camp of the *burgher-like moderate Lutheran* reforms, attracted all the propertied elements of the opposition, the bulk of the lesser nobility, the burghers, and even a portion of the lay princes who hoped to enrich themselves through confiscation of church estates and wanted to seize the

24. *On Religion,* P. 101.
25. *On Religion,* P. 264–265.

opportunity of gaining greater independence from the Empire. As to the peasants and plebeians, they united in a *revolutionary* party whose demands and doctrines were most clearly expressed by Munzer.[26] (Italics in original).

The rising commercial class had to direct its attack against the conservative Catholic establishment and it did so first in Germany under the banner of the Lutheran Reformation. It must be understood at this point that the religious revolution which goes by the name of the Protestant Reformation was a reflection of underlying economic forces. We have already alluded to this fact but it is important enough to underline. For though its form was religious, and it was undoubtedly understood as a religious movement by most of those who were caught up in its passion, the Reformation can for a Marxist have no ultimate foundation in religiosity for the simple reason that religion is a part of the social superstructure and is therefore primarily an effect, rather than a cause, of social action. To put the matter crudely, what is progressive in religion does not, for Marx, derive from some inherent virtue in the religious mode of consciousness, but rather, from the fact that the economic forces which are the ultimate causes of the religious mentality, are entering a progressive stage. There often have been in history human religious movements directed at the reform of established religious institutions, but by and large these do not derive from any logic inherent in the spirit of religion itself, but from more basic social causes. This view is often stated by Marx and Engels but one or two references will have to suffice for our purposes:

> The new world religion, Christianity, had already quietly come into being, out of a mixture of generalized Oriental, particularly Jewish, theology, and vulgarized Greek, particularly Stoic, philosophy . . . The fact that after no more than 250 years it became the state religion suffices to show that it was the religion corresponding to the conditions of the time. In the Middle Ages, in the same measure as feudalism developed, Christianity grew into the religious counterpart to it, with a corresponding feudal hierarchy. And when the burghers began to thrive, there developed, in opposition to feudal Catholicism, the Protestant heresy . . . The Middle Ages had attached to theology all the other forms of ideology—philosophy, politics, jurisprudence—and made them subdivisions of theology. *It thereby constrained every social and political movement to take a theological form. The sentiments of the masses were fed with religion to the exclusion of all else; it was therefore necessary to put forward their own interests in a religious guise in order to produce an impetuous movement.*[27] (emphasis added)

The same fundamental observation is made by Engels in the course

26. *On Religion*, P. 103.
27. *On Religion*, P. 264.

of an analysis of the devoping role of Thomas Munzer. In tracing the growing boldness of Munzer's position, Engels notes that his

> philosophico-theological doctrine attacked all the main points not only of Catholicism, but of Christianity generally. *Under the cloak of Christian forms he preached a kind of pantheism* . . .[28] (emphasis added)

The nature of this pantheism was to exalt reason over faith, secular existence over some supposedly future heaven, and a communistic egalitarianism over the propertied hierarchy of the feudal church. But Munzer's protest was nevertheless "cloaked" in Christian phraseology.

In its early stages Luther's revolt was not yet definite in character; it had to rely on the unified opposition of a variety of elements. And it was violent in its demands, as in the following passage which Engels quotes from Luther:

> Since we punish thieves with the halter, murderers with the sword, and heretics with fire, why do we not turn on all those evil teachers of perdition, those popes, cardinals and bishops, and the entire swarm of the Roman Sodom *with arms in hand and wash our hands in their blood?* [29]
> (Italics in original.)

But Luther's revolutionary posture soon collapsed. From among the peasants, plebeians, burghers, lesser nobility, and lay princes who originally supported him, Luther had eventually to choose. "He dropped the popular elements of the movement, and took the side of the burghers, the nobility, and the princes. His appeals for a war of extermination against Rome were heard no more."[30] As he identified himself with burgher sentiment he came to rely more heavily upon peaceful change, moderate progress and political activity within the bounds of law. But the separation of Lutheranism from plebeian and peasant factions brought it more and more completely under the influence of the reformed princes. This regressive tendency finally culminated in Luther's reactionary violence in the face of the Peasant War, for when the princes and lords of Protestant regions were attacked by the peasants, Luther acted against them with unbridled vehemence:

> They must be knocked to pieces, strangled and stabbed, covertly and overtly, by everyone who can, just as one must kill a mad dog. Therefore, dear sirs, help here, save there, stab, knock, strangle them everyone who can, and should you lose your life, bless you, no better death can you ever attain.[31]

28. *On Religion*, P. 111.
29. Ibid P. 105.
30. Ibid P. 105.
31. Quoted by Engels on P. 107 of *On Religion*.

The result of the Lutheran movement was not only the destruction of the peasant revolt, but of the burgher aspirations as well, so that it was the secular princes who benefited, thereby removing Germany "for three centuries from the ranks of countries playing an independent active part in history." [32]

But while the bourgeois thrust of the Reformation was defeated in Germany it made much better progress under the influence of Calvin. In Geneva, Holland, Scotland and England it forced important changes in existing social institutions, playing, in the latter country, so important a part that it was largely incorporated in the restored Established Church of England. And although the Calvinists were suppressed in France in 1685 they led to a liberation of free thought which manifested itself in an expanding, secular, commercial class.

Marx clearly regarded Protestantism as the perfect religious expression of capitalism. In his view even the Calvinist notion of predestination was rooted in economic fact—that in capitalist competition, success or failure depended not on personal effort, but on economic factors that were beyond understanding or control. He even notes, in a striking passage, the affinity between Protestant asceticism and capitalism that was to form a later theme in the writings of Max Weber:

> The money cult implies its own asceticism, its own self denial, its own self-sacrifice—parsimony and frugality, a contempt for worldly, temporal, and transient satisfactions: it implies the striving for *everlasting* treasure. Hence the connection of English puritanism, but also of Dutch Protestantism, with money making.[33] (Italics in original)

Nor was Protestantism without its effect upon the development of capitalism. Marx notes that the process of "forcible expropriation" of property in the 16th century received "a new and frightful impulse from the Reformation, and from the consequent colossal spoliation of the church property." [34] The inhabitants of the monasteries were hurled into the proletariat and the subtenants of the church's estates had their land confiscated as they were themselves forcefully removed. Again, Protestantism supported the genesis of capital by "changing almost all the traditional holidays into work days." [35] But of course, in these and numerous other ways, Protestantism was merely carrying out the underlying thrust of the growing tendency of capitalism itself.

The great moral fact of Protestantism remains its alliance with the propertied oppressor against the proletariat. Colonialism and the

---

32. *On Religion*, P. 265.
33. Quoted in *The Political Economy of Growth,* Paul Baran, Prometheus Books, 1960 P. 49.
34. *Capital*—Marx—Modern Library Edition. P. 792.
35. Ibid P. 303 note.

institution of slavery are obvious instances of capitalist rapacity. Marx quotes from William Howitt's *Colonisation and Christianity,* the following passages:

> The barbarities and desperate outrages of the so-called Christian race, throughout every region of the world, and upon every people they have been able to subdue, are not to be paralleled by those of any other race, however fierce, however untaught, and however reckless of mercy and shame, in any age of the earth.[36]

Nor is the domestic situation any better. The " 'holy ones' . . . show their Christianity by the humility with which they bear the overwork, the privations and the hunger of others." [37] In another passage Marx refers to the Venetian monk, Ortes, who in the 18th century maintained that the antagonism between great riches and widespread privation was a natural law of social wealth. He contrasts with Ortes the view of the Protestant, Townsend, who in 1786 wrote in praise of the hunger of the poor, that it acted as a "natural motive to industry," served to assure that the most sordid and disgusting tasks of society would be fulfilled, freed the most delicate from drudgery, and concluded finally that the Poor Laws tend to "destroy the harmony and beauty, the symmetry and order of that system which God and Nature have established in the world." On the contrast between Ortes and Townsend, Marx then makes the following comment:

> If the Venetian monk found in the fatal destiny that makes misery eternal, the raison d'etre of Christian charity, celibacy, monasteries and holy houses, the Protestant prebendary finds in it a pretext for condemning the laws in virtue of which the poor possessed a right to a miserable relief.[38]

The bourgeoisie realized the importance of "the evangelization of the lower orders" as a means for anchoring them more securely to their oppression. For religion represents as much the spiritual force of oppression as the state represents its physical force. Religion is the opiate through which the proletariat is rendered incapable of protesting its own exploitation. "The mortgage the peasant has on heavenly goods gives guaranty to the mortgage the bourgeoisie has on the peasant's earthly goods." [39]

36. Ibid P. 824.
37. Ibid P. 291 note.
38. Ibid P. 701–710.
39. Quoted in Bober P. 156 Op. Cit.

38 ADAM SCHAFF
The Problem of the Individual

In a debate between such contrary philosophies as Marxism and Existentialism—I refer throughout to Sartre's variant, which has played so big a role in Poland—it is necessary to go straight to the main point of their differences. This concerns the concept of the individual, which is the central concept of every variety of Existentialism, and around which are grouped all differences of viewpoint between Existentialism and Marxism.

Does the individual create society, by choosing the manner of his behavior in complete spontaneity and freedom of choice? Or is it society that creates the individual and determines his mode of behavior?—These questions lie at the heart of the antagonism between Existentialism and Marxism. All others, including the problem of "essence and existence," are consequent upon the way they are answered.

Of course, the different points of departure by no means signify that Existentialism completely rejects the role of society, or Marxism that of the individual. But all varieties of Existentialism—which differ greatly in the areas separating Kierkegaard from Sartre—are united not only by the fact that their central problems concern the fate and experiences of the individual, but also by—and, indeed, primarily by—their conception of the individual as isolated, lonely and tragic in his senseless struggle with the alien forces of the world around him. Involved here are problems hard to grasp and even harder to express clearly.

This standpoint is ordinarily called subjectivism; and that it actually is, despite the Existentialists' protest against such a designation of their position. Only by taking off from the position of subjectivism can one arrive at such a strange and internally contradictory conception as that of the "sovereign" individual, completely free to make decisions which depend only on himself, who is at the same time defenceless and tragic in his hopeless struggle with malicious fate. The internal contradiction that appears here is that between a voluntarist variety of subjectivism and the concept of an objective fate, independent of human activity.

From Adam Schaff, *A Philosophy of Man: Marxism or Existentialism* (New York: Monthly Review Press, 1963), pp. 297–307.

Sartre's reputation is due to his skillful treatment of the central problem of all varieties of Existentialism, the problem of the individual and his complex relations with the world surrounding him. Sartre's has become the most typical variety of Existentialism. This is due not only to the atmosphere of helplessness and despair with which his whole philosophy is permeated, but to the concept which generates this atmosphere—the asocial concept of the individual who, being isolated and lonely, must determine his behavior entirely for himself and, with nothing but his own judgment to guide him, grapple with hostile living and nonliving forces. This is not a new idea, but it exerts a strong appeal in the conditions of moral chaos of the postwar world, in the conditions of the breakup of traditional systems of values while new social values take shape amid conflict and pain. Its appeal is all the greater when expressed by a great writer who is at the same time an excellent psychologist.

But this is only one Sartre. There is another who, in spite of the first, leans toward socialism in his practical activities and toward Marxism in his theoretical work. There is something droll in the fact that Sartre—the Existentialist moving toward Marxism—could in an article specially written for a Polish journal teach something to our Marxists who, moving toward Existentialism, had lost their knowledge of Marxist philosophy and its values. Sartre reminded them that Marxism is the only modern philosophy which has the perspective of further development. I said that there is something amusing in this—but it is at the same time perfectly understandable. When two contrary tendencies—one away from and the other toward Marxism—intersect at a certain point, they by no means come to an agreement there. They are moving in opposite directions, and cannot agree. This is why an Existentialist moving toward Marxism understands Marxism much better than a Marxist who is moving toward Existentialism.

While fully recognizing Sartre's stature and talents, one should not lose sight of the inner contradictions of his views, which do not decrease but rather increase with the development of his views. There is a contradiction between the Sartre who clings to traditional Existentialism and the Sartre who pays tribute to the philosophy of Marxism. This contradiction can be overcome only by abandoning one or other of the two antagonistic views he now holds. And it is concentrated mainly in his conception of the individual.

The young Marx, whom certain of his "admirers" in Poland wish violently to transform into an Existentialist, wrote in his famous *Theses on Feuerbach:* "The human essence is no abstraction inherent in each single individual. In its reality it is the ensemble of the social relations." This statement, aphoristic in form, was directed against Feuerbach, who in Marx's opinion did not understand the social individual and so committed a double sin: (1) against the *historical* conditioning of the individual, whom Feuerbach conceived abstractly as an isolated being; (2) against his *social* conditioning, which Feuerbach conceived in a naturalistic way in terms of the bonds uniting the individual members of a species.

Referring to Feuerbach's views on the individual's religious beliefs, Marx further wrote: "Feuerbach consequently does not see that the 'religious sentiment' is itself a social product, and that the abstract individual whom he analyzes belongs in reality to a particular form of society."

It requires no special keenness of mind to realize that what Marx said hits not only at Feuerbach but strikes with equal force at the mistaken approach to the individual of both modern naturalism and Existentialism.

Marx states that "the human essence is no abstraction inherent in each individual. In its reality it is the ensemble of the social relations." This statement goes to the heart of the problem—if we discount the fact that this would not be today the ordinary way of phrasing his thought. The human being, as an individual, is "the ensemble of the social relations," in the sense that his origin and development can be understood only in the social and historical context, in the sense that he is the *product* of social life. This social and therefore historical approach to the investigation of the spiritual life of man and his works is the indisputable and tremendously important theoretical content of Marxism, freeing it from the limitations of both naturalism and Existentialist subjectivism in the analysis of human affairs.

It is important to emphasize this point not only in opposition to Existentialism but also to the vulgarized interpretation of the position held by the young Marx. I have already referred to the causes which led our latest revisionists to plagiarize Existentialism. The same causes led indirectly to the distortion and Existentialist vulgarization of the young Marx. The great enthusiasm of some of our intellectuals for the themes treated by the young Marx—and this is, moreover, a broader phenomenon of international significance—can be explained by their quest for answers to their pervasive question about human affairs, their desire to "humanize" the problems posed by Marxist theory, to saturate these problems with a humanist content, to connect them with the fate of the individual. That theme and its inspiration are, of course, comprised in the works of the young Marx. It is important to deepen one's analysis of this theme, making use of the further development of Marx's thought. But that is a task by no means connected only with the immediate social stimuli which actually propelled the theme to the fore.

The very social causes and spiritual shocks which caused the defection of some intellectuals, formerly connected with Marxism, to Existentialism led to their misrepresenting the tenets of the young Marx in the spirit of Existentialism. When, in contradiction with historical facts, they vulgarized their interpretation of the views of the young Marx, it was by no means with them a question of an objective investigation. It is in this light that one may understand the ignorant attempts, made with such boastfulness and aplomb by our revisionists, to counterpose the young Marx not only to Engels but also to the older Marx. For such enthusiasts, Marx was finished somewhere around 1846.

And yet it is precisely in the teachings of the young Marx that we find a firm and decisive refutation of Existentialist views on the problems of the individual. The views expressed by Marx on these problems, already expounded in the *Theses on Feuerbach*, and developed in his later theoretical works, constitute a rejection of the theoretical foundations of Existentialism—subjectivism, the asocial and ahistorical conception of the individual.

The internal contradictions of Sartre's views are related precisely to this question. It is not possible simultaneously to pay tribute to the tenets of both Existentialism and Marxism on philosophical problems in general and the problem of the individual in particular, without falling into eclecticism and toleration of contradictions. If one approaches the problem of the individual in a Marxist way, that is, historically and socially, one must abandon the idealist, subjectivist foundations of Existentialism. One must reject the thesis that because the individual must make independent decisions in situations of moral conflict—true, a real problem is involved here—he is condemned to loneliness and consequently to helplessness and despair. On the contrary, Marxism shows that the individual, in making independent decisions and, in a certain sense, choosing between given attitudes and activities, always does so socially, in the sense of the social conditioning of his personality. Marxism teaches that the individual's attitudes are social products and that, in adopting the attitudes he does, the individual "belongs in reality to a particular form of society." In this light, the "philosophy of despair" has its basis only in the attitudes of certain social classes who lose their so-called eternal philosophical truths at turning points of history. There is a fundamental contradiction between Marxism and Existentialism. It is possible to choose between these two alternative points of view; what is not possible is to combine them into one consistent system of thought.

We may note here that even atheistic Existentialism is much closer to the tenets of religion on the problems of the obligations and destiny of individuals than would appear at first sight. This is the price of departing from the social and historical analysis of human affairs.

I have already pointed out that Existentialism contains a contradiction between the postulate of the "sovereignty" of the individual, who is supposedly the independent creator of his own destiny (in the deepest sense, this is the thesis that "existence" is prior to "essence"), and the whole content of the "philosophy of despair." For that philosophy proclaims that man is a mere pawn in the hands of fate. As Sartre indicates primarily in his plays, evil triumphs regardless of human choosing (this conception perhaps finds its sharpest expression in Sartre's play *The Devil and the Good God*). But this is precisely the antimony of religious moralists, especially those who derive their morality from the Mosaic religion, of which Christianity is a copy. The Judaic Jehovah and the Existentialist Fate are the one as spiteful as the other: they truly create man "in their own image." They give him, cunningly enough, the power to recognize good and evil, but only so that they may condemn him. This miserable worm, with such means of knowledge at his command as the Ten Commandments, racks his brains as to what to do in life's conflicting situations and lives in a state of discord and fear, only to earn condemnation at the end. And yet this miserable and helpless creature, worthy of both pity and contempt, is in the light of religion the sovereign individual, God's highest creation! Atheistic and religious Existentialism alike repeat the tale of the cruelty and maliciousness of the old Jehovah. They create their individual as supposedly sovereign in order to make him lonely. They condemn to helplessness and despair the wretched puppets who are the sport of malicious fate while wearing the hollow crown of "sovereignty." For it is clear that the separation of the individual from society does not give him any sovereignty. On the contrary, it deprives him of all real independence. This cannot be doubted if one reads Kafka's *Trial* and *The Castle,* or sees on the stage the fate of Sartre's hero in *The Devil and the Good God*. The "philosophy of despair" is humanism inside out; it is in essence amoral morality, dehumanized humanism.

But enough of that. What most concerns us here is that it is actually possible to choose between Marxism and Existentialism, but impossible to combine them into one. Sartre himself will, sooner or later, have to make such a choice. It is impossible to complement Marxism with Existentialism. This does not mean, however, that to be a Marxist one must give up the *subject matter* of Existentialism.

In his article on *Marxism and Existentialism,* Sartre stated that his Existentialism only fills in the gap which now exists in Marxism, and that the moment this is accomplished, Existentialism loses all reason for existence as an independent current of thought.

It all depends on how the above statement is to be understood. If it is a matter of "completing" Marxism with the theory and methodology of Existentialism, then Sartre's proposition is very doubtful, since fire cannot complete water. But if it is a matter of Marxism undertaking, on the basis of the Marxist method, a more thorough investigation of the problems of the individual, which it has tended to neglect and which have been monopolized by Existentialism, then we have here an important proposal.

If it is true that Existentialism has raised questions which profoundly affect people and we have neglected them, and if it is true that this neglect has had political consequences, then it becomes important to get clear, in the first place, about exactly what questions are involved.

The usual answer is: Marxism has neglected the problems of ethics, and so it is necessary to undertake a comprehensive study of the broad principles of morality. This is true; but it is a truth of the kind that says little. What exactly is the object of a comprehensive study of the principles of morality, and how is it to be done? When it comes to the point, little remains for such studies but fine phrases.

A serious analysis of what amongst the problems posed by Existentialism is of most concern to people today brings two complexes of problems of the fore:

(1) the problems of personal responsibility for one's actions, including political action and particularly in situations involving conflicts between opposing moral standards;

(2) the problems of the individual's place and role in the world, which have been rather hazily expressed as "the problem of the meaning of life."

These are not single problems, but complexes of problems. They belong to the sphere of the science of morality, broadly conceived; but unhappily they were not in evidence when the traditional themes of Marxist ethics were developed. Because of that, the demand for the general "development of Marxist ethics" cannot be considered satisfactory. For the whole difficulty lies precisely in the question of how the subject is to be understood, i.e., what is the range of the problems of this ethics. By picking on particular problems we shall not, of course, develop a whole theory of ethics; but we may at least say something definite.

When an Existentialist raises problems of the individual's responsibility, he does so in a rhetorical and abstract manner. And this he cannot help. For by removing the problem of the freedom of choice and responsibility of the individual from its social and historical context, he cannot but treat the individual and his responsibility as abstractions. Sartre understands very well the conflicting character of situations in real life which present the individual with a choice as to how he will behave— he has expressed this in his work *L'Existentialisme est un humanisme,** and in his literary works; but he considers this choice as the free act of the individual. We cannot accept this abstract way of posing the problem of the individual's responsibility.

How has this problem actually presented itself to us, arising from

---
* "Existentialism is a Humanism." See the Sartre essay.

recent experiences? The problem of responsibility for one's deeds did not present itself to us in a purely theoretical and abstract form, but in a most living and practical way in conflict between party discipline and one's conscience, and in judgment of those who, not motivated by any personal considerations, were guilty of evil deeds under the conviction that they were fulfilling their social obligations.

Existentialism cannot answer problems posed in this concrete way. Its abstract and subjectivist outlook is useless in relation to such problems. To deal with them requires the development of a whole complex of theories, and first of all the sociological theory of *the individual in Society* and, connected with this, the dialectics of personal freedom and the necessities flowing from social determinism. Here we find already a firm theoretical foundation in Marxism. But there arise also a number of more neglected questions, of which the chief is that of the definition of responsibility in its sociological, psychological and moral aspects. Finally, there arises the difficult problem of conflicting situations and the definition of responsibility in relation to them.

Standard theories of ethics tend to overlook the fact that in real life moral judgments often relate to conflicting situations. So standard ethics simplifies its tasks and promulgates *absolute* solutions of moral problems independently of time, place and social circumstances. All religious systems and most so-called lay codes of morals attempt to do this.

All absolute ethical systems, so called, erected on the basis of supposedly eternal and immutable moral truths, are helpless before the problems occurring most often in life, namely, situations of conflict in which doing what is thought to be right brings about evil consequences. Uncertainty here does not arise because the so-called sinner is ignorant of the moral norm obligatory for him in the given situation; the moralist may come forward with his pompous commandments and prohibitions, but that does not help, because the situation is connected with a clash of contradictory standards and the poor sinner cannot decide which has priority. This may be called an "Orestes" * situation. Such situations confound all "absolute" moral systems, religious or lay. Existentialism has the merit of having been aware of the problem, although it cannot solve it. Marxism has the best equipment for solving it, but has so far remained somewhat aloof.

The second main complex of problems relates to questions which are only reluctantly mentioned by philosophies pretending to the name of science. These problems, it is said, are so hazy and so burdened with tradition, that they should be regarded as belonging to the spheres of religion, mysticism or poetry rather than science. Such, indeed, is the

---

* A reference to Sartre's play, *The Flies* (1946), which retells in existential garb the story of the murder of Clytemnestra by Orestes and Electra. Confronted by Zeus and given the choice between forgiveness with slavery or freedom with torment, Orestes chooses the latter, Electra the former.

opinion of the Neo-Positivists,* who class them among "pseudo-problems." But as I have already pointed out, to call a problem a "pseudo-problem" does not abolish it; it merely hands the problem over to those least equipped to tackle it seriously. The traditional mystification of a problem does not abolish either the problem or the possibility of its scientific analysis. "What is the meaning of life?" "What is man's place in the universe?" It seems difficult to express oneself scientifically on such hazy topics. And yet if one should assert ten times over that these are typical pseudo-problem, problems would remain. Let us therefore consider what is behind the haze.

"Vanity, vanity, all is vanity!" These words, repeated in various forms in all philosophies of the East, seem to appeal to many who in old age begin to reflect on life and death. It is possible to shrug this off with a compassionate smile as nonsense. And yet the words echo a problem which cannot simply be ignored. Nor can the questions "Why?" "What for?" which force their way to the lips of people tired of the adversities and delusions of life. This applies all the more to the compulsive questions which come from reflection on death—why all this effort to stay alive if we are going to die anyway? It is difficult to evade the feeling that death is senseless—avoidable, accidental death especially. Of course, we can ask: senseless from what point of view? From the point of view of the progression of nature, death is entirely sensible. But from the point of view of a given individual, death is senseless and places in doubt everything he does. Religion has tried to counter this feeling of senselessness. The old and very wise religions of the East pointed to *nirvana* as the final goal, thus giving death a clear meaning. Other, more primitive, religions instil faith in a life after death. But what is to be done when religious belief itself loses all sense?

Attempts to ridicule all this do not help at all. The fact alone of some agnostics undergoing deathbed conversions gives much food for thought. Philosophy must take the place of religion here. It must tackle a number of diverse questions which have remained from the wreck of the religious view of life—the senselessness of suffering, of broken lives, of death, and many, many other questions relating to the fate of living, struggling, suffering and dying individuals. Can this be done scientifically, that is, in a way that is communicable and subject to some form of verification? It certainly can. True, not by following the same methods as in physics or chemistry—for this is not a matter of physics or chemistry. This is why the Neo-Positivists are wrong in their sweeping verdict that these are empty pseudo-problems. And so are those Marxists who fail just as dismally to express themselves on these questions, and who cover their scornful silence by concentrating attention exclusively on

---

* Those philosophers who attempt to introduce the methodology and analytic precision of the sciences into philosophical questions.

great social processes and their laws of development. These are undoubtedly very important and socially decisive matters. But they do not provide automatic solutions to problems relating to individuals.

Existentialized Marxism

Sartre's latest work, *Critique of Dialectical Reason,* covers 755 pages and is only the first volume of what promises to be a monumental treatise. It must regretfully be stated that, if Sartre were identified only with this strictly philosophical work, he would remain an obscure and relatively unimportant philosopher. What Sartre writes as a philosopher is terribly muddled and communicates little. Although he is a Frenchman, Sartre has managed to embody in his writings the worst traditions of German pedantry and obscurity. His pages resemble, not Descartes or Diderot, but Husserl and Heidegger. Luckily, there is another Sartre, who wields a different pen and contrives as a dramatist to make clear "what the author wished to say." Thus Sartre the dramatist and novelist formerly clarified and popularized the philosophy of *L'Etre et le Néant.** Perhaps he will do the same later for his new book—though it is hard to conceive how he will do it.

Let us leave aside, however, the question of the lucidity of Sartre's new book—few philosophers are lucid anyway—and apply ourselves to its contents. The wealth of problems posed compels selection. We are interested here primarily in those which bear on Sartre's relations to Marxism and exhibit the internal contradictions of his standpoint.

Sartre has traveled far from *L'Etre et le Néant* to *Critique de la raison dialectique.*† He of course continues on the line of Existentialist thought, but arrives at the conclusion—surprising for his creed—that Marxism is actually the great philosophy of our time. In the Introduction he writes:

> I consider Marxism to be the undated philosophy of our time . . . while the ideology of Existentialism and its method of cognition is an enclave of Marxism itself, which simultaneously gives birth to it and denies it.

From Adam Schaff, *A Philosophy of Man: Marxism or Existentialism* (New York: Monthly Review Press, 1963), pp. 307–14.
* *Being and Nothingness* (1943), Sartre's massive study of phenomenological ontology.
† Sartre's book on philosophical method, *Critique of Dialectical Reason* (1960).

This introductory declaration contains in a nutshell the contradiction to which my further analysis is devoted.

How Sartre interprets his own evolution toward Marxism is of considerable sociological and psychological interest. He was attracted by the force of the Labor Movement; as an intellectual, he was influenced by the rising class whose consciousness is molded by its own social position. Husserl and Heidegger officiated at the cradle of *L'Etre et le Néant;* but in the *Critique* Sartre had arrived at the conviction that Marxism is the philosophy relevant to our time ("undated"). Anti-Marxism, he states, faces the Hobson's choice of either returning to pre-Marxist ideas or of rediscovering ideas already refuted by Marxism. This is an excellent and terse expression of an important fact many times observed in practice. Various critics have believed themselves to be superseding Marx when in reality they were only harking back to his precursors.

Sartre's ideas on revisionism are of interest. The term is, he says, either a truism or an absurdity. It is a truism when it asserts the evolution of Marxist ideas. That evolution is a necessity even for those who wish to be the most faithful disciples, since Marxism is a living philosophy which changes and grows with the development of society. Revisionism becomes an absurdity when it sets out to make a change in philosophy—which in its opinion finds itself in a state of crisis—by calling in the advice of "experts." If there is a crisis, and if any change is needed, that fact reflects a deeper social crisis, which can only be overcome as a result of social development. A revision made by "experts" is only a mystification. This thought of Sartre goes far beyond the shallow but loud propaganda of the revisionist miracle-makers, and in my opinion deserves a deeper analysis.

So we see that Sartre not only avows Marxist philosophy but attempts to defend it from attack. He ends his introductory study with a far-reaching prognosis of the fusion of Existentialism with Marxism.

> When Marxist analysis accepts human dimensions [i.e., the Existentialist program] as the basis of anthropological science, Existentialism loses its reason for existence. . . .

Is this not too good to be true? Doubts are at once raised by what Sartre says in continuation:

> Absorbed, mastered and retained by an integrated philosophical movement, it [Existentialism] ceases to be a particular analysis in order to become the basis of every analysis.

Thus Existentialism will "disappear," not in the sense of being overcome by Marxism, which resolves the Existentialist problems in its own way, but by being taken over by Marxism as the basis of every analysis. This is not a case of "disappearance" at all, but of the promotion of Existentialism to the role of serving as the foundation of all Marxist theory. It is a question of "completing" Marxism by Existentialism.

Is such a "completion" possible without giving rise to internal contradictions within the system?

To a certain extent Sartre himself is aware of contradiction. Indeed, in a polemic with Lukacs he once charged the latter with not seeing the contradiction.

> We were at the same time persuaded that historical materialism provided the only correct interpretation of history and that Existentialism remains the only concrete approach to reality. I do not intend to deny the contradictions inherent in his position. I only say that Lukacs did not suspect them. Further, many intellectuals and many students have lived and still live under the pressure of this postwar exigency. Where does this come from? It results from a circumstance of which Lukacs was well aware but of which he could not say anything at that time: Marxism—which attracts us as the moon does the tides, which has transformed all our ideas and eliminated for us the categories of bourgeois thought—could not satisfy our speculative needs; on the particular ground we occupied it had nothing new to tell us, since it was retarded in its own development.

Sartre is right, of course: there *are* contradictions here. Historical materialism understands human actions and motives as socially conditioned, whereas Existentialism seeks the true source of social phenomena in the autonomous, free individual. These are two diametrically opposed conceptions which cannot be united. Nor was this accomplished by Sartre, who perhaps managed to insinuate a little Existentialism into Marxism while trying to transform Marxism into a variety of Existentialism. It is not surprising that this new system splits at the seams under pressure of its internal contradictions. In a review of Sartre's book in *Prévues*, under the significant title *Marxism Existentialized*, Aimé Pari rightly remarked that Sartre had sacrificed none of his own doctrines for the sake of the "undated" philosophy, and that his position simply subordinates what he calls Marxism to Existentialism.

The discoveries of Historical Materialism advanced socialism from utopia to science. The discovery of the real mechanism of social development, and in particular of the determining role of the mode of production for the whole of social life, demonstrated the necessity of socialism and identified the social force which could bring it about. The guiding thought of historical materialism, and of the whole conception of scientific socialism, was historical determinism, which interprets the behavior of social classes and of human individuals in the light of the discovered laws of social development. Historical materialism does not deny the role of the individual in history. On the contrary, it strongly emphasizes that history is made by people. But it brings out the role of other factors, which determine in the last analysis why people think and act in one way and not in another. Materialism differs from idealism in understanding human thinking not as the primary but as a secondary and derivative factor in making history. True, in taking up this idea, so-called sociological materialism does involve the recognition of historical determinism and its corollary—the derivative character of the mode of thought in relation to the mode of production. Sartre, however, who declares his avowal of Marxism in the form of historical materialism, rejects what is the foundation stone of that materialism, namely, historical determinism, with its specific conceptions of the laws of social development, of the derivative character of social consciousness, and of the dialectic inherent in understanding the individual as both the product and at the same time the maker of society.

Is Sartre therefore dishonest in his pro-Marxist declarations? Nothing of the sort. It is simply a matter of contradictions in his views and personal convictions. He gets along with these the easier because he practices philosophy "artistically"—which means with complete carelessness regarding the precise meaning of the words he uses. With deep conviction he declares that vagueness should be the characteristic of every analysis. For the Polish reader, reared in the cult of temperance, clarity and precision of thought—and perhaps for the English reader, too—such playing with words is often unbearable.

Here is how Sartre conceives the subject matter of Existentialism:

> The subject of Existentialism—consequent upon the avoidance of the matter by Marxists—is the individual person in a social environment . . . the alienated individual transformed into a mere object, mystified, who was created by the division of labor and exploitation, but who struggles against alienation with insufficient means and, in spite of everything, patiently climbs to ever new positions.

It must be acknowledged that this is a proper subject for analysis, and we cannot object if Sartre takes this point of departure for his investigation of dialectical reason, since he clearly stipulates that the individual must be understood socially and as socially conditioned. However, when Sartre proceeds from general declarations to the concrete application of his intentions, he arouses serious misgivings. He clearly formulates these methodological intentions in the chapter entitled "Dogmatic and Critical Dialectics."

Here he is concerned with the problem of the freedom of the

individual, basic for every variety of Existentialism, which he approaches from the aspect of the relations between the individual and society, the individual and his environment in the broad meaning of the term. There are certain necessities, says Sartre, which the environment imposes on the individual in the form of laws. But the individuals at the same time make history. Such is his dialectic. But inconsistency arises here, since Existentialism desires at all costs to preserve its doctrine of absolute individual freedom—which is at the very heart of Existentialism as a philosophy, and without which it loses its reason for existence. Sartre finds himself entangled in the inconsistencies of an Existentialism which recognizes, at least in words, the social conditioning of the individual personality. And he emerges rather too easily from this entanglement. He simply withdraws with his right hand what he grasps with his left. He recognizes social conditioning and the necessity flowing from it only in order at once to deny it—"dialectically." This is a poor kind of "dialectic," the defects of which are due, among other things, to the fact that he never even attempts to make precise for himself what he understands by "dialectics" and "contradiction," although he uses these terms incessantly.

> Man makes history on the basis of the conditions he finds at hand. If that statement is true, it definitively erases determinism and analytical reasoning as a method and rule of human history.

The above-quoted argument of Sartre contains an obvious *non sequitur;* for the statement that people make their own history on the basis of given circumstances does not lead to the erasure of historical determinism but rather to the specific interpretation of the mechanism by which that determinism operates. But Sartre desires at all costs to save the "freedom" of the individual, as understood by Existentialism, the conception of which is required to "complete" Marxism. On this conception of "freedom" rests his understanding of dialectical reasoning, which proceeds beyond what already exists to what does not yet exist but is projected by human activity. Sartre speaks of the dialectic of freedom and necessity, of the dialectic of the external conditioning to which we are subjected, as well as of the dialectic which we ourselves create. It is all terribly hazy and inconsistent. But it does express his intention, as does the following statement:

> There exists no dialectic that could be imposed on facts, as Kant's categories were imposed on phenomena; dialectical development, if it takes place, is the individual adventure of the particular object.

This is a poetic rather than a philosophical statement. But its intent is clear. Talk as much as you like about "social conditioning," but without the "freedom" of the individual, in the sense of his being free from the action of determinism, Existentialism simply ceases to exist as a philosophical current. This is why determinism must go!

In the name of Existentialism, Sartre demands recognition of the details of historical events, rejecting the idea of laws governing historical development. But without recognizing such laws there is no Marxism, no historical materialism. Sartre does not particularly care how loose his language is, although the subject requires accuracy of expression. He says further:

> Historical materialism exists, and the law of that materialism is dialectics. But if, as certain authors maintain, by dialectical materialism is understood some kind of monism which wishes to direct human history from without, then it must be stated that there does not exist, or does not yet exist, any dialectical materialism.

Sartre is, of course, aware that the Existentialist individual with his "freedom" cannot be derived from any Marxist conceptions. Instead, he tries to make the transition from that individual to society, from freedom to necessity, from Existentialism to Marxism, by dragging in the concept of scarcity. He speaks of *rareté*—but the literal translation of the word as "rarity" does not express what he actually has in mind, namely, the lack or inadequacy of means to satisfy human needs. And here there arises a very serious misunderstanding; for Sartre—in all good faith, no doubt—now replaces Marxism with a version of social Darwinism:

> Certainly, [writes Sartre] however it may be with people and events, they have thus far appeared only within the framework of scarcity, i.e., within the framework of a society still incapable of freeing itself from the domination of its needs, and hence of nature, and which in this connection possesses limited techniques and instruments; a society torn asunder, overwhelmed by its needs and dominated by production, arousing antagonism between the individuals composing it; abstract relations between things, commodities and money, etc., are the premise and condition of direct relations between people; in this manner, implements, the circulation of commodities, etc., determine economic and social development.

Here Sartre tries to make economic scarcity the foundation of the whole mechanism of social development, including the class struggle. Human activity, he says, is carried on within the framework of scarcity of the means of subsistence; hence there is a surplus of population, and people naturally find themselves in antagonistic relations of competition with others for the division of the scarce means of satisfying their needs. The affinity of this with social Darwinism and Malthusianism is evident—but Sartre mistakes it for Marxism, with which it has nothing whatever in common. The Marxist conception of exploitation and surplus value is based on the fact that the worker produces *more* than the minimum amount required for his own satisfaction according to his historically determined living standards. The social problem in the United States today, for example, where the full employment of existing productive capacity would make possible the immediate transition to the Communist principle of distribution according to need, does not consist of any inadequacy in material means; and the class struggle there is certainly not waged within any framework of scarcity. Marxism opposes the ideas of social Darwinism and Malthusianism, and sees in them merely the apologetics of capitalism which imposes poverty amidst plenty.

The proposed marriage of Marxism and Existentialism cannot, then, be celebrated. Materialism and idealism cannot come together, and no kind of "dialectic" can unite them. Sartre has suffered the fate of many "completers" of Marxism before him, and has entirely failed as a "renewer" of Marxism.

But the fiasco of this marriage does not alter the fact, emphasized earlier, that some of the problems posed by Sartrist Existentialism are important problems. The failure of Sartre's hopeless attempt to reconcile the irreconcilable does not make their discussion any less urgent. Marxism cannot become one with Existentialism, but it can and must defeat it by tackling on its own ground those problems which constitute the vital part of Existentialism.

39 HERBERT MARCUSE
A Biological Foundation for Socialism?

In the affluent society, capitalism comes into its own. The two mainsprings of its dynamic—the escalation of commodity production and productive exploitation—join and permeate all dimensions of private and public existence. The available material and intellectual resources (the potential of liberation) have so much outgrown the established institutions that only the systematic increase in waste, destruction, and management keeps the system going. The opposition which escapes suppression by the police, the courts, the representatives of the people, and the people themselves, finds expression in the diffused rebellion among the youth and the intelligentsia, and in the daily struggle of the persecuted minorities. The armed class struggle is waged outside: by the wretched of the earth who fight the affluent monster.

The critical analysis of this society calls for new categories: moral, political, aesthetic. I shall try to develop them in the course of the discussion. The category of obscenity will serve as an introduction.

This society is obscene in producing and indecently exposing a stifling abundance of wares while depriving its victims abroad of the necessities of life; obscene in stuffing itself and its garbage cans while poisoning and burning the scarce foodstuffs in the fields of its aggression; obscene in the words and smiles of its politicians and entertainers; in its prayers, in its ignorance, and in the wisdom of its kept intellectuals.

Obscenity is a moral concept in the verbal arsenal of the Establishment, which abuses the term by applying it, not to expressions of its own morality but to those of another. Obscene is not the picture of a naked woman who exposes her pubic hair but that of a fully clad general who exposes his medals rewarded in a war of aggression; obscene is not the ritual of the Hippies but the declaration of a high dignitary of the Church that war is necessary for peace. Linguistic therapy—that is, the effort to free words (and thereby concepts) from the all but total distortion of their meanings by the Establishment—demands the transfer of moral standards (and of their validation) from the Establishment to the revolt against it. Similarly, the sociological and political vocabulary must be

From Herbert Marcuse, *An Essay on Liberation* (Boston: Beacon Press, 1969), pp. 7–22.

radically reshaped: it must be stripped of its false neutrality; it must be methodically and provocatively "moralized" in terms of the Refusal. Morality is not necessarily and not primarily ideological. In the face of an amoral society, it becomes a political weapon, an effective force which drives people to burn their draft cards, to ridicule national leaders, to demonstrate in the streets, and to unfold signs saying "Thou shalt not kill," in the nation's churches.

The reaction to obscenity is shame, usually interpreted as the physiological manifestation of the sense of guilt accompanying the transgression of a taboo. The obscene exposures of the affluent society normally provoke neither shame nor a sense of guilt, although this society violates some of the most fundamental moral taboos of civilization. The term obscenity belongs to the sexual sphere; shame and the sense of guilt arise in the Oedipal situation. If in this respect social morality is rooted in sexual morality, then the shamelessness of the affluent society and its effective repression of the sense of guilt would indicate a decline of shame and guilt feeling in the sexual sphere. And indeed, the exposure of the (for all practical purposes) naked body is permitted and even encouraged, and the taboos on pre- and extramarital intercourse are considerably relaxed. Thus we are faced with the contradiction that the liberalization of sexuality provides an instinctual basis for the repressive and aggressive power of the affluent society.

This contradiction can be resolved if we understand that the liberalization of the Establishment's own morality takes place within the framework of effective controls; kept within this framework, the liberalization strengthens the cohesion of the whole. The relaxation of taboos alleviates the sense of guilt and binds (though with considerable ambivalence) the "free" individuals libidinally to the institutionalized fathers. They are powerful but also tolerant fathers, whose management of the nation and its economy delivers and protects the liberties of the citizens. On the other hand, if the violation of taboos transcends the sexual sphere and leads to refusal and rebellion, the sense of guilt is not alleviated and repressed but rather transferred: not we, but the fathers, are guilty; they are not tolerant but false; they want to redeem their own guilt by making us, the sons, guilty; they have created a world of hypocrisy and violence in which we do not wish to live. Instinctual revolt turns into political rebellion, and against this union, the Establishment mobilizes its full force.

This union provokes such a response because it reveals the prospective scope of social change at this stage of development, the extent to which the radical political practice involves a cultural subversion. The refusal with which the opposition confronts the existing society is affirmative in that it envisages a new culture which fulfills the humanistic promises betrayed by the old culture. Political radicalism thus implies moral radicalism: the emergence of a morality which might precondition man for freedom. This radicalism activates the elementary, organic foundation of morality in the human being. Prior to all ethical behavior in accordance with specific social standards, prior to all ideological expression, morality is a "disposition" of the organism, perhaps rooted in the erotic drive to counter aggressiveness, to create and preserve "ever greater unities" of life. We would then have, this side of all "values," an instinctual foundation for solidarity among human beings—a solidarity which has been effectively repressed in line with the requirements of class society but which now appears as a precondition for liberation.

To the degree to which this foundation is itself historical and the malleability of "human nature" reaches into the depth of man's instinctual structure, changes in morality may "sink down" into the "biological"[1] dimension and modify organic behavior. Once a specific morality is firmly established as a norm of social behavior, it is not only introjected —it also operates as a norm of "organic" behavior: the organism receives and reacts to certain stimuli and "ignores" and repels others in accord with the introjected morality, which is thus promoting or impeding the function of the organism as a living cell in the respective society. In this way, a society constantly re-creates, this side of consciousness and ideology, patterns of behavior and aspiration as part of the "nature" of its people, and unless the revolt reaches into this "second" nature, into these ingrown patterns, social changes will remain "incomplete," even self-defeating.

The so-called consumer economy and the politics of corporate capitalism have created a second nature of man which ties him libidinally and aggressively to the commodity form. The need for possessing, consuming, handling, and constantly renewing the gadgets, devices, instruments, engines, offered to and imposed upon the people, for using these wares even at the danger of one's own destruction, has become a "biological" need in the sense just defined. The second nature of man thus militates against any change that would disrupt and perhaps even abolish this dependence of man on a market ever more densely filled with merchandise—abolish his existence as a consumer consuming himself in buying and selling. The needs generated by this system are thus eminently stabilizing, conservative needs: the counterrevolution anchored in the instinctual structure.

1. I use the terms "biological" and "biology" not in the sense of the scientific discipline, but in order to designate the process and the dimension in which inclinations, behavior patterns, and aspirations become vital needs which, if not satisfied, would cause dysfunction of the organism. Conversely, socially induced needs and aspirations may result in a more pleasurable organic behavior. If biological needs are defined as those which must be satisfied and for which no adequate substitute can be provided, certain cultural needs can "sink down" into the biology of man. We could then speak, for example, of the biological need of freedom, or of some aesthetic needs as having taken root in the organic structure of man, in his "nature," or rather "second nature." This usage of the term "biological" does not imply or assume anything as to the way in which needs are physiologically expressed and transmitted.

The market has always been one of exploitation and thereby of domination, insuring the class structure of society. However, the productive process of advanced capitalism has altered the form of domination: the technological veil covers the brute presence and the operation of the class interest in the merchandise. Is it still necessary to state that not technology, not technique, not the machine are the engines of repression, but the presence, in them, of the masters who determine their number, their life span, their power, their place in life, and the need for them? Is it still necessary to repeat that science and technology are the great vehicles of liberation, and that it is only their use and restriction in the repressive society which makes them into vehicles of domination?

Not the automobile is repressive, not the television set is repressive, not the household gadgets are repressive, but the automobile, the television, the gadgets which, produced in accordance with the requirements of profitable exchange, have become part and parcel of the people's own existence, own "actualization." Thus they have to buy part and parcel of their own existence on the market; this existence is the realization of capital. The naked class interest builds the unsafe and obsolescent automobiles, and through them promotes destructive energy; the class interest employs the mass media for the advertising of violence and stupidity, for the creation of captive audiences. In doing so, the masters only obey the demand of the public, of the masses; the famous law of supply and demand establishes the harmony between the rulers and the ruled. This harmony is indeed preestablished to the degree to which the masters have created the public which asks for their wares, and asks for them more insistently if it can release, in and through the wares, its frustration and the aggressiveness resulting from this frustration. Self-determination, the autonomy of the individual, asserts itself in the right to race his automobile, to handle his power tools, to buy a gun, to communicate to mass audiences his opinion, no matter how ignorant, how aggressive, it may be. Organized capitalism has sublimated and turned to socially productive use frustration and primary aggressiveness on an unprecedented scale—unprecedented not in terms of the quantity of violence but rather in terms of its capacity to produce long-range contentment and satisfaction, to reproduce the "voluntary servitude." To be sure, frustration, unhappiness, and sickness remain the basis of this sublimation, but the productivity and the brute power of the system still keep the basis well under control. The achievements justify the system of domination. The established values become the people's own values: adaptation turns into spontaneity, autonomy; and the choice between social necessities appears as freedom. In this sense, the continuing exploitation is not only hidden behind the technological veil, but actually "transfigured." The capitalist production relations are responsible not only for the servitude and toil but also for the greater happiness and fun available to the majority of the population—and they deliver more goods than before.

Neither its vastly increased capacity to produce the commodities of satisfaction nor the peaceful management of class conflicts rendered possible by this capacity cancels the essential features of capitalism, namely, the private appropriation of surplus value (steered but not abolished by government intervention) and its realization in the corporate interest. Capitalism reproduces itself by transforming itself, and this transformation is mainly in the improvement of exploitation. Do exploitation and domination cease to be what they are and what they do to man if they are no longer suffered, if they are "compensated" by previously unknown comforts? Does labor cease to be debilitating if mental energy increasingly replaces physical energy in producing the goods and services which sustain a system that makes hell of large areas of the globe? An affirmative answer would justify any form of oppression which keeps the populace calm and content; while a negative answer would deprive the individual of being the judge of his own happiness.

The notion that happiness is an objective condition which demands more than subjective feelings has been effectively obscured; its validity depends on the real solidarity of the species "man," which a society divided into antagonistic classes and nations cannot achieve. As long as this is the history of mankind, the "state of nature," no matter how refined, prevails: a civilized *bellum omnium contra omnes*,* in which the happiness of the ones must coexist with the suffering of the others. The First International was the last attempt to realize the solidarity of the species by grounding it in that social class in which the subjective and objective interest, the particular and the universal, coincided (the International is the late concretization of the abstract philosophical concept of "man as man," human being, *"Gattungswesen,"* which plays such a decisive role in Marx' and Engels' early writings). Then, the Spanish civil war aroused this solidarity, which is the driving power of liberation, in the unforgettable, hopeless fight of a tiny minority against the combined forces of fascist and liberal capitalism. Here, in the international brigades which, with their poor weapons, withstood overwhelming technical superiority, was the union of young intellectuals and workers—the union which has become the desperate goal of today's radical opposition.

Attainment of this goal is thwarted by the integration of the organized (and not only the organized) laboring class into the system of advanced capitalism. Under its impact, the distinction between the real and the immediate interest of the exploited has collapsed. This distinction, far from being an abstract idea, was guiding the strategy of the Marxist movements; it expressed the necessity transcending the economic struggle of the laboring classes, to extend wage demands and

* The war of all against all.

demands for the improvement of working conditions to the political arena, to drive the class struggle to the point at which the system itself would be at stake, to make foreign as well as domestic policy, the national as well as the class interest, the target of this struggle. The real interest, the attainment of conditions in which man could shape his own life, was that of no longer subordinating his life to the requirements of profitable production, to an apparatus controlled by forces beyond his control. And the attainment of such conditions meant the abolition of capitalism.

It is not simply the higher standard of living, the illusory bridging of the consumer gap between the rulers and the ruled, which has obscured the distinction between the real and the immediate interest of the ruled. Marxian theory soon recognized that impoverishment does not necessarily provide the soil for revolution, that a highly developed consciousness and imagination may generate a vital need for radical change in advanced material conditions. The power of corporate capitalism has stifled the emergence of such a consciousness and imagination; its mass media have adjusted the rational and emotional faculties to its market and its policies and steered them to defense of its dominion. The narrowing of the consumption gap has rendered possible the mental and instinctual coordination of the laboring classes: the majority of organized labor shares the stabilizing, counterrevolutionary needs of the middle classes, as evidenced by their behavior as consumers of the material and cultural merchandise, by their emotional revulsion against the nonconformist intelligentsia. Conversely, where the consumer gap is still wide, where the capitalist culture has not yet reached into every house or hut, the system of stabilizing needs has its limits; the glaring contrast between the privileged class and the exploited leads to a radicalization of the underprivileged. This is the case of the ghetto population and the unemployed in the United States; this is also the case of the laboring classes in the more backward capitalist countries.

By virtue of its basic position in the production process, by virtue of its numerical weight and the weight of exploitation, the working class is still the historical agent of revolution; by virtue of its sharing the stabilizing needs of the system, it has become a conservative, even counterrevolutionary force. Objectively, "in-itself," labor still is the potentially revolutionary class; subjectively, "for-itself," it is not. This theoretical conception has concrete significance in the prevailing situation, in which the working class may help to circumscribe the scope and the targets of political practice.

In the advanced capitalist countries, the radicalization of the working classes is counteracted by a socially engineered arrest of consciousness, and by the development and satisfaction of needs which perpetuate the servitude of the exploited. A vested interest in the existing system is thus fostered in the instinctual structure of the exploited, and the rupture with the continuum of repression—a necessary precondition of liberation—does not occur. It follows that the radical change which is to transform the existing society into a free society must reach into a dimension of the human existence hardly considered in Marxian theory —the "biological" dimension in which the vital, imperative needs and satisfactions of man assert themselves. Inasmuch as these needs and satisfactions reproduce a life in servitude, liberation presupposes changes in this biological dimension, that is to say, different instinctual needs, different reactions of the body as well as the mind.

The qualitative difference between the existing societies and a free society affects all needs and satisfactions beyond the animal level, that is to say, all those which are essential to the *human* species, man as rational animal. All these needs and satisfactions are permeated with the exigencies of profit and exploitation. The entire realm of competitive performances and standardized fun, all the symbols of status, prestige, power, of advertised virility and charm, of commercialized beauty— this entire realm kills in its citizens the very disposition, the organs, for the alternative: freedom without exploitation.

Triumph and end of introjection: the stage where the people cannot reject the system of domination without rejecting themselves, their own repressive instinctual needs and values. We would have to conclude that liberation would mean subversion against the will and against the prevailing interests of the great majority of the people. In this false identification of social and individual needs, in this deep-rooted, "organic" adaptation of the people to a terrible but profitably functioning society, lie the limits of democratic persuasion and evolution. On the overcoming of these limits depends the establishment of democracy.

It is precisely this excessive adaptability of the human organism which propels the perpetuation and extension of the commodity form and, with it, the perpetuation and extension of the social controls over behavior and satisfaction.

> The ever-increasing complexity of the social structure will make some form of regimentation unavoidable, freedom and privacy may come to constitute antisocial luxuries and their attainment to involve real hardships. In consequence, there may emerge by selection a stock of human beings suited genetically to accept as a matter of course a regimented and sheltered way of life in a teeming and polluted world, from which all wilderness and fantasy of nature will have disappeared. The domesticated farm animal and the laboratory rodent on a controlled regimen in a controlled environment will then become true models for the study of man.
> Thus, it is apparent that food, natural resources, supplies of power, and other elements involved in the operation of the body machine and of the individual establishment are not the only factors to be considered

in determining the optimum number of people that can live on earth. Just as important for maintaining the *human qualities* of life is an environment in which it is possible to satisfy the longing for quiet, privacy, independence, initiative, and some open space. . . ."[2]

Capitalist progress thus not only reduces the environment of freedom, the "open space" of the human existence, but also the "longing," the need for such an environment. And in doing so, quantitative progress militates against qualitative change even if the institutional barriers against radical education and action are surmounted. This is the vicious circle: the rupture with the self-propelling conservative continuum of needs must *precede* the revolution which is to usher in a free society, but such rupture itself can be envisaged only in a revolution—a revolution which would be driven by the vital need to be freed from the administered comforts and the destructive productivity of the exploitative society, freed from smooth heteronomy, a revolution which, by virtue of this "biological" foundation, would have the chance of turning quantitative technical progress into qualitatively different ways of life—precisely because it would be a revolution occurring at a high level of material and intellectual development, one which would enable man to conquer scarcity and poverty. If this idea of a radical transformation is to be more than idle speculation, it must have an objective foundation in the production process of advanced industrial society, in its technical capabilities and their use.

For freedom indeed depends largely on technical progress, on the advancement of science. But this fact easily obscures the essential precondition: in order to become vehicles of freedom, science and technology would have to change their present direction and goals; they would have to be reconstructed in accord with a new sensibility—the demands of the life instincts. Then one could speak of a technology of liberation, product of a scientific imagination free to protect and design the forms of a human universe without exploitation and toil. But this *gaya scienza* is conceivable only after the historical break in the continuum of domination—as expressive of the needs of a new type of man.[3]

2. René Dubos, *Man Adapting* (New Haven and London: Yale University Press, 1965), pp. 313–14.
3. The critique of the prevailing scientific establishment as ideological, and the idea of a science which has really come into its own, was expressed in a manifesto issued by the militant students of Paris in May 1968 as follows:
  "Refusons aussi la division de la *science* et de *l'idéologie,* la plus pernicieuse de toutes puisqu'elle est sécrétée par nous-mêmes. Nous ne voulons pas plus être gouvernés passivement par les lois de la *science* que par celle de l'économie ou les *impératifs* de la technique. La science est un art dont l'originalité est d'avoir des applications possibles hors d'elle-même.
  "Elle ne peut cependant être normative que pour elle-même. Refusons son impérialisme mystifiant, caution de tous les abus et reculs, y compris en son sein, et remplaçons-le par un choix réel parmi les possibles qu'elle nous offre" (*Quelle Uni-*

The idea of a new type of man as the member (though not as the builder) of a socialist society appears in Marx and Engels in the concept of the "all-round individual," free to engage in the most varying activities. In the socialist society corresponding to this idea, the free development of individual faculties would replace the subjection of the individual to the division of labor. But no matter what activities the all-round individual would choose, they would be activities which are bound to lose the quality of freedom if exercised "en masse"—and they would be "en masse," for even the most authentic socialist society would inherit the population growth and the mass basis of advanced capitalism. The early Marxian example of the free individuals alternating between hunting, fishing, criticizing, and so on, had a joking-ironical sound from the beginning, indicative of the impossibility anticipating the ways in which liberated human beings would use their freedom. However, the embarrassingly ridiculous sound may also indicate the degree to which this vision has become obsolete and pertains to a stage of the development of the productive forces which has been surpassed. The later Marxian concept implies the continued separation between the realm of necessity and the realm of freedom, between labor and leisure —not only in time, but also in such a manner that the same subject lives a different life in the two realms. According to this Marxian conception, the realm of necessity would continue under socialism to such an extent that real human freedom would prevail only outside the entire sphere of socially necessary labor. Marx rejects the idea that work can ever become play.[4] Alienation would be reduced with the progressive reduction of the working day, but the latter would remain a day of unfreedom, rational but not free. However, the development of the productive forces beyond their capitalist organization suggests the possibility of freedom *within* the realm of necessity. The quantitative reduction of necessary labor could turn into quality (freedom), not in proportion to the reduction but rather to the transformation of the working day, a transformation in which the stupefying, enervating, pseudo-automatic jobs of capitalist progress would be abolished. But the construction of such a society presupposes a type of man with a different sensitivity as

---

versité? Quelle Société? Textes réunis par le centre de regroupement des informations universitaires. Paris: Editions du Seuil, 1968, p. 148).

["Let us also reject the division between *science* and *ideology*, the most pernicious of all, since it is secretly perpetrated by ourselves. We wish no more to be governed passively by the laws of science than by those of economics or by the *imperatives* of technology. Science is an art whose originality lies in the fact that it has possible applications outside itself.

"It cannot, however, be normative except for itself. Let us reject the mystifying imperialism, guarantee of all abuse and reaction, inherent in it, and replace it with an actual choice from among the possibilities it offers."—VC]

4. For a far more "utopian" conception see the by now familiar passage in the *Grundrisse der Kritik der Politischen Ockonomie* (Berlin: Dietz, 1953), pp. 596 ff., and p. 49 below.

well as consciousness: men who would speak a different language, have different gestures, follow different impulses; men who have developed an instinctual barrier against cruelty, brutality, ugliness. Such an instinctual transformation is conceivable as a factor of social change only if it enters the social division of labor, the production relations themselves. They would be shaped by men and women who have the good conscience of being human, tender, sensuous, who are no longer ashamed of themselves—for "the token of freedom attained, that is, no longer being ashamed of ourselves" (Nietzsche, *Die Fröhliche Wissenschaft,** Book III, 275). The imagination of such men and women would fashion their reason and tend to make the process of production a process of creation. This is the utopian concept of socialism which envisages the ingression of freedom into the realm of necessity, and the union between causality by necessity and causality by freedom. The first would mean passing from Marx to Fourier; the second from realism to surrealism.

A utopian conception? It has been the great, real, transcending force, the *"idèe neuve,"* in the first powerful rebellion against the whole of the existing society, the rebellion for the total transvaluation of values, for qualitatively different ways of life: the May rebellion in France. The graffiti of the *"jeunesse en colère"* joined Karl Marx and André Breton; the slogan *"l'imagination au pouvoir"* went well with *"les comités (soviets) partout";* the piano with the jazz player stood well between the barricades; the red flag well fitted the statue of the author of *Les Misérables;* and striking students in Toulouse demanded the revival of the language of the Troubadours, the Albigensians. The new sensibility has become a political force. It crosses the frontier between the capitalist and the communist orbit; it is contagious because the atmosphere, the climate of the established societies, carries the virus.

* *The Gay Science;* see the Nietzsche selection.

40 WILHELM REICH
Truth versus Modju

The pestilent character is usually a very active, mobile emotional structure; his mobility, however, is *short-circuited,* as it were, in such a manner that all splendid ideas and good intentions somehow evaporate before they can concentrate enough to produce lasting results. This is a serious work disturbance which gains importance through the fact that the pestilent character most likely will turn out to be an *"abortive genius."* The short-circuit in performance renders the great abilities abortive and frustrates the individual who suffers from this inhibited ability. Thus, he suffers from chronic frustration which, like all biopathies, is based on a deep disturbance of the function of full genital gratification (*"orgastic impotence"*). Since every truth will increase the frustration within the structure, the pestilent character must hate truth. Since he could basically, but cannot factually live truth, he develops great ability in using the lie; not necessarily always the full, brutal lie, but most likely he will become a master in obtaining his goals by means other than open and frank procedure. Naturally, one will find all shades of lying, from the little innocent cheating in small matters to the BIG LIE of Hitlerian scope.

As a sexual cripple, the pestilent character who is endowed with more than average bio-energetic agility must develop channels to somehow live out his surplus energy. He will be a master in cunning, slyness, "know-how" in getting along with people *smoothly*. He will stand out little from the crowd. He will be a "good fellow," people will like him, he will appear honest and straight, and he will really mean what he says subjectively. But he will never quite overcome the feeling of being an abortive genius, gifted and crippled at the same time. This is strongly developed in him, and he has this trait in common with most average people. The people in general, however, have far less strained ambitions and are not as strong bio-energetically.

If, now, such a character joins a peaceful, hard-working group of people, he will smoothly fit in on the surface, but his inner frustration will sooner or later drive him to do underhanded mischief. Most spies

From Wilhelm Reich, *Reich Speaks of Freud,* edited by Mary Higgins and Chester M. Raphael, M.D. (New York: Farrar, Straus and Giroux, 1967), pp. 276–83.

who do not serve rational purposes probably are structured that way. To be hidden and to remain undetected has initially nothing whatsoever to do with the political or other kind of mischief. *The underhandedness is there earlier than the mischief.* It is the abortive genius, unable to accomplish lasting results, that drives the pestilent character to his underhanded actions on the public scene.

The pestilent character is basically a coward and he has much to hide, especially sexually. The hiddenness is essential to his social and emotional existence. It is safe to assume that such spies as Fuchs and others became fascist spies for dictators because fascism offers particular opportunities to integrate one's hidden character structure. It is clear that such pathological social phenomena as political movements which use and thrive on underhandedness are built on the foundations of such characters. It is clear from the history of the Russian Revolution why it was that a sly Djugashvili came to such power, riding high on the waves of the emotional plague. He shows all the character traits which characterize the pestilent character. But the riding to power and its misuse are not his fault or accomplishment. They are truly the result of the average character structure of multitudes of similar structures who feel incapable of the slowly grinding effort of lasting accomplishment, and, therefore, prefer the easy way of the politician who is obliged by nothing to prove his promises and contentions.

Djugashvili rides to power over millions, carried along by the very people whom he is going to suppress, supported and protected by what they have in common with him, be it ever so minute and little.

Let us briefly survey what public, pioneer, and administrator have in common with the pestilent character. Unless we find this common quality, we shall be unable to understand the great success of the emotional plague on the social scene; of the prevalence of the lie over the truth. No "congressional crime investigations" will ever change much on the social scene unless this point is brought to the fore and is understood. Otherwise, the actions of justice will only again hit the innocent, and lead to confusion and public panic. It is clear that the educator and physician instead of the politician and policeman should be in charge of these affairs of social pathology.

Every living human being has something to hide—the pioneer, every soul that constitutes "the public," and every single public administrator. They have no big crimes to hide; these are little personal affairs which must be kept off the public scene, which is governed to such a large extent by gossip and character defamation. The core of this social anxiety always has been and will be for a long while the so-called "private life," or, put bluntly, the *love of life* of the individual. Here an administrator has embraced a girl he knew in decency and honesty, but slightly out of range of what is considered "moral" by "the public."

Many knew it, of course, but since everyone has such little and perfectly decent secrets, there is a common bond, so to speak, among the people who constitute what is called the public. Everybody has a more or less pressing bad conscience, well hidden under a mask of righteousness. Fear of getting into trouble with the law is quite general. Conformism stems from this fear and from these little secrets. And there is nothing whatsoever in the social set-up to understand, handle, or protect such innocent little secrets against invasion by dirty minds.

Sexual guilt feelings are quite general. Who has never touched his genital, or has never played around with a member of the opposite sex, or has not strayed off the path of marriage, and who has never committed a little crime here or there? Everybody has, of course, and we should feel very humanly about it, since one of the first things we do in fighting the plague is alleviate the severe pressure which is exerted upon the people by the false righteousness of politically ambitious district attorneys or senators, looking for "a case" or to further a career, or of policemen or politicans who find a ladder to peaks of power by way of nuisance investigations.

It is all right to stop rampant cheating in the realm of public lotteries, but one can see no harm in a little gambling or a little fun at pinball machines. It is the pestilent character again who here, too, spoils the fun for the people by misusing and abusing freedom of action.

Thus, everybody has something to hide. And it is this weak spot in everybody where our pestilent character sets in with his misdeeds. One can easily observe that the innocent public school teacher or social worker or mental-hygiene administrator will cringe before a letter written by a "tax-paying housewife" who protests against this or that. Only very few have the courage and the directness to step up and tell the public crank off.

The emotional plague has in a masterly fashion found a way of building its protective devices. Not only does it cunningly hook up with everyone's guilty conscience; it has put into circulation high-sounding ethical rules, which are perfect in themselves, such as: "One does not pay attention to such things as slander," or "It always has been that way and always will be," or "Every pioneer had to suffer." That something evil that "always has been" also has to be, is just as much empty talk as that of the "naturally suffering pioneer." The "liberal mind" has gone off the beam in a very bad way as far as such tolerance is concerned. It will soon become quite clear that under the cover of this protection enjoyed by the plague, innumerable murders have been committed, multitudes of decent adolescents have been delivered to penitentiaries or lunatic asylums, millions of innocent babies and children have suffered agonies and have been crippled for life, and, if we ultimately include the wars of humanity among the misdeeds of the well-hidden emotional plague, millions have died on the battle fields in vain, for MODJU only.*

Thus, such slogans are more than empty. They are *murderous* talk, though innocently brought forth. However, this "innocence" itself will require clarification.

Those who talk that way mean it well. They are convinced of the ultimately decent nature of man. But, at the same time, they talk that way out of weakness and fear of the plague. They are factually hypnotized into immobility by the plague like a hen by the snake. Also, they certainly admire—at least some do—the apparent toughness of the pestilent character, his suavity, his cunning, and his "know-how."

All this protects underhanded, manifold murder.

The mass of people are held down by fear of speaking up, by actual immobility of the emotional organism, by fear of trouble, by other serious worries, and by latent sexual guilt feelings. This renders them easy prey for the pestilent character.

They fall prey in spite of knowing the truth, of understanding the importance of bodily love, in spite of a sense of decency deeply ingrained but rendered helpless by so much cunning and conniving.

And the pioneering men or women often fall prey to the mischief because they are too busy, too honest, because they do not wish to soil their hands with the evil stuff.

And the administrator is dependent on public acclaim just as he is bound down as a human being by his own little secrets.

* Reich's early theories stressed the importance of the "character structure" of the individual, and of discerning and pointing out to the individual the nature of his particular "character armor"—those resistances, and recurrent defenses used by each individual to ward off danger whether from their superego or their id. In his later years Reich developed an elaborate biophysical *orgone* theory of energy, a theory that evolved out of Freud's implicit "sex-economy" theories. Reich maintained that social problems emanated from psychosexual repression and inhibition of orgasm (the basic unit of energy); as a result, this energy had become perverted and aggressive. His interest in this area led him to formulate a theory of "Emotional Plague" or "Modju." In an interview in which he discusses how Freud changed from "a very alive strong-willed person" into a despairing one, he explains his theory of "Modju" and he explains how he coined the term: ". . . when he [Freud] discovered infantile sexuality, he was furiously attacked, in a horrible way, by Modju. . . . "Modju" is a synonym for the emotional plague or pestilent character who uses underhand slander and defamation in his fight against life and truth. That name "Modju" will stick to him for the rest of this century and far beyond. . . . It [the name] was derived from Mocenigo, a nincompoop, a nobody, who delivered a very great scientist, in the sixteenth century, to the Inquisition. That scientist was Giordano Bruno. He was imprisoned for eight years and then burned at the stake. This Mocenigo was a nobody who knew nothing, learned nothing, couldn't learn anything. He wanted to get a good memory function from Bruno, who had a marvelous memory. But he couldn't do it. Bruno couldn't give it to him. So what did he do? He went out and killed Bruno. You see? That's MO-cenigo. And DJU is Djugashvili. That's Stalin. [Stalin's real name was Josef Vissarionovich Djugashvilli, or Dzhugashvili.] So I put it together to make 'Modju.' And that is going to stick. They will never get rid of it. Never!"

Now the pestilent character has easy going. He is protected on all sides and can proceed safely, without any danger of being detected, put into the bright sunlight, or challenged in any other way. If he adds political power machinery to his already rather well-set position he can conquer whole continents.

A little slander, well placed, excellently formulated, will, without great effort, kill many an important truth right away in its infancy or it will deprive it of social effectiveness if it had the strength to mature under such social pathology. The public will not act or render any help to the truth. It will remain *"sitting"* silently and watch helplessly or even gloatingly any crucifixion of innocent souls. The public administrator will be frightened to bits and try to maintain public morals and order. The pioneer will be silenced or he may go psychotic or fall into deep depression. Nobody is served except the pathological emotion of a nuisance biopath, MODJU again.

It is truly as ridiculous as that. However, behind this ridiculousness there waits for us a terrific problem of human existence:

> *How could such ridiculous nuisance get into this world in the first place, and how could it, undisturbed, devastate human organizations of work and peace for ages?*

However tough such problems may be to solve, we cannot ever expect to even start solving them unless we *free ourselves from the nuisance interference with serious human work exerted by the pestilent character.* It is necessary first to achieve a certain amount of safety in doing the job of finding answers to questions of living life.

A few successful procedures in stopping such interferences in the bud are the following:

(1) Rely on the distinction between an honest and twisted facial expression.

(2) Insist on everything being above board.

(3) Use the weapon of truth wisely but determinedly. The pestilent character is usually a coward and has nothing constructive to offer.

(4) Meet the plague head on. Do not yield or appease. Master your guilt feelings and know your weak spots.

(5) If necessary, reveal frankly your weak points, even your secrets. People will understand.

(6) Help alleviate the pressure of human guilt feelings wherever you can, especially in sexual matters, the main domain of abuse by the emotional plague.

(7) *Have your own motives, goals, methods always fully in the open, widely visible to everyone.*

(8) Learn continuously how to meet the underhanded lie.

(9) Channel all human interest toward important problems of life, especially the upbringing of infants.

There can be little doubt that the ravaging plague CAN be mastered, even easily, if the force of truth is used fully and without restraint. Truth is our potential ally even *within* the pestilent character. He, too, is somewhere decent deep down, though he may not know it.

Basic Tenets on Red Fascism

(1) Communism in its present form as *Red Fascism* is not a political party like other political parties. It is politically and militarily armed *organized emotional plague.*

(2) This organized political and armed emotional plague *uses* conspiracy and spying in all forms, in order to destroy human happiness. It is not, as is usually assumed, a political conspiracy to achieve certain rational social ends, as in 1918.

(3) If you ask a liberal or a socialist or a Republican what he believes in socially, he will tell you frankly. The Red Fascist will not tell you what he is, who he is, what he wants. This proves that *hiding* is his basic characteristic. And only people who are hiding by way of their character constitution will operate in and for the Communist Party. It is *conspiracy and hiding for its own sake,* and not to use as a tool to achieve rational ends. To believe otherwise will only lead to disaster.

(4) Red Fascism as a special form of the emotional plague, uses its basic characterological tool, hiding (*"conspiracy"*), *"iron curtain,"* to exploit the identical emotionally sick attitudes in ordinary people. Thus the politically *organized emotional plague* uses the *unorganized emotional plague* to gratify its morbid needs. The political aims are secondary to this, and mostly subterfuges for emotionally biopathic activities. Proof: The political ends are shifted according to the "political," i.e., the emotional plague needs of hiding and causing trouble from ambush.

(5) The hiding, conspiring, conniving are there *before* any political goals are conceived, as draperies for the activities.

(6) The sole objective of the conspiring is *power* with no special social ends. The subjugation of people's lives is not intended, but is a necessary and an automatic result of the lack of rationality in the organization and existence of the emotional plague.

From Wilhelm Reich, *Reich Speaks of Freud,* edited by Mary Higgins and Chester M. Raphael, M.D. (New York: Farrar, Straus and Giroux, 1967), pp. 274–76.

(7) The organized emotional plague relies upon and uses consistently what is worst and lowest in human nature, while it slanders, destroys, and tries to put out of function all that threatens its existence, good or bad. A fact to the emotional plague is a fact only if it can be used to certain ends. It does not count on its own behalf, and there is, accordingly, no respect for facts. Truth is used only if it serves a special line of procedure or the general existence of the emotional dirtiness. It will be discarded as soon as it threatens or even contradicts such ends. Such an attitude toward fact and truth, history and human welfare is not specifically a characteristic of Red Fascism. It is typical of all politics. Red Fascism differs from other political disrespect for fact and truth in that it eliminates all checks and controls of the abuse of power and drives the nuisance politician to his utmost power. To believe that "peace negotiations" are meant as such is disastrous. They may and they may not be meant, according to the momentary expediency. Red Fascism is a power machine using the principle of lie or truth, fact or distortion of fact, honesty or dishonesty, always to the end of conspiracy and abuse by human malignancy.

(8) No one can ever hope to excel the pestilent character in lying and underhanded spying. Espionage and counter-espionage may belong as part of present-day social administration: It will never *solve* the problem of *social pathology*. *Using truth* in human affairs will burst open the trap and the unsolvable entanglement of spying and counter-spying. In addition, it will be constructive in establishing the foundation for life-positive human actions.

41 VIKTOR E. FRANKL
Basic Concepts of Logotherapy

THE WILL TO MEANING

Logos is a Greek word which means "meaning." Logotherapy or, as it has been called by some authors, the third Viennese school of psychotherapy, focuses on the meaning of human existence as well as on man's search for such a meaning. This striving to find a meaning in one's life is, according to logotherapy, regarded as the primary motivational force in man. That is why I speak of a *will to meaning* as over against the pleasure principle (or as we could also term it the *will to pleasure*) on which Freudian psychoanalysis is centered, as well as over against the *will to power* which is stressed by Adlerian psychology.

The will to meaning is fact, not faith. And if there were still need to give evidence for my assertion, such proof would be offered by a public opinion poll which was conducted a few years ago in France. The result of this statistical survey was that 89% of the people polled thereby admitted that man needs something for the sake of which to live; and 61% conceded that there was something in their own lives, or someone, for whose sake they were even ready to die. I repeated this poll at my clinic in Vienna both among the patients as well as the personnel, and the outcome was practically the same as among the thousands of people screened in France; the difference was only 2%.

EXISTENTIAL FRUSTRATION

Man's will to meaning can also be frustrated, in which case logotherapy speaks of "existential frustration." The term "existential" may be used in three ways: to refer to (1) *existence* itself, i.e., the specifically human model of being; (2) the *meaning* of existence; and (3) the striving to find a concrete meaning in personal existence, that is to say, the *will* to meaning.

Existential frustration can also result in neuroses. For this type of neuroses, logotherapy has coined the term "noogenic neuroses" in contrast to neuroses in the usual sense of the word, i.e., psychogenic neu-

From Viktor E. Frankl, "Basic Concepts of Logotherapy," *Journal of Existential Psychiatry*, III (1962), 111–18.

roses. Noogenic neuroses have their origin not in the psychological but rather in the "noological" dimension of human existence. This is another logotherapeutic term which denotes anything pertaining to the spiritual core of man's personality. It must be kept in mind, however, that within the frame of reference of logotherapeutic terminology "spiritual" does not have a primarily religious connotation but refers to the specifically human dimension.

NOOGENIC NEUROSES

Noogenic neuroses do not emerge from conflicts between drives and instincts but rather from conflicts between various values; in other words, from moral conflicts, or, to speak in a more general way, from spiritual problems. Among such problems existential frustration often plays a great role.

I am very indebted to *The Bradley Center* whose research team is just now working on a program in order to develop tests which should enable a doctor to differentiate between noogenic neuroses and psychogenic ones.

It is obvious that in noogenic cases the appropriate and adequate therapy is not psychotherapy in general but rather logotherapy; a therapy, that is, which dares to enter the spiritual dimension of human existence. In fact, *logos* means not only "meaning" but also "spirit." Spiritual issues such as man's aspiration for a meaningful existence as well as the frustration of this aspiration, are both dealt with by logotherapy in *spiritual* terms. They are taken sincerely and earnestly instead of being traced back to unconscious roots and sources, thus being dealt with in *instinctual* terms.

Logotherapy regards its assignment as that of assisting the patient to find the meaning of his life. Inasmuch as logotherapy makes him aware of the hidden *logos* of his existence, it is an analytical procedure and process. To this extent, logotherapy resembles psychoanalysis; however, in its attempt to make something conscious again it does not restrict its activity to *instinctual* facts with the individual's unconscious but also cares for *spiritual* realities such as the potential meaning of his existence to be fulfilled, as well as his *will* to meaning. Any analysis, however, even when it refrains from including the noological dimension in its therapeutic endeavours, tries to make the patient aware of what he is longing for in the depth of his self. Logotherapy deviates from psychoanalysis inasmuch as it considers man as a being whose main concern consists in fulfilling a meaning and in actualizing values rather than in the gratification and satisfaction of drives and instincts, in compromising the conflicting claims of id, ego and superego, or in the adaptation and adjustment to society and environment.

NOO-DYNAMICS

To be sure, man's search for meaning and values may arouse inner tension rather than inner equilibrium. However, this is precisely that which is an indispensable prerequisite of mental health. There is nothing in the world, I venture to say, that would so effectively help one to survive even the worst conditions, as the knowledge that there is a meaning in his life. There is much wisdom in the words of Nietzsche: "He who has a *why* to live for can bear almost any *how*." I see in these words a motto which holds true for any psychotherapy. In the concentration camps one could witness what was later confirmed by American psychiatrists both in Japan and Korea, that those who knew that there was a task waiting for them to fulfill were most apt to survive.

Thus, it can be seen that mental health is based on a certain degree of tension, the tension between what one has already achieved and what he still ought to accomplish, or the gap between what he is and what he should become. Such a tension is inherent in the human being and therefore is indispensable to mental well being. We should not, then, be hesitant about challenging man with meaning potentialities for him to actualize, thus evoking his will to meaning out of its latency. I consider it a dangerous misconception of mental hygiene to assume that what man needs in the first place, is equilibrium or, as it is called in biology, "homeostasis," i.e., a tension-less state. What man actually needs is not a tension-less state but rather the striving and struggling for some goal worthy of him. What he needs is not the discharge of tension at any cost, but the call of a potential meaning waiting to be fulfilled by him. *What man needs is not homeostasis but what I call "noo-dynamics,"* i.e., the spiritual dynamics in a polar field of tension where the one pole is represented by a meaning to be fulfilled and the other pole by the man who *has* to fulfill it. And one should not think that this holds only for normal conditions; in neurotic individuals, it is even more valid. If architects want to strengthen a decrepit arch they *increase* the load which is laid upon it, for thereby the parts are joined more firmly together. So if therapists wish to foster their patients' mental health they, too, should not be afraid to increase that load which is brought about by a reorientation toward the meaning of one's life.

After having shown the beneficial impact of meaning orientation I turn to the detrimental influence of that feeling of which so many patients are complaining today, namely, the feeling of the total and ultimate meaninglessness of their lives. They are lacking the awareness of a meaning worth living for. They are haunted by the experience of their inner emptiness, a void within themselves; they are caught in that situation which I have called "existential vacuum."

THE EXISTENTIAL VACUUM

The existential vacuum is a wide-spread phenomenon of the present time. This is understandable; it may be due to a two-fold loss which man had to undergo since he became a truly human being. At the beginning of human history, man was deprived of the basic animal instincts in which an animal's behavior is embedded and by which it is secured. Such security, like Paradise, is closed to man forever; man has to make his choices. In addition to this, however, man has suffered another loss in his more recent development inasmuch as the traditions which undergirded his behavior, are now rapidly diminishing. No instinct tells him what he has to do, and no tradition tells him what he ought to do; soon he will not know what he wants to do. All the more he will care for what others want him to do, thus falling prey more and more to conformism.

A cross-sectional statistical survey conducted by my staff in the Vienna Polyclinic of the patients and the nursing personnel in the neurological department revealed that 55% of the persons questioned showed a more or less marked degree of existential vacuum. In other words, more than half of them had experienced a loss of the feeling that life is meaningful.

Recently, I repeated the same investigation among the students attending my lectures on logotherapy both in English and German, namely, for Americans as well as Europeans. It turned out that 40% of the European students had at least occasionally experienced a complete lack of life's worthwhileness. The percentage of the occasional occurrence of existential frustration in American students was 81, i.e., twice as much.

One can observe again and again that certain types of feed-back mechanisms and vicious circle formations have invaded an existential vacuum wherein they then continue to flourish. In such patients, what we have to deal with is not a noogenic neurosis. However, we will never succeed in having the patient overcome his condition, if we have not supplemented the psychotherapeutic treatment with logotherapy. For by filling the existential vacuum, the patient will be prevented from further relapses. Therefore, logotherapy is indicated not only in noogenic cases, as pointed out above, but also in psychogenic cases, and in particular the somatogenic (pseudo-) neuroses.

Viewed in this light, a statement once made by Magda B. Arnold is justified: "Every therapy must in some way, no matter how restricted, also be logotherapy." And in a paper presented to The Royal Medico-Psychological Association, E. K. Ledermann declares that at least "existential psychotherapy" which "should enable the patient to achieve a meaningful life . . . for this purpose . . . must be spiritually-rooted logotherapy."

THE COLLECTIVE NEUROSIS

Every age has its own collective neurosis, and every age needs its own psychotherapy to cope with it. The existential vacuum which is the mass neurosis of the present time, can be described as a private and personal form of nihilism; for nihilism can be defined as the contention that being has no meaning. As for psychotherapy, however, it will never be able to cope with this state of affairs on a mass scale if it does not keep itself free from the impact and influence of the contemporary trends of a nihilistic philosophy; otherwise it represents a symptom of the mass neurosis rather than its possible cure. Then, however, psychotherapy would not only reflect a nihilistic philosophy but also, even though unwillingly and unwittingly, transmit to the patient what actually is a caricature rather than a true picture of man.

First of all, there is a danger inherent in the teaching of man's "nothingbutness," the theory that man is nothing but the result of biological, psychological and sociological conditions, or the product of heredity and environment. That which is a product, however, is a robot, not a human being. This neurotic fatalism, however, is fostered and strengthened by that psychotherapy which denies that man is free.

CRITIQUE OF PAN-DETERMINISM

Psychoanalysis has often been blamed for its so-called pan-sexualism. I for one doubt whether this reproach has ever been legitimate. However, there is something which seems to me to be an even more erroneous and dangerous assumption, namely, that which I call "pan-determinism." Thereby I mean that view of man which disregards man's capacity to take a stand toward any conditions whatsoever. However, man is not fully conditioned and determined but rather determines himself whether he succumbs to conditions or defies them. In other words, man is ultimately *self-determining*. Man does not simply exist but always decides what his existence will be, what he will become in the next moment.

By the same token, every human being has the freedom to change at any instant. Therefore, we can only predict his future within the large frame of a statistical survey referring to a whole group; the individual personality, however, remains essentially unpredictable. The basis for any predictions would be represented by biological, psychological or sociological conditions. However, one of the main features of human existence is the capacity to rise above such conditions and transcend them. By the same token, man is ultimately transcending himself; a human being is a *self-transcending* being.

Apparently pan-determinism is an infectious disease which has been inoculated also in educators and even adherents of religion who are seemingly not aware that thereby, they are undermining the very basis of their own convictions. For either man's freedom of decision for or against God, as well as for or against man, is recognized, or religion is a delusion, and education an illusion. Freedom is presupposed by both, otherwise they are misconceived.

A pan-deterministic evaluation of religion, however, contends that one's religious life is conditioned inasmuch as it depends on his early childhood experiences, and that his God concept depends on his father image. In contrast to this view, it is well known that the son of a drunkard need not become a drunkard himself; and in the same manner, a man may resist the detrimental influence of a dreadful father image and establish a sound relationship with God. Even the worst father image need not prevent one from establishing a good relationship with God; rather a deep religious life provides him with the resources needed to overcome the hatred of his father. Conversely, a poor religious life need not in each case be due to developmental factors.

A cross-sectional statistical survey conducted by my staff at the Vienna Polyclinic, revealed that about one third of those patients who had experienced a positive father image, turned away from religion in their later life; whereas most of those people screened who had a negative father image, in spite of this, succeeded in building up a positive attitude toward religious issues.

As soon as we have interpreted religion merely in terms of a resultant of psychodynamics in the sense of unconscious motivating forces, we have missed the point and lost sight of the authentic phenomenon. Then psychology of religion has become psychology as religion, inasmuch as psychology is then worshipped, is made an explanation for everything.

THE PSYCHIATRIC CREDO

There is nothing conceivable which would so condition a man as to leave him without the slightest freedom. Therefore, a residue of freedom, however limited it might be, is left to man in neurotic and even psychotic cases. Indeed, the innermost core of the patient's personality is not even touched by a psychosis.

I am reminded of a man of about 60 years of age who was brought to me because of his acoustic hallucinations of many decades. I was facing the ruin of a personality. As it turned out, everyone in his environment regarded him as an idiot. Yet what a strange charm radiated from this man! As a child he had wanted to become a priest. However, he had to be content with the only joy he could experience, and that was singing in the church choir on Sunday mornings. Now, his sister who accompanied him, reported that sometimes he grew very excited; yet in the last moment he was always able to regain his self-control. I became interested in the psychodynamics underlying the case, for I thought there was a strong fixation of the patient to his sister; so I asked how he managed to regain his self-control, "For whose sake do you do so?" Thereupon, there was a pause of some seconds, and then the patient answered: "For God's sake." At this moment, the depth of his personality revealed itself, and at the bottom of this depth, irrespective of the poverty of his intellectual endowment, an authentic religious life was disclosed.

An incurably psychotic individual may lose his usefulness but yet retain the dignity of a human being. This is my psychiatric *credo*. Without it I should not think it worthwhile to be a psychiatrist. For whose sake? Just for the sake of a damaged brain machine which cannot be repaired? If the patient were not definitely more, euthanasia would be justified.

PSYCHIATRY RE-HUMANIZED

For too long a time, for half a century, psychiatry tried to interpret the human mind merely in terms of mechanisms, and consequently, the therapy of mental disease merely in terms of a technique. I believe this dream has been dreamt out. What now begins to appear in the dawn, are not the sketches of a psychologized medicine but rather those of a humanized psychiatry.

A doctor, however, who would still interpret his own role mainly as that of a technician, would betray that he sees in his patient nothing more than a machine; instead of seeing behind the disease the human being!

A human being is not one thing among others; things are determining each other, but man is ultimately self-determining. What he becomes, he has made out of himself. In the concentration camps, e.g., in this living laboratory and on this testing ground we were watching and witnessing one part of our comrades behaving like swine while others were behaving like saints. Man has both potentialities within himself; which one is actualized, depends on decisions but not on conditions.

Our generation is realistic for we have come to know man as he really is. After all, man is that being who has invented the gas chambers of Auschwitz; however, he is also that being who has entered those gas chambers upright, with the Lord's prayer or the *Shema Yisrael* on his lips.

42 HELEN MERRELL LYND
from On Shame and the Search for Identity

Special importance and difficulties of psychoanalysis

Psychoanalytic theory and psychoanalytic therapy stand in a special relation to the search for identity.[1] Psychoanalysis is of all professions the one most avowedly and directly concerned with the discovery of identity. It would be impossible to explore the meaning of shame and of identity without special reference to psychoanalysis. My special indebtedness to Erikson, Schachtel, Schilder, Sullivan, and other psychoanalysts has appeared throughout this discussion. I shall speak in more detail below of Erikson's study of identity.

Just because of the strategic position of psychoanalysis in relation to identity, however, and because of the position of psychoanalysis in contemporary American thought, it is necessary to speak of the particular anomalies and hazards of the profession. This is a difficult subject to discuss, in part because judgment about it tends to be submerged under the vehemence and in-group thinking of its supporters (and even of supporters of particular schools) and the equal vehemence of its critics, and also because one's own emotional involvements, though they enter into any appraisal, are particularly concerned in the appraisal of psychoanalysis. But psychoanalysis is a phenomenon of the contemporary world, and we must try to appraise it. Five hundred years from now it may be appraised very differently, but we must do what we can with the knowledge we have.

No profession has ever occupied a position or assumed a responsibility entirely comparable to that of psychoanalysis. The psychoanalyst has been compared to a surgeon. But because of the kind of intimate relation he has and encourages with his patient, his own character and

From Helen Merrell Lynd, *On Shame and the Search for Identity* (New York: Harcourt, Brace & Co., 1958), pp. 195-210.
1. Psychoanalytic theory and therapy cannot, I think, validly be separated as much as is sometimes done. Freud's theory grew directly from his observations in therapy and was continually modified by further observations. The way therapy is conducted is in turn modified in the light of changes in the theory. What appears in the free associations and in the dreams of patients in treatment, as well as the disappearance of symptoms, is frequently cited as proof of the rightness of the theory.

his personal values enter into his therapeutic methods in a way and to an extent that is not true for the surgeon. He has been compared to a priest. But the priest by the nature of his assumptions does not do the kind of detailed probing over a period of years that the analyst does; and, to many persons who seek psychoanalysis today, to speak with the voice of Science is more than to speak with the voice of God. This particular combination of intimacy and impersonal authority is, I think, without precedent. It gives to the analyst enormous power. The persons who come to him are vulnerable, and the process of analysis tends, at least in its initial stages, to increase their vulnerability. Both because of the methods they use and the content of their therapy, there is probably no group of persons today—with the exception of priests and some practitioners of "mental healing"—in a position to exercise as much power over persons with whom they come into professional contact as psychoanalysts. This power aims to be, and often is, a means of bringing to the individual seeking treatment greater freedom and fuller realization of himself. But it can achieve this aim only if the psychoanalyst recognizes the extent of his power and of its hazards. Freud clearly recognized this power and its hazards (as well as the difficulties involved in "countertransference"), and emphasis on such recognition is increasingly a part of training in psychoanalysis.

There would seem to be two situations in which the kind of opening of oneself that is an essential of the analytic treatment is possible: one where the relation is one of mutuality, and there is in trust and love the opening of two persons to each other; the other where the person to whom one opens oneself is the surrogate of God or of some higher power. The analyst is in neither of these situations; he is likely to stand first on one foot, then on the other, and few analysts seem to me to have confronted the full complexity of this problem. Sullivan insisted on the importance of mutuality and communication; but the analyst does not open himself to the patient as the patient is expected to do to the analyst. Freud and the early Freudians leaned toward the conception of the remote analyst, an embodiment of a higher wisdom; but no analyst, however skillful and however humane, is all-wise and all-good. The late Frieda Fromm-Reichmann [2] seems to me to have come nearest to seeing this problem in its full dimensions. She carried to amazing lengths the ability to be open to the patient, to adapt to his views, to see the world through his eyes, but she was quite clear that the analyst remains the expert; the relation is not, and cannot be, one of mutuality.

In the attempt to appraise psychoanalysis there must be consideration of both method and content: the method of psychoanalysis, the assumptions involved in the relation between analyst and patient, and the content of analysis—what a particular school of psychoanalytic

---

2. *Principles of Intensive Psychotherapy* and articles in *Psychiatry*.

thought or a particular analyst considers a desirable outcome of therapy. The general aim of the analyst—sometimes more fully, sometimes less fully, achieved—is to help the patient to be more secure and happy in the realization of his own identity, or at least to remove neurotic obstacles to such realization.

But the achievement of this aim through the methods of psychoanalysis involves the deliberate breaking down of one identity and replacing it by another, accomplishing this in part through the "transference" of the patient to the analyst and "overcoming the resistance" of the patient to the analyst's implicit or explicit ideas of what is desirable, healthy, mature, and realistic. Ruth Munroe reports that the aim of psychoanalysis "is fundamental change in the personality," to establish firmly "a basic shift in attitude."[3] If this is true, then the psychoanalytic process would seem to have something in common with the substitution of one personality for another in military training and with religious and political conversion. The analyst, of course, always, attempts to make the new identity that replaces the old what the patient "really" wants, just as the religious or political leader says that he is expressing the "real" wishes of the people. These interpretations may be valid. But, as in any human relation—teaching, therapy, political or religious leadership, or any other—complete "objectivity" is impossible and the values of the interpreter enter into the interpretation.

The similarity in these different processes of changing identity and the problems this presents is recognized by students most sympathetic to psychoanalysis and by psychoanalysts themselves. Joost A. M. Meerloo, a Dutch psychoanalyst now in the United States, in a study of methods of totalitarian mass coercion,[4] has pointed out that mental coercion is more effective than physical torture in breaking down personality;[5] that just as educational training can degenerate into coercive training, so therapy can degenerate into the imposition of the doctor's will on the patient;[6] and that since a psychological interview is in itself a coercive situation, the therapist must use enormous care and restraint not to exert his influence unduly.[7] He believes that psychoanalysts recently have become more aware of these problems and have taken greater care to avoid them.

One of the most arresting recent studies of the methods of psychoanalysis is that of William Sargant, President of the Section of Psychiatry of the British Royal Society of Medicine.[8] Using as a basis for comparison the experiments of Pavlov in inducing neuroses in dogs, he

---

3. *Schools of Psychoanalytic Thought,* pp. 326, 518.
4. *The Rape of the Mind.*
5. *Ibid.,* pp. 23–24.
6. *Ibid.,* p. 68.
7. *Ibid.,* p. 150.
8. *Battle for the Mind,* especially Chap. 4 and pp. 188–92.

examines in detail what he believes to be the common physiological and psychological processes involved in psychoanalysis and in methods of destroying political and religious beliefs which are of the essence of a person's identity, and of replacing them by others.[9] Sargant begins his foreword by saying that he is discussing only *methods* of changing personality, *not* the nature of the changes or the content of the beliefs imparted. "It must be emphasized as strongly as possible that this book is *not* concerned with the truth or falsity of any particular religious or political belief. Its purpose is to examine some of the mechanisms involved in the fixing or destroying of such beliefs in the human brain."

Sargant's analysis is, I think, open to question on a number of grounds: Granted that there may be common physiological and psychological factors involved in the different processes he describes, differences are more important than he indicates. Under extreme pressure almost every individual may have an ultimate breaking point, where he abandons "resistance" and human reason and becomes indistinguishable from a salivating dog,[10] but it makes a great difference where this point comes.[11] One thing that helps to determine the degree of resistance to pressure—the previous experience of the person—is more important than Sargant seems to recognize. A person who has never known poverty, social frustration, or injustice may be less receptive to Communist doctrines; a person who has not experienced a sense of sin and of the futility of earthly life, to the religious evangelist; a person who has not felt himself hampered by conflict and inability to direct his own life, to psychoanalytic interpretations. Sargant also underestimates the enormous differences between the psychological processes that are involved if a person has voluntarily sought out the Communist party or the church or the psychoanalyst or military training and those involved if he involuntarily finds himself in the concentration camp or in the army. Furthermore, the character and content of the beliefs and identity destroyed and those that replace them seem to me to be far more important in relation to the methods used than Sargant allows.

But with all these serious qualifications, the similarities in the experiences of psychoanalysis and of religious and political conversion are phenomena that no one interested in the theoretical and therapeutic possibilities of psychoanalysis can ignore. Examining these similarities is not equating psychoanalysis with religious or political conversion. It is simply saying that certain processes in some respects similar are involved in these different experiences, and that these similarities merit ex-

---

9. Cf. Anselm Strauss' statement that in all these situations—religious or political conversion or therapy—"the learner has something to unlearn, to cope with, or as the psychoanalysts say, 'to work through.'" (*An Essay on Identity,* p. 165.)
10. All that has been said earlier of the fallacies of applying animal experiments to human beings applies to Sargant's analysis.
11. Sargant, *Battle for the Mind,* p. 181 and throughout.

amination by anyone interested in the possibilities of psychoanalysis for increasing human freedom.

Sargant points out that in the initial stages of psychoanalysis, as of political and religious conversion, anxiety, humiliation, and guilt are increased—often augmented by physical fatigue and debility resulting from the anxiety aroused by the process itself—so that the patient becomes more and more dependent on the analyst.[12] "As the analysis proceeds, and emotional storms mount" these "transference situations" are built up so that the patient becomes increasingly sensitized to suggestions that he would earlier have rejected. Sargant gives illustrations of persons who dream dreams that conform to the doctrine of a particular analyst, and even of the same person dreaming dreams that differ according to the doctrines of successive analysts of different schools of psychoanalysis.[13] After abreactions [14] over a period of months or even years the therapist may be able to bring about changes in the patient's ideas and behavior without too much difficulty; [15] the patient "will sometimes 'box the compass' in his views on religion or politics, or in his attitude to his family and friends." [16]

A stage is finally reached "when resistance weakens to the therapist's interpretations of a patient's symptoms. . . . He now believes and acts upon theories about his nervous condition which, more often than not, contradict his former beliefs. . . . These changes are consolidated by making [his] behavior as consistent as possible with the new 'insight' gained." "Analysis is often considered complete only when the therapist's points of view have been thoroughly absorbed and resistance . . . to the therapist's interpretations of past events has broken down." [17]

Sargant says that terror and shame play a large part in "being re-made" in therapy, brainwashing, and conversion, that a person particularly responsive to other pressures [18] is also particularly responsive to analytic pressure [19] and (as Munroe and others have also said) that what is actually involved is the breaking down of one identity and replacing it by one that the analyst, on the basis of the patient's revelations, considers more desirable.

Important as it is to recognize the similarities that Sargant points

---

12. *Ibid.*, pp. 51, 55–57.
13. *Ibid.*, pp. 57–58, 167.
14. Abreaction is defined by Sargant, following W. S. Sadler, as "a process of reviving the memory of a repressed unpleasant experience and expressing in speech and action the emotions related to it, thereby relieving the personality of its influence." (*Battle for the Mind*, Heinemann, 1957, p. 42.)
15. *Ibid.*, p. 51.
16. *Ibid.*, p. 55.
17. *Ibid.*, pp. 57–58.
18. Here, I think, he does not sufficiently distinguish among the *kinds of* pressures to which an individual has been responsive in his previous history.
19. *Ibid.*, pp. 59–60, 145, 153, 188–91, and throughout.

out, it is also important, as I said above, to recognize the differences in these processes to which Sargant does not give adequate weight: the crucial difference between whether a person voluntarily seeks a change of identity or is forced into a situation that demands it; the variations in susceptibilities to pressure that result from previous life experiences; the content of the new identity considered desirable by the analyst and acceptable to the patient and its relation to these previous experiences of the person engaging in the change.

In regard to the content of psychoanalysis, analysts vary greatly in the extent to which they think that the changed personality that should be the outcome of therapy should embody adjustment to the norms of achievement and success that are the "reality" of contemporary society. For some, ego development turns out to be adaptation to present social norms. For others, the aim of analysis is helping the patient to develop the courage to deviate in his own way from accepted norms.

Fromm, Horney, and to some extent Sullivan take specific issue with some of these accepted norms. They, however, may underestimate the difficulties involved if, on the one hand, the repressions of contemporary society are as great as they say and, on the other, the individual is deemed unworthy if, in spite of these repressions, he is not an independent, productive, mature person. They urge the individual to "be himself" instead of cherishing an unrealistic, ideal self-image or following the dictates of custom and of authority; to have faith, but to make sure that it is a rational faith; in the midst of social coercions to discover his true self.

Fromm, like Goldstein, is chiefly concerned with the self-actualizing possibilities of human beings. In his view the chief threat to realization of identity lies in submission to irrational authority. He believes that, contrary to Freud's view, love and hate have different roots in the personality, and that, contrary to Calvin's view, self-love and love of others are necessarily complementary, not antagonistic. He deplores the "market-place psychology" that dominates contemporary life. For Fromm the chief terror is isolation, the chief sin is self-multilation, the chief virtue is spontaneous realization of individual potentialities through productive work and productive relations with others.[20] But what is this real, spontaneous self independent of romanticism and of all authority—or at least of all irrational authority—that we are exhorted to realize? If the psychology of the market place, of achievement, and of

---

20. *Escape from Freedom* and *Man for Himself*. Fromm's next two books, *Psychoanalysis and Religion* (Yale University Press, 1950) and *The Forgotten Language* (Rinehart, 1951), are less concerned with the extent to which man is a social being and with the social factors in personality development. *The Sane Society* (Rinehart, 1955) returns to interest in the social environment. *The Art of Loving* (Harper, 1956) is chiefly concerned with the individual. Cf. the writings of Karen Horney and Harry Stack Sullivan previously cited.

success are to be repudiated, what is the reality that we must accept and adjust to if we are to avoid the unrealities of sentimentality and insubstantial idealism? The difficulties of self-realization in the midst of these conflicts may be more profound than Fromm sometimes seems to recognize.

Marcuse is, I think, too sweeping in his condemnation of Fromm, Horney, and Sullivan as Freudian revisionists; and he does not discuss Fromm's recent book *The Sane Society,* which does precisely question the extent to which it is possible for individuals to achieve productivity and self-realization in capitalist, bourgeois society. Marcuse denounces the revisionist movement because in it, he believes, the regressive features of psychoanalysis have become dominant;[21] therapy is a course in resignation;[22] there is a commitment to this present capitalist society;[23] the individual is held to be personally responsible for failure of self-realization, a view that minimizes the role of society;[24] and the brute fact of social repression is transformed into a moral problem for the individual.[25]

But admonitions to be one's spontaneous, real self and at the same time to accept reality minimize the difficulties of the problems involved. Learning when to yield to a recalcitrant reality and when to try to change it is a main problem of life, one that must constantly be resolved afresh. The question is not whether to adjust to or to rebel against reality, but, rather, how to discriminate between those realities that must be recognized as unalterable and those that we should continue to try to change however unyielding they may appear. Our whole life is spent in an attempt to discover when our refusal to bow to limitations is romantic escape from actualities and when it is courage and rational faith. There were many who argued that acceptance of reality when Hitler came to power demanded adjustment to Nazism, and that any other action was romantic folly. There are many, among their number psychoanalysts, who argue that being efficient in terms of the money and success values of our achievement society is one of the requirements for realistic mature living. Working for peace or for any form of shared

---

21. *Eros and Civilization,* p. 245.
22. *Ibid.,* p. 246.
23. *Ibid.,* p. 257.
24. *Ibid.,* pp. 265–66.
25. Marcuse's basic criticism of the Freudian revisionists is essentially the same as his criticism of the existentialists that "Behind the nihilistic language of the existentialists lurks the ideology of free competition, free initiative, and equal opportunity. Everybody can 'transcend' his situation, carry out his own project. Everybody has his absolutely free choice . . . in Sartre's philosophy . . . 'Pour-soi' vacillates between . . . individual subject and . . . universal Ego or consciousness. Most of the qualities which he attributes to the 'Pour-soi' are qualities of man as a genus . . . *not* the essential qualities of man's concrete existence." ("Existentialism: Remarks on Jean-Paul Sartre's *L'Etre ET LE NEANT*," *Philosophy and Phenomenological Research,* Vol. VIII, No. 3, Mar. 1948, pp. 323 and 334–35.)

welfare or noncompetitive community life, or for socialism is condemned by some persons as unrealistic sentimentality. And yet—innovation of any sort, in the physical or in the social world, has always been regarded as ridiculous, as unrealistic romanticism. "The idea seems ridiculous, but I can find nothing wrong with it" said Kepler of his concept of infinity. Only the refusal to bow to accepted realities can bring new knowledge of the physical or the psychological world or a new stage of history.

So, too, our whole life is an attempt to discover when our spontaneity is whimsical, sentimental irresponsibility and when it is a valid expression of our deepest desires and values. Horney, Fromm, and even Sullivan at times, seem to assume that there is an already existent real or true or spontaneous self which can be evoked into active existence almost at will. There is a tacit assumption that somehow we know the dictates of the real self, and that we should live in terms of these rather than of a romanticized self-image or of the pseudo-self of others' expectations. But, like understanding of "reality," such a real self is something to be discovered and created, not a given, but a lifelong endeavor.

Marcuse condemns our present society—in terms as far-reaching but less specific than Fromm's; he believes that only a revolution on Marxian lines would be of any use in creating a more humane social order and that individuals cannot hope to escape the repressions of this society. But Marcuse, Fromm, and any social scientist who believes that a society more expressive of individual desires is a possibility must confront the question of how we get from here to there. They must recognize, as Marx did, that some individuals are freer than others from the coercions of their class and their historical situation and can therefore take a more aware and active part than the majority in the historical processes that shape the future.

Erikson's concept of identity and the guilt-axis and shame-axis approaches to identity

Erikson's explicit recognition of the present importance of the problem of identity was quoted earlier.[26] I shall here describe

---

26. "The Problem of Ego Identity," p. 57. Cf. Erving Goffman's use of self, ". . . I have implicitly been using a double definition of self: the self as an image pieced together from the expressive implications of the full flow of events in an undertaking; and the self as a kind of player in a ritual game who copes honorably or dishonorably." ("On Face-Work," p. 225.)

Max Scheler also describes the "I" as a "double antithesis" between the outer world and the thou. (Alfred Schuetz, "Scheler's Theory of Inter-subjectivity," in "Symposium on the Significance of Max Scheler for Philosophy and Social Science," *Philosophy and Phenomenological Research*, Vol. II, No. 3, Mar. 1952, p. 325.)

in more detail his hypotheses related to the meaning and conditions of the discovery of identity, and then go on to discuss the implications inherent in and the questions raised by his, Schachtel's, and similar formulations.

In using the word identity, instead of self or ego or any of their variations, Erikson deliberately selects a term that has a double direction, that clearly indicates that some sort of correspondence between the inner and the outer world is indispensable for a sense of identity. He uses the term identity with multiple connotations, which include: unconscious and conscious strivings for continuity of personality, a tendency toward synthesis beyond even unconscious striving, a criterion for the outcome of this striving and this tendency, a maintenance of congruence with the ideals and identity of one's social group, a conscious awareness of who one is.[27] By implication he includes in the meaning of identity the self as subject and as object, as observer and observed—meanings that are sometimes kept separate in an effort to make exclusive distinctions between the concepts self and ego.

This ambiguity, this multidimensional character, of the term identity is not, I believe, a drawback in its use. We may question a particular connotation Erikson gives to the term and still recognize that its very ambiguity, the surplus meaning it carries, makes it more accurately descriptive of the awareness of "I" that may emerge from the processes of integrating life experiences than the narrower conceptions of self and ego. In part because of his very use of the double-directed term identity Erikson seems to me to make a special contribution to the understanding of the way in which the various identifications and introjections of the developing individual are woven into the "I" and the "me." In his view the integration into the "I" is more than a sum or an integration of social roles, more than the *persona*,* although these are parts of the fabric.

Erikson regards the awareness of identity as a special characteristic of one stage of development and also as essential for maturity. He traces eight stages in the development of personality, each of which involves a conflict and a possible crisis. Each stage may give rise to special difficulties if its particular conflict is not resolved in a way that is constructive for the growing person, and each has special possibilities for enlargement of personality and increased strength of identity if it is so resolved.[28] Erikson's hypothetical stages of development are im-

27. Cf. Emily Dickinson's ways of describing the self: "The 'self' she variously designates . . . as the 'undiscovered continent' and the 'indestructible estate.' The solitudes of space, of the sea, even of death, she styles popular assemblies compared to 'That polar privacy—a soul admitted to itself.' " (Thomas H. Johnson, *Emily Dickinson,* Harvard University Press, 1955, p. 247.)
* Mask or role.
28. "Growth and Crises of the 'Healthy Personality,' " p. 189; *Childhood and Society,* p. 233.

portant in that they go beyond Gesell's theories of chronological maturation and Freud's theories of sexual phases of growth to explicit recognition of the importance of shifting social relations, and also of greater surplus energy in each stage.

In setting out this pattern of development, Erikson is careful to say that these different stages, and the possible crises and the potentialities for development each presents, are suggested formulations rather than given or proved entities, "I am going to propose a list of these criteria [of ego strength at various stages of development] without knowing exactly what psychological units we are dealing with." [29]

Each potential component strength of developing personality reaches its particular unique ascendancy in one of these stages of conflict and has its own particular vulnerability and possibility at that period. But none of these potential component strengths begins or ends in its period of special climax. Each begins potentially in some form at the beginning of life, and the resolution of conflict that each has found continues in some form throughout life.[30] Each conflict stage is conceived not only, as in the compensatory theory of personality, as a threat of a destructive crisis that must be coped with or overcome, but also as an opportunity for accrued strength.[31] Each stage involves both the inner self and its relation to the social situation in the outer world.

The characteristic conflicts of the eight hypothetical stages of development are: [32] trust vs. mistrust; autonomy vs. shame, doubt; [33] initiative vs. guilt; industry vs. inferiority; identity vs. identity diffusion; intimacy vs. isolation; generativity (the interest in establishing and guiding the next generation) vs. self-absorption; integrity vs. disgust, despair.[34]

Erikson regards these eight stages of development as supplementing, not replacing, Freud's theory of periods of development with its emphasis on sexual conflicts and maturation. In the diagrammatic presentation of his eight stages he relates them both to chronological age and to Freud's developmental stages. But he does point out the contrast

29. "On the Sense of Inner Identity," p. 352.
30. "Growth and Crises of the 'Healthy Personality,'" pp. 188–89.
31. "The Problem of Ego Identity," pp. 70–71.
32. The chart expressing diagrammatically these eight stages of development is presented most fully in "The Problem of Ego Identity," p. 75.
33. In this stage the child learns to delineate the area over which he has control and to develop self-esteem. It is the task of society to "back the child up" in his wish to "stand on his own feet" lest he be overcome by the sense of having "gone too far" (shame) or exposed to the mistrust of looking backward (doubt). ("Growth and Crises of the 'Healthy Personality,'" in Clyde Kluckhohn and Henry A. Murray, *Personality in Nature, Society, and Culture*, 2d ed., Knopf, 1953, pp. 199–200.)
34. Some statements of Erikson's might lead one to think that he regarded these stages of development as completed at adolescence. Elsewhere, however, he makes it clear that he regards the development of identity as something that continues, at least for some persons, throughout life.

between the stress in Freudian theory on typical danger situations and his own emphasis on maturation of function, between the Freudian view of the central importance of psychosexual development and his own view of the significance of psychosocial development.[35] At each stage of the developing personality, Erikson believes, there is an access of surplus internal energy and the possibility of enhanced support from social relations that makes it possible for the individual to meet the potential crisis in such a way as to incorporate the resolved conflict into a strengthened identity.

Since each component of the personality exists in some form, latent or overt, at each stage, it would be theoretically possible, according to Erikson, to trace through each stage its components of shame and developing identity. Identity includes, but is more than, what Erikson calls autonomy, since autonomy does not have the double direction of identity.

This tentative formulation of Erikson's which contrasts shame (and doubt of oneself) with autonomy as a stage of growth preceding the conflict of guilt with initiative is relevant to the question of the guilt axis and the shame axis in personality, and of the part each plays in the development of identity. From Erikson's analysis it would follow that shame and guilt are two distinguishable—although not *opposite*—experiences which may at times be linked together, but are not always so linked. Shame, which at least in our culture is often related to visual exposure (including sexual exposure), characteristically occurs, he believes, as an earlier experience than guilt, which is more often related to specific auditory admonition against violation of a code. Shame is doubt, including diffused anxiety, an overall ashamedness, a consciousness of the whole self, a feeling that life is happening to the individual.[36] Anxiety is peculiarly associated with shame. In every potential crisis of development anxiety is possible, and each new conflict may revive latent anxiety. But anxiety has special relation to the conflict between shame and doubt and the developing sense of what he here calls autonomy. It is not fear, nor anxiety faced directly, but unconfronted aimless anxiety that drives an individual into irrational action, irrational flight—or, indeed, irrational denial of danger.[37]

Guilt, in contrast to shame, is more related to specific acts, going against specific taboos. Basic trust in one's world and especially in the persons who are its interpreters is crucial to one's sense of identity. In shame there is a doubt, a questioning of trust. It is for such reasons as these that shame may be said to go deeper than guilt; it is worse to be

---

35. *Ibid.*, pp. 70–71.
36. *Childhood and Society*, p. 223.
37. *Ibid.*, pp. 360–63, and "The Problem of Ego Identity."

inferior and isolated than to be wrong, to be outcast in one's own eyes than to be condemned by society.

The following comparison simply brings together some of the differences between the guilt axis and the shame axis in personality that have been noted earlier. They are in no sense polar opposites. Both the guilt axis and the shame axis enter into the attitudes and behavior of most people, and often into the same situation. But there are for different persons different balances and stresses between the two, and it does matter whether one lives more in terms of one or of the other. The particular comparisons listed are only suggestive; no two persons would experience these contrasts in exactly the same way. The differences are presented in this way only for the sake of comparison; in experience shame and guilt are usually not so sharply separated.

Guilt Axis	Shame Axis
Concerned with each separate, discrete act	Concerned with the over-all self
Involves transgression of a specific code, violation of a specific taboo	Involves falling short, failure to reach an ideal
Involves an additive process; advance to healthy personality by deleting wrong acts and substituting right ones for them	Involves a total response that includes insight, something more than can be reached by addition
Involves competition, measurement on a scale, performing the acts prescribed as desirable	Involves acting in terms of the pervasive qualitative demands of oneself, more rigorous than external codes; each act partakes of the quality of the whole
Exposure of a specific misdemeanor, with emphasis on to whom exposed; exposure of something that should be hidden in a closet	Exposure of the quick of the self, most of all to oneself; exposure of something that can never be hidden in a closet, is in the depths of the earth or in the open sunlight
Concern about violation of social codes of cleanliness, politeness, and so on	Concern about unalterable features of one's body, way of moving, clumsiness, and so on
Feeling of wrongdoing for a specific harmful act toward someone one loves	Feeling that one may have loved the wrong person, or may be inadequate for the person one loves
Being a good, loyal friend, husband, wife, parent	Having an overflowing feeling for friend, husband, wife, children which makes goodness and loyalty a part of the whole experience with no need for separate emphasis

Guilt Axis—Continued	Shame Axis—Continued
Trust built on the conception of no betrayal, no disloyal act, as a preliminary to giving affection	Trust that is a process of discovery which gradually eliminates fear of exposure, which is not the result of an act of will but unfolds with the unfolding experience
Feelings of anger, jealousy, meanness for certain socially recognized causes	Inwardly deep feelings of anger, jealousy, meanness in outwardly slight situations known to oneself only
Emphasis on decision-making; any decision is better than none	Ability to live with some indecisiveness (multiple possibilities) even though it means living with some anxiety
Feeling of guilt toward someone who has denounced one for adequate or inadequate cause	Feeling of shame toward someone who trusts one if one is not meeting that trust
Emphasis on content of experience in work, leisure, personal relations	Emphasis on quality of experience, not only on content
Surmounting of guilt leads to righteousness	Transcending of shame may lead to sense of identity, freedom

This comparison, as well as Erikson's analysis of stages of development, would seem to suggest again that a sense of identity cannot be reached along the guilt axis alone, that more is needed than discarding specific wrong acts and substituting specific right acts for them. Can confronting experiences of shame full in the face be one clue to the discovery of what this something more is?

We cannot know, but it is interesting to speculate on what Emily Dickinson meant when she wrote:

> Shame need not crouch
> In such an earth as ours;
> Shame, stand erect,
> The universe is yours!

43 FRANTZ FANON
The Negro and Recognition

A. THE NEGRO AND ADLER

From whatever direction one approaches the analysis of abnormal psychogenic conditions, one very soon finds oneself in the presence of the following phenomenon: The whole picture of the neurosis, as well as all its symptoms, emerges as under the influence of some final goal, indeed as projections of this goal. Therefore one can ascribe the character of a formative cause to this final goal, the quality of a principle of orientation, of arrangement, of coordination. Try to understand the "meaning" and the direction of unhealthy manifestations, and you will immediately come face to face with a chaotic throng of tendencies, of impulses, of weaknesses and of anomalies, bound to discourage some and to arouse in others the rash resolve to penetrate the shadows at all costs, even at the risk of finding in the end that nothing has been gained, or that what has been gained is illusory. If, on the other hand, one accepts the hypothesis of a final goal or of a causal finality, one sees the shadows dissolve at once and we can read the soul of the patient like the pages of a book.[1]

It is on the basis of similar theoretical positions that, in general, the most stupendous frauds of our period are constructed. Let us apply Adler's individual psychology to the Antilleans.

The Negro is comparison. There is the first truth. He is comparison: that is, he is constantly preoccupied with self-evaluation and with the ego-ideal. Whenever he comes into contact with someone else, the question of value, of merit, arises. The Antilleans have no inherent values of their own, they are always contingent on the presence of The Other. The question is always whether he is less intelligent than I, blacker than I, less respectable than I. Every position of one's own, every effort at security, is based on relations of dependence, with the diminution of the other. It is the wreckage of what surrounds me that provides the foundation for my virility.

From Frantz Fanon, *Black Skin, White Masks* (New York: Grove Press, Inc., 1967), pp. 210–21.
1. Alfred Adler, *Le tempérament nerveux*, p. 12. (Originally, "Der nervöse charakter," in *Festschrift William Stern,* Leipzig, Barth, 1931).

I should like to suggest an experiment to any Martinican who reads this book: Find the most "comparative" street in Fort-de-France. Rue Schoelcher, rue Victor-Hugo—certainly not rue François-Arago. The Martinican who agrees to make this experiment will share my opinion precisely insofar as he can objectively endure seeing himself stripped naked. An Antillean who meets an acquaintance for the first time after five or six years' absence greets him with aggression. This is because in the past each had a fixed position. Now the inferior thinks that he has acquired worth . . . and the superior is determined to conserve the old hierarchy. "You haven't changed a bit . . . still as stupid as ever."

I have known some, physicians and dentists, who have gone on filling their heads with mistakes in judgment made fifteen years before. It is not so much conceptual errors as "Creolisms" with which the dangerous man is belabored. He was put in his place once and for all: nothing to be done about it. The Antillean is characterized by his desire to dominate the other. His line of orientation runs through the other. It is always a question of the subject; one never even thinks of the object. I try to read admiration in the eyes of the other, and if, unluckily, those eyes show me an unpleasant reflection, I find that mirror flawed: Unquestionably that other one is a fool. I do not try to be naked in the sight of the object. The object is denied in terms of individuality and liberty. The object is an instrument. It should enable me to realize my subjective security. I consider myself fulfilled (the wish for plenitude) and I recognize no division. The Other comes on to the stage only in order to furnish it. I am the Hero. Applaud or condemn, it makes no difference to me, I am the center of attention. If the other seeks to make me uneasy with his wish to have value (his fiction), I simply banish him without a trial. He ceases to exist. I don't want to hear about that fellow. I do not wish to experience the impact of the object. Contact with the object means conflict. I am Narcissus, and what I want to see in the eyes of others is a reflection that pleases me. Therefore, in any given group (environment) in Martinique, one finds the man on top, the court that surrounds him, the in-betweens (who are waiting for something better), and the losers. These last are slaughtered without mercy. One can imagine the temperature that prevails in that jungle. There is no way out of it.

Me, nothing but me.

The Martinicans are greedy for security. They want to compel the acceptance of their fiction. They want to be recognized in their quest for manhood. They want to make an appearance. Each one of them is an isolated, sterile, salient atom with sharply defined rights of passage, each one of them *is*. Each one of them wants to *be*, to *emerge*. Everything that an Antillean does is done for The Other. Not because

The Other is the ultimate objective of his action in the sense of communication between people that Adler describes,[2] but, more primitively, because it is The Other who corroborates him in his search for self-validation.

Now that we have marked out the Adlerian line of orientation of the Antillean, our task is to look for its source.

Here the difficulties begin. In effect, Adler has created a psychology of the individual. We have just seen that the feeling of inferiority is an Antillean characteristic. It is not just this or that Antillean who embodies the neurotic formation, but all Antilleans. Antillean society is a neurotic society, a society of "comparison." Hence we are driven from the individual back to the social structure. If there is a taint, it lies not in the "soul" of the individual but rather in that of the environment.

The Martinican is and is not a neurotic. If we were strict in applying the conclusions of the Adlerian school, we should say that the Negro is seeking to protest against the inferiority that he feels historically. Since in all periods the Negro has been an inferior, he attempts to react with a superiority complex. And this is indeed what comes out of Brachfeld's book. Discussing the feeling of racial inferiority, Brachfeld quotes a Spanish play by André de Claramunte, *El valiante negro de Flandres*. This play makes clear that the inferiority of the Negro does not date from this century, since De Claramunte was a contemporary of Lope de Vega:

> Only the color of his skin there lacked
> That he should be a man of gentle blood.

And the Negro, Juan de Mérida, says this:

> What a disgrace it is to be black
> in this world!
> Are black men not
> men?
> Does that endow them with a baser soul,
>   a duller, an uglier?
> And for that they have earned scornful
>   names.
> I rise burdened with the shame of my
> color
> And I let the world know my courage . . .
> Is it so vile to be black?

Poor Juan cannot be sure any longer what saint to invoke. Nor-

---

2. In *Understanding Human Nature*.

mally, the black man is a slave. There is nothing of that sort in his attitude:

> For, though I be black,
> I am not a slave.

Nevertheless he would like to be able to flee that blackness. He has an ethical position in the world. Viewed from an axiological standpoint, he is a white man:

> I am more white than snow.

For, after all, on the symbolic level,

> What is it really, then, to be black?
> Is it being that color?
> For that outrage I will denounce
>   fate,
> my times, heaven,
> and all those who made me black!
> O curse of color!

In his isolation, Juan sees that the wish cannot save him. His *appearance* saps, invalidates, all his actions:

> What do souls matter?
> I am mad.
> What can I do but despair?
> O heaven what a dread thing
> being black.

At the climax of his anguish there remains only one solution for the miserable Negro: furnish proofs of his whiteness to others and above all to himself.

> If I cannot change my color
> I want Luck.[3]

As we can see, Juan de Mérida must be understood from the viewpoint of overcompensation. It is because the Negro belongs to an "inferior" race that he seeks to be like the superior race.

But we have a means of shaking off the Adlerian leech. In the United States, De Man and Eastman have applied Adler's method somewhat excessively. All the facts that I have noted are real, but, it should not be necessary to point out, they have only a superficial connection

---

3. My own translation from the Spanish—F.F.

with Adlerian psychology. The Martinican does not compare himself with the white man *qua* father, leader, God; he compares himself with his fellow against the pattern of the white man. An Adlerian comparison would be schematized in this fashion:

$$\text{Ego greater than The Other}$$

But the Antillean comparison, in contrast, would look like this:

$$\frac{\text{White}}{\text{Ego different from The Other}}$$

The Adlerian comparison embraces two terms; it is polarized by the ego. The Antillean comparison is surmounted by a third term: Its governing fiction is not personal but social.

The Martinican is a man crucified. The environment that has shaped him (but that he has not shaped) has horribly drawn and quartered him; and he feeds this cultural environment with his blood and his essences. Now, the blood of Negroes is a manure prized by experts.

If I were an Adlerian, then, having established the fact that my friend had fulfilled in a dream his wish to become white—that is, to be a man—I would show him that his neurosis, his psychic instability, the rupture of his ego arose out of this governing fiction, and I would say to him: "M. Mannoni has very ably described this phenomenon in the Malagasy. Look here: I think you simply have to resign yourself to remaining in the place that has been assigned to you."

Certainly not! I will not say that at all! I will tell him, "The environment, society are responsible for your delusion." Once that has been said, the rest will follow of itself, and what that is we know. The end of the world.

I wonder sometimes whether school inspectors and government functionaries are aware of the role they play in the colonies. For twenty years they poured every effort into programs that would make the Negro a white man. In the end, they dropped him and told him, "You have an indisputable complex of dependence on the white man."

B. THE NEGRO AND HEGEL

> Self-consciousness exists *in itself* and *for itself*, in that and by the fact that it exists for another self-consciousness; that is to say, it *is* only by being acknowledged or recognized.
> —Hegel, *The Phenomenology of Mind*

Man is human only to the extent to which he tries to impose his existence on another man in order to be recognized by him. As long as he has not been effectively recognized by the other, that other will remain the theme of his actions. It is on that other being, on recognition by that other being, that his own human worth and reality depend. It is that other being in whom the meaning of his life is condensed.

There is not an open conflict between white and black. One day the White Master, *without conflict,* recognized the Negro slave.

But the former slave wants to *make himself recognized.*

At the foundation of Hegelian dialectic there is an absolute reciprocity which must be emphasized. It is in the degree to which I go beyond my own immediate being that I apprehend the existence of the other as a natural and more than natural reality. If I close the circuit, if I prevent the accomplishment of movement in two directions, I keep the other within himself. Ultimately, I deprive him even of this being-for-itself.

The only means of breaking this vicious circle that throws me back on myself is to restore to the other, through mediation and recognition, his human reality, which is different from natural reality. The other has to perform the same operation. "Action from one side only would be useless, because what is to happen can only be brought about by means of both. . . ."; *"they recognize themselves as mutually recognizing each other."* [4]

In its immediacy, consciousness of self is simple being-for-itself. In order to win the certainty of oneself, the incorporation of the concept of recognition is essential. Similarly, the other is waiting for recognition by us, in order to burgeon into the universal consciousness of self. Each consciousness of self is in quest of absoluteness. It wants to be recognized as a primal value without reference to life, as a transformation of subjective certainty (*Gewissheit*) into objective truth (*Wahrheit*).

When it encounters resistance from the other, self-consciousness undergoes the experience of *desire*—the first milestone on the road that leads to the dignity of the spirit. Self-consciousness accepts the risk of its life, and consequently it threatens the other in his physical being. "It is solely by risking life that freedom is obtained; only thus is it tried and proved that the essential nature of self-consciousness is not *bare existence,* is not the merely immediate form in which it at first makes its appearance, is not its mere absorption in the expanse of life." [5]

Thus human reality in-itself-for-itself can be achieved only through conflict and through the risk that conflict implies. This risk means that I go beyond life toward a supreme good that is the transformation of subjective certainty of my own worth into a universally valid objective truth.

4. G. W. F. Hegel, *The Phenomenology of Mind,* trans. by J. B. Baillie, 2nd rev. ed. (London, Allen & Unwin, 1949), pp. 230–31.
5. *Ibid.,* p. 233.

As soon as I *desire* I am asking to be considered. I am not merely here-and-now, sealed into thingness. I am for somewhere else and for something else. I demand that notice be taken of my negating activity insofar as I pursue something other than life; insofar as I do battle for the creation of a human world—that is, of a world of reciprocal recognitions.

He who is reluctant to recognize me opposes me. In a savage struggle I am willing to accept convulsions of death, invincible dissolution, but also the possibility of the impossible.[6]

The other, however, can recognize me without struggle: "The individual, who has not staked his life, may, no doubt, be recognized as a *person,* but he has not attained the truth of this recognition as an independent self-consciousness." [7]

Historically, the Negro steeped in the inessentiality of servitude was set free by his master. He did not fight for his freedom.

Out of slavery the Negro burst into the lists where his masters stood. Like those servants who are allowed once every year to dance in the drawing room, the Negro is looking for a prop. The Negro has not become a master. When there are no longer slaves, there are no longer masters.

The Negro is a slave who has been allowed to assume the attitude of a master.

The white man is a master who has allowed his slaves to eat at his table.

One day a good white master who had influence said to his friends, "Let's be nice to the niggers. . . ."

The other masters argued, for after all it was not an easy thing, but then they decided to promote the machine-animal-men to the supreme rank of *men.*

Slavery shall no longer exist on French soil.

---

6. When I began this book, I wanted to devote one section to a study of the death wish among Negroes. I believed it necessary because people are forever saying that Negroes never commit suicide.

M. Achille did not hesitate to maintain this in a lecture, and Richard Wright, in one of his stories, has a white character say, "If I were a Negro I'd kill myself. . . ," in the sense that only a Negro could submit to such treatment without feeling drawn to suicide.

Since then, M. Deshaies has taken the question of suicide as the subject of his thesis. He demonstrates that the studies by Jaensch, who contrasted the disintegrated-personality "type" (blue eyes, white skin) to the integrated-personality "type" (brown eyes and skin), are predominantly specious.

According to Durkheim, Jews never committed suicide. Now it is the Negroes. Very well: "The Detroit municipal hospital found that 16.6% of its suicide cases were Negroes, although the proportion of Negroes in the total population is only 7.6%. In Cincinnati, the number of Negro suicides is more than double that of whites; this may result in part from the amazing sexual disparity among Negro suicides: 358 women against 76 men." (Gabriel Deshaies, *Psychologie du suicide,* note 23.)

7. Hegel, *op. cit.,* p. 233.

The upheaval reached the Negroes from without. The black man was acted upon. Values that had not been created by his actions, values that had not been born of the systolic tide of his blood, danced in a hued whirl round him. The upheaval did not make a difference in the Negro. He went from one way of life to another, but not from one life to another. Just as when one tells a much improved patient that in a few days he will be discharged from the hospital, he thereupon suffers a relapse, so the announcement of the liberation of the black slaves produced psychoses and sudden deaths.

It is not an announcement that one hears twice in a lifetime. The black man contented himself with thanking the white man, and the most forceful proof of the fact is the impressive number of statues erected all over France and the colonies to show white France stroking the kinky hair of this nice Negro whose chains had just been broken.

"Say thank you to the nice man," the mother tells her little boy . . . but we know that often the little boy is dying to scream some other, more resounding expression. . . .

The white man, in the capacity of master,[8] said to the Negro, "From now on you are free."

But the Negro knows nothing of the cost of freedom, for he has not fought for it. From time to time he has fought for Liberty and Justice, but these were always white liberty and white justice; that is, values secreted by his masters. The former slave, who can find in his memory no trace of the struggle for liberty or of that anguish of liberty of which Kierkegaard speaks, sits unmoved before the young white man singing and dancing on the tightrope of existence.

When it does happen that the Negro looks fiercely at the white man, the white man tells him: "Brother, there is no difference between us." And yet the Negro *knows* that there is a difference. He *wants* it. He wants the white man to turn on him and shout: "Damn nigger." Then he would have that unique chance—to "show them. . . ."

But most often there is nothing—nothing but indifference, or a paternalistic curiosity.

The former slave needs a challenge to his humanity, he wants a conflict, a riot. But it is too late: The French Negro is doomed to bite himself and just to bite. I say "the French Negro," for the American

---

8. I hope I have shown that here the master differs basically from the master described by Hegel. For Hegel there is reciprocity; here the master laughs at the consciousness of the slave. What he wants from the slave is not recognition but work.

In the same way, the slave here is in no way identifiable with the slave who loses himself in the object and finds in his work the source of his liberation.

The Negro wants to be like the master.

Therefore he is less independent than the Hegelian slave.

In Hegel the slave turns away from the master and turns toward the object.

Here the slave turns toward the master and abandons the object.

Negro is cast in a different play. In the United States, the Negro battles and is battled. There are laws that, little by little are invalidated under the Constitution. There are other laws that forbid certain forms of discrimination. And we can be sure that nothing is going to be given free.

There is war, there are defeats, truces, victories.

"The twelve million black voices" [9] howled against the curtain of the sky. Torn from end to end, marked with the gashes of teeth biting into the belly of interdiction, the curtain fell like a burst balloon.

On the field of battle, its four corners marked by the scores of Negroes hanged by their testicles, a monument is slowly being built that promises to be majestic.

And, at the top of this monument, I can already see a white man and a black man *hand in hand*.

For the French Negro the situation is unbearable. Unable ever to be sure whether the white man considers him consciousness in-itself-for-itself, he must forever absorb himself in uncovering resistance, opposition, challenge.

This is what emerges from some of the passages of the book that Mounier has devoted to Africa.[10] The young Negroes whom he knew there sought to maintain their alterity. Alterity of rupture, of conflict, of battle.

The self takes its place by opposing itself, Fichte said. Yes and no.

I said in my introduction that man is a *yes*. I will never stop reiterating that.

Yes to life. *Yes* to love. *Yes* to generosity.

But man is also a *no*. *No* to scorn of man. *No* to degradation of man. *No* to exploitation of man. *No* to the butchery of what is most human in man: freedom.

Man's behavior is not only reactional. And there is always resentment in a *reaction*. Nietzsche had already pointed that out in *The Will to Power*.

To educate man to be *actional,* preserving in all his relations his respect for the basic values that constitute a human world, is the prime task of him who, having taken thought, prepares to act.

9. In English in the original. (Translator's note.)
10. Emmanuel Mounier, *L'éveil de l'Afrique noire* (Paris, Éditions du Seuil, 1948).

By Way of Conclusion

> The social revolution ... cannot draw its poetry from the past, but only from the future. It cannot begin with itself before it has stripped itself of all its superstitions concerning the past. Earlier revolutions relied on memories out of world history in order to drug themselves against their own content. In order to find their own content, the revolutions of the nineteenth century have to let the dead bury the dead. Before, the expression exceeded the content; now, the content exceeds the expression.
> —Karl Marx, *The Eighteenth Brumaire*

I can already see the faces of all those who will ask me to be precise on this or that point, to denounce this or that mode of conduct.

It is obvious—and I will never weary of repeating this—that the quest for disalienation by a doctor of medicine born in Guadeloupe can be understood only by recognizing motivations basically different from those of the Negro laborer building the port facilities in Abidjan. In the first case, the alienation is of an almost intellectual character.

Insofar as he conceives of European culture as a means of stripping himself of his race, he becomes alienated. In the second case, it is a question of a victim of a system based on the exploitation of a given race by another, on the contempt in which a given branch of humanity is held by a form of civilization that pretends to superiority.

I do not carry innocence to the point of believing that appeals to reason or to respect for human dignity can alter reality. For the Negro who works on a sugar plantation in Le Robert, there is only one solution: to fight. He will embark on this struggle, and he will pursue it, not as the result of a Marxist or idealistic analysis but quite simply because he cannot conceive of life otherwise than in the form of a battle against exploitation, misery, and hunger.

It would never occur to me to ask these Negroes to change their conception of history. I am convinced, however, that without even knowing it they share my views, accustomed as they are to speaking and thinking in terms of the present. The few working-class people whom I had the chance to know in Paris never took it on themselves to pose the problem of the discovery of a Negro past. They knew they were black, but, they told me, that made no difference in anything. In which they were absolutely right.

In this connection, I should like to say something that I have found

From Frantz Fanon, *Black Skin, White Masks* (New York: Grove Press, Inc., 1967), pp. 223–32.

in many other writers: Intellectual alienation is a creation of middle-class society. What I call middle-class society is any society that becomes rigidified in predetermined forms, forbidding all evolution, all gains, all progress, all discovery. I call middle-class a closed society in which life has no taste, in which the air is tainted, in which ideas and men are corrupt. And I think that a man who takes a stand against this death is in a sense a revolutionary.

The discovery of the existence of a Negro civilization in the fifteenth century confers no patent of humanity on me. Like it or not, the past can in no way guide me in the present moment.

The situation that I have examined, it is clear by now, is not a classic one. Scientific objectivity was barred to me, for the alienated, the neurotic, was my brother, my sister, my father. I have ceaselessly striven to show the Negro that in a sense he makes himself abnormal; to show the white man that he is at once the perpetrator and the victim of a delusion.

There are times when the black man is locked into his body. Now, "for a being who has acquired consciousness of himself and of his body, who has attained to the dialectic of subject and object, the body is no longer a cause of the structure of consciousness, it has become an object of consciousness." [11]

The Negro, however sincere, is the slave of the past. None the less I am a man, and in this sense the Peloponnesian War is as much mine as the invention of the compass. Face to face with the white man, the Negro has a past to legitimate, a vengeance to exact; face to face with the Negro, the contemporary white man feels the need to recall the times of cannibalism. A few years ago, the Lyon branch of the Union of Students From Overseas France asked me to reply to an article that made jazz music literally an irruption of cannibalism into the modern world. Knowing exactly what I was doing, I rejected the premises on which the request was based, and I suggested to the defender of European purity that he cure himself of a spasm that had nothing cultural in it. Some men want to fill the world with their presence. A German philosopher described this mechanism as *the pathology of freedom*. In the circumstances, I did not have to take up a position on behalf of Negro music against white music, but rather to help my brother to rid himself of an attitude in which there was nothing healthful.

The problem considered here is one of time. Those Negroes and white men will be disalienated who refuse to let themselves be sealed away in the materialized Tower of the Past. For many other Negroes, in other ways, disalienation will come into being through their refusal to accept the present as definitive.

11. Maurice Merleau-Ponty, *La Phénoménologie de la perception* (Paris, Gallimard, 1945), p. 277.

I am a man, and what I have to recapture is the whole past of the world. I am not responsible solely for the revolt in Santo Domingo.

Every time a man has contributed to the victory of the dignity of the spirit, every time a man has said no to an attempt to subjugate his fellows, I have felt solidarity with his act.

In no way should I derive my basic purpose from the past of the peoples of color.

In no way should I dedicate myself to the revival of an unjustly unrecognized Negro civilization. I will not make myself the man of any past. I do not want to exalt the past at the expense of my present and of my future.

It is not because the Indo-Chinese has discovered a culture of his own that he is in revolt. It is because "quite simply" it was, in more than one way, becoming impossible for him to breathe. When one remembers the stories with which, in 1938, old regular sergeants described the land of piastres and rickshaws, of cut-rate boys and women, one understands only too well the rage with which the men of the Viet-Minh go into battle.

An acquaintance with whom I served during the Second World War recently returned from Indo-China. He has enlightened me on many things. For instance, the serenity with which young Vietnamese of sixteen or seventeen faced firing squads. "On one occasion," he told me, "we had to shoot from a kneeling position: The soldiers' hands were shaking in the presence of those young 'fanatics.'" Summing up, he added: "The war that you and I were in was only a game compared to what is going on out there."

Seen from Europe, these things are beyond understanding. There are those who talk of a so-called Asiatic attitude toward death. But these basement philosophers cannot convince anyone. This Asiatic serenity, not so long ago, was a quality to be seen in the "bandits" of Vercors and the "terrorists" of the Resistance.

The Vietnamese who die before the firing squads are not hoping that their sacrifice will bring about the reappearance of a past. It is for the sake of the present and of the future that they are willing to die.

If the question of practical solidarity with a given past ever arose for me, it did so only to the extent to which I was committed to myself and to my neighbor to fight for all my life and with all my strength so that never again would a people on the earth be subjugated. It was not the black world that laid down my course of conduct. My black skin is not the wrapping of specific values. It is a long time since the starry sky that took away Kant's breath revealed the last of its secrets to us. And the moral law is not certain of itself.

As a man, I undertake to face the possibility of annihilation in order that two or three truths may cast their eternal brilliance over the world.

Sartre has shown that, in the line of an unauthentic position, the past "takes" in quantity, and, when solidly constructed, *informs* the individual. He is the past in a changed value. But, too, I can recapture my past, validate it, or condemn it through my successive choices.

The black man wants to be like the white man. For the black man there is only one destiny. And it is white. Long ago the black man admitted the unarguable superiority of the white man, and all his efforts are aimed at achieving a white existence.

Have I no other purpose on earth, then, but to avenge the Negro of the seventeenth century?

In this world, which is already trying to disappear, do I have to pose the problem of black truth?

Do I have to be limited to the justification of a facial conformation?

I as a man of color do not have the right to seek to know in what respect my race is superior or inferior to another race.

I as a man of color do not have the right to hope that in the white man there will be a crystallization of guilt toward the past of my race.

I as a man of color do not have the right to seek ways of stamping down the pride of my former master.

I have neither the right nor the duty to claim reparation for the domestication of my ancestors.

There is no Negro mission; there is no white burden.

I find myself suddenly in a world in which things do evil; a world in which I am summoned into battle; a world in which it is always a question of annihilation or triumph.

I find myself—I, a man—in a world where words wrap themselves in silence; in a world where the other endlessly hardens himself.

No, I do not have the right to go and cry out my hatred at the white man. I do not have the duty to murmur my gratitude to the white man.

My life is caught in the lasso of existence. My freedom turns me back on myself. No, I do not have the right to be a Negro.

I do not have the duty to be this or that. . . .

If the white man challenges my humanity, I will impose my whole weight as a man on his life and show him that I am not that "sho' good eatin' " that he persists in imagining.

I find myself suddenly in the world and I recognize that I have one right alone: That of demanding human behavior from the other.

One duty alone: That of not renouncing my freedom through my choices.

I have no wish to be the victim of the *Fraud* of a black world.

My life should not be devoted to drawing up the balance sheet of Negro values.

There is no white world, there is no white ethic, any more than there is a white intelligence.

There are in every part of the world men who search.

I am not a prisoner of history. I should not seek there for the meaning of my destiny.

I should constantly remind myself that the real *leap* consists in introducing invention into existence.

In the world through which I travel, I am endlessly creating myself.

I am a part of Being to the degree that I go beyond it.

And, through a private problem, we see the outline of the problem of Action. Placed in this world, in a situation, "embarked," as Pascal would have it, am I going to gather weapons?

Am I going to ask the contemporary white man to answer for the slave-ships of the seventeenth century?

Am I going to try by every possible means to cause Guilt to be born in minds?

Moral anguish in the face of the massiveness of the Past? I am a Negro, and tons of chains, storms of blows, rivers of expectoration flow down my shoulders.

But I do not have the right to allow myself to bog down. I do not have the right to allow the slightest fragment to remain in my existence. I do not have the right to allow myself to be mired in what the past has determined.

I am not the slave of the Slavery that dehumanized my ancestors.

To many colored intellectuals European culture has a quality of exteriority. What is more, in human relationships, the Negro may feel himself a stranger to the Western world. Not wanting to live the part of a poor relative, of an adopted son, of a bastard child, shall he feverishly seek to discover a Negro civilization?

Let us be clearly understood. I am convinced that it would be of the greatest interest to be able to have contact with a Negro literature or architecture of the third century before Christ. I should be very happy to know that a correspondence had flourished between some Negro philosopher and Plato. But I can absolutely not see how this fact would change anything in the lives of the eight-year-old children who labor in the cane fields of Martinique or Guadeloupe.

No attempt must be made to encase man, for it is his destiny to be set free.

The body of history does not determine a single one of my actions.

I am my own foundation.

And it is by going beyond the historical, instrumental hypothesis that I will initiate the cycle of my freedom.

The disaster of the man of color lies in the fact that he was enslaved.

The disaster and the inhumanity of the white man lie in the fact that somewhere he has killed man.

And even today they subsist, to organize this dehumanization rationally. But I as a man of color, to the extent that it becomes possible for me to exist absolutely, do not have the right to lock myself into a world of retroactive reparations.

I, the man of color, want only this:

That the tool never possess the man. That the enslavement of man by man cease forever. That is, of one by another. That it be possible for me to discover and to love man, wherever he may be.

The Negro is not. Any more than the white man.

Both must turn their backs on the inhuman voices which were those of their respective ancestors in order that authentic communication be possible. Before it can adopt a positive voice, freedom requires an effort at disalienation. At the beginning of his life a man is always clotted, he is drowned in contingency. The tragedy of the man is that he was once a child.

It is through the effort to recapture the self and to scrutinize the self, it is through the lasting tension of their freedom that men will be able to create the ideal conditions of existence for a human world.

Superiority? Inferiority?

Why not the quite simple attempt to touch the other, to feel the other, to explain the other to myself?

Was my freedom not given to me then in order to build the world of the *You?*

At the conclusion of this study, I want the world to recognize, with me, the open door of every consciousness.

My final prayer:

O my body, make of me always a man who questions!

Dictionary of Terms

ANAGOGIA. The elevation of the mind to the celestial level. The mystical interpretation of words, especially of the Bible, in order to add a new mystical sense. In psychoanalysis, the term refers to the interpretation of dreams and symptoms as well as to the psychic forces striving toward progressive ideals.

ANARCHISM. The theory that equality and justice are to be attained only through abolition of the state and the establishment of free agreements between territorial and functional groups. Limitations on the freedom of the personality, which are the inevitable results of capitalism and private property, would be removed. Decentralized groups, based on the principle of free association, would carry on necessary production. Rooted in a profound belief in human good, anarchism sees the state as an intrinsic evil.

ANARCHO-SYNDICALISM. In France and Russia, a revolutionary socialist movement that stressed individual freedom as opposed to control by politicians and the state. The French social philosopher Georges Sorel (1847–1922), in his description of the method for overthrowing the capitalist state, saw a general strike of the proletariat as the chief weapon. The term is derived from Sorel's willingness to use the trade unions as the tool of revolution.

ANTHROPOLOGY. The study of man. The word, which probably originated with Aristotle, now refers to a contemporary science consisting of archaeology, linguistics, and physical, cultural, philosophical, and theological anthropology. Cultural anthropology is the study of man and his works; like social anthropology, it is concerned with the systematic study of social forms and institutions. Philosophical anthropology deals with man's essence and his distinctive character in the universe. Theological anthropology is the study of man's nature, with emphasis on man's creation and the relationship of body to soul.

ANTI-CATHEXIS. See CATHEXIS

ANXIETY. Fear, which is clear and particular, is usually distinguished from anxiety, which is vague and diffuse. Anxiety is expressed psychologically in apprehension and unpleasant feelings, and physically in nervousness and agitation. The most important cause of anxiety is the ego's inability to deal with a rush of stimuli either from outside—as when a person is suddenly beset with unresolvable debts and pressures—or from within himself—as when he is overwhelmed by sudden sexual feelings that threaten to break through social restraints.

APOLLONIAN. A term used by Nietzsche and derived, along with its counterpart, Dionysian, from Greek mythology. Apollo was the god of prophecy and divination as well as of the arts, both practical—of domestic animals and of all healing—and expressive—of music, poetry, and dance. For Nietzsche, he symbolized our experience of nature as appearance and order, a world characterized by beauty, restraint, lucidity, and harmony. In opposition to Apollo was Dionysus, the Greek god of the vine, of fertility, and of joyous life. Although associated by the Greeks with Apollo as a god of poets and musicians, Dionysus presented a strongly dual nature: of death and resurrection, of freedom and brutality. For Nietzsche, he signified primal energy, ecstatic release, mystical union. In art, the Dionysian strain rises to intensity in music, dancing, and lyrical poetry while the Apollonian strain emerges most clearly in sculpture, painting, and epic poetry. In his earlier writings, Nietzsche placed Dionysian and Apollonian tendencies in opposition; later he fused them into a new Dionysian impulse. Man's ideal, in life as well as in art, is to achieve a perfect synthesis of Dionysian and Apollonian elements.

ASCETICISM. Severe simplicity of life through abstinence and self-denial. At its best, asceticism is a rigid self-disciplining of one's sensual appetites in order to reach a higher spiritual or intellectual state. The term "ascetic" may be used to describe both those who reach higher spiritual states and those who merely deny the life of the senses.

BOLSHEVIKS. See MENSHEVIKS

BOURGEOISIE. The French term for the social and economic class whose origins coincide historically with the growth and development of towns in Europe from the twelfth century to the French Revolution and the era of Napoleon. Composed of merchants, master craftsmen, tradesmen and a few wealthy bankers, the class flourished through its commitment to thrift, hard work, and rationality as well as the elaboration of money economies, plus increasingly free movement of goods and persons from city to city and region to region. Later, as the middle classes (the bourgeoisie on all levels) triumphed in the nineteenth century in England, on the Continent, and in the United States, its earlier revolutionary impulse as a class gave way to an emphasis on materialism, conformity, reluctance to change, repressive labor legislation, and intensive exploitation of non-Western peoples. The bourgeoisie as a concept is central to the development of Marxist-Leninist thought.

CATHEXIS. The concentration of psychic energy upon a specific object or the investment of feeling and significance in the object. The term is used with a variety of prefixes depending upon the nature of the object, such as ego-cathexis when the energy is concentrated on the conscious self, and object-cathexis when it is attached to an object outside of the individual. Anti-cathexis is the shift of the emotional energy from the impulse with which it is associated to an opposite impulse, as when unconscious hate appears as conscious love.

CONSERVATISM. A political temperament and outlook that desires to maintain the existing order. Opposing wide reform, conservatism tends to value the wisdom of the past. It is somewhat more pessimistic than liberalism, and believes less in the basic goodness of man; it is suspicious of utopian proposals, and hostile to centralization. Though staunchly concerned with individual liberty, its reluctance to upset the status quo often leads it to support the claims of the society over those of the individual. See also LIBERALISM

DEISM. The belief in a personal God as the creator of the world and the laws by which it runs, but a God who remains detached from his handiwork. A favorite image is God as clockmaker who, having once wound the clock, plays no further role. He is not instrumentally involved in nature, history, or individual religious experiences. English Deism, which began in the seventeenth and lasted almost through the eighteenth century, attempted to construct a natural religion based on reason and devoid of mysticism. See also METHODISM; PIETISM

DETERMINISM. In its most sweeping and inclusive form, it is the belief that all events, absolutely without exception, are determined both in the physical universe and in the psychical by previously existing causes whose interconnections we may either perceive and understand or never perceive and never understand. When used in a more restricted sense, the term may be applied to inanimate and animated nature exclusive of man, and allow to man the possibility of free, unconditioned choice. See also FREE WILL

DIALECTICAL MATERIALISM. The official philosophy of communism, dialectical materialism employs the Hegelian dialectic of opposites (see HEGELIANISM) and modifies it to Marxist materialism, which took the following form. Life is a ceaseless struggle, for all elements contain opposing forces within them. Movement, growth, development are all determined by the nature and weight of the opposing forces according to laws as natural as those applying to physical bodies in motion. These laws are not, however, predetermined in isolation from man. They are arrived at through experience, yet they differ from natural law as it is usually conceived. For within dialectical materialism, human consciousness does not exist merely to discover nature, but has an impact on nature and thus modifies it. It is the conscious "antithesis" to nature's "thesis." The net effect is to destroy the separation of man and nature, to unify man with nature, to obliterate the division between physical reality—the material world—and man's consciousness of it. The dialectic is rooted in human activity, in the practices of men, as their environment shapes their consciousness. It is this interaction that is the dialectic.

When the dialectic is applied to history or sociology, it is also called historical materialism. The basic assumption of historical materialism is that all aspects of human life reflect the economic structure of society because man is ultimately motivated by economic concerns. Class struggle occurs because the class in control of the means of production attempts to exploit the other classes. Progress is the change that arises from this dialectical struggle of one class against another, of that thesis and antithesis forming a new force or synthesis. The individual's role in dialectical materialism is largely inconsequential, for the forces are so large that only collective action can effect change. See also MATERIALISM

DIONYSIAN. See APOLLONIAN

DYNAMIC. Theories are said to be dynamic when they deal with processes of change instead of with the fixed, static patterns of things. They are hence radical theories, in the sense of trying to get at root causes. Historical theories and studies, insofar as they attempt to perceive the evolutionary genesis of things, are also dynamic. Marx and Freud, different though they are in their methods and conclusions, may both be classed as dynamic theorists whereas traditional Christian thinkers may not.

DYNAMIC-CULTURALISM. A school of psychoanalysis, also called (by Marcuse and others) the "cultural school," to which Harry Stack Sullivan, Karen Horney, and Erich Fromm belong. Essentially neo- or post-Freudian in perspective, the dynamic-culturalists tend to reject Freud's libidinal theories, to stress cultural factors in the origin of neuroses, to emphasize interpersonal relations, and in general to be more affirmative than Freud about man's nature and possibilities.

EGO-CATHEXIS. See CATHEXIS

EMPIRICISM. A school of philosophy which has as a major premise the assumption that the ultimate source of knowledge is sensation, that knowledge independent of sensory data is impossible. Empiricism denies universal and absolute truths and is therefore opposed to Kantian theories of knowledge which hold that man has innate ideas and inborn knowledge, and that the mind has the power to shape reality. See also TRANSCENDENTALISM

EPISTEMOLOGY. The branch of philosophy concerned with the theory of knowledge, its nature, limits, methods, and the problem of assessing its validity. Epistemological questions— "How does one know?" "What can one know?" "What is worth knowing?" —and the answers to these questions give rise to the various schools of philosophy. See EMPIRICISM; IDEALISM; INSTRUMENTALISM

ESCHATOLOGY. The branch of theology which deals with final things—death, resurrection, the judgment, the immortality of the soul, the Second Coming of Christ. Early Christian eschatology stressed the imminence of the Second Coming and the Day of Judgment.

FALL. The Fall is the original alienation—man's alienation from God. In the Creation Myth, God created Adam, in Milton's words, "free to fall, but sufficient to stand" —that is, with the freedom to obey or not to obey, to love him or not. In obeying and loving God, Adam existed in a state of grace. To demonstrate his freedom and test his obedience, however, he was forbidden to eat from the Tree of Knowledge. But he did eat freely of the forbidden fruit of the Tree of Knowledge, and by knowing the nature of good and evil, the major and immediate manifestation of which in legend was carnal desire, he lusted after Eve and knew her in an animal way. As punishment for his "fall" from grace, he was stripped of his immortality and forced to leave the Garden of Eden and God's presence. The effect on his spirit was to create a disharmony, and on the universe to create disorder and cruel chaos. Nature lost her benevolence and man's reason was depraved. Instead of being ruled by love and reason, his baser emotions were permitted to gain sway over him. See also ORIGINAL SIN

FASCISM. The form of government which has appeared as a reaction to democratic and socialist egalitarianism. Fascism proposes no unified ideology, but it reveals a strong ideological preference for the corporate entity—the family, church, state—and for subordinating individual to corporate demands. Its world view is organic, tending to see individuals as part of a larger whole and performing specific functions necessary to preserve the whole. Just as the body needs limbs, liver, and brain, so a society needs plumbers, priests, and leaders, and it is the task of the leader to see that the needs of the state are provided for, even if it is at the expense of the individual. The following characteristics also appear consistently: use of law-and-order rhetoric to appeal to fear and insecurity; appeals to religious morality and national pride and prejudice; glorification of powerful leaders and suppression of intellectual dissent. The most recent examples of fascist states have been Hitler's Germany, Franco's Spain, and Italy under Mussolini.

FREE WILL. The power *to will* or *to choose,* without restraint from physical limitations or divine necessity; the ability to choose between alternative actions in such a way that choice and action are to some extent creatively determined. Free will is a major tenet both of Christianity and of existentialism.

GRACE. In Christian theology, man's salvation through Christ, given freely to sinful men who are without the ability or even the will to save themselves. It is God's way of allowing man to achieve more than man's helpless condition would otherwise allow. Paul, who was the first to stress the concept of grace, pointed out that it is because of man's sinfulness that he requires God's grace. Paul's view later became a universal Christian doctrine. Catholics believe in the sacraments as the channel for the bestowing of grace, while Protestants generally believe that personal faith is the only precondition for receiving God's grace.

HEGELIANISM. Georg Wilhelm Friedrich Hegel (1770–1831) was a German philosopher who attempted to achieve a unified philosophy by means of an absolute idealism (see IDEALISM), which would reconcile the opposition of the material (what is) and the ideal (what ought to be) into a higher, universal world-soul. All knowledge presupposes knowledge of the universal and begins with the universal world-soul. The entire process is dialectical, with a "thesis" (force) generating an "antithesis" (counterforce); the interaction of opposing forces creates a new force of "synthesis," which itself becomes a new thesis. The major dialectic occurs between "being" and "not being" (a thing is one thing, but it is also not its opposite), which generate a synthesis that results in "becoming." The basic realities are thus not things but the activity, process, or logic underlying their development; moreover, these realities are not above and beyond the material world but exist in and through it. As a result of this developmental process, knowledge advances.

Thus, for example, the conflict between external rightness (that which is accepted by society) and internal morality (one's conscience) results in a higher synthesis for Hegel: the State or the sum total of ethical life. The State is not a means by which the individual may pursue his private goals; it is the highest goal, the ultimate source of self-realization, and hence of freedom. The State is thus absolute totality above all individuals; it is itself a process having an organic nature and its own individuality. The highest level of development which the State can attain for the preservation of its unity is monarchy. War is a necessity, for it preserves the unique identity of the State. This absolutist, monarchist concept of the State offended Marx and the leftist Hegelians. Marx, however, acknowledged his debt to Hegel, though he modified him not only with respect to the nature of estrangement or alienation. Hegel was the first philosopher to elaborate on this concept. For the Marxian variant, see DIALECTICAL MATERIALISM and also Marx's essay "Alienated Labor" (pp. 279–89). See also DYNAMIC; IDEALISM; TRANSCENDENTALISM

HISTORICAL MATERIALISM. See MATERIALISM, DIALECTIC

IDEALISM. As opposed to materialism and positivism, which take as a starting point the physical world as perceived through the senses, idealism emphasizes the role of ideas and reason, and stresses the shaping power of the mind in creating reality. While Plato argued for a world of eternal ideas existing outside the mind, modern idealists have tended to attribute the origin of ideas to man's consciousness. Idealism gained major impetus in Kant who asserted a separation between the phenomenal world as conceived by the mind and the external world of independently existing things-in-themselves. He conceived of the mind as possessing a shaping power that makes it impossible for the mind to know, as it *really* is, any thing in the external world of things-in-themselves. The post-Kantians, Fichte, Schelling, and Hegel, denied the existence of any such real, unknowable, independently existing thing in-itself; for them, all reality was the creation of mind or spirit. Only mind and mental states exist. Hegel's idealism led to the belief that the material world is an expression of a higher universal world-soul. See HEGELIANISM; see also SUBJECTIVISM; SOLIPSISM; TRANSCENDENTALISM

IDEOLOGY. "A systematic set of arguments and beliefs used to justify an existing or desired social order. . . . Karl Marx popularized the term by applying it to the thought of the ruling class in society. In doing this he followed the principle laid down by de Tracy that all thought is based on sense perception [see EMPIRICISM; MATERIALISM]. However, Marx was concerned to show that this thought consisted of arguments and justifications used by the ruling class to defend the existing social system. [German idealism of the Hegelian absolutist monarchist kind seemed especially culpable to Marx.] From this it was but a short step to use the term to denote any partisan body of argument for an existing or desired social system." (Joseph Dunner, *Dictionary of Political Science* [New York. Philosophical Library, 1964], p. 251.)

INCARNATION. The Christian doctrine that Christ was at once fully God and fully man (without impairing the integrity or nature of either) rather than a temporary appearance of God in human form. The incarnation demonstrates the goodness of God who, for man's sake, was made flesh and suffered its infirmities. Christ's position as a mediator and man's dual nature—body bound to the earth, and his soul, a godlike spirit, destined for eternity—emphasize both the human nature of Christ's suffering and the spirituality available even within man's flesh.

INQUISITION. The organized pursuit of heresy and punishment of heretics by the joint action of church and state. The general tribunal for suppression of heresy (Holy Office) was developed under Popes Innocent III (1198–1216) and Gregory IX (1227–1241). Its aspirations were chiefly confined to Spain, Portugal, their dependencies, and Italy. The Holy Inquisition differed from the Spanish Inquisition, which was put under state control in 1480, and conducted its proceedings through the sixteenth century with great severity, especially while led by Torquemada. The Inquisition was abolished in France in 1772 and in Spain in 1834, but the Holy Office still exists.

INSTRUMENTALISM. The philosophical perspective developed by John Dewey (1859–1952) which holds that all forms of human activity are instruments that man has developed to resolve the unavoidable difficulties that surround him. Dewey went beyond pragmatism (see PRAGMATISM) in questioning the very nature of the relationship between ideas and facts. He held that we cannot understand the practical consequences of our ideas until we define our purpose, which, for him, is the desire to resolve our continual doubts and uncertainties. But ordered inquiry, by which doubt and uncertainty are resolved, is only possible by translating portions of our difficulty and distress into problems to which alternate solutions are possible. Brute facts thus necessarily impose limitations upon any problem, but facts are only one part of any problem, of which ideas are the other part. Facts and ideas interact and can never be perceived except as interacting; they are both essential ingredients in our defining any problem. The correctness of a proposed solution, however, is not subjective; a solution chosen to resolve a difficulty is "right," not insofar as it pleases us but insofar as it succeeds in removing that difficulty. Instrumentalism, unlike pragmatism or utilitarianism, is not concerned with subjective happiness as a criterion of truth. Like them, however, it denies any eternal reality. Ideas, in order to be useful, must change—on an evolutionary scale—as man encounters novel difficulties, tensions, doubts, and uncertainties. See the introduction to Marxism (fn. 2, p. 228) for additional remarks. See also UTILITARIANISM

IRRATIONALISM. "The doctrine that thought and behavior, both moral and political, neither are nor should be governed by rational considerations. Reliance is placed upon emotional and intuitive processes for the appraisal of values, and the possibility of a harmony of interests is denied. The sources of irrationalist political theory include the works of . . . Nietzsche . . . Freud" (Joseph Dunner, *Dictionary of Political Science* [New York. Philosophical Library, 1964], p. 270.)

KERYGMA. Preaching, especially proclaiming the gospel.

LIBERALISM. A political temperament and outlook whose primary beliefs focus on the value of progress and on the essential goodness of man. Liberalism emphasizes the rights of the individual and his welfare over that of the state; yet, in its efforts to promote individual welfare, liberalism of necessity promotes the power of the state over the individual. It advocates steady change, but prefers moderate evolutionary change to root changes or revolution. See also CONSERVATISM

MATERIALISM. The proposition that all phenomena—reality—can be explained in terms of physical matter. Unlike dualism, which accepts the existence of both mind and matter, materialism denies the existence of one half of the duality—mind or spirit. Thought becomes a complicated physical event, ultimately traceable to body chemistry; mental processes are determined by physical processes. Materialism is a respected theory dating from two Greek philosophers, Leucippus and Democritus, of the fifth century B.C. In our own time, materialism gained impetus as a reaction against post-Kantian idealism. It is a recurrent philosophy, especially attractive to scientific, technologically-oriented societies; but there are arguments against it, namely, the Kantian (see TRANSCENDENTALISM) that the mind's structure limits and conditions necessarily and universally the kinds of experience we have of matter. In the social realm, Marxists insist that every man's mental life is shaped by the nature of the physical means of production—their ownership as well as the distribution of their goods—which create his environment. They also admit the possibility that ideas characteristic of a given social class (or even those of an exceptional individual such as Marx) can influence the restructuring of a society's economic base and thereby lead to the reshaping of the mental life of future generations. See also DIALECTICAL MATERIALISM; DETERMINISM

MENSHEVIKS. A segment of the early Marxist party in Russia which favored caution in tactics and cooperation with all of the revolutionary elements in society. Though the majority party in numbers, the Mensheviks lost control of the party in 1903 to the Bolshevik faction, which was better organized and more single-minded in its aims. Gradually, however, the Mensheviks regained control of the party, and, after the February Revolution in 1917, they helped set up a provisional government under Alexander Kerensky. Russia's economic collapse because of her disastrous but dwindling participation in World War I and the Mensheviks' commitment to coalition politics, gave Lenin a chance to lead the Bolsheviks in a second revolution in October of 1917. Ousting the Kerensky government, Lenin placed the Bolsheviks, from whom the present regime in the U.S.S.R. has evolved, firmly in power. Unlike the Mensheviks, they believed strongly in withdrawal from the First World War and in the complete destruction of the old economic and social structures, both to be achieved by whatever force and violence seemed necessary to the party leadership. See Djilas (pp. 370–72).

METHODISM. A major branch of Protestantism, which began well after the other early major Protestant faiths had emerged during the period of the Reformation and Counter-Reformation. Founded in England by John Wesley in 1726, Methodism emphasized repentance, faith, sanctification, and free, full salvation for everyone. Its name derived from the stress placed on methodical devotion, regularity of pious conduct, and frequency of prayer. Along with Pietism it was a reaction against rational religion. See Weber (pp. 180–81).

OBJECT-CATHEXIS. See CATHEXIS

OEDIPUS COMPLEX. A child's attraction toward the parent of the opposite sex, which is often complicated by hostility toward the parent of his (or her) own sex. Freud considered it to be central to the workings of the unconscious, and the nucleus of all human relationships. For a full explication, see Herma (pp. 422–24).

ONTOLOGY. That division of philosophic inquiry which is concerned with the nature of being or existence.

OPPORTUNISM. The practice of taking advantage of situations and opportunities for immediate gain, usually with little concern for ethical standards or long-range consequences. It is a favorite epithet of communists for any Marxist revisionist who stresses non-violent, evolutionary change or shows pronounced democratic tendencies.

ORIGINAL SIN. The sin inherited by every individual at conception because of Adam's sin in asserting his will over God's. The doctrine was not explicitly formulated in the gospels, but found expression in Paul. In modern Christian doctrine this belief that man lost immortality and grace is usually balanced with the belief in Christ as the means of salvation. Apart from Christian doctrine, the concept of original sin has come to symbolize the origin of all human suffering and evil. See also FALL

PAROUSIA. A coming or advent; specifically the Second Coming of Christ.

Dictionary of Terms 887

PIETISM. A sixteenth-century religious movement beginning in Germany in reaction to formalism and intellectuality. Pietism stressed the individual's direct relationship to God, inward spiritual perfection, moral earnestness, other-worldliness, and personal religious experience rather than dogma. God's being and will is revealed to the believer in his reading of the Bible, without elaborate mediation. Pietism has exerted a great influence on American Protestantism. See footnote on Tillich (p. 742); see also METHODISM.

POSITIVISM. Two distinct and unrelated strands of philosophic inquiry bear this label. The first—which was predominant in nineteenth-century France in the philosophical writings of Auguste Comte (1798–1857) and in England a little later in the polemics of T. H. Huxley (1825–1895) as well as in the systematic writings of Herbert Spencer (1820–1903) —attempted to describe the laws and stages in the *evolution* of mankind's social relationships and scientific achievements. The second—which appeared in England before World War I in the work of Bertrand Russell and A. N. Whitehead as well as later in Europe (Vienna, Berlin) in the 1920's—focused on the *nature of language*, namely on the language of science, including mathematics, as well as the language of law, morality, and ordinary conversation. This second and new kind of positivism was distinguished from the earlier by the various terms, "logical positivism," "logical empiricism," "scientific empiricism." Its goal was clarity, an ideal expressed by Russell's remark that it is better to be clearly wrong than vaguely right. Logical positivism undertook the task of separating out of language those propositions that may at some point be verified as either true or false and of distinguishing them from those propositions whose terms or syntax, on the other hand, reveal them upon analysis to be meaningless, or "nonsense." On the side of the sciences, the model was mathematics, whose terms and propositions themselves were subjected to logical analysis. In the realm of value judgments, a distinction was drawn between *cognitive* meaning, or that part of value judgments which consists of verifiable propositions, and *emotive* meaning, which is the element in value judgments expressive of the feelings and attitudes of whoever expresses the judgment. (See Wilson, pp. 149–167)

Because the emphasis of modern positivism has been on form rather than on substance, it may, unintentionally or even in opposition to its own purposes, "have contributed to a 'myth of methodology': that it does not much matter what we do if only we do it right." (Abraham Kaplan, "Positivism," *International Encyclopedia of the Social Sciences,* ed. David L. Sills [New York: Macmillan & Free Press, 1968] 12:394.)

PRAGMATISM. A term first coined by C. S. Pierce in 1878 but made self-conscious and systematic by William James (1842–1910) to describe a traditional philosophical point of view that truth which claims to be independent of experience does not exist, that the truth of an idea depends on empirical observation and scientific experiment, on the "consequences" that that idea leads to. Pragmatism (James came to prefer the term "radical empiricism") insists that the function of thought is to guide action; it denies the traditional antithesis between theory and practice so beloved by "commonsense" amateur philosophers. Pragmatism attempts to distinguish the true from the false, the meaningful from the meaningless, faith from knowledge. It requires that all claims to truth be tested and valued or devalued according to the nature of their consequences. It thus opposes separations of truth from action, of pure science from applied science. Its clearest formulation is the phrase, "meaning depends on application." A notion that has no application is thus meaningless; similarly, two different notions that have the same application are said not to differ meaningfully. In the sense described above, Marx, in his analysis of society, is pragmatic, as is Nietzsche in his analysis of morals. See also INSTRUMENTALISM; UTILITARIANISM

PROLETARIAT. The lower or laboring class, the wage-earners with little or no property; Marx's revolutionary class. For a more complete definition see the first footnote of *The Communist Manifesto* (p. 241).

QUIETISM. A mystic school of thought that places prime and unique value on the individual's striving for inner peace and quiet. It was used to describe the post-Reformation sects of the seventeenth and eighteenth centuries. In reality, medieval mystics, who devoted their lives entirely to the contemplative life, were probably even more quietistic. Quietism was first propounded as such by St. Teresa and especially by Miguel de Molinos (1640–1697), a seventeenth-century priest condemned and imprisoned by the Holy Inquisition. He taught that spiritual perfection and peace are reached only by self-annihilation and openness to God through passive, absorbed, loving contemplation. The term is used to describe any belief that peace is the highest good and attainable only through destruction of the self, passive acceptance and surrender, pure love, withdrawal from the world, and divine transcendence. In psychological terms, it is the tendency to blunt all earthly feelings of desire in order to avoid pain; in politics, the tendency to endure injustice passively and patiently.

RATIONALISM. The belief that human reason, unaided, is sufficient to achieve objective truth. In its eighteenth-century form, it arrayed itself against religious dogma and held that all truth of society and science could be discovered by the human mind alone. Central to pure rationalism is a belief that reason as a source of absolutely certain knowledge is superior to sense perception, but the term is now used more loosely to indicate a sharply reasoned criticism of religious beliefs. Rationalism is a very old way of systematic thought which began in the Western world with the criticism of Greek mythology by the Ionian philosophers. It had a resurgence under the medieval scholastics (see SCHOLASTICISM), and again with the publication in 1637 of the *Discourse on Method* by René Descartes (1596–1650). By the exercise of his reason, Descartes sought to rid himself of all doubt by finding a single undoubtable premise, which proved to be the statement, "I think, therefore I am." He then proceeded to draw out the logical and unchallengeable consequences of that premise in order to construct a true and certain method of rational inquiry. In recent years, the term has taken on a pejorative turn suggesting something stale and scholastic.

REACTIONISM. Hostility to, or the attempt to bar, political progress.

REFORMATION. The movement that began in 1517 as a "reform" movement within the universal (Catholic) Christian church and resulted in the formation of Protestant sects. The impetus was Luther's rediscovery of the Pauline doctrine of justification by faith rather than by works of the law. Other points of controversy resulted from the denial of the doctrine of transubstantiation (that the bread and wine were transformed in the Eucharist into the actual flesh and blood of Christ), and from the refusal to venerate the Virgin and the saints, and to practice clerical celibacy. Also see headnote to Calvin (p. 137).

RESSENTIMENT. ". . . a sensitive yet powerful form of resentment coupled with a desire for revenge which—unable to find a chance for discharge—effects a subtle transformation of outlook among those who . . . experience it. Nietzsche claimed that Christian love is an inverted, transformed type of 'ressentiment' experienced by Jews and Gentiles after their conversion to Christ." (Joseph Dunner, *Dictionary of Political Science* [New York, Philosophical Library, 1964], p. 455.)

REVISIONISM. A term, generally derogatory, used to describe the philosophy of certain Marxist socialists who wish to modify Marxist socialism by stressing evolutionary rather than revolutionary aspects. See OPPORTUNISM

SCHOLASTICISM. A medieval school of thought that attempted to wed philosophy and theology. The term "scholastic" now has disparaging overtones, suggesting formal, pedantic, over-refined logical methods unrelated to factual evidence. See headnote to Aquinas (p. 127).

SCIENTISM. The methods, doctrines, and mental attitudes embraced by science. The term is usually used pejoratively.

SOLIPSISM. A form of extreme subjectivism; the belief that the self knows and can know only its own states and modifications—the self is the only existent thing.

SUBJECTIVISM. The theory that the individual consciousness is the final judge of good and evil, truth and untruth, and is the only real source of knowledge and experience. It is the cornerstone of existentialism and the arch-enemy of materialism, whether Marxian or not.

SUBLIMATION. Modification of an instinctual impulse in order to find gratification in ways that are acceptable to the individual and to society. It is not a case of the impulse being repressed, for the impulse is not denied but rechanneled by the ego into realistic satisfactions, for example, when aggression is used creatively and constructively in social reform.

TELEOLOGY. The study of design in the universe, of ultimate purposes or final causes. Everything, whether conscious or unconscious, is assumed to be striving toward its own appropriate end or state of fulfillment. All things in the universe, therefore, are guided to ultimate goals by which their values and meanings may be discovered. Both Christianity and Marxism are strongly teleological.

THEOCRACY. Rule of the state by the representatives of God—presbyters or priests.

THEODICY. The justification of God's purpose in permitting natural and moral evil to exist. Leibnitz originated the term in his attempt to prove that evil is necessary to the existence of the greatest moral good.

TOPOGRAPHY. The landscape of an object, consisting of its physical or natural features and their structural relationships. Freud's topography of the mind consists of the conscious, the unconscious, and the preconscious.

TRANSCENDENTALISM. A philosophical term used originally by Immanuel Kant (1724–1804) as "transcendental idealism" to describe the unique aspects of his philosophy, namely, that our individual minds possess, *prior* to all experience, certain forms which condition and limit our experience necessarily and universally. Foremost among our a priori ideas are those of space and time, which are not derived from our experience of things in space and time but permit us to experience things spatially and temporally. German philosophers who elaborated parts of Kant's philosophy abandoned his careful definitions about the structure of the mind and equated "transcendentalism" with the effort to demonstrate the reality of truths existing beyond nature and mind. In New England during the mid-nineteenth century, the term, as used by Ralph Waldo Emerson (1803–1822) and his circle, took on added political, social, and psychological overtones. It signified "a vague yet exalting conception of the godlike nature of the human spirit and an insistence on the authority of individual conscience; . . . nature conceived not as a vast machine demanding impersonal manipulation but as an organism, a symbol and analogue of mind, and a moral educator for the poet who can read her hieroglyphics; a sophisticated understanding of the uses of history in self-culture . . ." (Michael Moran, "New England Transcendentalism," in *The Encyclopedia of Philosophy,* ed. Paul Edwards [New York: Macmillan & Free Press, 1967] 5:480.)

TRANSFERENCE. In psychoanalytic therapy, the projection of feelings, thoughts, or wishes from the past onto the analyst, who has come to represent a figure from the past, such as a parent or a lover. Although the patient may display affection or aggression that is unwarranted by his present situation, it is this reenactment that allows him to understand the important events in his past which have shaped him. See Freud (pp. 431–33), Fromm (pp. 571–72).

UTILITARIANISM. The term, invented by Jeremy Bentham (1748–1832) under the label "The Principle of Utility," and elaborated by John Stuart Mill (1806–1873), has no very clear and distinct meaning. From a psychological and social point of view, the term is concerned with the happiness of the individual person, with maximizing the sum of his pleasures over that of his pains. The crux of morality is how the individual, as free as possible from externally imposed restraints, judges the pleasures and pains he sustains in his own acts and in the acts of others. The outcomes of any person's actions are thus morally good only insofar as they give him more pleasure than pain, provided that he refrain from inflicting pain on others. By the same token, he is not required to provide pleasure to others. Each person has responsibility for seeking his own pleasure within these broad limits. Mill, unlike Bentham, attempted to add a qualitative dimension to the quantitative balancing of pleasures over pains by introducing as a preferred standard the pleasure/pain judgments of a wise and experienced man.

All traditional moral precepts, such as the Ten Commandments, are defensible only to the degree that the past experience of mankind shows their observance, as distinguished from their violation, to produce a preponderance of pleasure over pain. The assumption is that men, because they are rational, will cooperate where possible and restrain themselves where necessary, all for the sake of their own well-being. In the utilitarian view not all of our customs and institutions have been built upon utilitarian considerations. Mill's and Bentham's claim is that they should be so rebuilt. "Ultimately, it is hard to see that Mill said more than that happiness is the life most worth living in the judgment of the wise and that we should have as our aim the provision of such a life for as many people as possible, which is as unrevealing as it is unexceptionable." (J. O. Urmson, "Utilitarianism: The Philosophy," in *International Encyclopedia of the Social Sciences,* ed. David L. Sills [New York: Macmillan & Free Press, 1968] 16:225.) See PRAGMATISM; see also ANARCHY

WELTANSCHAUUNG. A term elaborated by the German sociologist Karl Mannheim (1893–1947) shortly after the first World War. Mannheim's thesis is that every individual, class, society, and historical period has its own distinctive outlook on the world and itself in relation to what it understands of past, present, and future. The specific *Weltanschauung* or world outlook of any given intellectual work is thus a flowing together from many streams. In confronting any product of the human mind, one immediately enters into the realm of comparing, contrasting, and relating individual works to seek not only the resemblances and contrasts among them but also their historical, sociological, and psychological origins. A careful inventory and analysis of the "what" and "where" of a man's works help to build the basis for determining the range and complexity of modes of thought as well as the distinctive styles within each.

Glossary of Rhetorical Devices

ANALOGY. See ARGUMENT BY ANALOGY

APPEAL. See EMOTIONAL APPEAL AND PSYCHOLOGICAL ARGUMENT

ARGUMENT AND DEFINITION, CIRCULAR. A definition or argument that gains its point by preempting that point. That is, what is reached as a conclusion is no more than was first assumed in the premises of the definition or argument as starting points. The circle of reasoning, which may vary in diameter, consists of stringing together several statements to achieve a tautology. (What is being objected to is verbiage that is needlessly or confusingly repetitious: at the level of the phrase this kind of excess is usually called *redundancy;* at the level of statement, *tautology* [see TAUTOLOGIGAL STATEMENT]; and at the level of argument, *circularity*). One of the most famous examples of circularity is the ontological argument for the existence of God, which contends that "the factual existence of God is necessarily involved in the existence of the very idea of God," for the very idea of God presupposes existence as one of his characteristics, while his existence would inevitably lead to knowledge of it. This kind of argument also exists in many scientific fields: "If it exists, it is factually demonstrable, for all that exists is verifiable." Such arguments hope to gain their conclusion ("God exists," "all existent phenomena are observable") by asking us to grant what is to be proved in the premise ("if it exists, it is . . ."). In the ontological argument, the premise is an enthymeme, or suppressed premise, and may be recast in various forms, for example: "If the idea of God exists, he exists, for ideas are derived from experience, hence the idea of a thing presupposes the existence of a thing to be experienced." A premise, of course, is not a fact, merely an unsupported assertion. It need not and should not go unchallenged. Premises may be true or they may be false, but arguments that are completely dependent on granting an unestablished premise can scarcely command rational acceptance, though they may conceivably justify allegiance on other grounds. See also DEFINITION

ARGUMENT BY ANALOGY. To argue by analogy is to bring together two subjects that are not ordinarily thought of as similar, and to indicate in some point-by-point comparison how relationships that obtain within each are the same. An analogy, if it is to be persuasive and more than a metaphor or simile, must itemize structural features in one subject, which is usually complex, diffuse, and extensive, and assert that they truly resemble structures in another subject, one which is comparatively more simple, compact, and intensive. For example, a contemporary Japanese scholar, Wataru Hiraizumi, in summarizing what has happened to the culture of his country since 1868 when it turned to the West for science and technology, has gone beyond simple metaphor. "Japanese culture and tradition were deposited in the bank in 1868 and we have been continuously withdrawing from this account without making any new deposits."

The form of an analogy is usually reducible to one or more proportions, that is, "A is to B as C is to D" in which A and C are aspects of one subject, usually the more vast and intricate, and B and D aspects of another. Here, for example, the common ground that the two subjects share is "capital," cultural on the one hand and financial on the other. One is tempted, after recovering from the vividness of the analogy, to ask: What would a new cultural "deposit" consist of? How are culture and tradition "spent"? What kind of "interest" could or did accrue? And what was the nature of Japanese culture and tradition before 1868 that it could be treated as a "lump sum" by a whole nation?

The degree of persuasiveness of an analogy varies not only with differences between the understanding of one individual and those of another but also with differences between the perspectives of one culture and those of another. How ancient analogy is as an intellectual habit can be seen in folk sayings or proverbs. In Japan, at least until recently, the analogy implied in the following proverb was meaningful: "The nail that sticks up will be hammered down." That is to say, the individual who does not know and hold his appointed place in society will be forcibly driven back into his slot. In spirit this proverb is quite the opposite of one from another culture: "The squeaky wheel gets the grease." That is, the more an individual complains, the greater the effort to stop the complaint, not by force but by providing (often without regard for anything but the noisy protester) the satisfactions demanded. The folk wisdom of any proverb—and the same culture can produce contradictory sayings—is valid only within the tradition that creates and continues to reinforce the analogy that the proverb implies.

The appropriateness of the analogy is thus determined by the relevance and persuasiveness of the similarities proposed. A very common form of argument, it is nevertheless without weight in proving the argument. Analogies provide illustrations, provide probable lessons, even provide interpretation, but they do not provide proof. Their value in furthering argument lies in revealing possible relationships, principles, and directions, the weight of which must be left to interpretation by the individual. "If a plant cannot live according to its nature, it dies; and so a man." (56 J. S. Mill). The title of Marcuse's essay, "A Biological Foundation for Socialism?" entices with its ambiguity. Will Marcuse propose an argument by analogy, or will he describe in fact a biological base for socialism? The two sentences that conclude the piece not only extend biological metaphors to the pathogenic but also insert terms from the realms of space and weather: "The new sensibility has become a political force. It crosses the frontier between the capitalist and communist orbit; it is contagious because the atmosphere, the climate of the established societies, carries the virus" (832/26–29).

Glossary of Rhetorical Devices 895

The greatest value, however, lies not in furthering the argument but in creating suggestive, emotional ambiances favorable to one's argument. Thus Engels, who constantly seeks to suggest the scientific nature of communism and its discovery of natural law, makes the following analogy in *Socialism: Utopian and Scientific* (298/17–29):

> "The law that always equilibrates the relative surplus population, or industrial reserve army, to the extent and energy of accumulation, this law rivets the labourer to capital more firmly than the wedges of Vulcan did Prometheus to the rock. It establishes an accumulation of misery, corresponding with accumulation of capital. . . ." And to expect any other division of the products from the capitalistic mode of production is the same as expecting the electrodes of a battery not to decompose acidulated water, not to liberate oxygen at the positive, hydrogen at the negative pole, so long as they are connected with the battery.

For a more extended discussion see Patterns following the introduction to Marxism (pp. 236–38).

ARGUMENT, PSYCHOLOGICAL. See EMOTIONAL APPEAL AND PSYCHOLOGICAL ARGUMENT

ASSERTION, UNSUPPORTED. Not properly a fallacy, an unsupported assertion is merely a statement devoid of claims upon our allegiance, for, while ostensibly true, it provides us with no supporting evidence or argument. "There is no trace of utopianism in Marx in the sense that he invented or imagined a 'new society'" (Lenin). "The goal of life is death" (Freud). "God has no favorites" (Paul). "The crowd is untruth" (Kierkegaard). The failure to provide support has no bearing on the truth or falsity of the assertion, but only on its power to win our acceptance. It is wise to refuse to accept an assertion until evidence or argument is brought forth in support of it. This attitude is fundamental to critical thought and should be cultivated early. For a more extensive discussion, see Patterns following Niebuhr (pp. 203–4).

ASSUMPTION OF INFALLIBILITY. See ASSUMPTION, UNWARRANTED (9)

ASSUMPTION, UNWARRANTED. The tendency to assume a thing to be true or a relationship to be natural and inevitable when there is no warranty for such an assumption; the tendency to abstract particulars until they become general formulas; the overextension of one's argument from limited evidence. Generally unwarranted assumptions involve one or more of the following inaccuracies. (1) *Faulty generalization:* a generalization that contains either an implied tautology, or a buried assumption or definition not susceptible to rational debate: "All men are sinful"; "Fortune rules our destiny"; "There is no achievement without breaking down resistance. Every new deed of mankind signifies the conquest of a previous one. . . . Force determines the way of life. Right exists only when it is created and protected by power and force" (57 Hitler). (2) *Unsubstantiated causality* (see POST HOC, PROPTER ERGO HOC): the act of assuming that two related actions have a causal connection. (3) *Faulty analogy* (see ARGUMENT BY ANALOGY): the tendency to assert resemblances and similarities that are questionable or may not exist. (4) *Stereotyping:* the act of holding that what is true for a group in general is therefore true for all the individuals comprising the group. Both the initial generalization and the application may be faulty, as when one shows surprise at an unrhythmic person of black skin because "blacks have rhythm." Generalizations abstract qualities from a group; stereotypes compress a particular into an abstract mold. (5) *Reification:* the act of objectifying an abstraction, of transforming a universal into a discrete entity; it is the assumption that spiritual states or concepts have physical embodiments. At a simple level, a halo is the reification of sainthood, while sainthood is the reification of spirituality. The statement "God is love" involves a high-level reification of love. Many arguments based on natural law, natural reason, human nature, libido, the State, historical necessity, and many attacks made against imperialism, communism, and so on, involve reification, for they assume that these are *real* entities, not metaphors, concepts, and hypothetical constructions (see also HYPOSTATIZATION). (6) *Spiritualization:* the obverse of reification. The tendency to take a thing or person and disembody, idealize, and spiritualize it. The idealization or deification of a person is an obvious example; many stories have been written revealing how primitives turned on man-gods when they bled or otherwise were revealed to be flesh and blood. It often involves two steps: a faulty suppressed premise, "women are sensitive," "love is selfless and sublime," "mothers love children," and sterotyping—"she will be warm and beautiful when she has children," "she is too sensitive for such treatment." (7) *Perfectionism:* the demand that actions and proposals be measured not against realities but against ideal standards. The entire Christian concept of original sin may be charged with this tendency to measure man against a perfect norm. Quite often, perfectionism is used to forestall action, to create uncertainty, or to unbalance one's opponent. (8) *Relativism:* the assumption that there is no "real," objective reality that can be discerned and used as an enduring referent, and hence the assumption that follows for some that, as a consequence, all propositions are so compromised by subjectivity as to preclude any possibility of objectivity. Absolute relativism is almost unlivable in fact. The assertion that "it's all relative" or "everyone has a right to his opinion" breaks down when one is confronted with the stresses and choices of real life. Absolute relativism forbids anger at slander, makes crime exclusively subjective, utterly destroys the concept of responsibility to others for one's actions. Limited relativism, such as that employed by Marx in creating two self-contained value systems based on differing economic systems, is more acceptable but, in practice, it too breaks down. Marx does not accept one system: capitalism is evil, and about that there is no relativism. Even when one accepts two systems, as cultural anthropologists do, one does so in reality only with reference to means, not to ends; means that pursue patently destructive ends (mass slavery, mass extermination) fall outside the limits of permissible differences. (9) *Assumption of infallibility:* the obverse of relativism, which may become a refuge through systematic evasion, infallibility assumes that one has special access to the truth or the mysteries of the universe. Underlying relativism is the assumption that truth is so veiled, changeable, and mysterious that it cannot be glimpsed; underlying infallibility is the assumption that truth is clear, final, and immutable, and that one is in possession of it. Truth is not something that evolves, that we discover as we go along; it is fixed and we already have it in our possession. Extreme relativism and infallibility are especially dangerous attitudes, for they may result in self-serving, amoral individualism or authoritarian oppression. Both prevent dialogue, make discussion useless, are condescending, acknowledge no opposing claim, are impervious to argument, and hence, if widespread, are dangerously anti-social.

BEGGING THE QUESTION. The tendency to shift the basis of an argument by recourse to assumptions and definitions that do not really address themselves to the issue (see also ARGUMENT AND DEFINITION, CIRCULAR). "Dissent gives aid and comfort to the enemy and should be outlawed" is an example of assuming that dissent gives aid and comfort before such has been established. Thus a point is taken before it is given. Question-begging may continue throughout an entire system of thought. It is characterized by a steadfast reliance on fine verbal distinctions, a logical development that disguises the shaky premise, and resistance to observation and experience. Aquinas thus begs the question, "Is God's existence evident in and provable by nature and natural reason?" throughout the entire *Summa Theologica*. Marx begs the question, "How, by a historical dialectic involving action and reaction, does one arrive at the end of the historical dialectic?" In *The New Class,* Djilas provides us with an answer: one does not. The total effect of such evasions is to lead the reader to accept conclusions derived from an unestablished premise. A recognition of the shakiness of the foundation, of course, topples the entire edifice. For an extended illustration of question-begging, see Patterns following the introduction to Christianity (pp. 42–43).

CATEGORY, EXCLUSIVE. When all items in the universe are assigned to one or the other of two classes or groupings that are established by disregarding all points of distinction among their members except one and asserting it to be entirely sufficient and significant, exclusive categories are established. Hard-and-fast dichotomies carve up the world: "things are either black or white." The dichotomy may be disguised by many examples or arguments from the past to prove that no middle ground exists, say, between war and appeasement. The *either/or* structure (see CATEGORY, LIMITED) reveals the exclusive nature of the categories. "You're either part of the problem or part of the solution." For a more extensive discussion, see Patterns following the introduction to existentialism (p. 628).

CATEGORY, LIMITED. When individual items—concepts, beliefs, attitudes, aspects of human behavior—are distributed among a set of classes or kinds and the full reality and complexity of these items are denied, limited categories are established. Although the universe is not neatly divided into halves (see CATEGORY, EXCLUSIVE), points of similarity or difference among individuals which do not support the set of categories are ignored or brushed aside. "We responsible, hardworking, conscientious taxpayers are tired of supporting those shiftless, lazy unproductive people who live on welfare funds." But is everyone who pays taxes responsible, hardworking, and conscientious? Is every person who receives support from welfare funds shiftless, lazy, and unproductive? Does no one on welfare pay any taxes? Do those who pay the most taxes have the most or the least at stake in the present social and economic structure? For a more extensive discussion see Patterns following Mao Tse-tung (p. 342); following the introduction to existentialism (p. 628); and following Nietzsche (675–6).

CAUSALITY, UNSUBSTANTIATED. See ASSUMPTION, UNWARRANTED (2); POST HOC, ERGO PROPTER HOC

CIRCULARITY. See ARGUMENT AND DEFINITION, CIRCULAR

CONCESSION, RHETORICAL. The explicit granting of a point under contention for the purpose of disarming the opponent; in reality, a pseudo-concession made in order to strengthen an argument. An examination of the construction of the sentences in question, to see if they betray the "yes . . . but" structure, will frequently reveal the cursory nature of the concession as opposed to the lengthy explanation and justification that follows the "but." See EMOTIONAL APPEAL (7) for a variant of rhetorical concession.

CONCLUSION, IRRELEVANT. A conclusion which fails, upon examination, to reveal any necessary relationship to the argument's premises or facts. In all their forms such conclusions involve a faulty inference. (1) *Hasty conclusion:* the drawing of a conclusion from insufficient evidence. The hastiness may stem from a number of psychological tendencies, such as assuming the cause in advance (see POST HOC, PROPTER ERGO HOC), or drawing unwarranted generalizations based on too small a sample: "Stalin has revealed how treacherous all communists really are"; "Friendship between two nations, as is proved again and again by shifting alliances based on self-interest, is an illusion." (2) *Hypothetical conclusion:* the presenting of a conditional statement as though one is clairvoyant or omniscient and can see all of the consequences of an event, present or past. Although the verb tenses vary, the general form is identical: "If we do (do not do; did do or did not do) such and such, then this will happen (will not happen; would have happened or would not have happened)." For example, "If Marshall had not been Secretary of State at the time, we would not have lost China to the Communists"; "If law and order is not upheld by the courts, crime will increase." For a more specialized and extended discussion see NON SEQUITUR.

DEFINITION. A definition asserts the equivalence between the meaning of one word and the meaning of other words that are applicable to it and to nothing else. A good definition avoids the following faults: (1) *circularity,* that is, using synonyms (lie = prevarication) instead of analyses (lie = the deliberate making of, or concurring in, a false statement in order to lead someone to believe that the statement is true); (2) *metaphorical or obscure language* ("Religion is the sigh of the oppressed creature, the heart of a heartless world, just as it is the spirit of a spiritless situation. It is the opium of the people" [790/21–23]), which may mislead by implying more or other than is meant; (3) *negative terms,* unless the term to be defined itself implies a deprivation or negation (nonsense, sterility, bankruptcy). Learning how to define terms and concepts thus becomes an indispensable skill in learning how to learn.

Definitions are of two basic types: *intensive* (or *connotative*) and *ex-*

Glossary of Rhetorical Devices   899

tensive (or *denotative*). The intension of a term posits the sum of essential qualities of that term which are agreed upon within a given community ("a liar is one who deliberately makes false statements, or concurs in criminal falsehoods, in order to lead people to believe that such statements are true"). The extension of the term, on the other hand, points to specific and demonstrable instances wherein the intension is present (Mrs. Bridget Blifil, Miss Jenny Jones, Master Blifil, Mr. Thwackum). A term's intensive definition is thus simply the first of two moments whose second is extension. Hence a meaningful connotation implies the existence of denotable instances; and the existence of denoted instances implies a meaning shared among them.

Ideally, definitions are precise and unambiguous; in reality, they tend to two major defects in addition to the possible faults already noted: (1) *slack definition,* the tendency to loose, vague, incomplete definition that either moves from one general and abstract level to another, or that employs undefined abstractions as if their meaning were common knowledge, when in fact disagreement is possible; (2) *sliding definition,* the tendency to use a word in a sequence of sentences in more than one sense, for example, to speak of love first as charity or *agape,* then as passion or *eros.* Sliding definition is an extremely effective way of preempting a point gradually. Thus one might begin a talk on patriotism by defining it in fairly restricted, explicit, and acceptable terms, only to modify one's usage subtly, until patriotism becomes a shelter to house witchhunts. See Patterns after Cullmann's essay (pp. 191–2) for a fuller explication of slack definition. See also ARGUMENT AND DEFINITION, CIRCULAR

DISGUISED DISPARAGEMENT. The use of syntactical constructions, diction, and tone to create an illusion of relative balance, but at the same time permitting subtle but emotionally loaded commentary (usually, but not necessarily, of an adjectival or adverbial nature) for purposes of disparaging a position: "Bertrand Russell's prejudices on this subject are too violent to make his testimony against religion particularly weighty" (Niebuhr, 193/5–7).

> I have . . . come to postulate two fundamental attitudes, namely introversion and extroversion. The first attitude is normally characterized by a hesitant, reflective, retiring nature that keeps itself to itself, shrinks from objects, is always slightly on the defensive and prefers to hide behind mistrustful scrutiny. The second is normally characterized by an outgoing, candid, and accommodating nature that adapts easily to a given situation, quickly forms attachments, and, setting aside any possible misgivings, will often venture forth with careless confidence into unknown situations (58 Jung).

In disguised disparagement, a great deal of the emotional power of the commentary occurs through the use of undefined terms and unsupported assertions (Russell's attitudes are defined as "prejudices," as if they were so in fact and not in Niebuhr's opinion); through a double standard (one for Niebuhr, whose attitudes are not prejudices and one for Russell, whose are); and through the use of *non sequiturs* ("violence" and "weighty" are not related concepts; are less violent prejudices more "weighty"?); through the employment of emotionally loaded words (in Jung, "hesitant," "shrinks," "defensive," "hide," and "mistrustful" are unfairly opposed to "outgoing," "candid," "accommodating," "adapts easily," "quickly forms attachments" and "confidence"); through an apparently balanced structure and judicious tone suggesting an open mind.

By substituting key descriptive words, one can often discern the prejudices of the author and the intensity of his disparagement. Thus the definition of introversion could be recast to read: "characterized by a cautious, reflective, shy nature that is independent, indifferent to appearances, always slightly sensitive to hurt and prefers therefore to wait until he has observed and trusts the other person." The definition of extroversion could be recast to read: "characterized by a boisterous, simple and weak nature that is easily molded to a given situation, forms shallow attachments . . ." Obviously the meanings have been changed, but that is because so much of the meaning resides in Jung's attitude toward the two and hence in his tone as revealed by his diction. Jung created two *unequal* categories; our recasting erases that inequality but creates a new one. It is, of course, possible to pose equal polarities, but Jung did not wish to do so; he was less attracted to one polar attitude but was unwilling to acknowledge it. The result is disguised, and hence dishonest, disparagement. For another discussion of *disguised disparagement,* see Patterns following Paul (pp. 116–17).

DOCUMENTATION, QUESTIONABLE: The use of scholarly apparatus such as footnotes or references to give one's remarks an authoritative air. Close examination reveals the footnotes to be worthless because the source is questionable, biased, or weightless.

> Gus Hall, General Secretary of the Communist Party, USA, told Americans what to expect when the communists take over. Speaking at the funeral of Eugene Dennis in February, 1961, Hall said: "I dream of the hour when the last Congressman is strangled to death on the guts of the last preacher—and since the Christians love to sing about the blood, why not give them a little of it." (59 Stormer)

The quote is footnoted, "St. Louis Globe Democrat; May 12, 1963." Since its nature—editorial, article, or whatever—is not cited, and since the information appears in a paper whose political affiliation we do not know, *two full years* after the speech, and since the quote is taken out of context, it is scarcely documentation calculated to reassure us.

EITHER/OR. See CATEGORY, EXCLUSIVE

EMOTIONAL APPEAL AND PSYCHOLOGICAL ARGUMENT. A great number of rhetorical devices are meant to stir up emotions by (1) *ad populum* (Latin: "to the people") *appeals* that permit one to manipulate in a predictable way the biases of the vast majority of one's audience. Among the most common *ad populum* emotional appeals are the following. (a) *Stock appeal:* an appeal to a conditioned or stereotyped response—motherhood, patriotism and the flag, God and work, and so forth. (b) *Meaningless abstraction:* a word or proposition that is loaded emotionally but has lost its specific or historic referents and thus become an unarguable subjective response.

Glossary of Rhetorical Devices 901

"We cannot defeat Communism with Socialism, nor with secularism, nor with pacifism, nor with appeasement or accomodation . . . A 'soft' attitude toward communism can destroy us" (60 J. Edgar Hoover). (c) *Slanted argument:* sometimes extremely innocuous, slanted arguments all have as their end the calculated manipulation of information so as to create a desired favorable or unfavorable response. Here is an example: "Race hatred is not an ancient and inherent thing. On the contrary, all this prejudice, and the very concept of race, is the product of the modern era, of the era we call capitalism. There were other fears, other hatreds, other prejudices, but before the capitalist era man never discriminated against his fellow man because of his skin color." (d) *Abundant epithet:* The tendency to control response by using emotionally charged adjectives and adverbs that mold reader response merely by virtue of their frequency. For example: "Burly, helmeted highway patrolmen brutally removed the calmly singing students down the cold, hard marble steps."

Other devices are calculated to alienate the crowd by (2) damning the source of the argument as though the strength of an argument were not inherent in it, but derived from its source. "My opponent's argument that economic power is political power could have come out of a speech by Lenin"; "This is a very good example . . . of bourgeois journalism which differs from bourgeois science only in that the latter is less sincere . . ." (61 Lenin).

Another device is to damn the opponent by (3) personal, *ad hominem* (Latin: "to the man") *attacks* on him instead of on his arguments. Sir Winston Churchill's comment on a political adversary is brief, witty, and devastating: "He was a modest man, with much to be modest about." A more contemporary instance, but one that shows less style on all counts, might be, "I will listen to their arguments when they wash their toes and visit a barber shop."

An avenue that can be most effective under the right circumstances is (4) *appeal to tradition or authority.* Once again the implicit claim is that the argument's source is its most important aspect. "Indeed, those who excel in understanding naturally gain control, whereas those who have defective understanding, but a strong body, seem to be naturally fitted for service, as Aristotle says in his *Politics.* The view of Solomon is also in accord with this . . ." (134/17-20).

To limit the acceptability of certain facts for consideration is to determine the conclusion (5) *a priori* (Latin: "in advance"). "Anyone in America who wants a job can find one. If the Appalachian miners choose not to move to another area where jobs are plentiful, I do not see why we should involve ourselves." Here, of course, such factors as the cost of moving, financial and otherwise, or the lack of marketable skills, are ignored.

A whole range of (6) *diversionary tactics* can be used to throw an audience off the real issues at stake. One can direct the audience's attention elsewhere, change the subject, insist on irrelevancies, create misgivings, set up straw men (non-existent unpopular opponents), focus on alternatives, employ sarcasm or ridicule, analogy or anecdote, and finally intimidate by means of exasperation or personal accusation.

One way to forestall disagreement is to phrase sentences so as to (7) *neutralize disagreement* by casting indirect aspersions on those who disagree. This is done by using such introductory words as "clearly," "it is obvious," "everyone will agree," "no sensible person wants."

By means of (8) *reductio ad absurdum* (Latin: "reduction to absurdity") arguments, one can create amusement or fear in an audience and hence a confusion between the real situation and a hypothetical but fantastically senseless one. "If we continue to spend more on our space program than on urban transit, soon we will be able to reach the moon in less time than it takes to get to work."

For fuller discussions on the use of these devices in specific contexts, see Patterns following Matthew (pp. 85–86), Lenin (pp. 337–38), and Kierkegaard (pp. 706–707).

FAULTY ANALOGY. See ARGUMENT BY ANALOGY

FAULTY GENERALIZATION. See ASSUMPTION, UNWARRANTED (1)

HASTY CONCLUSION. See CONCLUSION, IRRELEVANT (1)

HYPOSTATIZATION. An assumption of omniscience and clairvoyance which consists in assuming that one has penetrated mysteries, made them objective, and imparted to concepts an independent existence, the secret of which one has discovered. "History shows" (as in Marxism), "science teaches us" (as in psychoanalysis), "Christianity reveals" (as in Christianity) are all examples of the tendency to assume that each of these—history, science, Christianity—is a monolithic entity speaking with one voice. In point of fact, they are all abstractions incapable of acting in any way; they are concepts, and concepts that have meaning and existence only as they are embodied in the thoughts and lives of their practitioners—historians, scientists, Christians—none of whom can be assumed to speak with one voice on anything.

HYPOTHETICAL CONCLUSION. See CONCLUSION, IRRELEVANT (2)

ILLUSTRATION, SELECTIVE. The tendency to select isolated, biased, or unrepresentative illustrations in support of one's argument. Example is an indispensable form of support and one of the most reputable kinds; as such it commands great allegiance. But it can be abused. Sometimes the bias is obvious in the illustration, but frequently it is impossible to discern the unrepresentative nature of the illustration unless one is well-informed. Special pleaders such as advertisers and lobbyists are most guilty of using selective illustration.

INSINUATION. See TONAL ARGUMENT

IRRELEVANT CONCLUSION. See CONCLUSION, IRRELEVANT

LOGIC CHOPPING. The tendency to resist the use of all general, abstract, and vague terms by requiring exhaustive, precise distinctions and definitions. Like relativism, it is often a method of attack. Logic chopping is difficult to combat, for it is almost impossible to communicate certain concepts such as "love" or "friendship" without recourse to high-level abstractions. To be required to define such concepts without using other abstractions in the process is to compel one to provide us with nothing but a series of illustrative incidents (see DEFINITION). Logic chopping, even when deserved, as it is when it is used against vague over-generalizations, has the effect of drying out and impoverishing the language. Concepts and metaphors (as well as most poetry) fall by the wayside. "Altruism is impossible. At heart all behavior is selfish. If a person behaves selflessly, it is because he receives a selfish pleasure from his apparently selfless act." The net effect, of course, is to destroy the concept "selfish" by turning it into a tautology. "All men are selfish" thus becomes somewhat meaningless, for it means merely that all men are what they are. Certain concepts require polar opposites, and the concept of "selfishness" is one of them.

NON SEQUITUR (Latin: "it does not follow"). A broad classification involving various forms of logical inconsistency, the most common being the drawing of faulty inferences or the development of inappropriate conclusions from inadequate premises: "If we prosper, it is because God loves us"; "Poor people are lazy"; "Communism is scientific; its victory is therefore assured." The *non sequitur,* however, need not exist within a single sentence; in fact, it often involves a chain of sentences. Paul, in his Letter to the Romans, is guilty of a lengthy one in his discussion on the purpose of God in history (107/9–26; 108/21–40; 109/12–20).

It is not only the analogy between man and a pot that is faulty (pots are not held to be responsible for their baseness, whereas man is); it is the development of Paul's argument. The *non sequitur* becomes inevitable when he tries to reconcile history as divinely ordered with human freedom, and when he destroys any possibility of justice in the relationship between God and man. He nowhere provides for both justice and mercy, as is usually provided for in law, and hence involves God in all actions, right and wrong. The result is a series of logical difficulties, for the very concept of mercy presupposes man's responsibility. If God makes people good or bad (treasured vessels or common ones) in order to serve his purposes, how are they then responsible? (Notice how the analogy between the potter and God continues to break down. The potter makes common pots because he must: better ones are too costly, or require more skill and patience than he has available. None of these obstacles apply to God, for whom practical considerations demanding compromise should be non-existent.) One may ask why, if God makes Jews stubborn in order to put them in the wrong, in order to show his mercy and thereby move gentiles to the faith, he should choose—since he can do all things—to destroy one thing in order to create another. Because he has such power, he need not destroy anything; but this line of thought is not really to the point. If God did not make them stubborn and they chose to be stubborn, then God's providential scheme is not final and complete, for God does not govern all actions. Either God compelled the Jews to be stubborn, and there is Providence but no freedom; or the Jews chose to be stubborn, and there is freedom but no historical order. One can, of course, abandon the logical attempt, acknowledge the illogicality of both, and confess to the inscrutability of God's ways, but then one should have confessed this at once and remained silent.

The *non sequitur* is perhaps the most common fallacy and the most exhausting to unravel. It is very persuasive because it gives the illusion of reasonableness and because it has about it a certain air of authority. Warning signs of its possible presence are the following constructions: "if . . . then," "had we . . . we could have," "given this . . . then this," "either this . . . or this," but as indicated in the examples, simple assertions themselves may contain a *non sequitur*. A means of assessing whether they do in fact contain a *non sequitur* is to convert the sentence into one of the above constructions and see if it withstands investigation. Thus, "poor people are lazy," can be restructured to read "if they are poor, then they are lazy." Many assertions are little more than enthymemes—logical units with the connective suppressed. Restructuring heightens the logical structure and is thus useful in revealing possible weakness.

PERFECTIONISM. See ASSUMPTION, UNWARRANTED (7)

POST HOC, ERGO PROPTER HOC (Latin: "after this, therefore because of this"), or ASSUMING THE CAUSE. The assumption that because two events follow each other the latter event is caused by the former. This fallacy is usually the result of inadequate observation stemming from careless methodology or from an emotional commitment to the relationship. *Post hoc* is a specific kind of *non sequitur* favored by politicians, the pious, advertisers, and persons emotionally committed in advance to assuming the cause. "Julie rinsed her mouth with Gargoyle mouthwash; she's getting married in June."

The more closely related in time and in resemblance to each other, however, the more likely one is to accept dubious causality. Many people who would smile indulgently at the above example would nevertheless accept the following without question. "Our failure to go all out in Vietnam caused the war to drag on." (We failed to go all out, therefore the war dragged on.) "Marx's poverty led him to become a Communist." (Marx was poor, therefore he became a communist.)

The *post hoc* error is very common and very vulgar, but very difficult to combat because argument and example are not persuasive against an individual who has an emotional investment in assuming the cause in advance.

PSYCHOLOGICAL ARGUMENT. See EMOTIONAL APPEAL AND PSYCHOLOGICAL ARGUMENT

QUESTION-BEGGING. See BEGGING THE QUESTION

REDUNDANCY. See ARGUMENT AND DEFINITION, CIRCULAR

REIFICATION. See ASSUMPTION, UNWARRANTED (5)

RELATIVISM. See ASSUMPTION, UNWARRANTED (8)

SLACK DEFINITION. See DEFINITION

SLIDING DEFINITION. See DEFINITION

SPIRITUALIZATION. See ASSUMPTION, UNWARRANTED (6)

STATEMENT, PSEUDO-FACTUAL. A statement which, because of its ostensible precision of detail, seems authoritative, but which, upon closer examination, is revealed to be improbable or foolish. For example, "The cold war is real war. It has already claimed more lives, enslaved more people, and cost more money than any 'hot' war in history. Yet, most Americans refuse to admit that we are at war. That is why we are rapidly losing—why America has yet to win its first real victory in 18 years of 'cold' war." (62 Stormer).

STEREOTYPING. See ASSUMPTION, UNWARRANTED (4)

TAUTOLOGICAL STATEMENT. A statement structured so as to be true by definition and hence devoid of new meaning. The tautology may be explicit—"Leaders have leadership ability"; "Either God behaves justly or he is not a just God"—or implicit—"Superior intellectual substances receive the influence of divine wisdom into themselves more perfectly, because each being receives something according to the being's own mode" (Aquinas). Translated, this means: superior intellects are superior because according to divine wisdom they receive more perfectly intellects in keeping with their superior being. It is empty utterance. Concepts that once had value are capable of being emptied of almost all meaning when two concepts become fused—for example, "Satan is evil." Tautologies indicate that the speaker believes final truth has already been found and thought can stop. Remarks like, "If it's communist, it's evil," or "If it's godless, it can't be good," are capable of being argued if they have not been converted into tautological equations. If they have been so converted, they cannot be. Thus, in many people's eyes there is no difference between the above remarks and the following: "If it's evil, it's communist"; "If it's good, it can't be godless." Tautologies are revealed by the interchangeability of their parts. See also ARGUMENT AND DEFINITION, CIRCULAR

TONAL ARGUMENT. Tone is an inflection of the written or spoken voice which expresses the author or speaker's feeling or attitude toward either his subject or his audience, or both. In conversation, we have no trouble recognizing a tone of heavy sarcasm. In writing, where we do not have the auditory reinforcement, we must rely on more subtle insinuations, such as syntax, diction, and rhythm, for tone is an instrumental device of persuasion. We are angered by an arrogant tone, irritated by a condescending one, pacified by a conciliatory one. What we fail to appreciate is that not only emotions are being conveyed by tone, but meaning itself. Depending on its context, the single word "great!" or "nice!" is thus capable of multiple meaning. Writers may either manipulate tone in order to ingratiate themselves with the audience, or to insinuate ideas they are unwilling to speak aloud (see Patterns following Jung, pp. 519–20); they may adopt a dignified, Olympian detachment in an attempt to allow the subject matter to gain the foreground (see Freud); or they may convey their vision through their passionate indignation (see Nietzsche). These differences are not matters of indifference; they are themselves expressive adjuncts of their vision. More importantly, the reader may react to tone without analyzing it to discern its purposes. He may thus be put off by Freud as well as by Nietzsche but warm to Jung without ever asking himself precisely why he does so. Is a warm, confiding tone appropriate to *Civilization and Its Discontents*? Should someone who is excoriating Christianity do so in a friendly, genial way? An uncritical response to tone can lead to a failure to discern the author's intentions. As a result, the reader overlooks the author's full range of rhetorical strategies and his skill in using them to achieve his purpose.

TONAL INSINUATION. See TONAL ARGUMENT

UNSUBSTANTIATED CAUSALITY. See ASSUMPTION, UNWARRANTED (2); POST HOC, ERGO PROPTER HOC

VERBAL ARGUMENT. Argument by stylistics, that is, discourse structured to gain a point by virtue of word choice, allusion, syntax, and so forth. To be sure, writers cannot have complete control over matters of style, for as the French say, style is the man. Even when dealing with extremely difficult concepts, however, writers can strive for simplicity and clarity by avoiding certain mannerisms that have an intimidating effect. Specifically, they can attempt to

(1) cultivate simplicity of vocabulary wherever possible, (2) avoid numerous Latinate polysyllabic words, (3) reject foreign words and jargon, (4) construct brief rather than relentlessly long, weighty paragraphs, (5) use self-explaining allusions that arise organically out of the subject, (6) employ a steady movement from high-level abstraction to low-level abstraction, (7) rely on illustrations and analogies whenever difficult concepts are involved.

The misconception persists that great authors are difficult; but a casual glance at the authors in this anthology reveals the falseness of that claim. The giants have both clarity and simplicity. Freud refrains from long sentences, from jargon. Compared to Adler or Marcuse, he is classical. He is organic and self-contained in his arguments and has few allusions, which are, in the main, nothing but redundant asides. Jung, on the other hand, is constantly creating gratuitous difficulties for the reader, and making allusions that have no function other than to impress. Few essays in this anthology, however, are as difficult as those in the average textbook for a first course in philosophy, psychology, or economics. This fact is significant. Great writers are not interested in verbal intimidation; they are secure, and eager to communicate; they wish to share their secrets in as simple and direct a fashion as possible. And, thus, even when matters of style are concerned, they may serve as models and give direction.

VERBAL INTIMIDATION. See VERBAL ARGUMENT

List of References

1. Richard Hofstadter, "The Unpopularity of Intellect," *Motive* (October 1964):29.
2. John Dewey, *The Quest for Certainty* (New York: Minton, 1929), pp. 347-48.
3. Sigmund Freud, *Beyond the Pleasure Principle* (New York: Bantam, 1959), p. 53.
4. Carl R. Rogers, "Toward a Science of the Person," as quoted in *Behaviorism and Phenomenology*, ed. T. W. Wann (Chicago: University of Chicago Press, 1964), p. 112.
5. John Keats, Letter to George and Thomas Keats, Sunday, December 21, 1817. (See Walter Jackson Bate, *John Keats* [Cambridge, Mass.: Belknap Press, 1963] pp. 242-44.)
6. Donald W. MacKinnon, "Conditions for Effective Personality Change," from *Nurturing Individual Potential*, ed. Harry Passow (Washington, D.C.: Association for Supervision and Curriculum Development, 1964), pp. 13-15.
7. John Dewey, *The Quest for Certainty* (New York: Minton, 1929), p. 349.
8. Shakespeare, *Hamlet*, III, ii, 351-52.
9. Terence, *Heauton Timoroumenos*, I, i, 25.
10. William Cozart, *The Power of Abstraction: Model-Building as Way of Life* (Pasadena: California Institute of Technology, n.d.), pp. 1-4.
11. Harry Emerson Fosdick, *A Guide to Understanding the Bible* (New York: Harper & Row, 1956), pp. 121-22.
12. Ernst Troeltsch, *The Social Teaching of the Christian Churches* (New York: Harper & Row, 1960), pp. 57-58.
13. Albert Camus, *The Rebel*, tr. Anthony Bower (New York: Random House, 1956), pp. 28-32.
14. George Eliot, *Middlemarch* (Boston: Houghton Mifflin, 1956), pp. 46-47.
15. Otto Hintze, "Kalvinismus und Staatsräson in Brandenburg zu Beginn des 17ten Jahrhunderts," *Historische Zeitschrift*, 144(1931): 232.
16. Walter Kaufmann, *From Shakespeare to Existentialism* (Garden City, New York: Doubleday, 1960), p. 206.
17. Karl Löwith, *Meaning in History* (Chicago: University of Chicago Press, 1949), pp. 184, 186, 188.
18. Walter Rauschenbusch, *Christianity and the Social Crisis*, ed. Robert D. Cross (New York: Harper & Row, 1964), p. 93.
19. Karl Marx, "Theses on Feuerbach," from *Marx & Engels: Basic Writings*

on *Politics & Philosophy,* ed. Lewis S. Feuer (Garden City, New York: Doubleday, 1959), p. 243.
20. Bruce Franklin, "Fictions of the Future," *Stanford Today* (Summer, 1966): 10.
21. Mao Tse-tung, "On Practice," from *Selected Works of Mao Tse-tung* (Peking: Foreign Language Press, n.d.), p. 296.
22. Mao Tse-tung, "Speech at the Meeting of the Supreme Soviet of the U.S.S.R. in Celebration of the 40th Anniversary of the Great October Socialist Revolution" (November 6, 1957), as quoted in *Quotations from Chairman Mao Tse-tung,* ed. Stuart R. Schram (New York: Bantam, 1967), p. 13.
23. Mao Tse-tung, "On Practice," from *Selected Works of Mao Tse-tung* (Peking: Foreign Language Press, n.d.), p. 296.
24. Erich Fromm, *Marx's Concept of Man* (New York: Ungar, 1961), pp. 2-4.
25. Lewis S. Feuer, ed., *Marx & Engels: Basic Writings on Politics & Philosophy* (Garden City, New York: Doubleday, 1959), pp. xiii-xiv.
26. Quinton Anthony, In *The New York Review of Books,* as quoted from the book jacket of Leszek Kolakowski's *Toward a Marxist Humanism* (New York: Grove Press, 1968).
27. Robert C. Tucker, *The Marxian Revolutionary Idea* (New York: Norton, 1969), pp. ix-xi.
28. Philip Rieff, *Freud: The Mind of the Moralist* (Garden City, New York: Doubleday, 1961), p. ix.
29. Herbert Marcuse, *Eros and Civilization* (New York: Random House, 1955), p. 229.
30. Ernest Jones, *The Life and Work of Sigmund Freud* (New York: Basic Books, 1957), 3:126.
31. Lawrence S. Kubie, "Research in Protecting Preconscious Functions in Education," from *Nurturing Individual Potential,* ed. Harry Passow (Washington, D.C.: Association for Supervision and Curriculum Development, 1964), p. 36.
32. Sigmund Freud, "The Dissection of the Psychical Personality," from *Great Ideas in Psychology,* ed. Robert W. Marks (New York: Bantam, 1966), p. 99.
33. Sigmund Freud, *A General Introduction to Psychoanalysis,* tr. Joan Rivière (New York: Washington Square Press, 1952), pp. 440, 442.
34. *Ibid.,* pp. 441-42.
35. *Ibid.,* p. 439.
36. Erich Fromm, *Psychoanalysis and Religion* (New York: Bantam, 1950), pp. 34-37.
37. Sigmund Freud, *Leonardo da Vinci,* tr. A. A. Brill (New York: Random House, 1947), p. 16.
38. *Ibid.,* p. 31.
39. *Ibid.,* p. 110.
40. Erich Fromm, *Sigmund Freud's Mission* (New York: Grove Press, 1959), p. 8.
41. Sigmund Freud, *Group Psychology and the Analysis of the Ego* (New York: Bantam, 1965), pp. 29-31.

42. Philip Rieff, *Freud: The Mind of the Moralist* (Garden City, New York: Doubleday, 1961), pp. xi-xii.
43. Abraham H. Maslow, *Toward a Psychology of Being* (Princeton, N.J.: Van Nostrand, 1962), p. iii.
44. *Ibid.*, pp. iii-iv.
45. Albert Camus, *The Myth of Sisyphus* (New York: Random House, 1955), p. 4.
46. Søren Kierkegaard, *Attack Upon "Christendom,"* tr. Walter Lowrie (Princeton, N.J.: Princeton University Press, 1944), pp. 120-23.
47. Walter Rauschenbusch, *Christianity and the Social Crisis*, ed. Robert D. Cross (New York: Harper & Row, 1964), pp. 91-92.
48. Albert Camus, *The Rebel,* tr. Anthony Bower (New York: Random House, 1956), p. 207.
49. *Ibid.*, p. 220.
50. Jean-Paul Sartre, "Portrait of the Anti-Semite," *Partisan Review,* 13 (Spring, 1946): 167.
51. Walter Kaufmann, ed., *The Portable Nietzsche* (New York: Viking, 1954), pp. 1-2.
52. Sigmund Freud, *The Life and Work of Sigmund Freud*, ed. Ernest Jones (New York: Basic Books, 1955), 2:344.
53. Friedrich Nietzsche, *"Ecce Homo"* from *Existentialism from Dostoevsky to Sartre,* ed. Walter Kaufmann (Cleveland: World, 1956), p. 111.
54. Søren Kierkegaard, "Concluding Unscientific Postscript," from *A Kierkegaard Anthology,* ed. Robert Bretall (New York: Modern Library, 1946), p. 201.
55. Jean-Paul Sartre, quoted by Maurice Cranston in *Jean-Paul Sartre* (New York: Grove Press, 1962), p. 10.
56. John Stuart Mill, *On Liberty,* ed. Alburey Castell (New York: Appleton-Century-Crofts, 1947), p. 59.
57. Adolph Hitler, Speech at Neustadt an der Aisch, January 15, 1928, as quoted by George H. Stein, ed., *Hitler* (Englewood Cliffs, N.J.: Prentice-Hall, 1968), pp. 22-23.
58. C. G. Jung, "The Problem of the Attitude-Type," in *Great Ideas in Psychology,* ed. Robert W. Marks (New York: Bantam, 1966), p. 107.
59. John A. Stormer, *None Dare Call It Treason* (Florissant, Missouri: Liberty Bell, 1964), p. 20.
60. J. Edgar Hoover, quoted by John A. Stormer on the book cover of *None Dare Call It Treason* (Florissant, Missouri: Liberty Bell, 1964).
61. V. I. Lenin, "Imperialism, the Highest Stage of Capitalism" from *The Essential Works of Lenin,* ed. by Henry M. Christman (New York: Bantam, 1966), p. 195.
62. John A. Stormer, *None Dare Call It Treason* (Florissant, Missouri: Liberty Bell, 1964), p. 7.

ENNIS AND NANCY HAM LIBRARY
ROCHESTER COLLEGE
800 WEST AVON ROAD
ROCHESTER HILLS, MI 48307